MW00378658

AmaBhulu

AmaBhulu

The Birth and Death of the Second America

Harry Booyens

Cliffwood Fogge
Vancouver
2014

Copyright © 2014 Harry Booyens

All rights reserved under International and Pan-American Copyright Conventions. No part of this book may be reproduced in any form or by any electronic or mechanical means, including information storage and retrieval systems, without permission in writing from the publisher except by a reviewer, who may quote brief passages in a review.

Published in 2014 by Cliffwood Fogge.
Printed in the United States of America

The moral right of the author has been asserted.

Cliffwood Fogge™
www.cliffwoodfogge.com

For permission to reproduce tracts of this publication, write to

Cliffwood Fogge,
1949 Cliffwood Road,
North Vancouver,
BC V7G 1S1,
Canada
e-mail: hb@cliffwoodfogge.com

Library and Archives Canada Cataloguing in Publication

Booyens, Harry, author
    AmaBhulu : the birth and death of the second America / Harry Booyens.

Includes bibliographical references and index.
Issued in print and electronic formats.
ISBN 978-0-9921590-1-6 (pbk.).

    1. South Africa--History. 2. Afrikaners--History. 3. Race relations--South Africa. I. Title.

DT1787.B66 2013   968   C2013-907373-6

Published in Canada
First Print Edition

To those many thousands who gave their lives
for the
Dream
of
Western Civilization in Africa.

Cover Picture: *The view over the plains of the Camdeboo and Lower Karoo from the vantage point of the "Valley of Desolation" lookout atop the Sneeuberg, immediately outside Graaff-Reinet; the crucible of South African history.*

• *"The discovery of America, and that of the passage to the East Indies by the Cape of Good Hope, are the two greatest and most important events recorded in the history of Mankind."*

Adam Smith,
An inquiry into the Nature and Causes of the Wealth of Nations (1776)

• *"As the colony improved and its peoples increased it would to us only prove a Second America and would more likely in time rob us of India."*

Rear-Admiral Thomas Pringle,
British Naval Commander at the Cape (1797)

• *"...this is our only motherland, we have nowhere else to go..."*

Hendrik F. Verwoerd
Prime Minister of the Union of South Africa (1960)

History is now repeating itself:

• *"If the reading public believe a hundredth part of the enormities which have been laid at the door of our people and Government, they must be irresistibly forced to the conclusion that this Republic is a den of thieves and a sink of iniquity, a people, in fact, the very existence of which is a blot upon humanity, and a nuisance to mankind...*

In this awful turning point in the history of South Africa, on the eve of the conflict which threatens to exterminate our people, it behooves us to speak the truth in what may be, perchance, our last message to the world."

F.W. Reitz
Secretary of State for the South African Republic (Transvaal)
From his book *A Century of Wrong* (1899)

Preface

The taxi driver hesitated for a second, and then told me that he thought every barkeeper in the south of England was now a South African. At Westminster tube station, three teenage boys walked past, obviously local friends, and they spoke Afrikaans to one another. On the bus, a young lady alighted at the door near the front where I was sitting, and two young men sitting in the back called out to her. They did so in Afrikaans. She joined them. At Heathrow, a young man served me in Afrikaans at the restaurant. This was the year 2000 and already a generation of young Afrikaners was growing up in England.

In Canada, in the North Vancouver Presbyterian Church, the minister mentioned that attendance would likely be low in the next few weeks, because so many parishioners would be going to visit family in South Africa in December. In this area, almost every locally born Canadian has at least one South African friend, colleague, or acquaintance. Nearly every classroom has one or two South African children. All this is in keeping with the reports that nearly one fifth of the white population of South Africa has left the country.

The singular characteristic of this present exodus is the large number of Dutch-German-French descended Afrikaners who have joined their English-speaking fellow-countrymen in saying goodbye to the tortured continent of Africa. In their case, it has been their home since the 1650s. This is the equivalent of the descendants of the Pilgrim Fathers abandoning the United States in horror. This work addresses who these people are, where they came from, how they became the White Tribe of Africa, the *AmaBhulu*, and why they are leaving by their hundreds of thousands the country they and their ancestors have built over twelve generations.

The future of the West is vividly etched into South Africa for all who would care to look beyond the tourist veneer and Western media bias. South Africa in the 20th Century and through two World Wars was as much a central part of the Western Allies as Canada and Australia. However, for practical purposes, the country is now lost to the West as we know it. The descendants of those Westerners who built it over 350 years are leaving. Those who remain are being systematically subjugated by a culture with a belief system that is anathema to the basic tenets and interests of Western Civilization.

The West is losing its place in the world and nowhere in the world are the consequences as vivid as in South Africa, the Western "canary in the coal mine." Failure to learn the correct lessons from this history will doom Western Man, because South Africa was to Africa what the United States has been to the world. In fact, in 1797 the British Naval Commander at the Cape of Good Hope called his new colony *"The Second America."*

Herewith, the reader is invited to join the author on his 350-year journey through the history of South Africa, the Second America, as seen through the eyes of his own ancestors, who lived the entire saga and who testify to the reader on the key events of their times.

Acknowledgment

I should like to acknowledge the help of many genealogists, both in South Africa and abroad, who tirelessly helped me to research and complete my own genealogy, that of my wife and those of some key characters in this work. I also had considerable help from Danish, Dutch, German, American and French genealogy groups and database facilities, including the Dutch Nationaal Archiev, the Danish State Archive, the French CNRS, and the British National Archives. Both the New York City Archives and the New York State Archives were very helpful.

Thanks are similarly due to the Library of Simon Fraser University in Vancouver for allowing me to take semi-permanent custody of large numbers of books, and to the good people at several museums and libraries in South Africa, all of whom went out of their way to help in different ways, even unlocking museums on Sundays. I trust the intense attention to detail shown in respect of this genealogy will give the reader cause to respect the historical facts described in this work, quite apart from the detailed reference sources provided.

I should like to thank David A. Lien and George R. Proto, both in the United States, as well as Chris Heiberg in Canada, for their encouragement, support, trial reading, and critique of the work over several years.

Lastly, thanks go to my wife, Jeanne Helen Basson, for her unwavering support throughout this long and arduous task. Her repeated critical reading of this work added immensely to its quality.

AmaBhulu

x

1

The Beginning

"The discovery of America, and that of the passage to the East Indies by the Cape of Good Hope, are the two greatest and most important events recorded in the history of Mankind."

Adam Smith (1776),
An inquiry into the Nature and Causes of the Wealth of Nations

Krotoa

The warning call of the sentry echoes against the massive cliffs that loom like a stone colossus against the southern skies. He has already vacated his post. The leader of the troop is casually making his way higher up the cliffs with his dutiful harem following behind. At the back follow the youngsters. The little ones are riding on their mothers' backs and the babies are clinging to their mother's breasts. The leader is doing his best to move in a stately fashion so that he does not betray any fear. If any of the other grown males were to detect fear, his position would shortly be challenged. Such is the reality of this continent. This is the continent of The Strong Man, a continent where weakness, real or perceived, means death, or banishment from the troop to a slow death from starvation.

Fig. 1-1 The landing of the Dutch - April 7, 1652

Several minutes later, the reason for the departure of the "Old Men of the Mountains" becomes apparent. Moving briskly towards a local prominence is a different troop of denizens of the area. These walk upright on two legs, rather than on four. The members of this new troop are tan colored, have prominent cheekbones, and their eyes have epicanthic folds. They have exceptionally sparse peppercorn hair curls. Some of them are partially covered in animal skins. The other inhabitants of these parts leave them alone, because they are wearing dried animal intestines around their necks as adornment and they are covered in animal fat and soot. The rancid smell carries on the wind for a long distance and serves as a warning to aspiring predators.

The members of the new troop are nattering all the time in peculiar click sounds. The smaller hyraxes and lizards that have stayed in the sunny spots for warmth after the baboon sentry gave his warning, now get out of the way of this new troop and scurry away into rock crevices. There are a lot of women and children among this troop of *Khoekhoe*[1], men of men, as these people are called. Towards the back of the group, a dainty girl in her early teens is skipping from rock to rock. Her name is Krotoa. She is the niece of

Autshumao, the leader of the troop, and is full of life. She has grand ideas for her future. After all, her sister has married the chief of another Khoekhoe troop that lives nearby.

Autshumao has another name, Herry. Strange looking big men with sickly white faces who came from over the Great Undrinkable gave him this name. These men called themselves "English." Some seasons ago they took him on a great wooden floating hut with big white wings to a faraway place and they taught him their language. Since then, more and more of these huge men have stopped here and have tried to barter cows from other Khoekhoe. They seem to speak different languages. Somehow, these strange visitors just will not understand that the animals are exceedingly precious and important to the Khoekhoe. The animals are a measure of their wealth and stature. They do not really want to exchange them for other things. However, metal rings are a different matter. These can be turned into spear points and are much prized by the women. They can also be traded with the big dark-brown Kobona people who live thirty days to the east at the characteristic Khoekhoe loping gait. Certain beads are also quite attractive. Generally, though, they prefer these visitors to just stay away. Autshumao's own troop does not have any cattle. They live from what they can hunt and scavenge from the rocks at the edge of the Great Undrinkable. They are Strandlopers (Beach Combers).

Suddenly Autshumao puts up his right hand. The whole troop stops and the children start to point and exclaim. Some of the women want to leave right away and start gathering their families to move to safety. Krotoa, however, wants to know more about these new things; so, she stays with Autshumao. Appearing out of the haze on the northwestern horizon are three of the floating wooden huts. And, from this moment Krotoa's life will be different, much different. And the name of this half-naked little entrails draped girl will live down through the centuries.

We should know; *Krotoa is our ancestor.*

April 6, 1652 – Cabo de Boa Esperança

The three ships are riding at anchor. Here, in the lee of the imposing Table Mountain that guards over this sheltering bay, the sea is calm. There is no comparison with the raging waters of the open ocean but a few miles south, where the westerlies of the Roaring Forties chase mountainous seas like foaming warhorses unimpeded over the South Atlantic. It is those very seas, and the frightening winter storms that rage over them with towering castles of cloud, that led explorer Bartolomeu Diaz to dub the southern tip of this peninsula Cabo de Tormentosa, Cape of Storms. Many ships have already disappeared along this frightening coast with its contrary currents and dearth of safe harbor. It took a man of some vision, King John of Portugal, to rename it more positively to Cabo de Boa Esperança, Cape of Good Hope. Appropriately, one of the three vessels is named the Goede Hoop.

The officers are gathered on the good ship *Dromedaris* where they are conferring on matters of the day. Commander Jan van Riebeeck has been instructed by the Lords Seventeen[2] to establish a refreshment station at this godforsaken place, which is bone dry in summer and suffers torrents of cold rain and gale force westerlies in winter. Thankfully, the expedition has arrived in April in the relatively wind-still autumn.

Everything points to war with the English. They have bases to the east of here and the control of this place is key in any naval conflict scenario. The key location of this stormy place on the way to India condemns it to be involved in the great feuds between nations.

The Portuguese created their commercial empire in the Far East in the years 1500, following the pioneering of the Cape Sea Route by Bartolomeu Diaz and Vasco da Gama, the man who first reached India by sea in 1498. Now, a hundred and fifty years later, their time is past. The Dutch have defeated them almost everywhere and they have been effectively eliminated as competition in the Far East trade. As the Portuguese have decimated the Moors, so have the Dutch and English decimated the Portuguese fleet.

The Dutch *Verenigde Oostindische Compagnie*[3] (VOC), created in 1602 and governed by the Lords Seventeen, is now undoubtedly the greatest power in the Far East. Much of this success has been due to their efficient and elegant ships, the *flutes*, named as they are after the equally elegant wine glasses. However, the fact that the Dutch destroyed Spain's naval power forever a few years ago has probably also played a huge role in disabling her Iberian little brother, Portugal.

The aggressive English are a different matter, though. On March 7 of last year, a delegation of 246 Englishmen appeared at the Hague with a suggestion from Oliver Cromwell, their Puritanical leader, that the Dutch and the English should divide the world between them; England getting the Americas and the *Nederlanders* getting the Far East and Africa in exchange for helping England conquer the Americas. Presumably the English thought that was a good idea since the two nations have so successfully banded together to defeat Spain and Portugal. However, even though the English are Protestants, like their closest cousins, the Dutch, they made the latter nervous when Cromwell ordered his own King's head to be cut off three years ago. When the Dutch did not accept their proposition, the English were offended and it became clear that war was now inevitable. Meanwhile, the English have started stealing Dutch merchant ships using their outrageous Navigation Act as an excuse. As a result, the Dutch have to make such preparations as are practical.

Five years ago the good ship *Haarlem* ran aground here in one of those terrible storms, so characteristic of this place. The men reached shore and some of them stayed here for a year to await rescue from *Nederland*. Their report led the Lords Seventeen to consider starting a refreshment station at the Cabo for VOC ships. Maybe it will be a great success. On the other hand, the little colonist settlement that the West Indies Company started thirty-one years ago at *Nieu-Nederland* in *Amerika* was such a disaster that the French-Belgian refugee governor from Wesel in Germany, Pierre Minuit[4], had to be recalled to Nederland. Then the settlers rose against his successor, the incompetent Willem Kieft. But, the new Director General, Pieter Stuyvesant, seems to have taken matters in hand and things are now better all the way up to Fort Oranje[5].

Tomorrow, the men will go ashore to start Van Riebeeck's fortified refreshment station. If it were to be successful, which many strongly doubt, it would certainly improve the lot of the VOC seafarers. The dreaded scurvy has taken a terrible toll of their sailors on the long journey to and from the Far East. The need for fresh meat and vegetables at this halfway-point of that voyage is quite dire as the Portuguese control the rest of the African coast here in the Southern Oceans. Everyone dreads having to deal with the outrageous Hottentotten[6]. The men can already see some of them on land through the spyglasses. The wide eyed young men are wondering whether all the stories they have been told about these reputedly terrible creatures are true.

*****

Here we rest the story of the settlement of the Cape of Good Hope for the moment. We shall return to it in Chapter 2. We now turn back the clock of history just a little bit; back to 1415 Portugal. From there we shall move forward to 17th Century Europe, North America, and Far East to collect the bloodlines that will weave through this work. These will provide us our witnesses to the history about to unfold. We shall follow these bloodlines in dedicated vignettes under the title "Nexus Familia." As we proceed through time, these vignettes will slowly converge to the author and his wife until they become themselves the witnesses to history. This is the history of South Africa through the eyes of those who lived it for three-and-a-half centuries.

The Land at the End of the Earth

Soon after defeating the Moors at Ceuta in Moroccan Africa in 1415, King João I of Portugal appointed his son Henrique as Governor of the Algarve. There, Henry set up his school of navigation at Sagres near the western tip of continental Europe. In so doing, he became Prince Henry the Navigator. Within five years he dispatched ships down the coast of Africa – the Portuguese Age of Discovery was launched. By 1483, Diogo Cão reached the Congo River. By 1484, he landed in Angola and in 1485 he raised a stone cross, a padrão, at Cape Cross on the frightening Skeleton Coast of what is now Namibia.

In 1487, in two linked missions, Bartolomeu Diaz set sail to find the sea route to India around the southern end of Africa, and Pedro de Covilhã was sent overland to the court of "Prester John" in Ethiopia. Before going to Ethiopia, Covilhã first made his way south along the East Coast of Africa as far as Sofala. When he finally arrived in Ethiopia in 1494, he was made Prisoner of State for the rest of his life, but treated exceptionally well. For his part, Diaz made his way south down the west coast of Africa and erected another padrão at Angra Pequena, the present day Lüderitz on the Namib Desert coast of Namibia.

In 1488, Bartolomeu Diaz rounded the Cape, having been blown badly off course into the Southern Oceans. Realizing he had somehow passed the southern tip of Africa in that storm, he sailed north and struck land at a bay they called Bahia São Bras, the present day Mossel Bay. Here he became the first Westerner to meet the Khoekhoe people the Dutch would later call the "Hottentots." The Portuguese tried trading, but the Khoekhoe just hurled rocks at them. Thereupon Diaz took a crossbow and killed a Khoekhoe; the first indigenous Southern African person to die at the hand of Western man. This was not a positive start to the relationship at all. It was to get worse, much worse.

Fig. 1-2 *Replica of Diaz's padrão at Lüderitz*

At Algoa Bay, now the city of Port Elizabeth, Diaz put ashore one of four West African women whom he had brought from Portugal. The notion was that she should sing the praises of Prester John and the King of Portugal. The mind boggles at the fate of this unfortunate woman, abandoned on the beach so far from what she knew. Four hundred and sixty five years later the author would be born within view of this spot.

When Diaz tried going further east, his men threatened mutiny. They believed that they might actually sail off the end of the Earth. So he planted a padrão and turned for home a few miles further east at a point known today as Cape Padrone, near Boknes, close to the mouth of what is now called the Great Fish River. The present day visitor can see a replica padrão at this point after a stiff walk through sand dunes.

In the decade following Diaz's discovery of the southern tip of Africa, Columbus sailed west and discovered the Americas. When Columbus returned from his first voyage, it was the intrepid Diaz who was sent by the Portuguese king to intercept him.

After major planning and preparation on the part of the Portuguese, strongman Vasco da Gama sailed past the Cape and reached India for Portugal on 14 May 1498, but not before firing a cannon at the Khoekhoe at the exact same Bahia São Bras where Diaz had used his crossbow. Clearly, the Portuguese and the Khoekhoe were not seeing eye to eye in matters of trade. Significantly, the first black people Da Gama met in southern Africa were found along the coast of present-day Mozambique. At the time, the southern limit of the Ba'Ntu peoples along the Southern African east coast was at the Umtamvuna River, which forms the present southern border of the Province of KwaZulu-Natal[7]. Either way, they found the black people in Mozambique helpful and friendly. The Arab chroniclers were much less happy with the arrival of the Portuguese in their home waters, a pivotal event in Western history:

> *"In this year the vessels of the Frank appeared at sea en route for India, Hurmuz and those parts. They took about seven vessels, killing those aboard and making some prisoner. This was their first action, may God curse them."*– Arab chronicler, Muhammad bin Umar al-Taiyab Ba Faqih (1503)

The Arabs simply had no answer to the Portuguese, among whom Francesco d'Almeida stood as a giant. Over this period, trading posts were opened along the east coast of the continent. On his final voyage back home to Portugal in 1510 as an old man, his son already dead, d'Almeida reached the Cape. Here his men were involved in a fight with the Khoekhoe. It would be a Khoekhoe spear in his throat that ended the great conquistador's life.

The Portuguese disaffection with the coast of present day South Africa and its Khoekhoe people was near total and they often sailed far south around the Cape. Despite their shunning the southern tip of Africa, they took the rest of Africa seriously indeed. They established a major post at Delagoa Bay[8] in Mozambique on the east coast in 1544 and the colony of Angola on the west coast in 1570. Further up the east coast, in what is now Tanzania and Kenya, it turned into an ongoing see-saw battle with the Omani Arabs for control of the east coast, the staging point for the last hop over the open ocean to India. It was important to the Omani Arabs for the same reason. Over the

Fig. 1-3 The point at Boknes where Diaz turned back

period November 22, 1575 to January 28, 1576, Perestrello, a Portuguese navigator sent by King Sebastian, found[9] that Natal on the east coast had rich soil and, as a result, was populous and well stocked with animals, both wild and domesticated.

By the start of the 1600's, the Portuguese were well settled along the Angolan and Mozambican coasts, but their maritime dominance had waned. That role shifted to the Dutch and the Spaniards, while the English were also in the running, mostly as privateers, better known as pirates.

Enter the Dutch

By the middle of the 1600's, the Dutch were clearly the player to beat at sea and the Portuguese dominion over the East Indies trade was waning rapidly. The joint effort of the Dutch and the English at the 1639 Battle of the Downs finally broke the power of the Spaniards and Portuguese at sea.

The new rulers of the oceans would be the Protestant Dutch. The Portuguese, for their part, were now rapidly fading from the picture. Somehow, the tale[10] of the ship *Santissimo Sacramento* serves as an appropriate epitaph to Portuguese sea power. This Portuguese galleon ran aground at the author's birthtown of Port Elizabeth in the first week of July 1647. The 72 survivors set off on a voyage overland to the Portuguese station at Delagoa Bay. Only nine of them reached their destination after a six-month and 800-mile walk through country populated by fierce Ba'Ntu tribes. After 150 years, the "Time of the Portuguese" was well nigh over. A bronze cannon salvaged from the wreck in 1977 is today the only testimony to Portuguese sea power in the region.

Up to this point, no one had paid much attention to the southern tip of Africa and its strange Khoekhoe people. In fact, the Portuguese preferred dealing with the black people of Africa further up the east and west coasts. However, with the creation in 1602 of the world's first multinational corporation, the Verenigde Oostindische Compagnie (VOC), or United East India Company, the picture rapidly changed. This Dutch business model exploded onto the scene on the back of the Calvinist movement in Northwest Europe. The Netherlands had become the home of the Renaissance. With it, came banks, stocks, and economic growth.

The Dutch were excellent seafarers and traders and, even while fighting the Spanish for control of the southern part of their own country, they built a strong economy and a huge fleet of their efficient flutes.

While these uniquely narrow ships were originally designed in that way to avoid taxes in the strait between Denmark and Sweden, they now defined the future for shipbuilding. In 1603, Sir Walter Raleigh famously complained, *"10 Dutchmen in a flute could do the job of 30 English sailors."* The Dutch East India Company (VOC) eclipsed all of its rivals in the Asia Trade. Between 1602 and 1796, a period of just less than two hundred years, the VOC sent 4,785 ships with just short of a million Europeans to Asia. In return, it brought home more than 2.5 million tons of Asian trade goods. The rest of Europe combined, from 1500 to 1800, sent only 882,412 people. In this period, the fleet of the English East India Company, the nearest competitor, sent only 2,690 ships, which carried only one fifth as much cargo. The VOC made huge profits from its spice monopoly through most of the 1600s. By 1650, the Dutch power at sea and in the East was at its greatest. The diamond in the crown of the Dutch was Batavia in what is now

Fig. 1-4 The ship's cannon from the Santissimo Sacramento

Indonesia. Much of the Dutch maritime economy in the 1600's revolved around Batavia.

Along the coast of Africa, there was major upheaval as the Dutch fought the Portuguese over Angola and Mozambique, and the Portuguese fought the Omani Arabs over the Kenyan and Tanzanian coasts. First, the Dutch took a whole lot of the West African Coast from the Portuguese. Then, the Portuguese took it back. Somewhere in between, the French set up shop on the coast of Senegal and the Swedes, not to be left out of the slave trade, took the Carolusburg fort on the Gold Coast from the Dutch. In the end, it all settled back to the Dutch being the undisputed masters at sea, the Portuguese controlling Mozambique and Angola and the West Coast, and the Omani Arabs controlling the Kenyan and Tanzanian coasts. The Ottomans had the Red Sea and most of the Mediterranean coasts. The other Europeans controlled little spots in various places. No one bothered with the southern tip of Africa, its desert, and its Khoekhoe people. They all preferred the physically stronger black people of West Africa and the Mozambique Coast as slaves for labor in the Americas.

The Dutch had to find a safe halfway house for

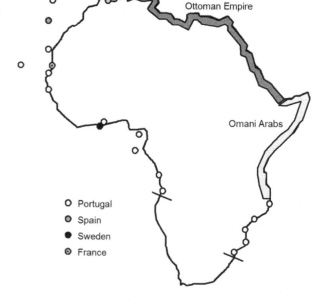

Fig. 1-5 Control of the African Coast by 1652

their long haul to the east. Given they were experiencing the English under Cromwell as a serious new threat, they had to make a plan. And that is how the three ships *Dromedaris*, *Reijger* and *Goede Hoop* came to the Cape. The Dutch had the sea, but the Portuguese had the land of Africa. And all the while the Ottomans and the Arabs continued their slave trade on the east and north coasts. The interior of the Dark Continent remained largely unknown to the Europeans. Most importantly, there was no taking of slaves in Far Southern Africa.

Nexus Familia 1: The men of John Company

On 26 April 1637, a man named Willem Bason registers as a *burgher* (citizen) of Wesel in the Dutch-controlled Duchy of Cleves in the Lower Rhineland, later to become part of Germany. He explains that he was a soldier under one Captain van Lier in the Dutch army that pushed the Catholic Spaniards out of this area some eight years earlier in 1629 during the 30 Years War. With this registration, Willem is allowed to practice his trade independently as a "Master Tailor." He married Elsken Boespinck earlier on May 9, 1634, when she was 24 years old.

In 1647, Willem and Elsken have a son whom they name Arnold Basson. Arnold will later write his name as "Arnout," suggesting that his father, Willem, is in fact a French-speaking Protestant Belgian Walloon, just like fellow Wesel citizen Pierre (Peter) Minuit of New York fame. On 31 March 1647, Arnold is baptized in the historical St. Willibrord Church, which was constructed between 1424 and 1526 and will still be standing in Wesel in the 21st century, despite two future wars that will rage across the entire planet and will reduce Wesel almost to rubble.

As a young man, Arnold joins the VOC, as do many young men from the Rhineland at this time. Arnold will introduce the name Basson to Southern Africa. He cannot know that one of his descendants, bearing the name of his father, will die a horrific death at the hand of a savage

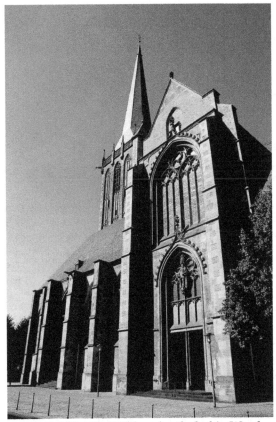

Fig. 1-6 *The St. Willibrord cathedral in Wesel*

African king and that another, bearing his own name, will take to the skies to fight once again in Europe. Many others will be ordinary wheat farmers who will develop a new country in Africa into the breadbasket of an empire, the quiet heroes of civilization.

• In Holland in 1657, Lambert Lambertsz Meijburg marries Aletta Albertsz. Aletta is from the historical Purmerend on the Purmer Lake in the Province of North-Holland. Lambert joins the Dutch East India Company, rising to become an official of that company. It will be Lambert who will introduce the name Meijburg to South Africa. Before entering our story, the couple has a first son, Jan Lambertsz Meijburg, born in 1658 in the Netherlands (*See Fig. 1-7 below*).

• On 9 November 1630, in the Bishopric of Cologne or *Köln* along the Lower Rhine, baby Jacob is baptized as the first son of Conradt and Catharina Klauten in the St. Vitus Catholic church in the village of Oedt. The State of Köln, a bishopric run by the bishop of Cologne, will later become part of Germany in the 19th century. The town of Oedt is on the border of the independent duchies of Jülich and Geldern. At home, Jacob speaks a Plattdeutsch language called Uetsch Plott. It is close to Dutch and Flemish and similar to the German of many Mennonites. He marries Sophia Radergörtges in the same church in Oedt on 31 May 1650. Their first two children, Gerrit (1651) and Elsje (1655), are also baptized there.

Like many young Germans from the Lower Rhine area, Jacob becomes an *adelborst* (cadet) in the Dutch East India Company. Jacob will earn a unique distinction in our story as not only the first of the author's European ancestors to arrive at the Cape, but also as Founding Father of the Afrikaner nation.

—*End Nexus Familia*

Fig. 1-7 Origins of four European ancestors of the author's family

 ## Nexus Familia 2: The Danes and the Vaudois

On the Eiderstedt peninsula of Denmark -1634

The Boyens family has been established for generations on the windswept reclaimed polder flats of the North Frisian Eiderstedt peninsula of 17th Century Denmark. The patriarch of the family is Boje Petersen[11], who is a prominent town councilor in the important harbor town of Tönning. The descendants of Boje will employ the patronymic family name Bojens or Boyens to indicate "Son of Boje."

Before 1650, there are quite a few Boyens family members living in the collection of quaint little towns. In 1603, the area suffered bubonic plague and then came the Thirty Years War. But it is really after the Second Great Drowning of 11 to 12 October 1634 that life becomes miserable. On this fateful night, a raging storm erases most of the island of Nortstrandt just north of the peninsula, along with 6,000 people on it. The dikes that the Dutch built for them a hundred years earlier give way everywhere.

On the Eiderstedt peninsula itself, 2,106 people drown. However, the real long-term disaster is that the soil has been rendered useless by the sea salt. Now, people truly struggle to make a living based on agriculture. Many move away; particularly the Dutch who earlier settled in the area in large numbers. But, life must go on, so some continue, like the Boyens family of Katharinenheerd. Many others join the Dutch fishing and whaling fleets that anchor at Tönning. At least one Boyens family member is on record as being referred to as Schiffer Peter Boyens; "Skipper" (Captain) Boyens of Tönning. The descendants of the Boyens family will also eventually have their lives intertwined with Jan Compagnie, but the people of Katharinenheerd could never dream where these descendants will go.

In the Aigues Valley of Provence, France – 1645

On the sunny southern slopes of the Lubéron Mountain chain of Provence, the Vaudois families Jourdan, Joubert, Mallan, Meynard, Courbon, and Grange have tended their vineyards, olive trees and fruit trees ever since 1495. They live around the cluster of villages of Cabrières-d'Aigues, La Motte-d'Aigues and Saint-Martin-de-la-Brasque in the Aigues ("water") Valley. Our wing of the Jourdan family, in particular, farms at Belle Etoile, a hamlet just north of Saint-Martin[12].

The Jourdan family is entrenched in this part of the world. The name can be found all over the district as suburbs (Les Jourdans in Cabrières d'Aigues), roads (Rue des Jourdans in Cabrières d'Aigues) and even towns (Bastide des Jourdans), along with the 1625 wall inscriptions of the Jourdan name of three relatives of our ancestor Pierre Jourdan. All of these landmarks and inscriptions will still exist in the 21st century.

Fig. 1-8 The polderlands of the Eiderstedt

It was in 1495 that some Vaudois—literally "Valley People"—moved to the Lubéron from their original country in the "lost valley" of Freisinnières, south of Briançon, at the foot of the Cottian Alps. In effect, they merely moved down the valley of the Durance River to where it makes a wide bow to the west. While some Vaudois have remained in the upper reaches of the Durance north of Embrum, the main body of these people lives west of Turin in the isolated valleys of Piedmont in what one day will be Italy, but is now (ca.1640) the independent Duchy of Savoy. The head of state in Turin is Duke Charles Emmanuel II. However, as he is just a child (born 1634), his mother Christine Marie of France is regent. The Protestant Vaudois have practiced their faith for centuries. They insist that they represent the original Christian Church before the implementation of the tenets of the Catholic Church.

Their oldest document, the Nobla Leyçon[13] speaks of the founding of their church in the year 317 AD in response to what they call "corruptions" during the time of Pope Sylvester[14]. In 1500, the Catholic Archbishop of Turin stated that the religion of the Vaudois ("Valdese" in Italian; "Waldensers" in German) originated in the time of Constantine the Great (274–337 AD). Certainly, the Roman Catholic Church has resented their very existence for many centuries and has coupled them with the Cathars of Languedoc, both being Occitan speaking groups. Their pastors are called "barbe," literally meaning "uncle" in the Vaudois idiom. They have the unique distinction of having initiated the first Protestant Bible in French in 1535.

The whole history of the Vaudois is one long litany of persecution at the hand of the Catholic Church and others in authority. In the middle of the 1850s, Alexis Muston will exclaim about the Vaudois of the Cottian Alps, describing their[15] persecution ever since the year 1209:

> *"There is not a rock in the Vaudois valleys which may not be looked on as a monument of death, not a meadow but has been the scene of some execution, not a village but has had its martyrs. No history, however complete, can contain a record of them all."*

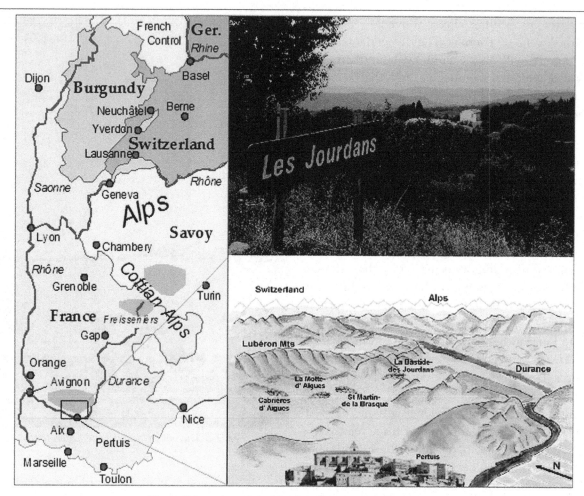

Fig. 1-9 *Location of the Vaudois Protestants of Provence*

In April 1545, the Vaudois in the Lubéron were massacred[16] by troops under the leadership of Jean Maynier, the Count of Oppède, the town on the Lubéron hills. Unspeakable horrors were repeated all over the Lubéron area as Maynier destroyed 22 villages and massacred the Vaudois. Mèrindol was completely destroyed. In the 21st century, the ruins will still hover over the new 17th century town at the foot of the hill. The horrors perpetrated upon these people in the 16th century are beyond description. In Cabrières d'Avignon, north of the Lubéron, the men were dismembered. Among the more merciful actions was filling their victims' mouths with gunpowder and igniting it. When the women and children sought shelter in the church, it was burnt down with everyone inside. It is against this background that several young women preferred to leap to their deaths from a cliff to being taken alive by the soldiers.

At the present time (circa 1645), there is relative calm in Provence, because Henry IV of France proclaimed the Edict of Nantes on 13 April 1589, in terms of which the Protestants in France were free to practice their religion within certain bounds. However, with the Dutch and German Protestants in the ascendancy, Rome is worried about dissenting groups in France. These include the Vaudois of Provence and Dauphiné, the Protestant descendants of the Cathars in the Cevennes fastnesses of Languedoc, and the more mainline Protestant Huguenots of Northern France. The Protestants fear a repetition of the Jean Maynier Massacres of 1545 in Provence and the St. Bartholomeu Day Massacre of 1572, when 10,000 Protestants were butchered in Paris and other major centers.

In 1645, Pierre Jourdan marries 18-year old Jeanne Marque, daughter of David Marque and Marie Grange. They continue to farm at Belle Etoile, directly across the road from some of the Joubert family.

In Cabrières-d'Aigues, the main town of the cluster of villages in the Aigues Valley, the villagers constructed a mule-driven olive oil mill in an enlarged cave at the center of the village in 1611. To this, they added an attic floor in 1626. Originally, the Vaudois of the Aigues Valley were allowed to use Catholic churches to hold their services. On July 21, 1632, the Parliament of Provence, located in Aix-en-Provence, forbade this practice. The townsfolk of Cabrières-d'Aigues thereupon converted the attic above the mill into a Protestant Vaudois meeting place.

In 1645, when their request to build a new temple in the town is refused, they convert the attic of the olive oil mill into a Protestant church. In La Motte d'Aigues the villagers build their own separate temple. This is where the Jourdans now attend their church services, about 1.5 miles from their farm.

— End Nexus Familia

 ## Nexus Familia 3: In the Far East

In the period around 1650, the VOC runs its operations at "factories" along the southwestern Malabar Coast of India and along its eastern Coromandel Coast, as well as in the Bengal area. In these areas, the Dutch trade in goods, but they also engage laborers. In many cases, people are so desperately poor that they present themselves for sale at the docks as "slaves" or indentured workers in order to have a living. The Dutch use only one term, "slaves," for all forms of such labor, whether forcibly enslaved or indentured. They name the slaves in terms of origin. So, for example, Angela from the Bengal area is called Ansela van Bengale, while Catharine from the Malabar Coast is called Catharina van Malabar. In time, their surnames become "van Bengale" and "van Malabar." This is no different from the way the Dutch name themselves. For example, a man named Jan van Deventer would be the particular Jan that comes from the town of Deventer.

The main base of the VOC in the Far East is Batavia. Many slaves and other laborers from India are taken to Batavia to work there for the company or in individual households. This is how we find the young Indian girl, Catharina van Bengale, originally from Pulicat on the Coromandel Coast of India, living as a slave in Batavia in the household of a lady named Maria Magdalena. Catharina is more popularly known in the community as Groote Catrijn ("Great Catherine"). She finds herself in a rather ugly abusive relationship with Claes van Malabar and is getting more and more frantic by the day about her personal situation. This simply cannot go on. Catherina has a compatriot named Ansela van Bengale, more popularly known as Maaij Ansela ("Mother Angela"), who is the slave of Pieter Kemp, a ship's captain. As her name indicates, she is also from Bengal. She works in Kemp's household.

Anthonij van Bengale, sometimes known as Anthonij Jansz de Later van Bengale, is a VOC employee in Batavia, and not a slave of the Dutch. Some say he is a Mardijker; a freed former slave. The Mardijkers have historically been released from slavery on condition of serving in the military when required. As a result, they form the backbone of the Dutch military in Indonesia. The Portuguese originally introduced this system, and the Dutch adopted it when they defeated the Portuguese in the Far East. The Dutch make quite a distinction between the Mardijkers and the indigenous people of Indonesia.

— End Nexus Familia

And in America?

On May 14, 1607, in what was later to become the United States, explorers of the Virginia Company from England landed on Jamestown Island to establish the Virginia English colony 60 miles from the mouth of the Chesapeake Bay. Matters were difficult for these folks until John Rolfe persuaded the Algonquins to stop their aggression through the expedient of marrying Pocahontas, daughter of a chief.

Not to be outdone, the Dutch started Nieuw-Amsterdam in 1614 on Manhattan Island as a fur-trading post. The Dutch West Indies Company founded the colony of Nieuw-Nederland in 1624 between latitudes 38 and 42 degrees, covering what is today part of Delaware, New Jersey, New York and Connecticut. The settlers were Dutch and Belgian. In 1625, Nieuw-Amsterdam was made capital of Nieuw-Nederland. In 1626, Pierre Minuit became director of the Dutch West Indies Company. Like Willem Bason, he was a Walloon

(French Belgian) refugee who also had settled in Wesel in Germany. His efforts were less than successful and in 1631 he was recalled. By then, it was clear that the infant settlement had turned into a financial disaster.

In around 1607–1608, a major part of the Separatist community in England fled to the Netherlands. Life there was not easy and so, in 1617, they started planning to settle in America and would eventually negotiate a "patent" from the English king to do exactly that. They sailed from the Netherlands in two ships and collected more members in Plymouth, England, where the crew sabotaged one of the ships to prevent it leaving.

They arrived in November 1620 at what is today Massachusetts on the remaining ship, the *Mayflower*, as the "*Pilgrim Fathers*." Of the 102 settlers, more than half had come from the Netherlands. By March 1621, only 47 were left alive and half of the *Mayflower's* crew had died. Not a good start at all.

As Jan van Riebeeck approached the Cape of Good Hope, the east Coast of North America therefore had two groups of disconnected English colonies with a Dutch one sandwiched between them. There was even a Swedish one further up the Delaware River, started by none other than Peter Minuit working for new bosses. None of these colonies had proved economically viable as yet. Certainly, none compared with Dutch Batavia.

Nexus Familia 4: Our American Ancestors

Adriaen Huybertszen Sterrevelt is a young man from Zegwaart east of s'Gravenhage (The Hague) in the Netherlands. In 1644, the 25-year old Adriaen is in the service of the Dutch West Indies Company on the island of Curaçao[17], off the coast of South America.

The island was only occupied ten years ago in 1634, so things are all a-hustle and a-bustle. The industrious Dutch under commander Pieter Stuyvesant are building their agricultural operations on the island group. At this time, Willemstad on the Schottegat inlet along the south coast, is the main center. A few years from now the Dutch will turn it into a major trade hub for the Atlantic Slave Trade from Africa. At this time, though, there is not much more than just Fort Amsterdam and a cluster of houses.

Adriaen has been away from home for a few years now and is dying to see his parents, Huybert Eggert Sterrevelt and Geertruyda Ariensz. His plan is to return to Holland as soon as he has saved up enough money.

In April 1644, Pieter Stuyvesant attacks the Spanish held island of St. Martin. There he is wounded. When he returns to the Netherlands, his right leg is amputated and he is fitted with an ornate wooden leg prosthetic. In May 1645, he receives the commission as Governor of Nieuw Nederland around the Hudson River in North America. On 11 May 1647, Stuyvesant, now fitted with his later-to-be-famous prosthetic, arrives in New Amsterdam. Ancestor Adriaen Huybertszen Sterrevelt is soon to follow.

—End Nexus Familia

-----ooOoo-----

2

The Cape of Good Hope

"A goodly Countrey, inhabited by a most savage and beastly people as ever I thinke God Created."

John Davis
Second Voyage with Sir Edward Michelburne in 1605

The Dutch at the Cape

When Jan van Riebeeck stepped ashore at the Cape on 7 April 1652, he did so with specific instructions to *not* start a colony. The focus of the refreshment station was totally on supplying the VOC Far East shipping traffic with fresh meat and vegetables. It was to be a VOC company operation with no colonial ambitions. In accordance with the commission of the Lords Seventeen, Jan van Riebeeck had to build a fort, a hospital for the sick, lay out orchards and vegetable gardens, prepare fields in order to provide the ships with grain, and obtain cattle by means of trade with the Khoekhoe tribes in the vicinity of the settlement. He succeeded in achieving all these goals. However, while the Dutch, Portuguese, and English had all traded to some limited degree with these indigenous Khoekhoe people for fresh meat, these encounters, as we have already seen, had often ended unsatisfactorily.

⛨ Nexus Familia 5: Table Bay – 1652

Fig. 2-1 Jan van Riebeeck, first Cape Commander

On Christmas Eve 1651, three ships leave the Dutch harbor of Texel, headed for the distant southern tip of Africa. The "fluit" *Reijger*, under captain Jan Hoogzaad, and the "jacht" *Dromedaris*, under captain David Koning, have both been to Batavia and back once before. Both are 560-ton vessels and typical examples of their respective designs. Simon Turver is the master of the third vessel, the "jacht" *Goede Hoop*. This is the first journey of the *Goede Hoop*. All three ships were built in the Amsterdam shipyard in the past five or six years and all three of them are sailing commercially for the Chamber of Amsterdam, one of the "houses" of the VOC. Initially, the *Dromedaris* is so top-heavy that the master fears she will capsize. However, as soon as they have cleared hostile waters, the guns are stowed below as ballast to stabilize the vessel.

On board the *Dromedaris* are 49 individuals destined to disembark at the Cape. Among them are the appointed commander of the planned refreshment station, Jan van Riebeeck, his wife, Maria de la Quellerie, daughter of a French Huguenot Protestant, and two nieces. On the *Reijger* are a further 28 members of the landing party[1]. The rumors that Jan has been caught in some form of misconduct are perfectly true. However, he has pressed for the creation of the refreshment station at the Cape after talking firsthand to the survivors of the 25 March 1647 wreck of the *Haarlem* at the Cape. Some are speculating that he volunteered for the role of commander in order to win the opportunity to clear his name.

With our ancestor Krotoa and her whole Goringhaikona clan of Strandlopers under the leadership of her uncle Herry (Autshumao) watching from the shore, the three ships arrive in Table Bay on 6 April 1652, after a three-and-a-half month journey. On 7 April 1652, Jan van Riebeeck and his party go ashore. Work on the building of a fort starts immediately. On April 15, the *Salamander* sails into Table Bay on the way from Batavia. When she departs on the 19th, she leaves behind[2] three men: a clerk, Frederik Verburgh, and two workmen. On the 24th of the month, Van Riebeeck moves permanently ashore with his family. The chief gardener, the aptly named Hendrik Boom (tree), and the sick comforter, Willem Wylant, are also accompanied by their wives and children. None of them will settle in this new country. On 7 May 1652, the *Walvis* and the *Witte Olifant* arrive from the Netherlands, having stopped in at Sao Vincente in the Cape Verde Islands. A full hundred and thirty people on the two ships have died en route and many are in a terrible state with scurvy. This illustrates the full horror of these long-range sea voyages in the seventeenth century. The decision is that the weakest fifty will be taken ashore, along with provisions for three months. Within one month of their arrival, the settlement party is already fulfilling its mission of caring for the sick of the passing VOC ships, though they cannot yet supply refreshments to those ships.

The *Walvis* and *Witte Olifant* leave again for Batavia on 16 May 1652 and the very next day the *Reijger* also leaves. On 25 May, the *Hof van Zeeland* arrives from The Netherlands having lost 37 men. She leaves within 7 days. On 28 May 1652, the *Dromedaris* finally departs, leaving the aptly named *Goede Hoop* (Good Hope) to do solitary point duty at the Cape. The *Goede Hoop* will stay until the next year. The founding party and their patients at the Cape are now alone at the mercy of the unforgiving rock of Africa, the tempestuous elements, and the reputedly barbaric and belligerent Khoekhoe. They are stuck in the haunt of the infamous[3] Flying Dutchman, doomed to forever challenge the Cape of Storms. It will no doubt appear in July, the southern winter with its terrifying gales and mountainous seas. It will be eight months before the party sees another ship and their morale will hit rock bottom when they realize that the annual return fleet from Batavia has actually passed them by, carrying the horses they so badly need.

Their misery increases by the day and, as the rainy season sets in, they systematically succumb to dysentery and scurvy. By 3 June, only 60 of the men are capable of work. They have no proper food and no proper shelter. All are cheered, though, by the arrival of the first baby of European descent born[4] at the Cape to Willem Barents Wylant, the *Sieketrooster* (Sick Comforter), on 6 June. However, the fate of the landed party is better than that of the three ships that brought them. None of the three will ever see home again. The ships sail away from the Cape to meet their respective dooms. The *Reijger* is blown up by its own powder on 19 October 1654 at Pulicat in India. The *Goede Hoop* stays on point duty at the Cape until 23 January 1653, and is then lost near Amboina in Indonesia on 13 July 1654 and the *Dromedaris* will stay in the Far East and be laid up there in 1661. The sad fate of these ships presages the ultimate destiny of the new country that will result from their journey.

— End Nexus Familia

The Infant Settlement

The settlement nearly went under in the first two years. For one thing, the Khoekhoe were not as forthcoming with cattle for trade as had been hoped. The fact that they were largely nomadic certainly did not help. For another, the rain in winter turned the little settlement into a quagmire. In fact, it was evident why the Portuguese, in their own 150 years of ruling these waves, had never created any settlement or refreshment station at the Cape. The place was beautiful, but harsh, and the Khoekhoe were a serious menace. It was also clear that Jan Compagnie[5] simply could not grow food fast enough here to supply the hungry ships rounding the Cape at the zenith of the company. They needed a better plan. So the ever-economically-thinking Dutch put their faith in Free Enterprise. At first, Van Riebeeck asked the Compagnie for some free men to work farms. When this failed, he petitioned for some of the existing Compagnie men to be freed from their obligations to the company in order to farm on a private basis. In 1655, the VOC granted this permission. The decision was implemented on 21 February 1657 when the first nine Free Burghers were given land along the Liesbeek River. By 1662, there would be sixty of these free men. Most became wheat farmers.

In 1657, Abraham Gabbema was sent to investigate the land to the north. He returned to report to Van Riebeeck the presence of a beautiful river flowing from the Hottentots-Holland Mountains over flat arable ground. They promptly named it the Berg River (the "Mountain" river).

Problems with the Khoekhoe started quite early on. On 19 October 1653, Autshumao, Van Riebeeck's interpreter who ate from his table as a friend, murdered the Dutch cattle-herd David Jans. He took off with almost the entire herd of the settlers' cattle. He was pursued but not captured. By 1657, with the station in its fifth year, the First Hottentot War broke out. It would appear that the Khoekhoe were unhappy about the VOC using their grazing land for growing crops. It was in this little "war" that the Dutch discovered the Khoekhoe had perfected the art of using war cattle. They could use whistles to guide the animals to stampede the lands, dwellings, and defensive positions of the Dutch. All in all, the "war" was a trifling affair and the Khoekhoe soon sued for peace. Nevertheless, on 4 May 1659 the Khoekhoe attacked again. At this point, Van Riebeeck realized he needed a better plan for the defense of the station and implemented the Commando system.

Commando! – Where it all started

During the 1659 war, the VOC soldiers found that they could not cope with the hit-and-run tactics of the Khoekhoe. So Van Riebeeck implemented what was to become known as the Commando system. In terms of this system, all the farmers were "called up for military service" in a militia, called a Commando. He imported horses from Batavia to pursue the Khoekhoe raiders and organized the burghers into groups that could be rapidly mobilized to conduct focused military expeditions. They also had to do annual exercises to prepare for all eventualities. The Commando system would last 347 years until 2006 and would have consequences around the globe.

In the year 2001, the millions of descendants of the people at New Amsterdam watched in astonishment as their own hardened and bearded Special Forces Commando men appeared on horseback in faraway Afghanistan, fighting alongside Afghan militia. It all started here with Jan van Riebeeck and the Khoekhoe "guerrilla" attacks in 1659. This was the moment that the term "Commando" was introduced into continuous use in British military history. The British would be impressed by the mobility and efficacy of South African Boer "Commandos" in the Boer War of 1899. In WWII, South African-born Lt Col Dudley Clark[6] suggested similar British units and the name, with support from Winston Churchill himself.

The US Rangers were subsequently based on the British model.

Nexus Familia 6: Free Burghers and Khoekhoe

On 10 April 1657, the VOC ship *Maria* leaves the harbor of Vlie, arriving at the Cape on 13 July 1657. On board is a 27-year old adelborst (cadet) named Jacob Cloeten (Klauten) (*NF1*). On 10 August 1657, Jacob becomes one of the first twenty[7] Free Burghers of the settlement at the Cape. On 10 October, he and one other man become the first to receive individual title[8] to land at the Cape. Three hundred years later, his farm will be known as the Cape Town suburb of Rondebosch.

On 22 October 1658, Jacob's wife, Sophia "Fijtje" Radergoertgens, her two children, Elsje and Gerrit, and her brother Pieter board the ship Arnhem under captain Jan Timonsz at the Dutch harbor of Vlie. When they arrive alive and well at the Cape on 16 March 1659, it is the first time in almost 4 years that Jacob sees his children again.

During the Khoekhoe problems of 1659, soon after Fijtje's arrival, Jacob Cloeten and Jan Martensz de Wacht are out tending their cattle when a raiding party of Khoekhoe appears. The womenfolk at the homestead see the Khoekhoe and run into the house, grab the front-loading muskets and help to beat off the attack. This is an early example of something we shall see again as the tough and stubborn "Dutch" women participate in the defense of their families.

On 4 April 1660, using the services of a chaplain on a passing ship, Jacob and Sophia baptize their first child born in Africa, Catharina, named after Jacob's mother in faraway Oedt. Jacob is the first European to cross the triple hurdles of (1) receiving his Letter of Freedom from the Company, (2) having his wife at the Cape and (3) conceiving and baptizing a child at the Cape. He sets the example to follow.

Willem Schalksz Van der Merwe is a haakbusskutter (arquebusier) on the ship *Dordrecht*. He arrives as an 18-year old in the Cape on this ship on 26 April 1661. He almost immediately makes use of the opportunity to become a Free Burgher, but two years later rejoins the VOC as an ensign charged with agriculture. On 9 September 1668, he marries Jacob Cloeten's eldest daughter, Elsje. By now, Willem has gained the respect of his colleagues as a successful farmer. Willem and Elsje will have thirteen children, of whom no fewer than five are in the ancestral pool of the author and his wife.

—End Nexus Familia

Nexus Familia 7: Ariaentje's New Amsterdam

One of the earliest things that Ariaentje can remember is the scary man with the stern face and the ornate wooden peg leg. He kept riding past their front door on his Flanders mare. She remembers she simply could not take her eyes off that leg. It looked like a fancy table leg. Now that she is much older, at four years of age, he does not seem quite so scary. Her father, Adriaen Sterrevelt (*NF4*), has explained that the man is the governor. She is not clear on what exactly that means, but it sounds important. Her father has also explained that many many years ago, she thinks maybe just after Noah built the Ark, he worked for that man on a faraway island with a funny name. Her father told her many stories about pirates and how the governor fought the Spaniards and lost his right leg. The man's name is Pieter Stuyvesant and her father said he is the bravest man he has ever known.

Ariaentje is every bit the four year old young lady; restless and inquisitive. Her new mother, Thysje, has told her not to go down the lane to the Waterside, but she simply cannot resist. That's where the naughty men have to stand with their heads and hands through holes in wooden planks. A little bit further along the shore is the Weigh House. Her mother has told her that place is totally out of bounds, because the rough sailors who work there with the boats must be avoided at all costs.

They have lived on Hoogh Straat[9] since the spring of 1663. They moved there when her real mother left one day in February. Ariaentje remembers her as a beautiful lady named Judith. That was the only time she has ever seen her father cry. She was also sad, but her father bounced her on his knee and told her that her mother was now with Jesus, so that was good. Her mother left them a new baby sister when she went away. Her father took the baby to the church in the fort. When he came back, he said that the *dominee* had baptized her Geertie. That was the name of Ariaentje's late granny in Holland, whom she never knew. Her grandfather is still living there in a town called Soetermeer (Sweet Lake). Her father was all fingers and thumbs with the baby. Only a few short weeks later her father brought Miss Thysje Gerrits to meet her and her sister, Neeltje. He married her soon after on 3 May 1664. This was all exciting, because Miss Thysje had four children of her own. So now they are a big family.

It was around the same time that her father took her and Neeltje to meet Mr. Aldert Coninck and Mr. Claas Visser. Mr. Coninck lives on Slyck Straat, the road behind their house. Mr. Visser lives further down Hoogh Straat, towards the Heere Gracht. Her father explained that the men in the Stadt Huys (City Hall) had said that the two gentlemen must be guardians for her, Neeltje and Geertie. Apparently, they have to look after the inheritance of the three girls from their mother, Judith. Ariaentje has no idea what that means, but the two uncles were nice to them; so that must be good[10].

Their front door on Hoogh Straat faces towards the East River, though there is one block of houses in the way. There are lanes leading to the East River from Hoogh Straat on either side of that block. The one on the left is the lane on which Mr. La Chair lives[11]. The one on the right is Stadhuys Laan[12]. Next door, to their left (her father says "east," whatever that means), lives Mister Wessel Evertsen. He must be a very old man, because Miss Thysje says that he got married in 1643 when Ariaentje's father was still on that funny island with Peg Leg and the many pirates.

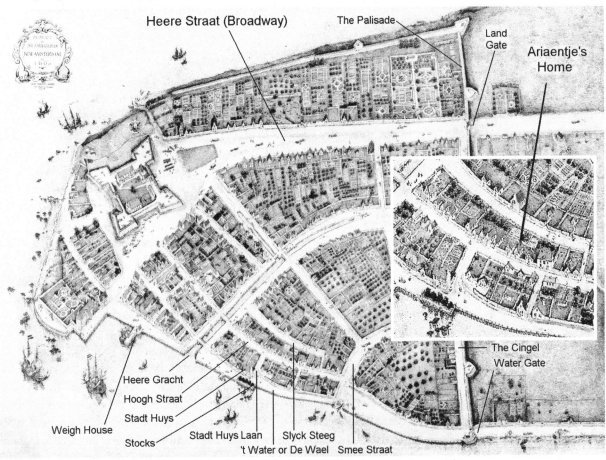

Fig. 2-2 New Amsterdam in the time of Ariaentje Sterrevelt

On their other side is the place of Mister van Vleeck. Her father says that Mr. Van Vleeck spends most of his time in the faraway village of Bergen catching bad men. Her father says he is the Sheriff in that town – whatever that is. Across the road lives the old Burgemeester, Mr. Van Cortland. Ariaentje likes him – he has grey hair and is wise indeed. Some days the traders bring their boats up the Heere Gracht and tie them to the bridge at the bottom of Hoogh Straat. Lots of people come from all over to buy and sell all manner of things. The Indians intrigue Ariaentje. They usually row up in their canoes, which is quite something to see. Ariaentje is fascinated by the strings of shells that everyone uses for money. They call it wampum, and Indians on Long Island specially make it from periwinkle shells. There are black ones and white ones, and the black ones are twice as expensive as the white ones. Miss Thysje was quite unhappy once when the men at the Stadt Huys told her that she must bring them wampum[13]. It had something to do with a thing called "Tax." Ariaentje has no idea what that is, but it made Miss Thysje extremely angry, so it must be really bad.

The other interesting thing is to go down Stadhuys Laan to the river. It is quite close – closer than what she can throw a rock. On the corner of the lane and the Waterside sits the City Hall. There is always interesting stuff happening there. The men look angry, and sometimes frightened, before they go in there. Her father says that is where grown-ups go to get their problems solved[14]. She should ask him again, because she has looked carefully at the men who come out of there. They do not look at all happy. Maybe that "Tax" thing lives inside the building.

Behind their house runs Slyck Steeg[15]. At the bottom end of that road, is Mister van Couwenhoven's brewery. Jochem the Baker is also on this road. However, the person she likes most on this street is Susanna, the black lady who owns a house with Mrs. Ruth Jacobsen, right next to Mr. Steenhuysen. She always gives Ariaentje something to eat when Miss Thysje is not looking.

One evening in August of this year, Ariaentje sees her father talking wide-eyed to Mr. Loockermans, the guardian for Miss Thysje's children. This is the moment Ariaentjie's life will change.

August 1664 - New Amsterdam

There are four English ships lying anchored off Nyack up the North River. Loockermans and the other leading men believe the English want to take New Amsterdam, but Stuyvesant is determined to fight them. There are several Englishmen living in New Amsterdam and others often come to trade from Long Island. In fact, Richard Smith and "Karel Verbrugge" (actually Charles Bridges) across the road from the Sterrevelts are both Englishmen. They are decent enough men, but the Englanders have never come with warships before. Adriaen tells his family that it may not be so bad for the Englanders to take over, because the West India Company has not been looking after its people in New Amsterdam. Perhaps the English will do a better job. The problem is the caliber of Englishmen from their colonies. They just want to plunder New Amsterdam. He does not trust the Company's own mercenary soldiers either.

By 5 September, the English commander, Colonel Nicholls, has lost patience. He puts some soldiers ashore at Breuckelen to join the colonial English who are eager for plunder. They have been eying New Amsterdam for many years. Then he sails two of his ships right under the fort. Thysje is frantic. Apparently, Stuyvesant is insisting on fighting. It seems he is standing on the ramparts at the fort and the gunners have lit matches ready to fire at the ships; the man does not frighten easily. *Dominees* Megapolensis Senior and Junior have gone to plead with him not to fire at the ships.

The next day, there is a huge commotion at the Stadt Huys near their house. *Dominee* Megapolensis seems to be the man who most men will listen to. They draw up a document and this is given to Stuyvesant later that day. It begs him, for the sake of the people, not to resist the English. Olof van Cortland, the previous burgemeester across the road from the Sterrevelts, is one of the signatories and so too is Loockermans, one of the family guardians. Soon the message makes its way up the street that Stuyvesant relented when he saw the name of his own son Balthazar among the signatories. He has asked a number of men, including *Dominee* Megapolensis and Olof van Cortland, to negotiate with the English.

The next morning, Saturday, everyone is on tenterhooks. The team from the town is meeting with the English at Stuyvesant's farm outside the palisades. And then comes the word – they have reached agreement. Stuyvesant will take his men and leave, and the English will take over the fort and the town and there will be no shooting. Most importantly, one of the conditions is that the people of the town will be able to commute between New Amsterdam and Holland for at least the next one year and six weeks.

Two days later, on Monday morning 9 September 1664, Peter Stuyvesant and his men march out of the Fort down Bever Straat under a Dutch flag. Then the English march in under an English one. Everyone is there to watch nervously, but Thysje keeps the children at home. All day her eyes are big as saucers. Later, the commotion moves nearer their house as the English officer Cartwright and his men take over City Hall. Ariaentje's father observes that the English have wisely left their colonial rabble on the Breuckelen side where they cannot do any mischief. It seems things may work out after all.

On 15 March 1665, Adriaen Huybertszen Sterrevelt advises the Orphan Chamber via the guardians of his children that he *"now no longer knows how to make a living."* He states his intention to return with his wife and children to Nederland. The next day he informs them that his father, Huybert Eggers, is still alive in Soetermeer while his wife has a sister in Alkmaar. One day later, on the 17th of March 1665, he sells their house on Hoogh Straat to Meindert Barentsen. Early in April he and Miss Thysje pay a security deposit to the Orphan Masters in order to access their children's inheritance. The only ship to Amsterdam recorded that year, the *Gekruyste Hart* (Crossed Heart) leaves soon after on 6 May 1665. They are likely on this ship, along with Pieter Stuyvesant who is sailing to Holland to clear his name in respect of the surrender.

On 29 October 1665, Adriaen Huybertszen Sterrevelt registers as citizen in Amsterdam, but we never hear of him or his wife Thysje Gerrits again. Ariaentje and Neeltje, on the other hand, shall return to center stage in our story two years later and 6,000 miles away.

Fig. 2-3 *Dominee Megapolensis and the women pleading with Pieter Stuyvesant not to fire on the English*

—*End Nexus Familia*

The "First Nations"

The matter of the indigenous peoples at the Cape constitutes the first enduring fallacy concerning South Africa. Many people in the Northern Hemisphere are under the misconception that black Negroid Ba'Ntu[16] people inhabited the Cape when the Dutch first arrived there in 1652. The original people at the Cape were in fact the Khoekhoe. It would take a full fifty years—two generations—before black and white would first meet overland, more than 500 miles further east. This is roughly the distance from Washington DC to Montreal in Canada, or from San Francisco to Boise, Idaho. In European terms, it is the length of the entire Britain or the distance from Bonn in Germany to Venice on the Adriatic Sea. In fact, one could fit all of New England, New York, New Jersey, Pennsylvania, Delaware and Maryland with space to spare into the area of the present South Africa not occupied by black Ba'Ntu people when the Dutch arrived.

Along the south coast of the country, the scenery is spectacular, but it is near-impassable territory with deep ravines and the Outeniqua and Knysna temperate forests with their towering trees. In amongst these are tree ferns and elephants. These forests are a result of the Tsitsikamma and Outeniqua mountain ranges. These forests and gorges formed a barrier to development well into the 20th century. They certainly separated the Western Cape Khoekhoe from the Ba'Ntu. Inland, behind these mountain ranges, the brutally dry Karoo offered almost no sustenance for livestock. This is quite similar to the situation along the US west coast, where the major forests hug the Sierra Nevada and it is bone dry in the lee of those mountains, with places like Death Valley. The South African mountains are much lower, but they are much closer to the sea, resulting in these unique coastal temperate rain forests.

The people who inhabited the dry western 45% of the present South Africa were the Khoi-San. The Khoi-San ethnic family is composed of just two members, the Khoi, or Khoekhoe (as they historically referred to themselves) and the San peoples, more popularly known as the Bushmen. The latter were made famous across the globe by the cult motion picture "The Gods Must be Crazy" from the early 1980s, which depicted the oddities of the culture clash between Western Man and the San.

The 300–350 mm summer rainfall line is the line of separation between the Khoekhoe and San people to the dry west and the black Ba'Ntu people to the moist east. This split still exists in the 21st century, as clearly shown by the 2002 South African voter registration list[17]. The uncanny correspondence between the rainfall distribution and the distribution of black Ba'Ntu people in South Africa is seen by comparing Fig. 2-5 with Fig. 2-4.

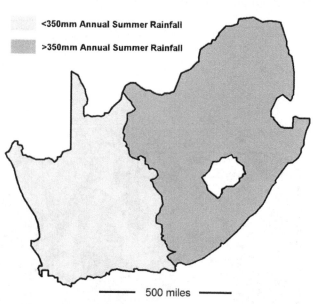

Fig. 2-4 Summer rainfall distribution in South Africa, excluding western mountainous orographic rain areas

The original Khoekhoe people constitute today the main stock of the so-called "Coloured" people of South Africa. It is therefore crucially important to understand the huge difference between the usage of the term "Colored" in the USA and the term "Coloured," as used by the 21st century government in South Africa.

The Khoekhoe tended to inhabit the slightly more moist regions nearer the coastline, while the San inhabited the desperately dry interior and the Kalahari Desert. The San inhabited all of Southern Africa at some point, as witnessed by the distribution of their characteristic rock paintings over most of Southern Africa. In fact, these paintings may be found as far north as Kenya in northeast Africa. As the black Ba'Ntu people migrated south, they pushed out these little people ahead of them until the latter remained only in the utterly marginal areas. The Khoekhoe appear to be a branch of the Khoi-San family that adapted some of the lifestyle of the Ba'Ntu, but not their agriculture.

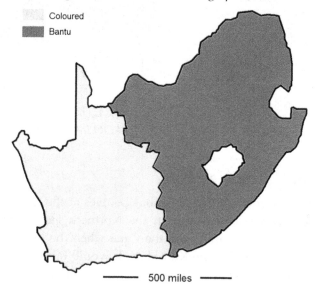

Fig. 2-5 Distribution of "Coloured" and Ba'Ntu South Africans by majority race per voting district

The Khoekhoe inhabited the southern coastal region of South Africa all the way to the Keiskamma River, some 600 miles east of Cape Town. Northward, they live all the way up through Namibia to roughly the Tropic of Capricorn. In Namibia, Ba'Ntu people, until recently, lived only north of the present Windhoek, where the rainfall increases abruptly due to a high plateau, allowing the keeping of cattle. It is important for the reader to comprehend that the Khoekhoe represent a historically important racial group in Southern Africa, predating the black Ba'Ntu people by millennia.

Fig. 2-6 A 1780s Khoekhoe man as sketched by visitor La Vallaint

Historically, the Khoekhoe were viewed by the Europeans as the most outrageously primitive people on Earth and best not engaged, unless really necessary. Their peculiar customs of removing one testicle from every male, covering themselves and their hair in reeking soot-saturated animal fat, eating raw animal intestines[18] still bearing some contents, did not sit well at all with Dutch Calvinistic sensibilities. Nor did wearing dried intestines around their necks or legs as adornment, and covering newborn babies in cow dung, as reported by Van Riebeeck[19].

At least thirteen contemporary reports describe them enjoying their own body lice[20] as a delicacy. These they extracted with much zeal from the untanned animal skins they wore. Visitors were also taken aback by the practice of the married Khoekhoe women of throwing their exceedingly pendulous breasts[21] over their shoulders to thereby suckle the babies borne in animal skins on their backs. It is difficult to imagine a greater cultural separation than between the 17th century Khoekhoe and the Europeans of that century. In 1616, Edward Terry[22] described the Khoekhoe as *"beasts in the skins of men, rather than men in the skins of beasts."* On 14 April 1653, one year and one week after the landing at the Cape, Van Riebeeck wrote[23] the Lords XVII and pleaded for a transfer to India away from the *"dull, stupid, lazy, stinking people."* At least he called them "people."

Up until the late 19th century, the term "Hottentot" was used in the English language as a definite pejorative, implying the lowest of human beings. The fact that these people had no writing had not discovered the wheel or the arch and, most particularly, had never developed any form of agriculture, certainly did not impress the Dutch, who had become the custodians of the Renaissance. After all, this was the time of Rembrandt van Ryn. Many visiting Europeans were also taken aback by the Khoekhoe ladies' practice of displaying their genitalia to all and sundry for some food or a roll of tobacco[24].

Much has been made in recent times of how Dutch and English writers of the 17th and 18th centuries either did, or did not, misrepresent these people to the European public. There is no doubt that many of the descriptions were, in fact, quite correct at the time, but the way in which these unique people were presented as the "nadir of mankind" was certainly inappropriate and did them a great disservice

The Khoekhoe, who cultivated no plants whatsoever, saw themselves as the owners of the land and the Dutch as the slaves to the land. They would not "demean themselves" by plowing the land like the Dutch[25]. The consequence of their philosophy was a lack of progress, but they had difficulty in seeing how the Calvinistic Dutch view of life offered improvement in their own lives. Through Dutch eyes, the Khoekhoe just lazed about.

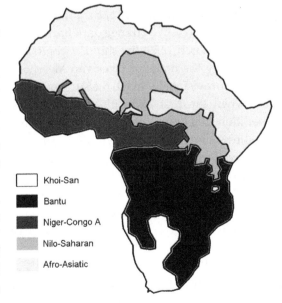

Khoi-San
Bantu
Niger-Congo A
Nilo-Saharan
Afro-Asiatic

Fig. 2-7 The ethno-linguistic groups of Africa

The semi-nomadic Khoekhoe kept sheep and cattle, though some, like Herry's Goringhaikona, were largely scavengers. They lived in temporary huts that consisted of slats that were tied together and over which animal skins were draped. The cattle were highly valued and seldom slaughtered. The Dutch notion of the Khoekhoe potentially being the source of an endless stream of fresh meat for passing Dutch ships was certainly fanciful. Ultimately, they could not keep up with the demand.

By contrast, the San or "Bushmen" were exclusively hunter-gatherers. They were called "AbaTwa" (the Twa people) by the Ba'Ntu peoples and "Obiqua" by the Khoekhoe. The Khoekhoe and the Ba'Ntu objected to the San preying on their domesticated cattle and killing those of their cattle they could not take with them. They hunted the San like animals to be killed on sight. The San, with their poisoned arrows and stalking skills returned the compliment, but their clan-based lifestyle placed them at a major disadvantage with respect to the more organized Ba'Ntu. Most fascinatingly, DNA-studies[26] strongly suggest that, of all present peoples on Earth, the San provide us with the most direct link back to our collective original human ancestors. They exhibit the earliest human Y-DNA haplogroup mutation on Earth, namely L0.

 Nexus Familia 8: Eva

Commander Jan van Riebeeck has been scratching his head about the difficulties in dealing with the Khoekhoe. He has instructions from the Company to maintain good relations with the indigenous people at the Cape. At the same time, he needs cattle from the Khoekhoe and they do have rather a nasty habit of stealing livestock from the company whenever they get the chance. They have this peculiar form of speech that consists of a series of click sounds; most strange. That is why everyone here calls them the *Hottentotten*. Their speech sounds like their name. The solution is to get an interpreter and the best one he can identify is the Khoekhoe girl, Krotoa, from the Goringhaikona nation. The Dutch rename her *"Eva."* Van Riebeeck therefore invites the teenage Eva to join his household[27]. Here she learns both Dutch and Portuguese, as well as how to conduct herself in "Western Society."

Eva is an enigma to the Van Riebeecks. She dresses in Western clothes in the Van Riebeeck household, but goes half-naked and wears a *karos* (animal skin) when visiting her uncle Autshumao, "Herry the Strandloper" (beachcomber). He is the chief of the Goringhaikona. Eva's sister is the wife of Oedesoa, leader of one of the other Khoekhoe clans living near Saldanha Bay. When Jean-Baptiste Tavernier visits the Cape in 1660, he meets with Eva and describes[28] her as being *"as white as one of our European women."* A few paragraphs later he states, *"She is white, and pretty, except that her nose is somewhat flat."* In October 1657, Eva tells Van Riebeeck of a strange dark brown "Kobona" people far to the east; the Ba'Ntu.

On 8 March 1659, the ship *Princes Royale* pulls into the bay. On board is a dapper young soldier from Denmark by the name of Peter van Meerhof. Before long, the young man impresses several senior officers and he is provisionally made the surgeon's assistant.

When the first expedition to the distant interior is launched in 1660, he is a member. While the expedition achieves little, Pieter again impresses, and is chosen as second-in-command of the second expedition under Pieter Cruythoff that leaves on 30 January 1661. This expedition is more successful and makes contact with the most advanced Khoekhoe group encountered thus far, the Namaqua. Van Riebeeck is keen to establish good trading relations with them, and the men notice that they have obtained gold somewhere. This becomes the start of several expeditions[29] to find the route to the legendary Kingdom of Monomotapa. Pieter van Meerhof will be on a total of six of these expeditions and a young man by the name of Cornelis de Cretzer will join him on one. Thereby they become close friends. None of the expeditions will find Monomotapa, but they will learn a lot about the more distant Khoekhoe groupings. Over this period, Pieter is finally promoted to surgeon.

On 3 May 1662, ancestor Eva becomes the first indigenous South African to be baptized as a Christian. The top governing structure at the Cape is much taken with Eva, and it is even minuted at their meeting how "fraei" (pretty) she is. She has supposedly demonstrated her loyalty by warning Van Riebeeck about the deceit of a Khoekhoe captain, but Van Riebeeck soon learns she is not to be totally believed.

On 6 May 1662, Van Riebeeck finally leaves the Cape and Zacharias Wagenaer takes over as Commander at the Cape. On 21 October, he dispatches yet a further expedition to the Namaqua people in the interior. Again, Pieter van Meerhof is part of the expedition as the number two, and again it is led by Pieter Cruythoff. While the expedition is generally a success, they are attacked one night by a group of what they suppose to be Sonqua Khoekhoe, who wound four of the Europeans. When Cruythoff wants to take vengeance by killing some women and children they find at a Sonqua dwelling, Pieter van Meerhof convinces the men to desist. For this dangerous resistance he is later commended.

On 2 June 1664, Eva marries with the minuted approval[30] of the governor the now accomplished young Danish surgeon and adventurer, Pieter van Meerhof from Copenhagen. The company even pays for Pieter and Eva's bridal feast at the house of the Cape Commander. By 1663, Eva has two children, Jacobus, who likely predates the relationship, and Pieternella.

On May 19, 1665, Van Meerhof is posted[31] to Robben Island in Table Bay as superintendent of the convicts there. Eva is now twenty-two years old. The child Salamon is born in 1666 on the island. Three-hundred-and-thirty years later the whole world will know about the famous prisoner, Mandela, on this penal island situated in view of the majestic Table Mountain. Now, however, it is a place of utter loneliness for the only woman on the island. Eva's life becomes one of boredom and depression. It is over this period that she takes to alcohol, the scourge of the Khoekhoe people, who seem unable to surmount its temptations.

Fate strikes out at her yet again when on 27 February 1668 news comes that her beloved husband has been killed in Madagascar, where he had accompanied a group of Dutch on a trading mission. The whole team of 8 men has been murdered by indigenous people; a tragic end for a brilliant man. On 27 February 1668, Eva and her children return to the Mainland. By virtue of Peter's death, Eva, the first indigenous person to be baptized a Christian, ironically becomes a slave-owner.

Eva's alcohol habit now gets the better of her. On 8 February 1669, the Church removes her children from her care and places them instead in the temporary care of Jan Reyndersz and his wife. Reyndersz is a former deacon in the Church. On 1 March 1669, the children are finally placed with Barbara Geens.

On Saturday, 29 July 1674, Eva Krotoa dies at the Cape. The next day she is buried inside the Castle. The blood of this Eve of Africa will run in the veins of many Afrikaner families despite the attempts of future race-preoccupied governments and families to deny this. Her daughter, Pieternella (*NF23*), survives her to become our ancestor. Several books will be written about her more than three hundred years later addressing her plight, stuck between two cultures.

Eva Krotoa's three orphaned children—Pieternella and her two brothers—are somewhat of an embarrassment to the Company. They are half-"Hottentot" and their parents have left them no means of support. They can clearly not be treated like slaves, nor are they regular settlers in the eyes of the community. The children are shuttled from foster parents to foster parents until, finally, the couple Borns requests[32] that they be allowed to take the Van Meerhof children to Mauritius with them.

This is clearly a heaven-sent solution to the commander at the Cape.

—End Nexus Familia

The Second Great Myth – Slavery

Many people in the Northern Hemisphere assume that, because there were black slaves in the United States and the rest of the Americas, and because their own nations traded in slaves, the Dutch or British in South Africa must have taken local black people as slaves. Nothing could be further from the truth. In fact, the black people of South Africa never knew slavery, except at the hand of their own. It is a point of some considerable frustration to white South Africans that they have to address accusations to the contrary, given that they actually have slaves among their own ancestors. To obtain a better picture of the slave trade as it relates to the Cape, we need to go back in time a bit again, to the 1500's.

The Portuguese took their first slaves in Africa in 1441. By 1612, they were exporting 10,000 slaves a year from Africa to Brazil. The English, in the form of John Hawkins, moved their first 300 African slaves from Sierra Leone to Hispaniola in 1562. He specialized in hijacking slaves from the Portuguese.

The leadership in England was much impressed with this and made him financial master of the Royal

Navy. By 1592, the English were not only participating in the slave trade, but were dominating it. Hawkins would write about the details of his third voyage in *An Alliance to Raid for Slaves* (1568) in which he commented on how trading and raiding were closely related in the English slave trade and how European success in the slave trade directly depended on African allies who were willing to cooperate.

Fig. 2-8 John Hawkins

Van Riebeeck had been pointedly instructed to refrain totally from involving any of the indigenous people in slavery. In fact, it would have been rank stupidity to do so. At the first opportunity, such a slave would have run off to rejoin his people. He would also have incited his fellow tribesmen against the Dutch. In the event, this principle was preserved through history and there is no evidence of indigenous South Africans ever entering slavery at the hands of Europeans. On the other hand, by 1658, six years after the founding of the station, it was clear that the settlers badly needed labor; but how to get it? The indigenous people were off-limits and the Dutch were too few. Van Riebeeck therefore tried to procure slaves from the Portuguese at Delagoa Bay on the East Coast of Southern Africa. This was unsuccessful[33]. On 28 March 1658, however, the ship *Amersfoort* arrived at the Cape with 174 Angolan slaves whom the Dutch had taken from a Portuguese prize ship.

The Company books routinely reported on slave traffic past the Cape, as they had to feed these slaves. The slaves who were brought to the Cape itself, came from Indonesia, Bengal in India, the Southern Coromandel Coast of India, Malaysia, Madagascar and the Guinea, Angolan and Mozambican coasts of Africa. Those from Madagascar were seen as excellent in agriculture and those from Angola in physical labor, while those from the East were particularly valued as superb tradesmen and artisans.

At the Cape, slaves could get their freedom upon application to the commander, provided they were baptized as Christians, could speak Dutch, and provided a replacement slave, or paid 100 guilders. Many of them did rather well for themselves at the Cape. As in the United States, several freed slaves also had some slaves of their own, as we shall see. The slaves from India seemed to feature particularly prominently among those who achieved their freedom soon after arrival at the Cape.

Despite the attempts of some South African governments to control racial purity, it is an incontrovertible fact that a number of the women from Bengal became ancestral mothers to many white South African families. Many slave women were wet nurses and gained their freedom on that basis, or it helped their cases for manumission. Certainly, South Africans of black Ba'Ntu stock cannot hold the matter of slavery against white South Africans; nor can black Americans, who may feel free to blame England and Portugal.

Many Americans' bloodlines are of Mozambican Ba'Ntu stock – a result of Portuguese slaving practices. South Africans did not enslave people for the Americas. Given the American experience of slavery, and the way it affected American attitudes towards South Africa in the 20th century, it is irony that it is the whites of South Africa that have ancestors that were slaves of the Dutch, and not the country's black population.

Nexus Familia 9: A friend enslaved!

In 1619, the English deliver their first African slaves to their Jamestown colony in North America. Therewith, quite ironically, Africans come to North America as slaves before the Pilgrim Fathers land as settlers! However, one should see the racially charged matter of slavery in context. The Moorish "Saracens" of the North African coast have raided the coasts of Europe and England for centuries, taking European slaves. In 1631, Barbary pirates abduct some hundreds of Irishmen from the village of Baltimore. While Jan van

Riebeeck is trying to establish his refreshment station at the Cape in 1652, there are endless collections at prayer meetings in England to raise ransom money to free English slaves who have been captured along the English South Coast and from hijacked ships.

By this time, there are 30,000 Christian slaves in Algiers alone. Even some European-descended Americans will end up as slaves. On the other hand, the English King is not above sending his own people into slavery in the West Indies. In 1662, Dutch Admiral Michiel de Ruyter reports from Algiers on the release on one occasion of sixty individually named Dutch slaves[34]. On two other occasions, he lists seventy others from as far afield as Hamburg, Bergen, and Rostock, some retaken from the Turks. He states that there are 1100 more Dutch slaves in Algiers.

By 1670, one of the leading individuals at the Cape is Cornelis de Cretzer, friend of Pieter van Meerhof (*NF8*), Eva's husband. De Cretzer joined Van Meerhof on an exploration expedition to the interior in the role of scribe or "journalist." Ultimately he becomes the *Secunde*; second in command to the governor. He is the stand-in for the governor if the latter were to be indisposed.

On 10 April 1671, he entertains a captain and passenger who are mutual rivals of long standing. Over some Cape wine, the two visitors enter into a brawl[35]. De Cretzer is forced to physically evict the captain. When the captain bursts back into the house, De Cretzer draws his rapier and runs the captain through. De Cretzer flees his own house and seeks sanctuary elsewhere in the settlement, eventually making his way onto a ship back to the Netherlands. In the end, the VOC finds him blameless, offers him his job back and pays for his return to the Cape. However, on the way past the Mediterranean, the ship is captured by Moorish Corsairs, and the intelligent and accomplished De Cretzer is last seen being dragged off as a slave to Algiers[36]. He is never heard of again. Many thousands of Europeans will ultimately share his fate up to 1816. The enslavement of white Europeans is therefore a real issue, not to be disregarded or trivialized. It is the fate of unfortunates such as Cornelis De Cretzer that will lead to the creation of the United States Navy (Chapter 6).

—End Nexus Familia

Nexus Familia 10: Sunday in Batavia

While Angela of Bengal (*NF3*) continues her work in the household of Pieter Kemp, matters finally come to a head for Catharina (*NF3*) around two o'clock on the afternoon of Sunday 8 October 1656 in Batavia. Catharina takes a pot of cooked meat to her husband, Claes van Malabar, who is going about his duties in the stable at Fort Rijkswijk. He attacks and sexually assaults her. Catharina (Groot Catrijn), being a person of some resolve, thereupon grabs hold of a nearby hay trestle and hits Claes with all her might, delivering the blow in the stomach above the genital area. Four days later Claes dies in excruciating agony from a burst bladder.

So it is that Catharina is brought before the Court in Batavia and is found guilty of murder. The usual punishment would be for her to be garrotted and that is indeed the sentence that is passed on 16 November 1656. Catharina, however, delivers a convincing defense that she has been the victim of assault. The judge decides to show clemency. Two days later he commutes her sentence to banishment for the rest of her natural life to the most far-flung outpost in the empire of the Dutch East India Company. Sixteen days later the frightened but unrepentant 25-year old Catharina is placed aboard a VOC ship bound for the place where she would live out the remainder of her life.

—End Nexus Familia

Nexus Familia 11: The Return Fleet

On Tuesday 21 February 1657, the autumn return fleet of six vessels from Batavia drops anchor in Table Bay on its way to the Netherlands. This fleet is under the command of Admiral Matthys Crab, vice-admiral Pieter Hackius, and Rear-Admiral Pieter Kemp. One of these six vessels is the 1200-ton *Prins Willem*. There is much public curiosity when the first-ever female convict for the Cape is brought ashore from this ship. This is an entirely new phenomenon at the Cape. The woman's name, apparently, is Groot Catrijn

(*NF10*) and she is reputedly one tough lady. Some say she is a murderer, but others tell a different story. She is immediately taken to the rather unimpressive fort of the Cape where she is told that she will henceforth be a washerwoman. In the same fleet is the *Amersfoort* and on board this ship is a slave girl belonging to rear admiral Pieter Kemp. Commander Jan van Riebeeck is not about to be upstaged by anyone else at the Cape refreshment station. So, he promptly buys Angela (*NF10*) from Kemp and takes her into his household where she becomes nursemaid to his children. Angela, our ancestor, clearly makes quite a big impression on the Cape Commander's family.

On 17 November 1658, a certain Pieter Everaerts arrives on the VOC ship *Harp* from Wielingen in the Netherlands. He is a highly placed official of the Compagnie and is made a member of the Council for Justice and Policy at the Cape. Everaerts immediately takes an amorous interest in Catrijn and soon a girl child is born. Catrijn certainly moves in high circles as she serves her sentence at the Cape.

On the 19th of April 1662, as he is about to leave for Batavia, Van Riebeeck sells Angela to Abraham Gabbema, second in command at the Cape and discoverer of the Berg River. Four years later, on the 13th of April 1666, when Gabbema is also promoted to Batavia, he signs a document liberating Angela and her three children subject to some six more months' service to another burgher. Herewith Angela becomes only the third slave to be freed at the Cape. Soon after gaining her freedom, she asks for and receives a parcel of land in the Heerenstraat (Main Street), 57 by 50 feet in area. In the 21st century, the deed will still exist in the Cape Archive. It is over this period that she meets her future husband from Europe.

Ten Years Later

It is, of course, normal practice to post guards at a critical and sensitive semi-military establishment such as the Cape refreshment station and one particular night in 1667 is no different. The soldier assigned to guard duty is Hans Christoffel Schneider from Heidelberg in Germany. Hans, however, is not at his post. After an extensive search, he is eventually tracked down to Groot Catrijn's quarters. For this dereliction of duty Schneider is sent to Robben Island on 30 July 1667 as punishment. And so he becomes our second ancestor and the third family member on the island. There is no punishment for the enchantress.

On Sunday 29 April 1668, Catrijn is baptized along with her best friend, Angela of Bengal. A year later, Catrijn has her baby Christoffel baptized as the son of a Christian and gives him the surname Snyman, a Dutch form of Schneider. Christoffel Snyman is to be the progenitor of all the future Snymans in South Africa, and they will be many indeed, including the author's family. The amorous Hans Christoffel Schneider, however, leaves the Cape and is never heard of again. His role in our story is done.

On 12 September 1670, the freeman Anthonij van Bengale (*NF3*), who has since also arrived at the Cape, is baptized. On 20 December 1671, he marries Catrijn. Her freedom from slavery is recorded in a letter of 6 January 1672. In this process, Anthonij takes full responsibility for young Christoffel and his older half-sister, Petronella, the daughter of Everaerts. Oddly, it transpires that none other than the distant and important governor of Batavia, Joan Maetsuycker, has personally issued the pardon for Catrijn. She most assuredly has influence in high places, or maybe the wheels of justice just grind slowly. One can only but speculate why and how so many powerful men in the VOC take such an interest in her well-being.

The muster roll of 1682 shows the entire family living happily together; mother, father, and two children. By 17 December of the same year, Catrijn, Anthonij and Petronella have all died, leaving Christoffel as the sole surviving heir at the tender age of fourteen. The new Governor of the Cape, Simon van der Stel, a much respected and competent man, approves the release of money from the estate to make payments for the funerals. So ends the fascinating life of Groot Catrijn, one of the author's most colorful ancestors and our son's eighth great-grandmother. To this day, it is not clear how this lowly slave woman could get governors in two countries to take special actions on her behalf, even in her death.

We leave our young ancestor, Christoffel Snyman, watching forlornly as his family's earthly possessions are auctioned off and he is committed to the mercy of the Masters of the Cape Orphan Chamber.

—End Nexus Familia

Nexus Familia 12: From slave to slave owner

Arnold Willemsz Basson (*NF1*) arrives at the Cape from Wesel in the Duchy of Cleves on a VOC ship and is listed as a Cape parishioner in 1665. He soon earns the nickname Jagt ("Hunt") and gets deeply involved in the seal hunting efforts in Saldanha Bay. It is said that his nickname refers not so much to his livelihood as to his disposition toward the ladies.

It is sometime after this that he becomes aware of the Indian lady living alone on Heerenstraat. He finds out that she is actually a freed slave and that she used to be the nursemaid to the children of the first commander at the Cape, Jan van Riebeeck, who has since left for Batavia. One thing leads to another, and on 15 December 1669 Jagt marries Angela van Bengale (*NF11*) in the Dutch Reformed Church at the Cape. On 31 August 1670, their first child, the first Basson ancestor born at the Cape, is baptized as Willem Basson. As the first son, he is named after his paternal grandfather in Wesel, Germany. Several children follow. The fourth is a daughter baptized as Elsje on 29 August 1667.

The intrepid Angela will outlive her husband "Jagt" and all her own children except for her eldest natural daughter. As a successful landowner, she will leave a considerable estate comprising several slaves. Son Willem is our ancestor. He is the start of a long legacy of wheat farmers who will establish themselves north of Cape Town. When we return to look in on the Bassons at the end of the 19th century, we will find them still living a peaceful agrarian life in the Western Cape.

—End Nexus Familia

 ## Nexus Familia 13: The Myburghs – Company men

In 1665, Lambert Lambertsz Meijburg (*NF1*) arrives at the Cape. With him is his wife Aletta Albertz and his 7-year old first born son Jan Lambertsz Meijburg. Lambert takes up a position as official of the VOC at the Cape. The jacket that Lambert wears in his capacity as VOC official, as well as a seal ring, purses, belt and shoe buckles will be treasured to survive to the twenty-first century within the family.

Some time after they settle in their new home, they get new neighbors. They are two sisters Sterrevelt from North America. The older one soon marries, albeit at the age of just 15, but the younger one is too young for that, being only 12 (*NF 14*). Lambert and Aletta baptize their second son, Albert, on 1 May 1672. Lambert dies in 1673, reportedly murdered by the Khoekhoe. Albert will marry Elisabeth, daughter of Willem Schalksz van der Merwe and Elsje, daughter of Founding Father Jacob Cloete (*NF6*). By the 19th century, all the Myburghs in South Africa will be descended from Albert and Elisabeth. We return to our branch of the family in that century when they will have moved to the east as wagon builders.

—End Nexus Familia

 ## Nexus Familia 14: Ariaentje of America

Fate has been less than kind to Neeltje and Ariaentje Sterrevelt from New Amsterdam (*NF7*). In the two and a half years since we have last seen them return to Nederland with their father and his new wife, they have lost both of their parents. The powers that be in Nederland have elected to send the 10 year old Neeltje and 7-year old Ariaentje to Africa. So it is that in December 1667 the two girls find themselves wards of the Church at the Cape of Good Hope. They have been placed with the recently widowed Geertruyd Meyntings.

When the ships *Poelsnip* and *Westwout* return from Mauritius and Madagascar on 27 February 1668 with the news of the death of the intrepid Pieter Van Meerhof (*NF8*), they also bring back governor Wreede. He has been removed from office at the insistence of the inhabitants of the island.

On 29 April 1668, Geertruyd Meyntings marries again and the two Sterrevelt girls are removed and placed with ensign Dirck Jansz Smient. And this is when fate intervenes yet again. The Cape governor now decides that the much-respected Ensign Smient should relocate to Mauritius as caretaking governor of the island. And this is how Neeltje and Ariaentje end up boarding the *Poelsnip* with Dirck Smient on 29 June 1668. Their stay there will last 18 months. The Cape church books have an entry dated 26 July 1668 stating that money is allocated *"for clothes for two orphans sent to Mauritius."* Smient then also refers to Neeltje by name later in 1669 and it is recorded in the church books. On 9 December 1669 the ship *Voerman* arrives back at the Cape with Smient and his extended family. The church books record on 22 December 1669 that Ariaentje is to be placed with a different family than her sister, Neeltje. On 7 July 1670, Ariaentje's foster family requests that the church take her back. She is placed with her sister.

Life has been unfair to our ancestor Ariaentje. First she lost her carefree young existence in New Amsterdam when the English took it away. Then she lost her parents. Then she was sent to Africa on a long and dangerous sea voyage. Then she was moved from Geertruyd Meyntings to Dirck Smient. Then she was moved to the island of Mauritius with Smient; and then she was moved back. Then she was separated from her sister and finally placed back with her. It has been an utterly disrupted life as a young orphan child living on the alms of the church. Her life as an adult would prove no better.

On 14 April 1675, the not quite 15-year old Ariaentje marries Heinrich Evert Schmidt, a young German soldier from Ibbenbüren. Heinrich left the Company in 1670 to become a Free Burgher and is now a trader in beer and tobacco in Cape Town. On 29 August 1667, the two of them are witnesses to the baptism of Elsje, daughter of ancestor Arnold Basson (*NF12*). On 25 April 1683, Ariaentje baptizes her third child, our ancestor Judith. She is named after Ariaentje's mother, Judith Robberts, who died in New Amsterdam twenty years earlier. Ariaentje's life is shattered again, when Evert dies soon after.

On 17 September 1684, Ariaentje marries Casparus Willers, the VOC company scribe. Ariaentje bears Caspar two boys. However, on 30 January 1687, Caspar Willers is banished[37] to Mauritius for six years for being chronically in arrears on his payments to the company. He is also sentenced to being flogged, but governor Simon Van der Stel stays that particular punishment, because Willers is an epileptic. The Master of the Court is also sent to Willers' house to seal it and attach all the goods.

Caspar Willers is never heard from again. Ariaentje's life is shattered yet again.

—End Nexus Familia

Nexus Familia 15: The storm gathers

Shortly after the crowning of Louis XIV in 1654, pressure on the Protestants of France and Savoy escalates dramatically. It is in the mid 1650s that matters boil over on the Italian side of the mountains in Savoy. Even intervention by Oliver Cromwell[38] ultimately fails to stop the persecutions.

Matters escalate

On May 4, 1663, the government commissioner orders the Protestant Vaudois citizens of Cabrières d'Aigues (*NF2*) to demolish their olive oil mill and their church with it. The same holds for the village of La Motte d'Aigues. The villagers are also ordered to build a church for the two Catholic families in town. In a final crackdown, the government bans the preaching of the Protestant Faith in the Aigues Valley. Over the following twenty-two years of Louis XIV's reign, life grows systematically worse for our Protestant ancestors in the Aigues Valley

The Jourdans of Saint Martin de la Brasque

When Pierre Jourdan dies in 1677, he leaves behind his wife, Jeanne Marque and 5 children, one daughter named Catherine having died young. The family now is composed of the widowed Jeanne Marque, her two married daughters Magdalene and Marie, married son Barthélemy, and two youngest unmarried sons, Jean and Pierre, who work the farm at Belle Etoile with her. Daughter Marie has provided Jeanne Marque with three granddaughters.

Elsewhere in France and its environs

Many French Huguenot families will contribute to the bloodline of the author's family, eventually accounting for around 25% of the author's ancestral origin; quite typical of the Afrikaner as a nation.

• On the River Loire, in the town of Suèvres near Blois, between Orléans and Tours, we find the family Foucher busy making a simple living on the farm La Bruslée. In 1656, Besnard Foucher and his wife Anne Bruére have their son, Philippe.

• Just north of Blois along the same River Loire, we find the family Rétif, headed by Jacques, born in 1637, whose descendants will play a major role in South Africa.

Fig. 2-9 Belle Etoile at the foot of the Lubéron Mountains

• In Poitiers in St.Lienart, Poitou, Jean Prieur Du Plessis is born in 1638 into a family of landed gentry. No fewer than three of Jean's grandchildren will be ancestors of the author. Jean's grandson, Jan, will become a pioneering settler in Africa and experience some unique events that will take his words all the way from Africa to the President of the United States. Jan's grandson, in turn, will lead the ancestors of the author's family safely through Hell on Earth. But, that all lies in the future.

• Fate smiles on young Protestant Philippe Naudé in the city of Metz when the Duke of Sachsen-Eisenach selects him as companion for his young son in 1667. Philippe eventually returns to Metz where his second marriage is in 1683 to the 20-year old Anne Isnard, daughter of the local doctor. Events surrounding his descendants will change the course of British policy in Africa 117 years later.

• Jean du Buis of Guines in the Pas-de-Calais is not an ancestor, but one of his descendants will become closely allied with the author's forefather and he will affect the power play on the eastern Frontier of the Cape settlement directly. On 6 September 1670, Jean and wife Isabeau have a son and eight days later they baptize him in Guines as Jean.

—End Nexus Familia

Paul Revere – The Huguenot roots

In Sainte-Foye-la-Grande, on the Dordogne River in the Aquitaine region, near the author's La Buscaigne ancestors, lived the Rivoire family. The Rivoire family later moved to nearby Riocaud, where Isaac Rivoire was born in 1660. His son, Apollos Rivoire, would also be born there in 1702 and Isaac would send him as an apprentice silversmith to America, where he would change his name to Paul Revere. His son, Paul Revere II, was to make a name for himself in the future of the United States of America and become immortalized in American history as the man who ensured that the defenses of the Republican citizenry were readied against the attacking English forces.

In both the United States and in South Africa, we see the keen influence of this staunch French Huguenot blood. These were men with strong convictions and depth of character. Their bloodlines would show up repeatedly in the future leadership of South Africa, and also in the United States. In South Africa, in particular, their bloodline would consistently produce leaders in both the military and the political arenas.

Nexus Familia 16: How tenuous the bloodline?

One of the more remarkable ancestors of our family is the indefatigable Trijn Ras. She started life as Catharina "Trijn" Oesting from Germany. She arrives at the Cape in 1662 as a widow. On 2 September 1662, she marries Hans Ras from Gelderland in the Netherlands. She will marry a total of five times and only her last husband will outlive her. Hans will be killed by a lion, the third husband will be murdered by Khoekhoe, and the fourth husband will be trampled to death by an elephant. The third child of the Ras couple will be Maria, our ancestor, who is baptized on 23 June 1669. By so tender a thread hangs the existence of this author, what with lion, elephants and murdering Khoekhoe all vying to extinguish the bloodline.

—End Nexus Familia

Nexus Familia 17: In the Danish Eiderstedt

In 1672, a young man named Joen Peter Boyens (*NF2*) is listed as illegally "hiring out" at Tönning, likely as a deck hand. Tönning, situated on the mouth of the Eider River, is the point of departure for all people going on major sea voyages, be it to the New World or to the burgeoning Netherlands. If a young man from nearby Katharinenheerd in the Eiderstedt were looking for a first job, here is exactly where he would come to hire out as an apprentice or *knecht* (servant). This is the typical thing to do in these parts at this time if you are a 14-year old boy. Some are even younger.

—End Nexus Familia

The Stavenisse and the distant Ba'Ntu

In the night of 16 February 1686, the Dutch flute *Stavenisse* was unsalvageably wrecked just off the mouth of the Umzimkulu River at the southern end of the present Kwa-Zulu-Natal. Sixty made it ashore. Forty-seven men decided to walk to Cape Town, almost one thousand miles away. Joining forces with shipwrecked sailors of two English ships, the *Good Hope* and the *Bonaventura*, the remaining Dutch sailors built a seaworthy vessel from the remnants of the Good Hope with which to attempt to reach the Cape of Good Hope. And so it was that a strange craft, named the *Centaurus*, sailed into Table Bay[39] on the afternoon of 1 March 1687. Its tale of no fewer than three shipwrecks was almost too incredible to believe.

On 10 November 1687, the same *Centaurus*, suitably improved and serviced, sailed in search of the survivors of the *Stavenisse*. Several of the shipwrecked Dutch and English were found, along with a young French boy, Guillaume Chenu de Chalezac[40], victim of a fourth maritime disaster. The survivors reported[41] some indigenous people as hospitable and friendly, but others as[42] "thievish and lying"(sic). A later voyage by the *Noord* rescued more castaways.

A picture was emerging of the coastal tribes. Starting from the north, the different Ba'Ntu people were the amaMbo, the amaPondomise, the amaPondo, and the amaThembu. The amaXhosa lived further south along the coast, separated from the other black nations by a group of Magryghas (Khoi-San). West of the amaXhosa lived San Bushmen whom the Ba'Ntu people considered sub-human and killed on sight. When some twelve of the *Stavenisse* survivors tried to cross that Bushman country, they were killed to a man. To the north, there was no such nation as the Zulu. Twenty-five years after the founding of Cape station, this was the first ever-useful Dutch intelligence on the then faraway Ba'Ntu people of Southern Africa.

In 1688, an Inqua Khoekhoe chief sent an emissary to the Cape to invite an expedition to his land. The expedition left on 14 January 1689 and found the chief's land near the present Graaff-Reinet[43]. The Inqua provided intelligence on Khoekhoe nations who lived bordering on the amaXhosa, five days to the east. The Inqua were constantly raided by San Bushmen, whom they killed on sight. By April 1689, the Dutch therefore knew that the amaXhosa people were some 600 to 700 miles to the east of Cape Town, somewhere beyond the Keiskamma River. Between the Dutch and the Xhosa was a whole string of Khoekhoe nations.

When the *S. João Baptista* ran aground between the Fish and Kei Rivers in late 1622, the survivors found Khoekhoe people there, rather than black Ba'Ntu people[44]. They were also attacked by San Bushmen, who stole the cattle the Khoekhoe had traded them. The survivors struggled northward along that coast for no fewer than thirty-nine days before encountering the first black Ba'Ntu people on 15 December 1622. There was no mention of amaXhosa people. They would only move south later. The area between the Keiskamma and Kei Rivers, in particular, was San Bushman country until the end of the 17th century and they remained there in large numbers for another hundred years, before being pointedly exterminated[45] in the area by the amaRharhabe clan of the amaXhosa, led by Rharhabe, who we shall meet in Chapter 4.

Since 2003, there has been an attempt by the present amaXhosa-dominated government of South Africa to resolve a long-standing and fascinating succession dispute among the Royal Houses of the amaXhosa. The testimony presented as part of that process by respected representatives of the two parties places the collective amaXhosa in the 17th century under the leadership of Tshawe at the Umzimkhulu River[46]. This is 735 miles as the crow flies and 800 miles in a smoothed curve along the coast from Cape Town. Here they fought, defeated and absorbed the local Khoekhoe people who lived there before them.

The Situation at the Cape by 1687

By the end of the first 35 years, the refreshment station had grown to a semi-military establishment with an associated settlement of non-company people and adjoining farming areas. It was still comprised of just the settlement at the Cape itself, and Stellenbosch, which was founded twenty-seven years after the landing at the Cape.

As we have seen, the first ten years, were characterized by the basic founding of the settlement, the freeing of some VOC officials to become farmers, and the importation of slaves. Some of the latter were imported from the east via Batavia. Others were West Africans, mostly taken from captured Portuguese ships. The first skirmishes with the indigenous Khoekhoe had also taken place. The decade was concluded with what came to be called the *First Hottentot War* with the Khoekhoe. It nearly destroyed the fledgling economy. In fact the Governor of Batavia, Joan Maetsuycker, wrote[47] to Van Riebeeck expressing his view that the Cape station was doomed and that he had never believed in its creation in the first place:

> "...*producing no return,* [it] *will always be a burden to the Company. We never entertained any high idea of the Cape scheme.*"

The next seventeen years were unstable due to a rapid succession of no fewer than nine commanders and care-taking commanders. It was only with the arrival of Commander Simon van der Stel on 12 October 1679 that some stability was brought to the Cape. It was also Simon Van der Stel who, on an inspection trip of his new domain of responsibility, camped along the Eerste Rivier (First River) and declared that a town should be built there. It would eventually become the town of Stellenbosch, which today remains the cultural capital of the Afrikaner nation. By 1683, the first school was built and a *landdrost* (magistrate) was appointed. In 1686, a Dutch Reformed Church was built in town and we see much of the historical focus move from Cape Town to Stellenbosch. In 1664, there were one hundred and seventy eight company officials at the Cape. There were twelve people stationed at various lookout posts, one master carpenter with sixteen servants, a master mason with twelve servants and fifteen people working in the granary. Seven persons served in the Company Gardens along with numerous slaves. Five souls were on Robben Island. By 1700, there would be only five hundred officials at the Cape. By 1687, the traffic in VOC ships past the Cape was typically thirty annually. They typically sailed in fleets for the sake of mutual protection and did so in particular seasons to avail themselves of the prevailing wind patterns and sea conditions.

The Cape settlement was not growing rapidly at all. The Dutch East India Company had no interest whatsoever in its growth.

-----ooOoo-----

3

Religious Persecution

"...we have, by this present perpetual and irrevocable edict, suppressed and revoked, and do suppress and revoke, the edict of our said grandfather, given at Nantes in April, 1598..."

Louis XIV, King of France
Revocation of the Edict of Nantes (October 22, 1685)

Enter the French Huguenots

On 30 April 1598, Henry IV of France proclaimed the Edict of Nantes, which granted the French Protestants, the Huguenots, a guarantee of safety in an otherwise Catholic country. He also designated certain places as safe havens for Huguenots. One such location was La Rochelle, a harbor town on the Atlantic coast of France.

On 18 October 1685, Louis XIV, Henry's grandson, signed the Revocation of the Edict of Nantes. So began the brutal persecution of the Huguenots in France. At the same time, the Huguenots constituted much of the intelligentsia of the country. Many of these staunch Protestants left France to settle elsewhere in Europe, rather than to abjure their faith. Some 200 Huguenots found their way to the Cape via the Netherlands. Here they found a unique little spot on Earth where the climate was Mediterranean just as in Provence, where many of them came from. The Cape had ample rains in winter and almost none in summer. This is ideal for viticulture, the art they had perfected over the centuries.

The arrival of these staunch folks also injected some much-needed moral fortitude into the Cape population. They had their fares paid to the Cape and were provided with land, implements and seed. They could return to France, if they wished, but they had to pay their own way back and would

Fig. 3-1 Louis XIV of France - the Sun King

have to leave behind any property they had accumulated at the Cape. Few, if any, had the necessary means to return to Europe. The Huguenots adapted relatively quickly and learnt to speak Dutch. However, they forever changed the Cape via their introduction of viticulture and their staunch Calvinism. To this day, the Cape proudly sports its typically French wine estate names, which found their way onto wine labels. Family names, such as Rétif, Celliers, and Joubert feature prominently in the military history of the country. The French heritage is a matter of great pride to South Africans of European descent and is carefully guarded and protected.

Nexus Familia 18: The King's soldiers are coming

On 18 October 1685, Louis XIV, King of France, revokes the Edict of Nantes. On the same day, the King's Dragoons enter Provence. The southern Protestants are a major concern for the king, given the long history of resistance in the area. Between 22 and 26 October 1685 the citizens of Cabrières d'Aigues are forced to abjure their faith en masse[1]. The same follows in the other towns. On 23 October 1685, the elderly Jeanne Marque's heart is broken when daughter Magdalene Jourdan and her husband and daughters abjure their Protestant faith at La Motte d'Aigues (*NF15*). The same follows for son Barthélemy and his wife and child.

Louis XIV now implements his infamous Draggonade. The King's dragoons and other soldiers are billeted en masse in the homes of Protestants and the unwilling hosts have to pay the soldiers until they deny their faith. The trauma in the Jourdan family of Belle Etoile is extreme.

Grandmother Jeanne Marque wants nothing to do with the abjuration, and her two young sons, Jean and Pierre, stand with her. Daughter Marie and her husband Jean Roux stay out of the argument. Older siblings Magdalene and Barthélemy try to reason with the two young brothers, hoping the two young men can be convinced to sway their mother. Meanwhile, Jeanne Marque is desperately worried about Jean (26) and Pierre (22), because they are of fighting age.

It is then that fate takes a direct hand. On 23 March 1686, Jean Roux dies, leaving Jeanne's daughter Marie a widow with her three daughters of ages ranging from 14 downwards. Marie thereupon moves back to her mother, Jeanne, at Belle Etoile.

Word reaches the Belle Etoile Jourdans that their friend Jean Meinard of Saint Martin de la Brasque is planning to flee the country with his entire family of pregnant wife, five children, and his mother-in-law, Marie Anthouarde. Apparently Pierre Mallan, his wife Isabeau Richarde and the whole extended Mallan family in Saint Martin, including the unmarried Jacques Mallan, will also be going. Jeanne Marque therefore decides that she and her two sons, Jean and Pierre Jourdan, will be going with Meinard. Daughter Marie tells her she has already decided to flee with her three daughters in the company of two other ladies. They are Suzanne Goirande, a spinster from La Motte d'Aigues, and Isabeau Long, a cousin of Suzanne from the same town. Paul Jourdan and Pierre Jourdan from Cabrières will also be joining. Pierre Joubert from La Motte d'Aigues is apparently making his own separate plans.

Elsewhere in the Lubéron, similar plans are being made. And this is how three groups of prospective refugees meet separately in secret to plan their escape[2]. The decision in almost all cases is to head overland[3] for Geneva in the Swiss cantons; the land of John Calvin, the Arch-Reformist. There are many Vaudois families along the way to give them aid and shelter. They just need to keep out of the way of the King's dragoons and any Catholic Church operatives. They will need to cross far northern Savoy around Chambéry. By Meinard's calculation, they will need at least three weeks for the whole 270-mile journey; perhaps four to five weeks in view of the children and elderly in the group. They also cannot delay too long, as it is already late in summer, and there is high ground to cross.

—End Nexus Familia

 ## Nexus Familia 19: To the end of the Earth

The Flight of the St Martin Protestants

When the St. Martin group leaves in mid-August 1687, the first short leg of the trek is southwards to the flat country of the Durance River valley. This takes them past La Tour d'Aigues to the vicinity of Pertuis. 330 years later a small country road south from St. Martin de la Brasque will still be known as the Chemin de Huguenots. This is countryside they know only too well, and there are many friends who help them on their way.

The first major stage of the journey is along the floodplain of the Durance to Sisteron where the river forces its way through a narrow gorge. It is the first place where a proper bridge exists over the river.

However, there is also a commanding fort overlooking the river. So, they make contact with the sympathetic Vaudois in town who help them avoid the King's dragoons. In fact, something of an "Underground Railroad" has been set up for fleeing Protestants and guides are available at several points. Once past Sisteron, the voyage is easier. They follow the Valley of the Durance, but leave the river at the town of Tallard, where the Durance swings dramatically eastward to the dead-ended Freissinières valley of their ancestors. Here they set off for the town of Gap, a few miles north of the bow in the river.

Up to this point, the journey has taken our Saint Martin refugees along the even path of the Durance. Along this route, they have now risen to 2,500 feet above sea level. Now they have to climb 1,500 feet over just a few miles out of the Durance basin to the plateau of the Forest of Saint Julien. This is bound to be difficult for Marie Anthouarde and the 60-year old Jeanne Marque. Jean and Pierre Jourdan are worried about their mother. However, she is as tough as nails, and surprises all of them by gaining the high ground without too much trouble. From here through the St. Bonnet area to La Motty the ground is fairly level. On their left, is the 8,000 foot ice-scoured mass of the Montagne de Féraud. When they go down the Col des Festreaux, they enter the physically most rugged part of the route. Three hundred and thirty years later, the undulating and winding road through this area will still be a spectacular route. Off to the right the Cottian Alps of Savoy loom.

Fig. 3-2 The Col des Festreaux area

As our little knot of refugees descends the highlands near La Mure, they enter the low country of Grenoble. Even though the mountains tower over the valley, the town itself is a mere 700 feet above sea level. They are now in the flat glacially gouged valleys that characterize this part of the world. Travel along these is infinitely easier than across the broken high ground they have left behind. However, this is a major population center and they again have to be on the watch for the King's dragoons. The Massif de la Chartreuse looms to their left as they make their way along this flat glacial valley towards Chambéry.

Finally, crossing the border of France, they enter Savoy. In the past, Chambéry was the capital of Savoy, but has been replaced by Turin. The town has a notorious reputation. Several Vaudois were martyred here. They reach Geneva along the same glacial valley on 12 September 1687. Here they are told that the groups from Cabrières d'Aigues and La Motte d'Aigues have passed through two days before.

Geneva, at the southwestern end of Lac Leman (Lake Geneva), is the hometown of the great Reformist Jean Calvin. This is the first truly safe refuge for the Huguenots. Many others will end their journey here and they will contribute significantly to the building of the Swiss watch industry. Our group from Saint Martin appeals to the Protestant Church in town for help. Here their names are duly recorded in the church books where they will still be in the 21st century. The same is true for the other groups.

After a suitable rest period, our little knot of refugees is ready to proceed onward. Their next stop is at Lausanne at the northern extremity of the lake. A large body of the Vaudois from the Italian valleys of Savoy elect to remain here. Two years hence, in 1689, men from this Lausanne "colony" will set off along footpaths over the Alps as an armed body of some 900 and, against all odds, retake their Piedmont Valleys from the Duke of Savoy.

From Lausanne, the St. Martin group systematically makes its way northeastward along the lower country of Switzerland. The next time we see our group specifically recorded in church books is on 30

September 1687, in the far northern Swiss town of Schaffhausen on the Rhine. Here they discover that the earlier groups arrived just one day ahead of them. From here on our three groups of Lubéron refugees travel together.

The ten major cities on the west bank of the Rhine were placed under the control of Louis XIV as part of the Treaty of Westphalia, even though this is Burgundy, a separate country. This does not make using the Rhine any easier. The Duke of Würtemberg controls the land to the east of the river and is fearful of Louis XIV. He is not particularly welcoming to Huguenots. For this reason most of the refugees elect to try the river rather than the long trip overland. After all, it is already almost November and winter is setting in. Near Mannheim and Heidelberg, they use the overland route again to reach Frankfurt.

They reach Frankfurt on 31 October 1687. Here they find Pierre Jaubert from La Motte d'Aigues, as well as Suzanne Reyne. All in all, forty-nine Protestant souls have managed to escape the hold of Louis XIV on the Lubéron and environs and are now all congregated at Frankfurt, the central hub of the Huguenot Diaspora. Here, their names are entered for a final time in the church books as they seek help at the French Protestant church. The church books of Frankfurt show that more than 4,000 families specifically state their destination as "Hollande," and our Lubéron group is indeed headed there. They admire and revere William of Orange, ruler of the Netherlands and soon to be King of England. He is their undisputed champion.

On 6 October 1687, the VOC in Holland decides they will specifically allow "Piedmontese or Dalluyden (Valley People – Vaudois), our co-religionists" to settle[4] at the Cape. An Oath of Allegiance is drawn up in French for any prospective Vaudois or other French refugees to sign if they wish to settle at that Cape. Seven weeks later our knot of refugees from the Aigues Valley is in Rotterdam in Holland. This is evidenced by a letter to the Cape of Good Hope written on 23 December 1687 by the Rotterdam Chamber of the VOC[5]. The letter identifies those "People of the Valley" who have stated their intent to sail on the ship China to settle at that faraway Cape.

Saturday, March 20, 1688 – Goeree, the Netherlands

A group of eight excited Dutch orphan girls watch from the deck of the ship as the huge sails are unfurled and the VOC ship China[6] gains way on its 4 month and ten day voyage to the far distant Cape of Good Hope under the command of Captain Samuel van Groll[7]. We note for later reference that one of the orphan girls is named Willemijntjie Ariens de Wit. But, our attention is really on another group of 28 people on the deck. They appear apprehensive.

As we move closer we realize that they are speaking Occitan; some call it Provençal. This is the language of the southern parts of France, such as Languedoc, Provence, and parts of Dauphiné. They are all Protestant Huguenot refugees[8] from the Lubéron region of Provence in France. They have no experience of the sea at all. As they stare in trepidation at the open ocean ahead of them, they experience the deep ache in the soul of those who know they shall never see the land of their fathers again.

The 60-year-old Jeanne Marque (NF18) has made it all the way from Belle Etoile outside Saint Martin in Provence to this point with the help of her two dedicated youngest sons, Jean and Pierre Jourdan. Now she looks at the setting sun, knowing that she shall never set foot on land again. But, she is at peace. She has saved her two youngest. That is all that really matters. So, she smiles reassuringly at the world-weary 64-year-old Marie Anthouarde.

The experienced sailors just look away uncomfortably. They know what will happen when the fresh cheese supply is finished two months into the journey and all the livestock on board has been slaughtered. That is when they shall have to break out the sickening brine-soaked meat, vinegar, and "ammunition biscuit" on which they shall have to survive for two months, along with reeking water. Yes, they know only too well.

The attention of the sailors immediately shifts elsewhere when the names are called out for the two different watches for the ship. This starts a ritual that will continue unabated for months until they reach the distant Cape at the End of the Earth. All will get used to the monotonous bell at every half-hour of the watch when the ever-patient hourglass is turned.

Wednesday, August 4, 1688 – Table Bay

As the *China* slowly enters the Bay under the striking cliffs of Table Mountain, a local boat goes out to meet her. Letters from Holland, instructions for the Cape Commander and the like are delivered to the boat, while messages to the captain, fresh water, fruit and meat are supplied from the refreshment post. The captain in turn reports on the human losses on the 140-day voyage. Data is available for 16 of these voyages in the particular season, and the average duration of these voyages is 125 days. The *China* has taken 140 days. This is not at all exceptional. The loss of life on the ship is also not exceptional, being 6.5% of the total number on board. However, the ship left Goeree with 305 souls on board, by far the largest complement in the season. Of the 267 crew and company soldiers, twelve have died. The Dutch orphan girls have all arrived safely, including Willemijntjie Ariens De Wit. The two regular passengers are also safe. One will disembark and the other will continue onward to Batavia. However, of the 28 Vaudois refugees no fewer than 8 have died – almost a third.

Jeanne Marque has succumbed to the privations on this ship. Marie Anthouarde also is no more. Marie Jourdane likewise has failed to survive, and so too her eldest daughter, Jeanne. Marie's two youngest daughters, Marie and Margarite, have been left orphans. Two of the six Meinard children have died. Suzanne Reyne, the 20-year-old newlywed, has died. She leaves Pierre Jaubert a widower within weeks of his marriage. Pierre Mallan has also died, leaving Isabeau Richarde a widow. It is largely the young men between 16 and 30 years of age who have most successfully survived the voyage.

On the 11th of August 1688, the survivors of the refugees and crew finally struggle off the ship and onto dry land. Some are committed to the hospital. Over a period of several months the other Huguenot ships arrive, bearing a total of approximately two hundred Huguenots. Among them (*NF15*) are Philippe Foucher and his wife, and Francois Rétif with his sister Anne. The three De Villiers brothers Abraham, Pierre, and Jacques arrive on the ship *Zion* bearing a special letter from the Netherlands introducing them to the governor at the Cape as experts in viticulture. Jean du Buis from Calais arrives on the *Oosterland*, as does Jean Prieur du Plessis with his wife and one child born en route.

As they take their first steps in their new country, the Huguenot families cannot know the epic future history that awaits their descendants. The Mallan and Foucher families cannot possibly comprehend the key roles their bloodlines will one day play in this new land. A few more will follow later; Jacques de la Porte from Lille, for example, will arrive at the Cape in 1699 with his new wife, Sarah Vitout. We shall meet her granddaughter, Sarah Delport, in due course.

—End Nexus Familia

Building a new life in Africa

For the first few years at the Cape, the Huguenots were placed on loan farms and some received financial assistance. Most were settled in a beautiful sheltered valley at the foot of the Hottentots-Holland Mountains, a jagged and solid barrier of imposing mountains separating the Khoekhoe-dominated interior of Southern Africa from the Dutch-controlled coastal region of the Cape.

At the tip of this flat sandy coastal plain, later to be known as the Cape Flats, was the rugged mountainous Cape Peninsula with its signature Table Mountain. Nearer the Hottentots-Holland, mountains the sterile sand abated and the soils became arable. The valley where the Huguenots were to settle became known as Franschhoek ("French Corner"). It was indeed uncannily like their beloved Lubéron. It was Mediterranean in climate and the mountains, in fact, were higher and prettier and the water supply plentiful. The soils suited viticulture. The Dutch had not lied.

The Huguenots took to this land like ducks to water and within a short space of time these staunch Calvinists, who had paid so dearly for their Protestant faith, had their own church parish, known as Drakenstein. They named their farms after their places of origin. Pierre Jaubert named his "Provence," for his Province of origin. The farm La Motte was obviously named after La Motte-d'Aigue.

As their descendants would do in the 19th century in the interior, and *their* descendants in turn internationally in the 21st century, these folks went about building their new life with total dedication and a spirit of devotion to their new country. They owned little, but they took their Protestant Work Ethic and their faith seriously indeed. Certainly, they brought with them their unique skills in viticulture and in growing soft fruit, but they also brought a sense of pride, duty and stoicism; attributes that may not have been in great supply in the 17th century Cape, given the polyglot VOC personnel who populated the place.

Where the Dutch brought a healthy pragmatism, the Huguenots brought a certain flair to create the unique collective character of the little nation that was starting to develop. Where the Dutch brought business sense and economic thinking, the French brought the ability to stand for a principle. Where the Dutch contributed a nature that is slow to anger, but dogged once roused, the French provided the fire and passion that would shape the future country.

Where the Dutch contributed the genetic structure of the tallest Caucasians on Earth, the French contributed a bloodline that produced, and still

Fig. 3-3 The Franschhoek Valley

produces, strikingly beautiful women, ever the subject of comment by visitors to the Cape. More than anything else, the French bloodline would in future assure a goodly supply of men with leadership qualities, for better or for worse. The history of South Africa is built on the blood of these strong-willed Protestant people.

 ## Nexus Familia 20: Abandoned!

In 1689, Joost Luns arrives at the Cape as a midshipman. He becomes a burgher at the Cape in 1690 and Ariaentje Sterrevelt (*NF14*) takes him as her third husband on 23 July of that year. They have one daughter, Elizabeth, who is baptized on 10 October 1690. Of course, Ariaentje still has two of her children from her first marriage, including our seven-year-old ancestor, Judith. There are also the two boys from the second marriage to Willers. One would love to tell a story here of a loving stepfather who takes his wife's children by her prior marriages into his family. The truth, however, is rather different and disappointing.

In 1690, Joost Luns, like previous husband Caspar Willers (*NF14*), ends up in big trouble along with Ariaentje. Ariaentje accused a certain Koenraad Hogenkamp of theft. Luns then bound his hands, suspended him from the rafters of their house and, aided by Ariaentje, assaulted him in an attempt to extract a confession. Hogenkamp ended up in hospital.

On 13 December 1690, the Court of Justice sentences Luns and Ariaentje to be flogged and banished to the island of Mauritius. The execution of the sentence is held in abeyance until mid 1692, when Joost and Ariaentje decide that the time has come to act.

Against this background, we note that the 1692 return fleet of nine ships from Batavia and Ceylon has been in Table Bay from the middle of May and has departed quite recently on 26 June. It is best if we quote here the words from a document[9] issued by the Orphan Chamber of the Cape some six weeks later on 29 July 1692. In the Cape, as in Holland, this body, despite its peculiar title, administrates the estates of the deceased, and also specifically manages any moneys left to minor children. The assets and goods of the deceased are auctioned off for the benefit of those left behind; in this particular case, the children:

> **Testators:** *Joost Lons, Arriaantje Sterrevelt, 29 July 1692*
>
> *Sale of the goods of the Free Burgher Joost Lons and his housewife Arriaantje Sterrevelt; who in all belief have run away with the return fleet; whose abandoned goods and children have been assigned on 23 July 1692 by the governor and the Council of Justice to the Masters of the Orphan Chamber; which goods have been auctioned to the highest bidder on 29 July 1692 in the presence of the undersigned master of the Orphan Chamber.*
>
> *Signed by* [among others] *Master of the Orphan Chamber: Adriane van Brakel.*

Ariaentje has abandoned her own children in Africa! She and her new husband have departed for Patria (The Netherlands), leaving all five her surviving children, including her youngest, Elizabeth, to the tender mercies of the Orphan Chamber.

However, fate has not quite finished with Ariaentje. A number of VOC ships join the return fleet under the command of Willem Kemp on the ship *Waterland*. We do not know which ship of the seven in the fleet carries Ariaentje and Joost, but the fleet makes its way up to the 45th latitude, southwest of the British Isles. Here they are intercepted by a French squadron on 12 September 1692 and the *Waterland* is sunk with all hands. Do Ariaentje and Joost lose their lives in this event? No one knows for certain. All we know, is that they are never heard of again. Through their daughter Judith, our family is descended from Adriaen Huybertszen Sterrevelt of New Amsterdam and his daughter Ariaentje.

At this point, we say goodbye to the Sterrevelt family whose name dies out at the Cape as their bloodline eventually joins that of our Western Cape Basson ancestors (*NF12*).

—*End Nexus Familia*

Nexus Familia 21: Obiqua! The San attack

The burghers have suffered ongoing cattle theft by the San since the 1670s, a good example being the theft from Gerrit Cloete, son of ancestor Jacob Cloete (*NF6*), and three other Free Burghers in April 1686[10]. In this era, the Dutch refer to the San as Obiqua, as though they are another Khoekhoe tribe. However, around 1700 it becomes clear to the settlers that there is a profound difference and they start referring to the San as *Bosjesman Hottentotten* (Bushman Hottentots).

The first serious trouble also starts with Gerrit when, in March of 1701, a band of Obiqua drive some forty head of his cattle off into the Obiquaberg[11] (Obiqua Mountain). Not only do they kill a herdsman with four or five poisoned arrows, but they also leave a message with a survivor that they will first destroy the farmers and then the Company[12]. The San Bushmen have turned political.

A first commando sent against the San fails. Next, a military post is established at the foot of the Obiquaberg, between the later Tulbagh and Gouda. The next month Gerrit loses another thirty cattle elsewhere. A second Commando is unable to track down the thieves. Soon after the Commando returns, a further 137 head of cattle are stolen from the first post. This leads to the permanent posting of six soldiers at each post and more at other key sites. Herewith starts a struggle that will last well nigh a century.

Since the Khoekhoe are also being raided by the San, they openly volunteer their help to exterminate the San. Governor Willem Adriaan Van der Stel is about to send out a Commando when he learns that Gerrit has formed his own Commando with the help of neighboring farmers and the willing Khoekhoe. Van der Stel calls off his own Commando and charges our ancestral brother Gerrit with starting an unsanctioned war; an accusation that will later again be leveled at our family (Chapter 4).

From this time on, our ancestors prefer to take the initiative, rather than to rely on the apparently ineffectual VOC Company government. Van der Stel hereupon decides to use only soldiers and no commandos. In September, one of these parties recovers a large number of cattle, but soon after the San steal more than two hundred head of cattle belonging to Henning Hüsing (*NF22*). In November 1701, the San kill their first European soldier. From this point, on the San are treated more ruthlessly.

Even though the Khoekhoe are distantly related to the Obiqua (San), the former consider the latter to be a scourge upon mankind. In February 1702, a Khoekhoe captain complains at the castle that the Obiqua have killed five of his wives and all of his children. It is interesting to note that the Khoekhoe demand protection from the governor against the San, implying that they now fully accept[13] the authority of the Dutch, even asking the governor to approve their captains.

—End Nexus Familia

 ## Nexus Familia 22: I am an Afrikaner

At the top end of the historic Dorpstraat (Town Street) in the town of Stellenbosch, inside the gate of the retirement residence Utopia, under one of those old oak trees that are so characteristic of this university town, there is a nondescript rock with a nondescript plaque. It reads in Dutch: *"Ik ben een Afrikaner"* (I am an Afrikaner). This memorial is dedicated to our ancestral brother, Hendrik Bibault, who gave our nation its name and died for it in banishment. The event has a background that sounds more than just a little like the prelude to the Boston Tea Party in America some 70 years later.

Before attending the event, we sketch the characters in the saga that will give a new nation a name.

• Governor Willem Adriaan van der Stel

Simon Van der Stel remains commander of the Cape from 12 October 1679 until 1 June 1691, when the settlement is formally made a Colony of the Netherlands, but still run by the VOC. He then becomes the first formal governor. Besides presiding over the settlement of the French Huguenots, he also mounts voyages of exploration into the north of the country. In this process, he amasses significant land and wealth. He also sends his son, Willem Adriaan, to the Netherlands for a formal education. There, Willem Adriaan serves as mayor of the center of the Dutch universe, Amsterdam. In this, he attracts the attention of the governors of the VOC, who decide that he will make a superb governor for the Cape.

On 11 February 1699, Simon retires to his Cape farm, Great Constantia, and Willem Adriaan takes over as governor, at first emulating his father by mounting voyages of exploration and involving himself in horticultural study. However, he soon starts alienating the settlers by competing outright with them. He starts scooping business away in front of their noses by virtue of his access to government information. Before long, he turns to nepotism and corruption, granting concessions to his favorites. His unpopularity increases when it appears that he is targeting the successful German immigrant and owner of the farm Meerlust[14], Henning Hüsing (See Nexus Familia 29).

By 1706, matters are out of hand. A corrupt van der Stel is running the Cape like a personal fiefdom. His close compatriots include the *landdrost* (magistrate) Starrenburg.

• Henning Hüsing

Henning Hüsing arrives at the Cape in 1672 from Hamburg. Twelve years later, he marries Maria Lindenhovius. Hüsing is regarded as the wealthiest burgher in the entire colony and serves on the Stellenbosch Heemraad (Regional Council) – a position of some considerable responsibility.

• Adam Tas

Adam Tas, son of Maria Lindenhovius' sister, finishes his commercial training in the Netherlands and emigrates to the Cape. Here he initially works as secretary and bookkeeper for Henning Hüsing on his farm, Meerlust. Though Jewish, he becomes a member of the Dutch Reformed Protestant community in Stellenbosch in 1703, marrying Elizabeth van Brakel on 7 June of that year and becoming thereby the owner of the lucrative farm Libertas.

• Jacob Louw

The widower Jan Pietersz Louw, an ancestor from Caspel-ter-Mare, arrived at the Cape on 16 December

1659. He became a Free Burgher almost immediately and obtained from the governor a farm on the Liesbeek River. Jan's son Jacob marries Maria van Brakel, sister of Elizabeth above, in 1702.

- **Hendrik Bibault**

Detlef Bibault arrives at the Cape in 1683 as a German soldier working for Jan Compagnie. Around 1685 he becomes a Free Burgher and practices as a surgeon. On 4 August 1688, eight young Dutch orphan girls disembark from the same ship *China* as our Huguenot ancestors (*NF19*). Among these young ladies is Willemijntjie Ariens De Wit. Detlef is quick to lay claim to Willemijntjie and marries her on 24 December 1688. The oldest of their four children is Hendrik, born on 28 May 1690. His sister, Maria, is our direct ancestor. However, it is Hendrik who will assume a unique position in South African history.

The memorandum of Adam Tas

And so it is in 1706, against a backdrop of continued excesses on the part of Willem Adriaan van der Stel, that Adam Tas draws up a memorandum of complaints against this governor. It is signed by sixty-three individuals, of whom thirty-one are French Huguenots, thereby raising Van der Stel's suspicions against the French at the Cape. Enough of the charges are actually true to make a convincing case against the governor. The plan is to send this memorandum to the Lords XVII with the return fleet. A first letter of complaint has already been sent the previous year, but up to now there has been no reaction.

As the return fleet arrives on 4 February 1706, the governor learns of the plan with the memoranda. Given that he cannot identify the authors of this "sedition," he draws up a memorandum of his own, praising his own virtues. He then "invites" the people of the Cape settlement to the castle. Once they are there, he "requests" them to sign this document, without great success. In desperation, he then sends Landdrost Starrenburg around the colony with an armed guard to induce colonists to sign. He manages to get 240 signatures by scraping the bottom of the Cape social barrel. Many absolutely refuse to sign.

In the Dark Hole

Early in the morning of Sunday 28 February 1706, armed dragoons surround Adam Tas' house, arrest him, and take him in chains to the Cape Castle. In his desk, they find a draft of the memorandum and a list of the intended signatories. Tas is dragged in front of a tribunal consisting of precisely the people he has indicted, including the magistrate Starrenburg. The tribunal convicts Adam and has him thrown into the *Donker Gat*, the Dark Hole, a deep and dank dungeon in the Castle with no natural light at all.

Van der Stel maliciously banishes the venerable Jan Rotterdam to Batavia for failing to show him adequate respect. Four others, including Henning Hüsing, are to be deported to the Netherlands. They are forced to leave almost immediately on a ship bound for Amsterdam. And then, Van der Stel seems to have a sudden change of heart. He sets off at maximum speed in his own galleot in pursuit of the ship bound for Amsterdam with the purported goal of reversing his decision. However, he fails to intercept it. Although he claims he wanted to free the men, his real motivation is totally different. The ship's doctor, who is sympathetic to the colonists, has smuggled the true, signed memorandum aboard the Amsterdam-bound ship. When the ship is clear of the Cape, he gives the memorandum to Henning

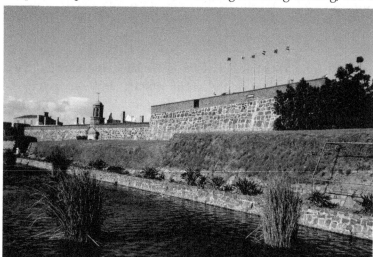

Fig. 3-4 The "Castle" in Cape Town – location of the Dark Hole

Hüsing. Ironically, Van der Stel has empowered Hüsing with the means to discredit him as governor. He has even unwittingly arranged for the fare for Hüsing to the Netherlands. Totally frustrated by his own folly, the anguished governor now lashes out in all directions.

Jacob versus the Magistrate

On 14 April 1706, there is a knock at ancestor Jacob Louw's door. Standing at the door is a detachment of VOC dragoons and the man in command orders Jacob to accompany them to the *Drostdy* (magistrate's offices). He has no choice but to obey. He says farewell to Maria and Elizabeth and leaves for the Drostdy. Jacob is shown into the office of Starrenburg, the *landdrost* (magistrate). Starrenburg proceeds to question him about the petition that he signed some months ago. Jacob steadfastly refuses to answer, maintaining that Starrenburg does not have the right to question him. That right belongs to the *fiskaal* (the prosecutor). When Starrenburg wants him to sign a recantation, he flatly refuses. Starrenburg thereupon orders the dragoons to put Jacob in jail. Other burghers soon follow. Four days later, on 18 April 1706, Starrenburg has Jacob brought out of jail and questions him again. If he will answer some of the questions, they will let him attend the baptism of his baby son. He answers two questions, and is then taken to the church for the event. Afterwards, he is returned to the jail, this time for two months until June 1706. He answers more of the questions, but still refuses to recant.

He remains in jail until September 1706. At this point, he is finally released to rejoin his anguished wife and family. Van der Stel then turns on the women and tries to force statements out of them, in return for which he promises to release their menfolk. However, the women are resolute and refuse to sign.

Civil Disobedience

Hereafter follows a period of civil disobedience. The governor issues subpoenas for a number of men to appear before the tribunal or "Court of Justice." The men reject the authority of the court, stating that they will react once the response to their memorandum comes from the Netherlands. The court thereupon sentences them in absentia to banishment to Mauritius.

On the morning of 18 September 1706, the farmers of three districts ride armed into Stellenbosch. To the roll of drums, they draw up in front of Landdrost Starrenburg's office. A major altercation arises between Starrenburg and the citizens. The women also speak their minds and declare that they will not submit to Starrenburg's tyranny. It is at this point that Landdrost[15] Starrenburg complains to Van der Stel:

> "...the wives are as dangerous as the men, and they are not still."

Two days later, some of the men under sentence of banishment to Mauritius return to town and jeer the magistrate in public. All respect for the Van der Stel government has disappeared. When Starrenburg tries to execute further arrests ordered by Van der Stel, his own officials warn the citizens and the soldiers end up empty-handed. At this point, the citizenry refuses to provide any further food to the soldiers or to Starrenburg. He is reduced to slaughtering his own goats for food for himself and his soldiers.

On 4 February 1707, a triumphant Jan Rotterdam returns from Batavia. The Batavian governor has rejected Van der Stel's transparently trumped up charges. He has treated Rotterdam with exceptional kindness, and has sent him home at the Company's expense. Clearly, Van der Stel's picture is crumbling.

I am an Afrikaner!

Adam Tas has been in prison for more than a year when, on 6 March 1707, a group of rowdy young men vent their anger by causing some commotion in the company's mill in Stellenbosch. One of them is Hendrik Bibault, a young man of seventeen years and brother of our ancestor Maria. At this point, none other than magistrate Starrenburg happens upon the scene. He goes at the young men with a cane. The others disperse, but Hendrik stands his ground. He defiantly shouts at the magistrate:

> "I will not go! I am an Afrikaner! Even if you beat me to death and even if you put me in jail, I will not stay quiet!"

To punctuate his position, he hits the magistrate with a bag of flour from the mill.

Hendrik Bibault hereby enters the history books as the first person of European descent at the Cape to publicly express his cultural association with Africa rather than Europe. It is clear that he sees the local "Afrikaners" as having been willfully disadvantaged by the "overseas" officials. This would be exactly the same as if, for the first time ever, a citizen of the English Colonies in America in 1707 were to yell *"I am an American"* at a British colonial judge. Herewith the new nation finally acquires a name and a voice. Henceforth we are to be Afrikaners, like Americans are Amerikaners, and for exactly the same reasons. It does not matter whether the person is of French, Dutch, German, Danish, Swedish or any other foreign origin, he or she will be an Afrikaner if his or her dedication is to the new country and the new community rather than to the mother country. For his pains, Hendrik Bibault is jailed along with his friends and they are thrashed in public outside the gate of the Fort in the Cape. Hendrik loses his future burgher rights, he is banished from the Cape. He dies in the Far East ten years later.

Fig. 3-5 *"Ik ben een Afrikaner" -The Rock*

Toppling the Governor

On 16 April 1707, the VOC ship *Kattendyk* anchors in Table Bay. As per instruction, the captain, Cornelis de Geus, delivers a letter to the Governor in person in front of suitable witnesses. The letter is dated 30 October 1706 and announces that governor Van der Stel, the secunde Samuel Elsevier, the clergyman Petrus Kalden and the landdrost Jan Starrenburg are removed from office and are ordered to return to the Netherlands. The governor's brother, Frans van der Stel, is to *"betake himself somewhere outside of the company's possessions."* The burghers deported to the Netherlands are to be sent home at company expense and those in jail are to be released immediately. Much more importantly, in future, no servant of the company is to own or lease land in the colony, or to trade directly in cattle, wine, or wheat. If those who now own property do not dispose of it with sufficient urgency, it will be confiscated. In addition, the Cape government is no longer allowed to interfere with the rights of the burghers to dispose of their cattle or produce in any way they see fit. Free trade is hereby finally established as an entrenched right.

It is a total, utter, and complete victory for the citizens, and this author can claim that his ancestors stood their ground for their new country and for their name: *Afrikaner!*

—*End Nexus Familia*

 ## Nexus Familia 23: Pieternella

Mauritius has been a Dutch possession for a long time, but it has been a continuous struggle to make a success of any settlement there. Now, at the end of the 17th century, there is a renewed effort underway. The Borns family, with Eva's children, Pieternella and Salomon in tow (*NF8*), is joining in this endeavor. However, the Borns appear to mistreat the children. Daniël Zaayman, a successful cooper, rescues Pieternella from this life by marrying her. Salomon dies a few years later in an epidemic on the island.

The folks on the island do their level best to make a success of the settlement, but they are tormented by cyclones, epidemics, slave revolts, and shifting market requirements from the VOC. In one of the slave revolts, the family of governor Lamotius is killed. Lamotius thereupon turns into a major problem and Italian-Swiss company man, Roelof Diodati, is sent in 1692 to arrest him and replace him as governor. Overall, Mauritius is just a problem for the VOC, which outweighs any benefit it is bringing.

Pieternella and Daniël live happily on the tropical island; the home of the dodo. Their eldest daughter, Catharina, marries the new Governor of Mauritius, Roelof Diodati. The second daughter marries a capable farmer. The family has come a long way indeed from the days of Eva and her primitive entrails-draped Goringhaikona Khoekhoe people. Pieternella's third daughter, Magdalena, marries Johannes Bockelenberg, a surgeon from Germany. Their first daughter, named Petronella after her grandmother, is our ancestor. Magdalena, however, dies on Mauritius during the birth of her fourth child.

In 1709, the VOC decides yet again to abandon the island. Pieternella and Daniël Zaayman go to the Cape with their family on the ship *Mercurius* and land back at the Cape on 26 January 1709. Four years later Pieternella dies in the greatest natural calamity to ever befall the Cape (*NF24*).

—*End Nexus Familia*

Smallpox!

On 12 February 1713, the Return Fleet of nine VOC ships from Batavia under Commander Johannes van Steeland on the flagship *Zandenburg* dropped anchor in Table Bay. As was the custom, the linen from the ships was sent to the slave lodge to be laundered. No one seemed to appreciate what they had done. A number of men on the ships had died from none other than the dreaded smallpox! An epidemic broke out in the settlement and spread like wildfire. In short order, two hundred of the five hundred slaves at the Cape had expired. The disease did not spare the Free Burghers at the Cape and many of them succumbed, including numerous members of our ancestral pool. One quarter of the colonists died.[16] Bodies had to be buried without the benefit of coffins due to a shortage of wood. The disease spread to the farmers in the rural areas but to a lesser degree than at the Cape itself due to their isolation. By the end of 1713, the epidemic had taken its course and, by 1716, the white population had recovered to 88% of its level before 1713.

The devastation among the Khoekhoe was much more far-reaching. In some cases, entire settlements of Khoekhoe died. Eventually, slaves were sent to clear these villages because the smell of death had started to pervade the entire Table Valley. By 1714, only 10% of the Khoekhoe population of the southwest Cape remained. Incredibly, those who fled inland were killed by their own people to prevent the spreading of the disease. This was the end of the Khoekhoe as a viable people in their own right in that region, marking the end of their existence as a distinct culture near the Cape Settlement.

The remnants of the Khoekhoe people essentially integrated into the Western culture of the settlement, mixing extensively with the population of freed slaves. These slaves originated from India, Indonesia, Madagascar, East and West Africa. This mix of people became a distinct group of people in South Africa, having Dutch-derived Afrikaans as their mother tongue. This formed the basis of the unique racial grouping known as "Coloured" in South Africa. The word bears little if any relation to the term "Colored" that was in use for some time in the United States. While the latter is today disparaged as a term, the former is in daily use by the "post-Apartheid" government of South Africa

 ## Nexus Familia 24: The Reaper's Bill

More than forty-three ancestral family members die in the 1713 Year of the Smallpox. Entire families are destroyed by the ravages of this terrible disease. Some of our direct ancestors who pass away in this year of bitter sorrow and suffering include:
- Pieternella van Meerhof, Eva Krotoa's daughter (*NF23*);
- Jacob Louw, who stood up to the corrupt governor (*NF22*);
- Maria Bibault, sister of the man who gave us the name "Afrikaner" (*NF22*); and
- Willem Basson (*NF 12*) and his wife Helena Clement.

—*End Nexus Familia*

Nexus Familia 25: First Contact

A family always in trouble

The Founding Father of the Bezuidenhout family was Wynand Leendertsz Bezuidenhout, who arrived at the Cape from the Netherlands back in 1666. Wynand took employment as master gardener at the Cape. On 23 September 1668, he married Johanna Gerrits from Amsterdam and they had four children, two of whom were boys. The one boy died young, and so it fell to Wynand Wynandsz Bezuidenhout, the last of the children, to be the only bearer of the family name.

Now, a generation later in 1702, Wynand is the leader of a group of forty-five men who set off eastward on an illegal hunting trip far beyond the eastern limit of the settlement. Theal records[17] that most of the men are *"fugitives from justice and men of loose character who had been imprudently discharged from the Company's service."* It is not known how Wynand, a regular citizen, has become their leader.

After some weeks, they find themselves in the vicinity of the Fish River in the land of the Gonaqua Khoekhoe nation (*See Fig. 3-7*). This is when they are attacked by a kind of people they have not seen before near the colony. They are black Ba'Ntu people and not Khoekhoe at all. In fact, these are men from across the Kei River, situated further east. They are the supporters of a rejected chief named Gwali together with the Tinde clan of amaXhosa people, all of whom have fled from the victorious and legitimate chief, Palo, the "Great Son" of chief Tshiwo (See the final section of this chapter). It is less than clear whether the hunters realize that this represents the first overland meeting of black and white in Southern Africa.

One white man is killed in the attack, but the group drives off the attackers. The hunters now go on the rampage and attack the innocent local Khoekhoe people. They will later attempt to defend this action as being reprisals. Ultimately few will believe them and this notorious party proceeds into future South African history perceived as bloodthirsty marauders. The settlers at the Cape are outraged at all of this. Few of the names of this hunting party, beyond that of "Bezuidenhout," will live on in South Africa.

From the Danish Eiderstedt to Blokzijl and the Cape

It is now twenty two years since a young man named Joen Peter Boyens hired out at Tönning near Katharinenheerd (*NF17*). On 10 September 1694, a mature bachelor named Joen Peter Boyens and his wife-to-be, Brechtje Molinerus, stand in front of the *predikant* (minister) of the Grote Kerk in the Dutch harbor town of Blokzijl in the Overijssel province (See *Fig. 1-7*). Brechtje is a widow with a son and daughter. Joen Peter Boyens provides attestation from Katharinenheerd in the Eiderstedt peninsula.

Their first child is a boy whom they baptize "Pieter" on 16 October 1695 in the same church. He is to be the Founding Father of the Booyens family in South Africa. He is named after Joen's father, Peter. Another son and two daughters follow.

In its heyday, around 1666, Blokzijl was a major port, but, by 1710, the town has become a backwater with little opportunity. And so, on 27 September 1710 a certain *"Joen Boeijens van Blockziel"* arrives at the Cape on the Dutch East India Company ship *Wijnendal*. Exactly one month later, the retired Governor Simon van der Stel arranges a sabbatical contract for *"Joene Boeijers van Blockziel."*

On 23 November 1711, Joen requests permission from the Governor to relocate to Stellenbosch. On 13 August 1712, "J.P. Boijens" is listed as a schoolteacher in the French Huguenot area

Fig. 3-6 *Blokzijl and its Grote Kerk*

of Drakenstein. The 1712 Muster Roll at the Cape reports Joen Pieter Booyens, but also a *"Pieter Boeijens"* as *knecht* (servant) in the Pieter Erasmus household in the Drakenstein Parish. Later muster rolls show both men with the Danish Erasmus family. When *"Joen Pieter Booiens uit Blozkziel"* leaves the Cape for Batavia on 22 February 1714 aboard the ship *Middelwout*, his son Pieter remains at the Cape.

Pieter marries Geertruid Blom in 1717 and by the time Geertruid dies in 1730, they have six children. Pieter will eventually become a lieutenant in the militia, a deacon in the church and a member of the Heemraad (Regional Council).

Of Pieter's seven own natural children, only Barend will propagate his family name, resulting thereby in the name remaining exceedingly rare in the country. Three of his other children will marry into the French Huguenot families of Jean Prieur du Plessis and Jacques de Villiers (*NF19*).

—End Nexus Familia

The San Bushmen

In late 1702, reports were received at the Cape of the illegal hunting party led by Wynand Bezuidenhout (*NF25*). This was the first contact ever between black and white overland in South Africa and occurred a full fifty years or two generations after Van Riebeeck had landed at the Cape. However, the black people far beyond the eastern limits of the colony were not at all a serious threat at this time.

The 1700s were to be the century of the Bushman Wars. The San people, better known as the Bushmen (Dutch: Bosjesmans) and part of the broader grouping of Khoe-San peoples, largely escaped the devastation of the smallpox epidemic because of their limited contact with the Khoekhoe and colonists.

From their refuges in the barren lands and mountainous terrain of the Cape interior they would form the next obstacle as Western Civilization started to spread eastward along the coast and into the interior. The mountain slopes from the west all the way to the river Kei were the home of the San Bushmen[18].

The Ba'Ntu – the Black People

By the end of the seventeenth century, when almost all of the activity at the Cape was still centered on Cape Town, Stellenbosch and Drakenstein, the amaXhosa Ba'Ntu people were expanding southwestward from the Umzimkhulu River, 800 miles to the east along the coast[19]. Tshawe, the successful integrator of the various amaXhosa peoples, was buried at Ntsibakazi, near the Umzimkhulu in the present day Kwa-Zulu Natal. He was succeeded by Ngcwangu and later Sikhomo.

Sikhomo led the amaXhosa southwestward down the coast and nearer to the sea. He was ultimately buried beside the Cumngce, a tributary of the Mthatha (Umtata) River in the Ngqeleni district. This placed the amaXhosa between the present day town of Umtata and the Indian Ocean in the early 1700s. There they would live for three generations of kings.

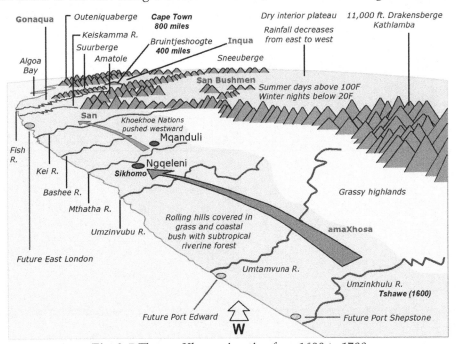

Fig. 3-7 The amaXhosa migration from 1600 to 1700

The rules of succession of the amaXhosa are important to understand. A king can have up to seven wives. Associated with each of these is a "House." Among these Houses, that of the primary wife (usually not the first in time) is the "Great House" and that of the "second wife" is the "Right-hand House." These are the two key "Houses." The first-born son of the Great House succeeds the father. The first-born son of the Right-hand House may establish a separate chiefdom elsewhere and can be semi-independent. However, he is of lower status and owes allegiance to the Great House. The new king, however, can only ascend the throne once he has undergone the initiation rite, including late teenage circumcision. If a king died before his first-born from the Great House is old enough to be initiated, a brother of the father can be appointed as regent.

Over time, a collection of Right-hand House spin-off chiefdoms was being pushed ever southwestward into Khoekhoe and San territory. At the same time, there trailed behind them a hierarchical fealty system that placed the Great King some distance behind the spin-offs from the Right-hand house and other sons. In principle, the spin-off chiefdoms were individually and separately subject to the heir from the Great House.

Togu was Sikhomo's "Great Son." He was the ruler at the time of the wrecking of the *Stavenisse* in 1687. His "Great Son," in turn, was Gconde. Gconde died in the general vicinity of the Mthatha River.

Gconde's sons will create for us the first split in the amaXhosa clans whom we meet later in the 18th century. His "Great Son" was Tshiwo, while UmDange was his first born from the Right-hand House. Herein we find the origin of the small but key imiDange grouping who will repeatedly influence the history of the Eastern Frontier. The third son was Tinde, founder of the amaTinde. His mother was from an unknown Khoekhoe nation. It is with these people that Wynand Wynandsz Bezuidenhout and his wayward hunting party clashed in 1702 (*NF25*).

In the early 1700s, the major clashes were among the amaXhosa clans themselves and between the various amaXhosa clans and the Khoekhoe, who were the original inhabitants of the eastern seaboard. The names of those Khoekhoe nations are now largely lost to us. However, the Gonaqua clan of Khoekhoe existed on the Eastern Frontier during the middle to late 1700s and will enter our story at various times into the 1800s, though they would in future intermix extensively with the black amaXhosa.

-----ooOoo-----

4

The Wild East

"The robbery and bloodlust of the Bushman Hottentots is continuing daily to such degree that our people [...] now do not know where to flee to next."

Joint meeting of Regional Council and Militia Officers,
Minutes of the Council of Policy of the Cape of Good Hope (1777)

Enter the Trekboer

By the late 1690s, it was clear that a new kind of burgher (citizen) had emerged, the *trekboer* (plural: *trekboere*). The word *"boer"* simply means "farmer" in Dutch. The term *"trekboer"* refers to the fact that these cattle stockmen would move their cattle to follow the grazing. Over time, the term has come to represent those who spread eastward across the southernmost part of the continent.

The pressure for this migration came from the fact that the pasture at the Cape was scarce in summer and the cattle ranchers had to find new pasture for their

Fig. 4-1 The Swartberg under spring snow

stock[1]. To most people, the Netherlands was now a far off place about which their grandparents might ramble on. The people in Cape Town had closer ties to Europe, while the frontier people considered Cape Town an almost foreign place, whence emanated little but rules and regulations. These families were totally committed to a new country forming at the southern tip of Africa, run by a company under a charter from the Dutch government. The burghers were also compelled to sell their produce to the company at controlled prices. One recognizes in this several of the elements that eventually led to the American War of Independence. For the frontier folk the main role of Cape Town became that of a place where they could purchase manufactured goods and lead, flint, and gunpowder.

The diffuse boundary of the colony systematically moved eastward, while the authorities at the Cape tried desperately to keep up. As time went on, they proclaimed the official boundary to be ever further east, and tried to prevent the trekboere from crossing it. In 1734, the Groot Brak (Great Alkali) River (See *Fig. 4-2*) was proclaimed the boundary. The expansion proceeded in an easterly direction for a very simple reason. To the north of Cape Town lay a desert coast and the inland territory grew barren very rapidly indeed as one proceeded northeastward beyond the Hottentots-Holland Mountain range. This is very similar to the climate and geography of California, with Death Valley situated in the lee of the Sierra Nevada.

Three major mountain ranges extend from west to east parallel to the south coast of the country. Within about ten miles of the coast runs a series of folded mountains. The only passage through them was at Attaqua's Gorge near the present Mossel Bay. Parallel to the coastal mountains, displaced inland by some thirty miles, runs the extremely rugged Swartberg (Black Mountain) range of similarly folded mountains. Approximately eighty miles north of the Swartberg is the Great Escarpment of South Africa.

The Orange River drains almost the entire country to the north of the Escarpment. This Great Escarpment has a number of names, being variously called the Nuweveld (New Country) Mountains, the Sneeuberg (Snowy Mountains) (See *Fig. 4-3*), or the Winterberg, again from west to east. To the north of this was the domain of the San Bushman. Along the south coast, expansion east of the Groot Brak River (near the present Mossel Bay) was well nigh impossible as the coastal strip is very narrow, covered in deep forest, and drained via impressive crevasses.

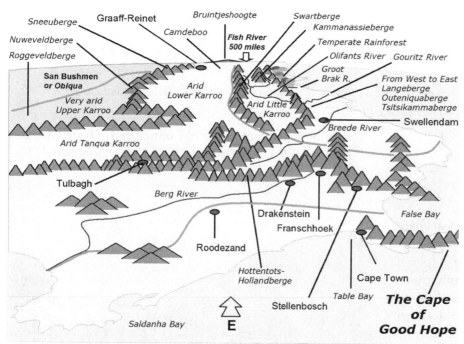

Fig. 4-2 A 500-mile view eastward from Cape Town

Throughout all this, the VOC saw the Cape as little more than a refreshment station and meat supply depot for its ships. It threatened the farmers with corporal punishment if they traded cattle with the indigenous people. Jan Compagnie had very little interest indeed in the wellbeing of the settlement and the people of the Cape knew it. The Settlers were merely a means to an end.

As the devoutly Protestant Christian Afrikaners expanded in an easterly direction, they created church parishes and towns. By the time of the 1713 smallpox epidemic, there were already towns and Dutch Reformed Church parishes close to, or north of the Cape. The founding of Swellendam in 1746 (See *Fig. 4-2*) was a major step eastward for Western Civilization in Africa. At this point, the Council at the Cape decided to administer the east of the country in two elongated east-west strips, as shown in *Fig. 4-2*.

The first, administrated from Swellendam, stretched between the Indian Ocean and the towering Swartberg Mountains. The second, administrated from Stellenbosch, stretched eastward along the north of the Swartberge to the abrupt start of the summer rainfall region at a nondescript escarpment known as Bruintjeshoogte (Bruintje's Heights; *Fig. 4-2* and *Fig. 4-4*).

Fig. 4-3 The Sneeuberg as seen from the Camdeboo plain

The plan to govern this vast territory was as grandiose as it was impractical. One can imagine the logistical difficulties in trying to govern such vast territories from two villages relatively close to Cape Town. On 26 April 1770, the eastern boundary was placed at the Gamtoos River (See *Fig. 4-4*) and on 11 July 1775 at the Upper Fish River and the Bushmans River[2]. In 1778, governor Van Plettenberg established the Great Fish River as the new eastern border after talks with some lesser amaXhosa chiefs such as Kobela of the amaGwali (See *Fig. 4-8*).

The Fish and Bushmans mouth out into the Indian Ocean near where Bartholomeu Diaz turned back homeward in 1488. In 1778, as in 1488, it would mark a major boundary in history. In 1786 the town of Graaff-Reinet was founded at the foot of the Sneeuberge (Snowy Mountains) in the northeast in an attempt to bring peace, law and order to the region, previously administered from faraway Stellenbosch.

The Camdeboo region at the foot of the Sneeuberge would become a spatial nodal point until 1803. It is in this area that the tough frontier farmer, his

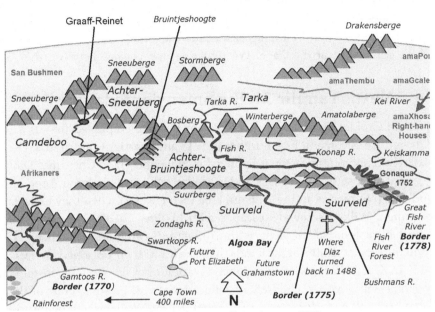

Fig. 4-4 The Eastern Frontier c.a. 1770

horse, and his trusty gun were all honed in confrontation with two other races and the bloody unforgiving harshness of Africa; the Wild East of South Africa. To the south of the Camdeboo is a world of peculiar succulent drought-resistant latex-bearing plants (See *Fig. 4-5*). It is a hard country that breeds even harder men. It abuts the Suurveld to the east. The area abounded in game such as the majestic kudu and herds of springbok antelope; a hunter's paradise even today. This is a world in which men learnt to ride and shoot from the saddle with a flintlock at an early age.

To the east was higher summer rainfall with herds of elephant for ivory, but also the formidable black Ba'Ntu people called the amaXhosa. On this frontier, a man slept with his flintlock next to his bed and he kept his powder dry at all times. These were not men to be trifled with. Nor were the proud amaXhosa. None of the latter had yet been encountered beyond the fateful Wynand Bezuidenhout expedition of 1702 (*NF 25*).

Fig. 4-5 Euphorbia and aloes south of the Camdeboo

The earliest reference to any formal dealings with respect to the Ba'Ntu people in the east is in the minutes[3] of the Meeting of the Council of Policy at the Cape held on 29 September 1722, a full seventy years after the landing at the Cape. It was minuted that a certain Nicolaas Gockelius wished to have permission to trade cattle with the *"very distantly situated Hottentots or Caffers"* (sic). This was a major request for a concession, as John Company saw the cattle trade as its own exclusive business.

On 2 July 1737, eighty-five years or three generations after the founding of the settlement, the Council minuted[4] that it had become aware of rumors that some Cape elephant hunters had been killed. These rumors proved true, and in fact a fairly large party of hunters had been murdered. The Council thereupon suspended elephant hunting expeditions *"leaving in the direction of Caffersland* [sic]*,"* in order to avoid provoking the Ba'Ntu people. Similar expeditions northward to the Namaqua Khoekhoe were still allowed.

It would be in the 1780s that matters would finally come to a head with the Ba'Ntu people, between five hundred and six hundred miles east of the Cape and some one hundred-and-thirty years after the founding of the settlement at the Cape. We first treat the clashes between the Afrikaners and the San "Bushmen."

 ## Nexus Familia 26: Bushmen depredations!

Johann Grobler arrives around 1708 from Prussia, employed first as a woodcutter and then as a transport driver. He becomes a Free Burgher in 1715 and marries Geertruyd Knoesen in the same year. Nicolaas, their sixth child and our ancestor, is baptized in Stellenbosch on Christmas Day 1723.

In August 1739, Nicolaas' older brother Willem is helping three other men to take some wheat, cattle and sheep to market in the Tulbagh area (See *Fig. 4-2*) when they are attacked with poisoned arrows by San Bushmen. Willem somehow escapes with his life, but the two other men are killed[5]. Two wagonloads of wheat have been stolen along with 210 head of cattle and 350 sheep. This is one of the earliest reports of civilian colonist deaths at the hands of the San and their poisoned arrows.

In 1753, Nicolaas marries Johanna Combrinck in the Drakenstein parish (See *Fig. 4-2*). Nicolaas and Johanna will have ten children, of whom eight will be sons. Four of them will enter our story. The eldest, Johannes, will be tortured to death. The third son, Willem, will be imprisoned as a rebel by the English. The second youngest, Cornelis, is our ancestor. The youngest brother, Michael, will provide two sons who will strike out northward to seek a new country, but they will both die horribly on that quest.

—End Nexus Familia

Obiqua! The San Bushman Wars

By the second half of the 18th century, the Dutch East India Company (VOC) was a waning force. It was a time of ascendancy for the French. However, in Southern Africa the trekboere were largely ignorant of the sweeping power play across the globe. They were involved in a struggle for the very existence of Western Civilization in Africa against the most unlikely of foes; a hunter-gatherer race of people of very small physical stature, but armed with a superlative knowledge of terrain, tracking skills, hunting craft and poisoned arrows; the San Bushmen or Obiqua. These little men would attack the isolated farmsteads and strike fear into the hearts of the thinly spread Afrikaners. The minutes[6] of the Council of Policy at the Cape of 5 June 1777 record a discussion of a letter dated 3 June 1777, signed by the combined regional council members and officers of the militia of Stellenbosch. One of the signatories was Johannes Albertus Meijburg, third son of our ancestor Albert Lambertsz (*NF13*) as a member of the Stellenbosch Regional Council. The report states:

> *...The robbery and bloodlust of the Bushman Hottentots is continuing daily to such degree that our people who have already fled from the Sneeuberg district to the Camdeboo, now do not know where to flee to next.* [...]
> *...requesting a cessation of farm loan payments and assistance with ammunition* [...]
> *...the last shipment of 400 pounds of gunpowder and 800 pounds of lead needs to be increased to 1500 pounds of gunpowder, 3000 pounds of lead and 3000 pounds of flint.*

The signatories proceeded to state their losses in each "watch" presided over by a Master of the Watch.

The list goes on and on with losses of the order of 200 sheep or 30 to 40 cattle per farmer. The report cautioned the commandos sent against the San were too small to effectively counter the San activities in the Sneeuberg region. It also reported on friendly Khoekhoe being killed by the San. There was a desperate plea for help from the government. The report sketched the existence of the San as a "bane on the land." The authors stated that they had been so impoverished by the depredations of the San that they could no longer afford to support their families, let alone pay their loans or buy gunpowder.

Another message had a more ominous tone. This missive referred to the fact that senior Commando leader, Adriaan van Jaarsveld, had tried and failed to raise a suitably sized commando to drive off the San, and had now moved away. He was living in an area beyond the all-important Bruintjeshoogte, where he said it was possible to live in a greater degree of peace. The signatories warned that more of them would follow suit in despair unless the government took action. It was signed on 17 November 1776 in the Sneeuberg district by no fewer than twenty-six senior leaders. The Council thereupon approved the supply

Fig. 4-6 *The Camdeboo Plain from the San position in the Sneeuberge*

of gunpowder, lead, and flint and instructed the Militia to not commit cruelties against the San women and children, or against their wounded, and to ensure that the Khoekhoe helpers did not do so either. Severe cruelty was nevertheless perpetrated on both sides.

While the campaign against the San was cruel, the San meted out their own atrocities. There are published accounts of farms being attacked and young Afrikaner girls being captured, stabbed with poisoned arrows and then stuck upside down in aardvark burrows to die a lingering death, kicking helplessly as they struggled against the infamously slow-working poison. Various visitors and observers also reported the wholesale slaughter of farm animals and their Khoekhoe herders by the Bushmen, who left nothing alive in their ravaging of the land. They truly did try to exterminate all human and domestic animal life. In 1792, they would murder the author's own ancestor, Casper Labuschagne, and his son[7].

During this "Bushman War" the Cape government turned to the use of the Commando system as the only plausible mechanism available to them to address the problem. On 29 July 1796, the Cape Governor would appoint[8] the author's own ancestor, Matthys Andries de Beer, as Commander of an expedition to drive the San from the Swartberg region of the South Cape. Despite everything the Cape government sent against the San Bushmen, they would remain a significant threat into the early 19th century.

In America — Attempted Genocide

The morning of 28 May 28 1754 sees Ensign Joseph Coulon de Villiers de Jumonville of Quebec leading his 35 French soldiers south from Fort Duquesne. At this point, they are suddenly attacked[9] by a force of forty Virginia militiamen and their Iroquois allies led by a twenty-two year old Virginiaman. Ten French soldiers are killed and twenty-one wounded are captured, including Joseph. The French wounded are summarily killed, except for Joseph and one who escapes. Even as Joseph explains that they were on a diplomatic mission, Seneca chief Tanaghrisson tells him *"You are not yet dead my father!"* and cleaves his skull open with his hatchet. Thus begins the French and Indian War in North America. It will spread across the French and English world into Europe, where it will be remembered as the Seven Years War. It will change the map of North America. The young Virginiaman who led the attack is a certain George Washington.

In Canada, British forces led by General Jeffrey Amherst take Quebec and Canada is henceforth British. The British, paranoid about the fact that the Acadian people are French descendants, decide to deport them all from Nova Scotia and neighboring territories. Thereby they consign these proud, devout, and industrious people to destitution and servitude. Here is where the legend of Evangeline is born. This is how people in the future state of Louisiana will get to know French-speaking folks, whom they will refer to as Cajuns (Acadians). In this war, France loses all its possessions in North America east of the Mississippi River. The war is over by 1763. However, the French are determined that such a calamity does not befall them again. They strengthen their navy and wait.

At the end of the French and Indian War, General Jeffrey Amherst institutes new policies toward the Indian allies of both the French and British in the area of the Great Lakes. These policies limit the supply of gunpowder and presents to the Indians. The gunpowder is needed for hunting and the new policy therefore directly affects the ability of the Indians to hunt and trade and have an income. The presents have been a key mechanism used in cementing alliances among the Indians. Furthermore, while the French have always been few and have treated the Indians with respect, the English now descend on the Indian territory in large numbers. The Indian population correctly feels that the English view them with contempt. Their conviction is that the English are actively disarming them in preparation for war. Under the leadership of the Ottawa chief, Pontiac, they start what will become known as "Pontiac's Rebellion." Initially, the Indians overrun a number of forts and besiege yet others. Many colonists are captured or killed. Others flee to the forts and yet others flee the frontier region altogether. This is the prelude to the first documented[10] attempt at genocide via biological warfare in modern history.

When Colonel Henry Bouquet at Lancaster, Pennsylvania, prepares to lead an expedition to relieve Fort Pitt, Amherst makes the following proposal[11] on or about 29 June 1763:

"Could it not be contrived to send the small pox among the disaffected tribes of Indians? We must on this occasion use every stratagem in our power to reduce them."

When Bouquet agrees on 13 July 1763, Amherst adds on 16 July 1763:

"You will do well to inoculate the Indians by means of blankets, as well as every other method that can serve to extirpate this execrable race."

It is not known whether this attempt at biological warfare actually worked. Eventually, the British forces get the upper hand and peace is agreed. In this process, presents are supplied to the Indians. Andrew Blackbird, the adopted son of an Ottawa chief, will eventually transcribe the oral account of what happens when the gift boxes are opened[12]:

"Accordingly, after they reached home they opened the box; but behold there was another tin box inside, smaller. They took it out and opened the second box, and behold, still there was another box inside the second box, smaller yet. So they kept on this way till they came to a very small box, which was not more than an inch long; and when they opened the last one they found nothing but moldy particles in this last box...

Pretty soon burst out a terrible sickness among them. The great Indian doctors themselves were taken sick and died. The tradition says that it was indeed awful and terrible. Everyone taken with it was sure to die. Lodge after lodge was totally vacated – nothing but the dead bodies lying here and there in their lodges. The whole coast of Arbor Croche... which is said to have been a continuous village some fifteen or sixteen miles long... was entirely depopulated and laid waste."

Bouquet later writes that by sending germs instead of British soldiers, he has "...saved the lives of better men."

Clearly, the indigenous population of North America has made use of the transition of power from French to English to attempt to overthrow the "occupying forces." Early in the next century, the change of colonial power in South Africa will result in a similar situation with consequences even more disastrous for ordinary people trying to survive on a frontier between civilizations.

The Cape and American Independence

When the frontier farmers signed the request to the Cape government for help against the San Bushmen, they probably had little idea that 8,000 miles away across the ocean in North America another drama was starting to unfold. Just as our ancestor Jacob Louw had stood up against bad government (*NF22*), so people in America were about to follow suit. Whatever the local symptoms, the core issue on both continents was the practice of European overlords treating their colonies as closed fiefdoms without granting the inhabitants the same benefits and rights as citizens of the home countries. Neither the inhabitants of New England nor those at the Cape had true citizen's rights. In the Cape, the Dutch East India Company was effectively the government, while the British government gave special concessions to the British East India Company. These included the right to sell tea in New England without having to pay the import duties that New England merchants had to pay. The tea provided by this august company would become the subject of the famous Boston Tea Party.

The American War of Independence was only but part of a wider international struggle for maritime supremacy between England on the one hand, and France, Spain, and Netherlands on the other over the period 1775 to 1783. When the War started in 1775, the American cause garnered enormous support from the Europeans who were hugely inspired by the advent of real democracy. People in the Netherlands were openly supportive of the American efforts to gain representative government. Of course, the fact that the people of New York were still to a large degree Dutch or Belgian may have played a major role in this support. Even a cursory look at the registry of citizens for the year of 1720 in the general area of Albany, New York, reveals that almost all the names on the list were still Dutch at that point, and this was to be the case for many more years. New York was still culturally a Dutch colony legally owned by Britain. This was particularly true of upstate New York, called New Belgium on period maps.

As soon as the Americans demonstrated their ability via a first nominal victory at Saratoga in 1778, the French signed a treaty of alliance with them and declared war on Britain. In 1779, the Spaniards joined against Britain and in 1780, the Dutch. The American Revolution had therefore started a World War with the Continental allies ranged against Britain. With all this support, the war was America's to lose. With the major navies of Europe jointly arrayed in war against the British, the latter found the international chessboard stacked against it. Britain had major commercial interests in the Caribbean and the Far East, but the French were already busy taking island after island from them in the Caribbean.

With its possessions everywhere under attack by the Allies, Britain was compelled to divert a major part of its naval strength to secure its crucial Far East holdings, which it considered most valuable. The key to protecting these holdings was Cape Town. This was the international maritime nodal point that controlled access to the Far East from Europe. Whoever held it, could dictate the great game. It was vital for the French and Dutch on the one hand, as well as for the success of the American Revolution on the other hand, that the Cape should stay out of British hands at all costs. The French strategy consisted of effectively blocking the British effort in America whilst threatening their Far East trade route by occupying the Cape.

Faced with this global threat, the British Admiralty redefined the war. It now viewed the contest in America as "*a secondary consideration*"[13] and the principal object was now "*distressing France*" and defending and securing Britain's own possessions against the French. Up to that time, the French had preferred Mauritius and the British St. Helena, but both islands required support from the Cape to operate. Britain realized that all now hinged on their control of the Cape. They needed to secure it for Britain. France thereby appreciated that to thwart the British they would have to control the Cape. In March 1781, both navies dispatched[14] significant fleets to take Cape Town. The French fleet was led by Baille St Tropez de Suffern, the "Nelson" of the French. Commodore Johnstone led the British fleet. Johnstone was not held in particularly high regard; in fact, the Americans had refused to negotiate with him, as he was considered "incompatible with their honor." Johnstone sailed first and had no fewer than thirty-five ships laden with troops in addition to his warships. De Suffern sailed nine days later. They both headed for the Cape Verde islands as a first stop.

Johnstone arrived at the islands on 11 April 1781 and proceeded to put his men ashore to procure supplies. He neglected to make proper defensive preparations. On the 16th of April, De Suffern also arrived and surprised the British, who were taking their leisure and making use of the brothels. De Suffern sailed straight into the harbor and did as much damage as he could while the English looked on helplessly. Then he withdrew and ran for the Cape. On 21 June 1781, he landed his troops at the Cape to reinforce his Dutch allies and went on to successfully attack the British in the Indian Ocean.

With this horrendous damage having been visited on the Royal Navy, France now had strategic control of the world's oceans. Soon afterwards, on 5 September 1781, French Admiral de Grasse assured victory for the Americans by cutting off all relief for the British commander Cornwallis across Chesapeake Bay. Cornwallis offered surrender at Yorktown on 17 October 1781. On 3 September 1783, the Thirteen Colonies could therefore forge a lasting peace arrangement and recognition of their new country.

This series of events, whilst working well for America, was to dramatically affect the future of South Africa. It was now evident to the British that control of the oceans of our planet hinged on their control of the Cape. This was a lesson they learned the hard way and would not soon forget. Back in America the rejoicing citizens probably never gave the subject another thought at the time. They had no way of appreciating the central role that the race for the faraway Cape had played in their victory.

After three years at the Cape, the French troops departed. The Dutch were still in control there, but in a greatly weakened state. The British had severely mauled the Dutch in the 1780-1784 Fourth Anglo-Dutch War, which is inseparably linked to the American War of Independence. Before that war, Dutch sea power had already been reduced to just 20 ships and after that it effectively ceased to exist. The Dutch East India Company was now near-bankrupt, and a mere shadow of its former self. The Netherlands had effectively been removed as a significant power. While Americans could glow under the protection of mighty France, the Cape went into decline under its much-humbled Dutch master.

While the events of the first few years of the 1780's were hugely positive for America, they spelled future misery for the citizens at the Cape. Now supported only by a weakened Netherlands, they were pitted against the Xhosa, an infinitely more formidable indigenous nation than what Americans would ever have to face on their own continent. Also, while the Thirteen Colonies faced Britain at a time when she was weaker and stretched to match the French, Spaniards and Dutch, our ancestors at the Cape would have to face that same country totally alone when she was at the peak of her strength, the first unassailable modern superpower. The next century would belong to the British.

Trouble in the amaXhosa World

The amaXhosa lived at Ngqeleni beyond the Umtata River during the reigns of three kings, being Sikhomo, Togu and Ngconde. Under the next king, Tshiwo, they moved over the Mthatha River to settle at Mqanduli (See *Fig. 3-7*). Tshiwo was succeeded around 1730 by one of the longest reigning kings of the amaXhosa, Phalo. He settled the amaXhosa further west at Tongwana, a short distance from the Great Kei River (See *Fig. 4-7*). Phalo's Great Son, the one who would succeed him, was Gcaleka. However, the first born of the Right-hand House, Rharhabe, was a very ambitious young man. His father, Phalo, therefore decided to give him the lands to the west beyond the Kei River to start his own chiefdom. The split that resulted between the amaGcaleka and the amaRharhabe resulted in war in 1750 and would last into the 21st century. The split is of profound importance in amaXhosa tradition, requiring a special commission[15] to address it in 2008.

On 29 February 1752, a formally sanctioned expedition[16], led by Ensign Beutler, departed the Cape for the Eastern Frontier. On 13 May, the party put up a sign marked VOC at the mouth of the Swartkops River, indicating possession by the Dutch East India Company. By 5 June, they reached the Keiskamma. Thus far they had encountered only Khoekhoe. At this point, the Gonaqua, who lived in large numbers between the Fish and the Keiskamma Rivers, were still of relatively pure Khoekhoe stock, but were on good terms with the amaXhosa.

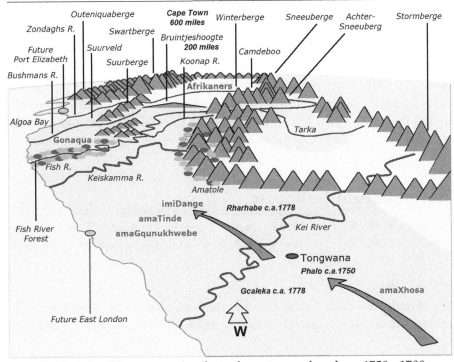

Fig. 4-7 AmaXhosa expansion down the eastern seaboard c.a. 1750 - 1780

Beyond the Keiskamma, near the coast, the expedition met the amaTinde. As they approached the Buffalo River (near where Rharhabe reputedly lived), their Gonaqua Khoekhoe guides started deserting them. This gives us an idea of the disposition of the amaXhosa in the 1750s and some insight into the power that Rharhabe wielded.

During the following 25 years, Rharhabe turned his attention westward. The notion that people such as the imiDange, amaTinde, and amaGqunukhwebe[17], west of the Kei, could be independent from him did not suit Rharhabe at all.

Even before his father Phalo died in 1775, Rharhabe started his attempts to force the amalgamation of these groups into his amaRharhabe empire, but the spin-off chiefdoms resisted. The result was a major upheaval which precipitated the imiDange, amaTinde, and amaGqunukhwebe not just over the Keiskamma into the Koonap, but right over the lower Great Fish River into the Suurveld. We shall refer to them in this work as the "Suurveld amaXhosa," a loose alliance of displaced imiDange (sometimes called Mandankees), amaTinde, amaGqunukhwebe, and other lesser-known spinoff chiefdoms such as the amaMbalu and amaGwali. Along with them, there were some remaining semi-Khoekhoe Gonaqua groups. Herein lies the root of no fewer than nine subsequent wars on the Eastern Frontier and the 21st Century political disposition in South Africa.

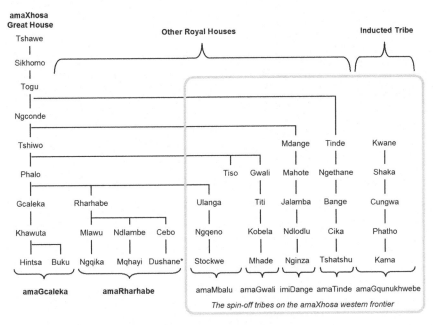

Fig. 4-8 Succession in the amaXhosa Royal Houses

To understand what happened subsequently, one has to visualize the Suurveld amaXhosa grouping squashed between the amaRharhabe across the Keiskamma and the Afrikaners in the west. Moreover, the amaThembu occupied territory vacated by the amaXhosa to the northeast of the latter along the coast, increasing the pressure on various amaXhosa groups to move southwestward.

The first reaction of the harassed imiDange in particular was to fall upon the cattle herds of the farmers near the Fish River. It would have been exceedingly difficult to try and convince a 1778 European-descended Christian frontier farmer to show understanding of the dilemma of these people. Through the eyes of the farmer, it was a simple matter of "black savage hordes" armed with *assegais* (throwing spears) stealing his cattle and threatening his homestead. The farmers at this point had little concept of the pressure exerted on the marauders assailing them. East of the Keiskamma, behind the Suurveld amaXhosa was the powerful Rharhabe with his ambitions to control the whole of the territory between the Kei and the Keiskamma. Even more distant, beyond the Kei River, was the amaGcaleka Great House kingdom – the heart of the amaXhosa Empire.

 ## Nexus Familia 27: Beyond Bruintjeshoogte

Our immigrant ancestor Hendrik Frederik Klopper arrives at the Cape in 1713 from Hoorn in the Netherlands and marries Catharina Botha in 1717. She gives him six children, of whom three hold interest for us.

1. Son Johannes is our direct ancestor.

2. Son Hendrik will soon be at odds with Field-Cornet Adriaan van Jaarsveld (*NF28*). Hendrik's daughter Elsie will marry Johannes, the eldest of our ancestral Grobler brothers (*NF26*) and experience the horror of the Eastern Frontier (*NF29*).

3. In 1742, daughter Maria marries Willem Prinsloo, grandson of immigrant Adriaan Gerritsz Prinsloo from Gouda in the Netherlands. Willem becomes a pioneering farmer on the eastern frontier.

Fig. 4-9 The Boschberg, site of Willem Prinsloo's farm

On 9 October 1772, the Cape Government advises[18] the magistrate of Stellenbosch that Willem has allegedly settled illegally beyond the formal Colonial border of Bruintjeshoogte. The information is correct. Willem has established a farm at the foot of the towering Boschberg (See *Fig. 4-4* and *Fig. 4-9*) beyond Bruintjeshoogte, at the site of the much later Somerset-East. On 10 November 1774, Willem and our ancestor Johannes Klopper, along with several other family members and farmers, successfully petition[19] the governor of the Cape to allow them to stay in Achter-Bruintjeshoogte (Beyond Bruintje's Heights).

When Swedish scholar Anders Sparrman[20] travels the area in December 1775, Willem is his host:

"The first place where we took up our lodging was at an old elephant hunter's, of the name of PRINTSLOO, who was the first that had migrated here, and at the bottom of a high mountain had selected the finest situation for a farm in the whole district, and, I had almost said, in all Africa."

Willem's son, Marthinus, marries Maria Margaretha Klopper, daughter of our ancestor Johannes Klopper above. The Kloppers and Prinsloos, together with a number of other frontier families, become something in the nature of a frontier clan, which we shall refer to as the "Prinsloo clan." Our ancestral Prinsloo clan and our ancestral Bezuidenhouts (*NF25* and *29*) will take center stage in challenging the authority at the Cape over the period 1795 to 1815, for better or for worse; mostly for worse.

Nexus Familia 28: The French bloodline goes East

We last saw Jean and Pierre Jourdan disembark at the Cape from the fateful ship *China* (*NF19*). Jean eventually married his fellow refugee from the Lubéron, Isabeau Le Long, in 1690. Now, two generations later, Jean's granddaughter, Maria Jordaan, has married Albert van Jaarsveld. Their son is Kommandant Adriaan van Jaarsveld, local commando leader on the Frontier.

Jean's grandson, Pieter, now lives near a hot spring[21] at the southern foot of the Swartberg (*Fig. 4-1*). Pieter's third son, our ancestor Pieter Johannes, is born in 1779. We shall follow his children to the kingdom of an African tyrant and unspeakable horror.

Isabeau Richarde (*NF19*), widowed by the death of husband Pierre Mallan on the *China*, married fellow refugee Pierre Jaubert. They settled in the Franschhoek (French "Corner") area near Stellenbosch. We shall be tracking Pierre Joubert's grandsons, brothers Isaac and Josua Joubert. Isaac's son, Pieter Schalk, is our direct ancestor and still lives in the Tulbagh area in the late 1700s. For more than a century brother Josua and his descendants will be at the heart of South African history.

Josua moves to the Camdeboo area near Graaff-Reinet before 1780 and becomes Master of the Watch in the militia; a rank later known as Field-Cornet. It is in this capacity that he calls out a commando in 1780 to pursue amaXhosa cattle raiders and kill several of them. They take the cattle back and seek approval for the actions after the fact[22] from the government in the Cape. The correctly anticipate that there will not be any more help from the Cape. The Council at the Cape approves of the raid, but insists it not be taken as precedent.

—End Nexus Familia

Xhosa! The First Frontier War

While the citizens of the Graaff-Reinet district were driving the San Bushmen out of the Camdeboo and the Achter-Sneeuberg, matters were going from bad to worse along the eastern border. In 1776, Anders Sparrman, the Swedish naturalist, traveled the Cape and met his first Ba'Ntu people at the Fish River[23]. He reported no amaXhosa west of the Fish River in the so-called Suurveld ("Sour country"). His Gonaqua Khoekhoe guides told him the black people lived much further east[24]. The very next year, 1777, black people were west of the Fish River en masse, while several farmers had driven their cattle across the Zondaghs River into the Suurveld for grazing. White and black had finally met territorially. It was now one-and-a quarter centuries, or five generations, since the founding of the Settlement at the Cape in 1652.

Since the 1730s, the VOC had been worried about elephant hunters and trekboere going beyond Bruintjeshoogte and, in particular, beyond the madly winding Fish River. In 1778, Governor Van Plettenberg toured the border himself, during which he declared the Fish River the formal boundary of the colony. However, by 5 November 1779 the farmers started fleeing the eastern border when the amaXhosa began to raid farms and steal cattle. The amaXhosa in turn accused the local Gonaqua Khoekhoe of raiding their cattle[25].

In 1780, came an important moment in history, often forgotten, when Rharhabe asked the frontier Afrikaners for their help in crushing his Suurveld amaXhosa opponents, offering permanent friendship and peace in return[26]. It is at this time that an experienced frontiersman by the name of Adriaan van Jaarsveld (*NF28*), was made *kommandant* in command of the border with both the San Bushmen in the north and the amaXhosa in the east. Located safely in the Cape, five hundred miles away from the boiling Fish River frontier, the Governor thought the amaXhosa a "timid people." He instructed Van Jaarsveld to use a strong Commando to persuade the Xhosa to move across the Fish River without using force. By now, some Afrikaners on the frontier had had their farms destroyed by the "timid" Suurveld amaXhosa. The Prinsloos had lost almost all (*NF29*). In May 1781, Van Jaarsveld set up his base at Marthinus Prinsloo's burnt-out farm, organized the families into protective *laagers*[27], and set out against the Suurveld amaXhosa, driving them back across the Fish River[28].

Despite the efforts of remote historians to describe events in Southern Africa as an unequal struggle between spears and guns, the two parties to the conflict were well matched. The amaXhosa had numbers and the Afrikaners had muskets. The amaXhosa were capable of holding their own, combining superior tactics with their less sophisticated weapons. These latter day historical experts and revisionist social commentators ought to be challenged to reload a flintlock with powder from a horn while being charged by an overwhelming horde of battle-crazed amaXhosa, each expert at hurling a spear with astounding accuracy, and each carrying a supply of 4 to 6 of these weapons.

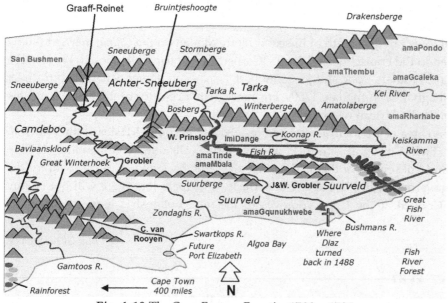

Fig. 4-10 The Cape Eastern Frontier 1780 – 1795

It had taken a full one hundred and thirty years from the founding of the Cape Settlement for the white man and the black man of South Africa to clash over matters of territory in the Suurveld. However, strategically the clash came at the worst possible time for the settlers. With the Netherlands now distinctly diminished, the VOC government at the Cape had become utterly enfeebled. It would get worse.

The independent-minded frontier people were becoming disenamored with what they saw as a distant and useless VOC government. That government was preoccupied with Dutch shipping schedules and political contests among white men in Europe, while the frontiersmen were locked in a three-way struggle for their own survival in drought ridden bush country next to the Great Fish River, five hundred miles away. Discontent was at an all-time high, and it would get progressively worse. Most of the trouble could be traced to two factors. A new nation was being run by a commercial company with essentially zero interest in their well-being, and that company was now nearing bankruptcy.

 ## Nexus Familia 29: The Troubled Frontier

The period that now follows was one of tremendous instability on the Eastern Frontier. A number of ancestral family members on that frontier were very directly involved.

1. The Unhappy Men of the Frontier

During the First Frontier War with the amaXhosa in 1781, Willem Prinsloo and his family lose all they have but six cows, and their new house is burnt down[29]. After the war, the Prinsloo and Klopper families become deeply unhappy with Field-Cornet Adriaan van Jaarsveld (*NF28*), as they feel they have not regained what they have lost. Van Jaarsveld, in turn, does not want to fight wars on two fronts at the same time; one with the amaXhosa in the east and another with the San Bushmen in the north. In his communications with the Cape government, Van Jaarsveld refers[30] in 1782 to the Prinsloo clan, as the "band of rebels." As a result of the frayed relations on the frontier, Van Jaarsveld asks for the appointment of a landdrost (magistrate) for the eastern districts. He subsequently withdraws from further action against the amaXhosa, but will return to center stage in the late 1790s.

2. The new Frontier District

On 7 May 1785, the British East Indiaman, the *Pigot*, puts ashore one hundred scorbutic passengers and crew near Algoa Bay and they are taken to a nearby farm. Some officers of the ship then make their way overland to the Cape, apparently doing surveys on the way. This so alarms the Cape Government that they decide to make Graaff-Reinet a separate district, covering the eastern sections of both the old Swellendam and old Stellenbosch districts up to the Fish River. In December 1785, the Cape Government appoints[31] Maurits Woeke as magistrate to the new district. Adriaan van Jaarsveld and Josua Joubert (*NF28*) are selected as members of the first Regional Council of Graaff-Reinet in 1786.

3. The drunken Magistrate

The Groblers (*NF26*) are right in the heart of the frontier crisis. They face multiple challenges. To their north are the tenacious San Bushmen who kill all living things. To their east, the Suurveld amaXhosa have started occupying land west of the Fish River yet again and are raiding the farmers' cattle at will. Since the First Frontier War Willem Grobler's own farmhouse has been completely burnt down once and set alight twice more[32] by the amaXhosa. At the same time, the magistrate they have asked for has turned out to be an incompetent and corrupt drunk. Many amaXhosa insist that Woeke has accepted cattle from them in a personal arrangement in exchange for them occupying the Suurveld. The farmers are inclined to believe this. This allegation will continually resurface[33] in the future. The farmers soon lose all faith in Woeke. Ancestral brother Josua Joubert is mentioned[34] as a witness in the complaint. On 31 October, Woeke is dismissed from his post[35]. Somehow, it never occurs to Governor Sluijsken to visit the frontier. The Suurveld amaXhosa are overrunning farms, but the Council at the Cape does not believe the complaints. In March 1793, the Cloete family from *Rissiesvalleij* (Pepper Valley) flees their burning farm under the leadership of Stephanus Abraham Cloete. They reach Willem's farmstead, but there Stephanus is murdered[36] by the amaXhosa.

4. The misplaced "Son of Jean Jacques Rousseau"

Into this intensely confrontational situation, on 29 April 1793, the VOC injects the new caretaking Graaff-Reinet Landdrost, Honoratius Maynier, the secretary to the dismissed drunkard, Woeke. This is the final straw for the frustrated men of the frontier. Maynier has passionately liberal convictions and sees in the frontiersmen all that is bad and in the Khoekhoe and amaXhosa all that is good; a true Son of Jean Jacques Rousseau and his naive "Noble Savage" theory. Here is a man who uses the three-word phrases *"otherwise peace-loving Caffers"* or *"otherwise peacable nation"* in nearly all of his letters; this while the same Suurveld amaXhosa are stealing the farmers blind and killing one another in large numbers. He strongly opposes the farmers he is supposed to protect. The Canadian historian, Theal[37], says of Maynier:

> *"It was one of the most injudicious appointments ever made in South Africa, for no one could have been more out of sympathy with the colonists than Maynier was. It seems almost impossible that any man living on the frontier of the Cape Colony could really have held the views concerning the simplicity and honesty of barbarians enunciated by the French philosophers..."*

The "Noble Savage" thinking is well exemplified by Francois le Vaillant, who travels the Cape around this time and writes[38] the following even as, unbeknown to him, the amaXhosa tribes are slaughtering one another in droves beyond the Fish River and the Khoekhoe kill the San Bushman on sight like wild animals:

> *"In every part, where the natives live entirely unconnected with the whites, their manners are mild and amiable; on the contrary, an acquaintance with the Europeans, alters and corrupts their natural character, which amazingly degenerates; and this remark, which is a melancholy truth, seldom admits of an exception."*

By 1793, Josua Joubert, now captain in the Commando, is at odds with Maynier. It is perversely ironic that Josua, a direct descendant of the Vaudois Pierre Joubert, is again set upon in Africa by a Maynier, just as Pierre Joubert's Vaudois ancestors were set upon by Maynier, the Count of Oppède, in 1545 Provence (*NF2*).

Ultimately, Josua simply abandons his responsibilities as Regional Council member for Graaff-Reinet[39]. He is entirely representative of the frustrated Afrikaner on the frontier. At Graaff-Reinet, Maynier believes the farmers to be lying about the depredations of the Suurveld amaXhosa.

5. A family forever where there is trouble

By 1793, we find three brothers, grandsons of Wynand Wynandsz Bezuidenhout (*NF25*), living on the frontier. Two of them, Frederik Cornelis and Johannes Jurgen, will later feature prominently in one of the fundamentally defining events in South African history. The third brother is our ancestor Coenraad Frederik. He and his cousin Coenraad de Buys (see below), along with friend Chris Botha, are in Xhosa territory. There they have sided with Ndlambe against the Suurveld amaXhosa, whom Ndlambe regards as renegade underlings (see Chap 4: *Trouble in the amaXhosa World*).

Umlawu was the first son from Rharhabe's Great House, but he has died before his father Rharhabe. Umlawu's son, Ngqika (commonly pronounced "Gaika"), is too young to ascend the throne, and hence Umlawu's Right-hand brother Ndlambe has been appointed regent for the young Ngqika. Ndlambe thereby temporarily commands all the amaRharahbe. He is using his temporary status as regent to improve his own political position in the collective amaRharhabe House. In keeping with his ambitions, he appoints one of his own sons, Dushane, as chief of the people of his brother Cebo, thereby effectively establishing control over all the amaRharhabe (See *Fig. 4-8*). He is a powerful man indeed.

The other spin-off royal houses near the Fish River are all wary of Ndlambe's ambitions and, as with his father Rharhabe before him, they are resisting his efforts. After all, they are Right-hand Houses of longer standing than the amaRharhabe. So it is that a number of Boer Masters of the Watch report[40] battles between Ndlambe and the amaGqunukhwebe. This is the internal amaXhosa tribal struggle in which the three frontier farmers have become involved. Ndlambe is their obvious ally, as he opposes the Suurveld amaXhosa (the amaGqunukhwebe, amaTinde, and imiDange) who continually raid Afrikaner farms. These wars between the amaRharhabe and the other Suurveld amaXhosa are pushing the Suurveld amaXhosa onto Afrikaner farms. The Suurveld amaXhosa see the Afrikaners as a distinctly smaller threat than the amaRharhabe.

It is not clear that magistrate Maynier understands any of these internal amaXhosa complexities and rivalries. The Bezuidenhouts and Prinsloos, living in Achter-Bruintjeshoogte closer to the amaXhosa, certainly do. So, most definitely, does Coenraad de Buys.

6. Cousin Coenraad – Hercules as bogeyman

Coenraad de Buys, great-grandson of Jean de Buis (*NF19*), is a first cousin of ancestor Coenraad Bezuidenhout. The mothers of the two Coenraads are two Scheepers sisters, Sophia and Christine. We shall soon meet the two ladies' eldest brother, Gerrit, and his family. Both Sophia and Gerrit are direct ancestors of the author. The 30-year-old Coenraad de Buys stands close on 7 foot in his socks. He is a very impressive man indeed. Hinrich Lichtenstein[41] says of him:

> "*...his great strength of body, a countenance full of courage and ardour, a daring and active mind, with superior eloquence of speech, [...]*
>
> *...the strength, yet admirable proportion of his limbs, his excellent carriage, his firm countenance, his high forehead, his whole mien, and a certain dignity in his movements, made altogether a most pleasing impression. Such, one might conceive, to have been the heroes of ancient times; he seemed the living figure of a Hercules, the terror of his enemies, the hope and support of his friends.*"

He submits to no man and subscribes to no societal norms. In a nation of independent-minded men, he more than anyone else is his own man. He has taken up residence with the young amaRharhabe heir to the throne, Ngqika. He knows how the amaXhosa Tribal House System works and he understands the game Ndlambe is playing. He also knows that the other amaXhosa look down upon the amaGqunukhwebe as "half-bloods." While the amaRharhabe regent Ndlambe wants to unite all the right hand houses under himself before Ngqika can ascend the throne, he resents the amaGqunukhwebe. Meanwhile de Buys has taken as concubine a girl[42] recently married to chief Ulanga of the amaMbalu Xhosa. This has incensed the Suurveld amaXhosa and they are venting their ire on the Frontier farmers.

7. Matters finally boil over

In frustration at the inaction of the authorities, the brothers Willem and Johannes Grobler, as well as Coenraad de Buys and Carolus Johannes Tregard[43], along with some other senior men in the area decide on independent action under the leadership of Barend Lindeque. Their aim is to retake the cattle stolen from them by the Suurveld amaXhosa. Willem, Johannes, and three more men are deputized[44] to discuss the matter with Ndlambe, regent of the amaRharhabe.

So it is that on 18 May 1793 the joint Boer Commando and amaRharhabe force attacks[45] the Suurveld amaXhosa, takes 1800 cattle from these tribes, and divides the booty 50:50 between Ndlambe's force and the Commando. In the last week of May 1793, the Suurveld amaXhosa retaliate. They fall upon the Christian settlers, while Ndlambe stays out of this fight, having got what he wanted. Theal reports[46] that, of the 120 farms in the Suurveld, 116 are laid waste.

All over the Suurveld, the Khoekhoe and Afrikaners now flee westward for their very lives. Johannes, oldest brother of ancestor Cornelis Grobler, along with several other men, dies a horrific death by torture at the hands of the Suurveld amaXhosa horde. He leaves his 31-year old wife, Elsie Klopper (*NF27*), and six little children, the oldest of whom is just 11. The Cape Government, hitherto actively misled by Maynier, finally orders magistrates Maynier and Faure to raise Commandos from Graaff-Reinet and Swellendam respectively. The Suurveld amaXhosa attempt to retreat to chief Khawuta of the amaGalecka for safety, but Ndlambe cuts them off[47] and crushes them, killing Shaka of the amaGqunukhwebe and capturing Ulanga of the amaMbalu. Ndlambe actually offers Ulanga to Maynier, who refuses the offer, letting Ulanga die in Ndlambe's hands.

Ndlambe is now at the peak of his power, but Maynier does not seem to comprehend any of this. Despite having failed to recover the farmers' cattle, he sets about making peace with the Suurveld amaXhosa. In effect, he has ceded the Suurveld to the collection of defeated Suurveld amaXhosa – he has given them victory. Through burgher eyes, Maynier is rewarding the amaXhosa on the frontier for attacking the farmers. Indeed, the ignominious peace made by Maynier leads to a series of cattle raids and murders by the Suurveld amaXhosa[48]. Maynier then gives instructions that the frontiersmen are not allowed to retrieve any of their cattle that they might identify among the amaXhosa herds and he threatens punishment if they were to leave their farms to seek safety, as he does not believe they are in danger. The burghers, led by Adriaan van Jaarsveld, now formally complain to the governor at the Cape about Maynier[49]. Among the accusations against Maynier is the allegation that he is making his own farmlands a refuge for disaffected Khoekhoe farmworkers, whom he then pays more. This places the government in competition with the poor frontier farmers.

In defense of Maynier, it needs to be said that the treatment of the Khoekhoe farmworkers at Graaff-Reinet is unacceptable and that he has rightly tried to do something about it. The simple frontier farmers are no match for the articulate Maynier who holds sway over the thinking of the distant government. However, the Dutch East India Company is basically bankrupt, has flooded the Cape with worthless paper money, and is unable to protect the frontiersmen.

8. The end of the VOC on the Frontier

On Friday 27 December 1793, the Council of Policy at the Cape discusses the murder of Stephanus Abraham Cloete by the Xhosa in May of 1793. Cloete's farm has been burnt to the ground by the amaXhosa[50], who have stolen all the cattle. The widow pleads to be released from rent payments to the VOC for the destroyed farm. Instead of discussing the raid by the Suurveld Xhosa, or assistance for the widow, the VOC dispatches magistrate Faure more than 400 miles to determine whether the widow truly cannot pay. On 31 March 1794, Faure reports[51] that the widow has been reduced to such a state of poverty that her late husband's brother is making collections in the community for her.

On 9 May 1794, a year after the amaXhosa incursion, the Council is confronted with an extensive letter of complaint[52] from magistrate Maynier of Graaff-Reinet. It is a comprehensive indictment of the Frontier Farmers with no attempt at balance in the matter. Maynier suggests that the frontier farmers are the engineers of their own misery, citing the unauthorized Commando led by Barend Lindeque, but more particularly, a litany of alleged outrageous actions on the part of Coenraad De Buys and our ancestor Coenraad Bezuidenhout as the causes of the amaXhosa incursion. He complains about insubordination by Burgher Lieutenant Carolus Trichardt. It seems that it was Trichardt's reaction to Maynier's refusal to believe his report that his district was being attacked by the Suurveld Xhosa. In Maynier's world view, Black people can do no wrong. The council instructs Maynier to discipline the men of the Lindeque commando.

The relationship between the farmers and Maynier has reached the point of no return. In February 1795, inspired by the little they know of the American and French Revolutions, Adriaan van Jaarsveld (*NF28*), Marthinus Prinsloo (*NF27*) and the local burghers, calling themselves the *Volkstem* ("Voice of the People"), confront Maynier, read him a list of complaints, and run him out of Graaff-Reinet, declaring their independence. The Governor sends a commission headed by Stellenbosch landdrost O.G. De Wet, but after some polite interaction, the burghers order him out of town as well on 16 June 1795. They want no more to do with the hapless Dutch East India Company (VOC), which they hold accountable for all their troubles.

In Swellendam near the southern coast, the burghers already know about the events in Graaff-Reinet. They plan to remove their VOC magistrate the next day. However, as always in the history of this tortured country, Fate has other plans for these sorely tried people.

—End Nexus Familia

The ship in the bay

It was on the night of 12 June 1795 that the Commissioner at the Castle in Cape Town received an interesting visitor. It was a purser from a British warship, the *Monarch*, at anchor in False Bay to the east of the Cape peninsula. He delivered a message from an Admiral Elphinstone, commander of a British Fleet in False Bay. The Council of Policy was convened in the middle of that night, and 200 infantrymen and 100 artillerymen were dispatched to False Bay. The message stated that the Admiral has important information for the Governor and Colonel Gordon, the Scottish-descended commander of the Dutch forces at the Cape [53].

Nexus Familia 30: The Government at Gunpoint

Paul Fouché, our direct ancestor, is the great-grandson of the original French refugee, Phillipe Fouché from Suèvres near Blois (*NF15*). Since their arrival at the Cape, the Fouché family has also spread eastward. Paul's father had a stock farm near the Breede River in the Swellendam district (See *Fig. 4-2*), and Paul has continued in his father's footsteps growing wheat and running a cattle ranch.

At this point in time, Swellendam is the capital and only formal town in the District of Swellendam. The District Council is in session on 17 June 1795 in the Drostdy (Magistrate's building) in town when Paul Fouché, accompanied by 11 other armed burghers, interrupts the proceedings. Paul delivers a message that the council is to stay in session and wait for a deputation that is on the way. Meanwhile Paul and his armed burghers ensure that the council members do not leave town.

Much later on the same day, the deputation eventually arrives in the form of some sixty armed and mounted burghers. The burghers dismiss the council members and officials from their posts and put men of their own choosing into those positions. The deposed officials are required to leave town.

After this brief moment in the center stage of South African history, Paul returns to his ordinary farming life. His descendants will eventually include the author's Fouché great grandmother, a lady with great pride in her French heritage.

Fig. 4-11 The Swellendam Drostdy

Meanwhile, a letter from the magistrate of Swellendam to the Governor in Cape Town bearing the news of the insurrection is speeding by lone horseman along the foot of the *Riviersonderend* (*River-Without-End*) mountain range between the two towns. But greater events will eclipse the message.

—*End Nexus Familia*

The Special Meeting

On the morning of Sunday, 21 June 1795, the Council of Policy of the Cape of Good Hope held an extraordinary meeting. The men present at this historic event were Robert Jacob Gordon, the military commander at the Cape, together with the Commissioner, Sluijsken, and three other senior officials, including Secretary Goetz[54]. First secretary Goetz tabled an urgent message from Landdrost Faure of Swellendam, signed 18 June 1795, reporting that he and his officials had been run out of the town (*NF30*). But, discussion on the subject of this letter had to be postponed. Another "missive" had arrived from Major General Craig and Admiral Lord Elphinstone of the British naval squadron of some nine men o' war at anchor in False Bay. The letter was the first news that those at the Cape would receive of the momentous events in their homeland. The men around the table were shocked, incredulous, and 6,000 miles from Europe.

The letter informed them that the Netherlands had been overrun by Napoleon and that the leader of the Netherlands, the *Stadtholder*, had fled to England. The exiled Stadtholder had purportedly agreed that the Cape be made available to the English forces to counter Napoleon. It went on to list supposed outrages in the Netherlands at the hands of the French Army, few if any of which were true. Nevertheless, the message was clear: *deliver your colony into our hands; or else.*

The end was at hand for the VOC rule at the Cape of Good Hope. The VOC had never wanted the Cape to be more than a refreshment post. It had managed it accordingly, intentionally stifling its progress. There had never been a real concern for the wellbeing of the people at the Cape. In fact, they had been left to their own devices in an extremely frightening place. Wilmot and Chase[55] quote Cape judge Watermeyer who summed up the VOC rule at the Cape of Good Hope as follows:

> *"The Dutch, as a commercial nation, destroyed commerce.*
> *The most industrious race of Europe, they repressed industry."*

The settlement at the Cape would become a frustrated and abused pawn as part of the impending struggle between Britain and France for supremacy at sea; the global pivot point of world marine power. In the eleven years to follow, it would earn its original name:

"Cabo de Tormentosa" – The Cape of Storms.

-----ooOoo-----

5

The Second America

"As the colony improved and its peoples increased it would to us only prove a second America and would more likely in time rob us of India."

Rear-Admiral Thomas Pringle,
British Naval Commander at the Cape (1797)

Enter the British

In 1788, the Dutch and the British had signed an accord of mutual assistance if the Asian or African possessions of either were threatened by a third European power. When war broke out again with France in 1793, Henry Dundas, the British Secretary of War, promptly suggested that his country take over the Cape to guard it against the French. The British had learned their lesson in 1781. The Dutch declined the ensuing "offer." However, when the French Army started making inroads into the Netherlands, the Prince of Orange fled to Britain, arriving there on 18 January 1795.

A mere twenty-one days later the British had extracted from the distraught prince an order to commanders of all Dutch territorial possessions to "be of assistance to" British ships and troops. Dundas thereupon sent a fleet of nine warships to the Cape under Lord Elphinstone and Major-General James Henry Craig. This was the fleet that precipitated the special Meeting of the Cape Council of Policy on Sunday June 21, 1795. Its mission was to keep the Cape out of the hands of the French by any means, fair or foul.

Fig. 5-1 Major-General James Henry Craig

VOC Commissioner Sluijsken in command of the Cape was in an incredibly difficult position. Firstly, the burghers of both the extensive Graaff-Reinet and Swellendam colonies had declared independence and run his government out of town. At the same time, the commander of the British fleet in False Bay was demanding that he should surrender the Cape, supposedly in the name of his own exiled sovereign. But, he had no hard evidence that his country had fallen. Eventually, an American ship would bring news confirming the Netherlands had become a client state of France, calling itself the Batavian Government.

When Sluijsken still refused to surrender the Cape after this, the British attacked and took the Settlement rather easily on 16 September 1795. It was, of course, less than clear that the Prince of Orange had indeed instructed the British to attack his countrymen. The truth is that Robert Jacob Gordon, the Scottish-descended commander of the Dutch forces, had been actively misled by the British into believing that he would be surrendering the Cape to forces acting in the name and under the flag of the Prince of Orange. As soon as he commanded his men to surrender, the British ran up the British flag and dropped all pretenses. The Dutch forces wanted to kill Gordon for his submission to this British subterfuge, but he spared them the trouble by committing suicide. This was a truly tragic end to a man who had done much for the Cape. It was a great and unnecessary loss of a good and competent man.

The new young King

Some 650 miles east of Cape Town, the new amaRharhabe heir to the throne, Ngqika, had come of age. He had dismissed an incensed Ndlambe as regent, and was ready to exercise his power. It is here that Coenraad de Buys (*NF29*) had done the "unthinkable" by marrying Ngqika's hugely influential mother, Yese. As was the custom, Xhosa kings married ladies from the amaThembu nation. Coenraad, the white Afrikaner, incredibly, was now Royal Advisor to the young amaRharhabe king. The amaXhosa by now accepted the Afrikaners as part of their reality; as just another tribe.

Coenraad made use of his new position of power. When Ngqika enquired as to who the strange new white men (the British) were, Coenraad explained[1] that English were the "*Bushmen of the Sea*" and had taken the "*cattlefold*" [Colony] from its rightful owners. Since the racial loathing of the amaXhosa for the San Bushmen was legendary, Ngqika now had a clear perception of the British. The British, however, had no concept of what they were dealing with in the amaXhosa.

Ngqika had managed to make Ndlambe captive. Ndlambe's chief general, Nyalusa (Jalusa), had escaped. He had moved into the Suurveld area, making common cause with the Suurveld amaXhosa. Ngqika not only managed to defeat the Suurveld amaXhosa, but also the amaGcaleka, taking captive the underage Great House heir, Hintsa, the future king of all the amaXhosa. Ngqika now reigned supreme in the world of the amaXhosa, but did not have the required cultural legitimacy to hold sway over the amaGcaleka. In the amaXhosa world, power is everything, but when it is at its greatest, it is often at its most fragile.

 ## Nexus Familia 31: The Spider Flag

When the British take the Cape on 16 September 1795, the burghers of Graaff-Reinet are still busy putting their little mini republic together. The new British military commander, Craig, has a misplaced and simplistic view of the convictions of the burghers in the eastern border area. To him they are[2] "*infected with the rankest poison of Jacobinism*" and, as for the rest, "*nearly every man in the Colony is our enemy*." As a result of the Reign of Terror in France between 1792 and 1794, the British are absolutely paranoid on the matter of French Revolutionary thought; what they term Jacobinism. The Burghers in the interior of the Cape have never even heard of "*Jacobinism*." Craig, however, is concerned that he needs to establish control, because Graaff-Reinet is the source of all the meat for the colony[3]. Against this background, General Craig sends Magistrate Frans Bresler, a devoted Dutch Orangeman, to represent British authority in the district. The Republicans of the district organize a full meeting of their elected representatives on 22 February 1796.

When the morning of that day arrives[4], we find around the table a collection of leading men from the district, including Adriaan Van Jaarsveld (*NF29*) and Christoffel Lötter, an ancestor of the author. Bresler is invited to explain his mission. He chooses this opportunity to read his commission from General Craig and announces that he shall hold a first meeting of the District Council in the afternoon. Bresler confirms that he is not allowed to acknowledge the elected Representatives of the People.

Two o' clock in the afternoon the bell of the *drostdy* (magistrate's office) is rung and Bresler instructs one of his Khoekhoe servants to hoist the British flag, in response to which all hell breaks loose. A number of people start crowding Bresler. Ancestral cousin Jacobus Joubert, son of frontiersman Josua Joubert (*NF28* and *29*) and son-in-law of Adriaan van Jaarsveld, orders Bresler to lower the "*Spider Flag*[5]." When Bresler refuses, Jacobus and two other men haul it down themselves and shove it back in his arms. Bresler then demands to know whether they will acknowledge the King of England as their sovereign, Major-General Craig as their governor, and himself as their *landdrost* (magistrate), and whether they will take the oath of fidelity. They respond by explaining that they have instructions from their elected leader, our ancestral brother-in-law Marthinus Prinsloo (*NF29*), to not take the oath. Marthinus has styled himself *"Protector of the Voice of the People"* (the *Volkstem*).

Marthinus is still living at the foot of the Boschberg (*Fig. 4-9* and *4-10*) on the original farm of his father, Willem. Bresler therefore waits another month until 22 March 1796, when Marthinus arrives to attend another meeting. Marthinus takes his seat and silences his compatriots to give Bresler a chance to speak. Bresler largely repeats the British position. The Republicans respond that they would love to live in peace with the British, would like to trade with them, will obey all laws, but have a major problem. Taking the oath will place them in an impossible situation when the British return the Cape to the Dutch, as the British are sworn to do. They

Fig. 5-2 The Graaff-Reinet Drostdy – a national monument and hotel

also present Bresler with a memorial in which they declare that they would much rather have as magistrate a *"born Englishman"* than a *"secretly partial Afrikaner."* They distrust Bresler, whom they view as one of Maynier's henchmen[6]. They do not hate the English, of whom they know little. They hate the VOC, and will not accept officials who used to work for that body.

Realizing that he is powerless, Bresler returns to Cape Town, where he reports the events to the governor. Bresler also echoes all of Maynier's original views to the governor, without having ascertained any of the facts for himself. The Graaff-Reinet men have judged Bresler's affiliations correctly. And here matters rest for a while, as the next act unfolds just north of Cape Town. On 12 April 1796, in an official letter[7] to Henry Dundas, the Secretary for War in London, Craig makes known his willful intention to use racist means to subjugate the Afrikaners. Naturally, he will not have to live with the consequences of his actions:

> *Amongst the measures which I have been anxious to carry into effect for some time past has been that of collecting and arming a body of Hottentots. Nothing I know would intimidate the Boors of the Country more [...]*
>
> *...I have assurance of near 200 who ought to have arrived some days ago [...]*
>
> *...I have promised to arm and cloathe them, to give them rations, and sixpence per week, on condition of their engaging not to quit His Majesty's Service for a year.*

This racist decision will ultimately cost the author's ancestors dearly. Some months later, the Naval Commander at the Cape, Admiral Pringle, will say the following about the Settlement and its people to Lady Anne Barnard, wife of the Cape Colonial Secretary[8]:

> *As the colony improved and its peoples increased it would to us only prove a second America and would more likely in time rob us of India.*

The Napoleonic Dutch, known as the Batavian Republic, have meanwhile agreed with the French to jointly retake the Cape. However, the arrangements are a disaster and the Dutch are hopelessly undone by the British at Saldanha Bay north of Cape Town on 17 August 1796. It is an inglorious end to Dutch naval ability. The British gladly enlist the German mercenaries of the Dutch into their army at the Cape, and they ship the Dutch sailors and seamen back home in ignominy. With this, the last hope for the men of Graaff-Reinet disappears and they send a letter of submission to General Craig on 12 November 1796, specifically entreating him not to select a magistrate from the old VOC government, and specifically not Bresler. Ancestor Johannes Jacobus Klopper and ancestral brother Willem Grobler are two of the signatories[9]. Craig has already dispatched an army of his newly enlisted Khoekhoe units to suppress the "Graaff-Reinet Jacobins," but recalls it and grants a general amnesty. On 27 December, Bresler, still at the Cape, sends a letter[10] to the Governor stridently badmouthing the Graaff-Reinet burghers, piling accusation upon accusation against them. Perhaps the poor man cannot anticipate what is about to happen next.

—End Nexus Familia

Nexus Familia 32: Jan and the American Captain

It is a day like any other in June 1796, some 600 miles east of Cape Town on the New Year's River, a tributary of the Bushman's River (*Fig. 4-10*) right on the outermost limit of Christian civilization, bordering on the territory of the amaXhosa[11]. Jan du Plessis is dressing two carcasses of animals his son shot the previous day. He is doing this immediately outside his mud brick and thatch roof house. Jan is a captain in the militia and a rather remarkable man for his time and place. While he lives on the far frontier, he is a literate man and his diary will survive into the 21st century. Jan is 64 years old; the grandson of the immigrant Jean Prieur du Plessis from Poitiers (*NF15, 19*). His younger sons live on the farm, and he has one daughter who is not yet married. When Jan looks up, he sees a sight that freezes the blood in his veins. Standing dead still some distance away are two Tamboekie[12] warriors, *assegais* (throwing spears) in hand. It is only three years since the last war with the vicious amaXhosa, and here he is now confronted with the Tamboekies. They live even further away to the east than the true Xhosa, and these two are totally out of place. He yells to his sons in the house, and turns to fetch his *schietgeweer*—his musket—and the powder horn. But then some disheveled white men join the Tamboekies. Their leader is an American ship's captain named Benjamin Stout. They have been aided by these two Tamboekie warriors all the way from the land of the Tamboekies where they were shipwrecked. Jan promptly dispatches his sons with a wagon to collect the rest of the shipwrecked men.

That evening, Stout discusses the state of the country with Jan, who makes it clear that the farmers distant from the Cape are disgusted with the VOC[13]. It taxes them, makes rules for them, does not understand their needs and then leaves them in the lurch in times of danger. They would welcome any decent liberal authority on the local coast and they would be happy indeed to trade with them.

At this point, Stout asks Jan the one question that has bothered him all day since their arrival:

"What on earth are the two massive carcasses you are dressing outside the house?"

Jan responds without blinking an eye:

"Two rhinoceros my son shot yesterday."

Jan arranges for the men to be taken to the distant Cape. Jan writes a note in Dutch for Stout and his party to show to all the farmers along the way, and which Stout will later immortalize in a book:

> *Good Friends,*
> *Be so good as to help these people forward towards the Cape. They are Americans, who have lost their ship beyond the river Biga. The Caffers have brought these people to me.*
> *Your friend, Jan Du Plessis, the elder.*

The survivors are taken by wagon to the Cape. One, a Swede named Peter Ernst Wahlstrand, elects to stay in the colony. He will become the Graaff-Reinet Court Messenger[14] and will eventually marry Maria Magdalena Olivier, niece of Anna Elizabeth Olivier, whom we meet in Nexus Familia 35.

—End Nexus Familia

An American Colony in South Africa?

On 16 June 1796, the American ship, the *Hercules*, was wrecked on the Suurveld coast. The Master of this ship was Captain Benjamin Stout. He was well treated by the amaThembu ("Tamboekie") subgroup of the extended amaXhosa nation, and was impressed by the countryside. He was equally impressed with the Afrikaner farmers who went out of their way to help his party get back to the Cape (*NF32*).

When Stout returned to Europe, he wrote[15] as follows to his relative, President John Adams, suggesting the establishment of an American colony on the Southeast Coast in the land of the amaThembu:

> *To the Honorable John Adams,*
> *President of the Continental Congress of the United States of America.*
>
> *Sir,*
>
> *If this Narrative be transmitted across the Atlantic, and should find its way to your hand, receive it as the voluntary homage of a native of America, who from his earliest life hath been taught to venerate and admire your virtues and your talents. [...] It has never been understood, when the Dutch took possession of the Cape of Storms, as it was originally styled by the Portuguese, that they also claimed a title to the whole of the southern part of Africa; such an undefined and unlimited claim must at once appear not only presumptuous, but preposterous; and on this ground I argue, that the people of any nation have an unquestionable right (provided the natives give their assent) to settle on such parts of the southern continent of Africa, as do not interpose with the lands already in possession of the colonists.*

By the early years of the 1800s, American ships were trafficking up and down the southeast coast of the present South Africa. Ever more American sailors were calling for an American presence in South Africa. Britain prized its trade route between Britain, the Cape and the River Platte in South America. Losing America was one thing, but conceding its trade routes to the Americans was another matter altogether.

In the event, Adams turned down Stout's suggestion. Thereby died the intriguing thought that, had he accepted, Nelson Mandela, the later South African president, might very well have been born an American citizen – Nelson Mandela is a Thembu; a Tamboekie.

Hate, Prejudice and Ignorance

On 5 May 1797, Sir George Macartney, a gout-ridden crotchety Irishman in semi-retirement, took over as civilian governor of the Cape Colony. He made his own views quite clear when he imposed an oath of allegiance to King George III on all heads of households and wrote home that[16]:

> *The best thing the Dutch inhabitants can do, is to become good English as fast as they can, for certainly they will never see their own flag fly in South Africa again.*

This was hardly a friendly occupation of the Cape by an ally of the Dutch. With Macartney came his personal secretary, John Barrow, a man afflicted with intense prejudice against the "Dutch" Afrikaners. His observations[17] vividly demonstrated his lack of experience at the Cape:

> *"A temperate climate, a fertile soil, a mild and peaceable race of natives, were advantages that few infant colonies have possessed."*

Our ancestral brother Johannes Grobler, had been tortured to death (*NF29*) by that *"peaceable race of natives."* Barrow was obtaining all his briefings from none other than Maynier[18], the very official whom the Afrikaners had previously run out of Graaff-Reinet (*NF29*). This, combined with Barrow's own prejudices against all things "Dutch," which caused him to write[19] about them that *"they cannot disguise the cloven foot,"* ensured a slanted view. Despite his self-confessed[20] ignorance regarding the whereabouts of Graaff-Reinet, and the plea of the Frontier Burghers for a magistrate who was a *"born Englishman"* rather than one associated with the VOC, Macartney foisted magistrate Bresler on the people of Graaff-Reinet. He dispatched his prejudiced secretary Barrow to accompany Bresler to that district where they arrived on 30 July 1797.

Here matters rested again for a while. However, it was vividly clear that the British were highly suspicious of specifically Adriaan van Jaarsveld, Marthinus Prinsloo, and Hendrik Krugel. The locals, in their turn, did not trust Bresler one inch. They had only just escaped the disastrous reign of the VOC and here the British were imposing the very same kind of official over them. The community insisted that they had been assured that the Cape would be given back to the Netherlands when the war with France was over, so how could it be that they needed to swear allegiance to the English king? Afrikaners were therefore deeply angered when the Commandant of Swellendam, Petrus "Pieter" Jacobus Delport, was banished without trial[21] from the colony for refusing to swear fealty to the English king. Pieter was the brother of the author's ancestor, Sarah Delport, who shall soon feature in *Nexus Familia 34.*

Fig. 5-3 Sir George Macartney

The British administration was one with a world-view that consisted of all matters English on one side, and all matters French on the other. As the Afrikaners were not British, they had to be French sympathizers and therefore *"Jacobin Revolutionaries."*

Nexus Familia 33: The Van Jaarsveld "Rebellion"

On 21 November 1798, Major-General Francis Dundas, the Lieutenant-Governor, takes over interim responsibility for the Cape and Macartney returns to England, having finished his contribution to the wholesale disaster that would be the First British Occupation of the Cape. Dundas is now the third in what would ultimately be a long line of British men to initiate problems in South Africa and then absent themselves, Major-General Craig having been the first and Macartney the second.

Dundas soon makes his prejudice[22] toward the frontiersmen known in no uncertain terms:

> ...*the Boors are the strongest compound of cowardice and cruelty, of treachery and cunning, and of most of the bad qualities with very few of the good ones, of the human mind*

Against this background, what now follows should come as no surprise.

Early in January 1799, the elderly Adriaan van Jaarsveld is summoned to Graaff-Reinet by the magistrate. When he duly and correctly appears there on 17 January, not suspecting a thing, he is promptly arrested by Bresler on charges of failure to appear for an earlier summons, that summons originally arising from a dispute about mortgage payments. He is to be taken to the faraway Cape. When three dragoons set off four days later with Adriaan van Jaarsveld to the Cape, they are intercepted by a commando led by Marthinus Prinsloo, leader of the Prinsloo clan and of the Volkstem (*"Voice of the People"*- see NF31).

Prinsloo overrides Van Jaarsveld's objections against securing his release, and makes it clear that the burghers anticipate foul play at the hands of the British. They believe that the British, under the influence of the likes of Maynier and Bresler, are using a trivial mortgage matter to ensure the incarceration and possible banishment of Van Jaarsveld. The dragoons surrender their prisoner under protest and Van Jaarsveld returns to Graaff-Reinet in the company of Prinsloo and his men.

Back in the town, they insist to Bresler that Van Jaarsveld should be allowed to go free on bail, given the trivial subject of the arrest. However, the Magistrate is adamant that Van Jaarsveld has to go 500 miles under guard to the Cape on a charge relating to a mortgage payment. The locals, fully aware of the true British feelings toward them, are convinced that the British are trying to rekindle the problems of 1796 in order to incarcerate or banish all of them, as has already been done to our ancestral brother Pieter Delport for refusing the British Oath of Allegiance.

The British at the Cape treat the events at Graaff-Reinet as an out and out rebellion, and they dispatch[23] General Vandeleur, along with Craig's special anti-Afrikaner Khoekhoe "pandours" and some further British soldiers, to confront these few frontier farmers.

When the men of Graaff-Reinet get wind of the governor's intentions, they escalate the situation. On 19 February, ancestral brother Willem Grobler walks into Bresler's office, handing the magistrate a letter written by Marthinus Prinsloo. The letter prescribes the conduct of the colony towards the amaXhosa, including that all communications should go via Coenraad de Buys, adviser to King Ngqika. The British will later call the letter "*insolent and threatening*[24]."

In the face of the lack of interest from most of the frontier farmers, the "rebels" eventually submit when Vandeleur promises that the government will be lenient. The "rebels" interpret this as meaning amnesty, considering that not a shot has been fired nor anyone hurt. When they duly surrender on 6 April 1799, they are rudely surprised when twenty of them are made prisoner by the King's new Khoekhoe soldiers. They are taken to Cape Town aboard the aptly named 16-gun sloop, the *Rattlesnake*, under the command of Lieutenant Alexander Mouat. The captives include Adriaan van Jaarsveld, Marthinus Prinsloo, and ancestral brother Willem Grobler.

The day after the surrender of the "rebels" Dundas declares Martial Law, cuts off the lead and gunpowder supply to the border region and, with few exceptions, orders all Afrikaner farmers in the frontier districts to hand in their personal arms and ammunition[25]. The leadership of the Afrikaners on the border has been obliterated, the people, whether "rebel" or not, have been disarmed, and they are now completely at the mercy of all who would assail them. Meanwhile, ancestor Coenraad Bezuidenhout (*NF29*) joins his cousin Coenraad de Buys at amaXhosa king Ngqika's Great Place. On 24 May, Vandeleur puts a reward of £200, dead or alive, on the heads of the two Coenraads and five others[26].

—End Nexus Familia

The Third Frontier War starts

Dundas' ignorance about the frontier and General Vandeleur's incompetence conspired so that they somehow did not comprehend that the 7 April 1799 disarmament of the Frontier Afrikaners had effectively destroyed the defenses of the colony. Vandeleur was completely obsessed about the letter claiming that the Afrikaners would be supported by King Ngqika. He did not comprehend the profound difference between Ngqika's amaRharhabe and the Right Hand House Suurveld amaGqunukhwebe. The latter were the enemies of both the amaRharhabe and the frontiersmen. As a result, he persisted in declaring in letters various that the Afrikaners were allied with the amaGqunukhwebe. These particular Suurveld amaXhosa under Cungwa had been raiding the frontier farmers again.

In early 1799, on his way north from Algoa Bay to Graaff-Reinet, Vandeleur had visited Cungwa near the Bushmans River to ask him to withdraw across the Fish River. Now, on his way back to Algoa Bay, Vandeleur found that Cungwa had ignored his instructions. Cungwa tried hard to explain, quite realistically, that he could not cross the Fish River, because Ngqika would kill him and his people. Vandeleur would not hear this. As Vandeleur made his way back to Algoa Bay his troops were attacked by Cungwa's amaGqunukhwebe. The latter had been placed in an impossible position by Vandeleur's demands – stay and be attacked by the British, or move across the Fish River and be attacked by Ngqika. They realistically elected to attack the small British force, not wanting to face Ngqika's powerful army.

Vandeleur chased Cungwa's warriors off with a few rounds of grapeshot from his cannon and made for the beach at Algoa Bay. Meanwhile, a group of Cungwa's men had also fallen upon a patrol of 20 British soldiers dispatched towards the Bushmans River under a Lieutenant Chumney. All but four of the British soldiers were killed. These two events constituted the first military clash between the British and the black people of Southern Africa. It was to get much worse, infinitely worse.

General Vandeleur had been attacked twice, 16 of his men had been killed, but somehow Barrow[27] attempts to couch the British flight to the beach as a humanitarian action. Ignorant of internal amaXhosa relations, he still found the opportunity to blame the Afrikaners who were allied with Ngqika against Cungwa:

> *However desirable it might have been to apprehend and punish the rebels, who had instigated the Kaffers to acts of hostility against the British troops, yet it was by no means advisable, in order to obtain that point, to wage an unequal contest with savages in the midst of impenetrable thickets, whose destruction would have added little lustre to the British arms, and been advantageous only to the very people who had urged them on. General Vandeleur, therefore, very prudently withdrew his forces, and marched them down to Algoa Bay, where part of them were embarked on board the Rattlesnake, and the rest intended to proceed to the Cape by easy marches.*

Somehow, it was very important for the British to punish the Afrikaners for a "rebellion" that never hurt a hair on any British head, but the amaGqunukhwebe who had killed 16 British soldiers were not worthy of similar British attentions.

The reality is that the ignorant, frightened, and incompetent Vandeleur had fled in the face of Cungwa's army. Vandeleur simply knew nothing about fighting in Africa. He would soon enough attempt to blame everyone else for his disastrous "campaign"; the Afrikaners, Magistrate Bresler, Magistrate Faure of Swellendam, as well as Governor Francis Dundas.

In suppressing the "Van Jaarsveld Rebellion," the British had committed a number of serious blunders. The first had been that of dispatching the Khoekhoe pandours under Brig Gen Vandeleur to confront the Afrikaner "rebels," thereby turning it into a racist issue with malice aforethought. The second had been that of disarming the frontier farmers, thereby destroying the defenses of the colony. The third had been cowardice in the face of the enemy, which is guaranteed to invite attack by that enemy in Africa. The country herewith faced something infinitely worse than one "difficult Dutchman" with bad English skills and a mortgage problem (Van Jaarsveld).

These actions, along with the well-documented[28] intense hatred of this particular bevy of Englishmen for the Afrikaners, had sent a loud and clear signal to both the Khoekhoe in the border area, and to the Suurveld amaXhosa. The frontier was ripe for the picking.

The Khoekhoe on the various farms, along with some from Vandeleur's own Hottentot Corps, now deserted their employers, stealing what guns and powder they could. Given the large Khoekhoe component in the makeup of the amaGqunukhwebe, the main body of the deserting Khoekhoe people made common cause with that tribe and started plundering and murdering the defenseless frontiersmen. However, Vandeleur and Barrow, together with the distant governor Dundas, were as yet unaware of this.

Barrow, who had volunteered to go to the frontier to ensure that the powder and flint remained cut off, was then on his way from Graaff-Reinet to Algoa Bay with a detachment of Vandeleur's men. Along the way he ran into a motley collection of armed Khoekhoe under a man named Klaas Stuurman. They were dressed in stolen clothes and had guns that they had taken from the Afrikaners whom they had raided and murdered. Incredibly, even when Stuurman confessed to Barrow that he had attacked and plundered the Afrikaner farmers, Barrow still held to his misconceptions. This is borne out by the following statement he makes in the very same paragraph of his book[29] :

> *"From lying and stealing* [...] *the Hottentot may be considered as exempt."*

This statement is quite incredible, considering that Stuurman had actually confessed the theft to Barrow. One concludes Barrow had given Stuurman every reason to believe he was speaking to an ally. In fact,

Barrow enlisted 100 of Stuurman's motley collection of plundering thieves and murderers into the British Forces[30].

With their leaders in captivity, all their means of defense taken from them, a British Army scared of the amaXhosa but hell bent on subjugating Afrikaners, the Suurveld amaXhosa on the rampage, and Khoekhoe murderers now marauding freely under the aegis of the very same British, the helpless Afrikaner farmers had to yet again flee westward for their lives. And this is when the author's ancestor and relatives found themselves in the path of the combined Khoekhoe and amaGqunukhwebe horde.

 ## Nexus Familia 34: Massacre at the Mountain

Ancestor Gerrit Scheepers was one of the first farmers in the east of the colony. His younger sisters Sophia and Christina (*NF29*) were respectively the mothers of our difficult ancestor Coenraad Bezuidenhout and his giant cousin Coenraad de Buys, both in exile at this time with King Ngqika (*NF33*). Gerrit's fifth son, Stephanus, was field-corporal at the frontier near the Bushmans River as long ago as 1779. He has since settled his family on *Doornrivier* (Thorn River) at the foot of the Great Winterhoek Mountain range (See *Fig. 4-10*). The 5,060 foot Round Mountain (*Fig. 5-4*) looms over the farm, which is a well-established stop on the

Fig. 5-4 Round Mountain - site of Doornrivier Farm

long road to Algoa Bay and the Eastern Frontier. In 1790, Stephanus accompanied Jacob van Reenen on the expedition[31] to the distant Thembuland coast to search for the abandoned survivors of the wreck of the British East India ship, the *Grosvenor*. In 1794, he was one of the men who testified[32] that the Suurveld amaXhosa blamed in his presence his own difficult cousin Coenraad de Buys for the instability on the border (*NF29*). That same year he informed the Cape Government that "*Hottentotten*" and "*Caffers*" were raiding the farmers. He had demanded action be taken[33]. As usual, under the hated Maynier, nothing had come of that request.

The 70-year old Sarah Delport, widow of Stephanus' late brother, Jacobus, lives on the farm in the care of Stephanus. She is our direct ancestor and none other than the oldest sister of the banished Commandant Pieter Delport (See Chap. 5: *Hate, Prejudice and Ignorance*). Sarah and Pieter are the grandchildren of Jacques de la Porte from Lille (*NF19*). When word comes in early 1799 that the deserting Khoekhoe farmhands have joined forces with Cungwa's people to attack the farmers, Stephanus invites his Janse van Vuuren in-laws and the neighboring farmers to join him at *Doornrivier*, to mount what defense they still can. On 27 July 1799, the following message reaches Magistrate Bresler in Graaff-Reinet from Field-Cornet C.J. De Jager[34] at Sondaghs River, beyond the mountains:

> *Sir, —With regard to Stephanus Scheepers we have made inquiries and unfortunately found 8 Individuals to be dead, viz., Stephanus Scheepers, Senior, Stephanus Scheepers, Junior, Lucas Scheepers, Lucas van Vuuren, Pieter Heyveld, the Widow of Jacobus Scheepers, Senior [ancestor Sarah Delport], the Wife of Stephanus Scheepers and a Daughter of Jacobus Scheepers; 20 Individuals are missing, viz. 6 men and 14 women with children;...*

This is the handiwork of Stuurman's bandits, whom Barrow is busy enlisting in the British Army. It will be the massacre of our Scheepers family and the obvious blunders committed by Vandeleur that will finally bring Governor Dundas to realize the scope of his own folly and prompt him to action.

Over the next few days, messages fly between various Field-Cornets, desperately pleading for armed help and for powder and lead. A panicked Magistrate Bresler, confronted with the direct consequences of his political campaign against the farmers, sends the following message directly to Governor Dundas:

> *Honorable Sir,*
>
> *I have received a report from the Field Cornet Carel de Jager at the Zondag's River, stating a shocking murder committed by the aforesaid Caffres and Hottentots on the Family of Stephanus Scheepers [...]*
>
> *...the most part, if not all of the Inhabitants, of the Southern parts have fled from the said Caffres and Hottentots [...] on the sole pretext of being destitute of Powder and Lead, so that should there not arrive a speedy succour, I am not secure but even this Drostdy may within a few days be attacked, [...]*
>
> *... the Hottentot Captain Willem Hasebek and two others, who belonging to the lately recruited Hottentots, have deserted from General Vandeleur, and are thus kept here in a secure confinement in order that any farther mischief may be prevented. From all this Your Excellency may be aware how my present situation is, and unless the requested supply of 500, nay was it even 600 or 700 lbs. Powder, 1000 or 1200 lbs. Lead, and a proportionate number of Flints speedily arrive, I can not answer for the further consequences,...*
>
> *(Signed) F. E. Bresler.*

Bresler, the man who must carry part responsibility for Dundas' ill-conceived decision to disarm the frontier, now stakes his own safety on the very Commando system that he denigrated before. Having helped to design the Khoekhoe people into a British Army unit pointedly created to subjugate Afrikaners, he now has to jail those very Khoekhoe *pandours* for desertion. Meanwhile Graaff-Reinet has been cut off from Algoa Bay by the joint invading force of Khoekhoe and amaGqunukhwebe.

—*End Nexus Familia*

The British General on the Beach

When Barrow reached Algoa Bay with his newfound *friend* Stuurman in tow, he found a collection of some one hundred Afrikaners on the beach, forlornly hoping for help from the infamous ship *Rattlesnake* lying in the bay. These people were incredulous when they recognized Stuurman and his roughly three hundred people partly embedded in the British Army. Barrow thereupon acquired a cannon from the *Rattlesnake* and positioned it on a swivel mount between the Afrikaner farmers and the Khoekhoe[35].

Stuurman, no doubt realizing that he had little hope of deceiving the British much longer as to the true nature of his group, quietly stole away[36] from the beach with his followers during one of the subsequent nights and disappeared into Cungwa's country. Here they were welcomed by the half-Khoekhoe amaGqunukhwebe because they had guns and powder and knew how to use them.

Barrow, now mysteriously silent in his book about his Khoekhoe entourage, waited for Vandeleur to arrive in his flight from Cungwa's amaGqunukhwebe army. Upon arrival, Vandeleur inexplicably dispatched part of his army to the Cape on the *Rattlesnake* while Barrow returned to Cape Town overland. He had finished his lamentable personal contribution to the disaster of the First British Occupation.

Of Western Civilization in the east of the Colony, there remained only the outpost of Graaff-Reinet, Vandeleur's huddle on the beach of Algoa Bay, and some farmers in wagon circles. A further detachment of forty British soldiers joined Vandeleur via the area of the massacre of our Scheepers and Delport ancestors. This brought Vandeleur's total complement of men[37] to two hundred. By August 1799, the British Army had therefore been driven onto the beaches of Africa through its own unique mix of hate, prejudice, and ignorance and was stuck in a problem entirely of its own creation. Its sole achievement had been the almost complete destruction of the frontier Christian society and the effective loss of nearly the entire eastern half of the colony. Five months before, on his way to Graaff-Reinet, Vandeleur had written[38] to the Governor:

> *...the Caffres, with what intentions I know not, are coming across the Fish River in great numbers; for the present it is our interest to keep them our friends...*

At that time, his prejudice against the Afrikaners and ignorance about the differences between the amaRharhabe and the amaGqunukhwebe had kept him from correctly assessing this as an amaGqunukhwebe activity. He clearly could not tell friend from foe among the whites, the Khoekhoe or the Ba'Ntu and his briefings at the time came from the likes of Maynier and Bresler, men with deep grudges against the frontiersmen and misguided perception of the reality in which they found themselves.

The horde of runaway farmworker Khoekhoe and murderers like Klaas Stuurman, backed up by Cungwa's amaGqunukhwebe, now swept into the colony, killing entire communities of farmers on their way (*NF34*). When Stuurman's horde came upon a party of fleeing Afrikaners, he killed all the men[39]. The joint amaXhosa-Khoekhoe assault penetrated to near the present day George, halfway to Cape Town.

Vandeleur did not comprehend the severity of the situation. Sitting near the beach of Algoa Bay, where Port Elizabeth would be founded some 20 years in the future, he wrote to Governor Dundas, criticizing and blaming the very farmers whom he had disarmed. Calling the situation "*a great reverse of fortunes,*" he described how he planned to escape back westward to Cape Town along the coast over the Gamtoos River mouth[40]. He was ignorant of the fact that the author's Scheepers family in the Winterhoek to the west of his position had already been massacred and that the country through which he aimed to escape had already fallen. A few days later in the greatest outrage of all[41], he railed against the disarmed Afrikaner farmers for fleeing, but then insists that the governor should commandeer their relations and friends to ride to his relief at Algoa Bay. He insisted on help from the two magistrates of Swellendam (Faure) and Graaff-Reinet (Bresler), somehow blaming them for the situation. Here was a general of the most powerful nation on Earth demanding protection from the brothers, cousins and friends of the farmers he was supposed to protect, but whom he had mere weeks before disarmed, assaulted and imprisoned. Finally, descending to one of the lowest points in the history of the justly proud British Army, he contemplated abandoning my ancestors, whose defenses he had destroyed under instruction from governor Dundas:

> *One of two measures must (in my mind) be adopted, viz. either to attack them with a strong military force assisted by the Boers so as to drive them completely over the Fish River, or to garrison the Block house and leave the Boers and savages to fight it out...*

The various letters eventually made their way to Magistrate Faure at Swellendam, who sent the following message[42] to Governor Dundas on 4 August. Faure made it clear that the much-vaunted British Army had failed and that he now demanded support in the form of lead and powder from the British governor:

> *Honorable Sir, — As the sad situation in which both His Majesty's Troops and the Inhabitants find themselves, so as appears from the enclosed Reports which I just now have received per Express from the Fieldwachtmeester at the Lange Kloof, absolutely require that speedy means should be adopted both to open the Communication with General Vandeleur and to defend our Country and the Inhabitants, I have been so bold as under Your Excellency's approbation to issue an order for a great part of the Inhabitants under the command of the Fieldwachtmeesters to arm and to proceed to give assistance, and that I should send after them the ammunition which I hope to receive from Your Excellency. I have &c.*
> *(Signed) A. A. Faure*

Faure was a much-respected man, and Dundas now finally realized that he has a disaster on his hands. Britain appeared to be losing the colony. The man was certainly no fool and was most likely starting to realize that all had been entirely his fault. He had to do something, but what? Meanwhile, our focus moves closer to Graaff-Reinet.

 ## Nexus Familia 35: Anna's Plea for Help

To the north in the Buffelshoek Valley, east of Graaff-Reinet, below the towering Sneeuberge, Anna Elizabeth Olivier is at this time writing a letter to her husband, Regional Councilor Stephanus Naudé. He is a very successful farmer with more than a thousand head of cattle and near 4000 sheep. He is a direct ancestor of the author and a descendant of French Huguenot, Philippe Naudé from Metz in Lorraine (*NF15*). Anna (actually Johanna) is his second wife. Stephanus' grandfather, Jacob Naudé, came to the Cape in 1713 and took a job as schoolmaster. On this night in August 1799, Anna is writing[43] to her husband who is away, likely at a Heemraad (Regional Council) meeting in Graaff-Reinet:

August 5th, 1799. Dear Husband, —

I am most speedily to acquaint you that Friday last the Caffres have been at the old Holts' and taken away 1100 head of Cattle and also taken the said Holts prisoner himself, who however at the intercession of one of the Caffres has been released, and they have thrown a number of assagays at the waggons of the flying Inhabitants, none of whom are however hurt. The last man has this night removed from Zwagershoek, so that there is no longer any Inhabitant there, and the men who are here won't continue longer than tomorrow night, when, if the party of Armed Burghers be not arrived all of them intend to remove, but if the said party arrive then they will stay. Further I know nothing to mention to you but our hearty wish that you my dear Husband and the party of Armed Burghers may speedily arrive. I with all your children greet you tenderly and remain your faithful wife till Death.

(Signed) Anna Elizabeth Olivier

The term "*Caffres*"[44] was used at the time to specifically denote the amaXhosa and associated nations. It has since assumed a derogatory connotation and has fallen from use. The *Zwagershoek*[45] is a mountainous region to the east of Graaff-Reinet.

—End Nexus Familia

Britain pays tribute to men with spears

Further to the south, the white population of Bruintjeshoogte abandoned their homes and followed Piet Prinsloo, Marthinus Prinsloo's nephew, better known as *"Piet Cafferland,"* in a wagon train up the Baviaansrivier Valley to the Tarka[46]. There they hoped to be safe from the Suurveld amaXhosa. They gathered at the entrance to the valley on 29 July 1799, where they were joined by a curious character we shall meet in depth in Chapter 6 of this work. As they proceeded up the ever-narrowing valley they were continually attacked by the imiDange Xhosa. On 3 August, having crossed onto the open Tarka behind the mountains, Piet Prinsloo and two others set off to king Ngqika of the Rharhabe amaXhosa to seek help against the imiDange.

On 14 August, Prinsloo returned from Ngqika with a promise of peace and aid. The very next morning four delegates from Ngqika arrived under orders to remain with the beleaguered fugitives of the frontier. When the imiDange again attacked on that evening, Ngqika's men addressed them and the imiDange departed. As always, the Suurveld Xhosa lived in fear of Ngqika's military power. Some weeks later General Vandeleur approved of this agreement arranged by Prinsloo, whose family he had imprisoned. On the 7th of August, a week before Prinsloo left for Ngqika's kraal, Governor Francis Dundas set off in person for the frontier, supported by various units to bring the British force to 800 men[47], a vastly larger force than Vandeleur had at his disposal. Dundas was surreptitiously trying to make peace at any price. He instructed Secretary Ross[48]:

August 5th, 1799.
Van der Walt's Kraal, 5 hocks from Zwellendam, 10th August 1799.

Dear Sir, —

...it is not my wish that the rather critical situation of affairs in Graaff Reinet should become the subject of general conversation [...] A Ship must now be procured at any price, having become indispensably necessary for transporting flour and provisions or necessaries to Algoa Bay, the country in the neighborhood of it being laid waste and depopulated by the Hottentots and Caffres [...]

...the safety of the Fleet, the Army, and the Colony, with perhaps eventually our possession of it, may possibly be at stake if we do not secure a permanent establishment for the protection of the Frontier of this too extensive Colony. I have desired Mr. Faure the Landdrost to assemble all the men of his District [Swellendam] capable of serving and bearing arms, with whom I hope we shall soon clear the country of every Vagabond and Savage, should the amicable measures which it is my intention first to try prove ineffectual.

(Signed) Francis Dundas.

Incredibly, the much-maligned Afrikaners, still without powder and lead, were now expected to ride to the rescue of none other than the British Army huddling pathetically on the beach of the author's future birthtown. By 13 September, these men had still not received ammunition, but Secretary Ross advised the incredulous Afrikaners that *"they will find plenty on the road to Graaff-Reinet"*[49]. No Afrikaner was going to believe this after what Dundas and Vandeleur had done. Vandeleur could quite rationally have been court-martialed. However, denigrating the failed general in public would likely have endangered Dundas' own position with London where his own uncle, Henry Dundas, was Secretary for War. We turn to Lady Anne Barnard's diary[50] for Dundas' views on the performance of Vandeleur, and for Vandeleur's reaction:

Before dinner General Vandeleur came to see me, arrived from the scene of the war, his mind full of vexation and irritations at the conduct of General D. [Dundas] he does not know I see how much he has raild aginst him [Vandeleur] behind his back for his misconduct, how much he has blamed him for the bad success of every thing – but tho he [Vandeleur] does not know the tenth part of what he has said he knows enough to make him angry to make him collect his proofs & his materials in case any investigation into his conduct should be necessary.

It is at this point that Dundas invited none other than the hated Maynier[51] to join him on the frontier. Maynier, now backed by the 800 British soldiers, was sent to arrange a "peace." In reality, the Khoekhoe and the Xhosa had fallen out over the division of the spoils[52]. The Khoekhoe had run out of gunpowder, had failed to take the British stores, and now were of no further benefit as allies to the amaGqunukhwebe. On the other hand, the British were weakened and forced to temporarily concede the Suurveld to the amaXhosa. It is difficult to improve on the description of the situation given by the great Canadian historian, Theal[53]:

"There was nothing left to plunder within reach of the insurgents and invaders. Under these circumstances it was an easy matter to persuade the Hottentot and Xhosa captains to give their word that they would abstain from further hostilities and not trespass beyond the Suurveld. They were promised that they would not be molested there, and large presents were made to them. To the conditions of things thus created Mr. Maynier gave the name of "peace," and the government gladly consented to the word being used."

On 16 October 1799, the British government announced, "hostilities had ceased." It is left to us to quote the later words[54] of Sir George Yonge, who would arrive as new governor in December of 1799:

Major General Dundas had recourse to the only expedient he thought left namely making Peace on any Terms. He has done so by paying tribute to the Caffres...

The amaGqunukhwebe, despised by the colony and the amaRharhabe alike, had humbled the most powerful nation on Earth. For two hundred years various white British and South African historians would attempt to paper over this history, but Governor George Yonge's summary stands – black on white. To add insult to injury, Dundas appointed[55] none other than the hated Maynier as High Court Judge, Bookkeeper of the Loan Bank, and Government Commissioner over the Afrikaners in both Swellendam and Graaff-Reinet. He was now the absolute master of the Afrikaners outside the Cape Town area.

Nexus Familia 36: The Birds of Prey

With peace, or what passes for it, having been established on the Frontier, the British now turn again on the frontier Afrikaners. The "Afrikaner rebels" are tried in Cape Town in June of 1800, having languished in the dungeon of the Cape Castle for more than a year after their surrender. They have been held 86 to a room without exercise or fresh air[56]. By now, a new governor, Sir George Yonge, is in command at the Cape, with Francis Dundas back in his original role as Lieutenant Governor. The prosecutor demands[57] that:

- [the first 8 prisoners] *"...be punished with the halter at the Gallows until Death ensueth, Further the Corpses of the four first prisoners, being dragged to the Out Gallows, there to be hanged again, in order so to remain until the birds of prey shall have consumed them away, and the Corpses of the 5th, 6th, 7th & 8th prisoners being laid in a Coffin, to be interred under the Out Gallows.*

- *"That the 9th & 10th prisoners Gerhardus Scheepers & Pieter Ignatius van Kamer each of them an halter round his neck exposed under the Gallows, be further with the 11th Prisoner Lucas Meyer and the 12th Prisoner Zacharias Albertus van Jaarsveld bound to a stake, severely whipped on their bare backs, branded and banished this Colony and the Dependencies thereof, during the time of their natural lives.*

- *"That the 13th & 14th prisoners Willem Grobbelaar and Jacob Johannes Kruger having witnessed the aforesaid Execution, be banished this Colony for a term of Twenty-five years."*

The first two prisoners are Adriaan van Jaarsveld and ancestral brother-in-law Marthinus Prinsloo. Prisoner 9, Gerhardus Scheepers, is a close relative of the Scheepers family massacred in July 1799 (*NF34*). Willem Grobbelaar (Grobler) is our ancestral brother (*NF33*). On 3 September 1800, they are finally sentenced. It is more appropriate for us to simply quote the sentences meted out to these men[58]:

- *"The 1st and 2nd prisoners Marthinus Prinsloo and Adriaan van Jaarsveld to be brought to the place where Criminals are executed, and being delivered over to the Executioner, to be hanged until death ensueth; that after that the 2 Corpses shall be placed in a Cofin and buried underneath the Gallows behind the lines.*

- *"The 3rd, 4th, 5th, 6th, 7th, & 8th prisoners, [names listed] to be also delivered to the Executioner blindfolded, & having kneeled upon a heap of Sand, he is to Sway the Sword over their heads for punishment, and then to be banished for the remainder of their days from this Government and its Dependencies.*

- *"The 9th and 10th prisoners Gerhardus Scheepers and Pieter Ignatius van Kamer to be also brought to the said place, and having been punished with the Sword over their heads, they shall be banished for life from this Settlement...*

- *"The 11th and 12th Prisoners Lucas Meyer and Zacharias van Jaarsveld, after having been present at and Eyewitness to the aforesaid Execution, to be exiled from this Colony for life.*

- *"The 13th and 14th Prisoners Willem Grobbelaar and Jacob Johannes Kruger to be banished as aforesaid for the Space of Ten ensuing Years, after they shall have seen the Execution.*

- *"The 15th and 16th prisoners Willem Venter and Paul Venter, the first mentioned to be imprisoned for the space of Two Years, and the last also for the time of One Year.*

• *"The 17th and 18th prisoners Gert Botha and Jan Kruger shall be set at liberty, in consideration of their long detention.*

• *"Condemning all the prisoners to pay the Costs of the process, and rejecting the further part of the prosecutor's demand. Done and sentenced at the Cape of Good Hope the 3rd September 1800, and pronounced the instant."*

Maria, sister to our ancestor, Johannes Klopper, is trying to come to terms with the death sentence that has been passed on her husband, Marthinus Prinsloo. Ancestor Cornelis Grobler has already lost his eldest brother, Johannes, seven years ago when he was tortured to death by the amaXhosa (*NF29*). Now his older brother Willem is to be banished from his own country for 10 years after witnessing the hanging of their friend Marthinus Prinsloo. In the event, because of the impending peace agreement with France and the Netherlands, the sentences are not executed and the men are again remanded in custody in the Castle.

—*End Nexus Familia*

The Afrikaner-amaRharhabe Friendship

In the middle of 1800, Sir George Young, the new Governor, sent Maynier and his understudy, Somerville, to the young amaRharhabe King Ngqika to discuss the matter of a peace treaty with the British. This happened during the period that Coenraad de Buys and our ancestor Coenraad Bezuidenhout were still with Ngqika. The two British representatives took every precaution to ensure that their messages went only to Ngqika and did not fall in the hands of the two Coenraads. Nevertheless, the answer that came back from Ngqika, who would not see them personally, is insightful. We quote verbatim Ngqika's response from the letter[59] that the two British representatives wrote to the Governor on 14 August 1800:

> *"...the Principal Grounds on which he would consent to make Peace must be the Release of the Prisoners confined in the Castle who he said were his Allies, & without this he could have no Faith in any Peace."*

This is the clearest evidence on record that the legitimate leader of the powerful amaRharhabe House of the amaXhosa nation saw the long-settled Afrikaners as his friends and allies. A simple understanding of the amaXhosa "House" system reveals why. At this time, Ngqika was much more powerful than the Great House of the amaGcaleka across the Kei River, while he experienced both his uncle Ndlambe and the various other Suurveld Xhosa minor right hand houses as rebels, this while these latter groups were a permanent threat to the Afrikaners. In the first decade of the 19th century, the British simply did not comprehend this very pragmatic position, but the frontier Afrikaners did.

Act One of the First British Occupation

It is clear that the British at the Cape were totally confused as to the realities of the frontier, unable to tell their friends from their enemies, totally lacking in any form of useful military intelligence, and beset by an anti-"Dutch" prejudice that bedeviled any pragmatic decision making. Most particularly, they kept assuming that the unhappy Afrikaners were allied with the amaGqunkhwebe, whom they could not tell from the far more powerful but (for now) peaceable amaRharhabe under Ngqika.

At this point, at the end of what we shall call "Act One" of the First British Occupation, ex-Governor Dundas had to have known that he had been massively in error. He must surely have been doing some serious thinking about his own future, and what he would do if he had a chance to do it all over again.

It is odd indeed how history works, but he would be granted that opportunity.

-----ooOoo-----

6

A Culture of Guilt

"How shall we hope to obtain, if it be possible, forgiveness from Heaven for the enormous evils we have committed..."

William Pitt, British Prime Minister,
House of Commons (2 April 1792)

The London Missionary Society

During the 18th century, England had something of a religious revolution under the leadership of what became known as the Clapham Sect. With the benefits of slavery having been reaped, the American slave market largely out of their ambit, and the infant Industrial Revolution having no need of slaves, Britain could comfortably develop a conscience on the subject at little cost to itself. It is a matter of some question as to whether the fate of the roughly 5,000 European slaves in Algiers ever occurred to those with their newfound conscience.

Led by such people as William Wilberforce, the reformers went from strength to strength as the British somehow convinced themselves that they now possessed the moral high ground of the human race. All Britain had to do was feel guilty and pay with some blood; preferably someone else's. As Protestants, they turned not to the Catholic Pope for absolution but to a communal sense of guilt, which they would carefully nurture.

Fig. 6-1 William Wilberforce

Given that they had championed the cause of African slavery, they now convinced themselves that Africa was where they had to go to atone and be absolved. Even their Prime Minister, William Pitt[1] joined in the national lament on 2 April 1792:

"How shall we hope to obtain, if it be possible, forgiveness from Heaven for the enormous evils we have committed, if we refuse to make use of those means which the mercy of Providence has still reserved for us for wiping away the shame and guilt with which we are now covered?"

The cynical might suggest that they could have made reparations to the people of West Africa where they had obtained their slaves to start with. Alternatively, they could have used their money from the slave trade to buy back slaves from the Americas to free. In fact, there was an extensive list of things they might have done to make good for the earlier inhumanity. Instead, the London Missionary Society was created.

This crusading "moral army" was filled with people from the lower rungs of society, consumed with religious zeal, but having little if any formal religious background and often no education. They were hell bent on assuaging their own national guilt, which they immediately extrapolated to all white men. Other people of their own race, caught in the middle of a fight for survival against "noble savages" became an easy emotional target for their guilt-ridden obsession. These men did not comprehend that Johannes Grobler was being tortured to death by "noble savages" even as they were lamenting their own guilt (*NF29*).

In an effort to address the wrongs of the past, or comfortably absolve themselves, depending on the point of view, the British "socially concerned" devised a unique plan. Starting in 1792, they would relocate their so-called "Black Poor" from the streets of London and from Nova Scotia to the coast of West Africa in what would later become Sierra Leone. The capital of the little settlement was appropriately dubbed Freetown. Here these poor people, who had been employed in various jobs, such as serving Britain loyally in the American Revolution, were left to make their way with the indigenous black people. Their only qualification for being in Africa was possession of a dark skin. However, the locals had nothing in common with them but that skin color, and that would eventually count for nothing, as we shall see in due course.

It somehow did not occur to anyone participating in this collective moral hair rending that they were actually expediently washing their hands of their resident "Poor Black" problem. These "concerned citizens" could not anticipate that two hundred years later they would, if logic and morality were to prevail, be considered extreme racists. Assuming people of the same skin color are all the same and could therefore happily integrate culturally must be one of the most misguided expressions of racism imaginable. It is equivalent to the Barbary Slavers depositing some hundreds of freed English slaves on the southern coast of France and expecting them to "re-integrate" with the French.

The issue was that Freetown was not an easy place whence to go forth into Africa and atone for the sins of one's society. This posed a major problem for the London Missionary Society. And so it was that this group of fanatics, drunk on the "*Noble Savage*" philosophy of Jean Jacques Rousseau, who had himself never met a "*savage*" in his life – "*noble*" or otherwise – elected to make the Cape their target for seeking their personal absolution from their nation's sins in Africa at any cost.

And this is how a grief-stricken Dutch cosmologist by the name of Johannes Theodorus van der Kemp, who had seen his wife and child drowned in front of his eyes by a waterspout on the Meuse in 1791, offered his services to the Society. Van der Kemp arrived at the Cape[2] on 31 March 1799 on his way to Graaff-Reinet. Perversely, the London Missionary Society was about to attempt atonement for British slavery in the single part of Black Africa where the indigenous population had never experienced slavery at the hand of Europeans.

Moreover, the British themselves had only just recently arrived at the Cape and had hardly had time to earn a guilty conscience for their activities with respect to African people there. But one should not let such trifling matters as truth or practical reality intrude on the well-intentioned plans of the uninformed zealous; especially when they can foist their philosophical excesses on a country whilst living off and enjoying the protection of the very Western people they seek to assail.

Pouring oil on the fire

On 28 May 1799, Van der Kemp and his party set off for King Ngqika's country with letters of commendation from the governor. Near Graaff-Reinet, he was assisted with accommodation, food, protection and draught oxen by four of the author's own ancestors, among whom was Stephanus Naude[3] (*NF35*). They advised Van der Kemp to travel to the Fish River over the Sneeuberg and helped him to do so, because the ImiDange Xhosa were in control of the direct route via Bruintjeshoogte.

At the start of the Baviaansrivier valley, he joined Piet Prinsloo's refugee party from Bruintjeshoogte, described in the previous chapter. With Graaff-Reinet nearly surrounded and cut off and the British Army driven onto the beach at Algoa Bay by Xhosa attacks, Van der Kemp asked Prinsloo's help in getting to "*the land of the Xhosa.*" The incredulous Afrikaners refused, but nevertheless allowed the British-accredited missionaries to travel with them for protection. To the disgust of these simple frontier folk, Van der Kemp refused to assist in the defense of the refugees. He claimed that he had no fight with the indigenous people, but nevertheless kept his own flintlock next to his bed. When indeed they were attacked, he sat on his wagon and refused to lift a finger in defense of his protectors, electing to salve his conscience by giving his flintlock to his Khoekhoe assistants.

Willing to accept the Afrikaners' gracious help and protection, he would soon proceed to vilify his protectors under the very banner of the God that the Afrikaners believed in so passionately. Piet Prinsloo was very distrustful of Van der Kemp, but subsequently made his peace with this man. Van der Kemp's London Missionary Society would soon find its raison d'être. It would "preach" to the Xhosa, "liberate" the Khoekhoe, and consign all Westerners to hell by any means, fair or foul, particularly if they were not British. The Afrikaners would never comprehend the thinking of these missionaries who assailed at every turn the very culture that protected their lives.

Fig. 6-2 Johannes Theodorus Van der Kemp

To the Shores of Tripoli

While the British were lamenting their slaving past, matters were going from bad to worse in the Mediterranean Sea due to Barbary Corsairs enslaving Europeans and Americans. The United States Congress passed the Naval Act of 1794 specifically to address the matter of the Barbary Pirates who operated from the coast of what is today Algeria and Libya. The United States initially agreed to pay tribute and ransom monies. This had worked in 1787 in the case of the pirates from Morocco, who had wanted only $20,000 as ransom.

Matters were more complex in the case of Algiers. In 1785, the Algerians had captured two US ships and held the crews ransom. They wanted $60,000 for the freedom of the men. While Adams was prepared to pay, Jefferson saw this differently. Matters were brought to a head when the Algerians captured a further 11 American ships and added one hundred more men to those already in captivity. On 5 September 1795, Joseph Donaldson Jr. signed an agreement on behalf of the United States with Hassan Bashaw, the Dey of Algiers, in terms of which the United States would pay $642,500 plus annual tribute, including presents to the Dey. The American captives were released and the Dey agreed to "protect" American shipping.

Similar arrangements were made with Tunis and with the Pasha of Tripoli. By 1796, the United States had to borrow money to pay these ransoms. The Barbary Slave States were busy bankrupting the United States. In terms of the Naval Act passed earlier, five frigates were already being constructed. The keel of the *USS Constitution*, in particular, was laid down on 1 November 1794 at Edmund Hartt's shipyard in Boston, Massachusetts.

By 1799, matters were out of hand. William Eaton, American Consul to the Pasha of Tripoli, wrote[4] on 15 June 1799 to the Secretary of the United States about the fate of the Europeans from the island Sardinia:

Fig. 6-3 The USS Constitution under sail

> *"On the eighth of September last [1798], five Tunissian corsaires, carrying nine hundred and ninety men, landed, in the grey of the morning, upon the island of St. Peters in the dependence of Sardinia, captured and brought prisoners to Tunis seven hundred women and children and two hundred and twenty men. The description given me, by the British Consul, of the barbarous and brutal conduct practiced upon these unfortunate, defenceless wretches, would shock a savage. The able bodied men of the island being at their vintages in the country, these people fell a feeble sacrifice to the merciless assailants. Decriped (sic) age, delicate youth and helpless infancy, were tumbled headlong from their beds, precipitated down flights of stairs, shoved out of street windows, driven naked in an undistinguished crowd, without respect to sex or circumstance, through the streets, and cramed (sic) promiscuously into the filthy hold of one of their cruisers; in this manner brought across the sea, and in this wretched plight goaded with thongs through the street of the city by their relentless captors, driven to the common auction square, and consigned to slavery."*

When the *USS Philadelphia* ran aground while chasing a Tripolitanian vessel, three hundred US officers and men were taken captive and the Pasha of Tripoli demanded $3,000,000 in ransom. On 27 April 1805, a rag tag army of Arabs and mercenaries led by William Eaton would storm the City under a barrage from three US warships and drive the defenders out. This would immortalize the words *"To the Shores of Tripoli"* in the culture of the U.S. Marines. However, it would not be the end of the Barbary Corsair problem.

Maynier and the Frontier

On 1 April 1801, George Yonge, Governor of the Cape, was removed from office in the wake of charges of corruption. Major-General Francis Dundas was once again to stand in as Governor[5]. Fate had provided him the opportunity to correct the tragic mistakes of his first term of office, not the least of which had been the appointment of Maynier.

By way of example, Maynier had issued a decree to the effect that no one was allowed to vacate their farms despite the depredations by the various amaXhosa and the renegade Khoekhoe under Stuurman. Against this background, the widow Hurter of the Graaff-Reinet region sent a letter to Dundas on 13th January 1801, petitioning the government for some indemnification for the "entire destruction of her property in the district of Graaff Reinet by the Kaffirs and Hottentots." She had remained on her farm in consequence of Maynier's order [6] *"that no person should abandon his place on pain of death."* She claimed she was unable to comply with Commissioner Maynier's injunction to return to her ruined place, and asked remission of rents. Dundas must have realized that something was seriously amiss.

Early in 1801, a rumor began circulating in the Graaff-Reinet area to the effect that the British would abuse the event of the annual census to press gang them into the British Navy. While the British had no such intentions, Americans know the issue very well and in fact would decide to go to war with Great Britain over exactly this matter ten years later[7]. The frontiersmen from the Achter-Bruintjeshoogte therefore took to arms and left their farms to withdraw far from Graaff-Reinet beyond the furthest northeastern limits of the colony.

When an enquiry[8] was held in August 1801 about the initial disturbances, Maynier insisted that no action was required as the farmers would soon enough realize their folly. He was questioned on his relationship with King Ngqika of the amaRharhabe and Chief Cungwa of the amaGqunukhwebe. Maynier reported excellent relations with both. As to how the Khoekhoe under Stuurman were behaving, he answered: *"Cannot be better."* He then asked on record that a further 400 "Hottentots" (Khoekhoe) be enlisted in the British Army for his use and be armed and fed by the government. When he was asked whether he needed a deputy, he stated that he knew of no suitable person. He also confirmed on record that he had spies among the frontiersmen. It is quite evident that his intention was to keep the frontiersmen in subjugation through the agency of the Khoekhoe.

On 12 October 1801, Dundas received the following instruction[9] from Downing Street:

"I am to signify to you the King's Commands that you are, on the receipt of this Dispatch, to abstain from the Commission of all Hostilities against the Subjects of France or of her Allies."

Upon this, Dundas elected to continue the detention of the men from the Van Jaarsveld rebellion (*NF33*) but did not carry out their sentences, despite having been ordered to do so by Lord Hobart in Britain[10].

Meanwhile rumors about Maynier and his intentions flew about the frontier. In late October 1801, the frontiersmen rode into Graaff-Reinet and surrounded the Magistrate's Office. Both sides fired some shots on 23 October, but the farmers withdrew. The British officers stationed at Graaff-Reinet under the authority of Maynier were quite taken aback when Maynier not only did not notify Cape Town of the disturbances, but also refused to build a blockhouse for their defense. On 21 November, two separate groups of farmers of the Graaff-Reinet area wrote letters[11] to Governor Dundas, reporting the depredations suffered, as well as the events of Nexus Familia 37, for which they held Maynier responsible. They had had enough of him.

Nexus Familia 37: Two deaths too many

The District of Graaff-Reinet is huge, being by itself much larger than all of New England. Graaff-Reinet, some 150 miles from Algoa Bay is still at this time the only town. In order to address what he fears might be another Afrikaner rebellion, Governor Francis Dundas has dispatched a British force of 300 men under Major Sherlock to Graaff-Reinet[12]. Sherlock is making his way from Algoa Bay to Graaff-Reinet in the first few weeks of November 1801.

Sherlock's first stop on his way to Graaff-Reinet is with Field-Cornet Cornelis Johannes van Rooyen at his farm on the Swartkops River, some 16 miles from the coast. Van Rooyen assisted Vandeleur some two years before. Cornelis is first cousin to our own ancestor who is also named Cornelis van Rooyen after their common grandfather. As fate would have it, the Field-Cornet's wife happens to be the sister of the murdered wife of Stephanus Scheepers (*NF34*). Cornelis no doubt tells Sherlock more specifically about the terrible massacre of his wife's relatives in the Winterhoek two years earlier. Cousin Cornelis reports to Sherlock that chief Cungwa of the amaGqunkhwebe seems to be keen on peace. Matters are less clear around the "Stuurman Hottentots," who were bought off with presents by Maynier and who are still lurking about the riverine bush along the Sondags River.

While Sherlock is on his way to punish the recalcitrant Afrikaners who have dared to hold a shoot-out with Maynier, matters on the frontier take a very serious turn. A few days after Sherlock's departure there is a knock on cousin Cornelis' front door at 2 a.m. When he opens it, he finds a gang of Khoekhoe from Stuurman's nearby horde. Without so much as a word, they shoot Cornelis through the left eye[13] and he dies in his own doorway. They chase his wife and children out of the house and burn the place down[14]. It is some time before Cornelis' widow, Johanna van Vuuren, can get word out to others. Sherlock will hear of this when he reaches Graaff-Reinet and it will dramatically affect his view of matters.

*****

Our ancestor Stephanus Naude (*NF35*) lives on a farm on the Sondags River in the county of Buffelshoek, east of Graaff-Reinet. He is a successful man and a member of the Heemraad. Matters in the district are unstable, but Magistrate Maynier has threatened dire consequences if they were to seek refuge in their protective wagon circles. Eventually, Stephanus decides that he and Anna will have to leave, because the Stuurman renegade Khoekhoe, forever protected by Maynier and bought off by the British, are lurking about. They have also been joined by the ImiDange Xhosa[15] from the Koonap River area. Maynier naively expects him to accept the "protection" of Khoekhoe Pandours. Stephanus hitches his wagon and he and Anna start out for Graaff-Reinet, some miles away to the west. Surely Maynier will see reason if matters were carefully explained to him. He might allow the farmers to focus on mutual protection and to put together a properly supplied commando. As they emerge into an open patch among the sweet-thorn trees, Stephanus and Anna see the men emerge from among the trees ahead; and Anna begins to pray out loud...

—End Nexus Familia

A British Epiphany

When Sherlock reached Graaff-Reinet on 27 November 1801, news arrived of the murder of Field-Cornet van Rooyen, whom he had spoken to mere days before. He also heard of the near-simultaneous murder of Councilor Stephanus Naude and his wife, Anna. He found that the British officers at Graaff-Reinet were also at their wit's end with Maynier. They detested the man. Just as he had refused to allow the farmers to protect themselves, so he had refused the soldiers the right to erect a blockhouse to defend themselves. Even the former magistrate Bresler had turned against Maynier. To make matters worse, Sherlock discovered that the soldiers had been four days without bread – an "unforgivable leadership sin" in the British Army.

Sherlock turned out to be a thinking soldier. He provided food for the Graaff-Reinet soldiers and sent a British dragoon to the unhappy farmers. He was surprised when the farmers sent a return delegation of two men, along with a message, which they maintained they had been trying to get to the Governor. And here, outside the little village of Graaff-Reinet in November 1801, the much-tried frontiersmen finally found that there had emerged from the poisonous welter of British hate, bias, arrogance, hypocrisy, and condescension a fighting man who actually listened and understood. As fighting men in a dangerous country, they could understand each other's concerns and views.

It is after this meeting that Major Sherlock wrote a letter to Governor Dundas that sealed the fate of the hated Maynier. Sherlock's letter[16] on 30 November 1801 stated that Maynier was *"detested by the Officers who have been stationed here"* and that against the British Government the frontier farmers have *"no cause of complaint, but many grievous against the commissioner* [Maynier] *which they will verify on oath. One paper containing several they have entreated me to forward to you..."*.

One of the charges brought against Maynier was that he had somehow had a hand in the murder[17] of our ancestor, Councilor Stephanus Naude (*NF37*). He was also accused of failing to prosecute the Khoekhoe men who were believed to have murdered Marthinus Prinsloo's eldest brother Nicolaas. Most important to the governor, was the accusation that Maynier had willfully concealed from the government the severity of the state of the district. Dundas knew well what had happened during his first term as interim governor, and promptly suspended Maynier from all his offices, pending an investigation.

He would eventually counter the charges, but this was the end of the detestable reign of Maynier; a much hated name that finally departs our ancestral history at this point.

On 7 December 1801, Governor Dundas issued a reward[18] of 500 Rixdollars for information leading to the capture of the murderers of Field-Cornet van Rooyen and Councilor Naudé (*NF37*). The deaths of two ancestral family members had induced a sea change in the attitude of the British at the Cape.

Boer and Brit finally find each other

During the next few months, Governor Dundas had a dramatic shift in personal conviction. Sherlock was the first Englishman with management responsibility to be placed in the east of the country and reported directly to Dundas. With this came a dramatic shift in policy:

1. There would be no punishment for the frontiersmen who had opposed Maynier, despite the fact that they had actually fired at the Magistrate's office.

2. This presented Dundas with a major conundrum. He had 18 frontiersmen languishing in the Castle for nearly three years, waiting to be executed (*NF36*) and banished for transgressions much lesser than those he had just forgiven. Accordingly, on 12 December 1801 Dundas wrote[19] to the new Colonial Secretary, Lord Hobart, in London:

> "... *feelings of humanity, by reason of their long imprisonment, give the Prisoners a claim to some modification as to the Capital part of their punishment, if not a full remission of their sentence.* [They] *obeyed without hesitation the summons to deliver themselves up together with their arms and ammunition, having assembled at the place appointed for that purpose, conceiving (as I have reason to believe they did) that they should meet with forgiveness from Government*
>
> [...] *all which considerations incline me to think that lenity ought, if possible, to be shewn to the Prisoners...*"

3. Aiming straight at Stuurman, Dundas demanded a policy on the matter of "*Vagrant Hottentots*" from the *Fiscal* (State Prosecutor), Van Ryneveld. The policy[20] was published on 31 October 1801. It stated:

> "*...no Hottentot is to be suffered to remain within the Boundaries of this Colony, unless belonging to one or other of the following classes, viz. :*
>   *1. The Class of Hottentots serving the Farmers.*
>   *2. To the licensed kraals or huts.* [living a traditional subsistence life]
>   *3. To the schools of the Missionaries.*
>   [...] *all wanderers and vagabonds ought immediately to be apprehended and placed either to the public works, or on Robben Island, there to labor for their bread. To which end every Hottentot in service, or belonging to the kraals, must always be provided with a certificate from the Landdrost of the District, and those belonging to the licensed schools with a certificate from one of the Missionaries, countersigned by the Landdrost, without which certificate, if found, they shall be liable to be considered as vagabonds, and taken up accordingly.*"

4. On 7 May 1802, with Stuurman's Khoekhoe, now joined by the ImiDange Xhosa, again attacking farms, Dundas called out[21] the Graaff-Reinet Commando, its officers now commanded by Government Commissioner Major Sherlock.

The British administration at the Cape had finally come to its senses. It finally understood what the Frontiersmen had known all along. Boer and Briton were finally fighting on the same side. All it had needed was a competent and experienced fighting man. But, alas, it was too late. On 30 April 1802, a letter[22] had already been sent from London to Governor Dundas. It read:

> "*Sir,- I have the honor to transmit to you herewith His Majesty's Royal Sign Manual directing you to deliver the Settlement of the Cape of Good Hope with the fortifications thereof in the state in which they now are, to such Person as shall be authorized to receive the same on the part of the Batavian Republic,* [...]"

Under the Treaty of Amiens between Britain and France, the Cape was to be given back to the Dutch Batavian government and be allowed to service all ships. The Afrikaner captives were all to be released; all except Adriaan van Jaarsveld. He had died in British hands, just as Marthinus Prinsloo had predicted in 1799 he would. Marthinus' stay in the Cape Town Castle dungeons earned him the nickname "Kasteel," a sobriquet that he would in time pass on to his son, Hendrik. Marthinus had survived his first "rebellion."

The British Empire, however, had a long memory – as we shall duly see in Chapter 7.

The First Great Abandonment

After the signing of the Treaty of Amiens, the previous Dutch leader, the Prince of Orange, remained an exile in Britain. The pro-Napoleonic bourgeoisie Dutch intelligentsia now controlled the Netherlands and called themselves the "Batavian Government."

In the east of the Cape Colony, the Khoekhoe bands again took to cattle rustling. Large numbers of vagrant Khoekhoe had also congregated at Graaff-Reinet. The London Missionary Society found a susceptible audience among this throng. In the view of the farmers, the missionaries were inciting the Khoekhoe against them, even using the farmers' very own church building for these purposes. When the farmers threatened Van der Kemp, he fled with a horde of Khoekhoe in tow. Most of them deserted this exodus and joined Stuurman's raiding band of Khoekhoe, turning on what remained of civilization on the eastern border. Van der Kemp would eventually settle the remainder on the Swartkops River north of Algoa Bay, at a place called Bethelsdorp.

For the frontiersmen the issue was that Van der Kemp kept interceding[23] with the Governor on behalf of Klaas Stuurman, the very man who had previously made common cause with the murdering amaGqunukhwebe. After all, he was part of the broader grouping of people who had massacred the author's own ancestors (*NF34*). Now Van der Kemp was protecting him.

Fig. 6-4 Fort Fredrick in Algoa Bay

In 1803, the British announced the withdrawal of their army from what was to be once more a Dutch colony. The renegade Khoekhoe and the Suurveld amaXhosa promptly went on the attack yet again and started laying waste to the eastern border region. As the British withdrew, the land was ablaze behind them. In late 1799, the British had erected a small square fort at Algoa Bay after a sea battle in the bay with the French frigate, the *Preneuse*. Around this little square fort, subsequently named Fort Frederick, would eventually grow the city of Port Elizabeth. Here the British left in charge Thomas Ignatius Ferreira, an Afrikaner Field-Cornet of the Langkloof area and a descendant of a 17th century shipwrecked Portuguese sailor, and then they simply departed. Ferreira penned this message[24]:

> *"We are stationed here, the Last Outpost of the Christian Empire."*

Soon enough, Van der Kemp and his Khoekhoe converts arrived, seeking protection from Ferreira. They had been attacked by renegade Khoekhoe, and had actually fought off the attackers using their own guns. However, once safe behind Ferreira, they refused to help with any defense and then accused him of abusing Khoekhoe people. Later, Van der Kemp would escalate this conduct.

In the interior, the Afrikaner farmers went back into their laagers for mutual protection and awaited the Dutch, abandoned by the British who had achieved nothing but the utter desolation of the frontier area. The interests of the Frontier Afrikaners had been practically destroyed by the advent of British rule. They were vastly worse off than before the British interregnum. The entire colony had been endangered and diminished. More than 35% of farms in the east had been destroyed and up to a third of the Afrikaner population had simply fled the border in despair.

The parallels with *Pontiac's Rebellion* (Chapter 4) in North America are clear. In both cases, a change in colonial power led indigenous people, who were former mutual enemies, to make alliances to rise against the new power. The first British occupation of the Cape had been an all-round colossal disaster, brought on almost totally by the British prejudice against the "Dutch" Afrikaner burghers.

This was the First Great Abandonment in which the Afrikaner nation was left at the mercy of the hordes that had been loosed by the hapless British involvement in Africa. The situation was made all the more dangerous by the meddlesome activities of the London Missionary Society. This body had yet to do something constructive about the slavery in West Africa that had led to the development of the British guilt complex in the first place. They inflicted the consequences and excesses of this guilt complex on the farmers who, unlike the French philosophers with their theoretical concepts, knew from bitter experience that there was no such thing as a "Noble Savage." "Savages" were people like any other, except that they had a vastly different culture. That is all. They were no more "noble" than anyone else; if anything, quite the contrary.

When the British had arrived in late 1795, they had made their dislike of the Afrikaner known in vivid fashion. They came with an assumed moral superiority that they thought would naturally help them resolve whatever they addressed. By the time they left, they had grudgingly come to associate with the Afrikaner's view of matters, even threatening the extermination of the amaXhosa and Khoekhoe in conversation. The Afrikaners had never suggested that. They had just expected realism and pragmatic government from the British, not attempted genocide, such as the latter had perpetrated in North America in 1763 during Pontiac's Rebellion.

The Afrikaners knew fully well that their destiny in Africa was intertwined with that of the Ba'Ntu and the Khoekhoe, and possibly even dependent on it. This is borne out by the fact that, throughout all of the troubles of the First British Occupation, relations between the Frontier Afrikaners and Ngqika's amaRharhabe remained excellent.

By the time the British had arrived in South Africa in 1795, the Afrikaners had been in the land no fewer than one hundred and forty-three years or about six generations. That is longer than most Americans can trace their ancestry in the United States even in the 21st century. The Afrikaners had been in armed conflict with the amaXhosa on and off for twenty years. Britain might have been well advised to tap that experience.

Dundas' last act as Governor was to absolve all non-British subjects from having to swear the oath of allegiance to his Majesty George III – exactly the point the Graaff-Reinet Burghers had made to Magistrate Bresler in 1796 after the British occupation (*NF31*) and the source of so much of the unhappiness.

A Dutch Interlude

In Afrikaans, the expression *"Die Kaap is weer Hollands"* (The Cape is Dutch again) is used in the sense of *"all is well and back to normal again."* It most certainly does not, and did not beyond about 1770, represent any belief on the part of Afrikaners that Dutch governance is necessarily in their interest. They had suffered one hundred and forty-three years of experience of Dutch East India Company (VOC) rule and had not considered it positive.

On 23 December 1802, a collection of Batavian officials, together with the 5th Waldecker regiment of German and Hungarian mercenaries, arrived at the Cape. The VOC had been dissolved in bankruptcy and it was now the actual Batavian government of the Netherlands that would administrate the Cape. On 19 February 1803, the Cape was formally handed over to the Dutch "Batavian" government, whose top structure at the Cape was a peculiar two-person leadership, generally referred to in South African history as simply "Janssens & De Mist." It comprised of a Governor, Lieutenant-General Jan Wilhelm Janssens, and a Commissioner-General, Jacob Abraham de Mist. The Batavians arrived with good intentions. Given that they were highly educated people, they put their faith in education. They were going to educate the populace and raise them to a higher level. This included the difficult frontier Afrikaners, who they believed would make better burghers if they were better educated. One of their first actions was to release the men who had been imprisoned by the British because of the "Van Jaarsveld Rebellion." This came too late for Adriaan van Jaarsveld. He had died a prisoner in the Castle.

Immediately before the transfer of power, the British had decided to call out a major Afrikaner Commando to stop the progress of the amaGqunukhwebe. When Batavian Commissioner-General De Mist came ashore, he promptly countermanded the order and insisted that the Afrikaner commandants make peace with the Khoekhoe and amaXhosa. Clearly, the Dutch were going to have to learn some hard lessons.

On 18 April 1803, a Dutch military force arrived by sea at Fort Frederick in Algoa Bay. It also concluded a peace without honor and it is later described as such by the British Colonel Collins[25].

Twice in rapid succession, first the British and now the Dutch, had made dishonorable peace with the amaGqunukhwebe. By now, the amaGqunukhwebe were calibrated. It clearly paid them to attack. When they then stopped, they received presents, and could also keep what they had stolen. Furthermore, no matter what they did, the Afrikaners would be punished – a most advantageous arrangement from the amaGqunukhwebe perspective. That would again be the operative paradigm in the late 20th century, with the Dutch and the British replaced by the entire Western World.

Fig. 6-5 Lieutenant-General Jan W. Janssens

Janssens & De Mist set out to stabilize the situation on the eastern frontier. Unlike the British, who had experienced great difficulty understanding the amaXhosa hierarchical structure, they soon discovered that there were three distinct groups of Xhosa, two of which had recently advanced into the Suurveld. In the Tyumie Valley, there remained the very powerful Ngqika, mortal enemy of the Suurveld amaXhosa groups. Janssens went to the Suurveld to personally negotiate with the Suurveld amaXhosa. He also managed to agree with Ngqika that his amaRharhabe would respect the Great Fish River as the border. We are fortunate to have the journal of General Janssens, preserved by Hinrich Lichtenstein. This journal, together with Lichtenstein's own observations on his tour with Janssens, makes a few things very clear[26]:

• Firstly, converse to what Barrow had speculated, Coenraad de Buys had not been involved in any instigation of attacks on the Colony. However, he had supported the young King Ngqika against the pretender, Ndlambe, who had attempted to usurp Ngqika's rightful throne while he had been Ngqika's regent. Ironically, De Buys could call on none other than missionary Van der Kemp to vouch for this. Both De Buys and our own ancestor Coenraad Bezuidenhout were with Ngqika. De Buys even built a house[27] for Van der Kemp no more than 300 paces from his own.

• Ngqika also made it clear that he set great store by the general counsel of Coenraad de Buys, and that he did not want to lose his services. Lichtenstein reports that De Buys in particular was quite clear about the fact that he personally resented British authority, but not Dutch authority.

• It was also clear that it had been Ndlambe and the other "right-hand houses" (the Suurveld amaXhosa) who had invaded the colony in the 3rd Frontier War and during the British Departure. Ngqika had not been involved. In fact, Ngqika styled the Colonists his allies against what he considered to be "rebel" right-hand houses.

It also becomes clear, upon studying Lichtenstein's descriptions, that the troubles on the Frontier since 1780 were the result of two major factors:

• The amaXhosa "Royal House" system, which pushed the Houses other than the Great House and the amaRharhabe ever more into Colonial territory; and

• The machinations of the amaRharhabe regent and "pretender" Ndlambe, who contrived every possible plan to unite the "right-hand houses" under his command in order to fight the legitimate amaRharhabe King, Ngqika. He alternately attacked these groups to subjugate and incorporate them or he allied with them.

The Afrikaner Boer Commando retaliatory incursions into amaXhosa territory may very well have exacerbated the situation, but were not the cause. On the grand scale of things, they were mere pinpricks.

On 30 May 1803, the new governor granted[28] Van der Kemp and his Khoekhoe flock a piece of land near the Swartkops River just north of the present Port Elizabeth. This Van der Kemp named Bethelsdorp.

The Batavian Government stabilized the border area. Janssens & De Mist soon assessed the London Missionary Society's efforts via Van der Kemp as not just a disaster, but a fundamental threat to the colony. Bethelsdorp was soon seen as a den of iniquity and an affront to civilization. Janssens had some first hand experience of the behavior of the Khoekhoe in the district of Graaff-Reinet. His fellow traveler, artillery captain Willem Bartholomé Eduard Paravicini di Capelli, noted[29] in his diary:

> *"Everywhere the Governor orders and requests Hottentots to be treated well. He sets the example by paying his own considerably better than good servants in Europe, and providing food and clothing generously. And yet they filch the food from our table."*

While the governor and his commissioner were themselves devout believers in the Enlightenment, they were not prepared to entertain a threat to the colony based on that philosophy. When Van der Kemp would not submit to Janssens & De Mist's rules, he was invited to the Cape in April 1805 and confined there. Janssens & De Mist comprehended the need for the Khoekhoe to be part of the economy, but they also realized that the burghers needed to be more disciplined. All in all this government did an excellent job in matters non-military. To administrate the Suurveld area, they created a new town at the foot of the mountains on the Swartkops River. This they named Uitenhage, after De Mist, whose full name was Jacob Abraham Uitenhage de Mist. Uitenhage was vastly closer to the troublesome Suurveld than Graaff-Reinet, and a mere twenty miles or six hours march from Fort Frederick at Algoa Bay, where the port city of Port Elizabeth would later be founded. The magistrate's office was erected on the farm of Gerrit Scheepers, the older brother of the murdered Stephanus Scheepers Senior (*NF34*). His widow was the Susanna Elisabeth van Leeuwen[30], better known as "Betje (Betty), the widow Scheepers"[31] and she lived there still. Their farm had been a long-established stop along the way from Algoa Bay to Graaff-Reinet.

In this new town, they placed their newly appointed district Landdrost, a very competent German soldier under the Batavian Dutch flag, namely Captain Johann Christoph Ludwig Alberti of the 5th Waldecker Regiment[32]. He is one of the small number of men who left us with reasoned and insightful information about the situation on the Eastern Frontier at the time. Alberti tells us, with reference to the conduct of the British Government at the Cape over the preceding period, that[33]:

> *"It is most probable that they endeavored at that time to increase their strength by excessively aiding and abetting the Hottentots, which was done in such an imprudent way that it resulted in a large part of the Colony being devastated. [...] Now all disputes between Colonists and Hottentots were decided in favor of the latter without regard for right or wrong."*

Ludwig Alberti was a man with great responsibility on the frontier and with an insight into the situation on the ground, infinitely greater than that of any present day historian, who is inevitably looking back at history though the heavily stained eyeglass of an all-powerful 21st century liberal hegemony in the Western World. By the above observations, Alberti bears out the picture presented in this work. He is nevertheless correctly critical of the "colonists" for their bad treatment of the Khoekhoe people.

Renewed conflict between Napoleon and the British would put an end to this government. Even as the British headed back home from the Cape in 1803, they received the news of renewed hostilities with Napoleon. The British would be back for more than a century, and the outrage would flare anew.

-----ooOoo-----

7

The amaBhulu

"A brave race can forget the victims of the field of battle, but never those of the scaffold. The making of political martyrs is the last insanity of statesmanship."

Arthur Conan Doyle,
The Great Boer War (1900)

Napoleon again – The British return

By 1805, the mounting activities of American ships around the Cape already worried the British, but it was when they heard that the French wanted to take the Cape once more that they decided to act. The man for the job was Commodore Sir Home Riggs Popham. A huge fleet of no fewer than sixty-one ships was assembled in secrecy, along with almost 7,000 troops, and set sail for the Cape in late 1805. This massive force arrived off Cape Town on Friday January 3, 1806. On 8 January 1806, the actual formal battle took place. General Janssens was opposed by a 6,500 man British Army. His motley collection of defenders was outnumbered, but it was the Waldecker mercenaries, drawn from the Austro-Hungarian Empire, who broke and ran.

Janssens surrendered on January 18, 1806 on extra-ordinarily lenient terms from a Dutch perspective. These included the fact that the Batavian soldiers would be returned to Holland at Britain's expense. The burghers' lives would be largely unaffected and all finances and currency would be maintained and guaranteed. At the Cape, the word "Waldecker" became synonymous with "coward." Many of these mercenaries simply joined the

Fig. 7-1 Jacob Cuyler

victorious British Army. The last representative of the one hundred and fifty-four year Dutch tenure at the Cape, albeit interrupted for a few short years by the first British Occupation "on their behalf," left Table Bay on March 6, 1807. The Cape would never be Dutch again. The British were back to stay and the Cape citizen was about to enter his darkest days until the excesses of the 21st Century. The British government of the Cape was a military one, a nature that would soon evidence itself.

 ## Nexus Familia 38: Angry Generals – happy dragoons

Our Myburgh family is directly exposed to the consequences of the British victory at Bloubergstrand over the Batavian Dutch General Janssens. After signing the surrender terms with the British, General Janssens is housed at Meerlust, the farm where the toppling of corrupt Governor W.A. van der Stel was initiated a hundred years earlier (*NF22*). Johannes Myburgh, grandson of the immigrant (*NF13*), bought Meerlust 50 years before in 1757. His son, our ancestral cousin Philip, is now the 69-year old patriarch and owner of the farm.

One good morning finds the brooding General Janssens sitting on the porch at the top of the staircase. This is when the commander of the Waldecker mercenary unit that had cost him the Cape, decides to pay Janssens a visit to offer his apologies. When the man finally gets to the top of the staircase, Janssens gets up and physically kicks[1] him to the bottom of the same staircase. This is naturally the end of the attempt at an apology.

The British now insist that all of the citizenry should take an oath of allegiance to the King of England. However, the elderly Philip Myburgh has no such intentions and bluntly refuses. As result, the decision is to emulate the French Sun King's actions of 1687 and to lodge a company of English dragoons with Philip in the house. They are under the command of a certain captain Story. This might just work, but the British commander at the Cape has overlooked one small detail. Philip, being a typical Afrikaner, cannot conceive of being rude to his guests, even under these trying circumstances. He therefore gives a warm welcome to the newly married captain's wife and lays open the wine cellar. So it is that when more senior officers appear on the scene some weeks later, they find the dragoons happily working the vineyards for the elderly Myburgh and taking their orders from him rather than from their captain. There is no record of Philip ever taking the oath to the English King.

—End Nexus Familia

America doubles in size

With the resumption of hostilities with Britain, Napoleon found himself in a difficult financial position. His profitable colony of Haiti had seen its African slaves revolt and, to the horror of all, the slaves had prevailed. With the loss of this profitable colony, Napoleon had to make a plan for money. At this point, the Spaniards threatened the American economy by suspending the arrangement that allowed Americans to store their trade goods at the port of New Orleans. Almost miraculously, it turned out that, according to the secret treaty of San Ildefonso between France and Spain, New Orleans was to revert to France. Interests coincided and Napoleon sold the entire stretch of land defined by the western tributaries of the Mississippi to the United States at the unbelievably low price of $15M. The Americans were now owners of a stretch of land that doubled the size of the United States. The deal was financed by the British Barings Bank and by Hope & Company of Amsterdam. So, ironically, the October 1, 1803 "Louisiana Purchase" financed Napoleon's war against Britain using British money. The United States was strengthened while Britain and France proceeded to weaken each other, a fact that would soon enough dramatically affect the Cape.

In 1806, the Lewis and Clark expedition was sent to explore the mysterious upper reaches of the Missouri River, which cut through the new territory. In a letter dated June 20, 1803, President Jefferson wrote to Captain Meriwether Lewis, leader of the expedition:

"The object of your mission is to explore the Missouri river, and such principal stream of it as by its course and communication with the waters of the Pacific Ocean whether the Columbia, Oregon, Colorado or any other river may offer the most direct and practicable water communication across this continent for the purposes of commerce."

Thirty years later, we shall meet its tragic equivalent in South Africa – also seeking an ocean.

The American and the proto-Marxist

In South Africa, Van der Kemp's joy knew no bounds when the British re-occupied the Cape. Now he would be able to return to the frontier to yet again attempt to "convert the amaXhosa, liberate the Khoekhoe and consign all Westerners to hell by any means, fair or foul." To his horror, he found that the new magistrate appointed at Uitenhage to administer justice in the *Suurveld* was one Captain Jacob Cuyler, late of the 59th regiment of Infantry. He was an American Loyalist from Albany and of 4th generation Dutch extraction with no concept of the British version of the Enlightenment whatsoever.

His father and grandfather had been mayors of Albany or, as the Dutch had known it, Fort Oranje. His father had fled to Canada at the time of the War of Independence, and had there been appointed a judge. Jacob had joined the British Army. History records that he brought with him his own gravestone, pre-inscribed with his date of birth. He was famously short-tempered and visited fire and brimstone upon the head of anyone who dared question his decisions in any matter.

As with both the first British occupation and the Batavian government, Cuyler very quickly came to the same conclusions as the Afrikaners on the matter of Van der Kemp and his Bethelsdorp LMS mission station. Lichtenstein[2], an independent witness, described the place as follows in his famous "Travels":

"This convenient mode of getting themselves fed attracted many of the most worthless and idle among these people. [...] ...nowhere the least trace of human industry: wherever the eye is cast, nothing is presented but lean, ragged, or naked figures, with indolent sleepy countenances."

Though it would be many more years before Karl Marx would formulate his thoughts on egalitarian Marxism, Van der Kemp was living it in its most raw form, sliding from Western Civilization into a lowest common denominator existence that would have insulted Eva Krotoa's original Khoekhoe beachcomber existence. Read, Van der Kemp's assistant, described their diet as:

"... a little milk and water for breakfast and tea, perhaps a little sour milk for dinner or some wild roots or berries when the old Hottentot women came home from the fields in the afternoon."

Certainly, the Protestant Work Ethic had no place at Bethelsdorp. This image of indolence remained with that desolate place into the 20th century. Read cemented his belief in this kind of existence by marrying a Khoekhoe girl whose entire estate, as reported by Van der Kemp, was two sheepskins and a string of beads.

At the other cultural extreme was Cuyler, who had the twin job of being magistrate of Uitenhage and military commander of Fort Frederick. Van der Kemp was ardent and inflexible in fighting for the continued existence of the peculiar culture in Bethelsdorp. Cuyler, for his part, maintained in a letter of 8 April 1807 to the Colonial Secretary that the Khoekhoe were being...

...*"enticed [...] through the arts and insinuations of Mr. Van der Kemp, to the great injury of the inhabitants of the country."*

Forced to live there, the British representatives with responsibility for security now agreed with the Afrikaners regarding matters on the frontier.

The "Hottentot Magna Carta"

It was while Van der Kemp was embedding this culture in Bethelsdorp in 1807 that the British abolished the slave trade. The Batavian Dutch government of Janssens & De Mist already banned the importation of slaves before the second British invasion, but the British step made it formal in the English world. As a result, slave labor was now becoming scarce and expensive. Meanwhile, Van der Kemp was actively withdrawing the services of the Khoekhoe from the colony by providing them with a life of vagrancy around the mission stations. Simultaneously he was doing his best to sketch the farmers as the embodiment of all evil. The situation erupted into a war of letters between Van der Kemp, the Governor and Cuyler, who demanded Van der Kemp be removed from the combustible frontier.

On 22 May 1807, came a new governor to the Cape: Du Pré Alexander, Earl of Caledon. Having studied the situation, his solution in October 1809 was simple. He guaranteed due process under the law for Khoekhoe people, but they had to register a fixed address. This measure was to stop the theft and vagrancy about which burghers were complaining. At the same time, Khoekhoe people employed by farmers had to be given proper contracts, but the Khoekhoe employees also had to have passes from such farmers if they were going to leave the farmers' premises. This system has been referred to as the *"Hottentot Magna Carta,"* but this

British invention was a form of indenture without choice. Here in 1809 we find again the British roots of the later infamous Pass Laws of South Africa. It made work on burgher farms essentially the only possible existence for Khoekhoe people beyond emigration from the Cape. Cuyler placed ever-tougher restrictions on the people at Bethelsdorp. Then, by a very nasty piece of subterfuge, he also arrested the last captain of the free Khoekhoe in the colony, David Stuurman (brother of Klaas, who had been murdered), at his "reservation" (to use an American term) on the Gamtoos River. David Stuurman was sent to Robben Island to work in chains.

And so it is that a Loyalist American was the man to erase the last trace of free Khoekhoe existence in the Cape Colony. It is here with the Khoekhoe that one sees the parallel between the experience of Native Americans and the Native African. The parallel is pointedly not with the black Ba'Ntu people of Africa.

On 30 August 1808, Read sent a message[3] to the London Headquarters of the London Missionary Society, over the head of governor Caledon. He attacked the Afrikaner burghers, lambasted Cuyler and Caledon, and generally described the white people at the Cape in such derogatory terms that a full two hundred years have not restored any modicum of balance to their image. He implored:

> *"...the friends to humanity in the Society [...] assist us [...] to use active means to discover and punish these crimes."*

Westminster asked that Caledon investigate. Read and Van der Kemp, having drawn blood, attacked again[4]:

> *"Major Cuyler who was unfortunately appointed to investigate the matter has married one of these farmers' daughters* [Maria Elisabeth Hartman]*, of course shutting his ears to the poor Hottentots."*

An outraged Cuyler summoned Read to explain, but Read appealed directly to the now very influential William Wilberforce, claiming *"upwards of a hundred murders"* had been committed by Afrikaner farmers. Wilberforce contacted the Colonial Secretary who said *"the honor of the British name"* demanded *"Exemplary punishment."* In response, Caledon constituted a Circuit Court to hear charges against Afrikaner farmers, and then left the Cape, like the string of governors before him who had absented themselves after instigating policies they would not have to account for. Before the so-called Black Circuit Court could set off, trouble on the frontier intervened.

The Fourth Frontier War

In July 1809, the strife between amaRharhabe regent Ndlambe and rightful heir Ngqika had come to a head and the Right-hand houses were pouring back into the *Suurveld*, encroaching on the colony. By the end of 1809, it was the same old story again. Khoekhoe herders had been killed and stock driven off by the amaXhosa. The Peninsular War against Napoleon was at its peak and the Cape was ill defended. The amaXhosa were brazenly trespassing on the colony and letter after letter by the frontier Magistrates make the dire situation of the colonists quite clear. Alone on their farms, the isolated men could not very well defend their families and farms against the massive hordes of amaXhosa that challenged them, simply doing as they pleased on their property. Some small groups of amaXhosa had penetrated halfway westward through the colony. The Swedish-Afrikaner[5] magistrate of Graaff-Reinet, Anders Stockenström, reported to the Cape[6]:

> *"I have no manner of doubt but some troops of kaffers* (sic) *will proceed to the Cape, if they are not already arrived"*

The success of the intimidation campaign by the amaXhosa was obviously stimulating their belligerence in primal fashion. It was in the middle of this dangerous situation that Governor Caledon resigned and left for Britain. He had done his bit. The two magistrates of the frontier districts — the "American Dutchman" (Amerikaner) Cuyler, and the "African Dutchman" (Afrikaner) Stockenström — appealed directly to the Cape Governor for help on a grand scale. The new governor, Cradock, was a tough, short-tempered military man who had been replaced by Wellington in the Peninsular Campaign. He was hugely upset at having been sent to this backwater away from the "real" action. He was about to take that out on the amaXhosa.

Cradock had made up his mind to remove Ndlambe from power, drive his people across the Fish River, and acknowledge Ngqika as paramount chief, though by now he was hated by many of the amaXhosa. In the year 2001, that would be called "Regime Change" and would have the same attendant problems. As overall commander, Cradock chose Lieutenant-Colonel Graham, who had arrived with the 1806 British invasion. Martial Law was declared and several hundred Afrikaner farmers were called up for military service within their established Commando structure under regional Field-Cornets. This recognition of reality was diametrically different from the British military reaction in 1799, and there were three reasons:

1. The British had finally realized the fallacy in cutting off the gunpowder supply to the very men who shared their interest in defending the border, as they had done in 1799.

2. They remembered and acknowledged their ignominious defeat at the hand of the amaXhosa in a form of warfare they themselves did not understand in the least, but the Afrikaners did after decades of fighting.

3. Earlier in 1809 the Government had sent an exceptionally brave, dedicated, competent, and accomplished man, Lt-Col. Richard Collins, to assess matters on the frontier. He came away with a very positive impression of the Afrikaner farmers. He returned with much more than his masters had hoped: a comprehensive plan for the military and political stabilization of the colony for the following 25 years. A key element in this plan was his recommendation[7] that the mainstay of the defense should be Jan Van Riebeeck's Afrikaner Commando system. British colonial interests would henceforth be defended and its policies imposed with Afrikaner blood:

> *"... they would be considerably more useful than regular troops. They are well acquainted with the country; are excellent marksmen; are accustomed to bear fatigues and privations, and are provided with horses fit for all the purposes of irregular cavalry, without being subject to the disadvantages of requiring stabling and dry forage...*
> *... the farmers should be made the principal instrument of hostility against that people* [the amaXhosa].*"*

It is a strategic tragedy that this unique man did not remain at the Cape to become governor. He was subsequently wounded in the Napoleonic War and provided with an extensive prosthetic. Despite his disabled condition, he insisted on returning to the fray, and was eventually killed in battle. This was a great loss indeed. Collins' report on the Cape Colony was a masterpiece of investigation, insight, analysis, and policy. History would have been very different indeed with this man at the helm.

Nexus Familia 39: Treachery at the Ridge of Thorns

The *Suurveld* is a transitional region consisting of stretches of sour grass country, through which rivers carve their paths to the Indian Ocean. The rivers are flanked by impenetrable thickets of acacia karoo thorn trees, red-flowering Boer bean, prehistoric-looking euphorbia, and flowering creepers like plumbago and brick red Cape honeysuckle. The *acacia karoo* tree has multiple-inch-long red-tipped spikes that will penetrate the sole of a shoe with ease. In more protected ravines, bigger trees like celtis africana ("stinkwood") grow, entwined with "monkey-rope" lianas.

Into this treacherous terrain Col. Graham's advance on the *Suurveld* amaXhosa is taking place on three fronts: The British Captain George Fraser is leading the bulk of the Khoekhoe Cape Corps up the middle, along with Lt.-Col. Graham himself. The Amerikaner magistrate of Uitenhage, Jacob Cuyler, has crossed the

Sundays (Zondaghs) River with his men along the coast, heading for Ndlambe's kraal or Great Place. On the third front, posted to the north of the *Suurveld* behind the Suurberg, is the Swedish Afrikaner magistrate of Graaff-Reinet, Anders Stockenström, leading a Boer Commando with orders to protect the farming community of Bruintjeshoogte and Graaff-Reinet. His son, Ensign Andries Stockenström junior, at this time a young officer in the Cape Corps, is his aide-de-camp.

One of the Boer Commando leaders implicitly trusted by Stockenström is Jacobus Potgieter. He is the great grandson of the original immigrant, Harmen Jan Potgieter who hailed from Nordhorn in Germany. Jacobus and Jan Christoffel Greyling, another Boer in this same Commando, are married to two sisters, Maria and Magdalena de Wet. Back on the farm in the remote Tarka, Jacobus' children include Jacobus Jr., more popularly known as "Koos Greatfoot," and his sister, Isabella. (See *Chapters 10, 11* and *12*).

When magistrate Cuyler, the Loyalist "Dutch Amerikaner," goes out on

Fig. 7.2 *The Suurveld bush can hide an army*

a patrol near the coast on the 26th of December 1811, he happens upon none less than Ndlambe himself in full battle regalia. Ndlambe steps forward out of the thicket, stamps his foot and shouts his famous statement[8]:

> *"This country is mine! I won it in war...!"*

Then he shakes his assegai at Cuyler, blows on an animal horn and his men yell and charge, but the battle fizzles out and the amaXhosa disappear into the dense bush. Ndlambe, by his own statement has just confessed that his people have not always lived there, as so many would have one believe. As a result of Ndlambe's demonstration, Graham now knows he is facing the main force of the Suurveld Xhosa army. The very next day Graham sends a unit of the Khoekhoe-based Cape Corps to ask Stockenström to join him with his Boer force on the central front.

Stockenström senior has meanwhile met with hereditary amaRharhabe Chief Ngqika beyond the Fish River. Ngqika has undertaken to stay out of the colony's fight with his uncle, Ndlambe, as long as the British force will not cross the Fish River. Stockentröm therefore has some faith in the power of parley. Two days later, on 29 December 1811, Stockenström, somehow accompanied by only a San Bushman helper and some 24 of the Boere[9], including specifically brothers-in-law Jacobus Potgieter and Jan Greyling, sets out to reach Graham. Graham is at this time some distance upstream from the mouth of the Zondaghs River. Stockenström takes the route via the so-called Suurberg Pass.

The Suurberg range is a severely folded mountain range, comprising two parallel east-west ranges with only one "neck"[10] joining the two. This unique spot is called Doringnek – the Ridge of Thorns. To its west flows the White River and to its east, the Coerney. And so it is that, on this fateful day, Stockenström is approaching the narrowest part of Doringnek from the north with his company of 25 men. However, the Boere are not the only people who understand the strategic significance of the ridge. The amaXhosa also know the lay of the land.

As they crest the range the Boer party sees a group of imiDange Xhosa at Doringnek. Jacobus warns Stockenström not to stop and that they should proceed along their way, keeping their arms at the ready. Stockenström, styling himself a diplomat after his earlier success with Ngqika, decides otherwise and commands the 25 men to stop and dismount. The Xhosa know Stockenström and they are impressed with his fearless behavior. A Khoekhoe helper of the imiDange is sent to fetch milk for the honored guest, as is the amaXhosa custom. The helper is Antonie, one of Stuurman's people who fought the British at the turn of the century. Quite a number of the late Klaas Stuurman's people are with the amaXhosa and are led by Klaas' brother, David, who has escaped from Robben Island (See *"The Hottentot Magna Carta"*).

Fig. 7-3 Doringnek on the Suurberg

Stockenström becomes absorbed in his discussion with the imiDange and waves away his men who warn him that they are being surrounded. He would know by now that it is fatal to ever show fear in a barbarous land like Africa. At this juncture, the Khoekhoe helper returns with the milk in one hand and his assegai in the other. As the Khoekhoe helper gives Stockenström the milk, he suddenly drives the assegai into the back[11] of the grey-bearded magistrate. This is the signal for the rest of the imiDange to fall upon Jacobus, Jan and the other Boere. All three of these men die in this treacherous act and so do 12 others. Eight of the men manage to reach their horses and escape southward toward Graham's camp in the *Suurveld*. Two cannot reach their horses, but somehow manage to hide in some dense thicket and make their way back during the night on foot. The San Bushman helper escapes to give the tragic message to young Andries Stockenström. Andries and the rest of the Boer force immediately set off for Doringnek, where they wreak a frightful vengeance on the swirling mass of imiDange Xhosa. Then they withdraw back to their laager.

In the *Suurveld*, Graham receives a request for parley from Ndlambe, who suggests that the foot of the Suurberg would be an ideal meeting place. Graham actually sets off to attend with a small contingent of mounted men. What follows is the usual process by which a white man stands in an open field and his interpreter calls out until a disembodied Xhosa voice finally responds from the bush. Having ascertained that it is safe to do so, Ndlambe appears and Graham's little force is surrounded. The elderly Ndlambe now expresses his belief that he legally bought the *Suurveld* from a Magistrate of Graaff-Reinet for a herd of oxen – an obvious reference to the Woeke story that has permeated frontier Boer society since 1793, back in the VOC days (*NF29*, section 3).

In the middle of this, two Afrikaner messengers calmly ride up out of the bushes, pass carefully among the stationary amaXhosa ring, and hand a note[12] to Graham without batting an eyelid. Graham also keeps his wits about him. He announces that the note is from the Governor of the Cape, telling him the land belongs to the amaXhosa and that he must withdraw. He salutes Ndlambe, tells his incredulous men to mount, and they leave the area with the bemused amaXhosa staring at them as they leave. When they have ridden a safe distance, Graham halts and reads the note aloud to his men. It relates how Magistrate Stockenström and 14 others have just been killed in exactly the kind of parley situation they have themselves been in minutes before. The men thereupon dismount and kneel to do prayer. They are in awe of the two brave Afrikaners who rode into the ring of death to deliver the message with such nonchalance to the British commander.

The treacherous murder of Stockenström, Jacobus Potgieter, Jan Greyling, and the other 12 men seals the fate of the imiDange. The amaXhosa will later explain that, during the meeting with Stockenström, word arrived that hostilities had already begun between Ndlambe and Cuyler. As far as they were concerned, they had the leader of their enemy in their hands and therefore they killed him.

In the weeks that follow, Graham shows no ounce of mercy to the various amaXhosa groups. He destroys and burns down everything, including their food, houses and pasture, driving tens of thousands of amaXhosa over the Fish River. The amaXhosa beg to be allowed to stay to bring in the harvest, but Graham orders the crops to be trampled by a herd of 600 oxen and the resulting mess burnt. He spends several weeks making sure of the total destruction of all Xhosa resources. Then he issues an order that any amaXhosa found in the colony is to be shot unless he has a pass from chief Ngqika, whom most Suurveld amaXhosa refuse to acknowledge. Britain is now the master of the Eastern Frontier and aims to impose its authority. A year later John Campbell, a LMS man[13], will visit the *Suurveld* and write:

> *"...now not a living soul is to be found, universal stillness reigns."*

The Fourth Frontier War was the first concerted British military effort against the amaXhosa. After this, British authority in the *Suurveld* was centered on a new town laid out on the burnt out farm of the Afrikaner Lucas Meyer, one of the men who had been sentenced to banishment for his part in the Van Jaarsveld Rebellion (*NF33*). The symbolism was not lost on the Afrikaners.

The Afrikaners were getting tired of being a protective human barrier for British interests, given the treatment they suffered in peacetime, and therefore did not rush to repopulate the region. The new town was to be known as Grahamstown, and the district of the *Suurveld* was henceforth to be known as Albany, named after none other than Albany, New York, Jacob Cuyler's place of birth in America. This was the first time that Britain practiced a "Scorched Earth" policy in South Africa. It was not to be the last.

—*End Nexus Familia*

British Prejudice and Frontier Reality

The extreme tactics of the British against the amaXhosa did not sit well with the Afrikaners, who understood full well that they would have to live with the consequences of the actions of British officers after they had retired to the comforts of England. At the other extreme of the spectrum, the activities of the London Missionary Society troubled them greatly. They realized that the LMS was inciting the Khoekhoe population against them. In the event, it would take another forty years for the British Government to come to this same conclusion when the Khoekhoe under the ministration of the LMS would go into open rebellion. As for British prejudice, the Loyalist American Cuyler initially described the frontier Afrikaners as *"all a set of vagabonds and murderers."* After he had lived with their daily challenges, however, he considered them *"neighbors and friends."* For his part, Graham had called them *"the most ignorant of all peasants"* when he originally arrived. After the Frontier War, he said[14]:

> *"Finer fellows there cannot be...much more hardy than I had any idea of [...] I never in my life saw more orderly, willing and obedient men than the Boers, and whenever they have been engaged have behaved with much spirit, and always most ready and willing to go upon any enterprise."*

So, the front line military leadership of the British at the Cape was much taken with the hardy *"Dutch"* Afrikaners.

Clearly, already in 1811, there was a problem in that people would come to South Africa with what can at best be described as self-righteous hypocritical condescension. They looked down upon the supposedly ignorant Afrikaner burgher whose Dutch name of "Boer" unfortunately sounded all too much like the English "Boor." After a few run-ins with the indigenous people of Africa, the visitor almost invariably came round to the Afrikaner's view of the realities of living in South Africa.

Significantly though, there would always be the London Missionary Society and its adherents. These people took out their racial self-loathing, created by their sense of guilt over English slavery, on whoever looked a bit like themselves and who happened to be normal, well-adjusted people, fending for their families on a desperately dangerous continent. All the time those critics who gathered comfortably in their clubs in

England remained deluded about being "humanitarians" when they dispatched a "Scorched Earth" army to Africa. In Africa, the Afrikaner saw these two dichotomous aspects of the English national psyche in the form of the heavy-handed British Army and the London Missionary Society.

Back in Europe the London Missionary Society spread the word[15] that:

> "*The Dutch peasantry at the Cape of Good Hope are among the basest, the most cruel and the most degraded beings on the face of the earth...*"

From the Afrikaner perspective, if the British Army did not have much insight into their predicament on the outer wall of Western Civilization, then at least it had adequate power and, apparently, the willpower to actually use it. This was an improvement on the hapless Dutch VOC rule that they had suffered before. Notions that the "Dutch" population resented the British authority because it was British are simply misplaced. They were desperate for competent authority, but they resented being oppressed and were utterly desperate for a say in their own destiny. Surely, Americans, in particular, could understand this.

The Black Circuit

The war on the encroaching amaXhosa having been successfully completed, and the Afrikaners having served the purposes of their British overlords in that war, the first of the "Black Circuit" Courts designed to assail them in the civil domain left Cape Town on 23 September 1812. Here we have the moment that the Afrikaner realized clearly that the "English" government at the Cape was not his protector but his persecutor. In the end, the Court brought charges against twenty-eight Boere, including some of murder. There were eight convictions for assault and several for illegal detention of wages. Every single murder charge was dismissed for lack of evidence. The accused had to carry all the court costs, whether innocent or not. The damage was done. The reaction of the judges is quoted by William Charles Scully[16]:

> "*If the reformers, Messrs. van der Kemp and Read, had taken the trouble to have gone into a summary and impartial investigation of the different stories related to them, many of those complaints which had made such a noise as well within as without the Colony, must have been considered by themselves as existing in imagination only.*"

Reporting on Bethelsdorp, the six judges said :

> "*The late Dr. van der Kemp established such an overstrained principle of liberty as the groundwork, that the natural state of the barbarians appears there to supersede civilization and social order...*
>
> [...] *Laziness and idleness and consequent dirt and filth grow there to perfection, ...*
>
> [...] *It is certainly not to be denied but that some of the Bethelsdorp Hottentots in former times suffered injuries from some of the farmers;* [...] *but at the same time it is not the less true that there are many Hottentots at Bethelsdorp who have had a considerable part in plundering, robbing, setting fire to places, and even murdering the inhabitants;...*"

The Afrikaners were incensed at this constant outrage fomented by the hate-driven missionaries of the LMS. They saw the whole exercise as an attempt to force them to the same lowly and degraded form of existence as that which Van der Kemp had promoted at Bethelsdorp. Some eight years before, Janssens of the Batavian Dutch government had personally warned Van der Kemp against his unthinking passionate hatred of the white Afrikaners, but he had taken no notice. With this "Black Circuit," as it became known, the focus of England, then the center of the Anglophone universe, was placed on race relations in South Africa. For the rest of the existence of South Africa that focus would remain there and it would remain as skewed as what Read painted it in 1808. The two proto-Marxist Liberation Theologists, Read and Van der Kemp, are responsible for what went wrong in South Africa. They brought racial hatred to the frontier in the name of God and promoted hatred of the Afrikaner in Europe. Their one-sided portrayal of the Afrikaner would never be lived down. They sketched the Afrikaner as the "Skunk of Civilization," and there he would remain to this very day, with never a voice or the smallest opportunity to correct the picture. And that picture would later be exported to the United States by parties who benefited.

History provided the rebuttal to the Black Circuit, in the form of the Hon. Henry Cloete. He was a young court reporter in those proceedings. Years later, in the 1850's he presented a series of lectures in which he made a well defined condemnation of the entire effort in his famous Three Lectures[17]. The problem is, the damage was done, and London had been left forever with a stereotype image of the Afrikaner. Van der Kemp, instigator of this perversion of justice, died on 9 December 1811 before the commencement of the infamous Black Circuit Courts. Had he lived, he might have seen the ravages his handiwork visited upon the Eastern Frontier. Nevertheless, the damage he had done survives to this day. To the Afrikaner, it had become clear that his own concerns would never be addressed by the British. Despite the comments of the judges, no serious action was taken to address the situation of the frontiersmen.

The Second Great Abandonment

In April of 1814, the Allies in Europe finally defeated Napoleon and forced him to abdicate. They exiled him to the island of Elba. On 13 August 1814, in a forgotten sideshow to the central thread of history, the Dutch finally recognized the permanent British ownership of the Cape and various other parts of their former empire in return for a payment of 3 million pounds sterling and free access to refreshment at the Cape. Just as the Amerikaners in New Amsterdam had heard in 1674 that the Dutch had traded them for Suriname, so it was now the turn of the Afrikaners. Ten years before Percival, who apparently detested the Dutch, had described them as follows[18]:

> *"Avarice is the only passion, and wealth the only merit in the United Provinces."*

Herewith the Dutch finally deserted their kin in exchange for coin. There was no attempt to guarantee Afrikaners' right to residence in Holland or anything of the kind. They were simply sold to the British – lock, stock and barrel. To this very day, the Dutch do not accept that Afrikaners, despite being their direct descendants, have any right of "return" to the country that placed them in Africa. As to the reaction in the Cape, we turn to William Wilberforce Bird[19]:

> *"If you tell a Cape-Dutchman, that, by the treaty of Paris, he and all his family were sold for thirty-three pounds sterling per head, that being the amount at which, as one of 90,000, he was valued, when three millions were paid to the King of the Netherlands, he becomes most indignant."*

At the same time, the very same people were paying several hundreds of British pounds[20] for a slave. Forgetting the justifiable outrage for a moment, it is crucially important for the reader to understand that since 1814 the Afrikaner has had nowhere else to go. That was the date on which he ceased to be a "settler" or a "colonist" or any of these phrases that black nationalists are so quick to use in the 21st century.

One is dealing here with a Western Judeo-Christian Caucasian nation that is permanently married to Africa until death do them part. At no point in the painful history of the country has a Western country ever offered residence to the Afrikaners as a group. When the French control of Algeria was to fail much later, the French settlers would be entitled to return to France. When the British colonies in Africa would become independent, the British descendants would be able to return to Britain. When the Portuguese colonies would collapse in the 1970s, the Portuguese would eventually fly eight hundred thousand of their people out.

For the Afrikaner there has never been anywhere else to go since August 1814. It is indeed true that the Afrikaner had to look at himself in the mirror in that year and say,

> *"I am become the forsaken White Tribe of Africa ...the amaBhulu."*

Slagtersnek – a place of infamy

On a bluff overlooking a bend in the Great Fish River, some few miles south of the drab little 21st century railway town of Cookhouse in the Eastern Cape Province, stands a neglected memorial. It represents the vital center of gravity—the *Schwerpunkt*—of South African history. For the next one hundred and fifty years people would point to events at this spot as the root cause of every wrong in the country after 1815.

On the heels of the Fourth Frontier War and the Black Circuit, Governor Sir John Cradock implemented a new quitrent system for measuring, working, and taxing farms. He wanted to consolidate the population into a more settled—read "English"—way of life so that they would "work the land." The frontier Afrikaners, however, had learned the hard way that poor soil quality and the hugely unreliable rainfall made herding cattle and keeping sheep on large stretches of land a more pragmatic existence than any form of agriculture. Sitting in Cape Town's lush vineyards in 1000 mm per annum rainfall, he had little concept of the southern Camdeboo with its less than 300mm per annum rainfall and tough drought-resistant vegetation (See *Fig. 4-5*). This would be equivalent to a British governor sitting in bucolic Pennsylvania countryside trying to force agriculture on the cattlemen of the dry American West. The British had little if any concept of the practicalities of ranching, and largely still do not today.

As with Caledon, who left before seeing the result of the first of his Black Circuit Courts, Cradock now retired to England before seeing the consequences of his farm registration and taxation process. The intrepid Colonel Graham of "scorched Earth" infamy likewise returned to Europe to join the renewed fight against Napoleon. Significantly, Jacob Cuyler, the Loyalist American magistrate of Uitenhage, remained.

To the British, the Cape was only of military significance. Hence the Cape saw a succession of military governors, all with either experience in fighting Napoleon in Europe or with aspirations of doing so, the latest being Lord Charles Somerset (See Chapter 8). The Cape was to them merely a stepping-stone to a better commission. One therefore had the Afrikaners living under the heel of the British military. London saw all clashes in the east of the Colony as "adventures" to be avoided as these diverted troops from the defense of the Cape. The frontiers Afrikaners were merely an irritation to the British. On the other hand, via their extensive cattle ranching these ranchers were the providers of the all-important meat for the British via the Cape. For their part, the Afrikaners had, like their distant "Jacobin" American cousins, long ceased to look at Europe as some form of "home." They knew it not, nor did they care for it anymore. To them, it simply seemed like a place from which rulers were sent to govern them to their detriment, even as they were stuck in a three-way struggle for survival against the elements, the San Bushmen and the amaXhosa and beset by "vagrant Mission Station Khoekhoe." Would there then never be a government that cared about their interests?

Already the British had imprisoned the best leader they had ever had, Adriaan van Jaarsveld, on charges relating to a mortgage. Van Jaarsveld had died under suspicious circumstances in British captivity in 1801. Therewith the Afrikaners had lost their "George Washington." Since then there had been the outrageous and scandalous Black Circuit and now the British were even attempting to instruct them how they should survive in a country they had known for one hundred and sixty years and on a frontier where they had already been settled for going on three generations. They had respect for the British, who had shown themselves to be vastly more competent than the Dutch VOC. However, the British seemed to oscillate between treating the Afrikaner as a private army on the one hand, but persecuting them on the other.

Moreover, the standing army at the Cape was the Khoekhoe-based Cape Corps and some highly suspect "British" regiments that were really mercenary and semi-penal units.

The American equivalent would have been a British magistrate employing only troops of Cherokee descent to haul European settlers to court in the early 1800s. Such a policy had to have been practiced with malice aforethought. Against this background, the bungled arrest of a gout-ridden farmer would poison history for close on two centuries.

Nexus Familia 40: Where men die Twice

The Baviaans River (Baboon River) Valley runs northeastward into the Winterberg from the Fish River. One can pass over the mountain at Groene Nek (Green Neck) to enter the Tarka, most distant part of the frontier. In the valley live a number of families in multi-family clusters. These include the families Bezuidenhout (*NF29*, section 5) and Klopper (*NF36*).

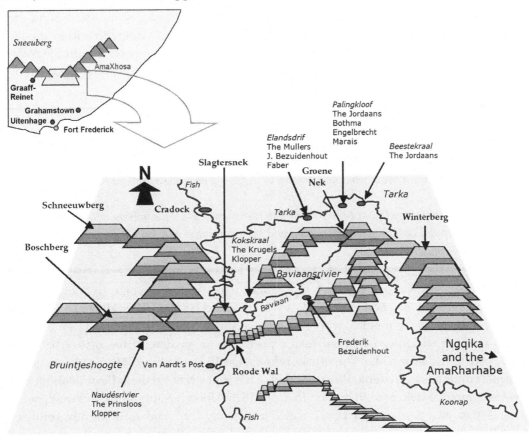

Fig. 7-4 *The vicinity of the Baviaans River Gorge*

At the foot of the Boschberg, live the Prinsloos (*NF36*), still on the farm of Willem the Elder (*NF27*). The family is under the leadership of the 62-year old Marthinus, better known as "Marthinus Kasteel (Castle)" who spent time in jail in the Castle in Cape Town for leading the Van Jaarsveld Rebellion of 1799 (*NF33*). Marthinus is married to the sister of Johannes Klopper, our direct Klopper ancestor. Marthinus' son, Hendrik Frederik, by now known as "Hendrik Kasteel," lives on the farm and so does Hendrik Petrus Klopper, who has married the widow of Marthinus' other son.

Our ancestor Pieter Johannes Jordaan (*NF28*) and his brother Johannes moved to the Tarka before 1799 and now reside on the farms *Palingkloof* (Eel Gorge) and *Beestekraal* (Cattle Corral). They have been in the Tarka since at least 1799. Pieter's first wife, Maria Snyman, gave him six children, including our ancestor Chris Jordaan, born 1808. When Maria died in 1814, Chris married Maria de Wet, the widow of Field-Cornet

Jacobus Potgieter, who was so treacherously murdered by the imiDange at Doringnek (*NF39*). Maria has brought eight children of her own, including son Jacobus Christoffel, who has a big future role to play in our story. Maria de Wet's sister, Magdalena, the widow of Jan Greyling who died in the same treacherous event along with Jacobus Potgieter, has recently married a man named Pieter Retief; who is destined to become a leader of the nation.

1. Making an example

It all starts in April 1813, with the dreaded Black Circuit Court uppermost in everyone's minds. The first of these LMS-instigated mobile Anti-Afrikaner "Inquisitions" left Cape Town recently on 12 September 1812. In the middle of this tense political situation, a Khoekhoe man named Booy complains to Deputy Magistrate Andries Stockenström Jr. at Graaff-Reinet about his employer, a certain Frederik Cornelis Bezuidenhout.

Frederik is none other than the 55-year old brother of our ancestor Coenraad (*NF 32*). Frederik lives on a farm overlooking the Baviaans River. His brother Johannes, two years his senior, also lives in the district. Johannes is married to Anna Elizabeth "Martha" Faber and has a son, not quite ten years old, named Gerrit. Andries Stockenström is the son of the murdered Magistrate Anders Stockenström (*NF39*) and used to be an Ensign in the Khoekhoe Cape Corps. Frederik Bezuidenhout lives on his farm with a Khoekhoe woman and his son, Hans, by that woman. When summoned[21] by the Magistrate in connection with the matter of Booy, Frederik Bezuidenhout responds with a letter to the Deputy Magistrate dated 28 June 1813, stating about the Khoekhoe Booy:

> *"...he and his wife still owe me two oxen, which they borrowed from me [...]*
>
> *He has made away with 21 sheep of mine, and one new spade he has destroyed; another he broke to pieces.*
>
> *Now, it is my friendly request that Mr. Landdrost sends aforesaid Hottentot again to me with a letter. If he comes back, I do not care much about what he owes me, or the loss which he has caused me: of both I will forgo a part.*
>
> *I would certainly come myself, but I cannot possibly leave home, as I have nobody with me except my son, of which the Field-Cornet also cannot otherwise testify, and I also hope that Mr. Landdrost will not take it amiss in me that I cannot come myself."*

After the district Field-Cornet, Philip A. Opperman, explains the situation to Booy, the latter happily engages with Bezuidenhout for another year. However, the feud between Bezuidenhout and Booy flares up again and drags on over several months, with the cantankerous Bezuidenhout at one point reputedly striking Booy with his walking stick. Bezuidenhout asks Opperman, to mediate in the matter before Booy again *"vilifies* [him] *before the Landdrost,"* but Opperman refuses. On 10 December 1814, the Messenger of the Court delivers a formal summons to Frederik. When the day of the trial starts, Frederik Bezuidenhout is absent from court. A final summons is delivered to him on 15 April 1815. Upon receipt of this, Frederik loses his temper and declares, *"What does Stockenström think? I care not for my life,"* and now bluntly refuses to appear. Stockenström thereupon writes to the Magistrate, a certain Fischer, that, *"in view of the protection* [he] *owe*[s] *the Hottentot"* and in view of the danger in *"overlooking all this,"* an *"example should be made"* of Frederik Cornelis Bezuidenhout.

In late September 1815, Hendrik (later Sir Henry) Cloete, at this time court reporter for the Black Circuit Court, takes an undated deposition from Field-Cornet Opperman. Opperman testifies to the feud between Frederik and Booy and also that he originally understood from others that Frederik was sickly, suffered from gout and walked with crutches, but that when he last saw Frederik, the latter was "hale and hearty."

The implication of this is that, specifically by Opperman's testimony, Frederik has no medical reason for being absent from Court. Frederik is therefore sentenced in absentia to one month in prison, with the rest of Booy's claims still to be heard. As is so typical of British authority at the Cape at this time, no attempt whatsoever is made to investigate Frederik's claims against Booy. Given the background of intense distrust and danger on the eastern frontier, what happens next has an air of inevitability about it.

2. Enter Andries Stockenström

When Deputy-Bailiff Johannes Londt sets out to arrest Frederik Bezuidenhout, both Field-Cornet Opperman and Field-Cornet Olivier refuse to have anything to do with this process. Opperman claims that he has already indicated his unhappiness to Deputy-Magistrate Andries Stockenström, and is seeking different instruction. Olivier insists it is not his jurisdiction but rather that of Opperman. Londt, a native of the Netherlands, then proceeds to two military outposts to obtain help. And so it is that a military troop composed of a Lieutenant Rousseau, Lieutenant Mackay, a sergeant, a corporal and 14 men set off. Most of the men are Khoekhoe of the so-called "Cape Regiment" in which Stockenström has been an officer. It is somehow considered appropriate to take 18 soldiers to support a deputy bailiff to arrest one sickly farmer. Not only that, but the soldiers are largely of the ethnic group that is the subject of the unhappiness on the frontier as well as in this particular dispute. The sergeant is a certain Khoekhoe, "Joseph," with no surname.

Matters take a distinctly sinister turn when this military troop refuses to identify its mission to farmers who question them along the way. When they arrive at Field-Cornet Opperman's farm at 10pm at night, they pointedly mislead him as to their mission, claiming they are on the way to Grahamstown. However, they do manage somehow to extract Bezuidenhout's Christian names from Opperman along with directions to the Bezuidenhout farm, all without Opperman supposedly realizing their purpose. Marching through the night, the troop arrives at 9 a.m. the following morning at Frederik's farm. Hans, Frederik's half-Khoekhoe son (the Court will later refer to him as *The Bastard Hottentot*), has warned his father that a veritable army of King's soldiers is approaching. As a consequence, Frederik has taken up a defensive position outside his house, aided by Hans and another resident of the farm, Jacob Erasmus.

When the soldiers approach, Frederik shouts to them to halt, or be shot. Lieutenant Rousseau then orders the soldiers to fix bayonets and to storm Frederik's position. At this point, Frederik fires about 12 rounds at them. He and his two helpers then retreat into two caves with their guns and ammunition. Eventually, the soldiers track them down. Erasmus surrenders, but Frederik and Hans remain in their cave and Frederik initially refuses to surrender. This is when sergeant "Joseph" climbs to the mouth of the cave and, perceiving a rifle barrel which he thinks is aimed at him, he fires into the confined space of the cave. Frederik dies in the cave. Young Hans promptly surrenders, and will later testify that Frederik did not aim his musket at sergeant "Joseph," but the court will pointedly ignore that testimony.

After the shooting stops, the military troop departs with its two captives, leaving Frederik's body on the farm. Along the way they are met by six local men, of whom five are armed and who inquire as to the shooting, asking whether there are problems with the San Bushmen or with Jalousa's amaXhosa. Jalousa's people are known to be raiding cattle in the district yet again. Under orders from Lieutenant Rousseau, the troop refuses to talk to the men. It turns out later that these are none other than five members of the victim's family, together with a Khoekhoe farmhand.

While Frederik has been vividly in contempt of court and has clearly resisted arrest, Stockenström, representing British judicial authority, has some matters to account for regarding his own actions:

1. He has sent Khoekhoe soldiers to arrest one white man in an already racially disturbed district smarting from the racist excesses of the pro-Khoekhoe Missionaries and upset by the Black Circuit Court.

2. He has actively bypassed the district Commando system, the trusted civil militia structure on which the men on the highly dangerous frontier depend for life and limb.

3. His men have deceived the family of the deceased as to the killing of their family member.

4. He has in effect punished Freek for Contempt of Court and Resisting Arrest by executing him, employing the army as the means to this end.

5. He has made no attempt to investigate Frederik Bezuidenhout's counterclaims against Booy.

6. He has left Frederik's body unattended for the shocked and uninformed family to find.

Certainly, having 18 soldiers charge one cantankerous, gout ridden farmer with fixed bayonets for refusing to appear in court would generally be considered "over-reaction" in most civilized societies, even in 1815. Also, hitting a farmworker with a walking stick hardly merits death at the hands of the King's soldiers. However, we are dealing here with Andries Stockenström, who is soon enough to make a name for himself and earn the everlasting ire of first the Afrikaner frontiersmen, and later the British Settlers.

Fig. 7-5 *The vista from where Frederik Bezuidenhout was killed*

3. Vengeance is mine!

At Frederik's funeral in the Tarka, brother Johannes is violently upset at what he perceives to be the extreme injustice of his brother's death. He announces openly to all that he shall seek revenge and makes it quite plain that he holds Field-Cornet Opperman and Lieutenant Rousseau directly and personally responsible for his brother's death. In particular, he feels that Opperman has lied about Frederik to Stockenström and thereby caused his death. In his ire, Johannes states that he will enlist the amaXhosa black people to kill the English, just as the English have enlisted the Khoekhoe to kill Frederik.

In the next few days, Johannes meets with Hendrik Frederik Prinsloo and with brother-in-law, Cornelis Faber, at ancestor Pieter Jordaan's farm, *Palingkloof.* The Bothma family also lives on the farm. Hendrik "Kasteel" Prinsloo (*Fig. 7-7*) has come all the way from his father's farm at the Boschberg (*Fig. 7-4*) to meet with the distraught Johannes. The two men subsequently meet on *Palingkloof* with some of Jalousa's men. Jalousa is one of King Ngqika's several uncles. He lives with his tribe near the Koonap River (*Fig. 7-4*). By now, the two Bothma brothers on *Palingkloof*, Stephanus and Abraham, have also become involved. When the Xhosa men inquire *"why the Christians do not go to speak to the chief,"* "Hendrik Kasteel" and Johannes Bezuidenhout deputize a four-man team to seek the aid of amaXhosa King Ngqika beyond the Koonap River. The men include Cornelis Faber, 21-year-old Adriaan Engelbrecht, Frans Marais, also known as *"The Frenchman,"* and a 12 year old Khoekhoe helper. Marais was born in Hungary and was a member of the Dutch Artillery who deserted at the Battle of Blaauwberg. He is now employed as a shoemaker. Johannes has enlisted the unfortunate Marais, who will claim that he simply stopped by the farm to obtain some tobacco.

The Field-Cornet of the Tarka, Stephanus van Wijk, gets wind of the plan when Engelbrecht's naive young wife talks about her husband's mission. Van Wijk tries very hard to make Johannes understand the implications of his utterances. He attempts to convince the aggrieved brother to use formal channels to obtain a proper investigation into his brother's death. Van Wijk eventually manages to convince Johannes Jordaan, older brother of ancestor Pieter Jordaan, to reason with Johannes Bezuidenhout and his group, but the group accuses him of being a traitor. Some individuals will eventually testify that members of the group even threaten to shoot Jordaan. Clearly, the time for talking is over.

4. We want Hendrik "Kasteel!"

When word of Johannes Bezuidenhout's plan leaks, Field-Cornet Opperman, promptly delegates his Field-Cornet role to Provisional Field-Cornet, Willem Frederik Krugel, and flees with his family for the safety of Graaff-Reinet. Krugel lives at *Kokskraal* (Kok's Corral) in the Baviaans River Valley. This is the farm of Jacobus Marthinus Klopper, cousin of our ancestor Johannes Jacobus Klopper (*NF27*). Jacobus Marthinus lives there with his two sons, Andries and Jacobus (*Fig. 7-7*).

At this point, a message from Landdrost Stockenström to Field-Cornet Opperman is delivered to Krugel in his capacity as Opperman's replacement. The message instructs the Field-Cornet to call out the Commando of the Baviaansrivier to guard against a possible amaXhosa invasion. Krugel executes the call-up order, but then shanghais the unsuspecting burghers to support Bezuidenhout's effort. The men of the Baviaans River Field-Cornetcy have hereby been added to the plot hatched in the Tarka. There will be much debate later as to whether Krugel actually understood what he was doing. Hendrik "Kasteel" Prinsloo has meanwhile been arrested based on intelligence already received. He is imprisoned at Captain Andrews' military post at Van Aardt's Post, overlooking a wide bend on the Fish River some miles south of the entrance to the Baviaans River Valley. His arrest is largely based on a letter he signed expressing that they:

> "...have resolved agreeably to the Oath they had taken to their Mother Country to remove the God-forgotten Tyrants and Villains" [the British].

The two Klopper brothers have set off to try and persuade the farmers of the Bruintjeshoogte to join in the effort, but return empty handed. Hendrik Petrus Klopper has joined Johannes Bezuidenhout's effort and rides over Groene Nek into the Tarka with Marthinus Prinsloo's other son, Nicolaas Balthasar (Fig. 7-7), to recruit more men. Bezuidenhout, who now seems to hold sway over Provisional Field-Cornet Krugel, tells all the men that the job immediately at hand is to proceed to Van Aardt's Post to enquire as to why Hendrik "Kasteel" has been imprisoned and to have him released into their custody. This is a similar decision to that which landed Kasteel's own father in the Castle with a death sentence over his head some 16 years earlier.

It is at this point that some of the men realize they have been shanghaied. When Bezuidenhout becomes aware of the dissent, he induces the hapless Krugel to have the men swear an oath of allegiance to their joint cause. Some do, and some abstain. Some remove their hats, some don't. At Van Aardt's Post, Captain Andrews refuses to deliver Hendrik Kasteel to this Commando. The Commando, not wishing to exacerbate the situation, prefers to withdraw at this point. Beyond the two brothers Bezuidenhout, ten members of our Prinsloo and Klopper families are by now involved in this whole exercise, along with the present author's direct ancestor, Coenraad, son of Coenraad Bezuidenhout (NF33, 34).

5. At Ngqika's Great Place

In Ngqika's territory, the rebel deputation is discussing matters with the amaRharhabe King. As testified later by King Ngqika's interpreter, Hendrik Nouka[22], Faber predicts that, if Ngqika does not help, then the British will attack first the Afrikaners and then the amaXhosa. He also asks that Hintsa, the paramount king of all the amaXhosa, should bring his men from beyond the Kei River, and adds:

> "Ndlambe and the children of Conga [Cungwa] should again get back the Suurveld, as also the cattle of the English and of the farmers who would not help, and further, the beads, brass, iron and pots, but that the guns, powder and shot were for the burghers who assisted [...] ... "when all was over and it was again peace, [the farmers were to] go and live off the veld of the Gonab [Koonap]..."

According to the interpreter, Ngqika answered, "it was good."

There will be much debate and outrage about this "pact" on the part of the burghers who are not part of the "rebellion." The "rebels" will become the subject of scorn in history books[23], but the plan is not nearly as outrageous as it is made out to be. We recall that Piet "Cafferland" Prinsloo, cousin to Hendrik "Kasteel," previously sought and indeed received Ngqika's help (Chapter 5: Britain pays tribute to men with spears), and that Ngqika has hitherto lived in total peace with the frontiersmen.

In fact, our ancestor Coenraad Bezuidenhout used to live with Ngqika (NF33, 34). For his part, Ngqika sends word to Ndlambe. Ndlambe responds noncommittally that it is "good that he is being informed." The deputation thereupon returns home, arranging with Ngqika that the rebels will send for help when they are ready to move. When that word comes, Ngqika should send his men to join the rebels at the Roode Wal (Red Bank) (See *Figs. 7-4* and *7-6*). Learning of Hendrik Kasteel's arrest, Cornelis Faber returns to Ngqika, accompanied by Marais and others, to obtain a formal response. And a response indeed he does get. However, it is not what he antici-pated, for by now even Ngqika has heard of Hendrik Kasteel's arrest.

6. The Rebellion that never was

Back in the colony, the Loyalist *Amerikaner* magistrate Cuyler has been fully informed of developments. He is approaching Van Aardt's Post with a 100-man detachment of dragoons and Khoekhoe soldiers and a 20-man Commando of Afrikaner burghers in support. The shanghaied Baviaans River Commando, having failed in securing the release of Hendrik "Kasteel," has withdrawn to the slopes of a mountain known as Slagtersnek (Butcher's Ridge) to obtain a better view over the approaches to Van Aardt's Post. Cuyler's group of some 130 now faces off with the shanghaied Commando on the slopes of Slagtersnek.

Fig. 7-6 Roodewal ridge on the Great Fish River near Cookhouse

It is at this precise crucial point that Cornelis Faber returns from Ngqika with the message that Ngqika will no longer be coming to support the "rebels." While many of the shanghaied Commando members have already departed upon realizing that they have been misled as regards their mission, a large number has stayed.

Upon receipt of Ngqika's message, eighteen of them surrender their weapons. Among these men is at least one Klopper. Provisional Field-Cornet Krugel also surrenders.

The "Rebellion that Never Was" falls apart at this point. A major group surrenders to another Field-Cornet. Of the ringleaders, Johannes Bezuidenhout, Faber, and the Bothma brothers make off up the Baviaans River valley to collect their families from *Palingkloof* and elsewhere in the Tarka. Theunis de Klerk, the last of the seven key players, also escapes into the mountains. Willem Krugel joins Hendrik "Kasteel" in jail.

7. Death in the Valley of the Baboons

Cuyler now calls up a further district Commando. Instead of relying on their skills, he tells these men that he only needs their horses, and he actually does not need them as men at all. This is a significant point, as we shall shortly see. Under the command of Major Fraser, the column of "British" Khoekhoe[24] soldiers, now with the benefit of the horses of the insulted commando, sets off in pursuit of the fugitives.

The fugitives collect their families from the Tarka farms and some of them proceed with their ox-wagons to Groene Nek at the head of the Baviaans River Valley, but there they decide to turn for *Schaapkraal* (Sheep Corral) back in the Tarka. However, unbeknown to them, Abraham Bothma has surrendered and has betrayed their location. The soldiers under Major Fraser have laid an ambush for them.

When the trap is sprung, most of the people surrender. Cornelis Faber does so after his gun malfunctions, but Johannes Bezuidenhout refuses. With the help of his wife, Martha Faber, and his (now) 12-year old son, Gerrit, he tries to fight back. The testimony will differ on what happens next. Abraham Bothma will later testify that Martha also fires at the soldiers. The soldiers will claim that young Gerrit also fires at them from among the wheels of the wagon. Martha will deny both statements. Her own testimony, as a twice-wounded widow and mother with a child in the middle of all of this, is rather compelling[25]:

> *"He first mounted his horse and wanted to gallop off, and on my asking him if he would leave me and my children, and allow me to be killed, he dismounted and came and stood by me behind the wagon, and spoke to the soldiers who stood in front of him, and I saw that one of the soldiers was going to fire at him, and therefore I pushed him away and warned him; at the same moment the priming of the soldier's gun burnt, and my husband fired at the soldier so that he was wounded and died afterwards [...]*
>
> *...he stood behind the wheel, and after he had fired, he loaded the gun again, and then he received a shot in the arm, which broke the bone above and below the elbow; he then fled to me in order to hide himself, and I called to the soldiers that they should lay hold of him, but when I covered him they wounded me and my husband then ran from me, when they shot him in the back; I thereupon ran up to him again and lifted him up, when I received the other shot. [...]*
>
> *...grief does a great deal, for my heart was sore, and we were there alone; my husband then said to the child* [Their 12-year old son], *'Go to them, and they will not do you any harm'; he thereupon went, but was wounded in his leg and under his foot..."*

All this happens near the Jordaan farm, *Palingkloof*[26]. On 30 November 1815, the widowed Martha Faber and her son, both wounded, are then also left[27] in the care of ancestor Pieter Jordaan, together with all the oxen. The dragoons and Commando set off looking for the remaining fugitives.

8. "Tears are my food"

With the vast bulk of the "rebels" in custody, a few were still evading capture. It was under these circumstances that Theunis Christiaan de Klerk wrote a message to one of the landdrosts:

> *"Dear and honored Mr. Landdrost,*
> *...I shall with a penitent heart come to you for pity, for I do not live as a human being, but as a beast of the fields and forests, and mountains, and tears are my food;..."*

Eventually, some 47 people, including Martha Faber, are jailed. After a trial that lasts from November 1815 to the end of January 1816 and gathers masses of interrogatories, 39 people are convicted and the conclusion and sentences that emerge are as follows for the individuals key to our story:

Prisoner 1: *Hendrik Frederik Prinsloo (32)* — *To hang by his neck until he is dead*

Prisoner 2: *Stephanus Cornelis Bothma (43)* — *To hang by his neck until he is dead*

Prisoner 3: *Cornelis Johannes Faber (59)* — *To hang by his neck until he is dead*

Prisoner 4: *Theunis Christiaan De Klerk (29)* — *To hang by his neck until he is dead*

Prisoner 5: *Abraham Carel Bothma (28)* — *To hang by his neck until he is dead*

The bodies of the above to be buried under the gallows at the place of execution

Prisoner 6: *Willem Frederik Krugel (49)* — *To hang by his neck until he is dead, His body to be delivered to his family*

Prisoner 7: *Frans Marais (29)* —*To be made fast by a rope around the neck to the gallows and exposed to public view and to witness, along with all the following prisoners (the twelfth excepted), the execution of the first six prisoners.*
— banished from the Colony and its dependencies for Life.

Prisoner 8: *Adriaan Engelbrecht (21)* — *Banished for seven years from the Colony and its dependencies*

Prisoner 10: *Andries Hendrik Klopper (24)* — *Banished for five years from the Colony and its dependencies*

Prisoner 11: *Nicolaas Balthasar Prinsloo (20)* — *To Robben Island to work in the public works for three years;*
— then banished from the frontier districts

Prisoner 12: Martha Faber (43)   *– Remove with her family from the district; take up abode more within the Colony*

Prisoner 14: Hendrik Petrus Klopper (28)   *– To Robben Island to work in the public works for one year*

Prisoner 22: Johannes Prinsloo (32)   *– 200 Rixdollar fine or four months local imprisonment*

Prisoner 28: Jacobus Marthinus Klopper (22)   *– 200 Rixdollar fine or four months local imprisonment*

During February 1816 Cuyler intercedes on behalf of the hapless Field-Cornet Krugel and the Governor, Lord Charles Somerset, reduces his sentence to Banishment for Life. They clearly realize that he was simply overwhelmed by the circumstances back in October 1815 and that his heart was never in it. Cuyler also asks for and gets clemency for the 18 men who surrendered at Slagtersnek. These are hugely important actions, in view of what now follows.

And so the infamous date of Saturday, 9 March 1816 inexorably approaches. As it does, Cuyler obtains two Khoekhoe carpenters from Van der Kemp's hated LMS institution at Bethelsdorp[28], of all inappropriate places in God's entire Creation, to build the gallows for the condemned white men.

9. When God speaks – The day that refuses to die

On Saturday, 9 March 1816, we find 300 soldiers lined up at Van Aardt's Post, the spot where the "rebels" had sworn their oath. At least 100 of the soldiers[29] are Khoekhoe men of the Cape Regiment, which will later be called the Cape Corps. Standing on the scaffold with the ropes around their necks, are Hendrik Prinsloo, Stephanus Bothma, his little brother Abraham, Cornelis Faber, and Theunis de Klerk, whose earlier written plea to the Landdrost has had no effect. Standing next to the scaffold, with a noose around his neck, is Waldecker mercenary Frans Marais, the Hungarian with a French name.

The rest of the convicted, except for Martha Faber, along with the local citizenry, have been forced to attend and watch the leaders of the "rebellion" die in public. The 300 soldiers have to keep them under control. Jacob Cuyler is in charge of the execution, but a number of other senior representatives of British Authority are in attendance, the most notable of which is Andries Stockenström, the man who insisted on "making examples" of the Afrikaners. He has since been promoted to the position of Landdrost of Graaff-Reinet. Five Field-Cornets are also present, as well as the collective Heemraad members and all the inhabitants[30] of the areas affected by the "rebellion." The Reverend Herold has been asked to attend the condemned. This is when the five condemned ask to be allowed to sing a hymn with their compatriots and families. Even the bitter and hard Jacob Cuyler, the American Loyalist, has to confess in his report[31] to the Governor that, "*it was done in a most clear voice, and was extremely impressive.*" Stephanus Bothma then addresses his friends from the gallows and cautions them to take a lesson from their example.

And this is the crucial moment when fate intervenes to embitter the future history of South Africa. Afrikaners are typically big people. An outdoor life on a dangerous frontier with a diet of meat builds big men. When one combines this with the fact that the Dutch are the tallest men in the Western world, one understands why British soldiers will for centuries refer to Afrikaners as "giants." When the fall is pulled from under the five men, four of them drop straight to the ground as their ropes break, even though those have been doubled as a precaution. We quote Cuyler himself[32], the man who is all-powerful when requesting death, but pleads powerlessness when called on for clemency:

> "*They all four got up. One attempted to leave the spot and rush to where the Collegie of Landdrost and Heemraden were. They all four spoke, and at this moment some of the spectators ran to me soliciting pardon for them, fancying it in my power to grant it. I cannot describe the distressed countenances of the inhabitants at this moment who were sentenced to witness the execution.*"

The fact is, Cuyler has already most desperately requested clemency for Willem Krugel, who previously served under him. He has not only obtained that clemency, but will ultimately obtain total amnesty for him. Peculiarly, he now claims that he is powerless to request instructions from the Governor, given the utterly extraordinary circumstances that present themselves. The extreme political impact of the event is obvious. In fact, the governor himself later will observe that he deeply regretted that the sentences were not commuted at this point.

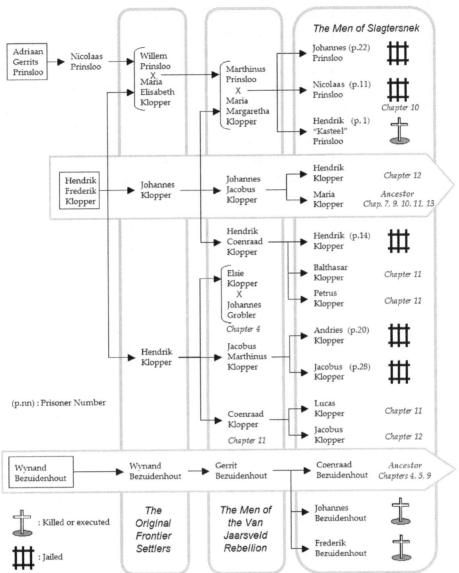

Fig. 7-7 *The Klopper, Prinsloo, and Bezuidenhout men of Slagtersnek*

This is the precise day that the British estrange the Afrikaner as a nation. Their agent in this is Jacob Cuyler, the American Loyalist. For these simple practical Christian farming folks, God has spoken and Imperial Britain is opposing His Will. From this day on, the British authority will never be trusted again. Cuyler, being ever the Loyalist Imperialist, simply sends for new ropes and hangs the men several hours later, with the body of their executed colleague still hanging next to them. This time the ropes do not break…

The gallows are duly broken down and a me-morial is erected more than a century later. As to Cuyler's perso-nal view[33] of the terrible debacle of the double hanging:

> [it] *"will more impressively mark its example on the minds of those inhabitants who saw it, as well as those who may come to hear of it."*

Indeed, this day will never be forgotten by Afrikaners, and we shall see the consequences.

10. And in the family

The trauma in the family is extreme. Our two Bezuidenhout brothers have been shot to death at the start and end of the sequence of events. Our sister has lost her son to the hangman. Several other family members are in jail and some await banishment. The entire region has been destabilized, first by the activities of the would-be rebels, and then by the events of the execution debacle.

It is over this period that a little girl is born to ancestor Johannes Jacobus Klopper and his wife, Maria Venter. They name her Maria Catharina, and she will be part of an epic quest, full of drama and danger and death (See Chapters 9 to 12), all to get away from this British subjugation. The seeds of that quest are sown in the frontier region with the execution of the five men. All that it will take is another event to set it all off. But, how can things get worse than they are? In fact, if the British Army and British missionaries are both involved, they most certainly can and will get worse.

Twenty days after the execution, news spreads that Marthinus Prinsloo and his family have been instructed to leave the frontier districts and move to the West Cape. The government is "calling up" his loan farm after all these decades and is clearly evicting the Prinsloos from the frontier. Soon, however, the word comes that all the men who escaped execution are to be freed. The only exception is Frans Marais, the Hungarian "illegal immigrant." He is to be deported.

Those still on the run can therefore come home. The beam of the gallows is removed and is used as a central beam in the roof of a nearby farmhouse for a very long time. Sometime in the future, it will be removed and committed to the State Archive. Afrikaners will raise the matter of this particular beam again in the year 1895 under ironically reversed circumstances. The British will then view matters rather differently, and again our family will be involved. Few events in the history of South Africa will be so central in the psyche of the Afrikaner as the terrible event of the men "dying twice" at Slagtersnek. It will become a symbol of British oppression of the Afrikaner and a political and cultural rallying point for more than a century-and-a-half.

11. And what are the British thinking?

The reason for the rebels being freed is purely political. Somerset, having realized the potential for military disaster on the frontier, has taken the advice of his Chief of Justice, J.A. Truter. We quote from Truter's letter[34] to the Governor, in which he explains that further instability caused by lengthy prosecutions will cause the Suurveld amaXhosa to invade opportunistically:

Fig. 7-8 The Slagtersnek memorial on the site of the execution at Van Aardt's Post

> *"...a political measure, corresponding with the act of grace already shown, cannot be said to be an infringement on the administration of justice...."*

The late Hendrik "Kasteel" told all who would listen that the frontier farms were overcrowded, that the quit-rent farming land system imposed by the British was not affordable, and that the British advantaged the Khoekhoe to the detriment of their fellow White Protestant Christians, the Afrikaners. There is therefore some merit in determining whether this man, who died for his actions, was right or wrong. Firstly, if the farming arrangement were sensible, then the Government at the Cape owes the people on the frontier some explanation of how it is that they have to live 8 families to a farm to survive, with grazing rapidly deteriorating. The unfortunate Willem Krugel's farm with seven other families is a good example. Cuyler's reaction to this fact is to say that Kasteel had no reason to talk about the affordability of the quit-rent system if he did not own a farm. Secondly, in the matter of the Khoekhoe we do not have to go far. We quote here from a letter[35] of 21 November 1815, just after the confrontation at Slagtersnek, to the Commission for Administering Justice from the very Jacob Cuyler who later hanged Hendrik "Kasteel." The reader can judge whether Cuyler has the best interests of the Christian citizens on the frontier at heart, or whether he sees himself as being there to impress by any means on them the power of the British Empire:

> *"As far as I can trace this affair, it appears to me to be the seeds of the former disturbances never properly weeded out, as all the families, which were then engaged, are now again implicated. This calls for Example, as in the first affair they were all pardoned."*

These first lines of the letter obviously refer to Marthinus Prinsloo, who led the 1799 Van Jaarsveld "Rebellion." Cuyler designed the example he so expressly desired. He then continues:

> *"1,000 men of the Cape Regt., 300 of them mounted, would always be a protection for this Frontier, as well as against the Kaffers, so as to support and enforce Government's influence among the Inhabitants; fancy to yourself a people of the description of the Boers, all marksmen, well mounted, and the knowledge of the country they possess! Foreign Troops cannot act against them.*
>
> *We now see when one Brother is brought against another, how he acts; whom, then, are we to depend on? The Hottentots are the only people. Instead of the 40 Dragoons I had with me the other day, had I had 40 Hottentots, who could have quitted their horses and entered the bushes, I would probably have been enabled to have secured some more of the mutineers."*

He is suggesting that the answer to subjugating the Afrikaner Boere is to use an army of 1000 men of the largely-Khoekhoe "Cape Corps." For him, the word "we" excludes Afrikaners. Unfortunately for any British attempts to plead the moral high ground, this evidence, directly from the pen of their Loyalist *landdrost*, shows that he views the Afrikaners inherently as an enemy. He certainly treats them as such. Imagine a Loyalist British magistrate subjugating American settlers using a largely Six Nations Indian army. Such matters count deeply in history and are not easily forgotten.

One is left with the clear impression that, despite the late Hendrik Kasteel's plans being hugely misguided, he was in fact no idiot. He read the situation accurately. Clearly, behind the Afrikaners' backs, the British government is considering them an enemy, this despite any words to the contrary that may cross their lips. If the Afrikaners were to know how callous the Empire could be toward its own British citizens, they may perhaps not feel so alone, oppressed and deserted. But that evidence lies exactly four years in the future. Eighty-four years after the executions, Sir Arthur Conan Doyle will say[36] about these events:

> *"A brave race can forget the victims of the field of battle, but never those of the scaffold. The making of political martyrs is the last insanity of statesmanship."*

Slagtersnek will come to deeply haunt the British Government a full 80 years later. In the year 2005, the beam of the scaffold, still bearing its bolt holes, will be removed from the South African Museum in Cape Town and returned to Somerset East, the nearest incorporated town to Slagtersnek.

The town will be on Marthinus Prinsloo's long lost farm at the foot of the Boschberg (*Fig. 4-10* and *7-4*).

—End Nexus Familia

The last White Slaves

While the London Missionary Society was doing its best to sketch the Afrikaner people as the skunks of Civilization and succeeding beyond their wildest dreams, the Barbary Pirates were continuing their practice of enslaving European people. This did not concern the dedicated LMS missionaries, who had found their entire raison d'être the cause of the Khoekhoe.

In fact, the practice of enslavement of Europeans only stopped when the Dutch and English jointly bombarded Algiers[37] on the "Barbary Coast" on 27 August 1816. Three thousand European slaves were freed after the bombardment, known as the Battle of Algiers. Ironically, this was almost a decade after Britain banned the slave trade in its Empire and started to enforce the ban at sea. At least the Americans had reacted sooner. After the War of 1812, the Dey of Algiers, Omar, ordered attacks on American shipping because U.S. tribute was supposedly overdue. The US Congress authorized military action against Algiers in February 1815. A squadron of nine warships under Commodore Stephen Decatur sailed for Barbary to end the shameful paying of tribute once and for all. They captured several of the Dey's ships and entered Algiers harbor on June 29, 1815. The next day Omar agreed to a peace treaty and the release of all American prisoners. In addition, Article II of the treaty stated,

"No tribute, either as biennial presents or under any other form shall ever be required by Algiers from the United States on any pretext."

Then the Americans demanded that Dey Omar pay the United States $10,000 as compensation for property taken from its citizens. Decatur proceeded to Tunis and Tripoli to do the same.

The joint Dutch-British attack in 1816 represented the death knell to the Barbary Coast problem.

The British eat the President's dinner

The War of 1812 was largely precipitated by Britain's attempts at blockading United States trade with France while they themselves were fighting Napoleon. The American President James Madison declared war on Britain on June 18, 1812. The reasons given were British constraints on neutral trade and anger at alleged British military support for American Indians against the colonists. Another factor was the impressment of American sailors into the British navy. This was precisely the issue that had created the instability at Graaff-Reinet in 1803 (See Chapter 6: *Maynier and the Frontier*). The war was characterized by unsuccessful attempts by the United States to invade Canada and by the British employing their power at sea to raid coastal areas of the United States. In one raid, the British attacked Washington and burned the President's House. One of the officers who sat down to eat President Madison's still warm dinner, was a daring young captain by the name of Henry George Wakelyn Smith, who wrote of this event in his autobiography[38] :

"...we were horrified at the order to burn the elegant Houses of Parliament and the President's house. In the latter, however, we found a supper all ready, which was sufficiently cooked without more fire, and which many of us speedily consumed, unaided by the fiery elements, and drank some very good wine also. I shall never forget the destructive majesty of the flames as the torches were applied to beds, curtains, etc."

After this war, the President's House was painted white. It would be President Theodore Roosevelt, who enters our story later, who would officially name it *"The White House"* in 1901.

The war ended inconclusively, after Britain and its allies defeated France. Britain lifted the blockade and the protagonists decided to leave the borders of the United States and Canada unchanged. Smith would become a central figure in South African history, and reputedly the inspiration for Gilbert & Sullivan's *"Thoroughly modern major-general."*

-----ooOoo-----

8

The British Settlers

"When our fathers and the fathers of the amaBhulu first settled the Suurveld, they dwelt together in peace"

Councilors for Xhosa chief Hintsa, referring to the Afrikaners,
Negotiations with British Commander Willshire (1819)

Lord Charles Somerset

The new governor of the Cape was yet again a military man on a purchased commission: Lord Charles Somerset. He set sail for the Cape with twenty-six people in tow, including footmen, butlers, chaplains, a "boy," various maids, a cook and laundry maid who was "of color." Somerset arrived on 5 April 1814. Here was a man who passionately hated and distrusted the men from the London Missionary Society. He quickly came to share the Afrikaner's view of that organization.

Even as he landed, the amaXhosa were raiding cattle again in the *Suurveld*. In response, Somerset did three things. He advised London that he needed 1,100 proper troops for the border; he insisted on a trip to the border to *"show the flag"* and intimidate the amaXhosa; and he embarked on an effort to politically destroy the missionaries in the country. Read of the London Missionary Society obliged him in this last goal by having an adulterous relationship with one of his convert Khoekhoe women at Bethelsdorp.

In showing the flag, Somerset insisted that Ngqika was to be the only spokesperson for the amaXhosa. Ngqika was now responsible for recovering all stolen cattle from other amaXhosa over whom he had no traditional authority. He also had to return all deserters from the colonial forces. This was a major issue for Somerset, because his "Royal African Corps" was composed of every manner of ne'er do well and criminal, most of whom had accepted this duty to avoid penal servitude.

Fig. 8-1 Lord Charles Somerset

"We are without milk!"

Somerset's interference in the power-balance among the Xhosa led in short order to a Xhosa civil war in 1818 in which Ngqika's army was massacred by Ndlambe's army at a place called Amalinde. For the first time ever, an amaXhosa army did not stop until all of the losing army was dead. As they had never done anything like this before, the assumption is that they had now learnt about Total War from the brutal British campaign in the *Suurveld*, or, as it was now known, Albany.

Ngqika asked for help from Somerset and got it. Somerset appointed the inexperienced Lt. Col. Brereton as leader of this expedition and instructed him to drive Ndlambe beyond the Keiskamma River, leaving a buffer between the Keiskamma and the Great Fish River.

Yet again, the Afrikaners were to be dragged into a colonial mess created by the British. They were to be led by Andries Stockenström Jr., with whom they had not exactly made peace after the ugly debacle of Slagtersnek. Stockenström, the Afrikaner Magistrate of Graaff-Reinet, was clear on the situation[1]:

> *"So sure as we take Caffer cattle, except when you force them to restore what they have taken...so sure must those from whom they are taken either plunder or starve."*

Stockenström had often been told[2] by the amaXhosa:

> *"We do not care how many Caffres you shoot if they come into your country, and you catch them stealing, but for every cow you take from our country you make a thief."*

Ndlambe hid his cattle in the deep riverine forests. This was the standard Xhosa response to a threat, their cattle being considered precious indeed. Brereton's response was to fire his cannon blindly into the forest. The amaXhosa scattered and their cattle stampeded. Brereton took an amazing 23,000 cattle.

Brereton warned Stockenström to be on his guard in Graaff-Reinet as the amaXhosa were likely to attack in revenge. He then gave 9,000 head of cattle to Ngqika, some to the Boer Commando members, and some to the Khoekhoe soldiers. The rest were sold by the British Army to defray the costs of the expedition.

In the amaXhosa society of the time, it was the social right of the vanquished to request from the victorious enough cattle to remain alive. It was, in fact, a measure of the greatness of the victor that he would grant such cattle. In this, there is possibly also a lesson to the Superpowers of later centuries in the difference between power and greatness. Hence, after the Brereton expedition, a Xhosa said[3] to a British officer:

> *"We are without milk and the new king* [Ngqika] *will not give us any, so we must get some from the white man's king* [the governor] *who has taken all our cattle and left us to perish"*

This seems to be plain, simple, and honest. The civil war had been an amaXhosa affair that had been no business of the white man. It had been brought on by Somerset's interference in Xhosa politics in the first place. The result was that the Ndlambe Xhosa were destitute. The now all-powerful Ngqika refused to honor the social code after what had been done to his army. What exactly were the Ndlambe Xhosa supposed to do?

The 5th Frontier War – Nxele's War

On Christmas day 1818, the amaXhosa once more started large scale cattle raids and the frontier started to collapse. Farmer J. Meyer, who was using his home as a refuge for surrounding farmers[4], sent a message to his Field-Cornet, Fourie:

> *"...the whole of Kaffirland is here. For God's sake please come to our assistance"*

One of the unique characters who had risen to power during the Xhosa Civil War was a pseudo mystic by the name of Nxele, also known as Makanna. To support his views, he had invented an entire religion, based on separate gods for white people and black people. By early 1819, he had swept up those amaXhosa beyond the Fish River into a frenzy.

On 22 April 1819, some 10,000 to 15,000 Xhosa attacked Grahamstown and almost took it. They were defeated, but it was a close run thing (See *NF41*). By the end of July 1819, an Army of 2,300 British soldiers and Boer commandos under Lt Col Willshire and Andries Stockenström left Grahamstown to force the Xhosa back beyond the Keiskamma River in a drive similar to that of Graham some years earlier.

On the evening of 16 August 1819, an amazing thing happened. Nxele walked into Stockenström's camp, accompanied by two of his wives. He had gallantly come to surrender himself in the hope that his people might be spared. He would to be sent to Robben Island. A few days later a Xhosa delegation approached Willshire and Stockenström's combined army and delivered one of the most majestic presentations ever recorded on the continent. Stockenström recorded how moved he was by it[5]:

"The war, British Chiefs, is an unjust one; for you are now striving to extirpate a people whom you forced to take up arms. When our fathers and the fathers of the amaBhulu [the Afrikaners] first settled the Suurveld, they dwelt together in peace."

They went on to ascribe most of the problems to the fact that the British favored Ngqika, despite the fact that he was treasonous and was also stealing the Boer cattle. They ended with the fateful words:

"...but Ngqika shall not rule over the followers of those who think him a woman."

The Afrikaners were much impressed with the presentation of the Xhosa delegation. Willshire, the British Army man, was having none of it. Stockenström was extremely unhappy with the slaughter that followed. Ultimately he managed to communicate with Captain Christopher Bird, the Colonial Secretary in Cape Town, and, with his help, got Willshire to stop the carnage. Nxele was captive, Ndlambe was destroyed and Hintsa, the paramount chief beyond the Kei River, had been cowed.

Ngqika, the treacherous ally, had gained all. At this point, Lord Charles Somerset sailed to Algoa Bay to personally meet with Ngqika to tell him that he too had to withdraw beyond the Keiskamma. Ngqika had cooperated with the British and had now also lost. He was allowed to keep his sheltered Tyumie Valley home territory west of the Keiskamma. All Somerset did by these actions, was to start the next Frontier War, albeit delayed by fifteen years. It would be fought by Ngqika's sons, Maqoma and Tyali.

It was against the background of these events that the next group of people arrived in the country to play their own unique role in the history of South Africa.

The British Settlers

After the war against Napoleon, the British economy was in a deep depression and into this market place streamed all the recently decommissioned men. His Majesty's government was not experiencing quite the "peace dividend" it had hoped for. Britain had developed a bloated example of what would be called a "military-industrial complex" in the 21st Century. With the arrival of peace, the bottom fell out of the market for coal, steel, and textiles. Matters in the socio-economic domain became heated, until it finally took the British Army to quell riots and uprisings. In the event, seventeen people were executed for their roles in these uprisings and many more were shipped to Australia as convicts.

It is useful to look at one small part of England during this period, such as Nottinghamshire. This was textile country and many people were framework knitters who worked from home, making socks using stocking frames. However, the industrial revolution was going full steam while the military demand for socks and other textiles almost disappeared. The workers found themselves literally begging from door to door. Children were dying from hunger. There were appeals for help to all who would listen and there was huge social unrest. The army was sent in. At the same time, there were large public funds raised and devoted to providing outdoor employment. From late 1819 until the following spring, many people were employed in civil projects, in clearing land and in planting potatoes. These were desperate times. Eventually, it was the Duke of Coventry who proposed that people from the shire should emigrate to the Cape Colony, and he duly started a fund to support this concept. Similar efforts were launched elsewhere in England.

The Cape Colony was presented to the people in England as a place of unlimited opportunity where one had but to strew seed on tilled soil to be successful. Various placards sang the virtues of the Cape. American Captain Stout's account of his shipwreck in 1796 was dredged up and re-published to motivate British people to emigrate to the *Suurveld*. The Colonial Office saw herein a major opportunity. Given that the Afrikaners, after so much plundering by the amaXhosa, were not at all keen to occupy the *Suurveld*, it might be possible to induce poor unsuspecting Englishmen to do the honors instead. The Afrikaners, for very good reasons, had not initiated much agriculture in the area.

The *Suurveld* is a treacherous country. Firstly, it was named "Sour Country" for a reason. The soil is not generally suitable for agriculture. Even in the 21st century, with all its associated technology, it is still not major agricultural country. But, the British had their minds set on wheat. Secondly, the rainfall is distinctly erratic. The area lies where the mountain ranges from the west stop and where the Summer thunderstorm zone starts. A slight shift in weather patterns, and both the marginal coastal winter rains and the summer thundershowers stay away for a year, leading to grinding drought. In years with good rains, the place is truly beautiful in fall. The honeysuckle and the plumbago and the aloes and boer bean and all the other shrubs, creepers and trees flower beautifully.

The Eastern Cape is the home of a wealth of plants found in gardens around the world today. The striking official flower of San Francisco, the Bird of Paradise, a form of dwarf banana (*strelitzia*), is indigenous to the area. Like all plants from the region, it is extraordinarily tough, because it pointedly has to be. However, this superficial beauty masks a hard and vicious soul sucking land that has broken many good men. In short, the place can look idyllic one moment, but can turn into a parched hell the next season; hence the tough vegetation.

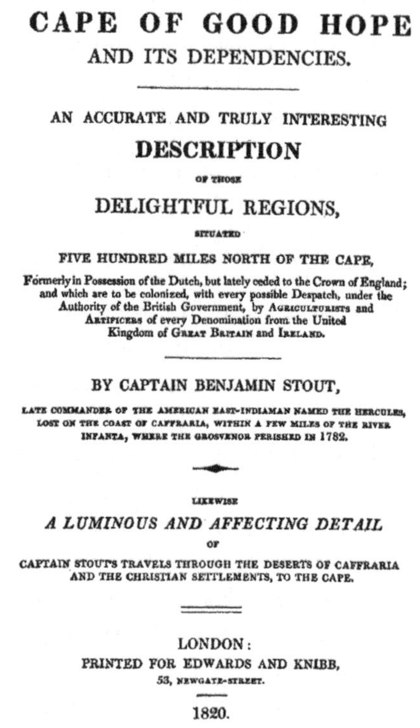

Into this misleadingly beautiful countryside, Lord Charles Somerset would now send the unsuspecting surplus population of Britain, who believed they were on the way to the land of milk and honey. And they came by their hundreds and by their thousands under leaders of parties. These leaders were either men of some sort of means, nominal and otherwise, or ex-military men. Eventually, there would be approximately 5,000 souls of whom some 3736 came as larger parties, sometimes numbering over 100 persons. The problem was that only a minority had any notion of agriculture. They were mostly city folks. A huge number came from London. In the early 19th century, there could hardly have been a place on Earth that could have worse prepared a human for the rigors of Africa than London! William Menzies led a small party from Kent.

They embarked on ships from all over the British Isles, and, after typically bad voyages, were disembarked at Algoa Bay, watched over by Fort Frederick, that *"Last Outpost of Christianity"* that we have encountered before (*Fig. 6-4*). The Government at the Cape was not properly warned and was inadequately prepared. There was no transport arranged for the 80 to 120 mile trip to their allotted areas. In the end, the authorities appealed to the long-suffering Afrikaners to come with their sturdy but ponderous ox-wagons to transport these folks. And that was how the ordinary Englishman first met the ordinary Afrikaner. The Afrikaners were incredulous that these folks would come all the way from civilized England to eke out a living in the *Suurveld*. How could it possibly be that people would volunteer for this life[6]?

A small number of the immigrants were disembarked on the west coast, north of Cape Town, to go to Clanwilliam and again the Afrikaners helped. As regards the preparations for the Settlers in the Eastern Cape Bird says[7]:

> *"No previous order had been given from home, to provide means of conveyance to Albany;... In the eagerness to get rid of a part of the redundant population of Great Britain, the limited powers of the Cape were entirely*

CAPE OF GOOD HOPE
AND ITS DEPENDENCIES.

———

AN ACCURATE AND TRULY INTERESTING
DESCRIPTION
OF THOSE
DELIGHTFUL REGIONS,
SITUATED
FIVE HUNDRED MILES NORTH OF THE CAPE,
Formerly in Possession of the Dutch, but lately ceded to the Crown of England; and which are to be colonized, with every possible Despatch, under the Authority of the British Government, by AGRICULTURISTS and ARTIFICERS of every Denomination from the United Kingdom of GREAT BRITAIN and IRELAND.

———

BY CAPTAIN BENJAMIN STOUT,
LATE COMMANDER OF THE AMERICAN EAST-INDIAMAN NAMED THE HERCULES, LOST ON THE COAST OF CAFFRARIA, WITHIN A FEW MILES OF THE RIVER INFANTA, WHERE THE GROSVENOR PERISHED IN 1782.

———

LIKEWISE
A LUMINOUS AND AFFECTING DETAIL
OF
CAPTAIN STOUT'S TRAVELS THROUGH THE DESERTS OF CAFFRARIA AND THE CHRISTIAN SETTLEMENTS, TO THE CAPE.

═══

LONDON:
PRINTED FOR EDWARDS AND KNIBB,
53, NEWGATE-STREET.

1820.

Fig. 8-2 Cpt. Benjamin Stout's book in British garb

overlooked."

Emma Lazarus had not yet been born, otherwise she might have written for these Settlers:

"Give me your tired, your poor, Your huddled masses yearning to breathe free, The wretched refuse of your teeming shore. Send these, the homeless, tempest-tost to me, I lift my lamp beside the golden door!"

But, there was no lamp or golden door, just the tantalizing but unforgiving *Suurveld* and the helping hand of the Afrikaners with their ponderous "12 miles a day" ox-wagons and open-hearted neighborliness. The Afrikaners knew full well what these folks were heading into. However, on the positive side, with British people now in the *Suurveld*, surely Britain would take more care of the situation and would be more inclined to act in the interest of these new colonists.

Possibly, this represented a greater degree of hope also for Afrikaners, who had started to despair of their own existence. It was now 168 years since their own ancestors had arrived in this tortured land. If these folks really had known what lay in wait for them, they would never in a million years have boarded any one of those ships. A year earlier the Reverend John Campbell had traveled through those parts and described[8] a scene in the *Suurveld*:

"Passed a farm belonging to Major Fraser, landdrost of Graham's Town, which had been destroyed by the Caffres, and had a gloomy aspect, the shells of the houses only remaining; the garden was overrun with weeds; there was a row of large orange trees completely stripped of their fruit by the Caffres and baboons. All was desolation."

 ## Nexus Familia 41: The British Bloodline

1. The First British Soldier in our Bloodline

In faraway England, William is the oldest of the eight children of William Misselbrook and Ann Hopkins of St. Faith near Winchester in Hampshire. The family has a long tradition as *cordwains*; makers of leather goods, particularly boots and shoes. In 1812, one year after the birth of William's youngest brother, their father dies, leaving Ann with the eight remaining children. The world the family knows now falls apart rapidly when Ann also dies in March of 1814. This leaves the 15-year old William the head of the family of eight children. The children are in a desperate situation and, in May of that year, the two youngest succumb and are buried in St. Faith on the same day, 2 May 1814.

On 1 January 1817, the eighteen-year old, 5 foot 5-1/4 inch tall William enlists in the British Army. His recruiter is paid 2 pounds 8 shillings and sixpence[9]. He is taken into the 38th Regiment of Foot, the *"1st Staffordshires."* These men have made a name for themselves in the Peninsular War at the Siege of San Sebastian in August 1813. William finds himself surrounded by men with reason to be proud.

The 1st Staffordshires are a *"blue blood"* unit. Not so the 60th Regiment or the Royal African Corps that join them to constitute the main British military force on the Cape Frontier. Already in 1816 Lord Charles Somerset advised London that it would be better to remove the 60th from the front due to its composition of *"foreigners and deserters."* By 12 November 1817, these two units have committed such acts as to force the governor to write[10] to Whitehall about them, desperate to avoid the total humiliation of British authority if he were forced to keep the units on the front any longer:

"...the outrages which it is evident they would commit would force me to arm the Burghers and form a Militia for the general protection of the Inhabitants against the Military..."

The thought of a British Governor having to arm Dutch Afrikaners to protect a British colony from the British Army proves to be too much for Whitehall to stomach. In August of 1818, the 1st Staffordshires set sail for the Cape of Good Hope to take over the duties of the 60th and the Royal African Corps at this key possession of the British Empire. This is the military strategic hub around which the empire and its vast navy rotate. Without the Cape, the sagging belly of the empire would be exposed. This is then also why the British have made haste to secure from the humbled Dutch permanent possession of the place.

William is hugely excited. Any Englishman worth his salt wants to see "The Cape", the only cape on earth known as simply "The Cape", the place that fundamentally defines the word. On 3 November 1818, after a two-month voyage, they sail into Table Bay. William is absolutely awed by Table Mountain. It sits like a massive wall across the sky. He has never even seen a mountain in his life. Hampshire is pretty, but it has no mountains. Mountains are things from storybooks.

On 21 February 1819, the commanding officer, Lt. Col. Willshire, receives instructions to proceed immediately to Algoa Bay with his men of the 38th Foot aboard the ship *Favourite*. Their stores are to follow on the *Alacrity*. At Algoa Bay, he is to meet up with Lt. Col. Cuyler, the American Loyalist Magistrate of Uitenhage, who will fill them in on the situation. The previous British Army commander in the area, Lt. Col. Brereton, is running away from the mess he has made with the amaXhosa. He has good reason. Brereton will later be court-martialed for other reasons and will take his own life.

On arriving in Algoa Bay, they unload their stores and march the 80 miles to Grahamstown where they garrison the town; and then they wait. And so it is that, on 21 April 1819, a Xhosa messenger from Nxele arrives in Grahamstown with a message for Willshire. The message reads that Nxele will *"have breakfast with him"* the following morning. Willshire believes this is a joke. He clearly has not dealt with enough amaXhosa yet to understand that this is no laughing matter. As a nation, the amaXhosa are not in the least given to levity.

In the early afternoon of 22 April 1819, the men look up at the hills around the town, and their hearts race for their stomachs. The sight is incredible. Lining the crest of the hills are some 10,000 to 15,000 Xhosa warriors, covered in ocher clay. They are moving into battle formation with excellent discipline. To the horror of the men, they can also tell that there are among the Xhosa some deserters from the infamous Royal African Corps, a regiment composed of British "undesirables" performing military service instead of penal servitude. These criminals have no doubt helped to train the Xhosa warriors. Willshire has no real defenses or prepared strong points at the town. Grahamstown has a total of 450 defenders, mostly the 38th Foot. However, the defenders also include a unit of some 82 Khoekhoe of the Cape Corps. Willshire has a few cannon, which he quickly ranges on the slopes near the town. He also prepares his grapeshot charges. Then he moves his infantry, including the 38th Foot, forward to draw the Xhosa. The latter, however, only respond when Nxele gives the order. Only Nxele's staggering arrogance and some amazing luck on the part of the defenders will save Grahamstown.

When the amaXhosa finally move, the hills come alive with a flood of ocher-colored bodies, yelling and screeching as they come loping down the hills. The guns mow them down, but they keep coming. Eventually, the shrapnel starts to take effect. However, the gunners are starting to slow down from fatigue and the ocher warriors can still take the day. It is then that the miracle happens. Onto the scene comes galloping the Khoekhoe big game hunter, Boesak, with 130 armed Khoekhoe men. These men are superb shots and quickly eliminate Nxele's key officers. Thereafter it turns into a rout. Among the dead lie two of Ndlambe's sons and many of Ngqika's people. Clearly, Nxele has had appeal from across the entire spectrum of Xhosa peoples.

The British dead include one officer and two men. Five men are wounded. This battle has been close, terribly close. The British soldiers have seen the real Africa and shall never forget it. It changes all who see it forever. They now realize that people overseas could never conceivably understand this place. One feels so uniquely alive here, because there is so much death and danger. This will remain a fundamental truth into the 21st Century, and Africa shall remain as imponderable to Americans in particular, a place foreign to everything they understand, believe, and imagine.

2. Our British Settler Blood

Richard Bowles is a native of the area around Dover. A branch of the Bowles family has lived in the area of Temple Ewell, River, and Dover for a century. On 20 July 1806, Richard and his wife Esther baptized their second daughter Esther in the parish of River, two miles from Dover.

By 1814, Napoleon is defeated and Richard is decommissioned from the Military. He still lives in River, doing odd jobs, but is finding it near impossible to keep body and soul together. When his wife Esther dies, he is left with the 12-year old Esther. His older daughter is already out of the house.

In Cheriton outside Folkstone, Elizabeth Taylor is married to Edward Amos, and they have three sons and four daughters. Fate also intrudes on Elizabeth's life when Edward dies, leaving her with seven mouths to feed in a severely depressed England. It is in mid-1818 that she meets widower Richard Bowles. On 5 June 1819, little Jemima Bowles is duly born. However, financially matters are desperate.

In mid-1819, William Menzies from the 91st Regiment tells Richard of the Emigration Scheme to the Cape of Good Hope. Menzies is collecting a number of ex-servicemen from the Dover area to join him in this venture and Richard falls in with this plan. Life has to be more promising in the new land in Africa that the government is telling them is so wonderful. Apparently, it even looks a bit like Kent.

Menzies has written a letter to the government asking to be considered for the emigration scheme. This simple, honest letter by the barely literate but devout Scot will still ring its unique tone from the British National Archives nearly two centuries later:

"Dover, 23rd July 1819
Sir,

Having seen in the news piper a grant for emigrants to go to the Cap of good pop your humble servent William MENZIS and John OLIVER solicty the faver from your honner to go under govinmant as Labrors or what you think proper to send us your Humble servent Wm. MENZIS has searved his King and Country 7 yeirs in 5 Company 91 Regt. Commanded by geinrl D CAMPBELL London & was descharged after the Battel of Watter Lou with a good Charitter if your honner Plise to mark I am master shoe maker Dover and John OLIVER is a man that I employ But as so much Confinment does not a gree with us and being a quinted with farming and moreover I have so many Bad debts and have no parish being a scotishman and being [illegible] offisers of Religon we wish to be Yousfill to our Country and our fellow Criatuers in workin with our heands defusing religous know Lige where eir we go we have both gott wifes but no Childring and young men and well a quinted with militry Dessipling and wishen to a bay all your commands as honist faithfull men to god and there Country if your honner will grant this faver and Lett your Humble servints know whin to geitt Reidy we will remnber you at a [Sermon?] of greace with the warmest of gratitude we Both remen your very Humble and obeident searvents.

William MENZIS; Jhon OLIVER, Dover
My a driss Wm MENZIS shoemakir oppiset St. Mary'is church, Dover. Kint"

Since the devout Menzies forces all the men to sign an agreement according to which they will conduct themselves in honorable fashion, never curse and never lie, Richard realizes that he'll have to do something about the fact that he is as yet not married to Elizabeth. Accordingly, the church books of St James' in Dover record the marriage of Richard and Elizabeth on 8 November 1819.

So it is that in mid-December 1819 the *Weymouth* lies ready in Portsmouth harbor on the south coast of England. Thirteen different emigrant parties are scheduled to embark. They include 55 people from Hampshire under Captain Alexander Biggar of the 58th Regiment, 51 from Kent under William Menzies, including Richard and Elizabeth Bowles, with Esther and Jemima and all seven Amos stepchildren, and no fewer than 167 people from Wiltshire led by, among others, Miles Bowker. In total, there are no fewer than 453 emigrants on board. There are to be 33 of these ships; two will make the trip twice.

On the ship *John*, departing from Liverpool, we find the farmer and party leader Samuel Liversage and family; Simon Biddulph of Bailie's party, his wife Ann and their five sons and one daughter, together with their 39-year old ex-Army servant, John Leech; the Cowies of Stanley's party; woolen manufacturer David Cawood of Hayhurst's party, with his wife Ann and their ten children; and Richard Halstead of the same party with his wife Ellen (21) and their three children, including his 9 year old son Thomas.

The people from Nottinghamshire are to go on the *Albury* under Thomas Calton, the surgeon. The butcher, Robert Robinson, with his wife Martha and 5 children will sail on the *Brilliant* under leadership of the baker James Erith. The youngest child is little William.

3. To the Cape of Good Hope

On 16 December 1819, the settlers from Hampshire, Kent and Wiltshire are ushered aboard the *Weymouth* in Portsmouth harbor. By 2 January 1820, they are still waiting in the harbor due to bad weather. On this day, the first Settler child, Thomas James, dies and his body is sent ashore for burial.

At 10:30 am on the morning of 3 January 1820, the *Weymouth* finally sets sail in a snow squall. She is commanded by Captain Richard Turner. At this point, we exchange our narrative for the captain's log of the *Weymouth*, as will be kept under number ADM51/3543 at the Public Record Office at Kew in England. It speaks volumes:

Sun 2 Jan: *Departed this life THOs JAMES (Settler's child); Sent body to be interred.*

Mon 3 Jan: *AM: Strong breezes with snow; 10:30: Cast off from the buoy and made sail out of the harbor.*

Wed 12 Jan: *Departed this life the infant son of SAMl JAMES (settler); [...] Port Santo S54W 532 miles*

Sat 15 Jan: *Departed this life SAMl DUGEBY settler's child. [...] Porto Santo S29W 310 miles*

Tues 25 Jan: *4: Short sail and hove to ; 8: center of the town of Las Palmas Gran Canary WNW*

Wed 26 Jan: *4 Do weather. Rec'd water from shore boats. Killed a bullock wt 342 lbs Rec'd 6 oxen and a quantity of fruit and vegetables for the settlers. Departed this life SARAH STAMFORD settler's child*

Thu 27 Jan: *Departed this life SARAH WHITEHEAD. Committed the bodies to the deep.*

Fig. 8-3 The approaches of Portsmouth: Early 1800s

Thurs 3 Feb: *Employed clearing decks and preparing for sea; 8: Weighed and made sail*

Sat 5 Feb: *9: Aired bedding; Departed this life SARAH HOBBS settler's child. Bearings and distance at noon S. Antonio Cape de Verde S36.47W 672 miles 8: Ditto weather. Committed the body of the above infant to the deep*

Tues 8 Feb: *Employed washing clothes; Departed this life JOHN COCK settler's child. Committed the body of the above infant to the deep*

Thurs 10 Feb: *Departed this life EMMA ROGERS settler's child. Committed body of the above infant to the deep*

Fri 18 Feb: *Departed this life MARTHA GODFREY settlers child. Committed the body of the above infant to the deep*

Sun 20 Feb: *Departed this life JOHN CROUCH and JAMES FARLEY settlers children. Committed the bodies of the above infants to the deep*

Mon 21 Feb: *Departed this life MARY RALPHS settler's child; Committed the body to the deep*

Tues 22 Feb: *Distance and bearings at noon St. Helena S34E 1242 miles.6: heavy squalls with thunder and lightning*

Thu 24 Feb: *Departed this life ELIZABETH STORTON settlers child. Committed the body of the infant to the deep*

Fri 3 Mar: *Performed the customary ceremony in crossing the Equator*

Sun 5 Mar: *Saw the Island of Annabona SSW 11 or 12 leagues*

Wed 15 Mar: *Departed this life JOSEPH PINNOCK settlers child. Committed body of above infant to the deep*

Fri 17 Mar: *Departed this life WILLIAM FORWARD settlers child. Body of the above infant to the deep*

Mon 27 Mar: *Departed this life SARAH FORWARD settler's wife. Committed the body to the deep*

Wed 29 Mar: *St. Helena NNW 24 leagues*

Thu 13 Apr: *Departed this life HOBBS (settlers child); Committed the body of the above infant to the deep*

Tues 25 Apr: *Saw the Table Land ahead; Employed working in for Table Bay; Anchored in 13½ fathoms.*

Wed 26 Apr: *Departed this life EPHRAIM DICKS settler*

Thu 27 Apr: *Sent the body of E.DICKS on shore to be interred*

Wed 3 May: *Departed this life JANE DICKS female settler*

Fri 5 May: *Disembarking settlers at Cape Town*

Sun 7 May: *Departed this life infant son of J SANDERSON settler*

Mon 8 May: *Committed the body to the deep*

Tues 9 May: *At anchor in Table Bay; 6: Made sail out of the Bay*

Mon 15 May: *At anchor in Algoa Bay*

Tues 16 May–Sat 20 May: Clearing hold of settlers luggage; Disembarking settlers and their luggage

4. The trek to the new home in Africa

On shore, numerous of the peculiar wagons, drawn by oxen, are lined up with men in blue tunics and extremely wide rimmed straw hats. The first thing that strikes the immigrants, is how big and tall these men are. They smoke long stemmed pipes and sit confidently on their disproportionately small horses or on the wagons. They always have their muskets close at hand. When they speak, which is not often, it is in a heavy lumbering English with an accentuated rolling "rrr," just like the Scots.

The rather flustered officials tell the settlers that these are the "Dutch" Afrikaners who have lived in these parts for some generations and who will take them to their allotted properties in the *Suurveld*, now named Albany. One of the officials mutters that the government has suggested that the Settlers be marched the 80-100 miles to their farms. Some of the folks are taken aback by that notion, but they do not believe it. Even worse, Richard Bowles has understood that he will receive seed and implements. He has assumed that to mean "for free." It now turns out they have to buy these basic necessities.

They eventually get underway on the lumbering ox-wagons, and, when they see the terrain, they realize that these heavy vehicles are ideal for this rough country. They notice the peculiar focus of the Afrikaner driver's eyes. They are constantly scanning the surrounding clumps of bushes, their attention never wavering for a moment. They seem to be looking through the bushes, rather than at them. This is weird and disconcerting. One hundred and eighty years later British visitors will still remark on the ability of South Africans to see animals behind bushes. However, these men are not watching out for animals. They are on the lookout for prowling amaXhosa warriors. The amaXhosa spies will by now have reported the commotion. However, the Afrikaners do not think it a wise thing to frighten the English Settlers.

With most wagons there are some other extremely peculiar looking people. They are generally barefoot and walk at the front of the wagon or behind it. They are quite short and have very sparse "peppercorn" hair, high cheekbones, and rather oriental eyes. Their skins are a light-brown color. The young Esther Bowles has never seen people like these before in her life. They are constantly conversing with the oxen and intermittently they crack the extraordinarily long whips. When young Esther asks their giant Afrikaner driver who these people are, he says:

"They are Hottentots, little missy."

She wants to take offence at the *"little missy,"* but then she looks straight into the man's face and sees the bright smiling blue eyes in the deeply sunburnt face, capped with blond hair. She recognizes a friend, and so she says,

"Well, they certainly look peculiar, mommy, don't you think?"

"Shush, child!," comes the answer from Elizabeth in the back. She is becoming more worried by the minute. Whatever made them do this idiotic thing? Richard Bowles is also worried, but is putting on an appropriately brave face for his family.

Fig. 8-4 *The Landing of the British Settlers at Algoa Bay*

They cover only about three miles in an hour. So they have to sleep over in the tent for several nights on the way. Their first day ends near the Swartkops River. That first night Esther crawls tightly up against Elizabeth when they hear an insane whooping and laughing sound from the dark, followed by a hysterical giggling. A heavy Afrikaans voice outside the tent says:

"Don't worry! That is just a wolf.... errr... hyena. They are cowards and will not bother you."

That certainly does not make Esther feel any safer.

The second night they stop at the Sondaghs River. A day or two later they reach a river running in the bottom of a gorge and their driver tells them it is the Bushman's River. Richard is worried:

"Mister Prinsloo, how will you ever get this wagon through there?"

"Don't you worry, Mister Bowels, just you watch. Please just take your family off the wagon."

"That would be 'Bowles', Mister Prinsloo, not 'Bowels'."

"Yes, sorry Mister Bowels!," comes the response.

Richard shrugs. It must be the language, he mumbles to himself. He gets the family off the wagon and watches in trepidation as Prinsloo and the team go down the precipitous road.

Richard is utterly amazed when Prinsloo negotiates the ford in the river without removing the pipe from his mouth where it appears to be permanently glued. He notices that Prinsloo consults the Hottentot *touleier* (literally: rope leader, *leadmaster*) in the process and seems to be talking incessantly to each individual ox. Nevertheless, these ox-wagons are quite remarkable. Now he can see the utility in the strange design.

Prinsloo patiently waits for the family to rejoin the wagon train. The trip is much slower than his usual 3.5 miles an hour.

"Where did you get your wagon, Mr. Prinsloo?"

"I bought it from Koos Myburgh up in the Achter-Sneeuberg other side Cradock, Mister Bowels! His family has been building wagons for as long as anyone can remember."

Richard assumes that he must mean Cradock, the town about 150 miles inland from Algoa Bay. They have been told it was founded only two years ago. These people seem to be used to incredible distances. In England, no place is more than 70 miles from the sea and people tend to die where they were born.

After several days of travel, Prinsloo abruptly stops in the middle of nowhere on a rise above a valley. The giant Afrikaner announces with a satisfied expression:

"There is your land, Mister Bowels!"

Richard's jaw drops as he realizes that he is looking at nothing but complete wilderness with towering monster-like prehistoric *euphorbia*. Elizabeth's eyes are as big as saucers, but Esther and the seven Amos children are off in a flash, before she can even rein them in. That is when Richard realizes that Elizabeth is crying:

"Please God, have mercy on us, what have we done?," she softly mouths through the tears. She has seen the burnt out cottages along the way.

"Aag, this is a good farm, Misses Bowels. You will be happy here," Prinsloo says, uncomfortably manipulating his hat in his hands, the tough-looking giant with the big heart and blue eyes not knowing what to do about the distraught English mother with the nine children on the African veldt near the warlike amaXhosa.

5. Settling down; or not

The above sketch is certainly fictionalized, but the ancestral Bowles family is quite real, and the Prinsloo character and his reactions are entirely typical. Even our ancestor, Jacobus Johannes "Koos" (pronounced "Quiss") Myburgh, is at this time a wagon builder who lives west of Cradock in the Agter-Sneeuberg ward of that district. The Bushman's River is roughly 45 miles from Port Elizabeth. The train of events is also quite typical and the travel schedule[11], as well as the directions past the burnt out Boer farms, is as prescribed by the British Government at the Cape.

There are still lots of hyena at the Swartkops River in 1820. Even the closeness of the relationship between these tough frontiersmen and the new arrivals is not unusual. Two of the Bowker sons, Miles and William, traveling in a different wagon train, will eventually marry two of the daughters, Barbara and Hester, of the Afrikaner driver of their wagon train, Piet Oosthuizen.

The Bowles family, like the other members of the Menzies party, is eventually placed at the site of their farm-to-be on the Kariega River, some 17 miles from the coast and 10 miles from Grahamstown. These lands on the Kariega are soon divided among the members of the Menzies party. The men proceed to construct rough shelter for their families to tide them over until they can build something more resembling houses. Some even start trying their hand at the agricultural side of things. However, these particular people are soldiers and sailors. They know little about agriculture. They also know nothing about the vagaries of the *Suurveld* climate and soil. The place is certainly pretty and the winter is vastly milder than in England. The winter storms barreling unimpeded over the open ocean on the winds of the Roaring Forties are impressive indeed, but there is no snow. Also, despite the dramatic behavior of the weather, there does not seem to be all that much rain. In fact, it is rather dry.

Slowly but surely, it starts to dawn on the Settlers exactly how tough this re-settlement thing is going to be. After a short while, some start to desert their farms and gravitate towards Grahamstown where they establish their former city trades and activities. The soldiers and farmers, having no other skills, persevere on the farms. They are actually running out of food. This is bad, very bad! And, it is getting worse.

On 25 February 1820, the Colonial Secretary writes[12] to the landdrost at Uitenhage:

> *"It is highly expedient that the parties, as they arrive, shall be marched without delay to the places on which they are ultimately to be settled."*

So, the rumors that the Government meant for them to walk the distance from Algoa Bay to their farms were true! Also, the Government has underestimated the number of Settlers by a factor of two.

The departure of the Settlers from the farms starts almost immediately the moment they get there. In response, the governor makes a rule that they have to get permission from the government in the Cape before they can leave the *Suurveld*. The Cape Government is attempting to confine these poor people to the farms against their will. The whole immigration scheme is collapsing on itself. The governor, as a dyed in the wool British Army man, actually suggests at one point that his immigrant countrymen are vagrants endangering his army! The crops fail in the first season, and then again in the second. This forces the government to provide the Settlers with rice to survive. With the crop failure in the second season, the Governor at the Cape instructs the landdrost at Uitenhage to hand out rice gratis to the settlers, but that no rice should be provided to *"any persons who are reported to him [...] not to employ themselves, or to have useful occupation which shall be calculated to assist in their own support"*[13]. The governor, not skilled in agriculture or in the vagaries of the *Suurveld*, actually goes so far as to suggest the Settlers plant potatoes. This only leads to the next crop failure. While potatoes flourish at the Gamtoos River, some 40 miles west of Algoa Bay, the *Suurveld* is not in the least potato country. Clearly, there is something the Afrikaners and the amaXhosa know about the *Suurveld* and the Settlers and British Government do not. This region is really cattle ranching and dairy country.

By 1822, only 552 of the original 1610 men are left on the farms that have been allotted to them. Some 451 other men are still registered at the *drostdy* in Grahamstown. Some 507 men have simply disappeared from the *Suurveld*. Many of those placed near the Fish River have fled their lands. Perhaps it is the depredations of the climate and bad harvests. It may be that they are simply not farmers. More likely, it is because they finally realize that the British government has placed them as a human barrier between the amaXhosa and the rest of the Colony. William Wilberforce Bird, the Customs Controller at the Cape, has the following to say[14] on the situation of the Settlers in 1822:

> *"...in truth, the most beneficial and rational advice, and that which every one really acquainted with the colony would have given, would have been to stay at home..."*

He will subsequently[15] pointedly state that the settlement plan has failed.

One consequence of this British immigration is that the new immigrants have identified with the plight of the Afrikaners on the border within a short space of time. From this point onward, the British authorities will have no choice but to take care of that frontier. It will consume ever more military power.

The immigrants are blessed in that the amaXhosa are living in apparent peace beyond the Keiskamma River. They will have 14 years of peace, a longer period than the Afrikaners have ever experienced. But, they have no concept of the horror that lies in wait. Their concept of a vicious foe is a fellow Christian Frenchman.

—*End Nexus Familia*

Napoleon and South Africa

After his defeat at Waterloo, Napoleon had been banished to the Island of St. Helena in the Atlantic, off the coast of Africa. While there, he had the company of the Count de las Cases. De las Cases describes a visit to Cape Town in which he obtains wine for the emperor from the Great Constantia estate, founded in 1685 by Governor van der Stel, and where a Myburgh ancestral family member made wine in the 1700s. Las Cases states[16]:

> *"... I had the inexpressible satisfaction of learning that the Constantia wine, in particular, had pleased the Emperor. It was reserved for his own use, and he called it by my name."*

Napoleon, the man who had made it possible for the United States to double its size, and whose mere existence had twice caused the Cape to be invaded, died on 5 May 1821, far from his beloved France. Ironically, this was the closest he had ever been to the Cape, which the British had denied him. Equally ironically, it would be in South Africa, the land that sustained him in his own last days, that his bloodline would finally end[17].

The English Afrikaners

Within three years of landing, James Erith's party disintegrated and they dispersed all over the Cape. Robert Robinson, the butcher, moved to Cradock where he ensured that his children were schooled. His youngest, William, became schoolmaster there and had his eye on an Afrikaner girl.

The Nottinghamshire people settled at Clumber near the Great Fish River. Their efforts at agriculture failed and they resigned themselves to the reality that the *Suurveld* is pastoral country. Cattle-ranching requires tracts of land greater than 100 acres to be economical for one farmer. So many left the area and returned to their original trades in the towns of the eastern Cape Colony.

The Hayhurst Party, including the Cawood and Halstead families, settled near the Nottinghamshire people. The land proved inadequate and Cawood was asked to lead a group of people even closer to the Xhosa people. The Cawoods soon set up the trading company of Cawood Brothers. As young men Samuel, James, Joshua, and David became famous big game hunters and ivory traders. In 1830, they went through Xhosa territory to Natal on a trading expedition and met the all-powerful king of the Zulu.

Fig. 8-5 *The Eastern Cape in 1820 at the time of the British Settlers*

The king treated them well while they were there, but after they left he sent an *impi* (army) to kill them. The Cawoods owed their survival to the rain that erased their spoor. The second oldest brother William Cawood eventually moved to Cradock to manage the Cawood Brothers business in that town. There his destiny would eventually intertwine with that of the author's Myburgh wagon-building family.

Richard Halstead's son, Thomas, left for the coast of Natal with the eccentric Lieutenant Francis Farewell of the Royal Navy. There they set up a trading operation and met the king of the Zulu, who struck fear into the hearts of all black people in Africa. In 1830, Thomas was back at Grahamstown with a certain John Cane and seven Zulus, bearing a shipment of ivory for the Cape Government as a present from the new King of the Zulu. In the world-view of the British authority, anyone this powerful had to be a potential enemy and would ultimately have to be put down. Halstead petitioned for British recognition of Natal as a colony in 1835, but was turned down. His destiny would be intertwined with his Afrikaner co-citizens, who were at this point still living in the East Cape border area.

Simon Biddulph's son, John Burnet Biddulph, an ex-Lieutenant in the Royal Navy, became an explorer in Bechuanaland (Botswana today) and in Natal. As was the case with so many British Settlers, he married an Afrikaner girl by the name of Wilhelmina Wahlstrand, the Afrikaans daughter of Peter Ernst Wahlstrand, who was shipwrecked with the American Captain Stout in 1796 (*NF32*). Younger brother Thomas Jervis Biddulph would throw his lot in with the Afrikaners, as would William Cowie, who married an Afrikaner girl, Magdalena Laas. British immigrants such as the Bowkers and the Biddulphs were all settling down locally with their Afrikaans-speaking families. Samuel Liversage and his English family would move to the Winterberg district and later join the Great Trek of the Afrikaners, thereby committing totally to the cause of the Afrikaner. John Leech married a young Afrikaner lady and settled next door to the Bowles family. Their son would rise to the occasion at a key moment in our story.

The Biggar family settled on a property, which they named "Woodlands," east of the Kariega River. The family's efforts at farming were so disastrous that Captain Alexander Biggar contemplated emigrating to Tasmania after the first few desperate seasons. However, after being granted his party's whole original allotment plus additional land, he decided to remain. Of their twelve children, only two were boys. They were Robert, who was seven years old during the trip on the *Weymouth*, and George, who was born on the *Weymouth*. The Sixth Frontier War would ruin the family and Alexander Biggar would relocate them to Port Elizabeth. From there he and his two sons would go to Port Natal, where they will enter our story again.

At the end of their tether

By 1834, fourteen years after the mass immigration, the visitor would have been hard pressed to tell the difference between the Bowker family, for example, and any of the long-standing Afrikaner families. Both were herding cattle and had given up trying the futile pursuit of agriculture in this drought-ridden countryside. Up north in the Tarka, Afrikaners like the Potgieters and Jordaans maintained good relations with the Xhosa paramount chief Hintsa, and he did business with them, leasing them land to graze their cattle. However, Lord Charles Somerset was keenly aware that the Dutch-speaking Afrikaners were by far the majority of European-descended people at the Cape. In support of his goal to convert them into Englishmen, he initiated a campaign of Anglification. Henceforth Afrikaners would have to defend themselves in English in court. He followed this up by banning Dutch in schools, including those schools that were serving only Afrikaner communities.

A period of caretaking governors followed Lord Charles Somerset's departure. It was in 1827 that the long-standing institution of Heemraden (Regional Councils) was abolished as a short-sighted means of saving money. It somehow escaped the Governor that he had therewith removed the last vestige of nominal representation for Afrikaners.

The major problem for all Afrikaners, and, as it would turn out, all British Settlers, actually arrived much earlier at in 1818 in the form of a new local leader for the London Missionary Society (LMS). He was a self-educated weaver's apprentice from Kirkcaldy in Scotland, Dr. John Philip; the title being an honorary one. He had changed his name from the original Philp to Philip around 1794, at which time he entered the Ministry. A Colony, populated largely by Dutch descendants and presided over by a British Military government, would in future be practically directed by this designing fanatic. Noël Mostert, in his seminal work on the amaXhosa, titled *Frontiers*, describes Philip as *"the rightful heir"*[18] to Van der Kemp.

Captain William Harris[19], writing in 1838, stated about the people in the east of the colony suffering under the London Missionary Society, the depredations from both the vagrant Khoekhoe around the LMS mission stations and the amaXhosa cattle raiders:

> *"...yet no unprejudiced person, who has visited the more remote districts of this unhappy colony, will hesitate to acknowledge that the evils they complain of actually exist. Long subjected to the pilferings of a host of Hottentot vagrants, whose lives are passed in one perpetual round of idleness, delinquency, and brutish intoxication on the threshold of the gin-shop, [...]*
>
> *"Far greater [...] are the evils that have arisen out of the perverse misrepresentations of canting and designing men, to whose mischievous and gratuitous interference, veiled under the cloak of philanthropy, is principally to be attributed the desolated condition of the eastern frontier; bounded, as it is, by a dense and almost impenetrable jungle, to defend which nine times the military force now employed would barely be adequate ; and flanked by a population of eighty thousand dire, irreclaimable savages, naturally inimical, warlike, and predatory, by whom the hearths of the Cape border colonists have for years past been deluged with the blood of their nearest and dearest relatives."*

Perversely, the interests of the Khoekhoe "vagrants" were now represented in London via the LMS, but the Afrikaner was left without a vote or a voice. They had to pay the tax and work under a British Military Government that treated them as cannon fodder. They were supposed to unquestioningly follow Magistrate Stockenström whom they had not yet quite forgiven for the Slagtersnek horror that he and Magistrate Cuyler had perpetrated (*NF40*). Through all of this galloped Somerset's son, Colonel Henry Somerset, constantly humiliating the powerful amaXhosa.

Fig. 8-6 *'Doctor' John Philip*

The Afrikaners thought Somerset, like Graham before him, was likely to go safely "home" at some point and leave the people of the colony with the mess he was making. Meanwhile they were dragged to court on trumped up charges on the say-so of the LMS, where they had to defend themselves in English and pay the court costs even if exonerated; this while the LMS incessantly sketched them as monsters in Britain, incited their workers against them, and allowing their supposed "congregation" of layabouts and vagrants to steal them blind. In these thefts, the farmers were largely left without legal recourse. The situation was untenable. Already a team of people had gone on an expedition to determine the suitability of Natal as a new home. This team included[20] not only Stephanus Maritz, Jacobus Uys, and Karel Landman, but also Evert Potgieter. Piet Uys, leader in the Boesmansrivier area of the Uitenhage district, and brother of the two Uys men, was a moving force behind this expedition, generally referred to as the Uys Expedition. They delivered a glowing report about Natal.

An American colony in Africa

The American Colonization Society was created in Washington on December 21, 1816 based on a number of divergent interests around the matter of slavery in the United States. The high profile individuals involved in this process included James Madison. Some supporters were truly supportive of a good future for American black people, while others wanted the freed slaves deposited outside the United States in order to avoid sharing the country. In one area, all the divergent views found common ground, namely the matter of a colony in Africa. As early as that same December the General Assembly of Virginia requested its governor to enter into discussion with the President of the United States about such a colony[21].

The Rev. Samuel J. Mills, charged by the Society with finding a suitable location for a settlement along the coast of West Africa, left us with intriguing notes. He relates comments from Sierra Leone to the effect that the local kings had a suspicion that those whom they sold into slavery might return and exact revenge[22]. Other kings were worried that the Americans would do what the freed slaves in Sierra Leone had done: make war on the locals and take their land. He also noted the advice[23] of the governor of the British Sierra Leone:

> *"that, in the first instance, white men of intelligence and good character should occupy some of the principal offices; [...]*
>
> *"...that one hundred men, with arms, and some knowledge of discipline, could defend themselves from the natives; [...]*
>
> *"...that it was particularly proper for the American government to commission an armed ship to this coast, to capture slave-trading vessels, as two thirds of them are, or have been American."*

Clearly the governor already knew something the philanthropists had not quite fathomed. Having a black skin and African ancestry did not make the settlers welcome. They no longer shared the culture of the people in Africa. Whether other Americans wanted to know it or not, these people were now Americans. They were not "African-Americans"; they were black Americans with no hyphenation required. As the events of 160 years later would prove[24], their differences with the indigenous people were already largely insurmountable. Eventually, with the able assistance of the threatening guns of the U.S. Navy, land was obtained at Cape Mesurado (now in Liberia) in 1822. The Missionary Register[25] of October 1822 reports:

> *"...It appears by the Treaty between Captain Stockton of the United-States Navy and the Kings and Headmen of Cape Mesurado, that the Natives agreed to accept the following valuable consideration for the Territory purchased:—*
>
> *"Paid in hand — Six muskets, one box of beads, two hogsheads of tobacco, one cask of gunpowder, six iron pots, one dozen knives and forks, one dozen spoons, six pieces of blue baft, four hats, three coats, three pair of shoes, one box of pipes, one keg of nails, twenty looking-glasses, three pieces of handkerchiefs, three pieces of calico, three canes, four umbrellas, one box of soap, and one barrel of rum.*
>
> *"To be paid — Three casks of tobacco, one box of pipes, three barrels of rum, twelve pieces of cloth, six bars of iron, one box of beads, fifty knives, twenty looking-glasses, ten iron pots, twelve guns, three barrels of gunpowder, one dozen plates, one dozen knives and forks, twenty hats, five casks of beef, five barrels of pork, ten barrels of biscuit, twelve glass tumblers, and fifty pair of shoes."*

And so the United States acquired a colony in Africa for what boils down to 18 guns and four barrels each of gunpowder and rum, the rest being trivial. By 1835, five more colonies had been started on the West African coast by other American Societies, and one by the U.S. government. The first colony on Cape Mesurado expanded along the coast, and also to the interior.

There soon were clashes with the indigenous people. The missionaries thought they were spreading The Word. The anti-slavery people thought they were fighting slavery. Some pro-slavery people were happy with a place they could send emancipated black slaves, as long as it was far from themselves. And the slavers, knowing that coast better than anyone else, continued to ply their trade.

In nearby Sierra Leone, the British used their piece of emancipation territory as the base for their worst soldiers, the Royal African Corp; a corps of men who chose to serve in the British Army instead of a life of penal servitude. Men from as far away as Canada were sent to this unit as punishment. They represented the worst that British society could produce and acted the part. These were the men who nearly cost the British the town of Grahamstown in South Africa in 1819 by training Nxele's amaXhosa to fight the British Army (*NF41*).

-----ooOoo-----

9

The Third Abandonment

"Why is there so much made of the Fingos, are they not my dogs? Cannot I do with them as I want?"

Paramount amaXhosa chief Hintsa,
In negotiation with Sir Benjamin D'Urban (1835)

The emancipation of the slaves

On 1 December 1834, the last slaves at the Cape were emancipated. They would have to render four more years of service, but the die had been cast; this more than three decades before it was done in the United States. The citizens of the colony had expected that the slaves would be freed. The trade in slaves had already been terminated decades earlier by the Batavian Dutch. It was mostly in the Western Cape with its wheat fields, vineyards, and fruit orchards that slave labor was used, rather than the eastern cattle ranching and sheep farming districts. However, there was nothing even vaguely like the plantation system of the United States. Says Bird[1] as Head of Customs of the Cape Colony:

Fig. 9-1 19th Century Xhosa warrior

> *"Of all the colonies belonging to England, there is not one where [...] emancipation could be so safely made as at the Cape of Good Hope. There are no indigo, coffee, cotton, or sugar plantations to be made desolate by labor suddenly withdrawn."*

Bird gives the exact numbers[2] of slaves for 1820 as being a total of 34,329 only 3,514, or roughly one in ten, were in the two eastern districts from where most people would leave on the Great Trek. Emancipation should certainly have been easier in South Africa than in the United States. However, there was a complication that modern liberal authors carefully keep from the reading public. Given the termination of the slave trade, slaves were hugely precious at the Cape and the price of a slave was a large fraction of the value of the typical farming property. As may be seen from the records of the Cape Orphan Chamber[3], a typical farming property was assessed at 3000 Rixdollars and a typical mature male slave could be around 1000 Rixdollars. When the government announced that the farmers would be reimbursed only a tiny fraction of the market value of their slaves, many established farmers technically went bankrupt. This was less of a factor in the cattle ranching east of the colony with its very few slaves.

The final straw came with the announcement that payment for the emancipated slaves would only be made available in Britain and that farmers had to make use of British agents to get this money. There were not ten Afrikaner farmers who had an agent in Britain. The British agents wanted 30% of the payments and the farmers were left with but a tiny fraction of the original market value of their legitimately purchased slaves.

The inevitable British "carpetbaggers" descended on the farmers and bought up their farms for next to nothing as the owners scrambled for cash to pay their debts called up in fear by their creditors. Many previously well-established farmers prepared to leave the Cape forever. Afrikaners were not against the actual emancipation of the slaves. They were dismayed specifically at the way in which it was done. Beyond the financial damage, they now faced having a loitering class of freed slave that would inevitably turn to crime, as they had experienced at the hands of the Khoekhoe for decades. And, the British insisted on protecting these new Freemen under the same Law as the burghers. This was simply too much for them.

Sarel Cilliers, of whom we will learn more later, would complain that he had slaves to the value of 2,888 Rijksdaler (Rix Dollars), but received only 500 Rijksdaler upon their emancipation. That is less than 17.5% of the true value. English slave owners fared better but were outraged. An example was Major Parlby[4], who lost £492 of the £830 he had paid. On behalf of his Afrikaner colleagues, he would later state:

"[...] *we* [the British Government] *have goaded them to desperation, we have plundered them of their property and they are leaving our territories in countless numbers execrating the name of England."*

The attempts by present day politicians and media to sketch this reaction as being directed against emancipation, is entirely willful and defamatory of a nation. Consider the hard numbers for the entire emancipation as provided not by an Afrikaner, but by English Notary Public, John Centlivres Chase[5] (all amounts in 1834 British Pounds Stirling):

Given that the government assessors had naturally assessed slaves far below the market value, the scope of the financial disaster is obvious to any responsible homeowner with a mortgage and basic mathematics. Coming after the excesses of Maynier and Van der Kemp, not to mention the first British Occupation and Slagtersnek, the reaction of the much-tried Afrikaners is wholly understandable. However, before these people could depart the Cape, matters on the frontier yet again interceded.

Total # of slaves (90% in the West Cape)	**35,745**
Value as assessed by government (Average of £85.08 per slave)	£ 3,041,290
Amount paid by government	£ 1,247,401
Less commission at 2.5%	£ 31,185
Less stamps & Postage	£ 10,722
Net amount made available in London	£ 1,205,494
Less 27% (some asked more) for agent	£ 325,483
Amount received by farmers (**29%**)	£ 880,011

Prelude to the Sixth Frontier War

In 1818, Lord Charles Somerset had appointed his son, Henry Somerset, as commander of the Cape Corps and deputy landdrost of Uitenhage under Jacob Cuyler. From this point on the British conduct of military matters was to be a long string of decidedly rough actions by Henry Somerset. These would be exacerbated by the presence of the London Missionary Society with their philosophy directed at the other extreme of conduct. The citizenry found themselves simultaneously confronted with the worst of heavy-handed military behavior and the worst of Far Left egalitarian Liberation Theology.

To the east beyond the Kei River was Hintsa, the Paramount Chief of all the Xhosa. Up to this point, he had managed to stay out of trouble. Remarkably, Afrikaners such as Hendrik Potgieter (*NF38*) found him a reasonable man and rented pasture from him in times of drought. Ironically, the Afrikaners in the Tarka, where British rule was only distantly felt, were able to co-exist with their amaXhosa neighbors on an amicable basis.

However, in the coastal border zone where Henry Somerset represented British authority, relations with the late Ngqika's sons, Maqoma and Tyali, were rapidly deteriorating. By 1828, there was a severe drought and the starving amaXhosa were yet again raiding Afrikaner farms. The Afrikaner ranchers wanted an end put to it, though their solution was a regular commando to retrieve stolen cattle. They specifically wanted Ngqika son Maqoma left alone. This was in line with their general philosophy of "live and let live"; each in his own place.

It was at this point in time that Stockenström obtained the support of the Governor to push Maqoma and his brother Tyali out of the belt between the Fish and the Keiskamma River, and to settle some Khoekhoe people in a buffer zone, calling it the Stockenström District. At the heart of this zone, was the Tyumie Valley, the ancestral home of Ngqika. This act on the part of Stockenström hugely upset the amaXhosa and provoked the ire of Paramount Chief Hintsa.

The Afrikaners warned that the Khoekhoe Settlement would inevitably lead to more problems with the LMS, which would be drawn to the place. They were correct. Before Stockenström could get the first missionary placed at this Kat River settlement, Dr. Philip and Read had insinuated themselves and all the old problems started again, with vagrant Khoekhoe congregating there and stealing from the farmers. This also, of course, bedeviled those Khoekhoe who were actually doing a good job at the Kat River settlement.

Two days after the emancipation of the slaves, a group of Xhosa warriors attacked a mixed British-Boer patrol and a British Ensign was severely wounded by a Xhosa assegai. Henry Somerset set out against Tyali, who was settled in the Stockenström district, counter to the Stockenström arrangement. Again the Xhosa attacked and in this skirmish a bullet grazed the scalp[6] of Ngqika's youngest son, Xoxo. It was a mere scratch, but it was enough. For the first time in their existence, the British Settlers would see the amaXhosa at war.

The Afrikaners had seen this no fewer than five times before.

Nexus Familia 42: The Little Church in the Bush

Since we last saw the Bowles family (*NF41*), they have added four sons to the family. Daughter Esther, much older than her Bowles stepsiblings, has since married John Openshaw, a discharged soldier from the much-lamented Royal African Corps and has borne him three children.

On a sunny day[7] during the Christmas week of 1832, the Rev. Munro, a missionary to some Dutch-speaking people of mixed descent in Grahamstown, is traveling by ox wagon from Grahamstown to the Theopolis Mission Station with his family. His route takes him through the Upper Kariega area. When they stop for lunch in the valley, they hear a man loudly remon-strating with some oxen. He is swearing like a sailor in a loud "stentorian voice." Mrs. Munro is quite put out by all this terrible language echoing around the place. Richard Bowles has been struggling all morning with the obdurate oxen on his land allotment where he has managed to keep life going after so many other British Settlers have simply given up farming and have left the region. His years under Lord Nelson in the Royal Navy have prepared his vocabulary well indeed for dealing with oxen. The last thing on Earth on his mind is the clergy and so he is startled when a calm voice behind him says:

Fig. 9-2 The little Kariega Baptist Church – now a national monument

"You swear as many times as there are stars in the heavens."

Turning, Bowles finds himself face to face with none other than a church minister. When Richard recovers, he asks Rev. Munro for a local church service, to which Munro responds that he needs a congregation. The story goes that Richard Bowles now goes from hill to hill, shouting from the hilltops in his stentorian voice the news of a service to be held. The service is duly held in the nearby home of Mrs. Eastland, another member of the Menzies Settler Party. Richard, having had something of a re-birth, proceeds to ask

Mr. Davies, the Baptist minister in Grahamstown, to become their minister at the new outlying parish. And so the only rural Baptist Church for white people in the Cape Colony has its origin with our ancestor. Among the letters received by the Baptist Missionary Society in London at the close of the year 1833, is one from the Rev. W. Davies, in which we find the following:

> *"I have one station in the country called Kariega, which I supply once a fortnight. There the seed has fallen into good ground. Three from thence have already been baptized, and we expect others to follow. Some of the individuals above referred to were formerly very immoral, but now they are living epistles, known and read of all men. Formerly they were drunkards, now they are sober. Formerly they made the hills echo with their drunken revels, now the wilderness and the solitary place are glad for them. The three baptized were Richard Bowles, his wife and daughter* [Jemima, born 1819 in Kent]."

The new parish needs a church building, and work is started on this in late 1834 when Mr. Davies lays the foundation stone. It is built near Bowles' farm on a sprit of land in a tight bow of the meandering Kariega River. On 21 December 1834, this work is interrupted by the invasion of the Ngqika's amaRharhabe.

—End Nexus Familia

From White House to Suurveld

On 21 December 1834, the Xhosa army invaded the Cape Colony on a 100-mile front stretching from the Winterberg to the sea. The discipline of the attack was taken as evidence that it had been planned well in advance. Henry Somerset was caught flat footed and fumbled in the face of concerted attack. The amaXhosa armies streamed past the helpless mission stations and those who were not missionaries were dragged out and killed. The Afrikaners knew how to defend themselves against these attacks using their wagon circle laagers, but the entire thing was new to the British Settlers. From a military perspective the "nation of shopkeepers" that had fled the Suurveld in the first three years for the comforts of Grahamstown was a frightened rabble.

In his epic work on the amaXhosa, *Frontiers*[8], Noël Mostert concedes that the Afrikaners were steady and controlled under these circumstances and that their confidence was rooted in their legendary shooting skills, knowing every shot had to count. As soon as they had beaten off the initial amaXhosa attack on their farm the typical Afrikaner family would retreat and join up with their friends in agreed places and run their wagons in the classic circle of the laager. There they would carefully prepare their collective defense, pour the lead to make slugs for their smooth bore muskets and lay out their fields of fire. They knew how to fight in Africa.

The British Settlers, for their part, were mostly ordinary civilians with zero military experience who had never fired a shot in anger, let alone faced a horde of battle-crazed amaXhosa. They were lost in the face of the onslaught. Now, when all was at stake, the supposedly "surly," "half-educated," "dour," "obstinate," "Jacobin," Calvinist Afrikaner Boer became the pillar of strength on whom all depended. At Fort Brown, on the Fish River, a mere 12 Afrikaners[9] joined the terrified British troops, who were new to all this, and beat off the amaXhosa attack through their sharpshooting.

On Christmas Day 1834, the amaXhosa fell upon the British Settlers themselves. They killed all the male settlers they could find, but, with some exceptions, spared the women and small children. The Settlers fled to Grahamstown, Bathurst, and Salem. The amaXhosa bypassed many military posts and focused on murdering the civilians. The British had only 775 military men in the entire border region, of whom two thirds were in Grahamstown. The message of the invasion reached the new Governor, Sir Benjamin D'Urban, during the 1835 New Year celebration party at the Cape. He dispatched the man who had been, from 1828 until that moment, the Deputy Quartermaster General at the Cape. Jumping from horse to horse to cover the six hundred miles from the Cape to Grahamstown came dashing none other than Harry Smith, he who had torched the American White House (See Chapter 7: *The British eat the President's Dinner*).

He first knocked some much-needed discipline into the population of Grahamstown and correctly concluded that Somerset was not an ideal military leader. Then he turned his attention to the amaXhosa.

He was at the Kei River on 15 April 1835 for the first ever crossing of a white man's army into the territory of paramount amaGcaleka chief Hintsa, who had always stayed out of any direct fighting. This was a strategic step, in comparison with which all previous military action was trivial. The amaXhosa had driven all the stolen cattle to Hintsa's land, as per agreement with him, and this had to be addressed. Hintsa was clearly and obviously complicit in the invasion of the Colony. It was also a clearer and more achievable objective than ineffectually chasing Maqoma in the Amatole Mountains, where the amaXhosa mocked the British Army.

At the front of the column, rode the Swellendam Afrikaner Commando under the white-bearded patriarch, Field-Commandant Linde. This venerable old campaigner was, according to Harry Smith himself[10], *"The finest old fellow upwards of seventy I ever saw, except my poor old Padre."* Captain James E. Alexander[11] described the Afrikaner Commando members as *"a Patagonian race, formidable with guns like wall pieces, and immense powder horns swinging at their hips."*

Fig. 9-3 Henry George Wakelyn "Harry" Smith

Harry Smith ensured that his personal armed escort consisted of twelve Afrikaners on Commando service, showing that the soldiers related to them and that they instilled confidence. Gone, for now, were the days of the First British Occupation and Slagtersnek.

The slaves of the amaXhosa

The British Army had hardly crossed the Kei when they saw of hundreds upon hundreds of black warriors in war dress and headgear marching towards them. These were the amaFengu (The Beggar People). They were ethnic Zulus who had fled the much-rumored tyrannical Zulu king further to the north. In exchange for refuge from the Zulu king, Hintsa and his amaXhosa had kept the amaFengu as slaves[12]. They had now fled slavery and were offering the British their assistance against Hintsa. The editor of the Grahamstown Journal, Robert Godlonton, wrote[13] of the amaFengu:

"The Commander-in-Chief having well weighed this question in all its bearings, came to the conclusion, that a compliance with their entreaty would be at once an act of the greatest beneficence in itself, as effecting the emancipation of 6,000 human beings from the very lowest and worst state of slavery,"

On 24 April 1835, Governor D'Urban declared the Fingo, as they would come to be called, British subjects and declared war on Hintsa. The Fingo freedom came into effect on 9 May 1835. They were the only indigenous nation of South Africa ever to be enslaved, and they were enslaved by their fellow black men. The Reverend William Shaw, Wesleyan superintendent for South East Africa in 1835, would later write that[14]:

"I now discovered that these Fingoes were regarded by the Kaffirs as a sort of slave; and hence I had to purchase Sigliki's freedom from his master by the payment of a quantity of buttons and beads to the value of five or six shillings!"

Harry Smith proceeded to burn Xhosa *kraals* (corrals: villages) and take their cattle as far as he went. Word was sent that he would only negotiate with Hintsa personally and not with any emissaries. Five days after the declaration of war, Hintsa arrived on horseback at Harry Smith and D'Urban's camp. Smith then proceeded to read him the typically unreasonable set of British demands. The strategic intent was to once and for all deny the amaXhosa access to the impenetrable Fish River Forest from which it was incredibly difficult to expel them. The Fish River was simply not viable as a practical border as it could not be militarily defended.

Hintsa apparently acquiesced, but already his people were moving. They started by killing those amaFengu they could find and taking their cattle. When Harry Smith threatened to kill two Xhosas in response for every Fingo killed, Hintsa uttered the infamous words[15]:

"Why is there so much made of the Fingos, are they not my dogs? Cannot I do with them as I like?"

The genocide of the amaFengu at the hands of the amaXhosa only stopped when Harry Smith threatened to hang Hintsa, whom he was effectively keeping as hostage after having invited him to negotiate.

The Death of Hintsa

With the Fingo situation stabilized, Hintsa agreed to accompany Harry Smith on a mission to retrieve the stolen colonial cattle. Then came the moment that Harry Smith probably regretted for the rest of his life. While on this cattle retrieval mission, Hintsa, bolted and was shot dead. To make matters worse, the British mutilated his body. Governor D'Urban declared the territory between the Keiskamma and the Kei to be the new Queen Adelaide's Province. The amaFengu would be settled there and the amaXhosa had to leave. The Fingo would now be the new human shield between the colony and the amaXhosa. In exchange, they were now British subjects and could call on the protection of Britain; or so everyone thought.

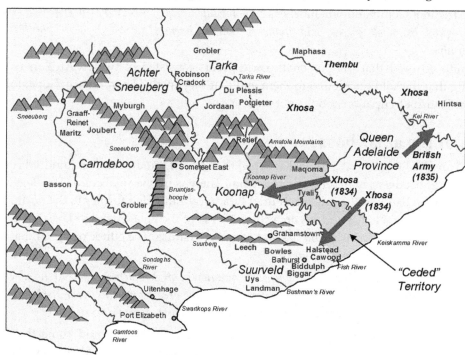

Fig. 9-4 The 6th Frontier war: Hintsa's War

Smith went off to the Amatole Mountain to give battle to Maqoma, who had earlier evaded him there. This became a long and drawn out affair with no victory on either side. The British response was to yet again burn their enemy out of their country, but it seemed to have little effect on the amaXhosa as a whole. The colony's own food supply was under threat and so, by August 1835, Smith released the Afrikaner farmers from commando service. They had been away from their farms for going on 5 months.

Almost concurrently with Governor D'Urban declaring war on Hintsa, the government in Britain changed, and with it came a new Secretary of State for War and Colonies, Lord Glenelg. He was a devout philanthropist and close friend of Fowell Buxton, who was promoting Dr. Philip's message in England.

Buxton himself had become heir to William Wilberforce as leader of the Anti-Slavery Movement in the British Parliament in 1825 upon Wilberforce's retirement. In early 1836, a Select Committee of the House of Commons was appointed to inquire into the treatment of aborigines in the British Colonies. This witch-hunt has to be one of the most disgraceful exercises in British colonial history. Says Notary Public Chase[16]:

> *"Biassed in favor of the Kafirs, and deeply prejudiced against the Colonists, every evidence on behalf of the latter, however respectable or trustworthy, was unheeded, while the wildest and most extravagant denunciations against them were favorably entertained, and even its very report was entrusted to be drawn up by the Rev. Dr. Philip, the least principled and bitterest accuser of the Colonists; a person who, to serve his purpose, did not hesitate in one case to suppress, and in another interpolate whole passages in public papers laid before the Committee, besides being guilty of the most shameless fabrications."*

The fervor with which Philip and his London supporters went about destroying the character of D'Urban, Smith, the Settlers, and the Afrikaners knew no bounds. Dr. Philip went off to England to introduce to parliamentarians his entourage of Diyani Tshatshu, son of a minor Xhosa chief, and the Khoekhoe, Andries Stoffels. The thought never occurred to him, as a supposed churchman, to include any Afrikaners, who still had no voice in anything whatsoever after all this time. Philip confessed[17] his true prejudice against his own blood in a letter to the American Board of Commissioners for Foreign Missions:

> *"[...] I consider the Caffres on the borders of the Colony as most decidedly superior to that portion of the refuse of English society that find their way to this country."*

He was not clear on whether he considered the *"refuse"* to exclude himself. One can only but wonder about the private thoughts of this all-powerful man on the subject of the voiceless Afrikaners whom he hated with a consuming passion.

It is not generally appreciated just how comprehensive, organized, and insidious this whole LMS cabal actually was. Philip's son-in-law, John Fairbairn, owned the *Commercial Advertiser* newspaper in Cape Town, which kept up an unremitting torrent of local attacks on the Afrikaners, the Settlers, and the Governor. He did not hesitate at publishing outright lies. In England, Buxton's family worked as a dedicated team to generate a key report to the Select Committee. In her recent book, Laidlaw[18] argues that the report was actually drawn up by Buxton's cousin Anna Gurney, with help from his sister Sarah, Buxton's daughter Priscilla, and Priscilla's husband, Andrew Johnston, who conveniently happened to be on the actual Select Committee.

This dedicated, obsessed, and disgracefully conniving team studied all colonial communications in detail and twisted it to their ends. Buxton unashamedly had his cousin Gurney edit the evidence. To ensure his view would succeed, he adjourned the Select Committee to keep matters stationary while waiting for Philip to arrive to testify, and then secretly primed Philip with all the prior confidential testimony. It was what in the 21st Century would be called a complete and utter "setup." The result was a foregone conclusion. The "Select Committee" only had ears for Philip and for Stockenström, who were called as witnesses. They blamed all the woes of the Cape on the British Settlers, the British Army and, conveniently, the ever-voiceless Afrikaners. Thousands of people were about to die because of Dr. Philip and his LMS coven.

The Third Great Abandonment

Lord Glenelg's reaction to the 6th Frontier War and his new province of Queen Adelaide was received at the Cape on 26 December 1835. A shattering communication that would have far reaching consequences to this very day, it said:

1. The "colonists" were themselves to blame for the war

2. The new Queen Adelaide Province was to be given back to the amaXhosa

3. Andries Stockenström was to be the Frontier Lieutenant-Governor

During the debate around the Select Committee in England it had even been suggested that Britain should give up the Cape Colony, bring their British Settlers back to Britain and consign the Afrikaners to "go and make their own way with the savages." The Afrikaners had known their second-class status as mere British subjects ever since 1795. The outrage of the British Settlers, however, knew no bounds. They had been attacked by the amaXhosa who had wanted to drive them into the sea. Nearly one hundred of them had been brutally murdered. The lives of the survivors had been ruined and their children were dead. Now their "Mother Country" on whom they had relied for support not only deserted them, but condemned them. And, to crown it all, Westminster inflicted the "turncoat" Afrikaner, Stockenström on them.

The Afrikaners had lived this kind of outrage for four decades. However, this was the first time that British-born people at the Cape experienced this profoundly sickening and demoralizing phenomenon. They were beyond anger. This was the key moment in which they became "English-speaking Afrikaners," members of the *amaBhulu*; the abandoned and disowned "White Tribe."

Governor D'Urban wrote three times to the hapless Glenelg on the subject, but to no avail. All the power at the Cape was in the hands of Dr. Philip and the London Missionary Society, aided and abetted by John Fairbairn's Commercial Advertiser. By the time of his third letter, the Governor had correctly concluded that the Cape was run by Dr. Philip. This is obvious from the letter itself[19], which we reproduce in excerpt here, as it also shows that D'Urban understood the frontier issues and the reasons for the Great Trek perfectly well. Moreover, it is clear from the letter that he had informed Whitehall and Glenelg on these matters before (author's emphases):

> "...I shall [...]... prepare the public mind for the relinquishment of the newly acquired province by the end of the present year; an information, indeed, scarcely necessary, since the intention of your Lordship in that regard seems to have been known here (I have reason to believe through the medium of the London Mission) [the LMS] **before I had received** your Lordship's despatch of December last on the subject.
>
> That this will be speedily followed by an extensive abandonment of Albany and Somerset on the part of the farmers, as predicted [...] I have [...] no legal power to detain them against their will and these persuasions [...] will at once cause an extensive emigration, along the whole Albany and Somerset border, or I am much mistaken."

Fig. 9-5 Andries Stockenström

For the first time the Englishman in South Africa felt the true depth of dismay, despair and the sense of desertion that the Afrikaner of that time had had to live with all of his mature life. The British settlers in the Graaff-Reinet district wrote to the King himself, stating that they now experienced first hand what had earlier been done to their Afrikaner countrymen by the likes of Maynier, Stockenström and Van der Kemp[20]:

> "...nothing short of actual experience could have [...] exposed [the British Settlers] to the same systematic misrepresentation which had been previously directed against your Majesty's Dutch-African subjects."

The local Frontier press reaction was violent. Godlonton, the press leader in the East Cape, called the amaXhosa[21]:

> "...the most barbarous savages, sunk to the lowest abyss of moral degradation."

The British Settlers, however, were still reasonably well off. The people who had suffered most ruin were the hinterland Afrikaners in districts such as the Koonap and Tarka. Even the son of the Afrikaner-hating Read confessed that the Afrikaners had been left destitute by the war. They traced their unhappy fate to the lack of say in their own destiny, the inconsistent policies of the British and the powers vested in LMS missionaries sent, in their view, by the Devil himself.

Governor D'Urban himself said of the activities of the LMS in the dark days of 1835, when the war was at its peak and the citizenry was intensely worried about the state of the country[22]:

> "...the dangerous efforts of some [...] to degrade the character of their fellow-countrymen, in defence of those of a savage and treacherous enemy; nor do they scruple even to pass over unnoticed, or to hold as trifling, the almost unequalled sufferings of the former in the barbarous invasion which laid the frontier districts in blood and ashes; while they earnestly invite all commiseration for the case of the latter. Whatever may be the real and ultimate object of this perversion of facts and inferences, its manifest and immediate tendency is, at home, to deceive and mislead His Majesty's government and the people of England"

For a word on the dismay and despair of the people themselves on the Frontier in 1835, we turn to Captain William Cornwallis Harris[23]:

> "...And whilst, during the unprovoked inroads of these ruthless barbarians, their wives and helpless offspring have been mercilessly butchered before their eyes; whilst their corn-fields have been laid waste, their flocks swept off, and their houses reduced to ruins, to add bitterness to gall, they have been taunted as the authors of their own misfortunes, by those who, strangely biased by ex parte statements, have judged them unheard, at the distance of several thousand miles from the scene of pillage, bloodshed, and devastation."

Lt-Colonel Elers Napier, on special services to the Eastern Border area, states[24] about the Afrikaners:

> "...victims of detraction and injustice in every shape — an oppressed people, who had been forced at length to abandon in despair the thresholds of their forefathers, and bury themselves in exile amidst the far wildernesses, and deserted wastes of the interior."

In the autobiography of Harry Smith, to which George Charles Moore Smith wrote supplementary chapters, the latter described the Afrikaner as[25]

> "...men shamefully abandoned by the British Government."

Philip's lies and Glenelg's actions lie directly at the root of most of what has been wrong with South Africa ever since. As leading an historian as Amery[26] calls Philip a "mischievous and unscrupulous person" and Glenelg "ignorant and incompetent." Afrikaners, unfortunately, did not hear about the luckless John Williams, LMS missionary to the New Hebrides, who in 1839 was consumed by his prospective congregation among his chosen "Noble Savages." Had they but known, they might have felt that there was some justice somewhere on Earth. The excesses of the London Missionary Society made one thing clear. The true enemy of the white man in Africa was not the black man in Africa. The true enemy of the white man in Africa was white men in Europe who lived in safety and comfort while they moralized about those of their fellow Western Christians desperately fighting for their own existence.

The Dominoes fall

On 14 September 1836, the irrepressible Harry Smith left the front, recalled to Cape Town as a result of his part in the death of Hintsa in what was now known as "Hintsa's War." Stockenström arrived in the border area in August 1836. On 5 December 1836, he not only returned Queen Adelaide Province to the amaXhosa as instructed, but also allowed them to move back into the region between the Fish and the Keiskamma, thereby giving them the refuge of the Fish River Bush yet again. This bush held the same strategic value on the Cape Frontier as the Golan Heights hold in the 21st century for Israel. See Figures *7-3* and *9-9* for the nature of this bush.

From that day, the British settlers saw Stockenström as a target that simply had to be destroyed. The Afrikaners, for their part, had started out by respecting Stockenström as a competent young military leader in 1811. Now, after the Slagtersnek affair and his new role, he was an outcast among his own, almost but not quite the "Benedict Arnold" of the Afrikaners. He entered into a most disgraceful exchange of letters with the highly respected Piet Retief (NF40), who had the onerous duty of being Field-Commandant on the frontier. Stockenström, a difficult man at the best of times, descended to a new low in attacking Retief's integrity while Retief maintained the high ground[27]. With all hope of pragmatism on the border lost, Retief resigned and hitched his wagons. Since Piet Retief was a man hugely respected by not only the Afrikaners, but also by the British Settlers and even the Governor himself, all in the East Cape took note. Governor Benjamin D'Urban's prediction had finally come true – the Afrikaner was on the move.

Governor Sir Benjamin D'Urban wrote Glenelg a letter so personally deprecating that Glenelg had no choice but to relieve him of his post as governor on 1 May 1837. D'Urban, who had been one of the best and most dedicated governors, would stay at the Cape until 1846 as a private citizen. He was a good man, but in London near criminal ignorance and an obsessive guilt complex over a slaving past reigned supreme.

In February 1838 Glenelg was himself forced to resign from his cabinet post for "being too indecisive," unfortunately only after appointing George Napier as new Cape Governor. Napier was to be the source of great heartache for the Afrikaners. Thomas Fowell Buxton, Dr. Philip's great protector, was out of parliament. The great Dr. Philip was alone. His English enemies gathered, and eventually this man, who forever conspired in the ruin of his own kin, would see his malicious power broken. However, all this would be too late for the Afrikaner.

Chase[28] describes how Stockenström met Napier, then on his way to the East Cape on his first ever tour of the frontier. He made sure that Napier's views were cemented in his favor:

"On the road he was met by Lieut.-Governor Stockenström, who, availing himself of the detention caused by two successive rainy days, imbued his mind with the highest opinion of his own new system, and tutored him into the belief that all the opposition he had hitherto encountered had had its rise among disappointed and factious individuals in the Eastern Province."

At this point, the British Settlers in the East Cape found their political stride. They set about systematically destroying Stockenström. They developed a charge of murder against him based on an event 25 years previous. They intimated that he had killed a Xhosa youth to avenge the murder of his father (NF34). Any pretext would do to rid themselves of what they considered a scheming enemy holding sway over them.

Stockenström went to Britain to clear his name, was rewarded with a baronetcy and a pension, and returned to the Cape an ordinary citizen. Even the British government appreciated that he had no more standing with the citizenry and that he was of no further use to them at the time. All the key players among the British had hereby departed the stage, and even Harry Smith would leave for India in 1840. No one, however, seemed to remember the promises made to the amaFengu, the Beggar People, who had just lost their new land to their former slave-masters, the amaXhosa; and this thanks to the involvement of the misguided and ostensibly anti-slavery LMS.

There cometh a time

The focus of South African formative history now moves away from the Suurveld to the interior beyond the Orange River. The Afrikaners, dismayed beyond redemption with the life they faced under their British overlords, streamed north into uncharted territory to a degree that utterly denuded the frontier. The Tarka, in particular, was almost emptied of people. A full third of the people that went on the Great Trek came from the Tarka. This is where the Trek was born, this is where it was formulated, and this is where it was largely launched from 1836 onward. The British authorities had to rush to put a basic defense in position for the area. British Settlers rushed in to buy up the farms for next to nothing.

The Afrikaner was heading into Africa to God only knew where, as long as there was no British Government. They had no quarrel with Englishmen, whom they considered honorable people. Their hatred was reserved for British Government. The only British authority they had ever known was a military one. They had never had a voice in their own destiny and now it seemed that their overlord was under the sway of the malicious London Missionary Society. Ordinary Englishmen and English soldiers were merely fellow Christians and generally "decent fellows," though they hated the English carpetbaggers from Grahamstown and Port Elizabeth who fed like vultures off their destitution. The Reverend Shaw alludes to this with typical British understatement in his book[29] about his mission:

> *"The British settlers in Albany were quite alive to the opportunity that was thus presented for obtaining extensive sheep farms."*

That the actual British Settlers, as opposed to land speculators, were as one with the suffering Afrikaners, is made clear by the signatures on the *Address of the Winterberg and Koonap Farmers* given to Stockenström by Pieter Retief[30] in late 1836. This painful document was signed by such British Settlers as Robert Wesson, Robert Sully, W. Potter, John Vaughan, William Bear, R.J. Painter, and James Edwards.

Had the Afrikaners waited but a few months, the history of South Africa would have looked drastically different. Even as their wagon trains started rolling slowly toward the Orange River for the so-called Trans-Orangia, a young lady was assuming the burden of monarchy in faraway England. Victoria liked the romance of Empire. She was not about to abandon the colony, as some in London had suggested.

The Afrikaners would know nothing of this. They had finally been wronged too much. This is a nation that is exceptionally slow to anger, but that anger, once awakened, is near impossible to quell. It was time for these descendants of the French Huguenots and Dutch-German founding fathers to leave the land of their birth they had known for 185 years; seven generations. The Crown had yet again become their tyrant under a cloak of religion, just as with their French Huguenot forefathers. With a foreign ruler that had abused them for two generations staring at their backs, a vast skeleton strewn prairie in front of them, and a towering 11,000 foot mountain range between them and the promise of a possible new life, they placed their faith in their God and the Bible, hitched their wagons, prepared the lead and powder, and rolled forth into Darkest Africa. Some of their freed slaves and servants elected to stay behind; others elected to accompany them. They had always been part of the broader community and were simply continuing the lives they had known. Many were hugely loyal and dedicated, like Regina, who had looked after Trek leader Jan du Plessis' mentally incapacitated sister (*NF43*) ever since her birth 28 years before.

Most of their British Settler friends stayed behind. They had more faith that Britannia would come to her senses. They were also subject to British Law outside British territories since the vast majority of them had been born in Britain. The Afrikaners, as people not born in Britain, could not be made subject to British Law outside the borders of British territory, though they had not known that until Stockenström obligingly told them during his disgraceful discourse with Piet Retief.

Nexus Familia 43: The Eve of Exodus

We are now at a crucial moment in the history of South Africa; the very eve of a national exodus that shall become known internationally as The Great Trek. It is the specific event that will introduce the word "trek" into the English language and introduce the Zulu to the media of Europe.

We have fetched our British ancestors and have placed them in the Suurveld, where they have been overrun by the amaXhosa. Their own government in Britain has deserted them and, at the instigation of the London Missionary Society (LMS), has accused them of being the cause of the war that has destituted them. They are angry, but they can ultimately rely on the support of their countrymen and they know this. There is merit for them in raising their voices to fight the situation politically, both locally and in London.

For our Afrikaner ancestors the situation is much worse. They have no one to speak on their behalf and they have never had a decent hearing in Britain. Yet, via the LMS both the amaXhosa and the Khoekhoe have representation in London. The Afrikaners are mere voteless and voiceless "subjects." We now sketch their situation and use the opportunity to take stock of the various families that are to play a role in the rest of this work. We also map in detail some of the ancestral threads spun earlier, before they start to spread across South Africa. The need for the detailed maps will become lamentably clear in the next chapter.

1. In the Tarka before Hintsa's War

We last saw Pieter Johannes Jordaan (Pieter the Elder) at the time of Slagtersnek (*NF40*), when he was living on the farm Palingkloof in the Tarka. His two sons by his late first wife, Maria Snyman, are now our focus. The older is Pieter George and the younger is our ancestor, Chris. Via their late mother they are descendants of slave ancestor Groot Catrijn (*NF11*). They are much under the influence of Pieter's brother-in-law, Piet Retief. Retief is the highly respected Field-Commandant for the Winterberg (See The dominoes fall) and another descendant of Pierre Jaubert from Provence in France (*NF19*).

Fig. 9-6 A wet winter in the cattle country of the Tarka

By 1834, just before Hintsa's War, the 31-year-old Pieter George Jordaan has been married to Isabella Potgieter (daughter of the murdered Field-Cornet – *NF39*) for about nine years and they have six children. Pieter's stepbrother, Jacobus Christoffel "Koos Greatfoot" Potgieter is provisional Field-Cornet in the Kei River district of the vast Tarka. Susanna, Pieter's 28-year old sister, is married to Jan du Plessis, grandson of the Jan du Plessis who helped American Captain Benjamin Stout in 1796 (*NF32*). Jan is also a provisional Field-Cornet in the region. Chris Jordaan, our direct ancestor, is married to Maria Klopper (*NF40*) and they already have two children.

From around April 1834 the farmers in the region suffer great losses due to extensive horse theft by the men of Chief Maphasa of the amaThembu.

The Jordaans, the Du Plessis family and Isabella Potgieter's cousin, Hendrik Potgieter, all suffer in this way. Hendrik Potgieter[31] tracks the spoor[32] of the animals to Maphasa's *kraal*, where the chief denies responsibility. Potgieter eventually induces Koos "Greatfoot" as provisional Field-Cornet to put together a commando to retrieve the animals from Maphasa. Brother Pieter George Jordaan is one of the men on the commando. After tracing the spoor of rustled animals repeatedly to Mapahasa's *kraal*, Koos impounds some of Maphasa's cattle, the animals to be returned when the horses are returned. On the way home, the men come across a farmer looking for his stolen sheep. Yet again, the spoor leads directly to Maphasa's place. When they follow the spoor, they are attacked by some of Maphasa's amaThembu warriors. Five of the Thembus die in the process.

Maphasa lays a complaint against Koos Greatfoot, who is dismissed as Provisional Field-Cornet. The cattle are returned to Maphasa. Such is justice in the Tarka for Afrikaners.

Pieter the Elder, the father of our Jordaan family in the Tarka, dies on 24 October 1834. The appointment of Andries Stockenström and the return of the new Queen Adelaide Province represent the final straw for the Afrikaners on the frontier. In the Tarka, in particular, it means huge dislocation for the Afrikaners since at least 162 families are stranded and deserted on the "wrong" side of the new eastern border. They have all had enough.

The man in the Tarka who takes the early lead in the Trek is Hendrik Potgieter. Pieter Georg Jordaan, despite being a neighbor and a childhood friend, does not trek with Hendrik Potgieter at the end of 1835, because his wife Isabella, cousin to Potgieter, is 5 months pregnant. Instead, Pieter baptizes his seventh and last child, Elsie, on 4 July 1836 in Cradock and then joins[33] Piet Retief's trek, which moves through the Cradock hinterland in February 1837.

Younger brother Chris, our direct ancestor, delays a little longer and then joins the Potgieter-Du Plessis trek put together by his older step-brother Koos "Greatfoot" Potgieter and his brother-in-law Jan du Plessis. Chris and his wife Maria Klopper leave on the Great Trek with four young children.

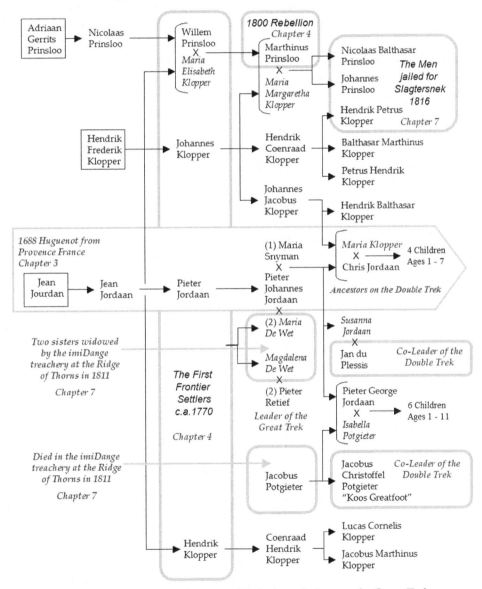

Fig. 9-7 *The Jordaan, Klopper and Prinsloo relatives on the Great Trek*

Maria's cousin, Nicolaas Balthasar Prinsloo, brother of the Hendrik "Kasteel" executed for the Slagtersnek debacle (*NF40*), is one of the first to leave. He actually departs along with Louis Trichardt (*NF43*). Maria's uncle, Hendrik Coenraad Klopper, leaves with "Hendrik" Potgieter in 1836. His three sons, Hendrik, Balthasar, and Petrus, prefer to wait for Pieter Retief and join his Trek instead. Maria's brother, Hendrik Balthasar, leaves with her and Chris on the Potgieter-Du Plessis "Double Trek." Maria's Klopper second cousins, Lucas Cornelis and Jacobus Marthinus, along with their father, Coenraad Hendrik, leave with Piet Retief. The detail is shown in Fig. 9-7, to which we return later with lamentably good reason.

2. The Groblers

The Grobler brothers (*NF29* and *36*) are really too old to go on the Great Trek. Their sons from the Camdeboo and the Tarka leave in separate treks, though. The Grobler family provides a superb glimpse into the statistics, drama and family splits of the Great Trek. Consider just the descendants of our ancestor Nicolaas, son of the original immigrant. In 1837, there are 52 male members between the ages of 20 and 60 in this group, of whom no fewer than 28 leave on the Great Trek. This includes practically all the Groblers in the Tarka. By way of example, all twelve mature male descendants of eldest brother Johannes Grobler trek northward. This gives us a representative picture of the impact of the Great Trek.

Our ancestor Cornelis' younger brother, Michael (*NF26*), dies in the Suurveld in 1832. We shall follow his two eldest sons, Michael and Reynier. These two Grobler men from the Tarka are married to two van Dyk sisters. Michael is married to Susanna van Dyk and they have four children. Reynier is married to Maria van Dyk. They have just one child, Michael, when they leave the colony. When Piet Retief's trek moves through their district, the two brothers and their families join him, along with their friend Pieter Georg Jordaan. Ancestor Cornelis Grobler himself dies early in 1837. His 26-year old son, Izak, is our direct ancestor. Izak elects to remain in the dry scrub country of the Camdeboo, but two of his older brothers decide to join the exodus.

3. The Jouberts

Our ancestor Pieter Schalk Joubert the Elder, son of Isaac Jacob (*NF28*), is now 53 years old and lives on a farm in the Uitenhage district. His wife, Johanna Lötter, is the daughter of Christoffel Lötter who was at the table of the Graaff-Reinet Drostdy in 1795 (*NF31*). Their third son, named for Pieter Schalk himself, is our ancestor. They will not be leaving with the 1837 Trekkers. They plan for a later departure.

The three cousins of Pieter Schalk the Elder are still living at Buffelshoek at the foot of the Sneeuberg. Cousin Jacobus who shoved the "spider flag" in the arms of the British magistrate (*NF31*), is now 62 years old and all his children are grown up.

Josua and his wife Elizabeth have two young boys. Adriaan has married Susanna Roos and they have five children. Abraham has recently married Anna Roets, whose pa-

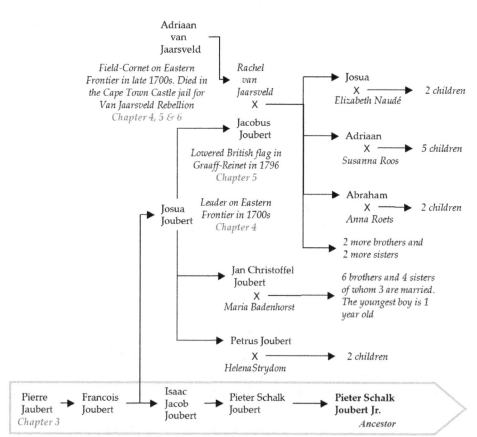

Fig. 9-8 The Buffelshoek and Winterberg Joubert family on the Great Trek

rents and siblings are also on the Great Trek, one of whom will narrate for us later. Abraham has a one-year-old boy and the second is on the way.

Jacobus' younger brother Jan Christoffel is now 56 and has no fewer than 10 children. The oldest four are all girls of whom three are married. The youngest of the married daughters is Anna (22). The rest of the siblings are all boys, ranging from 18 down to the very youngest, Jan Christoffel, at just 1 year of age.

The third cousin we are tracking is 51-year old Petrus. Helena, mother of his 9 children, has died, and he has remarried to Susanna De Beer. They will only leave[34] on the Great Trek in 1838.

This entire Buffelshoek and Winterberg Joubert clan, with the exception the married daughters, joins Piet Retief's Trek. These people have simply had enough. Surely, there must be hope also for them somewhere in God's Creation. We depict these individuals in Fig. 9-8, because they will be at the heart of an epic drama revolving around a key set of events in history.

4. The Booyens Family of Tortoise Bone

By the late 1700s, Barent was the only son of immigrant Pieter Booyens (*NF25*) to have surviving sons of his own. His wife, Elizabeth Strydom, was the great-granddaughter of the indefatigable Tryn Ras (*NF16*). They had three sons, of whom Matthys was the only one to have children. Around the time of the American Revolution Matthys and his brothers settled in the Swartruggens (Black Ridges) south of Graaff-Reinet. On the death of father Barent, Matthys relocated southward with his wife, five sons, and four daughters to the farm *Schilpadbeen* (Tortoise Bone) at the eastern limit of the Great Swartberg. Matthys died in 1816 and his widow Anna now runs the farm.

By 1836, our interest is in four of Matthys' five sons. The eldest is ancestor Pieter Johannes, born 1783. He lost his first wife Susanna Human on 21 October 1820. Their meager joint estate at the time of her death will one day be available in exquisite detail in the original Dutch on the Internet[35].

Pieter has subsequently married Sophia Snyman, the granddaughter of Coenraad Bezuidenhout who was accused by Maynier of precipitating the Second Frontier War (*NF29*). Coenraad's two brothers were killed by the British during the Slagtersnek event and his sister-in-law and her son wounded (*NF40*).

The second son of interest is Barend Matthys. In 1823, his eldest daughter, "Jenny," married a Scottish soldier in the British Army named Nehemia Wright. By contrast, her younger sister, Anna, is married to one of the Bezuidenhout men and they are preparing to leave on the Great Trek.

The third son of interest is Matthys Stephanus, who bears his own father's name. By 1834, Matthys Jr. has seven children, but our concern in this work will be with his later children. Matthys Stephanus will turn out to be quite a man, but we have to wait a little while for events to take shape in his life.

The fourth son of interest is Daniel Jan Andries, whose five own sons will trek north in the 1850s. A later special hell awaits them at the hands of Great Britain (Chapter 17). We shall be following these men and their children forward through history.

5. The Myburghs of Roode Taaijbosch

By the 1830s, the leader of the author's Myburgh family (*NF13*) is Jacobus "Koos" Johannes. By 1817 they were already in the Achter-Sneeuberg. By 1824, he obtained for his family a farm named *Roode Taaijbosch* (Red Tough Bush) in the Achter-Sneeuberg Plateau northeast of Graaff-Reinet, and west of Cradock. Now, in 1836, the family is still on that farm.

Fig. 9-9 The high snowy sheep country of Roode Taaijbosch

This is snow country and can be bitterly cold in winter, temperatures around -9 degrees Centigrade being regularly attained. The two nearest towns of Graaff-Reinet and Cradock are both situated at lower altitude and generally report considerably higher temperatures.

In the 20th and 21st Centuries, snow will cut off Roode Taaijbosch from Graaff-Reinet at least twice a season. The area is uniquely suited to sheep farming, but Koos has another strength. He is a wagon-builder (*NF41*); a skill he has been teaching his eldest son Albert (Albertus Jacobus) who is now 21. Albert is our ancestor. He will ultimately become the great grandfather to the author's mother. As the Achter-Sneeuberg is not cattle country, the amaXhosa have left them largely alone during the Sixth Frontier War, but the men have had to serve on commando against the amaXhosa.

6. The Basson Family

In the West Cape around the parish of Swartland, the Basson family is led by Matthys "Thys" Michiel Basson, a 5th generation descendant of Arnold "Jacht" Basson and his wife, the slave lady Angela (*NF12*).

His mother, in turn, was the great-granddaughter of Judith Schmidt, the abandoned daughter of Ariaentje Sterrevelt (*NF20*) of New Amsterdam in faraway America. As with generations of Bassons before him, Thys focuses on growing wheat. After all, he lives in the breadbasket of the Colony.

Two of his second cousins, Willem and Matthys Basson, live in the Swartruggens (Black Ridges) area of the Uitenhage District, not very far from the Groblers. In the 21st century, the mountain at their farm will still be called Bassonsberg, but it will not bear witness to the horrors that will befall these men.

They will join the Great Trek under Piet Retief.

—*End Nexus Familia*

The Settlers' Bible Farewell

"The inhabitants of Graham's Town and its vicinity, hearing of your arrival in this district, with the intention of quitting for ever the land of your birth, have entered into a public subscription to purchase this Bible; and I am deputed, with the gentlemen who accompany me, now to present it to you. We offer it to you as a proof of our regard, and with expressions of sorrow that you are now going so far from us.

We regret, for many reasons, that circumstances should have arisen to separate us; for ever since we, the British settlers, arrived in this colony, now a period of 17 years, the greatest cordiality has continued to be maintained by us and our nearest Dutch neighbors; and we must always acknowledge the general and unbounded hospitality with which we have been welcomed in every portion of the colony.

We trust, therefore, that although widely separated, you will hold us in remembrance, and that we wish allways to retain for each other the warmest sentiments of friendship."

W.R. Thompson, spokesman for the British citizens of Grahamstown, handing a Russian leather bound Bible[36] to Jacobus Uys, elderly leader of the Uys Trek (1837)

-----ooOoo-----

10

The Great Trek

"...men shamefully abandoned by the British Government"

George Charles Moore Smith,
The autobiography of Lieutenant-General Sir Harry Smith (1902)

Fig. 10-1 *On the Great Trek*

Exodus

Not since Moses led the Israelites from Egypt had there been a more emotive journey of a nation of Believers, fleeing from an authority in whom the people saw the parallel of the biblical Pharaoh. And "Pharaoh" was now apparently under the sway of the "Antichrist" himself in the form of the canting Dr. Philip and his London Missionary Society masters, who apparently wanted the Afrikaners dead. But, who is to be "Moses," and where is the "Promised Land"? And would "Pharaoh" send his "chariots" after them? The abandoned and forsaken Afrikaner was headed into the Dark Continent to parts unknown as the White Tribe of Africa, the amaBhulu. This epic migration provided the English language with the word "trek" and thereby the cult Science Fiction TV series *Star Trek* with its name, but its parallel is closer to the original television series *Battlestar Galactica*. In that series, the world of the people is destroyed, as was that of the Afrikaners, and they set out into the universe to seek a new home under fractious leadership, threatened on all sides, with an empire in pursuit bent on their destruction. The parallel fits exactly.

In preparation for the Great Trek, three so-called "Commission Treks" were sent out. The first, the Uys Expedition, went through amaXhosa territory to visit the area of Natal near Port Natal (the later Durban). Finding it to be clear from Ba'Ntu tribes and to be superb grass country, they returned with an image of the

British-free interior of Natal as a good choice for their future. The second, under a man named Scholtz went northeastward to the Soutpansberg (Salt Pan Mountains). The third under Johannes Pretorius went northwest to the so-called "Thirstlands," proving that only desert lay in that direction. All of these treks gathered information about the state of the interior, possible migration routes, hunters, missionaries, and itinerant trekboers.

There are many studies of the Great Trek and the present work cannot hope to dwell on all the details. However, it is useful to first stop and consider the leaders of this national migration. Their goals and motivations differed and these differences will clarify some of the events that follow.

The first grouping was composed of typical frontier folks; difficult and tough people. For them it was a case of getting as far away from the British as they possibly could. Leaders, such as Louis Trichardt, Hendrik Potgieter, Koos Potgieter, Jan du Plessis, and Pieter Georg Jordaan had proven that they knew how to co-exist with the amaXhosa before the British arrived to turn their world upside down. Their problem lay particularly with the British authority, which they regarded as criminally incompetent and haplessly self-contradictory. Their conviction was that they should stay away from the sea, because, where there was sea, the British Crown would sooner or later be. The trek leader Hendrik Potgieter can be viewed as their representative icon. Many of these tough and independent men came from the Tarka, the most outlying region of the colony.

The second group was composed of men of some accomplishment as settled citizens of the Eastern Districts of the Frontier. They came from Albany, Somerset, Graaff-Reinet, and Uitenhage. They were less the fractious frontier type. Their leaders were people like Piet Uys and Karel Landman of Uitenhage district, Gerrit Maritz, successful farmer and wagon builder from the Graaff-Reinet community and Pieter Retief, a highly respected farmer and businessman from the Albany and Somerset districts. Uys is described by Capt. (Sir) James Edward Alexander[1] as *a fine specimen of the manly character.*

In 1832, Retief sold his farm *Mooimeisiesfontein* (Pretty Girl Fountain) near Riebeeck Oos and moved to a new farm deep in the Winterberg near Stockenström's Kat River Khoekhoe Settlement. Retief so impressed Governor D'Urban as Commando commandant in the 6th Frontier War that he named the military strong point on Retief's farm after the owner. Retief lost all in that war. Robert Godlonton, the editor of the *Grahamstown Journal* newspaper, referred to Retief as[2] *"one of the most intelligent men on that part of the frontier."* Retief had hoped for things to settle after the war, but his abortive meeting with Stockenström on 20 September 1836 convinced him that all hope was lost. This was the occasion on which Stockenström suggested that those who wished to leave, should leave. They did. They had had altogether enough of him and his pseudo-philanthropist "anti-Christian" British masters.

Both groups of Trek Leaders were conscious of the need for their new country to have ports. Retief and Maritz considered Natal the obvious option in this regard, but Potgieter wanted nothing to do with anything even vaguely British. Retief and Maritz also accepted that they would have to deal with the British at the Cape Colony. These men had more concept of the potential economics and relations of the future country. Retief, in particular, had strong support from the English Press of the British Settlers in Grahamstown. A number of British Settlers actually joined their quest for a new homeland. Piet Uys was a somewhat different character, but commanded great loyalty. Right from the start, he and Retief would never really see eye to eye, possibly because he, Uys, had been to Natal on one of the original commission treks. Uys admired America.

The first of the formal large treks to leave was that of Hendrik Potgieter from the Tarka. However, while he was a bold leader, he took the precaution of dispatching his good friend Louis Trichardt to the north to reconnoiter the interior. In the meantime, he, Potgieter, was to slowly move his people northward through the interior of the country. The Tarka men started packing their wagons when they came back from Commando duty in the 6th Frontier War, and set off on the Great Trek..

A world strewn with skulls

The basic distribution of the indigenous black people of South Africa is simple. Moving south systematically over centuries were the so-called Nguni people, strung out like a sequence of beads on a string down the coast all the way to the Fish River, where they clashed in the 1780's with the white people moving eastward.

Along the east of the mountains and arrayed down the coast were the amaSwazi, the amaZulu, the amaPondo, the amaThembu, and the amaXhosa. In present times, the last three nations are all grouped together as being Xhosa people. All three speak the Xhosa language – isiXhosa.

Separating them from the other major ethnic group, the Sotho people, one finds the 11,000-foot Drakensberg, as significant a natural barrier as the Rockies that separate the Plains Indians from the Salish Indians of the West. It is unclear which Sotho people originally lived exactly where, because the depredations of the Zulu, Matabele, and Mantatee totally scattered the demographics of the interior.

By 1836, however, the Sotho peoples lived in a huge crescent around the perimeter of the central Highveld Prairie. These people may be seen as the Ba'Tswana to the west and northwest, the Ba'Pedi to the north and the inaptly named Ba'Sotho in the mountains to the east, where they had found refuge. The Ba'Sotho were a generally peaceful people who lived in smaller clans, each with a dedicated totem. So, for example, the Ba'Taung were the People of the Lion (Taung).

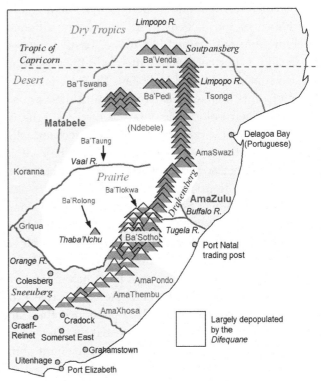

Fig. 10-2 *The demographics of 1836*

The Matabele, being Zulu-derived Nguni people driven from their home in Zululand, lived totally out of position to the west of the Northern Prairie. They had driven out the local seTswana speaking Ba'Rolong people, who settled in 1832 with the Rev. Archbell in a little spot around the Hill of Thaba'Nchu in the dry southern half of the Trans-Orangia region.

Similarly, the Sotho-speaking Ba'Tlokwa, who originally lived near the headwaters of the Vaal River, found themselves stuck right in the path of both the Zulu and the Matabele, and kept getting caught in the "crossfire" between these two warlike nations. They relocated to the northern Drakensberg Mountains bordering the present day Lesotho. But, they have a longer story to tell later, for they were at one point the Mantatee Horde. A glimpse of their world in 1836 may be found in a letter from the Rev. John Edwards[3]:

> "The accounts of their wars and bloodshed would affect the most hard-hearted. Here is wrath unmingled with one ray of mercy. One Tribe seeks to annihilate another. Poor women and innocent children are destroyed with savage cruelty: no cries, no tears, can move the heart of a savage, hardened with reiterated crimes. This country may be termed the Golgotha of South Africa. Thousands of human skulls strew the land. [Visitors are] principally 'Barimo' (or cannibals), of the Bashuta [Ba'Sotho] Nation, and speak the same language as the Mantatees. [...]
>
> About 35 miles south from the Mantatees, in the direction of Port-Natal, are found large Tribes of the Barimo, consisting of about twenty-five villages."

Of the Ba'Sotho "Barimo" James Backhouse, a missionary of the London Missionary Society, had the following to say[4]. His information came from the Rev. Allison stationed with the Mantatee in the 1830s:

> "...they stole around the neighboring kraals in the night, surprised, killed, and ate the inhabitants, until they gained such an appetite for human flesh, as made them more terrible than the lion or the wolf."

In Natal, the territory to the south of the Tugela River and to the west of the Buffalo River had also been largely denuded of people by the Zulu, who styled the region north of the Tugela and east of the Buffalo River as their territory and treated the surrounding area as a kind of no-man's land buffer zone.

North of the Ba'Pedi lived the hugely different Venda people, with a language and culture quite different from any named heretofore. Lastly, scattered as a small nation over the northeastern Highveld Prairie and its northern slopes, there was the mysterious Ndebele (not to be confused with the Matabele who are also sometimes called Ndebele). They are famous the world over for their incredible beadwork and the stacks of rings their women wear around their arms and legs and particularly their necks, which become extended. Their colorful angular painted patterns on their homes are equally famous. This small, but culturally distinct nation speaks a Zulu dialect and tells stories of being used as slaves by the Zulu.

North of the AmaSwazi and east of the Ba'Pedi, in the tropical Lowveldt, lived the Tsonga or Shangaan people, who are also very different. They had been conquered by yet another renegade Zulu by the name of Shoshangane. The upheavals by the Zulu King Shaka in Zululand therefore had massive and widespread repercussions all over Southern Africa. These led directly to the denuding of the central Highveld Prairie as the various Ba'Sotho nations scattered to avoid the Nguni armies and the Mantatee with their Warrior Queen, about whom we shall learn more later. Ultimately it would lead to instability all the way up to the Zambezi River. The net effect of all of this is that the Highveld Prairie was, for all intents and purposes, denuded of residents by 1836. In fact, at some point before the Great Trek, seventy-two householders who possessed no land visited the northern parts of the land between the Orange and Vaal Rivers and found the area to be devoid of inhabitants[5]. They then petitioned the Cape government to be allowed to settle there, but the petition was refused. Few people existed there beyond the Ba'Rolong, who were living at Thab'Nchu with the Rev. Archbell. And this is really south of the limit of the true Highveld Prairie. The Ba'Taung survived to the north of the Vaal River.

This Ethnic Cleansing by the Matabele, Zulu, and Mantatee is known variously as the *Difaqane, Difequane, or Fitcane* (*Mfecane* in isiZulu: the "Crushing"). Today, it would be called Genocide. In reality, it was much worse. In 21st Century terms, it may be described as a post-Apocalyptic world of extreme barbarity, wholesale starvation, armies like locusts, and rampant cannibalism; a place where life was held worthless.

John Centlivres Chase provides details[6] on 28 particular Ba'Tswana "tribes" of 384,000 souls who were destroyed by the amaZulu incursions between the Vaal and Limpopo Rivers, starting 1822. William Boyce[7] wrote in 1839:

> *"Within the last thirty years, at least sixty populous and powerful tribes have been exterminated by the Mantatees, Fitcani, and Zulus. The process is yet going on,..."*

The picture would be incomplete without describing the Griqua, who were people of mixed White, Khoekhoe, and Tswana descent who had earlier been known as the "Bastaards," before the missionaries changed their name to something more reasonable. They lived near the confluence of the Orange and Vaal rivers. They practiced a western way of life and had big battles of their own with both the Matabele and the Mantatee. Their relationship with the black nations was not good. In 1828, according to Stockenström[8], they destroyed two Ba'Tswana tribes by stealing their cattle, murdering the people and driving them to actual cannibalism. They used the Dutch language or a variant of its modern derivative, Afrikaans. To their northwest lived the Koranna, the last independent Khoekhoe nation in what was to become South Africa. They lived north of the Orange River, west of the Vaal River and southwest of the Tswana people. The last range of mountains before the Kalahari Desert is still known today as the Koranna Mountain.

Nexus Familia 44: The Louis Trichardt Trek 1

Louis Trichardt is the leader of about thirty Afrikaner families living in peace with the amaXhosa in Hintsa's land. He is the grandson of an immigrant flagman in the Dutch East India Company. Louis' father, Carolus, used to farm at the southern foot of the Swartberg, not far from the Booyens family (*NF43*).

Carolus was the Burgher-Lieutenant who was at odds with magistrate Maynier in the 1790s at the time of the Second Frontier War (*NF29*).

The British authorities intensely resent Louis' presence among the amaXhosa and soon enough they accuse him of being complicit in cattle rustling. During the disastrous 6th Frontier War of 1834, colonel Harry Smith accuses him of inciting the Xhosa to war and offers a reward of 500 cattle for the apprehension of this 'villain of a Boer'. Louis therefore moves across the Orange River. He knows Hendrik Potgieter well, as both have dealt with Hintsa and both have made use of grazing across the Orange River. The two men have a dream of a new homeland for the Afrikaners far away from the British military government and their attendant Afrikaner-hating London Missionary Society. Trichardt agrees to undertake an exploratory trek to the far north to find this Eldorado.

In early 1836, he hitches his wagons and sets off northward with his family, including his wife Martha, sister of the author's ancestor, Johanna Bouwer. He is to go a certain distance to the north and wait for the rest of the Trekkers from the long-suffering Tarka. He is asked to send out reconnaissance parties to explore routes to the Portuguese ports of Mozambique. They deliberately disregard the Natal ports as they believe the British will never allow them to live in peace in their own country. Trichardt's goal of finding a route to the Indian Ocean parallels the mission of Lewis and Clark to find the route to the Pacific.

The Trichardt expedition is composed of seven Boer farmers, their wives, and thirty-four children. They travel in the company of another trek, led by an elephant hunter called Jan van Rensburg and his companions, who include Nicolaas Balthasar "Klaas Nuweveld" Prinsloo (*NF43*, Fig. 9-7), son of our ancestral Klopper sister and brother to the executed Hendrik "Kasteel" (*NF40*). Trichardt is accompanied by his son, Carel. With them go their massive herds of 925 head of cattle, 50 horses and more than 6,000

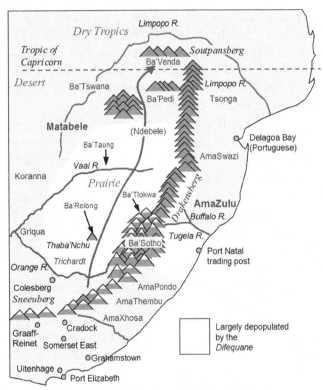

Fig. 10-3 The first leg of Trichardt's route

sheep. For their defense, the Trichardt trek has all of just nine men. The combined Trek crosses the Vaal River in January 1836, passing safely between the deadly armies of Mzilikatse and his Matabele to the west and Dingane with his Zulu to the east. Mzilikatse is the terror of the Prairie who kills all in his way.

At the site of the later Pretoria, the Prairie, treeless and sub-freezing in winter, ends abruptly as the altitude drops 2,000 feet to the hot dry frost-free African Savannah studded with acacia trees. Some distance into this Savannah or Bushveld, the two parties split up and the Van Rensburgs go their own way in an easterly direction towards Mozambique. With them go Nicolaas Balthasar Prinsloo and his family.

Trichardt goes north as agreed with Potgieter and establishes a base at the foot of the Soutpansberg (Salt Pan Mountains). There he finds the Buys people, the mixed-race descendants of none other than the giant seven foot Boer, our cousin Coenraad de Buys (Chapter 6 : *NF33, 34* and *A Dutch Interlude*), who had left the Colony many years before. These people will still live there in the 21st century. It is here that Hendrik Potgieter joins up with Trichardt and they debrief on the exploration thus far. Potgieter explores some distance into the present Zimbabwe, but eventually returns. He finds no trace of the Van Rensburgs either. Potgieter thereupon returns to his people and their wagons far to the south.

We leave Louis Trichardt for now at his temporary base. What his trek has discovered, is that the useful cattle country ends south of the Soutpansberg and that a deadly cattle sickness reigns to the north and east. What they cannot fathom is what has happened to the Van Rensburg Trek and "Klaas Nuweveld" Prinsloo.

—End Nexus Familia

The American from Ten Mile Creek

On 3 December 1834, a barque named the *Burlington* set sail from Boston, Massachusetts. On board were six American missionaries in two parties. The one party, referred to as the *"Maritime Party,"* consisted of Newton Adams, George Champion, and Aldin Grout, together with their wives. This team was to proceed to Zululand. While we shall meet them again, it is really the second group, the *"Interior Party,"* that we are interested in at this time. This group consisted of Dr. Alexander Wilson, Henry Venable, and Daniel Lindley, with their respective wives. On 6 February 1835, they dropped anchor at the Cape, full of expectation. Here they discovered that the Sixth Frontier War had broken out soon after they had left Boston. Therefore, the Maritime Party would remain in Cape Town until the war had been settled. The Interior Party set out for the country of the fierce Matabele King, Mzilikatse. None other than Dr. John Philip had suggested that it would be fertile ground for their labors.

Daniel Lindley[9] was born in the Ten Mile Creek area of Ohio, a countryside steeped in early frontier history. His father was acquainted with the vagaries of life in such a place and the dangers implicit in life when another civilization lurks nearby. Here Daniel grew up as a tough and athletic young man, a good horseman, and good shot, thoroughly capable of putting a ball through the head of a squirrel at the top of a tree. He knew cougars, wolves, deer, bears, and wild turkeys. He also knew how to select a good horse. Daniel subsequently attended Ohio University and eventually became Presbyterian minister to the parish of Rocky River in North Carolina. On 9 December 1833, Daniel wrote to the interdenominational American Board for Commissioners of Foreign Missions (AMBCFM), offering his services as missionary. He was the eldest of the six men of the missionary team. He was also the only one with ministerial experience.

Now, in early 1835, Lindley, Venable, and Wilson found themselves on a classic Boer ox-wagon slowly wending their way to the dangerous country of the despotic Mzilikatse. They were staggered by the dryness of the country they passed through – the Karoo. Afrikaners helped them with oxen along the way. They stopped for some time at Griquatown near the Orange River for the oxen to recover and to learn the language of the Ba'Tswana. In January 1836, they set out on the final stage to Mosega, the capitol of Mzilikatse. There they restored the house of earlier French missionaries and settled in to the slow business of dealing with Mzilikatse.

Shortly after 14 July 1836, coming back from a long trip to Robert Moffat at the Kuruman Mission to the southwest, the Lindleys encountered their first real Matabele warriors. They learnt that these were scouts on the lookout for a "Dutch Commando." This was the first inkling they had that something was up. Soon after, the entire party was struck down by a fever with tremendous associated pain, likely rheumatic fever. Wilson's wife died on 18 September 1836 as a result. Wilson himself was the only one capable of burying her at the time, the others being bed-ridden and in tremendous pain. It is here, soon after the death of Wilson's wife, that we shall again meet the missionary party.

Nexus Familia 45: Captain Harris' Wagon

When Captain Cornwallis Harris, author of *Narrative of an Expedition into Southern Africa*, reaches Graaff-Reinet in 1836 on his expedition to Mzilikatse, he finds it extremely difficult to purchase a wagon. It would appear that this is because none other than Gerrit Maritz, the main wagon builder in town and senior leader in the Great Trek, has purchased all the wagons he can find and is busy building more.

It is at Graaff-Reinet that Harris secures the help of Lt. John Biddulph, whom we met earlier as the son of British Settler Simon Biddulph and brother to Thomas Jervis Biddulph. John has married into the Afrikaner community. He introduces Harris to our Naudé family living outside Graaff-Reinet. Harris purchases an excellent ox wagon and a span of oxen from our family. This wagon will last him the entire trip and will witness all manner of things in the land of Mzilikatse. The oxen will not return, and Harris will learn the hard way what the Bushman Wars were all about.

Elizabeth Johanna, the 28 year-old daughter of Stephanus Naudé Jr. (*NF37*) of Graaff-Reinet is the great-grandmother of the author's own grandmother, who will still be named for her at the end of the century. Elizabeth's cousin, Elizabeth Maria Naudé is married to Josua Joubert (*NF43*) and lives in the Winterberg area where Piet Retief is the Commando commandant. Josua and Elizabeth Maria are about to join the Great Trek.

—End Nexus Familia

 ## Nexus Familia 46: The Horror Begins

1. Massacre on the Prairie

Andries Hendrik Potgieter is a red-brown haired and blue eyed 6 foot 2 inch Afrikaner who loves wearing a large straw hat and blue clothes. When life collapses in the Tarka in 1835, he makes the decision to leave this tortured land. The white-bearded 80-year old Hendrik Coenraad "Hendrik the Elder" Klopper (*NF43*), brother to ancestor Johannes Jacobus, leaves with Potgieter. His three sons, Hendrik Jr., Balthasar, and Petrus, decide to wait and see if matters will improve. The elder Hendrik, however, desperately wants to live his last few years of life without the British overlord.

The elderly Hendrik's first misgivings intrude early in February 1836 when they get to the Orange River, swollen with summer rain from the Drakensberg in BaSotholand. He thinks to himself that he is too old for this stuff. However, this hurdle is soon overcome by floating the ox wagons across.

A collection of Trekkers from Colesberg, led by the true "fire-and-brimstone" Sarel Cilliers, joins them soon afterwards. Sarel Cilliers is a man who combines the gun and the Bible in a way no one else will, a true proponent of "Praise the Lord and pass the ammo."

Their first major stop is with Chief Moroka of the Ba'Rolong clan. Grandpa Hendrik takes an instant liking to Moroka. The chief has suffered much at the hand of Mzilikatse's Matabele who chased his people until Rev. Archbell led them to the mountain called Thaba'Nchu. Moroka is therefore happy to provide support to Potgieter in exchange for protection from Mzilikatse.

Having stayed a while with the friendly chief, Potgieter and Grandpa Hendrik and the rest of them set off north past the *kraal* of chief Makuana of the Ba'Taung clan – The People of the Lion, who also receives them hospitably. This is where Grandpa Hendrik notices white things lying around in the veldt. When he goes closer to look, he realizes to his horror that he is looking at sun bleached human skeletons. They are absolutely everywhere. In fact, Mzilikatse has been maintaining a reign of utter terror on this Prairie. In May of 1836, the trek stops for several weeks to graze the worn out cattle beyond the halfway point between the Orange and Vaal rivers, near the later town of Theunissen.

On 25 May 1836, Potgieter and ten other horsemen, accompanied by a light wagon, prepare to set off to make contact with Louis Trichardt, as promised. Grandpa Hendrik asks Potgieter to inquire with Trichardt about his nephew "Klaas Nuweveld" (*NF44*), brother to the executed "Hendrik Kasteel." Nicolaas received that appellation after being forced by the British to move to the Nuweveld region after the Slagtersnek debacle, in which he had participated. Nicolaas recently left the Colony with Trichardt and Van Rensburg.

Potgieter and his men ride for a full 18 days through a totally deserted Prairie, punctuated with burnt out *kraals* that have suffered the ravages of Mzilikatse and Dingane of the amaZulu. Human skeletons are everywhere. These are the consequences of the Difequane. It is from this horror that the Fingos have fled and have chosen slavery under Hintsa's amaXhosa instead.

Meanwhile, back south, some of the Trekkers decide to split off from the main Potgieter Trek and move north. One party, composed mostly of the Liebenberg family, wants to cross the Vaal River while another larger group aims to camp next to the Vaal River. Grandpa Hendrik tries in vain to stop them.

Concluding their business with Trichardt, and finding that the Van Rensburg trek has simply vanished, the Potgieter party returns on 28 August 1836 to a nightmare. On 21 August, an independent hunting party under a certain Stephanus Erasmus was attacked by 500 Matabele. The Matabele took two of Erasmus' sons while he was out hunting. On the 23rd, the Liebenbergs were practically wiped out. A lady and a child were pinned to the ground with assegais through their arms. The child has survived but the lady has died. Their English schoolteacher, Mr. MacDonald, has also been killed. Fourteen of the party and 12 of their servants have been killed. The Matabele have taken two young white girls and have absconded with the wagons and livestock of both encampments.

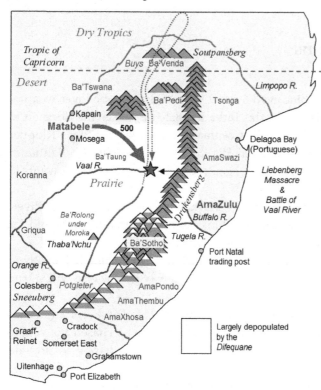

Fig. 10-4 *The Potgieter Trek*

On the same day, the Matabele attacked a group of farmers' laager at the Vaal River. Here the Matabele horde was beaten off. One young trekker died in this clash, but at least 50 (some say 150) Matabele lay dead around this camp. When the Matabele broke, a Commando went after them in the direction of the Liebenberg trek. There they rescued the few survivors and killed another Matabele who was trying to make off with a white child. At Erasmus' hunting camp, the tracks lead directly to Mzilikatse's *kraal* of Mosega – the place of the American missionaries.

Herewith, Potgieter is faced with the reality that, not only have the Van Rensburgs in the far north probably been killed, but now, on top of this, part of his own trek has been brutally massacred. A total of 53 men, women and children have perished in the three Matabele attacks. In response, Potgieter consolidates his people into one cohesive trek. His experience in dealing with Xhosa, also an Nguni nation, has taught him that a massive attack by the combined Matabele army is now inevitable. No other group on the Highveld Prairie has ever survived such an attack, as testified by the masses of human skeletons they had seen.

Grandpa Hendrik thanks God that his sons have elected to stay behind in the Colony, because he himself will surely die in what is to follow. However, he resolves to give a good account of himself.

2. The Captain, the King and the American Missionaries

At around this time, Captain Cornwallis Harris (*NF 45*) is approaching New Lattakoo (Kuruman), the mission station of Robert Moffat of the London Missionary Society on his expedition into Mzilikatse's territory. This is the same Robert Moffat whose daughter will later marry the famous David Livingstone. Harris reports[10]:

"At Koning on the 25th, we had the unexpected pleasure of meeting Captain Sutton of the 75th Foot [...] who was returning to the Colony from a successful expedition against the Elephants. [...] we obtained from this gentleman the first unwelcome intelligence that Moselekatse was embroiled with the emigrant Farmers."

Harris now proceeds to Mosega, Mzilikatse's capital, where he meets the American missionaries, Daniel Lindley, Alexander Wilson, and Henry Venable. Mrs. Wilson has died of what appears to be rheumatic fever in Mosega a few days before Cornwallis Harris' arrival. Harris reports[11]:

"We received a hearty welcome from Dr. Wilson, one of the American fraternity. [...] This gentleman likewise gave us accounts of the capture of several wagons, the property of a farmer named Erasmus, who

was hunting on the Vaal river. This was the event to which Captain Sutton had referred, but Dr. Wilson further informed us, that a very large Commando under Kalipi, the Minister and Governor of Mosega, had already been some days gone to the river Vaal, to complete the destruction of the emigrant farmers..."

Dr. Wilson, will later write[12]:

> ... *"these attacks by Mzilikazi were unprovoked on the part of the farmers. [...] We believe, however, that he was moved by avarice"...*

The Missionaries' situation is rather precarious. Mzilikatse has forbidden his people to take up any employment with them and the missionaries are not allowed to minister to the people. From here Harris now sets out[13] to meet Mzilikatse:

> *"Leaving the Mission house on the 22d October, and repassing the town of Mosega, within the fence of which we saw Erasmus's captured wagons [....] We saw comparatively few men, the larger proportion of the able bodied being absent with Kalipi on the Commando against the emigrant farmers. The Missionaries estimated this force to consist of near five thousand warriors."*

Harris finally meets with Mzilikatse and gives one of the best surviving descriptions of this despotic monster. He describes the discussion with the king and the problems of speaking to him through a series of translators from Zulu to Tswana to Dutch to English. In this he has the help of their Khoekhoe guide, Andries, whom they totally distrust; correctly, as it will turn out.

Fig. 10-5 Mzilikatse as sketched by Cornwallis Harris

Mzilikatse parades his harem for Harris, and they see among the women "Truy" (Geertruyda), the captive daughter of the leader of the mixed-race Griqua, Peter Davids. Later that evening, Mzilikatse sends Truy to them to try and relieve them of more of their supply of beads, having already obtained a huge number earlier in the day. In tears, she asks that they please tell her father that she is safe. She also tells them that her cousin Wilhelm, also a captive, has been sent to take two captive white Dutch girls, abducted during the recent raid on the Afrikaners near the Vaal River, away to a distant *kraal*. She confirms that the king has gone to great lengths to hide these girls from Harris and his fellow travelers. Nothing will ever be heard of these two girls again. Erasmus' two sons have apparently tried to escape on their way to Mzilikatse and have been summarily killed.

Upon leaving the King's *kraal*, Mzilikatse provides Harris' group with a guide, Lingap, a warrior who took part in the attack on the Erasmus camp. Harris writes[14] :

> *"His eyes glistened as he spoke of the pleasure he had derived from feeling his spear enter white flesh. It slipped in, he said, grasping his assegai and suiting the action to the word, so much more satisfactorily than into the tough hide of a black savage, that he preferred sticking a Dutchman to eating the King's beef."*

3. The Battle of Vegkop – dead men don't sweat

Grandpa Hendrik knows how Potgieter's head works. While some of his people have fled back south to Thaba'Nchu with their wagons, Potgieter himself simply does not fit this mold. He will make a stand. After the unprovoked murders, the Prairie is clearly not big enough to hold both Potgieter's people and the Matabele. Mzilikatse has a hitherto undefeated army of some 6,000 warriors, the fiercest that white men have yet encountered in Africa. He has repeatedly defeated Dingane's infamous Zulu when they have attacked him. After all, Mzilikatse has told Harris that he views the British king as possibly the *"second most powerful"* in the world after himself. Hendrik grins wryly when he adds up Potgieter's men and realizes that he has only 33 men and 7 boys. This includes Hendrik himself. He does not think they have much of a chance, but he is ready to sell what is left of his life as dearly as he can. He knows full well that he is still a deadly shot.

With the typically keen eye for terrain, so characteristic of the Afrikaner, Potgieter now chooses a nondescript hill on the prairie, just south of the future town of Heilbron, and places his mobile fort near it on barren ground that slopes away from the wagons. This will provide two things; a nominal height from which to see the Matabele approaching to provide adequate warning, and an unobstructed field of fire for his little band of 40 men and boys, with nowhere for any Matabele to hide. Grandpa Hendrik nods approvingly while pulling at his great white beard.

Fig. 10-6 *Acacia Karroo – Sweet thorn*

While the Afrikaners have repeatedly employed their laagers as sanctuaries since the end of the 1700s, Hendrik now helps to perfect it into an instrument of war, the likes of which the world has never seen before. They pull the wagons in a circle and run the pole of each wagon under the wagon in front. They lock the wheels and chain them together between successive wagons. Then they wedge acacia karroo branches between and under the wagons. These trees are excellent for this purpose. The branches are studded with long needle sharp spikes. Young South Africans know well the pain induced by these gum-tipped spikes.

At two opposing points in this mobile ring-fort, Potgieter now asks the men to construct shooting-pens. They also leave two openings through which men can charge on horseback, should the occasion warrant. They can close these portals quickly by running two wagons into the openings. In the middle of the wagon fort they place a tight circle of wagons, their tilts temporarily reinforced with animal skins, to serve as tenders for the wounded and to keep the gunpowder safe. Because he has too few wagons, Potgieter cannot keep his cattle inside the laager and is forced to place them some distance away, knowing that he will probably lose them all. He hopes to recover them afterwards. Then the men take a large number of oxen and flatten the grass around the laager. Hendrik is convinced that Potgieter knows what he is doing. They are now ready for the Matabele under the famous general, Kalipi – the wait begins.

Soon enough, news comes that a 6,000 strong Matabele *impi* (army) has crossed the Vaal River and is rapidly approaching the *Vegkop* (Fight Hill) laager, as the place will come to be called. The women and children cast the lead ball and slugs and the gunpowder supply and small fatty cloths are readied for the muskets. Each Trekker has two or three guns, and the women and children stand ready to load at high speed under the attack without fumbling. Pickets are posted. That night Grandpa Hendrik cannot sleep.

On the morning of 19 October 1836, the Trekkers hear the unearthly hiss on the cool Prairie breeze. It is the sound made by the thousands of Matabele as they approach, rattling their assegais against their shields. Sarel Cilliers leads a quick church service and then all the men – Hendrik included – are led out by Potgieter and Cilliers to meet the Matabele some six miles from the laager.

There is merit in trying to reason with the Matabele, but they are not Western men – they are Matabele. Potgieter tries once to parley with the Matabele, but they just scream *"Mzilikatse!"* And then they attack. Potgieter orders a volley to be fired and then the men fall back a distance out of assegai range to reload and fire another volley. In this way they systematically erode the Matabele front as they fall back to their defensive laager. Once at the laager, Sarel Cilliers leads a last prayer. Then the women and children are asked to be quiet.

When the Matabele reach the laager, they surround it. Hendrik expects the savage horde to charge, but they do nothing of the kind. In fact, they simply sit down some distance from the laager. Then they herd about 80 head of the Trekkers' cattle together and slaughter them right there, eating the meat raw with the blood dripping off their faces in full view of the laager. Inside the laager the 33 men and roughly 60 women and children silently watch this savage feeding frenzy. Off to his side, Hendrik sees the ten-year old Paul who had helped earlier to position the sweet thorn branches between the wagons. He is from the farm *Bulhoek* (Bull "Corner" or Place of the Bull), south of Colesberg. The boy stares at the Matabele army with grim determination. Hendrik can only wonder what is going through his mind, but smiles at him through his great white beard. He can see the boy is frightened to death, but is trying bravely not to show it.

Hendrik realizes that they cannot allow the Matabele to just sit there and wait for Afrikaner morale to crumble. When he looks around, he sees Potgieter tying a rag to the end of a wagon whip. Then he waves it above the laager to goad the Matabele. That does it! The Matabele yell *"Bulala! Bulala!"* (Kill! Kill!), and they charge. The Trekkers hold their fire until they know every shot will count...and then they fire. They fire massive slugs that vary from four to six to a pound. That means that each round penetrates a few Matabele. The women and children pass a steady stream of loaded guns to the fighting men.

The first charge of the Matabele is incredibly frightening. It almost overwhelms the little laager. Having been thwarted, the frustrated Matabele now jerk at the wagons and at the thorn branches. One Matabele almost worms his way into the laager. The next moment Abraham Swanepoel's wife runs screaming past Hendrik with an axe in her hands and promptly chops off the warrior's hand. The screaming Matabele falls back. Other women and children are now actually shooting. The fighting

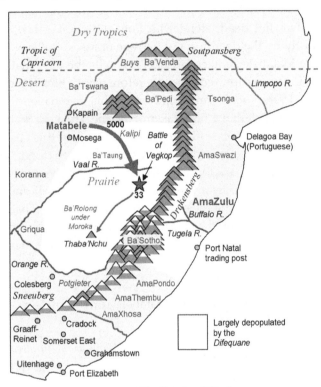

Fig. 10-7 The Battle of Vegkop

becomes so frenzied that some do not feel pain anymore. When one Matabele manages to thrust his assegai into Sarel Cilliers' thigh, Hendrik sees how the tough "blood 'n guts" Trekker pulls the assegai out of his own body and kills his Matabele attacker with it. The shooting has become so furious that there is no longer time enough to tamp down the charges in the barrels of the guns with push rods, so the men take to keeping lead ball shot in their mouths, spitting the balls down the barrels and banging the butts of the muskets on the ground to set the charges. Then... as suddenly as the attack started ...reprieve!

The Matabele withdraw a distance beyond the range of the guns to regain their breath. Potgieter immediately calls the men together, leads them out of the laager and orders them to shoot the wounded Matabele that are lying on the ground, yelling *"Dead men don't sweat!"* He simply cannot afford for any of them to jump up later and join in the expected second charge. This is a fight to the death – kill or be killed. There is no place for mercy in this transaction, because the men know what these savages have done, so they kill those that they find alive. Then they return to the laager, because the Matabele are on the attack again. Hendrik is not convinced they can withstand another charge.

This time Kalipi changes his tactics. Before charging the laager, he orders part of his Impi to loose a barrage of assegais high into the air to plummet almost vertically down onto the people in the laager. More than a thousand razor sharp assegais come whistling down onto the Trekkers, and several people are wounded in this volley. Several assegais barely miss Hendrik. When the second frenzied charge comes, it is somehow also beaten off with deadly Boer fire, a single slug downing up to five Matabele at a time. This is the point at which Kalipi himself is shot through the knee. Then, as dramatically as they arrived, the Matabele turn and leave.

Grandpa Hendrik sinks to his knees in prayer with his hands folded around his trusty *Sanna* (English: "Suzie") – his trusty musket. He suddenly feels old, so terribly old. That is when he sees young Paul Kruger looking at him, and he realizes that he had better put on a brave face for the benefit of the boy.

Potgieter orders the portals to be opened and half of the Trekkers pour out on horseback. They pursue the Matabele and kill as many as they can, but they cannot recover their herds. While they were fighting for their lives, other warriors drove off all the animals of the Trekkers. Inside the laager Nicolaas, Potgieter's brother, lies dead, along with Potgieter's son-in-law, Pieter Botha. Fourteen Trekkers are badly wounded, mostly by the deadly aerial barrage of assegais. They recover no fewer than 1115 assegais inside the laager. One Matabele is taken prisoner. He tells the men that his life will be forfeit if he returns to Mzilikatse after having been captured. They therefore recruit him as a guide. Already, Potgieter is planning his next step.

In the short term, Potgieter and his men have lost everything except their lives and their main wagons. The Matabele have now taken from the Trekkers 96 horses, 4,671 cattle and 50,740 sheep and goats, along with nine muskets and four wagons[15]. Beyond this being an economic catastrophe, the immediate problem is that they have no transport and almost no food. Potgieter's other brother, Hermanus, is sent off to Thaba'Nchu to ask for help. They have to survive for two weeks before oxen, milk cows and food arrive from the helpful Wesleyan missionary James Archbell and their loyal ally, Chief Moroka of the Ba'Rolong, at Thaba'Nchu. Using these oxen, they move back to Thaba'Nchu in two stages.

All in the land are glad that the power of the "invincible" Mzilikatse has been countered. For the first time ever it seems that it is possible to beat the Monster of the Prairie.

4. Near Mzilikatse's capital

Cornwallis Harris sees the Matabele army returning with the cattle of the Potgieter trek as he rides out from Mzilikatse's *kraal*:

> "*The appearance shortly afterwards of several hundred Matabili warriors in their war costume explained the riddle, and we knew that these must be some of the cattle taken from the unfortunate emigrants* [...]
>
> *The Hottentots looked aghast, and Coeur de Lion* [a most ironically nick-named Khoekhoe expedition member]*, in a state of extreme agitation, fainted when he saw a number of wounded warriors borne past on the shields of their comrades, whilst others groaned under the weight of accoutrements that had been stripped from the bodies of the slain.*[16]"

The American missionaries at Mosega will report[17]:

> "*...thirty-five Boers prepared to defend themselves, their wives, and their children, against the whole force of Moselekatsi. Every one under the influence of a martial spirit must exclaim, How gallant their determination!* [...] *...they now rode into the circle they had formed, and prepared, under cover of their wagons, to resist the assault of what they supposed one hundred and fifty to one!* [...] *We at first thought that in this affair Moselekatsi had lost the half of his fighting men; we now think about one third of them.*"

—End Nexus Familia

Gerrit Maritz — Democracy at last!

Even as Potgieter was fighting the Matabele at Vegkop, Gerrit Maritz, wagon builder and senior businessman from Graaff-Reinet, was leading the next major group of Voortrekkers over the Orange River. They left the Cape Colony in mid-September 1836 and arrived at Thaba'Nchu, home of Chief Maroko of the Ba'Rolong, from 19 November 1836 onwards. The new arrivals had one hundred wagons and made a big impression on the people already there as being numerous, prominent and influential.

Where Hendrik Potgieter was a tough frontiersman of few words and direct action, Maritz was the urbane and sophisticated townsman. He traveled with a library of books, including his collection of law books. Where Potgieter brought dogged toughness, Maritz brought organization to the Great Trek. It was here that the Voortrekkers or United Emigrants, as they called themselves, did a rather remarkable thing. Considering that these people had never experienced representative government in their entire history, they emulated the United States and elected seven men as their legislative, executive and judicial authorities. Hendrik Potgieter, who had so ably demonstrated his ability in the military domain, was elected Laager Commandant, while Maritz was elected as President and Judge.

One other interesting personage was Erasmus Smit. This enigmatic Dutchman had come to the Cape in 1804 by a circuitous route via New York. He was a member of the hugely distrusted London Missionary Society (LMS). He had set up a mission station for San Bushmen at the site of the later Colesberg, but this had eventually been shut down by the British government at the Cape and around 1822 Smit and the Society parted company. When the Great Trek became a reality, he joined his brother-in-law, Gerrit Maritz. Since the Western Cape based Dutch Reformed Church of the Cape Province was strenuously opposed to the Great Trek, it refused to provide church ministers for the Trekkers. Filling this obvious and serious void, Erasmus Smit offered his unordained services. He was never quite accepted by the Trekkers for two reasons. Firstly, he could never provide evidence of being properly ordained, and hence many Trekkers objected to him serving communion or baptizing their children. Secondly, many never quite accepted him because of his earlier connection to the London Missionary Society, which they detested with every fiber of their being as the primary source of all their woes. In the event, it would be Erasmus Smit who would baptize the members of the author's family on the Great Trek. His is the only comprehensive diary of the Great Trek that has survived.

Americans in the eye of the storm

On 3 January 1837, Gert Maritz and Hendrik Potgieter set out from Thaba'Nchu at the head of an Allied Commando of 107 Afrikaner burghers, 35 mixed-descent Griqua under Peter Davids, 5 Koranna Khoekhoe, and 60 of Chief Maroko's Ba'Rolong. These are four distinct nations of differing Southern African races—Black, White, Khoekhoe, and Mixed—cooperating against a tyrant. One of their guides was Chief Matlabe, a former captive of Mzilikazi. Another was the Matabele warrior who had been taken captive at Vegkop and whose life was now forfeit in the hands of Mzilikatse (*NF46 – Section 3*). Davids had a score of his own to settle with Mzilikatse, who kept his daughter Geertruy in his harem (*NF46 - Section 2*). From the Vaal River the Commando continued on horseback, and, instead of going directly to Mosega, they first feinted northeastward to the vicinity of the present Pretoria. Then they turned due west and headed straight for Mosega, approaching the settlement from a direction that blindsided Mzilikatse.

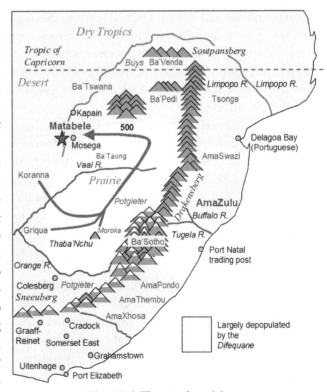

***Fig. 10-8** The attack on Mosega*

The Mosega Matabele settlement consisted of 15 villages surrounded by the Kurrichane Hills. On the night of 16 January 1837, the Commando reached the hills and dismounted. Maritz's sharpshooters took up firing positions in the hills and Potgieter's unit entered the first village at daybreak on the 17th. The surprise was complete. As the Matabele emerged from their huts they were shot down in droves. The Commando raced from one *kraal* to the next, burning everything as they went and driving the panicked Matabele headlong to the north. No mercy was shown and no quarter was given; not after what the Matabele had done. Most had a score to settle except Maritz, whose men held the hills for the others to have their way with the monstrous Mzilikatse's people.

The American missionaries to Mzilikatse were in the eye of the storm. Dr. Wilson wrote[18]:

> *"Early in the morning I was awakened by the firing of guns; I arose and looked and saw the farmers on horse-back, pursuing and shooting the natives, who were flying in every direction. [...] These white men had come to our house and had treated us kindly.[...] We decided to leave the country under their protection."*

Rev. Daniel Lindley was awakened by an anxious Stephanus Erasmus seeking news of his missing sons. Afterwards, Lindley and his fellow missionaries wrote[19]:

> *"The Boers attacked and destroyed thirteen, some say fifteen, kraals. Few of the men belonging to them escaped and many of the women were either shot down or killed with the assegai. [...]*
> *"The Boers took away with them about six thousand head of cattle and made our field of labor a desolation."*

The Commando drove hard at the Matabele, never giving them a chance to rally, otherwise their own small numbers would be too easily overwhelmed. Not a single Afrikaner, Griqua or Koranna was harmed, but two of Maroko's Ba'Rolong died clearing the huts.

When Potgieter explained to the three American missionaries that it was his intention to keep attacking Mzilikatse until he had left this land altogether, they decided that there was no more point to staying with the Matabele. So, they and their remaining two wives departed with the Allied Commando. Their lives would anyway have been forfeit if Mzilikatse had come back to find them unharmed, as indeed they were. Lindley would get an entirely new Calling from this event. The 6000 head of cattle that the Commando took that day, was nowhere near the total livestock haul that the Matabele had taken from Potgieter at the earlier Vegkop and Vaal River attacks.

Potgieter wanted to immediately press another attack on Kapain, the seat of Mzilikatse. However, Maritz would not support him in this. Potgieter therefore took his people and moved back north to the upper reaches of the Vaal River in the general area of the present Heidelberg. Potgieter, a man of his word, then set out to visit Louis Trichardt in the far north. However, after he had traveled more than halfway, word came that Trichardt was already on the move to Delagoa Bay. Potgieter therefore turned his soldier's mind to the matter of how to undertake a second strike at the "Monster of the Prairie."

Nexus Familia 47: The Louis Trichardt Trek 2

Louis Trichardt goes to look for the lost Van Rensburg Trek. He follows the trail to the renegade Zulu chief, Shoshangane, of the so-called *Bloot Kaffers* (Naked Kafirs [sic]), who lives where the Olifants (Elephant) River and the Limpopo join in the later Mozambique. The chief is quite hostile, and tells Trichardt that the trek passed through there but has not been seen since. Trichardt does not believe him and suspects that Shoshangane has murdered the Van Rensburgs. He is afraid that he will meet the same fate, and withdraws after telling Shoshangane that he will go and get all his wagons and cattle and then leave it all in Shoshangane's care. He himself will then continue the search for the Van Rensburg trek.

Shoshangane's avarice gets the better of his bloodlust and he lets Trichardt leave. Some years later Trichardt's son will discover the bones of the Van Rensburg trek-members near Shoshangane's *kraal*, all murdered at one spot in one night by Shoshangane's naked warriors. Here died Nicloaas Balthasar "Klaas Nuweveld" Prinsloo (*NF44*), along with his whole family.

By late 1836, Trichardt starts moving his people about to avoid the dreaded cattle sickness, Nagana, carried by the Tsetse fly. He is still waiting for Potgieter, who is embroiled in his own life-and-death struggle with the Matabele. He starts to build wattle-and-daub houses and even puts up a school for Daniel Peffer and his 21 students.

Trichardt, however, becomes more anxious by the day. Potgieter is not coming and his cattle are dying and his people have the fever, malaria, caused by who knows what. He decides to write to the Portuguese at Delagoa Bay. He tries three times and the second attempt makes it to the Governor at Delagoa Bay, carried by none other than a mixed race son of the tough old Boer, our cousin Coenraad de Buys (*NF44*). De Buys junior explains the predicament of the people at the Soutpansberg, and on 7 August 1837 he arrives back with two Portuguese lascars named Lorenço and Antonio.

On 23 August 1837, the trek starts out for Delagoa Bay; not via the route advised by the lascars, but further south to avoid the murderous "Naked Kafirs" of Shoshangane. This is the message that Potgieter gets when he sets out to meet with Louis Trichardt. On 30 November 1837, Trichardt stands atop the northern Drakensberg escarpment.

We leave Trichardt again at this point at the start of the last leg of his journey, with our ancestor's sister Martha, his faithful wife, by his side on the ox-wagon; headed directly for deeply malaria infested country. The carrier of the dreaded malaria fever will only be identified much later after 1880 as being the anopheles mosquito, so prevalent in that region.

—*End Nexus Familia*

The Retief Trek

While Hendrik Potgieter was the consummate soldier of few words and tough actions, and Gerrit Maritz was the sophisticated man of good government and administration, Piet Retief was to be the Voice of the Afrikaner and almost the embodiment of their aspirations. An articulate man of good standing in the Cape Colony, commanding respect from all who knew him, including the outgoing British Governor, he would be the one to draw up the Emigrant's Manifesto, which carefully listed the reasons for the Great Trek. On 2 February 1837, his good friend and admirer, Robert Godlonton, the British Settler editor of the *Grahamstown Journal*, published the document (overleaf).

The rest of the Trekkers at Thaba'Nchu could see why it was that people from all walks of life had followed Retief. He had a quiet authority, presence and urbane polish. People said it was his French heritage showing. He was the very model of all that their leader should be, and so, within a few days, Retief was elected Governor and Commander-in-Chief of the United Emigrants, the *Voortrekkers*.

Retief, older than any of the other leaders, accepted the role rather reluctantly, as one sees from his letters[20] back to the Cape:

> *"Were it to please the Almighty, my anxious wish is to be released from this burden, that I may spend the short period I have yet to live free from such important cares and responsibility. But I may not and will not murmur."*

Maritz retained his role as Judge and chairman of the Council of Policy. Most peculiarly, Hendrik Potgieter, the obvious choice for some form of senior military role, was not elected in any capacity at all. It also did not help when Retief appointed the unordained ex-LMS missionary Erasmus Smit as minister to the United Emigrants at 600 Rix-dollars a year. This hugely upset Potgieter's ultra-conservative followers.

Retief did, however, agree with Potgieter that the next order of business was to complete the assault on Mzilikatse. This plan was derailed, however, by rumors of an impending attack by the Griqua, who felt threatened by the 1,000 wagons and thousands of white people.

This attack did not materialize.

The Graham's Town Journal, 2 February 1837

Numerous reports having been circulated throughout the colony, evidently with the intention of exciting in the minds of our countrymen a feeling of prejudice against those who have resolved to emigrate from a colony where they have experienced for so many years past a series of the most vexatious and severe losses; and as we desire to stand high in the estimation of our brethren, and are anxious that they and the world at large should believe us incapable of severing that sacred tie which binds a Christian to his native soil, without the most sufficient reasons, we are induced to record the following summary of our motives for taking so important a step; and also our intentions respecting our proceedings towards the Native Tribes which we may meet with beyond the boundary.

• We despair of saving the colony from those evils which threaten it by the turbulent and dishonest conduct of vagrants, who are allowed to infest the country in every part; nor do we see any prospect of peace or happiness for our children in a country thus distracted by internal commotions.

• We complain of the severe losses which we have been forced to sustain by the emancipation of our slaves, and the vexatious laws which have been enacted respecting them.

• We complain of the continual system of plunder which we have ever endured from the Kafirs and other coloured classes, and particularly by the last invasion of the colony, which has desolated the frontier districts, and ruined most of the inhabitants.

• We complain of the unjustifiable odium which has been cast upon us by interested and dishonest persons, under the cloak of religion, whose testimony is believed in England to the exclusion of all evidence in our favour; and we can foresee as the result of this prejudice, nothing but the total ruin of the country.

• We are resolved, wherever we go, that we will uphold the just principles of liberty; but whilst we will take care that no one shall be held in a state of slavery, it is our determination to maintain such regulations as may suppress crime and preserve proper relations between Master and servant.

• We solemnly declare that we quit this colony with a desire to lead a more quiet life than we have heretofore done. We will not molest any people, nor deprive them of the smallest property; but, if attacked, we shall consider ourselves fully justified in defending our persons and effects, to the utmost of our ability, against every enemy.

• We make known, that when we shall have framed a code of laws for our future guidance, copies shall be forwarded to the colony for general information; but we take this opportunity of stating that it is our firm resolve to make provision for the summary punishment of any traitors who may be found amongst us.

• We purpose, in the course of our journey, and on arriving at the country in which we shall permanently reside, to make known to the native tribes our intentions, and our desire to live in peace and friendly intercourse with them.

• We quit this colony under the full assurance that the English government has nothing more to require of us, and will allow us to govern ourselves without its interference in future.

• We are now quitting the fruitful land of our birth, in which we have suffered enormous losses and continual vexation, and are entering a wild and dangerous territory; but we go with a firm reliance on an all-seeing, just, and merciful Being, whom it will be our endeavour to fear and humbly to obey.

By authority of the farmers who have quitted the Colony,
(signed) *P. RETIEF*

Nexus Familia 48: The Retief Trek – Salomé's Diary

When Piet Retief's trek reaches the Tarka to the east of Cradock, Pieter Georg Jordaan (*NF43*), older brother of our ancestor Chris Jordaan, packs his belongings, puts his family on the wagons, and joins Retief. With him is his wife Isabella and their children, who now number six. Isabella, we recall, is the daughter of Field-Cornet Jacobus Potgieter who was so treacherously murdered by the ImiDange at *Doringnek* (*NF39*). Michael and Reynier Grobler (*NF43*), the two cousins of our ancestor Izak Grobler also load their wagons and families and join Retief's trek. They travel together as an extended family. After all, the two brothers are married to the two sisters Susanna and Maria van Dyk respectively.

Michael's foursome is a handful. The 8-year old Helena, cute as a penny, cannot sit still for a minute, so Susanna keeps her busy with all manner of activity. The 6-year old Michael Junior is on and off their wagon repeatedly until his father lets him walk with the *touleier* (literally "rope leader"), the Khoekhoe man who leads the oxen at the front. Little sisters Elsie and Susanna Junior are likewise kept busy by their mother. On Reynier's wagon, his wife Maria is occupied with the one-year old Michael. Having joined Retief beyond Cradock, Willem Basson, and younger brother Matthys, second cousins to our ancestor Thys in the West Cape (*NF43*), are both from the Swartruggens area of the Uitenhage district. They also travel together, because they too are married to two sisters, their distant cousins Johanna and Maria Salomé Basson. Willem's oldest son, Matthys Junior, is on horseback as they travel. He is of fighting age (18) and does not ride on the wagon, except to take over the driver's role from his father some of the time. The two younger brothers, Nicolaas (14) and Willem (12) take on the touleier job at the head of the team of oxen. At ten years of age, little Maria Salomé (Junior) is in the wagon with her mother, Johanna. Maria Salomé (Senior), Johanna's sister, is on Matthys Senior's wagon with their children. There she meticulously keeps her diary. Whenever there is a stop of a day or more, she gathers a horde of children to present her school lessons, because she is the schoolteacher of the trek. The men take her very seriously indeed. This is a much-respected lady.

In Piet Retief the three men, Pieter Jordaan, Reynier Grobler and Willem Basson, see a man one can follow anywhere. Retief has proven himself as military commander and as general leader in the Winterberg area where he previously had magisterial authority. He has good friends in the British Settler community and counts Robert Godlonton, the leader of the free press in the East Cape, as a friend.

Given the general standing of Retief in the broader community, a number of British Settlers have also joined the Great Trek. These include Samuel Liversage and his all-British family who lived in the Baviaansriver area near Retief, Thomas Jervis Biddulph, the young English schoolmaster from Cradock, the family of John Leech and the one and only John Montgomery, an Irishman who came to the Cape to seek adventure and operate as *smous* (trader) to the Trekkers. And then there is William Cowie and William Robinson, the youngest son of British Settler, Robert Robinson. They end up with Retief at Thaba'Nchu.

Before leaving the colony, John Leech sold their farm next door to that of our ancestral family Bowles (*NF41, 42*) to the family Webber, who will look after the little Kariega Church for three generations. The family Leech spent a night of terror during the 6th Frontier War, huddled in fear in the dark of their cottage at Kariega, while the amaXhosa warriors stole all their cattle outside[21].

Pieter Jordaan's ox-wagon is quite typical of the wagons in which the Trekkers travel. It is lighter and narrower than the prairie schooners of their American "cousins." It measures eighteen feet in length and six feet wide. It can carry more than a ton. The wheels are saucer-shaped, being concave to the outward. The large wheels at the back are shoulder high and have fixed axles with fourteen assegai wood spokes. The smaller front wheels run on an axle fitted to a turntable and have ten spokes each. Drawing all of this is typically a span of ten oxen in two rows of which the two hindmost oxen are yoked directly to the *disselboom* (pole) of the wagon. On the wagon is everything of value that they have and everything they think they may need for their future lives. Some families even have their pianos on their wagons. All have carefully stowed on board a precious Dutch Family Bible. The gunpowder wagons travel separately.

The crossing of the Orange River is uneventful, and the convoy of 100 white-canopied wagons and 400 souls makes quite a sight as it approaches Thaba'Nchu on 8 April 1837. Pieter Jordaan is surprised to see a dust cloud up ahead. It turns out to be a collection of horsemen under Gerrit Maritz, the leader of the United Emigrants already at Thaba'Nchu. They have heard that Retief is coming and they have ridden out to meet him in a show of respect. Clearly, Retief's reputation has preceded him. Pieter finds the deference shown by Maritz to Retief quite remarkable, considering the collection of rough and tough frontier folks involved out here on the prairie. Clearly, expectations are high. The Afrikaners have a new "George Washington."

—End Nexus Familia

Dreaming of America

Retief now moved the entire United Emigrant group northward to an area just south of the Vaal River. This positioned them for all eventualities. From here, they could attack Mzilikatse, or cross the Vaal River to settle there or set out eastward into the Natal area, if so required. Then scouting parties were sent to search for suitable passes down the Drakensberg to Natal, in case they were to go that way.

He negotiated formal treaties with Moroka of the Ba'Rolong, Moshesh of the Ba'Sotho and with Sekonyela of the Ba'Tlokwa more to the northeast. These treaties cleared his route back to the Cape Colony. From this point onwards, there was constant travel backwards and forwards through the Trans-Orange back to the Cape.

Over this period, the Uys Trek of 100 wagons under Piet Uys arrived from Uitenhage (See Chapter 9). Uys was an accomplished man, but steadfastly refused to fall in with Retief and his new government. He preferred to keep his laager far to the south and drew up his own manifesto containing the important statement[22]:

> *"We propose to establish our settlement on the same principles of liberty as those adopted by the United States of America, carrying into effect, as far as practicable, our Burgher Laws"*

Retief's scouting parties to the Drakensberg returned with good news and Retief wrote on 9 September 1837 to Andries Stockenström, who was then still Lieutenant Governor in the East of the Cape Colony[23]:

> *"Having, however, sent out a party to ascertain whether there was no probability of crossing it, they returned, after an absence of twenty-five days, with the glad tidings that, at five different points, the whole encampment might cross this formidable barrier without difficulty or danger. [...]*
>
> *I proceed in person with a party of fifty men to Port Natal, and to the residence of the Zoola King, Dingaan, having heard more from that quarter than I exactly like. I leave this on the 16th inst... [...]*
>
> *I have not as yet ascertained anything respecting Trechard. Reports have, however, reached me that Matzalikatse has completed preparations for another attack upon us...[...]*
>
> *I have not left my native land to live in obscurity with the British government, or my countrymen who are left behind, but my anxious desire is to have free intercourse with them."*

He then included copies of letters sent to the Cape Governor and to the leaders of the Koranna and the Griqua, who had started to attack Afrikaner trek parties and who were apparently scheming to raid Mzilikatse to take the remaining Afrikaner cattle from him. He told the latter two groups to stay out of the fight between the Trekkers and Mzilikatse and to leave the cattle alone. He also mailed the newspaper copies of the rules of conduct (Laws) for the Trekkers relating to treatment of servants or San Bushmen and other issues. All this was done to show the Cape government that the London Missionary Society had been lying when it had insinuated that the Trekkers were leaving in order to practice slavery.

Hendrik Potgieter, on the other hand, was not at all supportive of the idea of going to Natal. His view remained that where there was sea there would be British Military Government, some time or other; and that in August 1836 the British Government at the Cape had enacted the *"Cape of Good Hope Punishment Act"* that placed any criminal actions south of the 25th latitude under their jurisdiction. This law was squarely aimed at the Trekkers. Therefore, since Natal was distinctly south of the 25th latitude, Potgieter insisted on being north of the Vaal River, which, despite being still south of the 25th latitude, would hopefully place his people clear of British designs. After all, there was all of Africa north of that latitude.

On 4 October, Erasmus Smit comments in his diary on a report of the previous day from Barend Liebenberg that some 50 Ba'Tlokwa men had passed their encampment with a large number of cattle, sheep and horses, coming from the direction of Dingane's country. Erasmus states that the future will reveal whether this is an issue to be concerned about. All believed that the animals had been rustled from the Zulu.

The American Missionary's warning

On 5 October 1837, Piet Retief eventually set off with just 14 horsemen and 4 wagons to Dingane's capital of Umgungundlovu, Place of the Great Elephant. On the way there, he first visited the British at the Port Natal outpost where his party was warmly received. The presence of the Trekkers meant that the British would now have a more solid line of communication back to the Cape and potentially a whole new life. Until this point, they had been living in fear of Dingane in Zulu reed huts, maintaining a basic existence. John Cane and Alexander Biggar looked forward to obtaining security through an Afrikaner occupation of the country. After all, they actually knew these people personally in some cases. Thirteen settlers out of the thirty-eight at Port Natal went so far as to sign an address of welcome to Retief, and Alexander Biggar, the accepted leader of the community, wrote[24] thankfully to the Grahamstown Journal:

> "The arrival of Mr. Retief [...] was hailed by us as a matter of no small moment. The conviction that we shall for the future be permitted to live in peace has infused a lively spirit among us. We can now proceed with confidence, and an assurance that our future exertions will no longer be cramped by doubts of our stability; but be rewarded by the fruits of our industry."

Having arrived at Port Natal, Retief wrote a letter to Dingane in which he honestly expressed the hope to settle the land to the south of the Zulu and to live in peace with them, and that he would like to discuss this land and how it might be settled with Dingane's blessing. Dingane responded by sending Retief some sheep he had captured from Mzilikatse and which he believed might belong to Retief. So, both parties were apparently doing their best to be courteous. However, upon the final deputation of Retief, Barend Liebenberg, Roelof Dreyer and interpreter Thomas Halstead arriving[25] at Dingane's *kraal* on 5 November 1837, things suddenly did not go well at all. We shall see later why not.

After delaying to see the visitors for two days, Dingane finally appeared. Retief was accused of stealing Dingane's cattle. Dingane insisted that the rustlers had been on horses, had worn Western clothes, and had had guns. They had also yelled to their Zulu pursuers that they were "Boers." Retief explained that those had to have been Sekonyela's men, who rode horses, wore Western clothes and had actually been seen herding the cattle past the Trekkers' encampment some time before! It was thereupon agreed that, if Retief were to retrieve the cattle for Dingane and "*If possible, send* [him] *the thief,*" then Dingane would grant the Trekkers the land. Retief understood this to be the area that Dingane had utterly desolated with his impis "*to the north, south and west of Port Natal.*" Retief had seen the desolation in that region as he had traveled to Port Natal. He therefore agreed to this herculean challenge. Bearing in mind his manifesto, he was duty and honor bound to properly negotiate land with the indigenous population, lest he should develop problems with the Cape Government.

There was a bad "snake in the grass," but Retief had no inkling of the real depth of this. In fact, he had a letter from Dingane via the good offices of the Reverend Owen, saying[26]:

> "To go on now with the request you have made for land, I am quite willing to grant it"

Given the bitter experience with the London Missionary Society back in the Cape, one is staggered by the fact that Retief trusted Owen, who likely was a completely innocent participant in the unfolding disaster. However, his protector, Captain Gardiner was most definitely not, and the other Englishmen at Port Natal were equally suspicious of Gardiner. History to that point had proven the LMS to be the *Serpent enveloped in the Cloth*, and a leader of the stature of Retief might have been expected to *not* trust British Missionaries. On the other hand, Owen did attempt to warn Retief of Dingane's duplicity, suggesting Dingane's had already given the land to the British.

On his way back to the Trekker camp, Retief stopped in with the American missionary, Rev. George Champion, who actually warned him that Dingane was likely leading the Emigrants into a trap. Retief refused to accept that. Herein he showed the same peculiar naive trust in his fellow man that had cost him so dearly in his business initiatives. His blind Christian faith in his fellow man seemed to intrude on his logic at the worst possible times. Here, ironically, we had an actual Christian missionary warning him, and he as ordinary man preferred simple faith in his fellow man.

Meanwhile, the Trekkers had started approaching the Drakensberg Escarpment. The point where they finally reached the escarpment was dubbed *Kerkenberg* (Church Mountain) by Erasmus Smit, because the gallery of sandstone rocks at that point reminded him of a church. On 11 November 1837, messengers from Retief reached the party at *Kerkenberg* with the news of the negotiations.

On 12 November 1837, Deborah Retief, Pieter's daughter, painted her father's name on one of the rocks. It was his 57th birthday. When Retief, his men and an assortment of Zulus to identify cattle at Sekonyela's *kraal* arrived back with the main body of the Trekkers on the 27th of November 1837, around one thousand wagons had made it down the Drakensberg and collected in loose groups in the general vicinity of a hill they named *Doornkop* (Thornhill).

The Battle of Kapain

Soon after the great "Meeting of the Nation" on 13 September 1837, Hendrik Potgieter and Gerrit Maritz trekked north and crossed the Vaal River to laager at a range of hills known as *Suikerbosrand* (Sugar Bush Ridge). Here they prepared for a final blow against Mzilikatse. Around the 6th of November Piet Uys arrived with his people, having asked Retief to delay further meetings with Dingane until he, Uys, had returned from the campaign against Mzilikatse. With all the combined treks at that point, they had around 185 wagons and just over 1000 people, of whom some 295 were men of fighting age. Eighteen Ba'Rolong guides sent by Moroka had already arrived earlier around 14 October 1837.

In November 1837, the Commando finally set out, minus the services of Maritz who had taken ill and was entering the last year of his life. Gert Rudolph, his nephew who had been on the original commission trek to Natal, led Maritz's men on the Commando. Potgieter and Uys each led their own men. They rode first to Mosega, which was still deserted, and from there north, initiating a series of running battles that pushed the Matabele further and further north through three gorges in the hills. In the process, the Matabele used their trained battle oxen with sharpened horns, but this backfired when these animals panicked, turned and mangled their own masters. Finally, the Matabele broke completely.

There had not been a single loss on Afrikaner side, but the Matabele had lost somewhere between 500 and 3,000 men. Sources differ on this point. The Commando took some 4600 cattle and the power of Mzilikatse in South Africa was broken forever. The Commando arrived back at Maritz's camp at the Suikerbosrand at the end of the first week of December 1837. As the dust settled over the Kapain campaign, Potgieter issued a proclamation annexing all Mzilikazi's former territory by right of conquest. It comprised an area embracing the east of modern Botswana, three-quarters of the region between the Vaal and the Limpopo, and half of the territory between the Orange and the Vaal. Then, ever true to his word, he gave the Ba'Rolong chief a major share of the cattle taken.

To this day, there is dispute about the number of cattle taken, but the most recent studies reveal that Potgieter never regained the total losses in livestock his people suffered at Vegkop. Mzilikazi was bowed, but not totally broken, and led his people far northward over the Limpopo River into the present-day Zimbabwe. There they still live today in the area known as Matabeleland, which comprises the drier southwestern part of the country. They still speak Zulu as they always have. They made peace with Hendrik Potgieter after all this and the Afrikaners never had trouble from the Matabele again. However, the proud Matabele would later suffer terribly at the hands of first the British and then the new 20th century monster of Southern Africa, Robert Mugabe. He would orchestrate the murder of 40,000 Matabele after assuming power in 1980.

News was beginning to filter back out of Natal that Retief had achieved a major breakthrough in his talks with Dingane of the Zulu. Maritz and Uys therefore decided to move to Natal to join Retief. Hendrik Potgieter tried again to convince these people of the fallacy of their Natal plan, but when they would not listen, he bade them farewell. History would prove Potgieter's minority view correct.

 ## Nexus Familia 49: Through the eyes of a child

The Jouberts from Buffelskloof (*NF43*) have decided to emigrate in their own separate trek as an extended family. The main cluster is formed by two of ancestor Pieter Schalk Joubert's cousins, Jan Christoffel and Jacobus Joubert, and two of the sons of the latter, namely Adriaan and Abraham and all their family[27]. Ancestor Pieter Schalk will trek later. Jan Christoffel Joubert's three married daughters are not with the family, likely being part of their respective husbands' treks. The total complement with Jan Christoffel's wagon train is the three senior sons; Jan Hendrik (18), Josua (16) and Dirk (14) on horseback, with Jacobus (11), and Hendrik (9) as *touleiers* leading the oxen. Then, of course there is the unmarried Jacoba (23) and Jan Christoffel's baby, Jan Christoffel junior (1), who commands all the attention.

Grandfather Jacobus Joubert travels with grandmother Rachel, daughter of the famous Commandant Adriaan van Jaarsveld who died in British captivity, and two of his three sons, Adriaan and Abraham. Adriaan and Susanna with their five children, Jacobus (16), Gert (11), Josua (9), Susanna (6), and bubbly little Rachel (4) are on a second wagon. Abraham, with pregnant wife Anna Roets and little Jacobus (1) have their own wagon. Grandfather Jacobus' third son Josua and his wife, our ancestral cousin Elizabeth Naudé, are traveling elsewhere in the wagon train with their sons Jacobus (14) and David (11).

Also in this trek is Anna Roets' family, led by her father Johannes Roets, and a lot of his extended family. Her 8-year old little brother, Nicolaas Johannes will one day narrate this trek to author Deneys Reitz[28] in 1911. He will then be an elderly gentleman in his eighties and we shall call on him repeatedly from this point on as our wonderfully candid and unpretentious "reporter on the spot"[29]:

> *"I was born in the Cradock District of the Cape Colony on the farm Matjesfontein - my father had two farms, Matjesfontein and Bulhoek – he was born in the year 1797 – and my mother was the daughter of Flip [Philip] Schutte.*
>
> *Around 1834 a commission had trekked other side the Great River[30] and, upon their return, had given such a positive report that a general trek-spirit arose. The people were all so unhappy with the British government that I want to recall there being continuous little groups of wagons trekking past northward and everywhere the people sold their farms or just let their farms lie and trekked away.*
>
> *Then my father decided to also follow this stream in 1835[31]. I was then just 8 years old, but I remember well how we left the old farm and finally got to the Great River, where there was already a large number of wagons and the people were busy taking them one by one across the water. Abraham Joubert, who was married to my eldest sister, was also with us with his entire family, and also lots of other family of my father. There was so much livestock that the people trekked a bit further so that their animals would not get too mixed; so that at night one could see everywhere on the plains the little laagers where the different families were camped together.*
>
> *From the river onwards there was a remarkable amount of game, especially quagga [zebra] and eland, but it is such a long time ago that I cannot remember exactly how we trekked from there, but we did eventually get to Marokko's city[32] – there were many people who had come but the laagers were not big –*

each family trekked separately to keep its livestock separate. At Marokka's city we stood a long time and meetings were held of "foremen" and then Kommandant Retief trekked away across the mountains to Natal and commandant Potgieter also trekked away, I think to the Transvaal, and now all the laagers went forth, some to the Vaal River, but most in the direction of Natal[33]. "The largest part of the laagers were already gone when my father's trek left Marokko's city and we only caught up with the leading wagons when we got to the New Year's River[34], where they were waiting for Retief's return from Natal.

Retief had gone with a few horsemen over the mountains to Dingane to negotiate land for the people and shortly after we got to New Year's River he came back – that was actually on New Year's Day[35] and that is why the river was so named – Retief reported that a certain Makatees Captain[36] had stolen a large herd of cattle from Dingane and that Dingane wanted him to first go take the cattle off the Makatees Kaffers [sic] and bring them back to his city before he would part with land."

—*End Nexus Familia*

Fig. 10-9 *Rain on the Prairie near the New Year's River*

Nexus Familia 50: On the Double Trek

Ancestor Chris Jordaan (*NF43*) does not leave with his older brother Pieter on Retief's trek. Instead, he delays about seven months longer until around October 1837 and then joins the Potgieter-Du Plessis trek assembled by his older step-brother Koos Potgieter and his brother-in-law Jan du Plessis. Chris and his wife Maria load their wagon and leave the Tarka with four young children, Maria (6), Pieter (5), Anna (3), and baby Jan (1). Koos Potgieter also has the nickname Grootvoet (Greatfoot).

It is tradition among Afrikaners and the black people of South Africa to apply nicknames based on personal attributes without being malicious. One therefore can only assume that Koos has rather large feet, or small ones, as the Afrikaner humor tends to be ironic in nature. Maria's brothers, various friends, neighbors and extended family join them. By the time they reach Natal, the trek will consist of some 80 wagons and 100 men of fighting age. They will arrive with the most acute of timing at one of the most critical junctures in South African history, and help tip the scale. Jan du Plessis and Koos "Greatfoot" Potgieter will duly bring their side at many of the key events that are to follow. The tough men from the Tarka are clearly key in the Afrikaner history of this period.

—*End Nexus Familia*

Son of the Warrior Queen

The Ba'Tlokwa or "Wildcat People" originally lived on the Highveld Prairie directly above the Zulu near where the town of Vrede (Peace) is today. Their country therefore lay directly between the Matabele of Mzilikatse and the Zulu of Dingane. These two Zulu based nations so overran the Sotho-speaking Ba'Tlokwa in the 1820s during the Difaqane (Crushing) that the latter had to flee southwestward around the great bend in the Drakensberg. They then settled next to a flat-topped mountain named Imperani, where they were ruled by the Warrior Queen Ma'Ntatisi. From her name the other common name for the tribe was derived; Mantatee. The mere mention of this word would strike fear into all who heard it.

The Mantatee went on the rampage from the northeast of the Prairie, killing and burning as they went, terrorizing people as far west as Robert Moffat's mission station at New Lattakoo (today's Kuruman) on the edge of the desert. There they were at last defeated by the mixed-blood Griqua of Nicolaas Waterboer, and their power was broken. Eventually, Ma'Ntatisi settled down and her son, Sekonyela took over from her as ruler. He made his headquarters at Marabeng[37]. The aging Warrior Queen herself remained at the adjoining mountain, Joala Boholo[38]. In 1834, the Methodist missionary Rev. James Allison and his wife settled with the tribe to bring them the Christian message. Today, these people are known as the Ba'Tlokwa and few remember that they were once the most fearsome of all the Sotho people, the vicious Mantatee of the dreaded Warrior Queen.

By 1837, having been exposed to Western influence via Rev. Allison, the Ba'Tlokwa would don Western clothes and use guns and horses like the Ba'Sotho of the Drakensberg highland. It was these people, looking to the Zulu like white men with guns on horses, who had stolen the Zulu king's cattle. They had also shouted to the Zulu that they were "Boere" (amaBhulu), clearly trying to shift the blame and even intentionally herding the stolen cattle past the Trekker encampments to implicate them. It was to Allison's mission station at Imperani near the present Ficksburg, that Piet Retief was headed to retrieve the stolen Zulu cattle.

On 26 December 1837, a 50 man horse Commando, together with an interpreter, two of Dingane's Zulu captains, and eight other Zulu officers to identify cattle, set off to the Place of the Puff Adder, home of Sekonyela, the king of the Wildcat People; the Mantatee. Retief handed a smart leather satchel to one of the Zulu captains with letters for his king, Dingane. Retief kept Dingane well informed. To mark the occasion for the benefit of the king's men, Retief asked Gert Rudolph to fire off two rounds from Grietjie (Little Gretchen), the little home made cannon of the Trekkers over which Gert guarded like a hawk. Gert called it "The Little Set"[39]. This was a visible shock for the Zulus. Two days later, Retief followed the Commando with Thomas Halstead, the British interpreter from Port Natal, and a gun bearer named De Koker.

At first, Retief reasoned with Sekonyela about the wisdom of returning the cattle. When Sekonyela persisted in denying the theft, Daniel Bezuidenhout[40] put Sekonyela in handcuffs and told him: *"That is the way by which we secure rogues in our country."* Retief then told Sekonyela: *"In my name[41] you have done wrong. Send for the cattle which you have taken from the Zulus"*

A variety of authors have suggested that Retief fined Sekonyela and that the fine was supposed to be for the benefit of Dingane. We consult the very Daniel Bezuidenhout who put Sekonyela in handcuffs:

> *"On the first day, Sikonyela brought 150 head of cattle, and already there were some of the Zulus' cattle among them, which was a proof that Sekonyela was guilty. On the second day, Retief sent to have Sikonyela's herds collected. Sikonyela remained as a prisoner. On the evening of the second day, we brought together a great number of cattle, and amongst them the Zulus (Dingaan's men) recovered nearly all their stolen cattle."*

This statement is important in that it shows that the Zulu representatives were clearly still there. Some of those preoccupied with denigrating the Afrikaner keep repeating the untruth that the Zulu representatives disappeared when Sekonyela was put in handcuffs and reported the action to Dingane, to demonstrate to him how Afrikaners treat chiefs. This would then imply that they would do the same to him. Hereby these parties then seek to excuse Dingane's later actions. The fact is that they are wrong, as ably shown by Bezuidenhout's report. Bezuidenhout continues, proving that the Zulus remained to take their cattle:

> *"On the third morning, Retief said to the Zulus, 'Drive out those of the cattle that belong to you, and, if any are missing of the number, choose from those of Sikonyela as many as will make up the tally'. The Zulus did this. Retief further took from Sikonyela 53 horses and 33 guns, as fine for having made evil use of those horses and guns, and having, in our name, made a predatory inroad with them against his neighbours."*

The fine of the horses and guns was clearly for sullying the name of the Trekkers and for no other reason contrived later by those who desperately wish to revise history in order to sketch the Afrikaner in a bad light. The Rev. Allison protested vehemently at the treatment of his host, but Retief was not having any of that, given the challenges he was facing. Retief advised Dingane in a letter a little later that, to punish Sekonyela, he had forced him to deliver 700 head of cattle and also horses and guns, because without the guns he could not have accomplished the theft. This was a tragic mistake, because now Dingane would want the horses and guns, and there was no pragmatic way in which Retief could appease Dingane by giving guns and horses to the dreaded Zulu without endangering his own Trekkers. In addition, it would appear that when Dingane had said, *"bring me Sekonyela's head,"* he had meant it quite literally, as we shall soon see.

 ## Nexus Familia 51: Span in your oxen!

We return to our young "on the spot reporter," Nicolaas Johannes Roets, to tell us about Retief's return after retrieving Dingane's stolen cattle from Sekonyela[42]:

"He then trekked with sixty men over Retiefsnek [Retief's Ridge] and after three weeks he came back with the cattle that he had taken from the Makatees[43]. "He then held a gathering and even though I was still so young, I can clearly remember that he sat on his horse with a white blaze and with his hat pulled over his eyes, addressing us – it was on a white sandstone bank and he spoke from the saddle. He said:"

"Burghers, the trouble that there was, has been removed by God; span in [yoke your oxen] and come with me over these mountains and I hope to soon have an own country and an own nation."

"There was great happiness among the people and rounds were fired and hats were waved and then Retief rode away to go and hold gatherings at two other places and thereafter he came back to our laager to fetch the cattle and then trekked away to go and deliver the cattle with seventy men, and also a lot of Hottentot outriders, but Kafirs I did not see with him."

—End Nexus Familia.

 ## Nexus Familia 52: The Eve of Nightmare

The next three months in South African history will prove pivotal and will become one of the formative periods for the country. It is a period soaked in the blood of epic battles and massacres. It is a time of setbacks that will come close to breaking this people. It will be a time that will test people to the utmost of their faith and their character and their stamina. It will change them forever. After this point, no Western nation could ever again be so presumptuous as to claim to understand us. We therefore pause at this point where:

1. Louis Trichardt and his wife, our ancestral sister, start to descend the Northern Drakensberg into tropical country to reach the Portuguese at Delagoa Bay in the hope of finding an alternative port to Port Natal;

2. Retief is about to proceed in good faith to Zulu King Dingane with the cattle he has retrieved as per agreement, hoping to obtain the land as agreed and as per his manifesto in the *Grahamstown Journal*;

3. Many Voortrekkers start rolling their wagons down the Central Drakensberg into their "Canaan," Natal;

4. Our own direct ancestors, Chris Jordaan and his wife Maria Klopper, are approaching the Drakensberg escarpment to descend into Natal.

They will arrive on the eve of a nightmare that is not for the eyes or ears of the impressionable.

—End Nexus Familia

-----ooOoo-----

11

Descent into Nightmare

"Dingarn's conduct was worthy of a savage as he is. It was base and treacherous, to say the least of it - the offspring of cowardice and fear."

Rev. Francis Owen, missionary to Zulu king Dingane,
The Diary of Rev. Fracis Owen – the entry for 6 February 1838

The Monster of Umgungundlovu

The man who had united the Zulu as a nation, and who had honed their fighting skills into the most effective and dangerous army on the continent, was Shaka. He was monstrously cruel. We can get some idea of this monster, who is still revered by the Zulu today, from the journal of one of the earliest English Settlers on the coast of Natal, a Mr. Isaacs, as reported[1] by John William Colenso, the first Anglican Archbishop of Natal:

"Mr. Isaacs was himself present, when 170 boys and girls were ordered by the monster to be butchered for some imaginary offence. Nothing could equal the consternation and horror of these poor miserable and devoted wretches, who, surrounded and without hope of escape, knew that they were collected to sate some revengeful feeling of their tyrant, but knew not for what. Chaka began by taking out some fine lads, and ordering their own brothers to twist their necks. Their bodies were afterwards dragged away, and beaten with sticks till life was extinct."

Fig. 11-1 Zulu king Dingane

As is still the general practice in Africa today, leaders largely get changed only in coups or by dying one way or the other, usually prematurely. And so it was that Shaka had been killed by his half-brother, Dingane in 1828. Dingane kept a special hut empty in which Shaka's ghost was supposedly resident. He himself became paranoid about opposition or possible enemies, some of whom might conceivably be inspired by the ghost of Shaka. He also had a chief named Matiwane killed by driving pegs into his brain through his nostrils on a hill at his capital, Umgungundlovu. Matiwane was said to still dwell there and so Dingane joked that Matiwane could rule there while he ruled in the city. The hill became known as Kwa Matiwane (The Place of Matiwane).

Here Dingane regularly executed people to keep the Zulu nation suitably intimidated and subservient to his wishes. The bodies of the victims would be left there to putrefy and there were constant hordes of vultures circling the place. Dingane called them his "children." These feathered beasts would be so gorged on human flesh that they could hardly get off the ground after a typical execution feast and would just hop along the ground flapping their wings. The vultures were so used to the routine killings that they were said to attend the trials of people, anxiously waiting for their meal.

On October 10, 1837, the Rev. Francis Owen, an Anglican member of the Church Missionary Society, having been accepted as missionary by Dingane at the insistence of his friend, Captain Gardiner, arrived to settle at Umgungundlovu. With him were his wife, his sister, and a Welsh servant girl named Jane Williams. He unwittingly set up house within view of Kwa Matiwane, presumably without fully comprehending the purpose of the hill. He knew not what he had let himself in for. It is to Owen that Dingane would turn to act as interpreter and secretary, and it would put this utterly misplaced and timid Cambridge Masters degree mathematician in the midst of indescribable horror.

From his diary[2] we get an idea of how the truth dawned on this hapless man who had been enticed into hell by Gardiner. He laments the continuous executions on Hlomo Amabutho (the hill of execution) and the outcrop on top of it, the dreaded KwaMatiwane. (Page numbers from his diary):

- *"Two persons were put to death yesterday,"* (p. 71)
- *"The day before yesterday one of the king's women was put to death."* (p. 71)
- *"Just as we were commencing our English service another execution took place on the hill opposite our hut."* (p. 82)
- A woman was executed for being *"somewhat saucy to an indoona"* (induna: headman or captain); (p. 91)
- Then he laments the execution of an induna and that now *"...the ravens were devouring his carcase!,"* (p. 93)
- The same week: *"Two women were executed today for the alleged crime of witchcraft."* (p. 103)
- His interpreter, R.B. Hully, describes the killing of 60 young girls (p. 180)

And so the killings on Kwa Matiwane continued through just the last two months of 1837 and the anguished Owen records it all.

A Coil of Serpents in Paradise

One resident of Port Natal was much taken aback by Retief's visit to Dingane. He was Captain Allen Francis Gardiner, the fifth son of a Berkshire squire and ex-Royal Navy man. The only naval action in which he was ever engaged was on 28 March 1814, during the War of 1812, against the scourge of the Royal Navy in the South Pacific, the USS Essex under American hero David Porter. On that day, with its topmast downed by a squall, Porter had had no choice but to surrender to the HMS Phoebe off Valparaiso, Chile. Gardiner's ship, HMS Phoebe continued firing for 10 minutes at the Essex, raking her and killing four more Americans after Porter had struck his colors. Porter was captured, but escaped back to the United States to a hero's welcome, having destroyed millions of dollars worth of British whaling activity.

Gardiner eventually went back home and drifted into *"carelessness and godlessness"*[3]. Then, one day, suddenly, he made his services available to the newly formed Church Missionary Society[4] in England, which wanted to work in South Africa. After an expedition through Xhosa territory in 1834, he finally settled near Port Natal, writing a book on his experiences and detailing such matters as the cannibalism[5] of some of the seSotho-speaking tribes located inland to the northwest of the Zulu. He made the acquaintance of the Zulu King, Dingane, whose favor he won by turning over to him a number of Zulu refugees who had sought, and had actually received, his protection. Dingane promptly proceeded to starve them for his own amusement, and then killed them the moment Gardiner's back was turned. This misguided man therefore actually conspired in the killing of his own converts, whether intentionally or not, again demonstrating how, in Africa, the road to Hell is paved with the good intentions of white men from the Northern Hemisphere.

After this, Gardiner went to see the Cape Governor, Benjamin D'Urban. He was unhappy with the result of the discussion and went straight to London over the head of the Governor and testified before the Select Committee for the Treatment of Aborigines; a body wholly under the influence of the London Missionary Society — the body whose ill-considered decisions had led to the Great Trek to start with. To this collection of "concerned members of Parliament" he painted a terrible picture of the British at Port Natal.

The Cape of Good Hope Punishment Act was then passed in London pointedly and specifically for use by the Cape British Government to try and control the Afrikaners on the Great Trek, but was extended to cover the English people at Port Natal. Here was "Pharaoh extending his suspect hand over the Israelites beyond the Red Sea." Gardiner himself was "appointed as magistrate" over the English Settlers to administer this inapplicable Act to people who were not even in British territory and who utterly resented him.

He came back to Natal with the Reverend Francis Owen, whom he "posted" to Dingane. After this, he moved into a house he built outside Port Natal and foisted himself as supposed magistrate on the English people at the trading post. The modern mind simply boggles at the kind of character that could reconcile being both missionary and magistrate in a post-Reformation Protestant community; the ultimate integration of Church and State. Gardiner therefore tried to emulate in Port Natal the combined excesses of the British Colonial Authority and the Missionary Societies, precisely the two forces that had driven the Afrikaners from the Cape. The result of this, predictably, was that there was no love lost between him and the earlier English inhabitants who had been there since 1824 and who intensely resented his presumption.

The English Settlers at Port Natal responded with the following protest to the Cape[6]. These men trusted Allen Francis Gardiner not one inch and based their position on the following points:

---

1. That this country of Natal is not an acknowledged part of the British dominions, but a free settlement.

2. That this said country of Natal was granted to the resident inhabitants by Chaka, the late King, and confirmed to them by Dingaan, the present King of the Zulus, and styled by them "The white man's country."

3. That the power invested in Captain Gardiner is contrary to the principles of equity, inasmuch as it extends to British subjects only, not empowering the said Captain Gardiner to punish any act of aggression committed by the native population, or by other Europeans, upon the British residents of Natal.

4. That the said Captain Gardiner is not empowered to decide upon civil cases, which would much more have benefited this settlement...[...]

5. That the appointment of Captain Gardiner to take cognizance of criminal cases only might open the door to acts of tyranny and oppression...[he could imprison them while having to wait for decisions from the Cape]

6. That no mode of redress is pointed out, in the event of acts of oppression being committed by said Captain Gardiner, or his order, upon the inhabitants of this free country, and ruin might be the result to the person so oppressed.

7. That the said Captain Gardiner, before his leaving this country for the avowed object of soliciting the British government to take possession of and annex Natal, has materially injured the interests of the inhabitants by advising the King of the Zulus to stop the trade with his people, which fact has been communicated to them by Dingaan.

The protest further explained that the inhabitants wished for her Majesty's Government to appoint a magistrate to protect and encourage them, and not to hold out threats or to imprison them. These men clearly had the measure of Captain Gardiner.

Just before Gardiner's return to Port Natal, the relationship between the settlers and Dingane soured markedly. Dingane forbade them entry to Zululand and the Settlers started building defenses. Then, suddenly, Dingane became conciliatory, and sent the Settlers a message to tell them Gardiner had been the instigator of the policy of precluding them from entering Zululand (See point 7 of their protest).

When Gardiner returned, it was to this situation. Retief was no doubt apprised of the machinations of Gardiner by ordinary English residents at Port Natal, such as Alexander Biggar and Thomas Halstead. After all, these people had known Retief much longer than they had known the presumptuous Gardiner. In fact, before Retief arrived, Biggar had written that they had every intention of *"forming a government"* when Retief arrived in their settlement; this against the background of the Cape Government having rejected their own earlier overtures towards annexation.

To get a glimpse of what was happening at Dingane's kraal around the time of Retief's first visit, we turn to Reverend Francis Owen[7], a mere sixteen days after he had himself arrived at Dingane's kraal:

October 26th, 1837. — *"I read a letter to Dingaen, which he had received from the Dutch Boors, who have lately left the colony, expressing their desire for peace, and a good understanding with the Zoolu nation; to effect which, it was their wish to have, by means of their chief head, a personal interview with Dingaen, who would at the same time also arrange with Dingaen the place of their future residence, which is to be in some part of the uninhabited country adjoining the Zulu territories. The letter was dated from Port Natal, and signed by the chief of the Boors [Piet Retief]. Their party were dispersed in various parts of the country. The letter also stated the cause of their rupture with Umsilikazi, Dingaen's great foe, who, by means of the Boors and Zulus, is now said to be utterly vanquished.* [...]

November 3rd, 1837. — *Dingaen sent for me to write a letter to Captain Gardiner, to request him to come and advise with the King respecting the territory to be assigned to the Boors.* [...] [some four days before Dingane starts negotiating with Retief on his first visit]

November 4th. — *Intense cold prevented the children from assembling. The King sent for me to read another letter, which he had received from the Dutch. It was written in Dutch, a language I do not understand. But I observed that the Dutch would be here the day after tomorrow.* [...]

November 5th 1837, Lord's Day — *Dingaen sent early to say that, as it was so cold, they would not be able to attend divine service. In the afternoon the Dutch arrived. Dingaen sent for me to come and see them. I went. The Dutch expressed their disappointment that they did not arrive in time for service. The deputation consisted of four persons[8].* [...]

November 6th, 1837. — *Dingane afforded amusement to the Dutch by collecting a large body of men to dance. The Governor, Mr. Retief, dined with us. Dingane told him that pleasure must take precedence of business. The indunas, he said, had been asking the King to go once more against Umsilikazi, to bring his head. We were much pleased with the frank and open manner of our guest.*

November 7th. — *Dingane sent for me to witness the festivities in honour of the Dutch."* [Owen gives a long description of war dances]

On the 7th of November 1838, Dingane asked Owen to read for him the response letter from Gardiner, which complains that the particular land had already been granted *"to Britain."* Retief, in his turn, obtained a letter from Dingane, written in English by Owen, which he (Retief) could give to the nearest missionary to read to Sekonyela. Retief's belief was that Sekonyela would respond to Dingane's demands in the letter if his Boer Commando backed it up. This was in the best tradition of "speaking softly while carrying a big stick." This would get Dingane his cattle and the Afrikaners the new land they so desperately sought.

It would seem, however, that Gardiner also told Dingane (likely in his letter of 7 November) that the Trekkers were "deserters" from the territory of the English king. Gardiner knew well from past personal experience that Dingane killed all deserters. He also knew fully well the circumstances of the departure of the Trekkers from the Cape but chose to misrepresent it in this specific fashion. Owen, who has since been much suspected by Afrikaners of having had a hand in what followed, clearly trusted Retief enough to ask him to forward his journal to the Cape, while Retief clearly trusted Owen in the dealings with Dingane. Owen therefore appears as a helpless and anguished pawn in the events that were starting to unfold.

It is difficult to determine which of Dingane and Gardiner was more machinating. The weight of the evidence points to Gardiner as the informed and educated "Serpent in Paradise" and Dingane purely as just a pathologically murderous tyrannical king with a passion for extreme horror and torture. However, Owen would later describe Dingane as "perfidious." Of course Owen could not criticize Gardiner. Gardiner was, after all, his employer. Joseph Kirkman, the interpreter for the American missionary Champion, reported[9] that, some time after Retief left his kraal, Dingane instructed a certain chief Isigwebana to entertain Retief's party on the way back to the Trekker encampment and then kill them. Isigwebana refused to do that and, as reprisal, Dingane sent a large force to kill 600 of Isigwebana's people, women and children included.

There is no doubt that Gardiner knew what was going on, because he was in constant communication with Dingane who saw Gardiner as "his agent." Gardiner sent people to warn various parties, including the missionaries, as we see from Owen's diary:

> *November 27th. — Dingane sent for me to read a letter he had received from Captain Gardiner.*

> *December 7th. — Dingane sent, early for me to read some letters from Retief. In allusion to the ruin of the chief Umsilikazi,[10] Retief observed that his punishment was brought upon him by the righteous judgment of God.*

> *December 14th. — Dingane sent for me to write to Captain Gardiner. Messengers arrived from Gardiner to inform us of some secret machinations of Dingane in which the safety of ourselves and all the white people was concerned.*

Significantly, while Gardiner warned the British parties and the American missionaries, he specifically did not warn the intended victims of the planned massacre, the Afrikaners. More particularly, he did not warn Retief, the direct object of the subterfuge.

Nexus Familia 53: Trichardt – Land of the Silver Mist

Far to the north of all the happenings in Natal, Louis Trichardt and his little band of people are making their way through some of the most rugged mountains that can be found in Africa. On the wagon with him is his wife, Martha Bouwer, our ancestral sister. The ascent has been tough. The 3000 foot descent they now face with their ox-wagons is an even greater challenge. It is a terrible struggle, and it takes three weeks, but eventually they find their way down two days before Christmas 1837. This is due largely to Martha and the other womenfolk doing their own bit of reconnaissance and finding an easier route. They are now at the foot of the Northern Drakensberg, west of where the Kruger National Park will one day be. They are in a countryside totally different from any they have seen before. This is the Lowveld of South Africa – tropical Bushveld. They do not know it, but they have passed just south of the home of the Modjadji, the Rain Queen.

Many years in the future a man named H Rider Haggard will write a book under the title *She* about the queen of this unique small matrilineal tribe of Sotho people living on the wet slopes of the mountain. From here the Trichardt Trekkers set out across the veldt of what will later become the Kruger National Park. Many years later people will still refer to it as a "desert." In its northern regions, though in the tropics where the stifling humid heat saps the soul, it has hardly more rainfall than the Cape Karoo.

As they move towards the southeast,

Fig. 11-2 Standing water on Trichardt's route

they encounter more swampy areas. In these, they notice a kind of acacia tree that grows rather large with a comparatively straight green trunk that has a coating of what looks like yellow powder. It almost always stands in swampy ground, slightly tilted in the wet soil. This tree will ultimately become known as the fever tree, because travelers will associate its presence with malaria. They will think the trees are the source of the disease. They will be right to make the association, but the logic will be wrong.

In fact, the *anopheles* mosquito and the particular tree species prefer the swampy country for the same reason; standing water!...and there are lots of fever trees where the Trichardt trek is now traveling. The further south they move along the way, the wetter it becomes. They are starting to see pans of standing water. If only they could somehow be told that the dry season is relatively safe, and the rainy season deadly, they may be able to make it to Delagoa Bay in good health. However, they have chosen high summer, the wettest time of the year. We watch helplessly as their oxen plod slowly southeastward to the bay, realizing the party is constantly being bitten by mosquitoes. Some are just irritating; others are *anopheles*.

In the evenings, Martha listens to the ritual cycle of the sounds of the African Bushveld. It starts with the sounds of the black-backed jackal even before the sun sets. When it is suitably dark, one starts hearing the whoops of the spotted hyena, which sometimes collapse into insane giggles and cackles when they have found food to argue over. Later yet, one hears the deep grunts of the lion miles away through the dead still air, the notes starting high and descending to a deep rumble in the still air.

The animals are intelligent; they move around in the early morning and late afternoon. At the height of the day, they stay under the tree canopies. Almost all the days are over 100°F and many over 110°F. Some nights, though, low clouds and fog roll in from the east over this endless flat country. H Rider Haggard will later call it *"The Land of the Silver Mist."* But the cloud and fog burn away by 10 o'clock in the morning. Real respite is only brought by the rare towering thunderclouds of the late afternoon. These, however, seem to prefer to rain out against the mountains far to the west. This countryside is pure unremitting tropical hell.

And still the oxen plod on. Clearly this is no place to be. In fact, there are no natives either. They know better. Most of the cattle have died. The future of the Afrikaner assuredly lies behind them on the Highveld Prairie. But they cannot go back... must... go... forward... forward.... east... to the sea!

—*End Nexus Familia*

I say to you; not one of you shall return!

At the encampment below the Drakensberg in Natal, Retief sent the cattle retrieved from Sekonyela on to Dingane, as per agreement. His next step would be to go to Dingane to finalize the agreed land grant. He had no idea of the machinations of Captain Gardiner, nor had he been warned by Gardiner of any of Dingane's plans. Retief called for volunteers to go with him and he was inundated with candidates. After all, this was to be the crowning moment of their "Escape from Pharaoh." This was to be the moment that they would get their place in "Canaan." For a people so steeped in the Old Testament, it is remarkable that no one recalled that the Israelites actually had had to fight for their place in Canaan under a new leader and that Moses never dwelt in the Promised Land.

Eventually, sixty-five men volunteered while four young boys of about eleven years of age created enough of a rumpus to also go along for the big event. One of them was Retief's own 11-year old son, Pieter, the apple of his eye. Thomas Halstead (*NF41*), the English settler from Port Natal, again offered his interpreting services. This made a grand total of 67 grown men and 4 young boys. With them went 30 of their Khoekhoe outriders, horse grooms and gun carriers who had loyally trekked with them all the way from the Colony over these many months as an inherent part of the Great Afrikaner Exodus from the Colony. The general air was one of great expectation. They had brought their side of the deal. Dingane now had his cattle. This was now obviously down to the final handshake.

Gerrit Maritz, however, was deeply worried. He offered to go instead with just a few men, because he sensed his own end was near and he was concerned about the large number of males of fighting age being drawn from the encampment. He also worried about the effect that such a large cavalcade of horsemen would have on the fears of a primitive and savage king with a 20,000 man army. What made matters worse in the camp was old mister Malan, who was telling all who would listen that he had had a premonition of a terrible massacre. The younger men just smiled at his rantings. Maritz was hugely upset. He felt that Retief was not only exposing himself to too much personal risk, but that he was also endangering his people.

Eventually, the morning of 25 January 1838 broke. The men of the commission to Dingane gathered in

Retief's field tent for an early morning prayer session[11]. Erasmus Smit led the session and committed the expedition to the care and leadership of God. After singing the 4th and 6th verses of the Morning Hymn, the Rev. Smit blessed the commission. They all filed out of the tent and it was an enormous hustle and bustle.

Retief told his second-in-command, Piet Greyling, who would be staying behind to look after the trek, that he must ensure that the people stay together at their present site of Doornkop and to not spread out.

The experienced Maritz just looked at all of this with a heavy heart. Then he spoke the fateful words[12]:

"I say to you; not one of you shall return!"

The commission of 100 souls set off to Umgungundlovu with Maritz's words ringing in their ears. Evert Potgieter, who had done the original Commission Trek to Natal along with Piet Uys, also watched them leave. He was hugely upset. He had an excruciatingly painful toothache and had been ordered to stay. His frustration knew no end. He had invested four years in the effort, only to miss the crowning moment.

Nexus Familia 54: Departure for Umgungundlovu

The men who volunteer to go with Retief on his second visit to Dingane inlcude:

1. Pieter Georg Jordaan, brother to our ancestor Chris, who is at this time trying to make his way down the Drakensberg as part of the Jan du Plessis - Koos "Greatfoot" Potgieter trek from the Tarka;

2. Reynier Grobler, cousin of our ancestor Izak Hermanus back in the Camdeboo, and brother to Michael, who elects to stay at the laager to protect his family; and

3. Willem Basson, second cousin to our ancestor Matthys Michiel in the Cape wheat fields. Willem's brother Matthys Michiel Basson, who trekked with him, prefers to stay at the encampment with his family. The lady Salomé has talked him out of going. She duly records all in her diary.

4. The last two are Balthasar Klopper; and

5. his brother, Pieter Klopper, first cousins of ancestor Maria Catharina Klopper, the wife of Chris Jordaan. In fact, there are two more distantly related Kloppers on this commission, second cousin Lucas Klopper and his father Coenraad.

When the commission members exit the tent where Erasmus Smit has been conducting their prayer session on the morning of 25 January 1838, their families are there to say goodbye.[13] Pieter Georg Jordaan hugs and kisses his wife Isabella goodbye. She has the six kids with her. The three-year old Pieter Georg Junior is as busy as always and gets a hug from his father, and so does the six-year old Isabella. Pieter pulls the 7-year old Pieter Johannes against his leg and ruffles his hair. The two older daughters, Anna and Aletta are hugged together.

Willem Basson plants a big fat kiss on little Maria's cheek and then shakes the hands[14] of his three sons Willem, Nicolaas and Matthys. He gives his wife a huge big hug. Then he turns back to Matthys (18) and tells him: *"You're the man of the family now! Look after your mother."* Before Matthys can open his mouth, Pieter says: *"...and, NO! You cannot come with! We've been over that!"*

Matters proceed a little differently in the Grobler family. Maria really does not want Reynier to go. She has little Maria on her hip and another baby is on the way. She thinks it is a really bad time for Reynier to go on this adventure. As it is, she has a terrible feeling about all this. Old man Malan's premonitions have upset her mightily. She wishes the old man had just kept quiet. She was worried enough already. Reynier tells her that, whatever happens, she must stay at Doornkop with Retief's people and she must not move elsewhere under any circumstances. Reynier then walks over and shakes the hand of his older brother, Michael, who puts his hand on Reynier's shoulder and says: *"Mooi loop"*[15].

* * * *

And at Umgungundlovu the vultures circle over Hlomo Amabutho and Kwa Matiwane. They flap their heavy wings slowly as they scan the hill and glide on the updraughts of hot summer air. The savage Dingane waits, deep in thought, as the Reverend Owen flounders in his vain attempts at spreading the Word. Instead, he has been reduced to a scribe and witness to daily executions and tortures.

His talents in these two areas will soon earn him a unique place in South African history.

—End Nexus Familia

Nexus Familia 55: descent into the Promised Land

The Drakensberg is an imposing mountain range by any standards. Just to the south of where the Trekkers are crossing, this sedimentary range reaches heavenward 11,000 feet, forming a plateau on top. One of the highest waterfalls in the world, the Tugela Falls, drops over those cliffs, apparently out of the sky near 11,000 foot.

The Trekkers, however, are making their way down a few miles north of the high cliffs. Here the mountains are several thousand feet lower and a bit more forgiving. But they still have to maneuver ox wagons down that slope. So some Trekkers resort to engaging the brakes on the rear or removing the rear wheels entirely and attaching branches as friction skids.

Since leaving the Colony, Anna Roets has delivered their second child, and she and husband Abraham Joubert have named him Johannes Nicolaas Rudolph.

Fig. 11-3 The 11,000 foot Drakensberg mountain range

They now have two sons; Jacobus the toddler and newborn Johannes. We turn again to Anna's brother Nicolaas Johannes Roets[16] to tell us about the descent into Natal of the extended Joubert and Roets families:

> "*After he* [Retief] *left* [on the second visit to Dingane], *all the laagers started trekking toward Natal. We went over the mountain at Van Reenen's Pass, there was no path and it was very steep and difficult to get the wagons over. When we got to the top, my father and Abraham Joubert carved their names in a rock along the path of our descent.*
>
> *When we got to the bottom, many people were far ahead of us and some had already crossed the Tugela river and (already) stood at Moordspruit [Murder Stream] and others at Blaauwkranz [Blue Cliff], near the confluence of the Moordspruit and Blaauwkranz [Rivers]. The people were spread everywhere in little groups – here would be a little laager of a couple of wagons and a little further another, and so it was all along the Moordspruit. We trekked after them and when we got near Blaauwkranz my father drew his wagons together next to a stream a short distance before Blaauwkranz where there were some nice pools of water. But Abraham Joubert (NF43), who was married to my eldest[17] sister [Anna Roets], trekked a distance further to where the path went through Blaauwkranz (river), there where the people in the advance guard had made the drift[18]; his brothers[19], two brothers in law[20] and Flip Venter were also with him. They stood no more than 20 minutes from us, and because the countryside around here was so beautiful, the people decided to stay here and wait for Retief and to measure up farms.*"

The Van Dyk and the Bester families also travel along with the Jouberts[21] when the Jouberts get near Blaauwkranz. These include[22] the widow of Joseph van Dyk, and the wife of his brother Andries van Dyk and her 11 children. Andries is one of the volunteers who has gone with Retief to Umgungundlovu. The two Grobler brothers are married to two of the daughters of the third Van Dyk brother, Sybrand, and so Michael

Grobler with his wife and four children join forces with the Joubert trek. It seems that Reynier Grobler's wife and son indeed stay in the Retief laager at Doornkop, as Reynier has instructed her.

This is a good point at which to introduce another eye-witness. She is Anna Steenkamp (nee Retief), the daughter of Piet Retief's older brother, Francois. Francois left the Colony on the Great Trek in November 1836, but Anna's husband was ill at that time, and so they only left on 5 May 1837, after Piet Retief. With the daughters driving some of their wagons they finally caught up with the rest of the Retiefs after some really bad experiences. They are at this point encamped at Doornkop in the Retief laager, under Retief's second-in-command, Piet Greyling. Anna tells us in a later memorial[23]:

[Before leaving] *"Mr. Retief had cautioned us at Doornkop to remain by each other till he came back, as he was ill at ease; he also wrote to us later afterwards that we should not separate from each other, but the trouble we had with the cattle obliged many to proceed down the river with their families in small troops."*

She describes the actions of the dispersing Trekkers as representing *"disobedience and imprudence."* She continues:

"We were alone, feeling secure and contented. Mr. Retief left his wife at Doornkop with Mr. Smit..."

—*End Nexus Familia*

But for one man with a conscience and a horse

For a variety of reasons, including pressure due to the livestock being too confined, the lure of the most beautiful countryside they had ever seen, or anxiousness to select future spots for farms, the Trekkers below the Drakensberg started to disperse along the local rivers just as young Roets explained and as Anna Steenkamp lamented. This dispersal increased as Retief stayed away longer and longer. He had left on 25 January 1838 and had now already been away for three weeks with not a word of news.

It is the most despicable of facts that, by 16 February 1838, the Trekkers had not been informed of the events that had already happened at Umgungundlovu ten days earlier on 6 February 1838. A number of white men knew, and the reader shall find out soon enough. These included the Rev. Owen and the missionary Venable. Certainly the machinating Captain Gardiner knew or suspected the whole thing. One man with a conscience and a horse would have changed the history of Southern Africa.

On the evening of Friday 16 February 1838, the state of the Great

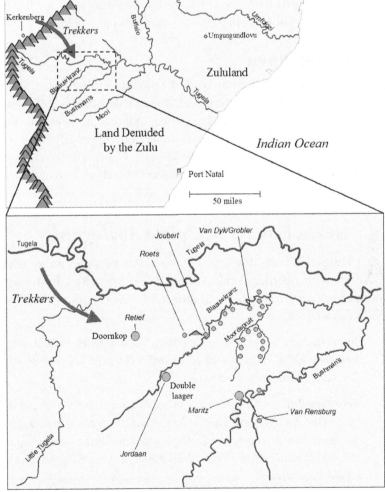

Fig. 11-4 *The disposition of Trekkers on 16 February 1838*

Trek was as follows (See *Fig. 11-4*):

• Piet Uys and Hendrik Potgieter were still on the Prairie above the Drakensberg with their treks.

• The laager of absent Piet Retief was located at Doornkop and, due to a constant influx of families, it had grown to some 78 wagons. His wife, Magdalena, aunt to ancestor Chris Jordaan, was located there in the care of the unordained minister Erasmus Smit.

• At this crucial point in time[24], the "Double Trek" of Jan du Plessis and Koos "Greatfoot" Potgieter arrived near the Retief laager. They formed a large party of around 100 wagons from the Tarka. Among them was our ancestor Chris Jordaan with his wife, two sons and two daughters.

•Many families were dispersed along the Bushman's River, the Moordspruit River, and the Blaauwkranz River. Among them was our joint group of Joubert, Grobler, and Van Dyk families, along with the Besters who trekked with them.

•Located along the Bushman's River was the separate laager of Gerrit Maritz and his deputy Gert Rudolph, with his pride and joy, Grietjie (*Gretchen*), the home made cannon. In anticipation of trouble, Maritz had maintained better control over his people and they had not dispersed quite as much.

• And, incongruously, somewhere between the Moordspruit and the Bushman's River was an enigmatic Italian lady, Teresa Viglione, with her wagons and three Italian men; traders dealing with the Trekkers.

We now turn back the clock by 13 days and join the 100-man Trekker delegation as they approach Dingane's capital of Umgungundlovu on 3 February 1838.

Umgungundlovu

Piet Retief and his men arrived at Umgungundlovu on the 3rd of February 1838. The next three days would be some of the most well documented of the 19th century by virtue of there being three British eyewitness accounts of what happened, none with any bias in favor of the Trekkers. One was by the Reverend Francis Owen, who was called on repeatedly in the process. Another would be by a young Englishman from Port Natal, named William Wood. The third was by Jane Williams, Owen's Welsh maid.

Rather than relate the events of the three days looking back from the future like historians, we turn instead to our own family and the documented eyewitness reports.

Nexus Familia 56: *Bulala Abatagati!*

At Dingane's kraal, the Rev. Francis Owen becomes an innocent and terrified witness to the events. We start with his diary on 2 January 1838, when Retief advises Dingane of the Battle of Kapain and the intended mission to Sekonyela to retrieve the stolen Zulu cattle. That mission already left one week earlier on 26 December 1837:

> *January 2nd.* — *Letter informed Dingane that the Boors had sent another commander against Umsilikazi, had slain 500 of his people, and captured 3,000 head of cattle. It informed him that they were going to retake Dingane's cattle from the Basuto.*

> *February 2nd.* — *Dingane sent for me to write a letter to Retief, who, with a party of Boors, is now on his way to the Zoolu capital. He said he was content because he had got his cattle again. He requested the chief of the Boors would send to all his people and order them to come up to the capital with him, but without their horses. He promised to gather all his army, to sing and dance in the presence of the Dutch, who, he desired, would also dance.*

> *February 3rd.* — *Large parties of Zoolus, in their war dress, entered the town. The Boors entered the town on horseback, with their guns, about sixty. The Boors showed Dingane the way in which they danced on*

horseback by making a sham charge at one another, making the air resound with their guns. This was something which the Zulu chief had never witnessed. In their turn the Zulus exhibited their agility in dancing. About noon I paid a visit to Retief. The answer which he gave to Dingane, when he demanded the guns and horses, was, to show the messenger his grey hairs, and bid him tell his master that he was not dealing with a child.

Pieter Jordaan, Reynier Grobler, and Willem Basson are in high spirits as their party of one hundred arrives at Umgungundlovu on Saturday 3 January 1838. Also with them is Andries van Dyk, whose wife and children have been left in the Joubert encampments, along with Reynier's older brother, Michael, his wife and four children.

This Zulu king with the really bad teeth seems to be alright as Nguni chiefs go. The men know that all the Nguni nations are culturally hyper-aggressive, but they are received well indeed. The messages that the king has sent Retief are also extremely encouraging. So, the men leave their guns and their 200 horses with their outriders under two big trees outside the king's kraal and proceed unarmed. They get to meet the Reverend Francis Owen, about whom Retief has already told them. Owen is a missionary and seems totally out of place; a strange fish out of water. The man seems quite neurotic, in fact, but stops short of saying what is worrying him. They also meet a bright looking young man named William Wood. He has recently arrived at Dingane's kraal after participating in a raid on another chiefdom at the request of Dingane. The Zulu king has taken to using the English at Port Natal as his own on-call personal rifle unit in his squabbles with other nations.

On this first day there is much dancing by the Zulus. Then the king asks that the Trekkers should dance. This is somewhat of a problem. There is no such thing as a rain dance or a war dance that is done by any white men that Pieter, Reynier, and Willem know of. However, Mr. Retief explains that what the king wants is for them to "dance on their horses." This is something they understand a bit better. So, they split into two groups and the two groups do a mock charge at each other, complete with the shooting of some rounds. This clearly hugely impresses the king. Reynier, as the youngest of the three family members, enjoys all this tremendously. Pieter, the oldest, quietly thinks to himself that it may not have been such a clever idea to do that. Many of the Zulu appear visibly frightened by the whole affair.

It turns out that his fears are well founded when the king promptly decides to ask for horses and guns. There is no way on Earth that any Trekkers are going to give this savage king any guns and horses. It would be suicidal. In the event, the King seems to forget about this demand and, amazingly, even tells them they can keep the cattle they took from Sekonyela. Then the two sides set about signing the much awaited contract, drawn up in English by the enigmatic Reverend Owen[25], with three of the king's men and three Trekkers also acting as witnesses to Dingane making a cross. Young William Wood[26], present through all of this, sums it up:

"Dingaan gladly received the cattle; but his attention was arrested by sixty horses and eleven guns which the farmers had taken from the enemy, and he told them he must also have them. Retief, however, told him that he could not comply with this demand, as the cattle were his property, but not the guns and horses.

With this Dingaan appeared satisfied, and, shortly after, told them that the cattle should also be theirs; likewise promising them a piece of land extending from the Tugela to the Umzimvubu. Retief accepted his offer, and a treaty was signed between Dingaan on the one hand and the emigrant farmers on the other."

And so dawns the morning of February 6, 1838. Pieter, Willem and Reynier, like all the other men, prepare to leave. The entire visit has been a tremendous success. Finally they are to have a country of their own. The alliance with the Zulu is also promising. This is when the message arrives that Dingane should like to have some parting festivity. They should come and drink some sorghum-beer with him and his men will dance for them. When they get there, Dingane has a lot of his men in the kraal and they dance in a ring around the Trekkers. This is an impressive dance in which the men dance ever closer to the Trekkers. In fact, Reynier finds it quite disconcerting. And this is when he realizes that they have been lulled into a trap. They have none of their weapons, and their outriders are in the kraal with them!

And then the king yells out the fearful words that will reverberate through the centuries:

"..Bulala AbaTagati!."..."...Kill the Wizards!"

William Wood:

"The farmers had been at Ngungunhlovu about two days, during which they walked about the kraal unarmed, but had taken the precaution to place their arms under the protection of their servants or after-riders, who had taken up their quarters under the two milktrees without the kraal. On the morning of the third day, I perceived from Dingaan's manner that he meditated some mischief, although from his conversation with his captains I could not perceive that he had given them any orders prejudicial to the farmers. I, however, watched my opportunity to warn them to be on their guard. This occurred when some of the farmers strolled into the kraal, and, having come near the place where I was standing, I told them I did not think all was right, and recommended them to be on their guard; upon which they smiled and said: 'We are sure the king's heart is right with us, and there is no cause for fear'.

A short time after this, Dingaan came out of his hut, and having seated himself in front of it in his arm-chair, ordered out two regiments. One was called 'Isihlangu Mhlope', or white shields, and the other the 'Isihlangu Mnyama', or black shields: the former were his best men, and wore rings on their heads, formed of the bark of a tree and grass, and stitched through the scalp: and the latter regiment was composed entirely of young men. These troops he caused to form in a circle, and, having placed his two principal captains on his right and left hand respectively, he sent a message to Retief, inviting him to bring his men, and wish the king 'farewell', previously to starting. Retief a short time after this entered the kraal, accompanied by the other farmers and all their servants, with the exception of one or two, who were sent out to fetch the horses; their arms being left unguarded under the two milk-trees without the kraal.

On Retief approaching Dingaan, the latter told him to acquaint the farmers at Natal, as soon as he arrived there, of the king's desire that they should soon come and possess the land he had given them; also to remember him to them. He then wished the party an agreeable journey to Natal, and invited them to sit down and drink some 'tywala' [corn beer] with him and his people, which invitation they unfortunately accepted. Retief sat by the king; but the farmers and their servants sat in a place by themselves, at a short distance from the king and his captains. After drinking some beer together, Dingaan ordered his troops to amuse the farmers by dancing and singing, which they immediately commenced doing.

The farmers had not been sitting longer than about a quarter of an hour, when Dingaan called out: 'Seize them!' upon which an overwhelming rush was made upon the party before they could get on their feet. Thomas Halstead then cried out: 'We are done for!' and added in the Zulu language, 'Let me speak to the king'; which Dingaan heard, but motioned them away with his hand. Halstead then drew his knife, and ripped up one Zulu, and cut another throat, before he was secured; and a farmer also succeeded in ripping up another Zulu. The farmers were then dragged with their feet trailing on the ground, each man being held by as many Zulu as could get at him, from the presence of Dingaan, who still continued sitting and calling out 'Bulala amatakati' [kill the wizards]. He then said, 'Take the heart and the liver of the king of the farmers and place them in the road of the farmers'.

When they had dragged them to the hill, 'Hloma Mabuto', [Mustering the soldiers] they commenced the work of death by striking them on the head with knobbed sticks, Retief being held and forced to witness the deaths of his comrades [including his 11 -year old son] before they dispatched him. It was a most awful occurrence, and will never be effaced from my memory. The Rev. Mr. Owen and I witnessed it, standing at the doors of our huts, which faced the place of execution. Retief's heart and liver were taken out, wrapped in a cloth, and taken to Dingaan. His two captains, Inlela [Ndlela] and Dambuza, then came and sat down by Dingaan, with whom they conversed for some time. About two hours after the massacre, orders were issued that a large party were to set off and attack the wagons that contained the wives and children of the murdered farmers, which were at a considerable distance from Ngungunhlovu, as Retief and his party had left them there, not wishing to bring their families into any danger.

A large body of men were immediately in readiness, and the captains, previously to starting, approached Dingaan singly, and made a mock attack on him, thrusting their shields and then their spears close to his face, and going through a variety of movements; at the same time giving him various titles and praising him, as all his people who approach him must do; and occasionally calling out, 'We will go and kill the white dogs !' A short time after the party set off with great speed in the direction of the wagons. The result of that attack is well known. The farmers who were guarding the wagons were taken by surprise, when many of them fell, and some hundreds of women and children were inhumanely murdered, but not without retribution, as a great number of the enemy were slain, and the remainder obliged to retreat with precipitation.

After the murder of the farmers, Dingaan sent a messenger, named Gumbu, to the Rev. Mr. Owen and me, telling us not to fear, as no harm should happen to us; informing us at the same time that the farmers were 'Tagati', or wizards, and that that was the king's motive for killing them. Mr. Owen told me to tell him that he had nothing whatever to do with the transaction, and could not help what had transpired. He then turned round and walked off. Knowing Dingaan's jealous and treacherous disposition, I did not give the messenger the answer of Mr. Owen, feeling assured that it would have caused our deaths; but I told Gumbu to tell the king that we considered that he had acted perfectly right in killing the farmers, as no doubt they would otherwise have killed us, as well as him and his people.

This answer pleased the king, and he sent us a present of an ox. Not long after, we saw between fifty and sixty men approaching the house; and it need scarcely be observed that this circumstance caused us not a little fear. When they came up to the house, they acquainted us that Dingaan wished to see us, and repeated the promise of the king that no injury should happen to us. We went immediately to him, and his first question was, 'Are you afraid?' upon which I saw that the opinion which we had formed of the king left no room for fear. He then laughed, and said we had acted as we should do. He then asked, 'Do you wish to return to Natal?' but we answered 'No'. He then dismissed us to our huts."

The Rev. Owen is at his house when all this happens, and describes it in his diary:

February 6th. — *"A dreadful day in the annals of the mission! My pen shudders to give an account of it. This morning as I was sitting in the shade of my waggon reading the Testament, the usual messenger came with hurry and anxiety depicted in his looks. I was sure he was about to pronounce something serious, and what was his commission! Whilst it shewed consideration and kindness in the Zoolu monarch towards me, it disclosed a horrid instance of perfidy - too horrid to be described - towards the unhappy men who have for these three days been his guests, but are now no more. He sent to tell me not to be frightened as he was going to kill the Boers. This news came like a thunder stroke to myself and to every successive member of my family as they heard it.*

The reason assigned for this treacherous conduct was that they were going to kill him, that they had come here and he had now learned all their plans. The messenger was anxious for my reply, but what could I say? Fearful on the one hand of seeming to justify the treachery and on the other hand of exposing myself and family to probable danger if I appeared to take their part. Moreover I could not but feel that it was my duty to apprize the Boers of the intended massacre whilst certain death would have ensued (I apprehended) if I had been detected in giving them this information. However, I was released from this dilemma by beholding an awful spectacle! My attention was directed to the blood stained hill nearly opposite my hut and on the other side of my waggon, which hides it from my view, where all the executions at this fearful spot take place and which was now destined to add 60 more bleeding carcases to the number of those which have already cried to Heaven for vengeance.

'There!' (said someone), 'they are killing the Boers now!'. I turned my eyes and behold! an immense multitude on the hill. About 9 or 10 Zoolus to each Boer were dragging their helpless unarmed victim to the fatal spot, where those eyes which awaked this morning to see the cheerful light of day for the last time, are now closed in death.

I lay myself down on the ground. Mrs. and Miss Owen were not more thunderstruck than myself. We each comforted the other. Presently the deed of blood being accomplished the whole multitude returned to the town to meet their sovereign and as they drew near to him set up a shout which reached the station and continued for some time. Meanwhile, I myself, had been kept from all fear for my personal safety, for I considered the message of Dingarn [sic] to me as an indication that he had no ill designs against his Missionary, especially as the messenger informed [me] that the Boer's Interpreter, an Englishman from Port Natal was to be preserved. Nevertheless, fears afterwards obtruded themselves on me, when I saw half a dozen men with shields sitting near our hut, and I began to tremble lest we were to fall the next victims!

At this crisis I called all my family in and read the 91st Ps., so singularly and literally applicable to our present condition, that I could with difficulty proceed in it! I endeavoured to realize all its statement and tho' I did not receive it as an absolute provision against sudden and violent death, I was led to Him who is our refuge from the guilt and fear of sin, which alone make Death terrible. We then knelt down and I prayed, really not knowing but that in this position we might be called into another world. Such was the effect of the first gust of fear on my mind. I remembered the words, 'Call upon me in the day of trouble and I will hear thee'. But of the Boers, Dingarn, the Mission, the Providence of God, I had other thoughts. Dingarn's conduct was worthy of a savage as he is. It was base and treacherous, to say the least of it - the offspring of cowardice and fear. Suspicious of his warlike neighbours, jealous of their power, dreading the neighbourhood of their arms, he felt as every savage would have done in like circumstances that these men were his enemies and being unable to attack them openly, he massacred them clandestinely!

Two of the Boers paid me a visit this morning and breakfasted only an hour or two before they were called into Eternity. When I asked them what they thought of Dingarn, they said he was good: so unsuspicious were they of his intentions. He had promised to assign over to them the whole country between the Tugala [Tugela] and the Umzimvubu rivers, and this day the paper of transfer was to be signed.

My mind has always been filled with the notion that however friendly the two powers have heretofore seemed to be, war in the nature of things was inevitable between them, but I dreamed of the ultimate conquest of the Boers who would not indeed be the first to provoke, but who would be the sure defenders of their own property, and the dreadful antagonists of the Zoolu nation, who could hardly be kept from affronting them, not to mention that real or imaginary causes of quarrel could not fail to exist between two such powerful bodies. The hand of God is in this affair, but how it will turn out favourably to the Mission is impossible to shew. The Lord direct our course.

I have seen by my glass that Dingarn has been sitting most of the morning since this dreadful affair in the centre of his town, an army in several divisions collected before him. About noon the whole body run in the direction from which the Boers came. They are (I cannot allow myself to doubt) sent to fall or to join others who have been ordered to fall unawares on the main body of the Boers who are encamped at the head of the Tugala, for to suppose that Dingarn should murder this handful and not make himself sure of the whole number with their guns, horses and cattle would be to conceive him capable of egregious folly, as he must know that the other Boers will avenge the death of their countrymen. Certain it is as far as human foresight can judge, we shall speedily hear either of the massacre of the whole company of Boers, or what is scarcely less terrible of wars and bloodshed, of which there will be no end till either the Boers or the Zoolu nation cease to be.[...]

At present all is as still as death: it is really the stillness of death, for it has palsied every tongue in our little assembly."

Jane Williams[27]:

"We had just done prayers when a Kafir messenger from Dingaan came running to us, covered with perspiration, and said that we were not to be frightened, that we were King George's children, and that the Boers were runaways from him. He also said that we would not be hurt. One of the Zulu maid servants said to me, 'They are taking the dogs away to kill them!' [...] Scarcely had the Zulus left the place of slaughter when the vultures swooped down on to the bodies of the victims."

It is the *"runaways"* comment that incriminates Gardiner as the driving force behind the mass murder and mutilation. Daniel Bezuidenhout (see below) claims that two specific settlers at Port Natal, Garnett and Stubbs, advised Dingane that the Trekkers were deserters after speaking to Gardiner.

Owen reports that Henry Venable, the American missionary who fled Mzilikatse with the aid of the Trekkers, arrives at Umgungundlovu on this very day at Dingane's request. When he sees[28] the results of the mass murder, he takes no action to warn the Trekker encampments. Ten days later, by 16 February, he and his colleagues are still desperately seeking permission from Dingane to leave. He eventually boards the schooner *Mary* and leaves for the United States with some of his colleagues.

William Wood:

"The next day[29] we waited on the king, when Mr. Owen asked permission to go to Natal, but was refused. A messenger came, however, the same afternoon, bringing the king's permission for us to depart, but not to take our cattle or servants with us. On the following day, he informed us that we might take both."

Fig. 11-5 *The keepers of Kwa-Matiwane*

The Rev. Owen:

February 9th. — *"The angel of death has been lately crying with a loud voice to all the fowls that fly in the midst of heaven, 'Come and gather yourselves together!' Numerous birds of prey flying over the hill whitened with the bones of men. The King sent for my interpreter soon after his arrival, and gave him a plausible account of the late unhappy affair. He said that if he had not despatched the Boors, they would have fired at him and his people before they left; and that when their guns were examined they were all found loaded with ball. The perfidious tyrant gave the following account of the manner in which they had been seized. He invited them all into the cattle-fold to take leave of him; his people were then ordered to dance, and forming themselves, as usual, into a half-moon, they came nearer and nearer to the Boors, till he gave the command to lay hold of the unsuspecting victims of his jealousy.*

Having duly reflected on our present situation, I determined to inform Dingane of my intentions. As war is inevitable we are not secure in this place. We see a storm coming. I took a present of red cloth to the chief, with which he was much pleased. I then said I was going (to leave) on account of the troubles that were coming. He told me to tell him what was in my heart. 'Was I leaving,' he asked 'on account of the Boors?' I said, 'That that was my reason, for I feared there would be war.' He asked, 'What war?' I said, 'Between his nation and the amaBhulu' (the Dutch). He was grave; he said he would wish me a pleasant journey. I told him I hoped to return. I fancy he anticipated my departure after his sad and wicked conduct."

William Wood:

"We remained four days longer without making any preparations for our journey, in order to show Dingaan that we did not expect any violence from him, and were therefore free from fear on that account, and not over-anxious to leave his kraal. Mr. Owen, who had two wagons, then commenced packing up his things; but in the midst of his work was interrupted by the arrival of a messenger from Dingaan, who told him that he must leave the best wagon, together with his cattle and servants, behind: to which orders Mr. Owen thought fit to submit; and everything being in readiness, we went and bade the king farewell, when he shook hands with us and wished us a pleasant journey.

I must here observe that Dingaan was averse to my going, and told me that during the time I had been with him I had received nothing but kindness; that I had been allowed to do as I liked; that he had given me a herd of cattle, and a number of boys as 'companions'; and he then asked why I wished to go away from him, telling me at the same time that I could do just as I liked, but he would much rather that I should stay. I told him that, having seen the farmers killed, I was so filled with fear that now I could not be happy any longer, and wished much to go to my father at Natal. 'Well', said he, 'I am sorry you are going; but if you are not happy, I will not detain you'.

A small party of Zulu's was sent with us to drive the wagon and take care of the oxen; and a messenger was sent before us to the different villages through which our journey lay, with orders that we should be supplied with everything we needed, and that every assistance we might require should be granted to us. When we had got about four miles from Megoonloof[30]*, Dinguan sent a message to Mr. Owen that he should come to him, and immediately afterwards another came, saying we might proceed. Having continued our journey to Natal, and not meeting with any further interruption, we rested for two days at one of the missionary stations, and then resumed our journey, being closely watched by two spies*[31]*, whom we supposed Dinguan had sent after us."*

—End Nexus Familia

Nexus Familia 57: The Umgungundlovu Death Toll

In the treacherous mass murder at Umgungundlovu, we have lost no fewer than eight family members among the one hundred slain:

• Piet Retief, Great Trek leader and brother-in-law to ancestor Chris Jordaan's father, has been murdered.

• Pieter Georg Jordaan, older brother to our ancestor Chris Jordaan, has been murdered.

• Reynier Nicolaas Johannes Grobler, cousin to our ancestor Izak Hermanus Grobler, has been murdered

• Balthasar and Pieter Klopper, cousins to our ancestor Maria Catharina Klopper, have both been murdered, as has her second cousin, Lucas, together with his father.

• Willem Johannes Basson, second cousin to our ancestor Matthys Michiel Basson has been murdered.

The men have been dragged to Kwa Matiwane on Hlomo AmaButho, clubbed to death, and impaled on two-inch stakes. Some die a more lingering impaling death on those stakes. This is the fate that is meted out to those who sought to treat with Dingane in respect. (See also *Fig. 11-8* and *11-9*)

—End Nexus Familia

Nexus Familia 58: Blaauwkranz – the ultimate horror

The English language has failed as yet in producing a descriptive enough adjective for what happens before dawn during the night of February 16th to 17th, 1838. We turn to Nicolaas Roets to relate for us the events of the early hours of 17 February, when the ultimate horror descends on his brother-in-law[32]. It will cement the white South African view of what the indigenous people of Africa are capable of when they have their way, and event after horrific event in Africa after that night will reinforce that view all the way into the 21st century:

Nicolaas Roets:

"After a while, Abraham Joubert decided to take his trek through the Blaauwkranz (River) and one afternoon[33]* he came riding along at sundown to ask my father to come and help him the following morning to get the livestock through the drift. My father promised he would come and so Abraham stayed that night with us to chat and visit. That same evening, around 8 o'clock, when we children were already lying under the wagon to sleep, gunshots started to fall beyond Abraham's wagons across the Moordspruit (River) where a few of Retief's wagons were under the guard of eight men. The gunshots started there and (moved) from*

there downstream as the wagons stood. After a while, a few shots fell at Abraham's wagons and from there again on this side up along the Blaauwkranz.

It carried on like this almost the entire night; there were not many shots, but we could hear that one after the other at each little group of wagons a few shots fell, and then again silence. My father and Abraham thought that Retief had returned from Dingane with his people and that celebratory shots were being fired at each laager, one after the other, as the news was being made known down the line. The shots went down along the laagte (glen) to the Tugela, but by the morning all was dead quiet.

When it was light, my father said to Abraham to take his horse and ride over to Retief and bring the news and after that we'd start to herd the sheep through. Abraham rode over the hill between his wagons and ours, but very soon he came charging back terribly fast and waved his hat from afar. When he got to us, he jumped off and just yelled:

"Kaffirs! Kaffirs! All murdered! All murdered...!"

My father let the servants fetch and saddle the horses and then we rode over the hill. I went with to hold the horses. We saw no Kaffirs when we got to the top of the hill and everywhere the little groups of wagons still stood apparently undisturbed, but when we rode down to Abraham's stand, which were the nearest wagons – there lay a terrible sight.

My oldest sister [Anna Roets], Abraham's wife, lay over the wagon chest half in the wagon and half out where the Kaffirs had murdered her, she was colored red with blood and torn apart and [had] almost no clothes on her body. Abraham's little children had all been stabbed to death and also his two brothers and his [two] brothers-in-law and Flip Venter and all the women and children, no, not one had survived, and it was bitter to see Abraham cry over his loved ones who lay there cut up and mutilated.

In the tent behind the wagons lay three of the women still clinging to one another where the Kaffirs had killed them in one heap. And the little children lay dead in the wagons and in the grass, but the Kaffirs had taken all the guns and the livestock, though they left the wagons undamaged.

And so it had gone at all the laagers; everywhere the people had been suddenly surprised in the dark and after a few shots they were all stabbed to death with assegais – all murdered, and also the black servants and cattle herds were dead, and we had only escaped this because our wagons were behind the hill and the Kaffirs had not come along there; and had missed us in the dark. Abraham was the only one of his family to escape because he had visited with us, and so he survived. We could not see any Kaffirs, but because they could perhaps still have been near, we rode back and my father spanned in [yoked the oxen] and we trekked away immediately to where the Moordspruit joins the Tugela, where a number of people who had escaped in the dark or who had been missed by the Kaffir Commando were camped against the hill.

All were very much in sorrow and depressed, because the loss was terrible and hundreds were dead, but that night they made defenses as best they could; though the Kaffirs did not come again; and the following day everyone trekked to Doornkop where there were many of the rearmost people who only now were arriving over the mountain; and here a proper laager was drawn and fortified with branches.

Fig. 11-6 The Massacre at Blaauwkranz

As there were now a considerable number of people, a Commando went out the next day to bury the bodies. My father and my brothers went with and so did I to tend the horses. The Commando went in small groups to wherever there were still deserted wagons standing; they made huge holes and laid the bodies to rest in those. My oldest sister with her children and Flip Venter and the brothers-in-law were all put in one grave – I shall never forget it as young as what I was - I had to hold the horses as long as the people toiled; so I did not see in the tents and in the wagons, but everywhere I looked I saw bodies lying on the ground; some in front of the wagons, others where the livestock was, or otherwise further away in the long grass where they had fled. My sister's smallest child [Johannes] lay on an ox yoke with his insides spilled out and many of the bodies were terribly mutilated. We went from the one laager to the next and everywhere it was the same; it was a bitter day and cannot be forgotten.

While the people were busy burying the bodies a horse patrol went out to spy but they came back when we were all already back at Doornkop, and they reported that the Kaffirs had gone to Dingane land with the cattle. Cattle was then collected from the new arrivals (rearmost people) and the wagons of the murdered were fetched and then everyone moved to Bushman's River where more and more people were coming over the mountains. Three men were sent by horse to hurry up the people who were still coming along, for reinforcements.

The three men who went were Abraham Joubert, Ignatius Maritz and my uncle Jan Schutte."

—*__End Nexus Familia__*

Blaauwkranz – *Oh, dreadful night*

Dingane's Zulu impi fell upon the unsuspecting Trekkers along the Bushman's and Blaauwkranz rivers on the evening of 16 February 1838 and into the morning of the 17th. The people were surprised in their nightclothes and in most cases could mount no more than a token resistance. The mindless barbarity of the Zulu had no limit. They took babies by their feet and dashed their heads against the wagon wheels and then they disemboweled them. Women were stabbed and their breasts hacked off and then they were cut to pieces. In some cases, they were thrown in heaps and riddled with assegais. They cut the unborn babies from their mother's wombs and cut the babies to pieces. They did whatever they could to inspire the greatest fear, such as draping poor little Johannes Joubert's disemboweled body over an ox-yoke. This was black terrorism in its most extreme form. It would not be seen again in South Africa until the 1960s. In most cases, the attacks were over relatively quickly. In a few cases, Trekkers put up a brave defense but succumbed.

In the middle of all of this, there were acts of great valor by the most unlikely of people. Teresa Viglione, the Italian lady, mounted her horse near Moordspruit and rode to as many laagers as she could reach in time, including that of Maritz, warning them of the Zulu attacks. Then she simply returned to the mists of history.

Marthinus Oosthuizen was rushing past a hill when he saw the Van Rensburgs surrounded on top of the hill. They yelled to him that their ammunition was nearly finished. So Marthinus fetched powder from some deserted wagons and charged right through the attacking Zulu to deliver gunpowder to the totally encircled Van Rensburgs. They beat off the Zulu. In fact, it is said that the Zulu thought his charge through the hundreds of assegais was sorcery and therefore broke off the attack. In the case of Maritz's laager, the Trekkers won the day and chased the Zulu into the river killing hundreds upon hundreds of them.

It is important to note that among those who died in this terrible night was George Biggar, the 18-year old younger son of Alexander Biggar, the trader of Port Natal. Both Alexander and his remaining son, Robert, would soon enough see action against the Zulu. The Biggar family remained the staunchest and most committed of supporters of the Trekkers to the ends of their lives. These were honorable men and deserve a much clearer place in our history as true English speaking Afrikaners.

As regards a strike against Afrikaner morale, it was a great success for the Zulu. As regards the immediate tactical success, the day certainly went to the Zulu. They had killed nearly 10% of the Trekker men of fighting age in the Tugela area, and they had taken 20,000 head of cattle. In doing so, they had left the Trekkers in imminent danger of starvation.

Strategically, it was a serious failure for the Zulu in the same sense that the attack on Pearl Harbor would one day be a serious failure for the Japanese. They had failed to realize exactly how large the Great Trek really was. They had failed to attack Doornkop and the Double Trek. At Maritz's laager, they found they could not manage at all once the Trekkers put up an organized defense. They had got the cattle and had dealt the Trekkers an enormous blow, but they had woken and consolidated a powerful enemy who had honestly wanted to live in peace with them.

Furthermore, there was no way on God's Earth that this savage massacre could go unanswered. Already embittered men like Abraham Joubert, who had lost his entire extended family, were on their way up the mountain to fetch more Trekkers to Natal. Abraham would have his vengeance. It would have to wait, but it would be all the sweeter.

We turn to some more first hand testimony of the events of that bitter night:

Daniel Bezuidenhout[34] :

Daniel was 24 years old at the time of the massacre and lost most of his family:

"The first assault of the Zulus was on Barend Johannes Liebenberg's bivouac [...] Of the Liebenbergs, four sons came forward; who, together with young [George] Biggar, went to meet the Kaffirs. All the other Liebenbergs were murdered. [...] Liebenberg's bivouac was the lowest down the Blaauwkranz kloof (gorge), and was thus first attacked.

The second attack was on Adriaan Rossouw, who was murdered with his wife and four children. We found two children badly wounded on the following day, but they were still alive. Elizabeth Johanna Rossouw had sixteen wounds, and died the next day. Adriaan Johannes, son of Adriaan, had thirty-two assegai wounds, and escaped with his life. He lived on my farm till his eighteenth year (he was my sister's child), and then died of one of the wounds, which had never been completely healed. [...]

The third attack was on my father's bivouac, consisting of five wagons and three skin tents; and there were three men with it – namely, my father, Roelof Botha (my brother-in-law), and myself.

It was about one o'clock in the night, and there was no moonlight. We stood on a rough hillock, near thorn trees. We had three or four bold savage dogs that would tear a tiger [leopard] to pieces without difficulty. I heard the dogs bark and fight, and thought that there was a tiger. I got up, having no clothes on my person except a shirt and drawers, and went to urge on the dogs; and, when I was 300 yards away from the wagons, I heard the whirr of assegais and shields, and perceived that we had to do with Kafirs, not tigers; and with the Kafirs the dogs were fighting.

I shouted to my father: "There are Kafirs here, and they are stabbing the dogs;" and I ran back towards the wagons to get my gun, for I was unarmed. But the wagons were already encircled by three rows of Kafirs. Still I strove to push with my hands, and struggle, to pass through the Kafirs to get at my gun. When I had in this way got through the three lines of Kafirs, I found that there was still a number within the lines closely surrounding the wagons.

As I was still advancing, I heard my father say, "O, God!" and I knew from the sound that he was suffocated by blood. He had a wound in the gullet above the breast. Roelof Botha had fired three shots, and there lay three Kafirs, struck down by his shots; then he too cried "O, Lord!" I heard no more and then I tried to make my way back from the wagons, through the three rows of Kafirs.

Then I received the first wound from on assegai on the knot of the shoulder, through the breast and along the ribs. A second assegai struck the bone of my thigh, so that the point of the blade was bent, as I found afterwards when I drew it out. The third struck me above the left knee – all the wounds were on my left side. A fourth wound was inflicted above the ankle, through the sinews, under the calf of the leg. Then I found myself among the cattle, and stood a moment, listening. I heard no further sound of a voice - all were dead; and the Kafirs were busy, tearing the tents, and breaking the wagons, and stabbing to death the dogs and the poultry. They left nothing alive.

Of the women murdered at my father's wagons, there were: My mother, Elizabetta Johanna, born

Liebenberg; my wife, Elizabetta Cecilia Smit; my mother-in-law, Anna Smit, born Botha; my sister, Susanna Margarita, married to Botha, her little child Elizabeth Johanna, about five months old; another sister, Maria Adriana Bezuidenhout; also my sisters, Rachel Jacoba and Cornelia Sophia, a little brother, named Hendrik Cornelis, my little daughter, Anna Bezuidenhout (she was eleven months old), who was murdered with her mother. My wife lay in bed with a little one, three days old, also murdered with the mother; and on the following day we found my wife with her breast cut off, and the corpse of my child laid at the blood stained breast.

There was also a brother of mine, Petrus Johannes, fourteen years old. He slept in my father's tent, and when I shouted "Here are Kafirs" he understood me to be saying the sheep were running off. He jumped out, and received only an assegai wound along the skin of the back, and then ran among the thorn trees. The next day late he arrived at Doornkop. He knew where the horses were running, had knotted his braces together, had caught and mounted a horse that was most gentle, and drove seven other horses before him, and thus had escaped.

From that place I went up along the Blaauwkranz River. The first family I came to was that of Sybrand van Dyk. This was bout two o'clock at night, and there was no moonlight. I had scarcely awakened the women and children and removed them from the wagons before the Kafirs were there. The second family that I roused was that of Scheepers, who had been murdered with Retief; there were only women and children there. The third was that of Hans Roets, Petrus van Vooren, and Karel Geer, with their families. This was the last. The day then broke, [...]

My father and I had had 7,000 sheep, and much money. All was gone. I had nothing left but a shirt and a pair of pantaloons. I had Johanna van der Merwe, little Rossouw, and two others to provide for; and I had neither food nor clothing. We had nothing but Kafir corn [millet or sorghum], *A little while after I bought a pistol; and with my wounded arm in a handkerchief, I rode after the eland, turned them in the direction of the wagons, and then shot and killed them. Then came the widows and orphans, and procured the meat. Had it not been for the abundance of game, we should all have died of hunger."*

Anna Steenkamp:

Anna, whose report we have consulted before, was in Piet Retief's laager where Piet Greyling had been left in command. This laager, situated at Doornkop, some distance rearward of the dispersed encampments, was not attacked at all. Anna describes the situation on the morning of Saturday 17 February 1838:

"Oh! dreadful, dreadful night! Where-in so much martyred blood was shed;

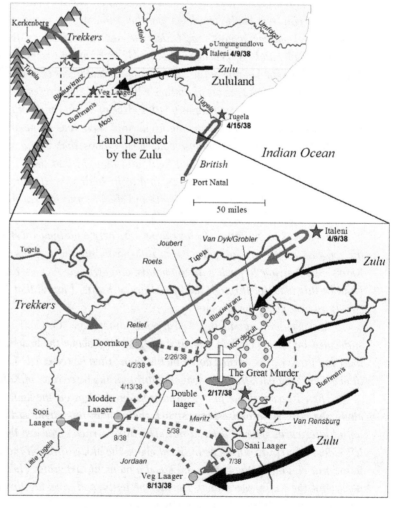

***Fig. 11-7** Natal from Feb. 1838 to Nov. 1838*

and two hundred innocent children, ninety-five women, and thirty-three men were slain, and were hurled into an awful eternity by the assegais of those bloodthirsty heathens. Excluding the servants, the number was over four hundred souls. Oh! it was well nigh unbearable for flesh and blood to behold the frightful spectacle the following morning. In one wagon were found fifty dead, and the blood flowed from the seam of the tent-sail down to the rim of the wheel. Oh! How awful it was to look upon all those dead and wounded. [...]

The day after our arrival there [at Doornkop], the wounded, the women and children who were left, arrived; some on foot, others on horseback, and yet another portion by wagon. Our field-commandant, Mr. Piet Greyling, carefully provisioned and strengthened our laager. He also took our sheep back from the Kaffirs, but our cattle were across the river, which was full. The commandant had the dead buried and the wounded attended to. On all sides one saw tears flowing, and heard people weeping by the plundered wagons, painted with blood; tents and beds torn to shreds; pregnant women and little children had to walk for hours together, bearing the signs of their hasty flight. Oh! How weary and fatigued were the poor women and children, and how awful it was to see the unborn children rent asunder by the murderous Kaffirs. When the women reached us, they fell upon their knees, and thanked God for their deliverance from the hands of the cruel tyrant. In our laager was nothing but lamentation and weeping. Every day we had to bury the dead bodies of the wounded. The spectacle, and the terrible circumstances, cannot be described by my pen."

Erasmus Smit:

Erasmus Smit, the unordained minister to the Trekkers was an agonized and fretful character, but benefited history tremendously through keeping a diary, most of which survived, including the section pertaining to the horrific events of Blaauwkranz :

Saturday, 17 February. — *"This night the most sorrowful night and present day of our long journey. In the early morning we were woken unexpectedly with a true alarm: that the Kaffirs had fallen upon the small laager-camp of W Bezuidenhout and B. Liebenberg [above], and had murdered and burnt all. Three white men and two black men escaped, of whom D. Bezuidenhout escaped with three assegai wounds. Quickly we pulled our wagons, and those that were nearby, into a threefold laager-ring to wait upon the enemy. God prevented his attack upon our laager! And so the Almighty let the enemy triumph over us, - we acknowledge that we doubly deserve God's punishing hitting hand, because our sins are big and many. Yet He shows us poor souls mercy in the Crucifixion and blood of Christ! Amen. His Will be done! Amen.*

And this is now possibly my last day of writing my Journal."

The voices of the strongest trembled

We turn to Johanna Fick, neé Landman, granddaughter of Piet Retief, who was in Gerrit Maritz's laager, where at the time she had her eye solidly fixed on a 17-year old young man named Hendrik Fick[35]. Hendrik and the young Leech[36] were close friends. She is telling her story to her descendants, quaintly mixing her tenses. She relates how the Zulu were beaten off at Maritz's laager on 17 February 1838, and how these simple ordinary farmers innovate grapeshot in the middle of a heated battle:

[..] *"The men go out to gather the cattle and meet an Englishman on a horse cart. He comes from the same direction from which Retief should be coming and they ask him whether he knows anything about them[37]. He says "no," he has not met people for days. They ask whether he has seen any Kaffirs, he says "no," he has not seen any Kaffirs either. And he rides further; reassured, the young men go on their way. Shortly thereafter they see a wondrous sight far away on the horizon. My husband later told me that it looked like a swarm of locusts. The sky itself got darker. He had never seen so many live things together.*

"Turn around! Turn around!" yelled Leech [...] The two boys, Leech and Fick were great friends and were always together. "Turn around!," everyone shouts to one another and they ride for their lives, because the assegais are starting to whistle around them.

My child, my husband arrives in the laager and he is so scared that he wants to roll up the legs of his pants right there and then and go back inland. But they quickly tell him that he will have to help fight.

The women quickly help draw the laager together, but they are in such a hurry that they cannot get it right. It is hard work. They draw it into a semicircle, but there is one place where they cannot get the wagons together, so there is a gap. But Gert Rudolph rides his little cannon [Grietjie], which was on wheels - the "little set" they called it - into the gap, and there the little cannon fired the first shot [in anger] in Natal. While they get everything together, a group goes out under Gert Maritz to try to deny the first stormers [sic] the crossing of the Bushman's river. My frightened young Fick was with them.

The Zulu go hand in hand through the strong river and our people shoot the one in the middle so he lets go and then the others wash away. Those standing on the other side of the river throw their assegais [at the Trekkers] to enable the passage. Then our men see that the Zulu have found a shallow area and are trying to cross there; now our little group will have to return to the laager. They run a distance while loading their guns, then they fire a round, run again and load again and fire again; and so it goes until they are at the laager. Meanwhile the little cannon puts a fright into the blacks. When a shot goes off, they fall flat and when the fright is gone, they carry on again. The cannon made the return to the laager possible, but we nevertheless lost seven men.

When Gert Rudolph noticed the effect his little cannon had, he was altogether unhappy. See, my child, the cannon balls go like tennis balls but they go only one place. So Gert Rudolph made a plan and the women brought all their peppermint tins together. The people took lots of peppermints on the Great Trek, my child. And they carefully saved all the empty tins. We never threw away anything because we could not buy anything. Gert Rudolph threw the mouth of the cannon—as they named its front—over backwards and threw a peppermint tin in. Then they put a bag of gunpowder in the tin, cut a slit in the bag so it can ignite easily. Then they throw in a handful of musket balls, tamp it all down well with the loading rod and, to keep everything from falling out, they stuff the mouth of the cannon with wadding. The mouth is turned back over and one man comes and sets off the cannon with a revolver shot, and it flies with peppermint tin and all.

The Kaffirs did not know what to do. Whoever was not shot, did not dare stand up for long. The peppermint tins were a great success. But my child, when the little cannon fired a shot, it would be lying on its back from shock, and the people actually had to laugh, however tough a time they were having. You can believe how tough a time they had. The people did not have time to look up or down, not even time to eat. The bigger girls help load the guns or they mind the smaller children. Gerrit Maritz had the actual Commando. He was already a little old, a distinguished gentleman with a long beard.

My child, the whole day the battle continued and when the sun sank away, the people [were] haunted [by] the terror of the night. How would they be able to protect the laager in the night; how would they be able to fight in the night? [...] and the joy when they saw that the hordes were moving way; the joy, my child, was too great! They fell into one another's arms and cried from sheer gratitude.

Later they capture a Zulu that is trying to flee and they want to know from him what happened to Retief and his men. He does not want to talk. They hit him; he must speak. Eventually they get it out of him. He tells how it all went and they are so horrified and feel so hurt and are so outraged that they kill him right there on that spot. This was the first news of Retief's death that came in. Later more Kaffirs confirmed the story. [...] It was a terrible day and then the news of the terrible—one can say insurmountable—disaster. When our little group started an evening hymn, the voices of the strongest men trembled."

—*End Nexus Familia*

Nexus Familia 59: The Blaauwkranz Death Toll

The large extended Great Trek family of descendants of the late Josua Joubert, the tough frontier Commando man and grandson of the original 1688 French Huguenot, has been utterly decimated. Along with it, the Van Dyk family on the Great Trek has almost ceased to exist, while the entire Grobler family encamped with the Van Dyks has been killed and their bodies horribly mutilated. Matters are sketchy under these horrendous circumstances, but this much we know:

1. The elderly Jacobus Joubert, who once shoved the British flag into the arms of the Graaff-Reinet magistrate (*NF35*), and his wife, Rachel, daughter of the frontier leader Adriaan van Jaarsveld, have both been brutally murdered. All but two of those of his descendants in his encampment on the Great Trek (See Figure 11-8), together with their spouses, have been murdered and their bodies mutilated.

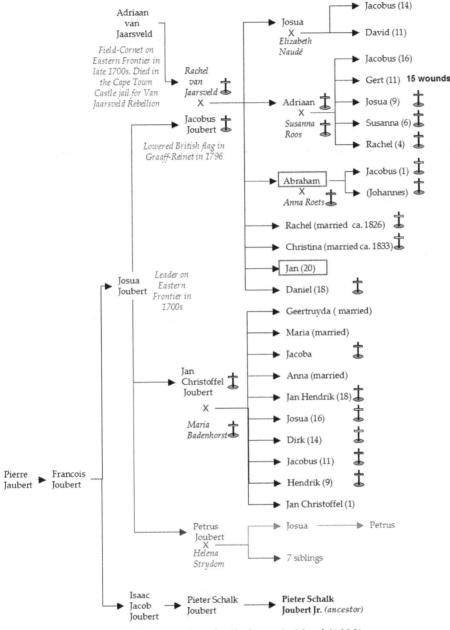

The babies have been swung by their feet to dash their heads against the metal of the wagon wheels and then they were disemboweled. The unborn babies have been ripped from their mother's wombs and then cut.

The only two of the encampment who we know for a fact have survived are Abraham Joubert, who was visiting his wife's Roets family, and young Gert Joubert, the 11-year old second oldest son of Adriaan Joubert and Susanna Roos.

The boy is in incredible agony, for he has 15 assegai wounds. Abraham's youngest brother, Daniel (18), who had been traveling with his father, is also no more. Abraham's recently married younger brother, Jan (20) has survived though, because he and his new young wife, Christina Meyer, were encamped elsewhere. Abraham's eldest brother, Josua, and his family were not part of the encampment, and survived. Josua and Abra-

Fig. 11-8 The Joubert family losses in Natal (1838)

ham will have their revenge for the murders of almost their entire family.

2. Jan Christoffel Joubert, brother of Jacobus, has been murdered along with his wife and all but two[38] of their children on the Great Trek. We know not, but daughter Anna has survived. The real miracle of Jan's family is that the one-year old Jan Christoffel has somehow survived in the heart of the massacre.

3. The Groblers and Van Dyks have been destroyed. Michael Grobler, our ancestral cousin, together with his wife Susanna Van Dyk, son Michael (6), and daughters Helena (8), Elsie (5), and youngest Susanna (3), have all been murdered and disemboweled by Dingane's impi.

In Figure 11-8 and Figure 11-9 we show in boxes the names of the men who will subsequently fight Dingane's army in remembrance of those who die in these terrible 10 days. Nicolaas Prinsloo died in the Van Rensburg Trek Massacre. A few months later the loss of the Grobler family will be specifically reported as follows in *The Grahamstown Journal* of 9 August 1838:

> *"names of men: Michiel Grobbelaar: Number murdered : Men (1), Women (1), Children (4)"*

Along with this will be reported the terrible loss in the associated Van Dyk family. The report in *The Grahamstown Journal* will read[39]:

> *"The following are the wives and children [now also murdered] of the men who were murdered earlier in Dingane's kraal: Andries van Dyk - Number murdered: Wife (1), children (10). One child left behind."*

Andries Van Dyk is uncle to Michael Grobler's wife, Susanna van Dyk, and they trekked together[40]. *The Grahamstown Journal* will also list the widow of Andries' older brother as having been murdered.

Having heeded the warning of her husband, Reynier Grobler, to stay in Retief's laager at Doornkop, the pregnant Maria Van Dyk and her son Michael have survived this night of terror. The same is true for the wives and children of Pieter Georg Jordaan and Willem Basson.

Our ancestor Chris Jordaan, his wife Maria Klopper and their children are safely in the large laager of Jan Du Plessis and Koos Potgieter, situated higher up along the Blaauwkranz River (See *Fig. 11-7*) outside the Ring of Death (the broken circle).

In the Prinsloo family, Joachim, cousin of the executed Slagtersnek Rebel Hendrik Kasteel (*NF40*), and son of Joachemus, has been murdered along with most of his family. Incredibly, his 15 year-old daughter, Grietjie, has survived, stabbed no fewer than 26 times by Zulu assegais. She is in terrible condition. She will live, but will be crippled for life. A number of Joachim's brothers are on the Great Trek.

—End Nexus Familia

Beyond death and despair

The Trekkers were in near total disarray after the wholesale slaughter by Dingane's Zulu. After burying the dead, nearly all but the Du Plessis-Potgieter "Double Trek" and Maritz consolidated back westward to Doornkop, where Piet Retief's distraught wife was placed under the ministration of Erasmus Smit. The people were in desperate straits. With the Zulu having gone off with most of their cattle, they are also staring famine in the face. Erasmus Smit sums up much with his diary entry:

> **Sunday, 18 Feb.**— [...] *The number of the dead, as far as we know, is of the white people on one day over 290, in all over 400 souls, men , women and children. [...] I could not manage a coherent prayer. It was sigh upon sigh, lamentation upon lamentation. Oh, God ! Oh, Lord ! How terrible, how great is your judgment upon us! The moans of the wounded, the fear and the fright of the others cry up to Heaven.*

> **Mon., 19 Feb.**— *Today some more trvelers* [his term for the Trekkers] *fleeing from the veldt drew into our laager. Pitiful was the sight and the bitter groaning of the wounded women and children, who have remained half-dead in life.*

> **Wed., 21 Feb.** — [...] *The Potgieters and G*[ert] *Rudolph were here to hold a meeting with the people on what the company should do under these circumstances.*

He relates how he spent his nights praying to God for dry weather in case Zulu were to attack again. Of course, their muskets were hugely unreliable in wet weather. He also traveled back and forth between the sub-laagers, doing service at the Potgieter-Du Plessis laager where our ancestor, Chris Jordaan, was camped. By late March, they had regained some of their stability. One of Smit's entries from this month is fascinating:

Thursday, 22 Mar.— [...] The patrol of the Du Plessis laager [where our family was] has captured two of Dingane's spies, who said that our Governor P. Retief and all [his] men were killed without them having their weapons with them, but that they had defended themselves with their pocket knives and had killed many Kaffirs; and that Dingane had let them all be killed, because the hon. P. Retief had not brought Sekonyela's head. One of the spies reported that there were no more Kaffirs on our side of the river, but that they have all gone back to Dingane, with some stolen cattle, and had said to him that they cannot fight against the horse- and fire people.

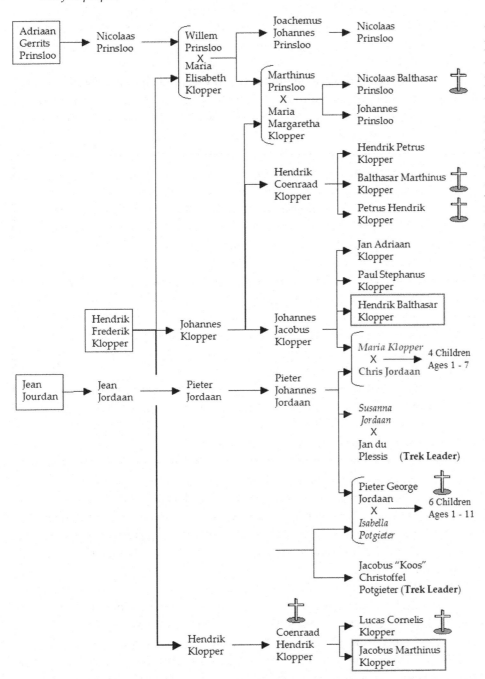

On 23 March 1838, they were visited by Robert Dunn of Port Natal, who also visited Maritz. This is clearly the visit during which the matter of an attack by the Port Natal English on Dingane was discussed. With Dunn was a certain John Stubbs. The problem is that Stubbs was one of Gardiner's supporters. It is less than clear whether the Trekkers realized this. Whether them knowing would have made any difference is also not clear.

By this time, all the Englishmen and Americans in Natal were gathered in Port Natal for the end game to Gardiner's intrigues. On 28 March, the Trekkers decided to make Piet Uys General Field-Commandant for the war that had to follow. On 2 April, they moved right up to a tributary of the Blaauwkranz River, directly across from the "Double" Laager, which included the wagons of Chris Jordaan under leaders Koos "Greatfoot" Potgieter and Jan Du Plessis. Their laager now had 80 wagons and 100 men.

Fig. 11-9 *The Jordaan-Klopper-Prinsloo family losses on the Great Trek*

On 6 April, the "Punishment" Commando set out against Dingane under Piet Uys, after a blessing by Erasmus Smit. Hendrik Potgieter, who had arrived from the far side of the Vaal River to help the people in

Natal, also went out on this Commando with his men. They had split command. One would have thought that Potgieter, who had won three battles against the Matabele (who were Zulu-based), would be made leader of this effort, but the vote of 28 March had been for Uys. This split would prove fatal. Also on the same Commando were Jan du Plessis and Koos Potgieter, and one would assume that the men from their trek are with them. The assumption is that Chris Jordaan is somewhere in among these men. However, on the 10th of April a very ill Jan du Plessis returned to the laager with two unnamed others.

On 10 April, 17 Englishmen and some 3000 Zulus, being refugees from Dingane, set off up the coast of Natal. A large number of these Zulu were armed with guns. They were to proceed up the coast to the Tugela and attack Dingane from there. This effort was intended to be coordinated with the Afrikaner Trekker assault. However, no real mechanism existed to truly coordinate the efforts. And that is when two messengers rode in from the battlefront with the terrible news that the Commando had failed at Italeni and had been defeated by the Zulu! Their new leader, Piet Uys, had been lured into an ambush and killed. He had managed to extract some of his men from the ambush, but could not save himself. His brave young son, Dirk, had turned and galloped to his father's side, and they had both died. The total death toll was eleven. We turn to the account written by Jacobus Boshof[41] in *The Grahamstown Journal*, 9 August 1838:

"Uys gallantly rushed in among the enemy with a mere handful of men and drove a whole regiment before him; but, on returning to join the rest of his men, another large body of Zulus, who had concealed themselves in the gullies on each side of him, rushed upon him and his few brave followers, and killed seven of them. By this time Potgieter had begun to retreat, and Uys and his son, a youth of about fourteen years of age, had as yet escaped unhurt; but as the former stopped his horse to sharpen the flint of his gun the enemy approached and threw an assegai at him, which wounded him mortally in the loins.

He, however, pulled out the weapon, and after this he even took up another man, whose horse was knocked up, behind him; but he soon fainted from loss of blood. Recovering again, he was held on his horse for some distance by a man on each side of him. At length he said he felt his end approaching, and desired to be laid on the ground. He then said to his son and the other men about him: 'Here I must die. You cannot get me any further, and there is no use to try it. Save yourselves, but fight like brave fellows to the last, and hold God before your eyes'.

They here left him, but not before they saw that to remain longer on the spot would be certain death to them. After galloping for about a hundred yards, the younger Uys, looking round, saw the enemy closing round his dying father in numbers, and at the same time he perceived his father lifting up his head. This was too much for the feelings of the lad: he turned round his horse, and alone rushed upon the enemy, compelled them to retreat, and shot three Zulus, before he was hemmed in by overpowering numbers and dispatched."

The news was even worse. According to the messengers, Hendrik Potgieter, who had outflanked the Zulu, had refused to go to Piet Uys' aid, though a few of his men disobeyed orders and did try. Over the next several days the Trekkers would accuse Hendrik Potgieter of cowardice. As a result, he took his men and left Natal, consigning to their fate what he considered to be a willful and unthinking heap of people messing around in the wrong place. As it was, he still did not believe in Natal as the realistic goal of the Great Trek. In the end, he would never return to Natal.

During the day of the 13th, the Trekkers remaining at the Double Laager moved the wagons through the river and joined with the Retief people directly across the river in an effort to improve the overall defenses. A few days later, the Trekkers received intelligence from two independent sources that a large group of black people was headed their way to seek safety from Dingane.[42] The Trekkers were having none of that and suspected more treachery from Dingane by such means. We turn to the Rev. Erasmus Smit for a picture of the state of mind of the people. He was beyond despair and diarizes leaving the laager to say a prayer:

Friday 13 Apr. — *[...] My heart was very anxious; I could find few if any words; only broken words, and sigh upon sigh. Oh God! Help, Help, Help; safeguard and protect now our laagers; desert us not; but save and deliver us, in Your name, for the Sake of Christ.*

On 2 May 1838, three of the men who had earlier set off for Port Natal, including the British Settler William Cowie, returned to describe the defeat of the British by Dingane. The English column that had gone up the coast had been completely routed. Of the seventeen Englishmen, only four made it back to Port Natal. Robert Biggar did not return. Nor did Stubbs, Gardiner's understudy. The entire white population of Port Natal had fled onto the brig *Comet* lying in the bay at the settlement[43]. The Zulu had finally driven the British

Fig. 11-10 The Natal-British defeat at the Battle of the Tugela

physically into the sea. They were destroying everything in Port Natal and were running around in the ladies clothes they had plundered.

Alexander Biggar, who had now lost his only two sons in clashes with the Zulu was on board. Also present was William Wood and his mother. William had lost his father and uncle in the battle. Among those sitting on the boat watching the proceedings were the missionary families of the Owens (British) and the Champions (Americans). Champion wrote as follows to his colleague, Aldin Grout[44]:

> *"All at the Point fled on board – women in their night dresses – Brother Owen with scarce anything on."*

And then there was the man who had had such a central hand in the machinations in Natal, Captain Allen Gardiner, and his wife. His entire mission in Africa lay in tatters and it was possibly entirely of his own making. After this, he would leave South Africa altogether and go to South America to try his hand at the natives of Patagonia in the Tierra del Fuego Islands. He would go there with an under-supplied and badly organized party. There he would eventually die slowly of starvation on the beach of a miserable island; a hugely tragic end for a man who had presumably tried to do well, but whose religious zeal always seemed to turn too quickly to political intrigue and power play.

Erasmus Smit records in his diary on 2 May the three men from Port Natal, including the Englishman William Cowie, reporting that Captain Gardiner hadearlier responded to an enquiry from Dingane that the king should do with the Trekkers what he would normally do with his own absconded subjects. To the savage Dingane, that meant killing the Trekkers, and Gardiner knew that full well.

Smit has a particularly picturesque way of describing the result for Gardiner:

> *"But here God was Judge! Captain Carner is fled into the sea..."*

The "Israelites in the Desert"

The trekkers were now consolidated in what would eventually become known as Modder Laager (Mud Laager). They were now full 500 wagons together. Over the next few months they would move from Modder Laager, because it was too wet and muddy for them to grow any crops. They would move first to Saai Laager (Sow Laager) where they could actually grow some crops, and then from there to a place they called Gats Laager (Hole Laager). They truly were the "Israelites in the Desert," moving around without entering their "Canaan." On 7 May, one hundred and fifty men with 26 wagons left for Port Natal to fetch whoever might be left at Port Natal and to obtain what supplies might be had from there.

Nexus Familia 60: And in the middle of it all... a child

On 20 April 1838, while the deeply despairing Trekkers roll into the rain-soaked Modder Laager (Mud laager) with their wagons, struggling to emotionally process all the shocking losses against the monster of Umgungundlovu, a new little face appears in Chris Jordaan's wagon in Koos Potgieter's trek. As the third son, the baby boy is to get his father's full name: Christoffel Johannes Petrus Jordaan. He is the fifth child of what will eventually be no fewer than fifteen. The Rev. Erasmus Smit will baptize him and write in his diary for the recorded baptism date five months later:

> *Sunday, 16 Sep.* — *In the morning the minister*[45] *preaches before a very large congregation in the laager of the Hon. Commandant Jacobus Potgieter; and baptizes 11 children.*

—End Nexus Familia

Nexus Familia 61: Trichardt—*All has been in vain*

When the little Trichardt Trek, now composed of 52 surviving members, trudges wearily into Delagoa Bay, they have been out of touch with civilization for two full years. The Portuguese Governor is hospitality itself, but these people are weary beyond all description. They have just done the impossible: They have covered one thousand miles of Africa in areas where no white man has gone before. However, they are almost all ill. If any mosquitoes have spared them thus far, the pestilential swamp that is Delagoa Bay now ensures that they all get malaria. One after the other they start to succumb. On 1 May 1838, Martha Trichardt, our ancestral sister, dies. Louis Trichardt dutifully records her last conversations in his diary and it is deeply moving[46]:

> *"Then I saw that my foreboding was all too true—that I would never see her well again. From that moment such sorrow took possession of me that I did not know what to do or say. The children wept with me and this made me all the more grief-stricken. I bade her farewell in this life, but thought to see her again in the Home of the Heavenly Father, and I did not reproach Him, but prayed to Him to come to my aid: The will of the Lord must be done. All our trouble and care has been in vain.*
>
> *About eleven o'clock the Almighty God took her away. I place my firm trust in Him, and I know that my dear love has entered into salvation. Nevertheless I am not consoled. Sorrow so overpowered me, that I nearly lost my senses. The Lord[47] and his wife did their best to console me, but for me there is no solace on this Earth.[...]*
>
> *My loving and precious troth has forever been taken from me."*

The tough, intrepid and wise Louis Trichardt leaves this world just less than six months later. His son Carolus now leaves on a journey of exploration of his own that will take him to all manner of places in East Africa as far as Ethiopia in search of a possible home for the Afrikaners, the forsaken amaBhulu, the White Tribe of Africa. Some insist that he is the first white man to see the Victoria Falls, many years before David Livingstone will presume that status. He returns through Mozambique and the Eastern South African Lowveldt and stumbles upon the bones of the lost Van Rensburg trek, of which Nicolaas Balthasar Prinsloo (*NF 44, 46*) was a member. He had survived Slagtersnek (*NF40*) to die like this.

—End Nexus Familia

Making a stand — Veg Laager

On Monday, 13 August 1838, while the Trekkers were encamped at Gats Laager on the Bushman's River, only just south of the present Estcourt in Natal, a 10,000 man Zulu impi was making its way toward them across the Tugela, this time with guns and horses. A lot of men were away at the time with the livestock in the Drakensberg and the camp had only 75 men of whom only two were Field-Commandants and two Field-Cornets. Two of them were Koos "Greatfoot" Potgieter and Jan Du Plessis, the two leaders of the Double Trek, of which our ancestor Chris Jordaan was part. Anna Steenkamp, whom we have consulted before, was there and we turn to her for a first hand description:

[...] *"we had but a few men of fighting age in our laager and the heathen could have easily overrun us, had God so wished it. Now you must think, my dear children, in what fear we women were when we saw the attack of the enemy—the largest part of the women were widows and orphans—because we could not believe that so few people could achieve a victory, but the Lord strengthened us and weakened the enemy.*

The Kaffirs charged on us in a ring until within firing range. Then they came in two points[48], so that our men were forced to position behind one another to shoot the enemy away; first on the one and then on the other corner of the laager. We had positioned our cannon such that they could not break in. The Kaffirs kept us busy for two days and two nights, and shot at us all the time, though none of us had any wounds from their bullets. [...]

We thanked God unanimously for sparing our lives, except for the loss of one man, who was murdered while out with his sheep."

For the specifics of the actual battle we turn again to our ever observant young on-the-spot "reporter," Nicolaas Roets, with his quaintly apt mixed tenses:

At daybreak we saw them coming across the heights. A few were mounted on horses they had taken from Maritz's murder[49] and some also had guns which they had got there, but most were on foot. They came to within 1000 paces of the laager and then sat down on their haunches for a few hours, made food and watched us. The people had already pulled together the wagons the previous day and had dragged branches everywhere between the wheels and in the openings and had tied these with thongs and chains so that the Kaffirs could not pull them out.

In the middle of the laager were placed four wagons with a huge sail over them to stop the assegais and in this all the women and children were supposed to go, and when the Zulu approached, we were all ordered to go into these central wagons; but many of the women refused and stood behind the other wagons to assist the helpers in loading the guns. I could see well where I was and I could clearly see the Zulu against the slope where they were watching us. They were all naked except for belts with riempies [leather strips] and they carried small shields, not the big ones.

By nine-'o-clock their captains start to blow on bone whistles and there all the thousands of Kaffirs jump up and charge down upon the laager from all sides - the Earth vibrates from all the feet as they come and many dance and make high leaps in the air while they come. Very soon they were close up and our people start to shoot at them from all sides. I did not stay in the central wagon but went forward to see. They charge right up to the wagons and then throw their assegais and yank at the branches or try to climb over and to get into the laager, but everywhere they are shot down terribly, we can almost not see from all the smoke, and the women throw rocks at them when they see that one is standing on the branches. Within a few minutes it was colored black with volk[50] around the laager, very many were dead and wounded. There is such a noise from the guns and from the screaming of the Kaffirs that the helpers inside the laager have huge problems to keep the horses from breaking out due to them being panicked by the noise.

After the first assault, when the Kaffirs see that they cannot break through and are being killed terribly, they flee a distance back but, before they have gone far the captains blow on the bone whistles again, and there they turn around and charge the laager again, running as fast as they can. They are shining from sweat, and scream and make a noise and dance, but they cannot break through into the laager, the men are shooting them dead too much and there is a black ring lying around as they have been hit, because our people are shooting with slugs, six to a pound, so that sometimes four and five Kaffirs are hit by one shot and however they throw with their "arrows"[51], and however they make a noise and try to get over the wagons, they do not get past, they are killed everywhere. They keep charging and retreating and charging again when the captains blow on the bone whistles, and so they did until the afternoon and then they fled up the heights where they sat and rested by the thousands, but this day they did not again come to us. The Kaffirs stayed there the whole afternoon and slept there, so that no one could leave the laager and the whole night we heard the moans and groans in the grass where there were wounded who were not taken away, but most of the wounded Kaffirs were taken away by their friends.

Early the next morning they are still there and we see how they are making food and are watching us. After a while, there is the blowing on the whistles and they charge us again, screaming and dancing like yesterday. They again get to the wagons and try hard to drag the branches away but our men stand fast and shoot them dead awfully. They retreat and charge a few times and then they fled earlier than yesterday and went and sat down on their haunches about 500 paces away to rest outside the range of our "Sannas" [muskets]. After that, they charge one more time and this time they came with the greatest force of all, but they could not make it – they now flee back up to the heights and do not start again this day. A few have guns from the murdered people, but they are stupid and shoot only a few rounds. We also saw that one of the horses they had stolen lay dead near the laager and the saddle was on back-to-front on the back and the rear cinch is fastened around the chest.

Fig. 11-11 *The women loaded the heavy muskets*

The entire afternoon we are still surrounded by the volk and they sleep around the laager and the following day they attack us twice, but they no longer have the same faith and they flee earlier than the previous day and it is no wonder, because surprisingly many Kaffirs are dead, but now they flee over the heights and we cannot see them anymore.

A patrol saddles up and an opening is hacked in the branches in one corner of the laager and the men ride out to see where the Kaffirs have gone. They report that the volk have gone in the direction of their land and now the laager is opened so that we can go out to see the dead Kaffirs lying in a ring around the wagons. There were also many wounded Kaffirs, legs and arms off or with slugs in the body, and these our men all killed. There was one lightly wounded creature who told one of the laager how it went with the murder of Retief; and he says there was a Missionary at the city of Dingane when Retief was there the first time and while he [Retief] was away to fetch the cattle from the Makatees Captain [Sekonyela], the Missionary said to Dingane that he must watch out for Retief and his men; they are just deserters and the English still want to have them captured, and thereupon Dingane got the idea to kill them. He tells that, when Retief and his men were inside the kraal, Dingane let his fighting Commando dance and then he stuck his head under his karos[52] and called out something and then the creatures started murdering the people.

Almost all our livestock had been sent away to the Drakensberg before the attack so that the Kaffirs could not steal them and so we now had to stand there with the wagons among all the dead Kaffirs until the oxen could be fetched. The oxen only came on the eighth day when the smell from the corpses was already unbearable, but meanwhile we obtained some cattle from Gert Maritz, brother of the late[53] Commandant, who stood on the other side of the Tugela with a few wagons; and so we therefore could get most wagons away before the stink was too unbearable."

Gats Laager was promptly re-dubbed Veg Laager (Fight Laager). However, the Trekkers did decide to relocate further westward to the Little Tugela. Here they surrounded their laager with sods which they dug. For this reason, this laager was renamed Sooi Laager (Sod Laager). It was here, some five weeks later, on 23 September 1838, that the Afrikaner Trekkers lost their last remaining leader of note, Gerrit Maritz. Erasmus Smit was with the redoubtable Trekker when he breathed his last[54] at the young age of 41:

"I prayed with him. He started singing hymn 123, which he kept up until the end"

Gerrit Maritz, the ever-sensible leader from Graaff-Reinet, whose solid leadership had protected his people for so long, was gone. Like Moses, he had seen "the promised land," but would not dwell in it. The Trekkers had lost Piet Retief at Umgungundlovu, and then Piet Uys at Italeni and now Gerrit Maritz. They had estranged Hendrik Potgieter and he had left them. The entire Great Trek was in jeopardy. However, Gerrit Maritz had sent to the East Cape for one of his old friends.

A new natural leader was headed for Natal. And he would serve them very well indeed.

 ## Nexus Familia 62: The name lives on

Maria van Dyk, wife of our murdered ancestral cousin Reynier Grobler, is now a pregnant widow with her 2-year old Michael in "Sod" Laager. Her sister, Susanna, and brother in law, Reynier Grobler, together with all four their children have been slaughtered by the Zulu Impi during the Blaauwkranz Massacre. When Maria finally delivers the baby, it is a boy.

Maria sees a parallel between the fate of her late husband, who was murdered on Kwa Matiwane by the unbelieving Zulu, and the first Christian martyr, Stephen, who was dragged to the gates of Jerusalem and stoned to death by those who would not believe. She therefore named the young man Reynier Nicolaas Johannes Stephanus Grobler for his martyred father and for the Biblical Stephen. And, he shall one day live a free man in the independent country that his father died finding.

—End Nexus Familia

God save the Queen!

As to any succor from the Cape Colony, it may best be judged based on the following. On September 10, 1838 the latest British Governor at the Cape, George Napier, issued the following proclamation[55]:

By His Excellency Major-General GEORGE THOMAS NAPIER, C.B., Governor and Commander-in-Chief of Her Majesty's Castle, Town, and Settlement of the Cape of Good Hope, in South Africa, and of the Territories and Dependencies thereof, and Ordinary and Vice-Admiral of the same, Commanding the Forces etc., etc., etc.

By virtue of the authority in me vested, I do hereby proclaim and make known […]

… not to permit or suffer the exportation or shipment of any goods whatsoever to any port or place between the mouth of the Great Fish River and Delagoa Bay, both places inclusive; […]

… nor to permit or suffer any gunpowder, firearms, or other munitions of war, to be exported coastwise to any place within the colony.

And whereas the schooner or vessel called the "Mary" is now lying in the harbor of Port Elizabeth, on her voyage to port Natal, having on board certain quantities of gunpowder, lead, firearms, and other munitions of war, destined for Port Natal, the Sub-Collector at Port Elizabeth and his assistants are hereby authorized and required to cause the said gunpowder [etc.] to be landed at Port Elizabeth before said vessel shall be allowed to proceed on her voyage.

GOD SAVE THE QUEEN!

Given under my hand and seal, at Cradock, the 10th day of September, 1838
(signed) GEORGE NAPIER

By His Excellency's command,
(Signed) H. Hudson
Secretary to Government

-----ooOoo-----

12

The Covenant

..."*should the Lord be pleased to grant us the victory, we would raise a house to the memory of His great name [...] to make it known even to our latest posterity, in order that it might be celebrated to the honor of God.*"

Jan Bantjes, scribe to Afrikaner Cmdt Gen Andries Pretorius,
On the first Church Service reciting the Covenant, 9 December 1838

Fig. 12-1 The Battle of Blood River

Ncome – The River of Blood

On 22 November 1838, there was great commotion in Sooi Laager. A large man, heavily armed, and with a sword on his side, arrived at the head of a column of 60 armed horsemen and a bronze cannon. New hope was at hand for the Voortrekkers in the form of Andries Pretorius. He had been a successful farmer in the Graaff-Reinet district and had led an 800-man Commando into the 6th Frontier War in support of Harry Smith. Here was a man born not only to lead, but who somehow also commanded respect with his persuasive approach. Three days after his arrival he was elected Commandant-General and two days later he led the Commando out of the encampment to deliver a knock-out blow against Dingane. Having gathered all the intelligence on the various Zulu attacks, and studied the tactics in detail, the Trekkers were ready to face off with the Zulu.

Most history books do not give the Trekkers suitable credit for their preparation. They clearly did their homework and Pretorius worked on the discipline of the entire operation. By now, the "horns of the bull" tactic of the Zulu had been analyzed and was understood. Their canny schemes to lure commandos into ambushes were now also understood. At Veg Laager, the Zulu had shown that they were incompetent in the use of both guns and horses, though by now they had a considerable number of both. It was also clear that, unlike the Xhosa, the Zulu did not primarily use their assegais as long distance throwing weapons, but rather as stabbing weapons for close-quarters combat.

It was clear that they used their less experienced troops as the "cannon fodder" in the two "horns of the bull," while their most experienced and fiercest warriors were held back to form the central head of the bull. The men in the different sections had differently colored shields. They had men to waste, and waste them they certainly did in the horns of the bull. It was also clear that the Zulu were hugely motivated, incredibly brave and savagely fierce fighters.

Lastly, military leaders like Zulu Generals Ndlela and Dambuza were not to be trifled with. These were competent military strategists and tacticians who could only be defeated by good plans, as the British would discover to their everlasting shock forty years later. In short, the Zulu Army was a serious army that had to be treated like a serious army and would have to be fought like a formal army with formal strategies and tactics; no savage rabble here. By now, it was clear why the Zulu Army had been considered invincible by all its opponents.

To address such a formidable foe, the likes of which Western Man had not faced in formal battle before, Pretorius realized he had to do a few specific things. He had to drum some discipline

Fig. 12-2 Andries Pretorius

into his own burghers while choosing the field of battle to frustrate the "horns of the bull" formation, which split the Trekker firepower. He also had to avoid close-in fighting and make it possible to switch rapidly from defense to attack. He needed to make sure he had enough men and enough help loading the guns. Previous commandos had tended to be too small to be effective against the well-oiled and experienced Zulu War Machine. He needed firepower, considering the Zulu now categorically had guns and had started learning to use them.

Even before Pretorius' arrival, the Trekkers had decided that scurrying around for branches to strengthen the laagers was both inefficient and dangerous. So they constructed wooden shooting frames which might be used to more efficiently and rapidly reinforce the laager. Erasmus Smit refers in his diary to Commandant Koos "Greatfoot" Potgieter making two of these on 18 October 1838, more than a month before the arrival of Pretorius. These shooting frames could be transported on the sides of the wagons. A total of 64 wagons were prepared for this campaign. The time for heroics was over. It was time for clear thinking, good planning, solid discipline, and smooth execution.

This Commando consisted of some 460 men. Alexander Biggar from Port Natal joined with some 100 of his anti-Dingane Zulu, armed with guns. Then there were still other helpers. Many of the men we have met thus far were in this Commando. They included Pretorius himself, Koos "Greatfoot" Potgieter, Jan Du Plessis, Hendrik Fick with young Leech, and Gert Rudolph with Grietjie, the cannon. Our various English-speaking Afrikaners[1] were also there, including Thomas Jervis Biddulph and William Cowie. Also with them were Edward Parker, recently arrived in Natal from Grahamstown, Robert Joyce and a certain J. Johnston. Pretorius explained carefully that this campaign was not about revenge, but rather to secure a lasting peace with the Zulu. Also, they were not to harm women and children. However, it is difficult to believe that the 28 men who had lost immediate family to the Zulu saw it the same way. One of them was Alexander Biggar, who had now lost both his sons to the Zulu.

Lost in thought in the column were Abraham Joubert, Sybrandt van Dyk and Daniel du Preez, all three of whom had lost almost their entire extended families in the Zulu attacks on the laagers at Blaauwkranz.

Nexus Familia 63: The Battle of Blood River

When the Commando rolls out of camp on 27 November 1838, it is with just over 330 white men and a number of outriders of mixed descent. The leadership is Andries Pretorius and Commandants Piet Jacobs, Koos "Greatfoot" Potgieter and Jan Du Plessis (*NF59*), Hans de Lange, and Stephanus Erasmus. They are traveling with 64 wagons, some 900 cattle, 500 horses and two little cannon. One of these is again the redoubtable Grietjie. The wagons move in 4 parallel rows of 16 wagons each over the open African grassland to ensure that the rows are short, thereby giving the Zulu little chance for splitting the force in an ambush. Both ends of the train are solidly protected by horsemen.

Like the other men, Abraham Joubert (*NF59*) is put through the process of drawing up the laager every single night and being posted as watch. The shooting frames are taken down from the wagons and chained between the wheels of the wagons, as well as between wagons themselves. These are designed with vertical members, spaced to prevent a Zulu from crawling through, but still wide enough to easily fire through. During the day, they hold exercises, divided into their Field-Cornetcies.

Andries Pretorius has insisted on strict discipline and is brooking no dissent or debate about what is to happen. He clearly believes that military discipline is required in this venture. As the men are sick to death of losing against the Zulu, they fall in line with this. This is true also for Abraham. The result is a remarkable discipline among these 330 difficult and fractious frontier farmers.

When they reach the Klip (Stone) River, they are joined by Karel Landman from Port Natal with a further 123 Trekkers, along with Alexander Biggar and his roughly 100 armed anti-Dingane Zulus. With them come Edward Parker and Robert Joyce. By 5 December 1838, they are at Elandslaagte (Eland Downs). Here a patrol by Hans De Lange runs into a formation of Zulu. When Pretorius goes after the Zulu with a 300-man detachment, the Zulus have disappeared. Clearly, they are now getting closer to real action. By 8 December, the Commando is at Waschbank (wash bank).

The Covenant

It is on Sunday, 9 December that an event takes place that will sear the coming battle into the souls of all Afrikaners. We turn the narration over to Jan Bantjes, scribe of the Commando[2]:

> *"On Sunday morning, before divine service commenced, the chief commandant called together all those who were to perform that service, and requested them to propose to the congregation 'that they should all fervently, in spirit and in truth, pray to God for His relief and assistance in their struggle with the enemy; that he wanted to make a vow to God Almighty, if they were all willing, that should the Lord be pleased to grant us the victory, we would raise a house to the memory of His great name, wherever it might please him, and that they should also supplicate the aid and assistance of God to enable them to fulfill their vow; and that we would note the day of the victory in a book, to make it known even to our latest posterity, in order that it might be celebrated to the honor of God.*
>
> *Messrs. Cilliers[3], Landman, and Joubert were glad in their minds to hear it. They spoke to their congregations on the subject, and obtained their general concurrence. When after this divine service commenced, Mr. Cilliers performed that which took place in the tent of the chief commandant. He commenced by singing from Psalm XXXVIII, verses 12-16, then delivered a prayer, and preached about the twenty-four first verses of the Book of Judges; and thereafter delivered the prayer in which the before-mentioned vow to God was made, with the fervent supplication for the Lord's aid and assistance in the fulfillment thereof. The 12th and 21st verses of the said XXXVIII Psalm were again sung, and the service was concluded with the singing of the CXXXIV Psalm. In the afternoon the congregations assembled again, and several appropriate verses were sung. Mr. Cilliers again made a speech, and delivered prayers solemnly; and in the same manner the evening was also spent."*

Abraham cannot help but notice that all the "Englishmen" on the Commando participate in the Covenant, but five Afrikaners abstain. Their reason is apparently that they fear the vengeance of God upon their families if ever their descendants were to dishonor the Vow. It also strikes him that Cilliers is a strange fish. He seems to be as keen for a fight as what he is keen to pull out his Bible. Without fail, Sarel Cilliers seems to be where the hardest fight is – a true proponent of "Praise the Lord and pass the ammo."

And then the fog descends

On 11 December, they reach the Buffalo River. Here an allied Zulu reconnaissance team under the leadership of Edward Parker stumbles upon a Dingane Zulu troop and kills one of the enemy. On the 12th, Pretorius again sends out Parker and his Zulu team, along with Hans de Lange. Parker again runs into a group of Zulu and takes captive one Zulu man and some women. The Zulu man tries to attack Parker, who kills him right there and then. Pretorius explains to the women: "*Afrikaners do not kill women and children.*" He gives them a message to take to Dingane:

> "*We have come to punish Dingane, but if Dingane is ready to cooperate, then we are prepared to consider peace. However, if Dingane prefers to fight, then he must realize that the whites will not give in, even if it takes ten years.*"

Pretorius signs his name on a white cloth to prove the authenticity of the message, gives it to the women, and they are sent off to Dingane.

Matters now escalate. On 13 December, the Commando sees a group of Zulu with a large herd of cattle. This "smells" just like the kind of lure that fooled Piet Uys at Italeni. On the 14th, Pretorius and 120 men go out to investigate and encounter some Zulu, some of whom are killed. The Trekkers, however, refuse to be drawn into the kind of ambush that the opposing general, Dambuza, excels at.

On Saturday 15 December, the Commando crosses the Buffalo River into distinct Zulu territory and stops at the Ncome River. Having reconnoitered some distance ahead, Pretorius instructs his men to draw up a laager in a very specific spot. Meanwhile, a reconnaissance party consisting of Hans Hattingh and Jan Robbertse reports that a massive Zulu army of some 15,000 men is half-an-hour by horse away from the Commando. The Great Moment has come. Dambuza and Ndlela have realized that the Trekkers cannot be drawn into another ambush. It is time for a straight fight.

While 150 men, specifically trained for the job, rapidly put up the shooting frames, Pretorius leads 300 men and his cannon to confront the Zulu. He splits his men into groups of fifty and parades them fifty yards apart for the Zulu to clearly see. Now it is Dambuza who will not be drawn. He is likely waiting for more of his army to arrive. Pretorius thereupon returns to the now ready laager.

Back in the laager, Pretorius orders candles lit on all the wagons, positioned high on long whip rods (See Figures 12-1 and 12-4). Then comes the opportunity for Sarel Cilliers to lead the evening service and repeat the Covenant. The guards are posted as the last reconnaissance troop returns with news that the Zulus are mere hundreds of yards from the laager. Those not on guard duty, go to sleep with their loaded guns by their sides. And then quiet descends upon the laager...and so does the fog!

Abraham is worried indeed. There has lately been fog every evening and night. This kind of damp is very bad for the guns, which use unenclosed dry gunpowder. It also provides the Zulu with cover, allowing them to close unseen with the laager. This negates the major strategic advantage the Trekkers have of a firing range that is much longer than the throwing range of an assegai. The fog is a massive and absolutely deadly disadvantage for the Commando. However, Abraham places his faith in his Covenant, his leader, his newfound discipline, and his shooting skills.

The disposition of the Laager

Abraham notes that Pretorius has chosen the location of their laager absolutely brilliantly. Figure 12-3 shows the disposition of the laager:

With its back to the flooded Ncome River and its one side next to a deep *donga* (erosion gully), it destroys any hope the Zulu have of effecting the famous Horns of the Bull. The Zulu will be forced to cross the river and then attack from the third side of the rough triangle of the laager. This effectively destroys any hope the Zulu have of a flanking movement, herds them neatly into a "killing field," and allows the Trekkers to concentrate their fire within a third of the laager circumference.

Every mechanism that concentrates the Zulu charge is in favor of the Trekkers. The massive shoulder-numbing muskets of the Trekkers are capable of shooting up to almost 3-ounce balls. These can penetrate up to five Zulus in one shot. Similarly, concentrating the Zulu in front of the cannon favors the Trekkers. The placement of the laager will nullify the "horns of the bull" tactic. This makes for a straight fight between the main experienced Zulu troops and concentrated Trekker firepower. Two wagons are in position as gates that can be opened rapidly for horsemen to charge out if the Zulu should falter.

Grietjie and the other cannon have been positioned to face the third side of the laager where the Zulu will be forced to concentrate. The oxen and horses are penned in the middle of the laager. It now becomes clear why 64 wagons have been chosen. This makes the laager the right size to keep the animals inside and gives space for the fighting men. The mistake of stranding the animals outside will not be made again. That lesson was learnt the hard way at Vegkop in 1836. For this reason alone, the Trekker Force has to be a certain minimum size, that size being fundamentally determined by the length of a wagon and the number of oxen needed to draw it; namely at least ten per wagon.

The area inside the laager is proportional to the square of the number of wagons. There is no way that twenty wagons can be circled to keep the required minimum of 200 draught oxen inside the circle and still leave space for the men to load, fight and keep the powder safe. However, a ring of 64 wagons can easily hold 900 oxen and 500 horses with suitable space. They also do not have to worry about any Zulu yanking out thorn tree branches anymore. They now have the chained shooting frames in position, which deny the Zulu access but provide a clear view for shooting. They have designed a reconfigurable mobile wooden fortress.

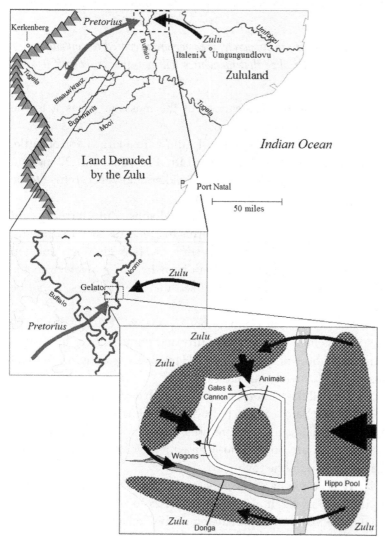

Fig. 12-3 Blunting the Horns of the Bull at Blood River

Abraham now feels a lot more confident. A lot of thought has gone into this campaign. Elsewhere in the laager, Hendrik, brother of our ancestor Maria Klopper, is lost in his own thought as he cleans his two Sannas. Tomorrow shall be the watershed, and he shall live or he shall die.

Dawn, December 16, 1838 on the Ncome River

Two hours before dawn, all the men are up and ready for the inevitable battle. Amazingly, the Zulu have not attacked during the night when they may have had the advantage. Abraham whispers a small prayer of thanks heavenward for this.

And then the first miracle happens. As the rays of the sun creep out from behind the hills in the East, the fog lifts! Abraham is convinced that this is a sign of Divine Intervention. The sight revealed is awe inspiring. Facing the laager are thousands upon thousands of Zulu warriors, the closest no more than 40 yards from the laager. They extend a thousand yards deep, arranged in rows in their regiments under their *indunas* (captains). They are all watching for the order from generals Dambuza and Ndlela. The discipline of these warriors is incredible; awesome. The moment is Shakespearean.

Says Jan Bantjies, Trekker scribe, looking from inside the laager:

"Their approach provided (though awful in view of the great force) a beautiful sight; they approach by regiment, each captain with his men behind him (so the patrols had also seen them coming the previous day) until they had surrounded us."

But, Dambuza is a worried man. He has failed to get his entire army in position in time before daybreak. He has a lot more men, but they are being hamstrung. The Ncome River is in full spate. Pretorius apparently realizes this and gives the order for a few rounds to be fired by all guns and by the cannon. All hell breaks loose as the giant Sanna smooth bore elephant guns with their four foot eight inch barrels roar from the shoulders of more than 300 Dutch-French-German descended Trekker "giants," spewing blue-white acrid smoke, which blots out the view. Grietjie also growls defiantly as she belches a huge cloud of smoke.

As the smoke rises vertically in the still damp air, they can see the Zulu have fallen back and are now arrayed 500 yards from the laager. The veldt in front of the laager is strewn with the dead and dying. Grietjie has cut a wide swathe through the *impi* [army or regiment]. But new reinforcements are joining the warriors now sitting in the distance beyond the useful range of the guns. The Zulu indunas have tested the fire by sacrificing many dozens of men. They now know that the Trekkers will fire at 40 yards and that they are safe beyond 500 yards. There are between 10,000 and 15,000 of them facing the 460 emigrant farmers, their English friends from Port Natal, their Khoekhoe and freed slave helpers, and some 100 refugee Zulu soldiers inside a ring of wagons. One is reminded of Thermopylae, but will this be a similar last stand?

Abraham can hear how the indunas are shouting orders in the distance. He can see the Zulu breaking the shafts of their assegais to make short stabbing weapons. The time has come.

The first charge

Then an unearthly rattling sound starts up. The Zulu are rattling their assegais against their shields as they work themselves up for the charge. And that's when the shouts of the indunas are heard, ordering the charge. The sound of many thousands of barefooted Zulu charging is like muted thunder. They whistle and shout and dance and leap high in the air as they come at full speed. It is a sight designed to shake the faith of the most steadfast soul. Abraham grins reassuringly at his younger brother, Jan, nearby. And then, rising over the din, he hears the voice of the redoubtable Sarel Cilliers, the man who has married the Bible and the gun like none other before:

"Here they come! Keep God before your eyes and do not be afraid! This day shall be ours! Wait until you see the whites of their eyes and make every shot count."

A strange calm descends on Abraham. Through the carefully set sight on his Sanna he sees the battle-crazed face of a Zulu warrior charging straight at him. He lowers the aim a tad and fires. As he

Fig. 12-4 The bronze Blood River monument near Dundee. Note the shooting frames on the furthest wagons

pulls the trigger he hears the distinctive double report of the gun, as first the cock of the gun strikes and then the powder ignites. The Zulu disappears for a second or two behind a cloud of gun smoke. No fewer than five Zulu have been dropped by his single round. He hands back the musket and his helper places his other Sanna firmly in his hand, before starting the process of efficiently reloading the first. He hears shouting behind him. Some men have run over to the corralled animals and are controlling them by firing their weapons. The animals have been spooked by all the noise. If they should break loose and stampede, it would be the end of the Trekkers.

The Zulu flanking movement

A huge number of General Ndlela's warriors now enter the *donga* (See Figure 12-3) in order to get as close as possible to the laager while out of the line of fire. However, this means they have to stand on one another's shoulders to climb out and attack under fire.

Pretorius sends Sarel Cilliers out of the laager to stand his men on the rim of the donga and annihilate Ndlela's troops there. The men are firing almost point blank into the donga. Ndlela must have thought the Trekkers would stay in the laager some yards from the *donga* and never come out. Pretorius also orders a cannon out to fire into the *donga*. Within minutes they have killed 400 Zulu in this natural trench. The survivors at the eastern end of the donga flee into the hippo pool in the river and those on the western end now join Dambuza's men. It is during this shooting at the donga that Philip Fourie is hit in the thigh by an assegai. He is carried off the field.

Fig. 12-5 Grietjie in the Voortrekker Monument

It takes Abraham a minute to understand Pretorius' logic. While the *donga* might very well be a "turkeyshoot," it is a distraction from the main battle, and Pretorius needs the Zulu as concentrated as possible in that central area. That way the Sannas and cannon can do the most damage.

The impi now retreats to the 500 yard line. There they sit down on their haunches and stare at the laager. And then Abraham sees a sight that is simply amazing. The ringheads[4] are calmly taking their snuff! *Snuff!* The martial culture of the amaZulu is something simply incredible. This is quite possibly the most disciplined, the most brave, and the most death-defying army the world has

The Ghost in the Gun Smoke

This situation does not suit Pretorius at all, though. He wants the Zulu in the killing field. So he sends out his own brother, Bart Pretorius, along with a handful of men and an interpreter. They proceed toward the Zulu and then Abraham hears the shout from the little knot of Trekkers in front of the massive Zulu army:

"We have come to fight men, not women and children!"

In response to this, the entire Zulu army hisses in anger. This is the most profound insult one can inflict on a Zulu. One does not ever equate a Zulu man to a woman. For this insult people are going to most assuredly die today. Incredibly, the discipline of the impi holds, and indeed all they do is hiss. Then the party fires a few shots in the direction of the Zulu. Still there is no reaction. Unbelievable! This Zulu Army is truly a thing of wonderment. As barbarous as they may be, they are something incredible to behold. One cannot but have total respect for them. In fact, it is an honor to fight against them.

Abraham just stares at the Zulu in quiet wonderment. When he looks to his side, he sees young Leech and Fick nearby. They are staring open-mouthed at this sight. The Englishmen Biggar, Joyce and Parker seem to be in their element. This is a day for men among men. They will tell their grandchildren about this day;

that is if they live. If Abraham were a learned man, he might have recited Shakespeare's version of Henry V's address before the Battle of Agincourt, but he is only a man begging God for a country where he might have some say in his destiny.

Andries Pretorius breaks the silence by ordering another round from the two little cannon. This gets the attention of the Zulu and the whole impi charges down on the laager again. This is the most concerted attack of the entire battle and it seems to last forever. The Zulu just keep coming and keep coming and keep coming. Each Trekker is now in his own world of smoke and fire and noise and assegais and screaming and whistling. Abraham's two Sannas are getting so hot that he is afraid the powder might self-ignite in his face. And still the Zulu keep coming and keep dying. He can now see the charging Zulu only when they are nearly right on top of him.

He wonders why he is struggling to see; and that's when he realizes that he is crying. He realizes that he is repeating, over and over, ..."*Annie, Kosie, Janneman......Annie, Kosie, Janneman....Annie, Kosie, Janneman...*" He is crying for his murdered wife and children. It is as though a huge weight is rolling off his soul as he aims and shoots. Shot after shot, four or five Zulus per shot. He is not thinking anymore. He has no idea what is going on anymore. He is just aiming and shooting at dim flailing figures in the smoke. The noise is utterly deafening and it is drumming against this head. But he is oblivious to anything and everything. There are just the figures in the smoke and his Sanna. Nothing else matters anymore. He has himself become but a ghost in the gun smoke.

Daniel Bezuidenhout[5], also in the battle, will later write:

"Of that fight nothing remains in my memory except shouting and tumult and lamentation, and a sea of black faces; and a dense smoke that rose straight as a plumb-line upwards from the ground."

And then, suddenly, it is over. As the immense pall of smoke lifts, it is clear that the impi has fallen back and has left thousands of dead and dying in the field. They have been fighting for two hours.

The Trekkers charge

Pretorius is a worried man. The rate at which they have used up ammunition is positively frightening. They simply cannot keep going like this. There is still a huge Zulu Army out there and it does not mind wasting Zulu lives to deplete Trekker ammunition. He therefore takes the initiative and decides to take the battle to the enemy. He orders Bart Pretorius out with roughly half of the men to charge the Zulu. So Bart takes his men between the wagons and the donga and tries to outflank the impi. These men go at the Zulu with all their might.

The frontmost lines of Zulu break under the assault, but run into the experienced men of the White Shields coming up from the back. Bart urges his men to shoot at the bundled Zulu tangled in a disorganized mess. But the Zulu captains are up to the challenge. They turn their men around and here they come again. Now it is Bart's turn to fall back with his men. The horsemen use the opportunity to reload. Then they turn and drive back at the Zulu ranks again, firing with deadly accuracy in the gallop. Again, the Zulu ranks break under the ferocious charge of horses and elephant guns. But again the Zulu rally and charge down on the laager. Two Afrikaner musketeer charges with maximal firepower have failed to break the Zulu impi.

In the laager, Andries Pretorius orders the men to fire with all they have at the charging Zulu. Again, Grietjie and the other cannon belch massive clouds of blue-white smoke and the elephant guns roar from within the laager. Abraham is shooting – loading – shooting – loading – shooting – loading. The nightmare is without end. And this is when Bart Pretorius makes his third charge. This time they penetrate right through the Zulu ranks. He turns around immediately and takes the Zulu army in the back with an almighty charge supported by fire from Grietjie, the homemade cannon. This finally starts breaking up the Zulu lines. Andries Pretorius rolls the two cannon out of the laager to loose a barrage into the front of the Zulu lines. The Zulu have the cannon ahead and the horsemen behind. At this point, they finally break and Bart charges his horsemen in among them and decimates the now disorganized warriors, who are trying desperately to flee.

The Chase

Andries Pretorius calls on another large portion of the Burghers to mount and they sally forth into the retreating Zulu, giving them no respite. This day is about killing as many Zulu warriors as God will tolerate. There is not to be another battle. This is to be the defining battle. It has to be utter victory. The "fire and brimstone" Sarel Cilliers now gets his sections mounted and they set off after the Zulu as well. Dambuza's frustrated regiments on the far side of the river see the failure of the proud Zulu army. They storm through the river to try and take the laager in the back. Some get across the drifts, but others wade right into the fast water. The remaining Trekkers line up to shoot them by the score in the river. Some of the wounded Zulu jump in the water to try and get away that way. In this process, the Ncome River starts to turn red with Zulu blood, thereby providing the river with its future name – Blood River.

The Zulu force is broken. A 15,000-man army is in headlong retreat. Behind them come 460 Trekkers who will hunt them to the end of that day. However, this has been an exceptionally desperate battle and the Trekkers are rapidly running out of ammunition. So it is that Gerrit Raath and one of the Hattingh brothers set off after the Zulu and come upon a wounded warrior. To save ammunition, they want to kill him with his own assegai, but the supposedly wounded Zulu suddenly jumps up and stabs Raath in the back with his assegai. Hattingh sees the fight and grabs the assegai and kills the Zulu. This is only the second assegai wound of the day.

Meanwhile, Andries Pretorius has one single big issue on his mind; he needs to send a message to Dingane and he needs a suitable captive to take that message. He finds a wounded Zulu, but the man stabs at him with his assegai. Pretorius shoots and misses. On the second shot, the gun malfunctions. He jumps off the horse and the Zulu stabs at him again. Pretorius wards off the assegai with the butt of his gun. The third time he has no choice but to ward off the assegai with his left hand and that is when the deadly blade goes right through his hand. Pretorius is a big man and he has the Zulu pinned to the ground, but the Zulu has his hands around Pretorius' neck and is doing his best to choke him to death. This is when Phillip Rudolph notices the one-handed fight, pulls the assegai out of Pretorius' hand, and kills the Zulu with it.

The Aftermath

Late that afternoon, the last dog tired Trekkers return to camp, having chased and shot Zulu all afternoon. It has been an unbelievable day and an epic battle. Strewn around the outside of the laager they count more than 3,000 Zulu dead[6]. Heaven only knows how many Zulu casualties are in the Ncome River, which promptly gets renamed to Blood River. Abraham Joubert is one of the last to return. Joseph van Dyk is with him. The two men do not say much. Having both lost most of their families at Blaauwkranz, they prefer not to talk about what has happened today.

That evening, Andries Pretorius calls the men together for a prayer of thanks led by Sarel Cilliers. Not a single man from the laager has been killed. There are only three assegai wounds, of which Pretorius' is the worst. The men consider this day a clear and irrefutable case of Divine Intervention. The odds were impossible and the result equally improbable.

Afterwards, Pretorius discusses going after Dingane in his capital. The Trekkers totally agree. The reasons are obvious. After all, standing in the group of men are Hendrik Klopper, Abraham Joubert, and the son of Piet Retief, who all lost family to Dingane. It is then also at this point that we say goodbye to Abraham's branch of the Joubert family, as he contemplates an empty future without his loved ones.

—End Nexus Familia

Oh, terrible torture death!

The Battle of Blood River is a seminal event in the history of South Africa. While there would be further battles, this was the defining one. This was the singular day that Western Civilization finally achieved the upper hand in South Africa. In terms of loss of life, it was the biggest battle fought between two nations inside the country in its 186-year history. Proponents of the Divine Intervention viewpoint draw attention to:

1. the lifting of the fog just before the battle;

2. the flood of the Ncome River; and

3. the impossibly light casualties on the Trekker side – three flesh wounds

The success clearly had much to do with good preparation, intimate knowledge of the enemy tactics, exceptionally brilliant placement of the laager, good discipline, and solid tactical leadership. The large slugs fired by the Trekkers also played a defining role. However, the unshakable religious faith of the Trekkers certainly inspired them to persevere in a titanic battle that could easily have gone the other way, as it would so spectacularly and awfully for the British Army at Isandhlwana 41 years later.

In later centuries, there would be increasingly desperate assaults on the history of that day. These assaults would typically take one of three forms:

1. Some will say that it was an "unequal and unfair struggle of spears against guns" and that the outcome was inevitable. Forty-one years later, a three times larger formal British Army, infinitely better equipped, was completely annihilated at Isandhlwana by a similarly sized Zulu Army using the same tactics. How is it then that the result at Isandhlwana was in favor of the Zulu? Over and above this, at Blood River the Zulu had hundreds of guns, which they had taken at Umgungundlovu and from the abortive British assault at the Tugela. They most certainly used those at Blood River. We quote Jan Bantjes[7]:

"The battle then became violent, even the firing from the muskets from our side as well as from theirs"

The total number of Zulu was likely between 10,000 and 15,000 and the number killed likely only just fewer than 3500, if those killed in the chase after the battle are included. In a Cape government notice[8] written by the English Colonial Secretary John Bell on 28 January 1839, he reports:

"It is stated that the camp of the commando was attacked on 16th December by a force of 10,000 Zulus, 200 being armed with muskets...."

2. Some will say it was an "evil massacre" that goes to prove "how evil white men are." The reader is invited to consider the description of the battle above. The Zulu were the attackers. Clearly they did not themselves consider it a massacre; otherwise they would have disengaged early on.

3. Yet others will warp the facts to the point of hilarity. Some high level political figures in South Africa have suggested the battle never even happened at all. An Internet website sponsored by the present South African government even recorded at one point that the Trekkers attacked the Zulu on 16 December 1838. This has caused Afrikaner commentators to muse sarcastically on the concept of "the high speed armored ox wagons of 1838."

The day after the Battle of Blood River, the Commando set off for Umgungundlovu and reached it on 21 December 1838. It was deserted and on fire. Dingane had fled and fired his capital. On this day, the men finally approached Kwa Matiwane, ten months and two weeks after the treacherous murders. Jan Bantjes gives a painful description of the scene of the killings on Kwa Matiwane. There were sticks and spikes lying all along the way the doomed men had been dragged. At each skeleton lay a heap of stones with which the men had been killed. Jan Bantjes, scribe of the Commando, continues in his unique style:

"Oh, terrible torture death! The now dead honorable gentleman Retief we could recognize by his clothing, though perished, pieces were still attached to the bones, together with which there were found other recognizable items, such as his valise, also almost perished, in which were still some papers, of which some were damaged and in pieces, while others were so well preserved, as though they had never been in the open air, among which also the contract between him and Dingane, about the distance of the land, so clean and undamaged as though it had been written this very day, besides a few leaves of clean paper, on one of which the Chief Commandant wrote a letter to J. Boshof the following day. All effort was now made to gather together these bones and to bury the same."

It was none other than Evert Potgieter (See "I say to you, not one of you shall return"), he who had escaped the fate of Retief by virtue of a toothache, who found and certified the document, which had been drawn up in English. It read:

Unkuginslouve[9],
the 4th February, 1838.

Know all men by this - that Whereas Pieter Retief, Governor of the Dutch Emigrant South Afrikans has retaken my Cattle which Sinkoyella had stolen which Cattle he the said Retief now deliver unto me - I Dingaan, King of the Zoolas as here by Certify and declare that I thought fit to resign unto him the said Retief and his countrymen (on reward of the case hereabove mentioned) the Place Called Port Natal together with all the land annexed, that is to say from Dogeela[10] to the Omsoboebo[11] River westward and from the Sea to the North as far as the Land may be usefull and in my possession which I did by this and give unto them for their Everlasting Property.

The mark XXXX of the King Dingaan

As witnesses:	As witnesses:
M Oosthûÿse,	Nwara,
A.C. Greÿling,	Juliwane
B.J Liebenberg	Manondo
	Lords of the
	Great
	Council

An attached certifying document reads:
    a True Copy:
    J. G. Bantjes, J.B Roedeloff

We certify that the annexed contract was found by us, the undersigned, with the bones of Mr. Retief in Dingaan's country, on the 21st day of December, 1838, in a leather hunting-pouch. If required, we are prepared to uphold this by solemn oath.

                    E.F Potgieter

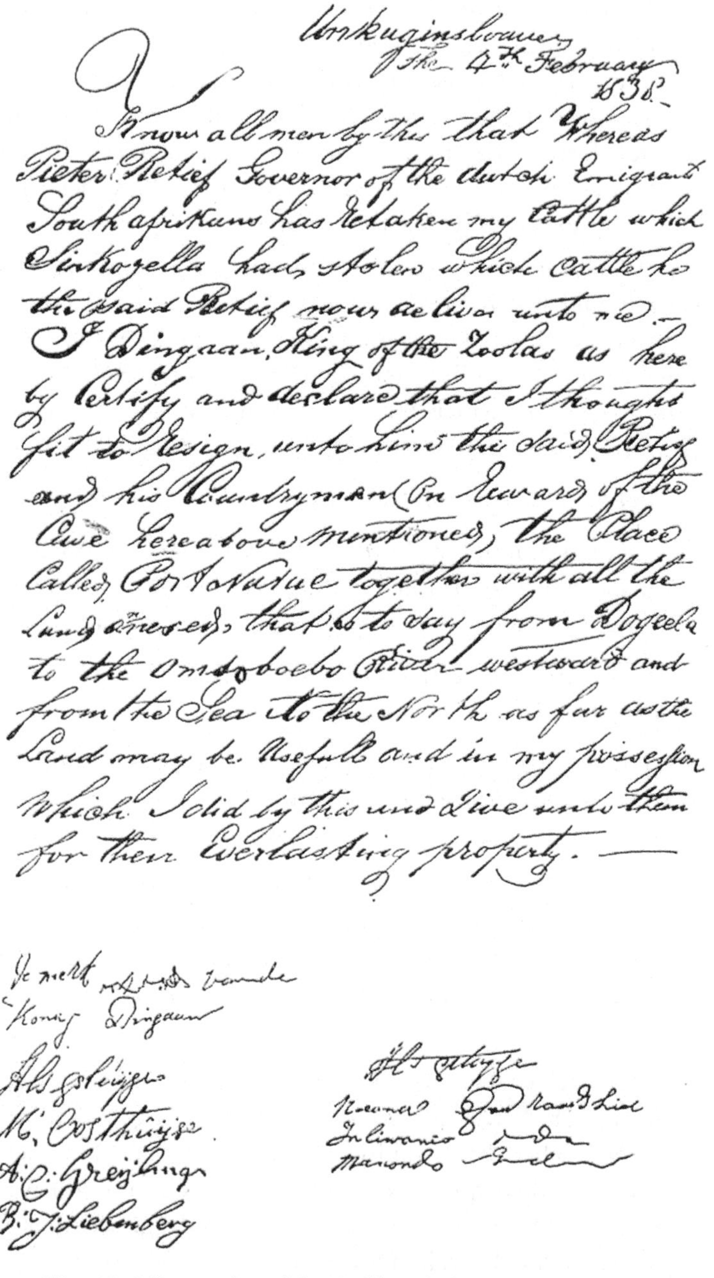

Fig. 12-6 Transcript of the Trekker-Zulu Contract.

On the 27th of December, a Boer Commando sent to investigate Zulu troop movements, became trapped in the valley of the White Umfolozi River and had to fight its way out from among the Zulu. In this process, five Trekkers were killed. It is at this event that Alexander Biggar, the last of the Biggar men, died along with 30 of his 70 or so unmounted free Zulus. He refused to leave them and died with them.

The distinctly English Biggar family had thereby sacrificed every single male of the family in the cause of the Afrikaner. They deserve much more recognition for this. Alexander Biggar's name lives on in the Biggarsberg, which will enter our story again. It is also good to remember the other British descended men who fought so bravely at Blood River, such as Robert Joyce, Edward Parker, William Cowie and young Leech. It is also a fact that enough credit has not been given in history to either the "Coloured" helpers of the Trekkers, or to the anti-Dingane Zulu who had fought valiantly. All of these people had one common goal; the removal of a monstrous tyrant. The victory at Blood River was a clear one of good over evil and did not have racial overtones at the time. Afrikaners see it as a triumph over a treacherous monster. For Afrikaners on the Great Trek and the English from Port Natal it was their very existence that was at stake. For the Free Zulu from Natal it was their liberation from a hated, murderous tyrant.

Given that the Afrikaners and the Zulu had fought each other so hard and so bravely, it is entirely appropriate that it should be an Afrikaner poet, C.M. Van den Heever, who would eventually pen an ode to *The Fallen Zulu Induna* (*Die Gevalle Zulu Indoena*). To the knowledge of the present author, it still remains alone in the world as an ode to a fallen enemy. It stands as a singular mark of mutual respect among brave men:

> *When the Indunas go to battle again, the hills alive with their wild dance, the shields rattle and the assegais flash high in the sun, then you still sleep, then you sleep deeply, your feathers scattered by the sun and the rain,...*

Some have called into question the authenticity of the contract signed by Dingane and maintain that it never existed. They point to its disappearance during the Anglo Boer War as a ruse. The reader may confirm the existence of the agreement as far back as 1852 by the simple expedient of reading the book[12] by The Hon. Henry Cloete, who represented the British Government. He quotes from the contract and then points out:

> *"These are the very words of the original document, which was found still perfectly legible, and was delivered over to me by the Volksraad* [the elected government of the Trekkers] *in the year 1843"*

It is also revealing to read the report[13] of Sarel Cilliers about their discovery at Kwa Matiwane:

> *"We found the corpses about 1,200 yards from Dingaan's dwelling. They had been dragged in one direction. Their hands and feet were still bound with thongs of untanned hide, and in nearly all the corpses a spike as thick as one's arm had been forced into the anus, so that the point of the spike was in the chest! They lay with their clothes still on their bodies."*

The Pharaoh's men arrive

Nothing in the history of the Afrikaner is quite as representative of his fate and experience as the series of events that unfolded on 16 December 1838. While the Trekkers were engaged in their epic battle to break the chokehold of Dingane on the land of Natal, the new British Governor of the Cape, George Napier, made his move. A small expeditionary force of Redcoats that had landed at Port Natal a few days earlier hoisted the Union Jack in the settlement on that very same day.

Napier was a political appointment by the hated and despised Lord Glenelg[14]. Being under the influence of the London Missionary Society, he had been watching the situation of the Trekkers in Natal. He had pointedly decided to move in on the Trekkers. Just in case anyone thought his motives were positive, he explained clearly enough in a letter to Whitehall[15]:

> *"One of my principal motives in taking possession of Natal was to mark my disapproval of the emigrants' proceedings by throwing such impediments in their way as I could."*

An American as Spiritual leader

The Trekkers preferred to ignore Napier's calculated and transparent provocation. They took no action that could strengthen his political hand. As it turns out, the two consecutive British commanders at the post actually had good relations with the Trekkers. In the event, Napier was forced by London to withdraw that unapproved occupation force some 13 months later in January 1840, because the British Government did not want any more extension to the Cape Colony at that point. It already had its hands full. This left Napier smarting badly indeed. When the British left, the Trekkers moved into Port Natal and hoisted their flag.

The little town of Pietermaritzburg had meanwhile been laid out as capital and the Trekkers had duly built the Church of the Vow there, as per the Covenant before the Battle of Blood River. It is at this point that the Trekkers, now Natalians, invited the American Rev. Daniel Lindley to become their minister at Pietermaritzburg. They had got to know him on the way back from the Battle of Mosega. He had shown the Afrikaners that he could ride and shoot and pick a horse as well as they could[16], and therefore they found him imminently acceptable; a man right after their hearts. Given his American upbringing, that was hardly surprising. Lindley understood Boere, because, in essence he was an American "Boer." Eventually, he would found the Dutch Reformed Church in three of the Provinces of the later South Africa.

The end of the Monster

After the Battle of Blood River, a two year period followed in which Dingane attempted to make peace with the Trekkers, using the British officers at Port Natal to intercede with the Afrikaners on his behalf. Captain Jervis did an excellent job of trying to get the two parties together. The trekkers demanded all the livestock Dingane had stolen from them in compensation. This he promised, but did not deliver. Of course the Trekkers would never really trust him in any negotiation again, given what he had done with Retief.

It is important to note that this attitude was purely with respect to Dingane and his two powerful generals, Dambuza and Ndlela (also called Umhlela or Hlela), and not towards the amaZulu as a people of some considerable honor. That the two indunas were key political figures in Dingane's regime is testified to also by Gardiner[17], who had not a care in the world for the Trekkers and opposed them in every possible way.

In October of 1839, Mpande, a son of Senzangakhona, like Dingane and Chaka before him, appeared on the southern side of the Tugela in violation of the treaty agreement that Zulus would keep north of the river. On 15 October of that year, he appeared in person[18] before the *Volksraad* (Council of the Nation) to plead for some land in Afrikaner territory south of the Tugela River in view of the fact that Dingane wanted to murder him. Apparently Dingane had attacked Sobhuza, king of the AmaSwazi, had been defeated, and wanted Mpande to bring reinforcements, because more than half of his men had died. Mpande asked for the land between the Umhlali and Umvoti rivers. This, the Afrikaners allowed him to occupy until such time as he had helped them depose Dingane, at which time he would be expected to go back to Zululand.

Mpande was as good as his word in this respect. From this moment starts a long history of alliance between the Afrikaner and the Zulu.

On 4 January 1840, the Volksraad met and instructed Andries Pretorius to lead a Commando against Dingane to demand the 40,000 head of cattle in restitution as had been agreed via the good offices of Captain Jervis of the British contingent at Port Natal. P.H. Zietsman was the appointed Secretary of War and documented[19] the entire campaign. He reports that, as agreed, Mpande provided his support with several thousand Allied Zulu warriors. Sobhuza, the king of the amaSwazi, sent a deputation of three captains to Pretorius, who told them, clearly playing on Dingane's earlier statement to Retief regarding Sekonyela:

"Well, I grant you peace, but on condition that you bring me Dingane's head!"

Early in the campaign, Pretorius was approached by a minor chief of the Zulu, Matuwane, who asked for some land so that he might be liberated from Dingane. He also wished to join in the fight against the Monster of Umgungundlovu. Soon after, chief Jobe made a request to be considered an ally and also joined the cause. Both Matuwane and Jobe stated that:

"...they only now experience the value of the invariable promises of the white men as allies, they now having no fear to be destroyed, along with their wives and defenseless children..."

They then joined the forces of Mpande and Sobhuza. In this campaign, the general for Mpande's army was Nonkalaza.

The joint forces of Sobhuza, Mpande, Matuwane, and Jobe numbered some 5,000. The Afrikaners were

350. The former would attack from the north and the Afrikaner horsemen would attack from the southeast. Daniel Pieter Bezuidenhout[20], who was on this Commando, reverses the roles of the two wings of the force. He also adds another chief, by the name of Hutsi, who offered alliance. Zietsman says of Matuwane's 450 men, who sang the praises of Pretorius as they marched:

"These men have a beautiful appearance in their parade dress [...] they all marched as regularly as the best drilled regiments."

While the Afrikaners were approaching Dingane's location, the latter sent a deputation in the form of none other than general Dambuza and another officer, Kambazana. Pretorius had no interest in any messages from Dingane anymore and promptly took the two men prisoner, knowing fully well the big role that Dambuza had played in the treacherous killing of the Retief party and the Blaauwkranz massacres.

It was on the 30th of January that Zulu messengers came bearing news that Dingane's plan was to link up with none other than his archenemy, Mzilikatse. To do this, he had to pass through territory of either the so-called "knob-nosed Kafirs" (who remain unknown to this day) or the AmaSwazi of Sobhuza. In the event, he chose the route through Swazi country. Obviously the link with Mzilikatse had to be stopped at all costs.

On January 31st, Pretorius convened a court-martial to hear the cases of Dambuza and Kambazana. Mpande was made part of the court-martial, representing the Zulu voice in the proceedings. The testimony by the Zulu in respect of the prior actions of Dambuza and Kambazana was overwhelming. Mpande insisted that Dingane made no decisions without discussion with Dambuza, and that the murder of Retief and the Blaauwkranz attacks were both instigated by Dambuza. His testimony was not significantly less damaging in the case of Kambazana. Zietsman[21] further reports that, when asked to plead, Dambuza said:

"Oh no! I have nothing to say against it. All that Panda has stated is true. I am willing to die for the many crimes I have committed; but this Kambazana, who is fettered with me, is not guilty, and does not deserve to die."

This was amazingly selfless behavior on the part of Dambuza. We turn to Adulphe Delegorgue[22], the Frenchman with the Afrikaner Commando, to describe the execution of Dambuza and Kambazana.:

"When the shots went off, both prisoners fell. Combezena died instantly, but Tamboussa was only wounded in the body. Then, as calmly as ever, and in spite of his suffering, he arose and stood steadfastly facing the guns, until the second round of shots rang out and he fell to the ground. These men know how to die..."

This was most certainly a savage and brutal man who deserved his fate thousands of times over. However, he was merely a product of his society, and no one could ever take from him the crowning moment of his life, when he died more bravely and with more honor than any man could comprehend. His executioners were much diminished in stature by this.

On the 2nd of February 1840 came word that Mpande's army had not waited for the Afrikaners to arrive and had engaged and defeated Dingane's army. One thousand of Dingane's men had died and 1,500 of Nonkalaza's men were wounded.

An event on 5 February serves to demonstrate the prevailing thinking in Zulu martial culture at the time. A party of Dingane's Zulu had taken shelter in a cave and Pretorius sent an interpreter with a message to offer them their lives spared if they would surrender. When no one appeared out of the caves, Pretorius ordered his men up to the caves to take the enemy. This hugely impressed Nonkalaza, who did not think it was possible to defeat an enemy so well-entrenched. After a few rounds had been fired into the caves, the men inside surrendered. We turn again to the independent Delegorgue[23]:

Immediately the fire ceased, and the men came out bringing with them fifty women and a number of children, who were all taken and kindly treated. But two hours later, when, with one accord the warriors attempted to escape to the nearby caves, they were shot down, more rapidly than they could ever have anticipated. The manner in which the Boers behaved on this occasion intrigued their Amazoulou allies, who were both admiring and disapproving. More than one spoke scornfully of the style of warfare practised by the white man.

"What," said Nonglas [Nonkalaza], "after forcing them to abandon so difficult a position, you spare their lives. This is not war; this is not profiting by your advantages. In war one must kill many; all if possible."

Officially, Dingane was never found. However, Daniel Pieter Bezuidenhout recorded[24] that Sobhuza, king of the AmaSwazi captured him. Considering Dingane's earlier atrocities against Sobhuza, his life was clearly forfeit the moment Sobhuza had him:

"He continually fled, till he reached the other side of the Umguza River, at Bamboesberg [Bamboo Mountain]. There, Sapusa took him prisoner.

On the first day (according to the statement of the Kafirs), Sapusa pricked Dingaan with sharp assegais, no more than skin deep, from the sole of his foot to the top of his head.

The second day he had him bitten by dogs.

On the third day, Sapusa said to Dingaan: 'Dingaan! Are you still the rainmaker? Are you still the greatest of living men? See, the sun is rising: you shall not see it set!' Saying this, he took an assagai and bored his eyes out.

This was related to me by one of Sapusa's Kafirs who was present. When the sun set, Dingaan was dead..."

Morris[25] suggests that Dingane crossed the Pongola River and was killed by a small group of Nyawo men on the advice of the Swazi, led by Sobhuza. Reputedly a centenarian who participated in his destruction died only in 1911. A pile of stones was made to mark Dingane's burial site and this was apparently rediscovered in 1947.

The message spread like wildfire all over the land of Natal and black people who had been driven from the land started coming back by the thousands. People of all the ethnic groups of South Africa had fought together to rid the land of an evil the scope of which the world has seldom seen. This great success belonged to all in the country. On 10 February 1840 Pretorius announced the accession of Mpande to the throne of the Zulu people. The border between Natalia and Zululand would be the Tugela and the Buffalo Rivers. Both sides respected this for decades and Mpande became the only Zulu ruler until 1880 to die a natural death in freedom. He and the Afrikaners maintained their arrangement for the rest of his life. This is more than can be said of any deal any British Governor ever made with any indigenous ruler or with the Afrikaners, as we shall see.

The removal of Dingane, and his replacement with Mpande, brought the Zulu the longest period thus far of sustained peace and represents one of the few cases in human history of a successful Regime Change. This fact was borne out by the streaming back into Natal of thousands upon thousands of black people who had been dispossessed and terrorized by the murderous despotic Dingane. In fact, in their very success lay the undoing of the Trekkers' dream of a country of their own. They were being swamped by black people streaming into their new country.

In future, the Zulu would repeatedly seek and get the help of the Afrikaners. In other key cases, they would rely on Afrikaner neutrality, and they would receive that as well. In fact, when South Africa became a Union in 1910, one of the first actions of its first Prime Minister, the Afrikaner Boer War general Louis Botha, was to release Zulu leader Dinizulu from the captivity in which he had been placed by the British. Even in the 21st century, the political leader of the Zulu Inkatha party, Mangosuthu Buthelezi, has warned the Xhosa-dominated ANC government to stop its constant attempts to humiliate the Afrikaner; an obsession with that government.

-----ooOoo-----

13

The Pharaoh steals Canaan

"The scene exhibited by about three or four hundred fathers of large families assembled and shedding tears when representing their position was more, I admit, than I could observe unmoved."

Sir Henry George Wakelyn Smith,
Meeting with Afrikaners leaving Natal after annexation by Britain (1848)

Battle between Boer and Brit

For George Napier, any excuse would do to regain Port Natal. Under the influence of London Missionary Society propaganda, he hated, detested, and despised the Afrikaner, as we shall see in due course from his letters published later. Thus, when Pretorius led a Commando against cattle thieves in the south of Natal, Napier pounced on this as the first available excuse. Again, British missionaries in Pondoland had inflated the story beyond rational scope. Upon instruction from Whitehall, Napier sent Captain T.C. Smith to the north of Pondoland in January 1841 to "protect the natives." Napier secretly told Smith to ready himself for taking Port Natal. The instruction to occupy the settlement came again from Whitehall in late 1841 and Smith was dispatched in March 1842.

Fig. 13-1 George Thomas Napier

At first, Pretorius made no direct challenge, believing that, if they did not provoke the British, they would go away again. Indeed, Britain had by now had quite enough of intrigues in colonies to last them a lifetime. However, while Whitehall had meant for this to be a simple demonstration message to the Trekkers, Napier had other intentions. Smith and Pretorius met several times, Pretorius asking the British Army to leave in peace, and Smith asking the Trekkers to submit to the Queen of England. In fact, Whitehall had never demanded that the Boers should submit to Britain. This was Napier's invention.

Eventually, on 24 May 1842, Smith decided to make a night attack on the Afrikaner town of Congella, some 3 miles south of Port Natal. He had wholly underestimated the Afrikaners. To make matters worse, he set off with his army on a bright moonlit night over soggy ground next to a mangrove swamp, with his howitzer being transported by boat. This was the first of many times that Boer and Brit were to formally give battle to each other over the following 60 years. After all the years of fighting together on the same side in dry country, here these two nations were finally squaring off incongruously in a mangrove swamp, of all places. It could all have been avoided, if not for Napier's blind hatred of the Afrikaner, induced by the London Missionary Society.

The British contingent under Smith blindly trudged straight into an ambush and was cut to ribbons by the Trekkers' long-range muskets, firing from concealed positions in the mangroves. The contingent scattered under the murderous fire, but the bulk of the men did make it back to camp. The all-time insult was that the

Boere intentionally shot the oxen used by the British to haul their cannon, thereby forcing the latter to abandon the cannon in the swamp. The British casualty roll was 34 killed, 64 wounded and 6 missing. There is no evidence of any casualties on the Boer side, though reports did circulate that the Trekkers may have had a man wounded. It was an inglorious military fiasco – the first of many through the following 60 years.

With this, Napier finally had what he had obviously been praying for; a disaster that was Heaven-sent and guaranteed to bring the full might of Britain to bear on the Afrikaner. He had finally completely compromised his superiors, thereby forcing their hand. Clearer minds in Britain might have recalled him, but that was not the style of Imperial Britain. This self-made disaster would now have to be avenged.

Captain Smith's problem was that he had no communication with the Cape. He had written a dispatch, but had no means to deliver it. Finally Dick King, one of the survivors of the abortive English sortie against Dingane in 1838, volunteered with his black helper to ride the 600 miles to Grahamstown to deliver the message. Dick King succeeded brilliantly in his Great Ride to Grahamstown and thereby became one of the heroes of South African history. Smith's sealed dispatch ended with[1]:

...I beg to urge the necessity of a speedy reinforcement, as I scarcely consider the troops at present stationed here sufficient for the performance of the duty to which they have been assigned.

I have the honour to be, Sir,
Your obedient humble Servant,
(Signed) T. C. SMITH, Capt. 27th Regt. Com.

The Natalian Trekkers gave the English women and children safe conduct out of the army encampment and provided them with safe conduct to board one of the British ships in the harbor, the Mazeppa. Smith made a point of stating that the Afrikaner treatment of the women and children had been superb[2]:

"...a flag of truce came to the camp to say that the women and children might leave the camp, and go on board one of the ships in the Bay. After a little consideration, Margaret consented to go with the children; for they could not be of any use in the camp; and how were they to live when we ran short of provisions? So they were escorted to the shore by some of the Boers. Part of the way they went in a large waggon: they were also very polite, and some of them wanted to know if Margaret was old Captain Smith's vrouw [wife]."

Fig. 13-2 *The Mazeppa slipping past the Boer guns*

Soon after, the Mazeppa, with the women and children on board, quietly slipped past the Boer guards stationed at the Point. The Afrikaners now sat down to a siege, using the captured British guns to lob a few shells at the British soldiers every day. Smith slaughtered the last oxen and horses, rationed his men, and waited. Now and then they had a skirmish. The Brits would try the odd bayonet charge and the Boere would fight back with their rifle butts. However, the gallant Captain Smith was rapidly running out of food.

We now turn again to our young Afrikaner narrator, Nicolaas Roets, for his quaint description of that siege and the ensuing events at the bay of Port Natal, later to be named Durban:

"... my brothers and brothers-in-law were therefore at the Bay. They cornered the English soldiers and almost let them starve until the troops even shot the crows when they flew over the camp and the horses were also slaughtered for food; but then the officer Cloete came over the sea and released the soldiers and so Natal was

given up to the English."

Captain Smith did indeed breakfast on a dead crow on the morning of 25 June 1842, but the above quote is essentially the story. Lieutenant-Colonel A.J. Cloete arrived with his reinforcements on 26 June 1842 and relieved Smith at 3 pm that day. The small handful of Natalian Afrikaners could not conceivably fight the British Empire. With the British arriving, the Natal black people had also resumed raiding the farmers. The Afrikaners elected not to "fight Pharaoh," especially as the "Pharaoh" came in the form of a "tame Afrikaner."

Josias Cloete was an Afrikaner like them and a descendant of Jacob Cloete, the author's own ancestor (NF1). This fact made it nearly impossible for the Afrikaners at Port Natal to fight. They were not going to attack "their own." Cloete's older brother, Hendrik or "Henry," would shortly afterwards be sent to head the Judiciary in Natal. The latter would become famous for his *"Three Lectures"*[3] on the subject of why the Great Trek had happened (See Chap. 7: *The Black Circuit*). He correctly summarized it as the matters of the *"1st, the Hottentot Question; 2nd, The Slave Question; 3rd, the Kafir* Question." So, he at least exhibited a modicum of sensitivity in the matter.

Hounding the Afrikaner

With Napier's raising of the British flag at Port Natal on Blood River Day 1838, a sequence of events started that was to repeat itself with monotonous regularity for the next 64 years. The Afrikaner would find a place to live, and the British Government would follow him and take it by force. This would happen no fewer than five times.

When the Government in London heard of the events at Port Natal, they approved of the relief of Port Natal, but refused to consider making Natal a colony of Britain. This certainly did not suit George Napier. When his bosses again instructed him to evacuate after the Battle of Congella, he refused and was entirely brazen about his reasons. He wrote a long rambling letter[4] to his bosses in London on 25 July 1842:

> *...I have never considered the colonization of Port Natal as, in itself, a desirable measure [...] ...in my despatch No _ , of the 18th May, 1838, I urged upon Lord Glenelg the imperative necessity of occupying Port Natal as the only means by which these contests could be checked, and the reduction of the natives to slavery could be prevented.*

The *"contests"* he was referring to were the events between the trekkers and Dingane. Mystically the murder of Retief and the massacre of Trekkers at Blaauwkranz transmute in his mind into slavery campaigns by the Trekkers. Prejudice is assuredly the true mother of invention.

Here we see clearly the hand of Dr. Philip of the London Missionary Society still on the tiller at the Cape with the help of his newspaperman son-in-law, John Fairbairn, owner and editor of the *Commercial Advertiser*. The reader can decide whether any of the Trekker's activity in the past few chapters had anything to do with the maintenance of slavery. Yet, this was still the view actively promoted in London by Dr. Philip. Napier had been totally convinced by his boss, Glenelg, who in turn had been totally, and willingly, misled by Dr. Philip and the LMS. In case they had missed anything in prejudicing Napier, none other than Stockenström met him halfway on his way to the East Cape on his first ever tour of the frontier, and made sure that his prejudices were cemented in favor of the London Missionary Society and Stockenström. Chase states[5]:

> *"On the road he was met by Lieut.-Governor Stockenström, who, availing himself of the detention caused by two successive rainy days, imbued his mind with the highest opinion of his own new system, and tutored him into the belief that all the opposition he had hitherto encountered had had its rise among disappointed and factious individuals in the Eastern Province."*

Napier continues in this rambling memorandum to summarize that his masters in Britain had offered the Trekkers an amnesty if they were to return to the Cape Colony. If they did not, then...

> *Her Majesty's Government will take every practicable and legal method of interdicting all commercial intercourse and all communication between them and the colonists; that if they should presume to molest, invade or injure the Kaffir tribes with which her Majesty is in alliance, her Majesty's Forces will support these tribes in resisting such aggressions; and lastly, if the laws of the colony are not sufficient, I am directed to propose to the Legislative Council the enactment of a law having for its object to oppose the most effectual obstacles which can be raised to supply to the emigrants of any articles of which they may stand in need, and especially of gunpowder, firearms, and other munitions of war.*

His letter therefore clearly shows that, while wanting the emigrants back, Britain was not ready for another colony in Southern Africa. However, this did not suit Napier who then lashes out in this letter against the Afrikaner with the most incredible statements; basically feeding Whitehall bare-faced lies, such as that the Afrikaners beyond the Orange River would welcome British authority. He gives argument after argument as to why the proposed British sanctions would not work.

He sketches emigrant Britons as people who want to better their situations, but emigrant Afrikaners as blood-soaked monsters who are hell bent on implementing slavery. His mind-numbing hatred of the Afrikaner is absolutely staggering in this letter. Anyone who ever blamed the Afrikaner for distrusting Britain, would have to concede they had solid grounds after reading this disgraceful document, which is simply too long to reproduce here. The author is convinced that any Briton with a modicum of honor who reads it, will be outraged.

Napier claimed, still in the same gigantic communication, that removal of the renewed military detachment from Port Natal, as instructed by Whitehall, would cause trouble:

> *...but by maintaining a post there, and if necessary, denying access to foreign vessels, whether Dutch or American, is the only way by which we can cut off supplies being furnished to the emigrants from without.*

Again the argument was for a colony in Natal. At least, now the reader knows that Napier wanted to keep the Trekkers from having contact with Americans, who were, after all, "fellow deviant Jacobins." He then openly accuses the Trekkers of practicing slavery and suggests that:

> *If the authority of the British Government is withdrawn from Natal, slavery will be there established.*

In this statement, he brazenly chooses to ignore the fact that the Cape Government had sent Field-Cornet Gideon Joubert to the Trekkers in Natal in 1838. Joubert had arrived at their encampment on precisely Monday 5 November 1838. His brief had been to investigate whether the Trekkers had illegally removed any emancipated slaves against their will and were keeping them in bondage, as claimed by the London Missionary Society. His task was to return any such people to the Cape Colony. The Reverend Erasmus Smit, himself an ex-LMS man, reports[6] that Joubert met with the ex-slaves in his encampment on 7 November. This was near the end of their 4 year apprenticeship, as per the Emancipation Act, which had taken effect on 1 December 1834, just before the outbreak of the fateful Hintsa's War of 1834-1835. Smit noted in his diary that:

> *"Today the erstwhile slaves (all well clothed and of sound mind) appeared before the gentleman Gideon Joubert and were questioned: With the exception of six, they declared that they were perfectly happy with their masters; that they had left [the Cape Colony] of their own free will; and that they did not want to return there."*

Theal[7] reports the overall numbers from all the encampments in Natal:

> *"Most of the apprentices had already been set at liberty, and when this was not the case they were without exception offered the choice of returning with Mr. Joubert or of remaining as servants with wages. Nearly all*

preferred to remain, so that Mr. Joubert brought back only eight men, eleven women, and twenty-one children."

Chase[8] reports the same number of 40 in 1843. It is hardly surprising that some would have wanted to return. After all, the Zulu had killed about 100 of their number during the terrible Blaauwkranz murders. Clearly the scheming London Missionary Society was not going to let a simple matter like the truth intrude on its plans. It had totally indoctrinated its pet governor to the extent that Napier preferred to totally ignore this finding commissioned by his own government. Lastly, just in case the reader or the British government somehow managed to miss his transparent real intentions, Napier wrote:

> The emigrants by their rebellion have forfeited much of the consideration; their proceedings have shown that it is dangerous to allow them to remain longer without control, and such of them as are unwilling to place themselves under whatever form of government might be conceded to them by the Queen, would of course retire into the interior of South Africa; but there they would be less troublesome to this colony, because, deprived of a seaport their consequence would be diminished...

After considering this document, dripping with his LMS-incited hatred of a fellow European-descended Christian nation who merely dared to be not English, Whitehall, on 12 December 1842, approved making Natal a colony of Britain. Britain would eventually deeply regret hounding the Afrikaner into the interior, as we shall see in due course in Chapters 14 and 15.

Canaan Lost

The man sent to Natal in May 1843 to convince the Afrikaners to return to British authority, was none other than Col. A. J. Cloete's older brother, Hendrik "Henry" Cloete, whom we have met before as the young Court Recorder during the Black Circuit. As an Afrikaner himself, albeit a Loyalist, he understood the Trekker people and certainly fully comprehended why they had left the Cape, even though it would have meant the end of his career for him to explain the reasons to Napier at the time. Napier was simply incapable of hearing that. Amazingly, confronted by a number of Commando units from across the Drakensberg on 7 August 1843, and battered by abuse from these men, Cloete managed to convince the Natal Volksraad (Congress) to submit to British authority. The highly unhappy Commando units withdrew from Pietermaritzburg. However, Cloete was clearly taken aback on the same day, when the women of the town sent a delegation which made their position clear indeed[9]. They had fought in battles with their menfolk, and insisted that, based on this, their husbands had given them a say in matters political. And their view was simple. They would rather walk barefoot back over the Drakensberg than give up their hard won liberty. None of this kept Cloete from explaining to the ladies that he considered it *"a disgrace on their husbands to allow them such a state of freedom."* To this, the women responded with a cry of *"Liberty or Death!"*

Clearly, Afrikaner women are not to be trifled with and did not confine themselves to tea and crumpets like their British counterparts. All in all, their view was to predominate, because the majority of the Trekkers would eventually leave Natal, despite Cloete's obviously genuine and dedicated efforts.

To Napier's credit, he testified[10,11] many years later before the House of Commons in England and conceded that he had been terribly wrong on the entire matter of the East Cape Border, whence the Great Trek had emanated:

> "I went out, if I had any prejudice at all, with a prejudice against the Colonists, and against that former occupation of the ground by Sir Benjamin D'Urban and Sir Harry Smith [...] My own experience and what I saw with my own eyes, have confirmed me that I was wrong, and that Sir Benjamin D'Urban was perfectly right."

This pious recantation just before his death was more than a decade too late. His prejudice before taking up the post as Governor, inspired by the London Missionary Society and Glenelg, had done all the damage it was ever going to do. The viciously prejudiced Napier left office on 18 March 1844 for the waiting comforts of England and the tender embraces of the London Missionary Society tea parties. The new Governor at the Cape was Sir Peregrine Maitland, formerly the governor of Upper Canada, followed a short year later by Sir Henry Pottinger.

Fig. 13-3 Sir Peregrine Maitland

In December 1845, the Afrikaners' hard-earned Republic of Natalia, for which so many of the author's family had died (See *Fig. 11-8* and *11-9*), formally ceased to exist. "Canaan" was no more. "The Pharaoh" had taken "Canaan" and the "Israelites" had to submit to his authority or be banished to the "desert" of the interior. Just to make sure that no other Afrikaners considered any ideas similar to those in Natal, the British placed a military detachment in the Trans-Orange south of the Modder River in 1845, effectively extending British control in all but name. At least, they left the people north of the Modder River largely alone (See *Fig. 13-5*). Those who did remain in Natal, mostly did so in the temperate rolling prairie interior at the foot of the Drakensberg, between the Tugela and Buffalo Rivers, far from Durban. This is the area generally drained by the Klip (Rocky) River, for which the district is named. The area remains mostly Afrikaans to this day. As with the people of the Alsace and Saarland in Europe, stuck between the French and the Germans, these people would be put through hell in future. Pietermaritzburg, with its Church of the Vow and its Voortrekker history, being close to Port Natal, became largely English.

For two years, Andries Pretorius tried to represent the case of his people to the new British Governor at the Cape, but he was not even granted an audience. Meanwhile, by way of example[12], on his own two farms in Natal, the influx of black people from elsewhere had been indulged by the British and had rendered £3,000 of improvements worthless. The government had taken his own sons' farms and they had not received any alternative land or compensation. This story was repeated for hundreds of farmers. In late 1847, Pretorius finally gave up, hitched his wagons, and started out toward the Drakensberg back into the "Wastes of Africa," which is ever where the British have wanted the Afrikaner, if anywhere at all. Exactly as Napier had hoped and prayed, the vast majority of the Afrikaners in Natal packed up their few miserable belongings, yoked their oxen and started leaving for the Trans-Orange region west of the Drakensberg. "Pharaoh" had again taken their liberty. The "Promised Land" was no more.

Hendrik Potgieter had been 100% correct – where there was sea, one could always sooner or later expect the British. Piet Retief, the hugely honorable man who had tried to "do things right," was dead and his dream of a land by the sea was lost. Given this experience, the majority of the Afrikaners would never trust the British government again – a statement as true today as in the 1840s.

At this point, we return to the Cape Eastern Frontier, where trouble was brewing, and now there were too few Afrikaners for London to blame.

The War of the Axe

Before leaving the Cape Colony on the Great Trek in 1837, the Afrikaners on the eastern border of the colony had warned Andries Stockenström about his policies towards the Khoekhoe settlement at the Kat River. They had also been incredulous when he not only returned the region between the Keiskamma and Kei rivers to the amaXhosa, as instructed by the British Government, but also gave the hard-won territory between the Fish and Keiskamma rivers to the amaXhosa for their use. This placed any Xhosa Army on the immediate border with the British Settlers in the Suurveld. It made the deep Fish River bush an instant Xhosa stronghold. In 21st century military strategic terms, Stockenström had "given the Golan Heights to the enemies of Israel."

This then was the strategic situation on 16 March 1846 when an ImiDange Xhosa, known by the Dutch nickname of Kleintje (Little One) was accused of stealing an axe at Fort Beaufort, the little fortified border town on the Kat River north of Grahamstown. Kleintje, together with two Khoekhoe offenders and a dragoon who had committed some or other offence, were then sent off under guard of four Khoekhoe soldiers to Grahamstown for trial. The four offenders were handcuffed in pairs. Kleintje was handcuffed to one of the Khoekhoe offenders.

Just before they left Fort Beaufort, local Xhosa chief Tola asked that Kleintje be delivered to him. When he was refused, Tola instructed his men to attack the escort and free Kleintje. A party of 40 Xhosa warriors attacked the escort some distance outside town, killed the Khoekhoe offender to whom Kleintje was handcuffed, and cut off his hand to release Kleintje. In the process, one of the Khoekhoe guards killed one of the attackers and then fled. From here, matters escalated until it developed into the Seventh Frontier War – aptly named The War of the Axe.

On 31 March, the burghers on the frontier were called to military service again. It was time yet again for the Afrikaners to fight for the British. Sir Peregrine Maitland, the aged governor of the Cape, then sent his entire army to the frontier. Colonel Hare, Lieutenant-Governor for the Eastern Frontier, brashly did not wait for the Boer Commandos to form up, and managed to lose a major part of a supply wagon train to the Xhosa.

After this disaster, the British decision was to retreat and consolidate. Taking all this as a sign of British weakness, the Xhosa under Ngqika invaded the Colony. It was a repeat of the 1834 Sixth Frontier War, except that this time the British Settlers knew to gather in groups for safety. However, the Ngqika Xhosa were destroying the colony as far as they went. With the British soldiers sitting inside fortifications, the Xhosa conducted wholesale raiding and taunted the soldiers to come out and fight. This war exposed some of the worst shortcomings in the British War Machine.

Maitland now saw firsthand that the posts along the Fish River were utterly useless as long as the Xhosa had access to the Fish River Forest. Governor Benjamin D'Urban and Harry Smith had been right all along. Stockenström had indeed "given the Golan Heights" to the Xhosa. Napier's Folly was utterly clear and undeniable. It had taken British lives to prove the obvious.

Fascinatingly, various Afrikaner burghers asked that Stockenström, of all people, be appointed overall commander of the Afrikaner forces. While they had no faith in his earlier policies, they respected him as commander in the field. Stockenström, for his part, realizing that his original policies had been an undeniable failure, now committed himself to restoring his name among his own people. Appropriately, he started by clearing the Tarka, the very area in which his countrymen had been most hurt by his earlier policy and from where the bulk of the Great Trek had proceeded. One of his main targets was Maphasa, the very man who had been the cause of Koos Potgieter's dismissal as Provisional Field-Cornet before the Great Trek (*NF42*).

Stockenström did a good job of clearing that area and then, due to an intense disagreement with the British Army, was dismissed again. At this point, this central figure, for better or for worse, departs the stage of South African history; another basically good man undone by the realities of Africa.

The main consequence of the War of the Axe was that it showed up the "Liberal Folly" for what it was. It now came to light that Dr. Philip's protégé, Dyani Thsatshu, whom he had taken to London to impress the Select Committee on Aborigines, was involved in open warfare against Britain. Finally Philip's machinations and his bile-dripping hatred of the Settlers and Afrikaners had turned on him in spectacular fashion. The British Settlers were absolutely baying for his blood. But, worse was yet to come for him.

The War of the Axe effectively turned when the Xhosa adopted a new and effective strategy that utterly confounded the British. They simply refused to fight. They would not even run away. They simply sat down in front of the approaching troops, realizing they would not be fired upon. The whole tribe could not be detained as prisoners. The women were busy making gardens, but as soon as the army approached, they and the children would throng around begging for food.

Eventually, Maitland granted Xhosa chief Sandile fourteen days to restore 20,000 head of cattle and give up his arms, in exchange for permanent peace. One day after the expiration of the truce, Sandile appeared with about 300 horses, three hundred cattle, and Kleintje ("Little One"), the stealer of the fateful axe. He also produced a man who allegedly had killed the Khoekhoe attached to Kleintje, but this man died before he could be questioned. After this, every Xhosa who surrendered a musket or six assegais was registered as a "British Subject." Some 300 inferior muskets were produced, but the good ones were obviously kept. The entirely competent and intelligent amaXhosa were making a complete fool out of the inept Maitland. In the middle of Maitland's efforts, London appointed yet another Governor.

Fig. 13-4 *Sir Henry Pottinger*

On 27 January 1847, Sir Henry Pottinger arrived at the Cape to take office. With him came a new military commander, Sir George Berkley. Pottinger was given the additional job of a "High Commissioner" for coming to an arrangement with the nations surrounding the Cape so as to reduce the burden on the British coffers of the incessant strife at the Cape.

While the doddering Maitland had canceled Martial Law and started recalling the soldiers from the frontier, Pottinger immediately countermanded the withdrawal of the troops and set about trying to raise a Khoekhoe force. He also appealed for volunteers from the Afrikaner Burghers and British Settlers. Systematically Pottinger built up an army of some 5,000 men. To this, he added a few hundred "Kaffir Policemen," drawn from among the amaXhosa. The Afrikaners warned strenuously about the loyalty of this particular force and wanted nothing to do with it. Most refused to volunteer if this force were involved.

Sandile, having had the benefit of his "peaceful stance," had now finished harvesting and was ready to fight again. The Xhosa are intelligent people and Sandile had learnt from Graham's outrageous Scorched Earth approach back in 1811. He had comprehensively fooled the British into leaving his people alone while he harvested the food needed for the next war. Hostilities renewed after the harvest, but eventually both Sandile and Kreli offered to surrender if their lives would be spared. Pottinger agreed, but subject to Kreli providing 10,000 cattle in restitution. Kreli surrendered, but could not or would not produce the cattle. At this point, all chiefs west of the Kei had submitted to Britain.

With the war in this state of incomplete resolution, the British Government finally turned to someone with some experience of the Cape Frontier. He was received in Cape Town to tumultuous welcome. The inhabitants of the Cape were ecstatic with joy; all, with the exception of the son-in-law of Dr. John Philip, John Fairbairn[13] of the *Commercial Advertiser*:

> *"The appointment of the successor to Sir Henry Pottinger in the government of the Cape of Good Hope, announced in the 'Gazette' of the 10th of September, carries back the affairs of South Africa exactly to the position in which they stood eleven years ago. This fact is well worth attention, in all its bearings. It is nothing less than the open abandonment of a great endeavour to reconcile the progress of British power with the principles of a humane system..."*

The "Thoroughly Modern Major General"

The new Governor of the Cape was none other than (now Major General) Henry George Wakelyn "Harry" ("Wackalong Smite") Smith, returned from India where he had meanwhile made a name for himself as the military hero of Aliwal. Here was a man who loved the Cape. Here was a man who secretly admired the guts of the Afrikaner; a man who understood at least to some degree what made them tick; a man who had fought a war with them by his side. Here was the man who had preferred them as escort over his very own British Army in the middle of Hintsa's War.

Harry Smith was honestly aghast and outraged at what had happened under Napier in particular. Furthermore, the Afrikaners' hatred of the London Missionary Society was exceeded only by that which Harry Smith had for this organization. In one of his letters[14] to the Earl Grey in London, he stated about Joseph Freeman, the Secretary of the London Missionary Society,

> *"...like all prejudiced men, he seeks for evidence to strengthen his own preconceptions, and loses sight of the general bearing and view of the subjects upon which he has so freely commented"*

Smith's first actions were to restore all that he and Benjamin D'Urban had done twelve years earlier in 1834. Literally within hours of arriving at the frontier, he re-annexed Queen Adelaide's Province and firmed up the border in the Tarka. Just for good measure, he added the rest of the country up to the Orange River (See Fig. 13-5). The new eastern border of the Colony followed a succession of rivers and mountain ranges, all the way to the Orange River, which river formed the northern border all the way to the Atlantic. The adjoining region between the Keiskamma River and the Kei he named British Kaffraria and declared it a separate Dependency of Britain. Smith then made a ceremony out of the whole process. He brought the surrendered chiefs out of captivity. Then he took a sergeant's baton and a wand with a brass head, and named the former the "Staff of War" and the latter the "Staff of Peace." He called the chiefs forward to touch whichever they chose. Naturally, each touched the Staff of Peace. He then gave them a long paternalistic address about what would happen if they broke that peace. Next, incredibly, Smith insisted they kiss his foot as a token of submission, which they did. Finally, to crown the occasion, the new High Commissioner then shook hands with all the chiefs and they were presented with a herd of oxen for a feast. Forts were put up in British Kaffraria and a strong military force was stationed there.

When all the division of land among the chiefs had been sorted out and all the commissioners appointed, Smith held another huge ceremony on 7 January 1848. Practically all the Xhosa chiefs were present, including the minor chief Diyane "Jan" Tshatshu, who had been to London with Philip and who had then turned on Britain. Then, to imprint his points upon their minds, Smith directed their collective attention to a carefully prepared wagon. Upon his signal, the wagon was blown sky high with explosives, and he announced that that was what he would do to them if they misbehaved. He then took a paper out of his pocket and tore it into many pieces, saying,

> *"There go the Treaties! Do you hear? No more treaties!"*

The Xhosa are a proud people. It is difficult to understand what merit Smith saw in humiliating them other than to ensure the next war. However, these antics did seem to have their short-term effect on the Xhosa. The War of the Axe was over — at least for now — and we follow the unique Sir Harry to the north.

A heart-rending scene

Having settled the Xhosa Frontier, however temporarily, Smith set off through the Trans-Orange to address in person the situation surrounding the desperately unhappy Afrikaners in Natal. While it was not possible for him to unmake the new Colony of Natal, he certainly could attempt to address the concerns of the Afrikaners. From the new little settlement of Winburg in the Trans-Orange he sent an urgent message on 27 January 1848 to Andries Pretorius who was leading the trek from Natal. Smith appealed to him to halt and grant him an opportunity to talk to them. We let Harry Smith speak for himself[15]:

> *"On my arrival at the foot of the Drachenberg Mountains, I was almost paralyzed to witness the whole of the population, with few exceptions, 'trekking'! Rains on this side of the mountains are tropical, and now prevail – the country is intersected by considerable streams, frequently impassable – and these families were exposed*

to a state of misery which I never before saw equalled, except in Massena's invasion of Portugal, when the whole of the population of that part of the seat of war abandoned their homes and fled. The scene here was truly heart-rending.

"I assembled all the men near me through the means of a Mr. Pretorius, a shrewd, sensible man, who had recently been into the colony to lay the subject of dissatisfaction of his countrymen before the Governor[16], where he was unfortunately refused an audience, and returned after so long a journey, expressing himself as the feelings of a proud and injured man would naturally prompt.

"At this meeting I was received as if among my own family. I heard the various causes of complaint. Some I regard as well founded, others as imaginary; but all expressive of a want of confidence and liberality as to land on the part of Government. I exerted my influence among them to induce them to remain for the moment where they were, which they consented to do.

"The scene exhibited by about three or four hundred fathers of large families assembled and shedding tears when representing their position was more, I admit, than I could observe unmoved. [...]

"To prove, if it be necessary, the faith which I place in their loyalty, I may mention that on one occasion when the little waggon in which I travel, and which they call 'Government House,' was nearly upset when crossing one of the tributary streams of the great Tugela, thirty or forty men on the bank stripped and sprang into the water, exclaiming, 'Government House shall not fall– it shall not fall!' and their efforts saved my only home from being carried down the current."

To his everlasting credit, Harry Smith immediately made a number of proclamations to address the concerns of the Natal Afrikaners. He told them that the future of Natal depended on its white population and he immediately appointed Andries Pretorius to the Land Commission (Pretorius afterwards declined this honor in view of subsequent developments). All of this played well to these much-abused people whom Smith experienced as *"his family."* To them, he and Sir Ben D'Urban had been the only Englishmen with any political power who had ever treated them with anything vaguely approaching true consideration.

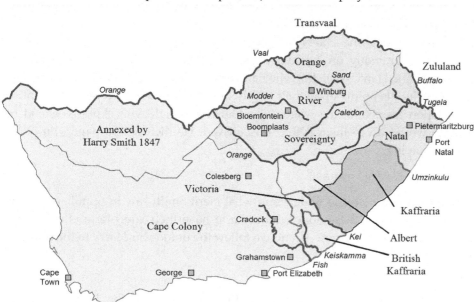

Fig. 13-5 The annexations by Harry Smith between 1847 and 1850

Andries Pretorius, as agreed with Smith, left the camp in order to determine the real feelings of the emigrant farmers in-land beyond the Drakensberg. It was Pretorius' understanding that Sir Harry had promised him that, if the general opinion of the settlers on annexation of the northern Trans-Orange was unfavorable, then the proclamation would not be issued. However, when Pretorius set off to do his bidding, Smith decided on 3 February 1848 to annex the rest of the region north of the Modder (Muddy) River and south of the Vaal River, calling the entire area the Orange River Sovereignty. To this day, no one fully comprehends on what basis he did that. Why it did not occur to him that he would anger the independent Afrikaners beyond the Modder (Mud) River is not understood.

These people had only just left Natal, and here he was condescendingly pretending to be their "father" and annexing the next place they had tried to move to after being expelled from their hard-won Natal by his very own masters. That made it three annexations within three years of areas that Afrikaners had lived in as independent men, Natal, the Southern Trans-Orange, and now the Northern Trans-Orange. Sir Harry maintained that his agreement with Pretorius only referred to the Boers north of the Vaal River, and so the territory they occupied was excluded from the terms of the proclamation. This totally avoidable misunderstanding sowed the seeds of problems to come. Nevertheless, confident in his measures and their reception by the Afrikaners, he sent the British troops back to the Cape. To their commander, Warden, he said[17]:

"My dear fellow, bear in mind that the Boers are my children, and I will have none other here for my soldiers; your detachment will march for the colony immediately."

It is said that the "Thoroughly Modern Major General" of Gilbert & Sullivan is based specifically on Henry George Wakelyn Smith. Given his mind-boggling arrogance one can certainly understand this. His heart was certainly "in the right place," but his actions often boggled the mind. Sensitivity was not a virtue he excelled at – and he would prove this yet again.

The Government in Britain reluctantly agreed to the creation of the Orange River Sovereignty. The measures taken by Sir Harry to induce settlers in Natal to stay there, and others to come there, were to a certain extent successful. However, he was wrong in the rather arrogant belief that the settlers in the northern part of the new Sovereignty, and particularly those across the Vaal, would readily accept British supremacy when offered them by one whom "they had known and trusted in the past." The sense of utter dismal wrong created by the Philip-Buxton-Glenelg-Napier-Stockenström policy could not be so easily undone.

Given his monumental ego, Smith's mistake was in thinking that the Trekkers' very real regard for him exceeded their desperate desire for freedom from England after all they had suffered at the hand of "The Pharaoh."

Boomplaats – designing an enemy

Having annexed all of the Trans-Orange and renamed it to the "Orange River Sovereignty," Smith thought the area stabilized. However, he had not reckoned with the outrage of the Afrikaners. Had he studied the outburst of the womenfolk of Pietermaritzburg to Henry Cloete, he might have understood matters. But his arrogance left no room for such understanding. On 8 March 1848, Harry Smith appointed none other than Thomas Jervis Biddulph as magistrate at Winburg. This would be the same man (*NF40, 44, 47*) who had, according to some sources, fought at Blood River. Author Noël Mostert refers to him as "villainous"[18].

The reaction of the Afrikaner burghers of Winburg to the sudden appearance of the British flag and a magistrate of that Empire was instant and total. It needs to be understood that the Afrikaners of the Transvaal, Trans-Orangia and Natal saw themselves as one body. In fact, they had had one Volksraad (Congress) for some ten years. When it became clear that he was being rejected by "his children," Smith turned to threats. In reality, the manifesto he issued was one of the strangest ever written, mixing pleas, threats and even proposing a new prayer. When Biddulph arrived on 22 May, the local population made it immediately clear that they would not submit. They went looking for Andries Pretorius.

When they finally found him, he was sitting at his wife's deathbed. She famously told him[19]:

"By staying here, you cannot save my life; your countrymen need your services, go and help them"

He left with his countrymen and never saw her alive again.

Pretorius approached the matter in stark black and white fashion. On 12 July, he chased Biddulph out of Winburg and published a notice that all who were not prepared to fight in this Freedom Struggle were to cross the Orange River into the Cape Colony before 20 July. A few Afrikaner parties who disagreed with Pretorius, preferred to go into laager. He let them be.

Then Pretorius rode up to the outskirts of Bloemfontein, the largest center, and met with Major Warden, commander of the British Forces in the Trans-Orange. The outcome was that that Pretorius courteously provided him with wagons and an escort out of the Trans-Orange. The British left Trans-Orange in perfect safety with all their property, private and public, as had been promised. Pretorius was a man of his word. He then drew up a memorandum to Harry Smith indicating that all this was a consequence of Harry Smith not accepting the voice of the majority of the settlers in the Trans-Orange, as he had said he would in their original agreement on the slopes of the Drakensberg. The Boer and Brit forces then stared at each other across the Orange River. This would not be the last time they would do so. Smith promptly mobilized all Imperial troopers in the Cape Colony and marched for the Orange River. He also placed a £1,000 bounty on Pretorius' head. Pretorius did his best to communicate with Smith, but the latter was not talking, he was threatening. By 16 August, all talk was over.

The British crossed the Orange unopposed and marched for Bloemfontein. Harry Smith was at the head of a formal army of 800 men, joined by 250 Griqua men under chiefs Adam Kok and Hendrik Waterboer. Smith provided the Griqua with horses and guns. Here we again have the British pointedly enlisting men of other races against their own kin; a pattern they would follow into the 21st Century. Theal[20] describes them as varying in appearance *from the pure savage in a sheepskin kaross to the half-breed in plumed hat and European costume.* The ensuing Battle of Boomplaats was well fought on both sides, but Pretorius' well thought out plan was frustrated by men who fired too soon when they saw Harry Smith himself in his colorful garb riding at the head of his troops into the ambush zone. At the end of the day, the Afrikaners were defeated. The British had 20 dead and 33 badly wounded. The Afrikaners suffered nine killed and five wounded.

Now followed an event that Smith probably regretted many times over afterwards. The British had captured two Republican stragglers; one a boy named Dreyer, the other an Irish deserter named Quigly. Smith promptly held a Court-Martial, condemned them to death and had them shot. The fact that the British had inspected young Dreyer's gun and that it had never even been fired, never entered their thinking. This kind of thing was not in the Afrikaner "playbook." They were utterly aghast. Their view of the British as oppressors was hereby affirmed. Many were angry at Pretorius for not having kept some of the British as hostages as a deterrent against this kind of British behavior, which they believed to be in character. His defense was that he had never expected this conduct from a Christian.

While there is no recorded evidence to support the statement, it has been said in Afrikaner circles for more than 160 years that Harry Smith, in his arrogant effort to ride at the head of the reconnaissance troop, had in fact been wounded in the buttocks and that his personal shame at this event drove him to this monstrous deed. That would certainly have been in keeping with his outlandishly arrogant character. And all the time, in the back of the picture, is the fact that Smith had insisted to the British Government that the majority in the Trans-Orange had actually wanted British government. It was bald-faced lie. It was going to be difficult for him to explain how it could be that he then had to invade the territory and fight battles to assert British Sovereignty. The Republican opponents of the British moved across the Vaal River into the Transvaal to bide their time. Their places were taken by that most "illustrious denizen" of the British Empire, the land speculator. And so the Trans-Orange also became formally British, at least for the time being.

We return again to the Cape for the next installment of Frontier Horror, courtesy of the London Missionary Society, the Unquestioning Liberals of their day.

The War of Mlanjeni

When farmers on the frontier saw their workers suddenly returning to amaXhosa territory in middle 1850, they knew war was brewing. Just as in 1819 with Nxele, the problem was an individual who claimed supernatural powers. This one's name was Mlanjeni. The amaXhosa were told to trust that charms he gave them, based on *pelargonium pulverulentum* roots, would cause British guns to shoot hot water and their powder to fail[21]. Naturally, this bolstered the amaXhosa morale for another war with the Colony.

When Governor Harry Smith invited all Xhosa chiefs to a meeting at King William's Town in the earlier

Queen Adelaide's Province on 26 October, not a single senior Ngqika Xhosa chief appeared. Only a few minor captains turned up. In reaction to this, Smith one-sidedly deposed Sandile as paramount chief of the amaXhosa; not a good idea at the best of times. Finally, in a staggering demonstration of the infamous Harry Smith arrogance, he decided on a tour through British Kaffraria to "Show the Flag," arrest chiefs who had not shown due respect, and generally attempt to intimidate the proud Xhosa. Smith himself, always eager to lead from somewhere near the front, occupied a strong point known as Fort Cox, on a foothill of the Amatole Mountain. So convinced was he of his dominance over the amaXhosa, that he gave standing orders for his men not to load their muskets for fear of creating an incident.

On 24 December 1850, a 650-strong army of British and Cape Corps Khoekhoe troops from Fort Cox wound its way down the slopes of the Amatole foothills. With them was a large contingent of the amaXhosa "Kaffir Police." These were the very people who the Afrikaner Commandos had given as reason for their reluctance to participate in the War of the Axe. The Afrikaners had firmly believed this ill-conceived British invention to be populated with Xhosa spies. When this army reached the Boomah Pass, they had to proceed in single file along the rugged defile. Thousands of Xhosa warriors suddenly appeared out of the forest. Twelve[22] men were killed and many more wounded. On their way back to Fort Cox, they found the mutilated remains of sixteen more men. The Eighth Frontier War, the War of Mlanjeni, had started.

Harry Smith, having positioned himself beyond the lines of the battle, now found himself isolated and surrounded at Fort Cox. Meanwhile the Xhosa descended on the settlers in the small military villages in the idyllic Tyumie Valley on Christmas Day. It was a massacre. As was their custom at the time, the Xhosa spared the white women and small children. But all men and older boys were murdered. Some forty men died in this event. The women and children were stripped of almost all their clothes and made to walk back to safety.

Fig. 13-6 The British Army assaults the Amatole Mountain stronghold

After a failed attempt to relieve him, in which another two officers and twenty men died, Harry Smith, at the head of two hundred and fifty Cape Corps Khoekhoe soldiers, dashed for safety through the Xhosa ranks. This was when he discovered that his "Kaffir Police" had deserted to the enemy. The Afrikaners had been horribly right yet again. This had become an established pattern. And then it became clear that the Khoekhoe of the Kat River and of the Theopolis Mission Station had also joined the Ngqika Xhosa. Both of these were London Missionary Society-dominated establishments. Finally the influence of the Society was clear for all to see. There was no more denying it. Scores of innocent British were dead, and, through the eyes of the Settlers, it was the indirect hand of the London Missionary Society that had killed them.

It is important to note that this "Hottentot Rebellion," as it was called, did not extend to the loyal Khoekhoe people from the West Cape. It was largely confined to those areas under the sway of the London Missionary Society and the Gonaqua. The Gonaqua were the last of the original East Cape Khoekhoe people who still maintained a modicum of tribal structure. These *"Gonas,"* as they were known, had intermingled with the Khoekhoe and half-Khoekhoe people at Kat River and with some of the amaXhosa. At Theopolis, the Rebel Khoekhoe mowed down the unarmed amaFengu black people who thought they were in a place of religious refuge. In the region adjoining the Amatole Mountain, Khoekhoe captain "Hermanus" led the rebel Khoekhoe in an attack on Fort Beaufort, but the inhabitants beat them off and managed to kill "Hermanus" in the process. He had been another Khoekhoe leader who had professed undying loyalty shortly before and who had the support of the LMS. Smith wrote home that[23]:

> *"These Hottentots are the most favoured race on earth, yet have a set of Radical London Society missionaries been preaching to them like evil spirits that they were an oppressed and ill-used race, until, encouraged by violent meetings all over the Colony upon the convict question, they have met with arms in their hands, arms given to them by us..."*

The War of Mlanjeni was the most expensive to that date in the colony. Significantly, the Afrikaner Commandos were not formally called up, but were asked to volunteer. They largely refused. Their distrust of the "Kaffir Police" and the Kat Rivier LMS Khoekhoe lay at the heart of this. Beyond the Amatole, in the Tarka, they did form up and quickly pushed Maphasa (*NF42*) and his Tamboekies from the area. Eventually, Harry Smith got the upper hand and slowly pushed the Xhosa back. The leaders of the rebel Khoekhoe were captured and jailed by the British. In late 1851, the British were still losing officers to the Xhosa on the slopes of the Amatole. At this point, Harry Smith received the inevitable letter[24]:

> *"It is my painful duty to inform you that...[...]...you have failed to show that foresight, energy and judgment which your very difficult position required, and that therefore the Government of the Cape of Good Hope and the conduct of the war should be placed in other hands."*

It is known that Harry "Wackalong Smite" Smith, Britain's Hero of Aliwal, he who put his foot on the necks of kings, kept a stoic face until in the cabin of the ship and then broke down. Clearly his exceptional arrogance had got the better of him. It was his arrogance that made him trust the "Kaffir Police," that made him try to humiliate the Xhosa, and that caused him to get cut off at Fort Cox. Similarly, in the Boomplaats affair, it was his arrogance that led him to annex the Trans-Orange and that led to his callous execution of young Dreyer. Both nations whom he had referred to as "his children" had taken up arms against Britain. Just too many difficulties seemed to be related to the singular arrogance of Sir Henry George Wakelyn Smith, the "Thoroughly Modern Major General."

Nexus Familia 64: The name on the lonely Obelisk

On 18 March 1851, our 31-year old ancestral brother Richard Bowles Jr. is trying to reach Grahamstown with his wagon and cattle from his home on the Kariega River[25]. He is the eldest son of the sailor-soldier Richard Bowles (*NF41*) by his new wife Elizabeth Taylor. Richard Jr. is traveling in the company of an escort. The farm is simply too unsafe to remain there any longer. His wife has already been removed to the safety of Grahamstown, along with a party of other Settlers.

When they reach the hill overlooking Grahamstown, widely known as Woest Hill, they decide to rest. A fire is lit and then the inevitable happens as the weary farmers fall asleep. Out of the dark of the night the Xhosa warriors appear. The little Xhosa servant boys around the fire are killed. One farmer is tortured to death with assegais; another is shot but is not mortally wounded. Richard is stabbed and left for dead. The cattle are taken—but Richard is not dead. With the aid of his gun and a staff, and a Xhosa woman of the party, he makes his way into town. Later that evening, Richard dies, becoming thereby the first direct member of our British family ancestry to die in war in South Africa.

An obelisk will one day be erected right next to the south wall of the

Fig. 13-7 The memorial obelisk

Anglican Settlers' Church in Bathurst. It will list the names of the settlers killed in the Border wars. Near the bottom one of those entries will read: *"R. Bowles 18-3-1851 Woest Hill"*

—End Nexus Familia

Death at sea and on land

When Harry Smith's replacement, Sir George Cathcart, arrived, he did so with massive military reinforcements and supplies. However, despite the fact that Harry Smith had been dismissed for his ineffectual war effort, Cathcart did not do anything different. Matters became more brutal and the War of Mlanjeni seemed to finally bring out the worst in the British psyche. They discovered that, when the Xhosa managed to capture any British soldiers, they exacted the worst of torture on these unfortunate men. The bandmaster of the 74th Highlanders was captured by the Xhosa. A witness later formally testified that the bandmaster had been brutally tortured[26] for three days, a joint being cut from each of his fingers and toes every day. His flesh was left hanging from his body. Then they gave him his own flesh to eat. Eventually, the poor man was shot.

The British were now discovering what the Afrikaners had known for a while. After all, the author's own ancestral brother had been tortured to death by the Xhosa earlier (*NF29*). Now the Xhosa were cutting off the heads[27] of British Settlers and sending these to Mlanjeni for ritualistic purposes. There were also rumors that live British captives had been slowly roasted to death. All tolerance was at an end.

The taking of body parts for ritualistic purposes and potions, so called *muti,* has been a long-standing aspect of life in Africa, and the amaXhosa are no exception. Even in the first decade of the 21st century Canadians were shocked to hear that children were being killed in Africa in order to make potions[28] for rituals. In 2004, war graves in South Africa were being dug up for the bones of the fallen for similar potion usage[29]. These aspects of Africa die slowly and may, in fact, never die at all.

The parties fighting on the British side south of the mountains were mostly regular British forces or volunteer units from among the British Settlers. The Settlers had been caught totally wrong-footed in the 1834 war, but now they knew the Xhosa and their behavior in war. These volunteer units now had no mercy, especially not after they saw how their civilian kin had been murdered and how captured British soldiers had been tortured, disemboweled and beheaded.

It was the influence of a certain Lieutenant-Colonel William Eyre that made the actual difference in the end. He drove his men like slaves and actively instilled cruelty as a systematic method. Harry Smith had not had the stomach for this, but nevertheless gave the order to start burning all Xhosa lands and food supplies in January 1852, even before Cathcart arrived. Finally faced with starvation, the Xhosa started suing for peace before the autumn harvest season, but just then Harry Smith was recalled and the twin-masted paddle wheel steamer *HMS Birkenhead* sank off Danger Point with the loss of 358 soldiers bound for Port Elizabeth and the front.

For the British this was the occasion of the first use of the principle of "Women and Children First," with the soldiers standing to attention as the ship sank. For the Xhosa it had a

Fig. 13-8 HMS Birkenhead - women and children first

totally different meaning: it caused them to believe that Mlanjeni's promises were starting to come true. So they fought harder, even as their people starved. When Cathcart arrived, he simply allowed the burning and the slaughter to continue and offered no peace. The final push came at the slopes of the Amatole Mountain.

By then, the Xhosa were walking skeletons. Eyre now added a new element to his horrors. He had his men hang the bodies of the Xhosa dead from trees as a warning to others. The war now assumed a dimension of horror that is best left described in the words of the British soldiers themselves[30]:

> *"They* [black auxiliaries] *shot several men, women and children, and took women and children prisoners, but they shot more than half of them before we got down the hill."*

During the last drive up the slopes of the Amatole, Captain W.R. King[31] reported:

> *"As we ascended, the evidences of the fight became more frequent; rolling skulls, dislodged by those in front, came bounding down between our legs ; the bones lay thick among the loose stones in the sluits* [ditches] *and gullies, and the bush on either side showed many a bleaching skeleton. A fine specimen of a Kaffir head, I took the liberty of putting into my saddle-bag, and afterwards brought home with me to Scotland..."*

The Xhosa never quite surrendered, but the war was in effect over. Mlanjeni, the man who had provided the impetus for the war and who would forever more be associated with it, died[32] in 1853, shortly after the collapse of the Xhosa war effort. He was just 23 years old. This war saw the end of the traditional royal leaders of the Xhosa as leaders in war.

The End of Dr. Philip

The War of the Axe, the War of Mlanjeni and the associated "Hottentot Rebellion" finally spelled the end of not just Harry Smith, but also of Dr. John Philip. His machinations, provocations, and political attacks on all English Settlers, Afrikaners and any responsible Cape Government had finally caught up with him. His family life also turned to horror.

In July 1845, John Philip's son William, who was a pastor of the "Coloured" congregation at Hankey near Port Elizabeth, was drowned along with Philip's grandson, John Fairbairn Jr. His wife, Jane, died in October 1847. A few weeks later, one of his granddaughters was killed in an accident.

Back in England, the directors of the London Missionary Society now finally had the insight and presence of mind to doubt his judgment. For his part, he felt that they were betraying their principles. By this time, he was reviled by Boer and Brit alike. He had consistently argued against their interests in nearly every domain. Both Boer and Brit saw him as the direct cause of the death of their families.

In the civil domain, the Settlers bayed for the blood of the London Missionary Society men. British Settler John Green[33], stepson of ancestor Richard Bowles (*NF41, 42*), wrote a letter to the *Graham's Town Journal* on 24 May 1851 at the time of the court case of Andries Botha of the rebel Khoekhoe:

Fig. 13-9 *The settlement at Hankey, where "Dr." Philip retired and died.*

THE REV. H. RENTON AND THE KAT RIVER.

To THE EDITOR:
SIR, — Much has been written about the rebellion in the Kat River by parties at a distance from the scene, and no doubt much more will be written. Perhaps it is matter of wonder that no eye-witnesses have written to any of the newspapers; but for my own part I have had my own reasons for my silence: the principal one being that I was waiting to see if the missionaries, or any of the six ordained ministers who were residing at Philipton, exclusive of Mr. Thomson, would come forward and state their own case.
The names of the missionaries I refer to are as follows :
— Mr. Renton, Messrs. Read (2), Mr. Niven, Mr. Cumming, Mr. A. van Rooy.

I was desirous of seeing whether any one of these would come honestly forward before the public, and declare, without partiality, the wickedness, the deceit, the robbery, and the murderous designs carried on in that settlement, and by that professedly Christian community and acknowledge fairly that they were deceived by their people. [...] Omitting to make any remarks (at present) on the evidence given by some of these rev. gentlemen, I do assert, fearless of contradiction, that they have done great discredit to their profession as preachers of the Gospel and professed servants of the God of truth.

I am one of the party that fled from Fort Armstrong on the 23rd of January. I can give reason that will satisfy the world why I stopped at Philipton. At that time, little did I think that that place was soon to become the harbour, or halfway house or hiding place, of any rebels who chose to stop there. I little thought that this would be allowed by their ministers, and that they would be permitted to act as they pleased. [...]

JOHN GREEN

The London Missionary Society squirmed every which way they could, but their hegemony was over. The Society was finally mortally wounded and from this day on it would never again have the voice it had had before. All of Western Civilization in Southern Africa breathed more easily. The elderly Dr. Philip had retired in 1850 and, to no one's surprise, had gone to live in the largely Khoekhoe-descended community of Hankey, west of Port Elizabeth. It is to be doubted whether he would have been welcome anywhere else. There, he died a broken man on August 27, 1851, and was buried by his Khoekhoe constituency. Thereby he came to rest among the people whose interests he had always put above those of his own people, and certainly above those of any Afrikaners, whom he profoundly hated and upon whom he made constant political war, both at the Cape and in England. During his entire life he never exhibited any understanding of the predicament the Afrikaner found himself in. Sadly, many welcomed his demise as much as that of Dingane. It is popularly said that God made his displeasure known at this man by causing a big tree to collapse on his grave and split his gravestone in two. The author has no evidence of the stone being split.

A deep and profound hatred of even the memory of this individual permeates Afrikaner history. Many lay the basics of Apartheid at his door. He promoted a solution for South Africa that consisted of Black, White, and, above all, Khoekhoe, sharing equally a common area controlled by Britain. However, in his model, whites should be forcibly excluded from any say in matters relating to events outside those areas from whence blacks, and now Khoekhoe, could attack the colony with impunity, given that he could not conceive of them as being aggressors. Thereby, many feel he implicitly recognized Black Homelands, the subject of later international obsession about South Africa. He was wholly incapable of conceiving of a life in a country controlled by the very people whom he steadfastly promoted. Adherents of his views today remain people beset by a strange form of racial arrogance. They consider their own culture so superior, that they cannot conceive of it being in any danger. Therefore they attack it, deride it and break it down around every corner even as they deeply rely on it to trumpet their views.

The deaths of those hundreds at Umgungundlovu, Blaauwkranz and the Tyumie Valley were laid at his door, with considerable justification. He was the root cause of the Great Trek. To this day, many Afrikaners see him as the true embodiment of Prime Evil masquerading behind the Cloth. He was no doubt a man with good intentions, but few men in history so avidly paved the way to Hell with those intentions and harried his own kin along that path to oblivion with such devotion.

The major negative impact of the London Missionary Society disappeared with him, but they had done their damage and South Africa would suffer for it to this day. Considering how laudable their goals had been, it is sad indeed that this organization had become such a suppurating sore in the side of civilization. And yet slavery, the basis of their creation, persisted elsewhere in Africa. They had achieved nothing but the deaths of their own. It would be the impact of the horrific Indian Mutiny some five years later that would finally ring their death knell throughout the British Empire. After that, the British government would drop the pretense of fostering Christianity when it was actually fostering Empire.

Reflection on the "Hottentot" Rebellion

While the "Hottentot Rebellion" was an infinitely more serious event than the earlier Slagtersnek Rebellion on the part of Frontier Afrikaners, it was also not without cause. While the role of the LMS in the Kat River Rebellion was undeniable and unforgivable, it remains true that what had happened to the people of that settlement prior to the rebellion had simply been inexcusably wrong.

Stockenström had meant for the Kat River Settlement to be a defense mechanism between the Colony and the Xhosa. However, before he had been able to get any decent missionaries placed there, Dr. Philip had insinuated the LMS there, had created Philipton, and had started convincing "his" flock that they were oppressed. As we have seen, he had then represented them and the Xhosa in London, thereby managing to get Governor D'Urban dismissed and causing the Great Trek and all the associated murders in Natal. He had also earned the mortal hatred of the British Settlers whom he had accused of being the cause of Hintsa's War. He had even managed to convince London of that.

However, it is true that both British Commissioners Bowker and Biddulph had despised the very people they were supposed to care for. Whether they had had reason to is a separate debate. What is clear is that there were entirely decent people in the Kat River Settlement, but there were also some truly lamentable characters who were attracted to the place. Many of the latter were Gonaqua from outside the Colony. While the core of the people was diligent and devoted, the layabouts they attracted were bound to cause a problem as was always the caution of the Afrikaners. The latter had by now known the "Vagrant Khoekhoe Problem" for centuries and had predicted what would happen. Now it had happened, and none of those who had designed the problems were there to take responsibility for their actions, except Stockenström.

To this needs to be added the conduct of the "Kaffir Police" who were brought in by the commissioners to remove some "squatters" from the settlement, and who then proceeded to indiscriminately burn the decent Khoekhoe out of their homes. This understandably turned many Khoekhoe into rebels. However, as the Afrikaners had already learnt, it did not matter how realistic your grievances were, the British Government would not listen. But, if you dared lift a finger against them, they would hang you; twice, if they could.

The Kat River Settlement had been a well-intentioned idea that had gone quite predictably wrong.

Free at Last!

Even before the War of Mlanjeni was over, George Cathcart led a major fraction of his British Army north into the Trans-Orangia. As Captain W.R. King, who went on this expedition, put it:

> "The object of the expedition was to demand satisfaction from the Basuto Chief, Moshesh, whose 'Great Place' lay some hundred miles beyond the Orange River, for the constant and increasing depredations and attacks of his tribe, and of the neighbouring minor Chiefs, his vassals, on the Boers of the Orange River Territory, and on the Barolong Chief, Moroko. The latter was a staunch ally of our Government, but did not dare alone attempt reprisals on a Chief so much more powerful, while the former, as being under British rule and protection, were prohibited from avenging themselves."

There is an irony, bordering on hilarity, in these proceedings. The Afrikaner had left the Cape Colony because the British would not protect them. Britain had then put every conceivable impediment in their way and even stole their country three times in a row. Now Britain was sending its army into territory the Afrikaner had secured in the Great Trek to recover the Afrikaners' stolen cattle from Moshesh's country, and no Boer commando was required. The Trans-Orange Afrikaners must have been not a little bemused.

The Ba'Sotho fought well in the single battle of the campaign, were entirely undefeated and were actually in command of the situation. It was a large and visible loss for the Victorian British Army in a colonial war, and London noticed. The wily old King Moshesh read the situation perfectly correctly, and so, on the night of that single battle, Cathcart received the following diplomatic masterpiece of a message[34]:

> *Thaba Bossigo,*
> *Midnight, December 20th, 1852.*
>
> *Your Excellency, — This day you have fought against my people, and taken much cattle. As the object for which you have come is to have a compensation for Boers, I beg you will be satisfied with what you have taken. I entreat peace from you. You have shown your power; you have chastised; let it be enough, I pray you, and let me no longer be considered an enemy of the Queen. I will try all I can to keep my people in order for the future.*
>
> *Your humble servant, MOSHESH.*

Truthfully, this was a clear Ba'Sotho victory, known as the Battle of Berea, but the pompous Cathcart declared it a sound British victory and marched back to the Cape. The fact is, he had secured all the "punishment" cattle he was going to get before the battle. The entire battle achieved nothing but the deaths of 38 brave British soldiers whose bodies had to be left behind. Cathcart ap-pealed to Moshesh to in-

Fig. 13-10 *Thaba Bosigo, the Ba'Sotho stronghold*

ter the bodies after receipt of the letter. Today, the Basotho are proud of this battle and rightly so. Cathcart left them in command of their own destiny. In truth, he had done no better against South African indigenous opposition than the unfortunate Harry Smith, and more likely worse.

Earlier in the same year, on 17 January 1852, the British signed the Sand River Convention, which recognized the region beyond the Vaal River as autonomous. Cathcart's escapades with the Ba'Sotho had raised the visibility of the colony in Britain. By now, it was clear that Harry Smith, in his arrogance, had misrepresented the situation to the Earl Grey in London. While he had suggested two thirds of the population of the territory supported British rule, it now appeared that a full nine tenths opposed it. In the British parliament, the Undersecretary of State for Colonies, quoted what Adderley had said of the region[35]:

> *"It secures no genuine interests – it is recommended by no prudent or justifiable motive – it answers no really beneficial purpose – it imparts no strength to the British Government, no credit to its character and no lustre to its crown."*

While history would eventually prove the words *"no lustre to its crown"* dead wrong in the most direct fashion possible, it came as no surprise to anyone in 1853 when Sir John Pakington decided to implement the Earl Grey's earlier decision to abandon the territory. On 11 March 1854, the flag of England was saluted for the last time in Bloemfontein, and lowered. As though fate wanted to make a point on this subject, one of the British soldiers attending promptly made history by dropping dead[36].

The Trans-Orange became the "Republic of the Orange Free State." The territory beyond the Vaal River became the "South African Republic." The two were more popularly known as the "Vrystaat" (Free State) and the "Transvaal." The Afrikaners finally had their freedom from British rule and two Republics of their own. For the next twelve years they could focus on living in honorable friendship with chief Moroka and his Ba'Rolong and tend to their cattle, corn and wheat. In fact, the Free State became a model agrarian state while the Transvaal became the "Wild West" of Southern Africa.

In 1854, the Cape Colony was finally granted Representative Government – eighteen years too late for the Trekkers.

Nexus Familia 65: In the Aftermath of the Great Trek

After the epic trials and horrors of the Great Trek, what follows is a period of comparative stability that allows us to take stock of the families we have been following and to tie together several hitherto separate ancestral lines. We also use this opportunity to place the family characters on the chessboard of history for the next set of momentous events that will leave their lives torn asunder.

The Jordaan–Klopper–Prinsloo Clan of Natal: In the path of war

After the annexation of Natal, relatively few Afrikaner families remain in Natal, despite Harry Smith's desperate efforts to stem the flow of "his children" as he calls the Afrikaners. The majority of those who remain do so in the region between the Tugela and the Buffalo Rivers. This is undulating grassland, known as the Klip River District (Rocky River), and is much better suited to corn and cattle ranching than the lowlands of the Natal colony, which are too tropical for these people from a dry country.

One of the families that remain in this area is that of Chris Jordaan. His extended family now includes the wife and the children of Pieter Georg, his older brother who died a horrific death by impalement at Umgungundlovu (*NF56*). They all live on a farm just north of the later Dundee in a valley on the Biggarsberg, named for Alexander Biggar (*NF63* and Chapter 12: *Oh terrible torture death*). The farm will later be surveyed and named Prestwick. The younger of these "Rocky River" children have been baptized at the Church of the Vow in Pietermaritzburg. For the first few years the honors have ironically been done by none other than the American, Reverend Dan-iel Lindley from the Rocky River parish of North Carolina, who so dramatically fled from Mzilikatse's land with Hendrik Potgieter after the Battle of Mosega in 1836. The minister from Rocky River in America is now baptizing the chil-dren from Rocky River in South Africa.

Fig. 13-11 Pietermaritzburg in 1854

The location of the family Jordaan will place them near the heart of future military conflicts in South Africa. Like the people of the Alsace and the Saarland in Europe, they will pay heavily for that. In the meantime, the Colony of Natal enters a period of peace until 1879.

By 1860, Chris Jordaan and Maria Klopper have no fewer than 11 children. Four others have died, including the baby boy born in Mud Laager (*NF60*). The second last child, Margaretha Johanna, is born in 1855 and baptized in the Church of the Vow the following year. She is our ancestor. Her much older sister and brother, Susanna and Johannes, both marry descendants of the tough old frontier settler, Willem Prinsloo, from the middle 1700s (*NF43*). The links within the Jordaan-Klopper-Prinsloo Clan are thereby again strengthened.

The Lötter–Naudé–Joubert and Grobler Families: The Lötter Rebel Blood

In 1860, on a farm in the Jansenville district of the *Noorsveld* (See *Fig. 4-5*) a little baby girl is born to parents Stephanus Smit and Susanna Sophia Lötter Joubert. She is baptized Johanna Catharina Smit in the Dutch Reformed Church in town. Johanna is the great grandmother of the author.

Father Stephanus counts among his recent ancestors Field-Cornet Stephanus Naudé, whose murder helped precipitate the demise of the hated Magistrate Maynier (*NF37*). It was also Stephanus' mother's family who provided the wagon that went to Mzilikatse with Captain William Cornwallis Harris in 1836 (*NF45*). Another of his ancestors is Johanna Bouwer, whose sister Martha succumbed to malaria with her husband Louis Trichardt in Delagoa Bay at the end of the fateful Trichardt Trek (*NF44, 47, 53,* and *61*).

Mother Susanna counts among her ancestors Pierre Jaubert from the Lubéron region of Provence in France (*NF19*). Her father was Pieter Schalk Joubert Jr. whose Joubert relatives were massacred by the amaZulu (*NF59, Fig. 11-8*). Another of her ancestors is Casper Labuschagne, who was murdered along with his son by the San Bushmen (Chap. 4: *Obiqua!*).

This marriage of staunch French Huguenot Joubert blood with the unyielding Dutch-Afrikaner patriotism of the Lötters will make young Johanna a staunch republican. Susanna's brother Corrie has also married a Lötter lady. Family members still talk with pride of Chris Lötter who confronted the British Magistrate at Graaff-Reinet about the British "Spider Flag" in 1796 (*NF31*). When the time comes, it will be yet again the Lötters who will step to the fore and be counted for the Afrikaner nation. The Lötter name will echo through the British Houses of Parliament, where lesser men will disgrace their justly proud nation.

For Johanna and her mother all that still lies in the future. Right now, the life of a little girl on a sheep farm in the Jansenville-Pearston region is a simple one. The extended family fills its days with all the various activities required to take care of the sheep. These range from dipping or shearing sheep to shooting the horrendously damaging *rooikat* (caracal) and *rooijakkals* (black-backed jackal). They also have to guard against black eagles that target the lambs. Wind pumps have not yet been introduced and the farmsteads are therefore located near the few natural springs that occur in this arid semi-desert countryside.

On a farm in the nearby Vogel River area, lives the family of Johanna's future husband. Nicolaas Johannes is the sixth son of ancestor Izak Hermanus Grobler. Izak's oldest uncle, Johannes Grobler, was tortured to death by the amaXhosa in the Second Frontier war of 1793 (*NF29*), while his younger uncle, Willem Grobler, was imprisoned by the British in reprisal for the Van Jaarsveld Rebellion and threatened with banishment from the country (*NF33, 36*). Izak's cousin Reynier was impaled by Zulu King Dingane (*NF57*) while Reynier's brother Michael, together with his wife and all four of their children, was massacred by the Zulu at Blaauwkranz (*NF59*).

Because Izak elected to remain in the Cape Colony and did not join the Great Trek, he has had to serve on Commando under Harry Smith against the amaXhosa. Young Nicolaas' family also has very close ties with their Lötter relatives. That is why the witnesses to his 1855 baptism in the Jansenville Dutch Reformed Church were his oldest uncle Nicolaas and his wife Johanna Susanna Sophia Lötter. All of the farmers in this desperately dry region of less than 300mm rain per annum have meanwhile turned to sheep farming. The lower lying plains of the district are simply too dry for cattle ranching. However, while the countryside looks like Nevada, this Southern Karoo region is blessed with the nutritious Karoo scrub, which provides good pasture for sheep and a unique and much sought after flavor to South African lamb. By the second half of the 19th century, the focus of these farmers has turned to the all-important wool. It is the wool farms of this area that have now made Port Elizabeth into the biggest export harbor of the country. Of course all the wool is transported the 150 miles by means of the ubiquitous ox wagon.

The Myburghs – Life in the Achter-Sneeuberg

In the Achter-Sneeuberg (*NF43*), Albertus Jacobus "Albert" Myburgh is in his 40s and is married to Renske from another branch of the Myburgh family. By the end of 1860, Renske has given Albert six children. The fourth child is Albert Jr., the author's great-grandfather, who was born in March 1857 in the Quaggashoek (Zebra 'Corner') area of the Achter-Sneeuberg, west of Cradock. By the end of 1861, the family is still living on the farm Roode Taaijbosch. Albert Sr. now runs the wagon building enterprise on the farm, having taken it over from his father Koos (*NF41*). Albert is the preferred supplier of wagons of different types to the much-respected Cawood Brothers Stores of Cradock. At this time, the Cawoods (*NF41* and "*The English Afrikaners*") are a leading British Settler family in the Cradock district.

Life on Roode Taaijbosch is uncomplicated and settled for young Albert Jr. His mother, "Renschie" as everyone calls her, has her hands full keeping him away from the workshop. Young Albert is fascinated with the wheels and in particular with the dramatic process of fitting the heated iron rims on the wooden wheel frames. He particularly loves the chilling process when the rims are cooled with water and clouds of steam erupt to the cracking of the spokes setting into the frame. This appeals to a young boy's mind. Young Albert has to be constantly evicted from Albert Senior's workshop when the dangerous 200 lb. bags of Smith's coal and the iron and wood supplies are offloaded. In the 21st century, the estate documents of Albert Sr. in the Cape Archives will provide a detailed record of the purchases for the wagon making enterprise, all bought on consignment at Cawood's in Cradock. The young man grows up surrounded by these bags of Smith's coal, bags of chaff and the sounds of the wagon building workshop. The unique smell of steam and coal smoke is part of his existence.

Albert notices that his father sometimes has difficulty breathing, what with the chaff he uses to stoke the fire for his forge and coal dust and fumes from the forge. Some nights he can hear his father coughing and wheezing. Albert Sr. has been ordering classic Lennon's Dutch phytomedicines from Mr. Engels' little country pharmacy down the mountain in the hamlet of Petersburg to address his problem, but it is rapidly getting worse. The fact that Roode Taaijbosch is located high up on the snowy plateau behind the Sneeuberg does not help. The combination of thin air, floating chaff dust, coal smoke and steam is taking its toll on Albert's lungs and heart. The list of medicine from Mr. Engels is appropriate for someone suffering from heart-lung problems. On 1 October 1862, Albert Senior can no longer breathe properly. Mr. Engels' medicine is no longer helping. Renschie anxiously sends her oldest son, the 12-year old Hendrik, for Dr. Grey in Cradock. The doctor gets as far as the Doorn River with his horse-'n-buggy. Here he receives the message that Albert has finally succumbed to his heart-lung problems at the age of only 47. Doctor Grey's £5 invoice for his abortive mission will be duly entered in the records in the Cape Archives. It is at this sad juncture that the fortunes of the Myburgh wagon-maker family of the Achter-Sneeuberg start to steadily decline.

In 1863, just outside nearby Graaff-Reinet, Martina Fouché is born, destined to be little Albert's wife. She is a direct descendant of Paul Fouché who held the VOC government at gunpoint in 1795 (*NF30*). Her bloodline is almost 100% French.

The Bassons – In the Cape and in the Transvaal

The Cape Bassons (*NF43*) are still growing their wheat and making their wine in the district of Swartland around Malmesbury, the breadbasket of the country. They are now represented by 38-year old Pieter Abraham Basson. Pieter's 17-year old son, yet another Matthys Michiel, is the great-grandfather of the author's wife. He is named for Matthijs Michiel Clement who arrived from Sweden some 18 years after the founding of the Cape settlement. Clement's daughter Helena married "Jacht" Basson's eldest son, Willem (*NF12*), on 14 September 1670.

The Great Trek Bassons, whom we have followed all the way from the Swartruggens in the East Cape

(*NF43, 48, 54, 56, 57,* and *59*), are now represented by Marie Salomé and her husband, Matthys Michiel. They have elected to leave Natal where Matthys' brother, Willem, was murdered by Dingane (*NF56, 57*), and have moved to the Transvaal Republic. They eventually settle on the farm Rhenosterfontein (Rhino Fountain) in the Marico district of Western Transvaal, not far from Mosega, where Hendrik Potgieter defeated Mzilikatse (*NF46 - section 3*). Marie Salomé has carefully preserved her Great Trek diary in a solid wooden chest.

The Booyens family – On the chessboard of History

The Booyens family in the South Cape is now represented by Pieter Johannes Booyens Jr. (born 1824), son of Pieter Johannes senior (*NF43*) and great great grandson of immigrant Pieter Booyens (*NF25*). Pieter and his brothers live on the farm Rietvley (Reed Valley) in the Little Karoo, between the two parallel ranges of the Kammanassie Mountains and the rugged 7,000-foot Swartberg (Black Mountain) near the later town of De Rust. This is dry country along the Olifants (Elephant) River. The Swartberg and Kammanassie Mountain ranges either side of the farm both collect snow in winter. The unique combination of dry climate and good water makes for excellent mixed farming. The activities range from ostrich farming to cultivating fruit under irrigation. All fruit seems to be sweeter here. Away from the river it can be hell, but where water touches the ground in this part of the world, it is transformed into a fruit orchard or vineyard.

Pieter Johannes married Maria Stander in 1855 in the Dutch Reformed Church in George. She is a descendant of Jacob Louw who opposed the Cape Governor in 1707 (*NF22*). George is the nearest major town, situated on the coastal side of the parallel mountain ranges.

The descendants of Pieter Johannes's two Booyens uncles, Matthys Stephanus and Daniel Jan Andries, will feature prominently in future. We shall follow a few of them: Pieter Johannes' uncle Matthys Stephanus trekked with his family to the Free State in the 1850s where his first wife died in 1857. He has since remarried at the advanced age of 71. Not only that, but his much younger second wife has given him two sons. Our interest is in the second son from this marriage, Barend Matthys Johannes, who is born in 1861 in the Bloemfontein district. Because Barend is born so late in his father's life, he is a massive 48 years younger than his oldest half-brother. In fact, he is 11 years younger than his oldest Booyens nephew. Among those nephews we shall follow Johannes Hendrik Booyens, whose father, Pieter Adriaan, is the second son of Matthys Stephanus. Johannes Hendrik is in fact three years older than his uncle Barend Matthys Johannes.

Fig. 13-12 *The aloe studded slopes of the Kammanassie Mountain near the Booyens farm Schilpadbeen*

Pieter Johannes' uncle Daniel Jan Andries has several sons who left the Cape Colony in the 1850s and settled in the Transvaal and Free State. We shall follow the three eldest and their sons in turn:

• Eldest son is Matthys Jacobus. He and his sons have settled in the cattle and corn country of Ventersdorp in the Western Transvaal district of Potchefstroom. Matthys' second son, Tjaart, together with his own sons, will participate in an epic battle that will be the turning point of the greatest war to ever be fought in the country.

• Second son Jacobus Frederik has settled in the area of Heilbron in the northern Free State – right there where the Battle of Vegkop was fought in 1836 against Mzilikatse (*NF46*). He will suffer the consequences of a special British-designed hell, as will his eldest son named Daniel Jan Andries.

• Third son of Pieter Johannes' uncle, Daniel Jan Andries, is named Daniel Jan Andries after his own father. He has settled on the farm *Blesboklaagte* (Blesbok Flats) near Heidelberg in the Southern Transvaal. In 1857, Daniel Jr.'s wife Judith presented him with a son whom they named Adam Johannes. Adam will help to deliver a key victory in the darkest of times.

The Bowles–Misselbrook–McCusker family: The English family in the East Cape

The 43rd Monmouthshire Regiment of the British Army, better known as the "43rd Foot," leaves Cork on the ship "Vulcan" for South Africa on 12 October 1851 under the leadership of Lieutenant-Colonel Henry Skipworth[37]. One of the enlisted men on board is a 29-year old rifleman, James "Mac" McCusker, an Irishman from Dublin. He is reputedly one of six brothers, of whom 3 have gone to America and one to Australia. The ultimate destination of the regiment is the Eastern Cape, where they are to fight the amaXhosa in Mlanjeni's War. The Vulcan arrives in Simon's Town on 8 December 1851, and then proceeds to East London, arriving 9 days later. The unit disembarks and immediately marches for King William's Town, where they meet Sir Harry Smith. The unit had served with him in the Peninsular War. Forty-two men of this unit are also aboard the ill-fated HMS Birkenhead when she departs Simon's Town for Port Elizabeth and hits a submerged rock at Danger Point on 26 February 1852 to create the legendary principle of "Women and Children First."

While this war has some hard-fought battles, it is also a hugely distasteful one in which the 43rd Foot spends much of its time burning down the cornfields of the Xhosa, dooming them to starvation. The units also duly follow Governor Cathcart to fight King Moshesh of the Ba'Sotho. It is on the march to Thaba Bosigo that they go through the Tarka and the "New Hantam" north of it. These much drier districts they experience as "Boer Country:" The soldiers of the 43rd note[38] that:

> "[...] *the Boers are an uncommonly fine race of men, and showed every civility to the troops*"

They they were encountering the first Dutch-descended Afrikaner ladies since disembarking.

After the war is over, the 43rd Foot leaves South Africa on 28 November 1853, but Mac seeks a discharge from the Army and stays in the Cape Colony. On 5 November 1855, he marries Caroline, daughter of William Misselbrook and Esther Bowles (*NF42*) in the Catholic Church in Uitenhage. Mac settles in Graaff-Reinet where he works as a shoemaker and keeps a canteen. By 1858, Mac is a sergeant in the local Volunteer Rifle and Cavalry Corps. By middle 1861, Caroline has given him four boys, of whom James Elijah and Thomas will play a role in our story. Mac is elected to a committee of five to canvass more men for the Corps.

The year 1861 sees him as the sergeant-major of the unit, responsible for keeping the district free of amaXhosa cattle thieves. The unit develops a brass band that will become an establishment in the town for a number of years, providing a means for Caroline's sons to exercise their musical talents.

—End Nexus Familia

The Xhosa National Suicide

On a day in April 1856, young Nongqawuse and Nombanda, who lived in chief Mhlakaza's village just beyond the Kei River, went to the crop fields to scare away the birds. And it was here that "the people" "spoke" to them. And "the people" told Nongqawuse that the she must tell all the amaXhosa to destroy all their cattle and their corn fields, because then the white man will disappear back into the sea. Everything the English had and that the amaXhosa wanted, would come up out of the ground. Furthermore, everything the amaXhosa had was impure and had to be disposed of; clothes, copper rings, cooking utensils, crops, cattle...everything. "The people" explained that they were the "great ones" that Nxele and Mlanjeni had spoken of. At first, Mhlakaza did not believe what Nongqawuse told him, but when she saw "The People" a second time and they called for him by name, he went to speak to them. And this was when he recognized his dead brother, the father Nongqawuse never knew. His departed brother spoke to him through Nongqawuse. From this moment Mhlakaza was convinced. The real impetus for the killing of all the cattle of the amaXhosa, however, came when Sarhili, paramount king and son of Hintsa, declared himself a believer. He was said to have seen the "new People" who would come to establish the independence of the amaXhosa. From this point on these events assumed religious overtones and, to the horror of the missionaries, some of the amaXhosa said that Mhlakaza had a New Word from God. The amaXhosa were heading into national suicide.

Finally the day of 18 February 1857, Mhlakaza's Day, broke. Hundreds of thousands upon hundreds of thousands of amaXhosa sat and watched the sun rise. And they watched it move across the sky. By the end of the day, they knew it had all been a lie and they were already dead. Some were found dead at the empty corn pits they had dug and which were supposed to have filled up again with magic corn from the ground. Others died in groups together. While cannibalism is the strictest taboo among the Xhosa, it was reported repeatedly. Thousands of the amaXhosa flocked into the Colony to offer labor in exchange for food. The amaXhosa were a broken people. The population of just British Kaffraria alone dropped from 105,000 to 37,500 during 1857, some having died and others having fled. Hundreds upon hundreds of parents sought refuge for their children at mission stations. To make matters worse, Sir George Grey, the new Governor, believed that the Xhosa kings and captains were to blame and that they were trying to stir up a war against the colony using national suicide. As a result he imprisoned 900 chiefs, including Maqoma, who had fought the British in so many wars. We close with Sarhili's words to the Anglican Bishop of Grahamstown:

"Tell the governor I am dead"

More than a hundred years later the National Party Government of the Apartheid Era, in a sign of respect for the history of the Xhosa, would use a navy destroyer to return what were believed to be the bones of Maqoma and Sarhili from Robben Island to their name descendants in a major traditional ceremony.

Liberia becomes independent

Meanwhile, far to the northwest along the tropical coast of West Africa, the American Colonization Society was busy populating Liberia. By 1842, four of the other American colonies were incorporated into Liberia, while one was destroyed by indigenous "natives." The colonists were soon referred to as Americo-Liberians. Most of the colonists were still coming from Virginia and its neighboring states. There was a peak in colonist immigration in the period immediately following the slaughter of 55 white Virginians in Nat Turner's Rebellion[39] of August 21-22, 1831 in Southampton County. The white population of Virginia turned on the black population with a vengeance in the wake of this miserable episode. Liberia was one of their options. Between 1820 and 1843 the American Colonization Society sent 4417 black Americans to Liberia. Of those, 1608 (36%) were from Virginia, of whom 53% had been manumitted[40].

By the late 1840s, the American Colonization Society was bankrupt and decided that the best way forward was for Liberia to become a sovereign independent state. This eventually happened in 1847. The first president of the independent country was Joseph Jenkins Roberts of Norfolk. His father had been a freeman in Virginia and his mother had won her freedom in that state.

This all sounded nice, but the troubles of Liberia were far from over. After a generation of settlement, they were no nearer to gaining the acceptance of the local indigenous tribesmen. While the missionaries and agents of the American Colonization Society reported on all the great happenings of their pet project, the reality on the ground was that matters were never quite settled between the "Immigrants" and the "Natives." Ironically, the immigrants from the United States were now the "amaBhulu of West Africa"- the American Black tribe of Africa. As history will show, they fared no better in terms of integration than the European White Tribe of Africa. They were, after all, Black Americans with values, customs and a culture that now differed dramatically from the indigenous people.

And herein lies the subtlety that the so many in the Northern Hemisphere simply cannot see.

-----ooOoo-----

14

Greed and Imperialism

"The furtherance of the British Empire, for the bringing of the whole uncivilized world under British rule, for the recovery of the United States, for making the Anglo-Saxon race but one Empire."

Cecil John Rhodes,
Summarizing the central goal of his life (1877)

Daniel and the shiny stone

In the museum of Colesberg, the hot little Northern Cape Province town that was once the mission station of none other than Erasmus Smit, is an old window pane. And on this windowpane are scratched the letters "DP." This simple windowpane changed the history of the British Empire.

As fate would have it, the story starts in the one small section of the Orange Free State where territorial matters had not been completely settled when theBritish lowered their flag in 1854. Any reasonable person who considers the map of Southern Africa would think the Orange Free State is clearly defined as the piece of land between the Orange and the Vaal Rivers. In fact, this is not the case.

Fig. 14-1 The Big Hole at Kimberley

In 1867, a small section in the west of the Orange Free State was in the hands of the mixed-descent Griqua. However, many Free State farmers farmed there as per agreement with them. There was no formal British presence in any shape or form. At this time, a man named Schalk van Niekerk lived in the Cape Colony, just across the Orange River from this part of the Free State.

One day, while visiting his neighbor Daniel Jacobs, he noticed Daniel's little daughter playing with a shiny stone. She was pretending it to be a lamp in her doll's house. When the child tired of the game, Daniel gave Schalk the stone. Some time later, D.P. O'Reilly, a trader on his way south from a hunting trip, spent the night at Schalk van Niekerk's farm, *De Kalk* and saw Van Niekerk's bright stone. When O'Reilly tried to buy it, Van Niekerk wanted to simply give it to him. But, O'Reilly felt sure that this stone was valuable. So, they agreed to split whatever it fetched. O' Reilly took his find to Colesberg where he reputedly talked about his stone and showed it around. Tiring of O'Reilly's tales, one of his drinking mates reputedly threw it out the door of the local "watering hole" onto the dusty road outside. Fortunately, or unfortunately, it was recovered. O'Reilly took it to the Civil Commissioner, one Lorenzo Boyes, who scratched the initials "D.P." on the window pane with it, thereby concluding that it was a diamond. O'Reilly, heartened by this evidence, then sent it to Dr. W. Guiban Atherstone in Grahamstown to be tested. Then he sent it to Mr. Herite, the French consul in Cape Town, for a second opinion. They both pronounced it to be a 21¼-carat diamond.

Hearing the news, people began searching near the confluence of the Orange and the Vaal Rivers, and soon several more stones were discovered. However, when the massive "Star of Africa" was found in the possession of a Ba'Tlapin witch-diviner in 1869, all hell broke loose across the Anglophone world. The diamond diggings started to spread along the Orange, Vaal, and Harts Rivers.

British avarice – designing an enemy

In the area north of the Vaal River, the South African Republic of the Trekkers was something akin to a Dutch version of the early Texas, a rough and tumble frontier state with lots of European-descended cowboys plagued by indigenous Ba'Ntu tribes on the west, north and east that regularly "went on the warpath."

In 1871, diamonds were discovered east of the Vaal River in what was Orange Free State territory. Napier, the Cape Governor in the 1830s, had once hoped that the Afrikaners would leave Natal and settle in the out of the way interior where, *"deprived of a seaport their consequence would be diminished."* However, soon after the discovery of the diamonds Britain was beset by a newfound altruistic concern for the territorial and other rights of the Griqua against the Afrikaners; this despite the fact that the latter had been living in peace with the Griqua up to that point. Soon enough, an unscrupulous[1] British individual named David Arnot, styling himself "agent" of the Griqua chief Nicolaas Waterboer, made a claim to a huge tract of the land in this area on Waterboer's behalf. Not content with peace in that area, the British then made use of their well-exercised skills at subterfuge. Witness for example Lt. Gen. Hay, who was supposedly negotiating "in good faith" with President John Brand of the Free State, in a letter[2] to the Secretary of State and Colonies:

> *"The governments of the two neighbouring republican states [...] have, since the discovery referred to, assumed an attitude towards the Griqua people and other aboriginal inhabitants which plainly indicates an intention of seizing [...] the whole of the Griqua and adjacent other native territory"*

This was a lie and a manipulation of the situation in favor of the British diamond hunters who had descended on the area. However, the damage was done. To see how insidious the disinformation of the London Missionary Society had been regarding the ever-fictitious slavery, we find that a full 19 years after Dr. Philip's death, and despite all the mountains of evidence to the contrary, the Secretary for State and the Colonies, a man in a position of great responsibility, nevertheless states the following[3]:

> *"Her Majesty's Government would see with great dissatisfaction any encroachment on the Griqua territory by those republics, which would open to the Boers an extended field for their slave-dealing operations."*

The hatred the LMS had fomented in Britain against the Afrikaners had now become ingrained. The leading slaving nation of the planet in the 18th century would keep accusing the Afrikaner repeatedly of exactly that which they knew themselves to have been guilty of — slavery. They made the completely innocent Afrikaner the international whipping boy for the historic excesses burdening their own conscience.

When the Free State and Transvaal entered into negotiation with the Cape Colony on the subject of the diamond fields, a totally farcical commission was set up, duly headed by the obligatory Englishman. The chairman, who happened to be Lieutenant-Governor of Natal, was named Keates. It obviously, predictably, and conveniently ruled in favor of Waterboer. Naturally this required a British presence to "protect" Waterboer. Soon enough, the area was incorporated into the Cape Colony to get it totally under British control. Waterboer and his people were soon forgotten. Of the diamonds they had no benefit. Britain got that.

For one Englishman who had lived in the disputed territory for two years the outrage of what Britain had done proved too much to stomach. He was Captain Augustus F. Lindley[4], and he took the entire British machination apart, point-by-point. He expresses his disgust in the preface of his work:

"As an Englishman, I am jealous of England's honour and prestige, and rank myself with those who hate to see her people blindly dragged into a petty, cowardly and unworthy policy."

The Keates Award joined the double hangings of Slagtersnek, the disgraceful 1837 Glenelg decisions that led to the Great Trek, and the brazen theft of Natal as building blocks in the edifice of ingrained Afrikaner hatred of the British Empire in whatever form it might present itself. They fully comprehended the French outcry of "Perfidious Albion." Again a part of the Afrikaner's country had been taken from them by the British.

The British had taken the Cape in 1795, then they had taken it again in 1806, then they had taken Natal in 1839 and then they had taken the Orange Free State in 1840. Now they had taken part of the Orange Free State and Transvaal. To the Afrikaner, Britain was like a disease that followed them wherever they went; the political equivalent of the Black Death with artillery and a navy.

This had been the second time the British used their transparently non-existent concern for the rights of the indigenous people to take land the Afrikaner had won by negotiation or by their own blood. There was neither slavery nor slave taking operations among the Boere in these states at this time or ever, but in Natal the Afrikaners were supposedly going to "turn the Zulu into slaves," thereby "necessitating" the taking of Natal. Now they were supposedly going to "enslave" the Griqua, "necessitating" the taking of the Western Free State and far western Transvaal. As we shall soon see, the Zulu too would suffer under the British Imperial style, just as the Afrikaner and amaXhosa had.

It is in this period that the Afrikaner learnt the hard way that, when Europeans express concern for third parties, Afrikaners should not believe a word of it and check behind their backs for a knife heading their direction. This instilled in the Afrikaner as a nation a deep seated and enduring distrust of any foreign nation professing humanitarian concern for a third party. Imperial Britain was all too much like a wolf expressing concern for the rights of sheep. There appeared to be a consistent and direct correlation between British "concern" and the desirability of what the sheep had.

Overnight the "Interior of South Africa" to which Governor George Napier had willfully hounded the Afrikaner (See Chapter 13: *Hounding the Afrikaner*) had mystically become important to Britain. It turns out that the part of the country that the British Parliament thought would *"add no lustre to the crown"* (See Chapter 13: *Free at last!*) contained exactly the lustre they wanted in the crown. Ironically, it would be the South African diamond fields that would eventually provide the most significant Royal Jewel. It would eventually lead British governments to conduct Total War and invent Concentration Camps in a desperate attempt to get their hands on the riches of the place that they had said in their own parliament *"secures no genuine interests," "is recommended by no prudent or justifiable motive"* and which *"answers no really beneficial purpose."*

British treasure-seekers streamed to Kimberley by their thousands and started to dig the biggest hole yet made by human hand and shovel.

The Vicar's Son

In 1877, a gangling boy of seventeen with one collapsed lung and an irritating squeaky voice disembarked from a ship at Durban in the British Colony of Natal. He was the son of a poor vicar in Hertfordshire, England. His father and aunt hoped that the warm dry climate of southern Africa might do him good and possibly even cure him. He would die a bachelor, bequeathing his fabulous riches to the University of Oxford, which was to fund a scholarship in his name. It was destined to become the most well known scholarship in the world. It is less well known that he advocated the restoration of the United States to Britain[5]. He summarized the central goal of his life as:

The furtherance of the British Empire, for the bringing of the whole uncivilized world under British rule, for the recovery of the United States, for making the Anglo-Saxon race but one Empire.

Never before him, nor after, would there ever walk upon the face of the earth a more devoted British Imperialist than Cecil John Rhodes. His life was devoted to the concept of British domination of the planet and he would stop at nothing to achieve it. Cecil's brother, Herbert, had already staked out some claims in Kimberley, and, before long, the brothers decided to exploit these claims. Cecil set off on a wagon with a shovel, a pick, and copy of the Greek classics, as he was preparing for the Oxford University entrance examination. Herbert's claims were on the farm of two Afrikaner brothers De Beer who were interested in farming, not in diamonds. The brothers De Beer soon sold their farm to the horde of prospectors and moved, leaving behind them one of the most well known, respected, and feared names in the commercial-industrial world, De Beers.

In the encampment, there were some 50,000 fortune seekers milling like ants over a low oblong hill of some thirty feet in height; in reality an extinct volcanic diamond bearing pipe. Rhodes soon decided that digging for the diamonds was a hit-and-miss affair and turned instead to servicing the needs of the 50,000 fortune seekers. First he imported ice cream, then water for the laborers. However, those were demand-limited markets. Rhodes' mindset needed a supply-limited market. He soon realized that, as the diggers went deeper, the seepage of groundwater became the major problem. It was threatening the works and assailed all the diggers equally. He took all of his worldly money and invested it in buying what was only the second steam pump in all of Southern Africa.

Soon, all the diggers desperately needed the services of his pump and were willing to pay nearly anything for it. Rhodes followed this up by buying more pumps. He was subsequently accused of sabotaging the pumps of his competitors. He systematically raised his prices and when mining parties could not pay he accepted shares in their companies. Soon he was the biggest mining magnate. He merged his efforts with two existing mining syndicates to form the De Beers Mining Company with himself as the major shareholder.

Armed with this arrangement, he obtained from the British government a charter giving De Beers the right to not just mine, but also to build railroads, recruit armies and install governments in Africa. The last organization that had had such rights had been the British East India Company two centuries earlier. Over this period, he also consolidated essentially all of the Kimberley diamond operation under his control and obtained a degree from Oxford. In all of this, he developed the support of the Rothschild banking family in London – the most close and intense relationship between Capitalism and Imperialism the world has ever known. Dissident shareholders eventually took him to court, claiming the company charter entitled them to "undertake warlike operations." They were dead right. Before the decade of the 1880s was out, Rhodes also controlled the Dutoitspan and Bultfontein mines in Kimberley.

By 1890, he would control 95% of the world's diamond production.

The Spider Flag again

The government of the Transvaal was inefficient and haphazard and it was often bogged down in in-fighting. On one occasion, civil war was only narrowly averted. By the late 1870s, the Transvaal was involved in a military struggle with the Ba'Pedi chief, Sekhukhune, who persistently raided Boer farms from his fortress in the Lulu Mountain. The Afrikaners in that country had bluntly refused to follow President Burgers into battle against Sekhukhune when they discovered that he was actually a Deist[6]. Through distant British eyes, this seemed to be cowardice that endangered all of Southern Africa. The devout Calvinistic Afrikaner thought supporting Burgers would be un-Christian and would invite the wrath of God.

The Native Commissioner in the British Colony of Natal saw all this through Imperial British eyes. As is often the case, the lapdog is more rash, obsessed, and vociferous than its master under whose protection it barks at all that moves. And so it was with Theophilus Shepstone, a locally raised arch Imperialist. After four decades of service, he was seen in Britain as the authority on all matters Boer and Zulu. In reality, both of those parties had little respect for him. The Zulu called him "Somtseu," after a Xhosa hunter; they despised the amaXhosa and still do today. He ran Zululand like a king, sitting on special chairs like Julius Caesar, taking snuff while chiefs had to sit down to be lower than him. The man clearly had delusions of grandeur.

On 5 October 1876, in London, Shepstone was secretly appointed by the British Government as British commissioner to ostensibly investigate the War of Sekhukhune in the Transvaal, but actually to annex that country if "a sufficient number of inhabitants agreed." When Shepstone returned to Natal, he put pressure on Cetshwayo, King of the Zulu, to threaten[7] the Transvaal or to induce Sekhukhune to attack. He needed an excuse to annex the Transvaal.

When this did not work, Shepstone simply went to Pretoria to tell the Afrikaner government, over their overly polite protests, that Britain was taking their country. On 12 April 1877, none other than staunch imperialist, H. Rider Haggard, secretary to Shepstone and author of novels such as *King Solomon's Mines* and *She*, personally hoisted the British flag and read the Annexation Proclamation in the sleepy capital, Pretoria. The 13th regiment of the British Army, at the head of 4 guns and 50 artillerymen, then marched unopposed to Pretoria. In this simple step, the hard won independence of the Afrikaners in the Transvaal disappeared. The Transvaal was British, and, except for some unpaid government employees, Shepstone had consulted not one single Afrikaner in the process, let alone tested whether the majority of inhabitants wanted British rule.

Shepstone's self-delusional plans went haywire almost immediately. Britain, and Shepstone in particular, had always disapproved of the Afrikaners trying to dislodge Sekhukhune. Now Shepstone insisted on trying to do just that in the name of Great Britain – this just as Sekhukhune had finally decided to live in peace with the Boere. Shepstone put together a mixed mercenary-volunteer army. The Afrikaners refused to have anything to do with these men. The discipline of Shepstone's force was a nightmare and their allies feared them more than their enemies. The inevitable happened. The campaign was a massive failure and the twice-wounded leader had to quell a mutiny by training a cannon on his own rank and file. Now the earlier Afrikaner dispersal when faced with Sekhukhune's impregnable position and President Burgers' suspect religious convictions no longer seemed so outrageous. The commander of the British forces in Natal, Lord Chelmsford, decided that decisive action needed to be taken. Twelve hundred professional British soldiers and six hundred cavalry of the renowned Frontier Light Horse, all led by Colonel Rowlands, were sent to punish Sekhukhune and his equally militaristic and murderous sister, Legolwana. This same force would have the added benefit to the British Imperialists of ably demonstrating to the restless Afrikaners what would happen to them if they dared rebel against British overlordship.

And this is how it came to be that a formal British army[8] marched into the dry bush of Africa with cavalry and infantry, headed straight for territory infested with horse-sickness in summer. It would appear that the British Army simply never did its homework. Rowlands occupied the four deserted forts that had previously been erected to keep Sekhukhune in check. Then set off with his army to teach Sekhukhune that he was now dealing with the disciplined army of all-mighty Great Britain.

To the shock and dismay of all of those in authority in the British dominions in Africa, Rowlands took one look at Sekhukhune's fortress and retreated. And that was the end of the "illustrious" First British Sekhukhune campaign. Sekhukhune and Legolwana were left in their mountain fortresses and Britain turned its Imperial appetite to other prey. Naturally, the Afrikaners now also had the measure of the British Army. Theophilus Shepstone's career was all over bar the shouting. The British would eventually defeat and capture Sekhukhune in late 1879, but only after a sobering lesson at the hand of the amaZulu army.

It is after Rowlands' ignominious retreat that Sir Bartle Frere, bearing the grandiose and highly anticipatory title of "High Commissioner for South Africa," essentially gave up on his dream of a federation of Southern African states and turned his beady eye to Zululand.

We now have to step back in time a little to make sense of what happened next.

Isandhlwana!

On 2 December 1856, the most outrageously savage royal succession plan on record was acted out on the banks of the Tugela River in Natal. That river formed the border between the Colony of Natal and the essentially independent Zululand. Mpande had been unable to resolve the matter of which of his numerous sons would succeed him as king upon his death, and so he told his two leading sons, Umbalazi and

Cetshwayo, to resolve the matter as they saw fit. And this is how, on this terrible day, 5,000 followers of Umbalazi died at the hands of the followers of Cetshwayo. The Tugela was filled with blood and corpses. This was an example of what the amaZulu refer to as "The washing of the spears."

In February 1861, Cetshwayo offered the Afrikaners of the Utrecht district (See *Fig. 14-3*), then loosely associated with the Transvaal, a large tract of land in the interior of Natal, adjoining their district, if they would return his brother, Mtonga, who had fled for safety to the Afrikaner "amaBhulu" of Utrecht. The Afrikaners agreed, subject to the condition that Mtonga would not be harmed. Mpande also approved of these dealings. When Mtonga subsequently fled again, this time to British Natal, Cetshwayo considered the arrangement with the Afrikaners void and wanted his land back. The Afrikaners explained that contracts did not work that way. This started a long-standing disagreement over the location of the northwestern boundary between Zululand and the Transvaal.

There would often be scares associated with Cetshwayo's powerful army, but in practice he never really seriously threatened the Afrikaners or the British in Natal, though the burghers in Utrecht on occasion moved into laagers for protection. The peace concluded between Mpande and the Afrikaner republics after the removal of Dingane in 1840 had essentially always held. The two parties did not necessarily like each other, but they respected each other. Both knew how to fight effectively in Africa. The amaZulu understood they could be defeated by the "amaBhulu."

In 1872, Mpande died after the longest reign of a Zulu King unto this day. The support the Afrikaners had given him in 1840 against Dingane had created stability in Natal for more than a generation. In 1873, Theophilus Shepstone formally recognized Cetshwayo as King of the Zulu, showing his base disrespect by literally placing a tinsel crown on the head of this striking man who commanded total loyalty from his Zulu nation.

Before stealing the Transvaal, Shepstone had always supported the Zulu territorial claims against the Transvaal. In fact, he had also tried to get Cetshwayo to attack the Transvaal. However, now that he had the Transvaal as a new fiefdom to lord over, his attitude towards Cetshwayo changed. By 1879, Shepstone and Sir Bartle Frere were worried about Cetshwayo's army of 40,000 trained warriors. Through Imperial British eyes Cetshwayo's power had to be broken simply because it existed.

What happened next simply cannot be defended. Certainly, the Afrikaners in Natal, Transvaal, and Free State were horrified and called it what it was: "unrighteous." This description would soon be deservedly followed by another: "incompetent."

Fig. 14-2 King Cetshwayo of the amaZulu

Unlike the Afrikaners, Imperial Britain had no experience of fighting the hugely disciplined amaZulu. Given the staggering arrogance of Imperial Britain, it hopelessly underestimated the Zulu war machine. What is much more unforgivable, is that Theophilus Shepstone, who had grown up in Natal among the Zulu, could so badly misjudge the amaZulu. On 4 December 1878, Major General Evelyn Wood of the British Army met in Utrecht with leading Afrikaners from the Disputed Territory. These included Pieter Lafras Uys (See below) and Pieter Willem Jordaan, the cousin of our ancestor Chris Jordaan. Pieter had also been on the Potgieter-Du Plessis "Double Trek" of 1837 from the Tarka with Chris. Wood wanted their help in the impending war with the amaZulu, and held out the possibility that the boundary dispute would be settled in favor of the Afrikaners.

For the sake of brevity and clarity, we may dispense with the detailed events leading up to the Great Zulu War and merely consider the situation on the banks of the Tugela River on 11 December 1878, when a British delegation met with a Zulu deputation on the British side of the river. Here the British announced their agreement as regards the fluid border between Zululand and the Transvaal in favor of the amaZulu, which, of course, cost Natal nothing to concede. Henceforth Britain would recognize the Blood River as the northwestern boundary of Zululand. This meant that the Afrikaners lost a major tract of land and the British lost the support of people like our Jordaan family.

This was much more than the amaZulu had hoped to attain. However, the British then delivered an ultimatum based on a set of demands so ridiculous that Cetshwayo could never conceivably agree. This included disbanding the amaZulu Army, delivering up certain chiefs, and more. Of course it was purposefully designed and calculated to be impossible to comply with and to willfully provoke a war. The British had already bought up all the wagons and every team of oxen they could lay their hands on, not just in Natal but also in the Free State and Transvaal. They had even sent men to the United States to buy mules. They had amassed a huge army to invade Zululand. This was Imperial Britain at its most outrageous extreme to that date. They left Cetshwayo no choice. War was now inevitable and there followed the usual posing of imperial gentlemen for photographs before they were to go off to "teach the savage heathen rabble a lesson."

British officers did their best to attract Natal, Transvaal, and Free State Afrikaner volunteers. However, the vast majority now wanted absolutely nothing to do with what they saw as a totally dishonorable and un-Christian enterprise to brazenly steal the country of the amaZulu, with whom they had lived in peace for more than a generation. Ironically, it was one of their stalwart families that gave its support to the British. This was Pieter Lafras Uys, who had lost his father Piet Uys and brother, brave young Dirkie, to Dingane's amaZulu at Italeni in 1838 (Chapter 11: *Beyond death and despair*). He wrote to his family in the Cape[9]:

> "I fight in good faith and in a righteous cause. I must avenge the death of my father and brother, although in doing so I am almost sure to lose my life."

When Major-General Evelyn Wood approached Marthinus Wessels Pretorius, the hugely influential former president of the Transvaal, author of the first Transvaal constitution and son of the late Afrikaner leader Andries Pretorius, he was told in no uncertain terms that the British could solicit help from the hugely experienced Afrikaner burgher commandos only when the latter had regained their independence. Pretorius also warned Wood that the amaZulu would defeat the British and that in his opinion the debacle of Rowland's expedition had demonstrated the incompetence of the British Army. Wood was clearly impressed by Pretorius, whom he described[10] as having "*a remarkable face, resolute and unyielding.*"

At the time, Wood seemed not to understand that he had walked in on a meeting of men who were designing the end of British domination in the Transvaal. Pretorius apologized for the surly behavior of his other guests and said it was because they "*detested the sight of Englishmen.*" Under the circumstances, Pretorius was the master of understatement, given the depressing history these people had lived under the British.

And so it was that Britain trotted out its next arrogant Imperial General, Lord Chelmsford, to conduct the war with the amaZulu. He had the foresight to obtain Andries Pretorius' diary of the campaign against Dingane, and to study the same, but in his arrogance he took all the wrong lessons from it. The Afrikaner effort had been characterized by careful discipline, solid doctrine and excellent tactics, including the drawing of laagers every night, the careful anticipation of the "Horns of the Bull" and the proper use of concentrated firepower, not to mention the wise choice of battleground. Chelmsford, however, concluded that, if a bunch of Boer farmers with flintlocks and two small brass cannon could defeat the amaZulu army, then his much larger and much better equipped formal British Army should be able to dispatch Cetshwayo with ease.

Chelmsford divided his invasion columns into three. One column was to enter Zululand from the Utrecht district of the annexed Transvaal in the northwest towards the mountain, Hlobane; the second was to proceed up the coast to Eshowe; and the third and main thrust was to be roughly along the path followed by Pretorius some forty years earlier, crossing the Buffalo River at Rorke's Drift. This nondescript ford would gain fame in news media around the world and ultimately start the career of motion picture actor Michael Caine. Pieter Uys rode out in support of the Hlobane column.

On 11 January 1879, Lord Chelmsford crossed into Zululand at Rorke's Drift (Ford). The wheels were now in motion for one of the most analyzed battles in the history of the British Army; the annihilation of a formal British Army at Isandhlwana by men with spears, and the subsequent brave defense of Rorke's Drift on 22 January 1879. The latter would see no fewer than eleven Victoria Crosses awarded; seven of them to one unit, and to this day the largest number for one engagement by one unit (the 24th Foot) in all of history.

Isandhlwana is a place every British man should take time to visit, if just to pay proper respect. There can be few places on earth where the silence is so overwhelming, but where the ground screams deafeningly at any soul that will listen. No fewer than 1,350 men were slain and their bodies horribly mutilated at this lonesome spot. The vast majority died while running for the Buffalo River. There are two areas where brave knots of men made a stand, but to im-mortalize this as the dominant feature of the battle, as in some famous paintings, is to willfully deny the true depth of the horror of the day and to absolve the commanders.

The outrage was not so much in the mindless disembowelment of the fallen by the Zulu, as in the criminally arrogant negligence on the part of the commanders of this ill-conceived and disastrously exe-

Fig. 14-3 Natal and the Zululand-Transvaal border region in 1879

cuted invasion. The Afrikaners had justifiably called it "unrighteous," but the fact that all their advice, based on bitterly hard experience, had been cast to the wind remains unforgivable. The callousness with which messages about the massacre were ignored in disbelief is even worse. Five days before the battle, on 16 January 1879, Pieter Uys' older brother, J.J. Uys, who had fought at Blood River many years earlier, had specifically visited Chelmsford and had warned him[11]:

"Be on your guard and be careful. Place your spies out, and form your wagons into a laager."

Not one of these four truly simple points had been heeded. Any one of them alone could have prevented the ensuing disaster.

The column under Lieutenant-Colonel Charles Pearson, approaching Zululand along the coast, had some nominal success, but then received notice of the disaster at Isandhlwana along with instructions to defend themselves as best they could, as there would be no help forthcoming. They ended up in Eshowe, cut off from civilization under a month long siege by the Zulu Army.

The disasters at Intombi Drift (12 March 1879) and Hlobane (28 March 1879), which were inflicted on the Northern invasion column, are less well known. It was at Hlobane that Piet Uys died, as he himself had predicted. The British had arrested his mother for no good reason in the middle of the 6th Frontier war in 1835, while his father was actually on commando in support of the British. It had been the particular reason for the family joining the Great Trek. The British had then taken his father's country of Natal. After his brave and untimely death, the British finally recognized the gray bearded Pieter Uys as a hero and awarded his family a pension. There cannot be many Afrikaners ever recognized in this ironic way. The honor and respect was belated.

Sir Bartle Frere, fully realizing that his dreams of Southern African Federation had died with Shepstone's brazen 1877 theft of the Transvaal, sent emissaries to the various Afrikaner leaders and communities soliciting help. None would be forthcoming. The Empire had lied, cheated, and connived once too often for these staunchly Christian people. In a desperate bid to gain some support from the Afrikaners, Frere then cynically reversed his previous decisions about the Natal border and gave the disputed territory to the Transvaal, then still under British control. This also had no positive effect with the Afrikaners. In fact, when a

Fig. 14-4 The soulful site of the Battle of Isandhlwana

group of Afrikaner farmers in the Disputed Territory found some cattle the British had taken from the Zulu, they promptly returned the animals to the amaZulu[12].

The Afrikaner rejection of the "unrighteous" British war was utter, total, and complete, from the Disputed Territory, through the Transvaal and to the Free State. Rather, they saw every reason to rise against the obviously hapless British whose bubble of invincibility had been spectacularly burst by Cetshwayo, a king with whom their own quarrels were distinctly trivial in comparison with the mindless antagonism the British had always seemed to show them as Afrikaners. On 29 March 1879, the day after the Hlobane disaster, the British finally had a victory at nearby Kambula. They employed the basic approach that the Afrikaners had used to such good effect in the past, forming a hexagonal laager. It was a great success For once the British did the right thing, burying the slain Zulu warriors with military honors.

Four days after Kambula, Chelmsford defeated an 11,000 man Zulu army at Gingindlovu and lifted the siege of Eshowe. The final battle was at the capital of Ulundi on 4 July 1879, where the British employed Gatling guns against the Zulu.

Fig. 14-5 Gen. Frederic Augustus Thesiger, 2nd Baron Chelmsford

Cetshwayo was captured two months later and locked up for three years in the Cape Town castle. Then he was taken to London and was shown off on the public circuit. The British public was much taken with the physically impressive king and showered him with presents. However, as with the Afrikaner, all he had ever wanted was to live his life in peace in his own country. He was eventually returned to Zululand, but died within a year of his return, some say poisoned by the British.

All considered, the Zulu War had been an unmitigated disaster for Britain. The British Army had been roundly defeated by the Zulu Army in every engagement until Kambula. They had had to retreat out of Zululand with their American mules to lick their wounds and resupply themselves to try again. It effectively ended the careers of Bartle Frere, Lord Chelmsford, and Shepstone, who was replaced in Transvaal by Sir Owen Lanyon. The myth of British invincibility had been very brutally shattered.

However, no one had yet won a war against the British Empire, the Superpower of the planet, in the 19th century. The disaster in Natal did, however, contribute significantly to Benjamin Disraeli's Conservative Government being replaced by Gladstone's Liberals in 1880.

Africa drinks Napoleon's last blood

At the end of the Franco-Prussian War of 1870-1871, Napoleon III, better known as Louis Napoleon, went into exile in Britain along with his wife, the empress Eugénie and his son, Louis Napoléon Eugène Jean Joseph. Louis Napoleon died in England on 9 January 1873. The Prince Imperial, Napoleon IV, was allowed to study at the Royal Military Academy, Woolwich. When the Zulu War broke out, nothing could keep him from going to South Africa. This placed quite a responsibility on the British officers, particularly since the Prince Imperial was a rash young man.

And so it was that the young Prince Imperial went out on patrol near the end of the Zulu War with his "minding" officer, Lt. Carey, a French speaker from the island of Guernsey. The party scouted ahead rather further than they should have done, into an area not too far from the farm of the Jordaan family (See *Fig. 14-3*). There was a sudden rush of Zulu who "came from nowhere." The Prince was killed and disemboweled in full view of Carey and the others, who fled no more than 50 yards and then helplessly watched the proceedings. There naturally was an outcry in Britain, and Carey was court-martialed, but eventually allowed to return to his unit. He lived a pariah until he died some six years later in India. He was never forgiven.

And so, Napoleon Bonaparte's bloodline came to a final rest in the African Bush. Napoleon had drunk the blood red wine of Africa in exile, and now Africa had drunk the blood of his last descendant.

Fig. 14-6 Napoleon IV: The Prince Imperial

Striking back at the Empire

After Theophilus Shepstone's outrageous annexation of the Transvaal, a three man team was deputized to discuss matters with him and to take the case of the Transvaal Afrikaners to the Cape Parliament and to Britain. This team comprised men like Paul Kruger and Piet Joubert. Paul Kruger was the young man who had fought at Vegkop (*NF46*) against Mzilikatse. Piet Joubert, whom we have traced[13] from his ancestor Pierre Jaubert in France in 1687, was now the Commandant-General of the Transvaal.

The deputation soon enough realized that no Empire Englishman would ever listen to a white man who spoke a language other than English. Also, the earlier pernicious and perfidious propaganda of Dr. Philip had so poisoned the British view of the Afrikaner that there never was any hope of any understanding for their position. Shepstone had been replaced by Sir Garnet Wolseley, who had so little regard for the fighting ability of the Afrikaners that he moved most British troops in the Transvaal back to Natal.

On 2 July 1880, Major-General Sir George Pomeroy Colley took over as High Commissioner for South Eastern Africa and Governor of Natal. Thereby he became responsible for matters in the Transvaal. Meanwhile, in England, Gladstone succeeded Disraeli as Prime Minister. As he had earlier made it clear that he thought that the annexation of the Transvaal had been a mistake, this gave the Transvalers hope.

Now that Gladstone was in office, he proceeded to back away from his earlier position on the matter of Transvaal Independence. He now only hinted vaguely at future self-government. All political avenues had been exhausted for the Transvaal and the inevitable followed. How Britain could not understand the gravity of the situation begs all logic.

In the week of 8 to 14 December 1880, between five and six thousand armed burghers attended a gathering on Marthinus Wessels Pretorius' farm, *Paardekraal* (Horse Corral), near Krugersdorp, southwest of Pretoria. They swore to stand together, to the death if necessary, until their independence had been restored:

> *"In the presence of Almighty God, the searcher of all hearts, and prayerfully waiting on His gracious help and pity, we, burghers of the South African Republic, have solemnly agreed, as we do hereby agree, to make a holy covenant for us and for our children, which we confirm with a solemn oath.*
>
> *Fully forty years ago our fathers fled from the Cape Colony in order to become a free and independent people. Those forty years have been forty years of pain and suffering. We established Natal, the Orange Free State, and the South African Republic, and three times the English government has trampled on our liberty and dragged to the ground our flag, which our fathers had baptized with their blood and tears.*
>
> *As by a thief in the night has our republic been stolen from us. We neither may nor can endure this. It is God's will, and is required of us by the unity with our fathers and by love to our children, that we should hand over intact to our children the legacy of the fathers. For that purpose it is that we here come together and give each other the right hand as men and brethren, solemnly promising to remain faithful to our country and our people, and with our eye fixed on God, to cooperate until death for the restoration of the freedom of our republic.*
>
> *---So help us Almighty God."*

As proof of their adherence to this national movement, each burgher placed a stone on a cairn, which was to be a lasting monument to their national pledge. It was decided to set up a Triumvirate, with full power to act, consisting of Paul Kruger, Piet Joubert, and M.W. Pretorius. Marthinus Wessels Pretorius was the former president of both the Free State and the Transvaal; the stony-faced and resolute man who had so impressed Major-General Evelyn Wood in 1879 when he sought Afrikaner help against the Zulu. In this event was born the First Boer War or First War of Independence.

The first shot in the war was fired at Potchefstroom on the commemorative date of the Battle of Blood River, 16 December 1880, when a Republican Commando patrol ran into a few British soldiers. A British force of 257 men was promptly dispatched towards Pretoria from Lydenburg in the east. As this force approached Bronkhorstspruit east of Pretoria on 20 December 1880, it was confronted by a Republican force of the same size led by Piet Joubert himself. Joubert sent Paul de Beer under a white flag to the British commander, Lieutenant-Colonel Philip Anstruther. De Beer delivered a message asking Anstruther to return to Natal, as the Transvaal was now an independent state again. Anstruther refused. Within a handful of minutes sixty-two British soldiers lay dead, four officers and eighty-six men were wounded[14]. Only one officer was not wounded. Anstruther, himself heavily wounded, directed the unhurt Army transport conductor to raise the white flag. The Republican fire ceased instantly. The transport conductor and a sergeant were allowed to proceed to Pretoria under the regimental flag in order to obtain medical aid, the Republican militia having nothing of the kind to offer.

The British were about to discover that the men who had been so constantly vilified in Britain had been decent compassionate Christian gentlemen and entirely honorable all along.

We quote Anstruther himself[15]:

> *"Immediately after the flag of truce was hoisted, Commandant Joubert came forward and shook hands with me, saying he was sorry to see me wounded. He then ordered the remainder of the men to surrender their arms, accoutrements, &c, together with all the wagons, to proceed to their camp, some distance off, promising, however, that all the private baggage should be returned; he also allowed 18 men to be left to attend to the wounded."*

On the Republican side, two men were killed and four wounded. In this war, the British would repeatedly experience these extreme casualty ratios. Naturally, the 34 wagons of supplies came in handy indeed for the Republican forces. Considering the fact that, unlike the Afrikaners, the British had the benefit of repeating rifles, no amount of praise for the Boer sharpshooting could be enough. The Transvalers besieged all the British forts in their country. The major focus of the war then moved to the natural line of defense formed by the Drakensberg mountain range between Natal and Transvaal, and to the area immediately south of it in the British Colony of Natal. This is the general vicinity of the Buffalo River and the Kliprivier District of Natal, near the Jordaan family farm, *Prestwick*.

When word of the disaster reached Queen Victoria, she commented[16]:

"The Boers are a dangerous foe, and we shall have to support Sir G. Colley strongly."

George Pomeroy Colley now entered the fray with every soldier he could find in Natal. With this force he approached Laing's Neck, the natural route into the Transvaal. On 28 January 1881, the battle opened with Colley directing six field guns and two rocket launchers at the Republican defensive positions. Then he launched a force of more than 1,100 men against the few hundred Republicans manning the pass.

The Battle of Laing's Neck stands recorded as yet another failure of British arms. They left 83 men dead, including seven officers and one hundred and eleven wounded before they retreated down the mountain. Colley had lost a full sixth of his entire force. The Republican casualties were fourteen killed and twenty-seven wounded. Colley retreated to his camp to wait for reinforcements. This was the last time[17] in British history that a regiment carried its colors into battle.

A few days later, Colley learnt, to his consternation, that a party of Republicans under Commandant Nicolaas Smit had infiltrated behind his lines and was busy cutting him off at the Ingogo River outside Newcastle. The British Army now discovered that, strangely, the Republicans dared to have initiative and tactical know-how. To counter this, Colley set off with five companies of infantry, 38 mounted men, and four artillery pieces, directly away from the Transvaal, in an attempt to stop the Republican activity behind his line.

When Colley left the field with his men this time, seven officers were dead and so were sixty-nine men. Three officers and sixty-four men were left behind, as they were too heavily wounded to flee. The Republican losses were eight killed and six wounded. It was evidently a bad idea to get into a straight shooting match with men who lived daily by their ability with a rifle and who were descended from men who had done so for more than two centuries. This clash would be recorded in history books as the *Battle of Schuinshoogte* (Cantered Heights) and is sometimes referred to as the *Battle of Ingogo River*.

Sir Evelyn Wood, who had played such a big role in the few successes of the Zulu War had by now arrived at Port Natal, or Durban, as it was now called. A number of other reinforcing units had also arrived. However, with the reinforcements had come a message to settle matters with the Transvalers. They were to be offered an armistice and invitation to negotiations on independence. Clearly, Shepstone's annexation had been a monumental blunder born of arrogance, and Gladstone had grievously compounded the situation with his own volte-face on the subject of independence.

Majuba – The Hill of the Doves

London had reckoned without the arrogance of its imperial officers. Whilst pretending to negotiate with the Republican Transvaal Afrikaners, Colley decided on his own initiative to try and obtain a commanding position over the Republicans encamped on the Drakensberg escarpment, perhaps thinking to make up thereby for his trail of blunders thus far.

Majuba, the Hill of the Doves, sits like a rook at the corner of the military chessboard, right where the north-south and east-west mountain chains of the Drakensberg escarpment join. It is some 2,000 foot higher than the surrounding country, and has total command of the entire escarpment in the vicinity.

On Saturday evening, 26 February 1881, Colley set off with 600 men up a goat path to the top of Majuba Mountain. The intention was to dig in up there on the Sunday to be in position for the Monday when Kruger's time for a response would expire.

By every textbook, Colley had pulled off a masterstroke. However, what followed was possibly Britain's most ignominious military defeat ever, and in his arrogant and willful subversion of his direct orders, Colley sowed that day the seeds of the next war. We cannot do the battle justice here, but merely highlight its salient points.

When the British troops reached the top, they did not dig in, they did not fortify the position, but they did find time to arrogantly taunt the Boere from their commanding position overlooking the Republican encampment on the escarpment far below them. When little groups of Transvaal Commando volunteers started climbing the mountain in full view of the British, the latter still did not understand what was happening. They could not comprehend why "The Boers were shooting at the grass seeds." The ordinary British Tommy had no concept of cover fire ("overwatch" is the term often used today in the United States military). One Transvaal unit would provide cover fire, "shooting at the grass seeds," while another would claw its way to the next terrace on the side of the mountain.

Fig. 14-7 Afrikaner Commandant-General Piet Joubert

Unlike the British, Americans are familiar with the layered structure of sedimentary mesas. The Transvalers were using the mesa terraces of Majuba as cover from the British fire from above, and it worked superbly. Add to this the fact that the regular Tommy had not had much in the way of shooting practice. It never occurred to them that they had to adjust the sights of their rifles if they were going to fire downhill. In any case, their shooting was perfunctory and dismissive. So, the Boer volunteer Commando climbed the mountain under British fire that mostly went over their heads, likely because of the unadjusted sights. After four hours of climbing, the band of volunteers was just below the flat summit of the mountain.

Colley had been warned on several occasions during the day that the Transvalers were scaling the mountain, but he dismissed the information and eventually the messengers were told that the General was sleeping and they should not bother him. The Transvalers had meanwhile taken a knoll on top of Majuba. They fired a volley from there, which killed some of the British soldiers, but the rest started forming up to defend.

When the next volley of Boer fire came, sixteen British dropped. Then a knot of Boere charged out of the smoke, firing from the shoulder. And the British broke and ran. Colley finally woke up to the problem when the Boer commandos came pouring out of the smoke, driving his soldiers before them.

While there were one or two efforts on the part of individuals to resist, the bulk of the British soldiers fled, even though they outnumbered the Boere and were better armed. Many ran headlong down the mountain. To his credit, Colley was last seen walking steadily towards the Boer force, revolver in hand, until he was felled by a bullet through the forehead, though descriptions vary on this point. Some British reports state that he was waving a handkerchief in surrender.

Thomas Pakenham[18] gives a description of those last few moments based on the testimony of Thomas Carter, a Natal newspaperman on the mountain. Carter heard a *"sudden piercing cry of terror"* behind him and a wave of fugitives broke past him as panic stricken men and officers tried to flee back down the mountain. It was a complete and utter rout of the Imperial British Army by a handful of farmers.

The news reached Britain on Monday 28 February 1881. There had been no gallant last stand. Unlike Isandhlwana most men had not died, but were taken prisoner by the Boere. 96 were dead and 132 were wounded, but 65 were hale and healthy and captive. The rest had run down the mountain for their lives, officers included. There was no Rorke's Drift for which to hand out medals and hide the mess. It had been a spectacular and undeniable failure of British arms and Britain's reputation stood massively dented.

First came the news that Afrikaners in the Free State were flooding to the Transvaal to help and that those in the Cape were finally exhibiting their displeasure at all the deceit and subterfuge on the part of the

British toward their cousins in the Transvaal. Then came the news that the British agents in the Transvaal had been lying all along about the extent of support in the Transvaal for British occupation. Finally the news came that Kruger had accepted the offer of peace negotiations before Colley had gone up the mountain and come down a corpse. There was absolutely no place for British politicians to hide. Not even rampant jingoistic Imperialism offered any credible psychological refuge. The Republic would have to be given back to the Afrikaners and Britain would have to learn to leave them alone — at least for a while.

The little band of sharp-shooting Transvaal Afrikaners had been the only people anywhere on Earth to win a war against Victorian Britain, the "unassailable" superpower of the nineteenth century. The British Army slunk off to lick its wounds and ignore all the tactical lessons as usual. It also swore revenge and proceeded to wait. The civilized world would eventually be outraged by its despicable concept of revenge. In London, the British press finally dredged up the depth of character to be more evenhanded[19]:

> "..it would be ungenerous and unworthy of Englishmen not to respect the patriotism and valour of those with whom they contend. The example of courageous determination and active zeal for the cause of their national freedom which has been set by these simple Dutch farmers, untrained in the modern arts of warfare, unprovided with artillery and military stores, and without any regularly drilled troops or professionally skilled officers, will not soon be forgotten."

The British prisoners did not understand why their captors exhibited such humility, until they learnt that the Calvinistic Afrikaners felt that the British had lost because they had dared to start a battle on a Sunday. What few knew, was that the men who so bravely climbed the mountain to take it from the British, were none other than those dubbed "cowards" by the British in the earlier confrontation with Sekhukhune.

The Afrikaner-Zulu Bond of Respect

Matters became so unstable in Zululand during the banishment of Cetshwayo, that the Transvaal Republicans repeatedly asked Britain for the restoration of Cetshwayo to the throne of the amaZulu; not because they approved of his bloodthirsty methods, but because he ensured stability in a country that now had no proper hereditary leader in a culture that obviously respected nothing else.

On 29 January 1883, the British returned Cetshwayo to the Zulu, but they so reduced his powers that little authority remained to him and confusion set in across Zululand. They also divided Zululand up into a part ruled by petty chiefs Sibebu and Hamu and the like, a part that they kept as Crown territory, and finally a part for Cetshwayo. The Zulu elders objected strongly to what they saw as the degradation of Cetshwayo, their hereditary king. Hardly was Cetshwayo back in the saddle or he was deeply involved in battles of tens of thousands of warriors with petty chiefs Sibebu and Hamu. Unfortunately for Cetshwayo, it turned out that Sibebu was the better tactical general. Cetshwayo was repeatedly defeated and had to flee to the deep Nkandla forest. The British went looking for him, because his mere presence caused a flood of refugees into the Natal Colony.

At this point, a number of farmers from the Transvaal Republic visited Cetshwayo at his forest refuge, because the eastern districts of their republic were being disturbed by the upheavals in Zululand. They found the Great King in a pitiful state. He solicited from them a promise to look after his Number One Son, Dinizulu. And this thing the Afrikaners respectfully did for the fallen king. Dinizulu took refuge in the Utrecht district of the Transvaal Republic and was protected there. The "Sons of Pretorius" had kept their word to the Son of Mpande.

On the 8th of February, the Great King of the Zulu died as "guest" of the British at Eshowe, but really as a political prisoner. Of the four supreme chiefs of the Zulu tribe, Cetshwayo had been beyond dispute the best. His collection of wives insisted that the British had poisoned him. One's first inclination is to ignore the comment, until one realizes the length of the list of national leaders who had died in British custody; from Napoleon, through Adriaan van Jaarsveld, Hintsa, Sarhili, and Maqoma to Cetshwayo.

Bayete! Bayete! The King lives

Zululand came apart when Cetshwayo died. Angry supporters of the departed king attacked the home of the British Commissioner and then the people of the various petty chiefs started fighting among themselves. The decision was actually made in London to not get involved, but to just strengthen the army. The various groups of defeated Zulu would repeatedly flee to the Afrikaners in the Transvaal for protection. In the end, the Transvalers had no other choice but to get involved, if only to stabilize matters in their own territory. And this was when the departed Cetshwayo's chief general, Mnyamana, approached the Afrikaners on behalf of Dinizulu, Cetshwayo's Number One Son.

Fig. 14-8 The young King
Dinizulu ka-Cetshwayo

And so it came to pass that, on 21 May 1884 on the Ngwibi Mountain the Afrikaners of the Transvaal placed the royal youth, Dinizulu, in front of 8,000 of his people to shouts of "Bayete! Bayete!" This is the highest form of recognition in the Zulu culture, reserved for the King of Kings. There were no tinsel crowns from arrogant condescending British imperialist "commissioners." The matter was treated as it had been by Andries Pretorius with the young man's grandfather, Mpande, forty-four years earlier. These were white men of Africa and black men of Africa treating one another with respect.

The Afrikaners of the Utrecht district made their position clear. They were unhappy with the British decision of 1877 to take part of their land away in favor of the Zulu. They wanted that land back in full and perpetual possession. In exchange, they would assist Dinizulu against the pretender, Sibebu. The Zulu leaders agreed to the cession of territory equal to eight hundred farms of 3,000 morgen each to obtain this support. The Utrecht Afrikaners' committee then sent word throughout Southern Africa for competent men to join in helping the Zulu in exchange for the negotiated land. And the men came from all over, including one hundred and fifty Afrikaners from the British colony of Natal. Among them was a striking young Natal man with violet-blue eyes, named Louis Botha whom we shall meet more closely in Chapters 16 -18. Within two weeks an army was ready.

When the battle started, Sibebu's army turned and ran at the first assault of the Boer group. Dinizulu's Usutu, as they were called, were mad with joy[20], as they had lost all previous engagements. The other important petty chief, Hamu, now submitted to Dinizulu. There was finally a proper hereditary king in Zululand. The Zulu did not cede all the land that had been expected, but the Afrikaners made peace with that. They awarded the larger farms to earlier recruits and smaller farms to the later. In large part, all parties had kept their word, proper respect had been shown by all for all, and there was peace in the land.

The British take the Great King

The concept that the Afrikaners of the Transvaal could have a working arrangement with the legitimate hereditary King of the Zulu was an outrage to British imperial thinking. On 19 May 1887, some three years after the Afrikaners had helped the Zulu to stabilize their country under Dinizulu, Britain declared Zululand a British Dominion. Naturally, Dinizulu and his chiefs objected and rose up in arms.

This was exactly the excuse the British were looking for to try them for treason. They were all found guilty and sentenced to imprisonment for excessive periods of time. This sentence was commuted in Britain to banishment to the island of St. Helena, where Napoleon had died in British hands more than half a century before.

The British had yet again taken the Great King of the proud Zulu people.

Nexus Familia 66: Convergence of the families

The Jordaan–Klopper–Prinsloo Clan: In the path of war

Our Jordaan family on the farm *Prestwick*, with 11 brothers and sisters, is quite a clan. Some of the men have moved out to other farms in the general vicinity of Dundee, such as *Bergvliet* further south. Their cousin, Pieter Willem, has moved into the Utrecht district of the Transvaal Republic, the part of that country that lies below the Drakensberg between the Blood and Buffalo Rivers.

In 1864, a son, Daniel, is born to ancestor Margaretha's older sister Susanna and her husband, Joachemus Prinsloo. Their second son, Joachim, is born in 1883. This little family eventually moves to a farm named *Schoongezicht* (Pleasant View), near Waterval-Boven in the Carolina district of the Transvaal Republic. Their nearest big town is Middelburg. Daniel and his farm will take center stage in our story later at the turn of the century.

On 4 December 1878, Major-General Evelyn Wood speaks to a number of Boer men, including specifically cousin Pieter Willem Jordaan, about obtaining their help against the Zulu. Pieter simply does not understand the British obsession with Zululand, which is not ideally suited for either cattle or general agriculture. They are interested when Wood suggests that Britain will ensure that the area they know as the "New Republic" will be incorporated in the Transvaal. However, when the announcement comes that Britain has decided to give the area to the Zulu, Pieter and his friends simply go home and let the British stew in their own juice.

On 12 January 1879, the day after Lord Chelmsford crosses into Zululand with his army at Rorke's Drift, Margaretha marries William C. Milward, who is resident English teacher to the many children on Prestwick farm. Over the next few weeks the talk over coffee on the porch on *Prestwick* is about the British debacle in Zululand. The Jordaans and Prinsloos are not in the least surprised at the defeat of the British on all fronts – a result they openly and confidently predicted. They were much irked earlier when the Colonial British ranted about the Transvaal Afrikaner's aborted attempt on Sekhukhune. In Jordaan eyes, a few hundred of Sekhukhune's Ba'Pedi sitting on a mountain with delusions of grandeur after a battle not joined is one thing. An army of 40,000 highly trained and disciplined Zulu warriors eviscerating a large British army and sending its general out of Zululand with his tail between his legs is something entirely different. The Jordaans feel the British have endangered everybody through their arrogance. Nevertheless, they generally stay out of this fight that Queen Victoria's men have pointedly picked with the Zulu.

On 15 August 1880, Margaretha has a daughter and, considering husband William's Welsh background, the couple names her Neve Constance. She is the maternal grandmother of the author's wife.

The British and the Transvaal Afrikaner's clash in the First Boer War takes place a short distance north of the main town of the district, Newcastle. The English in town, who have so confidently anticipated a British victory, are dumbfounded when the dejected British Army trudges back into town from the defeat at Laing's Neck. On 6 February 1881, the people in Newcastle hear the fighting all day long at Ingogo River outside town. Yet again they learn that it is a hopeless British defeat.

Many shop owners in town are suggesting the town be surrendered to the Boer forces, because the British Army has said it will not defend the town[21]. These men are worried that their businesses might be affected afterwards if they were to resist the Boer forces. Eventually, however, the Transvalers withdraw back to their country. The Jordaans rejoice when the Transvaal regains its independence after the fourth serial defeat of the British at Majuba.

It may be the politics of the republican-minded Afrikaner Jordaan family, or something to do with the actual relationship between the English schoolteacher and the Afrikaans farm girl, but on Christmas Eve 1881 William Milward unceremoniously deserts his family and disappears into the Afrikaner-governed Orange Free State Republic. He leaves Margaretha three months pregnant with her second daughter and last child. Margaretha names her Mary Elizabeth. This decidedly Afrikaans lady now has two daughters with typically English names, Neve Constance Milward and Mary Elizabeth Milward.

Margaretha's older brother, Pieter Johannes, helps her to launch a divorce case in 1883, but the deserting husband then flees the Free State arm of the Law for the Utrecht district of Transvaal, where justice is less organized. There he disappears. Twenty-six years later, in 1909, a simple hand-scribbled death notice in the far northern Soutpansberg district of the Transvaal will read:

"William Milward, recent prospector, 56, English"

Margaretha tells her daughters that their father died when they were babies, and no one in the family ever talks about the desertion again until 125 years later. Margaretha will never marry again.

The McCusker–Callanan family: The Irish family with the Republican heart

In 1863, the McCuskers acquire a small lot of land on River Road in Graaff-Reinet. However, financially things are difficult for the family McCusker. By the end of 1864, James is at his wit's end and decides to relocate his family to the harbor town of Port Elizabeth to open a small retail shop. This, however, is a financial disaster and, after getting deeper into debt, he uproots the family again a mere 4 months later and returns to Graaff-Reinet to try his hand at a retail shop there.

On 19 July 1865, James dies; his neck broken when he is thrown by his horse during a hunt. He leaves Caroline with an insolvent estate, five children to raise and a sixth on the way. When the trustees finally settle the estate, the family is essentially destitute and the trustee pleads with the creditors to leave Caroline her furniture and at least give her £5 a month from the insolvent estate to feed her family.

Faced with this harsh reality, the intrepid Caroline, who marks her name with a cross, obtains a trade license with the help of the trustee of their insolvent estate, and opens the Traveller's Rest Hotel in town. On 11 July 1866, less than a year after the death of McCusker, she marries Michael Charles Callanan, an Irishman from Galway. He has reputedly taken a discharge from a Royal Dragoon regiment. Family notes of more than 140 years later will still record that Michael is *"very handsome and spoke with an Irish brogue."* He was the signatory on McCusker's death notice a year before.

Unfortunately, Caroline's own efforts at running a business are as hapless as her late husband's, and by 1868 she once again faces bankruptcy. However, this time there is Michael Callanan's independent estate they can rely on to some degree, though Caroline's creditors in town try desperately to attach his estate, ultimately without success.

From 11 April 1867 onwards, Caroline gives Michael eight children. Among these Callanans we shall follow three of the young men, being Joseph (the oldest), Michael (the grandfather of the author's wife) and Harry Ambrose (the naughty youngest surviving brother).

Traveller's Rest Hotel,

Market Square, Graaff Reinet,

By M. CALLANAN.

EVERY attention paid to Travellers and Families.

☞ Good Stabling and Excellent Forage.

Graaff Reinet, Nov. 20th, 1868.

Fig. 14-9 *Advertisement in the Graaff-Reinet Advertiser for Caroline Misselbrook's inn.*

In 1879, Henry McCusker, Caroline's eldest son by "Mac" McCusker, dies at the age of just 24. In 1881, her third McCusker son, James Elijah, starts the *De Graaff-Reinetter* newspaper in Graaff-Reinet and steers it in a Republican direction, quite strongly opposed to the growing British Imperialism and the colonial jingos. It is the first Afrikaans newspaper in the east of the colony. James Elijah eventually becomes a leading light in the *Afrikanerbond*, the political voice of Afrikaners in the Cape Colony; he is the "Irishman" with the Republican Afrikaner heart. History will record that the grinding poverty of his youth has set his political views and made him an Afrikaner. Thomas, the youngest McCusker, meanwhile becomes a typesetter, as does Joseph, the oldest Callanan son. The printing business is clearly in the family blood.

One day in April 1882, Michael Charles Callanan simply deserts his wife and the children still in her care. She does her best to keep her family going using her boarding house, but it is to no avail. By early 1886, she is completely bankrupt. In July of 1886, she files for divorce with the Supreme Court in Cape Town, stating that Callanan was on the Kimberley diamond mines, earning between six and seven pounds a week. He has never responded to any of her letters and has never contributed to the upkeep of the seven children still in her care. The older McCusker boys are, of course, already out of the house and married. Two townspeople of Graaff-Reinet testify in affidavits that Caroline *"does not have five pounds"* to her name.

The divorce is granted after Callanan proves impossible to locate on the Bultfontein Mine where he is believed to be working. However, it is in Kimberley, in the rough and tumble environment of 1880's open pit mining, that Michael Charles Callanan is killed on 3 September 1886 in a horse and cart accident on Cecil John Rhodes' Dutoitspan mine. Since her youngest McCusker son, Thomas, has also moved to Kimberley with his wife, Emma Simpson, Caroline and her young Callanans now move in with this family. By the end of the 1880s, the Callanan family and some of the McCuskers are therefore living in the Kimberley diamond fields.

The Basson families: Life in the West Cape and Transvaal

In the wheat and wine country of the West Cape, the Basson grandfather of the author's wife is born in 1879. He is also named Matthys Michielse Basson and grows up in the wheat fields of Malmesbury on the farm Babylonstoren (Babylon's Tower).

In the Transvaal, Maria Salomé Basson still carefully protects her wagon chest with her memoirs and diary of the epic Great Trek at *Rhenosterfontein* in the Marico district of the Western Transvaal.

The Booyens family: Life in the Little Karoo and Free State

In the Booyens family in the Little Karoo region of the Cape Colony, Pieter Johannes and his wife Maria (*NF65*) baptize their son Pieter Johannes in 1871 in the new Dutch Reformed Church in Oudtshoorn, the central town of the Little Karoo. The infant Pieter is the great grandfather of the author and grows up on the farm *Rietvley* (Reed Valley) at the foot of the Kammanassie Mountain.

In the Free State and Transvaal, the Booyens families are still farming in the areas where we placed them around 1863 (*NF65*). Barend Matthys Johannes from Thaba'Nchu, now 18 years old, joins the tiny Free State Artillery on 15 September 1879 under Captain Albrecht, a German officer. On 1 January 1883, he is promoted to the rank of sergeant. On 5 August 1884, he requests and is given an honorable discharge from the unit. With it goes a positive testimonial from Captain Albrecht. Barend is the only Afrikaner among all our ancestral family and relatives at this time to have any formal peacetime military training.

The Lötter–Naudé–Joubert and Grobler families: Life in the East Cape

Johannes "Hans" Lötter is born in 1873 in the Pearston district. While he is younger than our great grandmother Johanna Catharina Smit (*NF65*), he is second cousin to Johanna's mother, Susanna Sophia Lötter Joubert. Hans will leave his indelible mark on the soul of the Afrikaner nation and the British Parliament.

On 31 January 1881, shortly before the dramatic defeat of the British at Majuba, Nicolaas Grobler (*NF65*) marries the beautiful Johanna Catharina Smit in the Dutch Reformed Church in Jansenville in the East Cape. Herewith, the long and tortured paths that have been walked by the Joubert, Lötter, Naudé, and Grobler families have finally merged. The respective wings of their families have survived the horrors and bloodshed of the Great Trek by the simple expedient of staying under British dominion in the East Cape. For that they have had to fight three more Frontier Wars against the Xhosa—the Seventh, Eighth and Ninth—as Boer Commando men chafing under British masters.

The Myburgh family: To the Rhenosterberg

In 1863, Renschie (*NF65*), mother of our great grandfather Albert, marries Gerhard Viljoen from the adjoining Colesberg district. Gerhard has no fewer than eight children of his own, more or less contemporaries of the seven Myburgh children. There are now fifteen children in the family. As part of the settlement of his father's estate, Albert sees the farm Roode Taaijbosch pass out of the hands of his family. They move to Gerhard Viljoen's farm *Klipfontein* ("Rocky Fountain") at the northern foot of the Sneeuberg. Here, Renschie and Gerhard add two more children to the family, but only the boy Ignatius survives.

In 1865, Gerhard joins his friends in the Orange Free State in a war against King Moshesh of the Ba'Sotho. He fights at the Battle of Thaba Bosigo, where Moshesh defeats them by yet again relying on his impregnable fortress-like position. Soon afterwards, however, the Republicans defeat Moshesh anyway by laying siege to his fortress. When Gerhard returns, he tells the young Albert all about the battles. The story about how they had to climb the mountain to fight Moshesh will be passed on through the generations to the author's mother, and thence to the author.

In 1872, disaster hits the family once again when Gerhard Viljoen (58) also dies. Only six of the sixteen children are over 20 at this time, leaving ten children of ages from 6 to 19 for the 42-year old Renschie to worry about, including great-grandfather Albert. Somehow, she copes with the help of the older children and never marries again.

On 13 November 1882, in Middelburg, Albert marries Martina Fouché (*NF65*). Over the next few years, Albert and his younger brother Willem work together on various farms in the Middelburg district of the East Cape. *Hoeksplaas* (Corner farm) in the Rhenosterberg mountain north of their old family farm of *Roode Taaijbosch* is where they spend most of their time. Over this period a strong bond is created between the Myburghs and the strongly Republican-oriented Erasmus family of the district when three of Albert's brothers marry three Erasmus sisters.

—End Nexus Familia

The American Civil War in South Africa

During the middle third of the 19th century, the Slavery Debate raged back and forth across the United States. For many Americans it was a fundamental moral problem that the author of their nationally defining Declaration of Independence had written the famous words "*We hold these truths to be self-evident, that all men are created equal, that they are endowed by their Creator with certain unalienable Rights, that among these are Life, Liberty and the pursuit of Happiness*" even as he himself had owned slaves.

For reasons varying from the moral to the social to the economic, and despite various agreements, arrangements and compromises, the nation systematically moved towards war. It fell to Lincoln to declare it formally. Seeing in the Northern Union an inherent competitor, while seeing in the Southern Confederacy a raw materials source and market, the ostensibly anti-slavery Great Britain backed the Confederacy, which was held up to Northerners as fighting to preserve slavery.

Early in 1862, a fast boat, 220 foot long and simply bearing the number "*290*" was launched at Laird Brothers Yard in Birkenhead, England. Then she disappeared, to emerge as the British "*Enrica*" at a lesser-frequented island in the Azores. Here, under the noses of the Portuguese authorities, she received her guns and American officers. She was at this time manned mostly by contracted[22] British seamen. On the morning of August 24th 1862, Captain Semmes, dressed out in full Confederate uniform, read his commission handwritten by Jefferson Davis, emphasized it with a round from the guns, dropped the British flag and ran up the Stars and Bars. The Atlantic was about to be introduced to the Confederate cruiser *CSS Alabama*.

After interception of no fewer than 60 "Yankee" ships in the North Atlantic and Brazilian waters, she turned for the west coast of Southern Africa to raid Union shipping in the area for two months from early August 1863 to end September. By now, the Union Navy was out in full force, searching for the raider that had essentially brought Union cross-Atlantic shipping to a shuddering halt. The North labeled Semmes and his men "pirates" and blamed Britain for the depredations the Union was suffering. The Hunt for the *Alabama* turned into the 19th century equivalent of the famous Hunt for the Bismarck of WWII.

The fame of the *Alabama* had preceded her and her reception in the capital of the Cape Colony was an ovation. South Africans cared not about the reasons for Christian Americans fighting one another – that was their business. On 5 August 1863, the whole Cape Town came to a halt to excitedly watch the *Alabama* overtake the beautiful Union bark *Sea Bride* almost at the 1 league line from the shore, the limit of international waters at the time[23]. The town went wild with excitement and the next day the raider, having docked, looked more like a human circus than a warship. The whole Cape wanted to be on board. On 24 September 1863, eleven men from Simon's Town near Cape Town were hired as crew for the raider.

The escapades of the famous steamer soon became the subject of popular songs. In the Afrikaans culture, no child grows up without knowing the folk song *Daar kom die Alabama* ("*There comes the Alabama*"), a particularly popular tune with the Coloured[24] participants in the so-called Coon Carnival through the streets of downtown Cape Town on January 2 of every year. The *Alabama* itself was eventually destroyed within sight of Cherbourg, France, by the armored Union warship the *Kearsarge* on Sunday June 19th, 1864. The *Kearsarge* struck a Caribbean reef and sank on 2 February 1894. The ensign from the *Alabama* is in the Cape Museum.

Fig. 14-10 *The CSS Alabama*

There seem to have been very few winners from this awful war, marked as it was by excessive carnage and brutal strategies. The barbaric burning of tracts of the South by Sherman would be repeated by the British in South Africa a generation later and Sherman would be referred to in the process.

The historic parallels between the United States and South Africa are obvious: founding by the Dutch, a company government, invasion by the British, fights for independence from an imperial master, a frontier society from all over Europe and clashes with indigenous people. However, significantly, there is one area in which they differ deeply and profoundly, and that is the matter of the relation between races. And it goes back to this particular period of U.S. history. Given the deep emotions surrounding the American Civil War, Americans wrongly apply their historical experience in the matter of slavery to South Africa.

While the abolition of slavery was the justification the Union gave for the war, the miserable lot of the American Black people for the following hundred years hardly seemed to lend credence to the argument. In fact, after an initial euphoria and particularly after the so-called Reconstruction of the South, the position of these people would get progressively worse. This trend in "faraway America" was to eventually affect South Africa extremely directly.

In this civil war and its aftermath in the South, we may find much of what would eventually drive the policy of the United States towards South Africa in the 20th century. While the relationship between White and Black in the United States was that of master and slave, that in South Africa was one of competing civilizations and cultures. The American experience does not apply in Africa, nor is it understood there. But any American sense of guilt certainly is eagerly exploited on the Dark Continent. This would eventually cause American Liberals and African Monsters to become the strangest of bedfellows.

One hundred years after this war, American politicians would attempt to link the American experience to the South African experience without having any insight into the realities of Africa. It would eventually lead to enormous human misery in South Africa and the loss of South Africa as an integral part of the West.

-----ooOoo-----

15

The European Rape of Africa

"I do not want to miss a good chance of getting us a slice of this magnificent African cake."

King Leopold of Belgium, cousin to Queen Victoria of Great Britain,
To his London ambassador after the Conference on Africa in September 1876

Doctor Livingstone, I presume!

Already back in 1876, King Leopold of Belgium, cousin to Queen Victoria of Britain, had decided that his little country needed some greatness. An empire was just what was required. And so it was that, when the newspaperman-turned-explorer, Stanley, found missionary-turned-explorer David Livingstone and spoke the immortal words, "Doctor Livingstone, I presume" in 1871 at Ujiji, a series of events was set in motion that would lead to the so-called Scramble for Africa. It would achieve the exact opposite of what Livingstone, yet another well-meaning London Missionary Society man, had originally had in mind for the Dark Continent. Livingstone had discovered that the Arab slave trade was alive and well in Africa in the second half of the nineteenth century and had wanted European involvement in stamping it out. He was to get their involvement, but it would be on terms he could never have imagined. Ironically, he would be to blame.

When the news of Livingstone's death in April 1873 reached Lieutenant Verney Cameron at Tabora in today's Tanzania, not far east of the great lakes, he arranged for the body to be transported to Britain, but then set off westward, making for the Atlantic across Africa. Almost two years later in 1875, he staggered onto the

Fig. 15-1 David Livingstone

beach near Benguela in the Portuguese backwater colony of Angola. He sent his notes[1] to the Royal Geographic Society:

"The interior is mostly a magnificent and healthy country of unspeakable richness...might be utilized, and from 30 months to 36 months begin to repay any enterprising capitalist that might take the matter in hand."

In Belgium, King Leopold, desperate for a suitable colony somewhere, had increased his inheritance by investing in Ferdinand De Lessep's scheme for building the Suez Canal. He was intrigued by the possibilities of Central Africa. Leopold was much taken by Cameron's reports. He promptly called a "Geographic Conference on Central Africa" to create an "International African Commission" to "fight slavery" and open up Africa. He was ready to spend his personal fortune on this, sparing the Belgian public the costs.

In Brussels in September 1876, after the Conference on Africa, Leopold said to his Ambassador to London[2]:

"I do not want to miss a good chance of getting us a slice of this magnificent African cake."

Livingstone would have been dismayed had he known what his close companion, Stanley, was doing in 1876. Stanley, finding his way down the Lualaba headwaters of the Congo blocked, resorted to asking the help of none other than Hamed Bin Mohammed, the most notorious of slave traders, better known as Tippu Tib. This man had ridiculed Livingstone's entire life as a pointless and aimless waste.

Nine hundred and ninety-nine days and 7,088 miles after leaving Zanzibar, Stanley arrived with his remaining Swahili bearers at Boma, the huddle of European "factories" (trading stations) on the estuary of the Congo River. He had proven that the Lualaba River was in fact the Congo.

Between Cameron traversing the territory along its southern perimeter and Stanley doing so along the massive northern bow of the Congo River, they had defined the land we would all eventually know as the Heart of Darkness, the Congo. The very mention of that word sends shudders down the spines of people in Africa, and of the pitifully few in the Northern Hemisphere who care about not repeating the mistakes of history. However, like Cameron, Stanley reported the Congo to be a treasure trove.

Fig. 15-2 King Leopold II

In mid-November 1877, the news of Stanley's achievement reached Britain. It also reached King Leopold. When Stanley tried to induce Disraeli's Conservative government in Britain to take control of the Congo, he found them hugely reluctant. The reason for the lack of interest in Britain was dead simple. As is clear from the previous chapter, Britain had bitten off considerably more than she could chew in both Southern Africa and Afghanistan, and simply had no more appetite for colonial intrigues and escapades. She was about to start the carefully contrived Zulu War and was mired in Afghanistan[3]. Eventually, in June 1878, Stanley gave up on Britain and threw his weight in with King Leopold, who was hugely interested.

Carving up Africa

When Leopold of Belgium started arranging for his personal colony in the heart of Africa, Britain, France and Germany scurried to acquire territory of their own. Avarice is a terrible thing, especially when the object of desire is vague. The parties involved are then apt to make the most extensive grab in order to miss nothing of value. In this process, the competitors simply had to have part of whatever it was and they had to limit, entrap, forestall, and generally bedevil one another to the best of their abilities.

It is against a backdrop of mounting rivalry for possessions in Africa and the danger of a destructive confrontation that might precipitate Europe into war that the wily chancellor of Germany, Otto van Bismarck, came up with his master plan. His real goal was to create division between France and Britain, and the two naturally antagonistic nations fell for it hook line and sinker. Bismarck quickly claimed the harbor of Lüderitz in the present Namibia for Germany and then expanded this possession to cover more than a thousand miles between the Orange River on the northern border of the Cape Colony, and the Cunene River in the tropics. Then he added Togoland, Cameroon and Tanganyika, the Tanzania of today. After this, he called the "Berlin Conference" and invited to it all countries interested in the "well-being" of Africa.

Without the participation of anyone from Africa, least of all the Christian Afrikaners of the two republics in Southern Africa, or the citizens of the Cape Colony and Natal, or of the indigenous black people of Africa, the conference proceeded to carve up Africa into spheres of influence where any signatory to the deal merely had to establish a presence to be recognized by the others. The United States too was present at the table; this ostensibly because of its concern for the anti-slavery effort and the rights of the indigenous people. This was the most illustrious den of scheming thieves the world had ever seen. A small huddle[4] of European, Turkish and American representatives, pored over a map of Africa in Berlin, between November 1884 and February 1885, carving up the future of the entire African continent without so much as a thought to the future of the people on that map.

Fig. 15-3 Otto von Bismarck

It is in this smoke filled room, with Bismarck preening in delight, and particularly the British, French, Italians, Portuguese, and Turks bent over the map that the patchwork political hellhole we know today as "Black Africa" was spawned. Unbeknown to the two Afrikaner Republics and the people in the Cape and Natal Colonies, Britain was granted all of Southern Africa as its exclusive sphere of interest. The partners to this brazen conspiracy are listed in the table in Figure 15-4. Britain, France, Portugal, and Belgium would have the major share of the continent. In the next tier, came Germany, Turkey, Italy, and Spain in the general category of "also ran," while Sweden, the Netherlands, Denmark, and Austria-Hungary participated but lost out.

The United States and Russia would largely abstain from demanding a sphere of influence in Africa, but would pretend in the 20th century to have been against the whole thing. There is no evidence that they spoke up for the people of Africa—white, black, or otherwise—at the conference. Any American should think through the implications of the delegates of European states gathering in, say, Brussels, discussing exactly how they are going to carve up the present North America without any Americans, indigenous, settler, or otherwise being present to have a say in the matter.

Essentially, the British had been given a green light to paint Africa red from the Cape to Cairo, while the French got their way in most of Central and West Africa. All of them granted Leopold his private colony, the Congo. Germany's control of Tanganyika (Tanzania or German East Africa) and the Arab occupied island of Zanzibar, as well as Togo, Cameroon and Namibia (German West Africa) was acknowledged. Despite all the fancy words about slavery, no one cared one iota about it or about the people of Africa.

The true horror and disaster of Africa was not, is not, and has never been slavery, in which its own people had been willing suppliers. The true horror was this event that carved up the continent without the least regard for the demographic distribution of the people or any of their interests. Martin Meredith[5] aptly points out that, by the time the Scramble for Africa was over, some 10,000 polities had been amalgamated into just 40 colonies of which the borders cut right through at least 190 culture groups.

Of course, the two "Dutch" Afrikaner republics with their cattle and cornfields barred the northward expansion route of British Imperial control to Cairo. Britain had been granted an Imperial Expansion Highway up the east of Africa, and the Afrikaners, in their trusting ignorance, were sitting astride it minding their own business, quite as helpless as any other inhabitants of Africa.

When the next big discovery came, British Imperial avarice simply could not be controlled anymore.

Colonies! We must have Colonies!

After the Conference of Berlin, the various European participants rushed to get their "piece of the pie." Before 1880, the true colonizing of Africa had been largely restricted to Portugal's slave trade colonies of Angola and Mozambique, the British occupation of South Africa and French efforts in Algeria. In South Africa, the Afrikaner "amaBhulu" were at the vanguard of the African effort at self-determination.

1400s–1600	1600–1700	1700–1800	1800–1850	1850–1880	1880–1900	1900–1922
					Congo	
					Rwanda	
					Eritrea	
					Somalia	
					Tunisia	
					Namibia	
					Cameroon	
					Togo	
					Tanzania	
					Guinea	
					Mali	
					Brazza. Congo	
					Burkina Faso	
					Benin	
					Madagascar	
					Cen. Afr. Rep.	
					Gabon	
					Malawi	Libya
					Zimbabwe	Burundi
					Zambia	Morocco
Cape Verde					Kenya	Mauritania
Angola			Côte d'Ivoire	Djibouti	Uganda	Chad
Mozambique	Guinea Bissau		Liberia	Senegal	Botswana	Niger
Equa. Guinea	Mauritius		Algeria	Lesotho	Egypt	Nigeria
Gambia	South Africa	Seychelles	Sierra Leone	Ghana	Sudan	Swaziland

Fig. 15-4 The European Scramble for Africa (1880–1900)

As we have seen, they had already expressed their opposition to British Imperialism at the time of the Slagtersnek "rebellion" of 1815. By 1834, this had turned into an Exodus in the form of the Great Trek. However, the British had constantly pursued them and taken their hard won land from them. Earlier, the British had used the Afrikaner in their effort to get a hold on amaXhosa territory, when the Afrikaners had been quite clear that they had no designs on that land. The Afrikaners had only recently won their independence back from Britain in the Transvaal.

It is important to understand the profound difference between the white "amaBhulu" of South Africa, Afrikaner and English, and the Colonialist British government. The former wanted to live in peace in their own country, the latter wanted to own Africa from the Cape to Cairo.

Anyone with any doubts in this matter need but refer to Figure 15-4, where the mad avaricious Scramble for Africa is mapped out as a time line. The sudden rush for Africa is evident in the twenty-year period 1880-1900, immediately after the Berlin Conference.

And this was when the best and the worst thing in South African history happened.

Gold! Gold! We must have the gold!

They say it was in March 1886, but the historical records say differently. There are at least two documents in the State Archive of the old Transvaal relating to the subject. One, dated 23 July 1886, is in the name of George Harrisson who discovered the gold-bearing reef on the farm *Langlaagte* (Long Flats). The other, dated 24 July 1886, is in the name of the owner of the farm, Gerhardus Cornelis Oosthuizen.

President Paul Kruger's government in nearby Pretoria, thinking that the reef would soon be exhausted, made a small parcel of land available for the mining activity. However, it soon became clear that it was the mother lode of all mother lodes; a deposit of gold-bearing rock, the scope of which was unimaginable. So much for consigning the Afrikaners to the "Wastes of the Interior."

This was vastly bigger than the 1873 discovery of gold in the East of the old Republic. And they came from England by their tens and by their hundreds and by their thousands and by their tens of thousands. And they started to dig and build, and soon a city started to grow on the spot. Within a tiny few years, it was the biggest town in all Southern Africa. And they called it Johannesburg.

Fig. 15-5 President Paul Kruger

President Kruger and his Volksraad (National Council) became apprehensive of this stream of immigrants. They were largely British and their sympathies were most certainly not with the people of the Transvaal. They were fortune seekers and drifters and men of such ilk, most out to make a fast buck, though some were of more stable stock. Nevertheless, it was clear that there were now two communities in the Transvaal Republic, the Afrikaner farmers and the English miners, each with its associated smaller groupings of professionals and administrators.

Kruger was doing his best to import Hollanders to serve as administrators and officials for his government and a considerable number came. None of that, however, was going to stop the so called "Outlanders" from insisting on voting rights in the country; and this they certainly did. Behind them, in the shadows, schemed and conspired people like Cecil John Rhodes in Cape Town, aided and abetted by his bankers, the Rothschilds, in London. These were people who were unimaginably rich and had dreams of Empire – hugely extremist dreams of Empire.

The annexation of the diamond bearing area by Britain, and the denial of any of the rights of the Free State in the area some years earlier, had made Rhodes staggeringly rich. Now he was planning the ultimate theft, supported by the shady agreement in Berlin, the Rothschilds, and the newly victorious Conservative Party in England. It would be a mere ten years before the British would use force to try and take the Transvaal. Any pretext would do. The greater the presumed outrage the better. The more moralistic the contrived argument, the more plausible it is. If it could be made to sound as though the "rights" of a third party were involved, it would be even better. That plays ever so well to distant audiences in London. And, as usual, the public would fall for it hook, line, and sinker and forget every decent principle their mothers must surely have taught them.

When gold walks in the front door, morality walks out the back door. Kruger knew this much.

Rhodesia – about chameleons and flies

Having attained his financial goals in life, Cecil John Rhodes chose the year of 1881 to formally enter public life as a member of the Parliament of the Cape Colony. For this he chose the constituency of Barkly-West in the diamond fields. Beyond his business activities and his parliamentary activities, he also involved himself in the annexation of Ba'Tswanaland. This was divided into two parts: a southern part that was annexed to his Cape Province, and a northern part that was turned into a "British Protectorate," to be "protected" from the Afrikaners of the Transvaal Republic. Ironically, Rhodes, the man that was doing the "protecting," had written in June 1877, with reference to the English[6]:

"I contend that we are the first race in the world, and that the more of the world we inhabit the better it is for the world."

He pledged himself to work for :

"The furtherance of the British Empire, for bringing the whole uncivilized world under British rule, for the recovery of the United States, for the making of the Anglo-Saxon race into one Empire."

In 1882, General "Chinese" Gordon, who had put down the Taiping rebellion in China, was sent to South Africa to resolve the troubles with King Moshesh's Ba'Sotho people, who were a constant frustration to the British ambitions. In this process, he met Rhodes and was most impressed with him. When Gordon was subsequently posted to Khartoum, he invited Rhodes to join him. The history of all of Southern Africa would have been vastly improved if Rhodes had accepted.

In the event, Gordon (as later portrayed by Charlton Heston in a motion picture) was killed by the Mahdi's men on the steps of the governor's residence in Khartoum in 1885. A then little known General Kitchener arrived too late to save him. These events spared Rhodes to do vast and irreparable damage to Southern Africa and its people. Along with Rhodes, it also gave us Kitchener of Khartoum, whom we shall soon meet; a man whose legacy has to date managed to avoid the tarnish born by the later Nazis, whose inhuman excesses he directly inspired.

In the mid 1860s, a German prospector had found indications of gold north of the Limpopo river, the northern border of the Transvaal Republic. He named it the Land of Ophir, the place where the biblical Queen of Sheba was said to have obtained her gold. While stationed in the annexed Transvaal during the period 1877 to 1881, H. Rider Haggard heard of this and gave birth to the classic novel, *King Solomon's Mines* (also the subject of motion pictures). In the late 1880s, Kruger's government did its best, via the efforts of a trader named Pieter Grobler, to rekindle the old arrangements between Boer and Matabele, based on Hendrik Potgieter's 1830s post-Vegkop peace arrangement with Mzilikatse. Commandant-general Piet Joubert warned Lobengula, Mzilikatse's son and king of the Matabele, of British Imperialist intentions. His characteristically colorful African description[7] of the British threat has survived the test of time:

"When an Englishman once has your property in his hand, then he is like a monkey that has its hands full of pumpkin seeds – if you don't beat him to death he will never let go."

When Rhodes' group of friends learned of Kruger's efforts in the trans-Limpopo, they rushed to convince the British High Commissioner at the Cape that Britain desperately needed to possess that land. The local missionary, John Moffat, son of Robert, the missionary host of David Livingstone, was induced to offer Lobengula "British Protection." Meanwhile John Moffat had openly stated his view in the Cape Colony that Lobengula's Matabele empire had to be destroyed. So much for British missionaries.

No sooner had Lobengula accepted Moffat's entreaties, than Grobler was murdered on the Limpopo River border. Kruger maintained to his death that it was Rhodes who arranged the assassination and the canny old president was more than likely right.

Lobengula and his Matabele were about to become a "pumpkin seed" in the "monkey's hand." Piet Joubert had been right. Kruger had merely wanted a mutual defense treaty with Lobengula, but the British wanted Lobengula's land. Rhodes soon set about extracting from King Lobengula a mining concession. Lobengula eventually granted it under duress on 30 October 1888 in exchange for weapons and some money. Lobengula also sent two emissaries to London to go and find out if there really was a queen. He was wary indeed of Rhodes' men. He summed up their deceit entirely correctly in terms well understood by all[8]:

"England is the chameleon and I am that fly"

In London, Rhodes literally bought off all his opponents and misled the British government, the end result of which was a charter to essentially do as he pleased via an entity they named the *British South Africa Company*. Meanwhile, back at Bulawayo, Lobengula's capital, the supposed main Matabele negotiator of the "land for arms" deal was executed by the Matabele and Rhodes' representative fled for his life with only the clothes on his body. The Matabele nation was quite rightly in uproar.

The next event was inevitable, as the Afrikaners knew only too well. The "tongue of the chameleon" emerged into open view and the "hand of the monkey closed."

Under the leadership of Rhodes' close friend, Dr. Leander Starr Jameson – actually a real medical doctor – a column of 17 civilians, 186 volunteers and 500 paramilitary police, called the British South Africa Police, crossed the border into Lobengula's land on 27 June 1890. With them moved two Anglican priests – reminiscent of the Spanish Conquistadors in the Americas 400 years earlier.

On 17 July 1890, Rhodes became Prime Minister of the Cape Province. Three months later, on 13 September 1890, the Jameson operation hoisted the British flag in the trans-Limpopo, fired a 21 gun salute and gave three cheers for their queen. Soon enough

Fig. 15-6 Cecil John Rhodes

Jameson invented a disagreement with Lobengula, assembled his army, and destroyed Lobengula's impis using his machine guns. Then he put together a "Loot Committee" and divided the spoils. In 1894, the British government formally recognized the authority of the *British South Africa Company* over the territory – Rhodesia was born, effectively belonging to Cecil John Rhodes, Prime Minister of the Cape Colony, in his private capacity. This was no different from Leopold II's ownership of the Congo.

Lobengula committed suicide. He had never done Britain any harm. Rhodes had wanted a war, had got his war, and had won it. War became a new arrow in his imperialist quiver. He had now learned that it works, especially if the government in Britain tacitly approved of everything and the Rothschilds financed it.

His next target was the Transvaal, which was now the main obstacle in his quest to paint Africa red all the way to Cairo.

Nexus Familia 67: The Jameson Raid – Prelude to War

Young Harry Ambrose has always been the rambunctious one of the Callanan brothers and the one most likely to get into trouble. And, as a young adult, it is to be no different. In 1892, his mother, Caroline, marries for a third time in Kimberley. This time the gentleman is a Cornishman by the name of Edwin Head. However, within a month he too dies in an accident on the De Beers mine. Caroline never marries again. Three husbands lost to accidents is one too many.

At this point, Thomas McCusker, with whom Caroline and her Callanan children have been living (*NF66*), moves to Pretoria, capital of the Transvaal Republic, where he takes a job in the Government Printing Office. He thereby becomes a British employee of Paul Kruger's government. The oldest Callanan brother, Joseph, also takes a job in that office. Shortly afterwards, Michael Charles Callanan, grandfather of the author's wife, joins the *Nederlands Zuid Afrikaansche Spoorweg Maatschappij* (The Dutch South African Railway Company) which inaugurates its Delagoa Bay line to Mozambique on 2 November 1894. As one of the first engineers, Michael receives a silver watch that will still be in the family in the 21st century and one of only five in the world. Caroline, now in her late fifties, moves in with Michael. Eventually, they move to Standerton, headquarters of the railway company southeast of Johannesburg.

Meanwhile, back down south in the Cape Colony, his older stepbrother James Elijah McCusker is using his newspaper, *De Graaff-Reinetter*, as a weapon against the excesses, abuses, and machinations of Cecil John Rhodes. Rhodes, however, has secretly bought off the Afrikanerbond, the political party with which James has been associated, and they start distancing themselves from James' paper. He becomes more and more isolated and is mystified as to why the Cape Afrikaners in the Afrikanerbond party cannot see through Rhodes' imperialist schemes.

It is Harry Ambrose, however, who commands our attention at this time. He gravitates towards the excitement of Johannesburg. And that is exactly where he is eventually recruited by one of Cecil John Rhodes' men representing a certain Dr. Leander Starr Jameson. He is to join a unit called the British South Africa Police. This is just the kind of excitement a young man of eighteen craves and Harry becomes one of Jameson's Boys. The unit is to be based west of the Transvaal border in what will later be Botswana. By the time he finds out the real intent of the unit, it will be too late. The deception of Slagtersnek will have repeated itself[9]. But, this time the shoe is on the other foot and, unlike at Slagtersnek, shots will actually be fired.

Jameson and the Uitlanders

By 1895, matters have come to a head between President Paul Kruger and the British immigrant mining community in Johannesburg, generally referred to as *Uitlanders* (Outlanders). The Uitlanders are fully aware that their large numbers threaten Kruger's republic. They do their best to present themselves as "reformers" and launch a "Reform Committee," ostensibly demanding that there be no "taxation without representation." However, unlike their American counterparts in 1776, they actually WANT British control and despise Kruger and his Afrikaners, whom they consider backward peasants.

This is the situation that Rhodes sets out to exploit in 1895, when he extracts from the little leadership team of the Reform Committee a letter essentially pleading for military intervention. The letter is given to the flamboyant Leander Starr Jameson, who, contrary to Rhodes' attempts to attack in careful steps, initiates an invasion of the Transvaal using his British South Africa Police. Among their number is young Harry Ambrose Callanan. Harry is attacking his own home country where his mother lives.

The expectation is that the Uitlanders in Johannesburg will rise and join the invaders. However, the Uitlanders get cold feet and try to retrieve the incriminating letter. At the same time, Jameson does a shoddy job of cutting the telegraph lines to Pretoria and word reaches the Transvaal government of the invasion by some 600 men with several cannon and Maxim machines guns.

For an insight into what follows we turn to none other than Mark Twain[10], who arrives in the Transvaal shortly after the ensuing mess.

> *I have got at the truth of that puzzling South African situation, which is this:*
>
> *The capitalists and other chief men of Johannesburg were fretting under various political and financial burdens imposed by the State (the South African Republic, sometimes called "the Transvaal") and desired to procure by peaceful means a modification of the laws.*
>
> *Mr. Cecil Rhodes [...] set himself the task of warming the lawful and legitimate petitions and supplications of the Uitlanders into seditious talk, and their frettings into threatenings--the final outcome to be revolt and armed rebellion. If he could bring about a bloody collision between those people and the Boer government, Great Britain would have to interfere; her interference would be resisted by the Boers; she would chastise them and add the Transvaal to her South African possessions. It was not a foolish idea, but a rational and practical one. [...]*
>
> *By the middle of December 1895, the explosion seemed imminent. Mr. Rhodes [...] was helping to procure arms for Johannesburg; he was also arranging to have Jameson break over the border and come to Johannesburg with 600 mounted men at his back. Jameson--as per instructions from Rhodes, perhaps-- wanted a letter from the Reformers requesting him to come to their aid. [...]*

He got the letter--that famous one urging him to fly to the rescue of the women and children. He got it two months before he flew. [...]

From that time until the 29th of December, a good deal of the Reformers' time was taken up with energetic efforts to keep Jameson from coming to their assistance. Jameson's invasion had been set for the 26th. The Reformers were not ready. The town was not united. Some wanted a fight, some wanted peace; some wanted a new government, some wanted the existing one reformed; apparently very few wanted the revolution to take place in the interest and under the ultimate shelter of the Imperial flag [...]; yet a report began to spread that Mr. Rhodes's embarrassing assistance had for its end this latter object. [...]

Jameson endured postponement three days, then resolved to wait no longer. Without any orders-- excepting Mr. Rhodes's significant silence--he cut the telegraph wires on the 29th, and made his plunge that night, to go to the rescue of the women and children, by urgent request of a letter now nine days old--as per date,--a couple of months old, in fact. [...]

Jameson would have to ride 150 miles. He knew that there were suspicions abroad in the Transvaal concerning him, but he expected to get through to Johannesburg before they should become general and obstructive. But a telegraph wire had been overlooked and not cut. It spread the news of his invasion far and wide, and a few hours after his start, the Boer farmers were riding hard from every direction to intercept him.

As soon as it was known in Johannesburg that he was on his way to rescue the women and children, the grateful people put the women and children in a train and rushed them for Australia. In fact, the approach of Johannesburg's saviour created panic and consternation there, and a multitude of males of peaceable disposition swept to the trains like a sandstorm.

The early ones fared best; they secured seats--by sitting in them--eight hours before the first train was timed to leave. Mr. Rhodes lost no time. He cabled the renowned Johannesburg letter of invitation to the London press--the gray-headedest piece of ancient history that ever went over a cable.

The new poet laureate lost no time. He came out with a rousing poem lauding Jameson's prompt and splendid heroism in flying to the rescue of the women and children; for the poet could not know that he did not fly until two months after the invitation. He was deceived by the false date of the letter, which was December 20th.

Jameson was intercepted by the Boers on New Year's Day, and on the next day he surrendered. He had carried his copy of the letter along, and if his instructions required him--in case of emergency--to see that it fell into the hands of the Boers, he loyally carried them out.

Clearly, Mr. Clemens ("Mark Twain") sees through Rhodes' ruse. It seems difficult to understand how the British government has taken 20 years to see through Rhodes, unless, of course, they have been in cahoots with him all along. Paul Kruger naturally assumes the latter, as do all people capable of independent thought in South Africa.

Mark Twain on the matter of the Jameson Raid

Militarily, the raid is a disaster. Mark Twain, a year later, proceeds to consider the First Boer War and then evaluates the Jameson raid against that backdrop[11]. He has it against the British tactics, which, in the First Boer War, by his information, cost them 700 soldiers for the loss of only 23 on Boer side:

...He had 8 Maxims--a Maxim is a kind of Gatling, I believe, and shoots about 500 bullets per minute; he had one 12-1/2-pounder cannon and two 7-pounders; also, 45,000 rounds of ammunition. He worked the Maxims so hard upon the rocks that five of them became disabled--five of the Maxims, not the rocks. It is believed that upwards of 100,000 rounds of ammunition of the various kinds were fired during the 21 hours that the battles lasted. One man killed. He must have been much mutilated. [He is referring to the only Boer battle death due to Jameson]

When Jameson raises the white flag on 1 January 1896, it is the fifth consecutive time that British forces surrender to Boer commandos. This attracts Twain's attention, and leads him to comment:

There is a story, which may not be true, about an ignorant Boer farmer there who thought that this white flag was the national flag of England. He had been at Bronkhorst[-spruit], and Laing's Nek, and Ingogo and Amajuba, and supposed that the English did not run up their flag excepting at the end of a fight.

[...] To retain the British method requires certain things, determinable by arithmetic. If, for argument's sake, we allow that the aggregate of 1,716 British soldiers engaged in the 4 early battles [of the First Boer War] was opposed by the same aggregate of Boers, we have this result: the British loss of 700 and the Boer loss of 23 argues that in order to equalize results in future battles you must make the British force thirty times as strong as the Boer force. Mr. Garrett shows that the Boer force immediately opposed to Jameson was 2,000, and that there were 6,000 more on hand by the evening of the second day. Arithmetic shows that in order to make himself the equal of the 8,000 Boers, Jameson should have had 240,000 men, whereas he merely had 530 boys.

Fig. 15-7 *Leander Starr Jameson*

The American author's words are prophetic. Britain will in the near future send 440,000 men to counter the total of roughly 40,000 men and boys that the Afrikaner Republics can put in the field at any one time.

The Callanans

Harry Ambrose Callanan is one of the prisoners among Jameson's men. He is wounded in the left side of the chest and is kept prisoner in Pretoria. His mother, Caroline, is angry and worried sick at the same time. She has two sons working in the Kruger government printing office, another on Kruger's Railway, and a third running a newspaper that is the mouthpiece of Afrikaner Republicanism in the Cape Colony, but her wayward youngest has to go and attack the very Republic they live in. What on earth was he thinking? Has that man Rhodes addled his brain?

In a short while, however, Harry is released unharmed and leaves for Natal to join the Natal Police.

Consequences of the Raid

It is at this time that the cry goes up to haul out the beam of the infamous 1816 Slagtersnek scaffold (*NF40*) in order to hang the leaders of the insurrection; preferably twice, as was done to the Afrikaners back then. Arthur Conan Doyle[12] states that the actual beam of the old Slagtersnek scaffold is brought to Pretoria for the purpose. In reality, Gen. Piet Joubert suggests that, if one manages to catch one's neighbor's dog in the act of raiding one's property, one does not shoot it. One hands it back to the neighbor and one asks for restitution. Cooler minds therefore prevail and the Afrikaners elect not to emulate the British military government of the Cape in 1815.

Kruger's government turns Jameson and his officers over to the British government for trial, and ships them to England. Next, the Transvaal government arrests 64 important citizens of Johannesburg as raid-conspirators, condemns their four leaders to death, and then commutes the sentences. Before the end of 1896, they are all out of jail excepting two, who refuse to sign the petitions for release; 58 are fined $10,000 each and the four leaders get off with fines of $125,000. One of them is exiled permanently.

Kruger promptly starts buying armaments from Germany and France. A collection of Krupp and Creuzot cannon arrives, as do 37,000 German Mauser rifles, firing the new smokeless rounds. Kruger knows full well that the Conservative Government of Lord Salisbury is behind the Jameson raid and that it is only a matter of time before Britain makes the next grab for the Transvaal.

As usual, the dour old man is right.

—End Nexus Familia

Nexus Familia 68: Five minutes to midnight

Everywhere in Southern Africa ordinary people can see the war clouds gathering. Britain clearly means to have the gold fields of South Africa and she is not going to let anything stand in her way. Any pretext will do. Given the most powerful nation in the history of mankind, with a queen who herself suggested that her title ought to be "Empress of India," a governing party hell bent on conquering Africa from the Cape to Cairo, and a license from the rest of the conspirators in Europe to do just that, the writing is on the wall.

The removal of Rhodes from the position of Prime Minister of the Cape after Paul Kruger releases the cipher letters that clearly show Jameson and Rhodes' conspiracy will change absolutely nothing. Britain will now stop at absolutely nothing. Mindless unthinking jingoism is now a national virtue. Victorian frenzy is at a level never seen before. No reason or appeal penetrates through the shallow patriotic fervor of the British nation at this time. It is on top of the world and brooks no input, advice, or view from anywhere. The ultimate in power has corrupted ultimately. Britain is now a nation that has lost all capacity for balance in its international policy. Even British Prime Minister Lord Salisbury seems helpless to stem the tide of warmongering insanity fomented by Colonial Secretary Joseph Chamberlain. Salisbury was weary of Chamberlain's machinations for war and the shallow British jingoism. He saw[13] the coming conflict as *"Joe's War"* and the jingoism as *"having a lunatic asylum behind one's back."*

So it is left to us to describe the situation of ordinary families as they stagger helplessly forth to a war that must, of necessity, destroy their lives in various ways – a war absolutely insisted upon by Britain.

In the Western and Southern Cape Colony

In the West Cape, Matthys Michielse Basson, paternal grandfather of the author's wife and 8th generation descendant of the original immigrant, is studying to be a magistrate. He is far removed from the impending struggles of the Great Boer War. However, a man from his district has moved to the Transvaal Republic and is at present the State Attorney of that Republic. His name is Jan Smuts, and he will play a major role on the world stage over the next 46 years.

Meanwhile, the author's own paternal great grandfather, Pieter Johannes Booyens, has married the neighboring farmer's daughter, young Elizabeth "Bettie" Snyman. Bettie is a 7th generation descendant of Christoffel Snyman, the son of the banished slave woman, Groot Catrijn. We last left Christoffel standing at the auction of his parents' worldly goods (*NF11*) on 17 December 1682. Bettie is also a descendant of Sara Delport who was murdered in the massacre that started the Third Frontier War (*NF34*)

Pieter's father died in January 1897 and his mother Maria has remarried to Barend Matthys Booyens, a cousin of his late father. Barend and Maria now live on Barend's farm, *Venterskloof* (Venter's Gorge) near the hamlet of Klaarstroom (Clear Stream) behind the *Swartberg*.

Pieter worries about his family in the north. He fully appreciates Britain's designs on the two Boer Republics. It is obvious that nothing but Afrikaner blood will now satisfy the Empress of India and her cabal of gold-crazed Tories. The loyal Cape Afrikaners are utterly dismayed at the duplicity revealed on the part of Rhodes and they now deeply distrust Britain, its true face having been revealed by the dour and canny old President Kruger. They feel they have been abused by both the conniving Rhodes and a Britain that clearly cares naught for them. Rhodes, the man who devoted his life to restoring the United States to Britain, has spawned a hatred that will last three generations.

In the Eastern Cape Colony

We have followed the Grobler and Joubert families from the original immigrants to this awful point in history. By 1897, Nicolaas Grobler and Johanna Catharina Smit have nine children. The second last child is a daughter, Elizabeth Johanna, who takes after her mother. From an early age, everyone calls her "Pretty Bettie." She is the author's maternal grandmother and grows up on the farm *Ezelsvlei* in the district of Middelburg, Cape. Nicolaas works as transport rider, covering the run from Colesberg to the Kimberley diamond mines. However, matters have become difficult because of the rinderpest epidemic. On nearby *Hoeksplaas* farm, Albert Myburgh and Martina Johanna Fouché have five children. Two later children have both died in infancy. The last surviving child is Albertus Jacobus Gerhardus, born in 1893. His triple name combines the names of his own Myburgh grandfather, Albertus Jacobus (*NF 65*), with that of his father's Viljoen stepfather, Gerhardus. Everyone will call him "Kotie." He is the author's maternal grandfather. His father, Albert, is a transport driver through the Karoo, from Port Elizabeth on the coast to Graaff-Reinet.

After the Jameson Raid, there is lively debate in the Grobler and Myburgh families about the situation in the distant Transvaal and both discuss this subject at length with their close friends and relations, the families Lötter and Erasmus. In the latter two families, feelings run high and there is little doubt as to where the 26-year old Hans Lötter, second cousin to Johanna's mother, stands on these matters. The family has a proud history of resistance. Their joint ancestor Christoffel Lötter resisted the British in 1796 (*NF31*). In anticipation of war, Hans' younger brother Zirk Daniel has recently arrived on the *S.S. Moravian* from Edinburgh in Scotland, where he has been studying medicine. Hans himself is now running a bar for Mrs. Elsworth in Naauwpoort, a railway junction some 19 miles north of Middelburg, Cape[14].

Sixty miles away in Graaff-Reinet, James Elijah McCusker now stands vindicated in his deep distrust of Rhodes. He, like all Afrikaners, believes in the principles on which the United States of America was founded as a country, and he deeply resents the British Imperialism that is suffocating the country.

In the Orange Free State Republic

The collection of cousins of Pieter Johannes Booyens in the Orange Free State realize that their well-run model republic will not escape the war. Some of them are attached to the usual commandos for their districts, but Barend Matthys Johannes Booyens of Thaba'Nchu joins the only formal military unit the little Republic has, the tiny Free State Artillery, in which Barend has served before (*NF66*). Barend becomes Sergeant-Major in the unit, led by Major F.W.R Albrecht from Germany. One of the sergeants in this tiny army is a certain Johannes Smith (See Nexus Familia 77 later).

The family under Jacobus Frederik Booyens on the farm *Weltevreden* outside Heilbron is now very apprehensive about where matters are headed. The fight is not primarily between the Free State and the British Empire, but the blood ties between the Free State and Transvaal do not allow the folks much realistic human choice in the matter. Of course, the Free Staters have to support the Transvaal.

Fig. 15-8 The entire formal Free State Army - The artillery. They had just three batteries of four guns each

In the Natal Colony

The Jordaans of Prestwick near Dundee find themselves directly in the natural path of the Commandos of the Transvaal and the British Army. In a sense, they occupy the "Belgium" or "Saarland" of South Africa. Theirs is the country where the big battles inevitably will have to be fought. While they also are burghers in a British Colony, and they have good British friends, their hearts run with Afrikaner blood. Their history has been so epic and there has been so much blood paid for their existence, that they cannot not be rebels. Two generations of Jordaans will join the cause of the Transvaal Afrikaners in their bitter and desperate struggle for independence from the Empress of India and her gold-crazed cabinet.

In the Transvaal Republic

The two Booyens families of Adam Johannes at Heidelberg and Tjaart Booyens at Ventersdorp both realize that war is inevitable. Adam's oldest son will join him in battle. Tjaart is a worried man. Six of his seven sons are of fighting age, ranging from just on 27 downwards to 17.

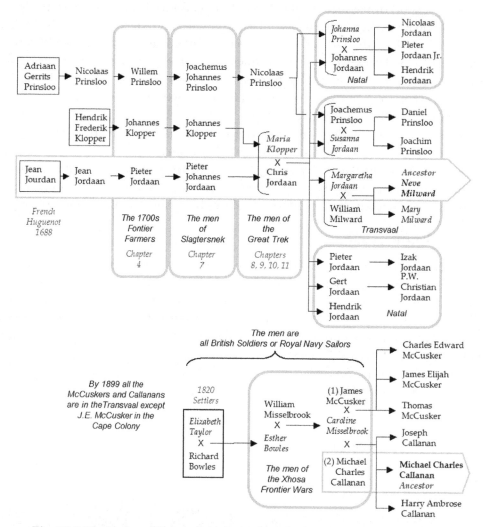

Fig. 15-9 The Jordaan-Klopper-Prinsloo and McCusker-Callanan families (1899)

In the far west of the Transvaal in the Marico district, Maria Salomé Basson (*NF65*), who had been on the Great Trek, passed away in 1890 and was duly buried in Ouma Salie's Cemetery at *Rh-nosterfontein*. Her treasured chest with the all-important Diary of the Great Trek is still carefully preserved on the farm by her children.

With the death of her brother, Pieter Johannes Jordaan, Margaretha Milward and her daughters, Neve Constance and Mary Elizabeth, leave his farm Prestwick in Natal and move to the Transvaal where they join Margaretha's older sister, Susanna and her husband, Joachemus Prinsloo on their farm *Schoongezicht* near Waterval-Boven in the Carolina district. In 1896, Joachemus dies and his son, Daniel, takes over the farming. He owns 400 morgen of this farm. His younger brother, Joachim, is still living on the farm with them. On the eve of the Great Boer War, Daniel is recently married to Susanna Van Rooyen.

Caroline Misselbrook, mother to the McCuskers and Callanans, is living with her third son, Michael Charles Callanan in Standerton where he is based as train engineer for Paul Kruger's railways. He is familiar with the run from Pretoria to Waterval-Boven and Waterval-Onder. From there, his friend and fellow train engineer, John van Graan, takes over for the run to the Mozambique border at Komatipoort. On 15 December 1898, Michael Charles takes Transvaal citizenship. He speaks English at home, is of half-Irish and half-English descent, and is now a "Boer"; an English-speaking Afrikaner.

Caroline's youngest McCusker son, Thomas, and her oldest Callanan son, Joseph, are both, quite ironically, typesetters for Paul Kruger's government printing office, but neither is a Transvaal citizen. In fact, they are British subjects, as is Caroline herself. Her youngest son, Harry Ambrose Callanan, has meanwhile left the Natal Police in 1897. He will later state that he also went to work as a train engineer.

* * * *

And so the scene is set and the chess pieces are in position for the greatest war yet on African soil – two small Republics of hardly 200,000 people, at best able to field around 40,000 farmers at a time with essentially zero military training, pitted against the mightiest empire the world has yet known. It will start as the Last Gentleman's War, but will end in the first Total War. And the world is watching as the British Cabinet schemes away in its smoky halls and the monocled money czars of London rub their hands together in glee at their handiwork.

In the last week of September 1899, the various Commando commandants send riders to the farms of their districts in the Free State and Transvaal to tell all able bodied men between 16 and 60 to ready their horses and their guns and a supply of flour, coffee, and biltong – the distinctively South African air dried unsmoked beef jerky that Mark Twain said he loved so much.

—*End Nexus Familia*

-----ooOoo-----

16

The Last Gentleman's War

"...the most formidable antagonist who ever crossed the path of Imperial Britain. Napoleon and all his veterans have never treated us so roughly as these hard-bitten farmers with their ancient theology and their inconveniently modern rifles."

Sir Arthur Conan Doyle
The Great Boer War (1900)

It is our country you want!

In 1897, Lord Alfred Milner arrived at the Cape as the new British High Commissioner for Southern Africa, and in May 1898 Paul Kruger was re-elected for a fourth term. Milner was quite clear that, if Britain were to win the "great game for the mastery of Africa" they would have to reckon with Kruger. Milner wrote to Colonial Secretary Joseph Chamberlain and made it quite clear that he intended war.

Kruger relented on the residency requirement for British subjects to be able to vote in the Transvaal, by reducing it to seven years. Milner, utterly hell-bent on having his war, then moved the goal post by demanding five years. This was the same Britain at work as the one that forced Cetshwayo into war in 1879. It would categorically not accept anything other than war. On 5 June 1899, during negotiations with Milner, the tears finally coursed down the craggy weather-beaten old face of Paul Kruger[1] as he told his adversary:

"It is our country you want!"

Fig. 16-1 *Alfred Milner, the poster boy of British Imperialism*

Ultimatum!

As usual, Paul Kruger was right. On 8 September 1899, the British Cabinet agreed to send 10,000 soldiers to South Africa. On 9 October 1899, Kruger presented the British government with an ultimatum to withdraw their troops from the border within 48 hours, otherwise a state of war would be considered to exist.

Milner and Chamberlain were jubilant. They had their war and could make it look as though they had not engineered it. Naturally, they expected the war to be a quick thing with a foregone conclusion. In Britain, people were hugely excited. They absolutely loved the idea of a war. They were sure it would be over before Christmas. They were going to teach these "upstart Boers" a lesson. However, ever since the Crimean, the British had been fighting "small wars" all over Africa and putting down mutinies in India or fighting the Afghans. None of these had been a serious challenge.

However, they had somehow not learned any of the clear lessons of the First Boer War. Other than the Crimean War, that had been their only clash with an organized and competent enemy with reasonable weapons, and they had resoundingly lost that war. Given their sheer might, there was no other conceivable outcome than a British victory, but they were about to start paying for this war with their very soul as a nation. After this war, Britain would never regain the moral high ground it had thought its exclusive domain. This war would start its demise as a viable Empire and would illuminate its shortcomings for all to see. And all were watching, particularly Germany, France and Russia.

Nexus Familia 69: A family divided – The Callanans

On 29 September 1899, a Transvaal Republic decree instructs all persons of the NZASM (*Dutch-South Africa Railway Company*) to perform those duties on the railway in the functions in which they are employed. They are also placed under the orders of the military. Those who wish to volunteer for military service are given leave without retention of pay if they can be dispensed with. Employees have to perform their duties for as long as possible, are not allowed to carry arms or to fight, and are discouraged from defending company facilities against a regular armed force. Should enemy occupation appear imminent, employees are to cease working and leave the stations, having put things in order.

Michael Charles Callanan, now a citizen of the Transvaal, ends up electing to fight "Ye Olde Enemie" of the Irish, the British. Michael's friend, John van Graan also remains train driver for the NZASM over this period. Michael's mother, his Callanan siblings, and his McCusker half-brothers are not Transvaal citizens. His brothers and half-brothers leave for the "Refugee Colony" at Port Alfred in the East Cape, where thousands of British subjects from the Transvaal are accommodated. So are "undesirables" from the colony, including the Members of Parliament for Cradock and Humansdorp and some Dutch Reformed clergy.

At first Michael's mother, Caroline, remains with him in Standerton, but when the war formally breaks out, she has no choice but to leave for the Cape Colony. She takes up temporary residence in Port Elizabeth. Michael is now the only member of his family actively fighting the British. His half-brother, James Elijah McCusker, is outwardly an English speaking Irishman. However, his heart is with the Boer anti-Imperialist cause. It is less than clear whether his life in the Cape Colony is as an "undesirable," or whether he joins the family in Port Alfred.

—End Nexus Familia

Nexus Familia 70: Off to War

In the East Cape

In February and March 1900, respectively, half-brothers Thomas McCusker and Joseph Callanan (*NF68*) join Nesbitt's Horse, a colonial unit of the British forces in Bathurst near Port Alfred. In the district of Middelburg in the Cape Province, the Myburgh family, headed by Albert and Martina, and the Grobler family, headed by Nicolaas and Johanna, do their best to stay out of trouble as British subjects who support the Independence Cause of the Afrikaner. At the outbreak of the war, they instantly find themselves civilians on the front line. The Republican Commando units are but a few miles away, between Colesberg and Naauwpoort railway junction. The hearts of the family members are clearly with their Transvaal and Free State cousins, but they are British subjects and will be treated as traitors and shot by the Empire troops if they join the Afrikaner Independence cause, however morally correct and justified it may be. One member does join the Boer forces, as we shall duly see.

In Natal

Several members of Margaretha Milward's Jordaan family in Natal join the Boer Commandos when they sweep into the Klip River district of Natal. They help the Transvaal Afrikaner Commandos in and around the Klip River district. Lots of British descended Natalians sympathize with the Afrikaners and join the Rebels.

This includes men like the 72 year old Peter Hogg and Peter, his 14-year old son; Tom and Mike Collyer; four of the Truscotts; Fred, Jim, and Tom Colling; Tom and John Bentley; Jim D'Arcy; and Joseph Hoolahan; clearly all names of British extraction. One specifically notes the Irish names that stand out so clearly. To the alarm of the British, the Reverend Prozesky of the Berlin Missionary Society also joins the Natal Rebels.

In the Transvaal

On the farm *Schoongezicht* in the Carolina district, Margaretha Milward (nee Jordaan) and her sister, Susanna Geertruyda Prinsloo, say goodbye to Susanna's son, Daniel Prinsloo, the main breadwinner of the extended family. By virtue of the fact that the farm is located in the Carolina district, he is automatically a member of the Carolina Commando under the leadership of his distant relative, Commandant Hendrik Prinsloo. At least, his younger brother Joachim is left on the farm for the moment.

At Ventersdorp in the Western Transvaal, Tjaart Johannes Booyens and five of his seven sons join the Boer

Fig. 16-2 Natal Rebels of the Newcastle district where the Jordaans were in 1899

Commandos under the leadership of General Piet Cronje, a veteran of the First Boer War. Cronje has biblical notions as to the conduct of wars. These will soon come to haunt the men under his command and will drive younger military leaders to distraction.

At the farm *Blesboklaagte* near Heidelberg in the south, Adam Johannes Booyens is joined by his eldest son, the 18-year old Daniel Johannes Andries, and they ride off to join the Boer Commandos. Adam is now Field-Cornet, and therefore has the responsibility for the mustering of the men of his district. In this farmers' army, his role is an elected one and not one that he is appointed to. This means that in normal life he is a man that has the respect of other men in the district.

In the Free State

As the only man within the family in a formal Boer army of any sort, Barend Matthys Johannes Booyens realizes that he and his artillery comrades will be facing the full brunt of the British Army. They are called up to service in the first week of September 1899. They have great confidence in their ability as artillerists. Barend's wife Ethresia is back on their farm *Maroko* near Thaba'Nchu.

On the farm *Weltevreden* in the Heilbron district, Barend's much older cousin Jacobus Frederik Booyens (75) is of the original Trekker generation and is too old to fight the British *Khakis*. He has to watch his sons and nephews saddle their horses and ride off to war, each with a spare horse.

—End Nexus Familia

Invasion – The First Phase

When the ultimatum expired at 5pm on 11 October 1899, the two Boer Republics, who had a mutual defense pact, had 35,000 Commando men on the Cape and Natal borders. The British had 20,000. Knowing fully well that they had no hope of prevailing against the incredible might of the superpower of their day, the two Afrikaner republics sought to strike hard with the hope of meanwhile gaining international diplomatic support to obtain a resolution similar to the First Boer War. They did not appreciate the fact that no single European government was going to dare challenge the British at the end of the 19th Century.

The Republican commandos poured over the borders in three places, correctly anticipating the inevitable three British thrusts. The first grouping crossed the Drakensberg into the Klip Rivier district of Natal, headed for towns like Newcastle, Dundee and Ladysmith. The second grouping crossed the Orange River from the Free State into the Northeastern Cape, occupying the part of the Cape Colony to the north of the Stormberg. They occupied Colesberg and placed men further south, just north of Middelburg, which now effectively became a front line town. The third grouping crossed the borders of the two republics to the west and occupied the part of the Cape Colony north of the Orange River, that is, the diamond fields.

The British Army was immediately pushed back on all fronts. To the west of the two republics, the British retreated south to the Orange River. However, instead of following up their successes, the Republican forces merely laid siege to Kimberley and Mafeking to its north, where Baden-Powell remained holed up. Based on his experience in Mafeking, he would later create the Boy Scouts. In Natal, the British were pushed beyond the Tugela River and further southeastward beyond Colenso. In this area, the Republican forces laid siege to Ladysmith. Many of the majority Afrikaner population of the Klip River district joined these Republican forces at this point. In the central theater of the war, the Republican forces pushed the British south of Naauwpoort and then held the line of the northernmost mountains of the escarpment, better known as the *Stormberg* in those parts.

In Natal, the fighting in the initial weeks was fierce. The British were also introduced to entirely new concepts in warfare. In his series of lectures[2] on "Psychology of War," Captain Le Roy Eltinge of the United States Army Service school describes the events at the Battle of Nicholson's Neck, near Ladysmith, where the British had occupied a hill and the Republican Boer commandos climbed up the hill to dislodge them:

"... the Boers crawled forward firing. The defenders fired also, but, while a storm of bullets swept over them, they could see the Boers getting nearer and ever nearer. The psychological effect of this uncanny crawling advance was so great that by the time the Boers were within 300 yards the British soldiers were individually showing white handkerchiefs. The Boers feared a trap and continued the attack. Soon the white handkerchiefs were almost universal. When the Boers came up to them, many of the British soldiers were weeping and their officers laid the trouble to the constant advance in the crawling line, against which the British fire seemed to have no effect."

Deneys Reitz[3], the 17-year old son of the Transvaal Secretary of State, was actually at that battle and tells a somewhat different story in his characteristically straightforward and honest fashion, with no references to handkerchiefs, 300 yards, or crying soldiers:

"Both parties were maintaining a vigorous short-range rifle contest, in which the soldiers were being badly worsted, for they were up against real old-fashioned Free State Boers for whom they were no match in sharpshooting of this kind. Time after time, I saw soldiers looking over their defenses to fire, and time after time, I heard the thud of a bullet finding its mark, and could see the unfortunate man fall back out of sight, killed or wounded. We joined in the fight and for the next hour we slowly but surely pressed the English to the far edge of the hill. [...]

"...we heard a bugle ring clear above the rifle fire, and at the same time a white flag went up. Hundreds of khaki clad figures rose from among the rocks and walked towards us, their rifles at the trail. We stood up to wait for them. The haul was a good one, for there were 1,100 prisoners [...]

"Shortly after the surrender I was talking to some of the captured officers when I heard one of them exclaim: "My God; Look there!" and turning round we saw the entire British force that had come out against us on the plain that morning in full retreat to Ladysmith. Great clouds of dust billowed over the veld as the troops withdrew, and the manner of their going had every appearance of a rout."

Tactical commanders such as the later to be legendary Christiaan de Wet were outraged at the elderly Kommandant-General Piet Joubert's refusal to send his horsemen after this British force to fully destroy it. It has been argued that Joubert was under instructions not to humiliate the British too much so as to make a political resolution more attainable. However, one hundred years of exposure to the British would have taught anyone that this was not the way to deal with the British. This was a nation that backed down only when totally and undeniably defeated, at which point there would be have to be provided some or other appropriate face saving process so that the British Army might go home with some pomp, ceremony and campaign medals. Joubert, having lived through the First Boer War, might have been expected to know this. And so, the student of history is left scratching his head.

Upon taking Glencoe, the confidential papers[4] of the British fell into the hands of the Republicans. In amongst this, was the correspondence showing the preparations for war on the part of Joseph Chamberlain immediately following the Jameson Raid. This was hard evidence of Chamberlain's intent to force a war.

Back in England, at the end of November 1899, the Empress of India entered a grand banquet in St. George's Hall on a litter borne by four bejeweled "Hindus" and sat down to a meal on a golden plate.[5]

The British Black Week

It was against the above background, some two months later, that the massive newly arrived British forces attacked on all three fronts in the week of 10-17 December 1899. Three consecutive battles combined to turn the particular week into the greatest military fiasco for British arms in the 19th century. Given the large number of texts on this war, we shall merely point out some of the major events and rather focus on the formative human experience within the family.

Fig. 16-3 *Some of the Republicans who fought at Stormberg*

The first disaster in the Black Week Trilogy was the *Battle of Stormberg*, northeast of Middelburg in the central theater of war in the Cape Colony. General Gatacre led 900 of the Royal Irish regiment and 600 of the Berkshire regiment, along with some artillery, engineers and volunteers straight into the Republican positions in a night march. The result was 25 British dead, 110 wounded and another approximately 600 taken prisoner. Republican losses were 8 men killed and 22 wounded.

This was followed immediately by the *Battle of Magersfontein* on the Western Front, right on the Free State-Cape Colony border, a short distance south of Kimberley. Here General Jacobus "Koos" de la Rey, a unique man whom we shall meet again, had taken careful note of the text-book bound British tactic of shelling entrenchments before attacking with infantry and then chasing with cavalry. He therefore had his men dig in physically in front of the base of a long range of rather low hills. The Afrikaner was about to teach the British the essentials of trench warfare.

De la Rey had been dead set against this war, but once it started, he aimed to fight to the finish. He, more than any other, embodied the stereotype Afrikaner character of "slow to anger, hard to quell." He had little tolerance of men who would start and stop wars easily. He was also the consummate gentleman and represented, for Afrikaners, all that is good about the decent and honorable fighting man. He was also a superb tactical leader, better known as "The Lion of the West Transvaal"; yet another French Huguenot descendant. He was facing Lord Methuen whose task it was to relieve Kimberley. Leading the infantry drive on the hills was Major-General Andy Wauchope of the Highlanders.

In the early morning of 11 December 1899, the British, entirely predictably, bombarded the hills with artillery, killing exactly zero Republicans, but destroying the Scandinavian Volunteer unit who had not followed the Commando example. When the British then attacked, the Highlanders under Wauchope marched directly at the hills, bent on performing what they thought would be largely a mopping up operation. Right in front were the Black Watch, followed by three Highlander groups. As these brave men came marching on in classic line abreast formation, the Republican fire was held under great discipline. When the British were 400 yards away, the Republicans opened fire from their camouflaged trenches. Given that practically every Republican was a marksman, it was an absolute "massacre."

Wauchope was killed by one of the first rounds fired and his men had no choice but to go to ground. They stayed flat on that piece of scorched semi-desert land all day, burnt mercilessly by the sun and tormented by huge biting ants that all South African children know only too well. And it was then that the Republican artillery first opened up. Methuen had no choice but to abandon his men to their fate. 136 men were killed, 756 were wounded, and 23 officers and 223 men were taken prisoner or reported missing. The Highlanders nevertheless made a huge impression on Afrikaners with their incredible discipline and bravery. To this day, the story exists in the author's family of the "Brave Scots with their little dresses" (kilts). This defeat caused consternation in Britain, where Wauchope had been a member of parliament.

The fact that British generalship was at an all time low was brought home vividly to all Britons nearer the end of that fateful week at the *Battle of Colenso*. General Redvers Buller was in overall command of the British Forces in South Africa, and it was in his Eastern Theater of Natal that the largest concentration of British forces was to be found. At the head of this, Buller now set out against the Republican forces barring his way across the Tugela River near the town of Colenso. His goal was to cross the Tugela River in a drive to relieve the Republican siege of Ladysmith. The disaster unfolded early on 15 December 1899, a mere four days after the debacle of *Magersfontein*. Due to faulty reconnaissance, Major-General Fitzroy Hart got his Irish 5th brigade stuck in a loop in the Tugela, with the other three regiments following behind. Facing him was the future first Prime Minster of South Africa, General Louis Botha, a name that may be traced to 17th century Germany. Botha, whose men were entrenched similarly to those at Magersfontein, had instructed his men to hold their fire until the British had crossed the river, but the milling brigade was simply too tempting a target. By the time the Irish were extricated, they had suffered 500 casualties.

The British Artillery was under the command of Major General Henry Hildyard. A detachment of two batteries of field guns under Colonel Charles Long moved ahead of the rest of the artillery. How and why will probably never quite be understood, but Long positioned his guns within rifle range of the Republicans. This level of incompetence in the face of an enemy that is a sharpshooter to a man, could not possibly go unpunished. The gunners came under intense fire and eventually deserted their guns to hide in a *donga* (arroyo, erosion gully). When some British soldiers tried to save the guns, a small knot of them was successful, but Lt. Freddy Roberts, the only son of Field Marshall Lord Roberts was killed. To the horror of the British, all but two of the guns were captured by the Republicans, who lost men in that effort. The British had 7 officers and 136 men dead, 47 officers and 709 men wounded, along with 20 officers and 220 men taken prisoner of war. On Boer side, Botha lost 6 dead (a seventh died later of his wounds) and 30 wounded as per Botha's report, where they are all listed in detail by name, down to splinter wounds. It is worth noting that two of the Boer dead were Graham and Shaw, both of British extraction.

At the end of the day, Buller dispatched the unavoidable letter calling for an armistice on the very day commemorating the seminal *Battle of Blood River*:

"To the Officer Commanding South African Republic Forces, Colenso.
Dec. 15th, 1899.
Sir,
I have the honour by desire of the General Officer Commanding British Forces South Africa [Buller] to request
that you will agree to an armistice tomorrow, Dec. 16th, 1899 in order that I may have an opportunity of burying
any men of any forces who were left dead on the field during today's operations. I would suggest that the armistice
hold good for 24 hours, from 8 a.m. tomorrow Dec. 16th, 1899.
I have the honour to be,
Sir,
Yr. Obedient servant, Fred. W. Stopford, Colonel, Military Secretary."

The final ignominy came when General Redvers Buller, as the master of Britain's might in Africa, signaled Sir George White in the besieged Ladysmith to,

"expend your ammunition, destroy your ciphers and make such terms as you can with the enemy."

An incredulous White rightly refused to obey the order.

The most incredible aspect of Colenso, not often discussed, was the light Boer losses as per Louis Botha's own report, where he lists them by name and includes "scratches" as wounds. Had the Irish managed to cross that river, it most likely would have been a total bloodbath for the British. More than likely, their blundering on the riverbank saved the British eastern army group from annihilation. On the western flank of the loop, were three more Commando units, and they never even fired a round.

In Britain, the shock and astonishment was total. The Imperial Superpower of the planet had been completely humbled by a bunch of farmers and their sons, fighting for home and country. However, in the Imperialist Jingo mindset, such an affront could not be left unavenged. But, what to do?

And this was when the call went out to the entire British Empire for men to fight the "Evil Boer" who had dared to defend his country against the rightful desire for the gold of Africa on the part of the war-obsessed cabinet of Her Royal Majesty, the Empress of India, Queen Victoria. This was also when the propaganda film was invented. Apparently shot on Dartmoor, it shows a supposed Boer rushing into a hospital tent with a smoking grenade to kill wounded British patients. It boggles the mind that thinking humans could believe such obviously unprofessional propaganda. Perhaps it convinced the British Jingos. Given the insanities they had already convinced themselves of, anything was possible. The sheer scope of the shock and disillusionment and actual fear in London is best gaged by considering some newspapers of the time. It is not at all evident that WWI or the Blitz of 1940 represented the same psychological shock for the nation as a whole. The concept of losing a war was something three generations of British since Napoleon had failed to comprehend. They had forgotten the First Boer War, which they had comprehensively lost.

In Continental Europe, people went delirious with joy at seeing the humiliation of the Imperialist British. Kaiser Wilhelm sent Paul Kruger a congratulatory letter. The French printed cartoons. The Russians actually wrote popular songs about the Transvaal. And, in America and Ireland, volunteers signed up to fight for the Republican Independence cause. They were joined by volunteers from Ireland, Russia, Italy, Scandinavia, Germany, France, and the Netherlands. These were all people who understood that Britain just wanted the gold and would do absolutely anything to get it. All of them had by then had quite enough of the excesses and arrogance of Imperial Britain. Shortly before, the Russian Czar had mused in a letter to his pro-Boer sister[6] about the possibility of moving his Turkestan Army to the borders of India (in effect, Afghanistan) to tie up the British Army in that sub-continent and stretch it too thin for escapades in South Africa. Had the Czar taken his planned steps, the entire outcome of the Great Boer War might have been different.

No one in Continental Europe realized just how thin the British nerve had in fact been stretched.

All the Queen's horses and all the Queen's men

Imperial Britain, clearly faced with the greatest challenge to its world stature in several generations, naturally recovered from the mind-numbing shock of the Black Week. The British Empire responded from all the Anglo-Saxon corners of its domain. They came from Rhodesia, Australia, New Zealand and even Canada. In the case of Canada, it was the first time that anything approximating a home-grown Canadian Army would serve outside that country. Some Canadian troops had already arrived just in time for Magersfontein, but Lord Methuen decided the Canadians were "too green" for this challenge. This spared the Canadians annihilation in their first battle. The pain was taken, instead by the Scottish Highlanders.

At Stormberg, it had been the Irish who paid in blood for the incompetence of the generals. At Colenso, it had also been the Irish who paid for Buller's haplessness. The actual Anglo-Saxon-Norman English, the core of the Empire, had yet to be properly blooded in a major battle in this war. Irish members of the House of

Commons would later point this out. We turn to American author Richard Harding Davis, who spent time with both the British and the Republican forces, for his view[7] of the obsessed British response at the resistance of, what he describes as, *"30,000 farmers"*:

> *"...the calmness and fairness with which the Boer regards the war and his enemy, in comparison with the hysteria of the Englishman on the same subject, are novel and unexpected developments. [...]*
>
> *"Even if the people of England have lost control of themselves and of their sense of perspective, her statesmen might be expected to keep their heads [...], But apparently, no one has any other thought than of South Africa. They have sent out the regular army, the reserves, the militia, the volunteers, three dukes, the Honorable Artillery company, the post-office clerks, the barristers from the Temple, the cashiers from the bank, the yeomen from the farms, the "special corps" of "gentlemen," the crofters and gillies from Scotland, the caddies from the golf links, the Canadian rough riders, the Australian mounted police, the New Zealand Light Horse, the Bengal lancers, the Indian coolies (sic) [...]*
>
> *"...they have sent all the way to Klondike to get an American to act as their chief of scouts"* [see below: *The Empress of India's American*].

The British High Command responded to the earlier disasters by replacing Buller as overall commander of British forces in South Africa. The man now in command was the very man whose son had just been killed by the Republicans at Colenso due to British military incompetence: Lord Roberts of Kandahar (the same Kandahar of the war in Afghanistan in the year 2003). Clearly, there was a death in the family to be avenged. With him, arrived General Horatio Kitchener, better known as "Kitchener of Khartoum". Here was the man who had won a victory at Omdurman in the Sudan by killing the Dervish in hordes with Maxim machine guns, as reported by an ecstatic young newspaper reporter, named Winston Churchill. Kitchener had overseen an inhuman slaughter of a totally outclassed and underarmed, but very brave foe. It was known that this was a man with no scruples or concept of humanity. He would amply demonstrate this in the months to come.

Fig. 16-4 Lord Roberts of Kandahar

The British forces now hopelessly outnumbered the Republicans and were vastly better equipped with artillery and the like. They had even stripped big naval guns from their ships to take on the Afrikaners. From this point onwards, the final outcome, in the absence of an international political solution, was a foregone conclusion. The British could field almost half a million men and thousands of cannon and machine guns against the 80,000 farmers and their sons who could field no more than 35,000 men at any one time – a ratio of more than ten to one. From the British perspective, it became a "rolling grind" in which even the women and children would not be spared. Ultimately, not even the animals would be spared the wanton Imperialist slaughter. From the Afrikaner Republican perspective it became a War of Attrition. It was based on making the British pay as high a price as possible, while risking as few precious lives of a small nation as possible, hoping and praying that God would take a hand in righting this travesty, for no country was prepared to.

Roberts had left Buller in command of the Natal front, and it is here that the most well known battle of this war was next to be fought on 23 January 1900. Since the author's extended family was present at this battle, known as Spioenkop, we shall treat that in Nexus Familia 70. It was characterized by the most intense fighting of the war, and by both sides believing the other had won. Both sides fought bravely. In the end, the battle went to the Republicans, largely because they made fewer mistakes, they knew the lay of the land better, and because the British simply gave up. Nevertheless, even as one works through the events of the battle one can clearly see that the war was strategically lost for the Republicans.

No significant help was coming. They stood alone against the mightiest Empire ever known.

The Empress of India's American

In January 1900, after the Black Week of December 1899, a telegram arrived in Skagway, Alaska. It was addressed to the 5-foot 4 inch "short 'n stocky" American, Frederick Russel Burnham, who had recently joined the Klondike gold rush. Within one hour he was on his way to the Cape, as the telegram read[8]: *Lord Roberts appoints you on his personal staff as Chief of Scouts. If you accept, come at once the quickest way possible.*

Burnham was already known to the British as a scout from his days in Cecil John Rhodes' infamous British South Africa Police, who machine-gunned the Matabele in Rhodesia. It would seem he was not aware of Rhodes' dream of regaining the United States for Britain; otherwise, his allegiance in this matter would be extremely difficult to rationalize. Clearly, the British were no match for the Boer abilities in the area of scouting and this was in invitation that Burnham could not resist, even though it allied him with the very Empire that had oppressed America.

He arrived in South Africa just in time for the Battle of Paardeberg and would do excellent scouting work for the British. Eventually, he was severely hurt blowing up the railway line between Pretoria and Portuguese East Africa beyond the front line of the war, but survived and was sent to Britain to meet and dine with the Empress of India. He would eventually be awarded the Distinguished Service Order cross by King Edward VII in

Fig. 16-5 *Frederick Russel Burnham*

person after the death of that Empress. He most certainly caught the attention of the Republican command.

To Burnham's credit, he appeared to be reasonably objective in his memoirs about the "Second Americans" he fought[9]:

> *"Their struggle for existence in this huge black continent, unsupported by the army or navy of a home country, makes one of the most romantic pages in history. [...]*
>
> *"Every inch of territory they gained was won against almost overwhelming odds – always some mere handful of men holding out against overwhelming hordes of savages. Through all the struggle with fierce and warlike tribes, the Boer had at the same time to contend with the most ferocious wild beasts and with almost equally savage and antagonistic natural conditions. Then, as a climax to his difficulties, he found himself threatened by the invasion of another race, similar to his own in blood and tenacity of purpose, but far superior both in number and in wealth."*

 ## Nexus Familia 71: The Battle of Spioenkop

The two Jordaan sisters Margaretha Milward and Gertruida Prinsloo said goodbye to Gertruida's son, Daniel, in October 1899 when he reported for duty in the Carolina Commando to serve under his distant relative, Kommandant Hendrik Prinsloo. It is now January 1900, the Black Week has come and gone, and the British have flooded South Africa with the largest army ever amassed under their flag in all of British history. New arrivals to Cape Town comment that there are so many ships that they simply cannot be counted. All this to take away a country from 35,000 farmers; a country to which the British themselves have effectively banished them with malice aforethought (See Chapter 13, Canaan Lost: *Hounding the Afrikaner*).

Daniel now finds himself near a misleadingly nondescript 1400 foot hill named *Spioenkop* (Spy Hill), which bars the way to Ladysmith in Natal for the relieving army of Sir Redvers Buller, now vastly bigger than the Republican forces. The hill is only just to the north of the Tugela River. Buller, still in command in Natal, is the man who oversaw the British disaster of Colenso during the Black Week.

Like all Afrikaners, Daniel has the highest regard for the ordinary British Tommy, whom he sees as not only brave in the extreme, but also as a decent human being. After all, they sing the same hymns, with the same melodies, only the words differing for language. This respect does not extend to the British commanders, who are regarded as basically inept and not worthy of the brave men they command.

So it is that the morning of 24 January 1900 opens as an overcast day, with the highland cloud base enfolding the top of Spioenkop. The Afrikaners of these parts know this kind of weather only too well. Later in the morning, the cloud base will lift as the summer sun heats the ground and the ridges on top of Spioenkop will be exposed. Daniel finds himself encamped, along with the rest of the Carolina Commando, on the plateau behind Spioenkop. On the other side of the hill runs the Tugela, 1400 feet below.

And this is when a message reaches General Schalk Burger of the Republican

Fig. 16-6 spioenkop as viewed from the plain below

forces that Spioenkop is in the hands of the British. 1700 British soldiers under General Woodgate have overwhelmed the Republican pickets and a handful of German volunteers on top of the mountain during the night. This is a crisis by any measure, and Burger immediately instructs Kommandant Hendrik Prinsloo to take 85 of his Carolina burghers up the mountain and to occupy Aloe Knoll (Little Knoll) on the right flank of the British, who do not grasp the significance of this hill. Before moving out, Kommandant Hendrik Prinsloo, subsequently to be hailed the Hero of Spioenkop, gathers his militia of Carolina farmers about him and tells them[10]:

"Burghers, we're now going in to attack the enemy and we shan't all be coming back. Do your duty and trust in the Lord."

Fig. 16-7 The view southward from atop Spioenkop

A unit of 30 burghers from Heidelberg in the Transvaal simultaneously heads for the British left flank. Meanwhile General Louis Botha is rounding up volunteers on the plateau behind the mountain and is herding them up the slope to attack the British in an uphill frontal assault. This includes members of the Pretoria Commando, one of whom is Deneys Reitz, the 17-year old son of the Secretary of the Transvaal Republic, F.W. Reitz.

Louis Botha takes overall command of the Boer effort, which he directs from a ridge to the north of Spioenkop. Botha has chosen well. From where he is, he can range his artillery on the British dug in on Spioenkop. Neither side knows exactly the movements of the other side, nor how large the opposing forces are at this point in time. As a straight matter of numbers, we have 1700 British regulars, dug in on a commanding hill, ranged against some 400 Republican volunteers (some sources put it at 300) faced with climbing the hill and dislodging them. We turn to young Deneys Reitz, who describes the view of the assault as he joins it from below the hill[11].

"Many of our men dropped, but already the foremost were within a few yards of the rocky edge which marked the crest, and [British] soldiers were rising from behind their cover to meet the final rush. For a moment or two there was confused hand-to-hand fighting, then the combatants surged over the rim onto the plateau beyond where we could no longer see them. [...] Apart from the Pretoria men, there were many other dead and wounded, mostly Carolina burghers from the Eastern Transvaal, who had formed the bulk of the assaulting column."

Fig. 16-8 Sketch Plan of Spioenkop with Aloe Knoll depicted as "Little Knoll"

In fact, Daniel's Carolina Commando has been brutally savaged in a charge that will establish their reputation for bravery for the next hundred years. Of their complement of 85, a full 55 have been killed or wounded. However, they have successfully taken Aloe Knoll and are pouring a devastating fire down the length of the British trench. Conical hill has also been taken. Meanwhile the British are sending up more men to ultimately bring their total to 2,000 on the confined plateau of the hill. Somewhere over this period a number of key things happen:

• Firstly, the African summer sun finally raises the base of the cloud and the British discover, to their great horror, that they have not occupied the highest area of Spioenkop and that the assaulting Boer Commandos have higher ground. Furthermore, the Boer field guns command their position. And these are exactly the guns that General Louis Botha now turns on them with devastating effect.

• Secondly, the British realize that the Boer guns at the weakly protected Twin Peaks are key to the battle. At least one of those guns is manned by the Orange Free State artillery. The British attack the guns successfully and the handful of Boer gunners desert their guns, but the British gunners mistake them for their own men and stop firing. The Boer gunners promptly return to their guns and the British manage to confuse their own signals. At the end of the exchange, the little knot of Boer gunners are back in command of the situation and are once more loosing a devastating fire on the 2,000 British troops pinned down on Spioenkop.

• Thirdly, General Woodgate is mortally wounded and confusion breaks out as to who of his three subordinates is in command on the British side, Thorneycroft, Coke or Crofton. A first messenger to Thorneycroft is shot dead before he utters a word. Finally, a second one reaches him with a simple message: *"You are a General."*

On the hill itself, it is utter hell. Deneys Reitz has stumbled on the body of the last of his tent mates. The rifle fire is intense and the opposing parties are mere yards apart. Of this situation, one may find the classic statement by Deneys Reitz in many treatises on this battle:

"The English troops lay so near that one could have tossed a biscuit tin among them..."

It is also over this period that a large number of the Lancaster Fusiliers start waving their white handkerchiefs in surrender. When the Boer riflemen stand up to accept the British surrender, Thorneycroft, assuming command, comes charging out of the scene of horror, famously yelling:

"I am the commander here, take your men back to hell, sir. There is no surrender!"

For the greater part of the day, the Boer riflemen cannot see the effect of their attack. They are only aware of their own losses, and these are grievous, painful, and telling by the standards of these ordinary men, unaccustomed as they are to Napoleonic bloodshed. In the midst of all this carnage, Commandant "Red

Daniel" Opperman does sterling work, moving from man to man in keeping up the morale.

But the battlefront is stagnant. The 400 Republican volunteers and 2000 British soldiers are mutually matched and checked, each with the support of their respective field guns. However, as the hours drag on in these few acres of hell, the Republican faith starts to fail while British discipline holds. We turn once more to Deneys Reitz:

"...around us were the dead men covered with swarms of flies attracted by the smell of blood. We did not know the cruel losses that the English were suffering, and we believed that they were easily holding their own, so discouragement spread as the shadows lengthened.[...]

"...when at last the sun set I do not think there were sixty men left on the ledge. [...]

"For a long time I remained at my post...[...]

"Afterwards, my nerve began to go and I thought I saw figures with bayonets stealing forward. When I tried to find the men who earlier in the evening had been beside me, they were gone. Almost in a panic I left my place and hastened along the fringe of rocks in search of company, and to my immense relief heard a gruff "werda." It was Commandant "Red Daniel" Opperman still in his place with about two dozen men. [...]

"At last Opperman decided to retreat, and we descended the hill..."

At this point, the men gather on the plain behind Spioenkop and ready themselves to leave, believing the British will come pouring through the gap they have won this day. Panic has clearly set in. But then the man of the moment takes center stage. We turn again to Deneys Reitz:

"There came the sound of galloping hoofs, and a man rode into our midst who shouted at them to halt. I could not see his face in the dark, but word went around that it was Louis Botha, the new Commandant-General, appointed in the place of Piet Joubert [Hero of the First Boer War] who was seriously ill. [...]

"...so eloquent was his appeal that in a few minutes the men were filing off into the dark to re-occupy their positions either side of the Spioenkop gap. [...]

"...we led our horses back to the [northern] foot of Spioenkop, to wait there.

"We woke with the falling of the dew and, as the sky lighted, gazed eagerly at the dim outline of the hill above [...] ...Then, to our utter surprise, we saw two men on the top triumphantly waving their hats and holding their rifles aloft. They were Boers..."

Incredibly, the 2,000 British troops have vacated the mountain in the night, believing they have lost. Not just that, but looking at the Tugela below, Reitz watches as the entire British Army in Natal moves back over the Tugela River in full retreat, vacating all the positions they have occupied on the north side of the river over the past several days. The 400 Boer militia fighters have managed to drive the 2000 British regulars from the mountain in an uphill assault, but they cannot believe their own victory.

When the burghers walk over to inspect the British trenches, they see the reason for the British retreat. The British dead are lying three deep in the shallow

Fig. 16-9 *The British dead atop Spioenkop after the British retreat*

trenches. This is the first moment that these simple farmers and townsfolk see the devastating results of their actions of the day, and they are horrified at the slaughter wreaked by the Boer guns and rifles. Again, Deneys Reitz:

"The Boer guns in particular had wrought terrible havoc and some of the bodies were shockingly mutilated. There must have been six hundred dead men on this strip of earth, and there cannot have been many battlefields where there was such an accumulation of horrors within so small a compass."

Later in the day, the Boer fighters will respectfully help the British to collect their dead from the mountain. The name "Spioenkop" enters the history of Britain and its Empire on this day. In the 21st century, tourists will find the name "Spion Kop" all over Britain and its Commonwealth at sports fields and the like. In both the United States and Britain, villages of that name will eventually be founded.

Below the hill, among the dispirited British troops, two men are going about their business. One is a reporter turned military courier, by the name of Winston Churchill, who reports on the devastation and horror on the hill. Many of the British dead have been shot through the head from the side; the work of Daniel Prinsloo's Carolina Commando. The other man is a quiet Indian stretcher bearer by the name of Mohandas Karamchand Gandhi who will also resist the British later. On top of the hill, the future first Prime Minister of a united South Africa watches as the British columns withdraw. His name is Louis Botha. Deneys Reitz himself will one day be the South African High Commissioner to Britain.

On Boer side, 58 have been killed and 140 wounded. On British side, 322 men lie dead on the hill, 563 are wounded and 300 are missing or prisoner.

Deneys Reitz's description of the scene, as they gathered the bodies of their own fallen after the battle, is both touching and telling:

"...when the Commando wagon came up we placed the bodies on board and escorted them to Ladysmith, whence they were sent to Pretoria for burial. So we rode behind the wagon which carried all that was left of our friends and companions, their horses trotting alongside with empty saddles.

I personally came home to a deserted tent..."

—*End Nexus Familia*

The Empire wins the second phase

The next major battle was as tough as Spioenkop, and again both thought the other side had won. However, in this latter case, the Republicans' nerve broke first, and they surrendered. It was the key turning point of the war for the British, as it exposed the entire western flank of the Boer Republics.

British history books make much of the Battle of Paardeberg of February 1900, where the British besieged General Cronje and his 5,000 men and 50 women and forced Cronje to surrender, amidst a cloud of flies from dead oxen and horses and knots of crying women, having shelled them mercilessly for 10 days. However, the surrender came only after Kitchener had refused the Afrikaners a truce to bury their dead – a refusal unthinkable to the Calvinist Christian Afrikaners, who had repeatedly granted the British truces under such circumstances, an example being Spioenkop, where they actually helped the British bury their dead. Kitchener also captured the Boer ambulance and refused to allow it to tend to the Boer wounded, enlisting it instead for his own men[12].

The legacy of Kitchener would have to live with this as the first in a long list of horrors against his name and that of Britain in this increasingly disgusting war that had started out as a Gentleman's War. One of the small recorded facts of this battle was that Cronjé, in stark contrast with Kitchener's behavior, protected his British prisoners of war with the Boer women in the safest possible positions. The surrender came only after 24 officers and 279 men on the British side lay dead and 59 Officers and 847 men lay wounded.

In terms of British casualties, it had been the costliest battle so far, but the British finally had a victory – be it a morally hollow one, achieved at a massive cost in blood and with massively superior forces. It does not appear among the list of British victories that bear studying for future reference. In fact, it has little to commend itself to military study. However, Cronje's own hapless tactical moves were no better on the Republican side.

A study of the battle reveals that Roberts was actually bent on withdrawing, which would have been the most inglorious debacle of British arms yet. However, this time it was the Boer nerve that failed first, more than likely a consequence of lack of suitable military discipline. A little more tenacity, a modicum of military discipline, and fewer women and children in the Boer train might have given them the day. Certainly, a number of Republican commanders were very frustrated with Cronje's prosecution of the battle and his refusal to make use of the opportunities of extraction they had presented him.

The inevitable outcome of this phase of the War, the western Republican front having collapsed, was the fall of the two capitals of the Free State and the Transvaal, Bloemfontein (13 March 1900) and Pretoria (5 June 1900) respectively. The flat Highveld Prairie offered little in the way of terrain for the Republicans to exploit in defense. However, if the British thought that the capture of the two capitals represented the end of the war, they were sadly mistaken. Lord Roberts certainly thought that the fall of the capitals heralded the end of the war, so he departed and left the "mopping up" to his subordinate, Horatio Kitchener.

The Afrikaners thereupon turned to guerrilla warfare. The three leading proponents would be Louis Botha, Christiaan de Wet of the Free State and Koos de la Rey of the Western Transvaal, all three of whom would fight the British to the final end of the war. In the immediate future, they would systematically fall back to the Mozambique border, and then double back around the north, disperse into smaller groups, and start making this war as expensive for Britain as possible. The 70-year old President Paul Kruger was sent off into exile in Europe via Portuguese East Africa. It was September 1900 – one year into the war and it was already four times as long as the British government and its Rothschild bankers had hoped.

Nexus Familia 72: Surrender at Paardeberg

On 27 February 1900, General Piet Cronje finally surrenders to Lord Roberts of Kandahar after the heaviest and most prolonged artillery bombardment of the war. With him are 4019 men and also 50 women. One battery of the Orange Free State Artillery is also surrendered in this process, along with its commander, German Major Albrecht, but Barend Matthys Johannes Booyens (*NF68*) is not serving in that battery. However, among the 4019 men are five of the seven sons of Tjaart Johannes Booyens (*NF64, 65* and

Fig. 16-10 In St. Helena Island POW camp

67), and also the father-in-law of one of them. The men are shipped to St. Helena Island Prisoner of War camp. They are to be kept there until the end of the war. This is the very place where the British had sent the Emperor Napoleon to die. Figure 16-10 shows these Booyens men in that camp, in front of a building constructed from beaten metal cans, the circular bases of which can clearly be seen. The group of buildings they named "Tin Town." All are sporting the customary beard as a "statement"; the youngest barely managing at age 17. The youngest of the seven brothers, Johannes Hendrik, is at this time a boy of thirteen years.

The men are as follows from left to right:

Back row: Christoffel Johannes, Daniel Jan Andries and Jan Adriaan

Front row: J. Yssel, father in-law of TJ Booyens Jr., Tjaart Johannes Jr., Matthys Jacobus, the eldest of the brothers

—*End Nexus Familia*

The American Volunteers arrive

A day or so before Kruger departs Pretoria, a train rolls into Pretoria station. On board is a group of American Irish volunteers from Chicago, led by Captain O' Connor. Also on the train is American author, Richard Harding Davis. The group will join the existing Irish Volunteer group led by Colonel Blake. President Kruger welcomes the Americans at his house. We are fortunate in having Richard Harding Davis' report on the welcoming address by Kruger[13]:

Fig. 16-11 Pres. Kruger welcomes the American Volunteers

"When Mr. Reitz [father of Deneys Reitz] came, the President walked out to the sidewalk, and Colonel Blake, the commander of the Irish Brigade, introduced Captain O'Connor of the Chicago contingent. The President said that it was to be expected that men should come from the country which had always stood for the liberty and for the independence of the individual; that the cause for which they had come to fight was one upon which the Lord had looked with favor; and that even though they died in this war they must feel that they were acting as His servants and had died in His service."

Davis, who started his visit to South Africa by moving with the British Army in Natal, now experiences a sea change in his views[14] when he reaches Pretoria:

"We all were with Great Britain as soon as her difficulties began. We had not forgotten how she came to our aid when, without her help, a coalition of the Powers might have put us to sore humiliation. But she must see now that her difficulties ran on for too long a time. The underdog at which 'the lion and her cubs' had been snarling and snapping made too strong, too manly, too intelligent a fight for his liberty for one to sympathize any longer with the lion's blunders and hysteria and rampant, impotent patriotism."

Noting the peculiar extremism and blood lust that besets the British when the specific matter of the Afrikaners is raised, he comments:

"It must be because the English are so conscious of the injustice of this war that they rail as they do at the Boer."

Of Kruger himself Davis says[15]:

"On the stoop, separated from the sidewalk by only a bed of flowers, you may at almost any hour you pass see the President smoking his pipe and sipping his coffee. This simplicity and democracy add infinitely to the interest he holds for you as a man."

On 29 May 1900, Kruger is ready to leave Pretoria by coach for Eerste Fabrieken, where he is to board a train for Machadodorp on the Eastern Escarpment of the Transvaal. Even as General Meyer and Mr. Reitz, the Secretary of State, urges him to depart, he insists on a last audience with some visitors. It is an American delegation consisting of Davis, Mr. Sutherland, James Archibald, the war correspondent, and a young man named Jimmy Smith. They bring three items. Jimmy delivers the first two.

The first is an embroidered flag of the Transvaal Republic, and the second a message of sympathy from twenty-nine hundred Philidelphia schoolboys, to be delivered by the red-headed young Jimmy Smith from

New York, the original home of the Sterrevelts (*NF4*). He is a member of the New York Messenger Service. The message[16], accompanied by 2,900 signatures, held that it was fitting that:

> "...the children of the city which had first declared for independence against Great Britain should send a greeting of sympathy to the leader of the people who were in their turn fighting for their independence against the same nation."

Before Kruger can make a statement of thanks, Mr. Sutherland also presents him with a locked box. When it turns out that Sutherland cannot get the box opened, the Secretary of War, Mr. Grobler, and the Secretary of State, Mr. Reitz, both get down on their knees next to Sutherland on the floor and try to help him, with President Kruger stepping closer to look interestedly over their shoulders. At this point, James Archibald asks Sutherland whether he does not have a key.

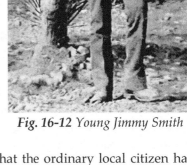

This is when Sutherland finally fishes the key from his pocket. Out comes a beautiful thick leather bound book. As Reitz lifts the book from the box, our minds go back to 1837 when the British Settlers presented Pieter Uys' father with a leather bound Bible as the family was leaving their country because of the British (See Chapter 9). Kruger himself had been a young lad of less than 10 years in the Trek of Hendrik Potgieter, when they fought the Matabele at Vegkop. This, no doubt, is a Bible from the sympathetic Americans to guide him on his way out of his own country yet again. Kruger beams in delight and says, *"It is a Bible!"*

We quote Davis directly:

> *"The mistake was so in character that, as we grasped it and heard the simple note of real pleasure in his voice, I believe every man in the room would have given half a month's wages to have changed that album into what Kruger believed it to be.*
>
> *"'No, a history of the war,' Reitz exclaimed, hastily, turning over the pages and showing the President pictures of himself, of Boer laagers, and of his generals.*
>
> *"But the President shook his head and closed the big volume."*

Fig. 16-12 Young Jimmy Smith

As the 70-year old President Paul Kruger closes the book, the calendar on the wall reads "29 May 1900." It is just over 105 years since the British invasion vanguard[17] arrived off the Cape in 1795. It is 105 years that the ordinary local citizen has dreamed of, fought for, and died for democratic independence.

And as the book closes, so effectively ends that precious hard won independence.

Nexus Familia 73: The End of the Beginning

We continue here the story of the families whom we last saw prepare for war (*NF68*). We consider each part of South Africa in turn, the different areas being affected in different ways.

Surrender in the Free State

On July 31, 1900, the *New York Times* publishes an article in which the surrender of General Marthinus Prinsloo in the eastern Free State outside Fouriesburg, near the base of the Drakensberg Mountains, is reported as a wise decision. Quoting directly[18] :

> *"The surrender of the Boer General Prinsloo with 5,000 men, as prisoners of war, will go far toward convincing people who have followed the events of the South African conflict that the days of the actual warfare in that territory are numbered; [...] To anybody but an insane person there was no option."*

The misreading of the situation by *New York Times* will soon be evident, and its suggestion that surrendering to the British is to be "reasonable" will be severely challenged by the victor's actions. Also, the number of men who surrendered with Prinsloo was closer to 3,000. Barend Matthys Johannes Booyens of Thaba'Nchu, along with others of the Free State Artillery, surrenders to the British at this point (30 July 1900) as part of General Prinsloo's army. For this, Prinsloo and his men will later be pilloried by their countrymen who expected them to fight on. Also surrendering on that day was Commandant Robert Crowther of the Boer Commandos, a good example of the many honorable men of British descent who had fought against the Empress of India for the independence of their country.

In the next chapter, we shall see what becomes of the family Booyens in the hands of the British. Of course, out here on the sub-freezing Orange Free State winter Prairie they are not subscribed to the *New York Times*. They trust in the thought that the British are reputedly honorable men and decent Christians.

Those they know indeed are.

Some of the men of the Free State Artillery refuse to surrender. They include a young sergeant by the name of Johannes Smith, who sets off to join the Free State Commando of a man named Kritzinger.

The last set piece battle

The last formal set piece battle of the war, the Battle of Bergendal (mountain and dale), starting on 21 August 1900, is fought right at *Schoongezicht*, Daniel Prinsloo's own farm. Even before the battle, Louis Botha has decided to pursue guerrilla warfare, as the conventional war is obviously lost to Imperial forces massively superior in number. For this battle, Roberts has over 19,000 officers and men, of whom 4,800 are mounted, 82 guns and 25 machine guns.

Against this, Botha has 7,000 men and 20 guns. The result is inevitable, but the Republicans withdraw in good order. Daniel goes back to his family and his farm, *Schoongezicht*.

Fig. 16-13 *The British Army enters Bloemfontein*

In the Southeastern Transvaal

With the British Army successfully crossing the Tugela and taking the Republican positions in February 1900, the Republican commandos fall back northward to the Southeast Transvaal. In Standerton, Michael Charles Callanan takes the next obvious step. After the bridges of the Railway Company are blown, he takes up arms as an Irish-descended burgher of the Transvaal. It is in this role that he is captured near the town on 22 June 1900, likely by the Canadian Strathcona Horse. He is thereupon transported to Green Point at Cape Town as *Prisoner of War No. 3368*. He is put in *Transvaal Camp 2, Tent 11*.

He is likely not aware that his brothers are under arms on the other side of this war.

Near the Mozambican border

In the Eastern Transvaal, Michael's Callanan's close friend, John van Graan, continues his work as train driver for Kruger's government as it withdraws eastward toward Portuguese East Africa. It is over this period that Frederick Russel Burnham, the American Scout in the pay of the Empress of India, blows up the railway line that John is trying to drive his train over in the Republican cause. However, Burnham is also badly wounded over this period and returns to Britain.

On 24 September 1900, after President Kruger has left for exile in Europe, the last formal Boer forces gather at Hectorspruit, the last station before the Komatipoort border post. Here the men who do not have horses are told they shall have to march to Komatipoort to await the British. Those with horses join Commandant-General Botha and several other senior officers, including Schalk Burger, the caretaking President of the Transvaal. This group sets off northward through the subtropical Kruger Park Lowveld to circle around the north of the British Army.

As a train driver with no horse, John van Graan is eventually taken prisoner on 22 December 1900 at Komatipoort. Therewith the British finally control all of the railways in Southern Africa outside Portuguese East Africa (Mozambique).

In the Eastern Cape

In the Eastern Cape, life goes on fairly normally. The British are holding their tea parties and drinking toasts to the Empress of India, singing, *"Britons never shall be slaves."* One is left wondering how 35,000 Boer farmers, few of whom had ever seen the sea, might have crossed 6,000 miles of ocean controlled by the mightiest navy the planet had ever seen in order to enslave several million Britons.

In the Bathurst area, the youngest McCusker and the oldest Callanan half-brothers are still serving in Nesbitt's Horse. Their lives are about to get more interesting.

* * * * *

In terms of bleeding the Empire and sickening its soul, the real Great Boer War is about to start. To borrow a later phrase from Winston Churchill, the fall of the two capitals represents not so much *"the beginning of the end as it does the end of the beginning."* It will turn into the most expensive war that Britain has ever fought to this date. Before the last Boer lays down his rifle, Britain will come to bitterly regret the mindset that had led it into this entirely contrived war. It will also learn that if it chooses to "bring democracy," then it should first determine who is the majority. In this process, Britain will lose all moral high ground it might once have claimed for itself.

Britain will lose its soul at the southern tip of Africa and will poison the entire 20th century in the process in South Africa. Furthermore, so many of the mistakes that Britain makes in the execution of this war will later be repeated by Western Powers that students of history will stand aghast at the willful refusal on the part of Western leadership to learn from history.

—*End Nexus Familia*

-----ooOoo-----

17

Total War

"...on the eve of the conflict which threatens to exterminate our people, it behooves us to speak the truth in what may be, perchance, our last message to the world."

F.W. Reitz, Transvaal Secretary of State and former Free State President
A Century of Wrong (1900)

Guerrilla Warfare

When President Kruger departed into exile, Commandant-General Louis Botha started planning his guerrilla war. The overall strategy was to bleed the British at the lowest possible cost to the Afrikaner until the Empire wearied of the war. The basic tactic was hit-and-run and live to bleed the British another day. There were to be no heroics, because those were not affordable. The basic target was the British logistics, because that was the lifeblood of the ponderous and oversupplied British Army, and because it would be the only source of supplies for the Republican forces.

This plan would eventually work so well, that it would drive Roberts' successor, Kitchener, to distraction and weary Britain of the most costly war ever fought against anyone in its entire history to that date, the United States, Napoleon and the Russians included. We cannot conceivably do justice to this subject in this present work, but merely touch on some major points that affected subsequent history with emphasis on those where we have family testimony.

The British Army itself would provide the ultimate testimony on the subject of the Boer guerrillas. At the start of WWII, the British Army would seek to emulate these Boer Commandos by

Fig. 17-1 Commandant-General Louis Botha

creating their own Commandos. On 10 June 1940, Lt Col Dudley Clark of the British General Staff, himself a South African by birth, would draw up detailed proposals for the creation of the British Commandos. He would declare[1]:

"Since the [Boer] Commandos seemed the best exponent of guerrilla warfare that history could provide, it was presumably the best model we could adopt."

We turn once more to Richard Harding Davis[2], the American author, for the reasons behind the British observation:

"With the exception of the capture of Cronje by Lord Roberts, which, after all, was the capture of 3,000 men

by 20,000, with 20,000 more hurrying up in reserve, there has not been in six months a single British victory except of a negative character."

He goes on to say[3]:

"...after forcing a war most insolently and barefacedly on one of the smallest governments on the globe, that smallest government was giving him for six months a severe and humiliating thrashing."

The reasons for this success may lie in what is possibly the most striking summary on the Afrikaner of the Boer War ever provided; that of one of the greatest of Imperialist Britons ever, Sir Arthur Conan Doyle[4]:

"Take a community of Dutchmen of the type of those who defended themselves for fifty years against all the power of Spain at a time when Spain was the greatest power in the world. Intermix with them a strain of those inflexible French Huguenots who gave up home and fortune and left their country forever at the time of the revocation of the Edict of Nantes. The product must obviously be one of the most rugged, virile, unconquerable races ever seen upon earth. Take this formidable people and train them for seven generations in constant warfare against savage men and ferocious beasts, in circumstances under which no weakling could survive, place them so that they acquire exceptional skill with weapons and in horsemanship, give them a country which is eminently suited to the tactics of the huntsman, the marksman, and the rider. Then, finally, put a finer temper upon their military qualities by a dour fatalistic Old Testament religion and an ardent and consuming patriotism. Combine all these qualities and all these impulses in one individual, and you have the modem Boer — the most formidable antagonist who ever crossed the path of Imperial Britain. Our military history has largely consisted in our conflicts with France, but Napoleon and all his veterans have never treated us so roughly as these hard-bitten farmers with their ancient theology and their inconveniently modern rifles."

From late 1900, Horatio Kitchener bore the full responsibility for the conduct of the War in South Africa, and Britain was getting more desperate by the day to see a conclusion to this costly exercise. As the Boer Commandos became ever more successful, so Kitchener's reactions became ever more desperate, until he finally crossed the unspoken line that sets the civilized apart from the barbarous.

Even as Roberts was leaving in 1900 under the naive impression that the war was essentially over, the British Army started implementing the intentional burning of Afrikaner farms in the Free State and Transvaal Republics to deny support for the remaining Afrikaner men in the field. It was to get worse – much worse.

What makes the subsequent actions of the British all the more difficult to comprehend, is a point well made by the great Canadian historian, Theal[5], about the Afrikaners:

Fig. 17-2 Lord Horatio Kitchener, "Kitchener of Khartoum"

"No people not of British descent ever offered such favourable material for conversion to loyal subjects. [...]

"They were men of our own race, of that sturdy Nether-Teuton stock which peopled England and Scotland as well as the delta of the Rhine. [...]

"They spoke a dialect which our great Alfred would have understood without much difficulty, which is nearer to the language of the men who fought under Harold at Senlac than it is to the English tongue of today. Their religion was that of the people of Scotland, of a considerable number of people in England."

Alas, the strident and malevolent propaganda of the London Missionary Society for the first half of the 19th Century, and the constant hounding by the cabal of empire-minded Conservatives and banking moguls in London in the second half of the century had taken its toll. They had painted the Afrikaners into depraved and corrupt monsters. For their part, the Afrikaners naively thought they would be seen as the decent devout Christian Westerners that they were. In reality, however, the average Tommy arriving in South Africa had somehow been led to believe, either intentionally or through sheer ignorance, that he was going to fight people akin to the Dervish of 1896 in the Sudan. The Afrikaner "Boer" sounded way too much like "Boor." And that is exactly how dehumanization starts. And dehumanization makes genocide an easy next step. And dehumanization is brought on by frustration. And frustration is brought on by failure. And Imperial Britain had failure aplenty in South Africa.

From here on out, the actions of the British Army and its allies would lead to generations of bitterness, both in South Africa and elsewhere in the Commonwealth, some of it as yet not quite spent in the 21st century. It is in the matters of *Slagtersnek*, the events surrounding the *Great Trek* and this third "Total War" phase of the Great Boer War that one may find much of the motivation for the subsequent history of South Africa. It therefore behooves us to consider this period and the men involved in more depth.

Christiaan De Wet

In the Free State, Christiaan De Wet, with the Free State President M.T. Steyn in his care, led the British Army all over this Prairie territory, striking hugely frustrating blows, and then simply evaporating as mist before the sun. The British Army became obsessed with catching him in particular, and failed to the end. And all the time the Empire bled lives and treasure, and, of course, vital supplies.

Fig. 17-3 General Christiaan De Wet

De Wet, an ordinary farmer with almost zero formal schooling, had made his name with one of the stunning victories at the beginning of the war at Nicholson's neck (See Chapter 16 – Invasion- The First Phase) and later at places like Sannaspos. He consistently outwitted his opponents. Even desperate warnings from Roberts' American scout, Burnham, could not divert the British from unerringly walking into De Wet's traps.

His most daring, spectacular, and hilariously humiliating blow against Kitchener and Roberts must surely be the attack of 31 March 1900 at Sannaspos[6], immediately following the fall of Bloemfontein. It was the kind of masterpiece that made him a household name in Britain and Europe and drove Roberts and Kitchener to distraction. De Wet placed his 350 men below the bank of a river near Sannaspos where the oncoming British escort force of a wagon convoy could not see them. Then he let his distant units open fire. The next moment the convoy of British wagons came charging along away from the fire. As each wagon descended the river bank to the water's edge, De Wet's men would calmly get on board and command the drivers to proceed out the other side of the river and to keep going and keep quiet. After this came bundling the British troops. They were utterly surprised when the Boer Commando men calmly told them *"Hands up!"* The guns dropped and hands all shot skyward.

Only after De Wet had hijacked a large number of wagons and captured more than 200 British soldiers without firing a single shot, did the remainder detect that anything was wrong. The formal battle then erupted and the day was won by De Wet. He took a total of 480 prisoners, 7 artillery pieces and 117 wagons.

On 5 June 1900, he repeated the honors by taking prisoner 200 Scots with 56 heavily laden wagons without firing a shot. Two days later he was engaged at Roodewal station where, after a daylong engagement, 27 British were killed or wounded and two hundred surrendered with a massive quantity of supplies. This secured for De Wet enough supplies to last him the rest of the war, which supplies he hid in a cave. Having looted Roberts' champagne supply in this process, all, including the British captives, were invited to celebrate Roberts' forethought. As a final humiliation to Roberts, he allowed the British prisoners of war to loot their own supplies and trudge off into captivity with laden arms. Then, taking what supplies he could from the huge booty, De Wet set fire to all that remained and blew a massive crater in the ground, courtesy Her Majesty, the Empress of India.

De Wet became a hero not only to Afrikaners, but even to the ordinary British soldier. He was to the Boer War what Rommel was to the Second World War; a leader admired and respected by friend and foe alike.

Koos De la Rey

In the Transvaal, it would be Koos de la Rey who would emerge as the leading exponent of guerrilla warfare. His had been the brain behind the success at Magersfontein during the Black Week, when he had suggested the risky placement of the trenches in front of the hills to fool the British. That had been the key to the Boer success. De la Rey's main theater of operations was the Western Transvaal. He had with him the ex-Attorney

Fig. 17-4 General Koos De la Rey

General of the Transvaal Republic, Jan Smuts, who would become a world leader in his own right in the following 15 years. Smuts would later be dispatched to the Cape with his own Commando and gain fame that way, striking at various places in the Cape.

De la Rey's most famous victory was at Tweebosch in the Western Transvaal where he roundly defeated his opponent, General Methuen, and took him captive. In one of the most famous acts of the entire war, he elected to return Methuen to the British lines, because the old British soldier needed treatment the Boer Commando could not provide; this despite the tremendous value of Methuen as a prisoner and despite the fact that Methuen had burned De la Rey's own house and evicted his wife.

Before news of the release of Methuen reached London, discussions in the British Parliament already centered on the belief among the British that De la Rey was an outstanding kind of Christian in whose hands Methuen would be safe. As will shortly be seen, while the British actively relied on the Christian decency and humane brotherliness of the Afrikaner, the Afrikaner would not be accorded the same consideration in British hands.

An interesting phenomenon in De la Rey's entourage was a unique character by the name of Siener (Seer) van Rensburg, reputed to be a clairvoyant of exceptional ability; the Nostradamus of South Africa. He made several predictions that were frighteningly correct. These include the outcome of the Battle of Tweebosch, the outcome of the war itself, the circumstances of the death of De la Rey and even the detail of his burial. And then there were his visions of the future of South Africa that have actually started affecting the behavior of some sections of the community in the 21st Century.

 ## Nexus Familia 74: The Natal Rebels

Several of Margaretha Milward's Jordaan nephews and her youngest brother, Gert, join the Boer Commandos when they sweep into the Klip River district of Natal. However, when the British eventually gain the upper hand, the rebels leave for the Transvaal, but are eventually captured and imprisoned on charges of high treason. The following Jordaan nephews and one brother of Margaretha are charged with high treason[7]. The dates of their sentencing are given (See also *NF68, Fig. 15-9*):

Sons of oldest brother Johannes Jacobus:

> Nicolaas Prinsloo Jordaan (26.9.1900)
>
> Pieter Johannes Jordaan (7.6.1901)
>
> Hendrik George Jordaan (7.6.1901)

Sons of Second oldest (deceased) brother Pieter Johannes:

> Izak J. Matthys Jordaan (7.6.1901)

Youngest brother Gert Jacobus (21.8.1901)

> His son Pieter W Christian (21.8.1901) of *Bergvliet*, Dundee (16)

What is more perplexing to the British in Natal is that they are faced with jailing so many British people who stand for the Boer cause. This includes men like the 72-year-old Peter Hogg, who dies in jail. His 14-year old son, Peter, also goes to jail. Others include Tom and Mike Collyer, John Donovan, John Gowthorpe, Stephen Brooks, George Shorter, Fred Brandon, four of the Truscotts, Fred, Jim and Tom Colling, Jim D'Arcy, John Wiggill, John Matthie, Tom Saddler, Tom and John Bentley and Joseph Hoolahan; clearly all names of British and Irish extraction.

The men are sentenced to varying times in jail, ranging from 4 months to 2-and-a-half years plus fines. Some of them have no choice but to sell their farms to raise the money to pay the fines. As a result, the English carpetbaggers move in on them yet again, just as the Voortrekkers had suffered in 1837. The last Natal man to leave jail as a Rebel prisoner is Margaretha's nephew, Nicolaas Prinsloo Jordaan. Again, we see that Prinsloo-Jordaan combination that comes all the way from 1799 in the Van Jaarsveld rebellion. He is totally ruined and ends up cutting sugar cane as a laborer along with indentured "coolies" from India to stay alive, having been a well-established landowner before the war.

—*End Nexus Familia*

 Nexus Familia 75: The Battle of Nooitgedacht

Adam Johannes Booyens (*NF65*) has become a Field-Cornet in the Transvaal Republican Commandos. Fighting by his side is his eldest son, Daniel. On 13 December 1900, Adam finds himself west of Pretoria, looking at the encampment of British General Clements at Nooitgedacht. The place is very aptly named for what happens next. In Dutch it means "never expected." It is actually named for the romantic waterfall in the mountain, but the name will take on another meaning today.

The Afrikaners have reserved a very special hatred for Clements. He is the man who has been meticulously burning their people out of all their farms along the upland valley that stretches from Pretoria to near Rustenburg. This stretch of land is a superb agricultural area known as the *Moot* (Gully), between the *Magaliesberg* Mountains to the north and the *Witwatersberg* (White Water Mountain) to the south. The Boer Commandos are ready to take on a major British Army.

Viewing the scene, we find General de la Rey. With him is Transvaal State-Attorney, Jan Smuts, together with rugby forward and lawyer-become-general, Christiaan Beyers. Also in attendance we find our "on the spot reporter," Deneys Reitz, and Adam Johannes Booyens with his eldest son Daniel. Clements cannot have chosen a worse spot if he had tried. The cliffs of the Magaliesberg rise about 600 foot over the valley at this spot. Clements has chosen this spot to put up a heliograph station on the mountain to communicate with General Broadwood in Rustenburg and to use the clear water from the falls. De la Rey is still flushed with his victory over a British contingent a few days before in which he made a massive haul of supplies, taking 118 wagons and 54 prisoners. He kept 15 wagons and burnt the rest. In this bonfire disappeared Broadwood's Christmas champagne supply.

The plan takes shape: Beyers will take 1500 men and roll up the fortified pickets along the mountaintop. Commandant C.P.S. Badenhorst is detached from De la Rey's command to attack the Clements camp down in the Moot from the west. Smuts and De la Rey himself will take the kopjes (hills) along the south of the Moot to block the escape. Deneys Reitz is part of Beyers' operation on the top of the mountain. Adam Johannes Booyens and his son Daniel are down below in the *Moot*.

The attack goes wrong almost immediately. Badenhorst has overestimated the distance to the camp. In the pitch dark, he blunders into the British pickets, prompting alarm too early. Beyers now goes on the attack on top of the mountain. We turn to Deneys Reitz[8] for what happens next:

> *"We had gone without sleep for two days and two nights, so that our spirits were low, and our advance at once came to a halt. Our line fell down behind rocks and whatever shelter was to be had, leaving General Beyers walking alone, his revolver in one hand and a riding-switch in the other, imploring us to go on, but we hugged our cover against the hail of the bullets lashing around us."*

These men are up against Captain Yatman and his 300 Northumberland Fusiliers in defensive positions on the crest of the mountain. Reitz now looks down on the camp below, where De la Rey's forces go on the attack. Among them are Adam Johannes Booyens and his son Daniel. At first, it seems to Reitz that the attacking Commandos will overrun the camp, but the British man their positions fast enough and the attack is initially beaten off within ten minutes with serious loss. On the mountain, the Northumberlands, who can also see the events below, break into cheering. This is one too many for the Boer Commando men opposing them. This collection of farmers and townsfolk jump to their feet and charge the British line, young Reitz among them. The laggards are also egged on by the biblically obsessed Beyers with his mighty lash. He is the 1901 incarnation of Sarel Cilliers, the "Praise the Lord and pass the ammo" leader of Great Trek fame. Thomas Pakenham[9] describes Beyers' charge as *"like veteran British infantry."* Again, Deneys Reitz:

> *"There was no stopping us now, and we swept on shouting and yelling, men dropping freely as we went. Almost before we knew it, we were swarming over the walls, shooting and clubbing in hand-to-hand conflict. It was sharp work. I have a confused recollection of fending bayonet thrusts and firing pointblank into men's faces; then of soldiers running to the rear or putting up their hands, and as we stood panting and excited within the barricades, we could scarcely realize that the fight was won. Our losses were severe."*

Reitz reports them shooting down 100 soldiers and capturing the rest. The Boer Commando has 25 dead and 70 wounded. They then discover the Imperial Yeomanry of London trying to make their way up the mountain along a gorge and they destroy the unit. In the midst of this carnage, ordinary men find time for mutual respect. Yet again, young Reitz:

> *"I also went to see the soldier whom I had shot. He had a very nasty wound, but he was bandaging it himself with the first aid pad which they all carried, and he said he could manage. He was a typical Cockney, and he bore me so little ill-will that he brought out a portrait of his wife and children and told me about them. I made him comfortable, and left him cheerfully smoking a cigarette."*

By seven o'clock in the morning, the Commandos are in control of the mountain overlooking the camp. They now have the camp within range of their plunging rifle fire. Soon after, Clements' camp falls under a renewed attack from De la Rey's men. However, the early blunder by Badenhorst has allowed Clements to escape to Pretoria with a major part of his force and his 4.7-inch naval gun.

Adam has led his men well and has taught the British a lasting lesson in how passionately the Afrikaner will defend his country. However, he has a very severe head wound. Daniel helps his father into the home of a black man who lives nearby. There they do their best to make him comfortable, but Adam pays the ultimate price for his country and people. He is believed to be buried in the communal grave that Deneys Reitz helps to dig. We turn once more to Deneys Reitz:

> *"General de la Rey was present and he addressed us in eloquent words that moved many to tears, for besides being a fighter he had a fine gift of simple speech."*

Jan Smuts[10] himself reports on the peculiar scene at Clements' lost camp that night. It was a pandemonium of psalm-singing, hilarity, and looting, punctuated with explosions from burning ammunition cases. Some were drinking British rum, while others were searching British materials for information. The veteran Reverend A. P. Kriel was conducting a service of thanks, with interruptions from exploding ammunition. On one side sat De La Rey, wistfully contemplating the whole scene.

From this moment onward, the British will never effectively control the Transvaal west of Pretoria. It will be the domain of the Lion of the West, Koos de la Rey; and he will eventually crown his career by capturing his opposing general; and then freeing him in an act of chivalrous mercy. The Battle of Nooitgedacht has demonstrated to the British that this war will not be over by this second Christmas either. They have now been at war for more than fourteen months, whereas the original plan had counted on four months. Eventually, it will endure far beyond the third Christmas.

Joseph Chamberlain's condescending acknowledgment of Afrikaner bravery in the House of Commons on 7 December 1900, as though by a victor, is very badly timed. He cannot dream that he will have to fight his pet war for another two Christmases and that the bill will more than double yet again.

—End Nexus Familia

And in the British House of Commons

By early December 1900, the British House of Commons was debating the terms of peace, thinking that the war was over. The Battle of Nooitgedacht was still a week in the future. The expenditure was already at £100,000,000 and various members of the House were commenting on the fact that there were now around 213,000 British Soldiers in South Africa. Trevalyan of the Opposition tried very hard to make it clear that some hope needed to be held out to the Afrikaners. Joseph Chamberlain as the man responsible for Colonial Policy tried hard to make it look as though he intended treating the Afrikaners in the two new colonies as respected men. He came up with such nicely phrased but transparently condescending statements as:

> ...."*they have carried on this war with great distinction, so far as personal gallantry is concerned, and also that they have shown the greatest consideration for the wounded and prisoners who have fallen into their hands.[...] They are brave foes, and they should be treated as brave foes.*"

He had no such intentions, nor did Kitchener. They were debating the appointments of the hated Milner as Governor in the two new colonies and were constructing concentration camps. At least, Timothy Healy, the later first Governor General of the Irish Free State, laid out brutally clearly the oppressed life the Afrikaner might actually expect, and then described the Afrikaner in 1900 exactly:

> "*They can lose nothing by fighting. You have bereft them of their liberty and independence. You have stolen their country and burned down their farms. What has the remaining Boer to expect—call him guerrilla, bandit, freebooter, what you like? Absolutely nothing. He is a free man, with a gun on his shoulder, and a horse under him, and I should like to know if any man with any ordinary independence, with any touch of spirit in his blood, would surrender that position and exchange it for the position of a British slave. I think these men seem to consider that it is better to be a Boer corpse than a British subject.*"

Herbert Henry Asquith, later Liberal Prime Minister, described the military situation:

> "*Your men are being captured by hundreds and shot by scores. A British convoy cannot move safely for any considerable distance in either of these conquered colonies. British garrisons are being besieged in places which six or seven months ago were taken from the enemy, and, in fact, you have throughout the length and breadth of these two newly-incorporated territories a state of war in the legal, practical, and popular acceptation of the term. Surely the first problem the Government have to solve is this—what are the means by which, at the earliest possible moment, that condition of things can be cured?*"

Burning a country to the ground

The scorched earth policy that the House of Commons debates were alluding to, started earlier in the year. With the British comprehensively unsuccessful in pinning down men like Botha, De la Rey and De Wet,

Roberts, before departing the country, decided to add yet a new dimension of horror to the growing list of what he already would have to explain at the Pearly Gates. He would now seek to emulate a man named Sherman whose actions instilled hatred in America to this very day. The author well remembers meeting a gentleman outside Charleston, South Carolina, in tears of anguish in 1980 at the very memory of this man from the 1860s. We leave it to Deneys Reitz[11] to describe events at the end of January 1901 in the Transvaal:

> *"During the course of the morning, pillars of smoke began to rise behind the English advance, and to our astonishment we saw that they were burning the farmhouses as they came. Towards noon word spread that, not only were they destroying all before them, but were actually capturing and sending away the women and children. At first we could hardly credit this, but when one wild-eyed woman after another galloped by, it was borne in on us that a more horrible chapter of the war was opening.[...]*
>
> *"The plain was alive with wagons, carts, and vehicles of all descriptions, laden with women and children, while great numbers of horses, cattle, and sheep were being hurried onward by native herdboys, homes and ricks going up in flames behind them."*

Thinking men of character will always recognize in such actions the hand of the incompetent coward. History, if it had real morality, would report such men to posterity in the coat of villainy they rightly earn for themselves. Regrettably, Britain would hail these men as heroes: the tormentors of innocent women and small children, the killers of dumb animals and the despoilers of civilization. In Canada, the horror persists to this day in that more than one town is still named after Kitchener, who gave the direct orders for the enforcement of this policy. In the Cape, he could not go around burning Britain's own territory to the ground, and so he reserved a special hell for the people there, as we shall soon see.

Fig. 17-5 Sheep killed by the British Army on an Afrikaner farm

Possibly the deeply Christian Afrikaners should have seen this coming. After all, the British had done this to the unfortunate Xhosa in the first half of the 19th century. However, they were incapable of believing that one Christian could do this to another. They clearly had no concept of the degree to which the British were capable of harnessing State Terror as an integral part of warfare. It would be left to the families in the Cape Colony to learn this, as they had been forced to do at the time of Slagtersnek in 1815. Amery[12] aptly sums up the reaction to the Scorched Earth Policy:

> *"The policy fitfully adopted after the beginning of June [1900] of burning down farmhouses and destroying crops as a measure of intimidation had nothing to recommend it and no other measure aroused such deep and lasting resentment. The Dutch race is not one that can be easily beguiled by threats, and farm-burning as a policy of intimidation totally failed, as anyone acquainted with the Dutch race and the Dutch history could have foreseen. Applying this system against a white race defending their homes with a bravery and resource which has rightly won the admiration of the world was the least happy of Lord Roberts' inspirations and must plainly be set down as a serious error of judgment..."*

Roberts had implemented the policy of dynamiting the homes and burning the farms of those Free State and Transvaal burghers who would not surrender after the fall of their capitals. Kitchener, however, now extended the concept to the destruction of entire regions of the country. This was to form part of his "drives" to try and herd the Boer commandos into fenced areas protected by blockhouses using long stretched out columns of men spanning entire horizons. Somehow, British Army plans consisted of plodding meticulous actions that could be outdone by simple actions. We turn once more to Deneys Reitz[13]:

"*General Botha directed all non-combatants, wagons, and livestock to make for Swaziland, and he ordered us to give way before the troops, and let them expend their blow on thin air. Owing to these measures the drive went to pieces during the next few days. The British could not maintain a continuous front over the increased distances, and the troops were left groping about after the elusive Boer forces, which easily evaded the lumbering columns plodding through the mud in the rear.*"

Fig. 17-6 Boer family outside their house burnt by the British Army

Kitchener would keep up these drives to the end. They would inconvenience the commandos, but would hardly break them. In this uninspiring generalship, one can detect the even less imaginative British tactics of WWI. The Republican victory on 13 December 1900 at Nooitgedacht was convincing evidence that this British intimidation tactic was nowhere near working. Throughout this war, Britain never controlled much more than the major towns, the railway, and a few strong points.

Nexus Familia 76: Destruction of the farms

To gain a glimpse into the destruction of the farms, we jump ahead in time just a little to 1903 to look at the documented claims for damages. After he eventually surrenders on 23 May 1901, Daniel Prinsloo will be confined to the Middelburg (Transvaal) Concentration Camp along with his family. His farmhouse and stables at *Schoongezicht* farm will be dynamited by the British Army in July 1901 in the presence of witnesses, as we see in his damages claim[14]:

Name of Applicant	*Daniel Jacobus Marthinus Louwrens Prinsloo*
Age	*38*
Farms	*Schoongezicht dist. Carolina*
Date of Surrender	*23rd of May 1901 to Imperial Troops operating under Major General Kitchener*
Oath of Allegiance	*10th day of January 1902 no. 2390*
Damages on Farm	*One Building on my farm Schoongezicht size 41 foot long by 20ft wide Iron Roof six Rooms used as a dwelling house destroyed by His Majesty's Troops on the blockhouse line at Machadodorp in the month of July 1901 In Presence of Ernest Walter Tawson of the farm Schoongezicht dist. Carolina and Archybald merchant in Township of Carolina. One building 25ft 20ft Iron Roof used as stables do.*
Valuation of Damages	*Dwelling House 41ft by 20ft* £150 *Stable 25ft by 15ft* £225
Witnesses	*Hendrik Francois Marais of the Farm Witkop district Carolina* *Ernest Walter Tawson of the farm Schoongezicht dist. Carolina*
Signed	*DJ Prinsloo* [Signed]

In the magistrate's office at Thaba'Nchu, in the Free State, Barend Matthys Johannes Booyens (*NF73*) will eventually file a claim[15] against the British Army on 18 April 1903. He will explain that he surrendered with General Prinsloo and signed "the declaration" (referring to an oath of allegiance) only to find that his farm had been burnt and ransacked by the British Army. He will claim as follows:

1 Cart with harness	£ 40 ' 00 ' 00
1 Bicycle	£ 20 ' 00 ' 00
Household furniture	£ 30 ' 00 ' 00
350 bundles of forage	£ 4 ' 07 ' 06
10 bags of wheat	£ 8 ' 00 ' 00
9 bags of Kaffircorn [millet/sorghum]	£ 9 ' 00 ' 00
6 bags mealies [corn]	£ 4 ' 16 ' 00
46 empty grain bags	£ 1 ' 14 ' 06
5 Zinc of 10 foot long	£ 1 ' 13 ' 04
1 harrow	£ 5 ' 10 ' 00
1 plough	£ 2 ' 00 ' 00
80 bags of wheat (destroyed on land)	£ 64 ' 00 ' 00
39 bags of potatoes (destroyed on land)	£ 28 ' 10 ' 00
TOTAL	£ 214 ' 09 ' 04

Barend will defer to his wife's testimony as regards the crops, taken down as follows by the magistrate who makes a point of ensuring that Barend's conquered country is now stated as being the "Orange River Colony." The Afrikaner has yet again been made a "subject" of the Crown:

> *Johanna Ephresia Booyens duly sworn states:*
>
> *I am the wife* [of Barend] *Mathheus Johannes Booyens. The 80 bags of wheat and 39 bags wheat* [should be "potatoes"] *which are growing crops. Three of horses were taken by the Boers. The other things were taken when I was removed to the refugee camp. The bicycle was presented to my son by a friend during the war. I have received no payment.*
>
> *Before me, at Thaba'Nchu ORC,*
> *18 April 1903*

The crops destroyed on the lands are eventually disallowed, but Barend is paid £109 to start life over without his two daughters, Susanna and Elizabeth, who die under British "protection" in their Springfontein Concentration Camp. Eventually, no fewer than 29 Booyens families in the Transvaal and Free State will file claims against the British Army for willful destruction of their property. In the 21st century, these claims will all be available in the Transvaal Archives in Pretoria and will be indexed on the Internet.

In the Marico district of Western Transvaal, the soldiers arrive at *Rhenosterfontein* farm where the Bassons have protected Maria Salomé's Diary (*NF68*) for a decade. They are under orders to burn the farm. When they leave, all is ashes. The late Maria Salome's precious Great Trek Diary has been destroyed.

—*End Nexus Familia*

She had a name – it was *Elizabeth*

After the two Boer capitals fell, Roberts instructed his officers to burn the farms of burghers who would not surrender. At first, they left the women and children on the burnt out farms on the icy southern winter Prairie, where the nighttime temperatures are of the order of 20 degrees Fahrenheit and snow is no stranger. Roberts soon realized that this would produce massive outrage not just in South Africa, but also in Britain. This is when he formulated the concept of Concentration Camps.

Attempts have been made to sketch the British concentration camps as somehow sensible and acceptable. However, such attempts fail to explain how it is that children of burghers who were still fighting received lesser rations than those of men who had surrendered. Fact is, Kitchener was attempting to force men to surrender by interning and starving their children. From this moment on, many Afrikaners developed the view that the British fight women and children. Of course, that is not true, but the British had themselves "saddled this horse" and now had to "ride it." All it did was to make the remaining burghers under arms even more dedicated. This accusation against Britain would be hauled out again in WWII after the firebombing of Hamburg and Dresden. British parliamentarian John Bryn Roberts would say it in so many words when he refused to support a grant of £50,000 to Kitchener on 18 June 1902 in a House of Commons debate.

Fig. 17-7 *British tented Concentration Camp in the snow*

When the news of the destruction of farms and the conditions in the concentration camps reached the Cape Colony in late 1900, it became one of the major reasons for ordinary law abiding citizens to join Rebel Boer commandos. As far as they were concerned, they were fighting a *Volksmoord* (literally: Murder of a Nation); the word "genocide" had not yet been invented. This outrage was new to the civilized world and had as yet no associated lexicon. The genocide of the Kurds by the Turks would happen later, and the Kurds would at least eventually see some justice meted out. For the later Jewish Holocaust there would also be justice. For the Afrikaners there would never be any.

Initially, the horror was not visible internationally. It would be Emily Hobhouse, an Englishwoman with a sense of honor, and a seven year-old Afrikaans girl, Elizabeth van Zyl, who would finally bring the true horror to the notice of the civilized world. Elizabeth, the daughter of an "Undesirable"—the British Army term for a man who refused to stop fighting for his country—was committed to the Bloemfontein British Concentration camp in November 1900 along with her mother and siblings[16].

Fig. 17-8 *Emily Hobhouse*

Fig 17-9 shows a photograph of the unfortunate girl after two months in the camp, as testified by Emily Hobhouse who saw her there at the time. Hobhouse found out in England about the existence of a concentration camp in the author's hometown of Port Elizabeth. Upon arriving in South Africa, she discovered there were some 32 more all over the country and she set out to investigate with the approval of Lord Alfred Milner. She sent the picture of Elizabeth van Zyl to Britain along with letters describing the circumstances. At the time, the photograph was considered too shocking to be published in Hobhouse's book.

On 17 June 1901, Leader of the Opposition in the House of Commons in London stood up in outrage and described the situation in the camps. Having brought the horror of the camps to the attention of the British public, Hobhouse was promptly restrained from further visiting the camps. When she again arrived in Cape Town on 27 October 1901, she was forcibly deported back to Britain on the *Roslin Castle*. A commission was set up to investigate the "allegations" and improvements were made.

It was too late for the author's relations. They were already dead. More than 25,000 children would eventually die in the camps. The total number of deaths in British concentration camps approaches the total number of 35,000 fighting men that the two republics could field at any one time. The British government would ultimately succeed in killing only approximately 3,700 Afrikaner men under arms in this war, but they would succeed in destroying 28,000 women and children – a massive blow to such a small nation. It would never completely recover.

South Africa is one of those unique places in the world where one may visit a war memorial to a member of the enemy, in this case the Lone English Lady, Emily Hobhouse, who, in a time of her nation's collective insanity, confronted her own people to do what was right. She rests at the foot of the Womens' Memorial in Bloemfontein in South Africa. A deeply grateful Afrikaner nation named the Free State town of Hobhouse for her.

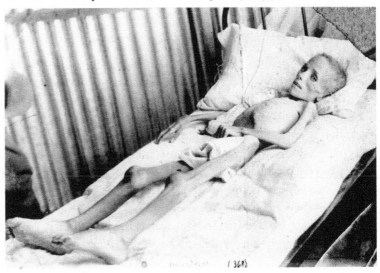

Fig. 17-9 Elizabeth van Zyl in the British concentration camp

Nexus Familia 77: Concentration Camp Horror

When Daniel Prinsloo finally surrenders to Kitchener's troops on 23 May 1901 on the farm *Jachtlust*, he is instructed to report to Wonderfontein station with his family to go to a "Refugee Camp"[17]. When they turn up at the station he is instructed to leave the horses, wagon and loose furniture he has brought and they are forced onto the train. He will later call witnesses to this event. On 29 May 1901, the whole family arrives at Middelburg[18] (Transvaal) Concentration Camp and they are registered by the camp secretary. The Milward family is with Daniel, but his mother Susanna is somehow absent.

Daniel and his immediate family are put in tent RT/ 210/ I 1065/ Block B. They are:

- Daniel Jacobus Marthinus Lourens Prinsloo
- Susanna Geertruyda Salomina Van Rooyen, his wife
- Joachim Johannes Prinsloo, Daniel's 17-year old brother
- Susanna Geertruyda Prinsloo, Daniel's 4-year old daughter
- Daniel's 9-month old baby Maria Johanna Prinsloo

The Milwards are put in the tent right next door; RT/ 210/ I 1066/ Block B. They are:

- Margaretha Johanna Milward, Daniel's mother's sister and our great grandmother
- Neve Constance Milward, Margaretha's 20-year old daughter, grandmother to our family
- Mary Elizabeth Milward, Margaretha's 18-year old daughter

By now, word of the horror in the British Concentration Camps has reached London. Joseph Chamberlain is practicing every form of denial he can manage, but it is not working in the face of reality. The British, a decent nation of some principle, is outraged at the de facto genocide being practiced in their name by an ineffectual British Army that demonstrably cannot subdue a nation fighting for its very existence. Already the rebels in the Cape Colony have cited this horror as their primary reason for rising.

In the House of Commons, matters reach a fever pitch by the middle of June 1901. On 17 June 1901, Lloyd-George thunders in the House that Kitchener has conceded the death rate in one camp is 450 per thousand. He complains that the food given to the inmates of the camps is less than that given to "criminals under hard labor" in Britain. He is outraged at the fact that children under six years of age have no flour, one-third the quantity of milk, and no meat at all on five days a week, because their relatives are on Commando.

John Ellis of Nottinghamshire reports that thousands of women and children sat in open train trucks for up to seventy-two hours, not allowed to leave these trucks, forced back at the point of British bayonets. He insists that:

"a more diabolical arrangement was never entered into by any civilized nation."

Broderick, the Secretary for War, actually stoops to suggesting that the retreating Boer Army should have taken their women and children with to feed a year earlier.

The genocidal conditions in the concentration camps prove to be too much for many of the people. On 9 December 1901, Daniel's 23-year old wife, Susanna, dies from peritonitis brought on by enteric fever. Two weeks later, on 23 December, Daniel's 17-year old brother, Joachim, also dies from the same causes. Despite every effort, baby Maria succumbs to infantile diarrhea 22 days later on 14 January 1901. In fewer than 5 weeks, over Christmas 1901, Daniel has lost his wife, his daughter, and his brother as "refugees" under British "protection" behind barbed wire in his own country. The only thing they are refugees from, is the willful destruction of their home and livelihood by the British Army under Lord Horatio Kitchener; future hero to many, with two Canadian towns yet to be callously named after him.

Eventually, matters will improve in the camps, but it will be too late for some 25,000 children and some 3,000 women.

The Booyens Family in the Concentration Camps

The author's Booyens family bears silent witness to the human toll in the British Concentration Camps. Their situation is wholly representative of what happened to all other Afrikaner families in the hands of the British Army. We consider the fate of just this single extended family in the Free State and Transvaal camps:

1. The Free State Concentration Camps

A total of twenty-eight Booyens family members enter the British Concentration camps in the Orange Free State, now named the Orange River Colony by their Imperial British Colonialist masters. They include a number of people we have met before:

• *Maroko*, the farm of Barend Matthys Johannes Booyens (*NF65, 66, 68, 70, 73 & 76*), is willfully destroyed and burnt down by the British Army. His family is herded into the dreaded Springfontein Concentration Camp in the middle of winter, his wife with a barely one-year old baby in her arms. This is the cold southern part of the Free State where snow in winter is not a stranger. Barend Matthys Johannes loses his two youngest daughters (***) in that camp.

• Barend's nephew, Johannes Hendrik Booyens (*NF65*), is also on commando, fighting for his country. When the British destroy his farm, they also put his mother Isabella, his wife Anna, and his children into the same terrible Springfontein camp. Johannes Hendrik loses his wife and daughter on the same day, and his mother succumbs in the week following the granddaughter that is named for her (**).

• Barend's much older cousin, Jacobus Frederik Booyens (*NF65, 68*) from the farm *Weltevreden* near Heilbron in the north, is now 76 years old. He and his second wife have been put in the Heilbron Concentration Camp. His son Daniel Jan Andries is on commando, but his immediate family is put in the Heilbron camp with grandfather Jacobus Frederik. Daniel Jan Andries loses all four his children under 11 years of age, as well as his father and mother (*).

The table below silently shows what happens to the broader Booyens family in those camps. Of the 29 Booyens family members from the Free State Republic who enter the six camps only three can reasonably be said to die of causes unrelated to the British policies. The only family members who survive the ordeal are nine of those who are in the Brandfort Concentration Camp. They are all from *Nieuwaanlegt* in the Hoopstad district. Nevertheless, five children of that family die. Fourteen of the twenty children in the various camps die. Not a single one of the 15 Booyens family members emerges alive from any one of the other five British Concentration Camps where they are recorded.

Name	Died	Age died	Camp
Miss Christina Elizabeth*	10.31.1901	11y	Heilbron
Miss Catharina Maria*	10.29.1901	2y 10m	Heilbron
Master Petrus Jacobus*	11.08.1901	5y 6m	Heilbron
Miss Maria Catharina*	10.30.1901	8y 8m	Heilbron
Mr. Jacobus Frederik*	08.18.1901	77y	Heilbron
Mrs. Aletta Elizabeth*	10.11.1901	48y	Heilbron
Mr. Matthys Christoffel	09.02.1901	57y	Kroonstad
Ms. Isabella**	06.11.1901	71y	Springfontein
Miss Isabella Petronella**	06.02.1901	8y	Springfontein
Ms. Anna Sophia**	06.02.1901	32y	Springfontein
Miss Susanna Catharina***	08.05.1901	3y	Springfontein
Miss Elizabeth Francina***	07.30.1901	1y 1m	Springfontein
Ms. Chatrina	Date unclear	70y	Vredefort Rd.
Master Jacobus Ockert	01.18.1902	2y	Vredefort Rd.
Miss Gezina Maria	11.20.1901	12d	Winburg
Miss Hendrietta Matilda	01.18.1902	12y	Brandfort
Miss Maria Elizabeth C.	01.21.1902	2y 2m	Brandfort
Master Johannes Sarel	10.20.1901	2y 3m	Brandfort
Master Mattheus Christoffel	02.03.1902	2y 5 m	Brandfort
Master Theunis Johannes	03.03.1902	6m	Brandfort
Mrs. Dorothea Elizabeth	Survived	-	Brandfort
Miss Johanna Margaretha	Survived	-	Brandfort
Master Nicolaas Johannes J.	Survived	-	Brandfort
Master Jan Christoffel A.	Survived	-	Brandfort
Mrs. Anna Sophia	Survived	-	Brandfort
Miss (baby)	Survived	-	Brandfort
Master Jan Christoffel A.	Survived	-	Brandfort
Mrs. Maria Elizabeth C.	Survived	-	Brandfort
Master Jan Christoffel A.	Survived	-	Brandfort

2. The Transvaal Concentration Camps

Matters are a little better for the Booyens family in the Transvaal, but only in the Middelburg and Heidelberg Concentration Camps. One of the families herded into Heidelberg camp is that of a nephew of Jacobus Frederik (*NF65 & 68*) by the name of Daniel Johannes Andries (*). Daniel is married to Aletta Elizabeth Thompson and they live on the farm *Uitkijk* in the Heidelberg district of the Transvaal Republic, which has now been razed to the ground:

Name	Died	Age died	Camp
Master Daniel Andreas	date unclear	2y	Johannesburg
Miss Maria Johanna M.	date unclear	10m	Johannesburg
Miss Johanna P	06.16.1901	5m	Potchefstroom
Miss Hester Cornelia	05.26.1901	1y 3m	Potchefstroom
Master Michiel Adriaan	06.05.1901	14y 1m	Potchefstroom
Master Albertus Johannes R	06.26.1901	2y 9m	Potchefstroom
Miss Petronella	06.16.1901	6m	Potchefstroom
Miss Helena A F	08.16.1902	9y	Standerton
Master P A	10.21.1901	2d	Standerton
Master Izaak Johannes	11.15.1902	3y	Vereeniging
Master Francois A.	11.11.1901	2y 4m	Nylstroom
Miss Martina Susanna	05.20.1901	11y	Heidelberg
Master Daniel Johannes A.*	02.10.1902	2y	Heidelberg
Miss Aletta Elizabeth*	Survived	-	Heidelberg
Mrs. Aletta Elizabeth F.*	Survived	-	Heidelberg
Master Barend Mathys*	Survived	-	Heidelberg
Miss Dertina Johanna*	Survived	-	Heidelberg
Miss Elizabeth Jacobina*	Survived	-	Heidelberg
Miss Hester Sophia*	Survived	-	Heidelberg
Master Willem Charles*	Survived	-	Heidelberg
Mr. Daniel Johannes A.*	Survived	-	Heidelberg
Mrs. Johannes Benjamin	Survived	-	Middelburg
Master Marthinus Gerhardus	Survived	-	Middelburg
Master Matthys Cornelis	Survived	-	Middelburg
Master Johannes Benjamin	Survived	-	Middelburg
Miss Susara Elizabeth	Survived	-	Middelburg
Miss Johanna Katrina	Survived	-	Middelburg
Miss Aletta Katrina	Survived	-	Middelburg
Miss Catharina Elizabeth	Survived	-	Middelburg

Twenty-nine Booyens family members enter the Transvaal camps. Only three are adults. Of the twenty-nine, only sixteen survive, including the three adults. Those who survive are in either the Heidelberg or Middelburg Concentration Camps. Thirteen of the twenty-six Booyens children die in these camps — exactly half. Not one of the 11 Booyens family members emerges alive from any one of the other five British Concentration Camps where they are recorded. The British burning of the farms and herding of women and children into concentration camps has cost the lives of 33 of the 58 Booyens family members listed in the dreaded camps in the two territories — more than half. Of the forty-seven children listed in the camps, twenty-seven die there — 57%.

—*End Nexus Familia*

The Second Invasion of the Cape

After Kruger left the country in September 1900, it was decided to take the war yet again to the Cape Colony in order to disrupt the British logistics and tie up more British troops away from the Transvaal and Free State. This task fell to three groups of men. The first was a Transvaal unit under a Cambridge Law student and former Attorney-General of the Transvaal—a man to later become famous in his own right on the world stage—General Jan Smuts. The second was a Free State group under Commandant Kritzinger. The third was a collection of Cape Rebel commandos. These groups were to do as much damage to the British rail traffic as possible and were to mobilize the Cape Afrikaners against the British to the best of their ability. The latter activity sought to increase political pressure on the British. Kitchener could certainly not afford for the majority of the Cape Afrikaner population to turn on his troops when they had such exceedingly long logistic lines running through the Colony.

In the Cape Colony itself, the British Army prepared to celebrate the New Year of 1901 with toasts to Victoria, the Empress of India. However, a Commando under Commandant Pieter Kritzinger of the Free State had already crossed the Orange River into the Cape Colony near Aliwal-North, named after Aliwal in India, ruled by that very Empress. The town was named by Sir Harry Smith to commemorate his own victory over the Sikh of India at Aliwal on 28 January 1846. On 30 December 1900, the attack by Kritzinger on a train transporting Colonial troops just north of Rosmead Junction near Middelburg, some 80 miles south of the Orange River, introduced the Cape to this newer, longer, and more expensive phase of the war. Ten days earlier, on 20 December 1900, Martial Law had been decreed in the Cape Colony.

A part of the Commando remained in the Middelburg and Graaff-Reinet districts, while another part moved south. On January 11th, there was a skirmish near Murraysburg. On the 16th, the commandos were at Aberdeen, and on the 18th at Willowmore, a full seventy miles away. Shortly after, they were seen at Uniondale, only thirty miles from the coast. They avoided contact with massed British troops, but attacked almost all British outposts and patrols. On February 6th, the King's Dragoon Guards and the Australians were defeated at Klipplaat. On the 12th, a patrol of yeomanry was overwhelmed at Willowmore.

Fig. 17-10 Rosmead Railway Junction in the Great Boer War

In a skirmish between Beaufort West and Aberdeen, (later captain) Lawrence Oates of the Inniskilling Dragoons was wounded, leaving him with one leg shorter than the other. He would later join Scott's ill-fated expedition to the South Pole, where he would become the hero who left the tent to crawl to his death on his birthday on 17 March 1912.

In the west of the Cape Colony, the Free State and Transvaal commandos, supported by Cape rebels, struck many hundreds of miles deep into the British territory. By 4 January, they took Calvinia in the West Cape and occupied it for a month. Then they moved on to Clanwilliam, the inland feeder town for the harbor of Lambert's Bay, closer to Cape Town. In the center of the colony, they pushed their outposts south to Beaufort West and Sutherland. By 15 January, Boer commandos were spotted around Touws Rivier. Cape Town finally woke up to the realization that the war was just 100 miles away.

In the Cape Midlands, as the Middelburg-Cradock region is called, the commandos moved south at some speed, taking towns like Pearston, far to the south. They never held onto a town. The purpose was to cause the British as much consternation as possible. This war was to be made as expensive as possible for the British. In response, the British created a number of mounted units to attempt to address the mobile Boer Commandos that were striking them with impunity. They also built forts and strong points almost everywhere. Instead of standing still to fight the British way, the commandos would merely fall back. After all, the purpose remained that of "Bleeding England." The United States would eventually experience this in Vietnam, Iraq and Afghanistan and live through the political psychology of this strategy.

Eventually, Jan Smuts would lead a Commando into the Cape Colony and occupy the northwest of the Colony to the end of the war. When peace negotiations started in March 1902, Transvaal Boer Commando men were splashing in the sea at Lambert's Bay north of Cape Town and controlled the Cape north of there.

Nexus Familia 78: The Cape Rebels – Martyred

When Kritzinger crosses into the Cape Colony with his Commando in late 1900, their first strike is at the railway line at Sherborne, just north of Rosmead station (See *Fig. 17-10*), outside Middelburg. This is where the author's Myburgh mother will be born just under three decades into the future, on a farm in the left hand background of Fig. 17-10. They seek to do as much damage as possible to British logistics. Rosmead is the critical junction of the railway line to East London with the line to Pretoria.

Getting started

The British have meanwhile moved the Coldstream Guards to Graaff-Reinet and Middelburg. They constitute one of the two oldest regiments in the British Army, having fought in the American War of Independence.

Given that the Afrikaners are largely farmers, the disappearance of some 120 of them from their farms and homes does not immediately attract British attention. When some of the local farmers ride over from Middelburg towards New-Bethesda, they come across a curious scene. They find some 120 men of the Middelburg, Graaff-Reinet, and Cradock districts with a collection of horses and rifles, fully in control of the foothills of the 8,200 foot Kompasberg (Compass Mountain), the highest mountain in South Africa outside the Drakensberg. It reaches skyward like a lone sentinel in this barren countryside, often bearing snow throughout winter.

Here, in a part of the country much like Wyoming, they have put up their headquarters. They have even managed to get the two winners of the local Bisley shooting competition to join their effort. The ages of the men vary from 16 to 60 and most of them have no experience of any form of warfare. A few of Kritizinger's Free State fighting men are with them. These are men from the southern Free State whose homes are in the district of Zastron. They include sergeant Johannes Smith, the colleague of Barend Matthys Johannes Booyens. Smith refused to surrender with Gen. Prinsloo (*NF72*).

The Myburgh and Grobler relations

The leader of the Commando is none other than Hans Lötter from Naauwpoort north of Middelburg (*NF68*), second cousin to Susanna Sophia Lötter Joubert (*NF65*), mother of the author's great grandmother Johanna Catharina Smit. He joined the invading Boer forces back in the days of the Battle of Stormberg in 1899. Ironically, before the war he actually helped the British build the defenses of the strategic Rosmead railway junction just outside Middelburg. He knows this part of the world like the back of his hand. He has already been captured once by the British, but has escaped. He has lived in the Free State for some years and claims he has Free State citizenship papers.

Nicolaas Johannes Grobler (*NF70*) and his family in Middelburg are not exactly surprised when they hear through the grapevine that Hans Lötter is now Kommandant Lötter, the leader of the local Cape Rebels. This is in keeping with the joint Grobler and Lötter ancestor, Christoffel Lötter, whom we saw confront the new British Magistrate at Graaff-Reinet a hundred years before in 1799 (*NF31*).

They are deeply worried, though. Hans is known to be an indifferent horseman and everyone knows that the hot headed 27-year old has a heart problem. Also with him is his younger brother, Zirk, the medical student returned from Britain.

The Erasmus men of Lötter's Commando are linked to Albert Myburgh by the marriages of no fewer than three of his brothers (*NF66*) to three Erasmus ladies. The links go further in that four of Albert's stepfather's Viljoen family (*NF66*) are also with Hans Lötter. Some British-descended men from the district also join in outrage at the willful British-instigated war, the scorched Earth tactics and the horrors recently revealed about the concentration camps. These men include Michael Watson and Robert Wilson. In British Army eyes they are now rebels and traitors to the Empire.

The men will later testify in court that they were driven to rebel by the concentration camp and farm burning outrages against their kin in the Free State and Transvaal. They regard it as *Volksmoord* (murder of a nation). The English term "genocide" will be invented much later. At this point in modern history, this sad British invention is new to the planet.

Fig. 17-11 The snowy 8,200-foot Kompasberg seen from the surrounding high country

Contact!

On 22 February 1901, the first contact of these men takes place with a British column under Gorringe, some four miles north of Kompasberg. On the 23rd, the British attempt to surround a group of men under the leadership of Free State Artillery sergeant Johannes Smith, a man we have met before as the colleague of Barend Matthys Johannes Booyens (*NF72*). He has come with Kritzinger's Free Staters.

The first major action by Lötter is on the next day, the 24th, when they attack the important Fish River Bridge train station. This incenses the British who start chasing up and down the line with armored trains carrying pom-pom guns. By now, the British are sending various additional columns to chase Lötter and Kritzinger's men. While the British are complaining that the Boere refuse to "stand and fight," they miss the actual point. The British Army is being tied up chasing men who can outrun them all the time. Every group so tied up, is a group not fighting in the Transvaal and Free State and assures a further waste of British taxpayer money.

It is at this point that Thomas McCusker and Joseph Callanan (*NF68, 70, 73*) also join the hunt as part of a column of *Nesbitt's Horse*. They eventually make contact south of Somerset-East, but the engagement, as always, is inconclusive. The next attack is at Waterford, the dusty little town near which great-grandfather Nicolaas Grobler was born. Sheldon station is next to be struck.

Gorringe's British columns are run ragged and eventually end up being called "*Gorringe's Light Oxen.*" The British are now totally frustrated. They already have their hands full with De Wet humiliating them in the Free State and De la Rey doing the same in the Transvaal. Now they are being tied up in the Cape Colony, which is supposed to be their fully controlled territory. No place outside a small radius around Cape Town is totally under their control anymore.

The British Army finally realizes the scope of its problem. The East Cape Afrikaners make no secret of their moral support for the Boer cause, which is why so many of them are confined to the "refugee colony" at Bathurst, where the British keep an eye on them. The fact that this is also the place of refuge for British subjects who have had to leave the Transvaal does not make matters any easier. Politically, the East Cape finds itself in an undeclared, largely non-violent civil war between the supporters of the British Empire and those of Republican convictions.

Just as the Nazis will do 38 years later, the British Army prepares lists of local individuals who they consider to be "undesirables." The list includes several Dutch Reformed Church ministers. As we shall see, they are preparing a special hell for these individuals.

Ordinary life in Lötter country

The ordinary citizens of the Cape Midlands region do their best to not make matters worse. However, the invading Boer Commandos, the Rebels, and the British Army all combine to make matters difficult. The Myburgh family takes to hiding its horses in a gorge in the *Rhenosterberg* behind *Hoeksplaas* farm. This is done in an effort to keep them out of the hands of both the Boer Commandos and the British.

The menfolk dig a deep hole near the house and hide their harvested wheat in it. It is covered over with a thick iron sheet and then covered with soil. For money, Albert Myburgh cuts firewood and rides it into Middelburg. He has to have a curfew

Fig. 17-12 Rhenosterberg Mountain at Hoeksplaas farm outside Middelburg

pass to do this, but possesses no such pass. Instead, he waves a piece of blank paper at the British soldiers who let him pass on every trip. Life is hard at this time. The Boer Commandos of necessity turn to the farms for their supplies, issuing the farmers useless Free State Government requisitions. Generally, though, the farmers, both Afrikaans and English, provide the needed help with some degree of grace. After all, these are not men who are natural enemies. In fact, quite the contrary; many know one another as friends and neighbors across the lines of this war.

One night a British patrol stops on the Myburgh farm. To the horror of the family, the troops elect to build their campfire right on top of the carefully disguised wheat larder. Fortunately, the *Tommies* get drunk that night and never uncover the hidden supply. The family breathes a sigh of relief as the Imperial Troopers move off the next day.

Escalation

By March 1901, the Boer commandos take the village of Pearston. Then fighting breaks out at Aberdeen to the west. The commandos move at high speed and strike left, right and center at the British all over the Cape Midlands. None of the blows are major, but they cause the British enormous frustration and cause them to waste massive amounts of resources.

18 months before, on 20 October 1899, Wyndham, the British Parliamentary Under-Secretary of State, explained in the House of Commons that Britain planned to send a field force of 47,000 men 6,000 miles over the sea, equipping and maintaining it for four months at £8,000,000. This was quickly increased to £10,000,000. That was the British concept of the war when they initiated it. They imagined it would be over not "by Christmas," but by at most two or three months afterwards. Now, on 28 March 1901, Bryce, an experienced parliamentarian and previous Under-Secretary of State, points out in the House of Commons that the war was now costing Britain between £1,250,000 and £1,500,000 every single week. In other words,

four months of war against a few thousand Republican farmers was now costing them between £20,000,000 and £24,000,000. They are now paying at three times the rate they had counted on and the war is already 4½ times as long as they had hoped it would be. And there is absolutely no end in sight.

Finally, on April 7th the Boer commandos in the Cape cut off a group of one hundred British Lancers and Yeomanry and seventy of the men are kept as prisoners of war for several days. British soldiers are now being taken prisoner of war in "their own" territory. They had never experienced anything like this before. As the war grinds at the British nerve and treasure, the Europeans cement their view of the British as something between a military laughing stock and a dangerous impotent giant. The British Army is at its wit's end. Germany, in particular, takes careful note for future reference.

At this point, the Cape Governor extends Martial Law from the coastal towns to the affected interior areas. Finally, on 22 April 1901, the British Army takes over the direct operation of the martial courts without the members of the court having a suitable background in Law. The new Law states that the Attorney General in Cape Town may comment, but cannot revoke the findings of these courts. Kitchener has to approve the death sentences. However, later an additional rule is made that gives officers on the spot the authority to execute men found in khaki clothes.

Charges that can carry a death sentence include "marauding," a term now used for such simple acts as commandeering fodder for a horse. Even the use of "abusive language" is deemed acceptable as a charge carrying the death penalty[19]. The consequences will be lamented in the British Parliament. While the horror of the concentration camps can still be partially passed off to the naive and gullible as an unintentional result of criminally incompetent management, what now happens in the East Cape is done entirely with malice aforethought and will produce the martyrs of this war in our family backyard among our relations.

For the next few months, the Lötter Commando has considerable success. On 20 June 1901, they have a major skirmish with the Midland Mounted Rifles (MMR), a Colonial Loyalist unit under the leadership of the German Captain Spandau. The Commando is desperate for the rifles, ammunition, clothes, and boots of the well-supplied British unit. The Commando men catch the MMR in crossfire and then call out to them to give them a chance to surrender. Spandau refuses. After a hot exchange, 14 MMR men lie dead and dying and a further seven are wounded. Trooper Davidson from the United States, fighting for the Empress of India, dies this day. Hans Lötter thereupon sends a cart to Cradock with a message for the British Commander there to come and fetch his men. As exchanges in guerrilla wars go, this is a heavy engagement.

The worst winter in decades now breaks over South Africa. While thousands of women and children die in their inadequate concentration camp tents amidst the snow (See *Fig. 17-7*), the Cape Rebels are having a torrid time of it. Their horses are failing them and fodder is difficult to find. Deneys Reitz, who has entered the Cape Colony under General Jan Smuts, tells more about the general struggle for clothes[20]:

> "...I unearthed an empty grain bag in which I cut a hole for my head, and one at each corner for my arms, thus providing myself with a serviceable greatcoat."

Later he adds,

> "Towards midnight it began to sleet. The grain bag which I wore froze solid on my body, like a coat of mail, and I believe that if we had not kept moving every one of us would have died."

Kitchener, meanwhile, issues a standing order that any Boers captured wearing khaki uniforms will be summarily executed. The British Army thereupon eagerly applies this rule and executes several of Jan Smuts' Commando members who are captured wearing khaki. Lt Col Scobell becomes the major British exponent of this particular form of conduct. Given the state of dress they find themselves in, as described by Reitz, the Commando men have little other choice but to wear khaki. Any excuse now seems acceptable to execute a man.

And yet, Imperial Britain has not plumbed the greatest depths of horror.

Innocent blood! Innocent blood!

Life becomes a daily misery for the ordinary people of the Middelburg district. General French of the British Army has made the town his headquarters with his contingent of Coldstream Guards. He has also obtained the services of Lieutenant-Colonel Scobell to suppress the activities of the Cape Rebels. However, these are not to be the men inducted to do the dirty work for the Empress of India. The British Army has other historically familiar ideas.

And so it is that one day, while great-grandmother Martina Myburgh (nee Fouché) is in the farmstead with 7 year-old youngest son Kotie (*NF68*), the author's grandfather, a troop of Cape Corps "Coloured" Khoekhoe soldiers in British uniform arrives. Yet again Britain has made the problems in South Africa into a racial matter. The leader of this troop screams at her:

"Where are the Rebels? Where are the Rebels?"

Not content to just do his job, their leader rides his horse onto the porch of the house, attempting to trample Martina while the frightened 7-year-old Kotie clings to her dress. They force their way into the house and start bayoneting the ceiling of their simple clay and thatch roof house with its dung floor. Eventually, they leave empty-handed, having instilled the fear, not just of Great Britain, but of the excesses of which these people had previously proven themselves capable in the eyes of all Afrikaners. The young Kotie will remember this to his dying day in the late 1960s. After 85 years, it is the time of Slagtersnek (*NF40*) all over again, but much worse.

When the lumbering Gorringe fails to engage the rapidly moving Kritzinger and Lötter as they pass Middelburg early in the second invasion of the Cape, his men arrest an ordinary farmer named Hendrik van Heerden of the farm *Sewefontein* (Seven Fountains), near where both maternal great-grandfathers Nicolaas Grobler and Albert Myburgh find themselves. The Army intends to have Hendrik questioned in Middelburg, so he dutifully saddles up to go with the British soldiers.

Fig. 17-13 Hendrik van Heerden

About 200 yards from the house, a volley of rifle fire rings out from a nearby *kopje* (hill). Van Heerden and two British soldiers are hit. Van Heerden is badly wounded and falls from his horse, but gets up and starts running towards the hill where the fire is coming from, waving his hat indicating that the shooting should stop. He is eventually taken into the house. Later, a military ambulance arrives for the lightly wounded British soldiers, but the heavily wounded Van Heerden is left in agony in the care of his wife.

The next day a British lieutenant rides up on his horse, barges into the house, physically kicks open the bedroom door where the wounded Van Heerden is lying, and announces that a British Military Court has found him guilty of treason, based on evidence by his black farm workers. He is to be executed and has eight minutes to make peace with his Maker and say goodbye to his family.

Van Heerden, in great pain, is pulled from his wife, thrown on a blanket and taken behind a corral where he is shot. Hendrik, still in his dying throes, is brought back to the house and is unceremoniously dumped on his bed to die in front of his distraught wife. Hendrik's last words are:

"My wife, my wife! Put on my grave: 'Innocent blood! Innocent blood!'"

The Cape Judiciary is rightfully outraged when they learn of the event, but in Pretoria Kitchener announces that he ratifies the sentence and that the "matter is closed." British Justice has just executed a wounded civilian who was not even present at his own trial. This is the Imperial Britain that the Afrikaner has fled all these years. The monster has finally shed all pretense and is strutting in the open over the graves of good men for all to see.

With this starts a litany of outrages; an organized terror campaign by the British Military. In June 1901, Colonel Scobell surprises a little camp of Cape Rebels and captures ten. Seven are sent to Bermuda POW camp, but three are to stand trial for their lives for having wounded a soldier. One of these is 16-year old Johannes Petrus Coetzee. After a brief trial, he is found guilty by a hastily composed Army Court despite the evidence, and the decision is made to promulgate the death sentence in public.

To this effect, the British Army, in the person of Major Wiseman Clarke, publishes the following note[21] in Cradock. The 16-year old is to hear in public that he is to die for fighting for his people:

NOTICE

All male adults in the township of Cradock are hereby ordered to attend in the Market Square tomorrow morning at a quarter to eleven to witness the promulgation of the sentence of death to be passed on Johannes Petrus Coetzee for high treason and attempt to murder.

TO THE CITIZEN

All places of business must be closed from half-past ten till after the promulgation of the sentence.

C. C. WISEMAN CLARKE, Major, Commandant Cradock District, Thursday, July 11, 1901.

Young Petrus, as he was known to all, is hanged in public in Cradock two days later on July 13, 1901. After the execution of the boy, the Rev. Reynecke who attends Petrus in his last moments of life, together with the community leaders, are summoned[22] to Clarke's office and told:

> "*The blood of Coetzee will be claimed from you and all the other Dutch ministers.*"

The British Army has finally descended to hanging children and threatening churchmen. In a final outrage, Petrus' father is denied his son's body. By 8 August of 1901, a copy of the above order is in the hands of the Irish members in the British House of Commons and Mr. Swift McNeill confronts the Financial Secretary of the Cabinet, demanding to know whether the order was sanctioned by Kitchener or not. McNeill's colleague, Mr. Leamy demands to know whether it is true that several individuals in the Dordrecht community, east of Middelburg, have been deported for refusing to attend the public hanging of Cornelius Johannes Claassen, one of the two colleagues of young Petrus. It is reported that villagers have been forced to watch and have had their heads wrenched back[23] by the guards if they looked away. Indeed, it is *Slagtersnek* all over again (NF40).

Fig. 17-14 The 16-year old Johannes Petrus Coetzee

Eventually, the British Army will execute 33 men in the Cape Colony. In some cases, they are hanged from windpumps, there not being a scaffold available. In most cases, they are tied to chairs and shot. Their bodies are deposited in graves dug by convicts and then covered in slaked lime.

Then the shots ring out from behind the hill

By August 1901, the Lötter Commando is on its last legs. Several Boer commandos have left the Cape Colony due to the winter depredations. Kritizinger has returned to the Free State, while the Transvaal Commandos under Smuts and his colleagues are in the west of the Colony. With all of the British troops in the east of the Colony now chasing them, the writing is on the wall. By now, Scobell has learned that the secret is mobility and he has obtained the services of some local Colonial Loyalists. The British have blocked all the paths down the Sneeuberg mountains onto the Camdeboo plain and have billeted soldiers on the farms to ensure that no one warns the Rebels. Johannes and his men are eventually forced to make their way down a precipice and, on 5 September 1901, they are cornered at the farm *Paardefontein* near the little village of Petersburg, where Albertus Jacobus Myburgh obtained his phytomedicines 40 years ago (*NF65*). They are hopelessly outnumbered by 450 well-fed, well-clothed, and well-equipped British soldiers and Colonial Loyalists. The rebels have hardly eaten anything in 8 days and are in terrible condition. After a grim 45-minute rifle battle, they surrender. Pieter Wolfaardt, the intrepid dispatch rider, is the last man to surrender. His comrades have to overpower him to force him to stop shooting.

Fig. 17-15 The wounded Hans Lötter after his capture

Thirteen of the men, mostly young farmers from the district, lie dead. They rose to defend their nation in the face of clear-cut evidence of the attempts at genocide by the British Empire, but they have lost. The scene inside the shed where the last group held out is terrible. The dead and dying lie everywhere and the place is swimming in blood. Johannes Lötter himself is wounded.

Over a period of one week between 17 and 23 September 1901, the vast majority of the rebels are tried by a Special Court in Graaff-Reinet. Some trials follow later. One hundred and seventeen of the men are sentenced to death. The sentences of 112 are commuted to penal servitude for life on foreign islands in the British Empire. A royal commission after the war will eventually reduce their sentences to typically two or three years. Some of the teenagers will be given strikes of the rod instead.

Johannes Lötter is brought before the court in Graaff-Reinet on 27 September 1901. He is charged with being in arms against the king (Victoria having died), with murder for having killed British soldiers during the battle in which he was captured, the murder of two native subjects (whom he shot as spies), the flogging of two men, the blowing up of the railway line at three places, and with "marauding" at Waterford.

The key to the case is the matter of his citizenship, the British insisting that he is a Cape Colony citizen and he insisting that he is a Free State citizen. He complains that the British have done away with his citizenship papers, which went astray on his date of capture. Two Free Staters captured with him testify that one of them carried his papers in a pouch. The magistrate of Colesberg insists that his name appears on the Colesberg voter's roll as Luther. Given the fact that all South Africans know the surname Lötter very well indeed, such a mistake is unlikely in the extreme. Johannes objects that he cannot defend himself in this respect because the witnesses to his citizenship are on Commando in the Free State.

It is all to no avail and he is carted by train with 15 other of the men to Middelburg, their truck covered over with sheep netting. Other men are sent to various towns in the region for public promulgation of their sentences. The British Army is seeking maximal intimidation of the public.

Middelburg is a typical Karoo town, where the main street is invariably named "Church Street" and leads directly to the front door of the Dutch Reformed Church. On 11 September 1901, Johannes is marched down the main street of Middelburg to the grounds behind the church where he hears his death sentence announced for the first time. Our family is forced to attend the promulgation event.

On 12 September, he is taken by cart to behind Ouberg, the little hill outside town, in the company of the Reverends Postma and Le Clus. There he is tied to a chair. Then the townsfolk hear the gunshots ring from behind the hill.

Johannes Lötter is no more.

Come let us sing!

On 15 October, it is the turn of Petrus Wolfaardt, the intrepid dispatch rider from Middelburg who had refused to surrender. As the cart with the condemned Petrus rolls down the street, it passes the family house where his aged Viljoen stepfather stands alone on the porch with his hat in his hands, the sounds of sobbing coming from inside the house where his mother is being consoled. When Petrus sees his father, he sits up straight on the cart and then his voice rings[24] out loud through the dry Karoo air:

"Come let us sing!"

Then his clear deep baritone fills the air with the inspirational Dutch Hymn[25] number 20, the text of which translates to:

"Let us stride emboldened forth,
  In fullest faith in His Word,
  Though our path leads through sorrow and fear,
  The end shall ever be salvation."

As the cart disappears around the hill, his voice is still heard clearly singing the nine verses one after the other as the British soldiers march next to him. When he finishes the hymn, there is a short pause, and then the rounds ring from behind the hill.

And then all is silent...

All in the district feel the loss. Wolfaardt's stepfather is related to Albert Myburgh's late Viljoen stepfather while Hans Lötter was the second cousin of Johanna Catharina Smit's mother, Susanna Sophia Lötter Joubert. Albert Myburgh's brother is married to one of the Coetzee ladies whose family lost young Petrus to the hangman, while the fate of the Erasmus men of the family is still unclear. The terror and trauma of the British intimidation campaign will leave a permanent mark on these people.

This is the community that will one day give South Africa its first two Prime Ministers in the later so-called Apartheid Era. Their hatred of all matters British will be total. Elizabeth Schoombee of the Middelburg District will one day marry

Fig. 17-16 *The men hear their sentences promulgated behind the church where they worshiped*

Hendrik Verwoerd, the architect of Apartheid, and be known to the world as Betsie Verwoerd. His successor, Balthasar Johannes "John" Vorster will himself be a product of the nearby Jamestown district, which is also at this time subject to similar treatment by the British. Ten members of the Middleburg Vorster family were part of Lötter's rebel Commando and two of them were killed during the final battle.

The men who rose against genocide

Fig. 17-17 shows some of the men in Lötter's Commando. Even across more than a century, the resistance is still there in their eyes for anyone to see as they await their fate in Graaff-Reinet in September 1901:

52. Gert Willemhardus Botha (22), Cradock - Death, commuted to penal servitude for life.

53. Hendrik Johannes Erasmus (25), Cradock – Death, commuted to penal servitude for life.

54. Albert Viljoen, Cradock (29) - Death, commuted to penal servitude for life.

55. Zacharias Gert Viljoen (--) - Death, commuted to imprisonment and 25 strikes of the rod.

60. Willem Johannes Joubert (--), Hanover - Death, commuted to penal servitude for life.

61. Louis Petrus Kruger (39), Cradock- Death, commuted to penal servitude for life.

62. Johannes Stephanus Kruger (21), Cradock - Death, commuted to penal servitude for life.

63. Johannes Jacob Kruger (19), Cradock - Death, commuted to penal servitude for life.

67. Dirk Christoffel Breedt (--) Bethulie, Free State Republic – Death. Executed 17 October 1901, Cradock.

68. Frederick Abraham Jacobus Pretorius (27), Cradock - Death, commuted to penal servitude for life.

69. Johannes Jurgens Lötter (17), Somerset East – Death, commuted to imprisonment and 20 strokes of rod.

At the end of the war, the sentences of penal servitude are eventually reduced to two or three years for all mature men in this picture. However, Britain has instilled a national hatred that will never go away.

Fig. 17-17 *Some of the Cape Rebels who rose against genocide*

—*End Nexus Familia*

To lose a war and win a peace

In around March of 1900, the British had made the first attempts at some form of peace agreement based on surrender of the Boer forces. The Boer leaders had turned it down. In March 1901, there was a second attempt that was promising enough to be sent to London for ratification. However, Chamberlain and his bevy of conservatives rejected the points that Kitchener himself had considered acceptable. By March 1902 Britain was the political skunk of the civilized world. Europe was outraged at what had happened in the concentration camps. No one in Britain could practice denial any further. Britain's casualties were approaching 50,000 and they had burned two entire republics to the ground. The bill for the war was now around £200,000,000. This was twenty times what they had anticipated, and it had now dragged on more than seven times as long as hoped.

In a final humiliation, on 7 March 1902, in a masterful piece of battlefield tactics, the much respected Koos De la Rey attacked a convoy led by Lord Methuen himself at a place named *Tweebosch* (Two Bush). All but the core of Northumberland Fusiliers and North Lancashires refused orders, broke, and ran. At the end of the battle, 68 soldiers lay dead, 121 were wounded and 205 taken prisoner[26], including Methuen himself. Back in London the master of the war, Broderick, confessed it was the biggest setback since Colenso in 1899.

After two years and six months of everything the entire British Empire could throw at this tiny nation, De la Rey had formally defeated his theater opponent, a senior general of the Empire, and had captured him to boot. Britain was incredulous. In Pretoria, Kitchener disappeared into his room and went off his food for two days[27]. Frank Maxwell, his secretary commented[28]:

> *"It floored poor K. more than anything else during the entire campaign and he didn't appear at five meals. [...] ...he volunteered the remark that 'his nerves had gone all to pieces' "*

On 10 March 1902, in a stunned House of Lords, Lord Roberts of Kandahar, still Commander-in-Chief of the British Army, stood up and stated, with a sudden newfound respect for his adversaries:

> *"I am sure, from the desire to act in a humane and civilized manner, which General Delarey has shown throughout the war, that Lord Methuen will be taken every care of by him"*

This stood in stark contrast to the conduct of his own commander in the field, Kitchener, when it came to the brave men whose executions he had defended, the more than 28,000 women and children who had died in his concentration camps and the hostages he had put on supply trains. There was also intense discussion about why British troops were constantly surrendering in droves, as at *Tweebosch*. The reason on the ground was that the soldiers knew they would be treated extremely well by the Boers and, mostly likely, simply be allowed to go back to barracks minus their boots. Already in a letter[29] of 14 December 1900 to his father, Maxwell noted:

> *"Hang this wretched surrendering, though I suppose sitting in an armchair it is easy enough to be brave; but it does seem to happen a bit often, doesn't it?"*

This was a source of major concern to the political masters in London, in whose picture the Boers had to be monsters to justify the war in the first place. Propaganda is very difficult to reverse in the face of the truth.

Then came the stunning news that De la Rey had in fact freed Methuen. Not only that, but De la Rey's wife had used the very last chicken she had available to prepare a meal for Methuen in the field – the very lady whom he himself had evicted from her farmhouse under Kitchener's orders. Mrs. De la Rey had even sent a letter to Methuen's wife to assure her that he was safe but needed British hospital attention. Commando men then took him into town under a white flag. Here the British Parliament was finally inescapably faced with the true nature of the Afrikaner whom they had vilified with such dedication for so long.

At the same time, Jan Smuts was now in control of the Western Cape north of the Olifants River and Transvaal Boer Commando men were splashing in the ocean north of Cape Town. In the House of Commons on 20 March 1902, Lloyd-George argued that if one looked at who controlled what exactly in South Africa on that date, then:

> *"the Boers have more territory in South Africa today than when the war began."*

It was entirely clear, though, that both parties to the conflict had by then had their fill. In a last amazing stupor of the war, a battle north of Pretoria saw a Commando of ordinary Boer farmers charging entrenched British positions like cavalry at the Charge of the Light Brigade. The particular Boer Commando was naturally essentially obliterated.

By this time, the British had learned to respect their foe, and Arthur Conan Doyle could finally write[30] about the two Boer Wars as:

> *"two costly and humiliating campaigns with men whom we respected even when we fought with them."*

A few weeks after the two above battles, Kitchener and Louis Botha hammered out a set of terms upon which peace was to be agreed. These terms were much more favorable than those of a year earlier. In summary, they read:

I	The burgher forces will lay down arms and recognize His Majesty King Edward VII as sovereign
II	All burghers outside the two ex-Republics will be brought back to their homes by His Majesty's Government
II	The burghers so surrendering or returning will retain all liberty and property
IV	No civil or criminal proceedings will be taken against men so returning. However, men who acted contrary to usages of war, as notified to the Boer generals, shall be tried by court-martial
V	The Dutch language will be taught in schools and will be allowed in courts of law
VI	The possession of rifles will be allowed in the Transvaal and Orange River Colony
VII	Military administration will at the earliest possible date be succeeded by civil government. As soon as circumstances permit, self-government will be gradually introduced
VIII	The enfranchisement of natives will be deferred until after self-government
IX	No special taxes will be imposed on the territories to defray the expenses of the war.
X	His Majesty's Government will place £3,000,000 sterling at the disposal of commissions for supporting returning farmers with shelter, seed, stock, implements etc. Receipt notes issued by Commandos of the defunct Republics for valuable considerations from farmers will be honored as war losses. His Majesty's Government will be prepared to make advances on loan for the same purposes, free of interest for two years, and afterwards repayable over a period of years with 3 per cent interest.

All in all, it was a better set of conditions than what the Frontier Afrikaner had ever lived under when ruled by Britain. Significantly, the representatives on the Boer side signed in their capacities as President of the Free State and the Transvaal Republics. This meant that the British acknowledged that their annexations were void and that they recognized those two Republican governments for the purposes of the Agreement.

Nowhere in the ten terms of the Peace of Vereeniging, as the above agreement became known, can the present author fathom any reference to the Uitlander Voting Rights over which Britain had ostensibly gone to war in the first place.

Reflection on the Great Boer War

For its part, Britain had fought the most expensive war in its entire history as a nation. It had been repeatedly humiliated in front of its European peers by what many saw as a rag tag bunch of "Dutch" farmers. In its frustration, it had sunk to a depth of barbarism that its own people could not stomach as decent Christians. And now it ended up with a bill to fix what it had broken, though hardly a significant sum compared with either the treasure spent or the real damage done. Britain had been more desperate for an end to this drawn-out and humiliating horror than what the Boer negotiators had ever comprehended.

Politically the Peace Treaty of Vereeniging was a hollow victory for Britain. The Empire had set out to create one country it could dominate out of the two colonies and two republics. This peace would eventually create exactly that, but among the White voting public the Afrikaner would be the majority and would dominate the picture from here on. Twice before, Britain had made this democratic miscalculation – first in annexing the Free State, then in annexing the Transvaal, and now in annexing both together. The so-called "Uitlanders," about whom Britain had ostensibly gone to war, had proven to be politically as nebulous as what they had been unreliable at the time of the Jameson Raid. Despite all the uproar these *Uitlanders* had created in 1895 before the Jameson Raid, the Afrikaner was the clear majority in the Transvaal. When the

Transvaal became a self-governing colony in 1906, the Afrikaner was immediately the voting majority.

Victoria, the Empress of India, never saw the end of the so-called "Great War" she had blessed. In the only war that Britain ever lost during Victoria's reign, the "Boers" had been the victors, and she did not live to see victory in the second. She died on January 22, 1901, right at the time that her nation had been dragged down a moral abyss by Kitchener's conduct of the war. At that time, young Elizabeth van Zyl was dying a wasting death in the Bloemfontein Concentration Camp. Victoria's adversary, Paul Kruger, outlived her by two-and-a-half years in Clarens in Switzerland. It was long enough for him to bless De la Rey's actions with respect to Methuen. He died in exile, having lost his beloved country, but holding the indisputable moral high ground in his remarkable but hopelessly unequal contest with the all-powerful Victoria.

Another key person died on 26 March 1902, before he could savor the surrender of the two Boer Republics. In fact, he departed this world just as the humiliating disaster at Tweebosch sank into the British psyche and all in England were praying that the De La Rey, the Boer, was a more decent man than the Englishman, Kitchener. The deceased was Cecil John Rhodes; mourned by few beyond his Rothschild bankers. Mark Twain, however, had also been unsuccessful in his goal of five years earlier[31]:

"I admire him, I frankly confess it; and when his time comes I shall buy a piece of the rope for a keepsake."

Donald Featherstone places the British "total reduction in Field Force due to casualties"[32] in the Boer War at 46,026. Of these, 10,698 died and 34,499 were invalided home. The military drain on Britain is best measured by the same author, who points out[33] that practically every infantry regiment in the British Army of the day bore the Anglo-Boer War Battle Honor. The only cavalry regiments not in the war were the 4th Dragoon Guards, the 4th, 11th and 15th Hussars—all in India—and the 21st Lancers, who were at home.

Colonel Blake[34] puts the number of Boer deaths at 3723; wounded unknown. The really painful loss was that of 25,000 children and 3,000 women.

In the House of Commons, John Bryn Roberts would oppose the grant of £50,000 to Kitchener, pointing out that, for a year and three quarters, he had had 300,000 to 400,000 men under his command to fight a force of 30,000 to 40,000. However, in that process he had resorted to tactics to which *"no other civilized army in modern times"* had. In this, he mentioned specifically the *"farm burning, the concentration camps and the murder*—[he] *could call it nothing less—of men like Scheepers and Lötter."* He suggested that these two men had but done what the British Army was doing, but, because they had been effective, these *"charges had been trumped up against them in order that they might be shot."*

In March 1900, the House of Commons had eagerly debated how they might tax the *"riches of the Transvaal"* to defray the costs of the war they had instigated. A year later they had balked at paying £2,000,000 in restoration support. Lloyd-George would never let Chamberlain forget that he had said he would never ever give the Boers any form of self-determination. They had also had major discussions about enfranchisement of people they called "natives."

Now, on 31 May 1902, they conceded on all their previous objections and raised the amount for restoration, although still a pittance. Earlier the British had insisted that rebels should lose their voting rights for life. Now a 5-year limit was acceptable. The Cape Rebels who were still alive came home, leaving everyone to wonder why it had been so important to execute 33 men and boys earlier.

A blot on the process was provided by the Natal Colonial Government, which was hell-bent on inflicting punishment on the Natal rebels. It was even discussed in the British House of Commons that the Natal colonial government seemed more focused on taking the farms of the Afrikaners than on a proper peace. This became a protracted exercise to resolve.

An interesting reflection on this horrible war is that Kitchener had been as anxious to have peace as what he had been brutal in executing the war. His notions of a reasonable arrangement seemed always to be more generous than those in London and certainly more so than those in the Natal Colony. One might speculate that, just as with the ordinary Tommy on the ground, he had developed a respect for his adversary.

It has become a common observation that *"the Empire had won the war, but the Afrikaners had won the peace."* From this point onwards, they would dominate the politics of South Africa for ninety years. However, for the immediate they were near destitute. Most men came back from distant Ceylon, Bermuda, India, and St. Helena to a pile of ashes and a mere pittance as restoration payment. The Empire had destroyed their country for no apparent gain and would have to account to the souls of 28,000 women and children.

Revulsion in England at the conduct of the war by the British Army, as laid bare in these present pages, led to a shift to the left in British politics, and therewith ultimately to the demise of the Empire. Leading historian Niall Ferguson discusses this revulsion and its political consequences in his seminal work, *Empire*[35]. It is that well-justified revulsion that was to lead to the much-abused Afrikaner taking over the leadership in South Africa shortly after the war.

In America – Jim Crow Laws

The victory of the Union forces in the Civil War had brought little in the way of true improvement in the lot of the black man in the United States. In reality, he no longer was an African man. His language was English, his culture was Western, his values were Judeo-Christian, and he was black. The last of these factors invariably doomed him to the lowest level of American society. He was now an American with very little in the way of effective rights.

As the Democratic Party built its power base among the white population of the former "South," they found it politically expedient to pander to the lesser instincts of some of the population. Starting with Mississippi, a series of laws was implemented that effectively governed the lives and rights of American people who happened to have black skins, purely in the basis of that skin color, there being no other presentable reason. This process was developed to a fine art, and by 1910 the complete edifice of so-called Jim Crow Laws was in position over a large part of the United States. In this process, not only black people, but also poor whites, became effectively disenfranchised. Being thereby essentially powerless, they became the last constituency to be considered in any matter.

This was a very far cry from the situation in South Africa, where black people had no identity crisis. A Zulu had always known what it meant to be one of the AmaZulu. He had always known that his language was isiZulu and it was quite distinct from the Tswana language and had nothing in common with English or Dutch. His culture was uniquely African and his value system in one of the world's primary Warrior Cultures had practically zero in common with the Judeo-Christian culture of the white AmaBhulu. He knew he lived in Zululand and he knew where that was. There might very well have been arguments about exactly what the extent of Zululand was, but he lived in Zululand. He had never been forced from his country against his will to cross an ocean in chains and work as a slave for another man with a different culture. He had never had his own culture whipped out of him and had never lost his language or been forced to be someone other than who he was. He had every reason to be a proud Zulu, and he was.

The same argument could be made for all the other black nations of South Africa. In the case of all the indigenous black people of South Africa, each arguably had his traditional territory, his language, and his culture. The only exception was the Matabele of Mzilikatse and Lobengula, who had now lived in Rhodesia for more than 60 years, having fled the Western Transvaal after their defeat in 1836 by Potgieter.

Certainly there can be all manner of argument as to whether the situation of the South African black man was good or bad or fair or otherwise, but he had no more in common with the black people of America than what the white people of South Africa had. In fact, the whites of South Africa had more in common with Black Americans – both had slave ancestors.

In faraway Liberia, though, the freed Black American slaves had a lot in common with the white people of South Africa, but neither party knew that – nor did any scholar feel obliged to point out any such parallels. In 1980, that reality would come crashing down upon the slave-descendants in Liberia (See chapter 21).

-----ooOoo-----

18

Under the Spider Flag

"You cannot — you must not — destroy a nation."

South African Prime Minister, General Louis Botha
On attempts to humiliate Germany in the formulation of the Treaty of Versailles

The boy with the violet eyes

On his way through Natal to annex the Transvaal in January 1877 (See Chapter 14), Theophilus Shepstone had stopped over with a Boer family named Botha near Greytown on the border of Zululand. Shepstone had discussed the annexation of the Transvaal with his host who had warned him strenuously against it. The annexation eventually delivered Victorian Britain's only lost war. Had the deluded Shepstone taken more notice of his surroundings, he would have noticed the keen attention with which a 15-year old boy in the family was listening to the debate, the piercing violet-blue eyes missing nothing. His name was Louis and he grew up to be overall leader of the Boer Forces against Britain in the Great Boer War of 1899. He also led them to peace in 1902.

In the aftermath of the war, the three undefeated Boer generals, Louis Botha, Christiaan de Wet, and Koos de la Rey visited Cape Town to tumultuous welcome. Britons had taken note of the adulation of all Afrikaners throughout Southern Africa for the three men, and correctly concluded that the future of South Africa did not lie in English domination. It was now clear that, rather than dividing and conquering the Afrikaner, the British had managed to unite all Afrikaners.

Fig. 18-1 *The Glorious Trio*

The three visited Britain to collect aid for their shattered people, but somewhere along the way they became The Glorious Trio. Their exploits were legendary and their moral leadership supreme. These were the men who had cost Britain £222 million – the most costly war in the entire history of the nation, Napoleon and the Russians included. And the British people showed that they were indeed the chivalrous people the Boers had originally assumed them to be, before the inhumanity of Kitchener and conspiracies of Joseph Chamberlain.

Here they met King Edward who specifically thanked them for the kindness and consideration with which they had treated the British prisoners of war. He offered them knighthoods[1], which they politely declined. In Continental Europe, their reception bordered on hysteria. They had to curtail their German visit because of violent anti-British demonstrations.

In early 1901, Milner had set himself up in Johannesburg as the benevolent dictator of the two former Boer republics. However, he found that he and the bevy of young men he had collected around him (known as The Milner Kindergarten) were no more welcome to the returning Uitlanders than old president Paul Kruger had been. The Uitlanders, whose role in the history of that province had not been all that savory and whose role in the war had brought them painfully little respect from Boer and Briton alike, now styled themselves the victors with a right to demand the spoils. In particular, they now demanded government jobs.

In reality, Afrikaners saw in Louis Botha their natural and default leader. He had eventually been the overall military leader in the war. In the absence of the pre-war leaders, removed either by death, as in the case of Piet Joubert, or by exile, as in the case of Kruger, the role fell naturally to Botha. He assumed it equally comfortably. Where Milner tried to generate immigration schemes to obtain a majority of British blood in South Africa, Botha was comfortable in transcending the differences between the groups. After all, the love of his life was his Irish wife, Annie Frances Emett. His sisters had married Englishmen and he had no family history of ingrained animosity to Britain. Milner, however, saw Englishmen as superior.

Jan Smuts was probably the man who most immediately identified Milner as a mortal enemy. He never let up until this man was destroyed politically. He realized that, for Milner, all revolved around Anglicizing South Africa by any means fair or foul, the war and its concentration camps being a good example of how "foul" he was prepared to operate. Milner was to Afrikaners the living embodiment of all that was foul about British Imperialism. When Milner announced that he planned to ship Chinese workers into South Africa to work in the mines, they knew he was already half beaten, because all parties would reject the idea.

The Transvaal people bore the irritation of this man with what grace they could muster; and they waited. The first political meeting of Afrikaners in the old Transvaal was held in Heidelberg on 2 July 1903, 13 months after the Treaty of Vereeniging. Louis Botha presided. The collective blood of the Afrikaner had started to stir again, but deployed around the gathering were 500 "special constables" appointed by Milner.

In England, the monocled Joseph Chamberlain resigned as Colonial Secretary in September 1903, to be replaced by a Milner protegé, Alfred Lyttelton. By now, Milner was under attack from Afrikaners and Uitlanders alike, both parties resenting his arrogant dictatorship. Milner's imperialist fanaticism was creating a hatred among Afrikaners of all matters English. Louis Botha detested him for his wartime conduct.

When Botha protested to Lyttelton about the importation of Chinese labor, the Secretary told him that he was not accepted as representative of the Afrikaners. That did it. It was time to form a formal political party. It would end up being called "Het Volk" (The Nation) and it would seek to unite all white South Africans, irrespective of origin or mother tongue, wherever they might be. On 23 May 1904, Botha prayed at the opening of the first congress of Het Volk in Pretoria[2]:

"May it please the Almighty Father to inspire all whites of South Africa with likemindedness, that hence one nation may be born."

Paul Kruger comes home

On Thursday, 14 July 1904, Paul Kruger died at his home of exile in Clarens on Lake Geneva. Queen Wilhelmina of the Netherlands promptly made available a ship to return his body to South Africa. The grand old man had been born under the British flag and had refused to die under it. In his last letter, directed to Louis Botha, he enshrined his most famous words as later quoted by King George VI:

"Take from the past all that is good and beautiful, shape your ideal therewith and build your future in this ideal."

Botha went to Cape Town personally to receive the body. He arranged for the train trip of a thousand miles to Pretoria, during which the train stopped wherever people had gathered or a light was shown in the dark. The grand old man was laid to rest in his beloved Pretoria on the carefully chosen date of 16 December 1904, the Day of the Covenant and first day of the First Boer War. The crowning feature of the Last Ride of Paul Kruger was the procession, led by his three undefeated Boer War generals, the Glorious Trio, on horseback: Louis Botha, Koos de la Rey and Christiaan de Wet, together with Schalk Burger, the care-taking president of his old republic during his exile.

Africa in the Scepter and the Crown

On a rainy 2 April 1905, Milner finally left South Africa, his dreams of empire in tatters and his ideas disregarded. He had done some considerable good in the area of administration, but all South Africa sighed in relief at his departure.

On 5 December 1905, the Scot, Henry Campbell-Bannerman, took over as Prime Minister of Great Britain at the head of a Liberal Government. The Conservative cabal that had plotted and schemed its way to war in South Africa had finally fallen, albeit 6 unfortunate years and several hundred thousand shattered lives too late. The Empress of India was dead. Cecil John Rhodes was dead. The whole concept of empire had been discredited in South Africa. From here it was to be downhill all the way for Great Britain. The Boer War had clearly mortally wounded the Imperial Beast in its belly.

The fiery Jan Smuts, not known in the least for his diplomacy, was dispatched to visit Winston Churchill, Lord Morley, and finally Campbell-Bannerman with a view to obtaining self-rule for the Transvaal. Churchill thought the idea of self-rule for a "defeated enemy" preposterous. Morley seemed incapable of decision making, but the all-important Scot listened. Smuts' message was characteristically simple and to the point. Did Britain want the Afrikaner as a friend or as an enemy? He felt the Afrikaners had already shown the quality of their friendship as honorable men. The alternative was for Britain to have another Ireland on its hands. Smuts spoke man-to-man with the leader, as Dutch Reformed Afrikaner to a Presbyterian Scot – there being no two closer denominations in the Protestant universe[3].

On 8 February 1906, less than four years after the last shots were fired in the Great Boer War between Boer and Brit, Campbell-Bannerman addressed his Cabinet on the qualities of the Afrikaner, the support they had given Britain in the past three years, and their brave fight for their freedom. He convinced his team that Britain needed allies of such caliber. Within minutes, the Cabinet decided on "Responsible Government." Self-rule for the Transvaal was implemented in December 1906 and a few months later for the Free State.

On 4 March 1907, Louis Botha and his cabinet, having been elected by popular vote, were sworn in as the government of the Transvaal, a colony within the British Empire. On 26 January 1905, the world's biggest gem diamond, the 3,106 carat Cullinan Diamond, had been found at the Premier mine outside Pretoria. This diamond was presented to the King of Great Britain as a token of thanks for the early granting of self-government. The two largest cut stones from this giant were then fitted to the British Royal Scepter (530.2 carat) and the British Royal Crown (317.4 carat), where they preside in state to this day.

The "wastes" of the "interior of South Africa" which, according to senior British Parliamentarians "added no lustre to the Crown" (Chapter 13: Free at Last) had, most ironically and literally, put the lustre in that very precise crown, but the men who had spoken those words were dead, gone, and buried.

The Bambatha Rebellion

In 1905, the Natal Colonial government passed a bill requiring every indigenous black man to pay a Poll Tax of £1. As soon as collection began, the situation turned violent. The next step was the declaration of Martial Law in the colony, followed by the suppression of the so-called Bambatha rebellion, named for its leader, a petty Zulu chief. The Natal Government suspected Zulu King Dinizulu, son of the great Cetshwayo, of instigating the murders of chiefs loyal to the government. On 9 December 1907, they arrested him, tried him for treason, and imprisoned him. Here he remained for the moment. The significance of the Bambatha rebellion is that it was the last tribally based opposition offered to Western government in South Africa.

Teddy Roosevelt and the Frontier clan

Theodore Roosevelt was the 26th president of the United States of America; a man who loved to project a heroic fighting figure. He ended his second term of office on 4 March 1909. It was after this that he decided that it was time to go on an expedition to Africa.

Fig. 18-2 President Theodore Roosevelt in East Africa

Kenya was on his itinerary, and it is here that his hosts included none other than members of the Klopper and Prinsloo families who had left South Africa after the end of the Great Anglo-Boer War. Just as their ancestors had populated the frontier in the 1770s at the Fish River in South Africa (*NF27*), these men had refused to live under British domination and had left[4] after the Great Boer War to find their freedom in German East Africa. However, they had suffered there with malaria and cattle sickness and had been forced to move even further north to Kenya. That had brought them again under British domination, but here the depredations of nature tended to level out the differences between Boer and Brit.

Roosevelt was most impressed with the farming arrangements of the Afrikaners in Kenya and described[5] them as follows:

"Those that I met, both men and women, were of as good a type as anyone could wish for in his own countrymen or could admire in another nationality. [...] It was a very good kind of pioneer life; and there could be no better pioneer settlers than Boers such as I saw."

Later in his book, he comments, using the term *"English Afrikaners"*[6] in the same sense as the author has used it in the present work:

"Already many Boers from South Africa, and a number of English Africanders, had come in; and no better pioneers exist to-day than these South Africans, both Dutch and English. Both are so good that I earnestly hope they will become indissolubly welded into one people; and the Dutch Boer has the supreme merit of preferring the country to the town and of bringing his wife and children, plenty of children, with him to settle on the land."

It is interesting to note that, in his discussions with his Afrikaner hosts, Roosevelt sang a Dutch song, which his mother had taught him. The author's own mother could still recognize the song, word for word, in the 21st century. Roosevelt, of course, was of Dutch extraction. The song has survived 350 years of separation between the Netherlands and South Africa.

The Union of South Africa

Jan Smuts, born in the Swartland wheat fields of the British controlled Western Cape, and Botha, born in the British controlled Natal, shared a dream of unifying South Africa into one single Federal system. This had been the dream of several Imperialist Englishmen before, not the least of whom had been Cecil John Rhodes. It would be no mean task. The Free State, being mostly Afrikaner based, did not take too kindly to Botha's reconciliatory approach with respect to pro-Empire English speaking South Africans. In Natal, where the vote was dominated by pro-Empire Englishmen, the leanings were in the opposing direction.

Nevertheless, the Union of South Africa came into being on 31 May 1910 and on 4 November Parliament in Cape Town was opened formally, with Louis Botha as the first Prime Minister of the new Union of South Africa. The new country was the envy of many. It controlled the critical Cape Sea Route, and it supplied almost all of the world's gold and most of its diamonds.

One of the first actions that Louis Botha took was to release from jail his friend of a quarter century, King Dinizulu of the amaZulu.

A deputation of the royal wives came to see Botha, whose wife entertained them with coffee and jam sandwiches. Of these simple things are built respect between honorable people.

In the context of the South Africa of the 21st century, the creation of the Union of South Africa is probably more significant for what it did not do, rather than for what it actually did. While Swaziland was hived off as a separate "British Protectorate," along with Ba'Sotholand (now Lesotho) and Bechuanaland (now Botswana), the all-important Zululand and the Transkei (land of the ama-Gcaleka, of the Xhosa "Great House," and of the amaThembu) were not similarly

Fig. 18-3 The Union Buildings – the statue of Louis Botha in front

given separate status. In fact, the Western Transvaal border sliced right through the Ba'Tswana nation while the Swaziland border also left a significant number of amaSwazi inside South Africa. The creation of such demographically illogical borders may be seen all over the globe where Imperial Britain once held sway. Three of the greatest danger spots on the planet, Iraq, Afghanistan, and Pakistan are prime examples. The border between Afghanistan and Pakistan leaves 80% of the Pashtun people on the Pakistan side of the border, while Iraq is an artificial combination of mutually incompatible Arabs and Kurds.

And so it is that the amaSwazi, Ba'Tswana and Shangane had the border of the Union slice through their distributions, while the amaZulu, amaXhosa and Ba'Pedi were wholly included in South Africa, but separate countries were nevertheless actively created for the Ba'Tswana (Botswana), amaSwazi (Swaziland) and Ba'Sotho (Lesotho). It is most odd that the international media would never refer to them as "Homelands."

South Africa in the 21st century is under the effective hegemony of a very unstable alliance between two ancient and deadly mutual enemies, the amaXhosa and the amaZulu, the other nations having little say in their own destiny – and it is this decision of 1909 that created the situation.

The first Black Nationalist stirrings

Before the creation of the Union of South Africa, it was possible for people of color to vote in the Cape Colony. Not many had used the opportunity, but it had been available. The South Africa Act of 1909, passed in Britain, entrenched no such rights for people other than whites, but it did have a grandfather clause on Cape non-white voting rights. It was effectively no better, or worse, than the situation in the United States, where the edifice of Jim Crow Laws effectively designed black people out of the national political process.

In 1910, a delegation of men of different "non-white" groups went to Britain to lobby the British government for the inclusion of voting rights for black, Khoekhoe and other people effectively disenfranchised by the South Africa Act. They were told to make their case to the South African government, as it was now an internal affair for South Africa. At this point was born the African National Congress (ANC), a political party designed largely around black people seeking a voice in national politics. It would later mutate into a much different body altogether. The 1910 delegation did not appeal to Britain for independence of the amaZulu or amaXhosa from South Africa. Had they done that, they might have achieved their goal. Swaziland, Lesotho, and Botswana had, after all, achieved theirs. The ANC had other goals.

The 1913 Land Act

The year of 1913 saw the first formal act by the new Union government directed toward addressing the matter of the majority Black inhabitants of the country. This particular act is often held up to the uninformed and untraveled as the "First Pillar of Apartheid," because its result was that 7.3% of the land area of the new Union of South Africa was specifically reserved for exclusive use by its Black people, who constituted two thirds of the population of the country as a whole at the time.

It is to this Act that the post-Apartheid Black Nationalist government traces its efforts in "land restitution." It uses this Act as the basis for all argument in the matter of land. For the present government it is a very useful tool to engender outrage in foreign countries and to thereby justify perpetrating its own outrages. However, the government steadfastly neglects to mention that the almost 50% of the country west of a line running north-northwestward through Port Elizabeth (See *Fig. 2-4* and *Fig. 2-5*, Chapter 2) is characterized by the following:

(i) It receives less than 300mm per annum summer rainfall in the interior;

(ii) It is incapable of sustaining cattle (the economic basis of Black culture); and

(iii) It never in the history of the country was the home of any indigenous Black population.

Fig. 18-4 The typical scrub Karoo west of the 300mm rainfall line

Furthermore, just as some White Supremacists, neo-NAZIs, and Islamic Radicals deny the Jewish Holocaust, so Black Racist Nationalists in South Africa endeavor to disclaim and deny the Difaqane, by which Black people largely abandoned the Prairie country of South Africa in the face of Zulu, Matabele, and Mantatee expansion (Chap. 10: *A world strewn with skulls*). Instead, they now try to present the events of the Great Trek and those surrounding Zulu King Dingane as a large-scale theft of land by Whites from Blacks. Fortunately, that history stands well recorded and we have relied on independent British and American missionaries as historic witnesses in the present work (See Chapter 10: *A world strewn with skulls*).

The real outrage of the Act never was in the matter of the ratios of area involved. It was in the detailed regulations that were implemented under its umbrella. These limited and controlled ownership of the land and the sizes of cattle herds and the like. The net effect was that it kept the Black people of South Africa poor and in that respect, it was a disaster. It remains important, however, that the student of history be careful about where and how any outrage is directed. The "percentage land" argument is and has always been a red herring by which to intentionally mislead the well intended. Nevertheless, white farming interests did indeed encroach on tribal land and land was wrongly lost. There are entirely legitimate claims to restitution, but a basis of demographic percentage is not a viable argument and is supported by neither history nor the potential yield of the land.

Figures 18-4 and 18-5 are quite representative of respectively the western interior of South Africa where the author's parents were raised and the southeastern interior, where the bulk of the Nguni nations (amaXhosa, amaThembu, amaPondo, amaBhaca, amaZulu and amaSwazi) maintained their cattle-based subsistence lifestyle. There is no comparing the two regions. Huge areas of the west of the country have zero agricultural value. Historically it was Khoekhoe or San Bushman country and black people had never lived there.

Fig. 18-5 *The typical countryside in the Transkei Black Homeland east of the 300mm annual rainfall line*

World War I and Rebellion

On his way back from "taking the waters" at a classical "Bad" in Germany in 1913, Prime Minister Louis Botha met with Winston Churchill in London, then First Lord of the Admiralty, and advised him that he was convinced that Germany was planning for war against Britain. Churchill himself reports[7] that Botha said, *"but you with the Navy, mind you are not caught by surprise."* Churchill implicitly trusted the practical intuition of the Boer War general.

By now, the other two members of the "Glorious Trio" had started to split with Botha. The complaint against Botha was twofold:

Firstly, all around the country many Afrikaners felt that Botha had become altogether too cozy with Britain and that he had become a "lackey of the Crown." His support from the English-speaking South African constituency was solid, but the rank and file Afrikaner had a very hard life and resented Botha's "hobnobbing with Royalty." Jan Smuts, who had become Botha's steadfast ally, labored under the same criticism. Smuts' view would later become clear in his statement that the British Empire was[8] :

"The widest system of organized human freedom which has ever existed in human history."

Significantly, Botha and Smuts were originally from Natal and the Cape Colony respectively, while De Wet was a Free Stater and De la Rey was the Lion of the West Transvaal. The latter two had seen the countries of their fathers reduced to charcoal by the British and could never forget that. The fact is, though, that Botha's family had suffered bitterly in the concentration camps and his sisters had been evicted from their homes which were burned to the ground.

Secondly, many have suggested that Botha had only managed to convince De Wet and De la Rey of accepting peace in 1902 after promising that they would all wait for Britain to be somehow weakened or at war with a third party, at which time that they could make another bid for their independence[9].

When War formally broke out, Britain expected South Africa to attack and take German West Africa (today's Namibia). Winston Churchill[10] insists that Botha himself had suggested it earlier. At the same time, the ordinary Afrikaner had absolutely no quarrel with the Germans and was still smarting from the Anglo-Boer War. They wanted nothing to do with British ideas of attacking the Germans. This sounded all too much to the ordinary Afrikaner like the British yet again wanting their Empire built on the much-abused Afrikaner blood. The very notion of fighting under the "Spider Flag" deeply upset many.

On the eve of the war, all eyes turned to the other two members of the Glorious Trio, Generals Christiaan de Wet and Koos de la Rey. Would they rise in rebellion, or would they support Louis Botha, who by now seemed to be wholly in the British camp? At this point, one of the most unfortunate events in the history of the country occurred.

While Christiaan de Wet was seen as the no-nonsense tactical fighter, De la Rey was seen as a pillar of moral strength and was respected with almost holy reverence. Whatever De la Rey said, that would be specifically the moral position of the nation. De la Rey himself certainly felt the weight of this responsibility. And so it is that he met with Louis Botha on 12 August 1914. The subject of discussion was quite incredible.

Siener van Rensburg, the famously accurate Boer clairvoyant (Chapter 17: *Koos de la Rey*), had visited De la Rey on his farm near Lichtenburg exactly a month before. In a vision or premonition, Siener had repeatedly seen De la Rey bareheaded; a symbol he recognized as a foreboding of death. He had also seen a white sheet of paper with the number "15" over Lichtenburg in the evening and the sky over the town had been of *"black crêpe,"* as though in mourning. He had seen many trains headed for Lichtenburg along with a Boer Commando from Schweizer-Reneke. He had come to warn De la Rey about the number "15."

In the meeting with Botha, De la Rey sought to hold Botha to the promised delayed bid for Afrikaner independence discussed 12 years before at the time of the Boer War peace negotiations. De la Rey automatically assumed that Botha would lead such a bid. To the shock and dismay of the venerable old general, Botha would entertain no such thing. Three other men were present in this meeting, including Jan Smuts, who described de la Rey as *"The whitest and noblest soul who ever lived."*

De la Rey was stunned at what he saw as a trust abused and a sacred agreement shattered. De la Rey had evidently never come across political expedience in his life, and Botha seemed by now to be an expert in that department. When De la Rey left, it was the death of the Glorious Trio. De Wet, the third of the Trio, was not a man given to talking. He would simply fight.

The 15th of August came and went. De la Rey addressed a political meeting on that day near Lichtenburg and all went well. In fact, a motion of confidence in the Government was accepted. De la Rey had clearly used his influence to calm the waters now that he knew that Botha was not prepared to rise against Britain. De la Rey made it quite clear, though, that he would fight neither for Germany nor for Britain, but for his own people – a position that most people in the United States also assumed at the time.

On 15 September 1914, General Beyers, Commandant-General of the Army, resigned. By now, Botha had in one way or another estranged many of his original Boer War subordinates and supporters and he realized he had a rebellion on his hands.

On the very same afternoon in Johannesburg, a group of common criminals, the so-called Foster gang, shot dead a policeman. Road blocks were set up to capture this gang. And so it was that late that evening, in the dark of the southern spring, the driver of a Daimler conveying Generals De la Rey and Beyers somehow did not notice one of these road blocks. A shot rang out. When the car came to a standstill, General de la Rey lay dead. It was the 15th of September. De la Rey's funeral in Lichtenburg was duly attended by a Boer Commando from Schweizer-Reneke and many trains conveyed people to the town for the funeral.

The *Siener's* vision had come horribly true.

Politically, this was the end of Botha. A large fraction of Afrikaners rose in rebellion at the notion of invading Duitswes (literally "German West," today Namibia) in support of British interests. Some, under general Manie Maritz, actually crossed over into Namibia to join the Germans. De Wet joined the rebellion, but was eventually captured. Botha himself joined the battles in the field, and eventually the rebellion was suppressed. Even Siener van Rensburg, who had joined his old comrades in rebellion, had been captured. In this process, General Beyers died when he tried to swim to safety through the raging Vaal River.

All would have ended reasonably well, had not Jan Smuts decided to refuse clemency to the leader of the rebellion in the region north of Pretoria. He was a much-respected fighter named Jopie Fourie. As with the executions by the British during the Boer War near Middelburg Cape (*NF78*), Fourie was executed seated on a chair against a wall singing a psalm. This was likely the mistake of a lifetime on the part of the over-militaristic Smuts. A significant fraction of Afrikaners would hate him with total passion to his dying day. To them, he was now an Afrikaans speaking British Imperialist; a "Benedict Arnold." More importantly, James

Barry Munnik Hertzog, one of the wartime Free State generals, broke with Botha over these events and started a party which he named the National Party, styling its focus as being on South Africa and not on the interests of the British Empire. This made him the Leader of the Opposition in parliament.

He promptly formed a Cape branch for the party and initiated a newspaper, Die Burger (The Citizen), for that constituency. A Dutch Reformed Church minister, Daniel Francois Malan, a descendant of Jacques Mallan of Saint-Martin-de-la-Brasque (*NF18, 19*), was appointed as editor and elected as Cape leader of the National Party. He would be elected to parliament in 1918. Malan was a true hardliner and would eventually initiate the road to ruin for the country, and it all started during the Rebellion.

With the 1914 Rebellion suppressed, Botha and Smuts could turn their attention to World War I. First on the agenda was Namibia, where the Germans maintained a considerable military presence and which had a very powerful radio transmitter located in Windhoek capable of communicating directly with Germany. More radios lurked along the coast for communicating with raiding German warships. The entire Namibia was taken with the loss of 114 dead and 318 wounded. This was partly attributable to a masterful outflanking movement which took a major force 690 miles from Kimberley along the dry bed of the Kuruman River through the Kalahari Desert to invade Namibia from the east. It is a pity that Hollywood has not made more effort to portray the drama of this war. The only motion picture that uses this particular theater of war as setting is the endearing story of a young German boy and his horse, entitled *"Running Free."*

After this, Jan Smuts took command of British Forces in East Africa and brought part of his Army up through Africa to tackle the Germans in German East Africa – what is today Tanzania. This effort, while more romanticized by motion pictures such as *"African Queen," "Shout at the Devil,"* and *"Out of Africa,"* was rather less successful. At the end of World War I, the Germans in Tanzania were still undefeated. It is again a pity that theater goers are not given more exposure to this fascinating war, what with its secretive Zeppelin flights, battleships hiding in tropical rivers, and gunboats brought 2,400 miles overland to African lakes. On the other hand, it was operationally characterized more by men succumbing to tropical disease than anything else.

Fig. 18-6 *The arrival signpost at Vanzylsrus in the dry bed of the Kuruman River in the Kalahari Desert*

The end of Kitchener

On 5 August 1914, in the first week of WWI, British Prime Minister Asquith asked a very particular man to be British Secretary of State for War. The man had most recently been Viceroy of India. He was none other than Horatio Herbert Kitchener, son of an English land baron in Ireland; the very man who had run the second half of the Great Boer War and implementer of the British Concentration Camps in South Africa. His was the famous face on the recruitment poster that read "Your country needs you."

By early 1916, his term had become something of an embarrassment to Britain, the crowning event being the terrible disaster at Gallipoli in Turkey, which ended in the largely Australian and New Zealand troops being evacuated in the face of stubborn German-led Turkish resistance. It was the first in a series of costly reverses for another man whom we met before as a newspaperman: Winston Churchill, now First Lord of the Admiralty. For Kitchener it was to be the last in a series of defeats in Europe while he was in office. These included Festubert, Ypres, Neuve-Chapelle, and Loos.

On 27 May 1916, the Russian Czar sent Kitchener an invitation to visit. The Secretary of State for War embarked for Archangel on his secret mission at Scapa Flow on 5 June 1916 on the cruiser *H.M.S. Hampshire*. It was decided to route the cruiser along the lee of the Orkneys and Shetlands to minimize the seas it would have to brave, thereby to make it more comfortable for the honored guest.

And so it was that at 7.40 p.m. a massive explosion cut the *H.M.S. Hampshire* almost in half and she sank within ten minutes. Eight days before a mine had been laid in the area by *U-475* under the command of Lt.-Commander Kurt Beitzen[11]. Kitchener did not survive, and his body did not wash up along with the many that did so. His passing was certainly not mourned by all in Britain by this time. The emotions in South Africa will be understood by anyone claiming to be a member of humanity. Kitchener would have to account to the souls of 28,000 innocent women and children – inmates of his horrific British Concentration Camps.

 ## Nexus Familia 79: Two Young Men and a War

When WWI formally breaks out, grandfather Kotie Myburgh has only just turned 21. He is called up for service in the 14th District Rifles, where he is assigned to C Squad. Six days after Germany declares war against Russia on 1 August 1914, the First World War starts in earnest – in Africa! Troops from Britain and France invade German controlled Togoland in West Africa from east and west simultaneously. An initial South African attack into South West Africa is badly cut up by the Germans at Sandfontein in the south of Namibia. When Jan Smuts, now Minister of Defense of the Union of South Africa, sends Coenraad Brits to reinforce Upington, Brits famously telegraphs back:

"Mobilization complete. Who must I fight? The English or the Germans?"

While Brits is famous for his sense of humor, these words said in jest actually summarize the South African situation very well. Kotie's family, for example, is very much against Louis Botha and Jan Smuts and sees them as "sell-outs" and "imperial toadies." Given what the family has experienced at the hand of the British in the Boer War they can hardly be blamed. Kotie's parents remember the execution of their family in 1901 by the British and Kotie remembers hanging onto his mother's dress as the King's Khoekhoe soldiers invaded their house, bayoneted the ceiling and threatened his mother (*NF78*). The entire concept of fighting for the British is repugnant to this family. However, they are not masters of their own destiny and the Germans make their own decisions in the matter of the war.

Kotie does not take part in the Rebellion of 1914. He simply does his best to get the war over with and hopes that he does not have to actually clash with the Germans, whom he has great difficulty viewing as an enemy. Initially, Kotie's unit is sent to Cape Town where they undergo basic infantry training; Boot Camp. Eventually, despite participation in the war supposedly being voluntary, his unit is sent to *Duitswes*. They are part of the force that moves into the German colony from the south. However, he is not required to fire a round in anger, because the Germans surrender soon after.

Kotie will resent unto his death his forced participation against the Germans in WWI. Later in life, he will consider both World Wars in Europe entirely insane. He will see them as White men stupidly destroying one another for no good reason and weakening his civilization while he struggles on its outer walls.

*****

By April 1915, Britain requests troops from South Africa for the European theater. And so it is that the 25-year old Ivan Merle McCusker, son of ex-newspaperman James Elijah McCusker (*NF69*), volunteers for service and is taken up in B company of the 3rd Regiment of the 1st South African Infantry Brigade. The 3rd regiment is known as the "Transvaal and Rhodesia" regiment and is one of four regiments in the Brigade. About 30% of the men of the Brigade are Afrikaners, despite the earlier rebellion issues.

As soon as he has been through Boot Camp, Ivan is assigned to a machine gun unit and it is in this capacity that he will serve in the war. On 29 December 1915, they embark on the Devonport Sexonia, to arrive at Alexandria in Egypt on 12 January 1916. Even though the Brigade is created to fight in Europe, their first assignment is in Western Egypt and Libya against the Radical Islamist Senussi who are supported by the Ottoman Turks. To this end, they embark for Mersa Matruh on 14 February 1916. Having completed the campaign successfully, they arrive back in Alexandria on 5 April.

Seven days later, on 12 April 1916, they are shipped to Marseille where they disembark on 20 April 1916. Ivan is about to take part in one of the most terrible encounters in one of the most terrible battles in the entire history of the Western World as a whole – the Battle of the Somme.

The assault on the German positions is launched on 1 July 1916 after a week of bombardment. By the 4th of July, the 1st South African Brigade is in the thick of things. After the first week, the brigade has suffered 537 casualties. However, the true hell of the Battle of the Somme, the Battle of Delville Wood, still lies ahead. It is here that Ivan's 3rd regiment is headed; an important forested salient into the German lines near Longueval. When the roughly 3000 men enter this forest on 15 July 1916, they are subjected to such a ferocious and unrelenting bombardment—up to 400 shells per minute—that the forest completely disappears.

The battle extends over several days of mindless hell. Having expended their ammunition, the men resort to hand to hand combat. When the Brigade is eventually relieved, a mere 142 souls stumble out of the devastation. Of the 121 officers and 3 032 other ranks who formed the Brigade on the morning of 14th July[12], only 29 officers and 751 other ranks are present at roll call after the battle. The resistance of the South African Brigade against the flower of the German Army has saved the southern part of the Allied line, but the toll is the worst in the history of the South African Army. British military historian Peter Liddle will later write[13]:

> *"The South African Brigade had fought steadfastly under such appalling and prolonged circumstances that in the grim litany of the Somme's savagery of sustained attack and counter-attack, Delville Wood stands unenviably pre-eminent."*

Ivan receives a gunshot wound in his left hand on 17 July and receives treatment at the field hospital at Rouen. However, two days later he is severely wounded in his left side. At Rouen, it is decided to transfer him to Tooting Hospital in England on the ship *Aberdonian*.

On 8 August 1916, Ivan Merle McCusker dies from complications arising from his wounds and is buried the next day in grave No.6F of Block 18 in Wandsworth, London; a young man who gave his life in what must surely rank as the most murderous and senseless of wars ever fought by man. He went all the way from South Africa to fight for the Allies, and gave his life in this orgy of mindless bloodletting that will most assuredly leave future historians aghast at the callous disregard of Western Europe for its own collective civilization as a family of nations.

Fig. 18-7 The trenches of Delville Wood in the Battle of the Somme

—*End Nexus Familia*

The World's first independent Air Force

The British were hugely impressed with Botha and Smuts. Jan Smuts was not only made a member of the Imperial War Cabinet, but also of the actual British War Cabinet. It was in this latter capacity that he was approached to assess and advise as regards the two British air arms, the Royal Flying Corps and the Royal Navy Air Service. There had been simply too much rivalry between these units and the British War effort had suffered for the arrogance of some of the players. Treating the war in the air as a subset of other defense arms also seemed unrealistic. The war in the air was now a reality and had to be treated as such.

Characteristically, Smuts proposed quite a direct and clinical remedy – combine the two arms into an independent air arm on a par with the Navy and Army, and brook absolutely no opposition in the matter. The resentment in both arms was intense, but the body that resulted from the merger on 1 April 1918 was called the Royal Air Force, the first independent national air force in all of history – it had an incredible 20,000 aircraft. It had taken an Afrikaner Boer farm boy from the wheat lands north of Cape Town, state attorney of the Transvaal Republic and Boer War general, to create it.

No fewer than 3,000 South Africans served in the British Royal Flying Corps in WWI. Forty-six of them became air aces, the leading one being Andrew Beauchamp-Proctor, with 54 victories – the fourth highest score in the entire British Empire. He was also the man who downed most observation balloons in that war. He was awarded the Victoria Cross, the Distinguished Flying Cross, and the Distinguished Service Order. Serving as officer commanding 45 Squadron of the Royal Flying Corps was Pierre van Ryneveld, a young Afrikaner from the Orange Free State[14]. He later assumed command of the entire 11th Army Wing. He had a total of five victories in the air, making him an "ace." Quintin Brand from Kimberley served as Officer commanding 154 Night Fighter Squadron with a total of 12 victories in the air.

As reward for his help to Britain in the war, Smuts was given 100 warplanes in 1920. It should not come as a surprise that South Africa had such a prominent role in military aviation history. The South African Flying Corps had already been created in 1912 as a unit of the Citizen Force under Jan Smuts.

This then provided the backdrop to the creation on February 1, 1920 of the world's second oldest independent[15] air force, the South African Air Force, under the leadership of Pierre van Ryneveld. On 14 May 1920, Van Ryneveld and Brand were knighted for completing the first ever flight from London to Cape Town.

Boer generals against designing WWII

On 18 January 1919, the first formal meeting of seventy representatives of the 21 Allied nations that had participated in WWI took place. Botha and Smuts were present. Also present was none other than their old adversary, Milner, now British Secretary of State for War. Of all the men in the room, Smuts and Botha, along with Marshall Foch of France, were the only ones who had actually faced the defeated enemy on the field of battle.

The eventual terms of the peace treaty were repugnant to Botha and Smuts. They had themselves lived through defeat and could not see what would be achieved by humiliating the proud Germans. It was during these proceedings that Botha stood up and made the statement of his life. Explaining how Britain had made an honorable peace with the Afrikaners at the end of the Boer War, and how that had strengthened the joint parties to that peace, he stated, with his hand significantly on Milner's shoulder:

"You cannot—you must not— destroy a nation."

However, France in particular, given their struggle in the war and their own humiliation in the Franco-Prussian War, seemed preoccupied with the concept of economic vengeance and humiliation of Germany. Smuts phoned Botha to tell him that he was not prepared to sign such a disgraceful document, but Botha talked him into signing. Smuts would comment:

"At that moment, when jubilation filled all hearts, he [Botha] heard the undertone of the ages and felt only the deepest pity for the fate of humankind."

The future would prove the two experienced generals right. History abounds with evidence that it takes a fighting man to make an honorable and lasting peace with a respected enemy. World War II was most assuredly designed by the ink drying on the paper of the Treaty of Versailles, and Hitler would never let the world forget that. In many things, he would be very wrong; but in this point, he would be very right.

Botha died of heart failure on 27 August 1919 and Jan Smuts became Prime Minister.

Designing the League of Nations

Long before the end of the war, Jan Smuts was very troubled by the events surrounding this conflict and the terrible toll it had exacted. In 1918, he published a treatise entitled The League of Nations: A Practical Suggestion. This came to be known as "General Smuts' Pamphlet." Not being a citizen of any of the "Great Powers" he was not mentally hamstrung by their particular needs, wants, desires and preoccupations. He went further than anyone else in formulating the eventual form of the League of Nations, the forerunner of the United Nations. He suggested far greater powers for this body than had previously been considered. He had seen what war had done to his Old Transvaal, he had seen the effects of Total War in his own country and the immense bloodshed in Europe, and now it was clear that France in particular, and to a very large extent also Britain, was hell bent on economically destroying the German nation.

When President Woodrow Wilson of the United States assumed the challenge of initiating the actual organization, it was to Smuts that he turned for the essentials of the new international body, just as Britain had earlier turned to the same Boer general to save it from Germany's air power. As a result, Wilson based the Covenant of the League of Nations on the work of Smuts. Charles Howard Ellis[16] explains that Wilson was greatly struck with Smuts' pamphlet and took the idea for the organization of the League from Smuts. He also took several other concepts from Smuts, as explained by Ellis.

When time came for the creation of the League of Nations Commission to hammer out the details of the organization, five Great Powers (The United States, Great Britain, France, Italy and Japan) and five small Powers were given positions on the Commission. It is considerable testimony to the standing of Smuts with the British leadership that the country made him one of their two representatives, the other being Lord Robert Cecil, who chaired in the absence of President Wilson.

Ultimately the League of Nations would fail to prevent the Second World War. In this respect, it most certainly did not help that the United States never ratified the Covenant of the organization, this despite the fact that Wilson was the leader of the effort to create the organization in the first place.

Wilson received the 1919 Nobel Peace Prize for his efforts. Eventually, many of the practical bodies created by this noble but vain effort would be taken over by the United Nations.

The young man from the Bashee River

Precisely five months before all the important men at Versailles met for the first time, a boy was born to tribal chief Gadla Mphakanyiswa in the nondescript village of Mvezo on the banks of the Bashee (Mbashe) River in the Transkei, some 800 miles east of Cape Town and 500 south of Johannesburg. This river, unknown to most outside South Africa, would be the source of momentous events, unrecognized around the world. This river would eventually become associated with a vision of hell and a glimmer of hope. The former would be unrecognized by the world at large, but would precipitate South Africa down a specific path to ruin. The latter would deliver an opportunity that the Western World would recognize, but would then turn its back on.

The young boy's father named him Rolihlahla – "Troublemaker," in the colloquial interpretation of his native isiXhosa (the language of the various amaXhosa peoples). The young man was a descendant of members of the amaThembu Left Hand House. In particular, the young man was a member of the Madiba clan, named for its reputed progenitor who lived in the 1700s. Chief Gadla rejected Christianity and subscribed instead to his tribal belief system in which Qamata is their all-powerful god. The chief was an unofficial priest within this community, presiding over the slaughtering of various animals at ritual ceremonies for planting, harvest, birth, marriage, and the like.

Soon after Rolihlahla's birth, his family moved to the slightly bigger village of Qunu, where his mother presided over three dwellings. They were built in the classic Xhosa style and equipped with a dung floor, just like that of the author's own family at Middelburg, Cape. By the age of five, in keeping with amaXhosa custom, Rolihlahla was given the responsibility to look after his father's cattle herd. The young man therefore grew up in a traditional amaXhosa society in which they lived their subsistence pastoral life as they had for hundreds of years – long before the advent of the white man. White men did not really enter his life, and he would eventually record[17] that their role in his life was distant. He regarded them as curious and remote figures.

Regarding the amaFengu, who had been kept in slavery by the amaXhosa, he would record[18] that the only rivalry at Qunu was between the Xhosa and the amaFengu, the "Fingos." Ironically, it would be one of his father's amaFengu acquaintances who would urge the chief to send his youngest to school. And so it was that the young Rolihlahla appeared at the little school behind the hill from Qunu, dressed in a pair of his father's trousers, cut off at the knees to fit his much smaller frame. On his first day at school, Miss Mdingane, the teacher, insisted that every student should have an English "Western" name.

And so, Rolihlahla became "Nelson"; Nelson Mandela of the Madiba clan.

Nexus Familia 80: The time of our grandparents

After returning from service in Namibia in WWI, Kotie Myburgh (*NF 79*) marries Elizabeth Johanna "Pretty Bettie" Grobler (*NF68*) from Ezelsvlei on 10 February 1919 in Middelburg Cape, in the Dutch Reformed Church, mere yards from where Hans Lötter's death sentence was promulgated by the British 18 years before. Whereas his father Albert has been a transport rider for the major part of his life, Kotie turns instead to the rigors of sheep farming. It is at this time that one of the Edwards brothers, a descendant of the 1820 immigrant[19], offers Kotie a job as foreman on his farm, *The Meadows*. This is a typical Cape Midlands sheep farm situated behind the mountains to the east of Middelburg.

Despite the fact that Kotie has done his bit to defend the British Empire that Mr. Edwards believes in so passionately, he has to go round the back door of Edwards' house, hat in hand, to obtain his agreed monthly meat supply for his family. Kotie is not convinced that this is the future that his parents voted for when Botha and Jan Smuts started running the country. Slowly but surely, he becomes more convinced of Opposition Leader Hertzog's view, which is based on a distinct identity for the Afrikaner. He can see that the notion of "one nation" as promoted by Botha and Smuts' South African Party is leading to his being a permanent second class citizen – one who has to plead at the back door for that which is his and who is not allowed to have his children educated in their mother tongue in his own country.

*****

In 1903 in the South Cape near de Rust, on the farm *Olienhoutskloof* (Olive Wood Gorge), nestled between the Olifants River to its north and the Kammanassie Mountain to its south, Pieter Johannes Booyens and Bettie Snyman (*NF68*) baptize their third daughter, little Annie. Annie is the author's grandmother. Her younger brother is Ben, born 1909. By 1911, there are eight children. On 5 March 1911, Bettie dies in childbirth. Soon after, with 8 children to look after, Pieter marries again – this time to his late wife's first cousin, also called Bettie. In fact, by virtue of the Dutch naming convention, the bride has the absolutely identical triple name – Elizabeth Petronella Wilhelmina "Bettie" Snyman. She is likewise a descendant of Sara Delport who died in the Baviaanskloof Massacre (*NF34*)

By the end of WWI in 1919, 16-year old little Annie attends a boarding school in the local main town of Oudtshoorn, the ostrich feather capital of the planet. Annie has to write her letters to her family in English, because the English school system forbids her to write to her parents in Dutch or in her mother tongue of Afrikaans. Generations later her family will still possess a letter in English imploring her father to come and fetch her for a long weekend at home.

Some time after finishing school Annie meets a dashingly handsome young man named Herman Stefanus Bosman. Herman is from a family with a strong tradition in the clergy going back to the arrival of the founding father, Hermanus Bosman in 1707. On his way back to Holland from Batavia, the latter elected to step off at the Cape, and stayed to become Sick Comforter. He "broke the first sod" for the Thatched Roof Church which will still grace the town of Paarl in the 21st century, and in which both Piet Retief and Louis

Trichardt's fathers were baptized. One thing leads to another, and in 1924, Annie and Herman are expecting their first child.

*****

Further to the west, Matthys Michielse Basson (*NF 68*) is already 40 years old and lives in Worcester in the winelands of the Cape where he has been magistrate for some years. In the middle of WWI, he marries Helena Loubser Burger. She is, like Matthys, a product of the wheat fields of the Swartland (Blacklands) around Malmesbury. By now, the two families represent some 250 years of wheat farming. They have lost contact with their distant Basson cousins, whose ancestor joined Piet Retief on the Great Trek and was murdered in Dingane's capital (*NF57*). Matthys is the paternal grandfather of the author's wife.

*****

In Waterval-Boven in the Transvaal, Margaretha Johanna Milward (*NF77*) dies in 1919. Immediately afterwards, eldest daughter Neve Constance, already 39, marries Michael Charles Callanan (*NF73*), son of the intrepid Caroline Misselbrook. Michael and Neve are the author's wife's maternal grandparents. Neve's sister, Mary Elizabeth, already married Michael's friend and fellow Boer War train engineer, John van Graan (*NF73*), shortly after that war.

—<u>End Nexus Familia</u>

In America – About Race in the North

In 1910, the Democratic Party took control of the United States House of Representatives. The public voted in Woodrow Wilson as President in 1912 and 1916. Wilson was by 21st century standards a devout white supremacist. He complained that in the post-Civil War era white teachers from the North, who were teaching American Black people in the South[20], "*seemed too often to train their pupils to be aggressive Republican politicians and mischief-makers among the races*"; and that "*the lessons taught in their schools seemed to be lessons of self-assertion against the whites.*" He also extolled on the virtues of the Ku Klux Klan. He complained of "*the intolerable burden of governments sustained by the votes of ignorant Negroes.*" He strongly supported segregation of the races and soon applied this to the Federal Civil Service. The entire Jim Crow process to limit the liberties and hopes of Black people, together with the associated Klu Klux Klan to intimidate them, were part and parcel of his view on matters of race. History would have to live with the fact that Jim Crow[21] had come to Washington under a Democratic Party banner.

By 1900, some 1.3 million American Black people had sought their destiny in the Northern States on what became known as the Great Migration. Northerners who had previously vilified the South and had steadfastly professed to be supporters of the aspirations of Black Americans now had to practice what they had preached. By 1915, racial conflict erupted in the North of the United States. Part of it was precipitated by the release of a silent motion film called the *Birth of a Nation*, based on the novel *The Clansman*. The film emphasized presumed outrages against whites in the South and generally vilified Black Americans. D.W. Griffiths, the author of the novel, had been a classmate of President Wilson's at Johns Hopkins University.

While public lynching of Black Americans had happened in the South before, it now became a feature of life in the North. In 1917, racial violence erupted in East St. Louis in Illinois. Various reasons have been advanced for the events, but the essential fact is that on 2 July 1917 a large crowd of white men descended on a Black area in the town and, after cutting the fire hoses, set fire to the place. About 100 Black people were killed.

On 8 September of that year, the mayor of East St. Louis and his private secretary were indicted on the subject[22]. This shows that senior members of Northern society were by now involved in anti-Black racial activities. Between 10 May and 1 October of 1919, public racial violence broke out on 34 occasions. This included the 5-day Chicago Riots in which hundreds of homes of Black Americans were destroyed. Lynching of Black Americans would remain a feature of American race relations for a long time to come.

It bears pointing out that never during the history of South Africa was there ever a Black man lynched by a White mob. This degree of naked street-level white racist action against black people is simply not within the South African experience. This point is made, not in an attempt to morally indict American society, but to explain that South Africans do not perceive themselves as carrying a moral burden of this nature, which still holds the United States psyche hostage in the 21st Century. Rather, the concern in the present work is that interested Americans simply presume that the same happened in South Africa and then judge the latter country on the basis of these fallacious assumptions.

South Africa would have severe enough problems in the future in the area of race relations[23], but enslaving of indigenous people, lynching of Black people, and White mob racial violence against Black people would not be among them. White South Africans would therefore not entertain a guilty conscience on those subjects. They would also struggle to comprehend why some sectors of American society would project their own guilty conscience in the domain of race relations onto white South Africans.

19

War and Poverty

"...I feel inclined to shift the intolerable burden of solving that sphinx problem to the ampler shoulders and stronger brains of the future."

Jan Smuts, at the Convention for the founding of the Union of South Africa
On political rights for Black South Africans (1908)

Smuts – Visionary or peon of Empire?

Even before the advent of the Great Depression, the Afrikaners were a Western Judeo-Christian nation in the deepest of distress. After the destruction of the two Boer Republics by the British Army, barely 50% of the fighting Afrikaner men of those two countries ever made it back to a life on a farm. They had to move to the towns and cities to secure a livelihood.

Their previous existence had been taken from them when the British Army burnt their countries to a cinder. However, the mining companies on which the wealth of the Transvaal in particular was being built, were now trying to import British workers. Some had strong socialist leanings. The mines were also recruiting indigenous Black people from their subsistence lives in their home territories to work in the mines. This left the Afrikaner economically disempowered in the Western country he himself had hacked out of the rock of Africa.

Soon enough, an Afrikaner under-class developed and one survey[1] showed three thousand white families to be living on the point of starvation. They had been actively made into second-class

Fig. 19-1 Jan Smuts

citizens in their own country. This led to intense resentment on the part of many Afrikaners against what they saw as British abuse of power in South Africa. In consequence, they turned on any proponents of Empire in the country. This now included Jan Smuts. The view of him among Afrikaners in the east of the country, away from his Western Cape origins and his supporters in the Transvaal was that of a man more interested in his position in the British Imperial hierarchy than in the actual problems of the country and those of his own people. As with Magistrate Andries Stockenström in the early 19th century, they respected him for having attained such a high position in the British Imperial System, but the respect ended there and in many areas of the country turned to active hatred.

Smuts' heavy-handedness also alienated many. In 1922, a particularly dangerous situation developed around a mining strike in the Johannesburg area that became known as the "Rand Revolt." The majority of mineworkers involved in this strike were poor Afrikaners. When matters threatened to get out of hand,

Smuts employed the Air Force to literally bomb the mineworkers; this after he had already used military force against a Black religious sect in the Cape Province. He had also used the same Air Force against a native uprising in South West Africa (Namibia), which was now administrated by South Africa under a League of Nations mandate stemming from the victory of WWI.

Smuts represented the kind of intellect that could help formulate a global body such as the League of Nations, an international body representing the first serious attempt to defend the interests of all of humanity on a level greater than that of individual countries. This being the case, it also means that Smuts had the international standing to have convinced the international community of a uniquely South African solution to the matter of the aspirations of South Africans of all colors. However, he actively avoided addressing the matter of political rights for Black people in South Africa. This would eventually cost his descendants any say in their own country. Never in history was there a better opportunity to address the political aspirations of black South Africans than when he ruled, yet he did not come to grips with the issue. In fact, he had already earlier commented to John X. Merriman[2]:

> "...I feel inclined to shift the intolerable burden of solving that sphinx problem to the ampler shoulders and stronger brains of the future."

While Smuts was avoiding the issue, a distant interested Power was not.

Communism in South Africa

On 10 April 1870, a year before diamonds were discovered in South Africa, a young man named Vladimir Ilyich Ulyanov was born in the Imperial Russian town of Simbirsk. In 1887, a year after his father's death, Vladimir's eldest brother was executed for his part in an assassination attempt on the Tsar of Russia. His sister, who had been with his brother at the time of the assassination attempt, was banished. Presumably the Tsar's security people had no concept of the tragedy they were inadvertently unleashing upon the planet Earth.

For a few years, Ulyanov practiced law in Samara on the Volga and gained insight into the social state of the downtrodden peasantry of Imperial Russia. The year when the author's Myburgh grandfather was born, 1893, Ulyanov moved to St. Petersburg and became involved in revolutionary propaganda, which led to him being imprisoned in solitary confinement for a year and then exiled to Siberia.

Here he met Georgi Plekhanov, the man who had introduced to Russia the socio-economic theories of a German Jewish philosopher named Karl Marx. By 1900, his exile over, Ulyanov launched the newspaper *Iskra* ("spark"). He experimented with various aliases and eventually settled on using his middle name together with a fictitious surname derived from the river Lena; he named himself Ilyich "Lenin."

Lenin, like very many other Russians, was captivated by the distant struggle of the small Boer *"nation of peasants"* against mighty Imperial ("Capitalist") Britain[3]. The very first issue of *Iskra*, which he published in Leipzig, Germany, featured two references to the Great Anglo-Boer War and he included many events in South African history in his *"Essayed Summary of World History Data after 1870."*

In 1903, his Bolshevik grouping was created from the split in the Russian Social Democratic Labour Party. One of the men who joined this organization was a certain Ioseb Besarionis dze Jughashvili from Georgia in the Caucasus. Jugashvili was known for his criminal conduct. This particularly unsavory creature would eventually take over the leadership of the Soviet Union after changing his name to Joseph Stalin. He would become one of the most ruthless mass murderers in human history.

While Lenin was in the process of assuming power in Russia in the Bolshevik Revolution, one of the world's earliest Communist Parties was in its formative stages in faraway South Africa. The International Socialist League of South Africa (ISL) dated from 1915 when it was formed from the left wing of the South African Labour Party.

In 1917, the ISL unconditionally supported the Bolshevik revolution in Russia. When Lenin formed the Communist International, better known as the Comintern, in 1919, the ISL promptly joined it. According to

Davidson et al[4] the Comintern dealt with its far flung member organizations via a vast secret network functioning under the guise of banks, industries, and trade companies, as well as youth, sports, women's, and community organizations. Secret schools such as the Communist University of Toilers of the East (KUTV) taught multiple disciplines relevant to the communist movement, from ideology to party building, military training, and subversion.

On 15 April 1920, a certain Mikhail Wolberg, a Russian expatriate, reported to the Comintern on his activities. He had been to South Africa as a visitor but had then elected to stay. He had opened a business representing manufacturers in South Africa and used it as a basis for political agitation. This is the oldest known[5] formal report to the Comintern on South African matters.

Fig. 19-2 Jughashvili (Stalin) and Ulyanov (Lenin)

In 1921, Lev Davidovich Bronstein, better known in history as Leon Trotsky, was all-powerful in the Soviet world. He asked David Ivon Jones in South Africa to respond to a questionnaire regarding the economic troubles in the United States and Europe and their bearing on South Africa. In his response dated 2 June 1921, Jones explained most instructively[6]:

"The economic crises that you mention in your questionnaire do not exist in South Africa as an independent phenomenon of its capitalist economy because there is neither the capital nor the slaves to subordinate it. [...]

"These native workers are a perfect material for the Socialist revolution. But they are all illiterate and for this reason they are out of reach of the Communist propaganda. Their mental awakening demands educational institutions of either Capitalism, or Communism – whoever will be the first."

On 1 August 1921, the South African Communist Party (SACP) was formally created[7] from the following constituent parts; its leadership dominated by Jewish immigrants from Latvia and Lithuania and a few immigrant Far Left British socialists:

1. the International Socialist League of South Africa, which convened the conference;

2. the Poalei-Zion, linked to the international Marxist Jewish organization of the same name;

3. the Jewish Socialist Party (Cape);

4. the Marxian Club (Durban);

5. the Communist Party (Cape), which had failed to get accredited with the Comintern; and

6. individuals from the South African Labour Party.

The Social Democratic Federation (Cape Province) and Social Democratic Party (Durban) rejected the conditions of membership stated by the Comintern.

Initially, the party was almost exclusively white, being dominated by the people who populated the above six organizations and by Jewish immigrants from the Baltic States – an ethnic influence that would remain with the organization. This soon led to strife in the party when this "old guard" tried to limit the powers and influence of new black members. Several members were sent to Russia to be trained at the KUTV.

The party was allowed to function legally in South Africa and soon attracted attention. Its attempt to hijack the miner's strike of 1922 brought it a certain degree of public notoriety and led to the imprisonment of a number of senior members. The party remained little more than an irritation for many years, but systematically its influence grew among the black population of the country.

Lenin took a particular interest in the developments leading to the Rand revolt in South Africa[8]. This interest of the Russian leadership in South Africa would grow systematically stronger for the following 60 years, waning only during Stalin's murderous purges. The Soviet regime would become preoccupied with South Africa, escalating its involvement into sporadic conventional warfare from 1975 onward. In 1927, James Laguma became the first Black South African member of the SACP to visit the Executive Committee of the Comintern (ECCI) in Russia. On his very next visit to the ECCI in the same year[9], he brought with him Josiah Gumede, the President of the African National Congress (ANC; founded 1912), the later governing party of the Republic of South Africa. In future, Black Nationalism and Communism would be bedmates.

American Communists and South Africa

In the late 1920s, the American Communist Party started playing a role in South Africa via the Soviet Union and the Comintern. The involvement of American Communists in South Africa before WWII has recently been revealed by the excellent work of Davidson, Filatova, Gorodnov, and Johns[10] in the actual archives of the Comintern.

Harry Haywood, a prominent African-American Communist was deeply involved in formulating the SACP strategy, basing his approach on what the Soviets called the "Negro Problem." In Moscow, the husband and wife team of William Patterson and Louise Alone Thompson worked on African affairs, then synonymous with South Africa, misleading folks in the United States to believe they were working on a movie. It is to be doubted whether the American authorities ever comprehended just how deeply this family functioned within the Soviet system. Thompson died in 1999 without her Soviet involvement becoming known. There was also George Clark. At least, that was his name in the U.S.A. In Russia, he was Georgy Samuilovich Shkliar. He was sent to South Africa in 1930. The American Communist Leader, Frances Waldron, better known under the alias of "Eugene Dennis," spent several months in South Africa in 1932 and reported[11] extensively on his work to the Comintern on 22 July 1932.

In the mid 1960s, Martin Luther King and Bobby Kennedy would continue (See Chapter 20) where the Comintern had pointed the way. The author prefers to believe they did not know the philosophical company they happened to be keeping in this venture. Nevertheless, both groups, some 40 years apart, would attempt to develop political capital by linking problems in South Africa and the United States that had nothing in common but the skin color of the parties involved.

During 1927-28, the Comintern came up with a goal for the Communist effort in South Africa. The country was to be[12] a "Negro republic independent from Great Britain" with "autonomy for the national white minorities." The SACP would struggle to interpret this concept for most of the next decade. All this theoretical gerrymandering of concepts ensured that the SACP remained confused and relatively ineffectual up to WWII. Many of those connected with the SACP would eventually die in Stalin's horrific purges. Meanwhile, racial conflict was tearing at the party. By the early 1930s, the indigenous black members of the SACP complained bitterly that the Party had become mainly a white man's affair, almost completely in the hands of the Jewish Worker's Club[13]. Meanwhile, the white members were hardly representative of the general white population. This much we can conclude from the testimony of David Ivon Jones[14], a founder member of the International Socialist League of South Africa, who referred to himself as a *"white colonist"* and suggested that, *"for some of us, the only tie with South Africa is the Communist movement itself."*

The mere fact that he saw himself as a "colonist" says all that needs to be said. As his surname suggests, he was indeed born in Wales and not in Africa, wherein he differs from some 10 generations of the ancestors of Kotie Myburgh, the author's grandfather, who was his contemporary. Jones' allegiance was quite obvious. Like the later master spy, Kim Philby, he would die in Russia and be buried there. He is today a great hero of the South African Communist Party, an organization that does not contest democratic elections, but whose members permeate the government of the country; a fact of which most Americans appear to be ignorant.

James Barry Munnik Hertzog

In 1924, Jan Smuts' own Afrikaner people finally turned on him and voted out his South African Party government. The new Prime Minister was James Barry Munnik Hertzog. He had been Leader of the opposition National Party in Parliament since the time of the 1914 rebellion. Like Smuts, he was a Boer War military commander. Like Smuts, he was of lesser impact than any one of the Glorious Trio. As a judge, he was essentially the Orange Free State equivalent of Jan Smuts, who had been Transvaal Attorney-General at the time of the Boer War. He had not been part of the 1914 Rebellion and had steered an independent course in that feud, though most would take it as read that his sympathies lay more towards the rebels.

Hertzog was known for his iron will and ability to stand for a principle, no matter how politically dangerous. Where Smuts had been trained as an attorney in Britain, Hertzog had been trained in the Netherlands and had gone on to study in France and Germany. While Smuts saw South Africa as a critical cog in the British Empire, Hertzog shared none of Smuts' admiration of matters British. Hertzog made no secret of his dream of independence for South Africa from the fetters of the British crown.

The period that followed Hertzog's entry into office was charac-terized by three factors:

1. a constant drive towards independence from Britain;

2. the Great Depression and its soul-grinding poverty among white people, particularly Afrikaners; and

3. a rise in Afrikaner Nationalism

Fig. 19-3 *James Barry Munnik Hertzog*

Hertzog steered a course that might be called pragmatic nationalism. He wanted the Afrikaner properly recognized in the country, but did not see any merit in harming the "English" constituency in the process. In the world of the 21st Century, he might be seen as akin to moderate French Québécois viewing themselves as an integral part of Canada but insisting that their culture and rights as a separate group be protected.

Initially, his view of the future was that of a South Africa in which there were "Two Streams," one for "Afrikaners" and one for "English." This was based on his perception that many British-descended residents of South Africa were in the country *"only for what they could take from it"* and that they remained "loyal to Home" rather than to South Africa; certainly many referred to Britain as *"home,"* though they had never been there. Later, in the 1930s, he would state his position quite succinctly[15]:

Our fight was not to obtain domination, but equality. Let those who yesterday wanted equality and today demand more remember this. Our word of yesterday is our word today and circumstances cannot change it.

Hertzog's credo was *"South Africa First."* He was vividly clear that South Africa would one day have its independence from the Monarchist Britain, *"even if it takes a thousand years."* To his one side was Smuts, by now a devoted Empire man and respected international statesman. To his other side, but within his own National Party, were the more rigid Afrikaner nationalists under D.F. Malan who cared little about other groups. Hertzog's was the voice of moderation in the country and it would remain so for most of the 1920s and 1930s. By 1926, Hertzog and Canada's McKenzie King finally managed to push Britain to issue the Balfour Declaration of 1926 in terms of which Great Britain recognized that the Dominions were[16]:

"...autonomous communities within the British Empire, equal in status, in no way subordinate to one another in any aspect of their domestic or external affairs, though united by a common allegiance to the Crown and freely associated as members of the British Commonwealth of Nations."

This represented for Hertzog a step along the road to true independence. A few years later, he pushed Parliament in Cape Town to accept the Statute of Westminster of 11 December 1931, which removed the dominance of British Law over ordinary laws made in the Dominions. This arcane legislative dominance device rested on the so-called Colonial Laws Validity Act of 1865, which granted British laws dominance if a "Colonial Law" conflicted with British Law. The Statute of Westminster repealed this disabling 1865 act, finally giving the British Dominions totally independent lawmaking powers in respect of ordinary laws. The major parties affected by this Statute were South Africa, Canada, Australia, New Zealand, Newfoundland, and the Irish Free State. Not all accepted immediately and in New Zealand, Canada, and Australia constitutional control remained with Britain until respectively 1947, 1982, and 1986. Newfoundland never adopted the Statute and elected to revert to British control until becoming a province of Canada in 1949.

Hertzog's attitude toward Britain is best summed up by an address he made at Smithfield in the Orange Free State on 5 September 1937. Referring to the fact that he had fought British Imperialism since he had been 14 years old and had now developed more friendly feelings since the Statute of Westminster, he said[17]:

"England has in an honorable and dignified manner made amends for her mistakes in the past."

Despite all his achievements, and possibly because of his experience in the Great Boer War, Hertzog could not bring himself to believe that an actual fully independent republic, like the United States, was attainable for his people. This particular dream belonged to his hardliner lieutenant, D.F. Malan. There was great appreciation among Afrikaners for the fact that Hertzog had made it possible for their children to be taught in their mother tongue again, and that Afrikaans was now an official language. For the rank and file Afrikaner, though, the Statute of Westminster was not independence. Like Americans, they wanted no king.

The Great Depression

When the contagion of the Great Depression of 1929 reached South Africa, it struck hardest at the level of the ordinary working white man, most of whom were Afrikaners. This soon developed into a major problem on two fronts. On the one hand, there was the very real hardship and need for social aid and economic growth, but on the other was the fact that it created a ripe field for political agitation.

The South African Communist Party attempted to recruit among the Afrikaners but never really received any significant support. The image of the Bolsheviks horrified the rank and file Afrikaner, eventually making the latter into probably the staunchest and most consistent anti-Soviet grouping on the planet. The horrors under Stalin sealed the fate of the Communist philosophy in Afrikaner minds. It was not so much the socialist philosophy as the total disrespect for religion and human life that created in the staunchly Calvinistic Afrikaner nothing but utter revulsion. Afrikaners saw Communism as the "Prime Evil."

It did not occur to poor Afrikaners to make their displeasure at their situation known by stealing en masse from their more fortunate countrymen, burning down their own schools, killing anyone whom they considered their oppressor, bombing the infrastructure of the country, or burning alive anyone among their own who did not agree with them. Bombing civilian apartment buildings and public restaurants frequented by schoolchildren, or mining farm roads similarly did not occur to them either. Such acts would have been considered utterly insane, inhuman and, more than anything else, un-Christian.

Their Judeo-Christian value system was that of any poor Midwest American in Dust Bowl times.

 ## Nexus Familia 81: The Childhood of our Parents

In the West Cape: The Bassons

On 26 August 1920, a baby boy is born in the Southwestern Cape town of Worcester to Magistrate Matthys Basson and his wife, Helen Burger. Soon after, the young man is baptized as Arnold Loubser Basson, bearing the first name of the original founder of the Basson Family in South Africa (*NF1*). "Nols" or "Bassie," as Arnold will become known, is my father-in-law. He grows up in Worcester and he takes it as read that he will follow in the footsteps of his father and become a small town magistrate. The family strongly supports Jan Smuts in whatever he does. This is because the Southwest Cape people, as British Subjects, were largely insulated from the Boer War horrors of 20 years earlier, and because they recognize in the present Prime Minister, Smuts, a man of some vision from their own district, even though he had fought as a Transvaal Boer War general.

In the Transvaal: The Callanans

A thousand miles away in Waterval Boven in the Transvaal, Michael Charles Callanan and Neve Constance Milward (*NF80*) are blessed with a baby girl on 30 May 1924. Margaret Caroline is named for Neve's late mother, the very Afrikaans Margaretha Johanna Jordaan, and for the intrepid Caroline Misselbrook, Michael's very English mother, who dies in that same year at the age of 86. "Molly," as the baby girl will become known, will one day be the author's mother-in-law. When Molly reaches school-going age, the family moves to the western suburbs of Pretoria. When she turns 13, she attends Pretoria Girl's High School.

In the South Cape: The Booyens family

On 11 April 1924, in the Dutch Reformed Church of De Rust in the Little Karoo, Annie Booyens (*NF80*) is attended by her parents when her baby boy is baptized "Herman Stefanus." He is named for his Bosman father who has deserted her, never to be heard from again, leaving Annie with a photograph and his name in the church books of De Rust. In view of the father's willful desertion, the boy is baptized with his mother's surname. The blond-haired and blue-eyed young Herman will become the author's father.

Fig. 19-4 *A male ostrich in the Little Karoo guarding its mate*

Herman's grandfather and grandmother, Pieter and Bettie Booyens, take on the role of raising him while Annie finds a job in nearby Oudtshoorn. The first 9 years of Herman's life are spent on the farms *Olienhoutskloof* (Olivewood Gorge) and *Fonteine* (Fountains) at the northern foot of the *Kammanassie* Mountain. He attends elementary school in the nearby town of Dysselsdorp. On the farm, he learns everything there is to know about ostriches, because he is now a rather unique kind of person; an ostrichherd.

In 1933, Pieter moves with his family from the Rietvlei area where the family has been for many decades. He settles just south of the little town of Calitzdorp, near his eldest son. This is bitterly dry pebble country. The farmers eking out a living in this barren land are subject to the vagaries of the inconsistent Gamka River. It is a hard life; very hard. He regularly fetches stray donkeys out of the *Rooiberg* (Red Mountain). It is on these trips that he discovers that there are "wild horses" on the mountain, but no one wants to believe him. More than 40 years later local conservationists will create the Gamkaberg Nature Reserve especially for the remaining 32 of the near extinct mountain zebra on this mountain. This rare threatened species now occurs only on the *Rooiberg* and on one other mountain plateau in South Africa.

When Herman reaches the age of 13, he is sent off to the Oakdale Agricultural School at Riversdal near the South Coast. Upon leaving school, he joins his mother's brothers, Pieter's first two sons, in growing alfalfa for seed purposes along the unreliable Gamka River.

In the Cape Midlands: The Myburghs

On 30 May 1929, just as the Great Depression breaks over the Western World, Kotie and Bettie Myburgh (*NF80*) have their third daughter. Nicolaas Grobler (*NF78*), Bettie's father, has lost all faith that there will be a second son to be named after him. He has used his not insignificant influence to force Kotie and Bettie into warping the Dutch naming convention. The daughter is named Nicola Elizabeth. Her first name is taken from Nicolaas, the second name being that of her mother. Nicolaas thereby takes from his daughter, Pretty Bettie, her right to name her own third daughter after herself. Ironically the daughter, who becomes known as "Nickie," will grow up to be the spitting image of Pretty Bettie.

Nickie is the author's mother, and will grow up in merciless grinding poverty; a true Afrikaner Child of the Great Depression. Some 18 months later she is joined by a younger sister, named Renschie Maria. By the Dutch naming convention, the child is named after the second oldest sister of her father, in turn named for Renske Maria "Renschie" of Roode Taaijbosch (*NF66*), Nickie's great grandmother.

As the Great Depression ravages the civilized world over the next few years, the struggling Afrikaners are pushed to the bottom of the scale of Western existence. Kotie has always left his monthly salary in the hands of his employer who was supposed to put it in the bank for him. However, it is at this juncture that Kotie discovers that the man has gone bankrupt. Herewith Kotie's job has disappeared, and so has his life's savings, entrusted—as he sees it—"*to an Englishman.*"

In a most bitter twist of fate, Kotie is struck down with trachoma right at this time, and goes blind. He cannot fend for his family. Eventually, via the help of the doctor in town, Kotie is sent to Port Elizabeth by train to have his eyes seen to in the big city of the Eastern Province. Pretty Bettie accompanies him with little Renschie on her arm. Kotie, the Poor White, is now a "patient of the state."

When Kotie returns with a cane and bandaged eyes, the family is left with little more than just the roof over their heads, but at least they have that much; a pathetic little house with a flat corrugated iron roof that leaks like a sieve. In fact, during a violent thunderstorm, one of the walls collapses onto the bed vacated by members of the family mere moments before. The family is now dependent on the mercies of the state and the church. It is over this period, during the southern autumn of 1933, that little Renschie develops whooping cough and complications set in. On 24 May 1933, Renschie dies.

When the lady from the Afrikaans Christian Women's Society appears at the gate some hours later with a piece of candle as a contribution to the family in their time of need, Kotie's father, Albert, freezes her at the gate with a penetrating stare and tells her:

"Just go away! ...The child is dead!"

After this day, Pretty Bettie will never be quite the same again.

The family is now in desperate straits. The barefooted Nickie goes with her two older sisters when they are sent off to the butcher in town to ask for meat on their government voucher for the poor. They are given the worst grade of meat the butcher has. But for the leaky corrugated iron roof over their heads, the family is essentially destitute. One year later Nicolaas Johannes Grobler, Nickie's maternal grandfather and our link to all the horrors of the old Cape Eastern Frontier, dies at the age of almost 80.

Life has dealt Pretty Bettie a miserable hand. Her husband is essentially blind, her youngest daughter and her father have just died and she has four other children to look after, the oldest of whom is just 14. Our Myburgh family has finally reached its lowest ebb.

During the Great Boer War, some of the Canadian soldiers said that winter in the northeast of the Cape Colony and in the Orange Free State was somehow the coldest they had ever experienced in their lives. The winter wind slices through marrow and soul in this 4,000-foot high country. It is over this period of the 1930's that the young Nickie freezes in winter, having just the thinnest of knitted sweater to wear for warmth. There is no money for fancy things like buying handkerchiefs. These are made at home, and so are the shoes and most of the clothes. They grow vegetables in the backyard in summer, but are beholden to the government and its vouchers for anything in the nature of meat, flour, sugar, or coffee.

In the middle of 1935, Nickie goes to school for the first time. This is in the so-called "Little School," covering the first three grades. The particular school was previously known as the "Poor School." Nickie has saved every penny that she could scrape together in her young life. She now has exactly £1 to put into a Post Office Savings Account that is kept for all school children to foster saving. At home, Kotie desperately fills in all the forms to try and obtain free hand-me-down school books for the children while Bettie struggles to put together clothes for her daughters to avoid the worst of the embarrassment at school.

In order to try and raise some money, Nickie is sent out after school to sell flowers door-to-door. But this is still the aftermath of the Great Depression, and flowers are not high on the agenda of the poorest white people on Earth. Neither the clothes nor the flowers entirely succeed, and human pride is trampled underfoot.

This period of grinding dust bowl poverty and simultaneous loss of life in the family will leave a deep imprint that will still engender tears in the family in the 21st century. The peculiar and malicious misrepresentation by the later Western Media of the Afrikaner as a supposedly rich nation with "slave estates" will leave this Calvinistic and much tried family altogether incredulous.

—*End Nexus Familia*

Afrikaner Nationalism

In 1935, Hertzog formed a coalition government with Smuts, the latter becoming Deputy Prime Minister. This eventually led to the forming of a new party that became known as the United Party. It is at this point that DF Malan and his right wing of the National Party parted ways with JBM Hertzog. DF Malan reconstituted the National Party, now the official Opposition, and moved it decidedly more to the right. It became the voice of conservative Afrikaners. He styled himself "the voice of the Poor Afrikaner," and painted Jan Smuts as "*England's pet Boer*" and Hertzog as a "*sell-out*." Given the atrocious economic condition of the rank and file Afrikaner, Malan's message easily found traction.

In 1918, Malan had formed a secret organization along the lines of the Free Masons, calling it the Afrikaner Broederbond. This organization was to be dedicated to economically and politically uplifting the Afrikaner and protecting his position in the country. The Broederbond now arranged a commemoration of the 1838 Great Trek – the Symbolic Oxwagon Trek. At first, it was met with scorn, but as the wagons and people in period dress made their way from the Cape northward, it slowly but systematically galvanized Afrikaners. It awoke a national spirit that people did not know they had.

This was the critical point at which the country started to turn decidedly in the wrong direction, dividing people rather than uniting them. While it was still possible to design a future in which Black South Africans could participate positively, the political direction was to actively exclude them and to dogmatically subdivide the white population into "*Real Afrikaners*" and "*The English.*"

Forgotten was the fact that many English speaking South Africans of European extraction felt their allegiance as being to South Africa in the first place and not to Britain. Many of them were of German extraction, but simply spoke English as a first language. The original concept of "Afrikaner" as someone of European descent who professed allegiance to Africa rather than Europe, was being adulterated. Forgotten was the fact that it was now more than four generations since the British Settlers had landed.

For Molly Callanan, the author's mother-in-law-to-be, it had been her great grandfather, William Misselbrook (*NF41*), who had been the soldier-immigrant in 1818 and her great great grandfather, Richard Bowles (*NF41*) who had immigrated as a retired soldier in 1820. Forgotten was the fact that "Englishmen" such as Leech, Parker, Joyce, and Biggar had fought bravely on the Trekker side at Blood River. Forgotten were the shared challenges of the old Eastern Cape Frontier. The parents and grandparents of many, such as our Callanans (*NF73*), had fought bravely on Boer side against Britain in the Great Boer War. Forgotten were Mike Hands, as well as Percy Wyndall and Edgar Duncker, or Jack Baxter, all of whom[18] had fought alongside Deneys Reitz in that war. In fact, the British had executed[19] Jack Baxter as a rebel (*NF78*). By rights, he should have been considered a martyr for the Afrikaner cause. Their descendants were now all somehow considered "English" because they did not speak Afrikaans at home.

As Europe marched inexorably towards another World War, White South Africa was divided largely along lines of language. The word "Afrikaner" had now come to mean only those white people who spoke Afrikaans as first language, and had lost the more inclusive sense of the North American parallel of

"Amerikaner." It is true that the Afrikaner had been horribly abused by Britain, but it is unfortunate indeed that the democratic politics of the country now divided along such nationalistic lines.

Clearly, the legacy of British abuses in South Africa ran very deep indeed, particularly in the Orange Free State and the Northeastern Cape – the two areas that had experienced the worst extremes of British human rights abuses in the Anglo-Boer War. The future would show that a major opportunity to accommodate the aspirations of Black people in Southern Africa was lost over this period while White democratic politics was fixated on independence from the British Crown, by far the lesser of the challenges, given that the British Empire was already collapsing in any case.

Human Rights elsewhere in the West

It seems entirely appropriate to stop for a moment and consider the state of human rights and franchise legislation elsewhere in the West at this point prior to WWII. Some of the countries that would have the most to say about South Africa two decades later were still embroiled in racial and franchise struggles of their own with decidedly less moral justification than South Africa.

In Canada, the franchise had been made universal in 1920, but aboriginal people and "minorities"[20] were still pointedly excluded. Over the same period as Hertzog and Malan were struggling with their policies the matter of franchise was again considered in Canada. The Canadian Dominions Elections Act of 1938 retained race as the basis for exclusion of citizens from the franchise. The Province of British Columbia specifically excluded Indians, Hindus, Japanese or Chinese people from the provincial elections to be held in 1940. Aboriginal people were nowhere near having voting rights.

Fig. 19-5 Separate Public Amenities for Black Americans in Durham county, N.C. – 1940

In the United States, the collection of Jim Crow laws was still in place and effectively excluded Black Americans from voting. In both Canada and the United States, as well as in Australia and New Zealand, white people were the unassailable majority of the population, thereby reducing the matter of franchise to a mere moral one, rather than a matter of survival as a nation, as was the case in South Africa.

Discrimination against Black Americans was vivid. Signs abounded forcing Black Americans, termed "Colored" at the time, to use separate public amenities. These signs would remain deep into the 1960s, even in the "North."

It is in this environment that a young black lawyer named Pauli Murray grew up in Durham County, North Carolina. She will enter our story again.

World War II – East Africa

At noon on Sunday 3 September 1939, Britain's ultimatum to Hitler expired and the country was formally at war with Germany. The very next morning James Barry Munnik Hertzog stood up in the South African parliament and moved that South Africa, like the United States, remain neutral, but honor the obligations toward Britain regarding the naval base at Simonstown. To Hertzog, it was a matter of whether South African interests were at stake in the war and he could conceive of no way in which a German invasion of Poland was the business of South Africa. The iniquities of the Treaty of Versailles were a matter for the conscience of France and Britain and the German designs in Poland could be traced directly to that treaty. He had warned the British government repeatedly about the long term implications of the treaty[21] and wanted to know why Britain was not now declaring war against Russia, which had also invaded Poland along with Germany. Hertzog knew only too well that there would be a political price to be paid in South Africa for involvement in the war in support of Britain. The 1914 Rebellion had shown that very clearly.

Fig. 19-6 Emperor Haile Selassie, "Descendant of Solomon"

Jan Smuts, without having discussed matters with his United Party leader Hertzog, stood up and moved that South Africa should declare war on Germany as this was the "honorable" thing to do and that it was in keeping with the position of the country in the British Commonwealth. The vote was 80 for war and 67 against. Hertzog felt that this did not represent the view of the voting public—the next election would eventually bear him out on this—and therefore asked the Governor General, Sir Patrick Duncan, to dissolve parliament and call an election. However, this representative of the King was not going to allow a British victory in the South African parliament to be snatched from his hands and turned down the request. Hertzog resigned the next day and Jan Smuts was the war leader in South Africa. Hertzog had discovered the hard way that his country was not really independent.

At first, parliament insisted that South Africans would only fight on African soil. South Africa was thereupon assigned the task of clearing the Italians out of Ethiopia and Somalia and the Vichy French out of Madagascar. What ensued in East Africa was the "War of a Hundred Days," during which the South Africans, with some support from other countries like Britain, Nigeria, Ghana, Rhodesia and Kenya, pushed the Italians out of Somalia and Ethiopia, forcing the Duke of Savoy to surrender. They thereupon returned the oldest independent country on earth, Ethiopia, to its "rightful leader," Emperor Haile Selassie.

It was South African aircraft, South African trucks, South African artillery, and South African soldiers who bore the brunt of the conventional war effort. Indeed, the diminutive black Emperor owed his position entirely to South Africa. Without the help of the South African soldiers, engineers, and materiel he would never have recovered his country. The majority of these soldiers were Dutch/French/German-descended Afrikaners, such as the author's family.

 ## Nexus Familia 82: World War II

The Booyens family

In the South Cape, my father's young uncle, Ben Booyens, volunteers for the South African Army and is sent to Egypt. The South African Army fights its way through Ethiopia and then moves on to Egypt. Ben takes part in the great drive against Rommel to the west through the Cyrenaica Desert of Egypt and Lybia.

By the time the U.S. Army makes its Torch landings, the air support it gets is often South African. In fact, there are eleven squadrons of the South African Air Force (SAAF) in the skies over North Africa, and only 5 American ones. This is the main theater of operations for the South Africans. Between April 1941 and May 1943, the South African Air Force destroys 342 enemy aircraft in North Africa in just on 34,000 sorties. A SAAF strike sinks Rommel's last oil tanker and he is eventually driven from Africa. Our Basson family is among the SAAF in the skies over North Africa (See below).

At this point, Parliament approves South African military service outside Africa and Ben Booyens is duly shipped to Italy to witness the American troops struggle on the beach at Anzio, south of Rome. The American and Canadian troops get used to the tank-busting South African Spitfires that support them from the sky as well as the 6th South African tank brigade, which ultimately is the first Allied unit to roll into the historic city of Florence. The Americans and Canadians probably mistake the South Africans for British most of the time. They are hard to tell apart, as the SAAF roundels look like the British ones, except that the dot in the middle is orange instead of red.

In Calitzdorp in the Little Karoo, my father, Herman, wants to become a pilot. He has seen the Commonwealth Pilot Training program at nearby Oudtshoorn. In fact, there are no fewer than 34 different Commonwealth Pilot Training bases in South Africa at this time. Within the British Commonwealth, only Canada has more. However, Herman's hopes are dashed when, while chopping wood, a thorn from a sweet thorn tree[22] penetrates his eye damaging it for life. It renders him medically unfit to serve.

Bassie Basson

By early 1940, Arnold "Bassie" Basson from Worcester in the West Cape, my father-in-law-to-be, is a young employee of the Government at the outpost of Sterkspruit, near the border of Basotholand, far from his West Cape family home. Sterkspruit is a government administration post on a piece of highland at the foot of the Drakensberg. It is occupied by a branch of amaXhosa people who are disconnected from the rest of their tribe further southeast. A group of the small amaHlubi nation also lives here, along with a few Ba'Sotho. Bassie is a young legal clerk in the administration of justice within the so-called Bantu Administration. The place and the job are both a disappointment to him.

1. Fighting Rommel

At Sterkspruit on 17 June 1940, the 19-year old Bassie volunteers for the South African Air Force and enrolls in the flying training program. He receives basic flight training outside Pretoria and at Kimberley, flying Tiger Moth, Hawker Hart, Hawker Hartebeest, and Curtiss Mohawk aircraft. In April 1942, he is on the ship *Empire Trooper* on his way along the east coast of Africa to Egypt to become a member of 7 Squadron of the South African Air Force. Here the squadron is equipped with already obsolete Hurricane Mk.1 tank buster aircraft.

Fig. 19-7 Flight-Lieutenant Arnold "Bassie" Basson" (ca. 1940)

Fig. 19-8 Bassie Basson and his captured German Messerschmitt Bf.109F "White 6"

They are sent to Haifa in Palestine, but are quietly pulled back to Egypt when someone in authority remembers they are supposed to only serve in Africa. Here 7 Squadron comes into contact with Heinz Joachim Marseilles' Jagdgeschwader 27 *Afrika*. Rommel's experienced pilots nearly wipe them from the sky. The older Hurricane Mk. 1 is not built for the hot and dusty Sahara and is simply no match for the Messerschmitt Bf.109 in experienced hands. The remnants of 7 Squadron are withdrawn. Bassie is one of the survivors.

On 9 September 1942, the squadron is re-equipped with Hurricane MkIID tank busting aircraft and pair up with 6 Squadron of the R.A.F. to become the well-known "Flying Can-openers" of the Desert Air Force. On 23-24 October 1942, they are heavily involved in the Battle of El Alamein in which Rommel is defeated and driven back towards Tunisia. 7 Squadron harries Rommel all the way along his retreat. This is the first major victory for the Allies in WWII. It is this event that leads Churchill to utter his famous quote:

"Now this is not the end. It is not even the beginning of the end. But it is, perhaps, the end of the beginning."

Fig. 19-9 White 6" in the South African Museum of Military History

During this campaign, 7 Squadron restores to serviceability a captured Messerschmitt Bf109F, "White 6" of no. 6 Staffel of I Gruppe, Jagdgeschwader 27 *Afrika*. Bassie qualifies on it and is very proud of his iconic aircraft, so distinctively German but clearly painted with SAAF roundels. This aircraft will eventually be flown to South Africa to participate in air shows to shore up morale and ultimately find its way into the South African Museum of Military History in Johannesburg where it will still be proudly on display in the 21st century, testimony to German engineering and the fighting ability of 7 Squadron S.A.A.F. at El Alamein.

In the first week of September 1943, Matthys Michielse Basson, at Somerset-West near Cape Town in South Africa, hears that the Allied troops, including the 6th South African Armored Division, have landed in Italy. On 8 September, he hears that Italy has signed an armistice. He is elated. However, on 12 October 1943 a telegram arrives at his home. It informs him that his only son, the 23-year old Flight-Lieutenant Arnold Loubser Basson, is "missing in action" on the island of "Cos, Italy." Matthys does not even know where this place called Cos is, yet it has apparently taken the life of his only son. This while he thought Bassie was safely in Egypt after Rommel's departure.

The telegram is followed by a formal letter three days later, on 15 October. It reads:

"IT IS WITH DEEP REGRET THAT I HAVE TO CONFIRM MY TELEGRAM OF 12 OCTOBER 1943 WHICH READ:

WRC.79/19806
DEPARTMENT OF DEFENCE ANNOUNCES WITH DEEP REGRET THAT YOUR SON 9336V LIEUTENANT ARNOLD LOUBSER BASSON WAS GIVEN AS MISSING ON 3 OCTOBER ON ISLAND COS STOP....

PS. YOUR LOCAL DEFENCE FORCE LIAISSON COMMITTEE WISHES TO ASSURE YOU THAT, IF YOU EXPERIENCE ANY DIFFICULTY WITH RESPECT TO THE FACT THAT YOUR SON IS MISSING, THEY WOULD GLADLY BE OF ASSISTANCE.
P.P.S. CABLE JUST NOW RECEIVED READS THAT YOUR SON IS SAFE AND WELL ON CASTEL-ROSSO ISLAND ITALY. CLASSIFICATION REMAINS "MISSING" UNTIL HE ARRIVES IN AFRICA"

Behind this letter is quite a story, and for this we return to the first week of September 1943:

2. The Dodecanese Adventure

On 3 September 1943, the Allies land on mainland Italy. On the same day, Italian military leaders sign an armistice with the Allies. It is formally announced five days later. No. 7 Wing of the South African Air Force herewith becomes the first Western Allied air power physically based in continental Europe. On paper, both my uncle Ben Booyens and my father-in-law Bassie Basson are headed for Italy, but none other than Winston Churchill will intervene.

On September 10, 1943, six pilots of 7 Squadron of the S.A.A.F under Captain H.E. Kirby and a handful of ground crew are secretly dispatched to the island of Cyprus in the Eastern Mediterranean. They are told to "travel light with clothing and rations for two weeks." They are told further flyers are to follow later. Arriving on Cyprus, they learn that they are to be part of Churchill's latest ill-considered secret plan, Operation "Accolade." Churchill has always had a preoccupation with the Dodecanese islands; ever since his debacle at Gallipoli in WWI. Now he is going to try the Bosphorus again by attempting to take the key Greek Dodecanese Islands off the coast of Turkey; this right under the noses of the Germans, who control the Aegean Sea. The focus is to be on Cos, Leros and Samos. Using Cos as base, the Allies are then to force the Germans out of Rhodes and Crete and open the Bosphorus so as to supply the Russians.

The Italians are in occupation of some of the islands. Others are garrisoned by German troops. The Luftwaffe is stationed on Rhodes. A poorly equipped Italian garrison of 4,000 is in command of the island of Cos with its fortress of the Knights of St. John, who were stationed there in the year 1306. And it is here that 7 Squadron is to head on an adventure into air space controlled by the Luftwaffe in a theater that Germany can hardly afford to lose at this time.

Eisenhower wants nothing to do with a venture his American staff considers to be classic British diversionary behavior, so no support will be forthcoming from that quarter. He has instructed that in no way is the Dodecanese "adventure" to influence the conduct of the rest of the war in the Mediterranean. He views it as a classic mistake in the making, but Churchill will not be dissuaded.

The men are intrigued but worried. The British have dreamed up this plan to send them into an impossible situation where they are utterly outnumbered by a very competent enemy. Moreover, the British planners have neglected to supply them with vital oxygen bottles for their Spitfires. This means they will be forced to stay below 15,000 foot to retain consciousness and alertness, and will be easy prey for any possible Messerschmitt 109s diving at them from high altitude out of the sun. They will also have no RADAR coverage to warn them of approaching Luftwaffe aircraft. Anti-aircraft protection will be extremely limited. And, last but not least, they will have very little fuel and will only be able to do highly selected patrols. They shall have to make do with what can be flown in through German-controlled skies.

In reality, Winston Churchill has sent a tiny handful of South African pilots on a suicide mission against the entrenched Luftwaffe.

*****

The process starts with the British Special Boat Service quietly occupying the Italian held island of Castelrosso, 2 miles off the south coast of Turkey while leaflets are dropped on Cos asking for assistance. A British intelligence officer and radio operator are parachuted in to make contact with the Italian commander and solicit his support. On the 11th of September, the Luftwaffe, concerned about the potential role of its former allies, attacks the Italian facilities on Cos and destroys two of their four aircraft at Marmari airfield outside Antimachia. While thirty-eight B-24 Liberator heavy bombers attack Rhodes to draw the Luftwaffe attention away, 48 British commandos go ashore on Cos on 13 September. On the same day, the first 7 Squadron S.A.A.F. flyers arrive at Marmari in their Spitfire Mk.V aircraft, fitted with long-range fuel tanks. The next day, they are joined by their squadron leader, Major Corrie van Vliet, and some more squadron officers, along with two R.A.F Beaufighters. The crews of the latter are to set up a radio station. Over the next several days the British will send a total of 1600 men, as well as some light anti-aircraft weapons that can be transported by air.

And so it is that, on the clear sunny afternoon of 17 September 1943, a flight of German Ju52 transports is making its way across the shimmering Aegean Sea, its Ju88 escorts far ahead and out of position. The next moment two Spitfires with prominent blue, white, and orange roundels appear from nowhere out of the sun. Smoke and flame erupt from one of the ponderous transports before the Germans can react and it plunges into the tranquil Aegean. This is the start of the Battle for the Dodecanese.

The very next day, a solitary Ju88 is found prowling around and is dispatched by Ray Burl and Lt. Fischer of 7 Squadron. However, it is likely that the pilot has managed to get a warning message off to base before falling in the ocean.

Retaliation is as savage as what it is swift. In the early morning of 19 September 1943, a lone Heinkel 111 circles Antimachia in the pre-dawn darkness. It drops a flare and a single bomb. Just after sunrise a flight of Messerschmitt Bf109G6 fighters from IV Gruppe of Jagdgeschwader 27 *Afrika* (JG27) comes winging low over the sea, sweeps in at treetop height and strafes the Spitfires parked in the open. The makeshift airfield has no RADAR warning and no anti-aircraft protection. IV Gruppe will later claim 5 Spitfire kills on this raid[23]. Next comes a low-level bombing and strafing run by Ju88s.

Fig. 19-10 Tank-buster emblem of 7 Sqn. S.A.A.F. during WWII with its isiZulu motto of "Kill the Wizards"

Meanwhile, one of the 7 Squadron flyers, Lt. I.M. Seel, has managed to chase a Bf109G6 right down almost to sea level. His eight Browning machine guns send a torrent of lead into the German plane, which goes down immediately. However, as Seel pulls up out of the high-speed chase, his plane suddenly just spins off a climbing turn and crashes into the ground in full sight of his comrades on the ground. The assumption is that the infamous Spitfire carburettor problem has taken a brave man's life. Unlike the German Bf109, the Spitfire has no fuel injection and tends to falter from fuel starvation in a high-g climb.

The place is now a total mess and the runway is cratered beyond usability. However, when the Germans disappear over the horizon, the engineers rush out and start fixing the runway. The aircraft are patched up as best possible. Work starts immediately on creating an alternative landing field at Lampi on the northern tip of the island. By the next day, the 20th, a landing strip of some sorts is ready for use.

On 23 September, a congratulatory note arrives from the British Secretary of State, reading[24]:

"We have been following the work of your squadrons. Particular congratulations to your Spitfires on the brilliant exploit of shooting down seven enemy aircraft over Kos coast yesterday."

To address the impudent challenge of these "Engländer" on Cos, Göring has sent to the island of Argos the very best of Germany: the famous Jagdgeschwader 27 *Afrika* (JG27), now under Gustav Rödel, who already has 79 "kills" to his name. III Gruppe of this geschwader is now under the command of Ernst Düllberg, who will survive the war with 45 "kills" to his name. At this time, he has 28 "kills." One of the men under his command is Harry Löffler. They arrive on the island of Argos on 23 September 1943.

Over the following ten days, the skies over the Dodecanese are ablaze as the little handful of South Africans and the mighty Luftwaffe are at one another's throats. In these actions over the island, 14 German aircraft will fall to the guns of "Corrie" van Vliet, "Bassie" Basson[25], "Ray" Burl, "Spuds" Kelly, "Van" van Deventer, "Gus" Ground, "Red" Taylor, Harry Kerby, George Wilkson and "Pitch" Inggs. Dakota transports desperately try to get fuel and supplies to the embattled band of flyers. However, the German bombing attacks on the airfield are so intense that the fighters can seldom take off. Only the most essential ground support men remain at the airfield. The fighter pilots themselves take up residence in a reedy ravine on the island where they cannot be spotted from the air and can at least survive the incessant onslaught. They race for the airfield to take off when there is an opening in the ground attacks and a usable run of field. In order to avoid the troubles being suffered at Antimachia, Corrie van Vliet, and Bassie elect to use the makeshift runway at Lampi.

The worst day[26] is 27 September 1943. This day starts out with seven Messerschmitt Bf109G6s of 9 Staffel JG27 approaching Cos. Corrie van Vliet and his wingman Bassie, on patrol off the island, meet the challenge; two South Africans to oppose seven of the best of Germany. Despite the numerical advantage, superior experience and altitude advantage of German flyers, Corrie, with Bassie covering his exposed back, piles into the Jagdgeschwader. Corrie manages to down one[27] of the Messerschmitts. Bassie, however, has no one covering his own back. Such is the fate of the wingman in aerial combat.

Bassie sees the tracer track past his cockpit and realizes he is in deep trouble. Van Vliet cannot help him at this time. Bassie tries desperately to shake the tenacious Bf109G6 off his tail. It is flown by Unter-offizier Harry Löffler. At this point, they are down to 300 foot above the open sea northeast of the island of Kalimnos and almost due north of the small island of Pserimos. This is when Bassie feels the entire aircraft shudder as the 0.51-inch rounds from the Messerschmitt's upgraded twin nose-mounted guns rake the Spitfire. The slab of armor behind his back protects his person to some degree from the German rounds. Everything around Bassie slows to a peculiar crawl as his life passes before his eyes.

*****

Back on Cos, Lieutenants A.A. Ground and K.W. Prestcott race their Spitfires down the runway to take off and chase a German formation. However, even as the two South Africans are retracting their landing gear a surprise inbound flight of Bf109G6s races down on them and both young flyers die in balls of flame[28] in full view of their friends. The lack of RADAR has cost them their lives. The Luftwaffe records will show a fourth Spitfire casualty on this day.

*****

A thin voice calls from far away. It does not really penetrate. Then, suddenly, Bassie is "back" in the cockpit of his stricken Spitfire and he hears Corrie's voice crackling through his headphones,

"Bassie! Bassie!... Bale! Bale! Bale!"

Bassie's training discipline kicks in; he pulls out his radio jack, slides open the cockpit canopy and inverts the aircraft. Then, as per the instructions, he pushes on the control column and undoes his straps. The stricken aircraft precipitates him neatly and safely past the deadly hurtling tailplane. The world is a mad rush as the high-speed air buffets him. As he tumbles, his parachute only just barely opens in time before he hits the strikingly blue water of the Aegean. Inside his Bf.109G cockpit Harry Löffler notes the time and position[29]. At debriefing, he will report:

"Spitfire - 11.18 am; 10-15km NW Insel Kos – 100m"

Bassie is Löffler's second "kill." Löffler will become a German ace and will down several American heavy bombers. He will eventually perish in the sky over the City of Paris, listed "Missing in Action."

The drama of the day is not yet over for Bassie. After being in the water for but a short time, a floatplane approaches. However, he knows that the S.A.A.F has no seaplanes nearby to rescue him. Then he recognizes the aircraft as a German Arado. The Germans set down on the water near him and try to make him get on

Fig. 19-11 Bassie was shot down just beyond Pserimos in the right hand background. Kalimnos is on the left

board. Bassie, however, has other ideas. He will later tell that he kept diving under the water whenever the Germans tried to get hold of him, doing his best to stay directly under the plane. Eventually, the Germans tire of the game and fly off, leaving him to his fate. It is quite some time later that a local Greek boat picks him up out of the water and takes him to nearby Kalimnos Island. Soon enough, he is back on Cos, and that is when he realizes that he has avoided the worst of the horror of the day.

The next morning, at 11:30 hours, 8 Spitfires of No 74 Squadron R.A.F. arrive to bolster the shattered defenses, but it is too little, too late. By 1 October, the squadron has only one single serviceable Spitfire left. When the Germans finally invade the island on 3 October, they find Cos to be the last resting place of six of the fourteen South African flyers and 15 of their ground crew. The officers are Cpt. Einar Rorvik and Lieutenants Harry Hynd, Ken Prescott, Alan Turner, Sonny Seel and "Cheese" Cheeseman. All of the squadron's Spitfires have been lost. In their reports, the Luftwaffe will claim a total of 12 Spitfires destroyed around Cos in September 1943.

Bassie himself has downed one Bf109F on this campaign.

3. Escape from Cos

When Corrie van Vliet goes to ask the British Army commander how the remaining aircraft-less South Africans can help with the defense of Cos, he is advised to make his escape with his men from the island to fight another day. They return to their peculiar tented headquarters in the reeds and destroy all the documentation. In this process, Bassie's treasured flight log is also destroyed. Future generations shall have to rely on Luftwaffe records of the combat to piece together this history. Around them, the German Stukas are dive-bombing every target they can find.

The group of 23 S.A.A.F. men now set out for the village of Kardámena on the eastern shore of the island. There are about 100 armed Italians in the village and panic is setting in. While evacuation transport has been arranged, the men have no faith that they will have any access. At the village harbor, they find that Italians have been seizing the available caiques and coracles. The men therefore seize a 20-foot caique at the jetty and, together with two Italians they accommodate on board, they try to set off. However, 23 landlubber Boere flyboys together do not constitute any significant knowledge of boats, and the odd Brit among them is no great help either. What is to follow is both hilarious and terrifying.

The typical Greek caique is designed to carry sail, but this one has none. A quick search of the boat reveals that there are no oars either. And so it is that, after having fought the Luftwaffe to their last aircraft, 23 South African airmen, two Italians and a smattering of Brits are paddling a 20 foot sailless Greek caique at a furious rate using their tin hats and any other flat object they can lay their hands on. They are just off the coast of the Dodecanese island of Cos, headed for Cape Creo in Turkey, 12 miles away. For a narrative of their predicament, we turn to a 1970s newspaper article by Ray Burl, the man who downed the first German aircraft in the campaign:

"We rowed virtually the whole night and collapsed exhausted when we thought we were well clear of the island. Came the dawn and we discovered that the current had carried us virtually the whole way back to Cos.

"After some frantic rowing, we managed to get clear of the island again, only to receive a bad scare about mid-morning when two Me109s showed up. We spotted them when they were still some distance off and everyone - bar two or three of us - who pretended to be locals - scuttled below deck. The Messerschmitts came down to about 15 metres and circled us for two or three minutes... seemed like two or three hours...while we pretended to be mending nets or fishing. We held our breath, not daring to look up, and eventually they buzzed off.

"a few hours later we had another nasty moment when we spotted a formation of RAF Beaufighters coming towards us at low level in attacking, line-abreast formation. One of the jobs of the Beaufighter in the Aegean was to shoot up caiques, which were widely used by the enemy for inter-island transport. It seemed as though we were to become the target of our own guns and the whole crowd of us leapt about madly on the

deck, shouting like banshees and waving uniforms, caps and anything else, that might be recognised by the crews of the Beaufighters. The formation was almost on us when suddenly it parted."

At three o'clock that afternoon, the bedraggled party reaches Turkey. Here they are spotted by two Turkish soldiers, who escort them all the way along the coast further to the east in order to cross over to Castelrosso Island. It is a tough walk of some days. Oddly, they are not interned, as has happened with other Allied soldiers who have ended up in Turkey. From Castelrosso they are taken to Cyprus and from there back to Egypt, where the remaining men gather to toast their fallen friends.

Some time later, the men learn that the Germans have executed the Italian officers who commanded the men on Cos, but the story is overshadowed by the simultaneous executions on Cephalonia[30].

4. Twice in a lifetime: Northern Italy

The squadron remains in Egypt for a few months, and then in April 1944, it rejoins No. 7 Wing of the SAAF in Italy, where South Africa provides the bulk of the Allied Air Power. Here the squadron takes part in fighter-bomber operations and flies armed reconnaissance and bomber escort. By the end of 1944, the squadron has flown 808 missions; a total of 4000 sorties. It is now an integral part of the slow grinding hell that is the Italian campaign. Bassie has meanwhile had his promised "R&R" break in South Africa with his family. Afterwards, he makes his way back to Egypt. This time he flies the distance as co-pilot on a transport aircraft. The trip is 4500 miles as the crow flies, but Bassie does it in 12 stages from Pretoria, which is itself 1,000 miles from Cape Town. The whole shuttle flight reads like a protracted walk through the adventure stories of the 19th century British Empire in Darkest Africa.

After a stay of some months with 41 Squadron, Bassie rejoins his old friends of 7 Squadron in Italy, where they are now supporting Allied troops in their attempts to breach Field-Marshall Kesselring's Gothic Line that stretches along the peaks of the Northern Apennines. The squadron is now flying much-improved Mk. IX Spitfires, configured to carry bombs for ground attack work. Their main business is close air support for the troops that have broken through the eastern Gothic line and who are now nearing the so-called Genghis Khan line that runs from Sant' Alberto on the southern shore of Lake Commachio to just south of Bologna. The Germans have strong Panzer units along this line.

And so it is that on 3 January 1945 the squadron is based at Forli, southwest of Ravenna on the Adriatic coast of Italy. By now, Bassie has survived many weeks of ground attack work, infantry support work and bomber escort sorties into Yugoslavia. He has also survived being intercepted by a vastly superior Me262 jet fighter based out of far western Yugoslavia.

On this particular day, Bassie, Lt. Peter Potter and Captain P. Hughes are tasked to bomb German tank units at Sant' Alberto and to then strafe the German lines of the 114th Jaeger Division facing the Allied Eighth Army. This sector along the Canale de Bonifica is assigned to the Canadians who are in desperate need of air support in their operation known as Operation SYRIA[31]. They include the Canadian Irish, the Perth Regiment, the British Columbia Dragoons and the Cape Breton Highlanders.

The bombing run is carried out successfully. However, as Bassie and Peter Potter descend towards the German entrenchments they are suddenly confronted with exceedingly heavy 40mm anti-aircraft and machine gun fire. Bassie and Potter's aircraft are both hit in the process. The unfortunate Potter is wounded in the forehead and can barely see out of one eye. This is when Bassie hears Potter's voice calling Captain Hughes over the R/T:

"Will you please take me back to base as I can't see where I am going?"

But Bassie himself is in a world of trouble. His Spitfire has taken 40mm hits in both wings. One of the shells through the port wing has exploded his ammunition box and a hole large enough for a man to crawl through has been blown in the wing. The hit on the starboard side has severed the aileron controls. This has placed the craft in a permanently banked orientation and Bassie therefore can only fly in circles through the anti-aircraft fire.

Hughes breaks off the attack to escort Potter back to base where he talks Potter down to a perfect landing. Having assured that Potter is safely down, Hughes returns to the front to find Bassie still circling. However, Bassie has managed to gain some altitude and has figured out how to turn the circular path into a painstakingly slow spiral path, by which means he is now slowly spiraling his way back roughly in the direction of Forli. Together the two edge their way towards base. However, it is clear that there is no way to save Bassie's Spitfire. They therefore decide that he shall have to bale out.

The closest to Forli that they can nurse the aircraft is Bertinoro, some miles to the south of the town. And it is here that Bassie gets ready to bale out; only to discover that one of his flying boots has become jammed in the cockpit during the beating his aircraft took. After some struggling, he manages to free his foot and successfully bales out.

As his parachute deploys he looks down. And this is when he realizes that he has managed to jump directly over the main local power cables. This is the start of a frantic struggle with the lines of his parachute. Afterwards, Bassie will say in a wartime South African newspaper article:

"That part of the trip was my biggest fright. It looked as though I couldn't miss the cable. I gave a terrific tug at the last minute and missed it by about three feet."

In the typically matter of fact style of so many airmen, Bassie writes in his logbook[32]:

"Potter hit in eye. Was hit twice by 40 mm & baled over Bertinore."

Bassie has hereby joined the small group of men who have saved their own lives by parachuting from stricken aircraft twice in a lifetime.

The next day Bassie is back in the air in another Spitfire, however it very soon becomes clear that he has seriously damaged his back during his parachute landing the previous day. Bassie is thereupon committed to the hospital in Rome. By March, he is back in his Spitfire. The rest of his time on the front is spent harassing the German forces on their retreat through northern Italy.

One of Bassie's last log entries laconically records how one of his colleagues is shot down by the Germans, bales out behind German lines and returns to base the next day with a number of Germans who have surrendered to him. Shortly afterwards, the German forces in Italy surrender while still in possession of much of Northern Italy.

—End Nexus Familia

The contribution to World War II

For devoted collectors of model military figures, one of their most prized pieces is a WWII Royal Air Force flying officer with his fox terrier mascot. It represents the flyers of Fighter Command of the Royal Air Force in WWII during the Battle of Britain. These were the men of whom Winston Churchill said:

"Never was so much owed by so many to so few."

In the defining Battle of Britain, a handful of Allied fighter pilots fought off Hitler's attempt to gain air superiority in the skies over England. If that Battle were to have been lost, Britain would most certainly have fallen to Hitler. Hermann Göring, himself a product of South West Africa (now Namibia) had, however, not reckoned with a young South African, a descendant of Jacques Malan of Saint Martin de la Brasque (*NF18 & 19*). He was Adolf Gysbert Malan, and the little model figure is of this young South African and his dog.

In keeping with the age-old tradition of Afrikaners, the young Adolf had learnt to shoot on his father's farm in the *Wagenmakersvallei* (Wagonmaker's Valley) of the Western Cape. What he learnt on that farm he brought to the warcraft of aerial combat. He would end the war as "Sailor" Malan, D.S.O and Bar, D.F.C. and Bar, Croix de Guerre (Belgium), Croix de Guerre (France), Czech War Cross, Legion d'Honneur and more. Not only did "Sailor" become "Britain's" leading ace, he but also wrote the famous and defining 10 Rules of Air Combat. He led no. 74 Squadron of the Royal Air Force through the crucial Battle of Britain, playing a critical role in denying Hitler's air superiority over the islands in preparation for invasion. "Sailor" Malan remains today the symbol of the WWII British fighter ace – but was in reality a South African farm boy, just like Louis Botha, Koos de la Rey, Christiaan de Wet and Jan Smuts.

The small nation produced more than 40 fighter aces[33], the top five of them, "Tom" Pattle, "Sailor" Malan, "Chris" Le Roux, "Dutch" Hugo and "John" Frost accounting for more than 136 enemy aircraft. Three of the five were of French Huguenot descent, again showing the depth of influence of the original two hundred refugees from France in 1688. South Africans also flew American built B-24 Liberator bombers in raids on Ploesti and in the Warsaw Drop. They did much of the reconnaissance for the USAAF in the East European theater. A full one third of all the men who set off on the mission to Warsaw never returned. A grateful Poland erected a memorial to the brave South African flyers who gave their lives to save the beleaguered Poles.

After the collapse of the Italian power in Ethiopia on 18 May 1941, the South Africans moved on to Egypt. Here they became part of the British "8th Army."

In the Far East, individual South Africans were also made prisoners of war by the Japanese after the invasion of Indonesia. One of these was Laurens van der Post, who would later become advisor to the British Prince Charles. The motion picture *"Merry Christmas, Mr. Lawrence"* is based on his books about those camps. The characters, John "Lawrence" and Jack Celliers (a common Afrikaans surname), were both based on the personal experiences of Laurens van der Post himself.

By 1 August 1942, the South African 1st Division under the leadership of Major-General Dan Pienaar held Rommel at El Alamein in the first encounter at that place. On 23 October 1942, followed the famous Battle of El Alamein. This was the first major Allied success of the war, with the South Africans right in the thick of it. It is at this battle that 7 Squadron SAAF provided their services (*NF82*). On 13 May 1943, the German Afrika Korps formally surrendered.

In April 1944, South African forces, in the form of the 6th Armored Division, landed at Taranto in Italy and joined in the long, miserable, and arduous drive up the spine of Italy. One of the most intense battles was around the hilltop cathedral of Monte Casino. At first, the South Africans served as part of the British 8th Army. After the U.S. Landings at Anzio, they fought as part of the United States 5th Army and became the first Allied forces to enter the ancient city of Florence. They formed the spearhead of the attack when the U.S. 5th Army captured Monte Caprara and Monte Sole, thereby enabling the breakthrough into the Po valley. On 29 April 1945, the German forces in Italy surrendered. Among the Allied forces on the ground was the author's uncle Ben Booyens and in the air was the author's father-in-law (*NF82*).

In the naval domain, South Africa manufactured launches for use by the British Royal Navy and some were pressed into service on the South African coast. While the South African Navy itself was minuscule, South Africa did second some 3,600 men to the Royal Navy. During the later stages of the war Britain gave three frigates to South Africa. One of these, the *HMSAS Natal*, made contact with a German U-boat while still on trials off Scotland and destroyed the enemy vessel, which turned out to be *U-714*.

It is in the domain of materiel, logistics, and training that South Africa has never received appropriate credit. The engineering for the Allied North African campaign relied heavily on South Africans while thirty-four Commonwealth Flight Training Schools were set up in South Africa for Allied pilots, second in number only to Canada. The country also set up numerous factories for munitions, armored cars, patrol boats, trucks, guns, small arms and the like.

Nexus Familia 83: World War II at home

The Callanans and Bassons

By now the Callanan brothers are all too old to serve, but the ever-energetic Harry Ambrose Callanan (*NF67*) enlists and is employed as camp guard for Italian Prisoners of War at Zonderwater east of Pretoria. This camp will become the leading international example of a well run P.O.W. Camp. At the end of the war, the superb treatment of these 67,000 men will earn the South African commander, the eldest son of Boer War Commandant Hendrik Prinsloo of Spioenkop fame, together with three of his officers, the Order of the Star of Italy at the hand of the post-war government of Italy. The Pope himself will confer on the commander the Papal Order of Good Merit. The Italian prisoners of war are allowed to volunteer to go to farms to work there in return for "room and board." In this process, many of these Italian men will fall in love with the country and its people (See below).

Michael Charles Callanan has settled with his family in the Western suburbs of Pretoria. Having finished her training at Pretoria Girls High school, his daughter Molly Callanan (*NF81*) has joined the Government Service and is a secretary in the office of the Quartermaster-General of the armed Forces. She is a devoted follower of Jan Smuts, the ex-Boer War general turned Empire man. Her roots as the granddaughter of a Great Trek Jordaan, and the daughter of Neve Constance Milward who had been consigned to the British Concentration camps have been almost forgotten. Much of it has been actively hidden from her and would only be revealed by later research. Molly is every inch the "Young English Lady."

It is while working for Jan Smuts that she meets the young returned WWII Spitfire pilot, Lieutenant Arnold Loubser "Bassie" Basson (*NF82*). Just less than four years later, on 5 March 1949, they marry in the St. Andrew's Church in Pretoria.

Bassie returns to his job as commissioner in the Department of Bantu Affairs, the direct South African parallel of the Canadian Department of Indian Affairs. The latter will still be functioning in the 21st century. In this role, he can be transferred anywhere in South Africa, and he is indeed soon transferred to Elliotdale in the heart of the amaXhosa territory of the East Cape. This is just ten miles from Qunu, where the young man from Bashee River, Nelson Mandela, attended school. Bassie is therefore now one of those men of whom Mandela would later describe as having a *"distant role"* in his life and whom he considered *"curious and remote"* (Chapter 18: *The Young Man from Bashee River*).

The Myburgh family

The author's maternal grandfather, Kotie Myburgh (*NF81*), has partially recovered his eyesight and has finally found new employment as manager of *Vleipoort* farm (Valley Gorge) for two Russian Jewish brothers who have fled Stalin's excesses in the Soviet Union. As a typical East Cape Afrikaner, Kotie is now a totally devoted follower of hardliner DF Malan and dreams of independence from Britain, the place that he feels designed and exported to South Africa all the misery in his life.

In his fervent resentment of Jan Smuts' policies toward the British Empire, he joins a group that calls itself the *Ossewa Brandwag* (Ox Wagon Sentinel). It is a rather reactionary organization and some of its members move perilously close to urban guerrilla activity in their bid to oppose South African participation in World War II. They oppose anything resembling support for Britain, the "ancient enemy." In this, they are no different than the Irish, who had similarly suffered some of the worst of Imperial Britain.

Kotie does not take part in any illegal activity, but one day the police turn up and threaten to commit him to a political internment camp for German sympathizers. Ironically, they are talked out of it by Kotie's new Russian Jewish employers who vouch for him. Eventually, Jan Smuts' Police only impound Kotie's trusty German Mauser rifle, to him the symbol of his allegiance to the anti-Imperialist cause. Elsewhere in the country, several politically active anti-Smuts individuals are interned. One of them is a man named John Vorster, from Kotie's general part of the country; a man who will take center stage in our story soon enough.

Near the end of the war, Kotie's third daughter, Nickie, leaves school and takes her first job at the farm store of a local farmer contracted with the Railways to provide water to its steam trains. Two Italian POWs from Zonderwater, Francesco Rizzo and Carlo Pantano, volunteer for this work. In this way, Nickie gets to know the two Italian gentlemen. Francesco and Carlo will both fetch their families to settle in South Africa after the war. Thousands will follow their example, thereby forming the core of the South African Italian community which will, true to their historic culture, play a major role in Civil Engineering in the country.

The Booyens family meets the Myburghs

By the end of the war, it is clear that growing alfalfa (lucern) next to the Gamka River outside Calitzdorp is not going to be a viable living for the Booyens family. The author's father, Herman Stefanus Booyens (*NF82*), and his uncles all join the South African Railways. In this process, Herman is stationed at what is called a "railway cottage" next to the railway line outside Middelburg Cape, right next to *Vleipoort* farm where Kotie Myburgh, his wife Pretty Bettie and their three daughters are farming.

Herman is a track patrolman. He has to patrol and inspect a specific stage of the railway track that runs past *Vleipoort*. If he should discover a problem, he has to place a detonator[34] on the track for any approaching train to set off so that the loud sound may warn the engineer of the problem.

It is on her way back home from working at the nearby farm store further along the railway line that Nickie first meets Herman, who soon comes calling. He announces his arrival in his own unique way by setting off a detonator at the front door. He makes himself very useful to Kotie Myburgh. He loves fixing all manner of things, some of which he knows nothing about, such as radios. He soon has a number of acid bottle accumulators set up in the house, to be charged by a primitive wind generator. The family can now listen to the news on the radio for the first time ever. He also expertly prunes the fruit trees, which immediately respond by bearing fruit as they had never done before. His standing with Pretty Bettie, however, drops precipitously when he mistakes her prize turkey's bobbing head in the young cornfield for that of a springhare. Herman, like most Afrikaners of his era, is a crack shot despite the damage to his eye, and he dispatches the "spring hare" at a range of several hundred yards.

Despite the setbacks presented by dead turkeys and a desperate lack of money, Herman proposes marriage to the young Nickie. On 27 August 1949, the Booyens and Myburgh families are joined by the marriage of the 25-year old Herman and the 20-year old Nickie, third daughter and spitting image of Pretty Bettie.

—End Nexus Familia

In the wake of the Second World War

With the European countries having collectively weakened themselves to near total destruction through WWII, that continent focused inward on rebuilding itself. To compound matters, the British public summarily voted out Churchill in a landslide victory for the Labour Party immediately after the war.

When the near-bankrupt United Kingdom under the leadership of Labour Party's Clement Attlee desperately required loan facilities, it was to the United States that they turned, but the price would be very great. In the aftermath of the war, the United States simply would not allow Britain, now heavily indebted to that country, to resume its Imperial practices. In future, it would be the United States that would effectively determine Britain's foreign policy, as we shall duly see. In the event, Britain would remain indebted to the United States for this loan until 29 December 2006.

Attlee oversaw the granting of independence to India, Pakistan, and other parts. The British departure left in its wake a string of festering political sores that would plague mankind for the next half century – Cyprus, Palestine, Aden (now in Yemen), Iraq, Afghanistan, Pakistan, and Bangladesh. Most of these problems had at their root a near total disregard on the part of the British for the demographic realities and histories of those territories. After more than 60 years, most of these remain serious problems. In the Greater India, they created Afghanistan from one quarter of the Pashtun people, leaving the other three quarters in another artificial country, which they called Pakistan. The demographic disaster of Afghanistan would later bleed first the Soviet Union and then the West for roughly a decade each when either could least afford it.

In South Africa, the white electorate roundly rejected Jan Smuts in the 1948 general election and voted in D.F. Malan's National Party. This party fed off the unhappiness of two generations of Afrikaners still struggling to live down the twin disasters of the Anglo-Boer War and the Great Depression, as well as a century and a half of British oppression. Politically, the National Party came with a ready-made philosophy of separate societies for the races. This very parochial new government had its focus on real independence from Britain and the hopeless imbalance in racial makeup within the borders of the existing country.

Meanwhile, Nelson Mandela from the Bashee River area had become a member of the ANC. His future colleague, Raymond Mhlaba, was a Rharhabe Xhosa like Maqoma, amaXhosa hero of the Frontier Wars. Ray had been raised on a steady diet of history of the amaXhosa and perceived injustices against the amaRharhabe by the British. After completing his eighth year of school, he had been sent to a classic traditional cultural initiation class[35]. Young Xhosa men undergoing that training are temporarily isolated as a group from their kin. They cover themselves in white clay and are referred to as abaKhwetha. Part of the process is circumcision. The young men are taught their responsibilities and expected social conduct as adults.

Neither Mandela nor Mhlaba had yet had much contact with the ordinary white population beyond mission schoolteachers. Mhlaba[36] stated in his later book that he occasionally encountered White and Coloured people in Fort Beaufort.

During the early 1940s, Mandela and Mhlaba both finally left their respective traditional amaXhosa territories to seek their fortunes in "The White Man's South Africa." Many years later Mandela described his excitement as he, then in his twenties, approached Johannesburg, some 600 miles from the world where he had grown up[37]. He commented that Johannesburg had always been seen as a city of dreams where poor peasants could transform themselves in to wealthy sophisticates.

In this, he shared the aspirations of any young Mexican who wanted to live in the United States. Raymond Mhlaba moved to the author's hometown of Port Elizabeth[38] in 1941 when he was 21 to join his father who had retired as rural policeman to take another job in the "Big City."

In Johannesburg, Mandela had met Walter Sisulu, yet another Xhosa man from the amaXhosa territory. Sisulu had managed to get Mandela a job as an articled clerk with a law firm based on his partially completed studies at the University of Fort Hare. He eventually enrolled in the Law School of Wits University in Johannesburg.

Here he befriended a bevy of white communists, including Joe Slovo. By 1947, he had finished serving his articles. In the same year, he became a regional executive of the ANC in the Transvaal province.

With the National Party (white nationalists) in power, and some key future members of the African National Congress (black nationalists) now located where they could have maximal influence, the author's unborn generation now had their lives painted into a corner from where they would have little hope of a positive long-term future.

-----ooOoo-----

20

Uhuru! Nowhere else to go

"..The wind of change is blowing through this continent..."
"..This is our only motherland, we have nowhere else to go..."

Harold Macmillan, U.K. Prime Minster, and
Hendrik F. Verwoerd, South African Prime Minster,
Macmillan's address to the South African Parliament (3 February 1960)
Verwoerd's response to Macmillan's address (3 February 1960)

The Flight from Empire

Britain and France had designed World War II in 1919 at the Treaty of Versailles[1]. Churchill had refused to contemplate any other outcome to World War II than the destruction of Germany. The inevitable result was now upon the leaders in London and Paris. Both nations would at first attempt to hold onto their far-flung empires. Yet, neither could afford those empires anymore. Their intense conflicts with Germany had destroyed both their economies. But, European colonialism had served its purpose and had become a liability. Europe, the original proponent of African colonialism, now developed an expedient guilty conscience on the subject, just as it had about African slavery at the end of the 1700s. In the 18th century, the British national guilt complex about Slavery had led to the creation of the London Missionary Society. The 20th century British national guilt complex about colonialism would be serviced with devotion by its liberal media.

The British media assault on white men in Africa would be ramped up at the start of the sixth decade of the 20th century and continue unabated into the 21st century. Again, as in the 1830s,

Fig. 20-1 Kwame Nkrumah of Ghana

innocent white South Africans would pay with their lives for this hate-filled bias and lack of balance and insight.

The Scramble out of Africa would largely be delayed to the decade of the 1960s, but it would be nothing short of a disgrace dressed up in pomp and ceremony. Britain in particular would throw its colonies to the wolves, or the nearest available tin pot dictator. Most were artificial concocted countries comprising various nations and tribes stuck within borders that had been drawn up at or soon after the Berlin Conference[2].

The departing European overlords believed that they could quickly "bring democracy" to the countries they were departing and that this would somehow engender economic success and stability. Perhaps one has to live for a time outside the heartland of Western Civilization in order to appreciate the degree to which that civilization is the true guarantor of democracy. Without that underlying set of Western values, democracy is at best a farce and more often than not a guaranteed recipe for war and bloodshed, so often seen in Africa.

In reality, there never was any hope that democracy represented a solution for the people of these new African countries. The Germans, French, British, Soviets, and Poles had been unable to vote over the matter of Hitler's designs in order to avert WWII. How then could the same Europeans think that foisting democracy on this unprepared and disparate collection of African peoples would ensure either peace or economic success? The differences between some of these groups are greater than those between the Germans and the French. Their histories of warfare are even longer. Expecting these conglomerations of different tribes, nations, and peoples to vote peacefully on running such artificial countries was beyond the ludicrous.

And so it is that Africa with its more than 2000 languages lurched haplessly towards independence with both the Ibo and the Hausa people caught inside Nigeria, the Hutu and Tutsi caught inside Rwanda, the Luo and the Kikuyu caught inside Kenya, and a welter of nations grouped together inside the Belgian Congo. The list of split nations and joint countries continues at length. Africa is a patchwork of hundreds of nations, some large, some small, all trapped and forced together behind borders created by a departed Europe.

The United States, for its part, saw itself as the bastion and guardian of worldwide democracy. However, it found itself embroiled in the escalating Cold War even before the fall of Berlin. There was little chance it would take a serious hand in Africa.

In 1951, Churchill returned to power at the head of the Conservative Party. This heralded a brief period in which Britain would attempt to reverse the flight from Empire initiated by former Prime Minister Clement Atlee. Churchill famously insisted that he would not preside over a "dismemberment" of the British Empire. However, Britain would now find that it could do nothing contrary to the wants and desires of the United States, to which it had mortgaged itself. The United States was in control of Great Britain via its effective hold over the value of the British Pound. The "British Bulldog" was indeed now "toothless," and economically in little better state than Germany; and quite possibly worse.

The United States would demonstrate its control over the United Kingdom soon enough.

The Korean War – helping America

Before the matter of African Independence absorbed the attention of the world, the Korean War intruded. South Africa was there to do its part in support of the West. The new National Party Prime Minister, D.F. Malan, was adamant that South Africa would militarily support any effort to counteract the Communist aggression in Korea.

South Africa's contribution in Korea was in the form of air power[3]. The highly experienced No.2 Squadron of the S.A.A.F., the Flying Cheetahs, did the honors. Most of the pilots were handpicked WWII veterans. The men were led by Commandant S. Theron, yet another descendant of the French Huguenot Refugees[4] of 1688. Repeating the South African-American arrangements of WWII, they were to fly as part of the 18th Fighter-Bomber Wing of the US Fifth Air Force along with the 12th and 67th Fighter-Bombers and the 39th fighter-interceptors of the U.S. Air Force.

The Cheetahs were supposed to train at Johnson Air Base in Japan on the way to Korea. The squadron was offended by the notion of having to "train" to be allowed to fly with the USAF. So Theron climbed into a P51 Mustang and proceeded to perform a series of acrobatic maneuvers. Upon landing, the American commander said:

"Commandant, we cannot teach you anything about flying."

Theron's classic response was:

"That's right, and every pilot in the squadron is as good as I am. Give us some Mustangs and let's get on with the war."

The squadron, in which a total of 862 men served during the Korean War, went on to distinguish itself as a ground attack unit. It destroyed 18 tanks, 160 field guns, 615 vehicles, 46 bridges, 49 fuel supply dumps and 3021 buildings. The members earned no fewer that 50 United States DFCs, flying first P51-D Mustangs and later F-86 Sabres. They were awarded the United States Presidential Units Citation.

On 20 March 1952, a flight of eight Flying Cheetahs in their P51-D Mustangs under Commanding officer Dick Clifton ran into an enemy aircraft in the form of vastly superior MiG 15s. Dave Taylor's aircraft was hit by the MiGs and went down. Taylor had been a young Citizen Force volunteer. Three other Cheetahs formed up with Clifton to attack the MiGs. They were Mac McLaughlin and his two Afrikaner colleagues, Hans Enslin and Joe Joubert, yet again a French Huguenot descendant. They hit and damaged one MiG and put the enemy to flight, despite the overwhelming mismatch in aircraft capabilities.

On 24 June 1951, a US Marine position was overrun. The US Marine citation to the SA Air Force reads:

> *"We were catching all hell because of an overwhelming Gook counter-attack. The tide of battle was leaving casualties in its wake like seashells cast upon a beach. It was then we saw four silvery streaks plummet from the skies with guns blazing. It was so wondrous a sight we completely forgot our whereabouts or line and just stood up in our foxholes and cheered. The Hall of Fame does not possess any greater men than those who flew that day."*

Their greatest honor came in the form of Policy Order No.13 of the 18th USAF Fighter-Bomber Wing[5]:

> *"In memory of our gallant South African comrades, it is hereby established, as a new policy, that at all Retreat Ceremonies held by this Wing, the playing of our National Anthem shall be preceded by playing the introductory bars of the South African National Anthem, 'Die Stem van Suid-Afrika'. All personnel of this Wing will render the same honors to this Anthem as our own"*

A total of 34 Flying Cheetahs gave their lives in that war. This was the third successive major war in which Afrikaners and Americans, both colonial descendants of the Dutch founders and French Refugees, fought side by side. Regrettably, the United States would soon forget this.

The systematic isolation of white South Africa from the rest of their international kin started immediately after this war.

Mau-Mau – A Nostalgia for Barbarism

The term "Mau-Mau" still sends chills down the spine of any White or Indian person who lived in Africa in the 1950s. It was the first openly genocidal campaign against Western Christian settlers by indigenous African people, but would not be the last. It came against a background of a teetering British Empire in which West Africa, the Gold Coast, the Sudan, Malta, Cyprus, Malaya, and Kenya were all in some state of unrest, amounting in some places to bloodshed.

Trouble started brewing in early 1952 in the British East Africa colony of Kenya, where there were approximately 30,000 European settlers. The secret Mau-Mau organization was based exclusively on the indigenous Kikuyu people of that country. The 1 million Kikuyu constituted roughly 20% of the total population of black African people in Kenya.

The Mau-Mau was an offshoot of the Kikuyu Central Association; an organization created by a man named Jomo Kenyatta and was already outlawed by the British in 1940 for its "subversive activities." It was violently anti-white and anti-Christian. With his first political vehicle suppressed, Kenyatta formed the Kenya African Union.

By October 1952, several people had been brutally murdered, including some chiefs who would not fall in line with the Mau-Mau. Cattle mutilations, a uniquely perverse African indication of rising unhappiness, were reported far and wide. The members of the Mau-Mau were bound by an oath to specifically attack white farmers. It was reported as follows in the British Parliament[6] on 16 October 1952:

"If I am sent with four others to kill the European enemies of this organization and I refuse, may this oath kill me. When the reedbuck horn is blown, if I leave the European farm before killing the European owner, may this oath kill me."

On that particular date, the Secretary of State for the Colonies, Oliver Lyttelton, reported in the House of Commons on the escalating violence and stated that the 74-year old retired British Lt-Col. Tulloch and his wife had been attacked. More than 30 murders had been committed and churches and mission stations attacked or burnt. With witnesses being intimidated by the Mau-Mau, the British Authorities responded with Ordinance 35, which allowed evidence purely by affidavit. In brief, Britain was learning what an African colonial revolution actually looked like.

On the night of 20 October 1952, a State of Emergency was declared and Jomo Kenyatta was arrested along with more than 100 other key individuals. This was timed to coincide with the arrival in Kenya of the 1st Battalion of Lancashire Fusiliers, flown in from the Middle East to provide military support for a crackdown on the Mau-Mau. On 7 November 1952, the Secretary of State for Colonies, Oliver Lyttelton, freshly back in the British House of Commons from Kenya, curiously aptly summarized the Kenyan situation:

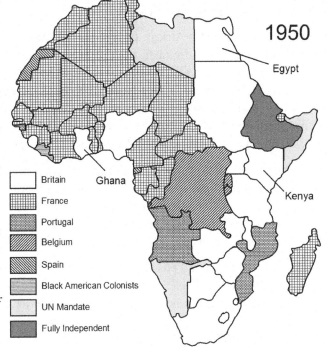

"Mau Mau is a secret society and feeds, not upon economic discontent, but is something far more sinister. It is the enemy of both white and Asian. It is the enemy of the law-abiding African. It is anti-Christ and it feeds, not upon economic discontent, but upon perverted nationalism and on a sort of nostalgia for barbarism."

These words may be taken as they stand and repeated for every single rising by indigenous African people in Sub-Saharan Africa since then.

Fig. 20-2 European control of Africa in 1950 before the Scramble out of Africa

All that has varied is the degree of barbarism and the degree to which the West has selectively closed its eyes to the horrors committed.

The uprising soon spread through the country and white farmers, particularly British ones, were attacked, and brutally murdered. One year later, on 16 December 1953, the British Secretary of State for Colonies reported in the House of Commons that 153,398 individuals (around 15% of all the Kikuyu) had been arrested in Kenya up to the 5th of that month. Of the security forces 213 had been killed and 196 wounded. After four years[7], 32 white settlers and some 2,000 loyalist Kikuyu had been killed. The official death toll of the rebels was given as 11,500. Others say it was higher. Some 80,000 Kikuyu were put in concentration camps.

The British authorities had rounded up some Britain blamed the insurrection on Jomo Kenyatta and he was found guilty after a trial in which the British Government, it was later revealed[8], paid off the witness. This perversion of justice is reminiscent of events after the 1815 Slagtersnek Rebellion in South Africa[9], when the Hendrik Nouka, interpreter to amaXhosa King Ngqika was similarly rewarded by the Cape Governor after testifying against the Afrikaner "rebels." The letter instructing the delivery of the "presents" survives to this day in the Cape Archives.

However, while the British managed to suppress the Mau Mau rebellion, they could not stop the drive towards independence, *Uhuru* ("freedom" in Swahili), as the locals called it. The majority of white British settlers left the country, while most of the small community of Afrikaners who lived at the town of Eldoret[10], which they had created on the Kenyan Highlands, made their way to South Africa.

Sixty or so miles to the southwest of Eldoret, in a village named Kogelo, a young Luo tribesman born in the village of Kanyadhiang was approaching his 20th year. His name was Barack Hussein Obama. His son would one day be the American President.

A small community of Afrikaners remained at Eldoret and they would maintain a Dutch Reformed Church until the 1960s, when most would leave. A solitary Afrikaner missionary remained at Eldoret in 2007. The post-election violence of 2008 would eventually make the town the scene of a massacre in which many people, including women and children, would be burnt to death in their church.

Ghana – leading the way

Few if any indigenous African people north of Rhodesia (now Zimbabwe) had the vaguest concept of any form of practical administration of national government or even day-to-day maintenance of any infrastructure. The Gold Coast (Ghana) was the possible exception. Even as events were starting to unfold in Kenya in 1952, Britain was already moving to grant independence to the Gold Coast. The new country would be named Ghana, to be led by the Prime Minister Khwame Nkrumah. In the British House of Lords, the debate about the task awaiting Nkrumah provides a telling glimpse into the British view of Africa, as articulated by Lord Milverton[11], ex-Governor of Nigeria:

"Only those who know the degree of unpreparedness of the Africans can fully appreciate the magnitude of this task. If we grant that there may be the top men of adequate ability to shoulder the responsibilities of government, even they lack experience and must initially be in need of friendly advice and guidance.[...]

"...at the present moment the Gold Coast could not dispense with the aid of European personnel in any of their Departments."

In reality, Ghana had possibly the best-trained indigenous black African administrators on the continent at the time, as well as a relatively strong economy. Naturally, none of that helped if the leaders decided on dictatorships or socialist schemes, and that is exactly what happened with Nkrumah.

Kwame Nkrumah had gone to the United States, not the Soviet Union, for his education. He had seen Free Enterprise at work in the heart of the Capitalist world. He had studied at the University of Pennsylvania and had been elected president of the African Student Organization of America and Canada. During his stay in the United States he had had extensive contact with various US Trotskyists, including Trinidadian C.L.R. James, Russian expatriate Raya Dunayevskaya, and Chinese-American Grace Lee Boggs. Nkrumah later explained that James trained him in *"how an underground movement worked."* In his new role in Africa, he would ably apply all the Communist theory and subversive practices he learnt from this cohort in the United States.

Nkrumah had a direct interest in South Africa. In line with the general drive of Uhuru, he wanted the white man driven from Africa. South Africa represented to him the bastion of white men in Africa. He would soon affect matters in the author's hometown, thousands of miles away.

The Cold War and McCarthy

By the end of World War II, the Cold War was already underway with the United States and the Soviet Union jockeying for position and international advantage. In the United States, suspicion levels grew around all people who had even the vaguest possible association with Communism. It eventually culminated in what is today known as the McCarthy Era. Fears of the influence of Communism grew in the United States, ultimately leading to the investigation of many Left-leaning individuals. While the hearings conducted against the "Father" of the Atom Bomb, J. Robert Oppenheimer, are possibly the most well-known of the McCarthy Era, it is the execution of Julius and Ethel Rosenberg on June 19, 1953 as convicted Soviet spies that concerns us in this work. Judge Kaufman made it quite clear that he held them responsible for endangering the country and providing benefit to the Soviets. There would be much subsequent debate as to the guilt of Ethel Rosenberg, but that is beyond the scope of the present work.

This history is raised here, not to question the validity of the case or the punishment, but to create a reference point for the reader in events that were shortly to follow in South Africa and which would affect U.S. policy towards South Africa for decades. The executions of the Rosenbergs clearly demonstrated the lengths to which the authorities in the most powerful Western country in the world were prepared to go in peacetime in their fight against the Soviet threat, personified by the inhuman extremism of Joseph Stalin.

In 1950 in South Africa, the National Party government passed the Suppression of Communism Act, which gave it sweeping powers to destroy anything vaguely resembling the promotion of Communism. The country was as staunchly anti-Communist as the United States. The United Nations would claim that the government was using this act to limit any political activity that it frowned upon, whether Communist or not. Then again, as we shall soon see, the country was facing a far more insidious internal Communist threat on own soil than the United States, which had the benefit of a massive population in which Western Caucasians were then the vast majority.

The thought of White Americans being threatened on their own soil by any part of their own national population was completely ludicrous. For white South Africans it was a daily reality.

Always the horror near Port Elizabeth

As we have seen in no fewer than six chapters of this present work, the Eastern Frontier near Port Elizabeth, Grahamstown and East London was the crucible of South African history from 1780 to 1835[12]. It was here that white and black first clashed. It was here that Great Britain clashed with the amaXhosa. It is from here that the Great Trek set out. It would again be here that the inevitable dying would start in the next installment of the horror epic that is the history of South Africa.

By 1952, the National Party government under D.F. Malan had implemented an array of blatantly racist legislation. Hendrik French Verwoerd, who became Minister for Native Affairs in 1950, marshaled much of this through parliament. Verwoerd had been born in the Netherlands of parents who emigrated to South Africa, after sympathizing with the plight of the Afrikaners during the "Great Boer War."

A large number of these pieces of legislation appeared on the Statute Book during the 1951 parliamentary session. These included the removal of the right of "Coloured" (mixed-descent, not black) people to vote for white candidates for parliament. Several acts addressed the matter of black people in what was seen as "white country"; that is, outside the homeland areas that had been reserved for them in 1913 and 1936. These roughly coincided with where they had lived for centuries. There were also laws, for example, limiting the right of black builders to work in such "white areas."

All in all it was a package of legislation that confined the civil rights of black people to being executed only in their home territories – always assuming they had such. However, by now there were many black people who had lost all touch with any original home territory and were living on the outskirts of the otherwise "white" towns. As objectionable as this legislation may have been for Black people, the fact is that it was the Coloured people who suffered the worst of it. They had no "home territory" to call their own, yet they were completely disenfranchised by this legislation. They were now truly "second class citizens with no say." The fully urbanized Black people were now effectively citizens of a place many of them had never seen, but at least they had a place called "home," albeit elsewhere. There is absolutely no way in which this legislation can be morally defended in any way, shape or form.

Among white people, the line of thinking as regards the Black people was the South African equivalent of the "send the illegal immigrants home" in the United States, and just as ill thought-through. The difference was that in South Africa the "illegal immigrants" completely outnumbered the "legal citizens."

It is against this background of patently unjust race-based legislation that the African National Congress (ANC) decided to embark on a campaign of civil disobedience[13], focusing on 1952 as the 300th anniversary of the arrival of Jan van Riebeeck at the Cape. The message in the choice of that year was obvious. June 26 was chosen as the day for action to be taken all over the country. Support for the general campaign came from a number of international leaders and sources. These included Chou-en-Lai of Communist China, Kwame Nkrumah of the Gold Coast and Paul Robeson of the Council of African Affairs in the United States.

Initially, it was simply public disobedience, as in the later United States Civil Rights Campaign. However, one starts to see the difference when one reads the statements of Florence Matomela, one of the ANC campaign speakers. Raymond Mhlaba, himself a key local black leader in the ANC at the time, records her sayin that[14] every white man is a Satan and should be treated as such. According to Mhlaba, she suggested that, if her audience had never seen Satan in Hell, then they ought to look at the white man, so they could say that they had "seen Satan."

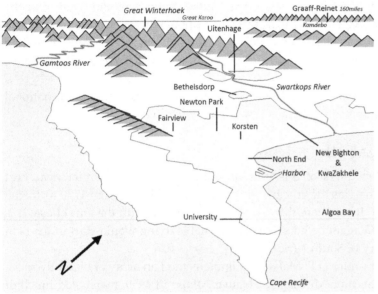

Fig. 20-3 Port Elizabeth

These were hardly the words of an organization that could claim to also represent white people in the country. Considering what was about to happen, they are ironic indeed. A number of people were arrested, and subsequently set free in this superficially peaceful campaign. They included Nelson Mandela and Walter Sisulu. However, the true racist nature of the campaign, as hinted at by the rhetoric from Matomela, soon showed. At this point, all parallels with the United States end. There would be attempts by the ANC to deny responsibility, but the irrefutable facts of the situation were that they started the campaign and that the following happened, the events being confirmed by Mhlaba himself in his memoirs[15]:

On 18 October 1952, the campaign turned into open riot in New Brighton, a black township of Port Elizabeth. The black crowd went berserk and targeted any white people who happened to be in the township. A white man named Rudi Brandt had a cinema called the Rio in New Brighton. The mob descended on the Rio and murdered Rudi and his two white employees, Gerry Leppan and Karl Bernard. In nearby KwaZakehle township, two white men, a Mr. Laas and a Mr. Isaacson, were killed by a similar black mob.

On 9 November 1952, two days after the British Secretary for Colonies referred in the House of Commons to the "nostalgia for barbarism" in Kenya, a black mob descended on a Catholic church in East London, the second biggest city in the East Cape. They burned down the church and killed a nun, sister Mary Aidan, and a white insurance salesman named B.J. Vorster.

It is this third event that had the greatest impact, its effects still being felt in East London in the 21st century. Time Magazine, referring to the relevant passbook laws as "Jim Crow Laws" and incorrectly to South Africa's Ba'Ntu people as "Negros," reported the killing two weeks after the fact[16], stating that that Sister Aidan had driven through the Police lines to greet her "Negro" friends. According to the paper, the howling mob dragged her from her car, slit her throat and burned her mutilated body, chanting *"Africa!."*

Actually, *Time Magazine* did history a disservice in refusing to report fully on this event that occurred in the black township of Duncan Village. One might forgive them, as the full story is probably too difficult for an American to credit. For those souls, black and white, who inhabit the continent of Africa, the truth of the day was only too real and recognizable. For a more complete version of the truth, we therefore turn to media sources closer to the event and more familiar with the realities of Africa.

In an editorial[17] of Friday 18 October 2002, commemorating the event after 50 years, the more than a century old East London newspaper, the *Daily Dispatch*, presented the facts of this horrific day:

The ANC party youth leader had obtained a permit to have a prayer meeting on this day, but the meeting had been turned into a political gathering as part of the ANC's "Defiance Campaign." Soon enough, two black youths came to warn the sisters of the Dominican order at the St. Peter Claver church that a mob was on its way to kill them. By the time matters reached crisis point, the Police and Father O'Malley, the parish priest, had already safely evacuated the personnel at the church along with the parish registers. At a certain point in the standoff between the Police and the crowd, when the Police executed a baton charge, an officer named Vogel received a grazing wound from a gunshot. This led to the Police opening fire and setting off after the mob and away from the church.

Sister Mary, a trained physician, was now headed back to the unprotected church in her black British Austin automobile, returning from attending a black woman of the parish in childbirth. A black man forced her car to a halt. The classic worked up black African mob then pulled her from the car and hacked her to death. Then they set her body alight and torched the church and other buildings. Over that day and the following night at least seven people were shot to death by the Police. Many were wounded.

On 21 September 2007, in an interview with author Cornelius Thomas, the taboo matter was raised that the paper had been too circumspect to openly address in the original 2002 article[18] – that of the attackers cannibalizing the body of 38-year old Irish born Sister Mary. This was based on testimony by Andrew Card, former mayor of East London and, at the time, the young detective who had to see the case through court. Fourteen individuals identified in the matter were convicted of "*devouring human flesh*"[19]. Card's biography describes the events in more detail[20].

The murderously racist Uhuru and its associated mindless inhuman savagery had somehow chosen the white people of the author's home town and nearby regions as its first racial target in Sub-Saharan Africa. Mobs of black people were killing the vastly outnumbered white people indiscriminately under the flag of the ANC during its ostensibly peaceful Defiance Campaign. All this *before* the first white man was killed in Kenya, the supposed home of Uhuru. In the minds of white South Africans, a monstrous tsunami of base savagery was rolling down the length of Africa in their direction – it could be Blaauwkranz[21] all over again. They could not conceive how this savagery could possibly be reasoned with. It held all the promise of debate that the Blaauwkranz Massacre had held in 1838; the events at Port Elizabeth and East London had certainly proven that much. It would naturally prove very difficult to convince rank and file white South Africans that the ANC cared one iota about their interests, future, or lives. The British Secretary for Colonies had indeed been right; Uhuru was "*perverted nationalism*" and "*nostalgia for barbarism.*"

It is hardly surprising that the government of the day reacted with draconian laws to clamp down on this entire campaign. These included the Public Safety Act and Criminal Law Amendment Act. The former allowed government to declare a state of emergency to gain extraordinary powers in order to address riots and the like. The latter took square aim at any form of political protest. In the face of this, the ANC called off the campaign in mid-1953. However, in his autobiography Nelson Mandela states that, at nearly that same time, he asked Water Sisulu to try and reach China to ask for weapons[22].

The immediate result of the events in South Africa was a flurry of international condemnation of the government and the start of a continuous war by the United Nations on South Africa. People in the United States did not at that time appreciate the true nature of the United Nations, but have since discovered it the hard way. In the early 21st century, Americans would sound remarkably like 1960s South Africans on the subject of that organization and its polyglot collection of banana republic leaders, tin pot dictators, despots, and mass murderers. In 1952, many in the West still naively had stars in their eyes about the organization. Within South Africa, the government increased its drive toward true independence from Britain, lest that country should attempt to sell out the white people of South Africa in a misdirected effort to assuage its guilty conscience over its own leading role in African Slavery and its recent Colonialist past.

The author was born into the world described above, with racially segregated public amenities in operation all over both the United States and South Africa and with Senator McCarthy at his peak.

Nexus Familia 84: Child of the Covenant

The Booyens couple "from the farm"

Soon after his marriage in Middelburg in the Cape Province, it becomes clear to Herman Stephanus Booyens that, if he ever wanted to progress beyond patrolling the railway track, then he would have to take some company exams for a better position. The Railways are apparently giving preference to demobilized servicemen. The country is also a favored destination for many young British men who cannot make their way in the horrifically depressed post-War Britain.

The best Herman has been able to do thus far is to have his track patrol role expanded to that of calling the train drivers and firemen for their shifts from nearby Rosmead junction. He and his wife Nickie are also still living on Vleipoort farm with Nickie's parents, Kotie Myburgh and Pretty Bettie. Herman therefore studies very hard to become a *laaimeester* (freight checker) on the South African Railways.

After passing this exam, he obtains a position as checker at Rosmead. Soon, however, his employer transfers him to a shunting yard known as "R site" near the Port Elizabeth docks. Herman is now the living embodiment of the newly urbanized blue collar Afrikaner farm-boy "working stiff." The major employment benefit is that any house he buys using a mortgage loan guaranteed by the S.A. Railways, would automatically be paid up if he should die. He also gets one free long distance return train trip per annum for himself and his family. For people with strong family ties up-country the latter is a major benefit.

The best he and his young wife Nickie can do for accommodation is a boarding room for some months. After this, they manage to rent two rooms from a family in the North End suburb, two streets up from the downtown Main Street area. They have no own bathroom or kitchen in their home. There is a shared bathroom in the little cemented backyard where there is also an aviary. Herman knows little if anything about electrical work, but he soon illegally converts the aviary area into a separate little building to which he routes some electricity from the rest of the house. This now serves as a makeshift kitchen.

There is no means to prepare food, so they buy a small spirit (methyl alcohol) stove, commonly known by its trade name of *Primus*. Nickie somehow manages to prepare their meals on this little *Primus*. However, it is abundantly clear that this family is going nowhere fast.

So it is that Nickie secretly applies for several jobs in town, finally obtaining an interview with a big South African publication distribution company. Nickie is offered a job as clerk – a 100% Afrikaans farm girl in a wholly English commercial establishment, complete with its collection of expatriate Englishmen talking about "*Home*" in England. Herman kicks against the concept of his wife having to work. He was brought up as a typical Dutch Reformed Church Calvinist with the belief that a man should earn his keep by the sweat on his brow and should provide for his wife and family. However, when it becomes clear that they might just be able to afford a pressure cooker on Nickie's meager salary, he relents.

Child of the Covenant

It is Wednesday, December 16, 1953. In keeping with the Covenant made by the Trekkers before the Battle of Blood River, this date is treated as a perpetual Sunday in South Africa (*NF63*). Early on this morning a new child enters this world. As with all other Afrikaner children born on this date, the child is referred to as a *Geloftebaba* ("Baby of the Covenant").

The child is born the great grandson of a wagon transport rider from the Cape Midlands and a farmer from the Little Karoo. He is the grandson of a sheep farmer of the Cape Midlands and a policeman who served in the Little Karoo. He is born the son of an Afrikaner farm girl from the Cape Midlands and an ostrich herding farm boy from the Little Karoo who has become a railway worker in a city. In terms of his descent, he is approximately 40% Dutch, 35% German, 20% French and 5% Other, including Danish, Belgian, Baltic, Irish, Italian, Indian, Indonesian and Khoekhoe. His family name is North-Frisian, from Schleswig-Holstein. He is born with a white skin in Africa, but with DNA anchored in the unforgiving rock of Africa.

With a 300 year bloodline in Africa that runs through the indigenous Eva Krotoa (Chap. 1: *Krotoa, NF8*) from before 1652—a bloodline that is verified back to Jacob Klauten of the Nether-Rhine area who arrived in 1657 (*NF1, 6*)—this child is a true Afrikaner with genetic credentials to one day speak with natural authority on their behalf. The very DNA in his blood carries those credentials. In this, he will be very different from endless British, European and latter-day immigrant South Africans who presume themselves experts on the matter of Afrikaners and sit in judgment on issues to which their ancestry, background, or culture could never bear witness.

The regional culture of his young mother Nicola is that of the Eastern Cape Frontier; the tortured country from which the Great Trek emanated in 1836. Her own ancestral sister was married to the very first Trekker, Louis Trichardt (*NF44, 47, 53, 61*). Her ancestors were murdered by the Khoekhoe (*NF37*) and killed with poisoned arrows by the San Bushmen (Chap. 4: *Obiqua!*). Her grandparents were terrorized by the British Army and their family members executed (*NF78*) by that army for rebelling against genocide of their kin. This was the country where her ancestor opposed the British in 1800 at Graaff-Reinet (*NF31*). She is a direct descendant of the man who held the Government at gunpoint in Swellendam (*NF30*). She has been raised with an in depth understanding of the background (*Chapter 9, NF43*) to the Great Trek, on which her ancestor's Grobler and Joubert cousins were massacred at Umgungundlovu (*NF56*) and Blaauwkranz (*NF58*).

The ancestral background of his father Herman includes the two brothers whose deaths at the hand of the British Army respectively started and ended the Slagtersnek Rebellion of 1815 (*NF40*). It includes the third of those brothers, his own direct ancestor, who was accused of starting a frontier war in 1792 (*NF29*), a man whose cousin married the mother of the amaRharhabe Xhosa king Ngqika and became the king's adviser (Chap. 5: *The new young King*). It includes Sara Delport who died at the hand of the invading ama-Gqunukhwebe and Khoekhoe in the Scheepers massacre (*NF34*) at the foot of the Round Mountain and whose brother was banished from his own country for refusing to swear loyalty to the occupying English crown (Chap. 5: *Hate, Prejudice, and Ignorance*). It includes Jacob Louw who was thrown in the dungeon in the Cape Castle for opposing the corrupt governor in 1707 (*NF22*). It includes the man who made the first overland contact with black people in 1702 (*NF25*). Of the Booyens family of his grandfather who entered the British Concentration Camps, a full 57% died there (*NF77*). He is a direct descendant of Catrijn, the Indian Slave woman who was banished to the Cape for killing her abusive husband in Batavia (*NF3, 10, 11*).

For the baptism, the family goes to Middleburg, 220 miles inland, where Kotie and Pretty Bettie Myburgh are dying to see their grandchild. The baptism takes place on Sunday 14 March 1954 in the Dutch Reformed Church in Middelburg, mere yards from where the death sentences were promulgated in public over the Boer War rebels of 1901 (*NF78*).

I am baptized "Herman," named after both my father and my absconded paternal grandfather. It is the name of the original immigrant progenitor of my paternal line, who arrived at the Cape on 18 April 1707, passed down over nine generations.

Child of History

In 1950, in Elliotdale in the Transkei region of South Africa, undisputed land of the Gcaleka amaXhosa, Bassie Basson and Molly Callanan (*NF83*) have their first baby girl, Marie Neve. The delivery is done in the hospital at nearby Umtata. Marie's second name recognizes her Great Trek-descended grandmother, Neve Constance Milward. The first language that Marie masters is not English, her mother's language, but rather isiXhosa. This she gets from the Xhosa woman who is employed as her nanny in this rural area.

Some time later the family moves to Krugersdorp, some 700 miles to the north, not far from Johannesburg in "White South Africa." Not long after, on 19 April 1954, the couple have their second daughter, Jeanne, who will eventually marry the author. Jeanne has a bloodline that reads like a time-line of the history of South Africa. She shares several ancestors from the 17th century with the author, including Eva Krotoa and Pieter van Meerhoff (Chap. 1: *Krotoa, NF8*), Jacob Klauten (*NF1, 6*), Lammert Myburgh (*NF1, 13*), Pierre Joubert, and Jean Meinard (*NF18 and 19*).

Jeanne is the granddaughter of a survivor of the British Concentration Camps (*NF77*), an Afrikaner magistrate (*NF80*) from a long-established wheat farming family of the West Cape, and an Irishman who fought for President Paul Kruger against the British (*NF80*). She is the daughter of a WWII Afrikaner fighter pilot who helped to defeat Rommel, fought the air aces of the Luftwaffe, and who was shot down over Italy even as he supported Canadian and American troops from the air (*NF82*). She bears the name of her Protestant Huguenot ancestor, Jeanne Marque, who fled 1687 France with her two sons as a 60-year old lady, only to die aboard ship on the way to the Cape of Good Hope (*NF18, 19*).

Her ancestry includes Ariaentje Sterreveld from New York (*NF4, 7, 11,* and *20*) and Angela, the slave woman from Batavia (*NF3, 10, 11, 12*). It includes Johannes Klopper, whose brother-in-law led the Van Jaarsveld Rebellion against the British and was jailed in the Cape Castle for it (*NF33*), and whose nephew was hanged for his role in the Slagtersnek Rebellion (*NF40*). It includes Pieter Jordaan, who was brother-in-law to Great Trek leader Piet Retief, and on whose farm the Slagtersnek Rebellion (*NF40*) was planned, whose son Chris, her direct ancestor, joined the Double Trek jointly led by Pieter's son-in-law and his stepson (*NF50, 52*), and whose son Pieter George was impaled by the Zulu king at Umgungundlovu (*NF56*). Her direct ancestors also include three British Army soldiers (*NF41, 42, 66*).

Jeanne will grow up to be an English-speaking Afrikaner.

—*End Nexus Familia*

Prelude to disaster

While matters were brewing in Kenya and in the future Ghana, the situation was not hopeful for the other European nations that had been party to the disgraceful Berlin Conference of 1884-1885. For France the process of decolonization would start in a faraway irrelevant country that no American would ever have thought about. The name of this forested backwater was Vietnam, and it would eventually consume more than 60,000 American lives, severely diminish the stature of the country internationally, and deeply affect the psyche of the American nation for decades.

On May 7, 1954, the French garrison at Dien Bien Phu in Vietnam was overrun by Viet Minh troops backed by Red China. More than 11,000 French troops were made prisoners of war. The vast majority died in captivity. Many of them had been recruited from Algeria and Morocco. This was the first time in history that a major European power lost a formal war in a colony against indigenous people not of European descent. It shocked the Western World. Clearly, Western Man was not invincible. Although the United States naturally denied it at the time, it did provide extensive help to the French in the battle. In fact, two of the contingent of American pilots who assisted the French died in the battle. They were CIA pilot James McGovern and co-pilot Wallace Buford[23]. Their efforts would only be properly recognized 51 years later in 2005 when they were posthumously awarded the Legion of Honor with rank of Knight by the French President.

The prestige of France was hugely diminished by this experience. The event provided the impetus to the Arab colonies of France to launch their own drives toward independence. In the same year, the National Liberation Front of Algeria, led by Ahmed Ben Bella, launched a guerrilla campaign against the French authority in the country. France was to be the first European power to suffer a major blow in Africa, Britain having overcome the horrific Mau Mau for the time being through sheer repression and military force.

Algeria was unique. France had made it a formal province of the mother country. Consequently, Algerians of European descent were citizens of France. Indigenous Algerians received no such rights. Like the White Christian Afrikaner "amaBhulu" of South Africa, they were mere "subjects." Between 1825 and 1850, some 50,000 French settled in Algeria. By the late 1950s, the European descended population had grown to more than a million. Some 200,000 indigenous Algerian Harkis served in the French Army, including at places such as the aforementioned Dien Bien Phu.

The United Nations mandate troops from Britain and France departed Libya in December 1951. Morocco and Tunisia obtained their independence from France in March 1956. With a million French citizens in Algeria, however, the future of that country was much more difficult for France to resolve. And so fighting continued unabated.

Britain would be first to provide the world with a long term African humanitarian disaster. It would come in the form of the Sudan. Ever since 1924 Britain had administrated the Sudan as two separate entities: a Northern Arab Muslim state and a Southern Black state. The Arab north was more powerful, but entirely under the influence of Egypt. Upon independence from Egypt and Britain on January 1, 1956, the two Sudanese territories were united into a single predictable sociological disaster. The consequences of this precipitate British decision would still be with the world in the 21st Century in the form of the humanitarian crisis in the Darfur.

The inauspicious mess of the Sudan comes nowhere near the horror that would be unleashed by later British decisions. What seems to be generally less well understood, however, is the direct hand of the United States in this process.

Suez – Lighting the African fuse

On paper, the first European colony in Africa to obtain independence from European masters was Egypt in 1922, but in reality it remained under British military dominance. In 1952, Gamal Abdel Nasser was instrumental in removing King Farouk as head of state. By early 1953, he discarded all pretense to democracy and announced a One Party State. By February 1954, Nasser ousted the very man he helped place in position and was made Prime Minister. In this, he set the example for similar coups in Algeria, Iraq, Syria, and Yemen. In the process, he became the "poster boy" for Arab Nationalism and One Party States. Nasser set about negotiating true independence from Britain. The last British troops would leave in 1956.

However, there was a complication. France and Britain had huge strategic economic interests at stake in the Suez Canal through which most of their oil came from the Middle East. Nasser knew this very well. When he decided to make an armaments deal with the Soviets and recognized the "Red Chinese" government, the United States and Britain withdrew their funding for the Aswan dam in the Nile. Nasser then used this withdrawal as excuse to nationalize the Suez Canal.

In reality, Nasser was concerned about the new arrangements that Britain's Prime Minister, Anthony Eden, had concluded with Iraq and Jordan. These arrangements challenged Nasser's inflated perception of himself as the leader of the Arab world, or rather, leading dictator of the Arab world. He had been steadily and intentionally picking a fight with Britain to enhance his stature with the Arab nations. Now he had that fight.

The joint British and French response to the nationalization was to make a secret deal with Israel to retake the canal. Israel would attack in the Sinai and Britain and France would then re-occupy the canal, ostensibly in order to protect it from Israel. The level of intrigue here is much smaller than that which classically accompanied British and French activities in their colonies, but the fact that they embarked on this course on 29 October 1956 without consulting the United States earned them the ire of United States President, Dwight Eisenhower.

The Soviet Union made various threats, on none of which it was pragmatically in a position to act. Nevertheless, the United States threatened to sell all its holdings of British bonds. British Chancellor of the Exchequer, Harold Macmillan, warned that the resulting fall of the British currency would depress Britain economically to the point where the country would not be able to feed its own population. He promptly challenged Eden's decision to intervene militarily in Egypt.

And so it came to pass that a petulant American government threatened Great Britain with economic destruction in favor of an Arab dictator with delusions of grandeur. Britain and France had no option but to withdraw. Both the French and the British Prime ministers departed the scene in the wake of the debacle. The United States government, in failing to consider the full consequences of its actions, had just seriously weakened two pivotal pillars of Western Civilization. The country had not yet assumed the role of "Policeman of the World" and presumably did not understand these consequences. Five years before, Dean Acheson, then Under-Secretary of State, had commented on the new role of the United States[24]. He believed that only two powers were left and that the British were "finished" and "through." He also commented that these events were striking the United States before it was "ready for it."

The United States may have bought itself some influence with Egypt and Saudi Arabia in this process, but forty-five years later that influence did not prevent the majority of 11 September 2001 terrorist attackers of the World Trade Center in New York from being from those two countries. Nor did it prevent the new friends of the United States from attacking Israel, its closest ally in the Middle East, in 1973, thereby precipitating the Oil Crisis of the 1970s.

It has been argued that the Six Day War, the Yom Kippur War and the consequent Oil Crisis would have been averted if the United States had supported Britain and France in 1956. President Richard Nixon claims that Eisenhower subsequently considered the Suez decision *"a tragic mistake"*[25], but it was too late. The US administration had done all the damage they were going to do. It has been suggested that they were distracted by the Hungarian Revolution, which took place simultaneously and seemed far more germane at the time. This may have made them more apprehensive in their dealings with the Soviet Union. In the event, their opposition to the Soviet repression in Hungary had absolutely no effect anyway and was at best a distraction from events at Suez.

It is in Sub-Saharan Africa that the true cost of this decision may be counted today. In the wake of the Suez debacle, both Britain and France prepared to hive off their colonies as fast as they could, the consequences be damned. They clearly could not afford to retain their colonies if the United States were to make further decisions of this nature. All of Africa watched as France and Britain were internationally humiliated and weakened by the United States. All of Sub-Saharan Africa would now push for independence. The sub-continent was primed for fifty years of abject horror from which it has yet to emerge.

The man who followed Anthony Eden as Prime Minister of Britain was Harold MacMillan. In coming to terms with Britain's dramatically reduced international stature, he would end up presenting a fateful address to the South African Parliament. It would echo loudly in the author's family home. Given MacMillan's earlier opposition to Anthony Eden in the matter of Suez, his actions should come as no surprise.

Uhuru! The Scramble *out* of Africa

Formal independence, generally confused in Africa with Freedom or Uhuru, arrived in haphazard and drawn-out fashion in the British colonies in Africa, but in rather more organized fashion in the French ones. With the exception of their hugely negative experience in Algeria, the French managed the independence process vastly better than the British. They also managed to retain a longer-term positive influence. Fig. 20-4 gives the years of independence of the various colonies from 1955 until 1968.

The French, in their inimitable fashion, developed a unique solution to the matter of independence for their Black African colonies. They maintained close relations and signed defense agreements with most of them. These agreements often also secured special access for France to key strategic minerals, such as the uranium of Niger for the French nuclear effort. Throughout the following decades France would maintain military bases, warplanes and several thousand soldiers as a quick reaction force at the following places: Dakar in Senegal; Port Bouet in Côte d'Ivoire; Libreville in Gabon; N'Djamena in Chad; Bangui in the Central African Republic and Djibouti in the Horn of Africa. Little happened in the French ex-Colonies without the tacit agreement of the French government. Parties who stepped out of line soon found themselves confronted by either the French Air Force or the French Foreign Legion. All in all, France played a superb stabilizing role in what is otherwise a continent synonymous with man-made disaster.

A good example[26] of a functional French base in Africa was Djibouti, a strategic location with huge capacity for shipping. In essence, Djibouti is the "Window of the West" on the Red Sea. Here, as recently as the 1990s, the French stationed a squadron of ground-attack Mirage F1-C aircraft and helicopters along with anti-aircraft missile units, howitzers, 155 mm guns, some two-dozen tanks, and 446 vehicles. Here they also placed half a brigade of the famed French Foreign Legion. The imposing slow 88 steps per minute traditional march of the legendary Legion also served to maintain the mystique so respected and feared in Africa. Africa took note that the French "meant business" and were "not to be messed with." On an innately barbarous continent, such symbolic messages are very important given that debate or negotiation is mostly perceived as weakness. We shall later meet another foreign legion in Africa with an equally impressive mystique.

Dates of Independence	1955–1956	1957–1958	1959–1960	1961–1962	1963–1964	1965–1966	1967–1968	Legend
			Mauritania					Spain
			Mali					Belgium
			Senegal					France
			Gabon					Britain
			Brazzaville					
			Central Afr. Rep.					
			Chad					
			Côte d'Ivoire					
			Burkina Faso					
			Niger					
			Benin	Algeria				
			Madagascar	Rwanda				
			Togo	Burundi				
			Cameroon	Uganda		Lesotho		
	Tunisia		Congo (Belgian)	Tanzania	Zambia	Botswana	Equat. Guinea	
	Morocco	Guinea	Nigeria	South Africa	Malawi	Zimbabwe	Swaziland	
	Sudan	Ghana	Somalia	Sierra Leone	Kenya	Gambia	Mauritius	

Fig. 20-4. A graphic depiction of the Scramble out of Africa by the European countries in 1955-1968

Based on this excellent distribution of bases throughout Black Africa north of the Equator, the French could project their comparatively limited military power with great efficacy, earning them huge respect on the continent. French presidents during the Fifth Republic always had a special civilia–n advisor for African affairs at the Élysée Palace: "Mr. Africa." The leading Mr. Africa was Jacques Foccart. He met with de Gaulle every evening to discuss events in Africa. France took Black Africa very seriously indeed. It intervened militarily in Françafrique, as they call Francophone Africa, no fewer than five times[27] between 1958 and 1968.

By comparison, the British departure from Africa was a disaster. Their legacy includes Zimbabwe with its murderous tyrant Robert Mugabe, Kenya with its Mau Mau and its 2008 uprisings and massacres, Sierra Leone with its civil wars and inhuman atrocities around blood diamonds, Uganda with its Idi Amin horror and Nigeria with its endless internecine fighting and civil wars. To their credit, their legacy also covers the two states in Africa that stand out above all others, South Africa and Botswana.

When all is said and done, the most stable state in Africa is Botswana, a country with a full multi-party democracy where white and black live happily together. Even South Africa cannot match that feat, despite its vastly bigger economy. Botswana has two major factors in its favor. Firstly, its population is largely composed of one single Black ethnic group, the Ba'Tswana. Secondly, its government has specifically followed a policy of leaving white people alone to build the economy and make a living. This is to be contrasted with the ANC government in South Africa and its brazenly racist Affirmative Action and Black Economic Empowerment policies, along with its focus on the willful destruction of white Afrikaner culture in particular.

The Belgian departure from Africa spawned the worst results of all. Their legacy includes the "Belgian Congo," the Rwandan genocide, and Burundi. The Congo will assume a unique place in this work and will be addressed in more detail. The events in the Congo would directly touch the author's family in South Africa.

One Party States, Genocide, and worse

Soon after gaining independence for Ghana from Britain on 26 March 1957, Nkrumah started to consolidate all the powers of government in himself. He set the example that practically every other newly independent African state would follow. With him, as leader of the first significant country in "Black Africa" to gain independence, the concept of The Big Man Government started and is with us still in the 21st century. Within two years of independence[28] he abolished regional governments and centralized power in his own hands. Black African states would offer endless explanations and justifications for why incumbent Black leaders had to remain in power outside the limits of Democracy. Grandiose theories would be advanced on their part as to why this needed to be so in Africa in particular and how European models of government were inappropriate. Leaders such as Julius Nyerere would excel at this Soviet style theory-mongering. By 1964, Nkrumah in Ghana had dropped all pretense of supporting Democracy and had turned the country into a one-party state. Britain conveniently looked away. Of the eight Black African British colonies that had democratic governments at independence, only Botswana would eventually retain that status[29]. The rest all lapsed into autocracy or worse. White people of the south wryly referred to Black Africa as a case of *One man, One vote, Once only.* They justifiably scratched their heads at how their kin in the Northern Hemisphere could expect them to submit to this concept of rule by indigenous African leaders.

Along with the One Party State came endemic corruption. Martin Meredith, as possibly the most insightful British writer in the 21st century on the subject of Africa, explains[30] the cultural nature of corruption and bribery in Ghana and Nigeria. Essentially, it was born from a perception that they were robbing the white man and that it was therefore acceptable; they were merely taking "their share." In fact, it would continue for generations after the departure of the Colonial powers and is today culturally inculcated. Africa now deservedly personifies the word "corruption." The well-known "Nigerian Scam" of the 21st century is an entirely natural next step. They are still taking from white men, the difference being that the white men are in the United States, Canada, and Europe. This would be an intriguing theory, if it were not for the fact that the leaders have robbed their own nations blind and squirreled away billions of dollars in places like Switzerland; all this while their own people languish in poverty.

With the advent of the One Party State came entirely predictable draconian laws aimed at squashing all opposition. Again, Kwame Nkrumah would be the poster boy for this corruption of the principles of Democracy when he introduced the Preventative Detention Act[31] in 1958. This Act allowed him to detain opponents without trial for 5 years. Often the next step in this cascade of horror would be a coup d'état or civil war or both. During the 1960s, and particularly after 1965, countries in Black Africa would reel from repeated coups. In later decades, various regions would lurch forth into Massacre and Genocide.

The ultimate horror would come with Emperor Bokassa of the Central African Republic. This man, who declared himself an emperor in the same vein as Napoleon, would literally feed his opponents to the crocodiles he kept in his palace pool. He would ultimately be removed by French troops brought in from Gabon and Chad. He would be charged with cannibalism when human bodies were discovered in his refrigerator – minus their heads[32]. His successor reported that human flesh had been a regular item on the menu at the Bokassa residence and had on occasion been served to ignorant foreign dignitaries.

The later decades of African independence would be characterized by massacres in Uganda and genocide in Rwanda. Through all this horror, the Northern Hemisphere democracies increasingly expected the typically staunchly Protestant Christian Western white South Africans to submit to the above. Through South African eyes the thought bordered on the criminally insane. It was clearly the "London Missionary Society" all over again, this time in the guise of the left-leaning Western Media and the *BBC* with its mysterious control board. Behind all this, the Soviets supplied various Communist-leaning countries in Africa with massive amounts of weapons and promoted their "International Communist Revolution." They would eventually help Cuba to send tens of thousands of troops to Africa. Along with these would come thousands of Soviet Bloc "advisors." This would turn to open warfare with South Africa in 1975.

With this 20-year sketch as background, we return to the period round about 1960.

The Year of Africa: Barbarity at Cato Manor

Inspired by the impending independence of many Black African countries during 1960 and emboldened by moral support from Communist countries and the British Communist Party in London, the ANC moved to politically exploit any confrontational situation. An appropriate opportunity presented itself on 23 January 1960 at a place named Cato Manor. It is a tragedy that the haplessly one-sided international media never raises this matter in addressing the Sharpeville event of a few weeks later. It is absolutely key and central to the events in the first half of 1960, but the troubles at Cato Manor had started much earlier.

Cato Manor outside Durban arose as an unregulated squatter area from around 1932 onwards. Many Zulu squatters moved in and Indians found that renting land and shacks to Zulus was more lucrative than other modes of commerce or business. By 1949, the population of Durban included around 250,000 blacks, 125,000 whites and 110,000 Indians, descendants of indentured laborers brought there by the British and at the time the largest community of Indians outside India; Mahatma Ghandi's original broader community.

By 1949, resentment among the Zulu toward their Indian landlords had reached an explosive level. The Zulu accused the Indians of slumlord tactics. When an Indian merchant in Durban City reputedly assaulted a Zulu boy, the unconfirmed event served as the spark to set off the powder keg. As is so typical of Black African mobs, there was no attempt to ascertain facts. They simply went on the rampage in the city and attacked any Indians they could find. Army and Navy units were quickly mobilized to drive the amaZulu horde from the city. However, the amaZulu mobs now directed their attention to the less well-protected Indians in Cato Manor. What followed was horrific. Time Magazine[33] described the Zulu horde as chanting their war songs and brandishing torches, iron spikes, and knobkerries. Whenever they spotted an Indian, the cry of "Bulala!"[34] followed.

The magazine reported seven of a family of eleven Indians dying in their burning shack. Seven others were thrown bodily from railway cars. Fleeing Indians were simply struck down. Others were pulled from their houses, beaten and raped. Police and soldiers tried to protect the Indians using improvised stockades, but some Indians bolted and threw themselves over a 500-foot cliff as the Zulu horde charged down on them with their shrill war cries. In the end, the Army put down the riots, but the death toll was more than 100. This was the Africa that the Afrikaner had known ever since first clashing with the amaXhosa on the Eastern Frontier in the 1780s. Despite politically expedient pretenses to the contrary, the culture of Black Africa and that of South Asia are utterly incompatible. In 1972, the Indian population of Uganda would experience the consequences of this mismatch when Uganda's new leader, Idi Amin, would expel almost all the Indians in the country, despite most of them having been born there. Today, many of them live in Britain and Canada.

On 17 June 1959, Cato Manor would again be the center of attention in South Africa. Over several decades, it had been the practice for local municipal authorities to brew their own beer and sell this to the Zulu population. It was both a source of revenue and an attempt to regulate the behavior of people who were capable of the group conduct described above. On the other hand, the brewing and selling of beer via so-called "shebeens" was also a traditional occupation of Zulu township women, so called "shebeen queens."

In 1959, the leader of the ANC women's League and Communist Party member, Dorothy Nyembe, and her protegé, Florence Mkhize, decided to target the government beer halls, ostensibly in support of the shebeen queens in Cato Manor. Both already had longstanding records as activists. They attacked the Zulu men drinking at the beer halls and left their mark on South African history in a unique way. Mkhize soaked her underwear in the beer and Nyembe urinated in the brew[35]. Nyembe would eventually receive the highest Soviet foreign honor[36], the "U.S.S.R. People's Friendship Award"; one of innumerable condescending trinkets handed out by that regime to parties in revolutionary movements useful to the U.S.S.R. the world over.

Some days later the Director of Ba'Ntu Administration of the government met with some 2,000 Zulu women to discuss their grievances. The whole event turned ugly when the women would not disperse after the meeting. The day ended with a huge crowd of Zulu men attacking the local police station and the police shooting to defend their own lives. Four people died in these riots and some 70 were injured.

Matters at Cato Manor came to a head on 23 January 1960. On that day, a crowd of Zulu men attacked a contingent of five black and four white policemen who had somehow got themselves separated from the bulk of the force that had arrived to undertake yet another so called "liquor raid." They were brutally hacked to death, their genitals were severed and stuffed in their mouths and their desecrated bodies were dragged through the Zulu township[37]. The event sent shockwaves through the country and particularly affected terrified policemen, both black and white. Their onerous duties constantly took them into areas such as Cato Manor, which had been the subject of ANC activism. The majority of the policemen killed in the Cato manor event were themselves black men.

With the country in this state of apprehension, the next blow fell a few days later in Cape Town. It would be delivered by the leader of Britain, the country that had paid with the lives of 10,698 soldiers and invented Concentration Camps in its single-minded insistence on taking Southern Africa by force in 1899.

The Wind of Change

The independence of Ghana in 1957 had already inspired some black people from elsewhere in the world to reconsider their own future. In fact, a considerable number of American black people elected to settle in Ghana[38].

One interesting individual was Anna Pauli Murray[39], a black lady lawyer from Durham Country in North Carolina with a Law Degree from Howard University in Washington, DC. She spent 18 months in Ghana to assist in training people for the new country. However, she quickly crossed swords with the regime of Kwame Nkrumah when the latter implemented the Preventative Detention Act to suppress opposition. The events in the Belgian Congo also brought her face to face with the fact that she could not possibly associate with the on-the-ground realities of the African Uhuru. She saw herself as an American first and "Black" second and, despite the discriminatory practices in the United States at the time, the reality of Africa was something that she could not associate with. She left Ghana after serving only half of her planned three years. Many years later, she would write[40] that the locals in Ghana called her "Oburoni," meaning "stranger" or "foreigner." She concluded that her dark skin and slavery history did not make her African enough for Africa. In the political parlance of the 21st century she, a Black American, was not "Black enough" for Africa. Very few Black South Africans shared Pauli Murray's kind of Western cultural background. Their cultural background was African. They would therefore not have perceived the problems that concerned her.

The government in South Africa was concerned about the potential effect in South Africa of the impending independence of no fewer than 17 African colonies in 1960. Fourteen of these colonies comprised the entire collection of French ones in Black Africa (minus Guinea, which was already independent). Two were British, being Nigeria and Somalia. However, the most worrisome one, and also the one closest to South Africa, was the Belgian Congo with its bad historical reputation and demonstrably weak "colonial master."

Many South African mining people, given their expertise as part of the world's most comprehensive mining industry, either worked or had worked in the Katanga area of the Congo. The author himself later worked with a truly brilliant scientist who had been a mining scientist in Katanga in this era. Many South Africans also had friends in the Congo. The railway line from South Africa ran northward through Botswana, Zimbabwe (then Southern Rhodesia), and Zambia (then Northern Rhodesia) and terminated in the Katanga Province of the Congo, famous for its copper mines.

Against this backdrop, and following a rebellion of amaPondo in the far eastern areas of traditional Xhosa territory of Trans-Kei in 1959, the visit of the British Prime Minister, Harold MacMillan, would prove traumatic in the extreme. On 3 February 1960, as part of a broader visit to Africa, Macmillan was set to address the South African Parliament in Cape Town. Instead of providing the white people of South Africa some sort of a sense of security in a difficult time on a bloodthirsty continent, he used the occasion to lecture the parliament of this as yet not independent country and did more damage to its future history than he could ever have imagined. His words would reverberate around the author's family dinner table and no doubt hastened the country's move to independence, and even more restrictive legislation. It would go down in history as the *"Winds of Change Speech."* This is the day that white people in Africa were told that they were doomed and deserted with nowhere else to go; mere sacrificial pawns in the Cold War. The excerpted salient points of this watershed Cold War speech were:

"No one could fail to be impressed with the immense material progress which has been achieved [in South Africa]. *That all this has been accomplished in so short a time is a striking testimony to the skill, energy and initiative of your people...*[...]

As I've travelled around the Union I have found everywhere, as I expected, a deep preoccupation with what is happening in the rest of the African continent. I understand and sympathize with your interests in these events and your anxiety about them. [...]

The wind of change is blowing through this continent,...[...]

... in the history of our times yours will be recorded as the first of the African nationalists.[...]

... the growth of national consciousness in Africa is a political fact, and we must accept it as such. That means, I would judge, that we've got to come to terms with it. I sincerely believe that if we cannot do so we may imperil the precarious balance between the East and West on which the peace of the world depends.[...]

The world today is divided into three main groups:

• *First there are what we call the Western Powers. You in South Africa and we in Britain belong to this group, together with our friends and allies in other parts of the Commonwealth. In the United States of America and in Europe we call it the Free World.*

• *Secondly there are the Communists – Russia and her satellites in Europe and China whose population will rise by the end of the next ten years to the staggering total of 800 million.*

• *Thirdly, there are those parts of the world whose people are at present uncommitted either to Communism or to our Western ideas. In this context we think first of Asia and then of Africa.*

As I see it the great issue in this second half of the twentieth century is whether the uncommitted peoples of Asia and Africa will swing to the East or to the West...[...]

What is now on trial is much more than our military strength or our diplomatic and administrative skill. It is our way of life. The uncommitted nations want to see before they choose."

It is to be doubted whether any nation in the history of man had ever been told so bluntly that it was being deserted and thrown to the wolves by the very Civilization of which the speaker confessed them to be a part. Possibly the Poles would have understood. They had been delivered into the hands of their archenemies at the end of WWII by the people who had ostensibly declared that war to free them. But at least the Poles had a country, and the Russians, for all the objectionable shortcomings of the Soviet model, were still members of Western Civilization. The Poles might very well be in bondage, but they always had hope.

The closest historical parallel for the whites of South Africa was the Romans absconding back to Rome, deserting the Britons in England and Wales and leaving them to the depredations of the Celtic tribes the Romans had fought for hundreds of years. It was worse, though, because the Romans at least did not side with the opposing tribes. Those who heard the speech wondered why the British had instigated the Boer War; what the generation before them had died for in the British concentration camps. Many of them wondered why they had fought World War II. They thought of the thousands of friends and family who had died in that war, and in World War I and in the Korean War. They stared into an abyss and knew they were totally on their own. As Macmillan's words fell, those listening knew only disgust. Macmillan might just as well have said:

"You are one of the Western Powers and part of the Free World, but you all be good chaps now and die to spare us all the bother. Your existence threatens my way of life."

No offer was made of citizenship in Britain. No recourse was offered to any means of maintaining a Western Nation in the face of the obvious threat. The French in Algeria would later know the same dismay, but they would in fact have French citizenship and receive help to return to France. The French Algerian Pieds Noirs would later attempt to assassinate de Gaulle for his actions in Algeria. Such options would not occur to the dyed-in-the-wool "Presbyterian/Dutch-Reformed" Afrikaner. Such acts serve no sensible purpose.

Hendrik Verwoerd, now the Prime Minster, rose to deliver his response:

> *"...this is our only motherland, we have nowhere else to go...[...]*
> *...we believe in balance, we believe in allowing exactly those same full opportunities to remain within the grasp of the white man who has made all this possible."*

Here was an Englishman with zero real experience of Africa trying to tell a nation that had lived on the continent for 310 years that the fate of the Western World actually depended on which way Darkest Africa would swing. That sounded as ignorant and analytically inane in 1960 to white South Africans as it might to Americans in the 21st century. Black Africa, the congenital "basket case" of the planet was now somehow in 1960 to determine the destiny of the United States, Germany, Britain, and France? The thought was insane. Nevertheless, based on that assessment, Britain was trying to force Westerners in South Africa to surrender to these savage forces. Perhaps the British government was still deluding itself into believing it could control Black Africa and maintain their minerals supplies via the traditional disparate British mix of pomp & ceremony and gunboat diplomacy.

The only conceivable way ahead for the white amaBhulu of South Africa was to,

a) recognize that Britain was no friend of Western Caucasian people in Africa; and

b) rid the country of the remaining British political influence as soon as possible to preclude them selling the nation out to the savagery of Black Africa, as they had already started doing elsewhere.

c) With the Soviets backing up the most vicious of groups on the continent, the traditional "laager" would have to be drawn and the powder kept dry, figuratively speaking; and

d) the country would have to wait and pray for a break in the "unholy alliance" of the ultra-savage African Nationalism and the Soviet Union.

Back in London, MacMillan's Colonial Secretary was already meeting with representatives of all the races in Kenya and unceremoniously told the stunned white Kenyan settlers' representatives that Britain accepted majority black rule for Kenya[41]. Given that the same British government had encouraged the settlement of these very same people a handful of years earlier, the dismay can certainly be understood.

British-descended people in Africa now found themselves facing the same position as that in which the Afrikaner had been for centuries. Suddenly everything looked different and "Britannia" did not seem such an honorable entity anymore. As had almost happened in 1835 in the wake of the 6th Frontier War (Chapter 9: *The Third Great Abandonment*), the British government had now indeed decided to withdraw from Africa. It had no choice. Fifty-eight years after the Boer War had showed up the Empire for what it really was, it was dead and spent. Britain was now just another country. Three years later MacMillan would leave office due to "ill health" in the wake of the Profumo Affair, in which it would be revealed that his Secretary of State for War, John Profumo, was sleeping with a lady who reputedly also shared the bed of the Soviet naval attaché.

Sharpeville – "Son of Cato Manor"

With Macmillan's detested speech ringing in the ears of white South Africans and the police still in shock after the horrific events at Cato Manor, the next outrage came on March 21, 1960 at a place named Sharpeville. The Pan Africanist Congress had been born on 6 April 1959, the anniversary of the landing of Jan van Riebeeck at the Cape in 1652. Its leader was Robert Sebukwe. While his father was of BaSotho stock,

Sebukwe's mother[42] was a Pondo, the northernmost of the isiXhosa speaking people. The young Sebukwe grew up in Graaff-Reinet. His cultural background therefore was heavily influenced by views emanating from the amaXhosa homeland. Pondoland, bordering on the province of Natal, was indisputably the territory of the broader amaXhosa grouping. This grouping included Raymond Mhlaba's amaRharhabe Xhosa, Nelson Mandela's amaThembu and Sebukwe's amaPondo, though the amaRharhabe had their own land south of the Kei – the so-called Ciskei.

The PAC was quite clear in its views. It rejected the ANC's purported multi-racial agenda and stood clearly for an "Africa for Africans only." They saw Whites and Indians as interlopers. This was an odd concept, given that among the Whites most Afrikaners could prove their presence in the country with suitable documentary evidence all the way back to the 1600s. At that time, the Xhosa peoples in particular were still living 800 miles from Cape Town. In this respect, the PAC therefore represented pure black racism.

In its search for a suitable issue to exploit, the PAC decided to focus on the hated passbooks that black people in "white areas" had to carry[43]. They arranged for massed demonstrations on 21 March 1960 in which black people would demand to be imprisoned for burning their pass books or for refusing to carry them. In most places, the call was not heeded, but in Cape Town and in Sharpeville it found traction.

The town of Vanderbijlpark on the Vaal River, south of Johannesburg, was founded during World War II around the main steel mills of South Africa. The company was the parastatal ISCOR, now named Mittal, and had been created to support the war effort. Thousands of black workers were employed in the operations of ISCOR and lived in the sprawling township of Sharpeville. It is here that the call by Sebukwe found its greatest response.

With Cato Manor and the horrific deaths of the policemen there still fresh in their minds, the twenty policemen at the local police station found themselves surrounded by 20,000 black people pressing forward to "be arrested" and chanting[44],[45] "Cato Manor! Cato Manor!" The terrified police barricaded themselves behind a 4-foot tangle of barbed wire and called in reinforcements. These soon arrived in the form of four British-made Saracen armored cars and 130 more police armed with WWII vintage British STEN submachine guns, making a total of only 150 policemen to control a crowd of 20,000 people. The result was entirely inevitable.

At 1.20 p.m., the crowd advanced on the police station and started throwing rocks at the police[46]. While the details and exact sequence of events in the following two minutes would be debated for many years to come, the agreed facts are that the police opened fire and, when the shooting died down, 69 people lay dead and more than 100 were wounded. The Western World erupted in outrage and the political isolation of the already physically isolated, frightened, and embattled white people of South Africa started in earnest. A few days later, the PAC led another march of 30,000 black people on the Parliament Building in Cape Town and Albert Luthuli, leader of the ANC, burned his passbook and called on all black people to stay away from work. The country was nearly paralyzed and the stock exchange fell precipitously.

On 8 April 1960, the government "banned" the ANC and PAC, driving both organizations underground, where they would ultimately do more damage. Much of the establishment in Afrikaner circles urged Prime Minister Verwoerd to ease up on the hurtful Pass Book system, but he was deaf to all entreaties. The leading Afrikaner newspaper, Die Burger, pleaded that the "Apartheid" policy had obviously failed.

On 9 April 1960, the Dutch-born Prime Minster, Verwoerd, was shot in the head by a deranged white farmer from Natal. The country appeared to be staggering from blow to blow. With South Africa in this stunned condition, the next event would play off some 2,000 miles to the north in the Belgian Congo.

Congo – The Heart of Darkness erupts

The Congo embodied the worst fears of white South Africans come horribly true in another African country, and it practically coincided with the horrors of Cato Manor and Sharpeville in South Africa. The Belgian Congo was and still is the Dark Heart of Africa. It had been the place where the worst of European colonial behavior had been implemented. The Congo under King Leopold had been the living embodiment of human cruelty.

As Belgium struggled to find her way out of the Congo in 1960 whilst simultaneously retaining control over the mineral riches of the southeastern Katanga region, matters started to boil over. Patrice Lumumba, a fervent Black Nationalist, had already been voted Prime Minister and independence had arrived on 30 June 1960. The Belgian head of the colonial army, General Janssens, had been retained as head of the new Army. However, Janssens refused to allow advancement of Congolese officers to senior positions in that army. This refusal became the spark for a mutiny five days later. The soldiers had seen the new black politicians in their fancy cars and they wanted their share of the "spoils."

The Congo was far from ready for independence. The Belgians had ensured that this would be the case, as there were no Congolese doctors, only 30 university graduates, and only 136 children completed secondary school in that year. South Africa was a heaven for black people in comparison with this disaster.

As the rebellion spread, the black Congolese specifically targeted whites, whom they humiliated, beat, and raped; priests and nuns being singled out for the worst treatment before being murdered. It was war on Christianity as a "white" institution. Such is Africa, as we have already seen in the ANC Defiance Campaign in the author's hometown of Port Elizabeth and in East London.

The white Belgian population started to flee en masse. When Lumumba refused to allow Belgian troops to take action to protect the Belgian nationals, the Belgian government ordered them into the field anyway. Lumumba thereupon broke off diplomatic relations and declared war on Belgium, considering his country under attack. He promptly Africanized the Congolese army and appointed a man named Joseph Mobutu as Chief-of-Staff. We shall meet him again.

The Belgians appreciated that the Congo was lost to them, but they sought to retain the key southeastern Katanga province with the minerals. On 10 July, a man named Moïs Tshombe announced that Katanga was seceding from the Congo with the full support of the Belgian Army. Tshombe also enlisted the help of a collection of white mercenaries from Belgium, Britain, Rhodesia, and South Africa. One of the mercenary leaders was a man named Mike Hoare, an Irish Gentleman[47] Mercenary who had served in the British Army and who lived in South Africa. Mike Hoare and Bob Denard, his French equivalent, would become the most famous mercenaries in the world and would elevate the occupation to a popular level seldom seen before.

Lumumba insisted on UN intervention. The UN was prepared to ask the Belgians to leave, but was not prepared to involve itself in a civil war, which it saw as an internal matter. This drove Lumumba systematically more frantic, leading him to ultimately ask for Soviet help. At this point, President Eisenhower of the United States made it clear that he favored the elimination of Lumumba. According to Larry Devlin, CIA station chief in the Congo, he received instructions, apparently issued by Eisenhower[48], to kill Lumumba and was provided with suitable poison.

Meanwhile Lumumba was removed from office by National President Kasavubu, a member of the Ba'Kongo tribe (See the next section). On 14 September 1960, Joseph Mobutu, with the full support of the United Nations and the CIA, announced that he was neutralizing all politicians and would assume power himself. He then ordered all Soviet and Czech personnel out of the country.

In 2001, a Belgian Parliamentary Commission[49] would confirm claims by author Ludo de Witte that Lumumba was shot by indigenous soldiers in the presence of Belgian officers. It took place at some time after 10pm on the night of 17 January 1961 in a clearing in the bush some 30 miles from Elisabethville[50]. The body was buried, then exhumed later, and hacked to pieces. It was then at least partially disposed of in sulfuric acid[51]. The West had won, but it had literally committed murder to do so.

The Soviets would not forget. They had learned that they needed votes at the UN. The battle for the many new African votes had started. Katanga and the rest of the Congo were eventually reunited in 1962.

Here the Congo would rest uneasily for now.

Angola – Horror on the Ides of March

As is so often true in Africa, the northern border between the ex-Belgian Congo and Portuguese Angola bisected a nation. In this case, it was, and still is in the 21st century, the Ba'Kongo people. On the night of 14-15 March 1961, an army of Ba'Kongo crossed the border into the coffee plantations of Northern Angola. They called themselves the União das Populaçoes de Angola (UPA: Union of People of Angola) and were led from an armchair in the Congo by an expatriate Angolan by the name of Holden Roberto, an admirer of Patrice Lumumba of the Congo. During a stay with Nkrumah, Roberto had decided on violence[52] as the way to independence. In 1959, he had visited the United States, meeting with (then) Senator John F. Kennedy, and the new Kennedy Administration now politically supported the Angolan independence drive[53].

On the morning of 15 March 1961, the drug-maddened attackers fell upon the villagers in the region with screams of *"Kill the whites! Kill the whites!"* and *"Lumumba! Lumumba!"* These men had all been treated by "witchdoctors" to believe that "white man's bullets would not harm them," a practice we have come across before among the amaXhosa in South Africa (Chap. 13: *The War of Mlanjeni*). What happened next would make the horrors of the Kenyan Mau-Mau and the 1952 cannibalism in East London, South Africa pale into insignificance. To white people in Africa, it became the indelible image of African Nationalism. There have now been more than five decades of attempts to rewrite this history to suit popular Socialist rhetoric, but the essential facts stand. The victims were horribly tortured[54] before being killed and mutilated. People were crucified and their eyes cut out. Machetes were used to slit open the wombs of pregnant women and their bodies were set alight. Children were reportedly burnt alive and men systematically chopped to death.

Sub-foreman Manuel Lourenço Eves Alves later described[55] the events to police. Some 400 terrorists attacked their coffee plantation village at M'bridge. He started shooting at them and his black helper tried to reach the next house to obtain more ammunition. He was caught, beheaded, his genitals cut off and shoved into the mouth of his disembodied head. The murderers then danced hysterically with these trophies in their hands, shrieking and whistling as they did so. The babies were thrown in the air to fall to their deaths. The men then played football with their bodies in front of their hysterical captive mothers. The children's bodies were dismembered and their body parts draped over the trees while the mothers were raped viciously by many of the men, who stuck sticks up their bodies as they died. The drug-crazed Ba'Kongo then cut the breasts off almost all the women; a mass psychotic obsession we saw at Blaauwkranz (*NF58*). Alves described the crucifixion of a pretty young white girl and how her severed breasts were placed in her hands.

According to some reports the UPA killed 42 white men, women and children in the village of Luvo, tying the dead and the still living lengthwise to planks and feeding them through the sawmill. In an interview[56] with Pierre de Vos of Le Monde a few weeks later, Roberto would confirm the massacre and torture of Portuguese men, women and children, stating *"why deny it?"* De Vos even met some of the men who had reportedly perpetrated the sawmill massacre and who said, *"we sawed them lengthwise."* Roberto tried to blame the events on a labor dispute, a common bogus theme to be used for decades to come by African Nationalists.

The Portuguese military reaction was understandably violent. However, it also spilled over into the civilian domain. *Daily Telegraph* reporter Richard Beeston describes[57] how, in the wake of the above, a mob of white Portuguese chased a black man onto a Luanda roof and then hurled him off the roof onto the ground right next to him. In a strange, almost medieval reaction, the Portuguese establishment also turned their anger on Protestant missionaries. Two years later Robert Kennedy[58] would instruct the CIA to provide Holden Roberto with financial assistance. Angola would never again be the quiet backwater it had been. .

Nexus Familia 85: Born in Fear

Port Elizabeth – 1955

One of the earliest things I remember of the world around me, is offering to carry the shopping basket if my mother, Nickie, would carry me. This is because I am so scared of the Xhosa people who are attacking trains passing through the New Brighton black township. I have no idea what exactly is going on in Port Elizabeth, but I am scared of Black people because I have been told that they have burnt churches, killed the nuns and any white people they could find and that they have even eaten them[59]. All the grownups walk around with big eyes. They say the "trouble is always around Port Elizabeth where the Xhosas are."

Fig. 20-5 Our 1950s family house on Kent Road with New Brighton Black Township in the distance

I am deeply aware of some or other scary thing called an "Uhuru" or a "Mau Mau" that somehow comes with black people who apparently go completely berserk and kill all people who are not black. However, the only black people I know are the two men who sell *Walls* and *Dairy Maid* ice cream from their tricycle ice cream carts. They somehow seem okay. I have looked really carefully at them and they do not seem berserk, though I do not quite know what to look for. Best to be careful, though.

My father seems to know these black people. He works with hundreds of Xhosa men from a faraway place called Transkei. He calls them "raw Xhosas." What I do know is that I cannot understand a word of what they say to each other, because they speak a really strange language. They speak very loudly and they continue shouting to each other at the top of their voices when they are quite far apart going in opposite directions. Nickie tells me the language is called isiXhosa. It has lots of loud tongue-clicking and sucking sounds with a lot of loud "oo," "ah" and "ee" sounds in between.

The corner shop is owned by people who look really strange. Nickie tells me they are Chinese. There I can use my penny that I sometimes get, to buy the very smallest *Cadbury's Dairy Milk* chocolate. Nickie says Chinese people do not go berserk, so they must be okay. Around the corner from us live some people who also look very different. When I ask Nickie why they look like that, she tells me they are Muslim "Malays." I have no idea what that means and no one really explains it to me either[60].

Sputnik – I want to be a scientist

My father, Herman, works at R-Site on the railways and walks the two miles to work every day, because we do not own a car. He takes along a lunch box my mother makes for him every morning. She tells me my father is doing his best to save some money by not using a bus. One evening he comes home, picks me up, and walks with me an incredibly long distance to a faraway place[61]. This is to show me a house he is planning to buy a few blocks away. I have no idea why he wants to do this. I am quite happy where we are and have no idea how other kids are growing up. I do not feel as though I am missing anything. I like our home, because I know where everything is; most particularly, I know exactly how to move chairs so I can scale the cupboard and steal the bottle of *Marmite* bread spread off the top shelf. Nickie tells me the new house is much better because it is a separate house, all just for us, and that it has an actual own bathroom and kitchen. That is good!

Soon after we move into the new house on Kent Road, it starts to rain and the roof leaks in torrents. Over this period, my two parents work very hard to put a new corrugated iron roof on the house by themselves. Nickie personally breaks rocks to make the gravel for a concrete lintel over the veranda. She tells me there is no money to pay anyone to help. It is at this point that I start to realize that money is quite important stuff and very difficult to get hold of. My father makes toys for me after hours in the Railway workshop, because there is no money for presents.

Our annual Free Pass on the S.A. Railways now comes in handy, as it allows Nickie and I to visit my grandparents, Kotie Myburgh and Pretty Bettie (*NF84*), on Vleipoort outside Middelburg. The train ride starts in the evening and we get to Rosmead station the next morning. At Rosmead junction, *Oupa* (Grandfather) Kotie comes to fetch us with his positively huge 1936 model *Studebaker*. At *Vleipoort* farm, he shows me how they shear sheep.

There are more black people on the farm than I have ever seen near our house in Port Elizabeth. I tell Oupa Kotie that they look different from the people that I see in Port Elizabeth. They also appear to be generally thinner than the Xhosa people. He explains that some of them are Ba'Sotho. He says they are very different from the Xhosa who "always make trouble near Port Elizabeth." In this way, I learn that there are different black people in different parts of the country.

Back in Port Elizabeth one evening, Nickie takes me to the grassy park diagonally across from the house. We call it "The Hill." She picks me up on her arm

***Fig. 20-6** Vleipoort farmstead outside Middelburg (ca. 1955)*

and points out a star. That is when I notice this particular star is moving. I have never seen that before. Then she tells me it is called *Sputnik*, and that some people called "scientists" put it up there a day or so before.

That settles it. I want to be a scientist. I am just on four years old and I know exactly what I want to do with my life. My dreams of being a train engineer, a fighter pilot like Sailor Malan, or a farmer like Oupa are shelved right there and then. My parents, however, do not look happy about this *Sputnik* thing at all. In fact, they look quite scared. They talk about "Soviet," but I do not quite know what that is. Perhaps it is another horrible scary thing like an Uhuru or a Mau Mau.

The abaKhwetha

The next big step in our little family is in the middle of 1959 when my father buys his first ever car. It is an early 1950's used *Leyland Morris Oxford MO* that he buys from Malcomess Motors on Main Street. The plan is to take this car to visit Oupa and Ouma in Middelburg. They now live on Church Street in Middelburg town, some two blocks from the fish & chip shop. Nickie tells me that Oupa is now too old to work on the farm and that is why they have moved to town.

As we leave Port Elizabeth on the national highway and pass over the Swartkops River (See *Fig. 20-3*), we enter an area with patches of stunted *Suurveld* bush. Suddenly some black men jump up near the road. They are almost completely naked, but are covered in what looks like white blotches that appear to be peeling off their skin. They look very, very scary indeed. They are yelling and waving *knobkieries* (fighting sticks) at us. My father laughs his head off at my consternation. He tells me those are harmless "Makwetas" (actually abaKhwetha) and that they are busy going through the amaXhosa ritual period for becoming young men. He says they are covered in white clay and have to live on their own out in the bush for a period and will be circumcised in that process. None of this explanation helps me much – I have no idea what "circumcised" means. When Nickie explains to me, I am even more terrified. Just now they do that to me and what then? Better to just keep away from these "crazy black savages" who "go berserk," sometimes "eat white people" and who now somehow seem to be everywhere.

Not very long after we pass the abaKhweta, my father pulls of the road. There is steam coming out of the front of the car. My father is angrier than I have ever seen him. He says something about a "block" being "cracked." I also look under the hood of the car. I know what blocks look like because I have had some of those, but there is definitely none of those in there. I elect not to ask my father, because he looks altogether too angry. Eventually, we get going again, but we have to stop frequently to put water into the car. One of the places we stop, is at the Slagtersnek memorial where I am told the history (*NF40*).

I am not very interested; I just keep looking behind us to see if the "Makwetas" are coming.

To speak English

Billy, the boy next door in Port Elizabeth, speaks only English, while I speak only Afrikaans. Nevertheless, we play together even though we cannot understand each other. So, it is obvious that I need to make a plan. I therefore take my monthly pocket money of three pennies and go down to Law's Stores, two blocks away. There I buy myself a copy of the local *Eastern Province Herald* newspaper, because I have decided that I need to understand English.

Things are not made easier for me when my parents and their friends burst out in raucous laughter at my attempts to read the paper. All this because I pronounce the word "people" as "poop-le." I learn to ignore them and carry on with my newspaper English. I will show them. These grownups are not helpful at all. They do not explain stuff and they just laugh at me.

Learning to use one's head

By the age of five, I am conversant in both Afrikaans and English and I am preparing to go to school for the first time. We have a huge radio and gramophone in the lounge and on this I hear music that varies from *Singing the Blues* (Guy Mitchell) to *Mary's Boy Child* (Harry Belafonte). My second youngest aunt, who now also lives with us, becomes a Jim Reeves fan in late 1959. So I am caught between strains of *"He'll have to go"* by Reeves and my favorites, the Everly Brothers, with songs such as *"Bye bye love."* All the teenage girls in the area are excited about a man called Elvis, but I have little idea why. It mostly just sounds noisy to me. My preference is to focus on the harmonies of the Everly Brothers.

In January of 1960, I report for school for the first time. I find it rather boring because they are not teaching me anything I do not already know. The teachers are very nice, and we get to play with clay and learn some simple maths. But that is all stuff that Nickie has already taught me at home. Ever since I said I wanted to be a scientist, she has scraped together all she could to give me educational toys and books.

Having placed me in school, Nickie takes a job at the publication distribution agency again. As part of this she is allowed to bring home books that have been returned unsold from the various stores supplied by the company. This facility is used to bring me mounds of educational books, some comic books and "picture libraries", many of them devoted to the Second World War. This is also when my parents hire a black lady to clean the house and to look after me during the day before they come home. At home, I have to hear all the time about Elvis being in the American Army in Germany and singing *"Wooden Heart."* In South Africa, everyone calls it by its German title, *"Muss i' denn."* Even Nickie likes that song.

Quite early that year, I keep hearing about "winds of change" on the radio. It has something to do with some or other Englishman named Macmillan. It is clear that most people around me are unhappy with this man, but I am not sure why. It also does not seem important to me at this point in my life. The grownups keep talking about this scary "Uhuru" thing and about black people and about places called Ghana, Kenya, Congo, and Angola. When we visit my grandparents in Middelburg, Oupa pretty quickly makes comments along the lines of *"To hell with the British. They do not care about us, they know nothing about Africa, and they can rather just shut up."* This man Macmillan seems to upset him quite a bit.

By now, I have learnt that Port Elizabeth is an industrial city and wool export port. Its most important role is as the "Detroit of South Africa." Both General Motors and Ford have huge manufacturing plants in town. The children are divided between Ford fans and Chevy fans. Volkswagens are manufactured in nearby Uitenhage. There are also tire manufacturers in the city, such as Firestone. There is a factory outside town that belches thick stinking fumes. It produces carbon black for the tire industry. Port Elizabeth is a polluted blue-collar industrial city at this time, but we have no concept of matters such as "pollution" or "blue collar."

Over this first year at school, I become friends with a girl named Juanita. Soon after, some of the boys start teasing me about my little girlfriend. One day during break, one of the boys insults her and that is too much for me. It ends in a fight, but I am a small guy and the other boy is one of the biggest. He just sits on me and I am pretty much helpless. On this day, I learn that I am not a good fighter and that I shall have to be more clever about these things. This is the day I learn to use my head, and not my fists.

Independence

In May of 1961, all the children in class are instructed to assemble in the schoolyard. A funny looking man in a black coat and top hat arrives and makes a speech. I do not have too much interest in this. Things do get a little more interesting when each one of us is handed a small national flag and a gold colored medallion. The event has something to do with the country becoming a republic. Apparently, Hendrik Verwoerd stays the Prime Minister, and we now get a president. I do not truthfully understand what all this means, but I do understand that our money is changing[62]. At home, a tune named *"Daan Desimaal, die rand-sent man"* (Dan Decimal, the rand-cent man) plays morning, noon and night on radio and explains that we shall no longer work with British pounds, shillings and pennies, but rather with rands and cents. All I know, is that the shopkeeper down the road is now demanding three cents for a chocolate when he should be asking two-an-a-half according to Daan Desimaal.

Uhuru comes through the front door

Seven hundred miles to the north in Krugersdorp, my future wife Jeanne (*NF84*) is growing up. Since Jeanne's mother is English-speaking, Jeanne is automatically raised as English-speaking. Her father, Bassie Basson, is in the government service and is often transferred to different locations. The family is soon transferred, first to Pretoria, and soon after to Pietersburg, a town just a few miles south of the Tropic of Capricorn in the Northern Transvaal. In this part of the world, English is seldom if ever heard outside school. This is Afrikaner heartland. Here they will stay until the second half of the 1960s. Her father, Bassie Basson, is now a Bantu Commissioner for the BaPedi nation.

In 1960, Jeanne turns six. In July of that year, she hears a knock at the front door. This will be the very first time she will open the door for a stranger. However, it is a white man and his family, so that should be okay. The slightly disheveled white man introduces himself and his family as friends of her father. The man is hoping to speak to her father. Every inch the young English lady, the six-year-old Jeanne entertains the family to tea while they wait for her parents to come home.

Jeanne does not quite understand the significance of the event. However, later that night her father explains that the man has just driven with his family all the way from the Belgian Congo. Her father is the only person the man knows in South Africa and he was hoping for some help and advice. They are now near-destitute refugees from the horror of the Belgian Congo.

Bassie and Molly, in attempting to shield the children from the worries about Africa, elect not to tell them much about all the events to the north, or in the East Cape near Port Elizabeth where I am growing up, or at Cato Manor and Sharpeville. In fact, they ban newspapers from the house.

When the day comes to vote for or against a republic, Molly and Bassie vote against it. They refuse to believe that Britain has sold them out. After all, Bassie laid his life on the line for Britain in World War II. Surely the British cannot be so callous as to deliver decent Western Christians into this mindless horror that is developing all over Africa. Molly and Bassie both think the National Party has gone overboard. They hanker back to the "good old days of Jannie Smuts" when "all in the West knew what Western Civilization was."

—End Nexus Familia

Africa by the end of 1960

By the end of 1960, just over half the surface area of Africa had been granted independence from their former colonial masters. Spain still held the Spanish Sahara and the "Cities" of Ceuta and Melilla on the north coast of Africa. Ceuta had been the first place taken by Europeans in Africa since Roman times[63]. Spain also held Rio Muni on the equator with its offshore island of Fernando Po. The latter two would later be combined to form Equatorial Guinea.

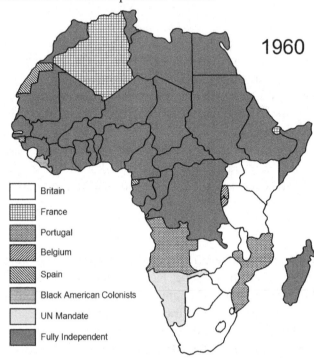

Fig. 20-7 *Africa by end 1960 - more than 50% independent*

Portugal still held all its colonies, of which the two large ones were Angola and Mozambique. Its other territory was tiny Guinea-Bissau in West Africa. Angola, along with its discontiguous enclave of Cabinda, was by far the most significant and prosperous. Besides South Africa itself, Britain still held British East Africa, comprising Kenya, Tanzania, and Uganda, and British Southern Africa, comprising Malawi (then Nyassaland) and the two Rhodesias, north and south.

In West Africa, Britain also still retained Sierra Leone. This was where the British had taken their first slaves in 1562 and where they had deposited their own black people in the second half of the 18th century[64].

In the North Africa, France was desperately hanging on to its colony of Algeria with its one million French settlers. It also retained the strategic port of Djibouti in the Horn of Africa. Some 42 years later, this French strategic outpost would enter the American lexicon as the African base of the U.S. military in the "War on Terror."

Despite their experience in the Congo, the Belgians retained their colonies of Rwanda and Burundi in Central Africa. Britain still held its three "protectorates" adjoining South Africa, being Bechuanaland, Swaziland, and Lesotho. Lesotho and Swaziland, in particular, were oddities. Lesotho was, and still is, totally surrounded by South Africa, while Swaziland was part of the Transvaal Republic until the Great Boer War, at the end of which Britain hived it off. Neither would ever be viable independent countries. Oddly, Britain had not done the same with either Zululand or the Transkei homeland of the amaXhosa, both of which were in British colonies at the time. Had they done so, the history of Southern Africa would have looked utterly different.

South Africa still had trusteeship of South West Africa (now Namibia) under a League of Nations mandate dating from the end of WWI.

-----ooOoo-----

21

Alone

"I came here because of [...] a land which once imported slaves, and now must struggle to wipe out the last traces of that former bondage. I refer, of course, to the United States of America."

Robert Kennedy
On a visit to South Africa (June 1966)

Republican Independence

The Cato Manor and Sharpeville events of early 1960 had a direct effect in swinging the vote of most white South Africans in favor of a republic. A substantial minority of English speaking whites now turned against the notion of British political influence in the wake of Macmillan's speech. It is therefore against a background of great unease inside South Africa, a complete collapse of order in the Congo, British desertion, and rapidly growing international isolation, that South Africa finally became an independent republic on 31 May 1961, six days after President Kennedy announced the intention to put a man on the Moon. The first State President was C.R. "Blackie" Swart and the first Prime Minister was the already incumbent hardliner, Hendrik F. Verwoerd.

The economy blossomed after independence and Verwoerd recovered very quickly from his wounds. He now likely saw himself as an Afrikaner martyr, but he was not really even an Afrikaner, let alone a martyr. He was a first generation Dutch immigrant with a pre -WWII German PhD in Psychology. And he was married to Betsie Schoombee, who was a product of the Boer War Cape Rebel country of the author's grandparents. Few, if any, Afrikaners of that part of South Africa trusted Britain one inch.

Fig. 21-1 The Voortrekker Monument

Verwoerd, the disarmingly soft-spoken implementer of the set of "Apartheid laws," became quite intransigent. The attempt on his life seemed to many thinking Afrikaners to have made him fanatical. The "Coloured" people of the West Cape had not been involved in any of the riots of 1960. Now, instead of incorporating them into a future for South Africa, he actively excluded them from any form of say in their own destiny. Having beaten down the ANC and PAC and won a reprieve from the threat of African Nationalist Uhuru, he failed to establish a pragmatic political way ahead for black people.

He systematically[1] worked to pull the Afrikaner press and the Dutch Reformed Church into his stark ideological world, and he was very good at that. It seemed not to matter to him that he was dragging the Afrikaner as a nation into a despised corner from where there was no recovery.

Anton Rupert was probably the most successful Afrikaner entrepreneur of all time on the international stage. He was chairman of the Rembrandt Group that owns many luxury brands worldwide. He was also a founding member of the World Wildlife Fund and was held in high regard by everyone whose life he touched. When Rupert suggested to Verwoerd that he consider giving black people property rights so they could own homes and become stable members of society, Verwoerd turned him down flat. The Afrikaans Chamber of Commerce suggested reforms of the hated pass laws for black people. He rejected this as well. Pieter Cillié, the influential editor of the most important Afrikaans newspaper, Die Burger, wrote at the time that Apartheid had vividly failed as a policy and could only turn Afrikaners into the political polecats of the world. He was ignored. L.J. Du Plessis, a very influential academic from the staunchly Afrikaans Potchefstroom University, proposed a complete revision of the democratic rights of black people. He was ignored and slunk off to join the ineffectual opposition. Three Cabinet ministers tried in vain to get Verwoerd to amend the hated passbook system. He rejected their overtures. He even organized the expulsion of "golden boy" Beyers Naude from the Afrikaner Broederbond "think tank" for standing by a set of Church resolutions that went against his policies.

Verwoerd would henceforth brook no dissent in his party, no broader discussion of issues, no real debate. He demanded utter conformance, something that often is in no short supply from those who do the least thinking. In the words of Pieter Cillié, Verwoerd had "summoned the Neanderthal" in the Afrikaner population.

While most white South Africans understood little of what was happening, a Dutch immigrant who could somehow swing their popular vote had totally polarized South Africa and set it on the road to destruction. These ordinary white people cared about their children and their jobs and their homes and had little notion of constitutional matters, and they were beset by fears about black people inside and north of the country.

It would be both easy and expedient today to say that he was completely wrong. However, in the Cold War world of 1961, with the Colonial Powers fleeing from Africa, the Soviets on the ascendancy, a wave of black race-based atrocities sweeping the continent to the north, and both the ANC and PAC building armies with Soviet and Red Chinese support, it would not have been easy to make such a conclusion. Any softening of policies might well have been read as weakness, as it indeed later was in the 1980s, with horrible consequences. It might have brought destruction down on the country despite the best intentions of the politicians, academics, editors, businessmen, and church leaders mentioned above.

Verwoerd had drawn the laager and the country was in it, for better or for worse. For the following fifteen years, the country saw relative stability and stupendous economic growth. On the face of it, Verwoerd's Apartheid appeared to have broadly worked compared with the general mayhem in the equatorial parts of Africa. But the price was to be incalculably high for white South Africans in the long term, and painfully obvious for other South Africans in the short term.

The Black Homelands

Having ensured full control in parliament, Verwoerd set about implementing his Black Homeland Policy. The concept was that there was a traditional homeland for each of the Black nations in South Africa. While lots of holes could be and were found in this policy, the basic historical facts supported Verwoerd's position.

No Black nation had ever lived in the bone dry and Mediterranean western parts of the country. Indeed, the very climate had made that impossible, as they needed a minimum of roughly 300 mm per annum of rainfall for their cattle herding culture. Nothing in the history or culture of the Black people of Southern Africa points to them gravitating naturally to areas with sub-freezing temperatures at any time of the year. In this respect, the Ba'Sotho people of the Lesotho Mountains only fled to their mountainous area in order to avoid the Difequane. Similarly, the Ba'Rolong people of Thaba'Nchu in the South-Central Free State were led there by the Rev. Archbell in order to escape the depredations of the Matabele under Mzilikatse. Both these groups, along with the Ba'Tlokwa (The dreaded "Mantatees" of old) were territorially disposed in rather odd locations.

In the end, a series of different homelands were identified for the different nations. Nine of these groups were wholly contained within the borders of 1960 South Africa and were given homelands of their own:

AmaGcaleka Xhosa, amaThembu, and amaPondo (all isiXhosa-speaking)	Transkei
AmaRharhabe and Suurveld Xhosa (See Chapter 4, 5, 6, 7)	Ciskei
AmaZulu	KwaZulu
Vha'Venda	Venda
Ama'Ndebele	KwaNdebele
Ba'Tlokwa	Qwa-Qwa
Ba'Pedi	Lebowa

Three other groups of people already had totally separate countries of their own but were granted further land for those of their people inside the 1960 South Africa:

AmaSwazi (already had Swaziland Protectorate under British control)	Kangwane
Ba'Tswana (already had Bechuanaland Protectorate under British control)	Bophutatswana
Shangaan (many lived in Mozambique separated by the Kruger National Park)	Gazankulu

A special totally non-contiguous area was set aside at Thaba'Nchu for the Ba'Rolong people of the long since departed Chief Moroka, who had helped the men of the Great Trek. This was to be part of Bophutatswana, as the Ba'Rolong were of Ba'Tswana culture and spoke the Tswana language.

While much can be found to criticize the plan, the basic underlying logic holds. Each nation would be assigned territory largely coinciding with the area they had inhabited before their mass inflow into "white" South African towns and cities. However, at the time of their creation these homelands consisted of impractically discontiguous pieces. The plan had as a goal exactly what the United States is supporting for the Palestinians in the 21st century. The stark difference was that, while the Gaza area is marginal desert, the Transkei area of the amaXhosa is possibly the most well-watered and beautiful part of South Africa. The international media would go out of its way, though, to attempt to depict it as a wasteland. Gazankulu, in turn, was the envy of many white farmers. Venda was blessed with lush subtropical mountain slopes and excellent rainfall in the tropical part of South Africa. Bophutatswana had two thirds of the world's platinum production[2]. Any one of these homelands was more viable than the Palestinian homeland proposed in the 21st century. By way of practical comparison, none of these homelands had the adverse climate of the areas where the author's family had to make their agricultural living. This has already been discussed at length in Chapter 18 (See figures 18–4 and 18-5).

Figure 21-2 shows the distribution of the resulting Black homelands in South Africa. The solid line indicates the westernmost point at which Black people formed the majority of population in voting districts in 2002, according to Statistics South Africa. As we saw in Chapter 2, this line corresponds exceptionally well with the 300mm annual summer rainfall line, the area to the west being drier.

As to whether the areas were appropriately chosen, we can consult Nelson Mandela himself[3] who so eloquently explained about white people in his life in the Transkei, the very place Verwoerd set aside for his own amaThembu people, the amaXhosa, and the amaPondo. He explains that he considered the white man's role in his life a distant one and he thought them "curious and remote figures." Many white South Africans would argue that, if he had his own country in the 1920s and 1930s where white men were "curious and remote figures," why did he have to come to "White South Africa" and demand civil rights there.

However, the practical issues revolved first of all around how to make the homeland areas usefully contiguous, given that white farmers held title to their farms and these had to be bought up. This is no different than the 21st century arguments about the Palestinian homeland consisting of two pieces, Gaza and the West Bank. Secondly, there was the problem of ensuring that these countries-to-be were economically viable. In Verwoerd's plan, "White South Africa" would put up border industries to induce development in the homelands. All in all, the plan seemed to have a distinctly more solid foundation than the later Israeli scheme revealed via the leak of Israel's infamous Koenig plan[4] in 1976.

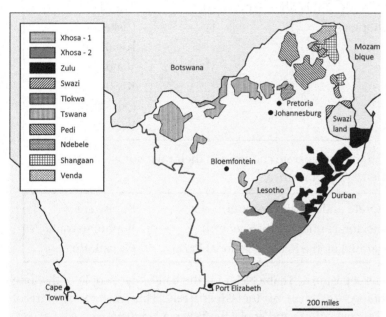

Fig. 21-2 *The distribution of the South African Black Homelands*

The moral dilemma lay in reversing the flow of Black people from those historic areas to "White South Africa." Opponents of the plan would naturally argue that there was no such thing as "White South Africa." This is the equivalent of arguing that there is no Israel, but only a single Palestine for all. And, as Jewish Israelis know only too well, if that conclusion were to be made, they would lose their own country due to the demographics of their situation and the much higher birth rate of Muslim Arabs. In a single unitary Palestine, the Muslim Palestinians would soon outnumber Jewish Palestinians.

There seems to be no essential difference between Muslim Palestinians crossing the border to work in Israel, but then staying there to outvote Jewish Israelis, and (for example) amaXhosa people crossing from their traditional home of Transkei into "White South Africa" and then demanding "human rights" tantamount to taking away the country of the White people of South Africa. The parallels become even more pointed when one realizes that the Transkei is one of the most stupendously beautiful and well-watered parts of Southern Africa.

The international resentment of the plan came about because of the predicament of those Black people who had moved away from the traditional homeland areas to "white South Africa" where they largely lived in shanties on the outskirts of the bigger cities, or in male dormitories in the case of formal migrant workers. Few had any of the formal low cost ultra-basic homes that had been erected by government. Almost none outside the dormitories had electricity.

The reality on the ground was that the government of the day simply was not looking after the interests of its Black citizens because it did not fundamentally regard them as citizens. However, many of these Black people had now lived in "White South Africa" for at least a generation; some longer. There was no genocide and no Balkan style Ethnic Cleansing. The government was busing people back to the homelands as fast as they could, but the return flow was just as fast; a situation understood only too well in the 21st century by authorities in states such as Texas, Arizona, and New Mexico with respect to illegal immigrants from Mexico.

Tanzania – African Socialism

With Ghana's Nkrumah leading the way, leader after leader in Black Africa would turn their countries into One Party States. Some would attempt to invent grandiose new philosophies, supported by various forms of "institutes for learning," to justify and promote their personal lust for power. Others would attempt to convince the world that African people have an inherent unique and mystical socially benevolent psychology that would somehow cause them to transcend the obvious shortcomings of a one-party state. Even in the 21st century in South Africa there is a major effort underway by the ANC government to "re-educate" white people in the workplace in an attempt to convince them that they are morally inferior. According to this school of thought, Black South Africans have a unique innate social morality, which they refer to as Ubuntu. Television images of innocent Zimbabwean immigrants being burnt alive by black South Africans in 2008 do not support this transparently racist view. Nor do either the repeated genocides or the insatiable appetite for horror elsewhere in Black Africa. Nor, in fact, do calls by Julius Malema, the 2010 leader of the Youth League of the ANC government of South Africa, for the slaughter of white South Africans.

One leader in particular embraced Communist Chinese Socialism like no other. He was Julius Nyerere of Tanzania, where the South Africans had fought the Germans in WWI[5]. Nyerere, always photographed in a Mao Tse Tung outfit, implemented collective farms and did all those things that Communists were espousing in the 1960s. More to the point, he also made his country available as a base for the South African ANC. Radio Tanzania would provide a carrier signal for the ANC to transmit to South Africa. At the same time, Radio Moscow and its less guarded understudy, Radio Peace and Progress, backed up these transmissions with their own vigorous and often insultingly transparent propaganda. In the background, Radio Peking would constantly repeat "Quotations from Chairman Mao" while attempting to influence Africa.

In this far-flung corner of the Cold War, a constant barrage of misinformation, disinformation, and propaganda was beamed at South Africa. The "wonders" of the Tanzanian Socialist Farm system was poured into the ears of all via shortwave radio. The Voice of America, the BBC and later Die Deutsche Welle, transmitting via Kigali in Rwanda, espoused the other side of the distant propaganda war on the airwaves.

Through all of this, the beautiful and highly distinctive signature tune of Radio South Africa would ring – the song of the *bokmakierie* bush shrike (*Telophorus zeylonus*) superimposed on a plucked guitar version of a mournful old folk tune. Naturally, this national institution transmitted its own particular version of the perceived truth.

The men from Bashee River

With the "banning" of the ANC and PAC in 1960 after the Sharpeville catastrophe, the two organizations went underground and each started building a military wing. That of the PAC was called Poqo. That of the ANC was called Umkhonto we Sizwe ("Spear of the nation" in isiXhosa, usually abbreviated as MK) and was led by a high command under the direction of Nelson Mandela[6]. MK operated from a 28-acre lot in the leafy rich-man suburban area of Rivonia, north of Johannesburg, known as Liliesleaf Farm. The property had been bought using money supplied by the Communist Party[7]. Mandela states in his own words[8] that he had the job of starting an army and that he recruited Joe Slovo, a devoted Communist of Lithuanian Jewish descent. With the help of Slovo, he recruited other Communists, because they had "resolved on a course of violence." Almost simultaneously, a warrant was issued for his arrest.

The date set for the ANC sabotage campaign was 16 December 1961, the date commemorating the Battle of Blood River[9] and the author's birthday. That night bombs exploded in the author's hometown of Port Elizabeth, and in Johannesburg and Durban. For the next eighteen months there were more than 200 attacks, including on people deemed to be "collaborators"[10]. This included policemen who happened to be black. Some 300 men were sent for military training in Cuba, China, Ethiopia, Tanzania, Algeria, and Ghana, including Mandela himself.

Nelson Mandela was eventually arrested in August 1962 after having, as he reports in his own words, visited Algeria, Liberia, Tanzania, and other countries, and having undergone 8 weeks of military training in Ethiopia[11]. The Police lacked the direct evidence linking him with Umkhonto we Sizwe, but he was nevertheless kept on Robben Island, indicating that they comprehended the significance of his role. There he would stay until the events described in the following section would reveal the full scope of his activities.

On 21 November 1962, between 200 and 250 Poqo members set off from the Mbekweni township outside Paarl in the West Cape. Their intention was to attack the local police station. They had gone through various rituals and had bathed their faces in various concoctions that were supposed to render them impervious to bullets – a behavior we have seen before in these pages. The Police, however, had early warning and drove off the Poqo horde with concentrated fire from automatic weapons. The horde then invaded a white suburb of Paarl and killed 21-year-old Frans Richards and a 17-year old white girl, Rencia Vermeulen.

The action of the police against Poqo was immediate, intense, and effective. Some 400 were arrested, 75 were tried, 13 went to prison, and three were hanged. The organization was soon broken as a force in the West Cape. However, the focus moved to the amaXhosa homeland of Transkei; the area beyond the Kei River.

In 1963, the PAC was ready to strike what it saw as a more concerted blow. Its concept of what such a blow should entail was barbaric in the extreme and invoked all the ghosts of the Mau Mau movement. Their activities were directed from the Cape Town townships, particularly Langa. Whites were targeted to be killed, because they had supposedly "robbed Africans of their country"[12,13]. The irony of them attempting to direct this from the one part of the country where black people had not historically lived apparently escaped them.

The true Mau Mau hell finally descended[14] on South Africa on the night of 4 to 5 February 1963. Norman Grobbelaar, an ordinary white road worker, was encamped at the Bashee[15] Bridge crossing of the river of the same name. With Norman, were his wife and his two daughters, Edna and Dawn. In a nearby trailer, was Derek Thompson. In the middle of this terrible night, a group of some 60 Poqo members fell upon this encampment of totally innocent people. Brandishing axes, pangas and assegaais they hacked the Grobbelaar family to death. Even the children were not spared. The Poqo horde then mutilated the bodies and torched the trailer. The following day Derek Thompson's body was found in his burnt out trailer.

The local magistrate described the attack as paralleling the Kenyan Mau Mau of the 1950s. He was personally threatened[16] with murder by Poqo; so were numerous black officials and headmen who dared testify against Poqo. Eventually, 23 Poqo members were sentenced to death for this murder. Fifteen of them were subsequently hanged.

Through the eyes of white South Africans, it was the same "Black African barbarity" at work that always seems to lurk just beneath the "sham humanistic exterior" held up to gullible people in Europe and North America. They had seen it in Kenya with the Mau Mau. They had seen it in Port Elizabeth and East London in 1952. They had seen it in the Congo in 1960 and Angola in 1961. Now they saw it again in South Africa in 1963, and it came from the very people among whom Nelson Mandela had been born, and the very area where he had been raised[17].

Few if any ordinary white South Africans were able to draw a distinction between the Pan Africanist Congress (PAC) of Robert Sebukwe and the African National Congress (ANC) of Nelson Mandela. In ordinary white households, these were Black Nationalist organizations that plotted their deaths. In simple terms, white South Africans had the same view of the PAC and ANC as what Americans have of Al Qaeda in the 21st century, and for the same reasons. Both the PAC and the ANC had been responsible for the deaths of South Africans and the PAC openly called for the killing of more white South Africans. The ANC was training its members in states aligned with the Soviets for the overthrow of the recognized government of South Africa.

Attacks would continue in the Transkei as Poqo attempted to destroy the government of the Homeland Leader Kaiser Daliwonga Matanzima, a member of the amaThembu royalty and nephew of Nelson Mandela. The effort failed. It simply was not possible to win this kind of war against the South African government or any of its structures. The Poqo effort faded, but the militant wing of the PAC would resurface many years later in 1993 in the most horrific fashion at the most unstable of times when they would attack a white church congregation[18].

Meanwhile, the ANC underground activities continued with Liliesleaf Farm as base. It is here that

Mandela had earlier joined Raymond Mhlaba and Lionel Bernstein, a Jewish communist. Together with Joe Slovo, they had formulated the constitution of Umkhonto we Sizwe, the military wing of the ANC.

Early in 1963, the following pamphlet[19] issued by the ANC appeared in the letter boxes of many whites in South Africa:

LISTEN WHITE MAN!

Five whites were murdered in the Transkei, another hacked to death at Langa... Sabotage erupts every other week throughout the country, now here, now there. The Whites are turning vicious and panicky... At this rate, within a year or two South Africa will be embroiled in the second, bloodier, more furious, Algerian war.

SABOTAGE AND MURDERS MULTIPLIED LAST YEAR.
SABOTAGE AND MURDER WILL NOT CEASE.

You now face an indefinitely long future of terror, uncertainty, and steadily eroding power. You will keep a gun at your side, not knowing whom to trust. Perhaps the street-cleaner is a saboteur, perhaps the man who makes your tea at the office has a gun... You will never be safe and you will never be sure.

YOU WILL HAVE LAUNCHED A WAR YOU CANNOT WIN

It caused the police to start taking an interest in the activities at Liliesleaf Farm in Rivonia.

On the way to the Sleepy Hollow Hotel

It was around 3 p.m. on July 11, 1963, that a dry-cleaning van pulled up to the gate of Liliesleaf Farm. The black guard at the gate approached the driver, who inquired as to the way to Sleepy Hollow Hotel. The driver then struck up a conversation. The next moment the van lurched forward toward the farmhouse and 16 men and a police dog tumbled out of the back and blocked all the exits of the buildings. So started the arrests[20] that would lead to one of the most famous of legal proceedings in international history.

Lieutenant Van Wyk, who was leading the squad, promptly recognized one of the men in the house as Lionel "Rusty" Bernstein, a known communist whom he had arrested before. Another one was Bob Hepple, a prominent lawyer. He also recognized Govan Mbeki from Port Elizabeth, whom he had previously arrested on charges relating to the illegal possession of explosives. Yet another one took a bit longer to identify, due to his extensive disguise, but van Wyk finally recognized him as Ahmad Kathrada, who had been active in Indian politics in the country. The greatest prize, however, was the light skinned black man with the thin Hitler moustache. He was Walter Sisulu, at that point the most well-known of the ANC leadership. Later in the day, with the police now secretly in occupation of Liliesleaf Farm, Arthur Goldreich, well-known artist, but actually an explosives and guerrilla war expert, drove up and was arrested. Some time later his wife arrived and was also taken into custody. One of the other men arrested in the initial raid was Raymond Mhlaba, the local ANC leader and key Communist Party member from the author's hometown of Port Elizabeth. But he was a new face to the police. The police team also managed to lift a fingerprint of Harold Wolpe of a legal firm in the city. Questioning of Wolpe's wife led to the arrest of her brother, James Kantor.

Wolpe and Goldreich managed to escape after bribing a young policeman. They fled to Botswana and from there to various destinations that were prepared to harbor communists. In Botswana, the British controlled authorities were sympathetic to them, but the local white population was strongly antagonistic, fully comprehending what these men represented.

While the haul of central ANC and MK (Umkhonto we Sizwe) leaders was significant, the documentation that was seized was possibly more so. Central among these was a specific document entitled "Operation Mayibuye." It was the ANC blueprint for a violent revolution, complete with weapons and other assistance from foreign countries. Right at the top of the list of places to attack was the rural area east of the author's hometown of Port Elizabeth – always Port Elizabeth.

The outline of Operation Mayibuye included[21] the landing by sea or air of four groups of 30 men, equipped to be self-sufficient for a month. They were to be joined by 7,000 guerrillas from the local population, some 2,000 to be from the Eastern Cape and Transkei (that is, amaXhosa territory), some 2,000 from Natal-Zululand, 2,000 from Northwestern Transvaal adjoining Botswana and 1,000 from the Northwestern Cape.

The notion of four squads of thirty foreign trained guerrillas flying unopposed into four South African airstrips near major centers is ludicrous. It would have entailed flying at least 2,000 miles from Tanzania over international waters and then dropping to below long range naval RADAR level to approach the southern coastline near Port Elizabeth. Given that there is no land anywhere to the east from which an ostensibly "innocent" airplane could have plausibly approached that coastline, the conclusions become entirely obvious for even the faint of intellect. The only way to insert these four 30-man squads would have been by sea, and the only plausible entity to have provided such assistance in 1963 was the Soviet Navy. That navy was already present in strength around the South African coast.

The "production requirements" for the operation were also outlined as constituting 150 tons of ammonium nitrate, 20 tons of aluminum powder, almost 20 tons of black powder, 48,000 land mines, 210,000 hand grenades and 1,500 timing devices for bombs.

The information found at Liliesleaf Farm identified Mandela as leader of Umkhonto we Sizwe, the military wing of the ANC. He was returned from Robben Island where he was still serving his earlier sentence. He joined the other accused on trial for their lives for the spate of 221 sabotage bombings in the country.

The Trial that Galvanized the World

The "Rivonia Trial" started on 3 December 1963 with Dr. Percy Yutar, Deputy State Attorney of the Transvaal, as State Prosecutor. Ironically, Yutar was himself of Lithuanian Jewish descent, just as Ronnie Kasrils and Joe Slovo, who were at the heart of the white Communist group that dominated the ANC. The lead attorney for the Defense was Abraham "Bram" Fischer, from a highly regarded Afrikaner family.

The trial has assumed quite a mythical status in the Western World. Consequently, there is merit in addressing this trial using the statements of the accused from the books they themselves wrote after they came to power in 1994.

First, let us consider the matter of the Defense maintaining that Operation Mayibuye was not taken seriously by the accused or that it was entirely theoretical. In this respect, Ahmad Kathrada, one of the accused, would state black-on-white in his memoirs[22] of 2005 that he only discovered during incarceration on Robben Island exactly how intensely his colleagues, who now included Nelson Mandela, resented his opposition to the plan, some even preparing to physically attack him. This was hardly the behavior of people who were not taking a plan seriously. Not having the benefit of later hubristic memoirs, the Judge concluded at the time that there was no direct evidence that a guerrilla war had finally been decided upon.

Mandela himself states on record[23] that Raymond Mhlaba was one of the leading figures in the ANC and MK in the Eastern Cape, but the State did not know that at the time and had little evidence against him. Mhlaba therefore simply insisted that he knew nothing about sabotage. He would later write in his memoirs[24] that he had been recruiting trainees for military training at the time of his arrest. He himself had already been to Communist China for military training.[25]

Bram Fischer, Chief Counsel for the Defense, was in reality a co-conspirator[26]. Fischer had written some of the incriminating documentation that the Prosecution was entering as evidence. His dual roles clearly made it possible to consolidate the defense strategy among the accused on more than one level. It is not clear whether the rest of the Defense Counsel knew about Fischer's double role at the time, but it was unlikely. If the Police knew, they did not let on. Bram Fischer would be targeted for arrest much later. In fact, he was the clandestine leader of the South African Communist Party and would later be awarded the Lenin Peace Prize.

Nelson Mandela was trained in the legal profession. He therefore appreciated the concern of the Defense Counsel that the accused would all receive the death sentence if he in particular were to be cross-examined. Hence, it was decided that he would not testify, but would read a carefully prepared speech[27] of more than four hours from the dock. The others would testify.

This then is the background to why Mandela made his much publicized speech. It seems that few people are interested in the second paragraph[28] in which he acknowledged that he was one of the persons who helped to form Umkhonto we Sizwe and that he had played a prominent role in its affairs until his arrest in 1962. He also confirmed that the ANC "admitted only Africans" as members[29]. However, he failed to mention that the official song of MK contained the words:

"*We have resolved to kill the amaBhulu*"- the Afrikaners[30]. In the 21st Century, it has come true.

He made his much-publicized address knowing full well that he was invoking his right not to testify, even as he was abusing the dock as pulpit for a political speech. He did so in a country that had a long and proud history of an independent Judiciary. Defense Counsel knew the Court would respect the choice. In fact, despite having had control since 1795, the British had never implemented their own legal system over the Roman Dutch Law of South Africa and it still pertains in the 21st century with some amendment.

In later decades, the international media and students of history would peculiarly only remember Mandela's last paragraph in which he expressed his willingness to die for a "*democratic and free society in which all persons live together in harmony with equal opportunities.*" These are fine statements to make, but in the 21st Century, white people in South Africa most assuredly do not experience it as a country in which they have an equal opportunity with Black people, there being legislation against equality.

It occurs to the informed student of history that this might be because the most damning evidence in the Rivonia Trial was never heard; and because the Counsel for the Defense was in fact in collusion with the accused rather than acting as their legal representative. Through all this, an admirably independent judiciary treated the accused with exemplary respect.

In one of the odd aspects of this singular trial that captivated the planet in 1963, Nelson Mandela passed the final exam for his LLB law degree as he waited for the verdict[31].

The main accused were duly found guilty on all four counts. The sentencing came on 12 July 1964 when Judge Quartus de Wet, himself an Afrikaner, announced a sentence not of death, but of life in prison. This he based on his conclusions that the war had not actually been started as such, and that the Prosecution had somehow not convinced him that the ANC and Umkhonto we Sizwe were one and the same organization, despite the accused being members of both organizations. He did point out that the Court did not believe the motives of the accused were as altruistic as they sought to convince that Court.

That night the prisoners were taken from Pretoria Central Prison to Robben Island. It was the start of a 10-year period of peace and quiet within South Africa, mute testimony to the role the prisoners had played in destabilizing the country. Mandela would become the world's leading "political prisoner" and would somehow be anointed "man of peace" by the Western media. It begs comprehension how he could have obtained this salutary status when he personally described in detail in his own autobiography, *Long walk to Freedom*, his efforts to convince the ANC leadership that violence was the way ahead in South Africa. He described at length his central role in turning the ANC into an organization that would be duly and correctly categorized as "terrorist" by the U.S. State Department. This included the sourcing of weapons and military training in Red China and Ethiopia. In few areas of human endeavor is the selective blindness and deafness of Western media as vividly clear as in the matter of their treatment of Rolihlahla Mandela.

Arms Embargoes

While the Western Nations made no attempt to comprehend, let alone respect the enormously difficult situation of the white people in South Africa, the Sharpeville shootings represented the poster event that the enemies of South African whites so desperately needed. Pressure was promptly brought to bear in the United Nations for a comprehensive international arms embargo against the country. In the United States, the Kennedy Administration was divided. The Assistant Secretary of State for African Affairs, G. Mennen "Soapy" Williams crowed "Africa for the Africans", thereby apparently implying Africa NOT for the Afrikaners. He failed to suggest where they should go if Africa were somehow not for them. He certainly never offered Afrikaners United States citizenship. On 12 June 1963, this man wrote[32] to Secretary of State Dean Rusk:

"In my view, the time has come to review our arms supply policy toward South Africa. I believe we should be thinking now in terms of a total arms embargo."

Williams later predicted the following consequences for the United States if a total arms embargo against South Africa were not implemented:

"... Loss of support in the UN on such questions as entry of Communist China in the UN";
"... Loss of military installations such as those in Morocco, Libya and Ethiopia";
"... Loss of scientific facilities such as those in Nigeria and Zanzibar";
"... Loss of communications facilities such as those in Liberia and Nigeria"

To even the most superficially informed, the list reads like a comedy of lost causes on the scrapheap of United States foreign policy. Ultimately the United States would in fact turn on South Africa[33], and it would still not avoid any of Williams' concerns. All of his fears came true, and it had nothing to do with South Africa. All of these countries, with the nominal exception of Liberia, were ill-disposed towards the United States to start with, and, as the United States would eventually discover, turning on one's few friends when they are under threat does not endear one to one's many natural enemies.

Dean Rusk, clearly a man with a vastly more balanced view of international matters and some notion of history and honor, responded[34] on June 15, recognizing the history thus far described in this work:

"... It has seemed to me, therefore, logical that we should not assist the Union of South Africa with the means of enforcing its Apartheid policy but that we should assist them in playing the kind of role which they have already played in two World Wars and which now is a part of a total confrontation affecting the life and death of our own nation."

Secretary of Defense Robert McNamara also rejected the call at the United Nations for comprehensive embargoes. This was the Cold War and the United States needed the cooperation of South Africa in keeping the Soviet "bear" from getting its claws on African minerals. The United States also needed the cooperation of South Africa via the Hartebeesthoek Satellite Tracking station near Pretoria. This NASA station was key to the United States' aim of landing a man on the Moon. Weapons were not the key in exercising pressure on South Africa. The spares required for South Africa's USA-made C-130 aircraft could be easily sourced elsewhere. No South African weapons initiative would be based on the United States as a significant supplier. The U.S.A. was already suspect as a partner. We had stood by the U.S.A. in war, but it would never openly stand by us.

The Heart of Darkness blows up

While stability returned to South Africa, to the north of the country the British Scramble out of Africa continued unabated. On 1964, on July 6 and again on October 24, Black Africa physically moved significantly closer to South Africa when Malawi (the former Nyasaland) and Zambia (the former Northern Rhodesia) became independent from Great Britain. The new head of Malawi was the archconservative Dr. Hastings Banda. He would become the epitome of the Benevolent Dictator, but would lose his job as President for Life many years later; another example of *One man, One vote, Once only*.

Matters were more complex in Zambia. The country had a white population of several tens of thousands, mostly associated with the copper mining industry, similar to the neighboring Katanga region of the Congo. While the independence of Zambia under Kenneth Kaunda went rather smoothly, it did not end positively for everyone (See Nexus Familia 86). Kaunda was a curious character who would regularly whip out a white handkerchief in public to wipe tears from his eyes while trying to convey a passionate point to his people. He too turned into a One man, One Vote, Once only wonder. And, as per the usual African script, he mismanaged the economy into the ground.

Fig. 21-3 Belgian troops on their way to Stanleyville

Early in 1964, after just two years of cohesion as a country, rebellion broke out in the eastern part of the (ex-Belgian) Congo. The rebels called themselves Simbas. Ironically, Moïs Tshombe, who had previously done his best to obtain the secession of Katanga with the help of mercenaries, was appointed as Prime Minister of the entire Congo in the middle of that year.

His first task was to stop the rebellion. Tshombe promptly called in the help of the Southern African white mer-cenaries who had helped him a few years earlier during the Katangan Secession. When the Simbas realized they were losing, they took 300 white people in the Stanleyville area hostage and held them in the Victoria Hotel. At this point, Tshombe turned to Belgium and the United States.

On 24 November 1964, C-130 transports of the 322nd Air Division of the United States Air Force dropped 350 Belgian paratroopers onto the airport at Stanleyville. By the time the paratroopers managed to release the hostages, some 60 had already been slaughtered. This was exactly the Black Africa that white South Africans were resolved to keep out of their lives. They fully realized that, if it were they who were taken hostage, there would be no obliging paratroopers coming to release them, because they were the amaBhulu, the forsaken White Tribe of Africa. Nevertheless, it was their family members who were fighting as mercenaries in the Congo and who had helped to save the hostages.

It was at this point, on 11 December 1964, that none other than the Cuban revolutionary hero Che Guevara addressed the United Nations General Assembly and denounced the Western intervention in the Congo. In April 1965, he followed up his speech by invading the Eastern Congo over Lake Tanganyika with a band of followers. It was a dismal failure and he had to retreat by November of that year.

On 25 November 1965, Mobutu en-acted another coup, with the full support of the US security establishment. Then, as per

Fig. 21-4 Bodies of murdered white hostages in Stanleyville

the standard African script, he declared a One-Party State with himself as head. In this format, the Congo would be comparatively stable for the next two decades and would remain in the Western fold. Mobutu would remain a staunch ally of the West through thick and thin.

The Rhodesian UDI

Given the experience of whites in the Congo and the ignoble exit of Britain from other parts of Africa, the white community of some 150,000 in Southern Rhodesia, now known only as Rhodesia, decided their own fate. Under the leadership of Prime Minister Ian Smith, they declared unilateral independence (UDI) at precisely 11 am (GMT) on 11 November 1965. The intent with the choice of the precise timing was to send a clear message to the British Government on the moment that Britain maintains two minutes of silence to respect the end of WWI and the sacrifices of its war dead. Ian Smith had been a Royal Air Force pilot in WWII.

Many white Rhodesians had died for Britain in that war and their kin now considered themselves deserted and sold out by Britain. The last significant community of whites outside South Africa and Namibia had finally realized what the country they used to affectionately call "Home" was doing to them. Afrikaners had known it for 165 years and had moved to obtain independence before Britain could sell them out.

On 20 December 1966, Harold Wilson, the Prime Minster of Britain, would confirm in the House of Commons in London that his country was bound to a principle of no independence before Majority Rule. Significantly, it was Lester B. Pearson, now Canada's Prime Minster, who pushed Wilson into adopting this policy. Pearson had not endeared himself to the people of Southern Africa when he joined the United Nations in loudly condemning South Africa in 1960. He did so mere days after his own country had finally given Canadian First Nations people the right to vote. By 1960, the First Nations of Canada had been reduced to a tiny permanent minority. Granting them voting rights had been an easy and politically useful decision. Furthermore, Pearson's personal role in the disaster that had been the Suez Crisis had not yet been lived down either.

To add to Britain's already dismal reputation in the eyes of white Rhodesians, Wilson appealed to the United Nations to impose sanctions on Rhodesia, which it obligingly did. Here was the "once great" Britain begging an organization composed largely of tin pot dictators, leaders of other basket case countries, communists and even the odd reputed cannibal (Emperor Bokassa of the Central African republic) to force loyal Englishmen to submit to people whose kin to the north were exhibiting every form of savagery imaginable. In Southern Africa, disgust with Britain knew no end. Ian Smith's government would hold out for another 14 years, building the economy in the process. When Black majority rule descended in 1980, the country would start to slide into an economic abyss until it became the international "poster boy" for political dictatorship, utter mismanagement and rampant inflation by the early 21st century.

Bobby comes to town

In June of 1966, South Africa grudgingly received an American visitor with a transparent agenda. He was Robert "Bobby" Kennedy, younger brother of the late President John F. Kennedy. Neither Kennedy commanded much respect from Western oriented South Africans. John Kennedy's handling of the Bay of Pigs Invasion and resultant Cuban Missile Crisis had led to an agreement whereby the United States could not invade Cuba. Within slightly more than a decade that result would predictably come to haunt both the United States and South Africa when Cuba would launch international military adventures.

The younger brother had made his views regarding South Africa clear in 1963 when he stated[35] that the United States ought to work via the CIA or students and intellectuals to support *"those individuals and organizations who are attempting to gain independence in Mozambique, South Africa, Angola, and Rhodesia."* Since South Africa was already independent in 1963, it is abundantly clear what he had meant with that comment.

Robert Kennedy was a strong supporter of the US Civil Rights Movement. His visit to South Africa took place against the background of that movement reaching a peak in the United States. Some weeks before, Martin Luther King had elected to work up the fervor in the United States by trying to draw inappropriate parallels between South Africa's race problems, which were based on huge cultural differences and demographic considerations, and those of the Civil Rights Movement in the United States, which were based on a legacy of slavery and color prejudice.

The key Civil Rights Act had been passed in the United States. The biggest issue in the upcoming US election was going to be which party would get the vote of the newly enfranchised Black Americans. Would it be the Republican Party, the classic champions for the Abolition of Slavery, or would it be the Democrats,

Bobby's Party, who had traditionally been "The Party of the South with its Slavery"? Obviously, the Democrats had to reposition themselves in the minds of American Black people.

Martin Luther King having made the inappropriate linkage, it was obvious that South Africa was the place where a leading Democrat had to be seen in order to position the party for the election. Bobby would oblige by making himself as visible as possible during the visit. At one point, in Johannesburg, he even jumped on the hood of his limousine to address a crowd. If there were any doubt as to his intentions with the visit and which audience he was actually addressing, the following excerpt from his speech in Johannesburg should put the debate to rest[36]:

> "I come here this evening because of my deep interest and affection for a land settled by the Dutch in the mid-seventeenth century, then taken over by the British, and at last independent; a land in which the native inhabitants were at first subdued, but relations with whom remain a problem to this day; a land which defined itself on a hostile frontier; a land which has tamed rich natural resources through the energetic application of modern technology; a land which was once the importer of slaves, and now must struggle to wipe out the last traces of that former bondage.
>
> I refer, of course, to the United States of America."

This misplaced public paroxysm of historic cultural guilt played very well to Black voters in the United States and it would be recorded as an example of a great address. However, Kennedy and Martin Luther King had hereby linked the Slavery legacy of the United States to the vastly more complex problem of opposing cultures and unmanageable demographics in South Africa. Even in the 21st Century, the author still found Americans erroneously accusing South African whites of enslaving indigenous Black South Africans.

Black Americans and Black South Africans have little in common beyond skin color, placing such parallels clearly in the domain of blatant racism. Ironically, the White South Africans and Black Americans in Liberia had more in common, both being Westerners, being located in Africa, having slave ancestors and being outnumbered by indigenous people within borders created by a third party. More ironically, the White South Africans had been in South Africa more than twice as long as the Black Americans had been in Liberia.

Death on the border

Namibia is the second most sparsely populated country on Earth. Its vast southern part contains two deserts, the Namib along the coast and the Kalahari in the east, separated by a bone-dry area in between. This is the nature of the country up to the capital of Windhoek. North of Windhoek, the climate rapidly turns more tropical, producing the northern tropical Namib Desert along the coast.

In the far north is a rather depressing flat chalky plain dotted with pans in the rainy season. The most famous of these is Lake Etosha, famed for its wildlife. North of Lake Etosha is the traditional home of the Ovambo people. It constitutes no more than 5% of the total land area of Namibia. South of Windhoek, and for some distance to the north in territory vaguely reminiscent of parts of Western Texas, the white population and the Herero tribe dominated the country. Ovamboland was treated as a controlled access area, and was respected as being the land of the Ovambo, much like the Transkei inside South Africa. Claiming its mandate from defeating Germany in 1914 in that territory, South Africa administered Namibia like a fifth province.

The Southwest African People's Organization (SWAPO) and its military wing, the People's Liberation army of Namibia (PLAN), were created inside Namibia in the early 1960s to oppose South Africa's mandate in the country. The insanely designed northern border left half of the Ovambo nation in Namibia and the other half in Angola. Even just half of that nation was enough to constitute the majority of the Namibian population. They formed the mainstay of SWAPO and PLAN. Many of the Herero also supported the organization.

On 26 August 1966, the first formal clash between the South African Police and SWAPO insurgents took place along the Angolan border. The fighting would systematically escalate, eventually melding with an independence war in Angola. It would involve a horde of countries, including the United States and the

U.S.S.R. It would eventually turn into the last conventional war of the Cold War before the Fall of the Berlin Wall.

One of the first young men who died on that border in 1966 came from the author's neighborhood in Port Elizabeth. The "Bush War," as it came to be called, would become a permanent feature of news in South Africa as time wore on. It would mean death for many Cubans and it would take the lives of several Russians. It would eventually cause South Africans to feel as though they were fighting the Cold War alone – to a large extent they were to do just that in respect of actual fighting.

The Verwoerd Assassination

In South Africa, matters were stable and the economy was going from strength to strength. This benefited everybody. In this respect, we can consult *Time Magazine*[37], never a magazine to have much positive to say about South Africa and its isolated white people.

On 26 August 1966, the news magazine commented on the fact that many urban black people could afford imbuia wood furniture, neat school uniforms, and sometimes a car. They also noted that countless thousands of black people from nearby countries flocked into South Africa to look for work. They also considered Verwoerd to be an able leader with a photographic memory, an analytical mind, and an endless capacity for work. They thought him a brilliant diplomat and inventive politician. This was rather an amazing summary, given the political situation and the history between the magazine and South Africa.

The stability that South Africa had been experiencing since the imprisonment of Nelson Mandela was interrupted on 6 September 1966. Shortly after Prime Minister Hendrik Verwoerd entered the House of Assembly in Cape Town at 2:15 PM, he was fatally stabbed by a deranged Court Messenger by the name of Dimitry Tsafendas. The assassin was subdued by other members of the Assembly. Tsafendas escaped the death penalty on the grounds of insanity. He was imprisoned indefinitely at the "State President's pleasure."

The new Prime Minister was to be John Vorster who had been interned in WWII for his anti-British position. Vorster, an attorney from Port Elizabeth, had since been the Minister of Justice. He came from the Jamestown district near Middelburg, likewise a region that suffered the worst of British Army intimidation in the Boer War.

Under Vorster it became more possible to question policies and Vorster himself sought to make contact with Black African states to the north. This coincided with a period over which several Black African countries, particularly in Francophone Africa, became disillusioned with the Communist ideal. Gabon and Senegal were good examples.

Vorster would develop relationships with Presidents Houphouet-Boigny of Côte Ivoire, Leopold Senghor of Senegal, Omar Bongo of Gabon, Mobutu of the Congo, Hastings Banda of Malawi, and Kenneth Kaunda of Zambia. These particular relationships would come into play soon enough at a critical point in African history. Strangely, Vorster also had good relations with the peculiar Emperor Bokassa of the Central African Republic. The northernmost effort at relationship building was with President Tombalbaye of Chad in order to keep Libya, in particular, at bay.

The relationships with the two ex-British colonies of Malawi and Zambia can easily be understood on the basis of their proximity and the fact that there were thousands of migrant workers from Malawi working on South African mines. In fact, Malawi had a formal labor representative in South Africa. Zambia made use of South African export routes.

The dealings with the ex-French and Belgian colonies stemmed from the involvement of the French via their Chief Government Advisor on Africa, Jacques Froccart. He played a huge role in keeping the Communist threat at bay in Africa while the United States, for better or for worse, was focused elsewhere.

Nexus Familia 86: Growing up in 1960s South Africa

A Lower Middle class Afrikaner Home

In September 1961, after having lived in Kent Road, Port Elizabeth, the southernmost city in Africa, for some seven years, we move again. This time it is to an entirely better and "faraway" suburb of Port Elizabeth called Newton Park. To its north is the "Coloured" township of Korsten and to its south, across the valley of the Baakens River, is Fairview – at this time another "Coloured" township. The townships for Black people are all much further away to the north of town, beyond Korsten and adjoining the industrial area of the city. Our street, 7th Avenue, is a direct thoroughfare between the two "Coloured" townships.

I have to complete the year in my original school, which is now six miles away near the city center. The result is that I have to take a municipal city bus all that distance. This is not an entirely easy or safe thing for a seven-year-old, but suburban South Africa is a safe world at this time where any murder is front-page news for weeks on end. My bus trip is on a signal red double-decker Leyland London bus, complete with a gray-headed British bus conductor who loves us kids.

At this time, Oupa and Ouma (Kotie Myburgh and Pretty Bettie) move to Port Elizabeth and come to live with us. The discussion at the dinner table often turns to worries about the country. Oupa is a fervent supporter of Dr. Verwoerd. When he says grace at the dinner table he always asks that God should be with the Prime Minister in this difficult time. He is very concerned about everything happening in "Black Africa" and considers the British a disaster for Western Civilization. He simply cannot believe that Britain can think that democracy will work in the hands of the Black people of Africa.

Diagonally across the road from us lives a staunchly Nationalist family. They often have the flag of the country flying in front of their home. The husband in that family is forever talking politics to my father, who refuses to let on what his exact opinions are. He just loves to argue with his neighbor, who, in his turn, cannot stay away from my father. Directly across the road from us lives an English family who can speak hardly a word of Afrikaans, while we can all speak fluent English.

At school, we start to learn things that help me understand a bit better what is going on in the country and also internationally. It is also during this period that Nickie brings home publications such as *Look & Learn, Knowledge, How and Why,* and *New Knowledge,* all part-work series publications of excellent educational value. She also brings me copies of *Scientific American.* I'm building quite a collection of educational publications. I lap up all that I can read and understand from these books. One of the things that these publications bring home to me most vividly is the subject of nuclear weapons. As a boy of around 9 years of age I am left with an overwhelming sense of horror at the thought of these weapons.

I follow the Space Race between Russia and the USA very closely. The US astronauts are my heroes because the Soviets frighten me. I know all the astronauts' names and keep a scrapbook of the various missions. Putting a man on the moon seems to me the ultimate goal of all mankind and I identify with it body and soul. I have also taken to using my pocket money to buy model airplanes and ships. I know most aircraft from WWII in detail. My interest is definitely in Science, Defense & Aerospace.

When I get inexpensive chemistry and electronics sets as birthday presents, I augment them with further chemicals and parts. Herman senior and Nickie are not impressed when they discover that their son has shot a chemical experiment against their bedroom ceiling. An inductive tap circuit to our first ever telephone is routed into our new "Hi Fi" radio set in the lounge. This latter act elicits a stern written warning from the Post and Telegraph people who point out that it is an illegal act subject to prosecution. Clearly my interest in science does not impress everyone.

Around this time, my father is transferred to a position on Port Elizabeth's docks. One day, most peculiarly, he brings home a visitor. They talk, look around the house, drink coffee, and then leave again. That night my father tells me that the man is captain of a British commercial ship. The captain apparently spoke to him at work and asked questions about why white people are rich and black people are poor in South Africa. So, my father took it upon himself to take time off and show the man around Port Elizabeth and bring him to our home to prove the realities of South Africa. Apparently, the captain says we are "Lower Middle class." I do not truly know what that means. It sounds like a British idea to me.

Khrushchev and Kennedy enter our home

On 23 October 1962, we learn in South Africa about President Kennedy's announcement of the Soviet nuclear missiles in Cuba. It dominates our news totally and I am frightened out of my wits. I know that, if the Americans and Russians were to attack one another, we in South Africa would be doomed to a horrible lingering death from radioactive fallout. My family does not seem to understand any of this stuff. Naturally, we are all on the American side in this matter – after all, we are the same people and culture and we have fought alongside them in three consecutive wars in defense of Western Civilization. As a child, I understand us to be natural God-given allies. I do not question it for one second. After all, Uncle Ben Booyens fought alongside them in Italy.

I discover the Beatles and Mozambique

One day, late in 1962, while playing with my silver *Corgi Toy* Mercedes sports car just outside our kitchen door, the strangest and most haunting song comes over the radio. It is by a British group calling themselves *The Beatles*. Soon after, they follow this up with an unremitting string of "hits." There is nothing else like them. I can hear how the music changes but do not know that these changes are called "chords." Despite this, I can musically construct entire songs in my mind.

My newfound interest in music soon gets me into big trouble when it turns out that the car tire tube that I cut up to use as velum for a drum is in fact a brand new one that my father recently bought. Nickie has to protect me from my upset father. So, I use some apple box planks, fishing tackle and a classic *Mazzawattee Tea* tin to make a guitar instead.

Some time around my 10th birthday, I have finally saved about $4. I undertake a secret bus trip downtown to buy a "proper guitar" at a jewelry store. The proprietor sells me a guitar that has a hole in the side, because I do not know any better. However, seeing my dedication to the subject, my father announces that, if I were to save another $4, he would provide a further $4 and I would be able to buy a "good" $8 guitar. A young man who lives up the road from us can play guitar, but has no instrument of his own. So he offers to tutor me if he can play my guitar. This arrangement works pretty well and, after living through the agonies of aching fingertips, I soon become quite a competent guitarist.

There are two radio music stations we can listen to. The one is Springbok Radio, operated on "Medium Wave" by the South African Broadcasting Corporation (SABC) from Johannesburg. The other is LM (Lourenço Marques) Radio, transmitting on "shortwave" from Lourenço Marques in Portuguese Mozambique. The latter plays almost non-stop pop music and the announcers are all English-speaking South Africans. At the top of every hour, announcements are made in Portuguese.

Rivonia, the Rhodesias, and the Congo

When the Rivonia case is heard, it becomes clear that there was a collection of white Communists at the heart of the conspiracy. These men, several of Jewish Lithuanian extraction, have links with the Soviets. Oupa Kotie is particularly perturbed by this, as he worked for a major part of his life for two Russian Jewish brothers (*NF83*) and now the country is beset by what he sees as "Jewish Soviet spies."

At this time, I have formed a little kiddie gang with three other 11-year-old friends. We call ourselves the Spider Gang, inspired by my *Spiderman* comic books. In my mind, I am a scientist and Peter Parker (Spiderman) is my hero. I am a little short on super powers, though. I have studied all the gadgets advertised on the back of the *Marvel* comics, but I have no clue how to order any of those from the United States, and they look rather suspect anyway. Our treasure is a bag full of broken armored glass pieces—"diamonds" to us—and a collection of used revenue stamps. However, we soon assign ourselves a new task.

The goal of the Spider Gang is now counter-espionage against the (totally innocent) Jewish gentleman next door. He is a radio ham and might just be a "Soviet Spy" and "part of the Rivonia Communists." Since I am the "scientist" of the team, I construct a crystal radio set from the educational electronics set I received recently as a birthday present and I figure out how to shift the frequency range of the unit. We stretch some cable the length of our 75-yard lot to serve as antenna. With this system, we try to eavesdrop on the "dreaded spy next door," but mostly we just pick up music from Lourenço Marques radio. Now and then, I hear other strange stations. Before the Spider Gang can make its much-anticipated breakthrough in "Western counter-espionage," our target inconveniently disappears one day in 1965.

The new neighbors are a British-born couple who have just fled from Northern Rhodesia. "Uncle Arthur and Aunt Daphne" are classic examples of the "Colonial English ex-pat," sipping the obligatory gin & tonic in the evenings. They have very little time for black people after having fled Kenneth Kaunda's independent Zambia, because, according to Uncle Arthur, a black man threatened his son.

My mother, Nickie, the 100% Afrikaner girl from the semi-desert Great Karoo, and the British expatriate neighbors become the very closest of friends. It seems the classic separation between "Boer" and "Brit" has disappeared. It seems the Brits learn reality soon enough when they actually settle in Africa.

Not long after, in 1965, it is announced that the white people in Southern Rhodesia have "done a UDI." It takes me a while to figure this out, but then I finally understand that it means they have declared themselves independent from Britain. Apparently, the British government is angry. According to Oupa Englishmen are "alright," but the British government is the *enemy of white people in Africa anyway. So, who cares what they think?* The newspapers have an article that shows how many white people there are in Southern Rhodesia. It seems to be around 150,000. There are very few whites in Bechuanaland Protectorate[38], Basotholand[39], and Swaziland. Everyone is nervous. When he says grace at night, Oupa now prays for our Prime Minister, Hendrik Verwoerd, and for Rhodesia.

We feel threatened and hemmed in.

Little Bull

During one of my school holidays, my father takes me along to his workplace at the docks. He explains to me about the intricacies of different kinds of cargo, including things such as grain silos that can explode and also radioactive cargo. He explains that he has not been able to get any of his Xhosa workers to go near the "radioactive"-marked cargo since he told them "their testes would shrivel up and drop off if they were to break the box." He shows me a cargo of clay sewage pipes marked "Gift from the Queen of Great Britain to the people of Bechuanaland." He scoffs at the British idea of Africa and wonders what the Queen expects the poor people of rural Botswana to do with these pipes, most of which are already broken.

Then he tells me to walk with him down the length of the pier. As we do so, the Xhosa men stop working and all look at me. I can see they are grinning and making comments, but I have no idea what they are saying. When we get to the end of the pier, I ask my father what they said. He explains that they were saying *"It is the Big Bull with the Little Bull."* When I ask him why some were laughing, he tells me that they are much intrigued with Little Bull's very white legs. I should clearly get more sun.

The Verwoerd assassination hits home

One day in 1966, my last year in primary school, I am sitting with Oupa Kotie in the lounge after coming home from school. He is listening to the SABC on the radio. Oupa is going blind and spends a lot of time in front of the radio, sitting with his hands on his rough carved walking stick which he props upright between his knees. In fact, being quite a bit of an artist, I have drawn pictures and made watercolor paintings of him in that pose. The next moment an S.O.S. beep signal interrupts the regular programming. Without a moment's hesitation, before any words emanate from the radio, Oupa says:

"They have killed him!"

True enough, the SABC announces that a Court messenger by the name of Dimitry Tsafendas has stabbed Hendrik Verwoerd and that he has died. As I look from where I am sitting at Oupa's feet, I see a single tear running down his tough craggy old face. Then he says in a broken voice:

"They have killed a great man. What will become of the country now?"

That night Oupa prays fervently for the country when he says grace at the dinner table. A cornerstone that I never knew was there has apparently been ripped from under many of the grownups. The mood is very somber. Everyone is frightened. Eventually, it is announced on the radio that a new man is to be Prime Minister. He is John Vorster, who was interned in Port Elizabeth by the British in WWII for his anti-British sympathies as member of the Ossewa Brandwag ("Ox Wagon Sentinel). Oupa Kotie was also almost interned as member of that organization (*NF 83*).

Like Oupa, Vorster comes from the Rebel country of the Northern Cape Midlands. Oupa tells me the Vorsters are a "good Afrikaner family" and that some of them were in the Lötter Commando (*NF78*). Apparently John Vorster used to be an attorney in our hometown of Port Elizabeth in the 1940s and lived in our own suburb of Newton Park at that time[40]. Apparently, this is why our neighbor across the road is such a fervent Nationalist with a South African flag in front of his house.

Oupa is quite pleased with the selection of Vorster, and if Oupa is happy, then it must be good; he should know. He is the one who knows politics in the family. It means little to the rest of us. I'm too busy with the *Beatles*, my guitar, and being a 12-year-old in the Spider Gang to care.

The Beatles and Mozambique – again

As a devoted *Beatles* fan who can recite all their lyrics and play most of their music on my guitar, I am dismayed to hear about John Lennon's comment about the Beatles being "more popular than Jesus." The result of this is that the SABC bans the playing of any of their music on its channels. The only option left to me now is to listen to Radio Lourenço Marques from Mozambique, long playing "vinyl" record albums being generally beyond my reach in price. I now record the *Beatles* on the tape recorder of a family friend. One particular day the LM Radio host, Paddy o' Byrne, is so taken with the Beatles' new *Paperback Writer* that he plays it twice in a row. I am now a devoted LM Radio fan. And that will give me a most peculiar "ear on the future" sometime in the future.

Praying for America

On the morning of 28 January 1967, in my first year in secondary school, I learn on the SABC's news transmission that three of my biggest heroes have been killed in a fire in Apollo 1. I know the details of each of these men. The loss of Edward White in particular has quite an effect on me, because he was the spitting image of my mother's much younger brother. That day I tune to *Voice of America* on short wave to find out what I can, but they are not much help. I eventually write to them, but, hardly surprisingly, I never get an answer.

Over this period I also know my greatest pride in being a South African when Chris Barnard performs the world's first successful heart transplant on 3 December 1967. It is evidence for me that my people are able to achieve anything they set their minds to. On top of it, Barnard comes from a typical Karoo town, just like both my mother and father.

At the beginning of February 1968, we learn of the Tet Offensive in Vietnam. Oupa Kotie is very worried. He is trying desperately to understand what is happening in Vietnam, but he cannot understand the maps we see in the newspaper because his eyesight has deteriorated too far. I therefore draw huge maps for him in heavy 1/4-inch black lines, showing the disposition of the various forces as best I can figure it out.

When Oupa Kotie finally understands the situation, he tells me:

"My child, we have to pray for the Americans. They absolutely must win this thing."

From 16 July 1969 I am glued to the radio[41], following the progress of Apollo 11. On 20 July 1969, I am one of countless millions listening to or watching the Moon Landing. It is the culmination of a dream I have had ever since my mother pointed out Sputnik in the night sky to me (*NF85*).

Shortly after, on 28 September 1969, Oupa Kotie Myburgh escapes this mortal coil when his heart finally fails him at the age of 76. He lived a full life:

- he grew up on the dung-and-peach-pip floor of a thatched roof Afrikaner cottage in the dry Karoo;

- he was intimidated as child by His British Majesty's Khoekhoe troops in the Great Boer War;

- he lived to experience mankind's first heavier-than-air flight;

- he fought under duress for the British King in WWI;

- he went blind and fell into abject poverty during the Great Depression;

- he narrowly escaped internment for his anti-British sympathies in WWII; but

- he finally saw his nation become a republic independent from the Britain he hated with such passion; and

- he lived to experience mankind land on the Moon.

Forty years later, I shall thank God that he did not live to see the future of his country and people.

We have nowhere else to go

Over the next two years, my interest in radio extends from Radio Lourenço Marques to cover the other "strange stations" we picked up when the Spider Gang tried to listen in on "the spy next door." And this is when it dawns on me that it is *Radio Moscow*, transmitting in an English so perfect that it puts the BBC to shame. I notice that, at a certain time every day, the Radio Moscow transmission stops, and another station takes over on the same wavelength. This one calls itself *Radio Peace and Progress* and it is quite strident, both in its screaming trumpet call sign and in its rhetoric, which is transparent, even to a 16-year-old.

On a nearby wavelength, I find *Radio Peking*, which is quite frightening because it has these doctrinaire "Quotes from Chairman Mao." The Russians still make some sort of a point, but the Red Chinese are completely alien. It occurs to me as a 16-year-old that, if we are ever to come up against them, we would have to fight to the death. They do not seem human.

One of the stations on a nearby wavelength is *Radio Tanzania*. At a certain time every day, it plays a very nice piece of music, after which the announcers identify themselves as the African National Congress of South Africa. On this channel, I hear for the first time ever about the ANC's Freedom Charter. They try to convey a picture of some general hope for all. However, they spend so much time verbally attacking white South Africans that there seems to be no way to ever reconcile with such people. As it is, a young man from our neighborhood has just become one of the first policemen to die in an insurgent raid on the northern Namibian border, and the ANC is identifying with the people who killed him. I also listen to *Voice of America*, the *BBC* and *Radio South Africa* with its *bokmakierie* signature tune. Having done German at school, I also listen to *Deutsche Welle*, which is transmitted via Kigali in Rwanda.

My mother Nickie now brings home copies of unsold news magazines such as *Time* and *Newsweek*. They are admittedly out of date by a week, but it is nevertheless clear to me that for us there is nowhere a single helpful or friendly party on the face of the planet Earth. The torrent of written attacks on South Africa is without end, and on the international radio waves it is worse.

This constant assault really hits home when one lives in Port Elizabeth, the southernmost city of Africa. This places one deeply under the impression of there being no place further south to flee to. All that is between the South Pole and us is the Soviet Navy. Even as a boy nearing the end of his school education it is obvious to me that the West is weakened and is not really standing up to the Soviets. Harold Wilson in

England has in fact recently withdrawn British naval and land forces east of Suez. At least, they have retained their military presence on the island of Diego Garcia; this much I know as a teenage boy nominally aware of international military matters.

Oupa was wrong; things are not right in this country

One day, near the end of my last year at secondary school, I am in front of the house when a Coloured man of clearly mixed white and Khoekhoe descent stops at the gate and asks me whether I might have a job for him. He says he has experience as a mason. So, I tell him that my aunt would very much like to have a proper aviary built in our backyard. We promptly agree on a price for the work and he duly turns up the next day. It is while the two of us are working on the aviary that he pauses. Then he looks at me with two blue eyes in his brown face and speaks the words that stop me dead in my tracks, affecting my social views for the rest of my life:

"You know, boss, I was almost a white man, but then my father went and married that black maid."

This is the moment that my own conscience tells me Oupa Kotie was wrong all along: things are not right in this country. They simply cannot be right if any man feels compelled to make a statement like that.

You are in the Army now

Soon after, I receive my "draft" papers for the army. At this point, military service is compulsory for all white males finishing school in the country. Immediately after Christmas Day, I report at Port Elizabeth train station. From there, we are transported to a base outside Kimberley on the edge of the Kalahari Desert. It is desperately hot country. What follows is an unremitting hell during which it seems every single member of our platoon collapses from heat exhaustion at some point or another, myself included. The young men with me mostly come from Grahamstown or East London and are headed for Rhodes University in Grahamstown. Practically all of them are English speaking and spend most of their time criticizing Afrikaners, the Army, and the Government. Not much of what they rant about holds any water in my view, but I conclude their anger is directed more to the hell they are living through along with me rather than to anything else.

When I eventually return home from the extreme climate of Kimberley, my own mother fails to recognize me. I am tanned deep bronze and I have grown muscles I never even knew I had before. I have feet that are a complete mess from forced marches and the like. Running with a 60-mm mortar base plate takes one's mind off the blood soaking through one's socks due to ill-fitting boots. In the event, it takes me several months to completely recover. The army is a tough place for small scrawny boys in a nation of large men.

This period certainly convinces me that I am not cut out to be a soldier. However, my interest in military history and military hardware remains as strong as ever. Having experienced ground attack aircraft making a straight run at me during training, my fascination with military aircraft is greater than ever.

University

I am still 100% resolved to be a Physicist and hence, while I have been training in the army, my mother Nickie has been wearing her soles through trying to find financial support for my university studies. Her dedication to my education has been total and utter from as far back as I can remember. To date, I have always been in the top 10% in my school classes and so I promise to be good university material, but there is no money in the family to pay for any of this. Eventually, it is South African Breweries, later to be SAB-Miller[42], who comes to our rescue. They provide me with a suitable loan that will be interest-free while I am studying.

During the first year of studies for a Science degree, I form a duo with a British immigrant and we do Simon and Garfunkel music at the local Folk Club. A bit later, I join a rock band as lead guitarist. This is one of the two top groups in town with some considerable track record. As part of this operation, we play at a rather seedy downtown nightclub every Wednesday, Friday, and Saturday night. I make only enough money to pay for lunch at university every day. Two of the other members are Chinese South African brothers. Their parents fled Mainland China with Chiang-Kai-Shek. We are beset by the usual female "groupies" and it is over this period that I turn a blind eye to the sexual relations that happen across the color divide. I consider it irresponsible, given the unhappy life that any possible children from such a liaison would have in the country. At the same time, I cannot see how something like that can be governed by a law that is ironically called the "Immorality Act." I consider the Act immoral, not the people transgressing it.

There is nothing romantic about being in a rock band. It is a very demanding way to make an existence and it takes its toll on me. I am not getting enough sleep. By the end of my second year at university, I stop my involvement in the band. The two Chinese members leave for London. They will return about two years later, because, as one of them will put it to me,

"the British are far more racist than the Afrikaners and, anyway, we like South Africa better."

It is in my second year of Physics studies that I fall head over heels in love with a brown eyed "English" girl in class whose parents have recently moved to distant Ovamboland, on the border of Angola; some 1600 miles away. Her name is Jeanne and her family name is a classic Afrikaans one – Basson.

In July 1974, Jeanne's parents invite me to travel with her to Ovamboland to meet with them. This will be a three-day train trip to Tsumeb in Namibia. Even more fascinatingly, they have arranged for us to travel with another South African family into Portuguese Angola as far north as Lobito Bay.

—*End Nexus Familia*

Nexus Familia 87: From South to Furthest North

In the Land of Rharhabe

Early in 1966, Bassie's job in the Department of Bantu Affairs yet again displaces the Basson family. This time it is to the traditional amaRharhabe Xhosa territory in the upper reaches of the Keiskamma River, near where King Ngqika used to live. Bassie is to be magistrate to the people of the area. The little town is called Keiskammahoek ("Keiskamma Corner"). It was originally a German settlement founded by German Hessian troops who fought for the British in the wars against the amaXhosa in the 19th century.

There are still many German families in town. There are few if any Afrikaans people in this part of the country. Apparently, they consider it the country of the amaXhosa and tend to avoid it. The lingua franca in these parts is English. The family duly moves into the "residence," the official home of the district magistrate. The setting on the slopes of the Amatole Mountains is idyllic and the twelve year-old Jeanne falls in love with the place. The residence next to the historic Keiskamma River has extensive grounds, with huge "Old World" fig trees, massive old oak trees and a lovely green field with cows behind the house. A watering furrow runs

Fig. 21-5 The lush Ciskei of the amaRharhabe near Keiskammahoek

in front of the house and the drinking water comes from a rainwater tank.

The inhabitants of the town are a fascinating mix of descendants of Hessian German soldiers, English descendants of the 1820 Settlers and a small handful of Afrikaners, of whom two are the only village teachers. The schoolhouse is an old style building in which the school bell is still rung with a rope and the toilets are in outbuildings. Once a week one of the ladies in the village unlocks the library and then Jeanne can borrow books. This includes periodical educational publications, such as *Look & Learn*, supplied from Port Elizabeth by none other than my mother, Nickie. Through all this move the amaRharhabe people from the surrounding countryside with their Xhosa culture and pride in the martial history of Ngqika and Maqoma from the Fourth to the Ninth Frontier Wars. For the last three quarters of 1966, Jeanne attends the little village school, where the two teachers teach the children of all grades.

At the start of 1967, however, she has to go to a boarding school in the district capital of King William's Town where she has to attend Kaffrarian High School. Her life in this boarding school is made a misery. In Pietersburg she was a little bit too English for some of the Afrikaans children, but now she is too Afrikaans for these descendants of the British Settlers who have somehow forgotten their own history and become obsessively anti-Afrikaans. Her father, Bassie, blames the influence of Rhodes University in Grahamstown and its extreme liberal tendencies. Despite his resentment of the National Party government, Bassie intensely distrusts the academics and personnel at that university who he feels are overly liberal London British. He believes them to lean towards Communism. He has particular objections to the ultra-left St Matthew's Mission and its Liberation Theology, which he traces to Rhodes University. Bassie has great sympathy for the amaRharhabe people who are suffering from all manner of malnourishment-induced diseases, brought on by unbalanced diet – they eat too much corn and too little protein and vitamin, even though they have cattle. Based on these convictions, he takes Jeanne to visit the hospital at St. Matthews to see how the amaRharhabe children are suffering. Kwashiokor and tuberculosis are rife and totally preventable by suitable education.

To the end of the Civilized World

After two years of life in Keiskammahoek, Bassie is yet again transferred. This time the family moves to the "Big Industrial City" of Port Elizabeth. Jeanne attends Pearson High School and finishes her school career with university clearance. She is an exceptionally brilliant student, with a particularly outstanding ability in mathematics, a subject that comes naturally to her. At the start of 1972, Jeanne enrolls at the Science Faculty of the local University of Port Elizabeth. It is clear that her first love is Mathematics, but one of her subjects is Physics.

Bassie meanwhile gets more and more disgruntled with his life at the office. He serves in the North End offices of the Department of Bantu Affairs in Port Elizabeth. He has to tend to the legal administrative woes of what appears to be an endless multitude of semi-urbanized amaXhosa, both legally present in the Port Elizabeth area and otherwise. Not long after, he is transferred to the most distant place he will ever work in Southern Africa: Oshakati in Ovamboland in far northern Namibia, near the Angolan border. Ovamboland has recently gained self-rule. Bassie is now 1600 miles north of Port Elizabeth. Here he is to be Secretary to the Minister of Justice, by the name of Taipopi. He has to take notes from and write speeches for the minister. To consult with the minister, custom requires that Bassie show respect by going through the very low opening in the minister's hut almost on all fours. Despite these oddities, Bassie is much happier here than in the big city.

Jeanne remains in Port Elizabeth, dedicated to her university studies, and it is near the end of her second year of Physics studies that she meets a young Afrikaans Physics student and Rock lead guitarist who grew up in Port Elizabeth. She realizes that, unless her parents get to meet this young man, they are definitely going to object to her having a relationship with a longhaired Rock guitarist; no matter that he comes from a conservative Afrikaans family. So, she makes a plan – have her parents invite him to Ovamboland.

—End Nexus Familia

Africa by the end of 1973

By 1969, the South African government had so broken the military hopes of the African National Congress that the Soviets were forced to airlift the 1500 members of Umkhonto we Sizwe to camps around Simferopol in the Crimean peninsula; some 4500 miles from South Africa[43]. Nevertheless, by the end of 1973 the ten-year period of relative peace in South Africa since the breakup of the ANC central ring at Rivonia was nearing its end. All that remained of the British presence in Africa was Ian Smith's Rhodesia, which had unilaterally declared independence to forestall being delivered to the murderous Robert Mugabe.

The French retained Djibouti and several military bases throughout Francafrique. They could strike within two days anywhere they chose in Francophone Africa. Britain had no such ability. The Portuguese still clung to their colonies. However, their army showed little appetite for the extended colonial war it was fighting in Angola and northern Mozambique. Of course, that army saw its home as being Portugal in Europe. In North Africa, Spain was in deep trouble in its colony of Spanish Sahara.

Early in 1969, while on a liaison visit to his Portuguese counterpart in Luanda, Angola, Major-General Fritz Loots of South Africa's Military Intelligence received a surprise visit at his hotel from two smartly dressed black men. The two gentlemen were representatives from Biafra in Nigeria[44]. Biafra, the largely Ibo province of that country, had recently unilaterally declared independence. Britain supported Nigeria, its former colony, but in this, it was keeping company with the Soviet Union. Such was the Socialist Britain of Harold Wilson, who had meanwhile applied an arms embargo against South Africa in December 1967.

France, on the other hand, supported Biafra and had also ramped up arms sales to South Africa to fill the void left by a far left leaning Wilsonian Britain. The Portuguese were ambivalent, but had directed the Biafrans to General Loots, who conveyed the detailed request for help to Prime Minister John Vorster. Eventually, South Africa agreed to join France to provide arms and training.

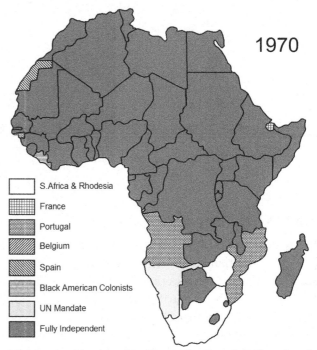

Fig. 21-6 *Africa in 1970 - Except for French Djibouti and Spanish Sahara, only Portugal retained its colonies*

One of the men who went to help was a Special Forces officer named Jan Breytenbach, whom we meet again later. It was all too little, too late. In January 1970, the Biafran quest for independence failed. It had opened for South Africa a tiny gap through which shone a glimmer of hope of a future. In addressing the matter of Biafra, the South Africans had found themselves on the same side as Gabon, Côte d'Ivoire, Zambia, and even Egypt. The white South Africans were talking to black Africans – and this without the usual condescending ex-colonial overlords complicating the process by imposing their ill-fitting concepts of how Africa should function.

The links with Gabon, Côte d'Ivoire, and Zambia were destined to expand and others would be developed further. From this beginning grew a quiet détente that would be of great significance in the following decade.

Guinea-Bissau unilaterally declared independence from Portugal in September 1973, but France was still holding onto the strategic Djibouti in the Horn of Africa.

On 20 March 1969, The United Nations adopted Resolution 264 by which the organization sought to end the control of South Africa over Namibia and to assume control for itself.

-----ooOoo-----

22

The Soviets are coming!

"Our aim is to gain control of the two great treasure houses on which the West depends: The energy treasure house of the Persian Gulf and minerals treasure house of Central and Southern Africa."

Leonid Brezhnev
In discussion with President Siad Barre of Somalia (1973)

The "White Enemy"

December 16, 1971, was the 10th anniversary of the creation of Umkhonto we Sizwe, the military wing of the African National Congress (ANC). On that day, the leader of the ANC, Oliver Tambo, made it vividly clear to white South Africans what his view was of their destiny. He called on his countrymen to "mobilize their black power" and to "arm themselves with the memory" of Moshesh, Sekhukhune, Hintsa, Maqoma in order to "liberate" themselves from "alien bondage." Then he made the key statement[1]:

"The white enemy in South Africa can and must be defeated."

That political party will still proudly display this communication on its promotional website after the first decade of the 21st century[2]. Clearly the organization viewed white South Africans as "enemies" and as "aliens." It was rather obvious that there could be no place for white South Africans in their own country if it were run by such an organization. After all, the official anthem of the military wing of the organization, Umkhonto we Sizwe, contained the fateful line:

Fig. 22-1 *"Christ the King", Sa da Bandeira, Angola (1974)*

"We have pledged to kill the whites" (bulala amaBhulu)

It is rather ironic to hear all this from people who have no way to prove their ancestry and whose own formally verified tribal history (Chapter 3: *The Ba'Ntu*) puts them a full 800 miles from the Cape when the Dutch settled there in 1652. There would have been vastly more justification in treating Oliver Tambo himself as a foreigner to the larger bulk of South Africa. This position of the ANC was based exclusively on a racial prejudice that simply presumes that Africa belongs to the Ba'Ntu. It also showed that their "multiracial" agenda at the time was nothing but a sham. It would seem that the ANC was leaving ordinary white South Africans no other choice but to regard the organization as their mortal enemy and to fight it to the death in order merely to live.

The position of the ANC above shows that the basic clash in South Africa was not in fact one of mere race, but one of competing civilizations to which the matter of race as understood by Americans had become hostage. In this particular communication, Tambo went to some length to ensure that he covered all the heroes of the different black nations in South Africa and none of the whites. Moshesh was the great leader of the Ba'Sotho who led them to victory over the British (Chapter 13: *Free at last!*). Sekhukhune of the Ba'Pedi had fought off both the Afrikaners and the British (Chapter 14: *The Spider Flag again*). Maqoma of the Rharhabe amaXhosa led the British on a hopeless chase through the East Cape mountains (Chapter 9: *From White House to Suurveld*). Hintsa was the overall Gcaleka amaXhosa king who was killed (Chapter 9: *The Death of Hintsa*) by Harry Smith's men. Tambo also invoked the name of Shaka, the bloodthirsty founder and tyrant of the amaZulu (Chapter 11: *The Monster of Umgungundlovu*).

This was a brazen declaration of racial war by the ANC on white South Africans.

The United States emasculates itself

The 1972 elections in the United States returned President Richard Nixon in a landslide victory, but both Houses of Congress were dominated by the Democratic Party, now united in its collective opposition to the Vietnam War. In June 1973, the Case-Church Amendment was passed, forbidding US participation in the Vietnam War beyond 15 August 1973. It sent an unmistakable signal to the rest of the world that the United States had lost its stomach for any war. The situation was sadly reminiscent of the Bay of Pigs disaster that inspired the Cuban Missile Crisis. The United States would continue to support South Vietnam beyond this date, but it became painfully clear that the United States would eventually divest itself of its Vietnamese allies. The Soviets had already started shipping advanced surface-to-air missile batteries to Egypt and Syria in 1972, correctly assessing matters in the United States. In the greater scheme of things, Communism was winning while the United States had lost faith and was turning in on itself.

On the holiest day of all

On 6 October 1973, Yom Kippur, the most holy day in the Jewish calendar, Syria struck across the Six Day War cease-fire line on the Golan Heights and Egypt crossed the Suez Canal into the Sinai Peninsula. It was Israel's turn to be caught by surprise. In the initial phase, the large numbers of anti-aircraft missile batteries decimated the Israeli Air Force, the protective umbrella that the ground forces and armor relied upon.

Initially, the Israeli Air Force was severely mauled by SAM-6 Gainful surface-to-air missiles in particular. This directly affected every domain of the war, as Israel relied on that air force as its main arm in any war. Moshe Dayan, as Minister of Defense, is known to have warned Premier Golda Meir that the nuclear option might have to be invoked.

In the end, the Israelis were on the way to Cairo along the Nile, when the US stopped them. Their victory against terrible odds was partly due to their own good soldiering abilities, partly due to satellite and overflight intelligence provided by the United States and partly through a massive resupply of weaponry by the United States. It is the last of these three factors that caused the next step in the international saga, despite the Soviet Union also resupplying Egypt and Syria[3]. The Soviets would remember that the United States had initiated the resupply build-up of Israel without consulting them.

When Kissinger got the Israelis to stop their assault, the Egyptian Army was cut off in the Sinai and their supply lines had been severed. They were already out of food. For the United States, it was a matter of sparing Sadat and his Egyptians utter humiliation. Somehow, Sadat misled the Egyptian nation to believe they had won. To this day, the Egyptians celebrate the war as a victory and no one appears to have the heart to disillusion them. However, they have never made war on Israel since then and have cooperated with Israel in isolating the Palestinians. It is most odd that Egyptians have not found this cooperation curious.

The student of history is left wondering whether the Soviets instructed Sadat in how to mislead his own entire nation. For the Israelis, the Egyptian self-delusion was a small enough price to pay for peace in the region. We would see this kind of utterly inverted nationally consumed propaganda, flying completely in the face of facts, again (See Chapter 25). Again, the U.S.S.R. would be involved.

The Arab Oil Embargo

In reaction to the United States' arms supply and other support to Israel in the Yom Kippur War, the Arab members of OPEC (Organization of Petroleum Exporting Countries) slowed their production of oil.

The immediate result was that the dollar price of oil shot up from below $12 per barrel to $50 per barrel (in real terms – 2008 dollars). This sent a shock wave through Western economies. South Africa was also affected and vehicle speed limits on open roads were reduced to 80 kilometers per hour (approximately 50 miles an hour). The price of oil did not fall below that level again.

Confidence had been shaken on the subject of oil, never to truly recover. More importantly, the five-fold increase in price created a global recession and destroyed the financial ability of South Vietnam to effectively use the massive amounts of weaponry the United States had provided it with when US troops were withdrawn. Enormous numbers of tanks and aircraft stood inoperable[4]. Despite South Vietnam's overwhelming superiority in weapons, it was now unable to match the performance of the North.

American disaster in Vietnam

On 9 August 1974, President Nixon resigned in the wake of the Watergate scandal and Vice-president Ford assumed leadership of the United States. This scandal also allowed the Democratic Party even greater success in the mid-term elections later that year. The Party now pushed for even harsher controls on spending in Vietnam, calling for a stop to all funding for Vietnam by 1976.

With no American forces to face, the North Vietnamese went on the offensive again. On 6 January 1975, one of the provincial capitals fell to the Communist forces. When President Ford implored Congress for funds to bolster the South Vietnamese effort, Congress refused. This desertion by their ally destroyed the morale of the South Vietnamese Army. On 23 April 1975, President Ford announced the end of the Vietnam War from an American perspective.

On 30 April Saigon fell and a horrified Western World watched as American Marines pushed away from rescue helicopters the very people America had promised to protect, given that their lives would be forfeit in case of a Communist victory. Television screens the world over showed American helicopters on the decks of aircraft carriers being pushed into the ocean by sailors to make way for more helicopters bearing fleeing Americans. Other helicopters simply "ditched" in the ocean.

A demoralized America had been driven into the sea in Vietnam and had publicly deserted those who had placed their faith in that country. A buoyant Soviet Union was going from strength to strength.

Angola and Mozambique

On 25 April 1974, with the United States already largely withdrawn from Vietnam and the Watergate scandal at fever pitch, a communist military coup dubbed the Carnation Revolution took place in Portugal. Much of it was precipitated by the costly guerrilla wars being fought in the African colonies of Portugal at the time. A staggering 69% of Portugal's 204,000 troops were tied up in these "bush wars." The South African Army already clandestinely supported both the Portuguese and the Rhodesians, but was less than impressed with the Portuguese Army as a fighting entity. In neighboring Mozambique, in particular the Portuguese seemed wholly ineffectual against the Soviet supported Black Nationalist FRELIMO guerrillas.

The Portuguese fared better in Angola. At the time, three guerrilla movements were opposing the Portuguese authority in that country. They were the semi-urban MPLA (*Movimento Popular de Libertação de Angola*) of Augustino Neto, UNITA (*União Nacional para a Independência Total de Angola*) of Jonas Savimbi in the south and the FNLA (*Frente Nacional para a Libertação de Angola*) in the north, led by Holden Roberto, husband to a sister-in-law of President Mobutu of the Congo. The FNLA is the old UPA that had perpetrated the horrors of 1961 (Chapter 20: *Angola – Horror on the Ides of March*).

In the wake of the revolution in Portugal, governmental authority in the colonies effectively collapsed. The MPLA was treated by the now communist government of Portugal as the "natural heir" to the colony, having in its midst some nominally trained people and also claiming the support of much of the "mixed blood" population of the country and many of the Mbundu people. The FNLA operated in the north, based mostly on the Ba'Kongo people of that region and the neighboring western part of Joseph Mobutu's Congo. The charismatic Jonas Savimbi of UNITA based his support mostly on the more rural Ovimbundu people of the south – for practical purposes the same basic ethnic group as the Namibian Ovambos. In line with the recent coup in Portugal itself, the Portuguese military leader in Angola had communist sympathies and supported the MPLA, which was strongly backed by the Soviet Union. On the other hand, as far back as 1963 Bobby Kennedy had arranged some nominal financial support for Holden Roberto and his FNLA[5].

The odd member of the three movements was UNITA. Savimbi had sought aid from Communist China. However, the Chinese effort in Africa during the 1960s and 1970s was something of a disaster, the consequences of some of which are still with us in the 21st century in the form of Robert Mugabe of Zimbabwe. Savimbi and his supporter, President Kenneth Kaunda of Zambia, both provided assistance to SWAPO in opposing South Africa inside Namibia. Even Nyerere was worried about the Soviet influence[6].

SWAPO had bases in Angola under the wing of UNITA and, in some cases, operated in tandem with UNITA. As the Portuguese authority collapsed in Angola, the FNLA and UNITA turned on the MPLA. At this point, the Soviets scaled up their support to the MPLA, heartened by a United States that had visibly lost the will to oppose them in the Cold War and had turned inward upon itself.

Nexus Familia 88: Angola – What will become of us?

Ovamboland

Just as we hear of the 1974 Portuguese Revolution in Europe, Jeanne tells me that that her parents have invited me to join her in visiting them in Oshakati near the Angolan border in July of that year. This would be the winter break of our third year at university in Port Elizabeth. We travel three full days by train to Tsumeb in northern Nambia. Here her father, Bassie Basson, collects us by car for the last leg of some hundreds of miles to Oshakati where Bassie is Secretary to Taipopi, the Ovambo Minister of Justice.

Oshakati is a strange little town, almost exclusively populated by government employees on assignment and by military staff. It is from Oshakati and nearby Ondangua that much of the effort is directed against SWAPO, the Communist supported insurgent group that is automatically preferred by the United Nations. By now, South Africans regard the United Nations as entirely equivalent to the Soviets, because it always assumes the same position as the Soviets as far as we are concerned.

Fig. 22-2 The Ovambo Legislative Assembly building at Ondangua

"A big ship in the harbor to take us home"

Soon we set off for Angola. This will be the very first time in my life that I leave South African controlled territory. My disappointment is quite big when the border is nothing but a few buildings and a cattle fence. This comes courtesy of the German surveyor who had mistaken his instructions and had drawn the border too far north, bisecting the natural territory of the Ovambo people, who live either side of the silly fence. Had this incompetent not made that mistake, the history of Southern Africa would have looked quite different, because the Ovambo people would not have been the dominating majority in Namibia and the SWAPO organization would have had very little manpower to draw on.

Fig. 22-3 Crossing the Cunene River at Fort Roçadas (later Xangongo)

There is only one major north-south blacktop road in the south of Angola at this time. It runs from the Namibian border to the regional capital of Sa da Bandeira. This road crosses the Cunene River, the biggest river for hundreds of miles, at a place named Fort Roçadas. We are equipped with tents for overnighting. However, at the end of our first day driving through Angola we arrive at a government surveyor's camp. He is a kind Portuguese gentleman who puts us up in a kind of Quonset hut for the night.

As we drive the next day, some bushes next to the road open up and out walk some stark naked black people with bows and arrows. They ignore us completely and disappear into the bush on the other side of the road. Bassie explains that they are Ovajimba people, the people on the lowest rung of the social ladder in Angola, and not to be confused with the cattle herding Ovahimba of far northwestern Namibia.

The second day ends at Sa da Ban-deira where we book into a caravan/trailer park. We are pretty much the only people there. The operator of the camp comes to talk to us and we inquire from him about the political situation. This man will be responsible for one of my enduring images of the decade; one that will haunt me for the rest of my life.

He explains that he knows that the time is now over for Portugal in Africa but that he is not worried, because there is *"a big ship in the harbor* [of Namibe] *to take them home"* and that *"the Portuguese Army will protect them."* Bassie and I look at each other and say nothing. I am looking in the eyes of a living man who is most likely already effectively dead. We instinctively know that these people are going to be deserted by their kin. The Portuguese whites in Africa have clearly not yet lived the Afrikaner experience.

The Collapsing Authority

From Sa da Bandeira, we set out through systematically drier countryside for Lobito on the coast, this being, in a sense, the northern wetter limit of the Namib Desert. Lobito is an odd place. Highly decorated tribeswomen are walking through the shopping area to have their photographs taken for a fee. There is not much economic activity in the harbor, the big freighters now being largely absent from this once hugely important port. There are still some fishing vessels.

At a crossroad in nearby Benguela, a traffic guard is directing traffic. He is standing on a red and white platform waving his arms at the traffic and blowing his little whistle, but no one is paying any attention to him. There is not really any traffic anymore anyway. Somehow, he becomes in my mind the enduring image of a pathetic collapsed authority, respected by none.

As we drive back to Namibia, we pick up the local AM radio

Fig. 22-4 Traffic guard in Benguela, Angola (1974)

stations. We do not understand what is being said in Portuguese, but the political faction acronyms MPLA, FNLA and UNITA are constantly heard. The locals tell us that all the fighting is in the north and there is nothing to worry about in the south. I come away from this trip with an overwhelming sense of foreboding.

Something dreadful is going to happen here, and it is headed our way. I cannot get the caravan park operator out of my mind. Even if a ship were to come for him and his people, there will never be a ship for us. There is no one on Earth who will take us in. We have no friends. We are all alone. We have no other home. In reading *Time* and *Newsweek* and listening to the *BBC*, it seems to me our own kin in Europe and America want to exterminate us. Either they have not the least understanding of our situation, or they are willfully playing stupid, or they just plain hate our very existence and want us dead.

Uhuru intrudes on the Beatles

September 7, 1974, is a perfectly fine and normal Saturday in Port Elizabeth. I am just on 21 years old and listening to my Beatles and other Rock music on my favorite radio station, Radio Lourenço Marques ("LM Radio"- *Radio Clube de Moçambique*).

My reverie is interrupted when one of the South African disc jockeys starts to speak in a most peculiar controlled voice. He announces that there are people with him in the studio and that they would like to make some announcements. What follows is a strange presentation in which a man explains that they are resisting the efforts of the Portuguese government to sell out the population of Mozambique to the African Nationalist Movement called FRELIMO. He then proceeds to read letters of support from various people in a range of places in the country.

The events that Bassie and I anticipated earlier the year in Angola have come home right on the South African doorstep. It seems obvious to me that military resistance on the part of the handful of Portuguese in Mozambique must end in disaster. The Western World holds 475 years of African slavery against them and they have not a friend on Earth besides us South Africans and the fewer than 150,000 white Rhodesians; and we have serious problems of our own. I have seen and heard the future and it looks bleak, terribly bleak. The Portuguese from Angola and Mozambique can go back to Portugal or flee to our open arms, but we have nowhere else to go. What will become of us!?

—End Nexus Familia

Retornado

While almost all Afrikaners in South Africa were born in that country and had no available alternative homeland, the Portuguese citizens in Angola and in Mozambique all had the right to return to Portugal. Approximately 800,000 of these so-called Retornados[7] would end up back in Portugal between 1974 and 1976. Many would settle in South Africa instead. It is important to note, though, that over 60% of the Retornados had been born in Portugal[8]. They truly were Colonial settlers. Many others would ultimately be flown out.

Many of the Portuguese in Angola located further from the capital of Luanda, would flee south as destitute refugees, desperately trying to reach the border of Namibia. There, they knew, the white South Africans in control innately understood their plight and stood ready to unquestioningly help their fellow Christians in their hour of need.

Those in Mozambique fled directly to the South African border, some 50 miles from the capital of Lourenço Marques. By 29 November 1975, some 200,000 Angolan Portuguese had been flown out of the country. Back in Portugal they would play a central role in restoring Portugal to proper democracy out of the hands of the Communist military revolutionaries. A number of the Portuguese men with military experience and strong roots in Africa elected to remain in South Africa and enlisted with the South African Army, offering their expertise which was lapped up in anticipation of trouble to come. A number of them would become singular heroes in what was to follow. They were a huge credit to their people – admired and honored in South Africa in the 21st century by those who fought and know brave men when they see them.

Angola – Henry Kissinger's War

The "Belgian" Congo, or Zaïre, as it was now known in 1974, is a uniquely strategic country at the heart of Africa. It straddles the equator and borders no fewer than nine other African countries. Together with South Africa, it represented the key to the mineral wealth of Africa. Since the Congo River is not navigable for commercial transport to the sea, and because the route to the Indian Ocean is prohibitively difficult, the country was, and still is in the 21st century, dependent on the Benguela railway line through Angola; one of those nine countries.

As African tyrants go, ranging from benevolent dictators to cannibals and genocidal maniacs, Mobutu was one of the better ones[9], even though he was busy destroying the economy, stealing his country blind, and squirreling the money away in Switzerland. Situated to the east of Angola and south of the Congo, is Zambia, the former Northern Rhodesia. In 1974, Zambia was ruled by Kenneth Kaunda. The Communist Chinese had helped him build a railroad to the Tanzanian Coast on the Indian Ocean, but it was never a totally reliable route. He eventually moved all these Chinese out of the country.

Both Kaunda and Mobutu knew that, if the Benguela railway line were cut, they would be totally dependent on South Africa for their mineral exports. Angola itself was inherently a very rich country, a major exporter of coffee, diamonds and a considerable amount of oil. The oil came from the non-contiguous enclave of Cabinda, situated to the north of the Congo River, beyond a narrow strip of Zaïre along that river.

Furthermore, if the Soviets were to obtain any form of military foothold in Angola, it would immediately place the key Cape Sea Route and its constant stream of oil supertankers headed for Western Shores within range of the massive long-range "Bear" (Tupolev Tu-95) reconnaissance aircraft of the U.S.S.R. The events of 1974 in Portugal and its two major African colonies were therefore of direct and immediate importance to greater Western interests. Naturally, the Soviets saw an opportunity in the United States' vividly obvious reluctance to become embroiled in another Vietnam-like debacle. The United States was also paralyzed by the Watergate Scandal and these were the last days of Richard Nixon's leadership.

As to why the Soviets had an interest in the region, we need but consult Soviet Leader Brezhnev himself who announced[10] in discussion with his ally, President Siad Barre of Somalia, that the Soviet aim was gain control of the two great treasure houses on which the West depends: The energy treasure house of the Persian Gulf and minerals treasure house of central and southern Africa.

In July of 1974, just as the author and his future in-laws, arrived in Angola (*NF88*), the CIA started clandestinely funding Holden Roberto's FNLA via the CIA offices in Zaïre, where their presence[11] was an open secret. The Soviets flew in arms for the so-called "African Liberation Movements" via Tanzania. It is recorded[12] that arms shipments went to the MPLA in Angola in August 1974. On 28 August, the press in the Congo reported[13] Romanian arms shipments to the MPLA. Mobutu, Kaunda, B.J. "John" Vorster of South Africa and the more moderate leaders further north in Africa watched the escalating events with increasing trepidation. It is clear that U.S. Secretary of State, Henry Kissinger, was worried and aimed to ensure that Angola stayed in the Western fold.

When the coup took place in Portugal in April 1974, there was a mass exodus of personnel from the Portuguese security police in Angola. In particular their unique San Bushman helpers, demonstrably the best trackers on the planet, were then killed in large numbers by their MPLA, FNLA, and UNITA enemies[14]; some suggest up to 25% of all Angolan San died in this process. Considerable numbers of them fled for safety to South African-controlled Namibia. There the military saw great potential value in their tracking abilities and set them up around September 1974 at what was then a secret base in the Caprivi Strip, later to be named Omega. The hope was to apply their legendary skills in tracking SWAPO insurgents. They were duly named Alpha Group and their numbers augmented with some Namibian San members. And so it came to be that Alpha was stationed at Omega.

Meanwhile, during a meeting in Lusaka (Zambia), the MPLA military leadership broke apart. Daniel Chipenda, the major military leader in the MPLA and a member of the southern Ovimbundu nation, broke[15] with his political bosses and joined the opposing FNLA with between 1,000 and 2,000 of his men. Roberto took them in but did not trust them. He therefore sent Chipenda and his men to Serpa Pinto in the south to try and neutralize the threat of Savimbi's Ovimbundu-based UNITA[16]. In what follows, we shall refer to them as the "Chipenda-FNLA," for sake of clarity.

Various texts on the Angolan War of 1975 attempt rather desperately to blame Henry Kissinger for the events, but the Soviet records show that on 4 December 1974 President Marien Ngouabi of the (formerly French) Brazzaville Congo approved a Soviet plan to airlift heavy weapons and ammunition to the MPLA via that country[17]. According to John Stockwell[18], the CIA was authorized to pass $300,000 to Holden Roberto on January 22, 1975. This clearly followed the first moves made by the Soviets.

Roberto moved his forces from Zaïre into Angola and attacked the MPLA the very next month. It became a see-saw affair, but the help of the Communist sympathizing Portuguese Army ensured that the MPLA was slowly getting the upper hand. Thus, by end of January 1975 the chess board of Angola was laid out as follows. Holden Roberto's FNLA was in the north, headquartered at Ambriz with his historical CIA support. He relied on support from Zaïre's Mobutu where the CIA office ran the American support from Kinshasa[19]. Savimbi's UNITA was headquartered in the central south around Silva Porto[20], with nominal support from Kenneth Kaunda of Zambia. Daniel Chipenda's new FNLA (but ex-MPLA) subgroup was located at Serpa Pinto[21], with a few hundred of his men in the far south at an old Portuguese Marines base called Mpupa. The MPLA's military wing, FAPLA, was firmly ensconced in the major western and northern towns and everywhere on the coast south of Luanda with Communist Portuguese and Soviet support.

The military events in Angola were about to assume an entirely new color and import. The consequences of decisions by the United States Congress over the following year would be felt all over the West into the 21st century. The conduct of that particular Congress over this period would create an image of the United States that would be perpetuated and would dictate the behavior of the world towards it during much of the subsequent 35 years.

Many Americans would later ask how their country developed such an unflattering reputation in the developing world. The answer can be traced back to the following 18 months in Angola. It would also affect South Africa very deeply by precipitating events and cementing attitudes. It is therefore most appropriate to address this war in some detail in order to fully appreciate what followed. Given that the Western media would fall hook, line, and sinker for Fidel Castro's propaganda, we shall provide some of the evidence that underscores what really happened in Angola.

Angola – Asking help from South Africa

In February 1975, Jonas Savimbi (personally) and Holden Roberto's London representative separately approached respectively the South African Head of Military intelligence in Pretoria and the South African Embassy in London. Both made the same basic offer[22], that of a future curtailment of SWAPO's incursions into Namibia in return for military assistance from South Africa. Roberto offered to allow South African hot pursuit operations 80km deep into Angola. These were significant offers, when one realizes that Savimbi had openly helped SWAPO before and that some SWAPO elements were in fact still operating with Savimbi at the time.

In March 1975, the Soviets resumed arms shipments to the MPLA and soon after[23] Fidel Castro of Cuba sent 230 military advisers to support the MPLA. They arrived[24] in May 1975. Secretary of State Henry Kissinger, with the benefit of all his intelligence assets, also confirms that the Cuban arrival in Angola predates South African involvement[25]. He states that the Cuban personnel was escalated to twenty times the number of men South Africa eventually would commit.

While the whole world lived pragmatically with the reality of the three way contest between the Soviets, Communist China and the United States, the introduction of Cuban Revolutionary Regime surrogate foot soldiers to Southern Africa was a completely new and outrageous move. Fidel's penchant for and obsession with fomenting Communist revolution wherever he could was well-established. The Cubans had no business whatsoever in Africa. For South Africans, Africa was their home and Angola was a neighbor. On the part of the Cubans, it was an attempt to export their failed Communist state to Africa using Soviet military muscle. This set off great warning bells all over southern Africa.

In April 1975, not to be outdone by Savimbi and Roberto, Daniel Chipenda flew into Rundu in Namibia without informing Holden Roberto, who was his boss. He offered to not just shut the border for SWAPO, but to actively assist South Africa in hunting down SWAPO insurgents. He claimed[26] he had offers of weapons from the CIA if South Africa would undertake to train his men. He also committed to work with UNITA to stop the MPLA. Around the same period Prime Minister B.J. "John" Vorster of South Africa was approached by at least five African heads of states[27] with a view to South Africa taking direct military action in Angola to forestall a Communist victory and a major Soviet or Cuban presence in Sub-Saharan Africa. These included[28] the heavyweights Joseph Mobuto of Zaïre/Congo, Kenneth Kaunda of Zambia, and the two respected elder African statesmen, Felix Houphouet-Boigny of Côte d'Ivoire[29] and Leopold Senghor of Senegal[30]. Seretse Khama of Botswana was possibly another. Some sources claim further leaders were involved. It most likely included Omar Bongo of Gabon with whom South Africa had ongoing contact.

The significance of this development cannot possibly be lost on the reader, given the history of South Africa up to that point. Here was a collection of African leaders and three senior political and military leaders from Angola all asking for urgent help from South Africa. Some of them were already on the payroll of the CIA and one, Mobutu, was practically synonymous with the agency in Africa. Usually the only subject on which the Organization of African Unity (OAU) had had any unity had been its rejection of South Africa. However, here now was a leading and highly respected segment of that body appealing to South Africa's supposedly pariah white government for urgent help. At the same time, the military leaders in Angola were offering to effectively shut down SWAPO.

The African countries, for their part, were on a knife edge in terms of which way to lean. They had to conduct their diplomacy by the way the wind was blowing, and then fall in line with the internationally "winning" side. Here, finally, was a realistic and practical issue where they had to set aside their prejudices and foibles about South Africa and make a pragmatic choice in the interest of the future of the continent.

In 1977, James Mancham, president of the Seychelles, would tell[31] Eschel Rhoodie, Secretary of the Department of Information of South Africa, that the OAU was divided on the matter of the Russian presence in Africa. He suggested that, if the South Africans had taken Luanda, and Savimbi had become president, the OAU would have split in two on the matter of recognition. Boigny would have led the moderates, and he believed they would have had a majority of perhaps two or three, Mancham's own vote included. Mancham commented that both Senghor and Boigny had told him they had sent urgent messages to Vorster to act swiftly and act strongly[32]. Even U.S. Secretary of State, Henry Kissinger, would later write[33] about his first experience of and surprise at the fact that Apartheid was no insurmountable obstacle for many of Africa's black leaders in cooperating with South Africa on the greater problems of Africa.

If the United States were to throw its weight in concerted fashion behind the Allies comprising Zaïre, FNLA, UNITA and South Africa, then the African countries would line up behind that grouping. If, on the other hand, the USA and the rest of the West were seen to vacillate and act in half-hearted fashion, they would be forced to go with the Soviet/Cuban/East Bloc/MPLA Axis as the more powerful group. Such were real politics for African countries in the Cold War. Africa idolizes power for its own sake and follows those who wield it[34]. At this point, the OAU was split straight down the middle on which side to support[35].

South Africa was clearly not the pariah that the United States media had painted it to be. However, South Africa could not possibly tackle the U.S.S.R and its proxies alone. Even the mighty United States had had to create NATO to face off with the Soviets.

Angola – South Africa responds

On 14 July 1975, with Cuban advisors on the ground in Angola and Soviet weapons being supplied at a considerable rate, John Vorster of South Africa decided[36] to support the FNLA and UNITA to oppose the Soviet-Cuba-MPLA Axis. A South African Bureau of State Security memorandum states that Vorster did so under American pressure[37].

It is highly instructive to note that Henry Kissinger confirms President Ford approved the United States action in Angola in the very same week[38]. The timing was clearly not coincidental, but the co-operation was secret in the extreme. Even though Henry Kissinger would later describe his diplomacy and actions in the ensuing war in some detail[39], he would carefully omit any reference to pressure on the South African government on the matter.

In his recent work, based on access to South African diplomatic communications from the office of the South African ambassador in Washington in early 1976, Odd Arne Westad of the London School of Economics and Political Science concludes that South Africa was expecting international political support from the United States for helping the superpower in the matter of Angola[40]. Ed Mulcahy, the acting Assistant Secretary of State for Africa, occupying at the time the highest post dedicated to Africa in the Ford administration, was not informed of Henry Kissinger's discussions with the South African government[41]. In a later 1998 interview with historian Piero Gleisejes, the head of the CIA station in Luanda, Robert Hultslander stated, with reference to the developments in Angola[42], that he had been unaware at the time that the United States would *"eventually beg South Africa to directly intervene to pull its chestnuts out of the fire ."*

On 29 July 1975, the first U.S. Air Force C-141 transport with CIA sourced weapons for Holden Roberto's FNLA took off from Charleston, South Carolina, and headed out over the Atlantic for faraway Kinshasa[43]. In the same last week of July, the Portuguese Army withdrew its men stationed at the Calueque barrage and pump station on the Cunene River, a short distance north of the Namibian border. This critical water supply for the parched Namibia had been a joint project between Portuguese Angola and South Africa. Now UNITA and the Chipenda FNLA faction were in charge of the facility, the MPLA was on the way and rumor had it that SWAPO was also headed there in the hope of strangling the Namibian water supply under the protection of what they assumed to be their ally, UNITA.

Against this background the first shots fired in anger[44] at South Africans in this war came, interestingly, from UNITA soldiers at the dam. This occurred when the South Africans approached the barrage to keep it out of MPLA or SWAPO hands. The UNITA group was simply chased off by the South African soldiers. Likely neither group of soldiers knew they were about to become allies. Ironically, the last exchange of this 13-year struggle between South Africa and the Soviet Bloc would also be at Calueque.

In August, John Stockwell was in Angola to meet with Holden Roberto. He also met Jonas Savimbi, the hugely charismatic leader of UNITA. Stockwell describes the strikingly positive impression that Savimbi made on him in comparison with Roberto, the armchair expatriate leader of the FNLA. The UNITA leader stated that if South Africa would give him the help he needed, he would accept. On 25 August 1975, Stockwell reported[45] his views on Angola in DC and during September and October of 1975 a total of 83 CIA officers were dispatched to various Southern African regional offices, a budget of $24.7 million being set aside.

Meanwhile, starting 4 August 1975, ex-professor and first term Democratic Party senator Dick Clark of Iowa, then chairman of the Africa Subcommittee of the Senate Foreign Relations Committee, was touring the Congo and Angola trying to gather information for himself. Clark was concerned[46] that the CIA was sending arms directly into Angola, that Americans were involved in the conflict and that the CIA was "illegally collaborating with South Africa." The hatred of left-leaning Americans towards conservative South Africa, isolated and surrounded by threats as it was, had by now apparently completely transcended their own strategic Cold War concerns. This particular obsession would eventually cost the whole Western world very dearly indeed and thousands of innocent Americans would die because of it in the following century.

On 30 August 1975, on the border between Namibia and Angola, Commandant Jan Breytenbach of the SA Defence Force, ironically the brother to liberal anti-government author Breyten Breytenbach, flew[47] into Mpupa to establish on-the-ground contact with Daniel Chipenda's faction of the FNLA. At that point, Jan was certainly one of the country's most experienced soldiers, having led specialist military operations in Biafra, Mozambique, Tanzania, and Angola on the South African equivalent of US Navy SEAL operations. He was accompanied by an Italian go-between for Chipenda, called Pelissa, who did all the communications in Portuguese. Jan described[48] the unit he found at Mpupa as the scruffiest, most underfed, worst armed, and most un-warlike body of troops he had ever seen in his life. However, the base commander gave him an elaborate salute, promptly turned his army over to Jan, and the rag-tag barefoot army of 300 grey-faced starved men excitedly yelled, "*Viva Carpenter!*" (Jan's nom de guerre).

When the flabbergasted Jan flew back to base to report on the contact, he had no idea how he was going to explain to Brigadier Schoeman back in Namibia that he was now somehow a "*commander in the FNLA*" and that, according to promises made by Pelissa, he and his 300 man army were going to "*conquer Angola.*" However, to his surprise back at base he was given food, uniforms and weapons for these men and set about training them to the best of his ability. They would be known as Bravo Group. This was the inauspicious beginning of one of the most remarkable fighting units the world has ever seen, later to be admired and feared as *32 Battalion* or "*Buffalo Commando.*" The relationships, and mutual loyalty unto death that it built between white men and black men from Africa have been even more remarkable, transcending all the subsequent changes in South Africa and the eventual politically inspired dissolution of the unit.

On September 11, 1975, Mobutu of Zaïre moved what he considered his "elite commandos" into Angola[49] in support of the FNLA, which had its headquarters around Ambriz on the coast, some 30 miles north of the center of Luanda. It was now a conventional war. Meanwhile it was decided in Pretoria that the military support for UNITA would take the form of logistical support and training of their personnel. On 24 September 1975, a SAAF (South African Air Force) C-130 landed at Silva Porto. On board was a collection of South African Defense Force (SADF) personnel to help "knock UNITA into fighting shape." Major Holzhausen of the South African training team promptly took over a disused airfield and began training 1,000 recruits and then placed the group in defense of Nova Lisboa, the biggest town in Angola outside the capital of Luanda.

The Americans were impressed with the South Africans. Stockwell, the head of the CIA's Angolan operation, reports[50] that the CIA admired the South African efficiency and that the agency liked the characteristically "*bluff, aggressive men without guile*" who somehow always managed to turn up throughout Angola to have "*just the correct gasoline and ammunition for an impending operation.*" UNITA was equally impressed[51]. Stockwell describes[52] how, after a flurry of cables between their headquarters and Kinshasa, a South African C-130 landed at Ndjili Airport in Kinshasa (Congo/Zaïre) on 20 October and how the CIA and South African Bureau of State Security men jointly oversaw the transshipment of supplies from a U.S.A.F. C-141 to the C-130 in order to deliver it to UNITA at Silva Porto in Angola.

The admiration was not entirely mutual[53]. The South Africans were dismayed at the very obvious disarray of the CIA effort and this raised a level of suspicion. One simple example was a set of recoilless guns for the FNLA which arrived without instructors or range tables. When instructors eventually arrived, they did not have the range tables either. This was clearly no way to fight a war in which speed and agility was of the essence. However, perusal of Stockwell's later book reveals that it was a consequence of the secrecy under which the CIA was operating, having to hide their efforts from a virulently hostile and war-shy Congress.

In September 1975, President Felix Houphouet-Boigny of Côte d'Ivoire, possibly black Africa's most respected head of state at the time, asked South Africa and the local moderate African states to intervene in Angola "on a massive scale"[54] in order to forestall the Soviet Union installing the MPLA as government using Cuban proxy forces.

Angola – The Fruit Truck War

Shortly after the training of UNITA started, the joint group at Nova Lisboa received warning that the MPLA's military wing, FAPLA, was on its way to the town in different columns from a number of towns. On 2 October, Major Holzhausen went on a personal reconnaissance and nearly ran into a FAPLA column advancing from Lobito. His advice was to attack before the different FAPLA units could join forces. The South Africans scrounged together a small force, later dubbed "Battlegroup Foxbat," and set off to face the enemy[55]. They had a handful of Jeeps and one serviceable *Panhard* armored car supplied by the French via Zaïre. FAPLA had Soviet BTR armored vehicles and 122mm Stalin Organ rocket systems. Battlegroup Foxbat ran into a prepared FAPLA position halfway between Nova Lisboa and Lobito on 5 October.

This was, as best can be ascertained, the first exchange of fire between SADF-advised (Angolan) UNITA forces and Cuban-advised FAPLA in the war. This was also the first conventional warfare for South Africa since Korea, and the first on land since WWII. The FAPLA unit was pushed back, losing some scores of dead. A Soviet BTR armored vehicle was destroyed — the first of this type seen in Angola.

The UNITA soldiers had broken and run under the first 122 mm rocket barrage, but Holzhausen had managed to maintain the fight with just his South African support personnel, one of whom died in the exchange. The other FAPLA columns withdrew. This was hardly a resounding victory, but the aim of turning FAPLA around had been achieved. The South Africans were convinced the FAPLA unit had been led or advised by Cubans. They were eventually proven correct.

The outcome of this contest was that the SADF officers insisted that they be supplied with armor – they could not very well be expected to use small arms, some Browning machine guns and one old semi-serviceable *Panhard* to oppose Cubans equipped with serious Soviet armor. The armored unit from South Africa was to be comprised of 24 Eland-90 armored vehicles, complete with South African crews. These were flown out[56], two at a time in a C-130, to Silva Porto between 13 and 20 October 1975. The officer on the ground in charge[57] of arranging all these machines, as well as other logistics support, was Commandant Willem "Kaas" (Cheese) van der Waals, previously South African military attaché to Angola. He knew his way around Angola. He was the "*very tall, flaxen-haired white man in khaki shorts and blue shirt*" at Silva Porto who was issuing "*crisp orders in Portuguese to a couple of black UNITA soldiers*" in the presence of the "*CIA's resident liaison man with Savimbi,*" as reported[58] by British journalist, Fred Bridgland who visited Silva Porto at the time.

At midnight on 15 October 1975, a very strange little army crossed the border from Namibia into Angola at Cuangar[59] on the southern border of Angola's southeastern corner. As the men rolled through Cuangar, the Portuguese refugees gathered at this remote town lined the road for 2 miles cheering them on. Task Force Zulu, as it was called, was led by Col. Jacobus "Rooi[60] Koos" van Heerden. It comprised Alpha Group, the ex-Angolan San Bushman unit, and Bravo Group, Daniel Chipenda's Angolan FNLA from Mpupa base. The two groups were under the leadership of Commandants Delville Linford and Jan Breytenbach respectively. Jan had installed a number of his former Reconnaissance unit colleagues as a leadership group, augmented with some of the really experienced Portuguese fighters from Mozambique[61] (See the present chapter : Retornado).

The men had surrendered their good South African *Mercedes Unimog* vehicles, uniforms and R1 rifles, and had been issued with equipment and clothes aimed at making them less obviously South African-armed. Their vehicles were now a collection of fruit and furniture trucks that had been used by refugees to escape Angola. In many circles, what was about to follow would be called "*The Fruit Truck War.*" They entered Angola on the understanding that they would leave before or on the Angolan Independence Day of 11 November 1975.

The San Bushmen of Alpha Group, which formed the lead of the operation, were quite incredulous and extremely unhappy. They had spent a lifetime fighting against the FNLA and now they were being told that they would be fighting not just along with the FNLA, but also with UNITA, both of which organizations had been their mortal enemies before. When they met up with the mostly black Bravo group[62], they immediately "locked and loaded." In fact, some distance along the road, on 18 October, UNITA unsuccessfully ambushed them in an attempt to settle old scores. Bravo Group's ex-MPLA (now FNLA) men from Mpupa under Jan Breytenbach were no less uncomfortable[63] when they heard that they were about to fight along with their most recent enemy, UNITA, against their former comrades, FAPLA.

The first clash of this unit with the real enemy, FAPLA, occurred on 19 October. On 20 October, two troops of Eland armored cars caught up with Zulu and dramatically strengthened the task force. On 23 October, Task Force Zulu took Sá da Bandeira[64], where the author had been the previous year. Here FAPLA lost more than 100 dead and many captured. Zulu took huge amounts of stores, as well as seven light aircraft belonging to FAPLA. These were promptly flown back to Namibia and some of these did sterling service for many years. Headquarters was advised to not send anymore supplies as they had quite enough.

Fig. 22-5 The Angolan War (1975)

Up to 13 November Task Force Zulu pushed back the FAPLA/Cuban forces until they were eventually stopped by the flooded Queve River. Here the bridges for some distance inland had finally been successfully destroyed by the hastily retreating Cubans. From the departure point of Rundu on the Namibian border to the Queve River, Task Force Zulu had moved 600 miles as the crow flies against opposition. They had removed the Cuban-FAPLA force in 33 days, during which time[65] they had undertaken 30 attacks and had fought 21 other skirmishes. They had killed 210 enemy troops, wounded 96 and had taken 56 captive. They had entered Lobito, the biggest harbor in Angola, to an unexpected tumultuous welcome as locals hailed them as liberators. They were strewn with flowers.

This performance was in the best traditions of the fast moving and hard striking Boer War commandos. Stockwell, with his military training and background in Vietnam, refers[66] to Task Force Zulu as "exploding" through the MPLA/Cuban ranks in a "blitzkrieg," which in November 1975 "almost won the war." He considered Task Force Zulu the most effective military strike force ever seen in Black Africa[67].

The commander, Koos van Heerden, had hereby earned for himself the nickname "Rommel." He had cleared the FAPLA-Cuban forces along the rump of Angola to within about 100 miles of Luanda. Several Cubans had been killed in this process[68]. The results certainly showed to what degree the Fidel Castro's Cuban advisers[69] had insinuated themselves in Angola. Reportedly it was the loss of Cubans at Benguela that moved Fidel Castro to take his next step.

Near Namibe, the Portuguese commanding officer came to protest to Koos van Heerden about the South African venture, stating he had a paratroop unit in town and a frigate in the harbor. Van Heerden was disgusted enough with the Portuguese Army's desertion of their own people to threaten this man that, if he did not take all his paratroopers and other personnel and leave Namibe ship-'n-all, he would sink the frigate in the harbor[70]. The next morning the frigate and troops were gone. Van Heerden had never had any actual means to sink it in the first place and the frigate could certainly have destroyed the Task Force Zulu column.

The Queve River, however, had stopped Van Heerden dead, as he had no bridge-building equipment. This was a consequence of the cloak of secrecy under which they had originally left Namibia in their fruit trucks. Eventually, they had no choice but to head back south, then east, and then back northward, meeting up with Battlegroup Foxbat. The next act in the war was about to unfold in the north of the country, while forces were afield in the United States that would destroy the position of the West in the entire venture.

Angola – Escalation

In the OAU, effectively the African United Nations, the support was split between the Allies and the Soviet-Cuban-MPLA Axis. If the last assault by the FNLA and UNITA on Luanda could be successful, the OAU would swing in their favor. However, this required commitment from the West. Also, much of the success depended on the ever-present support of the South Africans. However, if the assault folded, or if the Soviet Bloc shipped in major amounts of arms, supplies and troops, the OAU would immediately shift its support to the Soviet axis and then the classic Communist rhetoric about "Colonialists," "Imperialists," and "Racists" would be heard again all over Africa. It would also be obligingly and unquestioningly echoed in the US and British media. It would matter not one iota that South Africa was in Angola at the request of several senior African heads of state. That would be comfortably forgotten. It would matter not one iota that the *Racist Invaders*" were in fact largely Angolan black men and San soldiers. This would be conveniently ignored. Such are the vagaries of Africa and the left-leaning media of the West.

Fidel Castro in Havana and John Vorster in Pretoria both knew they now faced a major escalation in the war. In Washington, the CIA was struggling to maintain the veil of secrecy over its efforts. The Soviets maintained their air bridge and there were between 140 and 400 Soviet "advisers" with the MPLA[71]. Two staggering blows were about to fall in rapid succession. On 11 November 1975, the very day that Angola was to become independent, the main FNLA and Zaïrean force, actually amounting in fact to just 1500 men, was approaching Luanda along the wide and flat Quifangondo valley[72]. The South Africans and the CIA had both warned Roberto not to use this approach. He was sending his men in a motorized column with infantry on its sides along a valley that was a deathtrap commanded by entrenched Cuban-FAPLA positions equipped with devastating mobile 122mm Stalin Organ truck mounted rocket batteries. On the drive up Angola, the South Africans had dealt with these weapons and knew their efficacy. They had seen the FNLA and UNITA break under barrages of these rockets elsewhere in this campaign. More to the point, it was quite unnecessary to take Luanda at this point. The city could be brought to submission by other means by improving the hold on the surrounding territory.

Roberto, the armchair Ba'Kongo leader, considered himself superior in military judgment to all the professional South African and CIA men. He wanted to make a triumphant entry into the capital on its independence day. Having had their advice waved away, the South Africans and CIA men watched together in helpless resignation[73]. Four South African 5.5 inch artillery pieces had been flown in overnight, again demonstrating the South African knack for logistics. These were emplaced on a hill nearby, but were no real match for the Stalin Organs, which had double the range. There were two old 130 mm North Korean guns[74] with supposedly better range, but they were untried and were to be operated by Joseph Mobutu's Zaïrean soldiers backing the FNLA.

When the CIA and South African observers saw the first two salvos of Cuban rockets bracket the FNLA force, they knew it was all over. The next salvo rained directly on the little army. The CIA men estimated that 2,000 rockets rained down on the exposed men. They broke and ran, leaving vehicles, weapons and wounded comrades alike. It would become known as the Road of Death. The South African artillery was, as expected, completely outranged and therefore essentially useless in the larger scheme of things. The one North Korean cannon blew up on its first round, killing the entire Zaïrean crew and the other misfired, injuring its crew. This moment was the beginning of the end of Holden Roberto's FNLA. What remained[75] of the Zaïrean troops pillaged the country all the way back to the Congo and the FNLA ceased to be an effective fighting force.

Meanwhile the South African units with their white officers and their Black Angolan and San soldiers, supported by the South African-manned Eland armored cars, kept advancing at speed from the south with their Black Angolan UNITA allies. However, they were now encountering[76] rocket-armed Soviet helicopters, T-34 tanks, and long range cannon with better accuracy than the 122 mm Stalin Organs. It was turning into a regular conventional war.

The second and fatal blow for the Allies fell on 22 November many thousands of miles away. In Washington, all hell broke loose when British journalist Fred Bridgland's article about South African soldiers in the company of CIA operatives at UNITA's Silva Porto base appeared in the *Washington Post*[77]. His timing could not possibly have been worse for the future of Africa and the West. This was the moment that it became public knowledge that the United States was at war in Angola, allied with "Racist South Africa." Both the

United States and South African governments had hidden their efforts in Angola from their respective voting publics. A totalitarian Communist state with a dictator at its head like Cuba had no problem ordering its people into wars in distant places. Open societies with elected governments do not have such a luxury, and both the United States and South African governments, for all their shortcomings, were popularly elected bodies among their respective voting publics. Both Western governments now faced obvious problems.

In the very far north of Angola, the tiny handful of South African Army personnel had been working closely with the CIA in supporting the FNLA up to the disaster at Quifangondo. They had been promised by the CIA that the agency would provide them with a way home by air if the FNLA failed. When these *men without guile*—to quote the CIA's John Stockwell once more—arrived at the CIA base, the Americans had simply flown off[78], leaving them to their fate literally thousands of miles from home. Even worse, the South African contingent had key communications gear and cryptographic equipment, which could not be allowed to fall into Cuban hands under any circumstances. In a daring mission[79] on 27 November 1975, a South African Navy frigate extracted the knot of men from a beach near the northern Angolan village of Ambrizete in hostile waters now completely controlled by the Soviet Navy.

At this juncture, it was clear that Fidel Castro was shipping large numbers of troops and equipment into Angola, having made that decision[80] around 5 November 1975. Furthermore, the Soviet weapons supply to the MPLA was literally ten times as large as that of the United States to the FNLA and UNITA. To stabilize the situation and secure a victory, the United States would have to step up to the plate. Meanwhile the CIA was floating proposals to mine the harbor of Luanda[81] and use US submarines to prevent the Soviet arms shipments and Cuban troop disembarkation. It would later turn out[82] that the South African Minister of Defense, PW Botha, was relying on this help from Henry Kissinger. The CIA did not follow through.

On 8 December 1975, the United States Ambassador to the United Nations, Daniel Patrick Moynihan declared from the rostrum that[83] if only South Africa, and not the also the Soviet Union, were condemned, then the UN General Assembly would be on record as having found that invasion of African countries by some white armies [meaning the Soviets and Cubans] was perfectly acceptable. He failed to point out that the "South African invaders" were mostly Black Angolans who had actively sought white South African leadership and that the South African effort was backed by several leading Black African countries. In fact, the "invading" Task Force Zulu was mostly black Angolans under a small core of South African leadership, together with a few white soldiers in armored cars. Two days later, the African countries withdrew their proposed resolution to condemn only South Africa and by mid-December only 14 of the 46 member countries of the OAU had recognized the Soviet-backed MPLA government of the newly independent country. That represented much less than a third of the membership. The West could still win this thing. The OAU was still openly divided and watching carefully for a winner. The destruction of the FNLA at Quifangondo had been a far from fatal blow to the Allied effort and in the south the UNITA-South African forces were still moving northward apace. Everything now depended on the United States exhibiting resolve.

Against this background President Ford called Soviet ambassador Dobrynin to the Oval Office on 9 December and made clear his unhappiness about the escalated Soviet arms shipments to Angola. In the presence of Henry Kissinger, the president stated to Dobrynin that US-Soviet relations would be severely affected by the Soviet adventure so far from home. The next day, 10 December 1975, the Soviet arms shipments stopped[84]. This termination is also confirmed by Porter in his study of this conflict[85].

Over the same period Kissinger met with Giscard d'Estaing, president of France, who conceded that Angola was of great concern to France. He would therefore move Mirage fighter jets to Zaïre and supply helicopters armed with missiles for use in Angola. He would also send auxiliary troops of Moroccan or French-African extraction[86]. Kissinger was worried by developments in the United States Senate. Enraged[87] by what he would later call a "*McGovernite Congress,*" he warned his staff that he was concerned about...

> "...the African reaction when they see the Soviets pull it off and we don't do anything. If the Europeans then say to themselves, 'If they can't hold Luanda, how can they defend Europe?' The Chinese will say we're a country that was run out of Indochina for 50,000 men and is now being run out of Angola for less than $50

million."

He had already reported Mao's view of the United States to President Ford earlier on October 25, 1975[88]:

"We are the 'swallow before the storm'. We are ineffectual. What we say is not reliable."

Meanwhile, in the south central region of Angola the UNITA-South African advance still moved inexorably northward. Battlegroup Foxbat had been badly cut up in a Cuban ambush at a place named Ebo and a number of FNLA soldiers had been killed. An advance group of Foxbat had left the road and got their armored cars stuck in a quagmire, where they were badly shot up. The South Africans were outraged at the fact that the Cubans had gone about the battlefield systematically executing many of the wounded Angolan FNLA men[89]. This is the only battle against the South Africans in this war that the Cubans record as they never acknowledge a defeat in battle. Fidel Castro would have the reader believe that the Cubans retreated hundreds of miles under fire without losing a battle. Commandant George Kruys, now the leader of Foxbat, would have his revenge. Matters came to a head at what came to be called the Battle of Bridge 14; a battle that so profoundly worried[90] Fidel Castro that he even relocated it on the map in trying to hide the truth from his people. His official history of the war does not even mention it; such is media and respect for fact in communist dictatorships. Thirteen years later he would foist an even more extravagant mental gymnastic on the gullible Western media[91], but would not fool the US State Department. By the time the last Cubans would leave Angola around 1990, several thousand young Cubans, a disproportionate number of them blacks, would lie mysteriously dead without somehow losing a battle, if Castro were to be believed.

Battlegroup Foxbat, now having the benefit of sappers, built a eucalyptus log bridge over the Nhia River near Santa Comba while under fire from the Cubans across the river. Two men were lost to that fire. The Cuban force comprised[92] an infantry battalion supported by field guns, formidable BM-21 "Stalin Organ" 122 mm rocket batteries and also Sagger wire-guided anti-tank missiles. An elite South African "Recce" artillery spotter team infiltrated the commanding hill held by the Cubans, from where they directed artillery fire that annihilated a Cuban force attempting to cross the river southwards in a flanking movement. The leader of the Cuban expeditionary forces, Commandant Raul Diaz Argüelles elected to withdraw the Cuban forces from Ebo, thereby losing whatever they had managed to hold at the Ebo ambush a few days before.

Under cover of their own artillery fire the South African unit then crossed the log bridge on 11 December 1975 and attacked, immediately leaving the road[93]. This tactic disrupted the plans of the Cubans, particularly those of the Sagger operators, who had targeted the middle of the road. The FAPLA and Cuban defenders were routed[94] despite the intervention of Cuban Soviet helicopter gunships. Foxbat lost four men in this action, with twelve wounded, while independent parties reported that several hundred Cubans were killed[95]. The situation became surreal when the Cubans could not flee fast enough. In one documented case[96], a Soviet truck with twenty Cubans rushed away from the battle and indicated to an armored car also headed north that it wanted to overtake. The armored car allowed them to do so and then fired a 90mm round into the back of the truck killing all on board – it was a South African armored car that was already ahead of the fleeing Cubans and heading for the capital Luanda. The BBC reported truckloads of dead on the road to the north. Among the dead was the leader of the Cuban Expeditionary Force, Commandant Raul Diaz Arguelles, who had paid the ultimate price[97] when he had somehow driven into a minefield. Other accounts have him dying at the Battle of Bridge 14, and yet others claim he died when his armored car was destroyed in a river, likely the Bhia. The road to Luanda lay essentially open, only the town of Quibala remaining to be taken.

Before Kruys could advance again and retain Angola for the West, United States politics overtook the war and changed the future of Africa for the worse for a generation.

Angola – The Fourth Great Abandonment

Clearly, South Africa could not conceivably keep a war going alone against the mighty Soviet Union, especially given the shortcomings it had clearly identified in its own obsolete equipment, particularly in respect of longer range artillery and heavier mobile firepower. As it is, the country had already spent much more on Henry Kissinger's war than the United States itself – some $133M; four times what the Americans had spent. The Kinshasa and Pretoria CIA offices were clamoring for support for the South African forces. Proposals were eventually made to CIA head office for providing weapons directly to the South African forces[98] and Kissinger was using all his powers of persuasion to keep South Africa in the field. Yet his own government was vacillating on the subject.

Savimbi had flown to Pretoria on 10 November to beg John Vorster[99] to keep the South African forces in the field beyond the Independence date so as to clear the Benguela railway line. He obviously felt that would keep Kenneth Kaunda of Zambia "on-side." He asked that the troops should remain until the OAU could meet to decide which side they would support in the war. Anything was still possible. Vorster acceded to these requests, but the OAU meeting was delayed.

Meanwhile, the revelations about Angola in the media precipitated a closed debate on the Defense Appropriations Bill in the U.S. Senate Appropriations Committee around 15 December 1975. During the debate, which continued on the 16th of December, the Day of the Blood River Covenant that always seems to feature in South African history, Henry Kissinger's Department of State provided a briefing document[100] that contained two central truths that would be wiped aside in the debate:

> "Another factor we had to weigh was the effect of a Marxist-oriented Angola on future developments in Southern Africa. Our conclusion was that it would increase the prospects for violent rather than peaceful change and perhaps fatally undermine the incipient trend toward détente between South Africa and Black African States. [...]
>
> ...there is African sentiment; admittedly only in private but probably more extensive than we know, which accepts the necessity of South Africa's balancing intervention if a Soviet victory is to be prevented and the military balance necessary to achieve political compromise is to be maintained"

This was a huge understatement, and Kissinger knew it very well. On 17 December, he met in Paris with Mandungu Bula Nyati, State Commissioner for Foreign Affairs and International Cooperation of Zaire. Bula told him[101]:

> "We will be Machiavellian. Let the South Africans use their forces and we will then use this to get the Africans to get the Russians out. That's my opinion. Talk will not settle anything. The Russians won't leave. We'll continue to attack South Africa and we will condemn the Soviet Union too. Let the South Africans know that we will be attacking them as well as the Russians. We will be comparing the Soviets to Hitler in 1939. Let the South Africans know that this is just our way of showing up the Russians.
>
> "We are convinced the Soviet Union is trying to destroy us."

Back in Washington on the 19th of December, it was painfully obvious to the security attendees to a meeting with Henry Kissinger that they needed South African help as regards training and leadership of the pro-Western effort. However, their domestic political arena could not process that. The released (but sanitized) minutes of that meeting make deeply fascinating reading, but they are best summarized by the meeting notes[102] made by Robert S. Ingersoll, Deputy Secretary of State:

> "The key to keeping our side in Angola from collapsing is So. Africa. As far as Africans are concerned they would agree to have So. Africa clean up Angola, but we couldn't pay the domestic price in this country."

Ingersoll was proven correct. The problem lay not in Africa. It lay distinctly in the United States. Despite these central points explained above, John Tunney, the young liberal anti-Vietnam War Democrat from California, was instrumental[103] in having the $28 million earmarked for any anti-Soviet faction in Angola removed from the Appropriation Bill. This would become known as the Tunney Amendment. Therewith ended the Ford Administration's efforts in Angola. The House of Representatives would eventually vote 323 versus 99 for the Tunney Amendment on 27 January 1976. And therewith the United States faced away from the world and withdrew in upon itself to enter one of the lowest periods in its existence as a nation.

In Washington, dismayed by the actions of Congress, President Ford addressed[104] the press and spoke the prophetic words:

> *"The Senate decision to cut off additional funds for Angola is a deep tragedy for all countries whose security depends upon the United States. Ultimately, it will profoundly affect the security of our country as well. How can the United States, the greatest power in the world, take the position that the Soviet Union can operate with impunity many thousands of miles away with Cuban troops and massive amounts of military equipment, while we refuse any assistance to the majority of the local people who ask only for military equipment to defend themselves?*
>
> *"The issue in Angola is not, never has been, and never will be a question of the use of U.S. forces. The sole issue is the provision of modest amounts of assistance to oppose military intervention by two extra-continental powers, namely the Soviet Union and Cuba. This abdication of responsibility by a majority of the Senate will have the gravest consequences for the long-term position of the United States and for international order in general.*
>
> *"A great nation cannot escape its responsibilities. Responsibilities abandoned today will return as more acute crises tomorrow."*

The last sentence above would come to haunt the informed in the United States on September 11, 2001.

The Soviets and Cubans now correctly assessed the new American position as one of capitulation in the Third World and promptly resumed[105] their arms supplies and shipments of troops at an escalated rate on 24 December 1975. Secretary of State Kissinger makes the vividly clear strategic conclusion that, for the first time in the Cold War, the United States had capitulated to a Soviet-sponsored military adventure[106].

Angola – Consequences

As late as January 1976, there was still some limited hope for the West. At the 12 January 1976 meeting of the OAU the delegates were still split straight down the middle[107, 108, 109] at 22 versus 22. The Soviets failed to get the organization to condemn South Africa. Then Nigeria came out in support of the MPLA. It has been suggested[110] that the Soviets paid off the Nigerian delegation, a country that is known worldwide in the 21st century for its endemic corruption. The term "Nigerian Scam" is also well established.

Finally, on 11 February 1976, the bulk of the African states fell in line behind powerful Nigeria, including some that had asked South Africa to intervene in the first place. Such is Africa. Nevertheless, the vote was very far from unanimous, being only 27 to 19 in favor of recognizing the MPLA government in Luanda. Clearly, no fewer than 19 other Black African countries still had few qualms about the South African help to the opposing parties. But they had now been deserted by the United States and had to keep quiet. The Soviet ambassadors in their various capitals, however, were doing their jobs and pressuring their hosts. On 23 February, the OAU passed a resolution condemning South Africa while completely ignoring the influx of Cuban troops and the Soviet weapons buildup. It brazenly ignored the fact that its own leading members had sought the help from South Africa in the first place. It stated that the "People's Republic of Angola" was[111],

> *"a victim of an intolerable aggression by the troops of the racist and fascist Government of South Africa who are occupying part of its national territory."*

We were now "racists" and "fascists" again, even as young white South Africans were dying helping their black fellow Africans to keep the Soviet bear out of Africa. Stockwell explains[112] that the South African government realized that the United States was going to withdraw and therefore gave up in disgust and returned across the border as efficiently and quietly as they had originally entered Angola.

In Parliament on 17 April 1978, the South African Minister of Defence, P.W. Botha, stated[113]

> *"...we were ruthlessly left in the lurch."*

Shortly before his death on 31 October 2006 Botha granted a final interview[114] in which he emphatically stated that Henry Kissinger flew to Pretoria to speak to him after these events and that he told Kissinger:

"Don't hide behind your Congress. You know you left us in the lurch."

By the first week of January 1976, the South African forces started withdrawing.

The entire 1975/6 Angolan experience left great bitterness against the United States within the South African Defense community, and would color all future relations with the United States down to the avoidance of even the most insignificant American made parts in South African military equipment design. Ironically the United States would later have to purchase these designs for its 21st century war in Iraq.

The cooperation between the United States and South Africa would continue at arm's length in matters of intelligence, as we shall later see, but the trust would never be restored. The reader is referred to Chapter 20 (*The Korean War*) and to Chapter 19 (*NF82*) in order to comprehend the disgust and dismay.

PW Botha, South African Minister of Defense at the time, told parliament that the intervention by South Africa had been *"part of the involvement of the free world,"* but that South Africa was *"not prepared to fight on behalf of the free world alone."* It would now defend *"its own borders and those that it was responsible for."*

Kissinger's frustrated statement to President Ford had been proved correct[115]. Decades later Kissinger's dismay at the conduct of Senator Clark in particular was still vividly evident[116]. He insists Clark had been kept informed all along but, when the moment to be counted came, Clark denied being consulted.

The joint effort in Angola had potentially been a grand example of white and black working together in defense of Africa against overseas intruders. It could have set a positive tone for the next two decades. Unfortunately, liberal white men in North America had somehow found it incomprehensible that white and black in Africa could genuinely cooperate in resisting Soviet designs in Africa. They preferred to be cowed by their own self-made failure in Vietnam and swayed by their own unique historic race relations demons.

In May of 1976, according to Brand Fourie who led the Foreign Service for South Africa, Henry Kissinger advised[117] Prime Minister Vorster that South Africa could not rely on American assistance if the Soviets organized a military assault on the country. South Africa now knew where it stood after having fought alongside the United States in three major wars, WWI, WWII and Korea. We were completely alone on earth. On 29 June 1976, President Ford signed into law the infamous Clark Amendment[118] that forbade any military support for parties in Angola. On 22 November 1976, the "People's Republic of Angola" was recognized as the 146th member of the United Nations. It assumed its proscribed role on the shelf as Soviet Client State and springboard for World Communist Revolution.

As though to demonstrate just how truly ineffectual the United States had become against the Soviets under the post-Vietnam Democratic Congress, the Ford administration was reduced to making its displeasure known by calling off an exhibition baseball series[119] between the United States and Cuba. Kissinger experienced the effects of the US failure in Angola when the Brazilian Foreign Minister Antonio da Silveira told him to his face[120] that Brazil was no longer sure that it could rely on the United States.

Back in Angola a senior Cuban Intelligence officer took over the apartment that the CIA station chief, Robert Hultslander, had occupied in Luanda[121]. With the Cubans now settled in Africa, the wait for the next Soviet-Cuban move on the international chessboard would be very short indeed.

As the Bravo group moved back to Namibia, the Angolan soldiers of the group were left with instructions to report for service at posts in Angola near the Namibian border in January 1976, including at the original Mpupa. When Jan Breytenbach arrived back at Mpupa in Southern Angola in January 1976, he found, not 300, but several thousand[122] ex-FNLA Angolan black men with their families waiting for him. They would become known as 32 Battalion; "Buffalo"; *Os Terriveis*—The Terrible Ones—a sobering example of camaraderie between black men and white men of Africa in fighting the Communists who had flown thousands of miles from other continents to inflict their political model on the African continent. In future, the mere mention of *Buffalo's* involvement in an attack would cause opposing Angolan FAPLA troops to throw away all their equipment in panic and flee, as reported by Soviet advisers in Angola[123].

-----ooOoo-----

23

Adapt or Die

"...we are hardly free enough of sin to cast the first stone – or even the second."

Richard Milhous Nixon, President of the United States
about South Africa in *The Real War* (1980)

Exporting the Angolan War

Fig. 23-1 *US President Jimmy Carter*

In the wake of the American hesitation and failure in Angola, Africa swung dramatically and predictably towards a triumphant U.S.S.R. Cuba shipped several tens of thousands of troops into Angola, even using the airport of Gander in Canada[1]. Cuban soldiers, half of whom were reputedly selected to be blacks[2], were dressed in civilian clothes[3] and their weapons stowed in the cargo bay, an approach they used in flying via several different routes through the Caribbean in civilian airliners. Canadian authorities moved to shut down this route only after formal protests by the United States[4]. The far left-leaning Prime Minster of Canada, Pierre Trudeau, openly admired Fidel Castro, the totalitarian dictator of Cuba[5]. As though to emphasize his support, Trudeau paid a three-day visit to Cuba two weeks later on January 26, 1976, the first NATO Head of State to do so since the Missile Crisis; this while Cuba was militarily engaged against the West.

On Wednesday 28 January 1976, at the southern Cuban port of Cienfuegos, Trudeau infamously ended a 25 minute speech[6] with an enthusiastic cheer[7]:

"¡Viva Cuba y el pueblo cubano! ¡Viva el Primer Ministro Fidel Castro! ¡Viva la amistad cubano-canadiense!"

When Trudeau was confronted by the Opposition in the Canadian Parliament about his close relationship with Castro, he echoed:

"Long live Canada and Cuba..."[8].

This close friendship of a supposedly key Western leader left South Africans, such as the author's father-in-law who had defended the lives of Canadian soldiers against the Germans in the air in WWII (*NF82*), incredulous and outraged. As the Cuban presence in Africa expanded, the Canadian press finally realized the scope of the Cuban adventure their Prime Minister had indulged. The *Globe and Mail* newspaper openly accused Cuba of using Gander as a base for running "mercenaries" to Angola[9]. It seemed that ordinary Canadians comprehended that Trudeau was "hugging a monster," but he did not. When Castro eventually attended the funeral of Trudeau on 3 October 2000, he told Canadian reporters that there were still between 200 and 400 political prisoners in Cuba[10], but the Western media had no interest in opponents of oppressive Communism.

In faraway Africa, Jonas Savimbi retreated with his UNITA followers to the southeastern Cuando-Cubango Province of Angola, bordering Zambia and Namibia. From there he would continue a 27 year war. He would retain the support of Kenneth Kaunda of Zambia and Joseph Mobutu of Zaire who would secretly cooperate with South Africa to help him bleed the Soviets and Cubans.

The South African forces pulled unbeaten out of Angola in perfect order with a flag parade, the Cubans following very hesitantly[11] at a respectful distance, and the MPLA behind them at an even more respectful distance. The Soviets were now firmly established on the ground in Black Africa, complete with military personnel and supported by several tens of thousands of young Cubans as expendable cannon fodder.

A new president was inaugurated in the United States in January 1977 in the form of a Georgia peanut farmer, more recently State Governor, named Jimmy Carter. In a final moment that shall live in history to define the Carter administration, the new US ambassador to the UN, Andrew Young, announced[12]:

"There's a sense in which the Cubans bring a certain stability and order to Angola."

Hundreds of thousands of Angolans would eventually die proving him dead wrong. As for the South African relationship with the United States, John Chettle, the South African born United States director of the South Africa Foundation wrote[13]:

"We have more to fear from the United States than from the Soviet Union. [...] It is the United States with its volatile swings in opinion, its unassuaged yearnings for what it thinks of [as] idealistic action, its new administration with its debt to black votes [...] that is the truly unpredictable and potentially revolutionary force."

Militarily, the Soviets largely left South Africa alone in Namibia, no doubt realizing they would never win a proxy war against the South Africans using Castro's Cubans, given the emotional machismo culture of the latter. The South Africans were on home ground with excellent logistics and everything to fight for. The events in Angola had been a vivid demonstration to the Soviets of what the South Africans could achieve when allied with their Black African friends, despite their international isolation and very limited resources.

For Zaire, the American failure led in short order to an attempted invasion from Angola[14] on 7 March 1977. Mobutu blamed the Soviets and Cubans for this. The group involved was the Congo National Liberation Front (FNLC) and they set their sights on the mineral rich Katanga, now named the Shaba Province. This region generated 70% of Zaire's minerals revenues and contains the major source of cobalt for the world[15].

Historically, the FNLC were Mois Tshombe supporters (Chapter 20: *Congo*). They had first supported the Portuguese against the MPLA, and then later the MPLA against the other two Angolan movements that were supported by Mobutu of Zaire. The new Carter administration downplayed the Soviet and Cuban involvement in the invasion[16].

The French took the lead in opposing this invasion, again supported by the collection of African Heads of State who had requested South Africa's involvement in Angola. The invaders were driven back to Angola. The only involvement of the United States was in airlifting "non-lethal" supplies for the Western countries assisting Zaire. Having tested the United States more than once and found it wanting, the Soviets and their Cuban proxies now moved in on the Horn of Africa. To understand the background to the events, we have to retrace history some distance back to the Scramble for Africa in the 19th century (Chapter 15 : *Carving up Africa*).

The Italians were latecomers to that outrageous process and managed to secure southern Somaliland in the Horn of Africa; the southern part of the modern Somalia. When they then tried to invade independent Ethiopia in 1895, they suffered a tremendous defeat at the hands of a much larger, but ill equipped Ethiopian Army. Based on this success, the European powers condescendingly "granted" the Ogaden region to Ethiopia. As usual, they totally ignored the fact that the people in that eastern part of the country were culturally totally different from the largely Christian Ethiopians. They were in fact Cushitic speaking Moslem Somalis. During the 1930s Italy invaded and colonized Ethiopia and annexed the Ogaden to what was then Italian Somaliland. In World War II, the South Africans and some other British Empire troops liberated Somaliland and Ethiopia (See Chapter 19: *World War II- East Africa*). In Ethiopia, Haile Selassie was restored to his throne. At the end of the war, Britain attempted to maintain the Italian arrangement, but the United States put pressure on Britain who then gave the territory back to Ethiopia.

In 1974, Haile Selassie was deposed in a coup and Ethiopia was taken over by a group called the Derg. Their destructive management under a man named Mengistu Haile Mariam weakened Ethiopia. On 17 July 1977, a Somali force invaded the Ogaden in an attempt to restore the territory to Somalia. Sensing in Ethiopia a potential Communist government and useful future puppet, the Soviets supported the Ethiopians. After all, Mariam was a man after the Soviets' hearts – earlier that year he had walked into an Ethiopian cabinet meeting and shot all his colleagues[17]. The Soviets promptly linked the war to South Africa's "Apartheid" policies by suggesting that the war was instigated by Western Powers to divert the attention of Africa from that policy.[18] By September, the usual advisers were in the country along with some 200 Cuban Army men in support. Angola was replicating itself on the other side of the continent. By 13 November, the Americans were withdrawn from Ethiopia and the Russians from Somalia. This was followed by some 16,000 Cuban soldiers being moved into Ethiopia. The Soviets provided the equipment, logistics and body bags and the Cuban cannon fodder was to do the fighting and the filling of the body bags.

In Angola, the FNLC wanted to invade Zaire again, but, being under the control of the Angolan MPLA government and the Soviets, they were held off while the Ogaden War was first addressed, demonstrating the Soviet control over the attempts on Zaire. It was a relatively simple affair for the Cubans and by 5 March 1978, General Arnaldo Ochoa Sanchez stood victorious, having driven the Somalis from the Ogaden. President Carter had been tested far more directly than before and had failed spectacularly. Reality finally forced him to announce[19] that the Soviet Union was expansionist and the Cubans in Africa were Soviet proxy troops. The cynical reaction in South Africa at President Carter's sudden realization can surely be appreciated today.

With the MPLA and its Soviet-Cuban masters in control in Angola, SWAPO had gained bases in a number of places north of the Namibian-Angolan border from where they launched attacks into Namibia. In one hot pursuit operation, the South African Defense Force chased[20] SWAPO fourteen miles into Angola. By early 1978, the South Africans planned Operation *Reindeer* deep inside Angola on two SWAPO camps. One of these, Cassinga, was 200 miles inside Angola. It was the main SWAPO training camp. The other, Chetequera, was 17 miles inside Angola and was the transit camp for attacks on Namibia. They would be hit simultaneously.

The attack started[21] at 8 am on 4 May 1978 when some 257 South African paratroopers jumped near Cassinga. The South African Air Force initiated the attack with a run of 1,000 lb. bombs timed to coincide with the SWAPO morning parade. It was total devastation. The survivors of the bombing run fled into the attacking paratroopers and were cut to ribbons. The South Africans left[22] some 600 dead and 340 wounded SWAPOs at Cassinga. When the South African paratroopers tried to withdraw by helicopter, they were attacked by a Cuban formation. The Cubans were caught in the open in their vehicles on a road where an air-to-surface rocket attack by the South African Air Force left 60 Cubans dead.

The attack at Chetequera was similarly successful and left some 250 SWAPO dead. Taking a leaf from their Soviet masters' textbook, SWAPO sketched the camps as being populated by "refugees" and "elderly people." Of course the West believed this, quite ignoring the fact that the "refugees" were lined up in military formation at the time of the attack.

This event demonstrated to Fidel Castro that, despite his bottomless pit of military equipment from Mother Russia and his Soviet advisers, he would never be able to rest easy as regards the South of Angola. A major fraction of his troops were going to be tied up there, possibly forever. It was to become the Cuban Vietnam. Eventually, some 400,000 Cuban soldiers would be rotated through African states (mostly Angola) and more than 2,000 of them would die in Africa for this decision[23]. Cuba has steadfastly avoided making clear how many troops it had in Angola, but it is known that there were 26 distinct regiments[24]. Taking a regiment at 2,000 to 3,000 men, this makes between 52,000 and 78,000 men a realistic figure. At no point would South Africa ever have more than 5,000 men in Angola.

The Cuban soldier's perception of the ongoing war in Angola would register soon enough. For this we consult Jose Manuel Vigoa Perez[25], a highly trained 20-year-old First Lieutenant in the Cuban Special Forces; the Cuban Spetsnaz. Trained in the Soviet Union, he would eventually end up in the United States as refugee. He refers to the plethora of Soviet-Axis factions, advisers, and intelligence services. He explains that he was never as scared as in Angola, because it was never clear who was friend and who was foe. And then there were the lions. Finally he lamented the inexplicable presence of Cubans in Angola and Afghanistan.

The typical South African soldier would laugh heartily at this summary, cynically welcome the young man to Africa, tell him to forget about lions, but remind him of the lurking crocodiles, spitting cobras, deadly mambas, Gabon vipers, puff adders, and scorpions. They would enumerate the soul-sapping heat, powdery white dust, pans of stagnant water, and malaria. Subsequently, the South Africans would capitalize on the confusion of the Communist intelligence services that he refers to.

The above events paint a picture of a new paradigm for South Africa after the Angolan War. From now on there would be news reports of young men losing their lives *"in the Operational Area."* One took this to mean anywhere in Namibia or Angola. It was the new reality of life on the outer perimeter of Western Civilization in a world where the West was a joke and the United States was effectively absent, being now preoccupied with the Sexual Revolution while the Communist Revolution had its way with the world. To make matters worse, in May 1977 the Carter Administration insisted on "One man, One vote" in South Africa[26].

None of this kept the Soviets and Cubans from trying their hand at smaller ventures aimed at the dependence of the United States on minerals from Africa. Zaire and its cobalt supply was the softest attractive target in the subcontinent at the time. On 13 May 1978, the FNLC again[27] invaded Zaire from Angola. Most of the 2,000 white foreigners resident there, of whom 88 were Americans, were evacuated. Some, however, were taken hostage and 80 were killed. The impact of this invasion was far greater than the previous one. The French deployed their Foreign Legion and the Belgians sent 1200 paratroopers. This time[28] President Carter allowed the airlifting of Belgian troops and directly blamed Cuba in the matter of the Zaire invasion:

> *The Government of Angola must bear a heavy responsibility for the deadly attack which was launched from its territory, and it's a burden and a responsibility shared by Cuba. We believe that Cuba had known of the Katangan plans to invade and obviously did nothing to restrain them from crossing the border. We also know that the Cubans have played a key role in training and equipping the Katangans who attacked. [...]*
>
> *We want to take a careful look at whether our legislation and procedures are fully responsive to the challenges that we face today.[...]*
>
> *As for the Clark amendment, which prohibits action in regard to Angola, I have no present intention of seeking its modification.*

Possibly Carter had finally started to grasp the scale of the disaster precipitated by the ill-conceived Tunney and Clark amendments. The price for the glaringly obvious American failure of will in Angola would eventually turn out to be very high indeed for the United States and would exceed the worst nightmare[29] that Americans could conceive of, short of a nuclear war. The perception among Africans, Arabs and Persians of weakness and lack of resolve on the part of the United States started with the Tunney and Clark Amendments and is with us still in 21st century. That perception, and later inadequate responses to direct challenges in the last decade of the 20th century, led straight as an arrow to the terrible events of 11 September 2001. The trend set in in Angola in 1975 when the United States failed the acid test and literally deserted its allies on the field of battle; allies whom it had begged for help in the first place.

The effect on the Soviets was equally profound. Years later, Soviet Ambassador Dobrynin would write[30] that, having suffered no major international complications from its interference in Angola, Moscow had no scruples about escalating its activities in other countries, first Ethiopia, then Yemen, a number of African and Middle-Eastern States, and, to crown it all, Afghanistan.

Afrikaner historian Hermann Giliomee succinctly sums up the effect of the Angolan events on the South African government[31] by explaining that the US about-face in Angola had deeply shocked Vorster and that he was now so obsessed with the Soviet Threat that he gave little attention to reform.

The actions in the United States Congress in December 1975 had done more to destroy hope in Africa and strengthen the hand of the Communist Revolution than any action on any battlefield or any ill-considered social policy on the part of South Africa. For South Africa it was now a matter of survival and no risk could be entertained any further, especially risks urged on the country by those "allies" who thought nothing of abandoning it on the battlefield in the heat of battle.

It was hardly surprising that, when John Vorster resigned a few years later, he was replaced by the very hawkish Pieter W. Botha, the very man who had been Minister of Defense during the Angolan War.

Soweto and the "Total Onslaught"

After the withdrawal of the South African Defence Force from Angola, Black militant ANC members in South Africa started appearing in the streets yelling "Viva! Viva!," the only word of Spanish they would ever know in their lives. They would point directly at the events in Angola as evidence that the South African government could be toppled in short order. The immediate consequence was the Soweto uprisings of 1976, inspired by the Angolan events, and a South African government now more internationally isolated than ever. What was missing for the African National Congress was a suitable rallying issue with which to whip up support in the country for their revolutionary agenda. The National Party government would not disappoint them in providing a suitable issue. The ANC would also get the textbook deaths, martyrs, and emotional media visibility they were so desperately seeking. Such is the revolutionary textbook, which borders on the predictable and tiresome until it is one's own country that is at stake.

The area of so-called Bantu Education was already a subject with much to criticize as regards the quality of education for Black students. It was for reasons best known to himself that Andries Treurnicht, the Deputy Minister of Bantu Education in the governing National Party, decided to impose a rule of equal usage of English and Afrikaans in Black schools. He imposed a new ruling in terms of which Afrikaans would have to be used as the language for teaching Mathematics. There was no doubt that the matter of language use in school had in fact been politicized by the ANC. However, given the realities of the situation in the country, Treurnicht's action was bereft of any sound judgment.

On 16 June 1976, the streets of Soweto blew up in a student riot. Depending on which side the particular media supported, the students were either smiling and good-humored, or were attacking the Police. Experience suggests that both statements were simultaneously true in different places. As is so typical of mass protests by Black people in South Africa, matters got out of hand before the day was out. Someone – most likely the Police – had shot and killed a black student named Hector Petersen. As is usually the case for South Africa, the Western Media had a field day and the longer-term casualty of the media hate fest would always be the reasonable black and white people in the middle of the South African spectrum.

In one scene in Johannesburg, a small knot of white students from Wits University also took to the streets waving a banner reading *"Don't start the Revolution without us."* It remains one of the enduring images of Liberal White delusion in South Africa. Many of the Black students leading riots were members of the so-called Black Consciousness Movement for which an intelligent young Black man, Steve Biko, was spokesman. Biko had made it quite clear that he had no need of "White Liberals." In fact, he stated that white liberals who appeased their own conscience hindered the Black quest for freedom and fulfillment[32].

In one evening television newscast, an English speaking South African lady reported having a brick thrown through the windscreen of her automobile as she was shouting *"Don't throw! I'm English!"* She realized the profound absurdity of her screams even as the brick came through the windscreen. By October 1977, the deaths in the continued riots had risen to between six hundred and seven hundred. It is during this period that a new form of black leader emerged, exemplified by Bishop Desmond Tutu of the Anglican Church.

On 12 September 1977, it was announced that Steve Biko had died in police custody under very suspicious circumstances. It was later revealed that he had died from brain damage. He had obviously been beaten to death. This showed the white people in South Africa that something was profoundly wrong. It was no longer just a simple matter of outnumbered policemen being threatened by bloodthirsty Black crowds who would kill anyone and possibly even consume their flesh, as had happened to Sister Mary Aidan in 1952 (Chapter 20: *Always the horror near Port Elizabeth*). Something was clearly wrong on the side of the security forces as well. However, with not a friend on earth there seemed to the ordinary white South African no way forward but to hold out by any means, fair or foul, against this raging torrent of Soviet-Cuban supported Uhuru north, and now east, of the border. It was now down to sheer survival—life and death—and one assumed the government did what the government had to do to keep one alive.

As it is, Biko had earlier had a vividly clear message for white liberals[33], proving thereby that he had analyzed them perfectly correctly. He suggested that the limitations that had accompanied the involvement of liberals in the black man's struggle had been mostly responsible for arrest of progress in that effort. He suggested that, in view of what he called *"their inferiority complex,"* blacks had tended to listen seriously to what the liberals had to say. He stated that, with their *"characteristic arrogance of assuming a monopoly on intelligence and moral judgment,"* these *"self-appointed trustees of black interests"* had set the pattern and pace for the realization of the black man's aspirations.

After the suppression of the Soweto uprisings, many young black men left South Africa with the help of the ANC to undergo military training. In this process, ANC facilities were set up in a number of neighboring and near-neighboring countries, the prime example being Angola where they had Cuban protection. Some would later fight against the South African Defence Force in Angola under Soviet command[34] (See later Chapter 25: The War for Africa – 1). As to the link between the ANC, its military aspirations, and the unhappiness about Afrikaans in schools, we merely need to ask Oliver Tambo, leader of the ANC at the time. In an interview in 1978, he declared[35]:

Our struggle has developed in two basic directions. The main one is mobilization of the masses, workers, peasants and young people. The other is stepping up of armed action. In South Africa in 1977 mass action with workers and young people participating was combined with actions by the military formations of the African National Congress, and both types of action were obviously coordinated in time. This demonstrates, on the one hand, the support of the masses for the armed struggle that is needed to bring ultimate victory, and on the other, the reliance of our underground organizations on the support of the mass of the people.

In fact, this clearly demonstrates the reality of the situation, despite ongoing attempts in the United States to present the ANC as non-military in nature and the Soweto Riots as being purely an education language issue.

The assault on South Africa in the Western media reached fever pitch and would stay there for the following one-and-a-half-decades. It is instructive to analyze this in some more detail and to compare the attention given to social problems in South Africa over this period to that given other, typically non-Western countries. We are fortunate to have the results[36] of just such a study, published in November 1977 and covering the year of 1976. The study covered the *New York Times, Washington Post, CBS, NBC* and *ABC*. These five primary media houses had presented one single story about North Korea, only seven about Cuba, despite its thousands of political prisoners, sixteen about Cambodia and its Khmer Rouge horror. In the same year, they had published no fewer than 513 articles about South Africa.

It leaves the thinking reader with only one conclusion: there is something deeply and profoundly skewed about the news being fed to the American public and one cannot but suspect the true motives and affiliations of the parties involved. From this point onwards, the United States media would leave no stone unturned to sketch white South Africans as monsters. It would be the United States media, more than any other force, that would eventually destroy "White" South Africa. That media would assume the role towards South Africa that the London Missionary Society had in the 1830s, but with infinitely more devastating effect and with even less regard for fact, balance or even the vaguest pretense toward even-handedness.

On 4 November 1977, the unrelenting international political and media assault on South Africa finally led to United Nations Resolution 418 – obligatory military sanctions against South Africa. For years it would be celebrated[37] in the South African Defense technology community as the birthday of the South African "Military Industrial Complex."

When PW Botha became prime minister in 1978, he would talk of the "Total Onslaught"; a mix of pressure from Western Powers, destabilization inside the country, and Soviet sponsored troops on the border. It has become commonplace in the 21st century to refer to this as paranoia and fear-mongering. Inside South Africa in the second half of the 1970s it did not seem like paranoia and fear-mongering. It seemed very realistic. ANC documents reveal that Botha had a point, as may be seen from Tambo's statement above.

Military Self-Sufficiency

The international weapons sanctions, combined with hard practical experience against the Cubans and their Soviet weapons in Angola, laid the foundation for one of the most innovative military technology initiatives. During the campaign in Angola, a number of issues hit home. These included the fact that the South African artillery was completely outdated and of insufficient range. What artillery the South African troops did have, had been used with great effect. This was true even at the disastrous Quifangondo, where they had caused the Cubans to desert their Stalin Organs. Unfortunately, the FNLA had failed to exploit that opportunity to attack. Nevertheless, the army clearly needed new heavy artillery. Given the traditional technocratic mindset of the Afrikaner and his love of his rifle, such artillery would have to be of superlative range and superlative accuracy. After all, even in the Boer War the Afrikaners had proven themselves masters of the rifle and gun against the mighty British Empire.

Furthermore, the South African troops were much impressed with the Soviet "Stalin Organ" multiple rocket launchers. While these had had relatively limited effect on the few South Africans involved in the Angolan War, they had repeatedly caused the UNITA and FNLA troops to break and run. These weapons were not accurate and had more of a psychological effect than anything else, but their effect on undisciplined troops was very impressive. What if South Africa could have something similar of better range and accuracy?

There were challenges in the area of armor. A number of shortcomings had been identified regarding the Eland armored cars, a South African derived version of the French Panhard. These would need to be addressed. It was also glaringly obvious that South Africa did not have any tanks worth mentioning, but its soldiers had repeatedly faced Soviet tanks in the field. Other variants of armored vehicles were required with better armament and armor. South Africa's Mirage IIIC fighter aircraft were nearing obsolescence and plans would have to be made in that area. There were other demands in the air, such as better air-to-air missiles.

There were challenges in the areas of communications equipment, cryptography and allied electronic intelligence technology. The Army had developed a need for an innovative way to deal with the escalating use of anti-tank mines. These had been excessively used by the enemy and a solution was needed. The eventual solutions would be desperately simple and hugely effective. Lastly, while not often discussed, the ammunition supply had been severely drained by the war and plans would need to be made to ensure a goodly supply. Clearly an upgraded manufacturing ability would have to be established.

In one of the most impressive industrial adaptation processes yet in the Western World, South African industry stepped up to the plate and started building one of the most innovative high technology industries ever to address these wide-ranging demands. In Prime Minister (later President) P.W. Botha, the man who had felt so betrayed by the American withdrawal in Angola, this industry found a devoted supporter.

Some materials, goods, and expertise would have to be sourced overseas, and this ability was duly developed. It would lead to an interesting United States Public Broadcasting System television presentation on the subject. Copies of this would eventually be used as promotional materials by the South Africans[38].

Over the following decade this industry would grow to, for example, support three missile types, have two types in production and have five more under development; all at the same time[39]. Programs for different weapons systems would proliferate and the country would become an important exporter of arms, much to the chagrin of those who had imposed weapons sanctions. South African military engineers would later laugh cynically at the United Nations in the presence of the author, when the very organization that had imposed the sanctions on the country felt forced to purchase mine-proof Casspir armored personnel carriers from South Africa. These purpose-made vehicles had become a "symbol of oppression" in Soweto, but were grudgingly purchased by United Nations for use by "blue hats" in dangerous peacekeeping operations in Southeast Europe. By the 1990s, no other vehicle would be considered suitable to the task.

Eventually, South Africa would become the undisputed world leader in long range artillery, a key ability that it would use to drive the Soviets from Africa. Military analysts were intrigued, to say the least, with the devastatingly accurate South African G5 long range howitzer. They were even more struck with its motorized stable mate, the G-6. Simultaneously the country would become the world leader in mine/IED-proof vehicles.

The United States and Canada would eventually purchase this technology and it would save the lives of American and Canadian soldiers in Iraq and Afghanistan in the 21st century. By the year 2010, US-based companies such as Force Protection would be major suppliers of these vehicles and the engineers leading the development would be veterans of the South African defense technology fraternity. Ex-South African ballistic missile engineers would play key roles in the launch of important Canadian satellites in Russia in the 21st century.

Somewhere in the middle of all the turmoil, the old United Party of Jan Smuts finally died in 1977 (Chapter 19: *Afrikaner Nationalism*). The new Opposition in Parliament was the Progressive Reform Party (later named the "Progressive Federal Party"), led by an Afrikaner intellectual, Frederik Van Zyl Slabbert. The only problem was that they had so few seats that the government could basically laugh them off among the white electorate. However, the Progressive Reform Party cornered most of the leading Afrikaner intelligentsia[40]. Unfortunately, it was no longer a time for the intelligentsia. From September 1978, the country was run by P.W. Botha and the military and security forces of various types became the controlling force in the country. Gone was the political era of Vorster and his talks with Kaunda in a train coach parked on the bridge over Victoria Falls. Now it was "shoot first and ask questions later"- the unfortunate natural consequence of the West threatening the whites with their backs against a wall and nowhere to turn, or run, as the case may be.

Much has been made of how the government spurned the efforts of the Progressive Reform Party. However, a sober look at the realities of South Africa shows there never was any hope of a realistic political solution between black and white while the Soviet Union and its Cuban and Uhuru cohorts were hovering on the perimeter. The only practical strategic option was to hold out at any cost and wait for a break in the alliance between African Nationalistic Uhuru and its Soviet Communist underwriters. Meanwhile the best tactic within this strategy was to keep bleeding the Soviets and Cubans in any way possible, while keeping the opposing Southern African states on their hind legs in their own territories.

The "bleeding" would work supremely well. Cuba would end up spending around 11% of its meager budget on its African adventure over the following years and the Soviet Central Committee members would complain bitterly that they had to keep "protecting" Angola from the South Africans while the American company, Gulf Oil, continued to pump oil from Cabinda[41]. Such is the reality of a Communist system that could never represent a viable market for anything other than food. South Africa would continue to play this game until the Soviet Union collapsed, but other dimensions would be added to the mix.

The Sullivan Principles

Given the increasing industrial self-sufficiency of South Africa, it should come as no surprise that external pressure would be brought to bear in that arena. During 1977, the Board of General Motors included a Black American church minister by the name of Leo Sullivan. He was unhappy with the involvement of General Motors in South Africa and sought to implement an employment code that American companies should follow if they were to remain active in South Africa.

These principles seemed entirely reasonable and included the following: Non-segregation of the races in all eating, comfort, and work facilities; Equal and fair employment practices for all employees; Equal pay for all employees doing equal or comparable work for the same period of time; Initiation of and development of training programs that will prepare, in substantial numbers, blacks and other nonwhites for supervisory, administrative, clerical, and technical jobs; Increasing the number of blacks and other non-whites in management and supervisory positions; and improving the quality of life for blacks and other non-whites outside the work environment in such areas as housing, transportation, school, recreation, and health facilities. Eventually, of the order of 125 United States corporations active in South Africa adopted these measures.

A clear day in the Kalahari Desert

July 3, 1977, was a beautiful clear blue winter sky day over the Kalahari Desert region of the Northern Cape Province, south of Botswana. There are seldom clouds over the Kalahari in winter anyway. The men on the ground were packing up for the day. High above them, moving at around 17,500 miles per hour, a small ballistic object passed over. The Soviet area-surveillance Cosmos-922 satellite photographed the area[42] based on information provided by high-level Soviet Spy, Dieter Gerhard, at South African Defense Headquarters[43]. It did so again the very next day. The mission of Cosmos 922 ended around the 13th of July and the satellite was presumably recovered for analysis of its high resolution photographic results as per the usual Soviet practice. Immediately following this, Cosmos-932, a maneuverable satellite, was positioned to photograph a selected area more closely. This satellite was recovered on 2 August. Matters then developed rapidly.

On Saturday August 6, 1977, the acting head of the Soviet Embassy in Washington arrived at the White House. He had an urgent message for President Jimmy Carter[44], who was not available. William Hyland took the message from Leonid Brezhnev. The Soviet Union had detected preparations for a nuclear test in the Kalahari Desert of South Africa and wanted the help of the United States in stopping the process. On 7 August 1977, a light airplane overflew the site and no one could identify it or its origin or its destination. In fact, it was an airplane belonging to the American Military attaché in Pretoria[45]. The very next day, TASS reported that a Soviet satellite had identified a South African nuclear bomb test facility. Pressure was therefore now openly on the United States to induce South Africa to dismantle the operation. Some claim that the Soviets threatened to bomb the Pelindaba site west of Pretoria in a pre-emptive air strike.

Against a backdrop of betrayal, Soviet-Cuban forces on the Namibian border, a collapsed Mozambique right next door, a recent spate of internal violence, increasing sanctions by the West and a constant onslaught by the Western Media it is little wonder that the South African government gave the go-ahead for the sped up development of a nuclear ability. Steyn, Van der Walt, and Van Loggerenberg[46] provide a fascinating and insightful review of this process as viewed from the inside, free of the conspiracy theories, errors and blatant prejudice that usually accompany work on this subject originating outside the country.

In the 1970s and 1980s, South Africa, like Israel, played to perfection the game of keeping the world guessing as to whether or not it possessed a nuclear ability. In 1976, it had decided to establish a French-built nuclear power station at Koeberg outside Cape Town. As a nation it had no exploitable oil reserves but had a Western Free Enterprise economy with an insatiable demand for electricity. It was therefore fully justified in having a program for nuclear power. It also maintained a nuclear research facility about 10 kilometers west of Pretoria where another reactor called SAFARI was operated to produce, for example, medical isotopes.

Considering that this was the country that had developed the heart transplant, abilities in the nuclear medicine field were hardly surprising.

The country also had a uranium production program that had its origins in the original request of 1944 for help for the United States nuclear bomb activity of World War II. At the time, South Africa had been requested[47] by the British government to assist in identifying uranium sources. In fact, the United Kingdom and the United States had assisted in establishing the first uranium extraction plant outside Johannesburg in 1952. By 1978, South Africa's identified reserves of extractable uranium would be among the highest on earth at 462,000 metric tons[48] and the country would export[49] just on 4,000 tons of uranium oxide. The program of the Atomic Energy Board was mostly directed towards nuclear power, extraction and enrichment of nuclear materials, and control of the import and export of isotopes, such as those used in the medical field. In 1970, the Uranium Enrichment Corporation, UCOR, was established to drive the enrichment program. All was done quite in the open.

During the second half of the 1970s, the UCOR pilot plant for enrichment came on-line, also located at a site adjoining Pelindaba near Pretoria. While the plant was no secret, the technology was regarded as proprietary. One of the big drives in South Africa at the time was a "value-added" initiative associated with the extensive minerals base of the country. Enriching South Africa's vast reserves of uranium was an obvious industrial-commercial step and normal business in a technologically advanced country trying to pull itself up the "value-added-chain" by its own bootstraps in a commercially competitive world in which several European parties were anxious to be less dependent on the United States for fissile materials[50]. The first enriched uranium was produced in 1976.

Richardt van der Walt[51], at one point the general manager of the Atomic Energy Corporation, describes how the decision was made in the early 1970s to secretly explore the use of nuclear explosive devices in mining. By 1976, planning called for the first device to be tested at a remote military test site in the Kalahari region of the Northern Cape in late 1977. It was decided to make the test look like a normal military test of a conventional weapons system. This would be done by testing the earliest South African-designed version of the Soviet Stalin Organ multiple rocket launcher, a weapons system later to be named "Valkyrie." The design was derived from BM-21 "Stalin Organs" taken intact from the Cubans in Angola in one of those battles the latter "never lost." Though the particular nuclear device in question may not have been aimed at nuclear weapons, the international reaction to the event certainly impressed upon the South African government just exactly how powerful a political weapon a nuclear ability was. This would lead directly to a drive towards the fabrication of practical deliverable nuclear weapons[52].

Homeland Independence

In the 21st century, there is much debate about the so-called "Two-State Solution" for the "Palestinian Problem." The United States has been a staunch supporter of this concept, by which two non-contiguous pieces of land are to somehow become an internationally acknowledged Palestinian country. At the root of it all lies the hard fact that Jewish Israelis are rapidly headed toward minority status in their own country, formed only in 1948. If Palestinians in the West Bank and Gaza were to vote in Israeli elections, it would not be long before the Jewish population of Israel would be powerless. If the Israeli Jewish population were to hold onto power over a disenfranchised majority of Palestinians, the international world might treat them as South Africa was treated in the last quarter of the 20th century. The onslaught on the Israeli Jews would again be led by the likes of ex-President Carter of the United States who has already shown his colors.

In August 2005, the Jewish population[53] between the Mediterranean and the Jordan River fell below 50% and before the end of the second decade of the 21st century the higher Palestinian birth rate will assure for Israel the South African demographic dilemma. The Israelis realize this. All the Palestinians have to do is survive and procreate as fast as they can. Meanwhile the challenge for Palestinians lies in maintaining a living in the Gaza strip where there is little economic development and the rainfall is a mere 10 inches per annum in the south and barely reaches 20 inches in the far north[54].

It is instructive to consider the demographic situation in South Africa in the mid-1970s. The total population (1980 statistics) was approximately 30 million. Of these, approximately 21 million were Blacks, 5 million were Whites, 2.5 million were Coloureds and just below 1 million were Indians. Many millions of black people lived in the various homelands. In contrast with the Gaza Strip, the rainfall in the Transkei homeland[55], for example, varies from 400mm in the far southwestern interior to more than 1200mm in the northeast, as one might expect from a lush green subtropical coast. Nothing kept the amaXhosa inhabitants from turning this region into heaven on Earth, except themselves.

The Vha'Venda homeland was in beautiful countryside on the slopes of the northernmost *Soutpansberg* Mountains in the small true tropical zone of South Africa. The same was true of Gazankulu, the Shangaan homeland. Yet, as in most of Africa outside South Africa and Rhodesia, there was little in the way of economic farming. People in these homelands largely lived a traditional subsistence economy – that is, one in which the tenets of economic development are not given much thought. On the other hand, the government had also not done anything significant to create or foster such development.

In the case of Bophutatswana, the westernmost dry Bushveld Ba'Tswana homeland, they had fabulously rich platinum mines – the biggest in the world, accounting for a full two thirds of the entire world production. A number of other mines produced chromium, vanadium, manganese and granite. In December 1979, the Sun City fantasy resort was opened to much acclaim by hotel magnate Sol Kerzner in the Bushveld caldera of an extinct volcano crater in Bophutatswana. Kerzner would go on to develop such resorts as Atlantis in the Bahamas some twenty years later. Even Time Magazine[56], in a rare effort at balance on the subject of South Africa, conceded that this homeland had *"considerable economic potential."*

Given the problems the Government of South Africa faced in the second half of the 1970s, it moved to grant independence to four of the homelands. These were the amaXhosa/Pondo/Thembu homeland of Transkei (26 October 1976), the Ba'Tswana homeland of Bophutatswana (6 December 1977) and the Vha'Venda homeland of Venda (13 September 1979); the Ciskei homeland of the Rharhabe Xhosa people following a little later on 4 December 1981. These became known as the TBVC states, recognized by no country beyond one another and South Africa.

Most of the homelands were non-contiguous entities, just like the proposed 21st century Palestinian homeland in the Middle-East. However, while the Palestinians prefer to have all of Israel and generally do not accept the notion of two little enclaves to live in, several Western nations stand by this model. In South Africa in the 1970s, the Black Nationalists also wanted the whole country. In their case, though, they had never been present in most of the western half of the country, as already explained exhaustively in the present work. Ironically, the same Western nations that support the notion of a Palestinian homeland in the 21st century flatly refused to acknowledge the same homeland solution in South Africa in the 1970s. They specifically refused to officially recognize the four independent homelands – this despite the much more favorable land and economic possibilities than the pitiful split and semi-arid Palestinian homeland.

Meanwhile the Western media, such as the BBC, kept up the onslaught with movies such as Last Grave at Dimbaza. The viewer of that work is actively misled to believe that the homelands were wholesale misbegotten hellholes. While the actions of the government in relocating black people to settlements in those areas were disgraceful, the actions of the movie makers in neglecting to show, for example, the strikingly beautiful and green Transkei Wild Coast, were equally disgraceful. It is most interesting to note how the ANC government in the 21st century promotes that coast as a serene tourist destination, while it suited them to refer to the Transkei as an evil "dumping ground" of Apartheid in the 1970s.

Rhodesia – Kissinger takes a hand

Quite possibly the most sickening story in the history of modern Western Man is that of the transition to majority rule in Rhodesia, for which we have to retrace our steps slightly to 1976. What was done to this country is a disgrace for which Britain should be burdened with the full responsibility. The men who did it are essentially a club that presided over the diminishment of Britain. Britain is a country with a proud history.

It is the origin of many men who deserve the respect and admiration of the entire world. The men who destroyed Rhodesia are not among them and the man who started that was Harold Macmillan, the Chancellor of the Exchequer at the time of the Suez Crisis (Chapter 20: *Suez*) — the man who turned on his leader to become Prime Minister in the 1950s and who presumed to lecture the South African parliament (Chapter 20: *The Wind of Change*).

During 1976, in the wake of the successful invasion of Angola by Soviet armed Cubans and the flight of the United States from that war, Britain, the United States, and South Africa were all worried about a Soviet-Cuban adventure in Rhodesia. The 150,000 white Rhodesians, along with the many Black Rhodesians in the army, were doing a sterling job of keeping the Communist sponsored guerrilla groups at bay. But, the whole world was against them with the exception of South Africa, who was under constant pressure to assist in obtaining majority rule in that country.

The disposition of players was as follows. Prime Minister Ian Smith ran the Rhodesian government which was based on the 150,000 white people, mostly descendants of British colonists from the turn of the century, although there were also a few thousand Afrikaners, mostly farmers. The history of Rhodesia was that of a classic British colony, conquered by force of arms (Chapter 15: *Rhodesia*) and formally created as state in 1894. It had been part of Britain's dream of "painting Africa red" from the Cape to Cairo.

The whites in the country were the children and grandchildren, and rarely the great grandchildren, of the original settlers of the late 1800s. Many had settled from Britain after WWII, just as in Kenya. In this, it differed profoundly from the 350 year-old history of South Africa. The Rhodesians had supported Rhodes in his disastrous Jameson Invasion (*NF67*) of the Transvaal Republic in December 1895, a year after its founding. As a British Colony, Rhodesia had fought against the two Boer Republics in the Great Boer War (*Chapters 16, 17*). To the Afrikaners in South Africa, they were largely "Colonial Englishmen," but they were viewed as fellow Western White Men stuck in Africa for better or for worse. Thereby they were worthy of concerted support. To the rank and file white South African, Ian Smith was a hero for standing up against Britain's callous desertion of its own people in Africa.

Under Ian Smith's management, the economy of the country, heavily based on tobacco exports, had grown despite comprehensive international sanctions directed against the white minority. U.S. Secretary of State Henry Kissinger confirms that the Rhodesian armed forces were quite capable of defending the country against the Communist armed guerrillas unless foreign troops became involved[57].

Having seen that it was possible to deal realistically with men such as Kenneth Kaunda of Zambia, Joseph Mobutu of Zaire, Leopold Senghor of Senegal, Felix Houphouet-Biogny of Côte d'Ivoire, and Dr. Hastings Banda of Malawi (the former Nyassaland), John Vorster of South Africa systematically came to the conclusion that a moderate majority black government in Rhodesia might be a better solution than a white government under fire from the entire planet and based on a population of just 150,000 whites. Vorster therefore systematically moved Ian Smith in that direction.

Britain's role as ex-Colonial Power was cynical and callous in the extreme. Its concern was to ingratiate itself with Black Africa by the simple expedient of selling out its kin in Rhodesia. We can call U.S. Secretary of State Henry Kissinger as witness in this regard. He explains[58] that Britain did its best to avoid what was a completely hypothetical confrontation with the Cubans in Rhodesia by announcing a British timetable for majority rule in that country. When he discussed the future of the whites in Rhodesia with Sir Anthony Duff, the man responsible for Africa and the Middle East in the British Foreign office, this gentleman of the peerage ventured that the white Rhodesians might retain their businesses, but that their children would have no future[59]. In fact, Kissinger briefed President Ford in 1976 to the effect that the British preferred to overthrow Ian Smith and let the rest take care of themselves[60].

Kissinger, a man of proven ability, who would at least treat the Rhodesians with human respect, does not hide his disgust[61] at these British men whose existence detracted from an otherwise great nation. He also confirms that Ian Smith acted honorably in all his dealings with the United States, despite the image the British media created of him as a crook.

The United States became involved supposedly in order to forestall further Soviet-Cuban adventures in Southern Africa. Britain, by now a very poor shadow of the global hegemonic power it had once been, lacked the power to even address the situation in what it deemed to be legally its colony. The United States was another matter. While it had visibly demonstrated that it lacked the stomach for a fight in Angola, it did in reality have immense military and political power.

Kissinger, however, had to be careful that Britain did not hijack the power of the United States for its own purposes. The British party to negotiations was preoccupied with ingratiating themselves with Black Africa by selling their kin down the river. He describes how Anthony Crosland, British foreign Secretary, spent more time debating the possible overthrow[62] of Ian Smith, than any rational negotiation. Most likely this was due to the pressures on the British government from the left of their political spectrum — Britain was basically a prime example of a Western European socialist state at this point.

Kissinger soon discovered what the South Africans already knew, namely that Kaunda of Zambia, while a typical "African President-for-Life," was a relative moderate, and Nyerere of Tanzania a sponsor of Black African Nationalist radicals. Kaunda sponsored Joshua Nkomo, a member of the minority Zulu-speaking Matabele tribe of the dry western bush, while Nyerere sponsored Robert Mugabe, a member of the majority Shona tribe of the wetter eastern highlands. Robert Mugabe led the North Korean-trained Zimbabwe African People's Union (ZAPU) based in Mozambique and Tanzania and Joshua Nkomo led the pro-China Zimbabwe African National Union (ZANU) based in Zambia. Mugabe himself had done his early training in South Africa at Fort Hare University, and had then spent extensive time in Ghana where he was hugely influenced by Kwame Nkrumah, the "Father of Uhuru." It was also there that he met and married his first wife.

By late 1976, with the able diplomatic efforts of Henry Kissinger, Ian Smith accepted the advent of majority rule. Kissinger states[63] that the Americans felt a moral obligation to carry out the transition under the terms of the agreement reached. The British seemed not to feel any such obligation — their hatred of Ian Smith was visceral. Having put in all this effort, the Ford administration was replaced by that of Jimmy Carter, who elected to use his new United Nations ambassador to promptly start attacking South Africa, thereby destroying every incentive Vorster had had to cooperate with the United States. The American effort essentially fell apart at this point, but the momentum towards majority rule was maintained.

Ian Smith finally came to an agreement about an interim government with moderate black leader, the Reverend Abel Muzorewa in 1978. The latter was based inside Zimbabwe. This agreement came to be called the "Internal Settlement," which granted the whites in Rhodesia some degree of security whilst effectively giving black people control of Parliament. An election was to be held in early 1979 on this basis. However, interested parties in the U.N. Security Council insisted on tabling a resolution aimed at nullifying this agreement as the two Communist groupings based outside the country, Robert Mugabe's ZAPU and Joshua Nkomo's ZANU had not been involved in the process of the internal settlement. The UN Security Council passed Resolution 423 on 14 March 1978 condemning the Internal Settlement and refusing to accept the results of any impending election held under that agreement. Voting for the agreement were China, the U.S.S.R., Czechoslovakia, India, Nigeria, Venezuela, Mauritius, Gabon, Bolivia, and Kuwait. France, Britain, the United States, Canada and West Germany abstained. Significantly, neither Socialist Britain nor the United States under President Carter vetoed the resolution.

On August 14, 1978, Ian Smith did the previously unthinkable and flew to Lusaka where, with President Kenneth Kaunda of Zambia as host, he met with Joshua Nkomo[64] to try and hammer out an agreement by which the ostensibly more moderate Nkomo would become president. He obviously sought to avoid by any means possible having the extreme racist Marxist Mugabe somehow coming to power in the country. However, the Nigerians who had been part of the arrangements leaked the story of the meeting to Mugabe. Not only did this lead to a rift between Nkomo and Mugabe, but also between the moderate Kaunda and the extremist Nyerere, who was Mugabe's protector. Nkomo now had to "restore his revolutionary image."

Flight 825

Just after 5p.m. On September 3, 1978, Rhodesian Airways Flight 825 took off from Kariba and turned for the capital of Salisbury (today Harare). The four-engined turboprop Vickers Viscount was the workhorse aircraft of the Rhodesian airline. This particular aircraft bore the name Hunyani. Five minutes after take-off Captain John Hood announced an emergency, declaring that they had lost both starboard engines after an explosion[65]. The aircraft had been struck by a SAM 7 anti-aircraft missile fired by Joshua Nkomo's army, the Zimbabwe People's revolutionary Army (ZIPRA). This group was in alliance with the South African ANC's "army," Umkhonto we Sizwe – the organization with an anthem stating that they had pledged to kill the whites. The aircraft went down near the far eastern end of Lake Kariba.

A Rhodesian Special Air Service (SAS) commando troop that happened to be in the air at the time managed to parachute into the crash site. What they found horrified these hardened fighting men. Near the wreckage lay the bodies of ten women, children and babies who had managed to survive the fireball crash landing, only to be bayoneted, bludgeoned and shot to death. Five survivors had been spared when they happened to be away from the wreck to fetch water from a nearby black village. Three more had survived by hiding in the bush. Thirty-eight had died in the crash.

Joshua Nkomo appeared on BBC TV and, with a smile and a belly laugh[66], claimed responsibility[67] for shooting down the civilian aircraft but tried to convince the world that his men did not commit the murders. With this event died the efforts of Ian Smith to reach a settlement with either of the guerrilla groups based outside the country. The event simply demonstrated that black leaders in Africa collect political "brownie points" with their black constituency by killing white people. Robert Mugabe would eventually perfect that recipe in the 21st century. At the time of the creation of the present work, Flight 825 remains the only documented case of civilian aircraft crash survivors being massacred.

Five months later, Flight 827, also a Viscount on the same route and departing at the same time, was also shot down. This time the aircraft erupted in a fireball and plummeted into a ravine. None of the 59 people on board survived. The captain of the flight was Jan du Plessis, a descendant of Huguenot Jean du Plessis who eventually fled Louis XIV's France in 1687 (*NF15*). One of those who died was trainee air hostess Regina Chigwada, an innocent young Black Rhodesian woman.

On 13 April 1979 the Rhodesians struck at Nkomo himself in Zambia. A squad of their SAS attacked his home in a perfect raid. Nkomo claimed he managed to escape by squeezing his massive bulk through his toilet window[68]. It has long been argued that the Rhodesian Secret Services had been infiltrated by members loyal to Britain and that these men had tipped off Nkomo.

In March/April of 1979, the Rhodesian elections were duly held despite the United Nations resolution to not recognize these. Abel Muzorewa was set to become the Prime Minister in June 1979. However, it was clear that U.S. President Jimmy Carter would settle for nothing less than a government led by the violently racist Robert Mugabe.

 # Nexus Familia 89: To America!

In 1975, the South African Broadcast Corporation (SABC) finally starts the first test transmissions of television. South Africa thereby becomes the last Western nation to have television. My father, Herman, is so keen on this idea that he goes out and buys a Telefunken PAL television before there is anything to view on it. He rushes home over lunchtimes to see if indeed there is anything on TV.

One day the picture splutters, and suddenly there is a man named Riaan Cruywagen reading some bland news. My father promptly buys one of the earliest video tape recording systems, manufactured by Philips of the Netherlands. Soon we have some actual programming, and among the very first programs we see is The Brady Bunch ("Here's the story of a lovely lady..."). My father's preoccupation is an American Country Music artist named George Hamilton IV. He listens to this endlessly and drives the family to distraction with this music. It is over this period that we realize that something is wrong because his eyesight is systematically failing — he has diabetes.

By early 1976, I am ready to start working on my Masters degree in Physics. I am assigned an advisor for that degree. The head of our university Physics department has considerable experience in the U.S. Physics arena and wants to make sure that his post-graduate students do work that is on a par with the United States. My advisor has a Ph.D. from the University of Virginia in the United States and his name is George. George keeps a firm hand in guiding me and I learn a lot from him. He treats me as a mature human being, which I am not quite, and not as some person his junior, which I truthfully am. Of course we talk and argue and very soon I develop an image of George as every inch the Good American. George turns out to be a Democrat — a true blue Union Democrat. But George has realized that much of what he has been told by the United States media about South Africa is complete and utter rubbish.

We debate many things, including the similarities between South Africa's problems in keeping out black people who want to enter the country illegally into Apartheid, and the problems of the United States in keeping out illegal Mexican immigrants – a problem that would blow up spectacularly in the 21st century. George would eventually become my very best friend in the world and a huge influence in my life. It is George who caused me to develop my admiration for the Declaration of Independence. Shortly after I start work on my Ph.D. in Physics, George returns to the United States, his contract having ended.

My father Herman meanwhile does not look after his diabetes very well and systematically he develops all the classical symptoms of the disease. So it is that I receive a telephone call at the University in the first week of September 1977 to inform me that he has had a massive stroke. I am the last one to speak to him the night before he passes away on Tuesday, September 13. As though in recognition of his tough-but-fair management, his "raw Xhosa" dock workers approach the family and our church to ask to attend the *Big Bull's* funeral in a country that is in the deepest period of racially divisive Apartheid. On the day of the funeral, they come to the church to show their respect. I am very proud of the fact that in his death he can evoke this level of human respect across the vicious color divide of the country.

Given my late father's employment with the South African Railways, the family house immediately becomes paid up. The remaining family thereby has a roof over its head. When the estate is settled, my inheritance consists of my late father's Philips video cassette recorder, his collection of George Hamilton IV video tape recordings and his classic Gillette brass razor. I shall definitely have to build my own life my own way. With the loss of her husband, Nickie now becomes mobile and is offered the position of Provincial Manager for her publication distribution company in Natal, Eastern Free State and Southeastern Transvaal. She moves to the Durban offices of the company where her personnel are mostly South African Indians and Zulus. She moves into an apartment in the SANLAM tower building in the nearby South Coast tourist town of Amanzimtoti, placing her unwittingly at the epicenter of later developments in the country. She soon realizes that Western Civilization consists of a barely one mile wide strip along the coast south of Durban.

When PW Botha becomes Prime Minister, he is hugely disliked. The author in particular despises the man and his finger-wagging style. Finally, one day, I sit down and compose a song on my guitar containing the words *"He will turn the whole world black,"* sung to the tune of an old folk song.

When we finish our PhD degrees in early 1979, Jeanne and I graduate at the same ceremony and share a stage with none other than Ian Smith, the Prime Minister of Rhodesia, who receives an honorary doctorate on that occasion. Jeanne and I marry soon after on 24 March 1979.

We have been given an opportunity to work at IBM in New York. We are off to America!

—*End Nexus Familia*

Africa by the end of the 1970s

By 1979, only South Africa and Namibia had not succumbed to the Soviet supported wave of Uhuru. There were no more Portuguese colonial buffers and Rhodesia would soon be Zimbabwe under tyrannical Robert Mugabe. South Africa was all alone with Soviets and Cubans on our borders, internal unrest just beneath the surface, and insurgent bases in neighboring countries where they were protected by the Cubans in Angola. Moscow was clearly intending to hold onto control in Angola, Ethiopia and Mozambique and Mikhail Gorbachev would in fact make this particular statement to Fidel Castro as late as 2 March 1986.[69]

In the West, a virulently one-sided media complex was assailing the country morning, noon and night. From inside South Africa it became difficult to tell the BBC from Radio Moscow, the anti-South African rhetoric often being more extreme on the BBC and the formal English accent on Radio Moscow often better than on BBC. It was left to the ex-President of the United States, Richard Nixon, to state the simple truth[70]. He held that the sort of holy war that some African leaders preached would be bloody beyond the standards of Idi Amin. He pointed out that it took a century after the US Civil War to remove legislated racial discrimination. On that basis, in referring to the United States and its dealings with South Africa, he expressed the view that *"we are hardly free enough of sin to cast the first stone – or even the second."*

Unfortunately, President Nixon had no concept of just how deeply the liberal guilty conscience about slavery in America ran. Nor could he conceive of just how malicious that guilty conscience could be when harnessed by men with evil intent. It would take another five years for the depth of this cultural condition and its consequences to become vividly clear.

In Parliament in Cape Town, PW Botha stood up and told the nation that it would have to "adapt or die." But what did that mean? How were we supposed to avoid being

- hacked to death, burnt and eaten like sister Mary Aidan in East London in 1952;

- dragged through the streets with our genitals in our mouths as at Cato Manor in 1960;

- fed through sawmills like the Portuguese in northern Angola in 1961;

- held hostage and killed like Dora Bloch by Idi Amin in 1976,

- or perhaps just murdered like the whites in the Shaba/Katanga region of the Zaire in 1978?

A black government in next-door Rhodesia, potentially under Robert Mugabe, would be well-behaved only because it had "White South Africa" as neighbor, without which the likes of Mugabe would simply become another Idi Amin, as he indeed subsequently did after the disappearance of white rule in South Africa in 1994. Black leaders in South Africa would probably eventually follow suit. The ANC most certainly did not present to white South Africans any way to view a future. The few peculiar unrepresentative whites that revolved around its central power structure were mostly Communist Party members and people that ordinary Americans would consider Radical Far Leftwingers. After all, the United States quite correctly considered the ANC a Terrorist Organization and its military wing had sworn to kill the whites. It would eventually be formally listed as a Terrorist Organization by the State Department in November 1988 in a document[71] signed by Vice President President George Bush and Secretary of Defence Frank Carlucci.

The future looked very bleak indeed. We'd have to hold out, fight and pray for a "break in the bad international political weather" and for a crack in the alliance between the Soviets and the part of Black Africa that wanted us destroyed as people.

There was no other pragmatic choice.

-----ooOoo-----

24

You should just die!

"South Africa is not a totalitarian society. There is a vigorous opposition press, [...] outspoken protest and access to the international media that would never be possible in many parts of Africa or in the Soviet Union, for that matter."

United States President Ronald Reagan,
Press meeting in the Oval Office of the White House (10:30 am September 9, 1985)

A flash in the Southern Ocean

September 22, 1979, was a cloudy day over the Southern Indian Ocean, but for a brief period the clouds parted near Prince Edward Island, halfway between Africa and the Antarctic and 1500 miles from the author's home. In that short space of time, a United States Vela surveillance satellite detected a double pulse of green light near the island.

With the Soviets and Cubans on the Namibian border and mandatory arms sanctions against South Africa in force, it was clear that Prime Minister PW Botha was going to run the country as the military-oriented conservative that he was. Most people therefore assumed that it had been a nuclear test by South Africa, considering the prior Kalahari Desert event (Chapter 23: *A clear day in the Kalahari Desert*). Having learnt from that event that the mere perception of a country having a nuclear capability constituted a negotiating position, the South African Government wisely elected to be coy, conducting itself such as to create uncertainty regarding South Africa's nuclear arms status.

Many years later, Defense Minister Magnus Malan confirmed this approach to author Sasha Pulakow-Suransky in a face-to-face interview[1]. When a foreign journalist confronted a South African spokes-person in 1979 with the comment that he believed South Africa "had The Bomb," the response was[2]:

Fig. 24-1 Far Northern Namibia bordering Angola

"If we have, I would not admit it. If we do not have it, we want to keep you guessing."

In fact, the nuclear program of the country was nowhere near being in a position to undertake such a test[3,4]. Investigations would continue for some years in the United States, but failed to prove anything conclusive. Analysts and writers would obsess about this for several years more. Meanwhile South Africa's actual nuclear weapons program proceeded quietly in the background.

With the possibility of a South African test ultimately dismissed, speculation turned to the possibility that Israel, with the help of South Africa, had tested such a device off the South African controlled Prince Edward Island. Sasha Pulakow-Suransky[5] discusses this subject at some length and we shall not add to the speculation here. Soviet Spy Dieter Gerhard, at that point still entrenched as Commodore in the South African Navy, would claim many years later that the Prince Edward Island "incident" had been a joint effort between South Africa and Israel. The reader can decide whether to trust statements by Soviet spy Dieter Gerhard.

The enduring strategic point was that the Soviet Union had now been left guessing and would have to take greater care in its military ventures in Southern Africa.

From Angola to Afghanistan

On Christmas eve 1979, having got away with adventures in Angola, then Shaba, then Ethiopia, then Shaba again, and then Yemen (again), the Soviets invaded Afghanistan[6]. Some years later Mikhail Gorbachev would describe the Soviet presence in Afghanistan as necessary to help Afghan progressives defend themselves against Islamic fundamentalists who wanted to destroy schools, infrastructure, and cultural relics and who denied women any education and participation in society[7]. Ironically, the same arguments were to be presented by the United States some quarter century later for its occupation of Afghanistan. For their Afghanistan adventure, the Soviets used their own army rather than their Cuban proxies. However, they did allow some Cubans to participate in small numbers. These arrived[8] on 4 January 1980.

The United States would eventually ferry arms to the opposing Afghans and the Soviets would ultimately withdraw. However, it would leave the country awash with weapons and it would become the refuge of Osama bin Laden. From here his minions would plan the attack on the World Trade Center on 11 September 2001, setting the tone of the international world for the first decade of the 21st century.

Liberia – Being Black versus Black African

In Chapter 13 of this work, we considered Liberia, which had become independent by the mid 19th century. Since then, the country had been run by freed slaves relocated from the United States or by their descendants. By 1980, William Tolbert was the latest of these men of American slave descent.

As a minority of around 5% of the overall Liberian population, the so-called Americo-Liberian population had kept the indigenous black people in subjugation. The situation had earlier been so serious that the League of Nations had accused the country of slavery, leading to an international investigation in 1930. Black American sociologist Charles S. Johnson was sent to Liberia to investigate as part of an international commission. He wrote a text entitled *Bitter Canaan*[9] based on his findings.

The commission concluded that coerced indigenous black people from Liberia had been shipped to the Spanish owned island of Fernando Po under conditions *"analogous to slavery"*[10]. This happened under a 1914 agreement with Spain in terms of which Liberia would provide laborers. At the time, the revelations caused the resignation of the Liberian president Charles King in December 1930. *Bitter Canaan* remains a stark revelation of what can happen when people with Western background and values are placed in Africa, independent of skin color.

Now, many years later, on the night of 12 April 1980, Master Sergeant Samuel Kanyon Doe led a group of Liberian Army non-commissioned officers in a raid on the presidential mansion in the capital of Monrovia. There they killed President William Tolbert, the latest in the 133 year line of Americo-Liberian presidents. They proceeded to execute thirteen members of the country's ruling cabinet in public. Calling themselves the People's Redemption Council, they justified their actions by claiming that indigenous people had been marginalized by the ruling Americo-Liberian "freemen elite."

Uhuru had finally arrived in Liberia, proving that skin color was not the issue in Africa, but rather the culture. Americo-Liberians found that having a black skin was no guarantee of being acceptable to Black

African Nationalists. The Americo-Liberians had previously fought several wars against the indigenous population, but only from this key moment in 1980 onward did Liberia finally descend into the nightmare that is post-Uhuru Africa.

A first uprising against Doe was viciously put down with numerous executions. Soon enough, Americo-Liberian Charles Taylor, supported by individuals as barbaric as Doe and by some West African countries, seized power. American derived values were rapidly dissolving into the indigenous African horror. Taylor had descended to the same level of horror as his opponents. For the next two decades Liberia and the next-door British equivalent, Sierra Leone, would turn into the twin nightmares that would play off on the TV sets of horror-struck Westerners.

From this point onward, especially in the 1990s, the Western World would hear reports of child soldiers and children whose arms had been lobbed off to keep them from fighting for one side or another. At first, the world did not believe this, but the pictorial evidence would soon mount. The two countries would become the international "poster children" for African horror.

One of the few highlights in the miserable subsequent history of Sierra Leone would be the positive role played by South African security contractors who had learnt their skills in Angola – a subject to which we shall return later.

The Devil and the Peanut Farmer

With the advent of the Carter administration, the United States, instead of facilitating a peaceful path to majority rule in South Africa, became an ally of Black Uhuru in its worst form. Leading the charge was U.N. Ambassador Andrew Young. Carter pushed for a Rhodesia that should be ruled by Robert Mugabe, whose forces had committed some of the worst outrages in the east of the country. These included attacks on mission stations and the horrific murders of missionaries and nuns and the rape of the women involved[11]. Even *Time Magazine* commented that it was done to create panic among whites to scare them into leaving – that is, terrorism, but the magazine refused to employ the term. Mugabe's hatred of white people was legendary. The dismay and disgust of the threatened White people of Southern Africa at the perceived treachery of the Carter Administration was total. The concept of the United States associating with the likes of a monster like Mugabe was simply beyond the pale.

The White House now took guidance in its African policy from the likes of Nyerere and Kaunda, both of whom had dispensed with the idea of Democracy in favor of declaring themselves Presidents for Life. This somehow did not bother the Carter Administration. Considering the central role of the United States in the development of Western Democracy, it was peculiar indeed that this Administration had such difficulty in distinguishing between Dictatorship and Democracy. It appeared the only criterion of concern to them was that the people in charge in Africa had to be black, no matter how kleptocratic, dictatorial, or murderous. The US government was now enamored with a collection of "presidents for life" whose only qualifications were that they were black and opposed to white people in Africa. After all, despite the horrors Mugabe and Nkomo had committed, Andrew Young had suggested in a 22 May 1978 interview with the *Times of London* that Mugabe was very gentle man and that he could not imagine that either Nkomo or Mugabe could ever pull a trigger on a gun to kill anyone. Young had suggested that Ian Smith's supporters were *"the violent people,"* but that they would hopefully not *"be around for the new Zimbabwe."*

In 1980, the people of Rhodesia were forced by the Carter Administration to hold an election that specifically included Mugabe. The elections were a farce and Mugabe's men intimidated the electorate such that the other parties could not campaign in the east[12]. Even devoutly liberal British newsman Richard Dowden feels forced to point out that by now Britain would accept anything just to get out of Africa[13]. Turning a blind eye to the fear tactics of a monster did not bother them. News reached South Africa of Mugabe's men walking along the lines of voters waiting to cast their ballots and showing them little cardboard boxes. These uneducated, gullible, and superstitious people were made to believe these boxes allowed the despotic Mugabe to know how they were voting. Such is the Africa that the Northern

Hemisphere refuses to hear about. It prefers images of fly-encrusted starving black children.

Whites in Southern Africa wondered how long it would take Americans to realize the glaringly obvious. History records that it would take them one quarter of a century, a full generation, until they realized Mugabe's true nature around 2005. By then, tens of thousands of Zimbabweans had died at his hand.

Given this abject lack of judgment on the part of the Carter Administration, white South Africans were not in the least surprised by the general failure of leadership that it exhibited in other domains such as the Congo, Ethiopia, and Iran. It would take the population of the United States a few years to come to the same conclusion and wisely remove this disastrous administration from office after just one term. Young lost his job in 1979 for allegedly secretly meeting with the Palestine Liberation Organization; unfortunately too late for Rhodesia.

Nexus Familia 90: "You should just die!"

Arrival

Our arrival in New York in July 1979 cannot have been timed better to impress upon us the Hollywood image of the United States. The newspapers everywhere report the café shooting death of a Mafia leader and associates. It seems extremely frightening, but simultaneously exciting. Clearly we are in the land of Al Capone.

At IBM, I am at first overwhelmed by the sheer size of the research and development operation and the rows of unused equipment standing in the passages. When the first reactions wear off, it becomes clear that the surfeit of equipment also causes people to make odd decisions and leads to inefficient use of resources. I am left with the general impression that South Africans get more done with less than Americans.

On matters racial and geographic

In the domain of everyday life, I run into matters of race in the United States for the first time in my first week at IBM, and in rather amusing fashion. Whilst trying to rent a home near IBM in Westchester County, New York, a lady returns my phone call and, after hesitating a little, she asks the question that has clearly been weighing heavily on her mind:

"Harry, are you black?"

This is my introduction to a never ending train of questions along the lines of *"If you're from Africa, why aren't you black?"*

When a gentleman in his sixties helps me by advising me to put a bag of sand for weight in the back of my 1973 Ford Pinto, he somehow epitomizes the issue for me by saying:

"Yeah, I know South Africa. I served in the Mediterranean in the War."

He is a very dear gentleman, but he clearly has no idea where South Africa is. It is no better inside the hallowed halls of IBM. I know that there is a huge problem when a person with a M.Sc. degree comes up with the revealing question:

"Harry, I have a friend in Liberia. Perhaps you have met her. Her name is... ."

Liberia is as far from my hometown of Port Elizabeth in South Africa as what Argentina is from Florida.

I am deeply offended when a man turns up at my office, stating he has heard I am from South Africa, and then proceeds to tell a racially objectionable "joke" about the physiology of black people and food stamps. Another person turns up at my office with a picture showing a water trough for horses. It is marked with a sign reading: *"horses and coloreds."* This gets waved in my face along with comments about South Africa. I let the man finish, and then politely point out to him that the photo must have been taken in the United States, because we South Africans spell *"Coloureds"* with a "u" like the British.

The dumbstruck would-be socio-political commentator leaves my office trailing his pride. It occurs to me that I shall have to learn to be less polite in this society.

Yet another graduate female scientist politely but firmly criticizes me for the actions of Idi Amin in Uganda. This is when I realize that many Americans actually think that Africa is one state and the "nasty whites" must somehow be responsible for all that goes wrong in Africa.

I am simply dumbstruck by the ignorance of the ordinary American on almost all matters outside the United States. In fact, they seem to have little interest in anything that happens outside the USA. But, if a place is mentioned on CBS, ABC, or NBC television, then they magically have an opinion about it, ready-packaged and deliverable with sudden conviction.

This is extremely disconcerting. I have always looked upon the United States as the leader of the Free World, and I am now rudely awakened. This leader is hugely powerful, but knows frighteningly little of the world it is leading. My feeling is that such power in the hands of such self-imposed ignorance cannot be in the best interests of Western Civilization. It leaves me hoping and praying that someone in Washington is better informed than the highly trained people I deal with. Part of my soul tells me that is unlikely.

As to the relations between black and white in Mount Kisco where we live, the following possibly demonstrates it adequately. Every afternoon, shortly after we arrive home, another inhabitant of our building also arrives in his shiny black *Pontiac Trans Am*. Upon entering the parking area he always hits his horn without fail and it bleats out the first 11 notes of *Dixie*, the Southern anthem. One can set one's watch by his rendition of *Dixie*. I cannot help but notice the face of the black woman who on occasion shares the elevator with us when she hears this. Her face remains deadpan, but her eyes flash.

Over this period I realize that the United States is struggling with a uniquely toxic mix of ignorance, racial prejudice, and guilt. It is quite obvious that the American concept of race is one based on a history of slavery and prejudice, while the South African one is based on fear of a competing civilization and culture and centuries of armed conflict. I realize that South Africa will always be in trouble with United States politicians as long as Americans see the country through their peculiar "binocular lenses" of liberal guilt at the one end and racial prejudice at the other. The histories of the two countries on matters of race are profoundly different, but appear superficially similar to the prejudiced on either the liberal or conservative end of the spectrum. It is a bewildering realization that moves me in the direction of despair.

Ironically, the author's most welcome discovery is the "black" Americans at work. They are unfailingly friendly and helpful and they treat me with zero animosity. For me, dealing with black people who know no other language than English, have only one wife, no tribe, no AbaKhwetha (*NF85*), no witchdoctors, no muti[14] and are strongly Christian is a novel but heartening experience. It is also clear that they are proud to be Americans and do not see white Americans as an enemy to be driven from the continent of America. Here is a grouping of people who look at life the way I do, have basically the same values as I do and go about life the way that I do. The differences are trivial on my scale. I can converse with them as with any other American. As far as I am concerned, they are Black Americans—Americans who happen to have a dark skin—hardly an issue in the greater scheme of things. They may be black, but they're American, not African. I am the African in the picture; they are not. So, when asked to complete a national census form, I fill in my race under "Other" as "White African." I have some 330 years of evidence to back that up.

Technology

One of the first things I buy in New York is a little Tandy "home computer," sold by the ubiquitous *Radio Shack*. This thing cannot do very much, has extremely limited on board memory, and saves information using an ordinary cassette recorder. However, it gets me interested in computing for the ordinary consumer. I can see where this is headed, but somehow IBM, where I earn my daily living, appears oblivious to the obvious trend and scope of potential impact.

Much later that year, my manager walks into the office and tells me that Management has decided to see if these home computers *"can be made useful"* in some way or another, and could I please help by checking whether they could be used to control laboratory equipment. This leaves me with a permanent calibration as to the lack of vision of large US corporations. This experience also leads me to decide that I want to apply my science, rather than just do endless research at a University.

This decision will lead me in a very particular direction when I return to South Africa.

"You should just die"

My office at IBM is a tiny room into which two desks have been fitted for two people. The space is so limited that the person sitting nearest the door has to get up and leave the room to allow the other to get out. After a few weeks, a new office mate joins me. He is an engineering professor from one of the Scandinavian countries and is my senior in life by more than a decade.

The professor has a Northern European Socialist view of the world; my first ever encounter with this school of thought. He states that he is happy to pay more than 60% tax if it results in a peaceful community. He attempts to explain to me that the Soviets have corrupted the wonderfully principled concept of Communism.

Before long, the office conversation turns unavoidably to South Africa. My colleague has not the faintest concept of the realities of life in Africa, but intensely resents the white people of Southern Africa. I finally ask him whether he has actually ever been to Africa or met any black people from Africa, to which he answers that he has had one black student in his life who was the son of a diplomat. He has never been to Africa and has no intention of going there.

One Monday he arrives at the office and tells me that he feels ashamed, because he unexpectedly ended up in Harlem that weekend and felt compelled to turn up his car windows. It provides a clear view into the mind of people of these convictions. I cannot help liberal socialists who break out in a cold sweat when they meet black people. It is they who have the problem; not the black people, nor I.

When I finally confront him with the simple question as to what it is he expects white South Africans to then do, given their circumstances, he rants about Europe's slavery and his own country's colonialism and then, before storming out of the office, he utters the words that will define Western Liberal Socialists to me for the rest of my life:

"You are a sick anachronism and a blot on the name of Europe. You should just die."

If I ever had any doubt as to the fate liberals in the Northern Hemisphere had in mind for me and mine, this certainly makes it clear. But, I have no idea why I should die for what is vividly obviously their guilty conscience. Nevertheless, it clarifies for me that Afrikaners are destined to be the Galactic Whipping Boy for the guilty conscience of Europeans and Americans regarding Colonialism and Slavery respectively. For both groupings it is cheap and easy to redeem the "sins of their grandfathers" from the safety of their coffee shops. There are no real consequences for them in recommending the destruction of my society merely because I am to them a reminder of those "sins" to which my society and I personally bear no witness whatsoever.

The flash in the Southern Ocean

On 25 October 1979, we hear the first ABC TV report of a distinctive double flash in the Southern Oceans south of South Africa[15] a month earlier. The US TV reporters are adamant that it is a South African nuclear test. When I meet with my friend George who worked in South Africa in the 1970s (*NF89*), he delivers a fatherly speech about the responsibility that now rests upon South Africa. He specifically tells me that he believes I shall be part of the intelligentsia of the country when I return, and how it is important that I should comprehend the full implications of the country having this weapon. While I appreciate my mentor George's concerns, I am by no means convinced there really has been a nuclear test; let alone that it was by South Africa. Over the next few weeks the story disappears from our regular lives.

Iran & Afghanistan

On 4 November 1979, we hear the first confused news about United States Embassy personnel in Teheran having been taken captive by Radicals in Iran. This is of some concern to me as a South African, because the Shah of Iran has been one of the very few friends of South Africa and is the source of some of its oil. Iran is also a significant export market for automobiles manufactured in South Africa. This event is the start of a 444-day crisis. It will eventually become the defining aspect of Jimmy Carter's presidency and the unfortunate hostages will not be released until he leaves office. The influence of the United States in the Middle East is dramatically reduced in this process and the door is opened for further Soviet territorial adventures.

Since we have seen in Southern Africa how the Soviets exploit every Western weakness, I know they will now try their hand in the Southwest Asian region. It takes a mere 56 days before they do. The Soviet army invades Afghanistan on Christmas Eve 1979.

I have just barely turned 26, I'm 8,000 miles from home, and I'm shaking my head in dismay at the United States of 1979. My own country is in trouble, but I fear for the whole of the West. It has lost its way and its leadership is pathetic in the extreme.

In Kennedy Country

Our first significant trip outside New York is to Boston over a weekend around Thanksgiving 1979. As part of this, we see the *USS Constitution*. At this time, we do not realize that a key South African historical personality was a captive on that very ship[16] (See Chapter 7 : *The Black Circuit*).

At home in South Africa, I have the book *Roots* by Arthur Haley about the supposed Gambian roots of his slave ancestor, "*Kunta Kinte*." The first page of the book convinced me that it was a work of fiction. Nevertheless, I can understand the desperate desire of many Black Americans for clarity on their roots in Africa.

What is less understandable for me is that the city fathers announce during our visit that Roots is not to be screened in the city as it might incite racial violence. I find this both cynical and ironic in the extreme. Here I am in Massachusetts, the home territory of the Kennedys who earlier injected their own guilty conscience into the complex South African picture (See Chapter 21: *Bobby comes to town*) and presumed to judge us, but the series *Roots* may not be shown in their own territory. This convinces me that the condescending hypocritical trait that I have sensed in South African and British liberals is alive and well and living in Massachusetts.

Dixie

In Spring 1980, we take our 10 precious days of vacation to drive to New Orleans and back. The first part of the journey is along the back roads of New Jersey and then onward to the Blue Ridge Parkway. Shortly after crossing into Virginia, there is a stop for gasoline. An older white man appears out of the building to fill up the car. He is short and unshaven, and looks like he has low tolerance of any nonsense.

After hearing me speak, he asks the customary "*Where y'all from then?*" When I say "*South Africa,*" he just grunts dismissively.

As he is filling the car, a full sized early 1970s sedan pulls in for gasoline. Four large black men emerge from this sagging vehicle and stand silently next to it, looking pointedly at the man filling our car. At this point, he thinks it appropriate to remark:

*"So, you're from South Africa, then? Friend of mine just come back from down there; says he ain't going back there no more; too many G*******d n****rs down there!"*

I realize we have crossed the Mason-Dixon line. I just sigh in resignation and pretend not to hear, which is difficult, because he has raised his voice to ensure that the newcomers can hear him. The four black men just look at him expressionlessly. They must be used to this. I certainly am not.

The following night, the stop is just inside West Virginia. There, we decide to go to a drive-in cinema at least once while in the United States. A double feature of *Hair* and *Electric Horseman*, the latter with Jane Fonda in the lead, is showing. When the movie *Hair* reaches the point where there is reference to relationships between black men and white women, the cars shine their headlights full on the screen and make an awful din with their horns. The entire segment of the movie is thereby completely obliterated. We two supposedly "Racist White South Africans" are rather bemused by all this, but do not participate.

We make our way south along Route 59 to New Orleans via Tennessee and Mississippi, reaching the city on Easter Sunday. It takes us a while to realize that the reason we see so many Confederate flags along the way is because it is the formal state flag of Mississippi. I honestly did not know that. I make a silent "note-to-self" to not miss such key cultural points again. This kind of thing is important.

Along the way, we tune the car radio to the local FM stations and cannot help but pick up various stations with church services for black communities. We find the degree of moaning and wailing and lamenting and crying and general effusion of emotion desperately uncomfortable. The family is essentially Dutch Reformed and Presbyterian and we were brought up in a society that believes "religion is a dish best served cold." It is also clear that, despite any attempts to foster integration, this part of the United States is laid out along racial lines. However, we do not come across any of the "politically correct" hidden prejudice and condescension that was exhibited back in New York. Perhaps the visit is too brief to detect such matters.

When we make our way back to New York via the Florida panhandle and the East Coast, we stop at a motel a few miles west of Charleston. The owner tells us that it is possible to hike a distance into the beautiful forest behind the establishment to see some sights that hearken back to the Civil War. He then proceeds to tell us about General Sherman's pyromaniacal campaign in the Civil War and mentions how much was burnt down around his general area.

As he tells the story, the man chokes up and I realize how deep the feelings on this subject run. I decide it has to be an idiot who underestimates the depth of this hurt that has been done to the people of the South. This issue is unlikely to go away very easily. It has survived more than 100 years of Northern attempts to downplay it. This is something completely different from the gas station operator in northern Virginia and evokes my total sympathy. It is too close for comfort to our own experience at the hands of the British in the Boer War (Chapter 17: *Burning a country to the ground*).

America through 26-year old Afrikaner eyes

In my first few months in the United States, it strikes me that Americans have no concept of how they take certain matters for granted. They propose Democracy as a cure-all for all political situations, but seem to forget that the popular vote gave us Hitler. They are quick to talk with passion about Revolutions, but forget that it gave us the Bolsheviks and the mass murderer Stalin. Somehow, they seem not to realize that they are taking their underlying Judeo-Christian values for granted, and have absolutely no understanding of black people as a great majority with utterly different culture to theirs. Amusingly, they even call them "Minorities."

This nation has no concept of an existence in which one is under constant threat by a different civilization that wants to drive one into the sea. Americans have never had to defend their homeland against an invader since 1812 and have never lived as powerless subjects under a foreign master. Perhaps it is summed up by a single statement: they have never lost a war, so it is all theory to them. Their physical isolation, their riches, and their power shield them from the realities the rest of humanity has to deal with.

Return to South Africa

By the end of our year in the United States, we are badly homesick. New York's trees make it impossible to see the horizon. For two people who know the open plains of Africa and its uniquely blue skies, the hazy humid New York summers and miserable winters hold no attraction. More importantly, we have heard that PW Botha, contrary to my expectations, has started making positive changes in the racial policies in South Africa and the country is going through something of an economic boom on the back of a soaring gold price. The US dollar has dropped significantly against the South African rand. Things are looking up in South Africa and the future looks better for all.

When we return to South Africa, we are almost immediately bored by the tedium of lecturing at the University in Port Elizabeth. By September 1981, we accept positions in a high technology research and development organization located in the capital, Pretoria. It is the sister organization to the Canadian National Research Council. The challenge is to build the operations of the organization based on contracted research. Since the organization receives some funds from government for "blue skies" research, it remains nominally under the jurisdiction of the government, but that body has its hands full and shows essentially zero interest in the activities of scientists. We shall clearly have to build our future on industrial contracts, rather than government funding.

Significantly, one of the key industrial clients is De Beers, the major international supplier of diamonds. Among the other clients is Armscor, the national weapons procurement agency, which has learnt a lot of lessons from the original Angolan engagement. The role of our organization is in the research and analysis phase of conventional weapons development. Nuclear and chemical weapons are specifically outside our ambit. Our specific focus is on optoelectronic technology. This technology may in general be found anywhere from consumer products such as LEDs, TV remote controls and CD players to military target designators, air-to-air missiles and thermal imaging.

Changes are afoot in South Africa. I now deal with black PhD colleagues and black fellow physicists from Witwatersrand University. I never met any black scientists or engineers at IBM in New York.

—End Nexus Familia

America reawakens

A great nation can only wallow in its own misery for so long. Inevitably it has to restore its pride and self-respect and do something constructive. For the United States, the opportunity came with the presidential election of November 1980. Ronald Reagan, the governor of California and former movie actor, won in a landslide with George H. W. Bush as running mate. The Republican Party also took control in the Senate for the first time since 1958.

Bush had previously replaced Bill Colby as CIA director in the wake of the disastrous Vietnam-to-Angola period of the organization. In this role, he had served just under one year, to be replaced when Jimmy Carter took office. He was credited with restoring the morale of the CIA after the disastrous events of the early 70s. He also had a solid background on the events in Angola and therefore on South Africa's cooperation with the United States in opposing the Soviet Union. He was also of the generation that had fought World War Two, in which he had been the youngest aviator in the U.S. Navy. Bush was a kindred spirit with the author's father-in-law, who had similarly been an Allied fighter pilot (Chapter 19 - *Nexus Familia 82*) in WWII.

Fig. 24-2 U.S. President Ronald Reagan

Ronald Reagan represented the America the world had previously respected. His values were clear, his principles sound, and his humanity vividly evident. He had his shortcomings, but they were not in the area of principle. Here was a man who did not hesitate to call Muammar Gadaffi of Lybia a "*mad dog.*"

In the economic domain, President Reagan would become famous for his Reaganomics, based on reduced taxation, reduced regulation, and focus on small business. Internationally he would become known for the simple principle of taking a clear stand against terrorism and against the Soviet Union, which he named the "*Evil Empire.*" This somehow uniquely upset the Soviets who responded by calling Reagan's administration a "*Bunch of Hoods.*" The former epithet stuck internationally, but the latter did not.

On March 30, 1981, he survived an assassination attempt by a deranged obsessive named John Hinckley who had earlier stalked President Carter. This dramatically increased his popularity, especially when he told his wife: "*Honey, I forgot to duck!*" To white South Africans, he represented honor returned to the White House. He seemed like a breath of fresh air compared with the political odium of the Carter administration.

America was back on the world stage and the Southern African stage was set for Act 2 in Angola.

During the Carter period, South Africa had to square off alone against the Soviets and their Cuban proxies. In 1981, soon after Reagan entered the White House, his new Assistant Secretary of State for African affairs, Chester Crocker, developed a linkage policy, tying Namibian independence to Cuban withdrawal from Angola. South Africa had stalled any negotiations on Namibian independence in view of the Cuban-Soviet presence next door in Angola. Unlike the Carter team, the Reagan team saw the Soviet-Cuban presence in Angola, and not the South African presence in Namibia[17], as the problem.

The end of "Petty Apartheid"

PW Botha was a man who evoked one of only two human responses: admiration or hatred. The author confesses to hating this man at the time. In hindsight, this reaction was short-sighted. Possibly, it takes someone like Nelson Mandela to correctly judge the man who was at the helm of South Africa in its darkest days. Mandela would eventually write[18] about his first meeting with PW Botha on 5 July 1989 that PW completely disarmed him and that he was unfailingly courteous, deferential, and friendly. At the death of PW Botha in 2006, Mandela made a point of remembering[19] him for the steps he took to pave the way towards an eventual negotiated settlement in the country

So, if we can put aside the author's prejudices against PW Botha and the knee-jerk responses of many lesser men than Mandela, then it should be possible for the open-minded to proceed by looking at the facts.

Between 1980 and 1985 "PW" (pronounced "pieh vieh"), as everyone in the country called him, did a number of positive things that laid the foundation for a new South Africa:

- He ensured the country had the military ability to block the Soviet-Cuban adventure;

- He created governmental structures for Coloured and Indian South Africans;

- He normalized labor practice by approving labor unions for black people;

- He removed a number of the more petty and hurtful Apartheid Laws; and

- He stopped the removals of black people back to the Homelands

In the wake of some of these changes, the average black income in South Africa doubled[20] between 1979 and 1983, though inflation ate into that, as with everyone else.

It is true that PW left in place those pieces of Apartheid legislation that controlled voting rights for blacks and maintained the homeland structure, but Rome was not built in one day. It had taken the United States a century – one hundred years – to make its way from the Civil War, which had ostensibly stopped slavery, to the point of removing legislation that effectively kept black Americans from voting[21]. It seemed reasonable that it might take a while for South Africa to traverse the path between removal of petty discrimination and a multiracial democracy. After all, nothing elsewhere in Africa yet represented hope that any black nation of Africa could maintain the Rule of Law, let alone run an advanced country with a sophisticated industrial and commercial base and quite possibly the most advanced financial sector on the planet. Also, the Soviets and Cubans were still hovering on the border, the whole world had imposed weapons sanctions against South Africa and the military wing of the ANC, Umkhonto we Sizwe, was singing "*Kill the whites.*"

That is a bad position from which to negotiate. So, something in the constellation of forces arrayed against South Africa would first have to budge before black voting rights in a unitary democracy could be considered. Even if one assumed that those urging such a step on South Africa had meant the country well, which most certainly did not, it would have been brazenly naive to have expected "One man, One vote."

As a result of the new black unions, employment conditions for lower income urbanized black people improved markedly. For white South Africans this part of the decade of the 1980s was a period in which they saw major increases in taxes. In fact, by 1987 whites would be paying 32% of their incomes as tax[22], but would receive only 9% back in any form of benefit. At the same time, many black people were now upwardly mobile. Simultaneously there was a huge increase in black population and associated rising expectations.

It is against this background that David Lien, representing the Board of Regents of the Luther College in the United States, visited South Africa in 1984 on a fact finding tour and insightfully wrote[23]:

"In many ways South Africa is to Africa what the United States is to the world. It has been claimed that the prosperity is based on exploitation of the blacks. That's an easy charge to make, particularly out of context [...]

"But people migrate and stay only when they can improve their condition, so this must be better than where they came from. [...]

"I've never seen so many Mercedes anywhere, including, it seems, Germany. [...] They're as common as VW beetles used to be in the States. If the blacks driving them are all chauffeurs, they sure are chauffeuring a lot of other blacks around."

The simple test of this reality was that black people from neighboring countries were streaming into South Africa. Along the eastern boundary of the Kruger National Park with Mozambique, an electrified fence was erected stretching hundreds of miles. On the southern bank of the Limpopo River, extensive barriers of sisal were planted to deter Zimbabweans. All this was done to keep illegal aliens from neighboring states from "escaping *into* Apartheid." Along the Mozambique border, these people were braving prides of man-eating lion in order to reach the Eldorado of Apartheid South Africa[24]. None of this was ever mentioned in international news on South Africa. Only news portraying perceived oppression appeared in Western media.

This background of improved opportunity for black people was hardly conducive to a popular Communist revolution. The ANC would have to take a leaf out of its Soviet masters' handbook of revolution in order to create conditions suited to their goal of taking over the country.

Pressure was somehow required on South Africa if they were to be successful.

Meanwhile, in Angola

The situation on the northern border of Namibia with Angola had been steadily deteriorating. SWAPO now felt safe, having the protection of the MPLA and the Cubans. They were backed up by limitless supplies of equipment from the Soviets since the 1975/6 Angolan War[25]. The 1978 raid on Cassinga in Angola as part of Operation Reindeer has already been described (See Chapter 23: *Exporting the Angolan War*).

It needs to be mentioned though, that 32 Battalion, formed of the original Bravo Group assembled by Jan Breytenbach, had been quite active inside Angola since the war. These, however, were smaller operations generally aimed at keeping the MPLA a respectable distance from the Namibian border, or at disrupting SWAPO's infiltration efforts. Meanwhile the Soviets had increased their presence and by 1980 there were more than 500 Soviet personnel serving as *"advisers"* in Angola, led by Lieutenant-General V.V. Shahnovich[26], often wrongly referred to as Shaganovich.

On 14 April 1980, UNITA, still led by the redoubtable Jonas Savimbi, drove a 700 man FAPLA[27] force out of the town of Cuangar on the Kavango River[28] (See Chap. 22: *Fig. 22-5*). This was the first major strategic move by UNITA since the 1975 Angolan War. Savimbi formally approached South Africa and requested that the South African Army clear a supposedly understrength battalion of FAPLA out of Savate, some 43 miles north into Angola along the Kavango. All this was part of Savimbi's effort to wrest the southeast corner of Angola from the control of the Soviet-Cuban-MPLA Axis. Even a cursory study of the map of that area reveals the potential military security benefits to South Africa. Naturally, South Africa yet again could not be seen to be the party undertaking the action, and so the lot fell to 32 Battalion, which had by now become the de facto and exceedingly loyal Foreign Legion of the country, still commanded largely, but not exclusively, by white South African officers, who would participate with their faces covered in the ubiquitous *"Black is Beautiful"* facial camouflage.

The attack took place on 21 May 1980 as Operation *Tiro-A-Tiro* and was concluded successfully by the following morning. The South African force comprised just two rifle companies with one in reserve, one mortar platoon and a few Recces (ultra-tough South African reconnaissance specialists). It was a bitter fight and cost 32 Battalion 10% of the casualties it ever took in battle in its whole history. The reason was obvious by the second day. Savimbi had intentionally lied[29] to the South Africans, knowing full well that they would never have sent 32 Battalion up against what now transpired to be 1060 heavily armed and entrenched troops. The attack cost the lives of two South African captains, and two second lieutenants. Radio intercepts indicated that 558 FAPLA had been killed. UNITA duly arrived to take occupation and deny any involvement of South Africans to the media. This started a trend that would be maintained throughout the decade in which the South African units would do a lot of the actual fighting, but South Africa would deny its involvement, forced to do so by the previous behavior of the United States Congress (Chapter 22: *Angola – The Fourth Great Abandonment*).

On 10 June 1980, the South African Defense Force launched the largest scale attack of formal forces since World War II. In this case, there was no pretending as to their identity. The operation was aimed against SWAPO targets inside Angola as far north as Lubango. It would be known as Operation *Sceptic*. This time, SWAPO responded with anti-aircraft fire from Soviet equipment. The result was not an overwhelming strategic success for the South African Army and two precious Mirage fighter aircraft employed in the opening phase of the operation were damaged by ground fire[30]. However, huge amounts of equipment were captured. On the other hand, the Soviets seemed to have an inexhaustible supply. While the South Africans pulled back to the border, FAPLA was ill-advised enough to attack them and 90 FAPLA soldiers paid with their lives. By the end of the operation, the enemy losses were 380 and South African losses 17.

Strategically, the most important incursion into Angola between 1976 and 1984 was Operation *Protea* in August 1981. It comprised 4,000 South African troops and 138 aircraft. This time, the aircraft were met by heavy barrages of SAM-7 man-portable missiles. The ground forces were met with heavy fire from anti-aircraft guns operated in the ground-fire mode. The fighting was heavier than during the much-reported Angolan War. It resulted in 4 Soviet Russian advisers being killed at Ongiva, two of them being Soviet lieutenant colonels[31], proving that Soviet advisers were embedded with SWAPO. Soviet Warrant Officer Nikolai Pestretsov was taken prisoner guarding the body of his wife, who had been killed in Soviet Army uniform in the attack. He thereby won the admiration of the South Africans who treated him with the greatest of consideration. He was exchanged some 15 months later on 16 November 1982 for the bodies of three South African soldiers.

Time Magazine also reported that there were now 1,000 Soviet Advisers in Angola and anything from 400 to 2,500 East German advisers. Other sources state 2,000 East Germans focused on intelligence work.

On 30 August, UNITA troops finally arrived to take over control of Xangongo and present an image to the media of Protea having been a UNITA victory. SWAPO's command and control structure in the region had been effectively destroyed. A massive amount of equipment taken from FAPLA and SWAPO was destroyed. Some equipment was sent back to Namibia and South Africa. This included nine T-34 tanks, four PT76 amphibious tanks, various armored cars, two 122mm mobile multiple rocket launchers, 46 anti-aircraft guns, 94 SAM-7 anti-aircraft missiles, 43 fields guns, 165 cargo trucks and numerous other vehicles, along with 250 tons of ammunition and 18,000 small arms[32]. The bridge over the Cunene River at Xangongo, which the author had crossed in 1974 on his visit on the eve of war, was destroyed (See *Fig. 22-3*).

The above shows how the conflict was systematically escalating and how the equipment employed against the South African Army systematically increased in sophistication and volume. Strategically the risks were going up, but by supporting UNITA the South African Army had denied SWAPO almost half the border of Namibia and was keeping the Soviet-Cuban-MPLA Axis pinned a considerable distance from the border. It made good sense in terms of strategic risk and reward.

In the greater game of the Cold War, the situation also suited the United States, despite all the political fallout and denials, because the Soviets were now tied up in two wars and they were starting to bleed.

Operation *Daisy* in late 1982 was not big at all, but did represent the deepest penetration into Angola since the Angolan War. It is mentioned here, because there were gas masks[33] among the equipment captured. Given the Soviet history of disregard for the sanctity of human life, this was an ominous development indeed and word filtered back to the research and development community in South Africa to investigate means for detecting and protecting against chemical agents. It represented yet a further clear step in the escalating situation.

The 1983 Pretoria car bomb

On 20 May 1983, to complement the ramped up Soviet activity in Angola, an ANC car bomb exploded in front of the South African Air Force offices in downtown Pretoria. It was timed to explode just as most workers were emerging from the building, but did so prematurely. Nineteen people were killed and 217 injured, most of them black people. It would have been much worse if the attack had been executed as planned. Clearly the conflict with the ANC had assumed an entirely new dimension. The Government retaliation was swift and hard. Three days later, the South African Air Force bombed known ANC facilities in the capital of neighboring Mozambique, which had been operating as haven for ANC operatives and as a transit facility. As a direct consequence, President Samora Machel of Mozambique signed the 1984 Nkomati Accord with South Africa and expelled some 800 ANC personnel[34].

Richard Dowden, liberal British newspaperman, elects to call the South African response *"petty revenge"* for a *"pinprick"*[35]. It can only be speculated what that author would call the 9/11 attacks on the U.S.A. The question is relevant, because many in South Africa regard that day as "South Africa's 9/11," always remembering that South Africa's white population, the target, was not quite 5 million versus a US target population of 300 million in 2001.

The Soviets ultimately deserted Mozambique as a lost cause. Similar pressures on Lesotho and Swaziland led to more or less similar results. South Africa's policy of intentionally destabilizing bordering states that harbored the ANC was clearly working. In neighboring Zimbabwe, the despotic Robert Mugabe had much to lose by annoying South Africa. Practically all his imports came via South Africa. As a result, he was very careful not to openly assist the opponents of the South African government.

Over this period, Angola remained the major concern, given the tens of thousands of Cubans and several thousand Soviet personnel.

Cold War sidebar on West 44th Street

By early 1983, it was quite clear that the salutary effects of the blow struck against SWAPO two years earlier in Operation *Protea* had been eroded. A new strike was called for. It would be called Operation *Askari*. At this point, with the Soviets having learnt that war in Angola meant combat deaths for them and exceedingly costly losses of equipment, events took a new turn. From this point on there would be close linkage between events in Angola and events inside South Africa.

The Algonquin Hotel on West 44th Street in Manhattan is a most unlikely place for the more than 60 years of Soviet preoccupation with South Africa to reach a diplomatic climax, yet in November of 1983 that is exactly what happened. The event would set the stage for the ultimate defeat of the Soviet Union in Southern Africa. It is during that particular month that the United Nations, an organization by then completely and unquestioningly opposed to anything that South Africa might say or do, arranged a meeting between Soviet and South African representatives at this luxury hotel. Its purpose was for the Soviet Union to communicate directly with South Africa on the subject of Angola[36]. As for the United Nations, its supposed "impartiality" was laughable. This lamentable body had always been a useful and loyal agent for the Soviet Union. It even passed resolutions declaring the Soviet-supported Marxist SWAPO to be the only legitimate representative of the people of Namibia; this in the absence of an election.

At the Algonquin Hotel, the Soviets had a very vivid message for the South Africans: "Get out of Angola or else." They reputedly had satellite and "other" intelligence on South African preparations to attack

SWAPO bases in Angola. To emphasize their point, the Soviets dispatched[37] a powerful naval force to round the Cape of Good Hope. There would be later attempts to deny the link between the actions, but the message was quite obvious. The Soviets "meant business" in Angola. The South Africans obviously ignored the direct Soviet threat, as would the United States under similar circumstances. In fact, South Africa was indeed planning Operation *Askari*, as it would be dubbed. This operation in early 1984 is known not so much for its major strategic benefit as for an event that clearly revealed one of the enduring problems of exporting the Communist Revolution around the globe.

During the operation, South Africa's 32 battalion took the town of Tetchamutete, which they had found deserted by FAPLA. Meanwhile, the regular South African Defence Force was attacking nearby Cuvelai. During the night, some of the defenders of Cuvelai fled towards Tetchamutete along with a Soviet T55 tank. This resulted in a firefight during which the tank crew abandoned their machine. Of the twelve infantry with the machine, six were killed and six more fled without somehow informing their comrades elsewhere of the presence of their enemy in Tetchamutete.

The 32 Battalion men at the perimeter of the town were themselves Angolans dressed in combat fatigues not dissimilar to those of the FAPLA army and similarly armed with AK-47s. With some of the white Afrikaner officers and NCOs having been chosen for their rare ability to speak Portuguese, the scene was set for the event of the day[38]. FAPLA troops fleeing from Cuvelai soon began to arrive, greeting the men at the checkpoint under the impression that they were fellow FAPLA soldiers. The Angolans of 32 Battalion saw a major opportunity unfolding. After lamenting the events at Cuvelai, the new FAPLA arrivals were escorted, still armed, to the officers' area by the grinning 32 Battalion Angolans. The mirth of the checkpoint soldiers upset the FAPLA officer, and so, when they arrived at the headquarters building, he complained about the lack of respect from the lower ranks at the checkpoint.

Colonel Eddie Viljoen and Sergeant-Major Koos Kruger, both typical white Afrikaners, bearded and tanned by years of bush fighting, were rather bemused by the outrage of their visitors. They urged the men to sit down and even produced refreshments. The visitors then related all the details of the events at Cuvelai as experienced by the FAPLA forces suffering at the hands of the SADF. Finally, one of the FAPLA visitors asked whether the two South Africans were Cubans. When they answered in the negative, the FAPLA lieutenant ventured *"Russian?"*; when this produced a negative response, the question was *"East German?"*[39] This was when Koos Kruger told them, *"No, we're Boers!"* The stunned FAPLA men were disarmed and taken prisoner.

Beyond the evidence of East German participation, the event demonstrated the degree of confusion on the other side of the conflict. The Soviets had sent every form of Communist proxy nation to Angola and it was making matters difficult for the Angolan FAPLA soldiers. They were beset by white and mulatto Communists speaking German, Russian and Spanish in a country where the lingua franca is Portuguese. To the extent that South African electronic intelligence personnel had penetrated the command and control communications of the Soviets, Cubans and MPLA/FAPLA, they were aware of the Babel of confusion that arose on the Axis side of the conflict every time the South African forces moved[40]. This was fully exploited.

PW's "Total Onslaught" comes true

After some decades of being an issue that "bubbled under" on the American political scene, the situation in South Africa burst into full bloom on the U.S. stage in late 1984. The major promoters of the subject were Randall Robinson, founder of the TransAfrica foundation, and Archbishop Desmond Tutu of the South African Anglican church. In South Africa, Tutu was experienced as a hugely divisive force by many as his morality did not appear to be color blind. Many Afrikaners considered his moralizing to be suspect because of his liberation rhetoric and apparent anti-white, particularly anti-Afrikaner, racial bias.

Randall Robinson was hardly invested in making sure that matters came to a successful head in distant South Africa. He had his own agenda of self-promotion. It is not as though the reader needs to believe the author, who of necessity has strong feelings in this matter. We can turn to the Deputy-Secretary of State for

Africa, Chester Crocker, for his considered view as a man who had the job of engineering success in Southern Africa. He describes[41] Tutu entirely in line with the author's view as being a "prelate with a sharp tongue and a well-developed taste for liberation theology." He explains how Robinson would arrange demonstrations to make sure that celebrities would be arrested. The arrests were scheduled by appointment and coordinated with the media to ensure maximal coverage and impact.

The haplessly outclassed South African Government, utterly unprepared for this media frenzy, had not a fighting chance. They failed utterly. The so-called "Information Scandal" and consequent removal of key people like Eschel Rhoodie in the late 1970s had destroyed the only remote chance that South Africa had ever had to address this kind of media onslaught, suspect as the methods of that group might have been.

In his seminal book on the U.S. diplomatic effort during the Cold War in Southern Africa, Chester Crocker describes[42] how, on 4 December 1984, to avoid being upstaged by the Democrats, a group of U.S. Republicans threatened the South African Ambassador with termination of the Constructive Engagement policy of the United States with South Africa. It strikes the reasonable that they might have also considered pressuring the ANC to stop its own inhuman violence. Anyone reading Crocker's book will conclude that he was no friend of South Africa. However, in his book even he describes the behavior of the United States politicians towards South Africa over this period as being sanctimonious and self-righteous[43]. What was previously considered an outrageous demand even for the far left leaning Carter Administration just a few years before, was now peculiarly inadequate as even a starting point for a supposedly Conservative Republican in 1984. Few of these players if any had the vaguest idea of the realities of South Africa. Given the author's own experience in the United States (NF90), they probably could not place South Africa on the map despite its name, but they rushed to judgment and made local political hay from our misery. Crocker suggests that Reagan himself, now in his second term, was the target[44] of some of the U.S politicians.

In January 1985, Senator Ted Kennedy angrily berated Crocker about South Africa[45], implying that nothing had changed in South Africa since his dead brother's visit in 1966, which had initiated the facile parallels between South Africa and the United States. Ted Kennedy had never seen South Africa. The author had his own experience of matters racial in Kennedy's Massachusetts (NF90).

Starting in late 1984 and blooming in 1985, the ANC turned to violence in a spectacular fashion, emboldened by all the attention from the USA and by the international anger fomented by Robinson and Tutu. The ANC coordinated this with massively ramped up efforts by their Soviet sponsor in Angola (See Chapter 25). Most of this violence was directed not at the government or white people, but at the black people of South Africa whom they had to mobilize by any possible means against the government. However, some policies on the part of the government played straight into their hands.

One such example was the creation of locally elected urban management councils for Black people. These had all the powers and responsibilities of their white counterparts, but lacked any sustainable basis for revenue generation[46]. Much of that, such as the ubiquitous beer halls, had been destroyed in the Soweto riots of 1976. When these councils tried to raise funds from their communities for the services they received, they walked straight into rent boycotts. American author Adam Ashforth describes[47] this reality as lived by his friends and hosts, the Mfete family of Soweto south of Johannesburg. When PW Botha introduced 99-year property leaseholds for urban black people in 1978, they made sure they leased their own property. However, when the service and utility bill boycotts were forced on the black people of the country by the ANC around 1984, the Mfetes were part of the process.

So, the white people paid their taxes and service bills, but urban black people simply avoided paying because the ANC told them so, daring the authorities to cut the power and thereby cause a revolution. While whites were paying more than 30% tax, they were getting only a miserable benefit for their taxes. The whites were, in fact, paying for the upkeep of services to black people, not to mention the bread and corn meal subsidies; staples of many millions of black people. The close on 30 million South African blacks, whipped up by the ANC, were now openly exploiting the taxes on the 5 million whites. Unfortunately, this does not make news headlines and therefore never was reported on. The whites had to be the monsters in the tale.

The ANC turns to open Terrorism

In Parliament on 31 January 1985, State President PW Botha made an ill-considered public offer of freedom to Nelson Mandela if the latter would forswear violence in determining a future South Africa. Not only did Nelson Mandela reject this offer, but from this specific moment his African National Congress turned to open terrorism against innocent civilians. There is no need to agonize over the logic, morals or timing. We merely tabulate the actions of the ANC before and after this offer and treat the actions of that organization similar to what engineers call a "black box." One does not look into the internal workings of the "black box." One merely applies a signal to it and sees what it does. In this particular case, the signal was the offer by Botha and we consider the ANC actions before and after Mandela rejected that offer. These are given in the table below. The ANC attacks of the 1970s were so ineffectual that they are not worth tabulating.

Year	Attacks on the Military	Attacks on the Police	Attacks on Civil Structures	Terror attacks on Civilians	Comments
1980	0	2	5	0	
1981	3	4	20	5	
1982	2	3	15	2	
1983	0	0	33	7	
1984	3	8	11	4	
10 Feb 1985: Mandela refuses to swear off violence if released as part of deal with President PW Botha					
1985	7*	8	11	41	*: Including 4 anti-tank landmines
1986	7	16	7	30*	*: Including 13 anti-tank landmines
1987	6	25	2	32*	*: Including 3 anti-tank landmines
1988	3	23	18	37	

Fig. 24-3 The ANC turns to open Terrorism in 1985 - The numbers

Following immediately after the Botha offer, they turned dramatically to bomb and mine attacks on civilians, the rate increasing by a staggering factor of ten from the previous year. As fate would have it, the family of the author would find itself exposed to some of these events by sheer circumstance (NF91).

As a guerrilla group, the ANC was a dismal failure to the point of being an embarrassment to the term, their 31 attacks against the military being a litany of failures and a strategic joke. However, as a terrorist group they were clearly very active, being responsible for at least 158 attacks on civilians, not counting the 122 attacks on civil structures such as courts or infrastructure and the like. This new focus on the murder and terrorizing of civilians did not escape the attention of the US Central Intelligence Agency. In a Special National Intelligence Estimate[48] of 1986, dedicated to the ANC, it pointedly stated:

> *"Most ANC bombings since late last year have been directed against civilian rather than government targets. A recent ANC statement specifically noted that white farmers and urban white males were considered by the ANC as part of the government's "security forces" and were valid targets for ANC operations."*

This clarifies why the ANC was ultimately classified a Terrorist Organization by the U.S. State Department. It also explains why millions in South Africa do not support the unilluminated international impression that Nelson Mandela is a pacifist innocent, but rather an intelligent militant lawyer-figurehead with a self-confessed record of violence; a record for which he was formally convicted in open court and jailed as leader of the military wing of the ANC in 1964. It was his creation that was carrying out this horror.

Behind the planning of all this horror sat Joe Modise, the Operations Chief of the ANC's military wing, Umkhonto we Sizwe. This man will return later in this work to influence the life of the author quite directly.

With ANC terror bombings escalating dramatically as shown in the foregoing table, PW Botha announced a National State of Emergency on 21 July 1985, thereby giving the government greater powers in fighting the ANC.

Zulu political leader, Chief Gatsha Buthelezi pointed out[49] some time later that, after a quarter century of effort on the part of the ANC, every bridge in the country was intact and not a single factory out of operation. He used this to make his point that South Africa simply did not represent the kind of circumstances that facilitate winning anything by armed struggle. He was completely right; no amount of violence directed at the government of the country was ever going to succeed. Furthermore, while a handful of white people had indeed died in some of its efforts and more still would, the ANC had not even vaguely dented white power. Nor had the organization yet experienced a measurable fraction of the total power the government could have unleashed on them. However, Buthelezi and the government both completely underestimated the willingness of the ANC to direct its extreme violence at black people in order to intimidate them into falling in line with its agenda.

The Fifth Great Abandonment

By mid 1985, the pressures on the South African government were immense. Many countries had implemented sanctions and the United States was threatening to apply the same. There was much expectation that PW Botha would make a watershed announcement about a negotiated way forward in his speech to the Natal Congress of his National Party on 15 August 1985. The disappointment when he said nothing of any consequence in this so-called "Rubicon Speech" was profound.

The first blow came from Chase Manhattan Bank, which refused to roll over South Africa's short term loans[50]. In the United States, the Republicans and Democrats now vied with one another to run South Africa into the ground by any means fair or foul. We were now a helpless pawn in the United States' own callous internal politics. When Congress developed Comprehensive Sanctions legislation aimed against South Africa, one honorable man in the United States stood his ground. He was President Ronald Reagan and he was the one single man who internationally defended the simple truth[51]:

"South Africa is not a totalitarian society. There is a vigorous opposition press, and every day we see examples of outspoken protest and access to the international media that would never be possible in many parts of Africa or in the Soviet Union, for that matter."

It was all to no avail, the *Comprehensive Anti-Apartheid Act of 1986* was passed by both houses of Congress. President Reagan attempted to veto the law but was overridden by Congress (by the Senate 78 to 21, the House by 313 to 83). This marked the first time in the twentieth century that the veto of a president on a matter of foreign policy was overridden. Congress clearly intended to hurt South Africa.

To this moment in time can be traced the deaths of thousands of South Africans and the destruction of the lives of hundreds of thousands, if not millions. American foreign policy had come unhinged. Now emboldened by unthinking support from the United States, the ANC launched a campaign to make the country ungovernable, perpetuating the 1976 slogans of *"Liberation before Education."* This led to hundreds of thousands of young black men forgoing school on the assumption that they would somehow miraculously be great economic winners in a revolution. They provided the uneducated cannon fodder for the so-called *"Struggle"* of the ANC. The 1976 Soweto riots were the start of what would later be called the *"Lost Generation"*[52], but the 1980s continuation cemented it as culture, and the ANC is directly to blame.

PW Botha's much-mentioned "Total Onslaught" was now upon the country in no uncertain terms in the military domain in Angola, on the socio-political front within the country and on the international political front. International observers and authors can most certainly speculate, possibly even with some justification, that PW Botha turned his "Total Onslaught" into a self-fulfilling prophecy. However, that does not absolve the United States Congress from the fact that it pushed the button to actively destroy South Africa economically in its moment of greatest need.

The United States Congress can attempt to pride itself in fighting Apartheid in this process, but history mutely records its vote that fueled the consequences. Schools were burnt down and teachers were killed by the ANC (*NF91*). Black policemen were pointedly targeted for killing. We now stood completely isolated and all of mankind bayed for our blood to a drum beat that was now laid down in the United States and not the Soviet Union. It is most peculiar that the United States as a country, and Americans as a nation, would revere President Reagan later, but that they would not trust his correct judgment in the matter of South Africa at a time when he and George Bush senior were the ones with the actual proper "inside" intelligence on the situation, while Congress just had slanted newspaper reports. Perhaps a guilty social conscience trumps all in the end, especially if a suitably distant whipping boy, fighting for his existence, presents himself.

This represented the fifth time that the West had willfully abandoned us as a people.

Angola again

By 1985, the MPLA government, with all the help of the Cubans and Soviets, had produced four successive failed campaigns against UNITA, mostly because of well placed intervention on the part of South Africa. On some occasions, the intervention was quite open. On others, 32 Battalion was employed to masquerade as UNITA with the full cooperation of the latter. The Soviet Axis forces simply could not break UNITA, and could never take the southeast of Angola. The Soviets and Cubans were getting ever more desperate. However, events in South Africa itself were bound to create for them the opportunity they were looking for – at least, from their perspective.

Given the threats they had made in New York and the subsequent South African Operation *Askari*, the Soviets now obviously had to "put up or shut up," especially in view of the failure of the Axis forces to dislodge UNITA. The ramp-up of Axis forces started in July and August of 1985. No fewer than six brigades of FAPLA, each provided with seven Soviet advisers[53], were gearing up for the drive against UNITA. Two airports were strengthened and MiG-21 and MiG-23 aircraft brought in, along with anti-aircraft missile facilities. There were now several Russian pilots flying the fighter aircraft and on the ground the Russians were directly controlling much of the operations. Supply flights increased from 3 a day to 14 a day. This was to be the biggest drive yet against UNITA and the Soviets were leading it themselves. There was no conceivable way in which UNITA would be able to survive the impending Soviet-Cuban-FAPLA Axis campaign.

On 7 September 1985, the chief of the S.A. Army instructed the Namibian regional commander of the South African Defense Force to support UNITA. Again 32 Battalion would fight in UNITA uniforms. No fewer than 2500 UNITA troops were airlifted by the S.A. Air Force to positions from which to better oppose FAPLA, likely crossing the Zambian border in the process and equally likely with the approval of president Kenneth Kaunda. By 15 September, despite every effort of UNITA, the Axis army directed by Soviet advisers stood ready to take the key town of Mavinga south of the strategic Lomba River. At this point, the South African Air Force intervened and shot down four Mi 17 and six Mi 25 helicopters. However, the key turning point was probably when the Russians and Cubans upped and pulled out on a Mi 25 helicopter. FAPLA morale folded and they pulled back. Some 2,300 FAPLA lay dead. This campaign also cost the lives of six Russians. On the ground lay the wrecks of three MiG 21s and two MiG 23s. The customary hoard of captured weapons, including anti-aircraft equipment, tanks and other armor a made its way south. The War in Africa was not going well for the Soviets at all.

On 7 June 1986, Reuters announced that South African Recce forces had sunk a Cuban freighter and damaged two Soviet supply ships in the southern Angolan harbor of Namibe. Along with a joint UNITA-South African assault, it derailed the massive Axis campaign planned for 1986. The Soviets and the U.S. Media were equally unhappy. By now, that probably meant the South Africans had done something right.

Total Onslaught becomes Total Horror

There are many admirable traits about African culture, and, as with any other, there are objectionable traits. Possibly the most objectionable trait of the African culture is the dehumanization of people in acts such as "necklacing," in which some people of African background seem to positively delight[54]. "Necklacing" is the uniquely ANC-formulated method of hanging tires around a tied victim, dousing the person in gasoline, and setting it all alight. As the victim burns to death in indescribable agony, coated in melting flaming rubber, the participants dance and ululate. Not since the horror of the 11th century persecution of the Cathars had there been anything like this. The brutality of black-on-black violence in South Africa started to escalate to a level where one simply closed one's mind to it to avoid going insane.

On 13 April 1986, at Munsieville, a township of Krugersdorp (Birthtown of the author's wife (*NF84*) and childhood home of Desmond Tutu), Nomzamo Madikizela made one of her typical fist-waving speeches. In this tirade, she made the infamous statement that people will never forget nor forgive[55]:

"With our boxes of matches and our necklaces we shall liberate this country!"

Madikizela, better known as "Winnie," was the wife of the imprisoned Nelson Mandela. With this fist-waving tirade, she became the most well-known and most vocal proponent of this despicable method of torture-murder. The clear of mind is left to ponder the resulting values of the "children" of this so-called "Mother of the Nation." Her efforts would soon degenerate into further depths of horror when her home would become the nerve center of a campaign of intimidation, assault, and murder. The deaths of eighteen individuals would eventually be tied to her homes (See Chapter 25), some allegedly to her as person, according to witnesses. Meanwhile, the economic mathematics of the country was no longer working. The whole world had implemented extensive economic sanctions against the country, with Britain now almost the only exception. The country's loan facilities had largely ceased. The ANC was happy to facilitate the economic destruction of the country in order to get power and still clung grimly to its Communist rhetoric, threatening nationalization of the economy if they were to come to power.

And still the ANC sang: *"Bulala amaBhulu! Kill the Boers."*

Nexus Familia 91: Descent into the Valley of Death

Pretoria 20 May 1983

In the middle of a meeting in our boardroom at my R&D employee building in the suburban east of the capital city of Pretoria we feel a rumble and then hear a crack. Across the road from the Air Force building in downtown Pretoria a friend is thrown to the floor as her office windows implode. Everyone immediately knows that a huge bomb must have gone off somewhere. Soon enough, we get word that a massive car bomb has exploded in front of the Air Force Headquarters building in town, a building that I need to visit in the line of business. The carnage is terrible. Nineteen people lie dead and 217 lie writhing on the ground, black and white together, several severely maimed for life.

Later reports reveal that the two ANC terrorist bombers bungled their efforts and vaporized themselves. From this point onward any residual human consideration for the ANC evaporates. They have now shown what they truly are, and any pretense to any form of moral ground is just preposterous. The government now "takes off its gloves" in dealing with the ANC. Three days later, South African Air Force fighter-bombers strike at the ANC facilities in Mozambique. Mozambican president Samora Machel soon caves, signs an accord with PW Botha, and expels the ANC.

Watershed 1985 - "When the Soviet Union Collapses"

By 1985, our contacts in De Beers start using very interesting language. In their discussions, they talk about *"when* the Soviet Union collapses" and not *"if."* Of course, De Beers is kept from doing business in the United States because they are deemed to be operating a cartel, which they likely are. Nevertheless, their dealings with the Soviets on the subject of diamonds provides them with unique insight into the economics of what President Reagan refers to as the *"Evil Empire."*

Meanwhile, through my exposure to the military fraternity I learn that matters are heating up dramatically in Angola. The Soviets are hugely escalating the war effort and the SA Defense Force is under pressure in the domain of weaponry. However, by now the South African armaments industry has come of age and is particularly proud of its long range artillery system, the 155mm G5 howitzer, which has outstanding accuracy over the longest range of any such system on Earth. What we lack in air power, we make up for in artillery. Wide ranges of "bush bashing" mine-proof vehicles and armored cars have also been developed.

On TV, we hear day by day about the activities of some or other American called Randall Robinson who is inflaming the United States against South African white people. Furiously beating a political drum behind him is Desmond Tutu, radical black Anglican churchman in South Africa.

After Nelson Mandela rejects the offer by PW Botha in February, the ANC ramps up its civilian bombing and killing campaign. Major unrest starts in March, the month after Mandela's rejection. Marches are held in several places in the country. In April, the ANC attacks the buildings of the Anglo American business corporation, it launches two grenade attacks inside black townships in Pretoria, three bombs explode at the Brakpan police barracks and the Commissioner's Court in town is attacked. A military medical facility is attacked in the same month, as are the offices of the Southern Cross Fund, where fourteen people are injured. Attacks on the homes of policemen now become regular news. Soon after, attacks start on the homes of Indian politicians taking part in the tri-cameral parliament that PW Botha has instituted. A lot of the violence seems centered on the Durban area where the amaZulu are the main indigenous population.

The international condemnation of South Africa has reached fever pitch, and it just gets worse after PW Botha's much-lamented "Rubicon "speech (See this Chapter: *The Fifth Great Abandonment*). The author, for one is hoping to hear some sort of plan from PW Botha in the speech. Even Foreign Minister Pik Botha has drummed up the expectation. We are all glued to the TV to hear what "PW" will announce.

When no significant announcement follows, I just know that my country will suffer the hysterical wrath of the entire West. On the other hand, they are drumming us into hell anyway without any proper understanding of the situation. From the perspective of the Western Media, the ANC can apparently do no wrong despite "necklacing" and brazen terrorism, while South African whites can somehow only be evil. I am convinced the Western Media wishes us dead, because they never offer us any form of hope.

Emboldened by all the new support from Western countries and wailing outrage from the United States promoted by Desmond Tutu and Randall Robinson of the TransAfrica Foundation, the ANC turns to the bombing of Supermarkets in the last week of September. Limpet mines damage *OK Bazaars*, *Game Stores*, and *Checkers* and a further one is defused in a *Spar* supermarket. All these supermarkets are located in central Durban near where the author's mother, Nickie, works (*NF89*). It is in this month, in the middle of all this unrest, uncertainty, and bombs exploding left, right, and center, that our only child, a son, is born.

Starting in November of the year, the ANC turns to the use of anti-tank mines[56] in the northern farming region along the Zimbabwean border (See this Chapter: *PW's "Total Onslaught" comes true*). However, regular anti-vehicle mines are not considered good enough for the job of terrorizing the farming population. Instead, the ANC employs Soviet supplied anti-tank mines. In the second and third weeks of that month, farmers drive over these mines with terrible consequences. On 15 November, farmer Jan van Eck, hits a landmine near Messina. The carnage was extreme, given that it is an anti-tank mine. Five people die and five are severely injured. Three of the dead are children aged two, eight and ten. On the 19th of the month, another farmer runs his car over a similar landmine at Weipe, a few miles to the west.

Amanzimtoti, Natal: 23 December 1985

Nickie, the author's mother, lives in an apartment in the SANLAM tower building in the southeast coast tourist town of Amanzimtoti, some 18 miles south of Durban city, where she works. The building is the largest structure south of Durban and towers over the general area. It is home to a few thousand middle class white people, most of whom work in Durban. Part of the complex is an *OK Bazaars* supermarket. In Fig. 24-4, the supermarket is on the ground level, immediately adjoining the tower block. The apartment occupied by Nickie is on the 16th floor, right at the middle of the building, facing the ocean. She buys her groceries from the *OK Bazaars* supermarket on the ground floor every day.

Nickie works as regional manager of a magazine distribution company in Rossburgh, Durban, near the Bluff. On 24 October 1985, two black ANC operatives are killed and one injured when they bungle the setting of a limpet mine at the nearby Grosvenor Girl's School and the mine detonates prematurely.

Many, if not most South African factories shut over the Christmas period and the first week in January. This is high summer in South Africa. This is also the time when many mine workers go home to their countries various. Over this period holidaymakers stream into Amanzimtoti and every form of accommodation is packed with people. The shops are dedicated to making as much money as possible from the crush of visitors from the Johannesburg area.

So it comes to pass that, around midday on 23 December 1985, with the town of Amanzimtoti bustling with Christmas beach tourists, a young Zulu ANC trainee and an accomplice elect to bomb the mall at the OK Bazaars in SANLAM Center. During his trial a few months later, the terrorist bomber under the leadership of ANC "military" commander Joe Modise, will state quite openly in court[57]:

"... I had seen that the area had a lot of white people. Before placing the mine, I debated over it. But on Monday I decided to do it, racial as it was. I knew the people were innocent and had nothing to do with the government."

They set the timer on the Soviet limpet mine supplied by the ANC and place it in a trash can at the supermarket. When the device explodes, it instantly kills five women and children and maims and injures more than sixty others. The dead include two young white boys named Johan Smit and Willem van Wyk. The rest of the dead are white women who were doing grocery shopping for their families in the middle of the day. Over the next few days, wreaths mark the spots at the supermarket where the people died.

Two weeks later, on 9 January 1986, a bomb explodes at the Jacobs electrical substation near Nickie's workplace. When Police arrive to attend to the site, a second

Fig. 24-4 The SANLAM Center complex in Amanzimtoti

bomb detonates and kills one policeman, injuring another and two electricity workers. On 20 January, four limpet mines on a power pylon explode. Again, a fifth mine explodes afterwards, but this time there are no injuries. Early in February, another mine explodes at an electrical substation in Durban and then two police vehicles are destroyed in bomb blasts. This is clearly a terror campaign and it is sent against people like us by Joe Modise of the ANC.

On 10 February 1986, fewer than 6 weeks after the fatal bomb explosion in the SANLAM center, Nickie arrives at the *OK Bazaars* to buy groceries at the end of a busy day. The next moment she is hustled out of the building by the Police. A large ANC bomb has been discovered in the center and is being disarmed. This second event is recorded for posterity but is not much reported in the news. Bombings have become an everyday event and one routinely looks under one's car, because several limpet mines have been found, and some have exploded, under civilian cars. Black security guards with mirrors on 5 foot staffs are now a common feature at the vehicle entrances to public facilities.

In February 1986, the 19 year-old Andrew Zondo is arrested for the SANLAM center bombing and confesses. He reveals that he trained in Angola from August 1983 to late 1985. He states that he targeted the shopping center after deciding that he could not bomb the local police station alone. In April, he is duly given five death sentences and is hanged on 9 September 1986. The ANC will claim that they never really meant to kill people. It is difficult for a rational human to believe this statement. They were obviously encouraged by the carnage of the first bomb, reveled in the outrage of whites, and tried a second time with a more powerful device. We check the international news, but all we hear is unrelenting condemnation of the South African government and not a single word objecting to the actions of the ANC. Through the eyes of the Western Media the ANC can do no wrong.

The Western World has clearly lost all objectivity on the matter of South Africa. Just as Britain lost its moral compass in 1899 before the Boer War, the West has lost its moral compass 86 years later. We conclude they want us dead, just like the liberal socialist Northern European professor at IBM (*NF90*). Our mere existence is an affront to their efforts to assuage their guilty conscience. The South African government might very well be out of touch with reality, but the true base evil here is the mass psychotic guilt complex of the West, which it is taking out on us. It would have taken nothing for men of honor in the West to object to the ANC violence. However, Christians and so-called Liberals in the West have mysteriously lost their voices when white people die. Only the deaths of blacks are lamented.

The Zulu-Pondo War

In Amanzimtoti, Nickie has moved to a little two-story condominium in a building at the far western end of the village. It is, in fact, the westernmost residence in that area of the village. A road passes immediately to the west of the condominium. Across that road is the Umbumbulu Zulu territory where Chief Gatsha Buthelezi is the leader via his Inkatha Freedom Party. To the north of this piece of land lies Kwamakhuta, a sprawling Zulu township with lots of poor Zulu families. In short, the world of the amaZulu is right on her doorstep across a length of farming fence.

Fig. 24-5 ANC terrorist bombs set around Durban in 1985-1986

IsiXhosa speaking amaPondo men from the Transkei further south have started moving into this Zulu area. The Pondo are ANC supporters. Matters at first proceed peacefully. However, many Zulu men, mostly Inkatha supporters, work on the Johannesburg mines. When these tough traditional Zulu migrant mineworkers return home, they find the amaPondo on their territory. Later analysts will seek other explanations for the violence. They will ascribe it to an increased squatter population and disagreements[58] between the local Zulu Chiefs and the government of the Transkei Xhosa Homeland, of which Pondoland is the northern part.

When Nickie comes home one evening, she notices smoke rising in the direction of Kwamakhuta. At first, it does not strike her as significant, but after a while a peculiar smell becomes evident. She soon realizes that the smoke has increased a lot. Then she hears a peculiar rustling sound which shortly resolves into a rattling on the breeze. And then the black line on the horizon appears to come alive with thousands upon thousands of black men running. They are terrified amaPondo, running for their lives and they cover the entire field of view like a sea of ants. Between 20,000 and 40,000 Pondos are fleeing en masse[59].

Behind them, comes the traditional Zulu Army on the warpath, dressed out partly in western clothes and partly in various cultural animal skin adornments, wearing their distinguishing headbands. They have their cowhide shields and are rattling their spears against these, creating the intimidating rustle as they chase the frantic Pondos, just as when they attacked the Voortrekkers in 1838 (See Chapters *11* and *12*).

It is at this point that Nickie realizes that the peculiar smell is a mix of smoke and male perspiration from thousands of Zulu and Pondo bodies. It is the year 1986 and the Zulu Army of 1838 is rushing past her home at full tilt, called up by telephone! Behind it all the huts are blazing. And then, as though to complete the absurd tableaux, a little police van comes riding slowly along the road that separates her condo from this "19th century" Zulu War. In the back of the van is a policeman with a single mounted machine gun – this to separate Western Civilization from the "1838 Zulu Army" in full charge.

It is testimony to the incredible discipline of the Zulu that they leave the white people alone while they focus exclusively on attacking Pondos. The latter flee into the coastal white villages where the South African Police protects them and puts them onto trains that are rolled in specially for the purpose.

Some time later the Pondos are railed home to Pondoland to the south. However, since the coastal railway line down Natal only runs a limited distance, they have to be railed many hundreds of miles all the way through the Orange Free State around the independent Kingdom of Lesotho in order to arrive back in Pondoland, just a few miles down the road to the south of their starting point.

1986: Terrorism, terrorism, terrorism.

In Pretoria, the author's home is on a sloping hill immediately south of Silverton suburb. Beyond Silverton lies the black suburb of Mamelodi. In 1980, the ANC attacked the Volkskas bank in Silverton, near our home and killed two white women[60]. Our post office is in Meyerspark, little more than a mile to the east as the crow flies. On 24 April 1986, a limpet mine explosion rocks the building. No one is hurt in the explosion. The mine was placed in a garbage can mounted against a lamppost outside the office.

In May and early June, a number of anti-tank mines again are set off on farm roads, but these are now in the Volksrust area, much closer to Johannesburg. The mining of farm roads is therefore

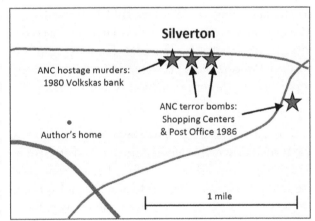

Fig. 24-6 *ANC terror attacks near the author's home*

no longer a matter of border regions and the ANC cannot claim that it is a guerrilla activity at the "perimeter of the enemy." In the same period, grenades are thrown into the house of the Wentworth School principal and he and his wife are injured in the explosions. Various supermarkets across the country suffer bomb attacks. In May, police disarm a 30lb bomb placed under an ordinary civilian vehicle in Durban. In the wake of all this, PW Botha announces a renewed State of Emergency on 12 June 1986. For this he is lambasted in the international media, but little if any mention is made of why he has taken this action.

Just two days later, on 14 June, a massive car bomb explodes at the Magoo's Bar at the Durban waterfront. The attack is carried out by three ANC terrorists under the leadership of a Coloured[61] man, Robert McBride[62]. He will later claim he saw this public bar as a military target. The dead are three young white women and sixty-nine people are injured. Nickie feels the vibration of the bomb where she works in the basement of a building 3 miles away. As usual, the main victims of ANC terrorism are yet again civilians. Fewer than three weeks later, on 4 July 1986, a limpet mine explodes at the Checkers supermarket in Silverton near our home. Twenty shoppers, mostly black people, are injured and maimed for life. Six days later, another ANC bomb explodes in Silverton injuring seven people.

We list here merely a few terrorist bombing events in order to illustrate the situation as it impinges on one white South African family that does not suffer direct injury in the attacks. These events happen against the background of constant attacks, bombings and anti-tank mine explosions which kill and maim innocents all over the country as per the table already provided. The international media still refuses to condemn the ANC's attacks on innocent people. We now simply ignore the world media, which is baying like rabid animals against the South African Government. We hope to remain as rational as possible in making our own decisions. This becomes extremely difficult when Winnie Mandela makes her murderous statement at Munsieville (See this chapter: *Total Onslaught becomes Total Horror*). In the same sick tirade, she makes veiled threats against white babies by suggesting their black nannies could have killed them but have not. Our son is a seven-month-old white baby and he has done this Mandela woman nothing.

Ordinary life and work

In our organization, we realize the country is undergoing major change. The government itself has completely lost interest in our research and development work. We are busy re-arranging the organization to become as self-funding as possible. My own dream is to get Defense Advanced Research Project Administration (DARPA) funding from the US Military. It is a forlorn hope under the circumstances, but it will remain a goal, and we shall return to this matter in this work. A small point of light is the announcement of the Dutch Reformed Church that it is finally breaking its links with Apartheid as a policy.

At this point, the United States imposes sanctions in nearly all domains on South Africa and stops all loan facilities. It effectively "cuts up the South African national credit card," "forecloses on its mortgage," and "stops it mortgage line of credit." Car manufacturers like Ford and GM flee the country and numerous other companies follow. The German (BMW, Mercedes, and VW) and Japanese manufacturers (Toyota, Nissan, and Mazda) do not follow suit. This is largely a massed American commercial exodus, having worked themselves into an anti-South African frenzy. South Africans buy the US holdings and some cleverly register trademarks such as "Macdonalds." However, it is the US financial sanctions that hurt. Credit is the Achilles Heel of any sophisticated western economy, as the United States would experience to its own enormous cost in 2009.

*****

On a visit to the United States in 1986, I am treated like an enemy. Requests to visit high tech companies are turned down and where I do get to visit, I am confined to sitting in the lobby like a Soviet visitor. It is so bad that a vice-president of a huge United States high technology corporation personally apologizes to me for the treatment and invites me to join him at his home in Pebble Beach for a weekend. In Britain, I have verbal abuse slung at me by a limo driver all the way back from the company I visit to the hotel. I elect to get out of the limo and walk the last mile. We are the skunk of Western Civilization. Nowhere outside South Africa do I detect even a glimmer of effort to comprehend what is really going on. The Western World has bought hook, line, and sinker into a narrative that exploits its guilty conscience at our expense.

*****

I am now a grown man with a responsibility to my only child that stretches beyond my own life and South Africa is literally a bloody mess. Soviet limpet mines and anti-tank mines are exploding everywhere, planted by the ANC. However, the words of De Beers people stick in my mind and give me hope:

"WHEN the Soviet Union collapses… ."

—*End Nexus Familia*

-----ooOoo-----

25

The War for Africa

"Mr. Gorbachev, tear down this wall!"

U.S. President Ronald Reagan
At the Berlin Wall, West Germany (June 12, 1987)

The United States rejoins the Fray

On 25 October 1983, the world knew that there was a new United States on the world stage. The superpower had invaded the little island country of Grenada, ostensibly to rescue some American medical students from the island's St. George's University. As a war it was hardly worth a mention. However, it demonstrated that America had regained some modicum of pride as a nation. It was ready to confront the U.S.S.R and its Cuban allies, who had had essentially a free hand internationally during the Carter Administration. Some 700 Cuban military personnel and 60 Soviet "advisers" had been sent to the former British colony of 100,000 people to bolster a coup to which the United States objected. This was also the first time that the world saw American soldiers with their new Kevlar helmets. The result was a foregone conclusion. Nevertheless, it showed that President Ronald Reagan was prepared to use military force for a suitable cause, albeit against a tiny and weak state.

By mid-1985, about the time that the anti-South African debate in the United States reached its apex, and with President Reagan in his second term of office, the United States had grown confident enough for Congress to vote for the lifting of the Clark Amendment (Chapter 22: *Angola – The Fourth Great Abandonment*).

Fig. 25-1 *US President Reagan delivering the Berlin Address*

Soon afterwards, covert weapons shipments to UNITA in Angola were resumed. This time, as in Afghanistan, it took the form of American FIM-92 "Stinger" shoulder launched anti-aircraft missiles[1]. There were strict instructions that these were not to fall into South African hands.

Association with South Africa was by now the international "kiss of death" and so the United States and South Africa cooperated independently with UNITA, essentially pursuing the same goal. The Axis campaign of 1986 against UNITA in Angola had been stopped before it could start by the simple expedient of damaging and sinking the supply ships in the harbor of Namibe (Chapter 24 : *Cold War sidebar*). However, at the strategic level the Soviets were hell-bent on scaling up the effort in Angola. This was done in tandem with the increased terror campaign of the ANC in South Africa initiated in 1985 and still very much in process.

In fact, the Soviets were building up for what would become the War for Africa. It was to turn into one of the nails in the coffin of the U.S.S.R., contribute in a big way to the Cuban "Generation of Disenchantment," and lead to the execution of a competent Cuban general. In particular, it was a key step in creating the "Break in the Weather" for which South Africans had prayed for decades.

Inside South Africa

The disenchantment with PW Botha among white people had been steadily growing. His finger wagging admonishing style did not endear him to anyone. People resented his apparently unthinking resistance to Western demands, as demonstrated in the much anticipated but disappointing "Rubicon" speech of 1985.

Against this background, a small knot of almost exclusively Afrikaner politicians and executives decided to meet with the ANC in Dakar, Senegal. PW Botha did not stop them, but called them "useful idiots." The leader of the delegation was Frederik van Zyl Slabbert, leader of the formal Opposition in Parliament. People with any degree of insight and pragmatism realized that the country was headed for a situation where the various parties would eventually have to negotiate.

At the strategic level, what was needed was that elusive break in the dangerous combination of external threat and internal unrest. Unless the Communist military threat on the border was disposed of somehow, there was no way an internal solution was going to happen. The matter of Namibia's independence was a side issue to this. Namibia was the buffer between South Africa and the Axis forces in Angola. If the threat from the Soviets and their proxy armies could be disposed of, independence in Namibia would be no problem.

This author today, with the benefit of hindsight, has absolutely no doubt that any potential concessions/negotiations announced by PW in the 1985 "Rubicon" speech (Chapter 24: *The Fifth Great Abandonment*) would have led to howls of feigned outrage by the Western Media and even greater masses of Soviet weapons on our borders. Nothing but our human destruction as a nation would have satisfied them anymore. However, in 1985 this author was still idealistic and thought PW should have announced a major plan. No one at the time, including the present author, seemed to give PW Botha any credit for what he had done. The international media preferred to only focus on the emergency measures and television scenes of police responding to the crowds, but never seriously reported on the removal of Apartheid legislation. So, let us enumerate for posterity exactly what positive changes this much criticized man actually implemented in South Africa, even if they did not go as far as some may have hoped. It can certainly be argued that it was too little too late, but that does not detract from the fact that he did implement these improvements.

- 1978: Introduced a 99-year leasehold right on property for black people outside the Homelands in so-called "White South Africa." By 1986, it was extended to full property rights;

- 1979: Repealed the injurious Bantu Education Act at the root of bad education for Black people;

- 1979: started repealing the acts limiting Black unions and access to jobs. Completed by 1983;

- 1980: Abolished the South African Senate and replaced it with a multiracial body catering for Whites, Coloureds, and Indians. Black people were still excluded;

- 1982: Introduced legislation to create local black authorities thereby acknowledging their permanence;

- 1983: Created separate Coloured and Indian parliaments parallel to the one for Whites. The United States parallel would have been three separate Houses of Representatives feeding into one joint Senate. Black people were, however, still excluded from this;

- 1984: Granted freehold property rights for black people outside the homelands;

- 1985: Repealed the "Immorality act" that forbade marriages and relationships across color lines;

- 1985: Allowed mixed-race political parties, but separate voter rolls remained;

- 1986: Repealed the laws that had governed the forced removal of people to homelands;

- 1986: Repealed 34 further laws that governed "squatting" by blacks and their removal to homelands;

- 1986: Repealed the historically hated passbook laws;

- 1986: Granted formal citizenship to blacks born in SA before their homelands became independent;

- 1986: Granted freehold rights and freedom of movement in South Africa for citizens of homelands;

- 1988: Repealed laws that barred access to some universities and their residences for black people.

While implementing these positive changes, the unrest in the country forced PW to declare a State of Emergency on a number of occasions. By now, the West was not interested in improving the lives of black people in South Africa. They wanted a black government. Nothing else would satisfy them anymore.

Eventually, it would be the much maligned PW Botha who would initiate the peace process with Nelson Mandela. Mandela would visibly retain more respect for PW than for his successor, De Klerk, and would be one of the more complimentary voices at the time of PW's death. Lesser political characters, including Desmond Tutu, criticized PW in death.

Nexus Familia 92: When the Soviet Union Collapses

About the future

In 1986, a man named Clem Sunter, a scenario planner with the De Beers-Anglo American business fraternity, makes a presentation to the Cabinet of the Government of South Africa[2]. In this presentation, he confronts his audience with a choice between a "high road" and a "low road." One of the integral aspects of this scenario map is the intriguing belief that the Soviet Union is on the verge of collapse. The close business relationship[3] between De Beers and the Soviets is well known and it is likely that this company has more insight than anyone else on earth into the strength of the Soviet economy, or the lack thereof. In fact, the U.S.S.R. is teetering on the brink, but even the CIA seems to not appreciate this[4].

By middle 1987, in the workplace of the author's research and development organization, we are reorganizing ourselves in terms of what we see as the most likely future scenario. The author is part of a scenario-planning group that concludes a scenario in which there is an ANC government by 1992, based on the Soviet threat having been disposed of. We specifically base this scenario on the input we have from De Beers.

By way of contrast, another group in our broader organization generates a scenario that predicts a conventional war along racial lines being waged at Middelburg Cape by 1992, the town where the author was baptized, and scene of the Boer War executions. The particular group, as might be expected, does mostly defense contracting.

We joke cynically about "peace breaking out everywhere," but the planning is very specific and painful. As part of the process, we redirect our efforts toward electronic engineering and the application thereof. Hitherto, our efforts have been directed more towards advanced electronic materials. We shall turn our attention toward electronic components, our aim being to serve the industrial electronics and mining sectors of the country, rather than Defense, a sector that we anticipate will dwindle. However, outside the door the country is in the throes of huge unrest and the South African Defense Force is entwined in a grueling war with the Soviet Axis forces in Angola.

About the border

Over this period, I receive an invitation to visit the "Operational Area." This is generally understood to be the northern border of Namibia. This visit starts at Waterkloof Air Force Base in Pretoria on a DC-4 *Skymaster*. The aircraft has been suitably modified to reduce the heat signature from its engines. In this comparatively large four-engined aircraft, we make our way straight over Botswana to Grootfontein Air Force Base in Northeastern Namibia. From there, we set off again in a northeasterly direction to land at Omega, the San Bushman base in the Caprivi Strip.

Here I have the privilege of meeting members of the amazingly efficient Bushman tracker unit, Alpha (Chapter 22: *Angola – Henry Kissinger's War*), who fought so well in Angola in 1975-6. Their entire lives are entwined with the South African Defense Force, which looks after their families with good facilities, hospitals, schools, and the like. Since they now all speak Afrikaans, I get to chat with some of them. They tell me the Botswana border guards often beat them up when they try to visit their family in neighboring Botswana. In 1987, Black African people treat the San Bushmen as animals and in Angola, it has verged on genocide.

When we make our way westward along the winding Okavango River to Ondangua in Ovamboland, the pilots drop to fifty foot above the treetops to foil SAM-7 anti-aircraft missiles. They take ten-minute turns at the controls. Flying a large lumbering passenger aircraft like a Douglas DC-4 fifty foot above a tree canopy is not a joke. It requires the utmost in concentration. Indeed, when one of the pilots gets a break, he relaxes with his head against the seat and his eyes closed. We are allowed to stand in the door of the cockpit, but are not allowed to distract the pilots.

At Ondangua, we receive an overview briefing. Obviously, we all know that South Africa is semi-permanently and intensely involved in the military conflict in Angola, but this is the first time that I realize just how serious the situation actually has been lately. An entire parallel world has been in operation here in the north about which most South Africans have only a vague idea. The Soviets have shipped in thousands upon thousands of tons of equipment. Their RADAR coverage in particular is intense. They have shipped in numerous supersonic MiG-23 swing-wing aircraft with their distinctive ventral fins. The MiG-23 is lighter, more versatile, and more maneuverable than the earlier American F-111 counterpart that inspired it. It completely outclasses South Africa's French Mirage F1-CZ fighters and custom Mirage F1-AZ ground-support aircraft dating from the early 1970s. I realize that the Cubans now have air superiority at the strategic level. This means that our men are likely fighting under dangerous skies. By contrast, American ground forces have taken air superiority for granted ever since World War 2.

The Cubans also have more sophisticated SA-8 surface-to-air missile batteries. I am told no country in the West has yet inspected one of these and all of NATO would love a good look at one. More Cubans have also arrived. They are considered much more competent than the FAPLA forces and often more so than the Soviets themselves, who tend to be doctrinaire as regards tactics. This is very serious stuff indeed. No wonder PW has been going on about the "Total Onslaught." The irritating man has been right all along!

It is here, in the officers' "watering hole" in the military town with its blinding white sand that I start to appreciate exactly what PW Botha has been carrying on about. Why does he not just tell the general public? They would stand behind him in a flash.

At Ondangua Air Force Base, we are taken to the Vernon Joynt[5] bar. The bar is named in Vernon's honor for his contribution to the ordinary fighting men of South Africa. In 1987, South Africa he is highly respected as the developer of mine-proofing technology. This is what gives South African military vehicles their distinctive look and ensures that very few if any South African troops lose their lives to anti-vehicle landmines.

While at the bar that night, a knot of very senior military officers walks in and they are visibly excited. This is when one of them volunteers with great satisfaction that "our boys up there" have now so thoroughly demolished the Soviets that the extent of their humiliation is actually a problem. His thinking is that we South Africans should now just "sit still" to allow the Russians to decide to leave while they still have some dignity.

He muses about the legendary machismo that might cause the Cubans to do something irrational under these circumstances.

It is a while before South Africans in general start hearing about the Battle of the Lomba River.

About home and holiday

By 1987, we realize that our son has not yet spoken a single word. He has not even said the word "mama." We are starting to fear what this might mean. When we have his hearing evaluated, the answer that comes back is that he has a large loss in hearing in both ears. The audiologists recommend that we immediately fit him with hearing aids.

****

One long weekend, we visit the far Northern Transvaal, near the border with Zimbabwe. We are particularly interested in finding the famous Mapungubwe Hill, where archaeological gold relics were found many years before. This is a rather mystical place and we do our best to find the route there. In this process, I take a dirt road that leads towards the Limpopo River.

As we drive along the base of a hill, a white soldier in characteristic "bush hat" materializes out of the dry tropical bush by the side of the road and waves me down. Addressing me using the classical Afrikaans title of "Oom" (uncle), he suggests that I turn around because this road is just too dangerous. This is when I look carefully at the bush from which he has emerged and realize that I am staring down the barrel of a mounted machine gun in an expertly camouflaged emplacement. At this point, I realize that I am on the Weipe road on which a farmer and his family lost their lives to an anti-tank mine some time earlier (*NF91*).

In our car are my wife and my two year-old son. We turn back.

—*End Nexus Familia*

The Cold War in 1987

By 1987, the Cold War was entering its final phase. President Reagan had promoted his "Star Wars" Initiative with gusto and the Soviets had taken the bait, spending far beyond their economic capacity to try and match the United States. In effect, it seemed Reagan had scared the Soviet regime into bankrupting itself on military spending. At the same time, the Soviets were stuck with two costly wars from the Brezhnev era; the "Oil Sector War" in the north in Afghanistan and the "Minerals Sector War" in the south in Angola[6].

In the Afghanistan, in what would later come to be called "Charlie Wilson's War," the Soviets were near impotent in their fight with an elusive enemy that whittled away at their morale. U.S.-made Stinger missiles were removing the much-vaunted Soviet Mi Hind helicopter gunships from the sky with impunity to shouts of "Allah u Akbar." Russian and Ukranian soldiers were deserting to the Afghan Mujahidin in frustration and dismay[7]. By 1987, the Soviets had already lost the vast majority of the 14,300 men they would eventually[8] lose in this war.

In the south, in Angola, in what would later become known as the War for Africa[9], they fought by proxy, using young Cubans as cannon fodder, who in turn squandered the blood of Angolans. However, in reality the costs came back to the Soviet Union and the Russian population was getting tired of carrying all this. After 12 years of war, the Soviets and Cubans were no nearer success than before, and distinctly worse off than in 1976 at the end of the original Angolan War. UNITA controlled the southeastern corner of Angola and could not be dislodged. Despite the inherent natural riches of Angola, the country was in ruins. The South African policy to keep the Soviets and Cubans hemorrhaging was working superbly.

By 1987, Star Wars plus the two actual wars combined with the inherent mathematical fallacy of Communism to put the Soviets in an economic quagmire from which they had to escape if they were to have a future. By this time, no one believed any further Soviet "Five Year Plans" based on the "work of the proletariat." The theoretical dream of a Communist nirvana had been proven to be exactly that; a theoretical dream. Something had to give in this strained Soviet picture. The moment of truth had come.

The War for Africa – 1. The massing of Soviet and Cuban forces

In early 1987, it became clear to the South African military that the Soviets and Cubans were building up for the most comprehensive assault to date in Africa. Crocker has suggested it was the Soviet Army and Communist Party that forced this campaign and that Gorbachev's Perestroika men were not involved[10]. The South African conclusion was that this drive was not just against UNITA, but likely was aimed quite particularly at the South African forces that had repeatedly intervened in favor of UNITA. By one account, there were between seventy and ninety Soviet "advisers" with each FAPLA brigade. One captured Angolan soldier reported that there were six Soviet advisers per FAPLA company.

Fig. 25-2 Angola 1987

In fact, the Soviet Foreign Ministry admitted that Soviet troops were manning[11] much of the hardware placed with the Angolan FAPLA units, including tanks, helicopters and, in particular, surface-to-air missile batteries, which now included very capable long range SA-8 "Gecko" systems. He was careful to insist they were not doing any fighting. South African officers told the author in private conversation that there were in effect three different RADAR networks, one each for the Soviets, Cubans and FAPLA, because none of the three parties fully trusted the competence or motives of the other two. It resulted in what was according to some, not just the densest RADAR coverage on the planet at the time, but also the most confused.

The first moves in the campaign were detected by South African Reconnaissance teams in March 1987. By July, the scope of the effort was clear. Bridgland states the South African command reeled in shock when it realized the scale of the Soviet commitment in weaponry[12]. Nevertheless, something had to be done.

Around the same time the CIA was providing intelligence[13] to the South African Defence Force based on the interrogation of senior Cuban Air Force Brigadier-General Rafael Del Pino Diaz who had defected to Key Largo in a light aircraft on 29 May of the year. He had served in Angola.

The Angolan theater of operations may be understood by reference to Fig. 25-2. UNITA's territory for some years had been defined by the Cuito River on the west, the Zambian border (the Cuando River) on the east, Namibia to the south and a huge "no man's land" to the north of the Lomba River and south of the Benguela Railway line. Ever since Portuguese days this parallelogram-shaped box of land had been known as the "Land at the end of the Earth."

Savimbi's headquarters was at Jamba, but he maintained an airstrip at Mavinga. It is here that the Soviet Axis force was headed, as it was obviously key to UNITA's entire defense. It was needed for supply flights from South Africa and Zaire. FAPLA maintained a forward air base at Cuito Cuanavale, and another at Menongue, the former Serpa Pinto. Cuito Cuanavale had been in Soviet Axis hands since the war of 1975/6 and had been the final launching point for most previous Axis campaigns.

The Cuito River is a major tributary of the Okavango River, which provides the supply of water for the world famous Okavango Swamp in the Kalahari Desert. The Cuito is large by Southern African standards. At Cuito-Cuanavale, it is joined by the Cuanavale River. Fig. 25-3 shows the size of this river at this strategic point. Except for an insignificantly small number of structures, the town lies as a sprawling collection of buildings on the western side of the river, joined to the No Man's Land by a mile long bridge.

It is immediately obvious why the Axis garrisoned this town and not some spot to the east of the river. The reverse argument held for UNITA. There would be no reason for UNITA to occupy the town, unless they were prepared to penetrate much further west to the next natural defensive barrier. If the bridge over the Cuito River were to have been blown, any UNITA army occupying Cuito-Cuanavale would have been trapped with its back against the mile wide river. Hence the town was important to any army based in the west, but was of much lesser value to a guerrilla movement based in the east, as long as it was not used as an air base against the latter party.

West of the Cuito River, the Soviets and Cubans generally remained north of the Lubango to Cuito-Cuanavale road that roughly coincides with the 15th parallel, 200 miles north of the Namibian border. They generally avoided clashes with South African forces in hot pursuit of SWAPO[14] guerrillas attempting to infiltrate Namibia. Since SWAPO, a Soviet client organization, was founded on the Ovambo people of central far northern Namibia, immediately north of the Etosha Game Reserve, it focused its activities to the west of Cuangar. This coincides roughly with the region in Fig. 25-2 where the border is the straight line through the sand drawn indiscriminately by the German Colonial Authority in the previous century. This border bisects the traditional territory of the Ovambo people. This part of the countryside within Angola was known to the Soviet-Cuban-MPLA forces as the "5th Military District."

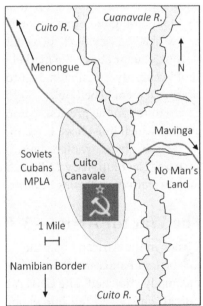

Fig. 25-3 Cuito Cuanavale - launch site of the Soviet offensive

The South Africans would go to great lengths to make it clear to the Angolans that their actions in this district were purely against SWAPO and not against Angola or the Soviets. Soviet adviser Igor Zhdarkin gives exquisite examples of this conduct, which included South African soldiers waving past a Soviet Intelligence officer before blowing up a road behind him[15].

The last element of note on the map (See Fig. 25-2) is the dam at Calueque on the Cunene River, which all parties had deemed off limits for the previous decade, as it supplied water and power to the inhabitants of Namibia, particularly the Ovambo people for whom SWAPO was ostensibly fighting with Soviet support.

By 1 August[16], the Soviets had armor in the form of T-55 and T-62 tanks and BTR-1 armored cars to a total of some 500 arrayed at Cuito Cuanavale. More MiG-23s and Sukhoi SU-22s had been supplied, bringing the total to 80 fighter aircraft. They had shipped in Mi 24/25/35 and Mi8/17 helicopters, bringing the total to 123. By this time, it was clear that FAPLA had a full eight divisions ready to launch the campaign, complete with their Soviet "advisers" in and on the aircraft, tanks, and surface-to-air missile systems. The Cubans were disdainful[17] of the Soviet strategic planning abilities after the 1985 rout (Chapter 24: *Cold War sidebar on West 44th Street*). Hence, they initially hung back in defensive duties, flying fighter-bomber sorties and freeing up FAPLA soldiers for the campaign. South African ANC members acted as scouts for the Soviet-led offensive[18], as did SWAPO members from Namibia.

The ideal plan for South Africa would have been to strike this advance in its flank from the southwest. However, that would have been impossible to hide in the more developed territory west of the Cuito River. South Africa was already reeling from international sanctions, particularly the financial sanctions from the United States. Ironically, the United States was now cooperating on the subject of Angola again. It was therefore decided to counter the Soviet initiative from the south through Savimbi's UNITA territory, the "Land at the end of the Earth."

On 5 August 1987, 32 Battalion again led the latest incursion into Angola from their beautiful game reserve headquarters in the northeast of Namibia under the leadership of Commandant Robert Hartslief. The

South African effort to stop and turn the final Soviet-managed campaign of the War for Africa would be named Operation Modular. The Soviets named their offensive *Towards October*, reflecting their own revolution.

Based on information supplied by Russian paratroop colonel Vyacheslav Aleksandrovich Mityaev[19], the man responsible for the planning of Towards October was Lieutenant-General Pavel I. Gusev. He was the Chief "Military Adviser" in Angola during the course of this war. Vanneman[20], quoting *Jane's Defense Weekly* and the *Washington Post*, disagrees and states that it was Lieutenant-General V.V. Shahnovich, assisted by general Mikhail A. Petrov. It seems only appropriate to respect the post-Cold War Russian source in this matter.

The War for Africa – 2. The talking starts

Up to July 1987, the United States, in the form of Deputy Secretary of State for Africa Chester Crocker, had negotiated with the Angolans, Soviets, and the South Africans. On July 27, he received a message from Fidel Castro that Cuba wanted to be part of the negotiations, and Castro later added that he wanted an "honorable" settlement[21]. He needed a face-saving way out.

The Cuban commitment in Angola had been more costly percentage-wise to the nine or ten million Cubans in blood and treasure than the Vietnam saga had been to the United States. The Angolans were also not maintaining their payments to Cuba.

Cuba was being kept economically afloat by the U.S.S.R. and by Soviet satellite countries buying Havana's sugar above the market price and supplying it with oil below the market price[22]; essentially a direct double subsidy of Cuba's adventures. The U.S.S.R. itself was strained beyond capacity to maintain this kind of arrangement. The Soviets had had enough. By 1987, they were curtailing[23] oil supplies to Cuba, causing Castro to ration the precious commodity. The new Soviet leader, Mikhail Gorbachev, was making Perestroika sounds, which must have been quite ominous from a Cuban perspective.

The Cubans wanted "out," but were now face to face with their own machismo culture and Fidel Castro's "Revolutionary Military Leader" personality. Unbeknown to the Cubans, Gorbachev's officials had already started contacting[24] South African officials directly at low level in early 1987.

The War for Africa – 3. "A stunning Soviet humiliation"

Back in the African bush, the decision of the South Africans was to let the Soviet-FAPLA force get as far as the Lomba River north of Mavinga and to then strike at them there, as their logistics supply line would be maximally stretched. The UNITA bases and the Mavinga airstrip were not far south of the river. The Mavinga airfield was not to fall into enemy hands under any circumstances, but the politicians in Pretoria were at some pains for the army not to get involved in a fight unless absolutely necessary. They had already engaged in negotiations earlier in 1985 with Chester Crocker and had accepted his basic proposals for withdrawal from Namibia[25]. However, this was all subject to Soviet and Cuban counter-performance.

Late on 24 August 1987, a South African commando team was inserted[26] 25 miles north of Cuito Cuanavale and they blew the key bridge (See Fig. 25.3) over the Cuito River, forcing the Axis to airlift all supplies over the river. This raid, however, is better known in South African circles for the fact that two of the frogmen had to battle crocodiles[27] irritated by Axis hand grenades thrown at the commandos in the floodplain of the river. Sgt. Beukman fought off a 10-foot crocodile with a knife and Maj. Wilkes had his scuba flipper bitten off.

By 29 August, the South Africans realized[28] that UNITA was in no position to stop the Soviet-led assault. It would be up to the South Africans to do the job and more forces were therefore committed. Colonel Deon Ferreira, former Commanding Officer of 32 Battalion, was brought in to lead the newly constituted 20 Brigade, which integrated its efforts with 32 Battalion and UNITA.

If any American ever thought that the U.S. Stingers were not available to the South Africans during this war, their illusions are addressed by author Piet Nortje, regimental sergeant major of 32 Battalion. He explains[29] that 20 Artillery regiment, pulled together for this defensive effort, comprised three batteries – Papa, Quebec, and Sierra. Four UNITA Stinger teams were attached to Quebec and two to Papa. In other words, the United States Stinger systems were deployed fully integrated with the South African forces. Had this been openly known in the United States at the time, there would have been the usual howls of outrage from the US media. One is left to conclude that US and South African operatives were simply more circumspect regarding the media in 1987 than in 1975 when Fred Bridgland's severely ill-timed report largely lost Black Africa for the West[30].

On 10 September 1987, the first T-55 tanks of FAPLA's 21st division attempted to cross the Lomba. They were confronted by South African Ratel 90 IFVs[31] equipped with ZT-3 anti-tank missiles. Three of the T55s were destroyed, stopping this first Soviet-managed attempt in its tracks. On 13 September, Papa and Quebec stopped FAPLA's 47th Division. At this point, it was decided that defensive actions would not be adequate and the South African forces would have to go on the attack. This was initiated on the 21st of September with three attacks by South African Mirage F1 fighter-bombers and heavier Hawker Siddeley Buccaneer bombers. On 27 September, the Soviet adviser contingent left[32] the field of battle by helicopter to Cuito Cuanavale and abandoned the FAPLA army to its fate.

On the night of 28 September, South African President PW Botha personally visited the front line on the Lomba River in Angola. The scope of the Soviet onslaught was finally comprehended at the highest level in South Africa. PW gave the order[33] to destroy the Soviet-FAPLA brigades east of Cuito Cuanavale.

The assault started on 3 October 1987, under attack from Cuban and Soviet piloted MiG 23 fighter-bombers. South African 61 Mechanized Battalion attacked the Soviet-FAPLA 47th Brigade with artillery and some air support. The description of the battle through Soviet eyes is extremely compelling. Lieutenant-Colonel Igor Zhdarkin recounted[34] the comments of his colleagues from the 47th Brigade, who said that they had never experienced horrors in Afghanistan such as those they encountered in Angola.

When the South African artillery barrages began, they became particularly terrified. And then came the South African Air Force while they, the Russians, had little space in which to reposition themselves. However, the most horrible for them was when the Angolans turned to flight and began to throw away their equipment. The Soviet advisors had to set fire to and abandon their armored troop carrier and then crawl, hugging the ground for one-and-a-half kilometers along the "shana"[35] to the other bank of the Lomba River. They were under South African fire all the way and threw away everything except their hand weapons. And then the swamps began.

We do not need to resort to South African sources to list the Soviet losses in this matter. Lt Col Zhdarkin, then one of the Soviet adviser group, states the 47th Brigade equipment losses in that single engagement as being eighteen tanks, twenty armored troop carriers, four D-30 (122mm) guns, three BM-21 "Stalin Organs," four OSA-AK (NATO SA-8 "Gecko") mobile surface-to-air missile (SAM) launchers, 2 Gecko transport vehicles, one P-19 RADAR system, heavy vehicles, radio transmitters, mortars, grenade launchers and 200 small arms.

Fig. 25-4 *SA-8 "Gecko" surface-to-air missile system*

It was as part of this assault that South African forces captured the first fully intact and operational SA-8 "Gecko" mobile SAM system ever to fall into Western hands. The system was quickly removed from the field of battle under fire from the enemy.

An American technical team[36] embedded with UNITA took extensive pictures of it at the time. The South Africans were surprised these units had operationally survived hundreds of miles of "bush bashing." This represented a major "catch" for NATO and the West, but South Africa got "first bite."

The SA-8 was the first mobile anti-aircraft missile system to have its own integrated target tracking RADAR system. The system was able to fire two missiles at one target and control both missiles at the same time. It was and still is a deadly threat to ground attack aircraft such as the South African Mirage F1-AZ.

The appearance of the SA-8 systems in the theater of battle foreshadowed the withdrawal of the lumbering 1950s vintage S.A.A.F. Canberra bombers. It became a battle of calculations – MiG-23s from Menongue or Cuito Cuanavale would take a certain amount of time to get to the area of the battle. The technologically outclassed S.A.A.F. aircraft would have to do their ground-support job in that period of time. They would also have to somehow evade the fixed Soviet Axis RADAR systems to get to the target area.

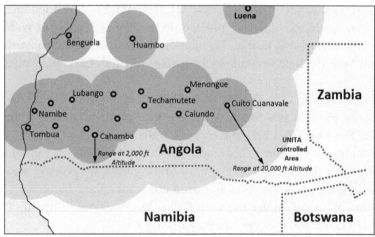

Fig. 25-5 The Soviet Axis RADAR coverage in Angola

The RADAR coverage of the combined Soviet, Cuban and FAPLA systems was very comprehensive, as shown in Figure 25-5. At 20,000 foot, their cover ranged into Namibia. To this, had to be added many batteries of Soviet surface-to-air missiles of different types, such as SA-2, SA-3, SA-7, SA-9 and SA-8. Yet, another dangerous variant was soon to make its appearance. According to Lt Col (then Lieutenant) Igor Zhdarkin these were all manned by Soviet "advisers"[37] because the Angolans simply could never come to grips with the control buttons that armed and directed the systems.

The fixed SAM batteries were arranged in so called *Kvadrants* of four mutually integrated launchers, all forming part of a countrywide system connected to RADAR and referred to as "*Pechora.*" The Soviets had clearly learnt from the 1973 Yom Kippur War against Israel how to effectively neutralize an entire air force using anti-aircraft missile systems. The Israeli Air Force had been all but eliminated in that campaign.

It is in these 1987 battles that the South African Air Force demonstrated their much-practiced toss-bombing technique. They would approach the target at very low level, in order to stay below RADAR. They would then rise very rapidly in a specific 45 degree path on approach, launching their bombs into an accurate ballistic trajectory. This usually resulted in total surprise for the enemy. The basic technique dated from earlier Cold War days as a means for delivering nuclear weapons. It gives the delivering aircraft the opportunity to escape the blast.

The South African aircraft were armed with proximity fused pre-fragmented bombs[38]. Each stick of eight bombs from a Mirage F1-AZ covered a swath of some 220 foot wide and 1300 foot long. Within that swath, everything but heavy armor took debilitating damage. The innately lower accuracy of the toss bombing technique was therefore entirely adequate to the challenge. The South African aircraft often raced home at 600 knots a mere 50 feet above the Angolan bush country[39].

South Africa was now the only Western country fighting the Cold War against the Soviets and, for its pains, it was treated as an enemy by the West. The country could not replace any of its front line fighter aircraft due to comprehensive weapons sanctions by the West. The pilots therefore had to be extremely circumspect in their flying to ensure that their precious aircraft came home. The French Mirages flown by the S.A.A.F. were roundly outclassed by the Soviet MiG-23 and their French air-to-air missiles were frustratingly unreliable[40]. When the Mirages were configured for ground support, they had a further increased drag factor which put them at a total disadvantage[41] with respect to the MiGs flying from nearby airstrips.

Ultimately, though, the real test of the South African Air Force was in how well it did its assigned job. We turn again to Lieutenant-Colonel Zhdarkin for his experience at the receiving end of the South African Air Force in its ground support role[42]. In his view, the South African artillery and aviation moved with impunity at all times, while their own aviation was afraid to show itself and, when it did so at all, remained safely at high altitude.

On the evening of 14 October, the South African long-range G5 howitzers were in position to start shelling Cuito Cuanavale 22 miles away and deny the Soviets and Cubans the key airfield. However, at this time several divisions of FAPLA forces were still on the "wrong" side of the river between the South Africans and the town. Sixteen MiG-23 and MiG-21 were stationed at the town, along with six of the infamous Mi-24 Hind helicopter gunships[43]. From the town it was a flight of just three minutes to threaten the South African front line. The South African Air Force, on the other hand, had to fly hundreds of miles from a makeshift base at Rundu in Namibia to the theater of operations. Their Time over Target was therefore limited.

In one of the best-executed electronic warfare deception operations in documented[44] literature, four S.A.A.F. Mirage F1-AZ aircraft[45] streaked northward toward Cuito Cuanavale at an altitude detectable by Soviet-Cuban RADAR. At a predetermined point, the Mirages dropped to below the RADAR detection altitude. At the same point, below them on the ground, Recces[46] released four special weather balloons with almost the identical RADAR signature as the Mirages. While the four Mirages streaked home at near ground level, the MiGs at Cuito Cuanavale were rolled from their protective concrete bunkers in order to "scramble." At this carefully timed moment, the shells rained down upon them from the G5 artillery some 22 miles away. One MiG-23 was destroyed and most of the others damaged.

Within the week, South African Recces had penetrated the perimeter of the Cuito Cuanavale defenses and were hidden in camouflaged "ratholes" near the airfield. From there they could radio-direct the artillery with devastating accuracy over their South African-made frequency-hopping radios (See Nexus Familia 93). Two Hind gunships were destroyed as they prepared to take off. By 28 October, the Cuito Cuanavale airfield had ceased to be operable[47]. The Axis MiGs now had to operate from Menongue, 110 miles away to the west. This bought the South Africans significant time before MiGs could be overhead after being scrambled.

During October, FAPLA consolidated its scattered forces in the north and tried again to advance south. By now, South Africa had moved its small collection of Olifant[48] tanks into position. On 9 October, there occurred the first classic combined tank and infantry assault by the South African Army since World War II. An Olifant versus T-55 tank battle erupted in which five T-55s were destroyed. When the South Africans broke through, they were attacked by flights of MiG 23 and Sukhoi 22 fighter-bombers executing heavy rocket attacks.

There is considerable evidence that the aircraft were flown by Soviet pilots.

Fig. 25-6 MiG-23 - wings in the extended low speed configuration

William Claiborne, reporting for the *Washington Post*, personally saw Cuban and Soviet pilots get into heavily armed MiG-23s[49]. By the end of that day, the FAPLA positions had been taken. Ten FAPLA T-55s had been destroyed, along with other armor and artillery. The customary heaps of Soviet weapons had been taken. FAPLA had lost 75 dead and four were taken prisoner. The South Africans had lost seven men and nine were wounded. One South African Ratel 60, much reported by the Cubans, had been destroyed.

On 12 November 1987, South African international spokesmen finally confirmed[50] that the South

African Army was fighting the Soviets and Cubans in Angola. That was the understatement of the decade. In reality, they were fighting the final clinching battles of the Cold War. By now, this was an out and out conventional war fought in a sea of bush in the "Land at the End of the Earth." The highest technology tactical weapons from both sides were by now deployed. The South African Air Force was about to deploy its new South African developed H2 TV-guided smart bombs, while the Soviets had moved in all their latest surface-to-air systems to suppress South African air attacks.

The South African and UNITA forces herded two Divisions of FAPLA, along with their Soviet advisors, into the small kill zone in the open floodplain of the Lomba River, reminding us of the Battle of Blood River of 1838 when Andries Pretorius had to make sure the Zulu were concentrated within the field of fire (NF63). Then the Mirages came in with their pre-fragmentation bombs. FAPLA was decimated and the Soviet plans lay in tatters with their carefully directed FAPLA army in disorganized[51] retreat. In his entry for 11 November 1987, Lt Col Igor Zhdarkin recounts[52] that the Angolans feared the South Africans "like fire," and when they heard that "Buffalo"[53] was part of an attack, they would throw away all their equipment in panic and flee.

The Soviet Colonel's description of the events of 15 and 16 November are certainly terrifying. He describes[54] the fate of the Angolan 25th Brigade, as well as the 21st, with which he was embedded. The South Africans had done thorough reconnaissance and the two Soviet-led Axis brigades walked into a nightmare of complete confusion and panic, with everyone running where they could. He describes his brigade as standing in the swamp with hands trembling and their eyes "squared" by fear, ready to throw away everything and run. They were hoping for relief from the 25th Brigade, but then he heard the chief Soviet adviser to that brigade over the radio, almost weeping as he swore at the Angolans who were abandoning all the equipment.

Apparently, the South Africans [who were in fact in a precarious position] had turned around and were cutting into the 25th Brigade. Again, when the FAPLA soldiers heard that they were being attacked by "Buffalo," they fled. The Colonel describes the hell of a South African bombardment. From his description, it appears to have been prefragmentation artillery rounds or tossed bombs. Whenever a round or bomb landed, they ran to that spot to stand there, in the hope that another round was not likely to fall there. He refers to the cries of the wounded and screams of horror, with shell and bomb fragments flying and whistling everywhere.

Fig. 25-7 The Soviet SA-9 "Gaskin"

U.S. Deputy Secretary of State for Africa, Chester Crocker, describes[55] how "*in a splendid paradox*" the Soviet Union had now become the major arms supplier to South Africa and UNITA[56]. Crocker proceeds to describe it as a "*stunning humiliation for the Soviet Union, its arms and its strategy*," especially given that they had shipped in $1.5 billion worth of arms for the offensive.

By February 1988, the South Africans were armed with captured Soviet SA-9 surface-to-air systems and Soviet 23mm anti-aircraft gun systems that they would use to protect Mavinga. Crocker maintains their FAPLA proxy army had suffered upwards of 4,000 dead and wounded. It had been the largest Soviet logistics effort to date, and it had failed in spectacular fashion.

It was at this point that the author happened to visit the Operational Area as an invited scientist (NF92). There he learnt of the events east of Cuito Cuanavale and officers suggested that South Africa would now largely just "sit still" and mostly ignore Castro's face-saving bluster that would no doubt follow. Their calculation was that the Soviets would "up and leave" and that would be the end of Castro in Africa.

The War for Africa – 4. The Incredible Vanishing Battle

At this point, Castro took direct command of the battle. The Soviets had yet again been trumped by the South African-UNITA army, which had completely destroyed the FAPLA offensive despite the help of one thousand Soviet "advisers" and technical air superiority. While the US Deputy Secretary of State for Africa was doing his shuttle diplomacy between the parties, Fidel Castro dreamed up a face-saving plan that could only conceivably succeed in a totalitarian dictatorship with no free press and among Castro apologists in the West.

While the South African Buccaneer bombers were attacking the bridge at Cuito Cuanavale with South African H2 TV guided bombs[57] to cut off the Axis supplies, and shelling the town's airstrip to deny it to MiGs, Fidel would attempt to turn this into the "Defining Battle for Angola." According to this myth, the South African plan was to invade the rest of Angola via Cuito Cuanavale. They had supposedly been stopped by the "Heroic Defenders of Cuito Cuanavale."

Castro went so far as to have special medals minted for this fictitious "heroic defense." The hilarity here is that the attack never happened. This is evidenced by the fact that the South Africans were in fact trying to destroy the bridge (See *Fig. 25-3*). The South Africans had no plan to take the town, because UNITA would never have been able to keep it when the South Africans inevitably withdrew, as always before. UNITA would have been stuck on the wrong side of the river with their backs against it. So, the only reason the town was an issue, was because of its airfield and because of its role as supply depot for the Axis armies to the east of the river. Furthermore, if the South African Army ever had any intention to take Cuito Cuanavale, they would have had to destroy the Soviet-Cuban air base at Menongue and turn the strip at Mavinga into a forward South African air base with RADAR cover. The presence of Axis air superiority aircraft such as the MiG-23 would have necessitated that. There is zero evidence of any attempt to render Mavinga useful to aircraft such as the Mirage F1. It was never anything more than a makeshift strip for covert shipments by transport aircraft. Tales of the harrowing nighttime transport flights into Mavinga abound, because the "runway illumination lights" were rows of UNITA soldiers with kerosene lamps[58].

Castro seemed to be taking a page from the tried and trusted British book on how to award medals. The Victorian British Army had made a massive issue out of the Battle at Rorke's Drift on the same day (22 January 1879) as the Zulu had slaughtered an entire British Army at Isandhlwana (Chapter 14: *Isandhlwana!*). In 1879 the Zulu had had no intention of taking any land beyond the Buffalo River (the river at Rorke's Drift) and had in fact been ordered by their king Cetswayo not to cross the river. The British had issued eleven Victoria Crosses for the Battle of Rorke's Drift; seven to one unit – the largest ever in history to one unit for one engagement.

Cuito Cuanavale would now fictitiously become the Cuban "Rorke's Drift," complete with "Victoria Crosses." This would make Cubans and the world at large completely ignore the "Isandhlwana" rout near the Lomba River that had effectively driven the Soviet-Cuban-MPLA alliance out of the UNITA territory in Southeast Angola. The only difference was that at Rorke's Drift the Zulus had actually crossed the river against orders and had actually attacked and the British had truthfully defended very bravely.

We do not have to believe the large number of amused South African officers who marvel at Castro's inventiveness. We may simply defer to U.S. Deputy Secretary of State for Africa, Chester Crocker, who naturally had the benefit of US satellite intelligence and no reason to love South Africans. He mocks the "heroic Cuban legend" as a case of claiming to a "credulous world" that Cuito Cuanavale was somehow the goal of the South Africans and then "crowing" about not losing it after having held it for a decade[59].

The logical reader will understand that a supposedly "invading" army would not blow a bridge across which it was hoping to invade the rest of Angola. However, in case that argument is too logical, we may also ask the Soviet soldiers stationed at Cuito Cuanavale what actually transpired during the supposedly defining "Battle for Cuito Cuanavale." We turn to Paratroop Colonel Vyacheslav Aleksandrovich Mityaev[60], who was one of the recipients of the Cuban *Medal for the Defence of Cuito-Cuanavale*. He describes how their BM-21 artillery had an ineffectual range of only 20kilometers, while the South African G5 and G6 artillery had (in his view) a range of 39 to 47 kilometers. He reports that the Angolans were the first to leave the town and relocate to a forest. Then the Cubans also left for the forest. They, the Russians, were left stranded in the town, as no one had arranged anything for them. So they stayed in their "little hiding-place."

Thus, according to a Soviet colonel who was there, the *"Heroic Defense of Cuito Cuanavale"* for which the medals were minted consisted of hiding in a forest from South African artillery bombardments. The disarmingly honest Lt.-Col. Zhdarkin is quite scathing about another Soviet commander who received the medal[61], stating that he "contemplated a warlike situation and made a speech."

By April 1988, the Boston Globe reported[62] what it called the *"Siege of Cuito Cuanavale"* in the context of the *"impending Soviet withdrawal from Afghanistan."* This shows how the Cold War in the South and the Cold War in the North were interrelated. The Soviets had finally had enough of the hot part of the Cold War. The routing of their biggest and best effort in Angola by the South Africans as part of what the newspaper described as *"one [of] the largest military engagements in modern African history,"* had brought matters to a head. In fact, the battles east of the Cuito River had been the biggest in Africa since El Alamein in WWII. Even worse for the Soviets, their defeat had occurred despite the much vaunted Soviet Axis air superiority which appeared to be very nebulous when it was actually needed. The series of engagements east of the Cuito River had certainly been the biggest land battle by far in the entire history of Southern Africa[63]. The Soviet generals back in Moscow would desperately try to escalate matters further with yet more weapons shipments[64], but Soviet Secretary-General Gorbachev saw the writing deeply etched on the wall.

Having effectively removed the Soviets as a threat and cleared southeastern Angola of MPLA and Cuban forces and pushed them north, the South African strategic position was to leave UNITA in charge of that area, withdraw, and settle the Namibian question from a position of strength. According to Russian editor Gennady Shubin, 107 Soviet generals and admirals, 7211 officers, more than 12,000 servicemen[65] (at least 30,000 in total if all personnel are included) had been cycled through Angola over the period from 1975 to 1987. It had all come to nothing for the Soviets. According to the unfortunate Soviet advisers[66] at Cuito Cuanavale, they had to withdraw westward through 180km of country that was now controlled by UNITA who had made no peace agreement. They were told to "look after their own security." This did not endear higher command to these much tried men.

All that remained to be addressed was the legendary Cuban machismo that bedeviled logic. In this respect, the Soviets even asked Chester Crocker to *"factor in Cuba's 'inferiority complex'"*[67] in his negotiations.

The War for Africa – 5. Castro's last bluster

Castro's plan was simple. He would sell this disaster to his own people as a great two-fisted strategy comprising a supposed "heroic defense" at Cuito Cuanavale, followed by a "victorious counter-offensive." To this end, he would:

- sketch Cuito Cuanavale as having been the main target of the South African counter-offensive,

- depict it as a victory for Cuba and the world at large against the "racist" South Africans, and

- make a dramatized demonstration towards the Western end of the Namibian border where the Western Media allowed him to operate openly, but where the "racist" South Africans would be predictably pilloried for "invading" by the same media.

For this he shipped more troops to Angola. Along with them came one of the most menacing surface-to-air missile systems yet, the SA-6 Gainful, which had so severely mauled the Israeli air Force 15 years before (Chapter 22: *On the holiest day of all*). Crocker[68] aptly refers to all this as being in keeping with *"Castro's 'strutting cock' school of grand strategy."*

The area of Angola that Fidel would now "take from South Africa" was really the occupied territory of SWAPO, the Soviet ally and United Nations favorite to run Namibia. South Africa certainly launched strikes into that area against SWAPO in hot pursuit operations. However, the South African commitment in men and materiel in that sector was not vaguely comparable to the scope of its commitment to UNITA in the east.

The only semi-permanent South African presence in the west was at the dam at Calueque, just across the border inside Angola. It provided the water for the people of Northern Namibia, particularly the Ovambo supporters of SWAPO, the ally of the Cubans. For several years South Africa had maintained a handful of men at the water scheme in far southern Angola where SWAPO had left them alone.

Nothing much came of this whole westward demonstration. Barring some minor exchanges, the South African forces simply pulled back across the Namibian border in that sector. The South African dynamic is best demonstrated by the last and most cynical event of the entire war. In a last glandular gush of machismo, Cuban MiG-23s appeared over the dam on 27 June 1988 and damaged it to no possible strategic purpose. Ten South African soldiers died when a single stray bomb hit their vehicle some distance from the dam.

South Africa did not respond in a major way, preferring to "sit out" Castro's "strutting cock" performance in this western sector, thereby allowing him to go home with his machismo in full bloom to

Fig. 25-8 Batteries of SA-6 surface-to-air missiles in the Middle East

delude his nation. After all, U.S. Deputy Secretary of State for Africa, Chester Crocker, had told Soviet Ambassador Adamishin that there was no way that South Africa was going to be *"bullied out of Angola"*[69].

Major Michael F. Morris of the US Marine Corps explains in his research analysis[70] of the War for Africa that a three thousand man mobile South African strike force defeated a combined Angolan/Cuban division size force bent on destroying UNITA. He is clear that the military outcome of the campaign convinced the Soviets and Cubans to settle for a diplomatic solution. Unfortunately, the Cuban nation, just like the Egyptians[71] in 1973, was left with a colossal lie and a set of cheap trinkets as reminder of the so-called "Heroic Defence of Cuito Cuanavale."

The Cuban soldiers did their jobs well enough in the battles that they did in fact fight, and generally won the respect of the South Africans. They had been clearly more competent and committed than the Soviet generals, who were doctrinaire, predictable in the extreme, and completely out of their depth in Africa. However, the brave Cuban soldiers are demeaned by this story concocted by Fidel Castro and doled out to gullible Third World leaders and his deluded admirers in in the West. Even Nelson Mandela, a man of some intelligence, was taken in by the ruse according to which Fidel was the "Savior of Africa" at Cuito Cuanavale.

Cuba suffered almost 15,000 casualties in Angola, Savimbi claiming 6,400 Cuban deaths and the defecting Brig. Gen. Rafael del Pino Diaz[72] claiming that 10,000 Cubans had died in Angola between 1976 and when he left. Of course, with his Soviet sponsors deserting Castro, their moderating influence also evaporated and the Cuban despot could say just what he pleased to his own nation. That nation desperately had to find a justification for the loss and suffering of such a massive fraction of its young men. Cuban parents would understandably cling to his invented story to make peace with the loss of their sons. The Castro government would tell them what to think and believe via a daily state newspaper called *Granma*. Other parents would flee Cuba to spare their sons being conscripted for what they themselves called the "Cuban Vietnam"[73]. The rest would shrug and believe the *Granma* tale.

In the broader human domain, it is a travesty. The long-suffering Cuban people deserve better. The ordinary South African soldier the author has met wishes the ordinary Cuban soldier nothing but the best.

They hope that one day Cubans will have a country that is truly free and a leader that is worthy of their expenditure in blood. Until then, that unfortunate nation will have to nurse a lie. The reader can decide whether to believe Fidel Castro on the one hand, or the U.S. Marine Corps, the U.S. Deputy Secretary of State for Africa, the Russian soldiers who were there, and South African soldiers who opposed them on the other.

The end of the Cold War

The War for Africa was all over bar the shouting and the South African military had done their country proud. In fact, the Cold War was over; the Soviet Union was imploding under its own bloated socialist weight. The "break in the weather" that South Africans had waited for, prayed for, and fought for, had finally arrived.

It would take a few more months for the results to percolate through the mire and mesh of international politics, but the results were obvious:

• The Communist revolution was now clearly a failure and the Russian nation and leaders knew it.

• The Soviet-Cuban assault on Southern Africa had failed, bled to death by the South Africans.

• The Soviet invasion in Afghanistan had failed, bled to death by the Afghans.

• Castro, the revolutionary "yapping lapdog" of the Soviets, was "up the creek without a paddle."

• Black Africa realized that it would have to deal with white South Africans as a permanent reality.

• The ANC faced a future without the bottomless support of the Communist Soviet Union.

• White South Africans had finally won their first ever pragmatic opportunity to create a country that was fair to all its inhabitants without having to fear for their lives or worse.

On 15 February 1989, the Soviet army finally crossed back into Uzbekistan[74], leaving Afghanistan behind. Fidel Castro proceeded to blame General Arnaldo Ochoa Sanchez for the disaster in Angola. Ochoa was the hero of several wars and leader of the Cuban army in the Ethiopia-Somalia War. On 12 June 1989, he was arrested. On 9 July 1989, in a Council of State meeting, Fidel announced that General Ochoa had been found guilty of racketeering. He was promptly executed by firing squad little more than three days later on the morning of 13 July 1989. The most powerful Cuban witness of the disaster in Angola, and the one most likely to air the facts, had thereby conveniently been removed. A deluded nation could rub the trinkets Fidel had handed out and would not ask him why he had wasted thousands of young lives and mountains of treasure.

In 1989, Soviet Deputy Foreign Minister Anatoly Adamishin met secretly[75] in South Africa with the South African government to discuss normalization of relations. Around the same time Cuba learned that it would no longer have a cozy "all fares paid" relationship with the Soviet Union. Castro was about to discover the difference between being the dictator of a fully paid totalitarian Soviet Client State and being a proper leader of his people. Unfortunately, his people, who had pointlessly spilled their blood in good faith in Africa to export his "revolution," would still be stuck with their geriatric despot, their cigars, and their badly outdated 1950s American sedans.

On 9 November 1989, the Berlin Wall finally came down and the Soviet Satellite governments of the East Bloc tumbled like dominoes. By one of those peculiar quirks of history, a newly united Germany now had in its Air Force the latest Soviet MiG-29 fighter jets. South Africa had heaps of captured Soviet equipment including several Soviet anti-aircraft missile systems. Several pieces of Soviet equipment ended up as targets on an artillery range in the western "desert" of the Cape Province. Communism had run its path and stood discredited by history. Similarly, Apartheid had run its course and stood discredited by history.

The time had finally come for the South African Government and the ANC to talk openly.

The inmate, the jailer, and the *Coca-Cola*

On 5 July 1989, four-and-a-half months after the Soviet Army rolled out of Afghanistan, PW Botha, the President of the Republic of South Africa, walked across the floor of his office with his hand outstretched. With a big smile on his face he shook the hand of his invited visitor. The visitor was none other than Nelson Rolihlahla Mandela, the jailed figurehead of the ANC, decked out in a new suit, a tie with neat double Windsor knot and nicely tied shoelaces. In order to understand the event and the curious[76] significance of the clothes, we need to retrace history just a little, starting at Robben Island in 1982.

Most people seem to believe that Nelson Mandela was incarcerated on Robben Island until his release in 1990. The truth is rather dramatically different. On 31 March 1982, after serving his life sentence for seventeen years and some months on Robben Island, Mandela and his fellow ANC prisoners were transferred to Pollsmoor Prison in the leafy Cape Town suburb of Tokai[77]. In 1985, Nelson Mandela was diagnosed with an enlarged prostate and required surgery. While in the hospital, the Minister of Justice, Kobie Coetsee, dropped in to visit. They only talked pleasantries, but it was a start. Upon returning to Pollsmoor prison after the operation, Mandela was placed in larger and better facilities, but separate from his ANC colleagues. During a formally requested visit with his colleagues, he explained to them that his new superior accommodations placed him in a position where he could talk to the government.

By 1986, the British Commonwealth insisted on having an "Eminent Persons" group visit with Mandela. This was arranged. Naturally, he told the group about the ANC Freedom Charter. In particular, he insisted to the group in the presence of Minister Kobie Coetsee that the white minority in the country should have a "sense of security" in any future South Africa. A few months later in June 1986 Coetsee and Mandela met again, but little happened. Then, on Christmas Eve 1986, the Deputy Commander of the prison, Lt. Col. Marx, asked Mandela if he would like to see Cape Town City. This resulted in a surprised Mandela, the lifetime prisoner, being taken on a tour through the streets of Cape Town by none other than his own jailer. In fact, they stopped at a shop where Mandela was left alone in the car while the Deputy Commander bought him a *Coca-Cola*. Mandela ignored the urge to flee and soon enough Lt.Col. Marx returned with two *Coca-Colas*.

This was to be the first of many excursions. One young warder even took Mandela to his home and introduced him to his wife and family.

"We do not want to drive you into the sea"

In May 1988, soon after the defeat of the Communist forces in Angola, the first formal secret talks started between Mandela and a core group of very senior government representatives, including Niel Barnard, the Chief of National Intelligence. Mandela was struck by the vehement resentment of Communism exhibited by these Afrikaners and their total distrust of the Whites and Indians that formed the core of the Communist Party in South Africa. He did his best to explain to them that the long-term goals of the ANC and the Communist Party did not coincide. Mandela records his words to his negotiation partners as being:

"We do not want to drive you into the sea."

When he took ill a while later, Mandela was committed to the Tygerberg Hospital in Cape Town. In American terms, Tygerberg is the "Johns Hopkins of South Africa." After being discharged, he was put up in the very upmarket Constantiaberg Clinic. He was receiving the very best care the country had to offer.

On the evening of 9 December 1988, the situation changed again and Nelson Mandela, the prisoner, was moved to Victor Verster Prison in Paarl in the winelands of the Cape. In fact, he was put up in a separate house within the compound, complete with swimming pool and all possible facilities of a normal home. There was one interesting addition; he was provided with a young white Afrikaner man to tend to his culinary needs. The young gentleman also had to clean up all the dishes. To crown it all, he was visited by Justice Minister Kobie Coetsee, who brought him a case of Cape wine as a housewarming gift and insisted on making sure he had all he needed. All in all, if Nelson Mandela was a prisoner, he must surely by 1989 have been the best cared for prisoner in the history of the planet.

The above series of events, as reported by Mandela himself in his own writing, proves that the interaction with the famous inmate was not spurred in the least by the campaign of the Cubans and Soviets in Angola. However, as soon as the Soviet-Cuban adventure had been neutralized as a threat, the discussions were elevated to a formal level. Fidel Castro will have the reader believe that his non-existent "Heroic battle for Cuito Cuanavale" somehow toppled the South African government.

Nomzamo Winifred Zanyiwe Madikizela - "Taking the dog away"

In 1986, PW Botha's government had allowed the wife of Nelson Mandela, Nomzamo Winifred Zanyiwe Madikizela, to return to her house in Soweto from her banishment in Brandfort in the Orange Free State[78]. She had promptly become an operative of the ANC's armed wing, Umkhonto we Sizwe (MK), and had started to assist MK "cadres" infiltrating the country from neighboring states. She provided accommodation[79] at her Soweto home to some disaffected youths from Soweto. By 1987, rumors abounded concerning the activities of these young people. The black community became incensed and torched her house on 28 July 1988. She thereupon moved to a new home in the Diepkloof extension of Soweto, complete with her gang of youths, who by now went under the name of the Mandela United Football Club (MUFC). By now, "Winnie" was assisted by US Civil Rights campaigner Robert Brown who had raised considerable funds in the USA for his activities in association with her[80].

The residents and associates of the Mandela household, including in some cases Winnie Mandela herself, would eventually be implicated directly or indirectly in a range of incidents, including assaults and abduction, and the murder and attempted murder of at least eighteen individuals. The abduction of four youths from the Methodist manse in Orlando West in late December 1988 and the murder of one of them, "Stompie" Seipei, in early January 1989, finally brought the matter to world attention. The Mass Democratic Movement, one of the synonyms for the part of the banned ANC operating in public, finally reached its tolerance limit for the outrages of the infamous "football club" and issued the following statement[81] in February 1989:

"...we are outraged by the reign of terror that the team [has] been associated with. Not only is Mrs. Mandela associated with the team, in fact, the team is her own creation."

The Truth and Reconciliation Commission (TRC) chaired by Desmond Tutu would eventually put on paper the following statement in 1998 in its report to (then) State President Nelson Mandela[82]:

"There can be no doubt that Ms. Madikizela-Mandela was central to the establishment and formation of the MUFC. Club members were involved in at least eighteen killings, for which many of them are still serving prison sentences. Many of the operations which led to the killings were launched from her homes. Witnesses who appeared before the Commission implicated her in having known of these matters, in having actively participated in assaults or in having assisted in cover ups and obstructing the course of justice. She denied all these allegations. In a number of incidents, people were labeled as informers, which 'legitimated' their execution by MUFC members."

With the benefit of the hindsight provided by the later report of the TRC, we focus on the period of January 1987 to February 1989. While there would be trials for the individuals concerned in the early 1990s, those would be actively and willfully starved of the truth. The later TRC hearings of 1997 would have the benefit of the confessions of the perpetrators who asked for amnesty. It would also have the benefit of statements by victims and their families. By then, these families would have no fear of any so-called "Apartheid Police." The most shattering revelations would relate to the closest confidantes of Ms. Mandela. She would later deny any knowledge of almost any of these incidents to the TRC. The only exception is the case of the assault on and death of Stompie Seipei (Case 9 in the table below), to which we return later. On that particular case, she would be charged. We address that court case in the next chapter.

From the cases listed below it is obvious that there was a culture of assault and murder permeating this group around Ms. Mandela. The killer-in-chief appeared to be Jerry Richardson, assisted by various members of the Mandela United Football Club. Within their culture, the word *impimpi* (informer) was equivalent to a death sentence. This term was apparently invoked for a number of different reasons; sometimes in respect of individuals who it was thought endangered Umkhonto we Sizwe, sometimes for brazenly personal reasons. An exceptional level of brutality seemed to permeate the group. On occasion, Ms. Mandela allegedly personally took part in the assaults and beatings. In one particular case, the father of a murdered young man would later testify that she went to the extreme of pointedly showing his badly beaten son to him before his death. We tabulate here the various assaults and murders associated with the Mandela United Football Club recorded by Archbishop Desmond Tutu's later *Truth and Reconciliation Commission*. We address only thirteen of the murders, not even counting the death of one policeman. The mere fact that a table is required to clarify even just part of the horrors of Ms. Mandela's "football club" speaks volumes.

1	**The murders of Xola Mokhaula and Mlando Ngubeni**
	Xola Mokhaula was executed in front of his family on the evening of 24 January 1987 and Mlando Ngubeni died in that process. One of the guns used in the killings was found in the bedroom of Ms. Mandela's daughter, Zindzi. Ms. Mandela's Audi was used in the killings. Three men were convicted for the killings.
2	**The torture and mutilation of Peter and Phillip Makhanda**
	On 26 May 1987, the Makhanda brothers, Peter and Phillip, were assaulted in the back rooms of the Mandela home in Orlando West. They had ANC slogans carved into their bodies and battery acid rubbed into their wounds. Two MUFC members and a driver of Ms. Mandela were charged in this case.
3	**The murder of Vincent Sefako and Susan Maripa**
	Sefako was deliberately killed by a car in Soweto in October 1987 and this event was witnessed by Susan Maripa. Later, Maripa was herself killed. The killings were tied to Mandela's MUFC.
4	**Assaults on Phumlile Dlamini**
	Ms. Phumlile Dlamini, claimed she had been assaulted by Mandela on more than one occasion, and that the MUFC had assaulted her for 5 hours in Ms. Mandela's house. Ms. Dlamini had a relationship with a certain Tau of the Mandela household, who had also claimed to have a relationship with Ms. Mandela.
5	**The murder of Thole Dlamini**
	Thole, brother of Phumlile (case 4) and one of the original members of the MUFC, was shot dead on 16 October 1988 for testifying against MUFC member Absolom Madonsela. Madonsela would later state to the TRC that he had given the order for Dlamini to be killed and would ask for amnesty. Later testimony would show an associate of Ms. Mandela, Sizwe Sithole, committed the murder.
6	**The deaths of Tebogo Maluleke, Sipho Mbenenge and Sergeant Stephanus Pretorius**
	Maluleke and Mbenenge were MK operatives who were accommodated at the house of MUFC "*coach,*" Jerry Richardson, a close confidante of Ms. Mandela. On 9 November 1988, Richardson tipped off the Police. In the ensuing police operation both MK members and Sgt. Pretorius were killed.

7	**The abduction and murder of Lolo Sono and Sibuniso Tshabalala**
	These two young men were (falsely) accused of being *"informers"* and executed. Sono's father would testify that Ms. Mandela brought his son for him to see in her car. The boy was badly beaten up. Mr. Sono senior testified that Ms. Mandela told him: *"I am taking this dog away. The movement will see what to do to him."* Mr. Sono never saw his son again.
8	**The murder of Koekie Zwane**
	Ms. Koekie Zwane, died of multiple stab wounds on 18 December 1988 inflicted by Jerry Richardson. Richardson would later apply for amnesty and would allege that she was killed on Ms. Mandela's instructions.
9	**The abductions and assault of Pelo Mekgwe, Thabiso Mono, Kenny Kgase and Stompie Seipei and murder of Seipei**
	On 29 December 1988, the four youths were abducted from the Methodist manse in Soweto, taken to the Mandela home. All four youths were viciously assaulted, but Seipei's condition was severe. In early January 1989, Seipei's body was found in a river-bed near Soweto. His body and head were riddled with injuries and he had been stabbed in the neck three times. His death was placed on 1 January 1989. Several MUFC members were arrested and charged with the assault and murder. Ms. Mandela herself was implicated.
10	**The murder of Dr. Abubaker Asvat**
	Dr. Abubaker Asvat allegedly examined[83] Seipei and advised Ms. Mandela that he would die if not immediately treated. Dr. Asvat was later shot to death in his medical office. Two men associated with Ms. Mandela were subsequently charged and convicted for Dr. Asvat's murder.
11	**The attempted murder of Lerotodi Ikaneng**
	Lerotodi Ikaneng and a man named Gift Ntombeni, both former members of the MUFC, would both allege that Ms. Mandela assaulted them and accused them of being informers. This related to Ikaneng making a statement to Police in another murder case (Case 5 above). Six weeks later on 3 January 1989 members of the MUFC and associates of the Mandela household tried to murder Ikaneng. Jerry Richardson (See cases 6, 7 and 8) would eventually confess to the TRC in 1997 that he led the attack on Ikaneng, and confirmed that Ms. Mandela and/or her daughter Zindzi had labeled Ikaneng an informer. Richardson would claim that he was congratulated by Ms. Mandela when he (erroneously) informed her that he had killed Ikaneng.
12	**The killing of Maxwell Madondo and attempted murder of Sibusiso Chili and Lerotodi Ikaneng**
	Madondo was killed on 13 February 1989. Members of the Chili family, Lerotodi Ikaneng (case 11) and two others were formally charged with murder at the time. They claimed it was self-defense and that Madondo had been sent from the Mandela house to kill Ikaneng and Sibusiso Chili. A man named Katiza Cebekhulu allegedly accompanied Madondo on a "mission" to kill Chili and Ikaneng on the instructions of Ms. Mandela. Several witnesses would later testify to the TRC that Ms. Mandela came to the scene after Madondo's death.

Both Cebekhulu and Richardson were key players in this sickening drama. Both will return to haunt the picture around Ms. Mandela a bit later, each in his own intriguing way. They would eventually produce startling revelations. By February 1989, the *Washington Post* was reporting on the situation.

The leaders meet as the violence continues

On 4 July 1989, Nelson Mandela was told he was to meet PW Botha the following day. On the morning of the 5th, Major Marais, commander of Victor Verster prison came to collect him, noticed his badly done tie, and tied it for him in a neat double Windsor knot. They stopped by Pollsmoor Prison where the commander's wife served breakfast for all of them. Arriving at Tuynhuis, the State President's residence, Niel Barnard, the "chief spook" of the Government noticed that Mandela's shoelaces were undone and knelt down to tie them for him.

From the description by Mandela in his book, it is evident that he and PW had clear respect for each other. Mandela's words in his book ring with historical clarity:

"Now, I felt, there was no turning back."

Nelson Mandela's faith in the future was possibly not shared by the operatives of his organization. Fewer than three weeks later, on the night of Sunday 23 July 1989, two young Umkohonto we Sizwe operatives set out to plant a limpet mine at a Magistrate's Court in the Cape Town suburb of Athlone. Polling nominations for an upcoming election were to be held there the following day and the ANC was opposed to these elections under the existing constitution. The ANC's approach to making its unhappiness known appeared to be that of bombing the relevant symbol of imperfect democracy.

The operatives were Robert Waterwitch, a BA student at Cape Town University, and Coline Williams, a drama student from the Bonteheuwel suburb. Across the road from the Magistrate's Court, an explosion went off. When the dust settled, the two young operatives, both from the local so-called "Coloured" community, had managed to blow themselves up with a limpet mine and their intended public target was unscathed.

Thereby, in order to protest an election among the very people it presumed to represent, the ANC had managed to blow up two of its own operatives behind a public toilet for that constituency; hardly an effective or inspiring way to oppose an election. To cover its technical ineptitude, the ANC would fall about desperately trying to get people to believe that the security services of the country had somehow adjusted the limpet mine to go off early. That way they could "justify" the deaths of the young people to the bereaved families, who were quite unaware of their children's activities. Tutu's later Truth and Reconciliation Commission would investigate the matter and would reach no conclusion as regards the government tampering with the devices.

By the standards of the West, people who bomb or attempt to bomb public courthouses are not guerrillas; they are terrorists, irrespective of their convictions or cause. This was also not the first time that a bombing effort of the ANC had gone wrong. The same had happened in Durban in 1986 (*NF91*).

*****

In August 1989, PW Botha resigned as State President, having suffered a stroke earlier in the year. This would be the key moment in exploiting the "Fall of the Wall."

Nexus Familia 93: Ordinary life among the chaos

One day in early 1989, while I am at home in Pretoria with our son, he suddenly starts to stagger and fall for no apparent reason. He recovers just as quickly. When we take him to the doctors and audiologists, it turns out he has lost most of his residual hearing. The doctor tells us to steel ourselves for a verdict of brain cancer. The verdict that comes back is that nothing is wrong beyond the loss of hearing. There is no real explanation forthcoming for the sudden loss.

While the audiologists advise us that there is no hope for our son's left ear, there is a little residual hearing on the right. They suggest that we put a hearing aid only on the right. The author, however, refuses to submit to this supposed reality and insists on the most powerful hearing aids on both sides. Peculiarly, our son's assisted hearing now improves in leaps and bounds, and he confirms the importance of the hearing on the left, however small. Since we realize the importance of having someone to talk to our son as much as possible, and since both parents are professional scientists with full time R&D jobs, the author convinces his mother Nickie to retire a few months early and to join the family in Pretoria.

*****

At work, most of the focus is on making our new organizational structure work. As part of the effort towards redirecting the organization as a whole, I am dispatched to the United States along with another strategic planning expert for a week around 4th of July 1989. Our task is to meet with various parties in the Research and Development field in order to investigate models for industrial financing of research and development. The visit is quite interesting, and all the parties we visit are quite helpful, but the most fascinating interaction is a totally unplanned event on Dulles Airport on the way to London, England.

Our British Airways flight has been delayed and, while walking around the airport building, I see my colleague in deep conversation with a stockily built gentleman with crew cut hair and a very military bearing. My colleague points at me and the man walks pointedly in my direction. I assume he is involved with airport security or some such function, but his suit seems very tight fitting for an American.

What follows is one of the more strange and simultaneously most gratifying conversations of my life. Without introducing himself, he states in a heavy northern British accent that my colleague has indicated that I have some friends in the South African Defense Industry. I confirm that. He then tells me that he was until very recently a member of the British Special Air Service (SAS) and that his last mission was in the Middle East. I can think of no recent involvement of the British in the Middle East. He then asks me whether I know anyone in the Grinaker electronics company in South Africa. I confirm that I do and that the company is quite close to my home. Then he puts his hand out for me to shake and says:

"When you get home, please thank those gentlemen on my behalf for their frequency hopping radios. One of those saved my life on my last mission."

On the way from London to Johannesburg, I sit next to an Alaskan trawlerman. He is on his way to South Africa to buy frequency-hopping radios, because the Russian trawlermen eavesdrop on the American trawlers' communications to locate the best trawling grounds.

It seems there is considerable scope for "beating South African swords into plowshares."

*****

Along with the rest of the world, we watch television in fascination in early November 1989 as the Berlin Wall comes down and East Berliners stream through to the West – a complete triumph for the Western Cold War warriors, including our own "Boys in the Bush," President Reagan and Mr. George Bush.

I fully realize that a key moment in history has arrived also for my own country.

—*End Nexus Familia*

-----ooOoo-----

26

The End of Apartheid

"Today we have closed the book on Apartheid."

South African President FW de Klerk
On the result of the 1992 referendum among whites

The end of Apartheid

On 20 September 1989, Frederik Willem "FW" de Klerk, leader of the National Party in the Transvaal Province, was sworn in as the seventh State President of the Republic of South Africa. He moved very quickly to remove the last vestiges of day-to-day discrimination associated with Apartheid as a policy. Mandela gives him credit for that in his autobiography[1].

Three weeks after assuming office, on 10 October 1989, FW announced that eight of Nelson Mandela's fellow ANC prisoners were to be released[2]. On 13 December, he and Mandela met for the first time, with Mandela still formally a prisoner in his peculiar jail with personal cook and swimming pool.

In the first week of January 1990, the apparently impossible happened quietly in Budapest, Hungary. South African Foreign Minister "Pik" Botha was received as diplomatic visitor. This was the first visit of a South African Cabinet Minister to a Communist state since the Iron Curtain came down on Eastern Europe. In the same month, Joe Slovo, leader of the South African Communist Party, penned an article[3] under the tile "Is Socialism dead?" in which he lamented the Budapest visit of "Pik" Botha. "Overnight" the world had become a very different place and Communists were an internationally threatened species.

Fig. 26-1 President FW de Klerk

On 2 February 1990, FW de Klerk stood up in parliament and announced the most sweeping changes in the history of South Africa[4]. Commentators all over the world were much taken with FW's announcements. This ostensibly heralded a new dawn in human relations in South Africa and a return of South Africa to the "Family of Nations" of the world. The announcements also represented a key moment in more than 300 years of Western history. They heralded the first permanent subjugation of a non-colonial Western nation to a non-Western one since the Turks were stopped at the gates of Vienna in 1688. To this moment can be traced the helpless condition of white people in South Africa in the 21st century, no matter how positive the changes may have been perceived at the time of their announcement in 1990. FW's announcements included:

• the ANC, PAC, SA Communist Party, and 31 other organizations were unbanned;

- members of those organizations jailed for non-violent activities were freed;

- the death penalty was severely restricted in its application; and

- a wide range of restrictions associated with the state of emergency was lifted.

In his address, he stated specifically that:

> *"The events in the Soviet Union and Eastern Europe, [...], weaken the capability of organizations which were previously supported strongly from those quarters. The activities of the organizations from which the prohibitions are now being lifted, no longer entail the same degree of threat to internal security which initially necessitated the imposition of the prohibition."*

Nelson Mandela himself states that[5], in one sweeping motion "FW" had virtually normalized the situation in South Africa. Significantly, Mandela was not released in that process. He had been jailed for his violence. FW would later add in conversation with Frederik van Zyl Slabbert that he made the announcements because he underwent a *"spiritual leap"* in which he *"accepted the moral untenability of Apartheid"*[6].

On 9 February 1990, Mandela was again taken to Tuynhuis to meet with "FW" and there he was told he was to be released the following day. After some discussion of the logistics involved, "FW" poured each of them a tumbler of whiskey. And so, with two tumblers of whiskey and a handshake South Africa took the first step on a path that would make it the extraordinary example the world had dreamed of.

The following day, the whole world watched as Nelson Mandela walked free from his special jail, leaving behind his exclusive house, his swimming pool and his personal white Afrikaner cook. Next to him strutted Nomzamo Winifred Zanyiwe "Winnie" Mandela with a grin on her face. One watched the seething mass of ululating black people around Mandela and remembered that it had been mobs such as these that had left in their wake burning bodies draped in melting gasoline soaked tires. More than a dozen crates and boxes of property that he had accumulated in jail followed Mandela separately. Oddly, no one now seemed to remember why he had been jailed in the first place and the myth was invented that he had been in jail for a quarter of a century for no good reason. The real history, as provided in this present text, would soon enough be rewritten by the Western media to erase Nelson Mandela's earlier dedication to violence. His own statements in his autobiography and later sanction of violence would simply be brazenly ignored by the media.

Nelson Mandela headed for the United States soon after his release, where he commented as follows[7] on Yasser Arafat, Muammar Qaddafi, and Fidel Castro, causing much raising of eyebrows:

> *"There is no reason whatsoever that we should have reservations about their attitude toward human rights in their own country. We have no time to look into the internal affairs of other countries."*

The end of the ANC "armed struggle"

In July 1990, the Security Branch of the South African Police uncovered a plan by the ANC, known as Operation Vula. It was aimed at the violent overthrow of the government by abusing the freedom of movement created by the negotiation process[8]. The individuals behind it were Jacob Zuma, Oliver Tambo, Siphiwe Nyanda, and core white Communists, Joe Slovo and Ronnie Kasrils. The exposure reputedly infuriated Mandela and his deputy, Thabo Mbeki, and led directly to the suspension of the ANC's so-called "Armed Struggle" on 6 August 1990. It had never amounted to anything significant.

Most white South Africans certainly did not comprehend what had been *"armed"* about the *"struggle"* of the ANC. Armed clashes between the ANC and the Security Forces between 1960 and 1990 were minimal. The ANC's own Soviet sponsors had lost all faith in the organization's so-called "armed struggle" by 1989, some in the U.S.S.R. calling it a *"glorified fund-raising exercise"*[9]. Data from the South African Defense Force (SADF) itself showed that only 4% of military engagements ever involved the ANC's Umkhonto we Sizwe, while General George Meiring of the SADF stated *"We never had one serious engagement with MK."*

The white population assumed that the ANC meant thereby that it would cease the necklacing of innocent blacks and the placing of limpet mines at supermarkets, post offices, schools, and restaurants. The later Truth and Reconciliation Commission, chaired by Desmond Tutu, would emphatically state that the armed wing of the ANC had in the end killed fewer security force members than civilians[10]. It seems the ANC's "Armed Struggle" had been against civilians, usually women or children, judging by the list of the dead.

Around the same time, de Klerk announced the shutting down of clandestine units such as the Police counter-insurgency unit based at Vlakplaas and the ridiculously named Civil Cooperation Bureau. Both of these had been revealed via special investigations and had been involved in murder. They had become like the enemy they were fighting.

South Africa returns to the World

At the opening of Parliament on 1 February 1991, F.W. de Klerk announced that the Land Act, the Group Areas Act, and the Registration of Population Act were to be scrapped. These were the lynch pins of the Apartheid policy of the previous forty years. On 16 February 1991, the Committee of Commonwealth Foreign Ministers, meeting in London, stated that sanctions against South Africa would remain until the promises were followed by concrete action. By 17 June 1991, de Klerk announced the actual repeal of these Acts, some with effect 30 June 1991. The supposed "Apartheid legislation" that still remained related mostly to political power and security, and not much to any practically executable racial discrimination. This seemed to be enough change to induce the USSR Chamber of Commerce and Industry to sign a mining development agreement with the South African Chamber of Mines on 15 June 1991. Perhaps this is what finally got the attention of the United States.

On 10 July 1991, United States President George H.W. Bush signed an executive order terminating the sanctions (Chapter 24: *The Fifth Great Abandonment*) against South Africa based on the determination that the South African authorities had met all five conditions set forth in the US Comprehensive Anti-Apartheid Act of 1986. It is worth remembering that President Bush had experience of the First Angolan War as CIA head. However, local and state sanctions remained, as well as the ban on arms and on support for International Monetary Fund loans to South Africa.

On the same day, the International Cricket Board granted full membership to the South African board. This meant more to South Africans than the insulting and irrelevant 2 May 1991 lifting of South Africa's suspension from competing internationally in (ice) hockey, of all ridiculous sports for a subtropical country like South Africa. Given the comments made to the author himself by his Danish colleague at IBM some 12 years earlier in New York (*NF90: "You should just die!"*), it came as little surprise that Denmark refused to lift sanctions, thereby effectively vetoing the European Union in lifting sanctions. The Nordic countries had been the first to impose sanctions the moment PW Botha had started making positive changes in South Africa in the very early 1980s. Sweden had donated several million $US per annum to the ANC.

On 24 July, Hungary re-established relations with South Africa. The USSR Deputy Foreign Minister Valeri Nikolayenko arrived in South Africa for a 5-day visit on 7 August 1991. Argentina, Turkey, Algeria and Czechoslovakia soon established diplomatic relations. Romania followed on 22 November 1991. The former Eastern Bloc was beating a path to South Africa's door (*NF94* later). On 23 January, Angola established diplomatic relations. The European Community lifted all sanctions on 27 January 1992. The Russian Federation dropped their support of the ANC and established formal relations with the South African government instead on 28 February 1992. By May, several African countries were opening embassies or commissions in South Africa. Zambia did so on 1 May 1992. For the ordinary white South African this was a peculiar time. For many, such as the author, international life had consisted of being treated like a pariah for the previous several years. Suddenly the international attitude was different. Everyone and his uncle wanted to visit South Africa.

Nomzamo – "Hamlet without the Prince"

On 2 November 1989, the horror of the Nomzamo Winifred Madikizela Mandela houses and the Mandela United Football Club finally made it into court when Jerry Richardson appeared on several charges, including the murder of "Stompie" Seipei. In the process, one of the young men abducted with "Stompie," Kenneth Kgase, testified that "Winnie" Mandela had been present during their assault and had actively participated. He testified that blood had been splattered over the wall of the bedroom and they had been forced to wash the walls themselves the following morning. Richardson was eventually found guilty on 25 May 1990 by Judge O'Donovan[11] and later sentenced to a term of life in prison.

On Monday 24 September 1990, "Winnie" Mandela was charged with four counts of abduction and assault relating to the disappearance and death of Stompie Seipei and the abduction of and assault on his three colleagues (*See Chapter 25: Nomzamo Madikizela*; Case 9). A number of other parties appeared with her on these charges. Journalists from the *Washington Post* and the *Christian Science Monitor* were present for part of the trial. Shortly before he was to testify in the court as co-defendant with "Winnie" Mandela, Katiza Cebekhulu (*See Chapter 25: Nomzamo Madikizela*; Case 12) was whisked out of the country by the ANC to Zambia, reputedly with the help of that country's president, Kenneth Kaunda. There, he was incarcerated without trial for three years to prevent him testifying against Mandela[12]. On 13 May 1991, after a trial of 14 weeks, Judge Stegmann found "Winnie" Mandela guilty of the kidnapping of Pelo Mekgwe, Thabiso Mono, Kenny Kgase, and Stompie Seipei[13]. She escaped the charges of assault and murder, but not a thinking soul in the country considered her innocent on those. The judge summed up the situation:

> "To imagine that all of this took place without Mrs. Mandela as one of the moving spirits is like trying to imagine 'Hamlet' without the Prince."

The judge was scathing on the subject of Mandela's testimony, which he described as

> "vague, evasive, equivocal, inconsistent, unconvincing and brazenly untruthful."

He stated that,

> "she showed herself on a number of occasions to be a calm, composed, deliberate, and unblushing liar."

The *Chicago Tribune*[14] would eventually point out that they could not find grounds for considering the prosecution to be politically motivated, and commented on the painstaking review of the evidence by the judge. The accused left court with a smile on her face and with her balled fist in the air. What had saved her was an alibi[15] that she had been out of town at the time of the assault. Outside the black ANC crowd erupted in a roar of adulation. Nelson Mandela, walking next to her, looked less comfortable. "Winnie" was sentenced to six years imprisonment for kidnapping and being accessory to assault, but appealed and was granted bail. Her sentence was eventually reduced to a paltry 15,000 rands fine. Justice had vividly not been served.

On 13 April 1992, Nelson Mandela announced his separation from Nomzamo Madikizela, who promptly started referring to herself as "Madikizela-Mandela." It would take the BBC a full eleven further years before it would finally refer to her as *"Mugger of the Nation"*[16].

Designing a new South Africa

By early 1992, FW de Klerk's ruling National Party had suffered three consecutive defeats in by-elections, each constituency going to the rightist Conservative Party which objected to the negotiations with the ANC. The last general election in which whites had had any say in their political life had been on 6 September 1989, and the ruling National Party had lost votes in that round. At this point in history, the ordinary white man in the street had no more say in his future than the average black man. A referendum was therefore called exclusively for whites. The question put to them on 17 March 1992 was:

> "Do you support continuation of the reform process which the State President began on February 2, 1990,

and which is aimed at a new constitution through negotiation?"

The voting turnout was a solid 85.1% and the "YES" vote was 68.73%. The "NO" vote lost even in the most conservative parts of South Africa. Only in one far northern district did they prevail. "FW" therefore had the mandate he had wanted and announced[17]:

"Today we have closed the book on Apartheid,"

while Mandela, for his part, said that he was "very happy." By May 1992, African countries were establishing diplomatic relations in droves. The future was now FW's to design. We would now all see whether this man had the leadership qualities, management acumen, depth of character, and fundamental intelligence to take South Africa where it so desperately wanted to go in negotiation with the ANC. The negotiation initiative would go under the title CODESA (Convention for a Democratic South Africa).

Nexus Familia 94: The Ghost of Patrice Lumumba

By 1992, South Africa is coming out of its international state of isolation. It has an immediate effect in the author's high technology workplace. With the Soviet-Cuban Communist threat removed, the emphasis of the technology world in South Africa moves from Defense related towards peacetime applications. This is an era of "beating swords into plowshares." Technology that previously went into making the formidable South African weapons now finds its way into products for application in supermarkets. Many parties in the international arena are quite aware of South Africa's high technology abilities and now come shopping. They sense that a nation that has defended itself so successfully against all odds must of necessity have some unique solutions to offer, and we do.

One of the more intriguing developments is that representatives from the old Eastern Bloc are now visiting South Africa. The country's independent technological and industrial base and its unique position on the edge of Western Civilization intrigues them. If little South Africa could remain standing for some two decades against the full economic might of the entire Western World, then there must be a lesson for the countries of the Eastern Bloc who now face having to reinvent themselves.

Against this background, I am tasked with receiving a visitor with technological background who happens to be a Member of the Russian Parliament. He is a bear of a man and he comes with a blond haired and pink faced young male interpreter. This being an international meeting, we conduct it in English. However, I have with me a colleague who insists on whispering in my ear in Afrikaans every now and then.

The conversation covers all manner of generalities in the area of technology. There is no way I'm going to be anything but diplomatic with the gentleman. There will not be significant technological information leaving our shores. After all, we have our own plans and ideas. I'm not about to train possible future competition for free, especially not after so recently finishing a war against them. When we finally get to the end of the conversation and are about to go to lunch, I tell my visitor in a closing diplomatic statement:

"The Russian people form one of the great nations of the world and I am sure they will be successful at whatever they set their minds to,"

and then I add the Afrikaans proverb,

"after all, 'n Boer maak 'n plan" (Eng: "a farmer makes a plan").

A silence descends on the table and my Afrikaans colleague punches me discreetly in the arm and says:

"You had better say that in English."

I do nothing of the sort and just stare at the interpreter with my best polite and diplomatic smile. Then the young man turns red as a beet and says something in Russian to his giant boss, who roars with laughter, and wags his finger at me. That is when I ask the young man where he learnt Afrikaans. When the embarrassed answer comes, it is intriguing in the extreme:

"Patrice Lumumba University. I studied Dutch and majored in Afrikaans."

So, the supposedly paranoid securocrats of the South African government have been right all along. The Soviets have indeed been preoccupied with South Africa. They have made sure over all these years that students attending their special university[18] for training their foreign revolutionaries in Marxist Doctrine are thoroughly competent in Afrikaans. We always suspected that, but here is the living proof sitting right in front of me. And that proof is young, blond, and red-faced, and is fidgeting uncomfortably.

*****

At home, our family now consists of my wife, our son, my retired mother, Nickie, and myself. We all play a role in the raising of our son. He is enrolled at an affordable private school where he can get adequate attention, given his profound hearing disability. The school is a multiracial and his friends include black children. Over this period we are doing everything possible as parents to raise our only child in a world that has no racial discrimination. When he has a birthday party, all his friends are there — his young black friends included — and dad has to walk all the children around on a hired pony and manage the jumping castle for the afternoon.

*****

We decide that the time has come to visit the family in Port Elizabeth. It is quite a long trip of some 700 miles from Pretoria to Port Elizabeth. This is the first in a number of such trips. One of the obvious stops on this route is Queenstown. This mid-sized town is situated immediately outside the northern part of the amaXhosa homeland, the Transkei. This homeland is at this time an independent state.

In sleeping over in the town, the issue is finding a place for the whole family to have dinner. The obvious choice is the Spur family restaurant in town, an affordable family steak house and part of a well known national chain. It is near the hotel and the fare is quite acceptable. It becomes our standard stop on these trips. Little do we know what the future holds for our favorite restaurant.

—End Nexus Familia

"Bulala amaBhulu"– Kill the white man, and dissenting blacks

One of the great peculiarities of Africa is that black politicians may say absolutely anything, however murderous or outrageous. They are never called to account for it by the Western Media. White politicians in Africa, however, are consigned to hell or worse by the Western Media if they dare say anything that does not befit the highest degree of liberal "political correctness."

Possibly the most brazen example of this in recent history took place on 8 September 1992 when Nelson Mandela and other ANC and Umkhonto we Sizwe functionaries participated in a wreath laying function. On that particular day, Nelson Mandela was televised with his fist in solidarity with his colleagues who were singing, *"We have pledged to kill the whites"*[19]. The author is somehow required to believe that, after reporting on the ANC for more than thirty years, the Western Media had not learnt the single most important word in isiXhosa or isiZulu, namely *"Bulala!"* (Kill!). Perhaps it really does not matter to liberal socialists[20].

The author is not aware of a single international Western journalist who ever questioned Nelson Mandela on this subject. At the same time, his ANC supporters were rushing through the streets in crowds of thousands singing songs with similar words, even identifying individuals by name and suggesting they be killed with axes. It is interesting that leading British journalists, who usually had a lot to say about what they referred to as the "Nazi"[21] whites of South Africa, were mysteriously silent on this subject.

The point here is that, just as in the early 1800s, the news from South Africa was managed mostly by British parties. These were often liberal news reporters, loathing their own culture and suffering from a guilty conscience about their country's history with respect to Colonialism, Africa, or black people in general[22].

As the strife between the ANC and moderate Zulu leader Chief Gatsha Buthelezi's Inkatha Freedom Party turned to open violence, these reporters became mysteriously deaf, dumb, and blind. Initially, the fighting was confined to Natal where Inkatha and the ANC fought low-level battles. It soon spread to the area around Johannesburg, where it became extremely bloody and somehow coalesced into what became known as Taxi Wars. Rival "Black Taxi" groups were fighting each other, but aligned along party lines. On the suburban trains transporting people from Soweto and other suburbs into the city of Johannesburg, people divided into ANC and Inkatha groups. Each party would command different coaches, and if a Xhosa ANC supporter entered a Zulu coach, he died. If an Inkatha supporter entered an ANC coach, he died. These people were simply thrown out of the coaches, leaving the employees of the South African Railways, now known as *Transnet*, to pick up the discarded bodies along the tracks.

It was a fight to the death for the heart, soul and, more than anything else, the fear and subservience of South Africa's black people. The three other major racial groups, White, Coloured, and Indian, watched this nightmare in trepidation. Instead of peace descending on the country after the removal of Apartheid, Black had turned on Black, mostly Xhosa versus Zulu, in a murderous bloodbath. The ANC accused the government of aiding Inkatha and all evidence points to this being true. However, at the same time the ANC was instigating coups in the black homelands, thereby destabilizing them and making them into bases for terrorist attacks on whites inside the rest of South Africa. There was an overabundance of pots calling kettles black.

Over this period, rumors about the ANC over many years were finally proven true. During his visit to London in 1990, Nelson Mandela was confronted with a letter by a man named Amos Maxongo and some colleagues about horrific abuses at the ANC's "correctional camp" Quatro in Angola. By middle 1992, the so-called Skweyiya Report (an internal ANC investigation) revealed Maxongo's statements to have been well founded. Several high ranking ANC officers, including members of Nelson Mandela's own bodyguard, were now implicated. Most of the evidence came from a group of Umkhonto we Sizwe mutineers who had resisted their own organization in 1984. Despite the subject receiving much attention during the late 1990s Truth and Reconciliation Commission hearings, chaired by Desmond Tutu, there would never be justice for these victims.

The Darkest Moment in a Dark Time

On 28 November 1992, terrorists attacked the King William's Town Golf Club in the Eastern Cape and four white people were shot to death. This attack on civilians carried a different trademark – open attacks with guns on white civilians in particular (*Chapter 21: The men from Bashee River*). This sounded like the work of the Azanian People's Liberation Army (APLA) (Chapter 20: *Sharpeville*), the so-called "military wing" of the openly black racist anti-white Pan Africanist Congress (PAC). Perversely, the PAC was party to the negotiations that were being undertaken by the Government and the ANC.

Five days later, on the evening of 3 December 1992, our favorite restaurant in Queenstown was packed with teenage white schoolchildren celebrating the end of the school year. Most of the servers at the restaurant were young white students. There were between 25 and 30 children present[23]. Three black people[24] walked in and sat down at a table. One of them put a leather satchel underneath one of the chairs. Some clients would later remember that the party of three got up and left after ordering a Hunter beer. Fortunately, most of the children also soon left. At this point, according to the owner, there were more black people than white people present in the restaurant. Another party, Mr. Les Barnes and a colleague, Jerome Pieterse, sat down at the table vacated by the black clients. Les worked at a bank in Port Elizabeth and they were on their way to Umtata in the Transkei.

At 11:10 pm, just as waitress Heidi Cunningham stopped at their table and leaned forward over the table, a large Russian SPM limpet mine in the satchel under Les' chair exploded. Les was blasted into the ceiling. All three of the individuals mentioned had severe injuries. Les had 33% burns and his body was riddled with shrapnel, including 6 inch nails. On Sunday morning, Jerome Pieterse died from his extensive wounds. Twenty other people were badly injured. This had been the work of APLA, operating out of the Transkei. They phoned a news agency to claim responsibility. By now, the ANC and PAC had bombed the author's neighborhood post office, local supermarket (twice), the complex housing the author's mother's local supermarket and apartment (Chapter 24: *NF91*), as well as the family's favorite restaurant in Queenstown. They had attacked the local bank in Silverton in 1980, where they killed two white women. These events are listed not because the author felt targeted in this regard, but because it is representative of what the so-called "liberation movements" did and what white South Africans were typically experiencing.

The darkest moment for South Africa came, not during the Apartheid years, but after Apartheid had been scrapped, proving that discrimination had nothing to do with the events and gaining power had everything to do with it. On 25 July 1993, during the 7:30 pm evening service in the St. James' Anglican Church in Cape Town, a team of APLA members burst into the church as a hymn was being sung. They threw M28 fragmentation grenades with tins of nails attached among the congregation of 1400 souls and opened fire with machine guns on the unsuspecting white parishioners. It would later be testified that they had been ordered to throw gasoline bombs into the church after the shooting. However, as is typical of this type of supposed "freedom fighter," they fled when one parishioner, Charl van Wyk, produced a 0.38 revolver and fired back at them, wounding one terrorist. Charl, with only his 0.38, pursued the heavily armed attackers and fired at their getaway car. When it was eventually found, one of its seats was heavily bloodstained.

Eleven parishioners were killed and fifty-eight wounded. 21-year-old Gerhard Harker died instantly when he threw himself on top of one of the hand grenades. His selfless sacrifice saved the lives of a large number of parishioners. His younger brother Wesley also died in the hail of bullets. Seventeen year-old Richard O'Kill died instantly when he flung himself across his two young friends to shield them. Among the eleven dead lay four visiting Russian seamen who had attended the service at the invitation of a member of the congregation, Marita Ackerman, who had also been killed. Possibly the most tragic victim was their fifth colleague, a young Ukranian seaman by the name of Dimitri Makagon. A grenade had landed in his lap and had blown off both of his legs, while one of his arms also had to be amputated. He was on this trip in order to earn money for his marriage. The PAC had managed to maim one and kill four people from countries where they had sourced their weapons and their earlier political support.

The commander of the terrorist team was identified as a certain PAC member[25], Letlape Mphahlele, then the local Director of Operations of APLA. In 1998, the men who executed the attack would ask for amnesty from Desmond Tutu's Peace and Reconciliation Commission. They would testify that[26]:

> "the slogan 'One settler one bullet' meant that 'any white person in South Africa was regarded as a settler and if we came across any settler during our operation, they had to be killed or injured'."

The end of South Africa's nuclear effort

In March 1993, FW de Klerk announced that South Africa had produced some six nuclear devices. The announcement was made in order to "come clean" and do away with the devices, now that there was no further credible threat from the U.S.S.R. For years the fear had been that the Soviets might arm a group of Black African states against South Africa, possibly combined with Cuban "boots on the ground." That threat had evaporated with the demise of the U.S.S.R. and departure of the Cubans out of Africa.

The delivery platform for the devices would most likely have been South Africa's 2-seat long-range Buccaneer bombers employing the toss bombing technique already described (Chapter 25: *The War for Africa*).

No statement was made regarding the much-reported "1979 flash in the Southern Oceans."

"One Settler, one Bullet" – Laughing at the death of an American

On 25 August 1993, an organization allied to the PAC held a meeting at the Langa High School. This grouping called itself the Pan African Student Organization (PASO). It associated with the aim of the PAC to render the country ungovernable via what they called *"The year of the Great Storm,"* thereby to pressure whites to *"return the land to the African people."*

We need to pause for a moment to consider the sheer insanity of the situation. Here we have a group of largely Xhosa young people in Cape Town, 600 miles away from their traditional territory in the East Cape. Their parents or grandparents most likely relocated to Cape Town since 1930 if not much more recently. They are discussing how to terrorize whites in Cape Town to "give back the land" to them. The very same whites, however, can trace their own history in the Cape back to 1652. If any, it is the Xhosa who are interlopers.

There were no classes being taught at Langa High School at this time. Instead, the students were being incited by local PASO leaders to much pumping of balled fists and shouts of *"One Settler, one Bullet."* A young man named[27] Ntobeko Peni was elected chairman of the PASO branch formed at the school. Also present were Mongezi Manqina, the equivalent chairman from the nearby Gugulethu Comprehensive School, and Mzikhona Nofemela, a PASO organizer at the Joe Slovo[28] High School. These three young leaders of the organization were between 18 and 22 years old and were accompanied by another student named Vuzumzi Ntamo. By the afternoon, having swept themselves up into a frenzy, the crowd set off down the streets, *toyi-toying*[29] and shouting *"One Settler, one Bullet,"* determined to put into effect what they had been urged to do.

At this point, a young white American student by the name of Amy Elizabeth Biehl was taking three black friends to their homes in the black township of Gugulethu. Amy was a straight-A Fulbright Scholar, associated with the Community Law Centre at the University of the Western Cape where she was pursuing her studies for a PhD in Political Science. Before coming to South Africa, she had worked at the National Democratic Institute in Washington, a body allied to the Democratic Party of the United States. She also acted as researcher for the ANC and helped the ANC Women's League, a body under the rule of Winnie Mandela.

As fate would have it, this is when Amy's path crossed with that of the PASO group. The killer mob ran toward her car and stoned it. The stones smashed the windscreen and side windows of the car. One of the stones hit Amy in her head, causing her to bleed so profusely that she could not continue driving. She got out of her car and ran towards a gas station across the road, but her attackers did not relent. They pursued her and continued throwing stones at her. Manqina tripped her and she fell. Peni would later admit to throwing stones at Amy at a distance of three to four yards. Manqina stabbed her with a knife in addition to throwing stones at her. Nofemela threw stones at her and stabbed at her 3 or 4 times. Ntamo threw many stones at her head from a distance of only one yard.

Here we finally had one American who learned the realities of Africa the most terrible way. Unfortunately, the PASO crowd only stopped their attack when the South African Police arrived on the scene. By then, it was too late. Amy died as a result of the injuries inflicted on her by the black mob. All of this was terrible and tragic enough, but the actual issue of historical note is what happened in the courtroom afterwards, when all in attendance already knew exactly who Amy had been. As Amy's friend Matsatsi Maceba recounted the details of how the promising young American girl had died, the black PAC supporting crowd in the courtroom laughed[30] – they actually laughed! This would happen again in 2008 when international reporters would scream in outrage at South African blacks laughing at Zimbabwean immigrants, fellow human beings, dying in excruciating agony in "necklace" murders[31].

The CIA's Frankenstein

Evidence would be provided[32] in 2005 that the Central Intelligence Agency had initially funded the infamous PAC, suggesting it had become "the CIA's Frankenstein." B.S. Nyameko directly stated that the CIA created the Pan Africanist Congress (PAC) in 1959 to undermine the ANC[33]. The author has no own independent evidence in this regard, but if it is true, then the CIA certainly has some matters to answer for. The author finds it difficult to make peace with the idea that the United States taxpayer would fund an organization that laughs about American girls being stoned to death.

In 1992, the USAID program listed that it was giving $4.8M to the ANC and some $2.6M to Inkatha. It remains a question who decided to suddenly turn all this funding into support for the ANC. It certainly is clear that a decision was made in the United States to effectively sideline the moderate Chief Gatsha Buthelezi and to support instead the ANC, which had so recently waged a terror and intimidation campaign; an organization still listed as a "Terrorist Organization" by the US State Department at the time.

Capitulation – The Death of the Future

During 1992, Mandela had put pressure on FW de Klerk about some elements of the Defense Force allegedly attempting to derail negotiations by fomenting violence via Inkatha. In response, FW had demoted the Minister of Defense and appointed Roelf Meyer instead to that portfolio. Up to that time, Meyer had been the Deputy Minister of Law and Order and Deputy Minister of Constitutional Development. Instead of using his highly successful and respected army as a negotiation strength, FW sought to minimize it in this inexplicable fashion. He also disbanded the highly respected 32 Battalion, which had meanwhile been dragged wrongly into urban security operations. They were "soldier's soldiers"; not a police riot squad. They had ended up killing civilians in one clash, leading to community resentment.

De Klerk finally stepped over the moral line of no return when he agreed to free Robert McBride, who had killed three young white women during his terrorist bombing of Magoo's Bar (*NF91*). It is worth noting that, according to his respected biographer, Martin Meredith, Nelson Mandela specifically insisted that this man be freed before he would return to negotiate[34].

The negotiation process with the ANC proceeded at a halting pace until late 1993, interrupted by several events. When the process was at its most tenuous, it was held together by the two chief negotiators from either side, Roelf Meyer from the ruling National Party and Cyril Ramaphosa, a Venda union leader on the ANC side. Several of the smaller parties would leave the process and rejoin at different stages. The two key men eventually became known as the "*Roelf and Cyril Show*."

According to the late Opposition Leader at the time, Frederik van Zyl Slabbert, Roelf Meyer was completely outclassed[35] by Cyril Ramaphosa. It is exceedingly difficult for the author to comprehend how FW de Klerk could have made a comparative "lightweight" like Roelf Meyer[36] responsible for the entire future of his nation. Meyer was reputed to have been a singer in an Air Force Choir during his military service. He was therefore popularly referred to as "The Canary," especially among those with practical military experience.

It is reported[37] that, when Meyer accepted the principle of straight majority rule, de Klerk told him "*My God, Roelf, you've given away the country!*"

Ramaphosa reputedly told Frederik van Zyl Slabbert that, when Meyer accepted this principle, the ANC team asked for a fifteen-minute recess to go and laugh their heads off. The fact is that FW had given Meyer the job and the two of them had simply capitulated. There were to be no checks on black abuse of power. The future of the author and his family in Africa had died but we did not know it. Three hundred and forty one years of dedication had been flushed away.

The end of "white rule"

On 27 October 1993, the office of the State President published Act No. 151 of 1993 to establish a Transitional Executive Council. It came into effect on 7 December 1993, and therewith, Western white people lost the last vestige of control of their own destiny in Africa.

In the early hours of 18 November 1993, the major political parties in the country adopted a comprehensive agreement on the way forward. This included an electoral act and an interim constitution giving legal basis for the transitional institutions and specifying non-negotiable constitutional principles. The agreement became the basis for South Africa's new fully inclusive democracy. Two parties on the left and two on the right were still absent. To the left were the PAC and the even more extreme AZAPO (Azanian People's Organization) and to the right were Zulu Chief Buthelezi's Inkatha and the AWB (Afrikaner Resistance Movement – Afrikaner Weerstandsbeweging).

In view of this agreement, Umkhonto we Sizwe, the so-called "military wing" of the ANC, was "disbanded" on 16 December 1993 – always that fateful date of the Battle of Blood River in 1838; ironically, the author's birthday. Since the organization had been created to fight white people, it meant the "struggle" was now among black people for control over the country. That fight was largely between the ANC and its myriad of associated organizations on the one hand, and the Zulu Inkatha Freedom Party on the other.

At this point, the fateful 19th century decisions of the British to take the countries of the amaXhosa and the amaZulu and incorporate them into the Cape Colony and Natal Colony had finally come to haunt the country the world knew as South Africa. Both these nations had been largely left to rule themselves in their respective countries, but the amaXhosa in particular had swarmed into the rest of South Africa and now dominated the political landscape in numbers. On the other hand, the Zulu, who were an ever-bigger nation, were more attached to their homeland of Kwa-Zulu. As a nation, they despise the amaXhosa and resent any political control by the latter.

Most oddly, both Swaziland and Lesotho stayed out of the fray. Lesotho is entirely surrounded by South Africa and is utterly dependent on it. In size, it is roughly the same as Vermont and Massachusetts combined and the vast bulk of it is uninhabitable mountain terrain ranging up to 11,000 feet. In 2001, there were no more than 1.7 million Sotho people in Lesotho, but more than 4 million in South Africa.

Swaziland used to be part of the Old Transvaal Republic and is the size of Connecticut. In 1993, there were 650,000 Swazis in Swaziland and one million in South Africa. The existence of the South African black homelands makes more demographic sense than that of these two countries. The author speculated at the time that the two countries feared Xhosa domination, and thus avoided incorporation into South Africa. Nothing has happened since to justify a different analysis.

Nexus Familia 95: The Train of Death

By 1993, the running battles between the ANC and Inkatha are intense. The trains running from Soweto to Johannesburg are brutal killing grounds. Even the train stations near Soweto become the territory of one or the other of the two groups. *Spoornet*[38] is at its wit's end as to how to prevent the murders on its trains. AK47s, Skorpion machine pistols, sawn off shotguns, and any other form of weapon is in use in what has become almost all out war occurring on the trains and in taxis.

It is over this period that a company in the industrial communications field approaches the author's organization. They are working together with Spoornet in search of a solution that will allow cameras inside the coaches to transmit imagery to a protected guard van on the train. Since there is no way to know which group would be the majority in a given coach on a given trip, ANC or Inkatha, they hope that by monitoring the coaches with closed circuit television cameras they might identify the various killers.

The optoelectronic technology of the research and development team, previously geared towards military applications, is now "beaten into plowshares" in the crime-busting field. Our solution is to communicate closed circuit television images via LASER from coach to coach along a LASER "daisy chain."

Our engineers manage to produce a design that satisfies everyone. However, when it is implemented, the *Spoornet* project manager invites me to his office. His goal is to "calibrate me" as to the severity of the situation. He explains the nature of this horrific Train War. He mentions that one train station has been completely demolished to the point where not one brick stood upon another, and the water was spurting vertically from the pipes in the ground. He maintains that it had all been destroyed in one night by people with their bare hands.

He probably sees the incredulity in my eyes, because he gets up without saying a word, disappears into an annex and returns with a train coach window. The *Plexiglass* window is absolutely riddled with bullet holes. The Spoornet manager sits down with a deadpan face, pointing out the different holes or sections of damage on the window, reading it like a catalog:

> *"This is an AK-47. Here you see a 9mm parabellum. This mess is a zip-gun. This series here is a machine pistol..."*

I stand duly calibrated.

—End Nexus Familia

Nexus Familia 96: "Affirmative Action"

At this stage, our organization is being pressed extremely hard to hire black professionals. *Affirmative Action* is now the imported American term that counts in management. I have major misgivings about employing American terms for issues in South Africa. Having seen how misconceptions about South Africa have dominated American thinking and decision making on our country, I am worried about how this will be interpreted in the United States.

While I am already working with at least two black PhD physicists in other organizations, there are no black post-graduate engineers in our own division. And so it is that a management colleague identifies a black engineer with previous experience at the South African offices of one of the largest American corporations. He reputedly comes with an excellent résumé.

My colleague hires him with great expectations and puts him onto a sub-part of a project in his area of our division.

In a management meeting a few weeks later, my colleague reports that the new hire is not working out as well as expected. Nevertheless, it is decided that every effort will be made to help the new employee perform the best he can.

After a few more weeks, my colleague reports that there is zero progress and the new hire is simply just not working out. He would like to terminate the employment, but is told that this cannot be done, given the circumstances in the country. Why not give the new hire something more definite and precise to do? How about him just writing up a report on what others have done on the project?

After another few weeks, my colleague is livid with frustration. The new hire is now a load on other people. He has given the man the task of writing up a report, but that also did not happen. He is now convinced the man is a complete fraud with a fabricated résumé.

The overall situation is a "political stalemate." The new man does no work, and yet he cannot be laid off for not functioning at all because of one simple fact: he is black. There the matter rests for the moment, with the load on the white professionals now increased amid the pressure to hire "Affirmative Action" candidates and make them useful. Our first attempt in this domain is a total irrecoverable disaster. We have to pray that the candidate leaves of his own free will.

—*End Nexus Familia*

Nelson Mandela: *"Even if they have to kill people"*

To the west of Pretoria and Johannesburg, the ANC was doing its best by March 1994 to topple Chief Lucas Mangope, president of the independent Ba'Tswana homeland, Bophuthatswana. They had already been successful in the Xhosa homeland of Transkei. The embattled Mangope, realizing that FW de Klerk's government was on its last legs and just doing the ANC's bidding, turned to none other than the White right wing group, the *Afrikaner Weerstandsbeweging* (AWB: The Afrikaner Resistance Movement). This badly organized redneck militia, often the target of jokes among most whites, set off to the Bophuthatswana capital of Mmabatho in the middle of March 1994 in a motley collection of light trucks. However, a combination of the South African Defense Force and the Bophuthatswana Defense Force routed them.

Somehow, two of the AWB men had been wounded and were lying against the side of their vehicle. They were filmed by an international television crew. And this is when a black soldier of the Bophuthatswana Defense Force walked up and killed the one wounded man, Nick Fourie, in cold blood in front of the international cameras. The reel was transmitted around the globe. South Africa was apparently coming apart for all to see. A few weeks later the Ciskei homeland government similarly collapsed. Both Bophuthatswana and Ciskei were put under interim management by the Transitional Executive Council.

The Western media flooded to South Africa in droves in anticipation of an "exciting" white bloodbath.

*****

In Natal and in the Johannesburg area, the fighting between the Xhosa dominated ANC and the Zulu

Inkatha movement continued as a constant backdrop to developments in the country in 1993 and 1994. So it came to be that on 28 March 1994, one month before the first ever all-inclusive elections in the country, Nelson Mandela was on one of the higher floors of the Shell House Building in the center of Johannesburg. In the street below, Chief Gatsha Buthelezi's Inkatha Freedom Party, opposition to the ANC, was holding a rally, marching past the building.

Here we had, to steal a phrase from Chester Crocker (US Deputy Secretary of State for Africa in the 1980s), a Splendid Paradox. For the first time ever the ANC was formally facing a black crowd that opposed it. It now found itself in the position that the Police had found themselves at the time of Sharpeville (Chapter 20: *Sharpeville*), for which the white government at the time (21 March 1960) had been committed to eternal damnation by the Western World.

The moment is critical in the history of South Africa. The test was what Nelson Mandela and the ANC would do in the face of this challenge. Would they respect the democratic rights of the crowd? Would they see it as the populace expressing its unhappiness? Here, finally, the moment of truth was upon the ANC, the darling of the Western Media. Here was the moment in which its much-vaunted "devotion" to multi-racial/multi-ethnic democracy stood before the tribunal of reality.

The "liberation movement" had bombed schools, apartment buildings, and restaurants and mined farmers' roads, but was seldom if ever criticized internationally for that. Now it was faced with a public demonstration by black men with ceremonial spears and shields in the heart of the capital of the country.

And this is when ANC members opened fire on the crowd with automatic weapons. When the firing stopped, at least 13 Zulu lay dead and many more were wounded. This was in the heart of Johannesburg. The Zulu King would later claim that 53 died. A "peaceful" ANC, safely ensconced on the upper floors of a protective building, was firing on the mass of opposing Zulu in the unprotected streets of Johannesburg.

This is rather different from the Police in Sharpeville in 1960 who found themselves directly threatened on the street with no protection other than their guns. The ANC was in reality located in what was effectively sniper positions and was firing down on defenseless black people in the street with no means to defend themselves. When police entered the building the next day to search for the weapons used, none other than Nelson Mandela himself prevented them[39]. On 7 June 1995, more than a year after being inaugurated as president, he would announce in a Senate speech in Cape Town that he had given the order to defend the building[40] *"even if they had to kill people."* In the final report of Desmond Tutu's Truth and Reconciliation Commission[41], the following conclusion was drawn based on the testimony of the applicants for amnesty for that shooting:

> *"...the Amnesty Committee found no evidence of an attack on Shell House by the IFP marchers. Objective ballistic and medical evidence indicates that the shooting was without justification as most of the deceased were shot after they had turned back. The applicants admitted that they might have shot at the marchers as they were running away."*

This had been the ANC's Sharpeville and the Western media did not even blink.

During a march on the Bophuthatswana embassy in Kimberley on 25 May 1993, the supposedly peaceful ANC marchers had thrown a hand grenade at the building[42], it had bounced back and killed their own people. The ANC men at Shell House therefore presumably thought Inkatha was as undisciplined as the ANC itself had been and might actually attack them.

There is something poignant about the proud King Zwelithini Goodwill ka Bhekuzulu speaking for his amaZulu nation a few days after the massacre, on 8 April 1994. It has the ring of an address from a distant century, but it still stands in the 21st century as a clear indictment of the ANC[43]:

> *"No words can express the horror I feel for the massacre of my father's people who were peacefully demonstrating for the restoration of the Kingdom of KwaZulu [...]*
>
> *"...three days earlier tens of thousands of ANC supporters had marched through Durban, a city divided between it and Inkatha. They went past Inkatha's offices, yet none was shot. When the Zulus did the*

same last Monday in Johannesburg, 53 of them were slaughtered.

"While it preached democracy, the ANC practices totalitarianism. It prefers to kill its opponents rather than use reason and argument. Its intolerance to criticism and its adherence to communist ideals means South Africa will be a virtual one-party state. As its officials gloated over its 'victory' last Monday, they refused to allow the police entry to their headquarters to gather ballistic evidence. [...]

"I want also, Sir, to say that I could go on for some considerable time to talk of the offenses to which the Zulu nation has taken exception, and to the many ways in which the ANC has shown disdain for the Zulu people.[...]

"It was my great, great-grandfather King Cetshwayo ka Mpande, who was in many respects the first new South African who saw that the old historic order of things in the sub-continent would have to be changed.[...]

"Mr. Mandela, I must inform you, Sir, that I reject the 1993 Constitution even as amended, because it extends the politically greedy arm of Pretoria right across the Zulu Kingdom."

The net result was that, nineteen days before the all-important first all-inclusive election, the Zulu nation withdrew from the process for a new South Africa. They withdrew because of the murderous conduct of the ANC and lack of respect the organization had shown the Zulu nation and throne. The amaZulu wanted an autonomous homeland; the very thing they had rejected when it was offered to them by PW Botha.

In a nutshell, while the white man ran South Africa the Zulu wanted to be part of it. However, as soon as a black Xhosa leader, Mandela, seemed headed for control of the country, the Zulu opted for independence. The amaZulu will never submit to the amaXhosa as long as the sun rises in the East and sets in the West. That is the way of Africa. At best, they will render apparent acquiescence and bide their time.

Both Henry Kissinger and Lord Carrington, British Foreign Minister, took a hand at this point in a major effort to induce the Zulu nation to participate in the polls. They both failed. However, Buthelezi did resume support for the election mere days before the election date.

Nexus Familia 97: The first all-inclusive elections

Shortly before the April 1994 elections, I visit an electronics company in Cape Town. To my surprise, I find that practically every Coloured woman in the company has a picture of FW de Klerk up on the wall in her work booth. When I ask one of them why, she says, *"He's my guy."*

When I ask why he has this unique status, I get an answer that is wildly suggestive and causes all the women on that floor to crow in delight. This is my first indication that everything is not going entirely the way of the ANC. Of course, the majority population in the Western Cape is Coloured, rather than Black, and my own Afrikaans is the home language of more than 90% of them.

*****

As we approach the election day of 27 April 1994, we watch the country slide into what seems like an abyss. The Zulu Inkatha and Xhosa ANC are killing one another like flies. Just for good measure, a bunch of white far right fanatics attempt to plant their own bomb to make their unhappiness known.

Nickie, the author's mother, quietly takes large empty plastic (PET) *Coca Cola* bottles, fills them up with water, and freezes them, just in case someone sabotages the water supply. We stare miserably at the TV as Nick Fourie is murdered at Mmabatho in full view of the world's TV cameras, as he lies wounded against the side of his truck. To white South Africans like us, it seems like a glimpse of the Armageddon we are facing with the first all-inclusive elections just around the corner.

The night before the election we go to the movies. The streets are deserted. An eerie silence has descended upon the land. Forty million people are holding their breaths while the world media salivates, readying their cameras for the bloodbath they are confidently anticipating.

*****

On the morning of Wednesday 27 April 1994, the sun comes up as usual. That is the first check on reality. The loerie, the famous Rainbird of South Africa, is singing its liquid call from a hiding place somewhere in the acacia tree outside our bedroom window. It always sings after the rain has passed, its song a melodic version of a bottle of water running out. A flock of hadeda ibis passes overhead, screaming their distinctive raucous "*Haaaahhh! Haaaah-deeeeh-daaaah!*" call.

All is normal so far.

Then I feel a churning sensation in my soul. I grab the TV remote and the TV switches on. No, no one has sabotaged the ESCOM power utility or the South African Broadcasting Corporation, as some had threatened. On the television, we find that there have been no major upheavals, no new major bomb explosions, and no new major terrorist attacks. Basically, nothing seems to have gone wrong. We are pleasantly amazed.

After breakfast, the family sets off to the voting station at a nearby school. The line is not very long and it includes both white and black people. At this voting station, however, it is mostly white people. Everyone is happy to stand in line and wait to vote. It is no different from any line at any other service in the country over the last ten years. In practice, day-to-day Apartheid has been long gone for most of a decade.

The first results come in on the same day, but we all have to wait for the drawn out process in rural Zululand. This is when the world is treated to sights of thousands of people standing in apparently endless lines to vote. Already on television BBC commentators are nodding in the classic condescending British fashion: "*How incredible,*" "*Amazing,*" "*A miracle,*" "*A great victory for democracy,*" and a myriad of other inane comments, while they are really saying "Thank God it's not in my backyard" (NIMBY).

In the rush for a scoop on a promised bloodbath, they are absent[44] from the story that is developing thousands of miles to the north in Rwanda. The reporters who should be covering that impending genocide are in South Africa in anticipation of blacks killing the whites and then turning on one another.

*****

When the results are made public, the ANC has won the overall election with ease, the Province of Natal has seen a clear win for the Inkatha Freedom Party of Chief Gatsha Buthelezi, Prince of KwaPhindangene and uncle of the Zulu King. Unexpectedly, FW de Klerk's National Party has kept the Western Cape Province, mostly thanks to the Coloured vote.

—<u>End Nexus Familia</u>

Nexus Familia 98: The New South Africa

On 10 May 1994, we watch the television, even though the inauguration of Nelson Mandela as president is taking place at the Union Buildings (*Fig. 18-3*) a paltry five miles from our house. As Mandela, flanked by Thabo Mbeki and FW de Klerk, appears the crowd goes wild, the whites cheering and black women ululating. Mandela's words to the "nation," which now overnight comprises all white Afrikaners, include[45]:

1. "*What is past is past,*" which he specifically also states in Afrikaans for emphasis; and

2. "*Never, never – and never again - shall it be that this beautiful land will again experience the oppression of one by another*"...[...] "*Let freedom reign, God bless Africa.*"

As he finishes, the South African Air Force does a dramatic fly-past in precision formation. A flight of puma helicopters trailing massive New South African flags flies over the Union Buildings. Moments later a flight of Impala ground attack fighters does a fly-past trailing the multiple colors of the new flag.

At home, we watch with a general feeling of "*What the hell, this might work.*" If everyone stands with this man, Mandela, then it can work. He started the bombings in the country in the 1960s, but perhaps the years in jail made him wiser about humanity and less bloodthirsty.

At one point in the proceedings, as though to signify the nature of the New South Africa, Mandela's *imbongi*[46] appears next to the podium and proceeds to sing his hero's praises for what seems like an eternity.

He is decked out in his leopard skins and "witch sticks" and the whole regalia. This, quite honestly, is a bit much for this Presbyterian family. The bemusement of a Western audience can only be imagined. It is one thing to have this as cultural entertainment at a concert hall in New York, and to then go home. It is quite another to experience this as the formal introduction of the leader of your country.

The author can only imagine the reaction of the entire United States if the U.S. President were to be introduced in such fashion at the start of a State of the Union Address. But we tolerate it in the interest of a future – there is nothing we can do about it anyway. We are completely powerless to influence our future. The West has forced us into the hands of these people whose behavior is as foreign to us as that of the cannibals of New Guinea are to an Australian. That is, we know full well about it, but cannot relate to it. I wonder silently whether parliament is from now on going to be opened by an *imbongi*.

As I sit there, I am asking myself how I should explain this experience to my American friends. Americans seem to be utterly, totally, and comprehensively ignorant in this particular domain. However, they flippantly inject the word "Democracy" as some sort of panacea with not the vaguest concept of what that word means when one's culture and values are not those of the majority of voters, and the majority sings songs that say *"One settler, one bullet"* and *"Kill the farmer, Kill the Boer!"*

The most directly equivalent experience the author can conjure up for an American is to imagine a collection of ordinary folks from the Midwest, most of them Presbyterian, Methodist or Lutheran, sitting in stunned silence, watching their new rulers—Osama bin Laden, Ho Chi Minh, Timothy McVeigh, and a collection of Jewish-American Cold War Soviet spies—grin like Cheshire cats from the stage as Malcolm X gets crowned leader of the country, and a Sioux medicine man stomps about the stage "speaking in tongues." To try and convince the author that this is somehow the real purpose of Democracy, is nothing but an extremely sick, cruel, and malicious joke. If they were to insist that the Israeli Jews submit to the PLO, Hamas and Hezbollah, then I might believe they have actually thought about what they are saying.

We are fully aware of the fact that many ANC politicians have been telling their constituencies that black men will be given white women and they will all get the white farmers' property. There is forever this mystical issue of "land" and its supposed connection to "forefathers" in the African political mystique (Present Chapter: *"One Settler, one Bullet"*). In the case of South Africa, the same black people have never in the history of Africa had any claim or residence in the western half of South Africa.

—*End Nexus Familia*

The New South African Government

When Mandela announced his new government, his new Minister of Defense was Joe Modise, the former operational chief of Umkhonto we Sizwe, the man who had sent terrorists to bomb civilians, including my mother's apartment complex, our supermarket, and our post office. Thabo Mbeki was appointed as the First Deputy President. By the transitional agreement, Mandela appointed FW de Klerk as Second Deputy President.

Two members of the Inkatha Freedom Party found their way into the main cabinet. The first was Chief Gatsha Buthelezi, leader of that party, who was appointed Minister of Home Affairs, and the other Dr. Ben Ngubane, who was appointed Minister of Arts, Culture, Science, and Technology. They were the only two Zulus in the Cabinet, despite the Zulu being the most numerous nation in the country. Also in the parade of characters was the new Minister of Housing, Joe Slovo, leader of the South African Communist Party. He was a Jewish Lithuanian immigrant – the stock ethnic base of white Communists in South Africa (See Chapter 19: *Communism in South Africa*), few if any of whom had three generations of bloodline in the country. Culturally they were foreign Communists.

Various far left fringe characters now seemed to crawl from the sidelines of civilization to occupy positions in the government as token whites. None of them represented any discernible constituency among whites except themselves. They were typically vastly further left than the Far Left in the United States.

The most objectionable appointment, however, was not that of Terrorist Boss Joe Modise, or the fringe white Communists, but that of Winnie Madikizela-Mandela as Deputy Minister of Arts, Culture, Science, and Technology. The very thought was revolting to many people. Learning to live with the idea that these creatures were now the government, and trying to convince oneself against all conceivable logic that they cared one iota for one's interests or rights was a massive challenge. At work, I would now report indirectly to Winnie Mandela. My disgust was total.

At least, there were a few honorable men in the government. The author would submit that Nelson Mandela himself was one, despite his violent history. Chief Buthelezi and his fellow Inkatha member, Dr. Ben Ngubane were others. The four white National Party cabinet ministers, members of the previous government, just sat there to no real benefit for man or beast.

Slowly, however, one got used to the idea that the new government was not going to put one up against a wall and shoot one, but they were just going to invent reasons every day why they had to somehow apply taxes with zero benefits. Financially it was not a dramatic change from the past. Already in the 1980s whites had got used to being taxed to death and getting little benefit (Chapter 24: *The end of "Petty Apartheid"*. By 1987, whites already paid 32% tax but got only 9% back as benefits) while the Black middle class grew apace and the broad mass of Black people got their services for free due to the boycotts in the black townships.

Slowly, white people started to muse about the "Transfer of Wealth Industry," but were prepared to credit the ANC with not behaving quite like the terrorist organization it had been.

There seemed to be some hope.

Little did we know.

Nexus Familia 99: The Boer, the Brit, and the Future

As I listen to the announcement of the new Cabinet ministers of the Government of the New South Africa, the trapdoor of my mind snaps shut at two specific points. The first is the appointment of Joe Modise, the ANC Terrorist in Chief, as Minister of Defense. It is a bitter pill to swallow.

The second is the appointment of the Deputy Minister of Arts Culture Science and Technology. It is none other than the Mother of the Necklace Killing Technique, convicted felon, and accessory to the disappearance of Stompie Seipei, Winnie Madikizela-Mandela. No fewer than 18 killings are associated with her Mandela United Football Club (MUFC) and household[47].

What makes it infinitely worse, is that the Mother of the Necklace is now my political boss, because the president of our organization reports to her.

*****

Shortly after the April 1994 elections, there is a management change in our Division. I am asked to take over the management of a group of engineers who have developed the most intriguing non-Defense technology I have yet come across. It only works because the engineers have approached the problem from a direction that would never have happened in any other country under different pressures. The electronics employed is a "swords-to-plowshares" idea taken from the pre-fragmentation airburst bombs used with such devastating effect in Angola (Chapter 25: *The War for Africa"*-Section 3).

As part of this development, we come to an arrangement with a British organization, which will license the technology internationally. One of my duties is to go to London to discuss some of the detail issues. And so it is that I, along with one of my South African colleagues, find ourselves at a formal lunch with the chairman of the British organization. Looking at the table in front of me, the array of "silver" cutlery on the starched white tablecloth conjures up images of the British Empire in its heyday. At the back of my mind, I wonder whether this chairman actually thinks this will impress me. As an Afrikaner, I appreciate Calvinistic simplicity, clear statements, direct talk, a proper Work Ethic, and the Rule of Law. I abhor overbearing pomp. In fact, as a nation, we tend to pride ourselves on our simplicity and openness. We probably actually are pretty much John Stockwell's "men without guile"[48] .

At a suitable point in the small talk process, this gentleman decides to announce how thrilled he is about developments in South Africa. This is supposedly a wondrous example for all. He thereupon proceeds to fawn on the whole election of 1994 without truthfully knowing a thing about it other than what he presumes from the skewed self-righteous and condescending BBC reports.

It feels as though a hot molten anger is spreading over my brain and down my neck. I have no idea whether my face and neck are turning red, but, presumably, they are. Here is exactly the kind of imperious pompous Empire Englishman that we have struggled against for all of our existence – the historic source of so much of our trouble. He is presuming to give my Afrikaner colleague and me a classic condescending hypocritical "not in my backyard you don't – I'm sitting pretty" speech. It sounded to my Afrikaner ears like Horatio Kitchener's inconsiderate words to the Boer Generals after they had just signed their own surrender at Vereeniging in 1902 and 28,000 women and children lay in the ground at the British Concentration camps:

"Oh splendid! Now we can all be friends again!"

Could it possibly be that these creatures truly have no idea what we are facing? Have they no concept of the sacrifice and the fear we have to swallow? I breathe deeply, get my emotions under control, and stare intently at the impressive collection of silver cutlery arrayed in front of me to steady myself.

Then I raise my head and look the Englishman in the eye, smiling as best I can, and I say,

"Yes. I imagine we now just have to sort out Northern Ireland and the Middle East."

I may as well have poured ice water over the table. The blood drains from one half of the chairman's face. The other two British company men fidget uncomfortably. They have actually been to South Africa and have some notion of what we have been through as a nation. The eyebrow of one lifts to his hairline and I detect a glint of satisfaction in his eye. The chairman just goes silent. There is not much more conversation over this meal; and it suits me just fine.

The relationship between the two organizations where it really counts remains acceptable and I will be working closely with one of their patent managers, who will become a family friend – the one who exhibited a glint in the eye. Our problems have never been with the ordinary Englishman or British soldier with whom we get along like a house on fire; it has always been their callous leaders and "upper classes."

—End Nexus Familia

 ## Nexus Familia 100: Shaking hands with the Devil

Early one morning, my telephone rings. It is a senior executive member of our organization. When I originally joined in January 1982 as a bright-eyed and bushy-tailed young research and development manager, I reported directly to him. However, he is a uniquely capable and ambitious man and has since progressed to a most senior position within the organization.

He sounds very perturbed indeed when he asks me about the Affirmative Action hire we made some time before in our division (*NF96*). I explain that I'm not the relevant manager and refer him to the manager in whose unit the AA hire "works." He has little interest in my attempt to refer the question to where it should rightly be posed. I therefore explain to him the troubles the division has had in dealing with this hapless hire. But I want to know the reason for the question.

And this is when this senior executive member drops a bombshell on me:

"Well, he is now my boss. I now have to report to Winnie Mandela through him."

• I should have known in this very moment that a South Africa under the ANC is not a workable solution.

• I should have known that the nature of this terrorist organization cannot be changed.

• I should have known that neither the National Party nor the African National Congress represent hope.

• I should have known right at this moment that the New South Africa is a sick farce.

However, it is amazing how the human soul will yearn for hope and embrace the slightest little glimmer of this desperately scarce commodity in the horror epic that is the history of South Africa. I have nothing to offer in mitigation for my naive hope and faith beyond a plea that I am but human.

*****

By the mid-1990s, South Africa is competing on the open market in the international Defense arena. There is great interest in South African products given the practical experience of the country in Angola and the battle proven status of much of its hardware. That fact that the weapons come with no political strings binding the operator to a European country or Superpower is hugely appealing to smaller or non-aligned countries.

Everyone knows about the phenomenal G5 artillery that turned out to be the nemesis of the Soviets and Cubans in Angola. The roughly one hundred G5s that were sold to Saddam Hussein during the Iraq-Iran War turned out to be a huge worry to the United States during the First Gulf War of 1990-1991.

One of the key efforts in the South African high technology arena in the mid-1990s is the *Rooivalk*[49] attack helicopter. Much of the South African high technology community is involved in some or other aspect of this intriguing project. Our organization is no exception. The main interest at this time is from the British, but there is much debate about the avionics. The British want the Rooivalk, but wish to have it equipped with American avionics. However, the United States refuses to provide the avionics if the British source the helicopter from South Africa; at least, that is what the South African negotiators tell us. Since this kind of deal is almost always part of a broader package of counter-trade agreements, a whole bunch of potential business deals now balance on this point.

One day a small handful of managers more or less on the level of the author are called to the conference center of our organization, a venue that is often rented out for high level meetings in the country. The subject is supposed to be the Rooivalk helicopter effort. When the author and his colleagues arrive at the center, they are asked to wait in the annex to the main meeting room.

After waiting a few minutes, there is a rustle as a rotund black man walks in. It is none other than Joe Modise, Nelson Mandela's Minister of Defense – founder member and former Operations Chief of Umkhonto we Sizwe, the "military" wing of the ANC – the ANC Terrorist Boss.

He puts out his hand and one by one, we shake it – I stare him straight in the eye.

In front of me stands the man who sent his operatives to blow up my mother's apartment complex, not once but twice, killing several people including two children in the first attempt and failing in the second. Here is the man who ordered his operatives to plant a limpet mine at our neighborhood post office and bomb our

Fig. 26-2 *Joe Modise on a formal visit to the United States*

supermarket. Here is the man responsible for the bombing of the Air Force offices in 1983, when 19 people were killed and more than 200 injured and maimed (*Chapter 24: The ANC turns to open terrorism*). Here is the man who arranged for the anti-tank mines to be placed in farmers' roads. Here is the Devil himself right in front of me and I have just shaken his hand.

I have no idea what the expression on my face or the look in my eyes is. Whatever it is, it causes Modise to keep staring at me as he speaks. He has peculiarly large and bloodshot eyes in a moon face. For the author this is finally the moment of truth as regards the New South Africa. And then Modise[50] speaks and says to us in English,

"Boys, now you've really got to help me. The damned Brits are trying to screw us!"

At this moment, something in my soul distinctly moves. It is as though a chessboard turns 90 degrees to confound the positions of the opponents. This man has just uttered the words *"help me," "damned Brits,"* and *"us."* Does this really mean he accepts we are all Africans on the same side? Can this be real?

It is in this key moment that I finally embrace the New South Africa despite all the fears, the horrors of Winnie Mandela, and the fact that I know the man in front of me sang a song with the words *"kill the whites,"* and launched at least five bombing missions against civilians that affected my family.

—End Nexus Familia

The world is our oyster

The period between April 1994 and 1996 will be recorded by many South Africans as "The Honeymoon," or the "Time of the Rainbow Nation." There was indeed a sense that the world was our oyster. Everyone wanted to meet with South Africans. Internationally, the election of April 1994 was seen as some sort of miracle and South Africa was now the international "cool" issue to fawn over. The white South African individuals with whom the author was acquainted did their best to make the New South Africa work; this despite their lack of practical representation in parliament. The world soon dropped all the sanctions that had been implemented against the country. The so-called "armed struggle" of the ANC was gone and the horrific murderous PAC, who murdered churchgoers, sidelined by the black population.

Possibly the most important project during the first year of the new government was the incorporation of the ANC's hapless Umkhonto we Sizwe (MK) and other undisciplined black militias like APLA with the hyper-professional South African Defense Force. This was a very painful process. The MK members supposedly in exile had returned to the country during the period before the election by agreement between FW de Klerk and Mandela. Many of them were really just ordinary criminals. Some of them defended their actions to Desmond Tutu's later Truth and Reconciliation Commission by claiming that while they were in exile they were looked after by the ANC, but upon returning they were instructed to undertake "military operations" without any financial support. Therefore, they felt compelled to rob and murder to get money.

By October 1994, thousands of these former Umkhonto we Sizwe members started to create problems at military bases. In a significant demonstration of leadership, Nelson Mandela berated them and warned they were now part of the army and, if they did not behave, they would be treated accordingly. When matters did not improve significantly, 4084 of them who had been absent without leave from the Walmansthal military base were court-martialed. On 7 November, more than 2000 of them were dismissed for failing to report for duty. The South African public saw this as a positive act, indicating the Army would not become the wholesale operational disgrace that Umkhonto we Sizwe had been.

On 17 February 1995, following violent student protests in Cape Town the previous day, President Mandela warned in Parliament he would not tolerate anarchy developing in the country. Through the eyes of the general white public, this was ironic in the extreme. After all, his ANC party had pointedly driven the country into anarchy earlier on a wave of student resistance and rent boycotts. He was starting to reap the harvest of the seeds his party had sown.

In one of the most positive moves of the young government, Winnie Mandela was dismissed on 27 March 1995 with effect mid-April. At first, she tried to ignore this and carry on as normal, having practically had a "free pass" to behave as she pleased since 1987. All this had led to the murder spree conducted out of her homes in Soweto. However, she finally realized that Nelson Mandela was quite serious, and she resigned a day before her dismissal would legally take effect.

The high point of this period was most likely the Rugby World Cup of 1995, portrayed by the movie

Invictus, based on the novel of the same title[51]. While the movie leans towards the ridiculous and perpetuates stereotypes that do more harm than good, it does capture the mutual goodwill between races of the period (See *Nexus Familia 101* below).

Nexus Familia 101: Invictus Redux

By late May 1995, we are very busy at work training five engineers from a large Japanese electronics corporation known in every Western household. This effort forms part of a technology transfer operation from our organization to theirs under a license agreement. This also happens to be the period of the 1995 World Rugby Cup. Japan is also represented on the field and we agree that we will cheer for Japan against its opponents and they will cheer for the South African Springboks in their games against other teams.

The later motion picture *Invictus* will suggest all manner of miracle relationship changes due to magic worked by Nelson Mandela wearing a Springbok jersey. I cannot substantiate these. What I do experience however, is the following:

On Friday 26 May, we put our Japanese visitors in a VW Kombi and drive them the 60 miles to Rustenburg's Olympia Stadium where Scotland is playing the Côte d'Ivoire. On the way, just as we enter Rustenburg town, our Kombi pulls up next to one of the typical Toyota Hi-Ace minivan Black Taxis at a traffic light. My white colleague in front of me turns down his window and gestures to his opposite number in the Hi-Ace to do the same. It is a roughly 28-32 year old black man. The man turns down his window and looks quizzically at my colleague.

Then my colleague asks him: "*Who do you cheer for – Kaizer Chiefs or Moroka Swallows[52]?*"

The man gives a broad grin and says: "*Chiefs!*"

At this point, my colleague suggests: "*OK! If you'll cheer for the Boks[53], we'll cheer for the Chiefs.*"

The occupants of both vehicles burst out laughing and the collection of black people in the Hi-Ace all show "thumbs up." It is not much, but, given what we have been through as a country, it is huge.

In the end, Scotland beats the Côte d'Ivoire 89 to 0. We all cheer for the black Côte d'Ivoire team.

*****

I confess to a lump in the throat as I watch Nelson Mandela on TV walking onto the field wearing his Springbok jersey. All my life I have had to watch as people of color denigrated the Springboks or cheered for their opposition, whoever it might be. On this day, all South Africans cheer for the Springboks for the first time ever.

When Joel Stransky kicks a drop goal in extra time to win the cup for South Africa against the almighty All Blacks from New Zealand, we certainly all go half out of our minds.

This is the highest point of the New South Africa – from here on it is all consistently downhill.

—*End Nexus Familia*

Nexus Familia 102: The proudest technological hour

One morning, my phone rings at work. On the other end of the line is a gentleman with an American accent and an imposing voice. He explains that he is visiting his son who is a missionary in Southern Africa. However, in his regular life he is the Director of the United States Defense Logistics Agency. His interest is in seeing a demonstration of our technology (*NF99*), if at all possible.

Since we have an agreement that a British agency will do all marketing, I tell him that I have to clear this, but that it should hopefully take just a few minutes. I phone the Brits who give me clearance to proceed and I advise the American gentleman accordingly.

Our visitor is physically as imposing as his voice. He reminds me of John Wayne. His business card duly reads "United States Defense Logistics Agency" complete with the right logo. When we do the demonstration of the technology, he stands there shaking his head in disbelief. At this point, the Director of the United States Defense Logistics Agency turns to this White African representative of the amaBhulu and says:

"Son, I'd like to shake your hand. Can you tell me how it is that we threw millions of dollars at companies in the United States to solve this problem and you boys pull it off down here with a PC and a supermarket cart"?

The incredulous American director then shakes hands with all the engineers attending the demonstration. There and then, he invites me to fly to Dallas to meet with his Deputy Director and do the demonstration in the United States. It may not be my original goal of doing a project for DARPA (*NF91 - Ordinary life and work*), but the USDLA is most certainly close enough and more practical. I have always thought that I would have to go looking for the USDoD. However, in a splendid paradox, they have come looking for us.

Some weeks later, I sit at a big table on the top floor of a high technology company in Dallas, a house-sized Star Spangled Banner flying outside the window. Next to me sits the deputy-director of the USDLA, armed with a satellite receiver connected to a laptop computer unit, demonstrating on the laptop the problem faced by the US Army and Air Force as regards supply logistics in the Gulf War. By the end of our sessions, the Deputy Director is convinced we hold the key via our technology and is talking to me about mechanisms via which our research and development might be funded.

*****

Some months later, we test the same technology in a different application relating to the management of munitions. The test, carried out at a firing range in the western desert of South Africa, consists of firing 155 mm rounds to which this technology has been applied. The interest this time is from the British Defense sector. As I stare out across the range, I see Soviet tanks and amphibious armor scattered over the field of view. The irony of the situation is not lost on me – the once proud Soviet armor is now a heap of rusting shot-up hulks used for target practice in the South African desert. However, the proud South African Army that had chased the Soviets out of Africa is being politically undermined from within by the ANC government. The ANC sees it as an employment agency for its uneducated black supporters — the ones whom they had taught to boycott schools and who were now, entirely predictably, unemployable.

—*End Nexus Familia*

The End of the Rainbow Nation

One of the earliest signals of change from the new government came on 14 July 1994 when Defense Minister Joe Modise announced the end of what he called "the special relationship with Israel." He compared Israel's policy with respect to the Palestinians with the earlier Apartheid in South Africa. Things turned much worse in August. On the 16th of that month, the monstrous Zimbabwean leader, Robert Mugabe, addressed the parliament in Cape Town to a standing ovation by the ANC members. Members of the opposition preferred to walk out. However, these signal events in 1994 were overshadowed at the time by the more positive things that happened that year.

By 1995, there were new signals when South Africa and Russia signed a military cooperation agreement on 14 July 1995. This made people like the author very edgy. On 15 August 1995, Iranian Foreign Minister, Ali Akbar Velayati, visited South Africa in connection with South Africa's agreement to store and market Iranian oil. This was done to assist Tehran in sidestepping sanctions imposed by Washington. On 19 September 1995, South Africa signed a memorandum of understanding with Iran on cooperation in the fields of mining and minerals. Iranian President Rafsanjani would visit the following year to strong US objections. South Africa under the ANC was associating with profoundly anti-Western players in the international arena.

On 29 January 1996, rank and file white South Africans were rudely awakened to the new reality when Nelson Mandela disclosed that he had invited Fidel Castro to South Africa. The National Party in parliament was dismayed and the United States "expressed its concern." Two weeks later, on 14 February, Mandela announced that he had similarly invited Colonel Muammar El Qaddafi of Lybia. Four days after that the Algerian government protested Mandela's meeting with a delegation of the Islamic Salvation front of Algeria. In fact, Algeria recalled its ambassador. Three days later Algeria rescinded that decision.

It is difficult to explain to an American what it feels like to see the president of one's country openly consorting with such vile international characters. But, no American can conceive of himself as being a helpless Western minority in his own country, as white South Africans now were. By April 1996, Foreign Minister Alfred Nzo was sitting in Tripoli expressing the *"thanks of the South African people"* for Libya's role in what was in effect the death of the future for the author. During Nzo's visit a cooperation agreement was signed in the economic, scientific, technical and cultural fields.

While many black people in South Africa likely felt they had a great say in their future, the author now had absolutely zero say in his. Signs were beginning to show of attempts to blame white people for all that was wrong in the country and credit them with nothing that was good. The Western media would amplify this to a crescendo that battered the now defenseless whites of the country morning, noon and night. All one could do was to sit there and "take it" as the Western media piled on accusation after accusation in its classic orgy of hate. Suddenly Apartheid was to blame for everything short of sunspots, and, of course, all Afrikaners were somehow to blame for Apartheid.

A new kind of international "sport" developed in which Afrikaners had to figuratively stand mutely like figures in a wax museum next to exhibitions of past issues as their history was completely trashed. Every character who had ever held an airplane ticket to South Africa now styled himself some sort of expert on the "horrors of Apartheid." Various characters with suspect credentials dubbed themselves "anti-Apartheid activists." If they had not been such activists themselves, then "their fathers" had somehow been such activists. One could now visit Robben Island to see the jail where Mandela spent 17 years. No one ever mentioned his time at Victor Verster Prison with his swimming pool and dedicated cook. One had to mutely listen to how he was "innocently imprisoned." Perversely, no one other than himself seemed to explain why he had been incarcerated, all others insisting he had been innocent. He became an icon of "Peace and Brotherly Love" and no one bothered to explain that he had been the leader of the military wing of the ANC. In fact, he had been the founder. Yet again, he had explained that himself, but the world did not want to know that. They had their image of who he had to be and he was going to have to be that; the truth be damned.

A distinct unreality was setting in. Oddly, when Menachem Begin became Prime Minister of Israel there was much reference to his involvement in the Irgun's 1946 bombing of the King David Hotel in Jerusalem. Mandela's much more expansive role in violence in South Africa was now internationally expunged. Through the eyes of the Western Media it just simply never happened. It was clear that the ANC was hell-bent on rewriting history in double quick time and the Western Media was bending over backwards to accommodate it. Those two parties had a symbiotic relationship. The ANC needed someone to blame for all that was wrong and the Western Media needed a "clear bad guy" as sacrificial "whipping boy." Afrikaners would do just fine for both. The first steps in genocide were thereby implemented with the aid of the Western Media. The Calvinistic Afrikaners were now the "Juden" of South Africa to the ANC's black Nazis.

On 9 May 1996, F.W. de Klerk announced that the NP would withdraw from the Government of National Unity at the end of June 1996 and move into formal opposition. He stated this was due to disagreements about lack of guarantees in the new Constitution and the growing financial crises as a result of the rapidly collapsing value of the rand, the national currency. Pretty much the only positive thing that could be reported by mid-1996 was the issuing of a White House statement on 26 July 1996 that a tentative agreement had been reached to not prosecute ARMSCOR over weapons sanctions busting before the 1994 election. The "honeymoon" of the Rainbow Nation was over. The world had lost interest in the "married couple" and the relationship was now "rape."

Nexus Familia 103: Idiots of either color

In early 1996, a business trip takes me to Philadelphia, PA. As fate would have it, the line I am standing in at Passport Control moves very slowly. Finally, I turn out to be the last person on our flight to pass through. The immigration officer at the desk is a black American. When he sees my passport, he asks,

"How are things going with the new government down there?"

I think for a moment and then I answer him as truthfully as I can:

"I think we have just replaced a bunch of white idiots with a bunch of black idiots."

He breaks out in laughter. I am quite some distance away when I can still hear him laughing. I imagine he thinks I was just being glib. It is already clear that the Rainbow Nation is a farce. Only ANC functionaries are seeing a rainbow. And they are rushing to the proverbial pot of gold at the end of that illusion.

—*End Nexus Familia*

The United States and Gothic Serpents

On 26 February 1993, a yellow Ryder van drove into the parking garage of the New York World Trade Center. The Kuwaiti man driving the van, Abdul Basit Mahmoud Abdul Kari[54], lit a 200 foot long fuse and absented the area. At 17½ minutes past noon, the bomb-laden van exploded, ripping a 100 foot wide hole through four concrete levels of the building, killing six adults and an unborn child. It destroyed the power system of the building and took out New York's TV and radio transmission systems for a week. More than a thousand people were injured during the evacuation of the building. The perpetrator left the country for Pakistan, an "ally" of the United States that would only be duly distrusted more than eighteen years later.

Somehow, the powers that be in the United States, then under the leadership of its next president, Democrat Bill Clinton, did not draw the logic through to its origins. The security establishment apparently failed to comprehend either the severity of the challenge or its roots in the international conduct of the United States at the time of the 1975 Angolan War and the series of Soviet and Cuban actions it had spawned (Chapter 22 : *Angola-Consequences* and Chapter 23 : *Exporting the Angolan War*).

*****

Fig. 26-3 U.S. Blackhawk helicopter over Mogadishu

In large part, the Somalis are a Muslim Cushitic people who have nothing in common with the Ba'Ntu people of Eastern and Southern Africa beyond the color of their skin. In fact, they used to enslave the black people in pre-colonial times. They do not even call themselves "Africans" and have a long history as North Africa's "toughest and meanest" fighters.

In December 1992, United States forces landed on Somali beaches in full view of television cameras in what was called Operation *Restore Hope*. British reporter, Richard Dowden, gives a striking account of the landing[55] of the first Navy Seals in the night of 8 December 1992. The initial purpose was to protect aid efforts directed towards the Somali citizens who were subjected to extremes in a never-ending civil war, also born in the wake of the 1975 Angolan debacle. By early 1993, it was clear that military action would have to be taken and this was sanctioned by the United Nations. The role of the US military therefore shifted distinctly from protector to participant.

In July 1993, US forces in Somalia made attacks on the stronghold of rebel leader Aidid. After the attack, four international reporters were murdered by mobs. By now, the United States had lost its innocence in the country.

On 3 October 1993, the United States suffered the horrors of the infamous "Blackhawk Down" event, more properly known as Operation *Gothic Serpent*. This was the heaviest fighting by U.S. Forces since the Vietnam War. It left 19 Americans dead and 70 wounded in a completely futile and disastrous effort to capture rebel leader Aidid. The next day the Somalis dragged the bodies of some of the Americans through the streets. That sight was enough to convince President Clinton to withdraw all US troops from Africa.

The United States just simply did not seem to get things right when it came to Africa. Unfortunately, they also failed to properly connect these events to the aftermath of the Angolan War, which had sealed the US reputation (*Chapter 23 : Exporting the Angolan War*). The Somali War, which had created the fertile ground for the advent of people like Aidid, had been a direct consequence of the Angolan War. Again, the US was reinforcing existing perceptions of the country in the military domain. It seemed the American "beard could be tweaked" with impunity.

That information was useful to a one-time U.S. ally in Afghanistan who had been living in exile in nearby Sudan since the previous year.

Osama bin Laden would come to dominate the United States national psyche eight years later.

-----ooOoo-----

27

The Rainbow hath no Color White

"This is not a country for a white man anymore."

Colleague from India to the author
Pretoria, South Africa 1998

Setting the scene

The three-year period of 1997-2000 set the scene for a South Africa that would spiral out of balance in the 21st century. Many of the results that were to be visible in the following two decades would ultimately be identified as natural consequences, or natural continuations of trends that were set up in the years 1997-2000 under the Mbeki regime. His obvious antipathy towards white people lay at the foundation of many of these problems. He forced the racial divide on the country, so let us consider it.

The United Nations claims[1] South Africa's economic condition in 1994 was such that, if one separated the "white economy" from the "black economy," then the whites had a standard of living just below that of Spain and the blacks compared more with Lesotho. This comparison is then employed to indicate how the wealth in the country was distributed in favor of whites. Even if one allowed for the UN data most likely being biased against the white people of Africa, the distribution was still one-sided.

As is so often the case in history, one merely needs to observe how people vote with their feet. In the case of South Africa, black people from elsewhere have always tried to illegally enter South Africa, even braving man eating lions on the Mozambique border

Fig. 27-1 The City Center of Pretoria through coral trees

in the process. During the so-called "Apartheid years" South Africa never had a problem keeping people inside the country. Its borders were configured to keep the aspiring foreign Black millions from escaping *into* Apartheid.

There is another way to view the same United Nations data. It merely proves the whites of South Africa were no better off than most other Westerners, Spain being hardly a match for Northern Europe, Canada or the United States. At the same time, the wealth of South African Blacks compared with their fellow Sothos in neighboring Lesotho. All that this United Nations data proves, is that Westerners in Africa develop Western economies and Non-Westerners in Black Africa keep to their old ways – mostly generating subsistence economies. The fact that no African nation in Black Africa has yet developed anything even vaguely comparable to the South African economy and industry, merely proves the point.

The pragmatic may then add to this the fact that in the preceding decade the country had suffered all out economic and financial warfare from the West, led by the United States; this while the country was engaged alone in a real war against the Soviet Bloc and its surrogates. Despite these burdens and immense internal destabilization, the country was among the world's twenty-five largest economies with a gross domestic product of $120 billion. The reader is left to imagine what this country is capable of if not constantly assailed, assaulted and undermined from without and within. Simply removing the external economic attacks on the country would have led naturally to growth.

The primary tax base of the government remained the individual Western White taxpayer, who was earning around 61% of all personal income in the country. By 1997, that white taxpayer was experiencing almost zero benefit for the 33% of taxes he was paying on his income.

Black people in Westernized South Africa provided the bulk of the unschooled labor and had very low salaries indeed. However, at home the public campaigns of the ANC during the 1980s and early 1990s resulted in few if any poorer black people paying for rent or utilities (See Chapter 24: *PW's "Total Onslaught" comes true*). Bread and the staple corn meal were subsidized by the state from taxes paid by Whites. The ANC, now that it was the government, could understand that this freeloading would have to stop. As described by American author Adam Ashforth, the Mfete family of Soweto now had to pay for their electricity and houses were no longer provided by the state[2]. They now had to have a mortgage at a high interest rate just like the white people did.

An entire generation of young black people in places like Soweto had not gone to school, thanks to the ANC's policy of *"No Education before Liberation"* since the 1976 Soweto Riots. Major parts of infrastructure in the areas where they lived had been destroyed by the urban warfare waged by the ANC on fellow black people. The major tax contribution by the black population was via the blanket General Sales Tax of around 6%.

By 1997, practical Apartheid in the workplace had been absent for more than a decade. At the same time, the 5 million whites, 3 million Coloureds and 1 million Indians could hardly have been expected to economically uplift to Western levels the aspiring mass of 30 to 35 million black people inside the borders of the country. The ANC had told the latter for years that Whites had "stolen" what was "theirs." They were now streaming into urban areas by the millions from the old homelands to collect "what was theirs." With little education, if any, these *"masses,"* as the Soviet-inspired ANC referred to them, were trying to emulate Nelson Mandela's great exodus to the Golden City (See Chapter 19: *In the wake of the Second World War*), only to end up in corrugated iron shacks. Unlike him, they had no legal training, helpful white Communist friends, or special connections.

The ANC made a bad situation worse by blaming every social or economic problem in the country on whites, thereby willfully setting the uneducated "masses" of black people on the whites. The trade unions now wanted their "piece of the pie" from the ANC for their earlier support. However, there was no pie. There was no tree on which money grew. Marxism had not prepared them for this reality.

It all comes down to simple mathematics. While whites were earning around 61% of the payroll in the country, they constituted about 5 million people in a country with some 30 to 35 million blacks. If all the salaries of whites were simply divided equally among the 30 million black people, they would on average have had one sixth of the income of whites, and, if tax tables stayed the same, would be paying little income tax, thereby destroying the tax base of the country. Black people who had school education and had joined the workforce during the time of Apartheid were now doing better than that financially. They were now buying houses in regular traditional "white" suburbs. However, the ANC had taught an entire generation – the so-called "masses" – that it could bomb, kill, murder, steal, riot, and terrorize its way to success. Issues such as Work Ethic and Study did not figure in the ANC rhetoric. The "masses" were now discovering that *"No Education before liberation"* actually led to *"No Job after Liberation."*

The State coffers were depleted because of the intense economic disruption by the ANC and years of economic warfare by the West on South Africa. So it turned out there was no pot of gold at the end of the Rainbow Nation's rainbow. Mandela must have realized he had saddled a horse that was crippled by his own party when he announced[3]:

"We must rid ourselves of the Culture of Entitlement."

As government, the ANC was now reaping what it had sown as a revolutionary organization during the twenty years since the 1976 Soweto Riots. Mandela's newfound awareness of economics was simply too late. The damage had been done by his own organization.

Truth and Reconciliation – Catharsis, Redemption, or Farce?

The much vaunted Truth and Reconciliation Commission promoted by Nelson Mandela started its proceedings on 15 April 1996 in East London under the chairmanship of Desmond Tutu. The members of this body were hardly representative of the political realities of the country. Firstly, there was the chairman, Desmond Tutu. He had initiated the political actions against South Africa in the USA. By no stretch of the imagination could he even vaguely be seen as independent in this conflict-ridden situation. His comments over many years had been quite extreme. At the very least he was, as the U.S. Deputy Secretary of State for Africa had earlier put it, a "prelate with a sharp tongue and a well-developed taste for liberation theology"[4]. He was infamous for comments such as[5], suggesting that he was thankful he was black, because, according to him, white people would have a lot to answer for at the last judgment.

Just in case one thought, quite reasonably, that the particular comment had been made in jest, he clarified his line of thinking a month later by musing to a Dutch newspaper[6] about the possible horror if "only" 30 percent of domestic servants in white households would poison their employers' food. In an interview with WNBC-TV in New York a few weeks later, he again raised the subject. In something as basic as an American jury selection process, a person with such statements on record would have been rejected outright as blatantly biased. In Canada, he would most likely have been prosecuted under the Hate Crimes Act. As chairman of a body as ostensibly key as the Truth and Reconciliation Commission the choice was beyond ludicrous.

When that choice was announced, Afrikaners in general simply wrote off the commission as a farce. They were understandably concerned this would turn into a witch hunt by the political victor, the ANC. The commission promptly received the Afrikaans sobriquet of *"Lieg en Bieg Kommissie,"* the rhyme and alliteration sealing it as practically the default name in Afrikaans. Significantly, it means *"Lie and Confess Commission."*

The ANC seemed to think anything it did was automatically justifiable, and it would therefore not have to testify. The Western Media had certainly created that climate for the benefit of the ANC. The ANC had burnt alive many black South Africans who disagreed with it and the Western media had not criticized it to any significant degree. Members of the security forces were convinced the commission was called into life merely to attack them. Certainly, few if any Afrikaners expected evenhandedness from this lopsided commission.

Considering that the 20-person commission presumed to sit in judgment on white people regarding the actions of a white government, its credibility was undermined by the fact that only four of the twenty councilors were whites. Of those, only two were Afrikaners, the nation everyone knew would be in the "accused dock." One was the co-leader of the opposition party in the last white parliament, Wynand Malan. He was a descendant of the French Huguenot refugee Jacques Mallan of Saint Martin in Provence, France (*NF2, 18, 19*). However, he was one of the Afrikaners who had flown to Black Africa to meet with the ANC earlier in the 1980s; the ones PW Botha had referred to as "useful idiots" (Chapter 25: *Inside South Africa*). That left only Advocate Chris de Jager, who had once been a Conservative Party member, but had later served in parliament as an independent. There was no one on the commission from the previous governing party or its institutions. De Jager was the only man who could be relied on to any degree to highlight the terrorism and murder by the ANC.

The other two white members were the left leaning Alex Boraine and Wendy Orr, who, to her credit, had stood up to the previous government about the conditions for prisoners in her care as district surgeon some years before. There were no established centrist or conservative white members on the Commission.

Based on its composition, most whites predicted a totally slanted view from this body. They were not to be disappointed. Years later in 2012 other nations, including the Irish, as hinted earlier by the author himself, would study this commission as a supposed success in "healing a nation." They are total and utter victims of the haplessly slanted Western Media. The only parties who obtained anything positive from the commission were those who finally found out how their loved ones had died, and those who sought to have the killers of their families look them in the eye. In that respect, they had some form of closure. As regards the supposed rainbow nation, the Commission simply flared open the wound and exacerbated the divide. It categorically achieved the opposite of healing.

Some distance into the proceedings, the Amnesty committee, in a fit of misplaced support for the ANC, simply granted blanket amnesty to the ANC leadership. Advocate De Jager promptly resigned in outrage, stating that he was clearly a powerless token. Eventually, even the left leaning Wynand Malan could not reconcile himself with the overall result and wording of the Commission's report. He elected to write a minority report. Therewith the whole concoction stood fundamentally rejected by all Afrikaners who counted in any way, conservative or liberal. PW Botha refused to have anything to do with it and called it a "circus."

Many individuals, singly and in groups, nevertheless eventually applied for amnesty to the Commission. The facts laid bare by the commission horrified the ordinary public. The sheer brutality of some of the acts was truly revolting. This held for both sides in the conflict. By the time of these revelations, the public had been aware for more than six years of the activities of shady security force units such as the cynically named Civil Cooperation Bureau and the Vlakplaas unit. Now, for the first time, ordinary white people heard the details of the horrors perpetrated by these units. What they were less familiar with, was the black-on-black brutality on the part of the ANC and Inkatha.

The reaction of rank and file whites to the revelations was the same level of disgust, dismay, outrage and sense of betrayal as what Americans felt when they learnt about the My Lai Massacre, the Abu Ghraib abuses, the World War 2 STD experiments on Black American soldiers or the 2012 Afghan mass murder by Sergeant Slade. The media devoted extensive time to the proceedings of the Commission, particularly on radio. After a while, one simply could not take it anymore. The revelations were too much to stomach and one's heart went out to those who suffered on both sides of the conflict.

Two special investigations of the Commission that attracted attention centered on the Mandela United Football Club of Winnie Mandela and on the Human rights abuses of the ANC at its Soviet-inspired correctional camps in Angola, particularly the Quattro camp.

What remains a travesty, however, is that, while the Security Forces of the National Party government distinctly targeted those who assailed the State, its institutions and its citizens, the ANC "struck back" by vividly targeting ordinary civilian whites and blacks, avoiding the Security forces like the plague. There is no equivalence between the ANC's bombing of a civilian Supermarket and a government to which they objected, but the children and women who died in the supermarkets had done the ANC no harm.

A mandate to kill

The revelations regarding the events around the Soweto homes of Winnie Mandela represented a key moment in the history of the Truth and Reconciliation Commission. During testimony by Mandela United Football Club members, it became clear that the supposed alibi (Chapter 26: *Nomzamo - "Hamlet without the Prince"*) that had protected Winnie Mandela against the murder-related charges in her earlier court case had been a fabrication. Wire tap information and medical records supported this conclusion[7]. Despite the 18 murders associated with her home, the utterly damning testimony by witnesses such as Cebekhulu (freshly returned from Zambia via Britain) that she had personally killed[8] Sepei, and the fact that her home was the scene of much of the sickening torture which outraged all thinking people in the country, she was never indicted for these crimes. The new regime was even more reluctant than the previous one to address the cloying stench of horror that spread from her house to envelop Africa. It remains a travesty to this day.

One of the most sickening moments was when Desmond Tutu, in desperation, tried to wrest at least an apology to the nation from the maw of this "Mother of the Nation." He simply could not extract any degree of contrition. Author Antjie Krog, present in the room, describes the sense of dismay and horror as Tutu finally descended to asking her to apologize by repeating after him a string of words[9].

Perhaps the single most revealing event of the entire proceeding was not one that took place in the hearings at all. In fact, it played out in front of the building where the commission was to hear Winnie Mandela that day. While those whose children and relatives died in her house of horrors sat rigid with fear of this woman in front of them, Mandela's old, wrinkled and poor ANC Women's League supporters physically danced outside the hall chanting[10] that Winnie Mandela had a mandate from them to kill.

Age does not always bring wisdom in Africa. They were applauding her for her alleged crimes.

 ## Nexus Familia 104: Confronting the past

When the Truth and Reconciliation Commission gets underway, left-leaning writer and poet Antjie Krog reports daily on radio for the South African Broadcasting Corporation (SABC), which has already become an ANC mouthpiece. Like most whites, I have shifted away from the SABC TV to the BBC, SKY or MNET via satellite TV and to newspapers. No one I know trusts the SABC anymore in any way.

As a rational human of some experience and considerable international exposure, I consider the Commission, based on its obvious witch-hunt-composition, to be a travesty. Having followed Desmond Tutu's progress through the international landscape and his statements over the years, I consider him to be biased.

On 1 December 1997, Tutu calls Albertinia Sisulu, wife of senior ANC leader Walter Sisulu, to the stand to testify in the matter of Ms. Mandela's possible role in the death of Dr. Abubaker Asvat. Sisulu had been Dr. Asvat's nurse on the day of his murder. While I bear Albertinia Sisulu no ill will, I find it revealing how Tutu invites her to the stand, because it leaves zero doubt as to how he views the clash between the two sides[11]:

"Thank you, I call Mrs. Albertina Sisulu. Good morning, Mama. It is lovely to have you. I am sorry that we have made you and your youngish escort come here so frequently, we are deeply grateful that both of you had been able to come and may I just take the opportunity of expressing our deep appreciation to you and to him for what you have meant to our nation, what you have meant to our struggle.

Both of you have been quite outstanding and I think one should say it goes also for your family. And we are just proud to have had you as one of the leaders of the struggle. I might point out to you that you had a great deal to do with making the United States Congress pass the sanctions legislation..."

I am forced to conclude the chairman of the Truth and Reconciliation Commission does not count me as one of his "nation." As for Albertina Sisulu, she played her role on her side of the South African divide largely honorably.

At the end of Sisulu's testimony, Winnie Mandela tries to approach her, but Sisulu rebuffs[12] her firmly and explicitly in isiXhosa.

As more individuals start confessing their activities in exchange for amnesty, the full horror of what has been done by operatives of the previous government becomes clear. It is frankly disgusting, and I feel morally betrayed and undermined. To date, it has been vividly obvious that the ANC was making war on civilians of all colors. They killed whites for the sheer sake of killing whites, and they intimidated the black public into submission by burning black opponents alive. They invented the flaming tire "necklace" in this process. People like Winnie Mandela appeared to revel in the fear they engendered. It seemed as though they lived to exert this life and death control over others by means of sheer terror.

Now it becomes clear that the secret services of the South African Police have been carrying out horrific torture and murder of their own. The ANC operatives sliced slogans into the flesh of their victims and burned them alive. The government men operated more quietly and targeted those who were attempting to overthrow the government. Both now revolt me. Those Americans who lived through the late 1960s when the My Lai massacre became public knowledge will have some perception of the overwhelming sense of betrayal and dismay that one experiences when confronted with such revelations.

In my way of looking at the world, the previous government has not just been incompetent; it now seems it actually sank to the level of inhuman barbarism of those it was fighting. I simply could not believe that people of my own Christian culture could do the things they were confessing. Where had these men grown up? For crying out loud, we are civilized Christian people! God, please help us! The details of the excesses of both sides will eventually be described in Antjie Krog's book[13]. I share her horror, anguish and dismay. But, I share little else with her other than my white skin and my language.

In the end, one switches off the radio. There is only so much one can process. In my mind, two heaps of miscreants from hell are in front of the Truth and Reconciliation Commission, asking for amnesty in exchange for a full confession. And their requests and confessions are presided over by Tutu who once mused to the newspapers about the poisoning of white children.

This is all insane; just plain insane! I do not know how much longer I can subject my family to this moral madhouse. I deeply love the country of my blood, but it has gone insane.

When Tutu finally persuades Winnie Mandela to repeat after him the lame sequence of words which he seems to believe will redeem her with people in the country, the Commission finally proves to me beyond any shadow of a doubt that it is a complete farce. From the intense emotions displayed during the hearings it is evident that the commission has played a role in creating a degree of closure between the perpetrators of abuse and murder and those who suffered at their hands. However, as regards healing the nation it is a spectacular and very public failure.

It has made things decidedly worse.

—End Nexus Familia

Exit Mandela

During 1997, South Africa changed drastically. In the period since the 1994 elections, Nelson Mandela had put in a major effort to allay White fears. There were few men who could do this as well as he. After all, North America had fallen for it hook, line, and sinker. He had gone out of his way to build good relations with his former opponents. Author Martin Meredith puts it well[14] when he states that Mandela's most loyal opposition had been his former enemies, the very conservative Freedom Front under previous Army boss, Gen. Constand Viljoen. There had also appeared to be a genuine sense of mutual respect between Mandela and PW Botha. However, this was distinctly absent from Mandela's dealings with FW De Klerk, whose standing also nose-dived in the eyes of whites. After leaving the Government of National Unity, the standing of De Klerk's National Party simply plunged. Whites in general, both to the left and to the right of the spectrum, felt betrayed by him – it was only the delay in coming to that conclusion that differed, the time-to-realization increasing from right to left across the white political spectrum. Of course, as long as the subject had been inanities that cost nothing, Mandela's platitudes had been an easy expedient. On 13 December 1994, in London, Mandela had stated[15] to SAPA and Agence France Presse:

"We had to allay the fears of whites to ensure the transition process took place smoothly. If we had not done so, the civil war that was threatening would have broken out."

However, according to his biographer[16], Mandela later stated that reassuring whites had involved no cost. Indeed, it had not. Everyone had been desperate for hope, and it had been cheap to provide. The reader can think through the true plan behind his words above.

Against this prior background, it was becoming clear by 1997 that the day-to-day business of the government was a mess. Mandela appeared distant and aloof from the business of governing. This he left to his Deputy President, Thabo Mbeki. It is the easiest thing in the world for politicians to make handouts and be popular. It is another thing entirely to manage a country, especially one in which 75% of the population had ridiculous expectations.

Mandela had made it clear as far back as 1996 that he had no intention of serving a second term. This effectively made him a lame duck president. By 1997, it was a matter of who would be the next president of the ANC. Whoever that was, would automatically become president of the country in the next election, given that South Africa was now effectively a standard issue Black African One-Party State, dressed up like a democracy for Western Media benefit. No party beyond the ANC stood the vaguest chance of winning an election for the foreseeable future. In this, it was no different from the ANC's mentor, the defunct Soviet Union. South Africa was governed not by Parliament, but by the Annual Party Congresses of the ANC. Parliament was a useless and irrelevant rubber stamp.

Mandela's choice for Party chief was Cyril Ramaphosa, the man who had been so effective in destroying the haplessly incompetent National Party in the 1993 pre-election negotiations. However, in December 1997, the ANC Party Congress elected Thabo Mbeki as leader. Mbeki had joined the ANC Youth League in 1956 and the Communist Party in 1961. In 1962, he had been one of 27 ANC students sent abroad for studies. He had done a degree at Britain's University of Sussex and military training in the Soviet Union. In this, he differed from Mandela, who had never been to the Soviet Union. A Soviet-trained ANC operative was now the shoo-in for the job of South African president. In the United States, those who should have noticed were too preoccupied with President Bill Clinton's new second term and the court case surrounding the Oklahoma City bombing to notice the tectonic shift in South Africa.

While white South Africans eyed these developments with a wary and weary eye, North America still fawned in adulation on Mandela and the ANC. If anything, analytical thought in the United States on this subject only decreased. South Africa was now "yesterday's news," and most Americans honestly thought Mandela was in command of South Africa. In fact, many would still think so twelve years later. Mandela remained State President, but only in name.

In all matters practical, Mbeki now ran the country, and he ran it his way. He soon presented his blueprint for South Africa in the form of GEAR, his Growth, Employment and Redistribution plan. Internationally it was welcomed as "investor friendly." The local business community carefully welcomed it. White employees distrusted it as a plan to work them out of their jobs and property. The ANC aligned Congress of South African Trade Unions (COSATU) and the Communist Party nevertheless screamed murder and treason. The honeymoon was now over and the real New South Africa was at hand.

On his way out as party president of the ANC, Mandela was forced to read a statement prepared by Mbeki. It set the tone that was guaranteed to destroy South Africa in the long run. There were references to whites undermining the government, Afrikaners in particular being blamed out of the blue. Business leaders were accused of intentionally resisting change in the workplace. It was a sudden and unjustified attack on white people. Here was the start of the open trend within the ANC government of blaming white people for all the failings of the ANC and intentionally sweeping up black people against white people.

From this moment on, white South Africans smelled a true blood-enemy in power over them, and those in the ANC who preached against him were even worse in their attitude toward white people. White people were no longer welcome in South Africa. Internationally no one seemed to notice. They were far too busy congratulating themselves on removing Apartheid to concern themselves about the growing disaster that had replaced it. Mandela deftly departed the scene before he could be personally blamed for the mess his party was devising.

Nexus Familia 105: Black Bwana come Africa

At work, in early 1996, our divisional director of some nine years transfers to another division and his position is advertised. As white men, we are told in no uncertain terms not to bother applying as the only acceptable applicants will have to specifically not be white. Any pretense to hiring people on the basis of competence has now been thrown out the window.

Soon enough, a devout young Moslem of mixed descent is hired and appointed as director over the collection of experienced managers. I get along with him well enough, but he seems to specifically target some of my colleagues to such a degree that I have to eventually confront him about it. After less than one year, he is forced to resign when it is discovered that he failed in his stated objective of meeting with our key clients in France on his visit to that country. Instead, he allegedly attended the French Open tennis tournament on the organization's account. Most of the female contingent in the division is very happy at this development, because they feel he let his religious convictions and associated attitude towards women intrude into the workplace. A caretaking white director from outside the organization is appointed in his place. By this event, the organization has now experienced at senior management level the same Affirmative Action problems we mid-level managers had already experienced "on the ground" (See *NF100*).

By 1997, our organization is under immense pressure to hire black candidates into professional positions, whether qualified or not. The performance of some of the black hires, especially among the women, is at least nominally acceptable. This is consistent with the gender roles in traditional African society, where all work, as understood by that concept in the West, is done by the women. So, the result should hardly come as a surprise. In this process of Affirmative Action hiring, one comes across some truly interesting phenomena. One of these is the advent of the "Helpful and Concerned Black American" visitor. I am assigned to act as liaison with one of them. As a person she is nice enough. She tries for a few short weeks to grasp what she is dealing with, but one morning I discover that she has absconded, or perhaps fled.

Africa has never been easy for Americans to grasp. Black Americans who believe they can relate to Africa on the basis of skin color are haplessly deluded. Liberia should have made that vividly clear, but they likely never noticed. Black Americans coming to Africa are like the white colonialists of the 19th Century. One of my colleagues cynically comments:

"Yes, now it is Black Bwana come Africa! Black Bwana go back America!"

—*End Nexus Familia*

The racial divide deepens

In many different pronouncements, Mbeki soon dispelled any notion that he would be evenhanded in matters racial. His conduct was that of an out and out Africanist. He clearly was not happy just to advance black people; he had to somehow actively disadvantage whites. The attitude promptly surfaced in the day to day workplace. Communication from Mbeki to the ordinary workplace seemed uncannily fast at the time. The reason would eventually become clear.

Soon, the local newspapers started reporting exceedingly savage torture murders of white farmers. On 14 March 1997, thousands of white farmers took part in a protest against the government's reluctance to investigate the extraordinarily high murder rate of farmers and the terrifying level of violence and torture involved in these attacks.

Some may argue that the white people were inheriting what their previous government had sown, but nowhere in Africa had any policy by whites, however positive, supportive or helpful, proven effective in preventing wholesale black savagery and ridiculous expectations. This was black racism at work. However, white Americans appear to perceive black people to be peculiarly immune to this human failing.

The whites of Rhodesia had thought a good education for their black people would make the difference. It had not prevented the horror of Flight 825 (Chapter 23: *Flight 825*) and the advent of Mugabe. The Portuguese had thought that assimilation would ensure a positive result. It had not. In fact, it had delivered even worse results (Chapter 20: *Horror on the Ides of March*). The British had thought that a pomp-and-ceremony handover of power would work, but it gave the world Idi Amin and the expulsion of hundreds of thousands of Asians.

Black Africa simply is what it is, no matter how much Northern Hemisphere white people wish it to be the "Land of the Noble Innocent." There is nothing wrong with the inherent abilities of the Black African. It is the culture that is at issue and Western Society has become too "politically correct" to discuss it, lest they should offend the black people who are exactly the ones who suffer most for the lack of Western honesty.

Respected Harvard University economics-historian Niall Ferguson has pointed out[17] that Western Civilization developed a set of "killer applications" which underpinned its economic success story:

(1) the Rule of Law;

(2) the Work Ethic;

(3) Competition;

(4) Modern Medicine;

(5) Modern Science;

(6) the Consumer Society.

Of all of these "killer applications," Black Africa has taken with gusto to the sixth concept while vividly failing to embrace the first three in any way that the West would recognize. In a television interview during 2011 on CNN with Fareed Zakaria, editor of *Time Magazine*, Ferguson added "Private Property Rights." This concept is brazenly ignored in Africa as Robert Mugabe instigates the killing of white farmers to steal their farms. A positive result on only the consumptive aspect, and none on the constructive aspects of the Ferguson List does not make for much hope as regards economic success. These shortcomings on the part of Black Africa have made it into the most enduringly backward society on Earth and may doom it to remain exactly that.

The emergence of economists such as Ghanaian Professor George Ayiteyyi and, more recently, Zambian born Dambisa Moyo, proves that Black Africans are thoroughly capable of identifying the problems faced by African societies. However, this handful of insightful people is not even vaguely representative of the bulk of the population of Africa; what the ANC refers to as "the masses."

Africa is about personal power above all else and that power is treated as simultaneously mystical, godlike, tangible, and all-determining; to be feared, revered, and desired at all times. Author Richard Dowden captures this issue well in his text *Africa - altered states and ordinary miracles*[18]. Westerners are "babes in the woods" compared with Africans when it comes to the subject of power: how to acquire it, usurp it, wield it, direct it, exploit it, or abuse it. Herein lies the root of the rampant corruption on the continent. It is by no means clear that the bulk of the population of Africa has any understanding of the Western concept of corruption. There is nothing in the history of the continent to give them any indication that it is not the default condition of man.

To the arguments maintained by Mbeki about disparity between white and black, there would usually be added comments about rampant joblessness. However, a subsistence society has zero formal employment and a 100% formal jobless rate. Why is it then a surprise that the relevant people, when transitioning to a formal employment-based Western economy, should have a high unemployment rate? To the author, this seems obvious and mathematically unavoidable. To move from a subsistence society with zero employment to 100% employment, one passes through some employment. But the Western Media prefers to talk of it in terms of "desperate unemployment." Perhaps the Western Media has no concept of what a subsistence society actually is.

One look across the border from South Africa to any neighboring state reveals the reality after many decades of African independence. In Black Africa, economic development is somehow consistently synonymous with the presence of white people, in whose absence it regresses. Next-door Mozambique is a vivid example and Zimbabwe makes the point rather painfully.

That is not a choice made by white people in Africa. It is a consequence of the choices made by the Black African people who are in control. They should look to themselves for the reason and not attempt to blame whites for having somehow "taken" something from them that they never had to start with. They've had thousands of years to develop advanced economies and have failed miserably. It has zero to do with the color of their skin, and everything to do with the issues listed above, so ably enumerated by Ferguson.

Unlike the industrious people of Asia, Africa has simply failed to "download" Niall Ferguson's "killer applications." It cannot be Apartheid, because there was no such policy outside South Africa where the condition of black people is still distinctly worse than in South Africa. That was why Africans from elsewhere were now flooding into the country and had previously tried to sneak in.

Fig. 27-2 Land decay under Black African management

To illustrate this point, consider Fig. 27-2. It shows a satellite image of the border region between South Africa in the west (left) and the completely independent Kingdom of Lesotho in the east (right). Lesotho never had Apartheid as a policy. It had the benefit of a homogeneous Ba'Sotho population of around one million and little history of tribal strife. Note how the border is sharply demarcated by the striking decay of the farming land on the Lesotho side. Lest the reader should think this is a matter unique to the Ba'Sotho people, the similarly decayed Herschel region south of the Orange River within South Africa has been for years under the control of the resident amaThembu, amaHlubi, and some Ba'Sotho people of South Africa. The decay of the land is so great that it is clearly visible from space. The same decay was now setting in within South Africa "proper" on lands appropriated by the Government from white farmers, whose role it had previously been to feed the nation. The defenseless and exposed white farmers were leaving their farms due to the extreme violence against them by black people. In 1994, there had been some 85,000 white farmers, the vast majority of them Afrikaners, but the number was now dropping precipitously.

It is against this background that matters in the South African workplace environment became systematically more difficult by 1997-1998. Perhaps people working in the private sector were still being shielded from the truth. However, in the semi-government environment where the author had built his career, matters were getting out of hand to the point of becoming a complete farce.

Nexus Familia 106: Ubuntu and the amaBhulu

By early 1998, our division management consists of a number of white Afrikaans speaking managers, three white English-speaking ones, including an expatriate Briton, and three black lady managers. One of the latter has spent much of her life in Communist Cuba.

Over this period, Thabo Mbeki's anti-white sentiments are injected with some vehemence into our workplace. We are herded into management meetings in which black spokesmen tell us that, as white men or amaBhulu, our culture is fundamentally "self-centered" (read "evil"), and that we need to be more like black people, who are "more socially concerned" (read "good"). There is much talk of a concept referred to as Ubuntu, in terms of which "one is a human being through others"; the morally confused African version of humanism. Left leaning author Antjie Krog describes[19] this matter based on a conversation with a black psychologist, who tells her that whites have a "self-centered, selfish, capitalistic" character.

I listen to this, but wonder where the live burning of black people by other "good humanistic" blacks, made infamous beyond our borders by Winnie Mandela (Chap. 24: *PW's "Total Onslaught"*), fits into all this "good" Ubuntu. I wonder about the rampant theft, financial abuse and corruption by several of our Affirmative Action hires. Most recently, one of the new black Human Resources managers, of all people, hired a car on the company account and disappeared without leave for a week-long holiday to Durban. He cannot conceive of how that is not his right, given his new Power – always this obsession with power and its abuse. I ponder how this stacks up against the much maligned whites who carry all the workload and are stressed out of their minds. This while they work themselves sick to get the black personnel trained up, fully knowing that they are to be replaced by the trainees. Thabo Mbeki is engendering nothing but intense racial hatred in the country – a hatred that is vastly greater than anything under Apartheid. Whatever Mandela started in 1994; it is now stone dead. Nelson Mandela is often quoted in this process, as though he represents the fundamental definition of humanity and the fount of all human wisdom. It is during one of these severely irritating "good Black Ubuntu versus evil White Man" sessions that one of the black lady managers softly elbows me in the side with a classic dead pan expression on her face and whispers the following in my ear:

"Mandela!? What the hell does he know? He sat in jail for twenty-six years!"

—*End Nexus Familia*

The rainbow hath no color white

By 1998, it was clear that there was no place in South Africa for white people if the ANC had its way. By now, it was obvious that the national rainbow contained no color white; only black, green and yellow, the ANC party colors. If you were not black, you were at best a "tolerated party." Your role as a white person was to produce money for the country and to be taxed. Otherwise your hope for the future was that you might be allowed to live as some sort of subservient powerless and mute drone with no means to affect your own future, or that of your children.

The psychology of the white people became an interesting study. Lots of instant white Anti-Apartheid activists now floated mysteriously upwards into public view. They competed with one another to promote their anti-Apartheid credentials, but somehow their competence was never a subject of discussion. Every nation has sycophants and the White South African is no exception. The country had a veritable infestation of self-styled "anti-Apartheid activists" who scurried about like rats at a cheese fest. These vividly transparent people were suddenly everywhere, their contribution to Post-Apartheid South Africa as nebulous as their previously invisible opposition to Apartheid. Those I met were truly unimpressive human beings and history would be well rid of them.

Perhaps the best demonstration of this phenomenon was made clear in a discussion between the author and his earlier half-Indian boss, who exclaimed in frustration:

"I absolutely detest these so-called Liberals who are suddenly running around trying to do good. I would much rather work with a straight up and down Afrikaner who disagrees with me and says so, and who does not try morning noon and night to ingratiate himself with me. I cannot ever trust these people! In the Afrikaner I know what I have."

Some Afrikaners who had previously leaned to the far left, now styled themselves *"The new voice of the Afrikaner."* They became very vocal, as though they had something new to add. Some appeared almost overnight on television, where most Afrikaners regarded them as "The ANC's Token TV Afrikaners." However, their story was spent. Several of them operated in what appeared to be a mode of *"ambient guilt."* They were attempting to emulate the sector of American White Liberals who personify the American Culture of Guilt, a phenomenon that paralyzes the United States to this day in the social and political domain. They simply could not conceive how forgiveness could not be forthcoming, given that they were being so "nice." This group included many previously viewed as "liberals." It included renowned Afrikaner authors.

In 1998, the ANC seemed to indulge them, but PW Botha's earlier words come to mind when viewing their moral desperation: "Useful idiots." The orthodox Stalinist leadership of the ANC must have found the moral gyrations of these people amusing in the extreme. It would take roughly ten more years for almost all of them to recant and realize they had been deluded. By 2008, some of them would finally give up on the ANC when their own families were attacked. By the time of this work going to print, it has become quite evident to all that the ANC will never, as long as it exists, ever stop blaming white people for all its own shortcomings. That is why it is part of the problem of South Africa and not a plausible part of the solution.

Some liberal voices were unique. One of these was the widow of famed author Alan Paton, who had penned the tome *"Cry the Beloved Country,"* based on his rejection of Apartheid. After fleeing to England, she wrote a letter to the London Sunday Times[20] describing what had gone wrong in South Africa. In fact, she suggested that it was in a certain sense fortunate that her husband was dead and could not see what had happened. This should have been a warning to others, but was ignored. Individuals like Anne Paton were at least principled in their stance.

Another sector of society was the ex-Rhodesians. They basically continued with their barbecues and rugby and fatalistically suggested: *"We told you this would happen. That's just the way Black Africa is. There's nothing you can do about it. Would you like another beer?"*

On the right of the spectrum, people came in two general groupings. Firstly, there were the militant or semi-militant groupings such as the *Afrikaner Weerstandsbeweging* (Afrikaner Resistance Movement) under people like Eugene Terre'Blanche. They had a following, but it was never significant and always did the image of the Afrikaner harm. Terre'blanche falling off his horse in public personifies the rank and file Afrikaner's view of his effort. He was never more than a village rabble-rouser with an incredibly dramatic and powerful voice and an even more dramatic turn of phrase. Intelligent people never knew whether to laugh or to worry when he spoke.

However, there were also the people whom the author would describe as ordinary genuinely decent "Midwestern American" Afrikaner folks. They were typically socially conservative, were steeped in the history of their farms and towns and had a genuine love for their country that would stand any nation in good stead. Those in the Free State province could be airlifted with their tractors, corn silos, and churches and deposited in Iowa (or Saskatchewan in Canada) without breaking their stride. They viewed what was happening with horror, and made sure they had their loaded rifles next to their beds, close to their Bibles. In American terms, they indeed *"clung to their Bibles and their guns,"* and they would be the men one would pray to have next to oneself in a serious battle. This author has the highest regard for them. They were specifically becoming the main target of the farm attack campaign.

And then there were the ordinary middle of the road urban white South Africans. They tried to protect themselves physically, financially, and mentally. The physical protection took the form of spiked fences and electric fences around their houses, comprehensive electronic security systems, hired security patrol services, 10-foot walls, and gated communities. The financial protection consisted of getting out of government related jobs, often starting their own small businesses. But, it is an unfortunate reality that not all humans are born entrepreneurial. Also, in a country where competence now rated less than a shoeshine, jobs that required competent engineers were being wrested from qualified people and given to the utterly incompetent. One of the ludicrous examples occurred when a senior white financial manager was removed to make way for a 19-year-old non-white gardener to be accountant for a local municipality in the South Cape.

The mental protection consisted of an ever more cynical and ironic sense of humor, combined with a philosophy of "shut up and suck it up; they'll eventually realize that they need us." In the 1970s and 1980s, there had been commercials on television for Chevrolet in which the jingle had the lyrics, *"braaivleis [barbecue], rugby, sunny skies and Chevrolet."* Much like the Rhodesians, these folks would prefer to drown themselves in this semi-fictitious parallel universe of the Carefree Chevrolet World over weekends. It was at work on Monday that reality would intrude, but then there was always the cynical and ironic sense of humor to protect one from insanity.

Another sector of the white population developed a form of National Stockholm Syndrome in which they formed a most peculiar association with the goals of their new oppressor to differing degrees. They had turned ingrained denial into a permanent way of coping psychologically. They would almost robotically defend patently ludicrous and racist government positions they would never have defended under Apartheid. To the author, it seemed as though people in this group had lost their mental discretion and had settled for "if you can't beat 'em, join 'em!" If one did not read the local newspapers, one would not know that thousands of farmers had been tortured and murdered and that someone on your own block had become the victim of a home invasion and rape. If one pretended it never happened, then it never happened, and so there is nothing to worry about – it seemed to the author a form of mass psychosis. The mind sometimes blots out terrible events to protect the psychology. These people appeared to be practicing this on a massive social scale. Presumably people from behind the old Iron Curtain know this condition well. Some in Canada have confirmed it to the author.

Now and then the white groups clashed vividly at the oddest of times and places. Most ordinary Afrikaners simply quietly watched the liberal creatures "dance on the corpse of the Afrikaner's history." However, sometimes it became too much to bear. This is well described by far left Afrikaner reporter, poet and author Antjie Krog in her interesting work entitled *Country of my Skull*. She describes how, about this period, the Truth and Reconciliation Commission had to undertake hearings in a small Free State town. When she tried to interview a local farmer about how he felt, he recognized her and loudly swore at her, describing in vulgar language exactly how she should depart.

Nexus Familia 107: No country for a white man

By 1998, three of my younger high technology colleagues have already left the country for Canada and the United States. Various companies in Canada have sent hiring teams to South Africa to retain the services of these individuals for the Canadian industry. The high technology community of the Western World respects the competence of their South African counterparts. Everyone wants South African engineers, scientists, doctors and pilots. By this stage, it is nothing strange to hear South African accents from the cockpits of many international air carriers, including in the Far East. On international flights, British Airways sometimes provides cabin services in Afrikaans, but Afrikaans becomes correspondingly rare on South African Airlines. The ANC government is clearly trying to kill the Afrikaans language.

In the early months of 1998, I relocate to the original High Technology Division I had helped found fourteen years earlier. For a few months I focus on the general research & development funding of the unit and on mentoring some of the Affirmative Action management appointees. At this point, I am tired of being the "fix-it guy" for the organization, but I do have a long track record of leading R&D groups out of financial trouble. It soon becomes clear that even the basic concept of something as simple as a budget is novel to some of these folks. One of the better managers I get to meet in this process is a citizen of India. We talk quite a bit about the situation in South Africa. One day, in the middle of a discussion, he tells me:

"Harry, you must be very careful. This is not a country for a white man anymore. There are people here trying to get rid of all white men. So far you are safe because your black personnel all vouch for you."

This is a novel concept to me. Apparently I am here merely by virtue of black people vouching for me; vouching for *what* about me? It takes a man from India to tell me that, as a White African umBhulu[21] with just on 350 years of proven bloodline in this country, I cannot take it as read that I am welcome in my own country? Is this a concerned colleague talking to me, or is this some hidden party giving me a veiled warning by proxy? I store this information away, but elect to proceed with my life as conducted to date. I have no idea how to do anything else anyway. I am now in God's hands; and, apparently, the hands of whoever is vouching for me in some invisible place to some invisible black power.

It soon turns out that the director of our division, as well as one of my white male colleagues, an Afrikaner umBhulu like me, have been cited on trumped up charges of racism in the workplace. It appears an invisible black employee "union" which denies its own existence, but is in communication with the President of the organization, is doing this. My concern is, given the obvious speciousness of the charges, how it can be that our Executive does not dismiss this chicanery out of hand. It seems the actual work the organization does is now of secondary concern. The prime concern is hiring black people and moving white people out of their jobs by any means.

It is over this period that the organization's clinical psychologist tells me the white male managers in the organization are all stressed beyond breaking point. She is no lightweight within the profession, and it is she who makes clear to me just how helpless our organizational Executive actually is. She describes it as caught between the ANC government to whom it reports, along with its secret "union" within our organization on the one hand, and the realities of running an international high tech R&D operation. The international clients are not interested in the ANC's efforts to force white managers out of their jobs and black candidates into jobs for which they are not qualified. They pay for results. This dichotomy at executive level places the competent and proven white managers under ever-increasing stress. While our Executive flails about ineffectually, the load of dysfunctional and deadweight Affirmative Action employees increases systematically, despite our fevered efforts to hire competent black candidates.

—*End Nexus Familia*

The rape capital of the world

The crime rate in the country had already escalated out of control. The Police were certainly not coping. Very few people if any had any faith in the Police anymore. It was widely rumored that members of the Police were themselves conducting some of the robberies, assaults and car hijackings. Car hijacking was the single most visible criminal act that affected the ordinary middle-of-the-road person. So-called "chop-shops" grew all over black suburbs, particularly Soweto. The situation was so out of hand that the rate of theft of automobiles from the existing base of some 4 million vehicles was a very large fraction of the production rate of new vehicles. Initially, the automobile manufacturers benefited hugely from this, but it soon secured them very bad press. By 1998, it was clear that insurance rates were climbing[22] as a result of the hijackings and this had started to affect sales.

The above is merely one reason why a number of businesses launched a joint initiative under the title of Business Against Crime. Its role was to help establish methodologies and techniques for combating crime, particularly the insanely high vehicle crime rate. South Africa had become the rape capital of the world. The 7th United Nations Survey of Crime Trends & Operations of Criminal Justice Systems[23] covers this period and is very revealing. Its results for 1999 are summarized in the following table. It would get much worse:

Per 100,000 population	South Africa	Swaziland	Zimbabwe	Zambia	United States
Major Assaults	1136	714	207	234*	355
Rapes	122	122	47	3**	34

*All reported assaults; **: rape is chronically underreported in Black African nations.*

By far most of this happened in the eastern half of the country where blacks were the dominant population group. Violence had become endemic among Black South Africans. The closer a country was physically to South Africa, the worse the problem. The comparatively low Zambian numbers demonstrate that it was not a racial characteristic. The problem had something to do with South African black people in particular. The ANC tried to blame Apartheid, but the violence had not been this bad under Apartheid. So that conclusion flies in the face of the facts. This had everything to do with an ANC government that had earlier legitimized violence and had actively created an entire generation knowing only violence as a means toward any goal. They wanted what they saw, and they were prepared to murder to get it. In fact, they seemed to believe they had a license to murder. And all the while the ANC party functionaries screamed :

"Bulala amaBhulu! Kill the Boers!"

-----ooOoo-----

28

The Death of the Second America

"Bulala amaBhulu! Kill the Boers!"

ANC party rallying cry after the Mandela government assumed power
1994 to present

The *Ongelykheid* Regime

When Mandela took office in 1994, there were around 85,000 white farmers in South Africa. Not long after, reports began to appear in the local newspapers of horrific torture murders of white farmers, particularly Afrikaans speaking ones. At first, one had hope that it was a passing phase and a consequence of political turmoil. However, the background screams of *"Bulala amaBhulu,"* *"Kill the farmers!,"* *"Kill the Boers,"* and *"One settler, one bullet!"* from people like Peter Mokaba, leader of the ANC Youth League, grew more intense.

By 1997, with Mbeki clearly in command of the day to day running of the country, South Africa entered an entirely new phase. Since the ANC had told its followers "whites stole this land," its policy was now to appropriate land for black people. However, 90% of the appropriated land promptly slid into disuse[1]. It is hardly surprising to find that by the end of the following decade the number of white farmers had dwindled[2] to 45,000.

With the advent of Thabo Mbeki as de facto political boss of the country, the government increasingly assumed the trappings of a Black Racist Regime. Where Mandela had done everything to create a multiracial country, Mbeki put all his effort into advancing

Fig. 28-1 Informal memorial to the genocide of white farmers

Black people. It seemed as though, if he could not do it specifically at the visible expense of white people, then it was not worth doing. He railed against Mandela for his efforts at reconciliation with white people, as described by author Martin Meredith[3]. Meredith accurately describes the effect of Mbeki's brazenly racist policies on whites. Where Mandela had respected Parliament, Mbeki reduced it to a rubber stamp for the ANC Party caucus. Opposition Party Leader Tony Leon suggested that Parliament had become a "branch office of the ANC."

Meredith confirms the author's view that white people were being drummed out of the government service and out of the para-statal organizations. Affirmative Action was being forced down on the country with an iron fist with no regard for logic or reason. If whites did not "get the message" and get out of the way fast enough, they were forced out via trumped up accusations of racism or worse in the workplace.

The term *"apartheid"* in Afrikaans means no more than "apart-ness." In the same spirit, the term *"ongelykheid"* (German: *ungleichheit*) means no more than "unequal-ness" or "inequality."

Since the Germans have been good enough to provide us with so much in the way of sociopolitical terminology, such as "Nazi," we turn to them also for guidance in respect of South Africa in the period since 1997. The German Nazis of the 1930 to 1945 period had been simultaneously Nationalists, Socialists, and Racists. By exactly the same three differentiating qualities, the ANC was now the Black Nazi Party; even its formal name making that quite clear: the African National Congress. Its doctrine was Socialist, and it was, and still is, in a three-way partnership with the South African Communist Party (SACP) and the Congress of South African Trade Unions (COSATU).

Where Hitler had railed against the Jews in public, the ANC now railed against white people in public. Hitler had swept up the Germans against Jews. Mbeki's party was now sweeping up his followers against white people. The Hitler Youth had been incited against Jews. The ANC Youth League was now being incited against whites by its leader Peter Mokaba, who yelled *"Kill the Boers"* and *"One Settler, one bullet."* The Jews had lived for centuries in Germany and had no other formal home at the time. The Afrikaners in South Africa have lived for centuries in South Africa and still have no other home. They have no Israel.

The 1948-1994 South African Government is often referred to as the *White Racist Apartheid Regime.* By the very same token, and based on the same principles, the government had now become the *Black Racist Ongelykheid Regime,* operated and controlled by the Black Nazi Party; the ANC. The Hitler Youth Handbook[4], more commonly known as the "Nazi Primer," stands in mute testimony on the following points:

1. *"The most important and influential facts in the life of nations are "blood and soil." He who understands their laws and effects in history can determine the future. The goal of this manual for the Hitler Youth is to build their political will according to the National Socialist worldview."*

2. *"The foundation of the National Socialist worldview is the knowledge of human inequality. No one will likely disagree with this as long as we stick to physical appearance."*

3. *National Socialism's first defensive measures therefore were aimed at driving the Jews out of our people's cultural and economic life.*

Mbeki was brazenly doing his best to drive white people out of the cultural and economic life of South Africa. His ANC Youth League was driving farmers off their soil yelling *"Kill the Boers"* and *"One Settler, one bullet."* The killers of American student Amy Biehl (Chapter 26 : *One Settler, One bullet*) had claimed that she died because they had been told to kill any white people they met. It is therefore peculiar indeed that *"Kill the Boers"* was now supposedly *"just rhetoric"* and *"cultural heritage."*

Ongelykheid was about to be enshrined in legislation.

Farm Attack

It was difficult in the bigger cities to keep the effects of Mbeki's actions from the prying eyes of the media. Therefore, the greatest price was soon to be paid in the rural areas. The number of murders of white farmers by black attackers is available from the Farmer's Union and it paints a very chilling picture indeed. We consider the

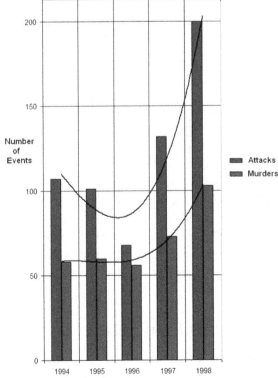

Fig. 28-2 Farm attacks and murders 1994-1998

attacks and murders per year over the period preceding Mbeki's ascension to effective control in 1997 and immediately thereafter. The result is shown in Fig. 28-2. The change in farm attack and farm murder rates upon Mbeki taking over effective control from Mandela in 1997 is striking. The mute graph cannot convey the true horror of these violent racist attacks. We shall later return to this subject to describe the situation more explicitly, so the reader might comprehend reality on the ground for the threatened white Christian Afrikaner.

Nexus Familia 108: To despair of one's country

In April of 1998, my wife and I decide to start exploring the possibility of emigration. We do not see a future for our hearing-disabled white son in the country of my twelve generations of forefathers. Three hundred and fifty years of bloodline in Africa count for nothing in the eyes of this black racist government if your skin is not black. This situation is blatantly and overtly racist. Apartheid at its very worst never did this to anyone. Even at the depths of Apartheid, white people did their best to create jobs for black people. Black people may well have complained they were fighting for a slice of the pie from a disadvantaged position. However, all nations have lived that problem at one time or another. My grandparents and parents suffered that. But the South African Black people were always moving up the economic ladder – never down.

Now it is black men doing their very best to strip white people of their jobs – it is done openly, it is overt, it is vivid, and it is "in your face." All of it is made infinitely worse by the "entitlement" behavior of new black hires who expect a salary for doing practically nothing. There is hardly even a pretense at performance on their part. Functionally, the black Affirmative Action employees have become a dead-weight financial overhead that loads the charge-out rate of the organization, causing the white employees to work themselves to a standstill to keep that charge-out rate competitive. Furthermore, if the white manager does not see to it that these AA appointees "achieve," then the white manager is marked down in his performance review. Fundamentally, the black employees have no incentive to work because they cannot be laid off, and they know it. White employees have been reduced to some form of worker drone that keeps the hive going while many black Affirmative Action employees merely consume the salary account. Some of the latter actually criminally loot the system, but, if the manager attempts any form of discipline, charges of racism are brought against him or her. The situation is untenable for any person subscribing to regular Western values.

By now, it has become tiresome to listen to supposed business leaders who attempt to sketch a rosy picture. They appear to have no concept of the realities on the ground. To the author, it seems as though the high level businessmen have reverted to the days of Cecil John Rhodes. The number of overnight rich ANC functionaries with sudden huge shareholdings in long existent industrial and financial establishments naturally leads one to conclude that the rich white industrialists and financial bosses have attempted to pay off the government. The large corporates themselves have squirreled away their company reserves in Britain. The ordinary working white man has been left to rot. This is no less than a disguised form of high-level slavery. And all the while the ANC yells: "*Bulala amaBhulu. Kill the Boers*" at the defenseless whites.

Later in 1998, I am asked to take over the management of the largest engineering unit within the division. With this, I am yet again involved in Defense related work; this time around jet turbines and related technologies. I drown myself in my work to try and relieve the anguish I suffer when I contemplate the future – I am now completely sure the country is ultimately wholly doomed under the ANC.

—End Nexus Familia

Nexus Familia 109: The Madness increases

In late 1998, I am selected to head up a new business unit in our organization. It is to be devoted to product development for South African industry, mostly in the metallurgical field. It is based on an agglomeration of earlier units of our organization, combined into a structure that is focused on the needs of the Manufacturing Industry. This new role also requires me to work more closely with the Government, from where we aim to obtain initiation funding. This new unit is to be launched 1 April 1999.

In this process, I am exposed to the technological aspects of a major and ultimately ill-fated South African arms procurement program. It will eventually gain infamy as "The Arms Deal"; a well of corruption that will spell the end of several careers, spawn several books, and will land a number of characters in jail. Our organizational role is the evaluation of metallurgical aspects of European weapons systems and the development of counter-trade project proposals to be presented to European companies who are vying to supply naval vessels and aircraft to the South African military.

Sweden, having been unquestioningly enthralled with the ANC over some decades and having never once questioned their terrorism, is bidding furiously via its SAAB aircraft industry. They are doing their best to sell South Africa their untried JAS39 Gripen fighters, while the British are equally active in promoting their BAE Hawk trainer. The former is to replace the now wholly outdated French Mirage F1 aircraft. The Swedish Gripen uses a Volvo-Flygmotor RM12 version of a General Electric (GE) turbine as power plant, and this combination is not wholly trusted technologically. In the process, I meet with the Swedes and the General Electric representatives.

The Air Force much prefers to stay with their French suppliers and purchase the Mirage 2000, because the French have proven to be reliable and honorable partners in Africa. The Air Force has no time at all for the Swedes. I am aware of the feelings on the ground in the Air Force, not just because I have some exposure to senior logistics officers, but also because my younger cousin has been until recently an aircraft maintenance technologist in the Air Force.

Meanwhile, in January of 1999 Tony Blair, Prime Minister of Britain, begets himself to Cape Town, to stand next to Mandela in the South African Parliament.

Fig. 28-3 The BAE Hawk

He obviously hopes that some of Mandela's charisma might rub off on him as he plays to his home TV audience in Britain. What receives less attention, are his labors behind the scenes at shoring up the British effort at landing another $1.6 billion in arms sales to South Africa in the rapidly developing Arms Deal.

In anticipation of our first full financial year, which is to start 1 April 1999, I need to raise the project funding to get the operation off the ground. We decide that I will make a presentation to the relevant Government Minister, Dr. Ben Ngubane. He is the only Zulu minister in the Cabinet beyond Chief Mangosotho Buthelezi. He is a member of Chief Buthelezi's Inkhata Freedom Party. Amazingly, I find that I like "Doc Ben," as he prefers to be called. It has something to do with him being a Zulu. I know the Zulu are more loyal to Africa than to some ridiculous spent idea from the long-defunct Soviet Union. This is something I can respect. If he cares as much for the country as I do, then things can possibly work.

I present the proposal downtown to the Minister, his two Directors and some Deputy Directors. To the horror of our divisional director, I elect to make use of props. More specifically, I demonstrate a Navaho clay pot, an item of Dutch Delft pottery, and a British Airways (BA) menu. The BA menu bears a distinctively South African Ndebele motif, because this is the period in which BA paints the vertical stabilizer of every aircraft in a distinctive national design of some country or other. My recent flight home from Heathrow was on the BA aircraft sporting the Ndebele motif from South Africa. The white directors get visibly unhappy with my presentation, but I do not care. They are no doubt expecting a regular *Powerpoint* and formal handout presentation, as in regular business. My plan is directed elsewhere.

I make a point of the fact that the two Ndebele ladies who did the paintwork design of the BA Boeing 747 were wined and dined in Britain, and then sent home, sans the rights to their work. BA now owned the intellectual property of the pattern on the tail of the Boeing 747. I use the Delft ceramic to show an example of something that is so characteristic that everyone with a house knows the ceramic is Dutch. I use the Navaho pot, by way of contrast, to show how easily one can mistake the origin of cultural wares – I know very well they all think it is South African. Minister Ngubane is clearly convinced when I look him in the eye and ask him to help me keep foreign parties like the British from ever again laying claim to our South African cultural wares, as per the vividly copyrighted BA menu, which I have just placed in his hand. This is the 100% Afrikaner technocrat asking the 100% Zulu leader for help in protecting their joint African country from the machinations of the original colonial power that had caused the ancestors of both such incredible misery.

Some weeks later we are granted several million rand to start our operation.

The above is recounted, not to give an expose of technology funding in South Africa, but to demonstrate the immense contradictory forces that one is subjected to under these conditions. On the one hand, there is the utter loss of all hope in the general workplace; yet, on the other hand, there is the above experience of national communality. It creates enormous stress; not just physical stress, political stress, and philosophical stress, but also moral stress. I love my country deeply, but it now seems to hate me. But, when I work with individuals in that very government, I have a better working relationship than ever before. Then I go home, read the news, and it says that very same government wants me dead:

"Bulala amaBhulu! Kill the Boers!"

—<u>End Nexus Familia</u>

Nexus Familia 110: The Past Intrudes

In preparing our building at work for its opening and dedication to Government Minister Ngubane, I have to ensure that its entrance and reception areas receive a "facelift." The entrance area is augmented with a succulent plant garden of aloes and the like, along with boulders, giving an African "look and feel." I have the plaque containing the Minister's name embedded in a huge boulder outside the front door.

Next, the attention is turned to the reception area. It clearly needs an overhaul, because it is little more than a face-brick research and development laboratory entrance. Our director, much to the chagrin of our financial manager, approves my plan to buy a sofa set and a collection of brushed stainless steel picture frames, the hope being to create a high tech impression at that entrance area.

To help me find the right furniture, I ask the assistance of our divisional public relations lady. She's a very sophisticated black lady and knows her stuff on this general subject. Given that I am going to have to dedicate this operation to Minister Ngubane, I want to make sure that it will all look good. We visit several downtown furniture shops, but nothing seems to want to work just right. As with any male forced into a buying spree, I am getting more agitated by the minute. I find the process severely vexing to the spirit. I know what I want and I cannot find it. My colleague agrees that what we have seen so far just will not work. We then agree to move our attentions to the suburb of Silverton, where there are some further furniture shops. One of them happens to be in the shopping complex where some ANC bombs exploded (*NF91*) in 1986. It also happens to be a socially very conservative part of Pretoria.

And so it is that I notice my colleagues' eyes getting bigger. She is also getting more hesitant to speak. When I look up at the smattering of shop assistants, I realize they are all staring at us. I have been so busy trying to end this buying torture that I have not realized that I have walked into a furniture shop and tried to buy lounge furniture with a black woman at my side. The salesperson helping us knows the circumstances, but the other sales personnel do not. Some things die slowly, but it is this kind of infantile petty nonsense that landed my country in the mess that it finds itself. And the pettiness clearly still survives. Stupid small-minded people like this pulled the world down on us until what it demanded was completely beyond the pale.

—<u>End Nexus Familia</u>

Nexus Familia 111: The Truth of the Cyclops

For the past several years, we have employed a gardener named John every Saturday. John is a member of the small Ndebele nation of some 300,000 souls – precisely the people who are so famous for their brightly colored designs, such as the pattern on the vertical stabilizer of the British Airways Boeing referred to in *Nexus Familia 109*. He is absolutely huge and has something that gains him immediate respect among black men – gray hair. John comes in on Saturdays to mow the lawn.

My mother Nickie is very proud of her garden and she and John often tend the garden together. We pay John better than the typical going rate, because he is very good in this job. While Nickie is certainly nowhere near senile, the relationship is not much different from that between the two central characters of the movie *Driving Miss Daisy*. John prefers to walk barefoot, taking off his shoes when he arrives at our home. Nickie secretly complains to me that John tends to not watch his feet really well, and his toenails slice off the heads of her marigolds. In truth, she finds it amusing. When we find him reading a tattered old Bible during his lunch break one Saturday, we feel compelled to buy John a new Bible.

John has a differentiating physical attribute beyond his enormous size. He lost one of his eyes in a fight as a young man. We therefore have, in a certain sense, the giant Cyclops working with us on Saturdays. But John is an innately good man and a member of the Zion Church of Africa.

One day, while he is mowing the lawn, John leaves the mower on the sidewalk while he fetches the gasoline to refill it. When he returns, two black men are trying to load the mower in their car. One look at the giant barefoot gray-headed cyclops coming in their direction is enough to dissuade the robbers. Later in the morning, John tells me in a very matter of fact way what happened. Just another day for him.

In June 1999, we face the first election since the Great Election of 1994. Mandela has departed the stage and Mbeki is in charge. A degree of dissent has set in among various black leaders, but there is nothing that can challenge the sheer overwhelming One Party State system of the ANC. They are Socialist at election times, and turn into a well of corruption as soon as they are elected. The classically fatalistic African psychology seems to automatically fall in line with the mystical regard for power. As a result they simply accept the corruption.

One of the welter of small parties that has emerged is the United Democratic Movement (UDM). It is a joint effort between Roelf Meyer, who had been the National Party negotiator in the disastrous National Party negotiation effort in 1993, and Bantu Holomisa. The latter is the rather impressive former Prime Minister of the Transkei Republic, the major amaXhosa Homeland. He was one of the first black senior officers trained by the South African Defense Force. He deposed his predecessor in a bloodless coup that South Africa indulged at the time. He was elected to the 1994 parliament as ANC member of Parliament, but has been booted out of the party for truthfully testifying as to the ANC corruption in the Transkei.

So, come one Saturday morning, I ask John how he sees the situation with the coming election and what might work. He says that the ANC has done nothing that will improve his life, and that the party officials are getting stinking rich while he stays poor. He no longer trusts them. Then I get the basic truth about South Africa from the friendly giant gray-headed Cyclops who had very little schooling and has never seen the sea:

"I am going to vote for that party that has the white man and the black man together at the top [the UDM]. *The Black Man cannot make South Africa work without the White Man; and the White Man cannot get the job done without the help of the Black Man – they need each other."*

But, the ANC does not understand this basic truth the Cyclops has spoken. Mbeki thinks Black South Africans can just take what the whites have uniquely created in all of Africa, and that blacks will thereby become rich overnight. Taking everything from white people has not worked anywhere in Africa. It defies understanding how Mbeki thinks it might work in South Africa – the mathematics simply does not work. And, of course, Ubuntu is "good" and white people are "inherently bad"; we are not allowed to forget this basic axiom of the ANC. And still the ANC yells: *"Bulala amaBhulu! Kill the Boers!"*

And still the farmers are being murdered in response.

—End Nexus Familia

Elections again

The first thing that struck one at the polling booths during the 1999 election, was that the elections officials were now all black – not a white face to be seen. It was obvious that white people had been largely trundled out of the Government Service. It had also been obvious when went to renew my passport some time before. It was not as though the more competent black people were getting these jobs. When I sought a new passport, the man attending the passport issuing booth at the government offices had sat fast asleep in the booth with a line of people in front of him.

The ANC won the election in a landslide. There was no feasible opposition to the Black Racist hegemony of the ANC. South Africa was now a One Party State in which the decisions for the country were not made in Parliament, but rather at the Party Congresses of the ANC party. The rest of the world had thrown off the shackles of the Kremlin, but we who had fought so hard against that foe and had driven it from the land, had, for our pains, inherited it in the guise of the ANC – the worst of both worlds. And yet the Western Media fawned on the ANC. It could simply do no wrong in the eyes of the Western Media. Jacob Zuma, the populist Zulu Deputy President of the ANC, was now made the Deputy President of South Africa.

The Sting of the Scorpion

On 1 August 1998, the Office of the National Director of Public Prosecutions had been established in terms of section 179 (1) of the Constitution of the country. This eventually led to the creation of the Directorate of Special Operations on 1 September 1999. This unit was to be the South African equivalent of the American FBI. It was specifically tasked with investigating organized crime and corruption. It was staffed with some of the best lawmen and investigators in the country. It was soon to earn its sobriquet of The Scorpions.

Those interested in Law and Order in a civilized country were thankful for the advent of The Scorpions. They seemed to take their work seriously, which was far more than could be said for the government itself. After all, the population was entertained with images of Members of Parliament sitting fast asleep in Parliament, large numbers being permanently absent. Of course, they knew full well that the actual decision-making about the country was happening at the ANC annual congress, and not in parliament. So those present might very well be forgiven for sleeping in their placeholder jobs. In keeping with the African concept of power, there was no need to be there. In fact, many could not be there, as they had to be elsewhere to flaunt and abuse their newfound power. They did turn up for visits of people like Robert Mugabe, though.

The Scorpions had a number of immediate successes. Given the ability of this grouping to wreak havoc within the heavily corrupt ANC, we should have known what would happen, but we were not yet cynical enough. We still dared to have a vestige of hope. It would all come apart spectacularly a few years later, as we shall see in due course.

Soviet style Political Officers

In Nexus Familia 100, the matter was discussed of a senior executive member of the author's organization having to report to Winnie Mandela through our first ever Affirmative Action appointee who had, to that date, exhibited zero useful ability. The relevant executive member had resigned soon after. It was lamented in that section that the author should have known right at that moment that the New South Africa was a farce that could not work. This point was to return with a vengeance in the year 1999. It was now a mere five years later and the misplaced nature of the author's hope for the New South Africa under the rule of the ANC was about to become vividly clear.

To provide some background, it is worthwhile studying the excellent work *"Europe, a History,"* by Norman Davies[5]. That work ought to be compulsory reading for all members of the Western Media. The present author would have been better prepared for what he was about to experience, if had read just pages 1093 and 1094 of Davies' work. In fact, had he read it, he would not have wasted five years of his life.

Davies addresses on those two pages the actual day-to-day working of the Soviet state. He describes how every department of the state had within it a parallel structure of the Communist Party that effectively policed the workings of the department to ensure that the department stayed within the dictates of the Party. Davies' warns that this arrangement was so alien to Westerners that Western political scientists were easily misled as to what was actually going on.

The author was about to see it for himself.

Nexus Familia 112: Soviet style Political Officers

By mid-1999, my part of our organization is supporting a department of the Government in setting up Small Business Support structures. Everyone now talks of SMMEs—Small and Medium Sized Enterprises—a kind of throwback to the Reagan Era United States. One of the Support Units is to be created in Bloemfontein in the Free State where it has the support of the three mayors of the three major central towns of the province, including the City of Bloemfontein. The Town of Thaba'Nchu is also involved. This is where Barend Matthys Johannes Booyens used to have his farm at the time when he served in the Free State Artillery during the Boer War (*NF66, 68, 70, 73,* and *76*).

My sense of abject unreality deepens in the first week of August 1999, when I am asked to go to Bloemfontein with a deputy director of the relevant government department. We hold a brief meeting in the heart of Pretoria in anticipation of the trip to Bloemfontein. I want to know about small businesses created by white people. Many of them have been forced out of their jobs by the government's Affirmative Action program in support of the overwhelming majority of Blacks who have all the political power in the country. And this is when the director in question, a Coloured South African, tells me verbatim:

"Harry, look, you know and I know that 'SMME' means 'Black businesses'"

I should have had a tape recorder.

A few minutes later a black man walks into the director's office. His eyebrows rise a little at my presence, but he seems to settle down when I am introduced. I am not told what his function or role is. I think it strange that I am merely offered a name, but I make my own conclusions and carry on with the discussion with the director. We are planning the visit to Bloemfontein, birthplace of the ANC in 1912.

A few days later in Bloemfontein, this particular director is supposed to present an opening address on behalf of her department of the ANC government. However, with the entire audience in position, including the three mayors in attendance, along with a hall full of dignitaries, the presenter of the address is nowhere to be found. Several minutes later the director arrives with an anguished expression, heads straight for me, and proceeds to plead very earnestly with me to do the opening address, utterly unprepared.

The man I am forced to assume is the director's relevant black ANC "political officer"—the man I met at the downtown Pretoria office; the one with no apparent function—is not around and somehow the opening address cannot be done in his absence. It would appear he has total control; control to a degree that engenders naked fear in the director.

This then is the basis of the director's point blank refusal to do the speech - debilitating fear at the thought of proceeding without the political officer. The "officer" in question is apparently asleep on the lawn outside! Can the lily white *umBhulu* – the author – please do the speech completely unprepared!

On the one hand, I am mystified by the abject terror of the director—a Deputy Director of a formal department of the Government of the Republic of South Africa—who is, significantly, a South African Coloured rather than a Black. On the other hand, I am annoyed at being thrown into the deep end of a totally unprepared situation in which I might make a complete public idiot of myself.

But it is the third consideration that turns me livid. I am about to start delivering an opening address on behalf of a government whose party operatives sing *"Bulala amaBhulu! Kill the Boers!"* at party gatherings. They want me dead, but I must open the proceedings on their behalf. This is utter madness, just madness.

I start the proceedings, speaking on behalf of said government that wants me dead.

After a few minutes, the director comes in, trailing the missing "political officer," and takes over the proceedings, now totally confident. The change is as day by night.

This is merely one day in the life of the hated amaBhulu, the white men of South Africa.

—End Nexus Familia

Nexus Familia 113: The White Communist

By late 1999, the process for the huge multi-billion dollar Arms Deal is in full swing. The team I am responsible for is in conversation with Rolls-Royce, General Electric, and SAAB on the subject of jet turbine technology. We have done metallurgical research work for Rolls Royce before. We most certainly get the attention of our overseas counterparts when we show them the specialized high-temperature superalloy blades we have cast for the engine of one of the most advanced fighter aircraft in the world – one not in the inventory of the South African Air Force.

Against this background we have the ANC-appointed Deputy Director of a government department at our facility for the morning, along with a number of men from the Armscor arms procurement organization. These are the men who looked after the weapons supply of the South African Defense Force all the way through the late 1970s and 1980s. I have great respect for these men who are proven in their field. These are the men who actually helped win the Hot Part of the Cold War when the whole of the West had turned against us. The Deputy Director, on the other hand, is a rare white ANC member. At a crucial point in the proceedings, when all the Armscor men are out of the room for a moment, the Deputy Director turns to me and says:

*"You know, I really detest these Armscor guys, but I have to tolerate them because each one of those b*****ds that gets a job keeps seven of my guys employed"*

This man has misread me completely as human being and, based on my command of the English language and lack of an Afrikaans accent, is taking me for a left leaning English-speaking South African. I do not object to his pragmatic mathematics. I *do* object most profoundly to the notion that the Armscor men are not also "his guys." Apparently, the only reason why government funding is to be put up for these acquisition projects is so his particular ANC party voters can have jobs. There is clearly no concern for the white technologists and engineers who just so happen to form the cornerstone of the economy. They must just be the helpless drones that keep the national teat going for the ANC Entitlement Society to suck at while it does nothing useful.

My country has been taken over by Communists who care not the least for its economy and well-being. As it is, I am amazed that these white ANC types actually think the black core of that party will ultimately tolerate them. I have just met a greater fool than myself for believing the New South Africa was possible. More than likely, he is going to end up a *dead* white fool with a picture of Fidel Castro in his pocket and a Che Guevara poster on his wall. These people actually think they can be successful by ingratiating themselves with the morally destitute.

—End Nexus Familia

Nexus Familia 114: Political Officers and Corruption

Not long after, I am in a meeting in one of the Armscor board rooms. The meeting is about counter-trade projects and products that the overseas suppliers of weapons systems are supposed to buy from South Africa. A penalty of 10% of the deal has been agreed with the suppliers if they were to renege on the counter-trade. It seems a ludicrous arrangement to me, as I'm sure these suppliers have raised their prices by 10% to cater for this trifling expense.

This is the Defense Technology market where prices are fluid as water and tax money is always involved, both on the supplier's side and on the buyer's side. Nevertheless, I have to put our counter-trade research project proposals on the table as required. In the grand scheme of things, our little bit of the picture is trifling to the point of amusement, but the situation is nonetheless irritating.

Two things strike me in the pre-meeting banter. Firstly, there is ever more intense reference to what sounds like "Chippy" Shaik, the character who has been put in charge of the procurement program ("Arms Deal") by the ANC government. His name is thrown around all the time to the point of it becoming irritating. I do not know who he is. I do not know what he is. I do not know how he got there. To me, he is just another of the endless creatures who appear to have been flushed up out of the drains of this new South Africa and who all rush about in Mercedes-Benz sedans as overnight millionaires.

The ordinary Black people refer them as the *amaBenzi* (The Benz People); the nuovo riche ANC sycophants who drive "Benzes," typically bought with suspect money, and who treat other Black people like dirt. Even if this man with a name that makes him sound like an Arab camel trader is in charge of the overall effort, there seems to be altogether too much personal involvement.

It takes me a while to realize that I am confusing two names. The one is "Chippy" Shaik, who is the Chief Procurement Officer for the Department of Defense, and the other is a certain Schabir Shaik. It eventually becomes clear that the latter is the brother of the former; two South Africans of South Asian extraction. Schabir Shaik operates a newly formed South African company called Nkobi Holdings, which has an indirect shareholding in African Defense Systems (ADS) via Thomson (PTY) (South Africa). ADS is tendering for some of the Navy work.

I get a distinct whiff of corruption wafting through the air conditioning. Fortunately, my team is not involved in work associated with acquisitions by the Navy and I don't have to deal with these Shaik characters.

The second thing is that, yet again, a key meeting cannot start until an apparent "political officer" arrives, dressed in what looks like a classic khaki-colored municipal cleaner's overcoat. The conversation in the room changes tone when he walks in. The chairman welcomes this black man and opens the meeting. The new attendee never speaks, never asks a question, and never writes anything down. Like the creature at Bloemfontein (*NF112*), he never makes any contribution whatsoever. He just sits there. I cannot help wondering whether it is because he has no role whatsoever, or whether it is because the results of any discussion are a foregone conclusion and the entire meeting is just window dressing. Experience has made me cynical enough to assume the latter.

What is unnerving is that it is now men whom I have respected for years (the chairman[6]) who are acting with strange deference to the new silent attendee. And then I consider the ineffectual conduct of our own organizational executive who are not taking action against the supposedly non-existent black union (*NF107*) that threatens white employees. More than likely they have their own ANC political officer to control them.

And now the earlier comment of our executive member, five years before in 1994, comes back with amplified clarity (*NF100*):

"Well, he is now my boss. I now have to report to Winnie Mandela through him."

—*End Nexus Familia*

The Boer War revisited

At the Centenary of the Great Boer War, on 11 November 1999, the Queen of Great Britain offered no apology for Britain's instigation of that War or for the pointed decision of the British Army to burn the farms of the Afrikaner farmers and put their wives and children in concentration camps. Instead she, expressed regret for the loss of life by all. And then she pointedly stressed that it was for the loss of life by all, black and white. The author has yet to find evidence of black farm intentionally burnt. So, yet again the British made it a racial issue.

The fact is that Britain had made war most specifically on the Afrikaners and had specifically burnt their farms, and had specifically herded their women and children specifically into concentration camps. They had specifically underfed the wives and children of those men still in the field against them. The author can find no record of such considerations entering into the thinking of the British Army as regards black people caught up in the process. By this statement, the queen finally lost all her credibility with Afrikaners. The

Throne was now part of the denial and the attempt to write genocide out of their history.

Given how seminal the Boer War had been in the history and culture of the Afrikaner, and given the fact that even Nelson Mandela had said that, if the British Concentration camps were operated today it would be deemed genocide, one might have expected the British authorities to – at the very least – *not* try and spin this event into a play for black support.

And so, even the greatest hurt ever suffered by the Afrikaner was not just disowned by its perpetrator, but was abused by that perpetrator at the time of this lowest ebb of Afrikaner history to curry favor with his oppressor. There was apparently no limit to British political expedience.

The Arms deal – the corrupt boil bursts

On 3 December 1999, the ANC government of the Republic of South Africa completed the so-called "Arms Deal." The whole package would cost the taxpayer R30 billion. In American terms, this is not a massive amount of money at federal level, but in South Africa it is equivalent to a very significant fraction of the GDP – the bulk of it from taxes paid by the salaried white people. Over the objections of the men who would have to use the relevant weapons, the ANC government decided to humor their leftist Swedish allies who had supported them for decades when they (the ANC) were foot-soldiers for the Kremlin's designs in Africa. The French and Italians were to lose out completely on the aircraft deals, as they had sold previously to the "wrong" South Africans, the white people.

The inferior, unproven, and more expensive British Hawk trainer was to be bought instead of the proven Italian Aermacchi product. The Aermacchi predecessor, the MB326, had done sterling work in Angola in the form of the South African built "Impala." It had been a superlative advanced trainer and light ground-attack aircraft. Impalas had even downed six Russian made Mi helicopters, some right under the noses of vastly superior Mig 21 fighters[7]. The South African Air Force now had two aircraft models foisted on it that it had never wanted.

However, the greater relevance of this armaments deal lies in an announcement three months earlier in Parliament in Cape Town. On 9 September 1999, the very vocal Patricia de Lille, a "Coloured" Member of Parliament ironically representing the Pan Africanist Congress, announced in Parliament that she had a dossier of evidence of corruption on a massive scale in the Arms Deal. At first, this was not taken seriously, because the lady had rather a reputation for extrapolation, hyperbola, and rabble rousing. However, her information would eventually prove damning. She handed over her dossier in November 1999.

It would take time, but the den of corruption would eventually be splayed open and Schabir Shaik would end up in jail. Joe Modise, the former head of the ANC's military wing, and later Minister of Defense, would die from cancer before he could be indicted for his central role in the corruption scheme. By the year 2012, all the players would still not have been fully prosecuted. What this whole escapade would prove beyond a shadow of a doubt was that the ANC was corrupt to its very core and to its highest offices.

More particularly, the investigation would expand to Europe where it would become clear that the Thomson CSF company of France had bribed senior members in the South African decision making process. The British Office of Serious Economic Offenses would become involved. There are enough texts and other information available on this subject and we shall not dwell on it further. We shall merely point out that, for those who thought until then that the ANC had any form of moral compass, their subsequent disillusionment can be traced to this well of corruption of the Arms Deal.

What is more odd, is that anyone would have expected any different. Africa does not even vaguely comprehend the concept of corruption. It is a word and concept brought to Africa by white people who deem it, apparently oddly through African eyes, to be wrong to exploit one's public office for one's personal gain. The giving and demanding of presents and favors to and by those in power is the norm in Africa, not the exception. The incumbent is expected to benefit from his or her position. If not, then the incumbent is deemed incompetent, not worthy of respect, and is most certainly not to be feared. "TIA" (This is Africa) as Leonardo Di Caprio's character indeed aptly says in his dying words in the later motion picture *"Blood Diamonds."*

Nexus Familia 115: The Silence of White 6

As a technology manager who serves at least some of the technological needs of the South African Air Force, I am invited to the annual South African Air Force event evening at the Air Force base. I am placed at a table with a senior logistics officer and a new senior black officer in the Air Force. The former introduces me to the latter, who parks a bottle of wine in front of himself and never manages much more than a grunt all night. As the evening progresses, the logistics officer and I end up disciusssing the Arms Deal.

The logistics officer reflects on the fact that the Swedes (he preceded the word with an expletive) are getting the fighter deal. He tells me of the discussions he had with the French from the Dassault company, the manufacturer of the famous, popular, and proven Mirage range of fighter aircraft – the mainstay of the French Air Force, the *Armée de l'Air*. He explains to me how demoralizing it has been for him to have to listen helplessly to the Frenchman with whom he dealt for decades telling him that the Swedish Gripen is a "*toy*" and not a suitable fighter aircraft "*for a man.*"

Fig. 28-4 *The Mirage 2000C in French colors*

The Air Force wanted the Mirage 2000, but the actual needs of the Air Force are now completely irrelevant. I am sitting at a table with a very senior officer of the second oldest air force on Earth; an air force with a stellar record of performance and achievement; an air force that has produced some of the greatest fighter aces (Chapter 19: *South Africa's contribution to World War II*) the world has ever seen. The man is practically in tears about what is happening to his beloved Air Force. And next to him sits the future with his bottle of wine; oblivious.

A few miles away "White 6" poses silently in the South African Museum of Military History – the captured Messerschmitt Bf109 that my father-in-law, Bassie Basson, had flown in WWII (*NF82*). My cousin, the SAAF aircraft maintenance technologist, has already resigned in disgust and is selling insurance for a living.

I am watching my country collapse while the West cheers in infatuated adulation of the ANC.

—End Nexus Familia

 ## Nexus Familia 116: The Final Straw

Near the end of the first quarter of 2000, our organizational division sets off to a resort in the aloe-covered rocky foothills northwest of Johannesburg for a strategy planning session for the coming financial year. Our management team includes a number of Black ladies, one Coloured man representing our Western Cape operations, one South African Indian man, and a few White managers of both genders. Naturally, in keeping with normal practice everywhere, the strategic planning excludes in principle any declared employment union members.

All proceeds just fine until our director brings in a Black gentleman to address us as a management team. The visitor presumes to talk to us about the shortcomings of White Culture and our supposed "unwillingness to change." Then he proceeds to explain that he can "help us" with the new government; this against a background where I have already negotiated several millions with the government and am getting along just fine with the relevant cabinet minister himself. Notably, though, that cabinet minister, even though a black man, is not a member of the ANC; at least, not yet. The key point here is that I am aware that the visitor is, in fact, the leader of the "invisible non-existent" Black union in our organization. Moreover, he is the husband of one of the black lady managers with whom I have worked in my previous division in the organization. More than likely he is our organizational president's "ANC political officer."

After a few minutes, I tire of his obsequious and patently transparent drivel. Either side of me are sitting two white managers, one male and one female. Both have recently been the subject of trumped up and unfounded charges of racism in the workplace. The case of the male manager has been such a farce that our organizational president has belatedly apologized to him in my presence, but the damage was done. The lady manager is currently in the middle of a similar hearing, brought on by her attempt to have a case of brazen fraud addressed properly. I am keenly aware of both cases, and I am also very much aware that the "invisible non-existent" black union is exasperated with not having something it can use against me. It might be that the visitor's wife, my former colleague, is "speaking for me." I do not know.

Against this background our visitor elects to tell my female colleague that he can "help her" in her problem of being charged with racism. Here is the leader of the actual party that is attacking her, suggesting he can "help" her. This has all the sincerity of Al Capone making "an offer that one cannot refuse."

A silence descends on the room. I can literally hear the labored breathing of my two colleagues as they struggle to control their rising anger. Then the female manager wisely says:

"I believe the case is sub judicae and I shall not talk about it here today."

I have had completely enough. As the man with the grayest hair in the meeting I demand to know right at this time who in this room belongs to the "invisible non-existent" Black union in our organization. In the absence of this clarity, I am not prepared to proceed one minute further with any planning with a team of people whose individual loyalties are now suspect. Our director splutters; trapped by his own ill-considered plan to bring this dangerous man into the room. It is to no avail. The focus of the team members is now on the prematurely gray headed man at this end of the table. I turn my head slightly to the left to focus on the black lady manager nearest me. As I look her in the eye, her eyes widen and her right hand slowly goes up in the air. This is followed by the black lady sitting on her far side. Then the Indian man's hand goes up. There is a bit of a delay, and then the hand of the Coloured man from the Cape goes up. He is the last one and looks desperately uncomfortable. Like me, he speaks Afrikaans to his mother. Yet he has joined this insidious cabal.

Clearly the meeting has to be recessed. In this break, I am approached by the group comprising all of the members of the team who are not white. The two black ladies seem wholly incapable of understanding why I am upset. The Coloured man is with them, but keeps a distance. Finally it is the Indian man, whom I had previously helped with the management of his unit, who speaks for them:

"I understand why you are upset. But, please don't be angry with us. [The organization president] knows fully well of this. Please be angry with him."

At this point, the visitor joins the little knot of people. I ask him straight out what the goal of his organization is. Is it to replace the president with a black man? If that is the case, then they can do it with my blessing, because he is clearly already been rendered totally ineffectual.

And this is when he looks at me and says in front of his bewildered "charges":

"No! It is to remove all white managers from the organization."

This is the exact moment that South Africa dies for me. This visitor's connection with the central structure of the ANC is by now well known and so I know this is the plan of the governing ANC. Perhaps some ignorant people in private enterprise who are not yet subject to these forces can delude themselves about the future. Perhaps some who support the ANC are well-meaning, but they are most certainly misguided. I have stared into the maw of this malicious monster and I have smelt its fetid breath. There is clearly no hope for a future. The time has come to leave the country of my ancestors and to create for my family a future elsewhere, as far away as possible from this monstrous insanity.

—*End Nexus Familia*

To lose one's country

The permanent loss of one's country is a process that is difficult for any man to describe. His relationship with the country of his birth is a very close one. Beyond his family, he is culturally expected to be prepared to defend his country to the death. That forges a bond that is not easily broken. When he leaves that country with the hope that his wider family and people will have a positive future, then it brings some comfort. When a man has to leave his country in the knowledge that there is no hope for his wider family and nation, it is infinitely more difficult. When he is then confronted with a Western Media that actually revels in the situation and insists on morally assailing his people even as they await their own death in terror, then the depth of dismay and revulsion cannot begin to be described.

In May of the year 2000, this was exactly the situation that the author faced. By that time, hundreds of thousands of White South Africans had already left the country. The author was just one of them and there is no great significance to his own departure, beyond being one of a stream of high technology people leaving the country in total dismay. However, some points surrounding that departure are useful in describing the general picture beyond just the personal situation. So we turn to the departure at work, and the departure from the country.

 ## Nexus Familia 117: To slaughter an ox

When I announce my impending departure for Canada in May 2000, the president of our organization insists on a meeting with me. He wants to know whether it is the organization or the country that is the problem, because my resignation after 18½ years is causing considerable instability. I tell him that it is both, because the organization is a microcosm of the country, is close to the government, and therefore represents the future direction the government will take the country, and that future is rubbish. I point out to him that the mere fact that he was asking the question already tells one there is a big problem with the country.

He is a British expatriate and will leave the country a few months after me. He is obviously just using me to confirm his own conclusions. He is good man, but he has forsaken his white Afrikaans-speaking employees on his way out the door. Perhaps the pressure on him has been beyond his bearing. I do not know. I just know the consequences. And the consequences are not to be proud of.

One of my South African Indian colleagues is a staunch member of the ANC, and was, ironically, an exile in Canada over the 1980's. On my last day at the organization, we talk about how we have enjoyed working together, and then his tone changes, and he says these key words to me:

"I don't know what to tell you. I was not white enough for the previous government, and it is now clear to me that I am not black enough for this one."

At my farewell party, one of the new young black engineers comes up to me, shakes my hand in the respectful limp-wristed way of the Venda people and says:

"Harry, I have not worked with you for long, but I know that where I come from, my people will slaughter an ox for a man like you."

The young man is a staunch Christian and a lay-preacher in his community. His comment means much more to me than the official presents and uncomfortable artificial "accolades" of the organization, but that's just me. I take it as my personal evidence that I have truly tried to make the New South Africa work. In a country historically labeled with white racism and now run by the party that swore to the world to do away with that racism, I am getting my strongest support from decent black colleagues, apologies from Indian ANC members who already feel betrayed, and more overt naked malicious racism from the machinery of the government than ever before in the history of the country.

—End Nexus Familia

Nexus Familia 118: Mooi loop! – Walk well!

It is a clear June afternoon in the year 2000 in Pretoria, South Africa. A prematurely gray man puts two suitcases, a sleeping bag, and a new notebook computer containing his family's information in a little rented Opel sedan. Then he turns to his family and kisses the womenfolk goodbye. He firmly shakes the hand of his 14-year-old son, telling him to look after the ladies, because he is now the Man of the House.

Then he turns to the diminutive Black Tswana woman who has worked with them for six years and he hugs her goodbye. And that, of all moments, is when he feels the strange stickiness on his face. He hopes his family does not notice.

The Tswana woman has no real understanding of what is going on. She just says,

"Die baas hy moet mooi loop." (The boss he must walk well).

Yes, I most certainly do appreciate the supreme irony in those precise words. They probably sum up the entire White Experience in Africa.

I look at our home of 18½ years and then out over the beautiful green-and-gold acacia-dotted African veldt in the distance. And, as Afrikaner, I silently say goodbye forever to the Africa of my birth – the country for which my ancestors fought their superpower enemy and I have opposed mine; the country that has carried 348 years of my bloodline since Eva saw the Dutch appear on the horizon in 1652; the country for which so many of my ancestral family paid with their lives. I know that I am making the right decision for my family, but will I ever be able to make my own peace with the decision?

I do my level best to smile reassuringly at my family, but I have no idea what that looks like. They will have to survive here for another two months while I try to set up life for us in Canada. My destination is Vancouver, almost precisely on the other side of the planet Earth, under different stars. Canada is a beautiful country with wonderful people, but it is not the Africa of my blood. Its skies have no Southern Cross. Its trees have no rainbird.

Then, I get in the car and drive the thirty miles to the airport through an unfocused blur.

—End Nexus Familia

-----ooOoo-----

29

God help the Rainbow Nation

"We are mighty! ....If they want to serve us, okay. If they want to go back, okay. Goodbye! You tell them goodbye!"

Muammar Gadaffi to Mandela, Mbeki, and Mugabe about South African white people
Durban, South Africa (9 July 2002)

To be known by one's friends

Ordinary Americans might be forgiven for not noticing the rapidly derailing situation in South Africa by the year 2000, as the signals were possibly not that clear to non-South Africans. Any such excuse evaporated on 1 September 2001, with the opening in Durban of a United Nations-sponsored racist hate fest under the title, *The World Conference against Racism*. It became better and more infamously known as *Durban 1*. Israel and all Jewish organizations were precluded from participating, and the United States and Canada wisely withdrew. South Africa now hosted and supported the likes of Mahmoud Ahmedinajad, the leader of Iran, who railed against Israel.

With the First Outer Wall of the West having been toppled in South Africa and its guardians disowned by the West itself, the forces that had toppled that wall now turned to focus on the next Wall of the West – Israel. The assailants accused Israel of racism and sought to equate it with the previous government of South Africa. That rhetoric had worked before. It likely would again.

Muammar Gaddaffi attended the July 9, 2002 launch of the new African Union in Durban, South Africa. His cavalcade consisted of 60 armored cars. The event was also attended by the likes of Charles Taylor of Liberia. Referring to the Whites of South Africa, such as the author, Gaddaffi stated[1]:

Fig. 29-1 Muammar Gadaffi of Libya – Key ANC supporter

"My brother, Mr. Mandela! My brother Mbeki! Forgive! My brother Mugabe! Forgive the whites. They are now poor. You are your own masters. Forgive them. You are free. We are bigger than them. We are mighty! ....If they want to serve us, okay! If they want to go back, okay. Goodbye! You tell them goodbye!"

He was drowned out by rapturous applause from the masses of black people in the stands.

By 2011, he would be a moldering corpse, dead at the hands of his own disgruntled people, and the Black people of South Africa would be suffering once more under their traditional masters: themselves. But the threatened White Western Christian Afrikaner would still have nowhere to "go back" to, sold in 1814 at

£33 a head as mere subjects by their own Dutch kin to the British victor of the Napoleonic Wars (Chapter 7: *The Second Great Abandonment*).

The ANC's concept of treating AIDS

The nightmare of AIDS in South Africa has been one of the most sordid subjects in the history of the country. Beyond his obvious humanitarian concern, the author had been involved in developing AIDS diagnostics based on X-ray technology applied to tuberculosis patients. In 2000, South Africa was the epicenter of the world AIDS pandemic, and the author therefore took a direct interest in the subject based on his earlier involvement in the battle against this horror.

The first outrage came with the failed local development of Virodene as a drug to battle the disease. It soon became clear that the ANC was more concerned with ensuring that stock[2] in the company set up to manufacture the drug should be given to the ANC elite than in treating actual patients. Development of the drug was terminated when it proved to be carcinogenic. The deeper concern was Mbeki's insistence on denying the link between HIV and AIDS – this while he was in charge of the spot on Earth that was poisoning the world with the problem. There was speculation that he actively chose that position so as to cause the greatest possible harm to his historic enemy, the amaZulu, who bore the brunt of the epidemic in the country. He did three things that sealed his fate in this area.

Firstly, he appointed to the position of Minister of Health the ANC doctor Manto Tshabalala-Msimang, a graduate of the First Leningrad Medical Institute and field doctor for the ANC in its Angolan camps in earlier years. This alcoholic kleptomaniac saw fit to tell the World that AIDS could be treated with concoctions of beetroot and garlic. Thereby she turned South Africa, origin of the heart transplant and the CAT scan, into a laughing stock and effectively signed the death warrants of some 330,000 South Africans with AIDS[3].

Secondly, Mbeki sent a letter[4] to President Clinton and other world leaders in April 2000 explaining his position on AIDS. Washington thought it a hoax. In Mbeki's mind, the insistence of the scientific community in linking HIV to AIDS was "a campaign of intellectual intimidation and terrorism," akin to "book burning." As ANC doctrine held that Whites are to blame for all the woes of Black people, Mbeki's provincial ministers insisted anti-retroviral medicines were "a plot to poison black people"[5].

Thirdly, via the hapless Tshabalala-Msimang, Mbeki refused to provide anti-retroviral drugs to AIDS patients. This outraged the thinking world. It would fall to Mbeki's successor and enemy to get rid of her in the face of Western pressure. By then, it would be clear that she had been banned[6] from neighboring Botswana for stealing an anesthetized patient's watch and wearing it to work. The authorities had also found other stolen property in her house. Before being dismissed, she would manage to jump the queue for a liver transplant, despite being fundamentally disqualified for a new one based on her alcoholism. She would eventually die[7] immortalized as "Dr. Beetroot" on 16 December 2009 – the Day of the Covenant (*NF63*).

None of this helped to address the very basic belief among a major proportion of black South African men that intercourse with a virgin cures AIDS.

Mugabe and White South African Farmers

With an impending general election in 2002 in neighboring Zimbabwe, the West assumed that ANC-led "democratic" South Africa would naturally guarantee that it would proceed properly. Unfortunately, Zimbabwe was destined to remain an enduring reminder of the fact that the Carter Administration had foisted the dictator Mugabe on that country.

Mugabe was exceedingly important to the ANC, and he knew it. Mugabe is the "bogeyman" the ANC uses to scare white South Africans "into line." Examples of ANC operatives telling South African farmers they would "do what Mugabe did" were legion. Thus there was no benefit for the ANC in destroying Mugabe, as they should have. Only tangible political pressure on the ANC from the West will ever do that.

Mbeki shipped "observers" to the election who ostensibly came back and reported the elections to be just fine. Mugabe won the election, but there were extensive outcries about it being rigged. Mbeki would hold to his supposed policy of "constructive engagement." There never was constructive engagement with Mugabe – only tacit support and everyone in South Africa knew that. The opposition MDC in Zimbabwe at one point completely rejected Mbeki as mediator, because they knew he was completely in Mugabe's camp.

Finally, six years later, on 14 May 2008, Business Day[8] would reveal that two black South African judges, sent separately to observe the 2002 elections, had provided a report to Mbeki at the time that cited a range of problems with the election. Those irregularities had allowed Mugabe to steal the election. Mbeki had quashed the report. The MDC had tried to get hold of it, but had backed off upon being threatened by Mbeki.

Mbeki would string the West along for most of the decade on this subject. It was tragic watching the monster Mugabe score political points off Tony Blair of Britain. Meanwhile people kept dying in Zimbabwe.

Angola comes home with a vengeance

On the morning of 11 September 2001, the Tunney and Clark Amendments, brought on by the events in Angola in 1975, came home with unimaginable horror. Almost 3,000 innocent Americans lost their lives in the single biggest act of inhuman Arab Islamic fanatic terror in the history of the modern world. And it was at this moment that President Jerry Ford's sage words of warning and Henry Kissinger's concerns in 1975 came true with a vengeance (Chapter 22: *Angola – The Fourth Great Abandonment*):

"A great nation cannot escape its responsibilities. Responsibilities abandoned today will return as more acute crises tomorrow."

Osama bin Laden, having observed President Clinton's reactions, or lack thereof, to the first bombing of the World Trade Center, the events in Somalia, the Embassy Bombings of 1998, and the later bombing of the USS Cole, thought the United States weak. The perfunctory lobbing of cruise missiles at a drug factory in Sudan and some mud huts in Afghanistan were ineffectual responses to the embassy attacks. After the strike on Afghanistan, Osama bin Laden had taunted President Clinton. There had been no response by the United States to the attack on the USS Cole. This litany of inadequate response was interpreted as weakness by the likes of Osama Bin Laden, who now struck at the heart of the United States.

For the sake of clarity, it is worth revisiting the comments of the former Soviet Ambassador to the United States, Anatoly Dobrynin, on the subject of Angola[9]. He holds that, having suffered no major negative international consequences from its Angolan venture, Moscow had extended its efforts to Ethiopia, Yemen, and various other African and Middle-Eastern States. Finally, it had launched its Afghanistan adventure, and the Russian adventures in Afghanistan and the Horn of Africa had given us Bin Laden.

In the wake of the 9-11 attack, the United States entered Afghanistan to find Bin Laden and punish his latest hosts, the Islamist fanatic Taliban, founded on the Pashtun population. Failing to corner Bin Laden in the mountains of Tora Bora, the United States settled in for a long struggle against the Taliban. The majority of that organization's Pashtun support base lived next door in Pakistan and moved freely between the two countries. This assured a future of "whack-a-mole" fighting until Bin Laden could be eliminated.

South African experience for the War in Iraq

With the United States and other Western countries bogged down in Afghanistan by 2003, the United States entered Iraq to depose the largely secular dictator Saddam Hussein. After removing Hussein, the US Military settled in for the occupation of Iraq.

In May 2003, the American Interim Minister of the Interior for Iraq landed in Baghdad, protected by South African Private Military Contractors[10] (PMCs). They would also protect the Al-Rasheed hotel the morning of 26 October 2003 when it was attacked while US Deputy Secretary of Defense, Paul Wolfowitz, stayed there. On that occasion, they would rescue US Colonel Elias Nimmer, who had been badly wounded by Soviet-made rocket fire. Five months later, to the day, Col. Nimmer was awarded his Purple Heart by

Wolfowitz and the American Forces Press Service reported on the event. The South Africans, who had dug Nimmer out of the rubble and carried him to safety, were written out of the story.

The U.S. Department of Defense and the British Ministry of Defense both made use of South African PMCs. Several formal South African Army members took leave in South Africa in order to join their colleagues in Iraq. By the following year, thousands of South Africans, many effectively barred from employment by the anti-white BEE law (See later in this chapter: Black Economic Empowerment) of the South Africa's ANC Ongelykheid regime (Chapter 28: *The Ongelykheid Regime*) were attracted by the offer of lucrative high risk contracts in Iraq. By 2005, South African PMCs constituted the third largest contingent of Western military men after the US and Britain.

The recruitment of South Africans assumed such proportions that the ANC government passed an Act in early 2005 barring South Africans from serving in such foreign wars. Ironically, the men who had been let down by their American allies in the Angolan bush in December 1975 were now the much sought-after hard bitten veterans and a new generation had grown up under their hand.

Despite the efforts of the ANC government, by the fall of 2005 some estimates[11] put the number of South African military contractors active in Iraq between 5,000 and 6,700. This time they

Fig. 29-2 RG-33 vehicles in Iraq; South African technology

were equipped with the best American weapons. They also got their part of the action. In Falluja, in April 2005, a dozen South African contractors, caught in an ambush, drove off sixty attackers, several of whom were killed. There were no losses on the South African side[12].

Fig. 29-3 US Special Forces sign on an RG-33

The South Africans were struck by the lack of anti-mine related technology on the part of the American forces. The much loved Hummers were particularly vulnerable. As losses to improvised explosive devices (IEDs) mounted, the United States turned to South African experience. And this was when 15 years of South African fighting in Angola brought the United States a direct benefit. It would eventually lead to the United States securing IED-resistant vehicle technology from South Africa and hiring experienced South African engineers and scientists.

American soldiers know these distinctively V-hulled vehicles as Cougars. Their oddly configured mine-removal partners are known as Buffaloes. During just the first eight months of 2007 alone the USDOD would order 6400 of these vehicles and they would be mass produced by US defense giant General Dynamics[13]. BAE Systems of the United States would eventually produce a version of mine-protected vehicle labeled the RG-33. It was based on a vehicle that had originally been developed in South Africa. At 23h00 on 2 April 2008, one of these vehicles would save the lives[14] of six US Special Forces men. They would express their gratitude by hanging a sign on the vehicle.

The US would eventually withdraw from Iraq in December 2011 after handing the country to the Iranian supported majority Shia community. The last US military vehicle out of Iraq on December 18, 2011 would be a mine-proof BAE Caiman based on a design by the South African company Land Systems OMC.

A self-confessed killer as Police Chief

In two previous sections in this chapter, we considered the decay in the health area and in the management of the Zimbabwean situation. We now turn to the decay in policing, a key function of government.

In 2003, in one of the most callous and ill-considered actions of its entire existence, the ANC appointed a convicted and self-confessed killer, the Magoo's Bar bomber (*NF91*) Robert McBride, as Police Commissioner for the region east of Johannesburg. In proportion to the white population of South Africa, this was the equivalent of making Oklahoma City bomber Timothy McVeigh the Police Commissioner in New York. It ensured that no white person could ever possibly trust the Police again. McBride told the BBC[15] that Nelson Mandela had congratulated him on his appointment. Whatever could be done to most outrage white people, was exactly what was most likely to be done by the ANC. They had 40 million black people from among whom to choose a Police Chief, but they had to choose a self-confessed murderer specifically to rub it in the faces of the South African whites whose daughters he had killed.

Since his amnesty he had been a high ranking official in the ANC Government's Department of Foreign Affairs. In that capacity, he had been arrested in Mozambique on suspicion of running guns from Mozambique to South Africa. The *New York Times*[16] reported the Mozambican police had discovered him with a pile of AK-47 assault rifles and $11,000 dollars on his person. He had spent seven months in jail in Mozambique, but was mysteriously cleared of all charges later[17]. The next year the media had connected him with an assault at an escort agency. Again he had walked free[18]. A charge of drunken driving, and a subsequent effort to defeat the ends of Justice would eventually lead to his long overdue dismissal[19] in 2008.

This kind of action on the part of the ANC is a good example of what they will attempt to inflict on the country unless confronted by people of principle in the West.

BEE – Black Economic Empowerment

In the next step of Mbeki's Downward Ethical Spiral, he turned his attention to the matter of Wealth Redistribution. The bulk of the Black South African population was evidently not getting rich quickly enough for him. In a normal liberal democracy, that would have been the motivation for major programs on economic growth. However, for the ANC it centered instead on how to take as much as possible from the 10% of the population that was white and to give it to the nine times larger "black" population. It bears repeating the earlier comment in this work that the South African Black people did not want "the same as what whites had." They wanted "*what* the whites had" (Chapter 27: *Setting the scene*). And the ANC fanned this fire.

On 9 January 2004, as though to publicly validate this last point, the Ongelykheid Regime (Chapter 28: *The Ongelykheid Regime*) passed a New Apartheid law entitled the "Broad-Based Black Economic Empowerment Act of 2003", better known as the "BEE Act." It was now some 15 years since the ignominious fall of Communism in the USSR and Eastern Europe, yet the ANC regime felt it necessary to write a preamble that started with classic Marxist rhetoric[20] :

> "*Whereas South Africa's economy still excludes the vast majority of its people from ownership of productive assets....*"

This infamous New Apartheid Act defined "Black people" as "Africans, Coloureds, and Indians," and therefore automatically defined white people as being Non-Blacks. It was the first fundamental Apartheid Act passed in South Africa since the early 1950s (Chapter 20: *Always the horror near Port Elizabeth*). It brazenly stated its goals as being:

"• *increasing the number of black people that manage, own and control enterprises and productive assets*";

"• *preferential procurement; and investment in enterprises that are owned or managed by black people*"; and

"• *achieving a substantial change in the racial composition of ownership and management structures and in the skilled occupations of existing and new enterprises.*"

Cyril Ramaphosa, the man who so ably destroyed the hapless 1993 National Party negotiation team (Chapter 26: *Capitulation – Death of the future*), sat on the core group of the committee that devised the BEE rules. This would ultimately make him the richest black man in South Africa.

Overnight, the BEE Act placed the racial composition of South African business in the hands of the brazenly racist ANC. Ten years after Nelson Mandela had wooed Americans, he had gone. Now South Africans were suddenly not equal. In a country with a GDP scarcely 1/25 that of the USA at the time[21], the government either controlled or could directly influence all the concentration points of capital flow and it was now hell bent on controlling who got jobs in South Africa.

The consequences were immediate and totally predictable. The larger companies in the country veritably fell over their own feet in their haste to find suitably "black" ANC members to appoint to their boards. When the first so-called "BEE Charters" for the various economic sectors were published, it spelled doom for the ordinary salaried white man who had by now been trundled out of his job and was trying desperately to start his own little business. It seemed the acronym BEE really stood for Black Economic Entitlement. It was little more than a legislated racist protection racket worthy of an Al Capone elevated to the US Congress.

The regime put numbers to its goals when it stated in its 2003 Financial Sector BEE Charter[22] that the intent was to have 20% to 25% black people at senior management level and 40% to 50% at junior management levels by 2008. Vastly more ominously, it insisted on a Financial Sector goal of 70% of all procurement being from BEE accredited companies by 2014. This put on record an open attempt by the government to put the majority of the economy beyond the reach of people based on their skin color. The only way for these white people to access the full economy was to give significant control of their business to "black" people. It is logically impossible to not see this as racist legislation.

The truly pernicious aspect of this Act was not so much in the anti-white discriminatory requirements placed on larger companies and organizations. Rather, it was in the prejudice that the desperate scramble for BEE "Brownie Points" engendered against small white business owners, such as the freshly jobless whites. If a white man starting his own business were now to try to get business from bigger companies he would find a mountain of odds stacked against him. When the BEE Charter for the Mining Sector leaked out prematurely in 2002, fifty two billion South African rands worth of stock value evaporated within 72 hours[23]. Meanwhile, individuals like Cyril Ramaphosa were gearing up for what inevitably had to follow. He had already formed his own investment holdings company, Shanduka, in 2001. He would become the BEE poster child.

In May 2004, the South African Mining and Petroleum Resources Management Act[24] of 2002 took effect making the retention of mining licenses contingent upon the Mining Industry attaining a 15% black ownership by 2009[25].

And in the pale blue Highveld sky the invisible vultures circled on the hot updraft from the sophistic Socialist rhetoric about BEE supposedly addressing "stolen resources" and "fair share."

The BEE flagship – the feeding frenzy starts

Just off Hyde Park Corner, at 4 Grosvenor Place, London SW1X 7YL, directly across from the corner of Green Park, we find the head office of Lonmin PLC, a British-incorporated company listed on both the London and Johannesburg stock exchanges. It is the world's third largest platinum producer and part of the Lonrho empire that operates exclusively in Africa. Lonmin's Lonplats mining operation includes the Marikana platinum mine outside Rustenburg, sited on the richest platinum deposit in the world.

On 6 September 2004, Lonmin announced a *"Broad-Based National Flagship for Black Economic Empowerment in the South African Mining Industry."* They named it Incwala Resources and referred to it as Lonmin's *"BEE Equity partner."* The majority share in Incwala was held by those whom the ANC defined[26] as "Black" in its BEE Act. Of this, a mere 2.8% was given to the Bapo Ka Mogale community of Tswana people on whose territory the Lonmin mine happened to be; a former part of the much criticized Bophutatswana Homeland (Chapter 21: *The Black Homelands*). The Bapo Ka Mogale community still lived there, as they always have.

Rick Menell was the man who set up many of these deals. He explained the scheme as follows to retired *New York Times* editor, Bill Keller[27]: The owner of a mine would sell a percentage of the mine to a party that was "suitably black"[28]. Since the buyer likely did not have any money, he could pay the owner back from his predicted profits. This is effectively a cashless transaction with the owner effectively lending the "suitably black" party the capital to buy most of the shares. The buyer would also be given a preferred dividend in order to have an income. The present author observes that all the buyer had to do was be "suitably black" and be associated with the ANC. In the case of Incwala, the purpose was to acquire 18% of Lonplats.

So, let us summarize the arrangement for what it really was: Lonmin was effectively giving the "suitably black" ANC-connected parties 18% of Lonplats plus a dividend. The "suitably black" party could pay Lonmin for that 18% if all went well. If not, then the risk devolved largely onto Lonmin.

The above *New York Times* article stated that BEE set aside government contracts for *"minority suppliers"* and "introduced" the *"previously dispossessed"* into the *"ownership class."* The *New York Times* reader is left wondering at what point South Africa's 90% "black" population became a *"minority"* and how a culture that never had mines was *"dispossessed"* of a mine.

Furthermore, how many Americans have received a share in a platinum mine plus a preferred dividend just because they were a *"minority"*? There also is no history of British mining magnates giving white Christian Afrikaners 18% of anything, let alone a dividend on top.

Fracture over Feeding Rights

On 20 February 2005, it was reported that Mbeki and his Deputy President, Jacob Zuma, had a major disagreement on the subject of the Scorpions, the "South African FBI"[29]. The Scorpions had clocked up a 93% conviction rate. In that particular week of 2005, the Scorpions had started prosecuting between 23 and 30 ANC Members of Parliament for fraud in what became known as Travelgate. The Scorpions had also investigated Zuma himself, the chief Whip of the ANC, Tony Yengeni, and the ever-active Winnie Mandela. Too many investigations were leading to the heart of the ANC.

By contrast, the general perception was that the Police were ineffective and corrupt, and it would subsequently be proved to be so at the very highest level. Zuma and others wanted the Scorpions incorporated under the Police. Mbeki wanted to keep the Scorpions independent. As Mbeki's fortunes waned in the ANC party, so did the survivability of the Scorpions.

Zuma and Mbeki were mutually exclusive characters. Mbeki, an inscrutable, serious, and self-conscious Xhosa, was of the school that believed in wearing Savile Row while destroying white men via BEE. Zuma, a guileless, extroverted, populist from the hyper-male-dominated Zulu society, was an Africanist of the leopard skin and potions variety; a classic African polygamist; every inch the future African Strong Man dictator; another Idi Amin in the making.

The trigger for the discord in the den was the Arms Deal in which a veritable mountain of tax money had been pilfered by various ANC members and hangers-on close to the top of the system. On 8 June 2005, Schabir Shaik, financial advisor to Zuma, was sentenced to 15 years in prison[30] for corruption and fraud. Zuma's name appeared more than 200 times in the judgment against Shaik.

There were multiple references to the money being used to fund Zuma's grand estate home at Nkandla[31], where he kept some of his many wives. By some reports, Shaik had paid some $186,000 to Zuma[32]. Exactly seven days later, on 14 June 2005, Mbeki relieved Zuma of his duties as Deputy President of South Africa and appointed in his place the wife of the head of the National Prosecuting Authority (NPA), governing body of the Scorpions (Chapter 28: *The Sting of the Scorpion*). Zuma was to be prosecuted on charges of corruption.

On 6 December 2005, Zuma was also charged with the rape of the HIV-positive daughter of a dead friend. Already in 1998 some 41% of pregnant Zulu woman at ante-natal clinics were HIV-positive and AIDS was the cause of 73% off Zulu female deaths[33] in the age group 15-49. Zuma had been head of the ANC government's National AIDS Council before being dismissed as Deputy President by Mbeki.

Zuma's rape trial started on 13 February 2006 in Johannesburg. He admitted to having intercourse with the woman, but maintained it was consensual. However, he felt it necessary to point out[34] that as a traditional Zulu man, it would have been a violation of her rights for him to have refused her intercourse.

When probed about the fact that he knew the accuser to be HIV-positive, he responded that he had protected himself by taking a shower afterward. As the civilized world shook its head at his jaw-dropping statements, in the streets outside the court his supporters yelled "*Kill the bitch! Kill the bitch!*" and pelted the accuser with stones[35].

Fig. 29-4 Supporting crowd at the Zuma rape trial

Ultimately the judge deemed the testimony by the Police suspect. Furthermore, the accuser had apparently leveled false charges of rape against others before. Zuma was acquitted of rape on May 8, 2006. In the streets of Durban, the Zulu population was delirious with joy; both male and female. Others were singing his political campaign song, "*Bring me my machine gun.*" The terrified accuser fled to the Netherlands where she was granted asylum.

In its May 10, 2006 report[36] on the trial, the *New York Times* correctly deemed Zuma "*unfit for office.*"

For those who knew Africa, the next few years would not be a surprise. It would follow the standard African script that the Afrikaner knew only too well and had always fought to be spared, but which the West had insisted he should be subjected to.

On 20 September 2006, the judge also threw out the corruption case[37] without shutting the door on later proceedings. The Zuma crowd went wild, but all thinking people in South Africa remembered that Zuma's name had been mentioned more than 200 times in the judgment against Shaik. This case was clearly not yet over. Nevertheless, Zuma's way was now open to contest Mbeki's leadership of the ANC and to thereby become the State President by default in 2009.

Corrupt to the very top

In 2004, Interpol thought it fit to appoint South African Police Commissioner Jackie Selebi to the post of President of the Organization. He was the first African to head the respected international police body. Selebi had been a Mbeki appointee who had previously been UN Ambassador. Before that, he had been the man on the ANC National Executive responsible for repatriating ANC exiles.

Rumors had been circulating for a while about Selebi being involved with a major organized crime boss, Glenn Agliotti, who had been implicated in murder. On Thursday 27 September 2007, it finally became clear that this most senior Black African policeman on the planet was about to be arrested by the Scorpions[38] on charges of corruption, fraud, racketeering and defeating the ends of justice.

On 5 October 2007, the Mail & Guardian ran an article[39] claiming that the Scorpions had obtained the arrest warrant on Monday 10 September and had followed that up on 14 September with search and seizure warrants for Selebi's home and his office at Police Headquarters. The warrants had been obtained from both white and black judges, just to be sure.

When the Scorpions chief advised the Minister of Justice of the warrant, Mbeki promptly suspended the chief and appointed a new man in his place, who personally attempted to get the judges to revoke the warrants. It was clearly an attempt by Mbeki and his team at perverting justice on a spectacular scale.

Selebi would ultimately be found guilty of corruption and sentenced to 15 years in prison[40]. He had links to organized crime and had accepted bribes[41] of $156,000. He would finally enter jail on 5 December 2011, but would be let out on supposed medical grounds a mere 229 days later.

Mired in fraud and corruption on all sides, with its government threatening its FBI and undermining its Justice System, the country lurched toward the all important ANC Party Congress of late 2007.

God help the Rainbow Nation

On Saturday 15 December 2007, Reuters reported that the Scorpions had filed affidavits[42] containing substantial new evidence against Zuma. In a last ditch effort, they were trying to reopen the corruption case against Zuma.

Three days later, on Tuesday 18 December 2007, the ANC delegates started gathering in Pietersburg for their three day Party Conference. The town had by now been politically renamed to Polokwane, just as the Bolsheviks had renamed St. Petersburg to Leningrad. Here they would elect their Party Leader, the man who would be a shoo-in for the President of the country two years later.

The fate of the country was sealed when Zuma defeated Mbeki by more than 60% to 40% of the delegate votes. All six top positions in the party went to Zuma team members. Zuma was now the president of South Africa in all but name. Mbeki would struggle on, but he was now a lame duck president.

The title of the British *Daily Mail* article[43] on the event aptly summed up the situation:

"Machine-gun man takes over ANC
– God help the Rainbow Nation"

-----ooOoo-----

30

When the loerie sings again

"...I just never thought that I'd be poorer now than I was. Yes racism still exists and we are faced with it from time to time, but today's oppression is from our own black government."

Retired Black South African nurse, Nomvula Ndlovu
29 August 2012

The vultures land

On 28 December 2007, Zuma was belatedly ordered to stand trial on charges of corruption, money laundering, racketeering and fraud relating to the Arms Deal, based on 93,000 documents seized by the Scorpions ("FBI"). In any civilized country, this would have ended the career of any politician.

Andrew Feinstein was the former head of the ANC's own internal "watchdog." In 2001, he resigned after the leadership of the ANC, including specifically Mbeki, refused to back his investigations. He fled to London. On 20 January 2008, he wrote in *Prospect Magazine*[1] that British and German investigators were looking into some $200 million of Arms Deal bribes paid to South African parties. According to Feinstein[2], who was cooperating with the investigators, at least £713,000 had been paid to the late Minister of Defence, Joe Modise, and there was evidence of up to £35 million pounds of such payments. Modise had been the closest of confidants of Thabo Mbeki.

On 12 February 2008, it was announced in parliament that the Scorpions were to be shut down and incorporated with the Police; this when the head of the Police was standing trial for corruption, fraud, racketeering, and defeating the ends of justice. In parliament, 252 votes were cast in favor of disbandment. ANC

Fig. 30-1 Jacob Zuma

members in the parliament literally applauded[3]. Some 220 of them, if not more[4], were by then under investigation by the Scorpions. Imagine the members of the Democratic Party cheering in the US Congress at the demise of the FBI. And while members of the ANC were enriching themselves from the state coffers, the party kept blaming the miserable state of South Africa's ordinary poor blacks on the white people.

The vultures had landed and were tearing at the entrails of what remained of Western Civilization. And if one listened closely, one could hear the drums of Africa beating on the wind, calling all to the kill. In response, Black people were pouring in from everywhere; Mozambique, Zimbabwe, Somalia, and Nigeria.

On 1 July 2008, the ANC was taken off the US Terrorist Designation list[5], their bombing and murder of civilians magically obliterated by a new liberal sun shining from the United States. A year before the

Canadian Government had correctly refused[6] a visa to the properly convicted common felon, Winnie Mandela.

And at the ANC party gatherings the crescendo rose:

"Bulala amaBhulu! Kill the Boers!"

The squabble at the kill

With Zuma headed for the Presidency, the Police chief under a cloud of indictment, and the Scorpions to be shut down for being too effective, our focus shifts to matters socio-economic. Zimbabwean refugees were flooding into the country in torrents of humanity, trying to escape Robert Mugabe, the man once physically hugged by Jimmy Carter as being the savior of his nation.

The contrast between the Zimbabweans and the local black people could not be greater. The Zimbabweans were often the more competent people from their country. The South African black people were being roundly outclassed by others of their own race, and it did not sit well. Here one had a refugee nation with excellent schooling and reasonable work ethic in search of opportunity for which they were prepared to work. They were up against locals indoctrinated by the ANC to believe they were automatically entitled to what white people owned.

In the early weeks of May 2008, several immigrant black people were killed using the horrific gasoline soaked tire technique immortalized by Winnie Mandela as necklacing[7]. By 31 May, some 62 foreign blacks were dead. Where the Western Media had averted its eyes from the horrors of the ANC in the 1980s and preferred to lay all wrongs at the door of Apartheid, the international community this time saw just exactly what it looked like when a human being died in flames. There was no Apartheid policy to blame this time[8]. The xenophobic violence was contained, but it was not the end of mobs burning people to death. On 5 August 2010, the *BBC* would report on a black mob burning to death three suspected power cable thieves[9].

This kind of horror was clearly premeditated. It had become cultural for South African black people.

Honorary Blacks and Poor Whites

On 18 June 2008, the Chinese Association of South Africa won its court case against the ANC Ongelykheid regime when it claimed that its members *"often failed to qualify for business contracts and job promotions because they were regarded as whites"*[10]. They provided several tangible examples, including tenders given preferentially to black people. The government did not oppose the application by the Chinese group to be redefined as "black." It seemed to escape the media that this public court case vividly showed how whites were being discriminated against on an institutionalized legislated basis.

The ironic gallows humor of Afrikaners had a field day. The largest part of the South African Chinese community in 2008 was immigrant based and had little if any experience of Apartheid, the supposed justification for the BEE Act. Now they were "Honorary Blacks," just as Japanese people had been ridiculously labeled "Honorary Whites" by the old National Party government. Legislated Apartheid was back, but appeared to be acceptable to the West when used to diminish a white minority.

In the wake of the BEE legislation, a new category of society therefore arose. These were the amaBenzi; a layer of ANC-connected deadwood, black opulence that draped itself like a bloodsucking cancer over the landscape. In view of the preference given to them in securing government tenders, they became known as *tenderpreneurs*[11], a uniquely South African term that, like *apartheid* before it, has found its way into Encyclopedias[12]. Staggeringly rich, these people did little constructive beyond vying for these black preference tenders. They rushed about in Mercedes-Benzes and Italian supercars, rubbing their opulence in the faces of less fortunate blacks while blaming white people for the woes of the country. South Africa was now solidly on the road to a formal kleptocracy.

White business owners now had to work harder to keep these ANC sycophants in honey. In order to secure business from larger companies, these white businessmen had no choice but to give blacks shareholding in their companies. It is difficult indeed to not interpret this as legislated economic entitlement for an ANC elite. No one was being "empowered."

Whites without a tertiary education rapidly descended the economic ladder. The majority of them were Afrikaans speaking, many of whom were historically employed in blue-collar jobs in Telecoms, Utilities, Roads, and Transport. They lacked the historic business culture of the Anglophone community. They had been forced out of their jobs by Affirmative Action applied in favor of the *majority* of the population – black people.

It was not long before white ghettos developed in the industrialized Johannesburg-Pretoria area. Their white skins had effectively outlawed these people from being employed in a country governed by the BEE Act. In July 2008, the *BBC* reported[13] on Jacob Zuma's first exposure to the true extent of white poverty. He was quoted as saying about the Bethlehem white ghetto:

> "*I am shocked by what I have seen here.*"

The Helping Hand charity organization stated that more than 130,000 whites were homeless by 2008; an increase of 58% since 2002, when BEE was first debated in detail. Given a white population of 4.5 million at the time, that meant that 3.3% of the white population—one in every thirty—was homeless. By 2010, a full 10% of the whites remaining in the country would be living under the poverty line[14].

The end of Mbeki – Zuma takes over

The corruption case against Jacob Zuma was dismissed on 12 September 2008. He had even personally flown to Mauritius to convince the authorities there to *not* help the South African investigation into his dealings. The Judge added that the episode seemed to have formed part of "*some great political contest or game*" between Mbeki and Zuma. In its report[15] on this ruling, the British newspaper, *The Guardian*, concluded that the Scorpions would "*come under great pressure*" not to file charges again.

One week later, on 20 September 2008, Mbeki agreed to step down as president of country, pushed to do so by his own party[16]. Several Mbeki cabinet ministers resigned their offices including the single demonstrably competent person in the Cabinet, the Finance Minister, Trevor Manuel. The parliament elected Kagalema Mothlante, a former trade unionist, as the stand-in president until Zuma could be technically elected to the post.

On 28 October 2008, parliament approved the disbanding of the Scorpions, as directed by the ANC Party. The fight to keep Zuma out of the South African Presidential office was all but lost. He had just seven months to wait. A few days later the disaffected members of the ANC announced[17] the formation of a new political party, the Congress of the People (COPE), a fractious muddle of newly illuminated ex-ANC members. On 6 April 2009, the expected announcement[18] came:

> "*It is neither possible nor desirable for the national prosecuting authority to continue with the prosecution of Mr. Zuma.*"

On 26 April 2009, parliamentary elections were held. The new splinter party COPE made little impression with just 7% of the vote – it was built on Mbeki supporters and thinking Black people of higher educational level. The bulk of the ANC did not harbor many of them. The existing Opposition party, the Democratic Alliance under Helen Zille, got 17% of the vote and 17 seats. The all-Zulu Inkatha Party got just 5%, but 18 seats. All the opposing parties together did not count for much in parliament, because there were 400 seats and Zuma's ANC had won 264. This was just short of the 67% needed to change the constitution.

The long battle was over and Lady Justice had lost. All that remained standing inside the country between the institutionalized abuse of the population of South Africa and their quasi-kleptocratic government was a local free press; the same free press that had so strongly opposed the previous Apartheid government.

The BEE flagship on the Sea of Reality

By September 2009, a perfect five years after the fanfare launch of the BEE flagship, Incwala, the venture was coming apart. The black "equity partners" were heading for default on their loan payments[19]. Lonmin was desperately[20] seeking a new "suitably black" partner with ANC credentials to have 15% Black ownership, according to the BEE goals, and thereby to retain its mining license from the ANC controlled government. By May 2010, Lonmin was issuing new shares[21] to raise cash for new BEE partners. The company attempted to woo none other than Cyril Ramaphosa, the BEE poster child. His fortune was by now approaching 100 million dollars on the back of BEE. He personified the concept of becoming a millionaire by simply being black in South Africa.

In Canada, investment funds bearing BEE companies' stocks were cynically being presented as supposed "*Ethical Investments,*" of all things. It certainly gives insight into the gullibility of Canadians. Given this attitude overseas, there was no hope that the ANC government would relent on this larcenous scheme. The Western World indulged the kleptocracy.

Ramaphosa surely must have known that he could simply sit back and let Lonmin "sweat." Lonmin reported:

> "*Following an extensive process in this regard, it has become clear that this objective can only be achieved with significant funding from Lonmin.*"

In other words, Cyril Ramaphosa would not become a BEE partner unless Lonmin itself put up the cash for him to buy his shareholding from Lonmin via his holding company, Shanduka. Lonmin duly gave Ramaphosa the loan of $304M at 5% interest rate at a time when the South African prime lending rate was 10%. The previous three Black BEE shareholders walked away with a profit despite their failure[22].

In September 2010, just as Lonmin emerged from this battle, the government made the game quite clear to the mining industry by increasing[23] the black equity goal for mining houses from 15% (by 2009) to 26% by 2014. With these BEE partners contributing nothing of value to these operations, it implied the owners were lobbing off 26% of their company to no other useful purpose than to please the ANC. Obviously the ANC government would simply continue to move the black equity requirement in the mines upward until the mines failed financially or until the present owners surrendered what was left to black equity holders.

By 2012, Incwala was in trouble yet again. If Ramaphosa defaulted, the shares would revert to Lonmin and they could walk away with a $300 million loss[24]. They would somehow have to make these numbers work in their offices in London.

Meanwhile, during early 2012, rivalry between the National Union of Mineworkers (NUM) and a new "upstart" union, the Association of Mineworkers and Construction Union (AMCU) had broken out. The AMCU apparently felt, with considerable justification, that the NUM was "too close to" management (read "Lonmin, Ramaphosa, and ANC"). Herein the ANC found itself confronted by a new grouping of angry blacks that was using against it exactly the same tactics the ANC itself had used against the white government before 1994. In that earlier era, the ANC worked through its union wing, the Congress of South African Trade Unions (COSATU), of which the NUM was the leading member. What goes around certainly comes around with a vengeance.

This then was the situation on Friday 10 August 2012, at Marikana platinum mine near Rustenburg. On this day, 3000 Marikana platinum rock drill operators affiliated to the AMCU started a new wildcat strike demanding[25] a 300% increase in salary. As always in South Africa, protest by Black people seemed to involve machetes, spears and sticks and often other weapons. Striking in the middle of a worldwide recession is never a good idea as it is a position of weakness. This is particularly true if one has an outrageous demand. Fighting soon started between NUM and AMCU members. On Sunday 12 August, two security guards were killed by the AMCU mob, who was now the majority. On Monday 13 August, a NUM member was hacked to death by the AMCU mob.

During later hearings on Thursday 8 November 2012, Lieutenant-Colonel Victor Visser, a senior white

Afrikaner Police Officer would testify[26] at the hand of video evidence in front of an investigating commission that the AMCU mob had used the services of an Inyanga (witchdoctor/traditional healer) to sprinkle them with *muti* (potion) so as to make them "invincible" on the Monday the 13th of August. On that day, the mob hacked two policemen to death and took their weapons. On Tuesday the 14th, Lonmin shut the mine. By the end of the sixth day, Wednesday 15 August, the strike had claimed the lives of 10 people.

The Marikana Massacre

As the sun came up on Thursday 16 August 2012 over Marikana, all the pawns of an inevitable tragedy were in position and were moving inexorably towards confrontation. On this day, the chessboard of history would witness a confluence of the key post-Sharpeville issues presented thus far in this work; the natural culmination of the actions and policies of the ANC to the date. BEE had run its larcenous course and had enriched a tiny top echelon of the ANC, represented by Ramaphosa, leaving millions of blacks poorer than in 1994, before Mandela's ANC had come to power. The "Socialist Revolutionary" ANC of the 1960-1990 period was now in command of the economy, and, more particularly, in command of the Police.

Before the sun would set on this day, the foregoing would become the setting for what future history will assuredly record as a watershed event in the history of South Africa. It would rival that of the Sharpeville incident in 1960 (Chapter 20: *Sharpeville*), which set South Africa on the road to worldwide condemnation and isolation. Lonmin had been pushed in a corner by a halted production and falling stock value. They had lost 15,000 ounces of production of "white gold" and announced that they would miss their annual goal. Their stock price promptly fell 6.6%. The company threatened to lay off the 3,000 black AMCU workers.

The AMCU had drawn blood and was now completely overcome with animal hubris as only a murderous black mob in Africa can be. Most of the AMCU crowd was armed with machetes, knobkerries or spears, but some had guns. And they were headed for the Police lines.

Fully five hundred mostly black Police stood ready with automatic weapons and armored vehicles near the mine. They were highly on edge, because two of their number had already been brutally hacked to death by this same AMCU mob a few days before. The 3,000 man AMCU mob represented a much lesser threat to the 500 heavily armed Police contingent at Marikana than the overwhelming crowd of 20,000 had represented to the initially 20 and later 150 badly armed policemen at Sharpeville. The Sharpeville shootings of 21 March 1960 had been preceded by the murder and mutilation of 9 policemen of all races at Cato Manor (Chapter 20: *The Year of Africa: Barbarity at Cato Manor*) on 23 January 1960. The majority of policemen at Sharpeville had also been black men.

Cyril Ramaphosa, former NUM union boss and a leading light in the ANC, now stood to lose millions if the mine folded – in essence a "rook that had changed color on the chessboard of history" due to BEE. The man who was so staggeringly rich that he bid $2.3 million on a prize buffalo bull warned the Minister of Police, Nathi Mthethwa, to "come down hard" on the strikers[27].

Elsewhere in South Africa, ordinary white men went about their lives, still blamed daily by an ANC government that spends its time trying to set mobs like the AMCU on the whites with bogus charges of being responsible for the situation in the country after almost two decades of destructive ANC rule.

And in the safety of London the moneyed masters of the chessboard rubbed their coins, sipped their gin, and charted their stock price, oblivious to the day to day realities on the ground in South Africa.

As the armed AMCU mob approached the Police lines, the Police attempted to funnel it using razor wire and by moving the armored vehicles into position on its left flank. When the mob rejected calls to disperse, the police fired teargas and rubber bullets. And this is when the Al Jazeera camera caught what was not caught at the Sharpeville event in 1960. A member of the AMCU mob pointed his gun[28] almost directly into the camera and fired at the flanking Police. At this point, the major body of Police being frontally approached by the mob opened fire with live ammunition.

At the end of the volley, thirty-four AMCU members lay dead and seventy-eight were wounded.

The ANC *Ongelykheid Regime* was now facing the same murderous mobs the *Apartheid Regime* had faced in the previous century. But, this time there were too many video cameras to bury the truth. Marikana had become the symbol of what was wrong with the ANC and had exposed BEE for exactly what it was – the personal enrichment of the ANC senior echelon at the cost of the entire country.

The ANC elite was now setting the Police on black mine workers and the black poor on the whites, while the President had been caught on camera (See this chapter: *Genocide*) singing[29] a variant of *"Bulala amaBhulu! Kill the Boers!"*

The reality for White South Africans

By early 2009, *Newsweek* reported that some 20% of the 1995 white population of South Africa[30] had already fled the country to destinations such as Britain, Canada, Australia, and New Zealand, and to a lesser degree the United States. In short, one in every five white South Africans had simply given up on the Great Lie that was the "New South Africa."

The main reasons were lack of personal safety and the difficulty in finding formal employment in a country where one was excluded from opportunity by the BEE Act and the Government's Affirmative Action policies. Both policies represented the international oddity of a vast majority of a population with total political power seeking to protect itself from competition with a 10% minority that happened to be white. The vast majority of those who left the country did so on work permits or permanent residence visas from other Western countries.

In 2009, the Canadian Immigration and Refugee Board granted refugee status to a young white South African man based on his *"well-founded fear of persecution on the ground of his race."* The board also stated[31] that the evidence showed a *"picture of indifference or inability or unwillingness of the government and the security forces to protect White South Africans from persecution by African South Africans."* This assessment was perfectly in line with what was being experienced on the ground in South Africa, as the following two exemplary cases will show.

On Monday night 3 November 2008 at around 11 pm Nick Lubbe, a 51-year old white Afrikaner, his daughter and her two young sons (11 and 3) were assailed[32] by robbers, who rammed their car from behind, jumped out and grabbed the daughter's handbag. Nick sped away and returned later to the same spot accompanied by a white police team, including a white policewoman. A black police inspector, who the news service *News 24* was prepared to identify by name, was already on the scene with the driver of the attackers' vehicle. The other three occupants of the attacking vehicle had somehow disappeared.

When Nick and the white police team joined the inspector, the latter turned on them and, according to witnesses, called them "white dogs." He told the white policewoman that he would,

"see to it that she was shot dead in a robbery."

Then he cocked his R5 assault rifle in Lubbe's face and told him,

*"it is time you whites packed your bags and ***** off out of the country."*

The wife of the attacking vehicle's driver then appeared on the scene, and emptied out Lubbe's daughter's bag and gave her back the empty bag. It is exceedingly difficult for white people to trust black policemen with their interests when this is the treatment they receive from the senior echelons of that force.

As to the matter of the willingness of the Police to protect white civilians, the following example might go some distance toward clarifying the situation. On Monday 6 June 2011, Jan Malan, a white Afrikaner, filed a complaint[33] with the Groendenne (Green Pines) Police Station to the effect that his dogs had been poisoned and he had received death threats. Jan lived on a homestead near Vereeniging, south of Johannesburg. The Police dismissed his complaint despite a report by the family's black housemaid that she had been *"told at church"* that Jan and his wife, Susan, *"would be next."* The couple had therefore hired a security firm to guard the house at night, at least until they got laser alarms installed on Thursday 9 June.

At around 9:30am on Sunday 12 June, the couple arrived home. Susan was overpowered by one of three intruders who held her fast. He would later testify that one of his accomplices instructed him to literally *"slaughter her,"* but that he could not do it. So, the accomplice slit her throat with a knife. Jan was assaulted with an axe and died near his wife. The Police, who belatedly involved themselves, could find no evidence of any theft[34].

Returning now to the refugee status granted to the young South African man; the ANC government of South Africa reacted by calling the Canadian Conservative Party government "racist." As anyone living in North America knows, this is the modern shibboleth for a white North American. The Canadian Minister of Immigration promptly took his own Refugee Board to court to get the young man's refugee status overturned and succeeded in doing so.

This present work has no opinion on either the granting or the overturning of the particular young man's refugee status. However, what is a serious issue, is that the office of the minister saw fit to issue a statement to the effect that the Refugee Board's decisions had been based on a *"jaundiced assessment of the country conditions"* in South Africa[35]. It is left to the reader to speculate where the Office of the Minister of Immigration of Canada gets its information, but it is not from Jan Malan and his wife Susan. They have already died proving the Minister's sources and lawyers dead wrong.

Land Redistribution

While the horrific farm torture-murder attacks started to surface in the international media, the focus of that media remained on how the "white 10%" of the population owned "90% of land" in 1994. It would have been closer to the truth to state that 80,000 white commercial farmers owned some or other large percentage of land in 1994 and that there were only a few black commercial farmers. By way of comparison, in the United States there were almost exactly 100 times as many white farmers in 1997 as black farmers[36]; a ratio about 25 times higher than the white-to-black population ratio would suggest.

The international media elects not to tell the reader that the vast majority of the western half of South Africa looks much like Nevada and is too dry to even support cattle (See *Fig. 18-4*). At best, it may be used for Angora goat farming and, further east, sheep farming. In fact, a mere 12% of the South African land surface is arable, and only 2.6% of land has high potential.

The indigenous black nations have no history of large scale commercial farming. The traditional African concept of agriculture is a few dozen square yards of corn or millet for own subsistence use (See *Fig. 18-5*). Yet the white farmer had turned the largely deserted South African Prairie with its comparatively poor soils into the breadbasket of Africa; the African equivalent of the US Midwest.

The ANC Government's target had been to distribute 33% of white owned agricultural land to black people. On 3 March 2012, the BBC finally reported[37] what everyone in South Africa had known for years; namely, some 90% of productive farms transferred from white farmers to black communities were now unproductive. The BBC quoted a remarkably honest ANC Land Reform Minister, Gigile Nkwinti:

> *"The [white] farms - which were active accruing revenue for the state - were handed over to [black] people, and more than 90% of those are not functional, [...] They are not productive, and therefore the state loses the revenue. We cannot afford to go on like that... No country can afford that."*

Indeed, no country can afford that. What a country can afford even less, is being turned from a net food exporter, which is what South Africa had been, into a net food importer, because half the productive farmers have been terrorized off their farms. The BBC failed to mention that the newly black held farms also generated no jobs through falling into dormancy. Eleazar Maahlo, the black treasurer of the Limpopo African Farmer's Union, put it well when he said that the government was more interested in putting (black) people on the land than in putting farmers in agriculture[38]. One would have thought the ANC might have learnt from the Zimbabwean experience.

But, learning from experience is not Africa's strong suit.

Twice as dangerous as Afghanistan

With the ANC yelling *"Bulala amaBhulu! Kill the Boers!"* from its party platform, the security of farmers had become impossible. The horrific farm attacks started around the time of the ANC taking power in South Africa in 1994 and escalated with Mbeki's ascension to de facto office in 1997. By 2012, it would eventually be reported that, after 11 years of warfare the United States had lost 2000 military personnel in Afghanistan. By the same date, more than 3,000 White South African farmers had been murdered, often horrifically tortured to death. This from among a community of only 45,000 farmers, whereas the USA had over 100,000 military personnel in Afghanistan. This made South Africa more than twice as dangerous for a white farmer and his family as Afghanistan was for a US soldier. The white South African farmers were by now the most likely group of people on Earth to be murdered.

Against this background we visit a farming family in the corn country of the South African Prairie in 2010.

Little House on the Prairie

When Deneys Reitz wrote his book about the Second Anglo Boer War (for example *NF71*), his introduction described life on a Free State farm. Life may have changed a bit in that the young farmer's son no longer rides a horse, but he is more likely to be behind the wheel of a 4x4 Toyota Hi-Lux. Otherwise he might be on a John Deere or a Massey Ferguson, plowing the land, which is to be used for dry land cultivation of corn to feed the country.

On Sundays, the family is in church, the Dutch Reformed Church, which seamlessly connects to the South African Presbyterian Church. In fact, many of the church ministers in the Dutch Reformed Church have classic Scottish names, such as MacDonald and Murray[39].

The local church steeple dominates the towns, followed by the local grain silo. The lady at the local co-op is also the greatest gossip and knows all that goes on in the district. It is a tightly-knit society. They stand together in the face of adversity, which often comes in the form of prolonged drought. At such times, they may even have to deal with dust storms eerily reminiscent of American Dust Bowl times. Prayer days for rain are a common feature of life. The farmers struggle with their loan payments to the bank, seed for the next season, and maintenance on their tractors and harvesters. But they do not despair; they pray. These are the "Midwesterners" of South Africa.

One could transplant an Iowa farming family to the Free State and they would fit right in, despite the change from a Ford F150 to a Toyota Hi-Lux truck and the differently accented English. The locals would move heaven and earth for them in any case, because "it is just simply what one does." These are people that any civilized member of Western Society would want to have on his side when the going gets tough. They are classic "sweat-of-the-brow Calvinistic Christians" who believe deeply in the Protestant Work Ethic. Like their Iowa counterparts, they are tough people with big hearts.

We are on the Prairie of South Africa – the breadbasket of the nation, covered horizon to horizon in corn. More particularly, we are in the Lindley district, some thirty miles northwest of the mid-sized town of Bethlehem. The town of Lindley is named for the American missionary, David Lindley, whom we met in Chapter 10 in 1836 when Hendrik Potgieter saved the missionaries from the wrath of Mzilikatse (See Chapter 10: *Americans in the eye of the storm*).

*****

It is here, in the December high summer of 2010 on the corn-covered Prairie, that we join the Potgieter family consisting of father Adam "Attie" (40), his wife Wilna (36) and their only child, little daughter Wilhelmina "Willemien"(not yet 3). Attie is the manager of the farm *Tweefontein* (Two Fountains). The farm is owned by Alex Macaskill who lives in the more distant town of Marquard. Attie's brother, Arno, works for Colyn van Tonder on a neighboring farm, *Van Tondersrust* (Van Tonder's Rest). Wilna is an assistant manager at the local branch of a farming services company in the nearest village of Arlington.

It is Wednesday 1 December, and it happens to be Attie and Wilna's seventeenth wedding anniversary. Attie has been to town to draw money for salaries for his farmworkers. Wilna and little Willemien are in the farmhouse. Wilna has tied a little pink ribbon in Willemien's hair. They have a plate of food in the microwave oven – just another summer day in the Northern Free State; God's Own Country.

As Attie approaches the house he is felled by a sudden blow to the head. He does not lose consciousness and realizes that his attacker is brandishing a panga (an African machete). Attie is a strongly built red-blonde Afrikaner, and tackles his assailant. He manages to wrestle the black man to the ground. But, then the assailant is joined by five others. They are all black men of ages varying between 17 and 33. They speak SeSotho to one another – the dominant Black language in the Free State.

Not satisfied to subdue or restrain Attie, they hack and stab at him with various weapons. The pathologist, Dr. Robert Book, will later testify that *the deceased was tortured to death* and *took many minutes to die.* Attie's broken body has no fewer than 151 wounds, 14 of which will be fatal; the rest represent torture that no human would inflict on an animal. Many of the wounds, the pathologist will testify, are from what appears to be a pitchfork. The attackers have a gun, but they do not use it on Attie's broken form; they prefer to torture him to death in front of his hysterical wife and daughter.

With Wilna looking on, some of the men carry his broken body to the fence. Only then do they turn on her. The State pathologist will later report that her body bore cuts to the head. Only then do they produce the gun and execute her with a bullet to the back of the head in front of little Willemien.

The attackers take the terrified little Willemien to an outside room. And this is when they put the gun to the back of her head and execute the innocent child. Then they take her lifeless body and throw it on top of her dead mother inside the house. Attie's body is left next to the fence in the open. They leave a firearm lying at the site of Attie's torture death.

When they leave, they stop at the gate to the farm. To the post they fasten a cardboard note bearing the following words in SeSotho:

"We have killed them. We shall return"

Inside the little house on the prairie, little Willemien lies still in death, sprawled on top of her murdered mother's body, the little pink ribbon still bound in her red hair[40].

*****

Later in the day, Chris, son of Colyn van Tonder on the neighboring farm, meets three black men coming from Arlington who tell him that their employer is lying dead outside his house; just another Afrikaner murdered, entirely expendable in the mind of a West that prefers not to notice.

Attie's torture death will eventually be referred to in overseas newspapers, but only after the obligatory pontification about the Apartheid policies, thereby apparently seeking to rationalize or even justify the murder.

There is but one problem: this event is not from 1990, but from 2010; a full twenty years after the end of the Apartheid laws. Attie was a mere twenty years old when Apartheid was taken off the Statute Books in 1990. At the time, the oldest of the murderers was just twelve. Wilna was just sixteen. Little Willemien was born a full thirteen years after Nelson Mandela became president, promising *Never, never – and never again"*[41]. The youngest of the murderers was born at the time when the great election of 1994 was being planned.

The only people who wish to inject Apartheid into this picture are the Western Media and the ANC; the former because it cannot justify its malicious prejudice without it, and the latter because it could not possibly exist without it.

The perpetrators provide the ignorant black racist muscle for the murder, the ANC provides the racist inspiration and incitement, and the Liberal Western Media provides the unthinking knee-jerk racist justification. It would seem that the Media deems murder and torture to be wrong, but somehow attempts to rationalize it when Afrikaners are the victims.

The torture aspect of the farm attacks would only get worse, including assaulting the farmer's wives with hot clothes smoothing irons, dripping flaming plastic on the farmers' bodies, pouring boiling water over the victims or down their throats, putting their feet in boiling water, cutting the soles off their feet and displaying the sliced-off soles on the table. The depravity would know no end. A characteristic of the savage is that his savagery increases, the more powerless the victim. As a result, there seemed to be a tendency for the depravity of the torture and violence to increase with the age of the victim.

The British saw this phenomenon in Kenya (Chapter 20: *Mau-Mau*). Back then, on 7 November 1952, Sir Oliver Lyttelton, British Secretary of State for Colonies, said in parliament about the Kenyan Mau-Mau:

> *"It is anti-Christ and it feeds, not upon economic discontent, but upon perverted nationalism and on a sort of nostalgia for barbarism"*

In South Africa, it was now no longer acceptable to just kill white people; they had to be tortured first. Death had to be slow, painful and preferably humiliating. If the perpetrators could make family members watch their loved ones being killed, then apparently all the better.

This was happening in a country that the US Media would have the American public believe is a model of the success of Democracy, a "major achievement" of the American Left. The British *Telegraph* newspaper would eventually[42] note the terrible fact of the farm murder statistics in 2012, but only because the latest victim would happen to be a British farmer who had been hacked to death.

By December 2012, the *Telegraph* finally addressed[43] the actual matter, but still sought to deny some of the facts. By then the murder rate among white farmers had risen to a staggering 99 killed per 100,000 compared with 32 per 100,000 for the general population and 4.5 per 100,000 for the USA.

While many would attempt to rationalize the situation, it is incumbent upon the distant observer to ask him- or herself what the relevant responsible government should do in such a situation. In any true democracy, there would surely be a national outcry. Politicians would fall over their own feet to hurry to microphones to position themselves as protectors of the farmers. Surely there would be major commissions of inquiry. Surely Amnesty International would show interest. Surely Human Rights Watch would react. Surely the left-leaning media, the self-appointed moral saviors of the West, would rush to express their horror and outrage and demand action.

There would be nothing of the sort. The Western Media, when interested at all, would actually descend to a new low of rationalization. Amnesty International ignored it. Human Rights Watch remained silent. And still Black politicians railed about the farmers owning too much land, and the ANC party apparatchiks yelled *"Kill the farmer. Kill the Boers!"*

But it was Thabo Mbeki's Black Racist Ongelykheid Regime that had by far the most callous and devastating response. They shut down the Commando system (Chapter 2: *Commando!*) (equivalent to the US National Guard) that had been the first line of defense of the farmers since 1659. They forced the farmers to return the weapons that had been issued to them under that system. This led to a fourfold increase in murder rate of farmers, as reported by Genocide Watch[44]. Mbeki's ministers suggested that the regular Police would be given responsibility, but nothing has ever come of that. In fact, quite the opposite has happened.

The underlying outrage was actually in 2007 when Mbeki's Black Racist Ongelykheid Regime took the most cynical step of all. They forbade the Police to issue statistics on farm murders[45], claiming it made the lives of farmers appear more important than the lives of blacks. This had the immediate effect of burying the 3,000 deaths out of 45,000 farmers among the murder statistics of the 40 million black people in the country, a thousand times larger population. The Police statistician left the country for Britain.

Genocide

One of the leading international authorities in the matter of genocide is Gregory Stanton, Research Professor in Genocide Studies and Prevention at George Mason University, Virginia. He was the founder and director of the Cambodian Genocide Project, founder and Chair of the International Campaign to End Genocide and was the President of the International Association of Genocide Scholars. During his service in the Clinton Administration he drafted the United Nations Security Council resolutions to create the International Criminal Tribunal for Rwanda and other related commissions. Professor Stanton also drafted the U.N. Peacekeeping Operations resolutions that helped bring about an end to the civil war in Mozambique. He served as Co-Chair of the Washington Working Group for the International Criminal Court. He is the founder and president of Genocide Watch. It would be difficult indeed to find on the planet a man better qualified to identify genocide in the making.

In mid-2012, Professor Stanton visited South Africa and promptly raised[46] the Genocide Alert Level on South Africa to Stage 6: "Preparation." The farmers most certainly believe that there is a campaign to murder them all. They point directly at the ANC and its legacy of singing "*Bulala amaBhulu!*"(Kill the Boers").

It is tremendously difficult to get the formal media to report properly and truthfully on this subject, but on 30 March 2010, the Reuters News Agency finally rose to the occasion when it reported[47] that the general Secretary of the ANC had formally defended the singing of the song. By then, the farmers being murdered in droves had known this for a fact for 15 years and some 3,000 of the 45,000 white farmers had been murdered. They also reported that 450,000 of the county's roughly 4.5 million white people were living in poverty; a full 10%, most of them Afrikaners, including some of the author's own family.

During 2011, the leader of the ANC Youth League, Julius Malema, was challenged in court by the organization Afriforum on the subject of his continual singing of "*Bulala amaBhulu!*" from public platforms, even as white people were being murdered at a frightening rate. The judgment eventually went against Malema and the judge ruled[48] it "Hate Speech." Yet President Zuma was himself caught on video on 8 January 2012 in Mangaung (Bloemfontein) singing a variant of the song at the centenary of the founding of the ANC. The result is a total loss of trust by white people in the president of the country; hardly surprising if he sings about killing them while he is supposed to be their leader. The equivalent would be the U.S. President singing "*Kill the Honkies*" at a Democratic Party convention while militant members of the Party dance around in front of him in camouflage outfits.

Professor Stanton of Genocide Watch reports the event[49]. However, despite numerous websites carrying the video[50], the formal media refuses to report on this event. Perhaps under these circumstances the utter disillusionment of the white people of South Africa with the international media can be understood.

North into Africa and Eurasia

Against the backdrop sketched here, it is hardly surprising that white farmers started looking outside the country for a future doing what they do best, which is to farm. Most fascinatingly, the greatest interest came from the rest of Africa. Countries further north in Africa had by now started maturing. They were getting over their "Revolution, Entitlement and Africanization" phases and were facing up to the reality that countries need management and proper economies and that people actually have to work to have success. Black people in South Africa, however, seemed philosophically trapped by the bankrupt Bolshevik rhetoric of the ANC while their own supposedly Socialist leaders were stealing the country blind.

A decade after the author had left the country, the AgriSA farmer union had interest from no fewer than 22 African countries. The British newspaper, *The Guardian*, reported[51] on 1 May 2011 that some 800 South African farmers had set up farms in Mozambique. Zambia would like them to grow corn. The Sudan wanted them to develop the growth of sugar cane. The biggest farming business deal was in the old Brazzaville Congo, where they had been offered free land, tax holidays, zero import duties on input materials and so forth. The first contracts for Brazzaville Congo (the old French Congo immediately north of the Congo River) had already been signed with 77 specific farmers for the use of 88,000 hectares. The financing for it had also been arranged. Power lines and roads were being promised. The banking world had noticed and was financing some of these agreements. British financing groups were also involved.

A paper presented at an international conference at the University of Sussex by Ruth Hall[52] pointed out that South African farmers were already active in Botswana, Malawi, Mozambique and Kenya, and that talks were underway with Angola, Democratic Republic of Congo (Zaïre), Egypt, Gabon, Guinea, Cameroon,

Senegal, Sudan, and Uganda. Given that several farmers had indicated they would continue to live in South Africa and hire managers to run the foreign farms, while securing third party funding and free land in these countries plus other help, the paper expressed surprise that Black Africa would do this if the farmers themselves apparently brought nothing tangible to the table. In this respect, the Brazzaville Congo had offered South African farmers a block of 200,000 hectares, with the option of expanding to 10 million hectares; twice the size of Switzerland. However, the paper eventually comes to the conclusion that these farmers are not going to the other countries to "grab land" for South Africa or even to produce food for South Africa. As Andre Botha, head of the Gauteng branch of AgriSA put it so clearly (quoted in the Hall paper):

"All over Africa the message we get is: 'We are looking for South African farmers', which is incredibly important to us. It means that our contribution to the future of this continent is valued."

But, in South Africa these farmers are tortured to death and the government tries to take their farms away. It proves the racial hatred is unique to the South African black people who are subject to daily indoctrination by an ANC that blames white people for the ANC's own economic failures. The entire "land redistribution" debate is a political red herring promoted by the ANC and lapped up by a gullible international media with a guilt complex about European Imperialism and Colonialism. Yet, these Afrikaner farmers' recent ancestors fought against this Imperialism and Colonialism in the First and Second Boer Wars.

In 1995, the author was host to a high level visitor from Rwanda who lamented the aid his country was receiving from Sweden. He described it as Swedish money for Swedish engineers to build Swedish telephone exchanges that only Swedes can run and maintain. As a result, within a few years, trees were growing through the disused telephone exchange and the locals were no better off. Then he said:

"This is why we come to you. To be honest, we do not like your politics, but we know that you are here to stay, that your heart and your blood is in Africa, and that you know how to do things we cannot do. So we would very much like to have your help."

In a nutshell, Black Africa had accepted the Afrikaner as an inherent and crucial part of Africa, but the ANC could only exist by turning Black South Africans artificially against white South Africans. Perhaps they could take a leaf from the book of a Nigerian visitor who wrote in his local paper[53] after visiting South Africa:

"South Africa is the potential and indisputable leader in Africa. Thanks to white South Africans...[...] I want whites back in Nigeria!"

A world away, the Agricultural sector of the former Soviet Republic of Georgia declined from 14.5% to just 8.3 % of the GDP between 2005 and 2009. As a result, the country came looking specifically for South African farmers[54]. To quote the Georgian Agricultural Minster:

"The South Africans have a long experience in large-scale farming and animal husbandry. They can set up such larger agricultural businesses in Georgia."

In response, farmers such as 68-year old Piet Kemp moved from the Highveld of Mpumalanga in South Africa, to ex-Soviet Georgia in March 2011. Kemp explained that he no longer had to spend his evening sitting with his gun and walkie-talkie on his porch, guarding his property. Pieter was one of ninety white South African farmers who toured Georgia in October 2010. His first crop was in the ground by mid 2011 and he expected about 2,000 tons of wheat and 3,000 tons of corn.

Perhaps it has helped that the President of Georgia, Mikheil Saakashvili, is married to a lady named Sandra Elisabeth Roelofs[55], a name that is as established in South Africa as apple pie in the United States. She is in fact Dutch born, but it does mean that she has a very direct cultural link to the White Afrikaner South African farmers, who, like the author, are typically 40% Dutch, 30% German, and 25% French in terms of their ancestral family trees. The Dutch and Afrikaans languages are thoroughly mutually intelligible.

The Economist belatedly published an article on the Afrikaners in Georgia[56] on 23 February 2012 describing the murder of 3,000 white Afrikaner farmers since Mandela took office in 1994. It neglected to describe the torture that usually accompanies the murders. It did describe the fact that less than half the arable land of Georgia is actually worked and that it was importing 70% of its food. By then, five South African farmers, including Pieter Kemp, had already settled there. Clearly the post-Communism Georgians comprehend something the Marx-addled ANC in South Africa cannot fathom.

The White South African Diaspora

Matters were getting progressively more miserable for white South Africans. No man who thought himself a member of Western Civilization could stomach South Africa anymore. The first people to leave were those of greater means or training. They could find their feet in Northern Europe or the USA, Canada, Australia and New Zealand more easily than their less fortunate countrymen.

A much favored destination was Great Britain for two reasons. The first was that many English speaking South Africans could still trace distant family in that country after several generations of separation, and secondly because until 2009 Britain was the one place that did not require a visa from South Africans.

For Afrikaans speaking South Africans the situation was different. After some 350 years in Africa, they did not feel like World Citizens. Their principles were basic – love of country, devotion to that country, and a sense of duty towards it. These are values Americans understand well, but Europeans have lost to a lamentable degree. While many indeed settled in Britain, it would be Australia, Canada and New Zealand that became favored destinations; and, to a lesser extent, the United States.

Canada held a special attraction as it offered a clear path to citizenship. This was an important factor to Afrikaners who knew that after 350 years there was no way back. Building a country as a citizen is fundamental to their cultural psyche. They needed another country to help build; a country to belong to. Their Calvinistic Protestant Work Ethic drove them in that direction.

Fig. 30-2 Scene in the author's mother's birthtown (2012)

While some of them would try to visit family in South Africa over Christmas time, they realized the country they had loved and built was no more. In its place was something of great evil that stalked them in their nightmares. Perhaps it is best exemplified by Figure 30-2 which shows the old fish & chip shop in Middelburg, Cape, the birthtown of the author's mother. It is located a few hundred yards from grandpa Kotie's house where the author had visited many times as a child (*NF85*). By 2012, the building had been turned into a Nigerian "Doctor's" muti (potion) shop. The name Yakubu, as seen in the photograph, is Nigerian and does not occur indigenously in South Africa. Given the horror we had grown up with in respect of the infamous *muti-murders*[57], this particular photograph strikingly presents the replacement of the "Christian Good" (real or perceived) with the African ancestor worshiping animist and potion brewing "evil" (real or perceived).

The loss of their country has been an exceedingly painful experience for Afrikaners. This is certainly true for those remaining in what has become the hollowed-out rotting carcass of South Africa. It is equally true for those who have to helplessly watch from afar as the country descends into a classic African "basket-case." It is made all the worse by a sense that the uninformed in Northern Europe and America actually lauds what is happening in South Africa and visits the tourist spots conveniently removed from reality.

To Afrikaners, it seems the West is actively enjoying their suffering. They see such Northerners as akin to a Roman amphitheater crowd cheering in bloodlust as Christians are being herded helplessly toward the hungry lion.

Cry the Beloved Country

As South Africa approached 20 years of ANC rule it had digested two decade's worth of news about beetroot concoctions to treat AIDS; about rape, corruption and fraud charges against the president of the country; presidential connivance to keep the monster Mugabe in power in Zimbabwe; jailing of the National Police Commissioner as a common crook; and apparently endless wives, mistresses and love children of the current president. South Africa was starting to look like a typical Failed African State.

One fifth of the 1994 white population had simply fled the country, the author included. The BEE policy had been shown up for what it really is – a racist plan to take away as much as possible from white people and give it to the ANC elite while their fellow blacks grow poorer in misery. The history of the BEE flagship company had shown what a debacle that ill-conceived policy actually was.

White farmers were living in abject terror on their farms, facing according to international experts a genocide, their numbers having declined by at least 50% since Mandela came to power in 1994. Some had fled to places as far afield as the ex-Soviet Republic of Georgia. The country had lost its position as biggest gold producer on Earth. Nigeria was about to overtake South Africa as the biggest economy in Africa and the country's ability to feed itself was in jeopardy. Yet the ANC government persisted in trying to take productive farmland from white people to give to black people; this while 90% of such transferred land fell into abject ruin by the ANC's own admission. Ironically, the new black landowners had sold 30% of transferred land[58]; in some cases to the previous white owners, revealing the entire land "restitution" issue to be a complete farce and red herring.

Even at this late hour the ANC persisted in thinking that one can take from the White 10% of the population to make the 90% Black population rich. The mathematics simply does not work and they will never be satisfied – why should they? By blaming whites for all the woes of the country, the ANC, including the country's president, persisted in setting the poor blacks upon the whites by chanting *"Bulala amaBhulu! Kill the Boers!"* It still had not occurred to the ANC to employ the 10% of the white population as a catalyst for growing the economy and raising black employment. It has been shown that the loss of every trained soul from the country leads to the loss of at least ten associated lower skilled jobs. By that calculation alone, the departure of the author's family of three professionals had deprived 30 South Africans, most likely ANC voters, of jobs. One retired black nurse, Nomvula Ndlovu, poignantly commented[59]:

> *"...I just never thought that I'd be poorer now than I was. Yes racism still exists and we are faced with it from time to time, but today's oppression is from our own black government."*

Now the country was dealing with a new "Sharpeville Massacre," massive joblessness, and news that its president Zuma had allegedly used a massive block of state funds to build his villa at Nkandla in Zululand. Thirty four people had been shot to death at Marikana to keep the ANC elite, the amaBenzi, in gravy as they rushed about as tenderpreneurs to exploit the Racist BEE Act. Against this background the ANC re-elected Zuma on 18 December 2012 as party president, and made BEE poster-child Cyril Ramaphosa the Deputy President of the Party.

As to the lost dream of Nelson Mandela's "Rainbow Nation," we turn to his former wife[60], Nomzamo Winfreda Zanyiwe "Winnie" Madikizela, on the subject of his relationship with the ANC:

> *"...they keep him as a figurehead for the sake of appearance."*

And in what remained of their once proudly Western Christian country the author's family pondered survival for one more year, and they prayed and pretended nothing was wrong. There was not much else left to do for the amaBhulu, the forsaken White Tribe of Africa.

No help was on the way. No one even acknowledged the crisis. No one in the West appeared to care.

May Alan Paton rest in peace, for he saw not the future.

May God have mercy on the Rainbow Nation.

Nexus Familia 119: At the furniture store

My wife and I are in a furniture store in Vancouver, Canada. On the previous day, we bought a recliner for my mother, but have since found that it does not fit our lounge arrangement. As a result, we are returning it.

And this is when I recognize a gentleman who was in the shop the previous day, but was busy with other clients at that time. When I leave my wife alone to complete the signing of the paperwork at the sales desk, this gentleman heads straight for me.

I'm certainly not ready to talk about more furniture purchases at this time. I would really prefer to just finish and leave. What happens next, however, proverbially "takes off my legs." When the gentleman gets close to me, he asks:

"Excuse me, but I could not help hearing you speak yesterday. Are you perhaps South African?"

When I confirm that I am, he responds with the following heartening comment:

"Well, I would just like to thank you for choosing Canada. You South African folks are exactly what this country needs. You are just the most ideal immigrants."

I thank him for the comment, but, just as I start wondering whether I am being set up for a sales pitch, he apologizes and says that he has a client to attend to. I am left standing in the store, wondering why Canadians can consider us to be just what Canada needs while the ANC *Ongelykheid Regime* of South Africa makes war on us in every domain under its control.

And then I remember the reality of my whole existence: the North American media will simply brand the sales representative a racist. They will never report on the South African doctors that have saved the provincial medical service of Saskatchewan. Contrast this with the fact that Ken Krawitz, Deputy-Premier of that province, personally shook my hand and thanked me for them a few years go, saying they saved the provincial health care system.

This has been our fate as nation for generations, and seems destined to remain that until we cease to exist – as was the wish of the learned Northern European Liberal Socialist professor (*NF90*) at IBM in 1979.

—End Nexus Familia

 ## Nexus Familia 120: When the loerie sings again

Every South African knows the liquid sound of the loerie – the rainbird of Africa. It is seldom seen, but always heard when the sun comes out after the rain[61]. Its call is imprinted on the mind of any person who has lived there and has cared to listen. It is the sound of the sun after the rain; the sound of the calm after the storm; the sound of hope after all has been lost. I have known the call of the loerie ever since I can remember. I have rescued its young, I have raised them, and I have protected them. I have set them free to be where God meant for them to be. And they are meant to fly free in Africa.

If only the Afrikaner could be so free in Africa and someone would help. But he is all alone.

*****

My eyes survey the courtroom. I am met by a veritable sea of inscrutable Asian faces, about three quarters Chinese and the rest South Asian. Other than us as a family, a single Caucasian man and a Somali woman stand out like sore thumbs. The Caucasian is from New Zealand.

When the judge takes the podium, he explains that Canada is a nation of immigrants; that they arrive here with no common language, no common religion, no common philosophy, no common culture. The only thing they have to keep them together under such circumstances is the Law. For this reason, Canadians are the most law-abiding people on the planet, otherwise the country would come apart. He explains that we all have equal rights, equal privileges, and equal responsibilities. I wonder silently whether he appreciates the true significance of these words. His Asian audience exhibits no emotion, no reaction – nothing. A large fraction no doubt does not understand a word he has said – there are schools in town that coach them in how to survive this event despite not comprehending a word of English.

Then the judge tells us to stand, and to say the oath of allegiance to the Queen of England after him, three words at a time, first in French and then in English.

And it is at this point that I feel the wetness rolling over my cheeks. I am crying for my Africa; for everything it could have been; for all the love I have given it, just to see it turned into a disgusting nightmare. Now I finally know how the old Bitterenders in the Boer War felt after surrendering. They broke their rifles in front of the British soldiers and cried as grown men at the loss of their country as they had to swear allegiance to the King of England. I really do my best to manage, but I am lost. I am swearing off everything my ancestors had fought and died for over more than 350 years and it is breaking me as a human being. But, I am an Afrikaner, a Child of the Covenant, and my word should be my bond.

I just keep looking the judge straight in the eye with the tears running uncontrollably. That is the least I can do with what remains of my pride, my dignity, and my courage. I croak along, with my right hand in the air and my Bible in my left. But I am smiling. At least, I think I am. I am going to wear my tears proudly, if that makes any sense, but I am obviously not as tough as I thought. The man who has had to be everyone's cornerstone for so long is obviously not that strong when it finally comes right down to it.

When the judge finishes, he says:

"Do you see those beautiful mountains out there?
They are now yours. Welcome Home!"

No one on Earth could ever imagine the power of those two simple words to people like us: *"Welcome Home."* We are home, dear God, home!… *Home!*

At the end of the ceremony, the judge comes straight over to us and pretty much puts his arms around us as a family. He tells me to take my family out that night and be happy. He is a decent man. He knows exactly where we are from and presumably understands why I struggled.

This is our first day as Canadians. And perhaps it is no major issue for the other new citizens who were sworn in with us, but for me it is everything. I have a country again that I can call "Home" and that I can love again and can help build and turn into something to be proud of; one that will understand when I commit to it; that will not damn me and recriminate me day in and day out for being white.

Perhaps we shall even have a government that does not scheme away day in and day out at how to hurt, disadvantage, and malign us further. I am a Canadian and I am so desperately thankful to the Canadians for allowing me to be one of them, even though they themselves likely have no idea how important that is.

Perhaps my son will know the wonderful feeling of pride in one's country and what it is to live in it with hope and without fear. For myself, I do not know. I think I shall die with my personal anguish. I simply wanted too much for South Africa. I believed too deeply and tried too hard. And I have been ever the fool for it. And I stand so proven before you.

For me, the loerie will never sing again.

—*End Nexus Familia*

-----ooOoo-----

Epilogue

We have presented in this work a history of the Afrikaner, whether Afrikaans or English-speaking, and we have traced a number of real families through that history. They were all ancestors of either the author or his wife, or near relations to those ancestors. We have done this in the hope that it will demonstrate to the reader that the Afrikaner is not some kind of "colonialist" or latter day "settler" as the ANC or ill-informed commentators would have the reader believe. The Afrikaner does not share the European history of Colonialism or the American history of Slavery. He fought two wars against British Colonial Imperialism, suffering the concentration camp nightmare long before Black Africa awoke and he typically counts early slaves at the Cape among his ancestors.

The vast majority of Afrikaners have a bloodline in South Africa literally centuries longer than the vast majority of Americans have in North America. Unlike the British, Italian, German, Portuguese, Belgian and French colonialists of the 20th Century, they have no European *"home"* to *"go back"* to. Africa is the only home they have known for centuries and no one anywhere has offered them a haven.

At this terrible juncture in time, we are witnessing for the first time in Modern History the destruction of an entire Western Christian nation, roughly as numerous as the Danes, the Norwegians or the New Zealanders. This is happening at the hand of an opposing civilization — that of Black Africa. The West is not just standing idly by. It appears to be engrossed in denying the hard facts of the situation, if not actively encouraging the process.

There is something inherently obscene about the West commending the destruction of its own first outer wall, even as it is preparing to sell out Israel, the guardian on its second outer wall. That country will soon be treated the same way the West treated "the Second America," and it will be morally assailed by the media. At the same time, the events of the first decade of the 21st century have forced the First America to question its own invincibility. The entire Western Civilization has lost its edge and is losing its place in the world. This work is a wake-up call to that Civilization; an opportunity to stare closely at the beast lying in wait.

We have quoted Deneys Reitz extensively in this work as an honest reporter on the Great Boer War. In 1899, on the eve of that war and its resultant British Concentration Camps, F.W. Reitz, father of Deneys and Secretary of the Transvaal Afrikaner Republic, wrote about his country and his Afrikaner people:

"If the reading public believe a hundredth part of the enormities which have been laid at the door of our people and Government, they must be irresistibly forced to the conclusion that this Republic is a den of thieves and a sink of iniquity, a people, in fact, the very existence of which is a blot upon humanity, and a nuisance to mankind...[...] In this awful turning point in the history of South Africa, on the eve of the conflict which threatens to exterminate our people, it behooves us to speak the truth in what may be, perchance, our last message to the world."

These words, written more than 110 years ago about the long-term vilification of the Afrikaner, again apply almost verbatim. Over the past 60 years, the Western Media has assailed with a passion a largely helpless Western Christian nation facing impossible odds, deserted by its kin. When these words were previously ignored, it led to the invention of Concentration Camps, and Britain consequently had to bear on its conscience the lives of more than 27,000 women and children. Will the West live with its conscience after the present situation at the southern tip of Africa has proceeded beyond the point of no return?

In Chapter 11 of this work, the author stated, *"but for one man with a conscience and a horse"* the history of South Africa might have been different. This statement was based on the events of February 1838, when missionaries elected to flee rather than warn the Afrikaner Trekkers about the Zulu army sent to massacre them in the night at Blaauwkranz.

In the same spirit, the author is forced to close this work with a simple phrase:

But for one reporter with a conscience and a pen...

Finis

-----ooOoo-----

Notes to Chapters

Notes to Chapter 1

1 Original inhabitants of Southern Africa, sharing primary DNA haplogroup L0 with the San Bushmen
2 The governing body of the Dutch East India Company
3 Dutch East India Company; also known as "Jan Compagnie" ("John Company")
4 Anglicized as Peter Minuit
5 Later Albany, New York
6 A term out of favor, used earlier to describe the unique original indigenous Khoekhoe people of S. Africa
7 George McCall Theal, *Records of South-Eastern Africa, Vol. 7,* (1901), p. 388
8 Now Maputo, the former Lourenço Marques
9 John Bird, *Annals of Natal, Vol. 1,* (1888), p. 24; Extract of the Decades of Joao de Barros
10 George McCall Theal, *Records of South-Eastern Africa, Vol. 8,* (1902), p. 297
11 The genealogical information in this section is obtained from the Danish State Archive and from the Lutheran Church Archive in Garding, Eiderstedt, Schleswig-Holstein, Germany.
12 Virginia Belz Chomat, *Cabrières d'Aigues et la Famille Jourdan, Edition Cabrières,* (2007), p. 207
13 William Stephen Gilly, *Narrative of an excursion to the mountains of Piemont,* (1824), p. xxiv
14 Some insist that they are followers of a religious sect started by Waldo in Lyon in the 12th century
15 Alexis Muston– translated by John Montgomery, *The Israel of the Alps, Vol. 1,* (1866), p. 106
16 Alexis Muston – translated by John Montgomery, *The Israel of the Alps, Vol. 1,* 1866; pp. 65-71
17 Berthold Fernow, *Records of New Amsterdam from 1653 to 1674 A.D., Vol. 3,* (1897), p. 412; Minutes of the Court, Nov. 20, 1661

Notes to Chapter 2

1 The detail per ship provided by J.R. Bruijn et al in *Dutch-Asiatic Shipping 1595-1795* clearly shows the numbers reported here: 49 on the Dromedaris, 28 on the Reijger. All ship information reported here is taken from this source.
2 George McCall Theal, *Chronicles of Cape Commanders,* (1882), p. 33
3 The Dutch town of Terneuzen claims to be the birthplace of "Captain Van der Decken" and dates the legend to the early 1600s. See e.g., *Het Verhaal van Zeeland,* (2005), by J. J. B. Kuipers and R. J. Swiers, p. 252
4 George McCall Theal, *Chronicles of Cape Commanders,* (1882), p. 36
5 The Dutch East India Ccompany (VOC)
6 Hilary Aidan St. George Saunders, *The Green Beret: The Story of the Commandos,* 1940-1945, (1949), pp. 21-24
7 H.C.V. Leibbrandt, *Precis of the Archive of the Cape of Good Hope, Vol. 13,* (1900), p. 264
8 H.C.V. Leibbrandt, *Precis of the Archive of the Cape of Good Hope, Vol. 13,* (1900), p. 319; the actual deed
9 Stone Street parallel to South William. Hoogh Straat was the direct route from the fort to the Water Gate at the eastern end of the palisade on the Cingel (Wall Street). The Sterrevelts bought Aris Otto's earlier tavern on the northern side of Hoogh Straat (Stone Street), a few yards north of Stadhuys Laan (Coentie's Alley). In 1664 Pearl Street was known as 't Water (the Water), the Waterside or de Wael. The Broad Street of today was the Heere Gracht canal, running inland and forking to the left along Bever Straat.
10 Inheritances of children from earlier marriages were carefully managed by the so-called Orphan Chamber until the children reached maturity. Parents were obliged to share and share alike among their children - great care was taken around this matter and guardians of the children's future rights were appointed.
11 The street along the water's edge, today's Pearl Street, was then more formally called De Wael, the Walloon (French Belgian) section where people such as the notary public, La Chair, lived. Generally it was simply called 't Water (the water).
12 Only the southern one of the two, Stadhuys Laan, remains – now Coentie's Alley; The section of Hoogh Straat between Coentie's Alley and the Heere Gracht (Broad Street) has also disappeared.
13 Thysje was indeed cited for tax arrears and her fine was stated in wampum
14 The City Hall, where the Court held session; the stocks were outside the door on the water's edge.
15 South William Street. In Ariaentje's time it was a lane, which turned 90 degrees to meet Hoogh Straat in a T-junction just north of their house. The lane that connected Slyck Steeg to Hoogh Straat is now Mill Lane. Slyck Steeg has been extended so South William now goes through to William Street (*Smee Straat* in her time).
16 People of DNA haplogroup L2; Spencer Wells; *Deep Ancestry-inside the Genographic Project,* (2007), p. 178

17 Courtesy Statistics South Africa; majority racial group per electoral district. (2002)

18 J. W. G. van Haarst, J. J. Meinsma, *De Opkomst van het Nederlandsch gezag in Oost-Indie, Part 2*, (1864); p. 301; *The Journal of Frank van der Does*; see also E. Terry, *A Voyage to East-India*, (1777), p. 17

19 D. Moodie, *The Record I*, (1960), p. 51; Journal of Commander Jan van Riebeeck for 20 May 1654

20 R. Raven-Hart, *Cape Good Hope 1652-1702*, (1971), p. 509; Detail index to thirteen individual visitor reports

21 R. Raven-Hart, *Cape Good Hope 1652-1702*, (1971), p. 512; Detail index to eleven individual visitor reports.

22 Edward Terry, *A Voyage to East-India*, (1777), p. 16; Reprint of 1655 book by Terry about his 1615 voyage

23 D. Moodie, *The Record I*, (1960), p. 32; Dispatch from Commander Van Riebeeck to the Chamber XVII

24 R. Raven-Hart, *Cape Good Hope 1652-1702*, (1971), p. 511; Detail index to nine individual visitor reports

25 Abraham Bógaerts, *Historische Reizen door d'oostersche delen van Asia*, (1731), p. 112; Second

26 Spencer Wells, *The Journey of Man: A Genetic Odyssey*, (2002), p. 56-60

27 George McCall Theal, *Chronicles of Cape Commanders*, (1882), p. 43

28 Jean-Baptiste Tavernier, *Travels in India*, Vol. 2, (1889), p. 394 and 398; A later English edition

29 George McCall Theal, *Chronicles of Cape Commanders*, (1882), p. 106

30 Cape Archives, *Resolutions of the Council of Policy of the Cape of Good Hope*, ref. C.3, pp. 16-26

31 D. Moodie, *The Record I*, (1960), p. 285; Extract from journal of Commander Wagenaar

32 Cape Archives, *Resolutions of the Council of Policy of the Cape of Good Hope*, ref. C.11, pp. 38-44 and 45-50

33 Now Maputo in Mozambique - the former Lourenço Marques of Colonial Portugal

34 *De Hollandtsche Mercurius*, Part 13, (1662), pp. 6-11

35 George McCall Theal, *Chronicles of Cape Commanders*, (1882), p. 166

36 George McCall Theal, *Chronicles of Cape Commanders*, (1882), p. 168

37 Cape Archives, *Resolutions of the Council of Policy of the Cape of Good Hope*, ref. C. 18, pp. 105-109

38 William Stephen Gilly, *Narrative of an excursion to the mountains of Piemont*, (1824), p. clxxxix

39 John Bird, *Annals of Natal, Vol. I*, (1888); Excerpts from the Journal of Commander Van der Stel, p. 27

40 His adventures are captured in *Guillaume Chenu de Chalezac: "The French Boy"*, ed. Randolph Vigne (1991)

41 George McCall Theal, *Chronicles of Cape Commanders*, (1882), pp. 247-257

42 John Bird, *Annals of Natal, Vol. I*, (1888): Excerpts from the Journal of Commander Van der Stel, p. 46

43 George McCall Theal, *Chronicles of Cape Commanders*, (1882), pp. 257-260

44 George McCall Theal, *History of South Africa under the administration of the DEIC*, Vol. 1, (1897), p. 113

45 George McCall Theal, *Ethnography and Condition of South Africa before A.D. 1505*, (1919), p. 198

46 S.A. Government, *Determination on amaRharhabe and amaGcaleka Paramountcies*, Article 81351, 28 April 2008

47 D. Moodie, *The Record I*, (1960), p. 197; Letter of Dec 15, 1659 from Joan Maetsuycker to Jan van Riebeeck

Notes to Chapter 3

1 Virginia Belz Chomat, *Cabrières d'Aigues et la Famille Jourdan, Edition Cabrières*, (2007), pp. 247-252

2 Nexus Familia 18 and 19 rely on the work of the following: M. Boucher in *French speakers at the Cape* (1981) and *Frankfurt am Main and the Cape refugees*, Bulletin of the Huguenot Society of South Africa, 19, p. 12 (1981); G. Botha in *French Refugees at the Cape* (1970 - original 1919) and K. Joubert, *Familia Vol. 19, no. 4*, (1982), p. 85-89, as well as the personal research of Virginia Chomat in France (private communication).

3 No documented account of their flight to Geneva exists, but the geography and political dispositions of the time provide convincing circumstantial evidence as to their likely route. Nice in Savoy no longer presented a plausible route for a larger group. The route north via Orange was extremely dangerous for Protestants.

4 C. Graham Botha, *French Refugees at the Cape*, (1970), p. 128 (Original edition was 1919)

5 C. Graham Botha, *French Refugees at the Cape*, (1970), p. 142 (Original edition was 1919)

6 J.R. Bruijn et al in *Dutch-Asiatic Shipping 1595-1795* list the name as *China*, not *Berg China*, as long thought.

7 *Bul. de la Comm. pour l'histoire des églises Wallonnes*, Vol. 1, (1885), p. 243

8 J.R. Bruijn et al, in *Dutch-Asiatic Shipping 1595-1795*, provide the total number of passengers, the number who died and the number who disembarked at the Cape. The passenger list of the *China* has disappeared. The names of the refugees on board must be deduced from other information.

9 Cape Archives, *Inventories of the Orphan Chamber*, Ref. MOOC10/1.4

10 Cape Archives, *Resolutions of the Council of Policy of the Cape of Good Hope*, ref. C.18, pp. 76-77

11 George McCall Theal, *History of South Africa under the administration of the DEIC*, Vol. 1, (1897), p. 385

12 Cape Archives, *Resolutions of the Council of Policy of the Cape of Good Hope*, ref. C.24, pp. 58-59

13 George McCall Theal, *History of South Africa under the administration of the DEIC*, Vol. 1, (1897), p. 387

14 Meerlust remains a leading wine label from South Africa

15 George McCall Theal, *History of South Africa under the administration of the DEIC*, Vol. 1, (1897), p. 403

16 George McCall Theal, *History of South Africa under the administration of the DEIC*, Vol. 1, (1897), p. 427

17 George McCall Theal, *History of South Africa under the administration of the DEIC*, Vol. 1, (1897), p. 391

18 D. Moodie, *The Record V*, (1960), p. 9; Note 1: Statement by 80-year old A. C. Greyling on Dec. 29, 1836

19 We rely on the work of a special commission of the new amaXhosa dominated government of South Africa, issued as *Determination on amaRharhabe and amaGcaleka Paramountcies*, Article 81351, S.A. Government, dated 28 April 2008. The more detailed history by S.M. Molema in *The Bantu – Past and present* (1920), pp. 70-74, differs on some points of early history.

Notes to Chapter 4

1 H.C.V. Leibbrandt, *Precis of the Archive of the Cape of Good Hope, Vol 13*, (1900), p. 144; Letter to Lords XVII

2 Cape Archives, *Resolutions of the Council of Policy of the Cape of Good Hope*, Ref. C.153, pp. 272-321

3 Cape Archives, *Resolutions of the Council of Policy of the Cape of Good Hope*, Ref. C.60, pp. 71-88

4 Cape Archives, *Resolutions of the Council of Policy of the Cape of Good Hope*, Ref. C.103, pp. 80-85

5 Cape Archives, *Resolutions of the Council of Policy of the Cape of Good Hope*, Ref. C.112, pp. 3-33

6 Cape Archives, *Resolutions of the Council of Policy of the Cape of Good Hope*, Ref. C.155, pp. 250-278

7 Cape Archives, *Resolutions of the Council of Policy of the Cape of Good Hope*, Ref. C. 202, pp. 196-383

8 British House of Commons, *Papers relative to the Condition and Treatment of the Native etc., Vol. 1*, (1835), p. 52

9 Richard White, *The Middle Ground*, (1991), p. 240

10 In the Russo-Swedish War (1710) the Russians reputedly tried to provoke an epidemic using cadavers of plague victims.

11 F. Parkman, *The Conspiracy of Pontiac and the Indian War After the Conquest of Canada, Vol. 2*, (1884), p. 39

12 Don Gillmor, Pierre Turgeon and Achille Michaud, *Canada: A People's History, Vol. 1*, (2000), p. 139

13 G.S. Graham, *Empire of the North Atlantic - 2nd Edition*, (1950), p. 210; from the Admiralty Out-papers

14 A.T. Mahan, *The Influence of Sea Power upon History 1660 -1783*, (1890), p. 421

15 S. A. Government, *Determination on amaRharhabe and amaGcaleka Paramountcies*, Article 81351, 28 April 2008

16 George McCall Theal, *History of South Africa under the administration of the DEIC*, Vol. 2, (1897), p. 126

17 A mixed Khoekhoe-Xhosa clan inducted as an amaXhosa tribe by Tshiwe and initially led by Kwane.

18 D. Moodie, *The Record III*, (1960), p. 14; Letter from Cape Gov. to Landdrost of Stellenbosch, 9 Oct. 1772

19 D. Moodie, *The Record III*, (1960), p. 39; Petition of Inhabitants residing beyond De Bruyns Hoogte

20 Anders Sparrman, *A Voyage to the Cape of Good Hope etc., Vol. 2* (1786), p. 140

21 C. P. Thunberg et al, *Travels at the Cape of Good Hope, 1772 – 1775*, (1986), p. 248; Originally published 1793

22 Cape Archives, *Resolutions of the Council of Policy of the Cape of Good Hope*, Ref. C. 158, pp. 225-236

23 Anders Sparrman, *A Voyage to the Cape of Good Hope, Vol. 2*, (1786), p. 253

24 Anders Sparrman, *A Voyage to the Cape of Good Hope, Vol. 2*, (1786), p. 147

25 D. Moodie, *The Record III*, (1960), p. 91; Declaration of Field Corporal Scheepers whom we meet later

26 D. Moodie, *The Record III*, (1960), p. 96; Records of Stellenbosch Heemraad -10 October 1780

27 Strengthened wagon circles laid out for optimal fields of fire, often with branches tied between wagons

28 George McCall Theal, *History of South Africa under the administration of the DEIC*, Vol. 2, (1897), p. 174

29 Anders Sparrman, *A Voyage to the Cape of Good Hope, Vol. 2*, (1786), p. 262

30 J.S. Marais, *Maynier and the First Boer Republic*, (1944), p. 11

31 Cape Archives, *Resolutions of the Council of Policy of the Cape of Good Hope*, Ref. C. 169, pp. 354-385.

32 J.S. Marais, *Maynier and the First Boer Republic*, (1944), p. 25

33 The British Colonel Collins still refers to it many years later: D. Moodie, The Record V, (1960), p. 10

34 Cape Archives, *Resolutions of the Council of Policy of the Cape of Good Hope*, Ref. C. 207, pp. 26-11

35 Cape Archives, *Resolutions of the Council of Policy of the Cape of Good Hope*, Ref. C. 208, pp. 32-91

36 Cape Archives, *Resolutions of the Council of Policy of the Cape of Good Hope*, Ref. C. 220, pp. 354-395

37 George McCall Theal, *History of South Africa under the administration of the DEIC, Vol. 2*, (1897), p. 258

38 F. le Vaillant, *Travels from the Cape of Good Hope, to the Interior Parts of Africa Vol. 1*, (1790), p. 306

39 Cape Archives, *Resolutions of the Council of Policy of the Cape of Good Hope*, Ref. C. 219, pp. 76-131.

40 J.S. Marais, *Maynier and the First Boer Republic*, (1944), p. 16

41 Hinrich Lichtenstein, *Travels in Southern Africa in the Years 1803, 1804, 1805 and 1806*, (1812), p. 210

42 Cape Archives, *Resolutions of the Council of Policy of the Cape of Good Hope*, Ref. C. 223, pp. 178-268.

43 Father of Louis Trichardt, whose travels to the tropics we later follow closely from Chapter 9 onward.

44 Cape Archives, *Resolutions of the Council of Policy of the Cape of Good Hope*, Ref. C. 223, pp. 178-268.

45 J.S. Marais, *Maynier and the First Boer Republic*, (1944), p. 41

46 George McCall Theal, *History of South Africa under the administration of the DEIC*, Vol. 2, (1897), p. 259

47 J.B. Peires, *The House of Phalo*, (1981), p. 51

48 George McCall Theal, *History of South Africa under the administration of the DEIC*, Vol. 2, (1897), p. 266

49 J.S. Marais, *Maynier and the First Boer Republic*, (1944), p. 71

50 Cape Archives, *Resolutions of the Council of Policy of the Cape of Good Hope*, Ref. C.220, pp. 354-395

51 Cape Archives, *Resolutions of the Council of Policy of the Cape of Good Hope*, Ref. C.222, pp. 433-485

52 Cape Archives, *Resolutions of the Council of Policy of the Cape of Good Hope*, Ref. C.223, pp. 178-268

53 Cape Archives, *Resolutions of the Council of Policy of the Cape of Good Hope*, Ref. C.231, pp. 141-144

54 Cape Archives, *Resolutions of the Council of Policy of the Cape of Good Hope*, Ref. C. 231, pp. 200-232.

55 A. Wilmot and John C. Chase, *The History of the Colony of the Cape of Good Hope*, (1869), p. 210

Notes to Chapter 5

1 Hinrich Lichtenstein, *Travels in Southern Africa in the Years 1803, 1804, 1805 and 1806*, (1812) p. 328

2 G.McCall Theal, *Records of the Cape Colony*, Vol. 1, (1897), p. 155; Letter from Maj. Gen. Craig to London

3 G. McCall Theal, *Records of the Cape Colony*, Vol. 1, (1897), p. 270; Craig to Henry Dundas, 27 Dec. 1795

4 This section based on G. McC. Theal, *Records of the Cape Colony*, Vol. 5, (1897), p. 7, unless stated otherwise.

5 Use of term acc. to Barrow in *An Account of Travels into the Interior of Southern Africa*, Vol. 2, (1804), p. 138

6 J.S. Marais, *Maynier and the First Boer Republic*, (1944), p. 88

7 G. McCall Theal, *Records of the Cape Colony*, Vol. 1, (1897), p. 354; Letter from Craig to Govt. in London

8 Anne Lindsay Barnard, *South Africa a Century ago: Letters written from the Cape of Good Hope 1797-1801*, Editor: W.H. Wilkins, (1910), pp. 53-54

9 G. McCall Theal, *Records of the Cape Colony*, Vol. 1, (1897), pp. 481-482; Graaff-Reinet Burghers to Craig

10 G. McCall Theal, *Records of the Cape Colony*, Vol. 1, (1897), p. 497, Letter from Mr. F.R. Bresler to Craig

11 Tributary of Bushman's River; J.S. Marais, *Maynier and the First Boer Republic*, (1944), p. 59, places Jan here.

12 AmaThembu, an isiXhosa speaking nation that has historically provided wives for the amaXhosa kings.

13 Jan was unaware the Cape had changed hands to the British in Sep. 1795; Stout discovered this later.

14 *The Missionary Magazine* for 1800, Vol. 5, (1800), p. 217; Recounted in Vanderkemp's missionary travels

15 Originally 1797. Republished in UK: Benjamin Stout, *Cape of Good Hope and its Dependencies*, (1820), see p. 2

16 Noël Mostert, *Frontiers*, (1993), p. 261

17 J. Barrow, *An Account of Travels into the Interior of Southern Africa (etc.)*, Vol. 1, (1801), p. 46

18 A. Wilmot and John C. Chase, *The History of the Colony of the Cape of Good Hope*, (1869), p. 220

19 J. Barrow, *An Account of Travels into the Interior of Southern Africa (etc.)*, Vol. 2, (1804), p. 102

20 John Barrow, *An auto-biographical memoir of Sir John Barrow*, (1847), p. 141

21 G. McCall Theal, *Records of the Cape Colony*, Vol. 2, (1898), p. 278; Letter from the Earl Macartney to the Right Honourable Henry Dundas, July 9, 1798. Macartney has the wrong first name for Delport; See also G. McCall Theal, *The History of South Africa (1795 – 1834)*, (1891), p. 24; Theal corrects the name.

22 G. McCall Theal, *Records of the Cape Colony*, Vol. 3, (1898), p. 58; Answers to questions proposed by Sir George Yonge relative to the District of Graaff-Reinet

23 G. McCall Theal, *Records of the Cape Colony*, Vol. 2, (1898), p. 366; Maj. Gen. Dundas to the Landdrost of Graaff-Reinet, 23 February 1799

24 G. McCall Theal, *Records of the Cape Colony*, Vol. 3, (1898), p. 293; Sentence of the Court

25 G. McCall Theal, *Records of the Cape Colony*, Vol. 3, (1898), p. 230; Criminal Claim and Conclusion made and demanded by the Fiscal versus Marthinus Prinslo and his Accomplices

26 G. McCall Theal, *Records of the Cape Colony*, Vol. 5, (1899), p. 49

27 J. Barrow, *An Account of Travels into the Interior of Southern Africa*, Vol. 2, (1804), p. 137

28 G. McCall Theal, *Records of the Cape Colony*, Vol. 3, (1898), p. 58;

29 J. Barrow, *An Account of Travels into the Interior of Southern Africa*, Vol. 2, (1804), p. 94

30 G. McCall Theal, *Records of the Cape Colony*, Vol. 3, (1898), p. 59; Dundas, briefing the new governor Yonge

31 D.C.F. Moodie, *The history of the battles and adventures of the British, the Boers, and the Zulus*, (1888), p. 66

32 Cape Archives, *Resolutions of the Council of Policy of the Cape of Good Hope*, Ref. C. 223, pp. 178-268.

33 Cape Archives, *Resolutions of the Council of Policy of the Cape of Good Hope*, Ref. C. 224, pp. 284-321

34 G. McCall Theal, *Records of the Cape Colony, Vol. 2*, (1897), p. 445; C. J. De Jager to Bresler, 27 July 1799

35 J. Barrow, *An Account of Travels into the Interior of Southern Africa, Vol. 2*, (1804), p. 129

36 G. McCall Theal, *Records of the Cape Colony, Vol. 3*, (1898), p. 51; Dundas to the new Governor, Yonge.

37 G. McCall Theal, *Records of the Cape Colony, Vol. 2*, (1898), p. 483; Dep. Secretary Ross to Henry Dundas

38 G. McCall Theal, *Records of the Cape Colony, Vol. 2*, (1898), p. 388; Letter Vandeleur to Maj.General Dundas

39 D. Moodie, *The Record V*, (1960), p. 14; Journal and report of Colonel Collins, (1809)

40 G. McCall Theal, *Records of the Cape Colony, Vol. 2*, (1898), p. 454; Vandeleur to Dundas, 31 July 1799

41 G. McCall Theal, *Records of the Cape Colony, Vol. 2*, (1898), pp. 457-458; Vandeleur to Dundas, 3 Aug. 1799

42 G. McCall Theal, *Records of the Cape Colony, Vol. 2*, (1898), p. 458; Letter from the Landdrost of Swellendam (Mr. Faure) to Major General Dundas, 4 August 1799

43 G. McCall Theal, *Records of the Cape Colony, Vol. 2*, (1898), p. 461; Mrs. Naude to husband, 5 August 1799

44 She is likely referring to the imiDange, who were active in the region at the time.

45 The county northeast of her in the Sneeuberg mountain

46 *Transactions of the Missionary Society, Vol. 1*, (1804) pp. 384 -388; Trans. of Dr Vanderkemp in the year 1800

47 G. McCall Theal, *Records of the Cape Colony, Vol. 2*, (1898), p. 482; Sec. Barnard to H. Dundas, 13 Sep. 1799

48 G. McCall Theal, *Records of the Cape Colony, Vol. 2*, (1898), p. 462; Private letter from Major General Dundas to Deputy Secretary Ross, Van der Walt's Kraal, 5 hours from Zwellendam, 10 August 1799.

49 G. McCall Theal, *Records of the Cape Colony, Vol. 2*, (1898), p. 491; Extract: diary of the Secretary's Office

50 Anne Lindsay Barnard, *The Cape Diaries of Lady Anne Barnard*, (1999), p. 21

51 J.S. Marais, *Maynier and the First Boer Republic*, (1944), p. 113

52 D. Moodie, *The Record V*, (1960), p. 14; Journal and report of Colonel Collins, (1809)

53 G. McCall Theal, *The History of South Africa (1795 – 1834)*, (1891), p. 46

54 G. McCall Theal, *Records of the Cape Colony, Vol. 3*, (1898), p. 89; Letter from Yonge to Henry Dundas

55 G. McCall Theal, *The History of South Africa (1795 – 1834)*, (1891), p. 47

56 G. McCall Theal, *Catalogue of Documents (1795-1803)* in the Cape Archives, (1880) p. 30

57 G. McCall Theal, *Records of the Cape Colony, Vol. 3*, (1898), p. 269; Criminal Claim and Conclusion made and demanded by the Fiscal versus Marthinus Prinslo and his Accomplices

58 G. McCall Theal, *Records of the Cape Colony, Vol. 3*, (1898), p. 295; Sentence of the Court

59 G. McCall Theal, *Records of the Cape Colony, Vol. 3*, (1898), p. 212; Extracts from a Report of the Commissioners Maynier and Somerville to Sir George Yonge, 14 August 1800

Notes to Chapter 6

1 William Pitt and James Phillips, *The Speech of the Right Honourable William Pitt*, (1792), p. 22

2 *Transactions of the Missionary Society, Vol. 1*, (1804) p. 365; Transactions of Dr Van der Kemp in the year 1800

3 *Transactions of the Missionary Society, Vol. 1*, (1804) p. 381; Transactions of Dr Van der Kemp in the year 1800

4 Charles Prentiss, *The Life of the late Gen. William Eaton*, (1813), p. 100

5 G. McCall Theal, *Records of the Cape Colony, Vol. 4*, (1899) p. 346; Enclosure to Letter from Sir George Yonge to Lord Hobart, 21 August 1802

6 G. McCall Theal, *Catalogue of Documents (1795-1803)* in the Cape Archives, (1880) p. 31

7 Intriguingly, an American who had been pressed into the Royal Navy had managed to escape at the Cape and had found his way to the east of the colony at just this time. He would later write a book on the subject.

8 G. McCall Theal, *Records of the Cape Colony, Vol. 4*, (1899), pp. 59-63; Questions proposed to Mr. Maynier relative to the disturbances (etc.) on and about the 20th July 1801, and his answers thereto

9 G. McCall Theal, *Records of the Cape Colony, Vol. 4*, (1899), p. 82; Hobart to Maj. Gen. Dundas, 12 Oct. 1801

10 G. McCall Theal, *Records of the Cape Colony, Vol. 4*, (1899), p. 480; Hobart to F. Dundas, May 1, 1801

11 G. McCall Theal, *Catalogue of Documents (1795-1803) in the Cape Archives*, (1880), p. 31

12 G. McCall Theal, *Records of the Cape Colony, Vol. 4*, (1899), p. 123; Letter Dundas to the Lord Hobart

13 J.S. Marais, *Maynier and the First Boer Republic*, (1944), p. 132

14 Hinrich Lichtenstein, *Travels in Southern Africa in the Years 1803, 1804, 1805 and 1806*, (1812) p. 334

15 J.S. Marais, *Maynier and the First Boer Republic*, (1944), p. 131, note 48

16 G. McCall Theal, *Records of the Cape Colony, Vol. 4*, (1899), pp. 98-101; Sherlock to Dundas, 30 Nov. 1801

17 G. McCall Theal, *Records of the Cape Colony, Vol. 4*, (1899), p. 303 ; Articles of Accusation against Maynier

18 G. McCall Theal, *Records of the Cape Colony, Vol. 4*, (1899), p. 112; Government Advertisement

19 G. McCall Theal, *Records of the Cape Colony, Vol. 4*, (1899), p. 114; Letter from Dundas to Lord Hobart

20 G. McCall Theal, *Records of the Cape Colony, Vol. 4*, (1899), p. 91; A Plan for amending the interior Police

21 G. McCall Theal, *Records of the Cape Colony, Vol. 4*, (1899), p. 330; Proclamation Lieut. General F. Dundas

22 G. McCall Theal, *Records of the Cape Colony, Vol. 4*, (1899), p. 282; Letter Lord Hobart to Dundas

23 *Transactions of the Missionary Society, Vol. 2*, (1806), pp. 83-84; Extract from Van der Kemp's Journal

24 J.S. Marais, *Maynier and the First Boer Republic*, (1944), p. 146

25 D. Moodie, *The Record V*, (1960), p. 15; Journal and report of Colonel Collins, (1809)

26 Hinrich Lichtenstein, *Travels in Southern Africa in the Years 1803, 1804, 1805 and 1806*, (1812); See, for example, p. 296; He was hired by Janssens as tutor to his son, and undertook his own travels to the frontier as attendant to Dutch Commissioner-General De Mist. In Chapter 22, p. 302 of this work he includes a section describing in detail Janssens' earlier voyage to the Frontier that started at Algoa Bay on 8 May 1803.

27 *Transactions of the Missionary Society, Vol. 1*, (1804) p. 413; Trans. of Dr Van der Kemp in the year 1800

28 *Transactions of the Missionary Society, Vol. 2*, (1806), p. 95; Extract of Letters by Van der Kemp

29 W.B.E Paravacini de Capelli and W. J. de Kock, *Reize in den Binnen-landen van Zuid-Africa*, (1965), p. 256

30 The only widowed "Betje" alive in 1803 who had been married to a Gerrit Scheepers (deceased - 1798)

31 George E. Cory, *The Rise of South Africa, Vol. 1*, (1921), p. 140

32 This regiment had earlier fought in the American War of Independence as the 3rd Waldecker Regiment

33 Ludwig Alberti, *Ludwig Alberti's account* (etc), [written 1807] Translated by William Fehr, (1968), pp. 100-101. The British were impressed with him and offered him every inducement to remain at the Cape. He left to support the Napoleonic (Batavian) Dutch and died on 12 June 1812, defending Java against the British.

Notes to Chapter 7

1 A.F. Trotter, *The Old Cape: A chronicle of its men and houses*, (1903), pp. 155-156

2 H. Lichtenstein, *Travels in Southern Africa in the Years 1803, 1804, 1805 and 1806*, (1812) p. 236 and p. 238

3 *Transactions of the Missionary Society, Vol. 3*, (1806) p. 206; the book wrongly attributes it to Van der Kemp

4 G. McCall Theal, *Records of the Cape Colony, Vol. 8*, (1901), p. 126; Read's own letter

5 Anders Stockenström had come to the Cape as a VOC employee and thereby predated the British invasion.

6 D. Moodie, *The Record V*, (1960), p. 60; Letter Stockenström to Acting Colonial Secretary; October 19, 1808

7 D. Moodie, *The Record V*, (1960), p. 17; Journal and report of Colonel Collins, (1809)

8 Noël Mostert, *Frontiers*, (1992), p. 382

9 G. McCall Theal, *Records of the Cape Colony, Vol. 8*, (1901), p. 236; Graham's communication to the Cape.

10 The term "neck" (Afr: nek) is used to describe a saddle between two mountains. Doringnek in effect connects two parallel ranges of mountains, creating a structure approximating an "H" turned on its side.

11 Noël Mostert, *Frontiers*, (1992), p. 384

12 Noël Mostert, *Frontiers*, (1992), p. 386

13 John Campbell, *Journal of Travels in South Africa Among the Hottentot and Other Tribes*, (1834), p. 57

14 G. McCall Theal, *Records of the Cape Colony, Vol. 8*, (1901), p. 237; Letter from Graham, dated 2 Jan. 1812

15 William Brown, *The history of missions, Vol. 2*, (1816), p. 358

16 William Charles Scully, *A History of South Africa, from the earliest days to Union*, (1915), p. 15

17 H. Cloete, *Three Lectures on the Emigration of the Dutch Farmers (etc.)*, (1852), pp. 7-8

18 Robert Percival, *An Account of the Cape of Good Hope*, (1804), p. 233

19 William Wilberforce Bird et al, *State of the Cape of Good Hope in 1822*, (1823) pp. 176-177

20 J. Barrow states up to £400 in 1797 in *An Account of Travels into the Interior (etc.), Vol. 1*, (1801), p. 46

21 H.C.V. Leibbrandt provides the complete court transcripts in *The Rebellion of 1815*, (1902). All facts here are from those transcripts unless otherwise indicated.

22 H.C.V. Leibbrandt, *The Rebellion of 1815*, (1902), pp. 743-745; Also known as Hendrik Nootka

23 It would serve neither the National Party government (1948 -1994) nor the post-1994 ANC government to acknowledge that Xhosa hero King Ngqika had repeatedly been allied with the White amaBhulu.

24 A. Wilmot and John C. Chase, *The History of the Colony of the Cape of Good Hope*, (1869), p. 259

25 H.C.V. Leibbrandt, *The Rebellion of 1815*, (1902), pp. 655-656; direct testimony from the court transcripts.

26 H.C.V. Leibbrandt, *The Rebellion of 1815*, (1902) p. 294; Court Transcripts

27 H.C.V. Leibbrandt, *The Rebellion of 1815*, (1902) p. 532; Court Transcripts

28 Noël Mostert, *Frontiers*, (1992), p. 404

29 Richard Cannon, *History of the Cape Mounted Riflemen*, (1842), p. 18

30 Noël Mostert, *Frontiers*, (1992), p. 404

31 H.C.V. Leibbrandt, *The Rebellion of 1815*, (1902), p. 824

32 H.C.V. Leibbrandt, *The Rebellion of 1815*, (1902), p. 824

33 H.C.V. Leibbrandt, *The Rebellion of 1815*, (1902), p. 823

34 H.C.V. Leibbrandt, *The Rebellion of 1815*, (1902), p. 837

35 H.C.V. Leibbrandt, *The Rebellion of 1815*, (1902), p. 147

36 Arthur Conan Doyle, *The War in South Africa, Its Cause and Conduct*, (1902), p. 4

37 William Shaler, *Sketches of Algiers* (etc.), (1826), p. 279

38 Sir Henry G. W. Smith, *The autobiography of Lieutenant-General Sir Harry Smith, Vol. 1*, (1902), p. 200

Notes to Chapter 8

1 Noël Mostert, *Frontiers*, (1992), p. 468

2 *Report of the Parliamentary Committee for Aboriginal Tribes*, (1837), p. 42; Testimony by Andries Stockenström

3 Ben Maclennan, *A Proper Degree of Terror: John Graham and the Cape's Eastern Frontier*, (1986), p. 179

4 George E. Cory, *The rise of South Africa, Vol. 1*, (1921), p. 381

5 Thomas Pringle, *Narrative of a Residence in South Africa*, (1840), p. 303

6 William Wilberforce Bird et al, *State of the Cape of Good Hope, in 1822*, (1823), p. 234

7 William Wilberforce Bird et al, *State of the Cape of Good Hope, in 1822*, (1823), p. 181

8 Rev. John Campbell, *Voyages to and from the Cape of Good Hope*, (1840), p. 166

9 National Archives (UK); As per the pay books of the 38th Regiment of Foot; Series WO 12/5186

10 G. McCall Theal, *Records of the Cape Colony, Vol. 11*, (1901), p. 404; Letter: Somerset to Earl Bathurst

11 G. McCall Theal, *Records of the Cape Colony, Vol. 13*, (1902), p. 172; The instructions require them to go via "the abandoned place of [ancestral brother] Johannes Grobler" - tortured to death by the amaXhosa in 1793 (NF29). See also Rev. John Campbell, *Voyages to and from the Cape of Good Hope*, (1840), p. 166

12 William Wilberforce Bird et al, *State of the Cape of Good Hope, in 1822*, (1823), p. 193; Extract of a letter written by the Colonial Secretary to the Landdrost of Uitenhage, dated Colonial Office, 25th February, 1820.

13 William Wilberforce Bird et al, *State of the Cape of Good Hope, in 1822*, (1823), p. 229; Annexure 22, Letter by Colonial Secretary Bird, November 15th, 1821

14 William Wilberforce Bird et al, *State of the Cape of Good Hope, in 1822*, (1823), p. 233

15 William Wilberforce Bird et al, *State of the Cape of Good Hope, in 1822*, (1823), p. 240

16 E.A.D. Las Cases, *Memoirs of the Life, Exile, and Conversations, of the Emperor Napoleon, Vol. 4*, (1862), p. 274

17 See Chapter 14: Africa drinks Napoleon's last blood

18 Noël Mostert, *Frontiers*, (1992), p. 512

19 Captain William Cornwallis Harris, *Narrative of an Expedition into Southern Africa*, (1838), p. 345

20 John Bird, *Annals of Natal, Vol. 1*, (1888), p. 230; Narrative of Willem Jurgens Pretorius; See also p. 549; Evidence of Evert Frederick Potgieter to the 1852 Native Commission

21 Gardiner Spring, *The Memoirs of the Rev. Samuel J. Mills*, (1820), p. 112

22 Gardiner Spring, *The Memoirs of the Rev. Samuel J. Mills*, (1820), p. 142

23 Gardiner Spring, *The Memoirs of the Rev. Samuel J. Mills*, (1820), p. 188

24 Chapter 24 : Liberia – Being Black versus Black African

25 *The Missionary Register*, (1822), p. 419; The full article pp. 416-419

Notes to Chapter 9

1 William Wilberforce Bird et al, *State of the Cape of Good Hope, in 1822*, (1823), p. 77

2 William Wilberforce Bird et al, *State of the Cape of Good Hope, in 1822*, (1823), p. 69

3 The government body responsible for managing death taxes and estates

4 John Centlivres Chase, *Natal, a re-print of all authentic notices (etc), Part 1*, (1843), p. 105

5 John Centlivres Chase, *Natal, a re-print of all authentic notices (etc), Part 1*, (1843), p. 43

6 Noël Mostert, *Frontiers*, (1992), p. 652

7 H. J. Batts, *The Story of a 100 Years, 1820-1920: Being the History of the Baptist Church (etc.)* (1922), p. 202

8 Noël Mostert, *Frontiers*, (1992), p. 667

9 Noël Mostert, *Frontiers*, (1992), p. 668

10 Sir Henry G. W. Smith, *The autobiography of Lieutenant-General Sir Harry Smith, Vol. 2*, (1902) p. 344

11 James E. Alexander, *Excursions in Western Africa, Vol. 2*, (1840), p. 58

12 Capt. W.R. King, *Campaigning in Kaffirland*, (1853), pp. 124-125; a scene of a Fingo with the British Army accusing a

Xhosa of Slavery: "You made us your slaves, Kafirs"

13 Robert Godlonton, *Irruption of the Kafir Hordes (etc.)*, (1836), p. 248

14 William Shaw, *Story of my Mission in South-eastern Africa*, (1860), p. 525

15 Noël Mostert, *Frontiers*, (1992), p. 720

16 John Centlivres Chase, *Natal, a re-print of all authentic notices (etc)*, Part 1, (1843), p. 47

17 *The Missionary Herald*, Vol. 29, (1833), p. 414; Letter of Philip to J.B. Purney, Cape Town, May 1833

18 Zoë Laidlaw, *Colonial Connections (1815-1845)*, (2005), p. 152

19 John Centlivres Chase, *Natal, a re-print of all authentic notices (etc)*, Part I, (1843), p. 77

20 Robert Godlonton, *Irruption of the Kafir Hordes (etc.)*, (1836), p. 276

21 Noël Mostert, *Frontiers* (1992), p. 777

22 Robert Godlonton, *Irruption of the Kafir Hordes etc.*, (1836), p. 208, Letter by Governor D'Urban

23 Captain William Cornwallis Harris, *Narrative of an Expedition into Southern Africa*, (1838), p. 346

24 Lt-Colonel Edward. H. D. Elers Napier, *Excursions in Southern Africa, Vol. 2*, (1850), p. 354

25 Sir Henry G. W. Smith, *The autobiography of Lieutenant-General Sir Harry Smith, Vol. 2*, (1902), p. 226

26 L.S. Amery, *The History of the War in South Africa, Vol. 1*, (1900), p. 31

27 John Centlivres Chase, *Natal, a re-print of all authentic notices (etc)*, Part 1, (1843), pp. 54-68

28 John Centlivres Chase, *Natal, a re-print of all authentic notices (etc)*, Part 1, (1843), p. 10

29 W. Shaw, *The Story of My Mission Among the British Settlers in South Eastern Africa*, (1872), p. 66

30 John Centlivres Chase, *Natal, a re-print of all authentic notices (etc)*, Part 1, (1843), p. 56

31 G.D.J. Duvenage, *Van die Tarka na die Transgariep*, (1981), p. 67

32 Literally "tracks" in Afrikaans; generally used to describe all trail signs used to track an animal or person.

33 J. Visagie, *Voortrekker Stamouers*, (2000), p. 105; Duvenage, in Van die Tarka na die Transgariep, p. 150 suggests the trek of A.H.Potgieter, but that is demonstrably wrong by virtue of the baptism reported in the present work.

34 G.S. Preller, *Joernaal van 'n Trek*, (1988), p. 144; Diary entry Mon. 25 June 1838; P. Joubert arrives in Natal.

35 Cape Archives, *Inventories*, MOOC8/67.13b; The Estate of Susanna Human

36 John Centlivres Chase, *Natal, a re-print of all authentic notices (etc)*, Part 1, (1843), p. 94

Notes to Chapter 10

1 James E. Alexander, *Excursions in Western Africa, Vol. 2*, (1840), p. 42

2 Robert Godlonton, *Irruption of the Kafir Hordes into the Eastern Province of the Cape of Good Hope*, (1836), p. 43

3 Rev. John Edwards in *The Missionary Register*, (1836), p. 544; Letter of 17 March 1836

4 James Backhouse, *A narrative of a visit to the Mauritius and South Africa*, (1844), p. 397

5 John Bird, *Annals of Natal, Vol. 1*, (1888), p. 252; The journal of Sarel Cilliers

6 John Centlivres Chase, *The Cape of Good Hope and the Eastern Province of Algoa Bay*, (1843), p. 12

7 William Binnington Boyce, *Notes on South African Affairs*, (1839), p. 174

8 John Centlivres Chase, *Natal, a re-print of all authentic notices (etc)*, Part 2, (1843), p. 253

9 Edwin W. Smith, *The Life and Times of Daniel Lindley*, (1949), pp. 1-54

10 Captain William Cornwallis Harris, *Narrative of an Expedition into Southern Africa*, (1838), p. 48

11 Captain William Cornwallis Harris, *Narrative of an Expedition into Southern Africa*, (1838), p. 90

12 *The African Repository*, Vol. 13, (1837), p. 250; Letter from Dr. Wilson, Grahamstown, 17 April 1837

13 Captain William Cornwallis Harris, *Narrative of an Expedition into Southern Africa*, (1838), p. 96

14 Captain William Cornwallis Harris, *Narrative of an Expedition into Southern Africa*, (1838), p. 172

15 John Bird, *Annals of Natal Vol. 1*, (1888), p. 364; Letter from Piet Retief to Dingane enumerating the losses

16 Captain William Cornwallis Harris, *Narrative of an Expedition into Southern Africa*, (1838), pp. 166-167

17 *The Missionary Herald*, Vol. 33, (1837), p. 417; Letter from Lindley, Venable and Wilson; 2 May 1837

18 *The Missionary Herald*, Vol. 33, (1837), p. 338; Letter from the missionaries; 17 April 1837, Grahamstown

19 *The Missionary Herald*, Vol. 33, (1837), p. 416; Letter from the missionaries; 2 May 1837, Grahamstown

20 Saxe Bannister, *British Colonization and Coloured Tribes*, (1838), p. 304

21 H.J. Batts, *The Story of a 100 Years, 1820-1920: Being the History of the Baptist Church (etc.)*, (1922), p. 205

22 George McCall Theal, *History of South Africa, Vol. 6*, (1964 Struik Edition), p. 316; Vol. 2 of the 1915 Fourth Edition by G. Allen & Unwin

23 Saxe Bannister, *British Colonization and Coloured Tribes*, (1838), pp. 303-309

24 John Bird, *Annals of Natal, Vol. 1*, (1888), p. 326; Letter by Alexander Biggar to the Editor of the Grahamstown Journal, dated 24 October 1837.

25 Gustav S. Preller, *Joernaal van 'n Trek, Uit die Dagboek van Erasmus Smit*, (1988), p. 103; Entry for Wednesday 13 Dec. 1837; the composition of the commission is given. See also the originally published Uit het dagboek van Erasmus Smit, (1897). Owen describes the arrival in his diary, given in The Church Missionary Record, Vol. 9, September 1838, p. 234. John Bird's Annals of Natal Vol. 1, (1888), p. 333. Owen confirms the commission consisted of four men.

26 Francis Owen and George E.Cory, *The Diary of the Rev. Francis Owen*, (1926); p. 63

27 The testimony of Nicolaas Roets shows them arriving at Thaba'Nchu long before the Jan du Plessis- Jacobus Potgieter "Double Trek." His father still baptized a child in Cradock after Retief's trek had already left the colony.

28 Boer War commando member, WWI leader, later Dep. Prime Minister, and High Commissioner to London in WWII

29 His reminiscences were published by Deneys Reitz in *Die Brandwag* in 1911.

30 Orange River

31 His recollection is faulty; it was 1837. His father still baptized a child in Cradock on 5 March 1837

32 Chief Moroka of the Ba'Rolong at Thaba'Nchu

33 Then 8 years old, he is referring to the schism between Potgieter and Retief about Natal as destination.

34 Site of the town of Harrismith, named for Sir Harry Smith, who re-enters the picture soon enough.

35 New Year's Day 1838. Other sources disagree on this date, making it earlier.

36 Ba'Tlokwa (Mantatee) chief Sekonyela. Today the term "Makatees" is considered derogatory.

37 Place of the Puff Adder

38 Place of the Big Drink

39 "Die Stelletjie" in Afrikaans

40 John Bird, *Annals of Natal, Vol. 1*, (1888), p. 367; Bezuidenhout's report: *Orange Free State Monthly Magazine*, (1879)

41 Translation corrected by the author. The John Bird translation reads "*Upon my word* [...]", which misses Retief's point concerning the Trekkers having been wrongly incriminated by Sekonyela's action.

42 His reminiscences were published by Deneys Reitz in *Die Brandwag* in 1911.

43 Sekonyela of the Ba'Tlokwa (Mantatee). "Makatees" is seen as a derogatory term today

Notes to Chapter 11

1 John William Colenso, *Ten Weeks in Natal*, (1855), p. viii

2 Francis Owen and George E.Cory, *The Diary of the Rev. Francis Owen*, (1926); pages as given in text.

3 Charlotte Mary Yonge, *Pioneers and Founders*, (1874), p. 255

4 Not to be confused with the London Missionary Society. See Thomas B. Jenkinson, amaZulu, (1884), p. 108; Gardiner's missionary organization is identified.

5 Allen Francis Gardiner, *Narrative of a Journey to the Zoolu Country In South Africa (1836)*; p. 185

6 John Bird, *Annals of Natal Vol. 1*, (1888), p. 320; Protest of the Inhabitants of Natal against the appointment of Captain Gardiner, R.N., as Magistrate over them

7 Thomas B. Jenkinson, *amaZulu*, (1884), pp. 115-119; Owen's diary is reproduced from the Missionary Register (September 1838 issue) on pp. 109-125

8 Other sources claim they were six, besides Piet Retief, being Coenraad Meyer, Lucas Meyer, Barend Liebenberg, Daniel Bezuidenhout, Roelof Dreyer and the interpreter Thomas Halstead, from Port Natal.

9 E. and J. Gledhill, *In the Steps of Piet Retief*, (1980), p. 189; based on interpreter Kirkman's letter reproduced in *The Diary of the Rev. Francis Owen*, (1926), p. 158. It is also discussed by D. J. Kotzé in *Letters of the American Missionaries*, (1950), p.232. The chief's name is variously spelled Isegwabana, Silwebana, and Isiguabana

10 Mzilikatse of the Matabele

11 Gustav S. Preller, *Joernaal van 'n Trek, Uit die Dagboek van Erasmus Smit*, (1988), p. 113; Diary entry for January 25, 1838. See also the originally published *Uit het dagboek van Erasmus Smit*, (1897).

12 Manfred Nathan, *The Voortrekkers of South Africa*, (1937), p. 194

13 This departure scene is fictionalized, but all the characters are historically entirely correct.

14 Like the British, Afrikaners typically shake hands among men, even in the family.

15 Literally, "walk well", as in "go thee well"

16 His reminiscences were published by Deneys Reitz in Die Brandwag in 1911.

17 Abraham Benjamin Joubert, son of Jacobus, was married to Nicolaas Roets' second oldest sister, Anna.

18 The term "drift" or "drif" is used instead of "ford" by all people in South Africa

19 Likely Adriaan (wife & 5 children) and Josua (wife & 2 children); see Nexus Familia 43 and Fig 9.8. Likely also their parents, Jacobus and Rachel. This (or a nearby) camp also included Jacobus' brother, Jan Christoffel (wife & at least 7 of 10 children).

20 Abraham had four sisters and two younger brothers. Older sisters, Anna E. and Maria M. were likely not on the Great Trek. Nicolaas is believed to be referring to the husbands of two remaining younger sisters.

21 Gustav Preller, *Voortrekkermense (V)*, (1938), p. 9

22 Deduced from *The Grahamstown Journal*, 9 August 1838 and De Villiers and Pama, *Geslagsregisters van Ou Kaapse Families*

23 John Bird, *Annals of Natal, Vol. 1*, (1888), p. 463; The complete Record or Journal (etc.) by Anna E. Steenkamp (née Retief), niece of Great Trek leader Piet Retief, extends pp. 459-468.

24 Gustav S. Preller, *Joernaal van 'n Trek, Uit die Dagboek van Erasmus Smit*, (1988), p. 116; The entry for 15 February 1838. See also the originally published *Uit het dagboek van Erasmus Smit*, (1897).

25 John Bird, *Annals of Natal, Vol. 2*, (1888), p. 202; H. Cloete to the Hon. J. Montagu, Secretary to Govt.,dated 4 July 1843. Cloete, Her Majesty's Commissioner to the Natal Territory, reports personally seeing the original.

26 John Bird, *Annals of Natal, Vol. 1*, (1888), p. 379. Detailed account by William Wood in pp. 376-387

27 D.C.F. Moodie, *The history of the battles and adventures of the British, the Boers, and the Zulus*, (1888), p. 426

28 *The African Repository and Colonial Journal*, Vol. 14, (1838), p. 243; General Letter by the Missionaries, dated Port Elizabeth, April2, 1838. The full letter: pp. 239-247. The American missionaries left behind Daniel Lindley, who would become minister to the Trekkers and establish the Dutch Reformed Church in the region.

29 February 7, 1838

30 Umgungundlovu

31 One assumes Dingane was doing his best to ensure that Owen or Wood did not warn the Trekkers

32 His reminiscences were published by Deneys Reitz in *Die Brandwag* in 1911.

33 Friday evening 16 February 1838

34 John Bird, *Annals of Natal, Vol. 1*, (1888), p. 371; Bezuidenhout's full report pp. 367-376

35 L. Rompel-Koopman, *In het Land van Piet Retief*, (1919), pp. 59-66

36 Chapter 8: The English Afrikaners

37 The Retief commission to Dingane

38 J.A. Heese, *South African Genealogies, Vol. 4*, (2006), p. 184; It notes that only Anna survived. Newer research adds Jan Christoffel (Jr.).

39 The author's research shows that there were 9 children and that the eldest son survived to marry in 1840.

40 The author can find no evidence that the Van Dyk father-in-law of the Grobler men was on the Great Trek.

41 John Bird, *Annals of Natal, Vol. 1*, (1888), p. 410; Boshoff's full report pp. 406-414

42 Gustav S. Preller, *Joernaal van 'n Trek, Uit die Dagboek van Erasmus Smit*, (1988), p. 131; The entry for Thursday 19 April 1838. See also the originally published *Uit het dagboek van Erasmus Smit*, (1897).

43 John Bird, *Annals of Natal, Vol. 1*, (1888), pp. 376-387; The detailed account by William Wood

44 John Bird, *Annals of Natal, Vol. 1*, (1888), p. 223; Letter of Champion to Grout

45 Gustav S. Preller, *Joernaal van 'n Trek, Uit die Dagboek van Erasmus Smit*, (1988) p. 161; Smit is referring to himself. See also the originally published *Uit het dagboek van Erasmus Smit*, (1897).

46 H.J.J.M. Van der Merwe, *Scheepsjournael ende Daghregister*, (1964); p. 243; Trichardt's Diary - translated

47 Some sources state this to be the Portuguese Governor

48 The famous Zulu "Horns of the Bull" formation, to split and thereby weaken the defense.

49 He is referring to the Blaauwkranz Murders that took place near Maritz's Laager. Maritz was still alive.

50 Literally "nation." An archaic term used to describe non-Caucasian people, typically in a farm setting, referring to the farm laborers.

51 Assegaais, spears

52 Animal pelt blanket

53 Gerrit Maritz, still alive at that time, was encamped at the Little Tugela river, not the (great) Tugela.

54 *St. Matthew Passion*, or *O Sacred Head now Wounded*. Nederlands and German: *Zie den Mensch* – translated: "*Is that, is that my King...*"; based on O Haupt voll Blutt und Wunden, composed by Johann Sebastian Bach in 1727 and sets Gospels 26 & 27 of St. Matthew to music. Adapted by Paul Simon for American Tune, the lyrics of which, though addressing US politics, are strikingly fitting to the sketch above. The original melody was by Hans Leo Hassler (1601).

55 John Bird, *Annals of Natal, Vol. 1*, (1888), p. 414; Proclamation by Cape Governor George Thomas Napier

Notes to Chapter 12

1 See The English Afrikaners, Chapter 8. Some question the presence of Thomas Jervis Biddulph, who reappears later in a decidedly different role. Major Chalmers, then recently arrived at Port Natal, would actually threaten Parker with murder

charges for his role in this commando. A gardener named J. Johnston arrived at the Cape as part of Moodie's immigrant party in 1817. Beyond that, Johnston has proved impossible to identify with total certainty. Robert Joyce had been with the 72nd Reg. of the British Army in Grahamstown around 1832 and had been living in the Natal region for some 5 years.

2 John Bird, *Annals of Natal, Vol. 1*, (1888), p. 445; The full report of Bantjes : pp. 438-452

3 Sarel Cilliers, the lay preacher of the Hendrik Potgieter trek of 1836, who fought so bravely at Vegkop

4 The isikoko was a ring of fibre, woven into the hair and coated with charcoal, gum and wax. It signified that they were senior married men. In their culture at the time, a young man could only marry if he had been blooded in battle.

5 John Bird, *Annals of Natal, Vol. 1*, (1888), p. 375; Bezuidenhout's report from the *Orange Free State Monthly Magazine*, (1879) extends pp. 367-376

6 Pretorius hinself reported they counted carefully and there were three thousand and "some hundreds."

7 John Bird, *Annals of Natal, Vol. 1*, (1888), p. 448; the full report of Bantjes : pp. 438-452

8 John Bird, *Annals of Natal, Vol. 1*, (1888), p. 500; Gov. Notice signed by Secretary John Bell, 28 January 1839

9 Umgungundlovu

10 Tugela River

11 Umzinvubu River

12 Henry Cloete, *Three Lectures on the Emigration of the Dutch Farmers (etc.)*, (1852) p. 47

13 John Bird, *Annals of Natal Vol. 1*, (1888), p. 247; Cilliers' full journal pp. 238-252

14 See Chapter 9: *The Third Great Abandonment*

15 John Bird, *Annals of Natal, Vol. 1*, (1888), p. 536; Letter by Governor George Napier to the Secretary of State, the Marquis of Normandy, dated 30 September 1839

16 Edwin W. Smith, *The Life and Times of Daniel Lindley*, (1949), p. 111

17 Allen Francis Gardiner, *Narrative of a Journey to the Zoolu Country In South Africa*, (1836), p. 34; The same text is also in John Bird, *Annals of Natal, Vol. 1*, (1888), p. 276.

18 John Bird, *Annals of Natal, Vol. 1*, (1888), p. 536; Minutes of the Volksraad of 15 October 1839 - an interrogatory of Mpande in person ("What did you come here for, and why did you cross the Tugela?"; Answer: "To escape Dingaan, and to seek for protection amongst you.")

19 John Bird, *Annals of Natal, Vol. 1*, (1888), p. 576; *Zuid Afrikaan* newspaper of the Cape, February 10, 1846

20 John Bird, *Annals of Natal, Vol. 1*, (1888), p. 375; Bezuidenhout's full report pp. 367-376

21 John Bird, *Annals of Natal, Vol. 1*, (1888), p. 576; *Zuid Afrikaan* newspaper of the Cape, February 10, 1846

22 Adulphe Delegorgue, *Voyage dans l'Afrique Australe, Vol. 1*, (1847), p. 229

23 Adulphe Delegorgue, *Voyage dans l'Afrique Australe, Vol. 1*, (1847), p. 237

24 John Bird, *Annals of Natal, Vol. 1*, (1888), p. 375, Bezuidenhout's report

25 Donald R. Morris and Mangosuthu Buthelezi, *The Washing of the Spears*, (1998), p. 153;

Notes to Chapter 13

1 W.C. Holden, *History of the Colony of Natal, South Africa*, (1855), p. 120; Also John Bird, *Annals of Natal, Vol. 1*, (1888), p. 711

2 William Clifford Holden, *History of the Colony of Natal, South Africa*, (1855), p. 128

3 Henry Cloete, *Three Lectures on the Emigration of the Dutch Farmers (etc.)*, (1852), p. 17

4 John Bird, *Annals of Natal, Vol. 2*, (1888), p. 46; Letter Gov. G. Napier to the Sec. of State, dated 25 July 1842

5 John Centlivres Chase, *Natal, a re-print of all authentic notices (etc)*, Part I, (1843), p. 10

6 Gustav S. Preller, *Joernaal van 'n Trek, Uit die Dagboek van Erasmus Smit*, (1988), p. 168; The entry for Wednesday 7 Nov. 1838. See also the originally published *Uit het dagboek van Erasmus Smit*, (1897).

7 George McCall Theal, *History of South Africa, Vol. 6*, (1964 Struik Edition), p. 379; Vol. 2 of the 1915 Fourth Edition by G. Allen & Unwin

8 John Centlivres Chase, *Natal, a re-print of all authentic notices (etc)*, Part 1, (1843), p. 43

9 John Bird, *Annals of Natal, Vol. 2*, (1888), p. 256; Letter of 8 August 1843 from Cloete to Governor at Cape

10 *Report from the Select Committee on the Kafir Tribes, ordered printed by the House of Commons*, (1851), p. 213

11 Henry Cloete, *Three Lectures on the Emigration of the Dutch Farmers (etc.)*, (1852), note on p. 35

12 George McCall Theal, *History of South Africa, Vol. 7*, (1964 Struik Edition), p. 251; Vol. 3 of the 1915/16 Third Edition by G. Allen & Unwin

13 *The Eclectic Review, Vol. 22*, (1847), p. 728; An excerpt from the *Commercial Advertiser*

14 J. J. Freeman, *A Tour in South Africa*, (1851), p. 254; Desptach from Governor Sir H. G. Smith to Earl Grey

15 Sir Henry G. W. Smith, *The autobiography of Lieutenant-General Sir Harry Smith, Vol. 2*, (1902), p. 234

16 The previous governor, Sir Henry Pottinger

17 Sir Henry G. W. Smith, *The autobiography of Lieutenant-General Sir Harry Smith, Vol. 2*, (1902), p. 236

18 Noël Mostert, *Frontiers*, (1992), p. 985; See also page 919 for his reasons.

19 George McCall Theal, *History of South Africa, Vol. 7*, (1964 Struik Edition), p. 280; Vol. 3 of the 1915/16 Third Edition by G. Allen & Unwin

20 George McCall Theal, *History of South Africa, Vol. 7*, (1964 Struik Edition), p. 285; Vol. 3 of the 1915/16 Third Edition by G. Allen & Unwin

21 Jeffrey Brian Peires, *The Dead will Arise*, (1989), p. 10

22 Jeffrey Brian Peires, *The Dead will Arise*, (1989), p. 11

23 Sir Henry G. W. Smith, *The autobiography of Lieutenant-General Sir Harry Smith, Vol. 2*, (1902), p. 272

24 Jeffrey Brian Peires, *The Dead will Arise*, (1989), p. 15

25 H. J. Batts, *The Story of a 100 Years, 1820-1920: Being the History of the Baptist Church (etc.)*, (1922), p. 208

26 Capt. W.R. King, *Campaigning in Kaffirland*, (1853), p. 92

27 Capt. W.R. King, *Campaigning in Kaffirland*, (1853), p. 119

28 Canadian *National Post*, 3 July 2009; Reports murders of children for the ritual use of body parts.

29 Canadian *National Post*, 4 April 2004; Reports desecration of Boer War graves to use bones for potions.

30 Jeffrey Brian Peires, *The Dead will Arise*, (1989), p. 26

31 Capt. W.R. King, *Campaigning in Kaffirland*, (1853), p. 271

32 M. Mabona, *Diviners and Prophets Among the Xhosa (1593-1856)*, (2004), p. 307

33 Andries Botha and William Buchanan, *Trial of Andries Botha (etc)*, p. 248; Letter by John Green, published in the *Grahamstown Journal*, May 24, 1851. John Green was the stepson of our ancestor Richard Bowles (NF41, 42), who married John's mother, Anne Rowney, in 1856 after the death of John snr. Anne had been a witness to Richard's marriage in Dover in 1819 (NF41)

34 Capt. W.R. King, *Campaigning in Kaffirland*, (1853), p. 322

35 T.C. Hansard, *Hansard's Parliamentary Debates*, (1854), p. 72; House of Commons debate of 9 May 1854

36 George McCall Theal, *History of South Africa, Vol. 7*, (1964 Struik Edition), p. 367; Vol. 3 of the 1915/16 Third Edition by G. Allen & Unwin

37 R. G. A. Levinge, *Historical Records of the Forty-third Regiment, Monmouthshire Light Infantry*, (1868), p. 251

38 R. G. A. Levinge, *Historical Records of the Forty-third Regiment, Monmouthshire Light Infantry*, (1868), p. 267

39 Nat Turner and Thomas R. Gray, *The Confessions of Nat Turner*, (1833), pp. 1-24

40 Philip J. Schwartz, i, (2001), p. 72

Notes to Chapter 14

1 J. H. Rose, *The Cambridge History of the British Empire, Vol. 8*, (1929), p. 432

2 A. Wilmot, *The life and times of Sir Richard Southey*, (1904), p. 337; Letter in appendix.

3 George McCall Theal, *History of South Africa, Vol. 8*, (1964 Struik Edition), p. 365; Vol. 4 of the 1915 4th Edition by G. Allen & Unwin

4 Augustus F. Lindley, *Adamantia*, (1873), p. iv

5 W.T. Stead, *The Last Will and Testament of Cecil John Rhodes*, (1902), p. 59

6 George McCall Theal, *History of South Africa, Vol. 10*, (1964), p. 263; Vol. 1 of the 1919 Edition under the title *History of South Africa from 1873 to 1884 : Twelve eventful years* by G. Allen & Unwin

7 Donald R. Morris and Mangosuthu Buthelezi, *The Washing of the Spears*, (1998), p. 251

8 H.W. Kinsey, *S.A. Mil. History Journal*, The Sekukuni Wars Part II, Vol. 2, No. 6, December 1973

9 Ron Lock, *Blood on the Painted Mountain*, (1995), p. 36

10 Ron Lock, *Blood on the Painted Mountain*, (1995), p. 33

11 Ron Lock, *Blood on the Painted Mountain*, (1995), p. 51

12 Ron Lock, *Blood on the Painted Mountain*, (1995), p. 97

13 See Fig. 11.8; Petrus Joubert, the grandson of Petrus Joubert and Helena Strydom

14 George McCall Theal, *History of South Africa, Vol. 11*, (1964), p. 119; Vol. 2 of the 1919 Edition under the title *History of South Africa from 1873 to 1884 : Twelve eventful years* by G. Allen & Unwin

15 Donald Featherstone, *Victorian Colonial Warfare: Africa*, (1992), p. 52

16 Thomas Pakenham, *The Scramble for Africa*, (1991), p. 97

17 B.G. Simpkins, *S.A. Mil. History Journal*, Tour of Schuinshoogte, Laings Nek and Majuba Battlefields, Vol. 1, no. 4 , June 1969

18 Thomas Pakenham, *The Scramble for Africa*, (1991), p. 105

19 *The Illustrated London News*, March 1881

20 George McCall Theal, *History of South Africa, Vol. 11*, (1964), p. 21; Vol. 2 of the 1919 Edition under the title *History of South Africa from 1873 to 1884 : Twelve eventful years* by G. Allen & Unwin

21 H. Rider Haggard, *Cetywayo and His White Neighbours*, (1896), p. 234

22 A.M. Goodrich, *The Cruise and Captures of the Alabama*, (1906), p. 16

23 A.M. Goodrich, *The Cruise and Capture of the Alabama*, (1906), p. 160

24 South African term for for people of mixed descent, usually with a strong Khoekhoe or Indonesian base.

Notes to Chapter 15

1 Edmund Burke, *The Annual Register: A review of public events (etc.), for the year 1876, Vol. 118*, (1877), p. 413

2 Thomas Pakenham, *The Scramble for Africa*, (1991), p. 22

3 History repeats itself with different actors. In the late 1980s a superpower of the day would again find itself in exactly the same predicament as all-powerful Britain in 1877. The U.S.S.R of the 1980s would also be mired in a war in Afghanistan and stretched to the limit of its tolerance in Southern Africa in its desire to control the natural riches of Africa. See Chapter 22

4 Niall Ferguson, *Empire*, (2002), p. 236

5 Martin Meredith, *The Fate of Africa*, pp. 1-2

6 Martin Meredith, "*Diamonds, Gold and War*", (2007), p. 127

7 Martin Meredith, "*Diamonds, Gold and War*", (2007), p. 209

8 Martin Meredith, "*Diamonds, Gold and War*", (2007), p. 218

9 At Slagtersnek, a legitimate commando was called up for duty, but then illegitimately applied (See Chap. 7)

10 Mark Twain (Samuel Clemens), *Following the Equator*, (1897), pp. 660-665

11 Mark Twain (Samuel Clemens), *Following the Equator*, (1897); p. 683

12 Arthur Conan Doyle, *The War in South Africa, Its Cause and Conduct*, (1902), p. 4

13 Miranda Carter, *George, Nicholas and Wilhelm*, (2010), p. 221

14 Taffy and David Shearing, *Commandant Lötter and his Commando*, (1998); p. 10

Notes to Chapter 16

1 William F. Butler, *Sir William Butler: an autobiography*, (1911), p. 432

2 Captain Le Roy Eltinge, *Psychology of War*, (1915), p. 120

3 Deneys Reitz, *Commando*, (1929), p. 34

4 Francis William Reitz, *A Century of Wrong*, (1901), Preface by W.T. Stead, p. 19

5 Miranda Carter, *George, Nicholas and Wilhelm*, (2010), p. 223

6 Miranda Carter, *George, Nicholas and Wilhelm*, (2010), p. 222

7 Richard Harding Davis, *With Both armies in South Africa*, (1900), p. 122

8 F.R. Burnham, *Scouting on Two Continents*, p. 271

9 F.R. Burnham, *Scouting on Two Continents*, p .273

10 Thomas Pakenham, *The Boer War* (1979), p. 303; Other sources replace "in to attack" with "in among"

11 Deneys Reitz, *Commando*, (1929), Chapter 9, p. 56

12 *New York Times*, May 6, 1900

13 Richard Harding Davis, *With both Armies in South Africa*, (1900), p. 141

14 Richard Harding Davis, *With both Armies in South Africa*, (1900), p. 137

15 Richard Harding Davis, *With both Armies in South Africa*, (1900), p. 139

16 Richard Harding Davis, *With both Armies in South Africa*, (1900), p. 151

17 See Chapter 5

18 *New York Times*, July 31, 1900

Notes to Chapter 17

1 T. Moreman and D. Anderson, *The British Commandos, 1940-46*, (2006), p. 9

2 Richard Harding Davis, *With both Armies in South Africa*, (1900), p. 133

3 Richard Harding Davis, *With both Armies in South Africa*, (1900), p. 138

4 Arthur Conan Doyle, *The Great Boer War*, (1900), p. 1

5 George McCall Theal, *History of South Africa, Vol. 6*, (1964 Struik Edition), p. 265; Vol. 2 of the 1915 Fourth Edition by G.

Allen & Unwin

6 Christiaan R. De Wet, *Three Years War*, (1902), p. 85

7 Johannes M. Wassermann, *The Natal Afrikaner and the Anglo-Boer War*, (2004) p. 456

8 Deneys Reitz, *Commando*, (1929), p. 106

9 Thomas Pakenham, *The Boer War*, (1979), p. 478

10 Jan Smuts, *Memoirs of the Boer War*, (1999), p. 150

11 Deneys Reitz, *Commando*, (1929), Chapter 9, p. 117

12 L.S. Amery, *The Times History of the war in South Africa 1899-1902, Vol. 4*, (1906), p. 494

13 Deneys Reitz, *Commando*, (1929), p. 118

14 Transvaal Archive, Reference CJC 354 and CJC226, filed later on 12 February 1903

15 Transvaal Archive, reference CJC 659 52, filed 8 April 1903

16 E. Hobhouse, *The Brunt of the War and where it Fell*, (1902) p. 213

17 Transvaal Archive, reference CJC 354 CJC226, filed 12 February 1903

18 Information from Anglo-Boer War Museum; The database may be found at http://www.lib.uct.ac.za/mss/bccd/index.php.

19 Graham Jooste and Roger Webster, *Innocent Blood*, (2002), p. 27

20 Deneys Reitz, *Commando*, (1929), p. 166 and p. 174

21 Walter Walsh, *The Moral Damage of War*, (1906), p. 376

22 Graham Jooste and Roger Webster, *Innocent Blood*, (2002), p. 40

23 Graham Jooste and Roger Webster, *Innocent Blood*, (2002), p. 38

24 T. and D. Shearing, *Commandant Lötter and his Rebels*, (1998), p. 42

25 Translated from great grandfather Albert Myburgh's Dutch hymnal (1884). p. 26

26 Arthur Conan Doyle, *The Great Boer War*, Final Edition (1902), e-book Chapter 38

27 Peter Trew, *The Boer War Generals*, (1999), p. 124

28 F.A. and C.A.H.O. Maxwell, *Frank Maxwell: his memoirs and a few letters*, (1921), p. 95

29 F.A. and C.A.H.O. Maxwell, *Frank Maxwell: his memoirs and a few letters*, (1921), p. 72

30 Arthur Conan Doyle, *The War in South Africa, Its Causes and Conduct*, (1902), p. 2

31 Mark Twain (Samuel Clemens), *Following the Equator*, (1897) p. 423

32 D. Featherstone, *Victorian Colonial Warfare - Africa*, (1992), p. 83

33 D. Featherstone, *Victorian Colonial Warfare - Africa*, (1992), p. 81

34 J.Y.F. Blake, *A Westpointer with the Boers*, (1903), p. 409

35 Niall Ferguson, *Empire*, (2002), pp. 278-282

Notes to Chapter 18

1 Johannes Meintjes, *General Louis Botha – A Biography*, (1970), p. 122

2 Johannes Meintjes, *General Louis Botha – A Biography*, (1970), p. 131

3 These two denominations seamlessly exchange ministers in many places. Scottish family names like Macdonald and Murray recur consistently among the South African Dutch Reformed clergy – now mostly Afrikaners.

4 Known today as Tanzania, the poster child of failed Soviet socialism in Africa

5 Theodore Roosevelt, *African Game Trails*, (1910), pp. 38-40

6 Theodore Roosevelt, *African Game Trails*, (1910), p. 352

7 W.S. Churchill, *A roving commission: my early life*, (1996), pp. 255

8 See, for example, Niall Ferguson, *Empire*, (2002), p. xx

9 Johannes Meintjes, *General Louis Botha – A Biography*, (1970), p. 214

10 W.S. Churchill, *A roving commission: my early life*, (1996), p. 255

11 Philip Warner, *Kitchener - The Man behind the Legend*, (1985), p. 198; Others also claimed responsibility.

12 Ivan Merle McCusker's name appears on this roll call.

13 Peter Liddle, *The 1916 Battle of the Somme*, (1992), p. 15

14 He would be succeeded by A.T. Harris – the later "Bomber" Harris, who had earlier lived in Rhodesia

15 An air force independent from other branches of the defense forces of a country.

16 Charles Howard Ellis, *The origin, structure & working of the League of Nations*, (1928), p. 82

17 Rolihlahla Mandela, *Long Walk to Freedom*, (1994), p. 13

18 Rolihlahla Mandela, *Long Walk to Freedom*, (1994), p. 14

19 See Chapter 9 : *The Afrikaners depart as a new Empress is crowned*

20 Woodrow Wilson, *A history of the American People, Vol. 5*, (1902), pp. 58 - 59
21 See Chapter 17: *In America - Jim Crow Laws*
22 *The New York Times*, 9 September 1917
23 See Chapter 20 onwards

Notes to Chapter 19

1   Hermann Giliomee, *The Afrikaners – biography of a people*, (2003), p. 33
2   Martin Meredith, *Diamonds, Gold and War*, (2007), p. 514
3   A. Davidson et al., *South Africa and the Communist International – (etc.), Vol. 1*, (2003), p. 3
4   A. Davidson et al., *South Africa and the Communist International – (etc.), Vol. 1*, (2003), p. 1
5   A. Davidson et al., *South Africa and the Communist International – (etc.), Vol. 1*, (2003), p. 35
6   A. Davidson et al., *South Africa and the Communist International – (etc.), Vol. 1*, (2003), p. 72
7   A. Davidson et al., *South Africa and the Communist International – (etc.), Vol. 1*, (2003), p. 69
8   A. Davidson et al., *South Africa and the Communist International – (etc.), Vol. 1*, (2003), p. 3
9   A. Davidson et al., *South Africa and the Communist International – (etc.), Vol. 1*, (2003), p. 5
10 A. Davidsonet al., *South Africa and the Communist International – (etc.), Vol. 1*, (2003), pp. 8-9
11 A. Davidson et al., *South Africa and the Communist International – (etc.), Vol. 2*, (2003) p. 35
12 A. Davidson et al., *South Africa and the Communist International – (etc.), Vol. 1*, (2003), p. 12
13 A. Davidson et al., *South Africa and the Communist International – (etc.), Vol. 2*, (2003), p. 51
14 A. Davidson et al., *South Africa and the Communist International – (etc.), Vol. 1*, (2003), p. 76
15 Oswald Pirow, James Barry Munnik Hertzog, (1958), p. 214
16 Not to be confused with thebetter-known Balfour Declaration of 1917 relating to Palestine
17 Oswald Pirow, *James Barry Munnik Hertzog*, (1958), p. 213
18 Deneys Reitz, *Commando*, (1929), p. 42, p. 154 and p. 193
19 G. Jooste, *Innocent Blood*, (2002), p.94
20 A parochial and revealing term, employed in North America to designate people other than Caucasians
21 Oswald Pirow, *James Barry Munnik Hertzog*, (1958), p. 247
22 See Fig. 10-6
23 John Weal, *Jagdgeschwader 27 "Afrika"*, (2003), p.98; He misidentifies the Spitfires as Royal Air Force
24 H.J. Martin and Neil Orpen, *Eagles Victorious*, (1977), p. 64
25 Bassie's logbook lists one Bf109F downed at Cos. He refused to ever discuss any aircraft he had downed.
26 We rely on detailed information from the Luftwaffe. The S.A.A.F logs were destroyed
27 The SAAF claims two Bf.109s between the two of them. Yet other sources credit only Bassie with one.
28 H.J. Martin and Neil Orpen, *Eagles Victorious*, (1977), p. 65
29 36 years later Bassie would tell the author one of the 9./III JG27 Bf.109Gs strafed him in the water.
30 Immortalized 58 years later in the motion picture *Captain Corelli's Mandolin* (2001).
31 Lt.-Col. M. Cessford, *Canadian Army Journal*, "Crack Canadian Troops", Vol. 1.1 (1998), p. 30 of the e-book
32 Bassie's flight log for the Italian campaign is in the possession of the family
33 Squadron leader D.P. Tidy, *SA Mil History Journal* ,Vol 1 No 2, June 1968 (SA ISSN 0026-4016)
34 Called a "torpedo" in the United States and Canada.
35 Raymond Mhlaba and Thembeka Mufamadi, *Raymond Mhlaba's Personal Memoirs*, (2001), p. 13
36 Raymond Mhlaba and Thembeka Mufamadi, *Raymond Mhlaba's Personal Memoirs*, (2001), p. 13
37 Rolihlahla Mandela, *Long Walk to Freedom*, (1994), p. 69
38 Raymond Mhlaba and Thembeka Mufamadi, *Raymond Mhlaba's Personal Memoirs*, (2001), p. 17

Notes to Chapter 20

1   See Chapter 18, *Boer generals against designing the Second World War*
2   See Chapter 15, *The Rape of Africa*
3   Peter Bagshawe, *Warriors of the Sky*, (1990), pp. 93-95 and 267-268. The events of this section are described
4   See Chapter 3
5   M.J. McGregor, *SA Mil History Journal*, Vol. 4, No.3, June 1978
6   See, for example, *Hansard* of the corresponding date for the British House of Commons
7   Martin Meredith, *The Fate of Africa*, (2005), p. 86
8   *Time Magazine*, March 16, 1959, The Roots of the Fig Tree

9 See Chapter 7: Nexus Familia 40: *Where men die twice*. HCV Leibbrandt, *The Rebellion of 1815*, (1902), p. 810; Nouka was rewarded with heifers, knives and tinder-boxes, and presents were sent to king Ngqika for providing his interpreter.

10 See Chapter 18: *Teddy Roosevelt and the Frontier clan*

11 See, for example, *Hansard* for the British House of Lords, 24 July 1952

12 See Chapters 4 to 9

13 M.P. Naicker, *The Defiance Campaign recalled*; United Nations Notes and Documents, No. 11/72, June 1972.

14 Raymond Mhlaba and Thembeka Mufamadi, *Raymond Mhlaba's Personal Memoirs*, (2001), p. 82

15 Raymond Mhlaba and Thembeka Mufamadi, *Raymond Mhlaba's Personal Memoirs*, (2001), p. 87

16 *Time Magazine*, Monday, 24 November 1952

17 *Daily Dispatch*, October 28, 2002

18 *Daily Dispatch*, The Joker in the Pack, September 21, 2007; an interview with author Cornelius Thomas about his new book based on the life of Donald Card

19 *Daily Dispatch*, Letters, August 16, 2007; Donald Card, responsible for seeing the charges through Court.

20 Cornelius Thomas, *Tangling the Lion's tail*, (2007)

21 See Chapter 11, Nexus Familia 58.

22 Rolihlahla Mandela, *Long Walk to Freedom*, (1994), p. 184

23 Bill McWilliams, On Hallowed Ground, (2004), p. 458

24 Norman Moss, *Picking up the Reins*, (2008), p. 66

25 Richard M. Nixon, *The Real War*, (1990), p. 79

26 Alain Rouvez, *Disconsolate Empires*, (1994), p. 124

27 C. Griffin, *French Military Interventions in Africa*; 2007 Conv. of the Int. Stud. Assoc., Chicago, IL, p. 35

28 Martin Meredith, *The Fate of Africa*, (2005), p. 165

29 M. G. Marshall, *Conflict Trends in Africa, 1946 – 2004*, (2005), pp. 20-21; report for the ACPP ; British Gov.

30 Martin Meredith, *The Fate of Africa*, (2005), pp. 173-174

31 Martin Meredith, *The Fate of Africa*, (2005), p. 175

32 Martin Meredith, *The Fate of Africa*, (2005), p. 230

33 *Time Magazine*, Monday 24 January 1949; Bulala!

34 Kill!

35 Allan Jackson, *Facts about Durban*, (2003), p. 45

36 South African Human Sciences Research Council; Women marching into the 21st century, (2000), p. 39

37 Some 30 years later Americans would see the bodies of their own men dragged through the streets of Mogadishu in the Horn of Africa, but that would be far away from their homes

38 Kevin Kelly Gaines, *American Africans in Ghana*, (2006)

39 See Chapter 19; Human rights elsewhere in the world

40 John Clay Smith, *Rebels in Law*, (2000), p. 162

41 *Time Magazine*, Monday 15 February 1960, Changing Wind,

42 Benjamin Pogrund, *How can man die better*, (1990), p. 6; Pogrund was a lifelong friend of Sebukwe.

43 In 2010,debate about such ID would rage in the state of Arizona with respect to illegal immigrants

44 L.K. Ladlau, *The Cato Manor Riots*, 1959-1960, M.A. Thesis, U. Natal (1975), p. 116

45 South African Democracy Education Trust, *The Road to Democracy, Vol. 1*, p. 106

46 *Time Magazine*, Monday 4 April 1960; The Sharpeville Massacre

47 L. R. Devlin, *Chief of Station, Congo*, (2007), p. 165 and 228, describes Hoare as well-educated & articulate

48 L. R. Devlin, *Chief of Station, Congo*, (2007), p. 95

49 Conclusions of the Committee: http://www.lachambre.be/kvvcr/pdf_sections/comm/lmb/conclusions.pdf

50 Martin Meredith, *The Fate of Africa*, (2005), p. 112; see also the original source: Ludo de Witte, pp. 97-142

51 Ludo de Witte, *The assassination of Patrice Lumumba*, (2001), p. 141; the disposal of the bodies is described

52 Hugh Kay, *Salazar and modern Portugal*, (1970), p. 135

53 Hugh Kay, *Salazar and modern Portugal*, (1970), p. 182

54 Hugh Kay, *Salazar and modern Portugal*, (1970), p. 222

55 B. Teixeira, *The Fabric of Terror*. (1965), pp. 97 -101; some editions provide photo-evidence of the massacres

56 Pierre De Vos, *Le Monde*, 5 July 1961

57 Richard Beeston & John Simpson, *Looking for trouble*, (2006 – paperback version) p. 70 [original 1997]

58 Arthur Meier Schlesinger, *Robert Kennedy and His Times*, (2002), p. 562

59 See *Always the horror near Port Elizabeth* – present Chapter

60 Indonesian-descended people who had retained their Indonesian culture and Muslim faith since the days of the DEIC in Batavia (Djakarta). None of them came from the country known as Malaysia.

61 Actually only around the corner and down the next street – a total of some two hundred and fifty yards

62 Britain would later decimalize, based on the positive experience in South Africa

63 See Chapter 1.

64 See Chapters 2 and 6, respectively.

Notes to Chapter 21

1 Hermann Giliomee, *The Afrikaners*, (2003), pp. 522-531; review of Verwoerd's quest, written by an Afrikaner

2 While the BBC never relented in attacking the white South African government on its Homeland Policy from 1960 until 1994, it would somehow recognize the great wealth of the local Ba'Tswana people due to this mine in the week of 17 October 2010, more than 16 years after the demise of that white government.

3 Rolihlahla Mandela, *Long Walk to Freedom*, (1994), p. 13

4 *Time Magazine*, Monday 11 October 1976; Pogrom at home?

5 See Chapter 18

6 Martin Meredith, *In the name of Apartheid*, (1988), p. 100

7 Martin Meredith, *In the name of Apartheid*, (1988), p. 100

8 Rolihlahla Mandela, *Long Walk to Freedom*, (1994), p. 325

9 See Chapter 12, the political reason for the choice was transparent;

10 Martin Meredith, *In the name of Apartheid*, (1988), p. 100

11 Rolihlahla Mandela, *Long Walk to Freedom*, (1994), p. 363

12 South African State Archives, Box 9/1/44: 1 COF; File C/12. Confession of Ndozi Tjulu and others.

13 South African Democracy Education Trust, *The Road to Democracy, Vol. 1*, p. 276

14 South African Democracy Education Trust, *The Road to Democracy, Vol. 1*, p. 282

15 See Chapter 18: *The young man from Bashee River*

16 South African Democracy Education Trust, *The Road to Democracy, Vol. 1*, p. 282

17 See Chapter 18: *The young man from Bashee River*

18 See Chapter 26: *The Darkest Moment in a Dark Time* & *"One Settler, one Bullet "(etc.)*

19 Lauritz Strydom, *Rivonia Unmasked*, (1965), p. 12

20 This description of events is based on *Rivonia Unmasked*, by Lauritz Strydom, (1965), pp. 24-36,

21 Lauritz Strydom, *Rivonia Unmasked*, (1965), pp. 66-75

22 Ahmad Kathrada, *Memoirs*, (2005), p. 159

23 Rolihlahla Mandela, *Long Walk to Freedom*, (1994), p. 440

24 Raymond Mhlaba and Thembeka Mufamadi, *Raymond Mhlaba's Personal Memoirs*, (2001), pp. 123

25 Raymond Mhlaba and Thembeka Mufamadi, *Raymond Mhlaba's Personal Memoirs*, (2001), p. 115

26 Stephen Clingman, *Bram Fischer - Afrikaner Revolutionary*, (1998), p. 305

27 Stephen Clingman, *Bram Fischer - Afrikaner Revolutionary*, (1998), p. 314

28 Rolihlahla Mandela, *Long Walk to Freedom*, (1994), p. 432

29 Rolihlahla Mandela, *Long Walk to Freedom*, (1994), p. 435

30 He would be filmed standing with a supporting balled fist raised in the air among a group of people singing this song after his 1990 release from prison.

31 Rolihlahla Mandela, *Long Walk to Freedom*, (1994), p. 443

32 State Dep. document; Memo from G. M. Williams to Secretary D. Rusk dated June 12, 1963; "U.S. Policy towards S. Africa." Ref. NLK -76-312. See also K. Mokoena, *South Africa and the United States*, (1993); pp. 54-55

33 See Chapter 22

34 State Dep. document; Response of June 15, 1963 to Memo from G. M Williams to Secr. Rusk June 12, 1963; "U.S. Policy towards South Africa." Ref. NLK -76-312. See also Kenneth Mokoena, *South Africa and the United States*, (1993), p. 57

35 Arthur Meier Schlesinger, *Robert Kennedy and His Times*, (2002), p. 562

36 See, for example, http://www.youtube.com/watch?v=KbNJVMtG2OA ; See also Josh Gottheimer, *Ripples of Hope: Great American Civil Rights Speeches*, (2003), p. 283

37 *Time Magazine*, Friday Aug 26, 1966; South Africa: The Great White Laager

38 Now Botswana, and then still run by the British, but with Sir Tseretse Kgama as head of the government

39 Now Lesotho, and then also a British "Protectorate"

40 John D'Oliveira, *Vorster – The Man*, (1977), p. 64

41 South Africa did not have any television service in 1969
42 The owners of Miller brand of beer in the United States in the 21st Century
43 Odd Arne Westad, *The Global Cold War*, (2005), p. 216; Source: Vladimir Shubin, Deputy Director of the Institute for African Studies, Russian Academy of Sciences
44 Peter Stiff, *The Silent War- South African Recce Operations 1969-1994*, (1999), p. 23

Notes to Chapter 22
1 See, for example, O.R. Tambo, *Sechaba, Vol. 6, No. 2*, (February 1972); Statement by OR Tambo to the People of South Africa on the 10th Anniversary of Umkhonto we Sizwe, 16 December 1971
2 Available on the ANC official website (16 October 2013) under the title "Statement by OR Tambo to the People of South Africa on the 10th Anniversary of Umkhonto we Sizwe", 16 December 1971;
http://www.anc.org.za/docs/sp/2010/sp0419a.html
3 William B. Quandt, *Soviet Policy in the October 1973 War*, (1976), pp. 23-26
4 Simon Dunstan, *Vietnam Tracks*, (2004), p. 190
5 Arthur Meier Schlesinger, *Robert Kennedy and His Times*, (2002), p. 562
6 James Barber and John Barratt, *South Africa's Foreign Policy*, (1990), p. 188
7 Andrea L. Smith, *Europe's Invisible Migrants*, (2003); p. 15
8 Andrea L. Smith, *Europe's Invisible Migrants*, (2003); p. 72
9 Lawrence R. Devlin, *Chief of Station, Congo*, (2007), p. 266
10 Richard M. Nixon, *The Real War*, (1980), p. 23
11 John Stockwell, *In search of enemies*, (1978), p. 67
12 Bruce D. Porter, *The USSR in Third World conflicts*, (1986), p. 162- A study of the 1975-6 Angolan War
13 John Stockwell, *In search of enemies*, (1978), p. 67
14 Peter Stiff, *The Silent War- South African Recce Operations 1969-1994*, (1999), p. 99
15 Kenneth Maxwell, The Legacy of Decolonization, Chapter 1 of *Regional conflict and U.S. Policy*, (1988), p. 21
16 Willem Steenkamp, *Borderstrike!*, (Edition 3), (2006), p. 16
17 Odd Arne Westad, *The Global Cold War*, (2005), p. 225
18 John Stockwell, *In search of enemies*, (1978), p. 67
19 John Stockwell, *In search of enemies*, (1978), p. 78
20 John Stockwell, *In search of enemies*, (1978), p. 139
21 Willem Steenkamp, *Borderstrike!*, (Edition 3), (2006), p. 16
22 Willem Steenkamp, *Borderstrike!*, (Edition 3), (2006), p. 20
23 Wayne S. Smith, The Cuban role in Angola, Chapter 5 of *Regional conflict an U.S. Policy*, (1988), p. 125
24 Bruce D. Porter, *The USSR in Third World conflicts*, (1986), p. 165
25 Henry Kissinger, *Years of Renewal*, (1999), p. 820
26 Peter Stiff, *The Silent War- South African Recce Operations 1969-1994*, (1999), p. 109
27 Piero Gleijeses, *Conflicting Missions*, (2002), p. 298; Gleijeses was given special access by the Cuban Government for this book and is exceedingly heavily biased against South Africa.
28 Willem Steenkamp, *Borderstrike!*, (Edition 3), (2006), p. 21
29 Peter Stiff, *The Silent War- South African Recce Operations 1969-1994*, (1999), pp. 111 suggests Houphoet-Boigny contacted Vorster only, or again in September 1975
30 E. Rhoodie, *The Real Information Scandal*, (1983), p. 142 ; Houphouet-Boigny is also identified by Rhoodie
31 E. Rhoodie, *The Real Information Scandal*, (1983), p. 142
32 James Barber and John Barratt, *South Africa's Foreign Policy*, (1990), p. 192; the authors confirm the request
33 Henry Kissinger, *Years of Renewal*, (1999), p. 910
34 Richard Dowden, *Africa - altered states, ordinary miracles*, (2009), p. 81
35 Willem Steenkamp, *Borderstrike!*, (Edition 3), (2006), p. 39
36 Willem Steenkamp, *Borderstrike!*, (Edition 3), (2006), p. 27
37 Odd Arne Westard, *The Global Cold War: Third world interventions and the making of our times*, (2005), p. 230
38 Henry Kissinger, *Years of Renewal*, (1999), p. 808
39 Henry Kissinger, *Years of Renewal*, (1999), pp. 791-833
40 Odd Arne Westard, *The Global Cold War: Third world interventions and the making of our times*, (2005), p. 231
41 Piero Gleijeses, *Conflicting Missions*, (2002), p. 298
42 National Security Archive, Interview with Robert W. Hultslander, former CIA Station Chief in Luanda, Angola;

http://www.gwu.edu/~nsarchiv/NSAEBB/NSAEBB67/transcript.html

43 John Stockwell, *In search of enemies*, (1978), p. 55

44 Willem Steenkamp, *Borderstrike!*, (Edition 3), (2006), p. 28

45 John Stockwell, *In search of enemies*, (1978), p. 158

46 John Stockwell, In search of enemies, (1978), p. 229

47 Willem Steenkamp, *Borderstrike!*, (Edition 3), (2006), p. 29

48 Willem Steenkamp, *Borderstrike!*, (Edition 3), (2006), p. 30

49 John Stockwell, *In search of enemies*, (1978), p. 163

50 John Stockwell, i, (1978), p. 187

51 Peter Stiff, *The Silent War- South African Recce Operations 1969-1994*, (1999), p. 112

52 John Stockwell, In search of enemies, (1978), p. 187

53 Willem Steenkamp, Borderstrike!, (Edition 3), (2006), p. 28

54 Peter Stiff, *The Silent War- South African Recce Operations 1969-1994*, (1999), p. 111

55 Willem Steenkamp, Borderstrike!, (Edition 3), (2006), p. 37

56 Peter Stiff, *The Silent War- South African Recce Operations 1969-1994*, (1999), p. 113; The dates vary: 13-20 or 17-22 October

57 Peter Stiff, *The Silent War- South African Recce Operations 1969-1994*, (1999), p. 112

58 Fred Bridgland, *The War for Africa*, (1990), p. 6

59 Willem Steenkamp, *Borderstrike!*, (Edition 3), (2006), p. 51

60 The color red, referring to his hair color

61 Sergeant Danny Roxo, for example was to earn great respect as the "Terror of the Bush."

62 Willem Steenkamp, *Borderstrike!*, (Edition 3), (2006), p. 50

63 Willem Steenkamp, *Borderstrike!*, (Edition 3), (2006), p. 51

64 The US National Intelligence Bulletin of Jan. 16, 1976 gives the date of the South African entry into Angola as 23 Oct. 1975. On the 23rd the South Africans were already busy taking Sa da Bandeira, deep inside Angola. They had already clashed with FAPLA on 19 Oct. The same bulletin states that 1500 Cuban military advisers were in Angola before 23 Oct.

65 Peter Stiff, *The Silent War- South African Recce Operations 1969-1994*, (1999), p. 119

66 John Stockwell, *In search of enemies*, (1978), p. 185

67 John Stockwell, *In search of enemies*, (1978), p. 185

68 Peter Stiff, *The Silent War- South African Recce Operations 1969-1994*, (1999), p. 117

69 John Stockwell, *In search of enemies*, (1978), p. 170

70 Peter Stiff, *The Silent War- South African Recce Operations 1969-1994*, (1999), p. 116

71 Peter Vanneman, *Soviet Strategy in Southern Africa*, (1990), p. 49

72 John Stockwell, *In search of enemies*, (1978), p. 213

73 John Stockwell, *In search of enemies*, (1978), p. 213

74 Communist China initially supported the FNLA and pushed the United States for more support against the Soviet efforts in Angola. The Chinese recruited some 50 North Koreans as part of this support and these men served in Zaire. See Odd Arne Westard, The Global Cold War: Third world interventions and the making of our times, (2005), p. 227

75 John Stockwell, *In search of enemies*, (1978), p. 215

76 John Stockwell, *In search of enemies*, (1978), p. 215

77 John Stockwell, *In search of enemies*, (1978), p. 202

78 Willem Steenkamp, *Borderstrike!*, (Edition 3), (2006), p. 111

79 Willem Steenkamp, *Borderstrike!*, (Edition 3), (2006), p. 116

80 Peter Stiff, *The Silent War- South African Recce Operations 1969-1994*, (1999), p. 121

81 John Stockwell, *In search of enemies*, (1978), p. 212

82 Television Interview of P. W. Botha by television journalist Cliff Saunders (2006)

83 Witney W. Schneidman, *Engaging Africa*, (2004), p. 216

84 Henry Kissinger, *Years of Renewal*, (1999), p. 822

85 Bruce D. Porter, *The USSR in Third World conflicts*, (1986), p. 173

86 Henry Kissinger, *Years of Renewal*, (1999), p. 824

87 State Department meeting of December 18, 1975. See, for example George Wright, *The Destruction of a Nation*, (1997), p. 69; also widely quoted in other texts.

88 Original Source: Ford Library, National Security Adviser, National Security Adviser Memcons, Box 16, July - October 1975. The document is a transcript of Henry Kissinger's briefing of President Ford on the subject of a diplomatic visit by

Kissinger to Mao Tse Tung. President Ford met with Kissinger and National Security Adviser Brent Scowcroft in the Oval Office on October 25, 1975 from 9:35 until 11:05am. The document is available online at http://history.state.gov/historicaldocuments/frus1969-76v18/d129; Memorandum of Conversation: Washington, October 25, 1975; Foreign Relations of the United States, 1969–1976; Volume XVIII, China, 1973–1976, Document 129:

89 Peter Stiff, *The Silent War- South African Recce Operations 1969-1994*, (1999), p. 138

90 Edward George, *The Cuban intervention in Angola*, (2006), p. 105

91 See Chapter 24 as relates to the Battle of Cuito Cuanavale

92 Helmoed-Römer Heitman, *Modern African Wars (3): South-West Africa*, (1991), p. 38

93 Edward George, *The Cuban intervention in Angola*, (2006) p. 103

94 Peter Stiff, *The Silent War- South African Recce Operations 1969-1994*, (1999), p. 140

95 Edward George, *The Cuban intervention in Angola*, (2006), p. 103

96 Edward George, *The Cuban intervention in Angola*, (2006), p. 103

97 Edward George, *The Cuban intervention in Angola*, (2006), p. 318

98 John Stockwell, *In search of enemies*, (1978), p. 218

99 James Barber and John Barratt, *South Africa's Foreign Policy*, (1990), p. 194; Also W. Steenkamp, Borderstrike!, (Edition 3), (2006), p. 106

100 See e.g., K. Mokoena, *South Africa and the United States*, (1993); pp. 219-225; US Policy toward Angola

101 Original Source: Kissinger Papers, Box CL 344, Department of State, Memoranda, Memoranda of Conversations, External, Sep - Dec 1975. Library of Congress, Manuscript Division. A transcript of a meeting between Kissinger and Mandungu Bula Nyati, State Commissioner for Foreign Affairs and International Cooperation, Zaire at the U.S. Ambassador's residence in Paris, Dec. 17, 1975 . The document is also available online at http://history.state.gov/historicaldocuments/frus1969-76v28/d149; Foreign Relations of the United States, 1969-1976; Volume XXVIII, Southern Africa, Document 149

102 Original Source: Kissinger Papers, Box CL103, Geopolitical File, Angola Chronological File. Library of Congress, Manuscript Division. Transcript of a meeting between Kissinger, Dep. Sec. of State R S. Ingersoll, and other individuals, including W.G. Hyland, Dep. Ass. Adviser to the President for National Security Affairs. The subject was Angola and South Africa's role was intensely discussed, with Kissinger making it clear that the South African involment was acceptable to the African states. The document is also availabe online at http://history.state.gov/historicaldocuments/frus1969-76v28/d156; Foreign Relations of the United States, 1969-1976; Volume XXVIII, Southern Africa, Document 156

103 See, for example, George Wright, *The Destruction of a Nation*, (1997), p. 69

104 Press meeting in the Briefing Room of the White House, Washington, DC, 4:58 pm, December 18, 1975

105 Henry Kissinger, *Years of Renewal*, (1999), p. 832

106 Henry Kissinger, *Years of Renewal*, (1999), p. 831

107 Willem Steenkamp, *Borderstrike!*, (Edition 3), (2006), p. 116

108 Edward George, *The Cuban intervention in Angola*, (2006) p. 106

109 James Barber and John Barratt, *South Africa's Foreign Policy*, (1990), p. 196

110 Willem Steenkamp, *Borderstrike!*, (Edition 3), (2006), p. 116

111 Res. 454 of the 26th ordinary session of the Council Ministers of the Org. for African Unity, Addis Ababa

112 John Stockwell, *In search of enemies*, (1978), p. 232

113 Piero Gleijeses, *Conflicting Missions*, (2002), p. 299

114 Television Interview of p. W. Botha by South African television journalist Cliff Saunders (2006)

115 The present chapter, *Angola – Escalation* : "We are ineffectual. What we say is not reliable."

116 Henry Kissinger, *Years of Renewal*, (1999), p. 828

117 Hermann Giliomee, *The Afrikaners – biography of a people*, (2003); p. 574

118 George Wright, *The Destruction of a Nation*, (1997), p. 69

119 Piero Gleijeses, *Conflicting Missions*, (2002), p. 365

120 Henry Kissinger, *Years of Renewal*, (1999), p. 913

121 National Security Archive, Interview with Robert W. Hultslander, former CIA Station Chief in Luanda, Angola; http://www.gwu.edu/~nsarchiv/NSAEBB/NSAEBB67/transcript.html

122 Piet Nortje, *32 Battalion*, (2004), p. 40

123 Igor Anatolyevitch Zhdarkin (translator: Tamara Reilly), *We did not see it even in Afghanistan*, (2008), p. 278 ; See also Chapter 25: *The War for Africa – 3. "A stunning humiliation for the Soviet Union"*

Notes to Chapter 23

1 Bruce D. Porter, *The USSR in Third World conflicts*, (1986), p. 167; Provides detail on the various flights

2 B. D. Porter, *The USSR in Third World conflicts*, (1986), p. 168; Disproportionate to its black population

3 Bruce D. Porter, *The USSR in Third World conflicts*, (1986), p. 166

4 *Montreal Gazette*, January 31, 1976; Also reported in other newspapers including the *New York Times*.

5 Castro and Trudeau were personal friends. Castro would attend Trudeau's funeral.

6 See, for example, Robert Wright, *Three nights in Havana*, (2007), p. 203

7 Viva Cuba and the Cuban people! Viva Premier Fidel Castro! Viva Cuban-Canadian friendship!

8 See, for example, Robert Wright, *Three nights in Havana*, (2007), p. 226

9 Robert Wright, *Three nights in Havana*, (2007), p. 241

10 Robert Wright, *Three nights in Havana*, (2007), p. 259

11 Piero Gleijeses, *Conflicting Missions*, (2002), p. 343

12 CBS television interview January 26, 1977; See for example *The Pittsburgh Press*, February 3, 1977

13 John H. Chettle, *Some suggestions for a new foreign policy for South Africa*, National Archives of South Africa, 144/1, Annex Jacket 1977. See also Odd Arne Westard, *The Global Cold War: Third world interventions and the making of our times*, (2005), p. 238 and 441

14 George Wright, *The Destruction of a Nation*, (1997), p. 78

15 See quote by Brezhnev at the head of chapter 22, reported by Richard M. Nixon in his text *The Real War*

16 Presidential News Conference, March 24, 1977

17 Thompson W. Scott, *American Spectator, Vol. 11, No. 11*, "The Soviets' African Waltz", November 1, 1978

18 Bruce D. Porter, *The USSR in Third World conflicts*, (1986), p. 189; Radio Moscow transmission July 27, 1977

19 Presidential Address at Fort Wake University, Winston-Salem, North Carolina, March 17, 1978

20 Edward George, *The Cuban intervention in Angola*, (2006), p. 133

21 Edward George, *The Cuban intervention in Angola*, (2006), p. 134

22 Edward George, *The Cuban intervention in Angola*, (2006), p. 135

23 Felipe Roque, Cuban Foreign Minster, addressing the African Union, Sharm El-Sheikh, June 26-27, 2008

24 Edward George, *The Cuban intervention in Angola*, (2006), p. 120

25 John Huddy, *Storming Las Vegas*, (2008), p. 39

26 *Time Magazine*, Monday, 30 May 1977; SOUTH AFRICA: Mondale v. Vorster: Tough Talk

27 George Wright, *The Destruction of a Nation*, (1997), p. 80

28 Presidential News conference, Chicago, Illinois, 25 May, 1978

29 The 11 September 2001 terrorist attacks on the World Trade Center in New York and on the Pentagon

30 Anatoliy Fedorovich Dobrynin, *In Confidence*, (1995), p. 403

31 Hermann Giliomee, *The Afrikaners – biography of a people*, (2003), p. 574

32 Hermann Giliomee, *The Afrikaners – biography of a people*, (2003), p. 564

33 Steve Biko and Aelred Stubbs, *I write what I like*, (1987), p. 66

34 Peter Vanneman, *Soviet Strategy in Southern Africa*, (1990), p. 56

35 O.R. Tambo, *World Marxist Review*, February 1987

36 Lewis H. Gann and Peter Duignan, *Africa South of the Sahara*, (1981), p. 106

37 Hannes Steyn, Richardt van der Walt and Jan van Loggerenberg, *Armament and Disarmament*, (2003), p.xvii

38 As related to the author many years later by a manager of ARMSCOR

39 Hannes Steyn, Richardt van der Walt and Jan van Loggerenberg, *Armament and Disarmament*, (2003), p.51

40 Hermann Giliomee, *The Afrikaners – biography of a people*, (2003), p. 610

41 Andrew Downer Crain, *The Ford Presidency: A History*, (2009), p. 229

42 Frank Barnaby, Nuclear South Africa, *New Scientist*, October 19, 1978, p. 168

43 Sasha Pulakow-Suransky, *The Unspoken Alliance*, (2010), p. 112

44 Sasha Pulakow-Suransky, *The Unspoken Alliance*, (2010), p. 112

45 Sasha Pulakow-Suransky, *The Unspoken Alliance*, (2010), p. 112

46 Hannes Steyn, Richardt van der Walt and Jan van Loggerenberg, *Armament and Disarmament*, (2003)

47 Hannes Steyn, Richardt van der Walt and Jan van Loggerenberg, *Armament and Disarmament*, (2003), p. 31

48 Ronald W. Walters, *South Africa and the Bomb*, (1987), p. 9

49 Ronald W. Walters, *South Africa and the Bomb*, (1987), p. 25

50 Frank Barnaby, Nuclear South Africa, *New Scientist*, October 19, 1978, p. 170

51 Hannes Steyn, Richardt van der Walt and Jan van Loggerenberg, *Armament and Disarmament*, (2003), p. 38

52 Sasha Pulakow-Suransky, *The Unspoken Alliance*, (2010), p. 113

53 Sasha Pulakow-Suransky, *The Unspoken Alliance*, (2010), p. 242

54 A.H. Al-Hallaq et al, *U. of Sharjah Journal of Pure & Applied Sciences*, Vol. 5, No. 2, (2008), p. 105

55 Food and Agriculture Organization of the United Nations, Fertilizer use by Crop in South Africa, (2005), p. 4; Rainfall http://www.fao.org/docrep/008/y5998e/y5998e06.htm

56 *Time Magazine*, Monday, 19 December 1977; SOUTH AFRICA: The Birth of BophuthaTswana

57 Henry Kissinger, *Years of Renewal*, (1999), p. 970

58 Henry Kissinger, *Years of Renewal*, (1999), p. 914

59 Henry Kissinger, *Years of Renewal*, (1999), p. 917

60 Henry Kissinger, *Years of Renewal*, (1999), p. 981

61 Henry Kissinger, *Years of Renewal*, (1999), pp. 958-1016

62 Henry Kissinger, *Years of Renewal*, (1999), p. 975

63 Henry Kissinger, *Years of Renewal*, (1999), p. 1014

64 *Time Magazine*, Monday, 18 September 1978; Seeds of political destruction

65 *Time Magazine*, Monday, 18 September 1978; Seeds of political destruction

66 Peter J. H. Petter-Bowyer, *Winds of Destruction*, (2005), p. 331

67 *Time Magazine*, Monday, 18 September 1978; Seeds of political destruction

68 Peter J. H. Petter-Bowyer, *Winds of Destruction*, (2005), p. 349

69 Odd Arne Westard, *The Global Cold War: Third world interventions and the making of our times*, (2005), p. 372

70 Richard M. Nixon, *The Real War*, (1980), p. 33

71 Terrorist Group Profiles: http://upload.wikimedia.org/wikipedia/commons/b/bb/Terrorist_Group_Profiles.pdf

Notes to Chapter 24

1 Sasha Pulakow-Suransky, *The Unspoken Alliance*, (2010), p. 141

2 Hannes Steyn, Richardt van der Walt and Jan van Loggerenberg, *Armament and Disarmament*, (2003), p. 68

3 Hannes Steyn, Richardt van der Walt and Jan van Loggerenberg, *Armament and Disarmament*, (2003), p. 92

4 Sasha Pulakow-Suransky, *The Unspoken Alliance*, (2010), p. 141

5 Sasha Pulakow-Suransky, *The Unspoken Alliance*, (2010)

6 Anatoliy Fedorovich Dobrynin, *In Confidence*, (1995), p. 403

7 Odd Arne Westard, *The Global Cold War: Third world interventions and the making of our times*, (2005), p. 371

8 John Huddy, *Storming Las Vegas*, (2008), p. 42

9 Charles S. Johnson and John Stanfield (Editor), *Bitter Canaan – the story of the Negro Republic*, (1987)

10 P. J. Johnson, Dissertation: *Seasons in Hell : Charles S. Johnson and the 1930 Liberian Labor Crisis*, (2004), p. 1

11 There is a long list of attacks on and murder of missionaries and nuns in Rhodesia. The very worst was the Elim Pentecostal Missionary massacre by Mugabe's men. Time Magazine failed abjectly to do their professional job in reporting fully on the horror of the deaths of the babies and women in particular. See Time Magazine, Monday 10 July 1978; Rhodesia: Savagery and Terror

12 Martin Meredith, *The Fate of Africa*, p. 327

13 Richard Dowden, *Africa - altered states, ordinary miracles*, (2009), p. 134

14 Potions to effect good or harm via spiritual intervention; See Ch. 13, British horror in South Africa

15 This Chapter: *A flash in the Southern Ocean*; See also Sasha Pulakow-Suransky, *The Unspoken Alliance*, (2010), p. 139

16 See Chapter 7 : *The Black Circuit*. The later Sir Hendrik "Henry" Cloete had tried to make his way home to the Cape from the Netherlands and UK on the frigate H.M.S. Java after his studies. Unfortunately for Cloete, this was in the middle of the War of 1812 and the H.M.S. Java was taken as prize by the U.S.S. Constitution. He eventually made his way home in 1813 where he became under-secretary of the Court and served as Court Reporter for the hated Black Circuit.

17 Chester A. Crocker, *High Noon in Southern Africa*, (1992), p. 43

18 Rolihlahla Mandela, *Long Walk to Freedom*, (1994); p. 659

19 *Mail & Guardian*, 1 November 2006

20 James Barber and John Barratt, *South Africa's Foreign Policy*, (1990), p. 303

21 Richard M. Nixon, *The Real War*, (1980), p. 33

22 Hermann Giliomee, *The Afrikaners – biography of a people*, (2003), p. 601

23 David Lien, *South African Diary #1*, http://southafr.tripod.com/trip1.html, entry for Saturday 3 March 1984

24 In the year 2010 this would be the subject of an episode of a popular American television show entitled *Rogue Nature* hosted by Dave Salmoni, set in the exact area.

25 Known as *Operation Savannah* in South Africa

26 G. Shubin, *The oral history of forgotten wars*, (2007), p. 43, Note 34; others refer to him as "Shaganovich"

27 The military wing of the Soviet-supported Angolan MPLA Government

28 Piet Nortje, *32 Battalion*, (2009), p. 147

29 Piet Nortje, *32 Battalion*, (2009), p. 153

30 Piet Nortje, *32 Battalion*, (2009), p. 156

31 *Time Magazine*, Monday 14 Sept. 1981; Marching to South Africa's beat; See also Fred Bridgland, *The War for Africa*, (1990), p. 300

32 Piet Nortje, *32 Battalion*, (2009), p. 176

33 Piet Nortje, *32 Battalion*, (2009), p. 179

34 Hermann Giliomee, *The Afrikaners – biography of a people*, (2003); p. 592

35 Richard Dowden, *Africa - altered states, ordinary miracles*, (2009), p. 141

36 Peter Vanneman, *Soviet Strategy in Southern Africa*, (1990), pp. 49-50

37 Peter Vanneman, *Soviet Strategy in Southern Africa*, (1990), p. 50

38 The description of the event is based on the work of Piet Nortje, *32 Battalion*, (2009), p. 198

39 This proved the rumors of the presence of East German personnel on the FAPLA side

40 Described to the author by SADF officers in Namibia (1987)

41 Chester A. Crocker, *High Noon in Southern Africa*, (1992), p. 258

42 Chester A. Crocker, *High Noon in Southern Africa*, (1992), p. 259

43 Chester A. Crocker, *High Noon in Southern Africa*, (1992), pp. 253-278; See specifically page 263

44 Chester A. Crocker, *High Noon in Southern Africa*, (1992), p. 257

45 Chester A. Crocker, *High Noon in Southern Africa*, (1992), p. 260

46 Hermann Giliomee, *The Afrikaners – biography of a people*, (2003); p. 611

47 Adam Ashforth, *Witchcraft, Violence and Democracy in South Africa*, (2005), p. 30

48 The African National Congress of South Africa: *Organization, Communist Ties, and Short-Term Prospects*, SNIE 73-86; July 1986

49 H. Giliomee, *The Afrikaners – biography of a people*, (2003); p. 593; See also Time Magazine, May 26, 1986

50 James Barber and John Barratt, *South Africa's Foreign Policy*, (1990), p. 324

51 Press meeting in the Oval Office of the White House (10:30 am September 9, 1985)

52 This generation still economically weighs down the country in the 21st century with their misguided and baseless sense of entitlement, similar to Robert Mugabe's so-called "War veterans" who still want their "spoils of the revolution."

53 The description of this campaign is based on the work of Piet Nortje, *32 Battalion*, (2009), p. 213-219

54 International reporters were outraged some two decades later in 2008 when South African black people laughed as they "necklaced" Zimbabwean refugees in South African black townships. Time Magazine suggested that the images would haunt the international imagination for years (*Time Magazine*, Monday 21 May 2008; South Africa's Wake-up call). In its 26 January 1987 article, however, it sought to rationalize it as as a consequence of Apartheid. By 2008, there was no Apartheid to blame. The legacy of horror of the 1980s ANC and the Tutu-Robinson campaign in the USA is still very much with the S. Africa in the 21st Century and the moral refuge of the Western Media on the subject of S. Africa is gone.

55 See for example *Time Magazine*, Monday 26 January 1987; South Africa - The War of Blacks against Blacks,

56 The ANC only reconsidered this campaign after 5 May 1987 when a truck with black farm workers set off a mine. Two were killed and twenty injured. Obviously their moral concerns were not color blind.

57 *City Press*, 27 November 2005; http://152.111.1.87/argief/berigte/citypress/2005/11/27/C1/27/03.html. The same verbatim quotation of his words may be found in the ANC's own fully documented statement to the Truth and Reconciliation Commission in 1996: http://www.anc.org.za/show.php?id=2639.

58 *Report of the Truth and Reconciliation Commission, Vol. 3*, (1998), p. 234

59 *Report of the Truth and Reconciliation Commission, Vol. 3*, (1998), p. 234

60 Somehow, the ANC seemed to kill mostly white women and children and relatively few white males.

61 A racial distinction that the ANC maintains in legislation in its policies as Government in the 21st century

62 McBride will enter our story again in a way that should leave incredulous any reader who claims to be human.

Notes to Chapter 25

1 Peter Vanneman, *Soviet Strategy in Southern Africa*, (1990), p. 53

2 Clem Sunter is a highly respected strategic scenario planner and was invited by the Central Party School of the Government of China to address them in 2006

3 De Beers, the arch-capitalist company, and the Soviets, the arch-communists, had an arrangement by which De Beers marketed the diamonds from both sources and ensured the highest possible price.

4 There would be considerable debate in 1990 as to how the CIA apparently did not anticipate the Collapse of the U.S.S.R.

5 In the 21st century Vernon Joynt became the Chief Scientist of an American company manufacturing IED-proof vehicles

6 See the quote by Leonid Brezhnev at the head of chapter 22, reported by Richard M. Nixon in his text *The Real War*.

7 J. Bruce Amstutz, *Afghanistan: The first five years of occupation*, (1994), p. 160

8 Dmitri Trenin and Alexey Malashenko, *Afghanistan – a view from Moscow*; p. 7

9 Fred Bridgland, *The War for Africa*, (1990)

10 Chester A. Crocker, *High Noon in Southern Africa*, (1992), p. 356

11 Peter Vanneman, *Soviet Strategy in Southern Africa*, (1990), p. 53

12 Fred Bridgland, *The War for Africa*, (1990), p. 44

13 Fred Bridgland, *The War for Africa*, (1990), p. 32; See Chap. 22: *The Angolan War 7*.

14 The Southwest African People's Liberation Army, deemed the government of Namibia by the UN in the absence of elections

15 I. A. Zhdarkin (translator: Tamara Reilly), *We did not see it even in Afghanistan*, (2008), pp. 324-326

16 Piet Nortje, *32 Battalion*, (2009), p. 234

17 Chester A. Crocker, *High Noon in Southern Africa*, (1992), p. 356

18 Peter Vanneman, *Soviet Strategy in Southern Africa*, (1990), p. 56

19 Gennady Shubin, *The oral history of forgotten wars*, (2007), pp. 5-25

20 Peter Vanneman, *Soviet Strategy in Southern Africa*, (1990), p. 54

21 Chester A. Crocker, *High Noon in Southern Africa*, (1992), p. 355

22 Fred Bridgland, *The War for Africa*, (1990), p. 374

23 C. McG Ekedahl and M. A. Goodman, *The Wars of Eduard Shevardnadze*, (1997), p. 57 and p. 313, note 58

24 Peter Vanneman, *Soviet Strategy in Southern Africa*, (1990), p. 23

25 Chester A. Crocker, *High Noon in Southern Africa*, (1992), p. 358

26 Dick Lord, *From fledgling to Eagle*, (2008), p. 396; Peter Stiff, *The Silent War- South African Recce Operations 1969-1994*, (1999); p. 545 states it was 40 miles

27 Peter Stiff, *The Silent War- South African Recce Operations 1969-1994*, (1999); p. 547

28 Piet Nortje, *32 Battalion*, (2009), p. 237

29 The general description of the battle is drawn from from Fred Bridgland, The War for Africa, (1990) and Piet Nortje, *32 Battalion*, (2009), pp. 240-244, unless otherwise referenced.

30 Fred Bridgland, *The War for Africa*, (1990), p. 11; see also Chapter 22: The Angolan War 5- Escalation

31 The Ratel Infantry Fighting Vehicle (IFV) is a lightly armored wheel-based South African design. Internationally, the Ratel was the first wheel-based IFV. In nature a ratel is an African honey badger, known for its outstanding toughness and aggression. One version mounted a three-tube anti-tank guided missile system with South African designation ZT-3

32 Peter Stiff, *The Silent War- South African Recce Operations 1969-1994*, (1999); p. 548; Likely the events described by Lieutenant-Colonel Zhdarkin in *We did not see it even in Afghanistan*, (2008), p. 254; One of them died and four were "shell shocked."

33 Piet Nortje, *32 Battalion*, (2009), p. 240

34 Igor Anatolyevitch Zhdarkin (translator: Tamara Reilly), *We did not see it even in Afghanistan*, (2008), p. 260

35 A clearing in the Angolan bush, sometimes with a pan of standing water in the rainy season. The term is sometimes also used to describe the open floodplain of a river, as in this particular case.

36 Peter Stiff, *The Silent War- South African Recce Operations 1969-1994*, (1999); p. 548; Stiff provides at least three very reliable witnesses

37 Igor Anatolyevitch Zhdarkin (translator: Tamara Reilly), *We did not see it even in Afghanistan*, (2008), p. 373

38 Dick Lord, *From fledgling to Eagle*, (2008), p. 399

39 Dick Lord, *From fledgling to Eagle*, (2008), p. 433 describes S.A.A.F. formation flying at 600 knots at 50 foot

40 Dick Lord, *From fledgling to Eagle*, (2008), p. 403

41 Dick Lord, *From fledgling to Eagle*, (2008), p. 439

42 Igor Anatolyevitch Zhdarkin (translator: Tamara Reilly), *We did not see it even in Afghanistan*, (2008), p. 373; The honest colonel's editor added a note claiming the Axis pilots avoided (high-G) stresses because of "poor nutrition." The editor was at some pains to explain that these were Angolan pilots and not Cubans or Soviets.

43 For Americans the Hind was the Soviet-piloted helicopter that hunted "John Rambo" in a motion picture. For Afghans and South Africans it was a very real threat in 1987. The one in the motion picture was a "dressed-up" French Puma.

44 Piet Nortje, *32 Battalion*, (2009), p. 179

45 A ground-attack version of the Mirage F1 unique to South Africa, equipped with custom electronics

46 Highly trained high endurance South African Reconnaissance Commandos; equivalent of the British SAS and US Navy SEALS. They specialise in long-range pentration and their physical endurance is legendary.

47 Piet Nortje, *32 Battalion*, (2009), p. 180

48 British post-WWII Churchill, much upgraded since their use by Israel in the Yom Kippur War of 1973

49 *Washington Post*, Rebels turn back major drive in Angola, October 4, 1987

50 *Washington Post*, South Africa Acknowledges Fighting Soviets, Cubans in Angola, 12 November, 1987

51 Chester A. Crocker, *High Noon in Southern Africa*, (1992), p. 360

52 Igor Anatolyevitch Zhdarkin (translator: Tamara Reilly), *We did not see it even in Afghanistan*, (2008), p. 278

53 32 Battalion of the South African Defense Force, also known as "Buffalo Commando"

54 Igor Anatolyevitch Zhdarkin (translator: Tamara Reilly), *We did not see it even in Afghanistan*, (2008), p. 285

55 Chester A. Crocker, *High Noon in Southern Africa*, (1992), p. 360

56 See Dick Lord, *From fledgling to Eagle*, (2008), p. 435

57 Peter Stiff, *The Silent War- South African Recce Operations 1969-1994*, (1999), p. 550

58 Dick Lord, *From fledgling to Eagle*, (2008), p. 351

59 Chester A. Crocker, *High Noon in Southern Africa*, (1992), p. 360

60 Gennady Shubin, *The oral history of forgotten wars*, (2007), p. 20

61 Igor Anatolyevitch Zhdarkin (translator: Tamara Reilly), *We did not see it even in Afghanistan*, (2008), p. 372

62 *The Boston Globe*, Rebels hanging on in key Angolan town battle (etc.), 24 April 1988

63 Peter Vanneman, *Soviet Strategy in Southern Africa*, (1990), p. 55

64 Peter Vanneman, *Soviet Strategy in Southern Africa*, (1990), p. 57

65 Igor Anatolyevitch Zhdarkin (translator: Tamara Reilly), *We did not see it even in Afghanistan*, (2008), p. 397

66 Igor Anatolyevitch Zhdarkin (translator: Tamara Reilly), *We did not see it even in Afghanistan*, (2008), p. 369

67 Chester A. Crocker, *High Noon in Southern Africa*, (1992), p. 361

68 Chester A. Crocker, *High Noon in Southern Africa*, (1992), p. 371

69 Chester A. Crocker, *High Noon in Southern Africa*, (1992), p. 385

70 Michael F. Morris, USMC Research Paper: *Flying Columns in Small Wars*, (2000), p. ii

71 Egypt and Cuba's military dictators rewrote history to save face. See Chapter 22: On the holiest day of all

72 *Los Angeles Times*, June 16, 1987 quoting Associated Press; 10,000 Cubans reported killed in Angola War

73 Virgil Suárez, *Spared Angola: memories from a Cuban-American childhood*, (1997); p. 60 an p. 81

74 Odd Arne Westard, *The Global Cold War: Third world interventions and the making of our times*, (2005), p. 377

75 Peter Vanneman, *Soviet Strategy in Southern Africa*, (1990), p. 23

76 Present chapter, *The leaders meet as the violence continues*

77 The descriptions given in this and the following section are based on Rolihlahla "Nelson" Mandela's own autobiography, *Long Walk to Freedom*, (1994); pp. 607-660

78 She is also known as "Winnie" Mandela

79 The information provided here comes directly form Desmond Tutu's Truth and Reconciliation Commission Report (1998) as presented to then President Nelson Mandela on 29 October 1998. See Volume 2, Chapter 6, pp. 555-582.

80 Martin Meredith, *Mandela, a biography*, (2010), pp. 374-375

81 *New York Times*, February 17, 1989; Anti-Apartheid Groups Cast Out Winnie Mandela, Citing Terror

82 *Report of the Truth and Reconciliation Commission (TRC) ; Volume 2*, Ch. 6 is dedicated to the MUFC hearings

83 *Washington Post*, Nov. 24, 1997; Winnie Mandela's Role in Mayhem Probed

Notes to Chapter 26

1 Rolihlahla Mandela, *Long Walk to Freedom*, (1994), p. 662

2 *Washington Post*, A voice for South Africa's blacks, 12 October 1989

3 Joe Slovo, Is Socialism Dead? *The African Communist*, January 1990

4 http://www.info.gov.za/speeches/1996/101348690.htm

5 Rolihlahla Mandela, *Long Walk to Freedom*, (1994), p. 665

6 Frederik van Zyl Slabbert, *The other side of history*, (2006), p. 28

7 See, for example, the *Los Angeles Times*, June 22, 1990

8 Frederik van Zyl Slabbert, *The other side of history*, (2006), p. 33

9 See, for example, Frederik van Zyl Slabbert, *The other side of history*, (2006), p. 34

10 *Report of the Truth and Reconciliation Commission, Vol. 6*, (1998), p. 648

11 *Beeld* (newspaper), 25 May 1990.

12 Revealed later in 1997 during the hearings of the Truth and Reconciliation Commission chaired by Desmond Tutu

13 *New York Times*, May 14, 1991

14 *Chicago Tribune*, May 14, 1991

15 The alibi would be disproved later by witnesses asking Truth and Reconciliation Commission for amnesty

16 BBC, 24 April 2003, Winnie: 'Africa's Evita'; the article followed her later conviction for fraud and theft.

17 See, for example, the British Broadcasting Corporation (BBC), 18 March 1992

18 The University was named for Patrice Lumumba. See Chapter 20: The Congo – The Heart of Darkness erupts; From the 1960s to the late 1980s there were irate references by the South African government to this specific university being used as a U.S.S.R training ground and indoctrination center for revolutionary operatives. On February 5, 1992 the university was renamed the "Peoples' Friendship University of Russia." It would eventually be the site of black students being murdered by white Russians.

19 www.youtube.com/watch?v=v4gv7isyXMI

20 In 2011 the pop artist Bono went so far as to suggest songs calling for the killing of whites in South Africa are entirely acceptable: *South African Sunday Times*, Struggle songs have a place – U2, February 11, 2011

21 Richard Dowden, *Africa - altered states, ordinary miracles*, (2009), p. 401; Compare with Chapter 19 of the present work in which the author's father-in-law fought against the Nazis.

22 Richard Dowden, *Africa - altered states, ordinary miracles*, (2009), p. 31

23 http://www.justice.gov.za/trc/hrvtrans/qtown/barnes.htm & http://www.justice.gov.za/trc/hrvtrans/qtown/vanwyk.htm Proceedings of the Truth and Reconciliation Commission

24 Edward F. Mickolus and Susan L. Simmons, *Terrorism, 1992-1995*, (1997), p. 235

25 President of the PAC at the time of writing and a member of the National Assembly of South Africa

26 http://www.justice.gov.za/trc/decisions/1998/980611_makoma%20mkhumbuzi%20mlambisi.htm

27 This description of Amy's vicious murder by a racist black mob is taken directly from the Amnesty Application AC/98/0030 to the Truth and Reconciliation Commission granted 28 July 1998 which summarizes it based on the confessions of the murderers.

28 The Lithuanian Jewish leader of the South African Communist Party and leading ANC member.

29 The mob dance routine that South African black people do en masse during public demonstrations.

30 Edward F. Mickolus and Susan L. Simmons, *Terrorism, 1992-1995*, p. 474

31 *Time Magazine*, Monday 21 May 2008, South Africa's Wake-up call

32 Richard Cummings, A diamond is forever, *International Journal of Intelligence and Counter-Intelligence*, Summer 2005 (http://www.namebase.org/diamond.html)

33 *The African Communist, No. 87, Fourth Quarter*, 1981, pp. 56-57

34 Martin Meredith, *Mandela, a biography*, (2010), p. 471

35 Frederik van Zyl Slabbert, *The other side of history*, (2006), p. 40

36 Meyer would later become a consultant on peace processes in Northern Ireland, Sri Lanka, Rwanda, Burundi, Kosovo and Bolivia, the Basque Region and the Middle East. He serves on the Strategy Committee of the Project on Justice in Times of Transition in New York.

37 Frederik van Zyl Slabbert, *The other side of history*, (2006), p. 41

38 The national para-statal railway company

39 Martin Meredith, *Mandela, a biography*, (2010), p. 509

40 *The Independent* (UK), 8 June 1995; Mandela: Why I Gave Shoot to Kill Order

41 *Final Report of the Truth and Reconciliation Commission (TRC)*, (2003), Volume 6, Section 3, Chapter 2, p. 302

42 *Final Report of the Truth and Reconciliation Commission (TRC)*, (2003), Volume 6, Section 3, Chapter 2, p. 298

43 http://www.info.gov.za/speeches/1994/230994029.htm

44 Richard Dowden, *Africa - altered states, ordinary miracles*, (2009), p. 239

45 See, for example, Rolihlahla Mandela, *Long Walk to Freedom*, (1994), p. 747

46 African praise singer, usually clad in traditional garb of various animal skins. They have the task of "singing the praises" of important leaders, usually ranting on for an indeterminate time with descriptions of great things done, or to be done, or presumed to to have been done, or imagined to have been done.

47 *Truth and Reconciliation Commission (TRC)*; Vol. 2, Chapter 6 is dedicated to the MUFC hearings

48 John Stockwell, *In search of enemies*, (1978), p. 187

49 Rooivalk: Red kestrel, a very effective raptor of the Southern African skies

50 Modise died from cancer on 26 November 2001. It was revealed he had been involved in major fraud around the Arms deal with several other countries that would be traced to the ANC leadership.

51 John Carlin, *Invictus*, (2009); Also published as *Playing the Enemy* (2008)

52 Soccer teams; in 1994 black people had no interest in rugby in S. Africa; soccer was and still is their game.

53 The Springboks – the S. African national rugby team, having no black players and one Colored member

54 Better known as Ramzi Yousef

55 Richard Dowden, *Africa - altered states, ordinary miracles*, (2009), p. 111

Notes to Chapter 27

1 Martin Meredith, *The Fate of Africa*, (2005), p. 648

2 Adam Ashforth, *Witchcraft, Violence and Democracy in South Africa*, (2005), p. 31

3 Address of president Nelson Mandela at the opening of the Second Session of the new Parliament. Cape Town, February 17, 1995. Available online at http://www.info.gov.za/speeches/1995/170595001.htm; See also, for example, Martin Meredith, The Fate of Africa, (2005) p. 651

4 Chester A. Crocker, *High Noon in Southern Africa*, (1992), p. 258

5 See e.g., the *Montreal Gazette*, October 17, 1984, All races stand equal before God says Nobel winner etc.

6 On 27 January 1987 the long-established Australian newspaper, *The Age*, discussed Tutu's interview of 15 November 1984 with the Dutch *Volkskrant* in which Tutu had made the fateful comment. On 24 February 1986 the equally long established *Lewiston Journal* (now defunct) in Maine, in a column by Jeffrey Hart, referred to a little reported interview Tutu did with WNBC-TV in New York in December 1984, shortly after the Dutch interview. In the WNBC-TV interview Tutu speculated that black domestics could be given vials of arsenic and he made sure to clarify that they looked after white people's children. Hart wryly commented that, *"Clearly, the bishop has given a good deal of thought to this kind of thing, arsenic-for-babies."* *The News and Courier* in Charleston ran the same column two days later on 26 February 1986.

7 Martin Meredith, *Mandela, a biography*, (2010), pp. 558-559; Meredith quotes the actual testimony

8 SAPA – 25 November 1997; http://www.justice.gov.za/trc/media/1997/9711/s971125j.htm

9 Antjie Krog, *Country of my Skull*, (1999), p. 338

10 See, for example, Antjie Krog, *Country of my Skull*, (1999), p. 332

11 TRC transcripts for 1 December 1997 : http://www.justice.gov.za/trc/special/mandela/mufc6a.htm

12 Antjie Krog, *Country of my Skull*, (1999), p. 334

13 Antjie Krog, *Country of my Skull*, (1999)

14 Martin Meredith, *Mandela, a biography*, (2010), p. 523

15 ANC press release, 13 December 1994: http://www.anc.org.za/show.php?id=4857. It is also more directly available at : http://www.e-tools.co.za/newsbrief/1994/news1213

16 Martin Meredith, *Mandela, a biography*, (2010), p. 525

17 Niall Ferguson, *Civilization*, (2011), p. 305

18 Richard Dowden, *Africa - altered states, ordinary miracles*, (2009), see for example p. 368

19 Antjie Krog, *Country of my Skull*, (1999), p. 213

20 Anne Paton, Why I am fleeing South Africa, *London Sunday Times* – DISPATCHES, Sunday, Nov. 29, 1998

21 Singular of "amaBhulu." A single white Afrikaner as opposed to the nation of Afrikaners or "Boere."

22 By 2007, one South African Insurance company would simply refuse to insure certain automobile models.

23 The United Nations Office on Drugs and Crime: http://www.unodc.org/pdf/crime/seventh_survey/7sc.pdf

Notes to Chapter 28

1 *BBC*, 3 March 2012; http://news.bbc.co.uk/2/hi/africa/8547621.stm

2 Data from the agricultural union, Agri-SA

3 Martin Meredith, *Mandela, a biography*, (2010), p. 578

4 Fritz Brennecke, *The Nazi primer*; official handbook for schooling the Hitler youth, (1938), Chapters I and IV

5 Norman Davies, *Europe, a History*, (1997), pp. 1093-1094

6 In a 2012 personal interview with the particular retired Armscor manager, who confirmed to the author that the political officer had been sent directly from the office of Joe Modise, and that, despite being one of the most senior men in Armscor, he had not been allowed to make a single significant decision without the consent of the political officer.

7 See the description by Tom Cooper, http://www.acig.org/artman/publish/article_183.shtml

Notes to Chapter 29

1 Martin Meredith, *The Fate of Africa*, p. 681; See also AllAfrica.com for 9 July 2002; Africa: *Launch Party (etc.)*

2 *New York Times*, AIDS in South Africa; A President Misapprehends a Killer, May 14, 2000;

3 The *BBC*, South Africa HIV-row minister Tshabalala-Msimang dies, 16 December 2009;

4 *New York Times*, AIDS in South Africa; A President Misapprehends a Killer, May 14, 2000;

5 *The Guardian*, How Mbeki stoked South Africa's AIDS catastrophe, June12, 2001

6 *The Guardian*, The minister and the liver transplant- South Africa's AIDS row gets personal, August 20, 2007

7 *Washington Post*, AIDS policy widely decried as disaster for S. Africa, December 17, 2009

8 *Business Day*, Mbeki 'threw toys out of cot' over Khampepe report, May 14, 2002

9 Anatoliy Fedorovich Dobrynin, *In Confidence*, (1995), p. 403

10 *The Washington Post*; September 17, 2006; based on *Imperial Life in the Emerald City(etc.)* (2007) by Rajiv Chandrasekaran, which provides the same text on p. 98 and the rocket attack is related on p. 200.

11 Al J. Venter, *War Dog*, (2006), p. 53

12 Al J. Venter, *War Dog*, (2006), p. 5

13 *USA Today*, The truck the Pentagon wants and the firm that makes it, August 1, 2007;

14 US Army Official Homepage, June 13, 2008; http://www.army.mil/article/9979/mraps-on-the-move

15 *BBC*, From death row to SA Police Chief, December 4, 2003

16 *New York Times*, Official's arrest puzzles South Africa, March 16, 1998

17 *New York Times*, World Briefing: South Africa- Arms mystery revived, February 11, 1999

18 *Independent Online News*, McBride of the hook in escort Fracas, July 10 , 1999

19 *Mail & Guardian*, McBride 'released' from his contract, September 26, 2008

20 South African Government Gazette, Vol. 463 No. 25899, January 9, 2004 p. 2

21 *CIA World Factbook (2004)*

22 1st Charter devised 2003, based on the Aug. 2002 NEDLAC Fin. Sector Summit; for implementation 2004

23 M. Creamer; *Mining Weekly*, South African mining movie rekindles nationalisation debate, June 24, 2011

24 Government Gazette Vol. 448, No. 23922, October 10, 2002; Act 28 of 2002

25 South African Government Information system (2012): http://www.info.gov.za/aboutsa/minerals.htm

26 Financial data from *Mining Weekly*; Empowerment Group buys $490m position in Lonplats, Sep. 7, 2004;

27 *NY Times Magazine*, Could Cyril Ramaphosa Be the Best Leader (etc.), Jan. 23, 2013

28 Author's terminology

29 *Sunday Times*, Mbeki, Zuma battle over Scorpions, February 20, 2005; http://www.armsdeal-vpo.co.za/articles07/battle.html

30 *BBC*, 8 June 2005; Jail term for corrupt Zuma aide; http://news.bbc.co.uk/2/hi/africa/4073720.stm; Case CC27/04-NB/CD

31 Zuma would not give up on targeting the coffers of the state for this purpose.

32 *New York Times*, South African Guilty of Bribing President Over Arms Sales, June 3, 2005

33 Victoria Hosegood et al, *Social Science & Medicine*, (2007), September; 65(6), pp. 1249–1259

34 *Daily Mail, Bring me my machine gun: That's the chilling cry of the '100 per cent Zulu boy' etc*, April 24, 2009

35 *Foxnews*, The "Bring me my machine gun" campaign, January 10, 2008

36 *New York Times*, The "She Asked For It" Defense Wins, May 10, 2006

37 *BBC*, Zuma's corruption trial collapses, September 20, 2006

38 *Mail & Guardian*, SABC: Arrest warrant issued for Selebi, September 27, 2007

39 *Mail & Guardian*, The desperate bid to shield Selebi, Oct. 5, 2007; Events described are based on this report

40 *Mail & Guardian*, Selebi sentenced to 15 years, August 3, 2010.

41 *BBC*, South Africa ex-police head Selebi guilty of corruption, July 2, 2010

42 *Reuters*, South African authorities file court papers against Zuma, December 15, 2007

43 *Daily Mail*, Machine-gun man takes over ANC – God help the Rainbow Nation, December 19, 2007

Notes to Chapter 30

1 *Prospect Magazine*, 20 January 2008; The ANC's awful choice

2 *The Guardian*, 13 November 2007; Former MP claims Mbeki killed BAE bribery inquiry

3 *The Guardian*; 12 February 2008; Row as ANC moves to disband South African "FBI"

4 Afesis-Corplan; *Transformer, Vol. 14*, No. 5, Oct-Nov 2008; Recent policy shifts in South Africa (etc.)

5 *BBC*, 1 July 2008; Mandela taken off US Terror List

6 *Globe & Mail*, 5 June 2007; Visa denial brings Winnie Mandela to tears

7 *Time Magazine*, Monday 26 January 1987; South Africa - The War of Blacks against Blacks

8 *Time Magazine*, Monday 21 May 2008; South Africa's Wake-up call

9 *BBC*, 5 August 2010; South African mob burns suspected cable thieves alive

10 *BBC*, 18 June 2008; S Africa Chinese "become black" http://news.bbc.co.uk/2/hi/africa/7461099.stm

11 *Engineering News*, 5 March 2010; Tenderpreneurs frustrating legitimate contractors

12 See e.g. Wikipedia and also, for more context, http://en.wikipedia.org/wiki/Corruption_in_South_Africa

13 *BBC*, 24 July 2008; Zuma 'shocked by white poverty'; http://news.bbc.co.uk/2/hi/africa/7524146.stm

14 *Reuters*, White poverty, http://www.reuters.com/news/pictures/slideshow?articleId=USRTR2C3ZV#a=1

15 *The Guardian*, 12 September 2008; South African court clears way for Zuma presidential run

16 *The Guardian*, 20 September 2008; Thabo Mbeki to step down as South African president etc.

17 *BBC*, 16 December 2008; New party to challenge ANC rule

18 *The Guardian*, 6 April 2009; Prosecutors to drop Jacob Zuma corruption charges

19 *Bloomberg*, Lonmin PLC LMI Update on Incwala Resources; 30 September 2009; http://www.bloomberg.com/apps/news?pid=newsarchive&sid=aBNydUIjONI8

20 *Bloomberg*, Lonmin PLC LMI New Ownership of Incwala Resources, 10 May 2010; http://www.bloomberg.com/apps/news?pid=newsarchive&sid=aSStx7Dt4OBM

21 *Bloomberg*, Lonmin Raises $241 Million (etc.), 10 May 2010; http://www.bloomberg.com/news/2010-05-10/lonmin-to-sell-shares-to-fund-306-million-rescue-of-incwala-resources.html

22 *The Mail & Guardian*, 7 December 2012; Lonmin unlucky in love

23 The SA Gov. Information System, Mineral resources; http://www.info.gov.za/aboutsa/minerals.htm

24 *The Mail & Guardian*, 7 December 2012; Lonmin unlucky in BEE love

25 *Reuters*, 16 August 2012; Lonmin shares tumble

26 *Independent Online*, 8 November 2012; Police: Marikana men queued for muti

27 *The Guardian*, 24 October 2012; Lonmin e-mails paint ANC elder as a born-agin robber baron

28 *e-NCA*, 20 August 2012; *New Evidence Shows Marikana Miners Shot First*; https://www.youtube.com/watch?v=t6guOlOFY7Q

29 See also http://www.youtube.com/watch?v=4NVkRmBTB7k

30 *Newsweek*, February 13, 2009; Fleeing from South Africa

31 Subset of the original documentation covering the reasons for granting of refugee status to Brandon Huntley. RPD File I No. dossier SPR : MA8-0491.
http://webcache.googleusercontent.com/search?q=cache:y9JOqVWzloUJ:www.cbc.ca/news/pdf/huntley-decision.pdf.

32 *News 24*, 6 November 2008; Cop: You whites must f*** off

33 *Die Beeld*, 12 June 2011; Vrou keelaf gesny (Woman's throat slit)

34 *Independent News Online*, 13 June 2011; Vereeniging couple murdered

35 *The Sunday Times*, 10 April 2010; SA 'refugee' faces ejection

36 US Department of Agriculture, Black Farmers in America, 1865-2000; RBS research Report 194, p. 24

37 *BBC*, 3 March 2010; South Africa black-owned farms 'failing'

38 Michael Aliber et al, *Trends and Policy challenges in the Rural Economy*, (2005); p.9

39 A. Murray Snr. from Scotland, and son Andrew, were key Dutch Reformed clergy in the 19th Century

40 Detail here is from the *News24* service (3 Dec. 2010 and 25 May 2011), *Independent Online News* (25 May 2011), *The Witness* (26 May 2011), *The Citizen* newspaper of 2 June 2011, and the Transvaal Agricultural Union

41 Rolihlahla Mandela, *Long Walk to Freedom*, (1994), p. 747

42 *The Telegraph*, 26 November 2012; British Engineer hacked to death on his South African farm,

43 *The Telegraph*, 1 December 2012; South African farmers fearing for their lives

44 Leon Parkin & Gregory H. Stanton, *Why are Afrikaner farmers being murdered in South Africa?*, Genocidewatch, 14 August 2012; http://www.genocidewatch.org/southafrica.html

45 *The Telegraph*, 1 December 2012; South African farmers fearing for their lives

46 Leon Parkin & Gregory H. Stanton, *Why are Afrikaner farmers being murdered in South Africa?*, Genocidewatch, 14 August 2012; http://www.genocidewatch.org/southafrica.html

47 *Reuters*, 30 March 2010; South Africa's ANC defends "Kill the Boer" song

48 *BBC*, 12 September 2011; ANC Julius Malema's Shoot the Boer ruled 'hate speech'

49 Genocidewatch, *South Africa - Official Hate Speech*, 12 July 2012; http://www.genocidewatch.org/southafrica.html

50 http://www.youtube.com/watch?v=4NVkRmBTB7k ;

51 *The Guardian*, 1 May 2011; South Africa's white farmers are moving further north

52 Ruth Hall, *The next Great Trek? South African commercial farmers move north*; International Conference on Land Grabbing at University of Sussex (6 -8 April 2011); http://farmlandgrab.org/uploads/attachment/RUTH%20HALL%20TREK.pdf

53 *This Day* (a Nigerian newspaper), 20 October 2009; My revealing South African Experience

54 Eurasianet.org, 9 June 2011; Georgia: Betting on Boers for an Agricultural Comeback; http://www.eurasianet.org/node/63647

55 Biography on the Georgian Government Website: http://www.president.gov.ge/en/President/TheFirstLady/Biography

56 *The Economist*, 23 February 2012; Boers in Georgia; http://www.economist.com/blogs/easternapproaches/2012/02/georgia

57 On 15 Nov. 2012 the premier of the Northwest Province, Thandi Modise announced that a 13 year old boy had been skinned and his tongue, throat and kidneys removed for muti http://www.info.gov.za/speech/DynamicAction?pageid=461&sid=32351&tid=90790. Two weeks before, a woman had been hijacked and murdered http://www.info.gov.za/speech/DynamicAction?pageid=461&sid=31877&tid=88915 and her right eye and private parts removed. All this happened at Mmakau village just outside Brits, near the South African capital, Pretoria. In a London (UK) case described by the *BBC* (http://news.bbc.co.uk/2/hi/uk_news/1899609.stm) and by CNN the British sought help from white Afrikaner South African police investigators. Nelson Mandela made a special appeal for information. He knew muti murders were a reality of Black South Africa and the ultimate horror for whites.

58 *Daily Mail*, 1 September 2011; Black farmers in South Africa cash in by selling land given to them (etc.)

59 *BBC*, 29 August 2012; Does race still matter in South Africa?

60 See, for example, the *New York Times*, March 11, 2010; Winnie Mandela's remarks Raise Stir

61 Pronounced "looree". Burchell's coucal; well known in Africa millennia before Burchell.

Bibliography

Format: Author(s), *Title*, (Date of Publication), Publisher/Imprint, Location, INSB-10, INSB-13 numbers.

Alberti, Ludwig, *Ludwig Alberti's account of the tribal life and customs of the Xhosa in 1807*, (Translation of *Die Kaffern auf der Südküste* etc by William Fehr), (1968), A. A. Balkema, Cape Town.

Alberti, Johann Christoph Ludwig, *Die Kaffern auf der Südküste von Afrika, nach ihren Sitten und Gebrauchen aus eigner Ansicht beschrieben*, 1815, Becker, Gotha.

Alexander, James E., *Excursions in Western Africa, and Narrative of a Campaign in Kaffir-Land on the Staff of the Commander-in-Chief Vol. 2*, (1840), Henry Colburn, London.

Aliber, Michael, et al, *Trends and Policy challenges in the Rural Economy*, (2005), HSRC Press, Cape Town, 0796921008, 9780796921000.

Amery, Leopold Stennett, *The Times History of the War in South Africa Vol. 1*, (1900), Sampson Low, Marston & Co., London. *Vol. 4*, (1906)

Amstutz, J. Bruce, *Afghanistan: The first five years of occupation*, (1994), Diane Publishing, Darby, PA, 0788111116, 9780788111112.

Ashforth, Adam, *Witchcraft, Violence and Democracy in South Africa*, (2005), University of Chicago Press, Chicago, 0226029743, 9780226029740.

Backhouse, James, *A narrative of a visit to the Mauritius and South Africa*, (1844), Hamilton, Adams and Co., London.

Bagshawe, Peter, *Warriors of the Sky*, (1990), Ashanti Publishing, Johannesburg, 1874800111, 9781874800118.

Bannister, Saxe, *British Colonization and Coloured Tribes*, (1838), William Ball, London.

Barnard, Lady Anne, *South Africa a Century Ago: Letters Written from the Cape of Good Hope* (1797-1801), (1910), Smith, Elder & Co., London.

Barnard, Lady Anne Lindsay, *The Cape Diaries of Lady Anne Barnard*; Edited by Margaret Lenta and Basil le Cordeur, (1999), Van Riebeeck Society, Cape Town, 0958411263, 9780958411264.

Barber, James and John Barratt, *South Africa's Foreign Policy*, (1990), Cambridge University Press, Cambridge, 0521388767, 9780521388764.

Barrow, John, *An Account of Travels into the Interior of Southern Africa in the Years 1797 and 1798 (First Edition) Vol. 1*, (1801), T. Cadell, jun. and W. Davies, London. *Vol. 2*, (1804)

Barrow, John, *An auto-biographical memoir of Sir John Barrow*, 1847, John Murray, London.

Batts, H. J., *The Story of a 100 Years, 1820-1920: Being the History of the Baptist Church in South Africa*, (1922), T. Maskew Miller, Cape Town.

Beeston, Richard & John Simpson, *Looking for Trouble*, (2007), I.B. Tauris & Co., New York, 1845112776, 9781845112776.

Biko, Stephen & Aelred Stubbs, *I write what I like*, (1987), Heinemann International Litera, Oxford, 0435905988, 9780435905989.

Bird, John (Editor), *The Annals of Natal 1495 to 1845 Vol. 1 & 2*, (1965), C. Struik, Cape Town.

Bird, William Wilberforce, *State of the Cape of Good Hope in 1822*, (1823), John Murray, London.

Blake, J.Y.F., *A Westpointer with the Boers*, (1903), Angel Guardian Press, Boston.

Bögaerts, Abraham, *Historische reizen door d'oostersche delen van Asia*; Second Print, (1731), Jan Daniel Beman, Rotterdam.

Boucher, Maurice, *French Speakers at the Cape in the first hundred years of Dutch East India Company rule: The European Background*, (1981), University of South Africa, Pretoria, 086981222X, 9780869812228.

Botha, Andries and William Buchanan, *Trial of Andries Botha, Field-Cornet of the Upper Blinkwater, in the Kat River Settlement, for High Treason, in the Supreme Court of the Colony of the Cape of Good Hope, on the 12th May, 1852*, (1852), S. Solomon, Cape Town.

Botha, Colin Graham, *The French refugees at the Cape* (3rd Edition), (1970), C. Struik, Cape Town.

Boyce, William Binnington, *Notes on South African Affairs*, (1839), J. Mason, London.

Bridgland, Fred, *The War for Africa*, (1990), Ashanti Publishers Ltd., Gibraltar, 187480012X, 9781874800125.

Brown, William, *The history of missions*, (1816), B Coles V.D.M., Philadelphia.

Bruijn, J.R., F.S. Gaastra and I. Schöffer, *Dutch-Asiatic shipping in the 17th and 18th centuries, 1595-1795, Vol. 2 and 3*, (1979), Nijhoff, Den Haag.

Burke, Edmund, *The Annual Register: A review of public events at home and abroad, for the year 1876, Vol. 118*, (1877), Longmans, Green, and others, London.

Burnham, Frederick Russel, *Scouting on Two Continents*, (2004), Kessinger, Whitefish, Montana.

Butler, William, *Sir William Butler: an autobiography*, (1911), Constable & Company, London.

Campbell, John, *Journal of Travels in South Africa Among the Hottentot and Other Tribes*, (1834), Religious Tract Society, London.

Cannon, Richard, *History of the Cape Mounted Rifles*, (1842), John W.Parker, London.

Carlin, John, *Invictus*, (2009), Penguin, New York, 0143117157, 9780143117155.

Carter, Miranda, *George, Nicholas en Wilhelm; Three Royal Cousins and the Road to Word War I*, (2010), Alfred A. Knopf, New York, 1400043638, 9781400043637.

Castelyn, Pieter (Editor), *De Hollandtsche Mercurius Part 13*, (1662), Pieter Castelyn, Haerlem.

de Chalezac, Guillaume Chenu (Ed: Randolph Vigne), *Guillaume Chenu de Chalezac, the French Boy* (Van Riebeeck Society Series, No. 22 of the Second Series), (1993), Van Riebeeck Society, Cape Town, 0620175249, 9780620175241.

Chase, John Centlivres, *Natal, a re-print of all authentic notices (etc) [Part 1] Vol. 1 and Vol. 2 bound together*, (1843), R. Godlonton and A.S. Robertson and J.H. Collard, Grahamstown and Cape Town.

Chase, John Centlivres, *The Cape of Good Hope and the Eastern Province of Algoa Bay*, (1843), Pelham Richardson, London.

Chomat, Virginia Belz, *Cabrières d'Aigues et la Famille Jourdan*, Edition Cabrières, (2007), Virginia Belz Chomat, Cabrières d'Aigues, 9782952960502.

Churchill, Winston Spencer, *A roving commission: my early life*, (1996), Simon & Schuster, New York.

Clemens, Samuel L. (Mark Twain), *Following the Equator: A Journey Around the World*, (1897), American Publishing Co. and Doubleday & McClure Co., Hartford, New York.

Clingman, Stephen, *Bram Fischer - Afrikaner revolutionary*, (1998), David Philip Publishers, Cape Town, 0864863187, 9780864863188.

Cloete, Henry, *Three Lectures on the Emigration of the Dutch Farmers from the Colony of the Cape of Good Hope*, (1852), J. Archbell and Son, Pietermaritzburg.

Colenso, John William, *Ten Weeks in Natal: A Journal of a First Tour of Visitation Among the Colonists and Zulu Kafirs of Natal*, (1855), MacMillan & Co., Cambridge.

Commission pour l'histoire des Eglises Wallonnes, *Bulletin de la Commission pour l'histoire des Eglises Wallonnes, Vol. 1*, (1885), Martinus Nijhoff, La Haye.

Cory, George E, *The Rise of South Africa Vol. 1*, (1921), Longmans, Green & Co., London.

Crain, Andrew Downer, *The Ford Presidency*, (2009), McFarland & Company, Jefferson, N.C., 0786441453, 9780786441457.

Davies, Norman, *Europe, a History*, (1997), Pimlico / Random House, London, 0712666338, 9780712666336.

Davis, Richard Harding, *With Both Armies in South Africa*, (1900), Charles Scribner's Sons, New York.

Delegorgue, Adulphe, *Voyage dans l'Afrique Australe notamment dans le territoire de Natal dans celui des Cafres amaZoulous et Makatisses et Jusque'au Tropique du Capricorne*, (1847), A, Ren, et Co., Paris.

Devlin, Lawrence R., *Chief of Station, Congo*, (2007), Public Affairs, New York, 1586484052, 9781586484057.

De Wet, Christiaan, *The Three Years War*, (1902), Archibald, Conatable & Co., Westminster.

Dobrynin, Anatoliy Fedorovich, *In Confidence*, (1995), Crown, New York, 0812923286, 9780812923285.

D'Oliveira, John, *Vorster- The Man*, (1977), Ernest Stanton Publishers, Johannesburg, 094999734X, 9780949997340.

Doyle, Arthur Conan, *The War in South Africa, its Cause and Conduct*, (1902), Mc Clure, Phillips & Co., New York.

Doyle, Arthur Conan, *The Great Boer War*, (1900), Mc Clure, Phillips & Co., New York.

Dowden, Richard, *Africa - Altered states, ordinary miracles*, (2009), Publc Affairs, New York9781586487539.

Dunstan, Simon, *Vietnam Tracks*, (2004), Osprey Publishing, Oxford, 1841768332, 9781841768335.

Duvenage, G. D. J., *Van die Tarka na die Transgariep: die emigrasie uit die noordoosgrensdele van die Kaapkolonie, 1835-1840*,

(1981), Academica, Pretoria, Cape Town and Johannesburg, 0868740950, 9780868740959.

Ekedahl, Carolyn McGiffert & Melvin A. Goodman, *The Wars of Eduard Shevardnadze*, (1997), Pennsylvania University Press, University Park, 0271016043, 9780271016047.

Ellis, Charles Howard, *The origin, structure and working of the League of Nations*, (1928), George Allen & Unwin LTD., London.

Eltinge, Le Roy, *Psychology of War*, (1915), Press of the Army Service School, Fort Leavenworth.

Featherstone, Donald, *Victorian Colonial Warfare* (Series) : *Africa, from the campaigns against the Kaffirs to the South African War*, (1993), Blandford and Bok Books jointly, Mbabane and Durban, 1874937435, 9781874937432.

Ferguson, Niall, *Empire: The Rise and Demise of the British World Order and the Lessons for Global Power*, (2003), Basic Books, New York, 0465023282, 9780465023288.

Ferguson, Niall, Civilization, 2011, Penguin Press, New York, 1101548029, 9781594203053.

Fernow, Berthold, *The records of New Amsterdam from 1653 to 1674 anno Domini V.3*, (1897), City of New York, New York.

Freeman, Joseph John, *A Tour in South Africa: With Notices of Natal, Mauritius, Madagascar, Ceylon, Egypt, and Palestine*, (1851), John Snow, London.

Gaines, Kevin Kelly, *American Africans in Ghana*, (2006), Univeristy of North Carolina Press, 0807830089, 9780807830086.

Gann, L. H. and Peter Duignan, *Africa South of the Sahara*, (1981), Hoover Institution Press, Stanford, 0817973826, 9780817973827.

Gardiner, Allen Francis, *Narrative of a Journey to the Zoolu Country In South Africa*, (1836), William Crofts, London.

George, Edward, *The Cuban intervention in Angola, 1965-1991*, (2006), Routledge, Abingdon, 0415350158, 9780415350150.

Giliomee, Hermann, *The Afrikaners*, (2003), University of Virginia Press, Charlottesville, 0813922372, 9780813922379.

Gilly, William Stephen, *Narrative of an excursion to the mountains of Piemont*, (1824), C. and J. Rivington, London.

Gillmor, Don, *Canada: A People's History Vol. 1*, (2000), Canada Broadcasting Corporation, Toronto, 0771033400, 9780771033407.

Gledhill, Eily and Jack, *In the Steps of Piet Retief*, (1980), Human & Rousseau (Pty) Ltd., Cape Town, 0798110880, 9780798110884.

Gleijeses, Piero, *Conflicting Missions: Havana, Washington and Africa, 1959-1976*, (2002), University of North Carolina Press, London, 0807826472, 9780807826478 .

Godlonton, Robert, *A Narrative of the Irruption of the Kafir Hordes into the Eastern Province of the Colony of Good Hope, 1834-5*, (1836), Meurant and Godlonton, Cape Town.

Goodrich, Albert M., *Cruise and captures of the Alabama*, (1906), The H.W. Wilson Co., Minneapolis.

Gottheimer, Josh, *Ripples of hope: great American civil rights speeches*, (2003), Basic Civitas Books, New York, 0465027520, 9780465027521.

Graham, G.S., *Empire of the North Atlantic: the maritime struggle for North America* (2nd Edition), (1950), University of Toronto Press, Toronto.

Griffin, Christopher, *French Military Interventions in Africa*, (2007), Convention of the International Studies Association, Chicago, IL, Chicago.

van Haarst, J. W. G. and Johannes Jacobus Meinsma, *De opkomst van het Nederlandsch gesag in Oost-Indië* (Part 2), (1864), M. Nijhoff, 's Gravenhage.

Haggard, H. Rider, *Cetywayo and His White Neighbours*, (1888), Trübner & Co., London.

Hansard, Thomas Curson, *Hansard's Parliamentary Debates Vol. CCCXX*, (1887), Cornelius Buck & Son, London.

Harris, William Cornwallis, *Narrative of an Expedition into Southern Africa*, (1838), American Mission Press, Bombay, 185532122X.

Heese, J. A. (Editor: Lombard, R. T. J), *South African Genealogies Vol. 4* (Genealogical Institute of South Africa), (2006), H. S. R. C. Press, Pretoria, 0796914915, 9780796914910.

Heitman, Helmoed-Römer, *Modern african Wars (3) : South-West Africa*, (1991), Osprey Publishing, Oxford.

Hobhouse, Emily, *The Brunt of the War and where it fell*, (1902), Methuen & Co., London.

Holden, William Clifford, *History of the Colony of Natal, South Africa*, (1855), Alexander Heylin, London.

Huddy, John, *Storming Las Vegas*, (2008), Ballantine Books, New York, 0345514416, 9780345514417.

Jackson, Allan, *Facts about Durban*, (2003), F.A.D Publishers, Durban, 0620304855, 9780620304856.

Jenkinson, Thomas B., *Amazulu: The Zulu, Their Past History, Manners, Customs and Language*, etc., (1884), W.H. Allen & Co, London.

Johnson, Charles and John Stanfield, *Bitter Canaan*, (1987), Transaction Publishers, 1560006307, 9781560006305.

Johnson, Philip James, *Seasons in Hell : Charles S. Johnson and the 1930 Liberian Labor Crisis*, (2004), Louisiana State University.

Jooste, Graham and Roger Webster, *Innocent Blood - Executions during the Anglo Boer War*, (2002), New Africa Publishing, Cape Town, 0864865325, 9780864865328.

Kathrada, Ahmad, *Memoirs*, (2005), Struik, Cape Town, 1868729184, 9781868729180.

Kay, Hugh, *Salazar and the modern Portugal*, (1970), Eyre & Spottiswoode, London.

King, W. R., *Campaigning in Kaffirland or Scenes and Adventures in the Kaffir War of 1851-2*, (1855), Saunders and Otley, London. Kinsey, H.W.,

Kissinger, Henry, *Years of Renewal*, (1999), Simon & Schuster, New York, 0684855712.

Kotz, D. J., *Letters of the American Missionaries,*, (1950), The Van Riebeeck Society, Cape Town.

Krog, Antjie, *Country of my skull*, (1999), Random House, New York, 0812931297, 9780812931297.

Kuipers, J. J. B. & R. J. Swiers, *Het Verhaal van Zeeland*, (2005), Uitgeverij Verloren, Hilversum, 9065508430, 9789065508430.

Laidlaw Zoë, *Colonial Connections 1815-1845: Patronage, the Information Revolution and Colonial Government*, (2005), Manchester University Press, Manchester, 0719069181, 9780719069185.

Las Cases, E. A. D., *Memoirs of the Life, Exile, and Conversations, of the Emperor Napoleon Vol. 4*, 1862, W. J. Widdleton, New York.

Leibbrandt, Hendrik Carel Vos, *Precis of the Archive of the Cape of Good Hope Vol. 13* , (1900), W.A. Richards & Sons, Cape Town.

Leibbrandt, Hendrik Carel Vos, *The Rebellion of 1815*, (1902), J.C. Juta & Co and P. S. King & Son, Cape Town.

Le Vaillant, F. (Editor: Elizabeth Helme), *Travels from the Cape of Good Hope to the Interior Parts of Africa Vol. 1*, (1790), William Lane, London.

Levinge, Richard George Augustus, *Historical Records of the Forty-third Regiment, Monmouthshire Light Infantry: With a Roll of the Officers and Their Services from the Period of Embodiment to the Close of 1867*, 1868, W. Clowes & Son, London.

Lichtenstein, Hinrich, *Travels in Southern Africa in the Years 1803, 1804, 1805 and 1806* (Translation: Anne Plumptre), (1812), Henry Colburn, London.

Liddle, Peter, *The 1916 Battle of the Somme: A reappraisal*, (1992), L. Cooper, London, 0850523494, 9780850523492.

Lindley, Augustus F., *Adamantia*, (1873), W., H. and L. Collingridge, London.

Lock, Ron, *Blood on the Painted Mountain: Zulu Victory and Defeat Hlobane and Kambula, 1879*, (1995), Greenhill Books and Stackpole Books, London and Pennsylvania, 1853672017, 9781853672019.

Lord, Dick, *From Fledgling to Eagle*, (2008), 30 degree south Publishers, Johannesburg, 1920143300, 9781920143305.

Mabona, Mongameli, *Diviners and Prophets Among the Xhosa (1593-1856): A Study in Xhosa Cultural History*, (2004), LIT Verlag, Berlin-Hamburg-Münster, 3825867005, 9783825867003.

Maclennan, Ben, *A Proper Degree of Terror: John Graham and the Cape's Eastern Frontier*, (1986), Ravan Press, Braamfontein, 0869752359, 9780869752357.

McWilliams, Bill, *On Hallowed Ground: The Last Battle for Pork Chop Hill*, (2004), Naval Institute Press, Annapolis, 1591144809, 9781591144809.

Mahan, Alfred Thayer, *The Influence of Sea Power upon History 1660-1783*, (1890), Little, Brown and Company, Boston.

Mandela, Rolihlahla, *Long Walk to Freedom*, (1994), Abacus, London, 0349106533, 9780349106533. Marais, J. S., *Maynier and the First Boer Republic*, (1944), Maskew Miller Ltd., Cape Town, ASIN: B001OZTRC2.

Martin, H. J. & Neil Orpen, *Eagles Victorious* (Volume VI of *South African Forces WWII*), (1977), Purnell, London,

0868430080, 9780868430089.

Maxwell, F. A. and C. A. H. O. Maxwell, *Frank Maxwell: a memoir and some letters*, (1921), J.Murray, London.

Maxwell, Kenneth (Editor: Bloomfield, Richard J.), *The Legacy of Decolonization; Chapter 1 of regional Conflict and U.S. Policy: Angola and Mozambique*, (1988), Reference Publications, Inc.091725645X, 9780917256455.

Meredith, Martin, *The Fate of Africa*, (2005), Public Affairs, New York, 1586482467, 9781586482466.

Meredith, Martin, *Mandela, a biography*, (2010), Public Affairs, New York, 1586488325, 9781586488321.

Meredith, Martin, *In the name of Apartheid*, (1988), Penguin Books Ltd., London, 0241124956.

Meredith, Martin, *Diamonds, Gold and War: The British, The Boers and the Making of South Africa*, (2007), Public Affairs, New York, 1586484737, 9781586484736.

Meintjes, Johannes, *General Louis Botha - a Biography*, (1970), Cassell & Company LTD, London.

Mhlaba, Raymond and Mufamadi Thembeka, *Raymond Mhlaba's Personal Memoirs*, (2001), HSRC Press, Pretoria, 0796919747, 9780796919748.

Mickolus, Edward F. and Simmons, Susan L., *Terrorism, 1992-1995*, (1997), Greenwood Press, Westport, 0313304688, 9780313304682.

Mokoena, Kenneth, *South Africa and the United States*, (1993), The New Press, New York156584081X.

Molema, S. M., *The Bantu- Past & Present*, (1920), W. Green & Son, Edinburgh.

Moodie, Donald, The Record I, III, V, 1960, A.A. Balkema, Amsterdam/Cape Town

Moodie, D.C.F., *The history of the battles and adventures of the British, the Boers, and the Zulus*, (1888), Murray & St. Leger, Cape Town.

Moss, Norman, *Picking up the Reins*, (2008), Duckworth Overlook, London, 0715636936, 9780715636930.

Mostert, Noël, *Frontiers: The Epic of South Africa's Creation and the Tragedy of the Xhosa People*, (1993), Pimlico, London, 0712655840, 9780712655842.

Moreman, Tim and Duncan Anderson, *British Commandos 1940-46*, (2006), Osprey Publishing, Oxford, 84176986X, 9781841769868.

Morris, Donald R., *The Washing of the Spears: The Rise and Fall of the Zulu Nation*, (1998), Da Capo Press, New York, 0306808668, 9780306808661.

Muston, Alexis, *L'Israël des Alpes Vol. 1*, (1854), Librairie De Marc Du Cloux, Paris.

Muston, Alexis, translated by John Montgomery, *The Israel of the Alps Vol. 1*, (1866), Blackie & Son, London.

Napier, E. H. D. Elers, *Excursions in Southern Africa Vol. 2*, (1850), William Shoberl, London.

Nathan, Manfred, *The Voortrekkers of South Africa: from earliest times to the foundation of the republics*, (1937), Gordon & Gotch, London.

Nixon, Richard Milhouse, *The Real War*, (1980), Warner Books, New York, 044651201X, 9780446512015.

Nortje, Piet, *32 Battalion*, (2004), Struik, Cape Town, 1868729141, 9781868729142.

Owen, Frances (Ed: George E.Cory), *The diary of the Rev. Francis Owen, M.A : missionary with Dingaan in 1837-38*; Vol. 7 of Publications of the Van Riebeeck Society, 1926, Van Riebeeck Society, Cape Town.

Pakenham, Thomas, *The Scramble for Africa: 1876 to 1912*, (1991), BCA, London.

Pakenham, Thomas, *The Boer War*, (1982), Futura, London, 0708818927, 9780708818923.

Parliament of Great Britain, *Report from the Select Committee on the Kafir Tribes: Together with the Proceedings of the Committee, Minutes of Evidence, Appendix, and Index*, (1851), House of Commons, London.

Parliament of Great Britain, *Papers relative to the Condition and treatment of the Native Inhabitants of South Africa within the Colony of the Cape of Good Hope or beyond the frontier of that colony Vol. 1*, (1835), House of Commons, London.

Paravacini de Capelli, W.B.E. & de Kock, W.J., *Reize in den Binnen-landen van Zuid-Africa*, (1965), pp. 162, 1965, Van Riebeeck-Vereniging.

Parkman, Francis, *The Conspiracy of Pontiac and the Indian War after the Conquest of Canada Vol. 2*, 1887, Little, Brown and Company, Boston.

Peires, J.B., *The House of Phalo*, (1981), Ravan Press, Los Angeles, 0869752146, 9780869752142.

Peires, Jeffrey B., *The Dead Will Arise: Nongqawuse and the Great Xhosa Cattle-killing Movement of 1856-7*, (1989), Indiana University Press, Bloomington, 0253205247, 9780253205247.

Percival, Robert, *An Account of the Cape of Good Hope*, (1804), C. and R. Baldwin, London.

Petter-Bowyer, Peter J. H., *Winds of Destruction*, (2005), 30 Degrees South Publishing, Johannesburg, 0958489033, 9780958489034.

Pirow, Oswald, *James Barry Munnik Hertzog*, (1957), Howard Timmins, Cape Town.

Pitt, William and James Philips, *The Speech of the Right Honourable William Pitt*, (1792), James Phillips & John Farb, London.

Pogrund, Benjamin, *How can man die better*, (1990), Johnathan Ball1870015339, 9781870015332.

Potter, Bruce D., *The U.S.S.R. in Third World conflicts*, (1986), Cambridge U. Press, 0521310644, 9780521310642.

Preller, Gustav S., *Voortrekkermense V*, (1938), Nasionale Pers, Cape Town.

Prentiss, Charles, *The Life of of the Late Gen. William Eaton*, (1813), E.Merriam & Co., Brookfield.

Pringle, Thomas, *Narrative of a Residence in South Africa*, (1835), Edward Moxon, London.

Pulakow-Suransky, Sasha, *The Unspoken Alliance*, (2010), Pantheon, New York, 0375425462, 9780375425462.

Quandt, William B., *Soviet Policy in the October 1973 War*, R-1864-ISA, (1976), Rand Corp, Santa Monica, CA.

Raven-Hart, R., *The Cape Good Hope 1652-1702 V.2*, (1971), A.A. Balkema, Cape Town.

Reitz, Deneys, *Commando: A Boer Journal of the Anglo-Boer War*, 1998, Jonathan Ball Publishers (Pty) Ltd, Jeppestown, 1868420663.

Reitz, Francis William, *A Century of Wrong*, (2008), BiblioBazaar, Charleston.

Rhoodie, Eschel, *The Real Information Scandal*, (1983), Orbis, Pretoria, 0620070579, 9780351179495.

Rompel-Koopman, L., *In het Land van Retief*, (1919), De Volkstem, Pretoria, ASIN: B0017V6TP6.

Roosevelt, Theodore, *African Game Trails*, (1910), Charles Scribner's Sons, New York.

Rose, J. H., *The Cambridge History of the British Empire Vol. 8*, (1929), Cambridge University Press, London.

Rouvez, Alain, *Disconsolate Empires*, (1994), University Press of America, Inc., Lanham, MD, 0819196436, 9780819196439.

Saunders, Hilary A. St. G., *The Green Beret: the story of the Commandos, 1940-1945*, (1949), M. Joseph, London.

Schlesinger, Arthur Meier, *Robert Kennedy and his Times*, (2002), Houghton Mifflin Harcourt, New York, 0618219285, 9780618219285.

Schneidman, Witney W., *Eganging Africa: Washington and the fall of Portugal's Colonial Empire*, (2004), University Press of America, Inc., Lanham, MD, 0761828125, 9780761828129.

Schwartz, Philip J., *Migrants against Slavery*, (2001), Univeristy of Virginia Press, Charlottesville.

Scully, William Charles, *A History of South Africa, from the earliest days to Union*, (1915), Longmans Green & Co., London.

Shaler, William, *Sketches of Algiers, political, historical, and civil*, (1826), Cummings, Hilliard and company.

Shaw, William, *The Story of My Mission Among the British Settlers in South Eastern Africa*, (1872), The Weslyan Mission House, London.

Shaw, William, *Story of my Mission in South-eastern Africa (the second book in the series)*, (1860), Hamilton, Adams and Co., London.

Shearing, Taffy & David, *Commandant Johannes Lötter and his rebels*, (1998), Privately Printed & published, Sedgefield, 0620227818, 9780620227810.

Smit, Erasmus (Ed: Gustav S. Preller), *Joernaal van 'n Trek Uit die Dagboek van Erasmus Smit*, (1988), Tafelberg, Cape Town, 0624026779, 9780624026778. Original published 1897 as Smit, Erasmus (Ed: H.F. Schoon), *Uit het dagboek van Erasmus Smit, predikant bij de Voortrekkers*, (1897), Townshend, Taylor & Snashall, Cape Town.

Smith, Andrea L., *Europe's Invisble Migrants: Consequences of the Colonists' Return*, (2003), Amsterdam University Press, Amsterdam, 905356571X, 9789053565711.

Smith, Edwin W., *The Life and Times of Daniel Lindley*, (1949), The Epworth Press, London.

Smith, Harry George Wakelyn and George C.M. Smith, *The Autobiography of Lieutenant-General Sir Harry Smith, Baronet of Aliwal on the Sutlej Vol. 1 & 2*, (1902), John Murray and E. F. Dutton, London and New York.

Smith, John Clay, *Rebels in Law*, (2000), University of Michigan Press, Ann Arbor, 0472086464, 9780472086467.

Smith, Wayne S., *The Cuban role in Angola; Chapter 5 of regional Conflict and U.S. Policy: Angola and Mozambique*, (1988), Reference Publications, Inc., Algonac, MI, 091725645X, 9780917256455.

Smuts, Jan (Ed: Spies, S. B. and G. Nattrass), *Jan Smuts: Memoirs of the Boer War*, (1994), Jonathan Ball Publishers, Johannesburg, 1868420175, 9781868420179.

South African Democracy Education Trust, *The Road to Democracy Vol. 1*, (2006), Struik, Cape Town, 1868729060, 9781868729067.

South African Human Sciences Research Council, *Women marching into the 21st century*, (2000), HSRC Press, Pretoria, 0796919666, 9780796919663.

Sparrman, Anders, *A Voyage to the Cape of Good Hope Towards the Antarctic Polar Circle and Round the World but Chiefly into the Country of the Hottentots and the Caffres Vol. 2*, (1786), Translated, London.

Spring, Gardiner, *Memoirs of the Rev. Samuel J. Mill, late missionary to the south western section of the United States, and agent of the American Colonization Society, deputed to explore the coast of Africa*, (1820), Francis Westley, New York.

Stead, T. W., *The last will and testament of Cecil John Rhodes*, (1902), Review of Reviews Office, London, 1920169008, 9781920169008.

Steenkamp, Willem, *Borderstrike!*, (2006), Just Done Productions, Durban.

Steyn, Hannes, Richardt van der Walt, and Jan van Loggerenberg, *Armament and Disarmament*, (2005), iUniverse, Lincoln, 0595356656, 9780595356652.

Stiff, Peter, *The Silent War- South African Recce Operations 1969-1994*, (1999), Galago, Alberton, 0620243007.

Stockwell, John, *In Search of Enemies*, (1978), W.W. Norton & Co. Inc., New York, 0393057054, 9780393057058.

Stout, Benjamin, *Cape of Good Hope and Its Dependencies: An Accurate and Truly Interesting Description of Those Delightful Regions*, (1820), Edwards & Nibb, London.

Strydom, Lauritz, *Rivonia Unmasked*, (1965), Voortrekkerpers, Johannesburg.

Suarez, Virgil, *Spared Angola: memories from a Cuban-American childhood*, (1997), Arte Publico Press, Houston, 1558851976, 9781558851979.

Tavernier, Jean-Baptiste, *Travels in India Vol. 2*, (1889), Macmillan & Co, London.

Terry, Edward, *A Voyage to East-India*, (1777), J.Wilkie, London.

Teixeira, Bernardo, *The Fabric of Terror - three days in Angola*, (1965), The Devin-Adair Company, New York.

Theal, George McCall; the following collection of texts:

   History of South Africa Under the Administration of the Dutch East India Company [1652 to 1795] Vol. 1& 2
      (Reprint of the 1897 original by Sonnenschein of London, UK), (1969), Negro Universities Press, New York.

   The History of South Africa 1795-1843, (1891), S. Sonnenschein & Co, London.

   Records of the Cape Colony from February 1793 to December 1796 Vol. 1, (1897), Gvt.of the Cape Colony, London.

   Records of the Cape Colony from December 1796 to December 1799 Vol. 2, (1898), Gvt.of the Cape Colony, London.

   Records of the Cape Colony from December 1799 to May 1801 Vol. 3, (1898), Gvt.of the Cape Colony, London.

   Records of the Cape Colony from May 1801 to February 1803 Vol. 4, (1899), Gvt.of the Cape Colony, London.

   Records of the Cape Colony from February 1803 to July 1806 Vol. 5, (1899), Gvt.of the Cape Colony, London.

   Records of the Cape Colony from March 1811 to October 1812 Vol. 8, (1901), Gvt.of the Cape Colony, London.

   Records of the Cape Colony from November 1815 to May 1818 Vol. 11, (1901), Gvt.of the Cape Colony, London.

   Records of the Cape Colony from January 1820 to June 1821 Vol. 13, (1902), Gvt.of the Cape Colony, London.

   Chronicles of Cape Commanders, (1882), W.A. Richards and Sons, Cape Town.

   Records of South-Eastern Africa Vol. 7 & 8, (1901 an 1902), Gvt.of the Cape Colony, London.

   Ethnography and Condition of South Africa before A.D. 1505, (1919), George Allen & Unwin LTD., London.

   Catalogue of documents from 16th September 1795 to 21st February 1803, in the collection of colonial archives at Cape Town), (1880), Saul Solomon & Co, Cape Town.

   The History of South Africa from 1795 to 1872 (V.6 of the Struik Series);
      Same as V.2 of 1915 4th Edition, George Allen & Unwin (London), (1892), Struik reprint 1964, Cape Town.

The History of South Africa from 1795 to 1872 (V.7 of the Struik Series);
Same as V.3 of 1916 3rd Edition, George Allen & Unwin (London), (1892), Struik reprint 1964, Cape Town.

The History of South Africa from 1795 to 1872 (V.8 of the Struik Series);
Same as V.4 of 1915 4th Edition, George Allen & Unwin (London), (1892), Struik reprint 1964, Cape Town.

The History of South Africa from 1873 to 1883 (V.10 & 11 of the Struik Series);
Same as V.1 & 2 of 1919 2-vol. Edition, George Allen & Unwin (London), (1919), Struik reprint 1964, Cape Town.

Thunberg, Carl Peter & Vernon Siegfried Forbes, *Travels at the Cape of Good Hope, 1772 - 1775*, (1986), Van Riebeeck Society, Cape Town, 0620109815, 9780620109819.

Trew, Peter, *The Boer War Generals*, (1999), Jonathan Ball Publishers (Pty) Ltd, Jeppestown, 1868420906.

Trotter, Alys Fane, *The Old Cape; a Chronicle of her Men and Houses*, (1903), A. Constable & Co., Westminster.

Turner, Nat and Thomas R.Gray, *The Confessions of Nat Turner*, (1832), Thomas R. Gray, Richmond.

Van der Merwe, H. J. J. M., *Scheepsjournael ende Daghregister (2nd Edition)*, (1964), J.L. van Schaik, Pretoria.

Vanneman, Peter, *The Soviet Strategy in Southern Africa*, (1990), Hoover Inst. Press, Stanford, 0817989013, 9780817989019.

Visagie, Jan, *Voortrekker Stamouers, 1835-1845*, (2000), U. of South Africa, UNISA, Pretoria, 1868880605, 978-1868880607.

Walters, Ronald W., *South Africa and the Bomb*, (1987), Lexington Books, Lexington, 0669141976, 9780669141979.

Warner, Philip, *Kitchener - The man behind the legend*, (1985), Hamish Hamilton, London, 0241115876, 9780241115879.

Weal, John, *Jagdgeschwader 27 "Afrika"*, (2003), Osprey, Oxford, 1841765384, 9781841765389.

Wells, Spencer, *The Journey of Man: A Genetic Odyssey*, (2002), Princeton U. Press, Princeton, 069111532X, 9780691115320.

Wells, Spencer, *Deep Ancestry - inside the genographic project*, (2007), Nat. Geo., Washington, 1426201184, 9781426201189.

Westad, Odd Arne, *The Global Cold War; Third world interventions and the making of our times*, (2005), Cambridge University Press, Cambridge, UK, 0521853648, 9780521853644.

White, Richard, *The Middle Ground*, 1991, Cambridge University Press, Cambridge, UK, 052137104X, 9780521371049.

Wilmot, Alexander, *The Life and Times of Sir Richard Southey*, (1904), Sampson Low, Marston & Co., London.

Wilmot, Alexander & John Centlivres Chase, *History of the Colony of the Cape of Good Hope: From Its Discovery to the Year 1819*, (1869), J.C. Juta, Cape Town.

de Witte, Ludo, *The assassination of Patrice Lumumba*, (2001), Verso, London, 1859844103, 9781859844106.

Wright, George, *Destruction of a Nation*, (1997), Pluto Press, Chicago, 0745310303.

Wright, Robert, *Three nights in Havana*, (2007), HarperCollins Publishers LTD., Toronto, 000200626x, 9780002006262.

Walsh, Walter, *The moral damage of the war*, 1906, Ginn & Co, Boston.

Wilson, Woodrow, *A History of the American People Vol. 5*, (1902), Harper & Brothers, New York.

Yonge, Charlotte Mary, *Pioneers and Founders or Recent Workers in the Mission Field*, (1874), MacMillan & Co., London.

Zhdarkin, Igor Anatolyevitch; Editor: Gennady V. Shubin, *The oral history of forgotten wars : the memoirs of veterans of the war in Angola*; See the section titled: *We did not see it even in Afghanistan* (Translation by Tamara Reilly), (2007), Memories, Moscow, 590311640X, 9785903116409.

19th Century Missionary Journals

Aborigines Protection Society (reprint for), *Report of the Parliamentary Select Committee for Aboriginal Tribes*, (1837), William Ball and Hatchard & Son, London.

The Church Missionary Record Vol.9, September 1838, (1838), Seeleys, Hatchard, Nisbet, Simpkin, Marshall, London.

The Eclectic Review Vol. XXII, (1847), Ward & Co., London.

The African Repository Vol. 13, (American Colonization Society), (1837), James C. Dunn, Washington.

The African Repository Vol. 14, (American Colonization Society), (1838), James C. Dunn, Washington.

Transactions of the Missionary Society Vol. 1, (London Miss. Society), (1804), Bye & Law, London.

Transactions of the Missionary Society (Vol. 2 & 3), (London Miss. Society), (1806), William & Smith, London.

Transactions of the Missionary Society in the Years 1803, 1804, 1805 and 1806 Vol. 3 (Vol. 2 and 3 bound together), (1806), Bye and Law, London.

The Missionary Herald Vol. 33, (1837), American Board of Commsioners for Foreign Missions, Boston.

The Missionary Herald Vol. 29, (1833), American Board of Commsioners for Foreign Missions, Boston.

The Missionary Register Vol. 24, (Church Missionary Society), (1836), L. & G. Seeley, London.

The Missionary Register, (Church Missionary Society), (1822), L. B. Seeley, London.

The Missionary Magazine Vol. 5, (1800), J. Pillans & Sons, Edinburgh.

Other Institutional Resources:

Cape Archives (ZA), Resolutions of the Council of Policy of the Cape of Good Hope and Records of the Cape Orphan Chamber and deceased estate information.

South African National Archives (ZA), Pretoria, Anglo-Boer War and deceased estate information.

Free State Archives (ZA); Booyens Estate and Death Notice information

The Graaff-Reinet Museum (ZA); Callanan and McCusker information

The Somerset East Museum (ZA); Slagtersnek information

The Uitenhage Museum and Cuyler Manor (ZA); Cuyler and Slagtersnek information

The Surveyor-General of the Western Cape (ZA); historical deeds and maps of farms

Anglo-Boer War Museum (ZA), Anglo-Boer War Concentration Camp information.

Danish State Archives (DK), Boyens Eiderstedt information.

New York State Archives (USA), Sterrevelt and New Amsterdam information.

New York City Archives (USA), Sterrevelt and New Amsterdam information.

Base de Données du Refuge Huguenot (France); Huguenot Refugee information

The City of Cabrières d'Aigues (France); Vaudois information

Oud Soetermeer Historisch Gemeenschap (NL); Sterrevelt genealogical information

Koninklijk Nederlands Historisch Geenootschap (NL) - Historici.nl; VOC Shipping information

Amsterdam Archives (NL); Sterrevelt information

Nationaal Archief (NL); Boyens information

Church Archives of Garding (DE); Boyens information

Stadt-Archiv Wesel (DE); Bason information

Landesarchiv Nordrhein-Westfalen (DE); Klauten information

The Historical Society of Oedt (DE); Klauten and Radergoertges information.

British National Archives in Kew (UK); British Army soldiers' data.

Olivetreegenealogy.com (USA); Sterrevelt information

Familysearch.com (USA); General genealogical information from archived documents

Burnaby Family History Center of the Mormon Church (CA); Church Book records

Kent Family History Society (UK); Bowles, Green, and Amos information

Cory Library at Rhodes University (ZA); Misselbrook and Bowles information

Genealogical institute of South Africa (ZA); Church Book records

University of South Africa Library (ZA); Church Book records

Voortrekker Monument, Pretoria (ZA); Great Trek information

The Genealogical Society of South Africa (ZA); General genealogical information

Image Credits and Sources

Unless otherwise stated, the photographs and graphics presented in this work are by the author, Harry Booyens, who claims copyright. Publication of the images in no way implies endorsement of the present work by photographers or copyright holders other than the author.

Images reproduced with the permission of copyright owners:

Fig. 4-11 and 10-6 with permission of photographer Bertus Steyn
Fig. 10-9 with permission of photographer Adel Myburgh
Fig. 14-1 photograph released to public domain by photographer with ID=Entropy1963
Fig. 16-6 photograph released to public domain by photographer Tom Giddings
Fig. 16-10 and 21-1 with permission of Belia van der Merwe & Family Booyens
Fig. 17-11 with permission of photographer J.P. Steynberg of Ganora Guest Farm
Fig. 18-3 with permission of photographer Patricia Truter
Fig. 19-7, 19-8, and 19-10 with permission of Margaret Caroline Basson
Fig. 19-9 with permission of photographer Nick Roux; from the S. A. Military History Museum
Fig. 19-11 with permission of photographer Batur Avgan of the Island of Cos; www.rlm66.de
Fig. 20-5 with permission of photographer John Magill
Fig. 20-6 with permission of Nicola Elizabeth Booyens
Fig. 24-4 Photography by the late John Hone; with permission of Art Publishers (PTY) LTD, Cape Town, South Africa.
Fig. 25-4 This image by author KGG1951 is published under a Creative Commons Attribution-Share Alike 3.0 Unported license, which may be found at http://creativecommons.org/licenses/by-sa/3.0/deed.en. Publication of the image in no way implies endorsement of the present work by KGG1951.
Fig. 26-1 with permission of the F. W. De Klerk Foundation.
Fig. 27-2 Copyright (2013) TerraMetrics, Inc. www.terrametrics.com, with permission; borders added by H. Booyens
Fig. 28-1 with permission of photographers Robbie Sandrock and Frank Fenner
Fig. 28-3 photograph released to public domain by photographer with ID=Arpingstone
Fig. 29-4 photograph released to public domain by photographer with ID=Gabbahead

Images from the United States Library of Congress:

Fig. 6-3; 15-1, 15-3; 16-5; 18-2; 19-5, 19-6; 23-1

Images from the South African National Archives:

Fig. 6-2, 6-5; 7-1; 8-1; 9-5; 15-8; 16-2, 16-3, 16-9, 16-13; 17-4, 17-5, 17-6, 17-7, 17-9, 17-15, 17-17; 18-1

Images from the United States Department of Defense, photographs by U.S. federal employees:

Fig. 21-3, 21-4; 25-6, 25-7, 25-8; 26-2, 26-3; 28-4; 29-1, 29-2, 29-3

Images from Museums, Libraries, and Information Systems

Fig. 14-10 from the U.S. Naval Historical Center
Fig. 17-8 from the Anglo-Boer War Museum
Fig. 17-10 and 17-16 from the Middelburg (Cape) Museum
Fig. 18-7 from the Imperial War Museum
Fig. 20-1 from the John F. Kennedy Presidential Library and Museum
Fig. 24-2 and 25-1 from the Ronald Reagan Presidential Library
Fig. 30-1 from the South African Government Communication and Information System

Images from texts in the public domain:

Fig. 2-6 from *Travels from the Cape of Good Hope etc.* by F. La Vaillant (1790)
Fig. 5-1 from *Canada - Empire of the North* by Agnes C. Laut (1909)
Fig. 8-2 from *Cape of Good Hope and its dependencies etc.* by Capt. B. Stout (1820)
Fig. 8-3 from *Views of Ports and Harbours etc.* by William Finden (1838)
Fig. 9-1 and 13-6 from *Campaigning in Kaffirland* by Capt. W.R. King
Fig. 10-1 and 13-10 from *Narrative of a visit to Mauritius and South Africa* by James Backhouse (1844)

Fig. 10-5 from *Narrative of an Expedition into Southern Africa* by William Cornwallis Harris (1838)

Fig. 11-1 from *A Narrative of a Journey to the Zoolu Country in South Africa* by Allen Francis Gardiner (1836)

Fig. 11-10 from *History of the Colony of Natal* by william C. Holden (1855)

Fig. 12-6 from *The First Annexation of the Transvaal* by W.J. Leyds (1906)

Fig. 13-1 from *Passages in Early Military Life of General Sir George T. Napier, KCB*, autobiography (1884)

Fig. 13-2 from *History of the Colony of Natal* by Rev. William C. Holden (1855)

Fig. 13-4 from *Illustrated History of the British Empire in India and the East, Volume 2* by Edward Henry Nolan (1858)

Fig. 13-9 from *A Tour in South Africa* by J.J. Freeman (1851)

Fig. 13-11 from *Ten Weeks in Natal* by John William Colenso (1855)

Fig. 14-2 from *The Ruin of Zululand* by F. E. Colenso and Lt. Col. E. Durnford (1885)

Fig. 14-5 from *Army and Navy Illustrated, Volume 2, No.15* (1896), with assistance of Charles Griffin of the Island of Cyprus

Fig. 14-9 from *The Graaff-Reinet Advertiser*, 20 November 1868; with thanks to the Graaff-Reinet Museum.

Fig. 15-6 and 15-7 from *Cecil Rhodes - Man and Empire-maker* by Princess Catherine Radziwill (1918)

Fig. 16-1 from *Lord Milner's work in South Africa* by W. B. Worsfold (1906)

Fig. 16-8 from *A Handbook of the Boer War* by Gale and Polden Limited (1910)

Fig. 16-11 and 17-1 from *With the Boer Forces* by H. C. Hillegas (1900)

Fig. 16-12 from *With Both Armies in South Africa* by R. H. Davis (1900)

Fig. 17-3 from *cover of L'Illustration* of Saturday 16 November 1901

Fig. 17-13 and 17-14 from *Hoe Zij stierven* by G. J. Jordaan (1904)

Images derived from other sources:

Fig. 1-1 from *Landing of van Riebeeck at the Cape of Good Hope, 1652* by Charles Davidson Bell (1813-1882)

Fig. 2-1 from *Jan Van Riebeeck* painted during van Riebeeck's life (1619-1677). Artist unknown

Fig. 2-2 derived from a redraft of the *Castello Plan of New Amsterdam* in 1660 by John Wolcott Adams (1874–1925) and I.N. Phelps Stokes (1867–1944)

Fig. 2-3 from a postcard published by The Foundation Press, Inc., 1932 by artist Jean Leon Gerome Ferris (1863–1930)

Fig. 2-4 and 2-5 are based on information from Statistics South Africa

Fig. 2-8 *John Hawkins*, artist unknown (1580)

Fig. 3-1 *Louis XIV* by Hyacinthe Rigaud (1701)

Fig. 4-8 is based on information from *House of Phalo* by J. B. Peieres (1981)

Fig. 5-3 Image of George Macartney, from *1st Earl Macartney; Sir George Leonard Staunton, 1st Bt (1737-1806)*, by L. F. Abbott (cropped) (ca. 1785)

Fig. 6-1 *William Wilberforce*, by Karl A. Hickl (ca. 1794)

Fig. 8-4 *The Landing of the British Settlers at Algoa Bay in the Year 1820* by Thomas Baines (1820-1875), painted in 1852; from the collection of the King George VI Art Gallery, Port Elizabeth

Fig. 8-6 John Philip; derived from an engraving by Thompson based on an original painting by Wildman

Fig. 9-3 derived from *Major-General Sir Henry George Wakelyn (Harry) Smith (1787-1860) of Aliwal* created 9 April 1846, Published by J. Hogarth, London

Fig. 11-6 *The Battle of Blauwkrantz* by Thomas Baines (1820-1875) in 1854; from the Collection of MuseumAfrica

Fig. 11-11 *The Women Loaded the Empty Guns* by Joseph Ratcliffe Skelton (1865-1927)

Fig. 12-1 Photographic rendition of a tapestry at the Voortrekker Monument, Pretoria

Fig. 12-2 derived form a painting of Andries Pretorius by G. Hauser (1848), also at Voortrekker Monument, Pretoria.

Fig. 13-3 *Sir Peregrine Maitland, KCB* (portrait ca. 1882-1883) by artist G. T. Berthon 1806-1892

Fig. 13-8 *Wreck of the Birkenhead* by Thomas M. M. Hemy (-1937), published 15 May 1893 by Henry Graves and Co.

Fig. 14-6 Photographic portrait of Napoleon IV (1856-1879) by unknown photographer before 1879

Fig. 14-7 Derived from a photographic image of Gen. Petrus Jacobus Joubert, sourced from the portrait Gallery of the Perry–Castañeda Library of the University of Texas at Austin; Also the South African National Archives

Fig. 14-8 Photographic portrait of Dinizulu Ka Cetshwayo (ca.1868-1913) taken by unknown photographer before 1900

Fig. 15-2 Photographic portrait of Léopold Louis Philippe Marie Victor of Belgium (1835-1909), Photographer unknown

Fig. 15-5 Paul Kruger (1825-1904), photograph taken by unknown photographer before 1899

Fig. 16-4 Photograph of Field Marshal Frederick Sleigh Roberts, 1st Earl Roberts (1832-1914) (retouched), photographer Poole of Waterford, England; taken in the 1880s after the Afghan Campaign

Fig. 17-2 Cabinet Photograph of Lord Herbert Horatio Kitchener (1850-1916) by Messrs. Bassano of London, 1899

Fig. 25-5 is based on information from *From fledgling to Eagle* by Dick Lord (2008)

Index

-----ooOoo-----

Made in the USA
Monee, IL
26 November 2020

49670139R00345